$16.60 MAY '77

P9-ECP-027

BUSINESS POLICY
Text and cases

BUSINESS POLICY
Text and cases

C. ROLAND CHRISTENSEN, D.C.S.
*George Fisher Baker, Jr., Professor of
Business Administration*

KENNETH R. ANDREWS, PH.D.
*Donald Kirk David Professor of
Business Administration*

JOSEPH L. BOWER, D.B.A.
Professor of Business Administration

All of the
Graduate School of Business Administration
Harvard University

Third Edition · 1973

RICHARD D. IRWIN, INC.   Homewood, Illinois   60430

Irwin-Dorsey Limited   Georgetown, Ontario   L7G 4B3

© RICHARD D. IRWIN, INC., 1965, 1969, and 1973

All rights reserved. No part of this publication may be reproduced, stored in a retrieval system, or transmitted, in any form or by any means, electronic, mechanical, photocopying, recording, or otherwise, without the prior written permission of the publisher. The copyright on all cases in this book unless otherwise noted is held by the President and Fellows of Harvard College, and they are published herein by express permission.

Third Edition

First Printing, November 1973
Second Printing, May 1974
Third Printing, September 1974
Fourth Printing, January 1975
Fifth Printing, May 1975
Sixth Printing, August 1975
Seventh Printing, November 1975
Eighth Printing, February 1976
Ninth Printing, July 1976
Tenth Printing, December 1976
Eleventh Printing, March 1977

Case material of the Harvard Graduate School of Business Administration is made possible by the cooperation of business firms who may wish to remain anonymous by having names, quantities, and other identifying details disguised while basic relationships are maintained. Cases are prepared as the basis for class discussion rather than to illustrate either effective or ineffective handling of administrative situations.

ISBN 0-256-01451-5
Library of Congress Catalog Card No. 73–82310
Printed in the United States of America

To
Edmund P. Learned
For reasons he knows well

Preface

THE AUTHORS believe that *Business Policy: Text and Cases* (Third Edition) provides the materials for a complete course in business policy. In this edition, building on the foundations established by earlier editions, we have incorporated a number of changes suggested by colleagues teaching in institutions throughout the world. We are appreciative of their interest in, and use of, this book. Their comments have helped us design a course which can be effectively taught at the undergraduate, graduate, and practicing management levels.

The basic administrative processes and problems with which business policy is concerned have been part of organizational life for centuries; the history of business policy as an academic field dates back less than six decades.

This volume builds on substantial contributions made by former policy colleagues; it carries their efforts further along the way to greater understanding and applicability. The specific core idea—the concept of corporate strategy and the organizational plan used in this book—began to be developed in the early 1960s under the leadership of Kenneth R. Andrews and C. Roland Christensen with the strong encouragement of now Professor Emeritus Edmund P. Learned. William Guth's skills in research helped convert this early conceptual framework into field case problems. Maintaining traditional course interests in a generalist–senior management orientation and in the administrative and organizational problems of the enterprise as a totality, the course concentrates on the determination of corporate strategy (Book One) and the implementation of strategy (Book Two). In this third edition we have added two subsections to our previous framework: one emphasizes the roles, functions, and skills of the general manager; the other emphasizes the process aspects of the generalist's task of formulating and implementing his firm's strategy.

Despite its incompleteness, the concept of corporate strategy provides both a teaching and a research framework. As coauthor Andrews has stated:

"This concept is far from complete. But its early development shows it to be an organizing perspective that makes possible the development of research projects which build upon one another, as for instance in a series devoted to the problems of scanning the environment. The process of planning thus defined can be studied in firms, in industries, or in the French economy, where the relation of the French national plan and strategic planning in private firms, for example, has been studied in detail. But besides providing a special focus and study for a general field . . . this framework allows all other fields to be brought to bear upon the highest function of the general manager—supervision of the continuous process of determining the nature of the enterprise and setting, revising, and attempting to achieve its goals. So far the development of organizational behavior fits well into the framework of implementation. The sophisticated developments in quantitative analysis are not yet readily available to policy problems, but if all goes well, this will come.

"The utility of the policy framework, which mostly articulates and raises to the level of conscious analysis the intuitive approaches developed over years of close attention to concrete situations, is such that some adaptation of it will surely remain after present attempts to develop and test it have been completed. It may prove, indeed, the answer to the conceptual need of the environmental studies. One alternative, at least, is to examine repeatedly the economic, social, technological, and political aspects of the American and international scenes from the perspective of the chief executive in an expanding firm in one industry after another, stressing constantly perception of relevant developments and opportunities for innovation. The skill exercised would be the imaginative identification of opportunity, something quite different from merely looking.

"The idea of corporate strategy constitutes a simple practitioner's theory, a kind of Everyman's conceptual scheme. It is nonetheless capable of including the most extensive combination of interrelated variables involved in the most important of all business decisions. It is a definition of the manager's central function, whether he is a staff specialist contributing in depth and detail to the identification of alternatives and to the predicted return on investment for each of these alternatives, or the senior executive who must finally make or complete the decision."[1]

And, of course, the business policy subject area continues to evolve and develop. The need for professionally trained generalists—the men who make our organized society's critical decisions—is great; our present efforts are limited. Sir Eric Ashby has put the challenge well:

"But the world needs generalists as well as specialists. Indeed you

---

[1] Kenneth R. Andrews, "The Progress of Professional Education for Business," unpublished remarks presented for discussion at the Centennial Convocation on Graduate Professional Education at the Episcopal Theological School, Cambridge, Massachusetts, January 27–29, 1967.

have only to read your newspaper to know that the big decisions on which the fate of nations depends are in the hands of generalists. I do not think that universities, American or British, are satisfied with the education they give to the man who is to become a generalist. Some believe he should have a rigorously specialist training in some field which he then abandons for life. Others believe he should have a synoptic acquaintance with the ways of thinking of humanists, social scientists, and natural scientists. And I suppose there are still a few antique persons who cling to the view that generalists need no higher education at all. We can with some confidence prescribe the minutiae of curriculum for doctors, physicists, and lawyers. The unpalatable fact is that we have no such confidence in prescribing curricula for men who will become presidents of industries, newspaper editors, senior civil servants, or Congressmen."[2]

We believe that the challenge will be met, at least in part, by all of us who work in the policy area in countless colleges and universities throughout this country and the world. And we hope this book will be of some help in meeting that challenge.

October 1973   C. ROLAND CHRISTENSEN
                                    KENNETH R. ANDREWS
                                    JOSEPH L. BOWER

---

[2] Sir Eric Ashby, Master, Clare College, Cambridge, "Centennial Convocation Address," delivered at the 100th anniversary of the granting of the charter to Cornell University, October 9, 1964.

Acknowledgments

THE AUTHORS of this book are in debt to former and present colleagues. Former colleagues—now numbering more than 100—cannot each be individually recognized but we are grateful to them for their multiple contributions. We wish to especially thank Professors Emeriti Robert W. Austin, M. T. Copeland, Myles L. Mace, Richard S. Meriam, and former dean Donald K. David, and acknowledge the major contributions of the late George Albert Smith, Jr. Professors John D. Glover, Abraham Zaleznik, and Raymond Bauer of our Harvard Business School faculty have continually aided us in our exploration of the general management process.

Present members of the Harvard Business School contributed to the constant developments in our field. We appreciate the help of our colleagues: Robert W. Ackerman, Francis J. Aguilar, Norman A. Berg, Ram Charan, Michael L. Lovdal, John B. Matthews, Robert W. Merry, John W. Rosenblum, Malcolm S. Salter, Bruce R. Scott, Audrey T. Sproat, Eoin W. Trevelyan, and Hugo E. Uyterhoeven.

Our sincere appreciation goes to the supervisors and authors of the cases included in this edition. To the following our thanks: Robert W. Ackerman for Xerox (B); Norman A. Berg and Charles W. Hofer for Aerosol Techniques and Heublein, Inc.; Peter Brengel for Solartron; Paul Donham and David C. D. Rogers for Multi-Products, Inc.; James Garrison for Crown Cork and Seal and the Note on the Metal Container Industry; John Grant for Stone Petroleum International; William D. Guth for the Olivetti series; Michael Hunt (assisted by John McMullen) for the Home Appliance Industry and Trade Association Notes and company case; and Edmund P. Learned for The Rose Company. Our thanks also to Michael L. Lovdal for the Raadgevend Bureau IR Berenschot N. V. series; Quinn McKay, Michael Farmer, and Charles B. Saunders for Heuer Leonidas; John Priedman (assisted by Robert C. K. Valtz) for the Note on the Portland Cement Industry and the Rugby series; John W. Rosenblum for Basic Industries, Industrial Products, and Richardson Company; Bruce R. Scott for American Motors; Audrey T. Sproat for J. I. Case Company, and the Drug Industry series; Howard H. Stevenson for Head Ski Company, Inc. and Dennison Manufacturing Company; Eoin W. Trevelyan for Sigma and Erikson Industries; Charles B. Weigle for Prelude Corporation and American Motors, Part II; H. Edward Wrapp (assisted by L. A. Guthart) for Texas Instruments; and Abraham Zaleznik (assisted by John M. Wynne) for the Saturday Evening Post case.

We are indebted to Kenneth Andrews for all of the text material found in this book. In those chapters—as in his pioneering volume *The Concept of Corporate Strategy*[3]—Professor Andrews brings us critical insights into the strategic decision-making process.

We owe special thanks to Julie Muenchen for her management of the production of this edition. She has carried out her assignment with efficiency and good humor. Winifred I. Barnard, Terry Cauthorn, and Josepha M. Perry have contributed much to the secretarial and editorial side of our venture.

Jean C. Corthesy, Chairman of Nestle Alimentana and Chairman of the Board of Trustees of IMEDE, and Dean Luigi Dusmet, Director of IMEDE, have been most generous in allowing our use of IMEDE cases. IMEDE has been the leader in developing policy field cases in Europe. We hope to continue our collaboration with IMEDE's policy research program.

This third edition of *Business Policy: Text and Cases* has a changed authorship group. Andrews and Christensen are joined in this effort by Joseph Bower. He brings new disciplines to our study of the policy process.

William Guth is now a senior professor of business policy at the New York University Graduate School of Business Administration. He maintains his strong research and teaching interests in policy; we look forward to further collaboration with him.

Edmund P. Learned, to whom this book is dedicated, is enjoying a very well deserved retirement. We acknowledge again his significant contribution to the policy area and his qualities of loyalty, integrity, and compassion which have made him such a great teacher and friend.

Dean Lawrence E. Fouraker and Associate Dean George F. F. Lombard together with their predecessors, George P. Baker and Stanley F. Teale, have provided steady support for our research and teaching programs. The McKinsey Foundation for Management Research and the Donaldson, Lufkin, and Jenrette Foundation have sponsored conferences concerned with teaching and research in business policy here at Harvard. These gatherings have been most productive for all concerned.

Andrew R. Towl, Director of Case Development and Director of the Intercollegiate Case Clearing House, Robert W. Merry, Director of Course Development, and Charles N. Gebhard, Director of Case Distri-

---

[3] K. R. Andrews, *The Concept of Corporate Strategy*, Dow Jones-Irwin, Inc., 1971.

bution have been most helpful in a wide variety of administrative matters.

We hope this book, in which the efforts of so many good people is compressed, will contribute to constructive concern for corporate purposes and accomplishments and to the continuing effective study and practice of business policy.

C. R. C.
K. R. A.
J. L. B.

Contents

The nature of the company's environment. Identification of opportunities and risks. Opportunity as a determinant of strategy. Determining corporate competence and resources. Application to cases.

The company and its strategists: Relating economic strategy and personal values 432

Strategy as projection of preference. Modification of values. Awareness of values.

The company and its societal responsibilities: Relating corporate strategy and moral values 578

The moral aspect of strategic choice. Relevance of the public good. Conflict of responsibilities. Corporate responsibility and individual self-expression. The problem of final choice.

BOOK TWO
IMPLEMENTING CORPORATE STRATEGY

The accomplishment of purpose: Organizational structure and relationships 673

Interdependence of formulation and implementation. Strategy and organizational structure. Subdivision of task responsibility. Coordination of divided responsibility. Effective design of information systems.

The accomplishment of purpose: Organizational processes and behavior 760

Establishment of standards and measurement of performance. Motivation and incentive systems. Systems of restraint and control. Recruitment and development of management.

Managing the strategic process 862

Strategy as a process. Managing the process.

Introduction

Introduction

BUSINESS POLICY AS A FIELD OF STUDY

THIS BOOK is intended as an instrument for the study of Business Policy. As a field in business administration, Policy is the study of the functions and responsibilities of general management and the problems which affect the character and success of the total enterprise. The problems of policy in business, like those of policy in public affairs, have to do with the choice of purposes, the molding of organizational character, the definition of what needs to be done, and the mobilization of resources for the attainment of goals in the face of competition or adverse circumstance. On occasions when more urgent but less important operating problems permit, policy is what the president of a country or a corporation is likely to think about at night.

In Business Policy, the problems considered and the point of view assumed in analyzing and dealing with them are those of the chief executive or general manager, whose primary responsibility is the enterprise as a whole. But while the study of Business Policy (under whatever name it may be called) should be the capstone of professional business education, its usefulness goes far beyond the direct preparation of future general managers and chief executives for the responsibilities of office. In an age of increasing complexity and advancing specialization, and in companies where no person knows how to do what every other person does, it becomes important that the specialist possess the ability to discern corporate purpose, to make recommendations for its clarification or development, and to shape his[1] own contributions, not by the canons of his specialization, but by his perception of the needs of the organization as a whole. The special needs of individuals and the technical requirements of specialized groups and disciplines inevitably

---

[1] Throughout this book, whenever *he* or *his* is used to refer to *person, specialist, student, manager*, etc., we mean (but wish to avoid the awkwardness of) *he or she* and *his or her*.

develop points of view that ultimately come into conflict with one another and with the central purposes of the organization they serve. The
specialist who is able to exercise control over this tendency in organizational life and to keep his deference to the conventions of his own
specialty subordinate to the needs of his company becomes free to make
creative contributions to its progress and growth. To be thus effective in
his organization, he must have a sense of its mission, of its character,
and of its importance. If he does not know the purposes he serves, he can
hardly serve them well. Most users of this book will neither be nor become corporation presidents, but virtually all can benefit from the
detachment implicit in the presidential point of view.

The purposes of organized effort, in business as elsewhere, are usually
neither clear, fixed, nor unchanging. Except in abstract language they
cannot be communicated once and for all to the variety of persons whose
effort and commitment are required. It is not enough, therefore, for
senior executives to issue statements of policy and for junior managers
to acquiesce and proceed. In each subunit of an organization and in
each individual, corporate purpose must become meaningful in ways
that announcement cannot accomplish. It must be brought into balance
with individual and departmental needs, satisfactions, and noneconomic
aspirations. But if corporate purpose is to be reconciled with rather than
subordinated to individual and departmental purposes, then there must
be widespread knowledge of the considerations on which corporate policy
is based, and widespread understanding of the risks by which it is
threatened. In addition, the adaptation of corporate purpose to changing
circumstances, to tactical countermoves by competitors, or to newly
identified opportunities, is assisted if there can be *informed* participation
in policy thinking by subordinate executives from different ranks and
groups. This advantage, however, can be realized only if these subordinates are capable of looking beyond the narrow limits of their own
specializations. Thus the study of Policy is not as remote from the immediate concerns of the apprentice manager or the student of business
as at first appears. In fact, whenever a person is challenged—in business
or out—by the problem of establishing goals *for himself* that will shape
a productive and satisfying life, he will find the study of the process of
determining strategy of central relevance. It is helpful to personal as
well as to corporate decision, and to the discovery of the individual's
own powers and the purposes to which they might well be devoted.

The study of Business Policy provides, therefore, a direct if distant
preparation for performance as a general manager, and a less direct but
more immediate broadening of the provincial perspective of the specialist. In addition, it may be viewed as resulting in certain *knowledge,*
attitudes, and *skills.* Some of these are unique to Policy studies. Others
may have germinated in other activities and learning. But the latter are
brought to fruition by examination of the most fundamental issues and
problems that confront the professional manager in the course of a
business career. It may prove useful to characterize briefly the expected
outcomes.

OBJECTIVES IN KNOWLEDGE

The choice of objectives and the formulation of policy to guide action in attainment of objectives depend upon many variables unique to a given organization and situation. It is not possible to make useful generalizations about the nature of these variables or to classify their possible combinations in all situations. Knowledge of what, *in general*, Policy is and should be is incomplete and inconclusive. The knowledge to be gained from Policy studies is therefore primarily a familiarity with an approach to the policy problems of business and public affairs which makes it possible, in conjunction with attitudes and skills to be discussed later, to combine these variables into a pattern valid for one organization. This pattern may then be examined against accepted criteria and tested for its quality.

The basic concept that the student of Policy will in time come to understand is the concept of *strategy*, since the design and implementation of strategy provide the intellectual substance of this study. What is meant by *strategy* and, more important, how this concept may be usefully employed in the choice and accomplishment of purpose is the subject of the rest of this book. Strategy will be the idea unifying the discussions in which the student will engage. These discussions will involve cerebral activities more important than simply acquiring information.

An abundance of information about business practice is, nonetheless, a by-product of the study of Business Policy—and other—cases. In their deliberately planned variety, the cases in this book encompass many industries, companies, and business situations. Although the information contained in these cases is provided mainly to permit consideration of policy issues, the importance of this incidental knowledge should not be underestimated. Breadth of exposure to the conventions, points of view, and practices of many industries is inoculation against the assumption that all industries are basically the same or that all men and women in business share the same values and beliefs. Thus consideration of the policy problems of a number of different industries guards against distraction by the particular in seeking out the nature of the universal.

For this reason it is hoped that the student—although he may be, or plan to be, an engineer in a utility or the vice president of a railroad—will not resent learning about the economics of the cement industry of England or the problems of allocating research funds in an electronics firm. Knowledge of the environment and problems of other industries and companies is something that the student may never consciously use. It will nevertheless widen the perspective which he brings to his own problems. It may stimulate the imagination he puts to work in introducing innovation into the obsolescent practices of his own industry. It should provide a broader base for his powers of generalization.

The study of strategy as a concept will be relatively systematic; the acquisition of information about the management problems of the many firms and industries whose strategic problems are presented in this book will be less orderly. Both are important. In particular the time spent in mastering the detail of the cases will ultimately seem to be of greater value than at first appears.

A considerable body of literature purporting to make general statements about policy making is in existence. It generally reflects either the unsystematically reported experience of individuals or the logical projection to general management of concepts taken from engineering, economics, psychology, sociology, or mathematics. Neither suffices. What people wise in practice have to say is often instructive, but intuitive skill cannot be changed into conscious skill by exposition alone. The disciplines cited have much to do with business, but their purposes are not ours. Knowledge generated for one set of ends is not readily applicable to another. Besides reported experience and borrowed concepts, the literature of the field also includes some first fruits of independent research, guided by designs derived from the idea of strategy. Such research has been for some time under way, but it is not yet advanced enough to make more than a modest claim on our attention. Thus, though we shall often allude to the expository literature of Policy and shall, where appropriate, acknowledge our considerable indebtedness to it, yet the most valid literature for our purpose is not that of general statements but case studies.[2] These present, not illustrations of principle, but data from which generalizations may to a limited degree be derived and to which the idea of strategy may be usefully applied.

OBJECTIVES IN ATTITUDES

Knowledge of either concepts or cases is less the objective of the study of Policy than certain attitudes and skills. What a manager knows by way of verifiable fact about management appears to us less important than the attitudes, aspirations, and values that he brings to his tasks. Instructors in Policy do not have a dogma which they force upon their students, but most of them, like their students, appear to be influenced in their analysis and conclusions by characteristic assumptions. Thus indoctrination is implicit in the study of the ideas and cases included in this book; this indoctrination—tempered by the authors' exhortation to the student to think always for himself—is comprised of some important beliefs of which the student should be aware.

The attitudes appropriate to the resolution of policy problems are several. First, the frame of mind which the student will be encouraged to adopt and which will influence the outcome of his thinking is that of the *generalist* rather than the specialist. Breadth, it follows, takes

---

[2] In addition to the cases in this book, the reader is referred to such volumes as G. A. Smith, Jr., C. R. Christensen, N. A. Berg, and M. S. Salter, *Policy Formulation and Administration;* E. P. Learned, C. R. Christensen, and K. R. Andrews, *Problems of General Management;* E. P. Learned, F. J. Aguilar and R. C. K. Valtz, *European Problems in General Management;* and H. E. R. Uyterhoeven, R. W. Ackerman, and J. W. Rosenblum, *Strategy and Organization: Text and Cases in General Management* (all published by Richard D. Irwin, Inc., Homewood, Illinois). Many other cases from a variety of sources are listed in the bibliographies of the Intercollegiate Case Clearing House, Soldiers Field, Boston, Mass. 02163.

precedence over depth. Since attitudes appropriate for the generalist are not always appropriate for the specialist, the two will sometimes come into conflict. Efforts to resolve this conflict in practice should help to prove that breadth which is shallow is no more satisfactory than depth which is narrow.

A second outlook encountered in the study of Business Policy is the point of view of the *practitioner* as opposed to that of the researcher or scientist. A willingness to act in the face of incomplete information and to run the risk of being proved wrong by subsequent events will be developed in the classroom as pressure is brought to bear on the student to make decisions on the problems before him and to determine what he, as the manager responsible, would do about them. Despite the explosion of knowledge and the widely heralded advance of electronic data processing, it is still true that decisions affecting the business firm as a whole must almost always be made in the face of incomplete information. Uncertainty is the lot of all thoughtful leaders who must act, whether they are in government, education, or business. Acceptance of the priority of risk-taking and problem-resolution over completeness of information is sometimes hard for students of science and engineering to achieve. Though natural and understandable, hesitation in the face of the managerial imperative to make decisions will impede the study of Policy. At the same time, rashness, overconfidence, and the impulse to act without analysis will be discouraged.

The third set of attitudes to be developed is the orientation of the professional manager as distinct from the self-seeking contriver of deals. The energetic opportunist sometimes has motives which are inconsistent with the approach to policy embodied in this book. This is not to say that quick response to opportunity and entrepreneurial energy are not qualities to be admired. Our assumption will be that the role of the business manager includes but goes beyond the entrepreneurial function. We shall examine what we acknowledge to be the obligations of the business community to the rest of society. We shall be concerned with the quality as well as the clarity of the alternative purposes we consider and of our final choice. Maximum short-run profit is not what we mean when we consider the purpose of business enterprise. At the same time it is assumed that profit is desirable and indispensable. It is one of the necessary *results* of business activity.

A fourth set of attitudes to be evoked is one that attaches more value to creativity and innovation than to maintenance of the status quo. We have grown accustomed to innovation stemming from new inventions and advancing technology. But suiting policy to changing circumstances includes also the application of a firm's long-established strengths to unexplored segments of the market via innovations in price, service, distribution, or merchandising.

In any course of study that has as its object enabling practitioners to learn more from subsequent experience than they otherwise might, the attitudes appropriate to the professional activity being taught are as important as knowledge. It is therefore expected that the student will take time to determine for himself the particular point of view, the values, and the morality which he feels are appropriate to the effective exercise of general management skills. Much more could be said about the frame of mind and qualities of temperament that are most appropriate to business leadership, but we will do better to let these exhibit themselves in the discussion of case problems.

OBJECTIVES IN SKILLS

Extensive knowledge and positive attitudes, desirable as both are, come to little if not effectively applied. The skills that a course in Business Policy seeks to develop and mature are at once analytical and administrative. Since even with a variety of simulation and the use of case situations drawn from life, the reality of responsibility can only be approximated in a professional school, we may look to make most progress in analytical power and to use it in actual experience to develop executive ability.

The study of Policy cases, unlike, for example, the effort to comprehend these expository notes, requires the student to develop and broaden the analytical ability he brings to the task from other studies. The policy problems of the total enterprise are not labeled as accounting, financial, marketing, production, or human relations problems. The student is not forewarned of the kind of problem he can expect and of which tool kit he should have with him. He must now consider problems in relation to one another, distinguish the more from the less important, and consider the impact of his approach to one problem upon all the others. He will bring to the cases his knowledge and abilities in special fields, but he will be asked to diagnose first the total situation and to persist in seeking out central problems through all the distraction presented by manifest symptoms.

The study of Policy, besides having its own jurisdiction, has an integrative function. It asks the analyst to view a company as an organic entity comprising a system in itself, but related also to the larger systems of its environment. In each diagnostic situation, the student must pull together the separate concepts he has studied in functional and basic discipline courses and adapt them to a less structured set of problems. He must be able to see and to devise patterns of information, activities, and relationships. If he deals one at a time with the facts he is given or the problems he observes, he will be overwhelmed.

Besides extending to the company as a multifaceted whole the knowledge and analytic skills developed in his less comprehensive studies, the student of Policy must acquire some additional abilities. These are abilities particularly needed to deal with the concept of strategy. Under the heading of thinking about strategy, the student will be asked to examine the economic environment of the company, to determine the essential characteristics of the industry, to note its developments and trends, and to estimate future opportunity and risks for firms of varying resources and competence. He will be asked to appraise the strengths and weaknesses of the particular firm he is studying when viewed against the background of its competition and its environment, and he will be asked to estimate its capacity to alter as well as to adapt to the forces affecting it. Finally, he will be asked to make a decision putting market opportunity and corporate capability together into a suitable entrepreneurial combination. At this point he will realize the full measure of the new skill required. The strategic decision is the one that determines the nature of the business in which a company is to engage and the kind of company it is to be. As such, it is the most important decision to be made for the company. It requires the best judgment and analysis that can be brought to it. Practice in making this decision while still safe from most of the consequences of error is one of the most important advantages offered by an education for business.

But analysis is not the whole of the task implied by the concept of strategy. Once the entrepreneurial decision has been determined, the resources of the organization must be mobilized to make it effective. Devising organizational relationships appropriate to the tasks to be performed, determining the specialized talents required, and assisting and providing for the development of individuals and subgroups are essential tasks of strategy and policy implementation. These tasks, together with those of prescribing a system of incentives and controls that will be appropriate to the performance required, and determining the impetus that can be given to achievement by the general manager's personal style of leadership, demand of the student that he bring to the discussion of Policy everything he has learned about administrative processes.

Administrative skills can be approached, though not captured, in the classroom. Patterns of action will be judged as consistent or inconsistent with the strategy selected according to criteria which must be developed. The student approaches the study of Business Policy with skills nurtured in his studies of accounting and control, personnel and human relations, financial management, manufacturing, and marketing; the balanced application of these skills to the accomplishment of chosen purpose in a unique organizational situation is the best test of their power. Any failure to see the impact on the program as a whole of a decision based on the tenets of a special discipline will be sharply called to its proponent's attention by the defenders of other points of view.

General management skills center intellectually upon relating the firm to its environment and administratively upon coordinating departmental specialties and points of view. Some students of business and even some students of Policy believe that these skills cannot be taught. General management is indeed an art to be learned in the last analysis only through years of responsible experience. And even through experience it can be learned only by those with the necessary native qualities: intelligence, a sense of responsibility, and administrative ability.

But if education means anything at all, a student with the requisite native qualities can learn more readily and more certainly from experience, and can more readily identify the kinds of seminal experience to seek, if he has at his disposal a conceptual framework with which to comprehend the analytical and administrative skills he will require and the nature of the situation in which he will find himself. If, in addition, he has had practice in making and debating the merits of policy decisions, he will be more likely to grow in qualification for senior management responsibility than if he is submerged is operational detail and preoccupied by the intricacies of technique.

This book is not a manual for policy makers or a how-to-do-it checklist for corporate planners. In fact it virtually ignores the mechanisms of planning on the grounds that they often miss their mark. The authors do not believe that the conceptual framework described here can take the place of informed judgment. All the knowledge, professional attitudes, and analytical and administrative skills in the world cannot fully replace the intuitive genius of some of the natural entrepreneurs the student will encounter in this book. Native powers cannot be counterfeited by book learning.

We do not even propose book learning in the usual sense. We plan instead to give men and women with latent imagination the opportunity to exercise it in a disciplined way under critical observation. We expect to prepare people for the assumption of responsibility by exposing them to the temptation of expediency. We plan to press for clarification of personal purposes and to challenge shoddy or ill-considered values. We expect to affect permanently analytical habits of mind in a way that will permit assimilation of all, rather than part, of experience. The ideas, attitudes, and skills here discussed are adequate for a lifetime study of one of the most vitally important of all human activities—leadership in organizations. Education is the prelude to true learning, which often does not take place without it.

The need for general management ability is far too acute to be left to chance. The ideas, attitudes, and skills that comprise this study are much in demand not only throughout our own economy but also—in this age of rapid economic development abroad—throughout the world. In addition to their utility, these ideas are their own reward. For those who wish to lead an active life, or to provide for themselves and their families the material comfort and education that make culture possible, or to make substantial contributions to human welfare, the acquisition of policy skills is essential. Not all who turn to business are called to leadership, to be sure, but all are affected by it. No one suffers from study of its place in business.

THE NATURE OF THE TEXT AND CASES

The vehicles here provided for making progress toward these objectives are the text and cases that follow. All the cases are drawn from real life; none is selected to prove a point or draw a moral. Accuracy has been attested to by the sources from which information was taken; disguise has not been allowed to alter essential issues.

The text is designed to assist in the development of an effective approach to the cases. Its content is important only if it helps the student to make his analysis, to choose and defend his conclusions, and to decide what ought to be done and how it can be accomplished.

The text is dispersed throughout the book so as to permit a step-by-step consideration of what is involved in corporate strategy and in the subactivities required for its formulation and implementation. The order of cases is only partially determined by the sequence of ideas in the text. Each case should be approached without preconceptions as to what is to come. To make conceptual progress possible without predetermining the student's analysis of the problem or the nature of his recommendations, the cases focus initially on problems in strategy formulation and later on problems of building the organization and leading it to the accomplishment of the tasks assigned. As the course unfolds, considerations pertinent to previous cases are included in the new cases. Students should not feel constrained in their analysis by the position of the case in the book; they are free to decide that an apparent problem of strategy implementation is actually a problem of strategy choice. However, the increasing complexity of the material provided will enable most students to feel a natural and organic evolution of subject matter, in keeping with their own evolving understanding, perspective, and skill.

The text suggests only that order is possible in approaching the enormous purview of Policy. The concept of strategy is an idea that experience has shown to be useful to researchers and practitioners alike in developing a comprehension of, and an approach to, policy problems. It is not a "theory" attended in the traditional sense by elegance and rigor. Only a very kindly "management scientist" will call it a "model," inasmuch as the relationships designated by the concept are not quantifiable. But in lieu of a better theory or a more precise model, it will serve as an informing idea to which we can return again and again with increasing understanding after dealing with one unique case situation after another. The idea is intended to sharpen the analytical skills developed in the process of case discussion, and to serve as the basis for identifying uniformities and generalizations that will be useful later on, in practice. Our energies should be spent not so much on perfecting the definition of the concept as on using it in preparing to discuss the cases and in coming to conclusions about their issues. The student will not really learn how to distinguish effective from ineffective recommendations and good from bad judgment by his study of the "word," but rather by active argument with his classmates. Such discussion should always end in the clarification of his own standards and criteria. The cases, we know from experience, provide stimulating opportunity for productive differences of opinion.

The president's job—roles, functions, and skills

WE POINTED OUT in the introduction to this book that Business Policy is essentially the study of the knowledge, skills, and attitudes constituting general management. *Management* we regard as leadership in the informed, planned, purposeful conduct of complex organized activity. *General* management is in its simplest form the management of a total enterprise. As we prepare to examine some cases which will present summarily the range of issues we will eventually consider more thoroughly, we should look at the general manager himself. The senior general manager in any organization is its chief executive officer, who for the purposes of simplicity we will usually call henceforth the *president*. As we said earlier, the role of the president in examining the situation of a company may be initially an uncomfortable assignment for students of some modesty who think themselves insufficiently prepared for such high responsibility. It is nonetheless the best vantage point from which to view the processes involved in (1) the conception of organization purpose, (2) the decision to commit an organization to deliberately chosen purposes, and (3) the effort required to achieve purposes decided upon.

We will therefore begin by considering the *roles* which a president must play. We will examine the *functions,* or characteristic and natural actions, which he performs in the roles he assumes. We will try to identify *skills* or abilities to put one's perceptions, judgment, and knowledge to effective use in executive performance. As we look at presidential *roles, functions,* and *skills,* we may be able to define more clearly aspects of the *point of view* which provides the most suitable perspective for high-level executive judgment.

The principal roles of the president can be viewed as being *organization leader, personal leader,* and *chief architect of organization purpose.* As leader of persons grouped in a hierarchical variety of suborganizations, the president must be taskmaster, mediator, motivator, and

12

organization designer. As leader his personal influence becomes evident as he plays the part of communicator, exemplar, or focus for respect or affection. When we examine finally the president's role as architect of organization purpose, we may see him behaving, if his organization is just being born, chiefly as entrepreneur or improvisor. If his company is long since established, the part he plays may be more accurately designated as manager of the purpose-determining process or chief strategist.

The point of this nontechnical classification of role is not its universality, exactness of definition, or inclusiveness. We seek only to establish that every general manager faces such an array of functions and must exercise so various a set of skills as to require of him a protean versatility as a performing executive. When you see Howard Head invent and perfect the metal ski, set up his company, devise a merchandising and distribution program of a very special kind, you see him in a role different from his arranging for the future of his business, his maintaining year-round production in a cyclical industry in order to meet the needs of his work force, his withdrawal from supervision of the company, and his selection of a successor. We make no claim to definitiveness in distinguishing executive roles as just attempted. It is essential to note, however, that the job of the general manager demands successful action in a *variety* of roles, which vary according to the nature of the problem observed or decision pending, the needs of the organization, or the personality and style of the president himself. The simpleminded adherence to one role—one personality-determined, for example —will leave the president miscast much of the time as the human drama he presides over unfolds.

We are in great need of a simple way to comprehend the president's total responsibility. To multiply endlessly the list of tasks he must perform and the personal qualities it would be good to see in him would put general management capability beyond that of a reasonably well-endowed human being. In truth his responsibility is formidable, no matter how one views it. The corporate president is accountable for everything that goes on in his organization. He must preside over a total enterprise made up often of the technical specialties in which he cannot possibly have personal expertness. He must know his company's markets and the way in which they are changing. He must lead a private life as a citizen in his community and as a family member, as an individual with his own needs and aspirations. Except for rare earlier experience, perhaps as general manager of a profit center in his own organization, he has found no opportunity to practice being president before undertaking the office. Very little, except in the study of policy for which this book is intended to be the basis, has been available for the training or education of general managers. The new president is obliged to put behind him the specialized apparatus his functional experience has provided him. The engineer, for example, who continues to run his company strictly as an engineer will soon encounter financial and marketing problems, among others, that will force his removal.

This book, together with the directed series of case discussions which will bring its substance alive, is intended to provide a way for the observer to comprehend the complexity of the president's job and for the president to put his past experience into the perspective of his new assignment and comprehend the world of which he has been put in charge. We will elaborate briefly the functions, skills, and point of view which give executive force and substance to the major roles we have just designated. This may lay a foundation for later discussion of the performance of presidents in the cases that follow. In due course we will have to identify an organizing perspecitve to reduce to practicable order the otherwise impossible agenda of the president.

THE PRESIDENT AS ORGANIZATION LEADER

The president is first and probably least pleasantly the person who is responsible for results attained in the present as designated by plans made previously. Nothing that we will say shortly about his concern for the people in his organization or later about his responsibility to society can gainsay this immediate truth. Achieving acceptable results against expectations of increased earnings per share and return on the stockholder's investment requires the president to be continually informed and ready to intervene when results fall below what had been expected. Changing circumstances and competition produce emergencies to upset well-laid plans. Resourcefulness in responding to crisis is a skill which most successful presidents develop early.

But the organizational consequences of the taskmaster role require the president to go beyond insistence upon achievement of planned results. He must see as his second principal function the maintenance and development of the organized capability which makes achievement possible. This activity leads to a third—the coordination of the specialist functions which enable his organization to perform the technical tasks in marketing, research and development, manufacturing, finance, control, and personnel, which proliferate as technology develops and tend to lead the company in all directions. If this coordination is successful in harmonizing special staff activities, then the president will probably have performed the task of getting the organization to accept and to order its priorities in accordance with the company's objectives. Securing commitment to purpose is a central function of the president as organization leader.

The skills required by these functions reveal the president not solely as taskmaster but as mediator and motivator as well. He should have ability in the education and motivation of people and the evaluation of their performance, two functions which tend to work against one another. The former requires understanding of individual needs, which persist no matter what the economic purpose of the organization. The latter requires objective assessment of the technical requirements of the task assigned. The capability required here is also that required in the integration of functions and the mediation of conflict bound to arise out of the values and provincialism of technical specialism. The integrating capacity of the chief executive extends to meshing the economic, technical, human, and moral dimensions of corporate activity and to relating the company to its immediate and more distant communities. It will show itself in the formal organization designs which he puts into effect as the blueprint of the structured cooperation that is required.

The perspective demanded of the successful organization leader embraces both the primacy of organization goals and the validity of individual goals. Besides this dual appreciation, he should have and exhibit an impartiality toward the specialized functions and criteria enabling him to allocate organization resources against their demands. The point of view of the leader of an organization almost by definition requires an overview of its relations not only to its internal constituencies but to the relevant institutions and forces of its external environment. A large order and a problem very demanding upon the conceptual solution which we will soon bring to it.

THE PRESIDENT AS A PERSONAL LEADER

The functions, skills, and relevant point of view of the president as leader of the organization hold true no matter who he is or who makes up his organization. The functions that accompany the president's performance of his role as communicator of purpose and policy, as exemplar, and as the focal point for the respect or affection of his subordinates vary much more according to his own energy, style, personality, and integrity. The president contributes as a person to the quality of life and performance in his organization. This is true whether he be dynamic or colorless. By his example he educates junior executives who seek to emulate him or simply to learn from his behavior what he really expects. He has the opportunity to infuse organized effort with flair or distinction if he has the skill to dramatize the relationship between his own activities and the goals of corporate effort. He sets in his own demeanor even more than in policy statements the moral and ethical level of performance expected. It is his function also to cultivate and embody a relationship between himself and his subordinates appropriate to the style of leadership he has chosen or fallen into. Students will have opportunity to argue warmly the need for or means of infusing a formally correct organization with an enthusiasm that comes not from the incentive system so much as from the sentiment which is provoked by the personal deportment of the chief executive. By the person he is, as much as by what he says and does, the president influences his organization, affects the development of individuals and the level of organized performance.

The skills of the effective personal leader are those of persuasion and articulation made possible by having something worth saying and understanding the sentiments and points of view being addressed. The maintenance of personal poise in adversity or emergency and the capacity for development as an emotionally mature person are essential innate and developed capabilities. It is probably true that some personal preeminence in a technical or social function is either helpful or essential in demonstrating leadership related to the president's personal contribution. Credibility and cooperation depend upon documented capacity of a kind more tangible and attractive than, for example, the noiseless coordination of staff activity.

The relevant aspects of the presidential point of view brought to mind by his activities in the role of personal leader are probably acknowledgement of his own needs and integrity as a person, and acceptance of the importance to others of their own points of view, behavior, and feelings. His self-awareness will acquaint him with his own personal strengths and weaknesses and keep him mindful of the inevitable unevenness of his own preparation for the functions of general management. These qualities may be more important in the selection of a general manager than in the study of general management. But students of the cases that follow will quickly see that the flamboyant Mr. Rojtman and the prosaic Mr. Grede influenced their organization differently as people, quite apart from their policy decisions. Similarly the personal contribution of George Romney to the survival of American Motors, the values of John Connelly in Crown Cork and Seal, of John Bolton in Solartron, or Sir Halford Reddish in Rugby Portland Cement will call to mind the validity and importance of the corporate leader's contribution as a person to the achievement and character of his company. To incorporate a practical consideration of all the implications of the functions of the president classifiable as personal will further test the utility of any concept purporting to relate the activities of the president in his roles of organization leader, as personal leader, and principal designer of corporate objectives.

THE PRESIDENT AS ARCHITECT OF ORGANIZATION PURPOSE

To go beyond the roles of organizational and personal leadership, we enter the sphere of organization purpose, where we may find the atmosphere somewhat rare and the going less easy. We think students of the companies described in these cases will note, as they see president after president cope or fail to cope with problems of various economic, political, social, or technical casts, that the contribution the president makes to the company goes far beyond the activities that clutter his days. His attention to his organization's needs must extend beyond answering letters of complaint from spouses of aggrieved employees to appraisal, for example, of the impact of his company's information, incentive, and control systems upon individual behavior. His personal contribution to his company goes far beyond personal attention to key customers and speeches at the Economic Club to the influence his own probity and character have upon his subordinates. We must turn now to activities even further out—away from immediate everyday decisions and emergencies and oriented toward maintaining the sustained development of the company over time and preparing for a future more distant than the time horizon appropriate to the roles and functions identified thus far.

The most difficult role—and the one we will concentrate on henceforth—of the chief executive of any organization, is custodian of corporate objectives. The entrepreneur who creates a company knows what he is up to. His objectives are intensely personal, if not exclusively economic, and his passions are patent protection and finance. If he succeeds, like Howard Head, in passing successfully through the phase of personal entrepreneurship, where he and his bankers or family are likely to be the only members of the organization concerned with purpose, he finds himself in the role of planner, managing the process by which ideas for the future course of the company are conceived, evaluated, fought over, and accepted or rejected.

The presidential functions involved include establishing or presiding over the goal-setting and resource-allocation procedures of the company, making or ratifying choice among strategic alternatives, and clarifying and defending the goals of the company against external attack or internal erosion. The installation of purpose in place of improvisation and the substitution of planned progress in place of drifting are probably the most demanding functions of the president. Where successful organization leadership requires great human skill, sensitivity, and administrative ability, and personal leadership is built upon personality and character, the capacity for determining and monitoring the adequacy of the organization's continuing purposes implies as well analytic intelligence of a high order. The president we are talking about is not a two-dimensional poster or TV screen portrait.

The crucial skill of the president concerned with corporate purpose includes the creative generation or recognition of strategic alternatives made valid by developments in the marketplace and in the capability and resources of the company. Along with this, in a combination not easily come by, runs the critical capacity to analyze the strengths and weaknesses of documented proposals. The ability to perceive with some objectivity corporate strengths and weaknesses is essential to sensible choice of goals, for the most attractive goal is not attainable without the strength to open the way to it through inertia and intense opposition, with all else that lies between.

Probably the skill most nearly unique to general management, as opposed to the management of functional or technical specialties, is the intellectual capacity to conceptualize corporate purpose and the dramatic skill to invest it with some degree of magnetism. As we will see, this skill can be exercised in industries less romantic than space, electronics, or environmental redemption. John Connelly did it with tin cans, Sir Halford Reddish with cement. Ralph Hart thought he could do it with beer because he did do it with Smirnoff vodka. No sooner is a distinctive set of corporate objectives vividly delineated than the temptation to go beyond it sets in. Under some circumstances it is the president's function to defend properly focused purpose against superficially attractive diversification or corporate growth that glitters adequately but produces only fool's gold. Because defense of proper strategy can be interpreted to be mindless conservatism, wholly appropriate defense of a still valid strategy requires courage, supported by detailed documentation.

Continuous monitoring, in any event, of the quality and continued suitability of corporate purpose is over time the most sophisticated and essential of all the functions of general management alluded to here. Because of its difficulty and vulnerability to current emergency, this function may not be present in some of the companies the student will shortly encounter in the pages that follow. Because of its low visibility, this activity may not be noticed at first in cases where it is properly present. The perspective which sustains this function is the kind of discontent called divine, which prevents complacency even in good times and seeks continuous advancement of corporate and individual capacity and performance. It requires also constant attention to the future, as if the present did not offer problems and opportunities enough.

ENORMITY OF THE TASK

Even so sketchy a record of what a president is called upon to do is likely to seem an academic idealization, given the disparity between the complexity of role and function and the modest qualifications of those impressed into the office. Like the Molière character who discovered that for 40 years he had been speaking prose without knowing it, many managers have been programmed by instinct and experience to the kind of performance which we have attempted to decipher here. For the inexperienced, the catalog may seem impossibly long.

Essentially, however, we have looked at only three major roles and four sets of responsibilities. The roles deal with the requirements for organizational and personal leadership and for conscious attention to the formulation and promulgation of purpose. The four groups of functions encompass (1) securing the attainment of planned results in the present, (2) developing an organization capable of producing both technical achievement and human satisfactions, (3) making a distinctive personal contribution, and (4) planning and executing policy decisions affecting future results.

Even thus simplified, how to apply this identification of presidential role and function to the incomparably detailed confusion of a national company situation cannot possibly be made clear in the process of generalization. The student using this text will wish to develop his own overview of the general manager's task, stressing those aspects most compatible with his own insight and sense of what to do. No modifications of the deliberately nontechnical language of this summary should slight the central importance of purpose. The theory presented here begins with the assumption that in the life of every organization (corporate or otherwise), every subunit of organization, every human group and individual should be guided by an evolving set of purposes or goals which permit forward movement in a chosen direction and prevent drifting in undesired directions.

NEED FOR A CONCEPT

The complexity of the president's job and the probable desirability of raising intuitive competence to the level of verifiable, conscious, and systematic analysis suggest the need, as indicated earlier, for a unitary concept as useful to the generalist as the canons of technical functions are to the specialist. We will propose shortly a simple practitioner's theory which we hope will reduce the four-faceted responsibility of the company president to more reasonable proportions, make it susceptible to objective research and systematic evaluation, and bring to more well-qualified people the skills it requires. The central concept we call "corporate strategy." It will be required to embrace the entire corporation, to take shape in the terms and conditions in which its business is conducted. It will be constructed from the points of view described so far. Central to this Olympian vantage point is impartiality with impact to the value of individual specialties, including the one through which the president rose to his generalist responsibilities. It will insist upon the values of the special functions in proportion to their contribution to corporate purpose and ruthlessly dispense with those not crucially related to the objectives sought. It necessarily will define the president's role in such a way as to allow delegation of much of the general management responsibility described here without loss of clarity. After students have examined and discussed the roles, functions, and skills evident or missing from the cases that immediately follow these comments, we will present the concept of corporate strategy itself. Our hope will be to make challenging but practicable the connection between the highest priority for goal setting and a durable but flexible definition of a company's goals and major company-determining policies. How to define, decide, put into effect, and defend a conscious strategy appropriate to emerging market opportunity and company capability will then take precedence over and lend order to the fourfold functions of general management here presented.

Despite a shift in emphasis toward the anatomy of a concept and the development of an analytical approach to the achievement of valid corporate strategy, we will not forget the chief executive's special role in contributing quality to purpose through the standards he exercises in the choice of what to do and the way in which it is to be done and through the projection of his own quality as a person. It will remain true, after we have taken apart analytically the process by which strategy is conceived, that executing it at a high professional level will depend upon the depth and durability of the president's personal values, his standards of quality, and the clarity of his character. We will return in a final comment on the management of the strategic process to the truth that the president's function above all is to be the exemplar of a permanent human aspiration—the determination to devote one's powers to jobs worth doing. Conscious attention to corporate strategy will be wasted if it does not elevate the quality of corporate purpose and achievement.

Aerosol Techniques, Inc.

IN JANUARY 1966, Mr. Robert Meyer, a 1965 Harvard MBA, joined Aerosol Techniques, Inc., as director of corporate development. While his immediate concern was the evaluation of numerous acquisition proposals that ATI had received, Mr. Meyer was also responsible for appraising over-all corporate strategy. Shortly after assuming his position, Mr. Meyer concluded that environmental trends might require a strategy change.

Founded in December 1955 by Mr. H. R. Shepherd, a chemist and biologist with aerosol R&D experience dating back to the end of World War II, ATI was a "contract filler," or producer and packager of items marketed to consumers by others. With 1965 sales of $47 million, or about 22% of the total contract filling market, ATI was the largest contract filler of aerosol products in the United States. Yearly growth since 1960 had averaged 46% for sales and 65% for profits. (For financial statements, see Exhibits 1 and 2.)

From the start, ATI's policy had been to emphasize service and development research for new products. As a result, about 95% of 1965 dollar volume was made up of products that ATI had developed in its laboratories either alone or jointly with customers. Mr. Shepherd indicated that ATI did not want to have to compete on a price basis, or to compete with customers by marketing products under its own name. Thus ATI's name was not on any products packed for other firms.

In 1965, ATI was the only contract filler with plants in each major section of the country. These provided an economic advantage over other contract fillers because of the relatively high cost of transporting filled aerosol containers. Nevertheless, Mr. Meyer was worried about ATI's strategy of developing and manufacturing aerosol products for national marketers because of several trends that had developed between 1960 and 1965. Of these, he felt the most important were a general decline in prices and profit margins for filling operations, and a tendency on the part of some national marketers to install their own aerosol filling lines as sales volume increased.

THE AEROSOL INDUSTRY

Aerosol products. The term "aerosol product" was used to describe any product packed in an aerosol container. The total item consisted of a pressurized container, a propellant to supply the desired pressure, the usable product fill, and a cap and valve combination that controlled the release of the product and propellant. While almost any product that was liquid or gaseous at ordinary temperatures could theoretically be packaged in an aerosol container, in actual practice it was often difficult to "marry" the product, the propellant, and the cap and valve into a workable combination. Nevertheless, by 1965 such diverse products as shaving cream, perfume, starch, furniture polish, hair sprays, and room deodorants were sold in aerosol containers.

Industry history and growth. The first aerosol product was the "bug-bomb" of which some 40 million units were produced for issue to servicemen during the last two years of World War II. When the war ended, the bomb was modified for civilian use.

While these first aerosols were high-pressure, refillable types which retailed for $3.98, myriad technical developments soon reduced both pressure and price. As a result, aerosol packaging spread to dozens of other products, as seen in Table 1. According to industry sources,

Table 1

	Year first marketed in aerosol packages
Room deodorants, lacquers, moth proofers	1948
Hair sprays, paints, automobile waxes	1949
Shave lather	1950
Whipped cream	1951
Perfumes	1954
Starches	1955
Glass cleaners	1956
Furniture waxes and polishes	1959
All purpose cleaners, antiperspirants	1962

aerosol packaging would continue to spread to other fields in the future.

Equally important to the rapid growth (about 17% a year between 1955 and 1964) of the aerosol market was the increasing penetration of aerosols as a packaging form in each of the above product areas. The percentage of room deodorants, shave lathers, and colognes packaged in aerosol containers increased from 0% in 1947 to 91%, 82% and 64%, respectively, in 1964 (see Exhibit 3). Moreover, some products, such as hair sprays, were made possible by aerosol packaging.

In 1964, total sales of all aerosol-packaged products reached over 1.3 billion units. All but 6% of this total was made up of nonfood items, of which 46% were personal products, 30% household products, and 24% miscellaneous products (see Exhibit 4). Table 2 gives examples of the types of products included in each category:

Table 2

Personal products	Household products	Miscellaneous products
Shave lathers	Room deodorants and disin-	Paints and
Hair sprays and dressings	fectants	coatings
Medicinals	Cleaners (all types)	Insecticides
Colognes and perfumes	Household waxes and	Automotive waxes
Personal deodorants	polishes	Veterinarian and
Other (shampoos, suntan	Starches	pet products
preparations, hand	Shoe and leather	Industrial products
lotions, etc.)	dressings	

Industry observers expected each of these major categories to grow at least 8% a year during the coming decade. Du Pont, for example, in a 1965 market report, forecast that between 1965 and 1967 sales of personal products would increase 14% a year, household products 12%, and all other nonfood products 10%.

Estimates of aerosol growth for foods were more uncertain. While sales of nonfood aerosols had increased more than 19% a year between 1955 and 1964, the sales of aerosol-packaged foods had increased less than 2% a year (see Exhibit 5). However, in 1963 and 1964, du Pont gained approval from the Food and Drug Administration for two new tasteless propellants. According to some industry sources, these promised to overcome previous technical problems and to open the way to aerosol packaging of a wide variety of foods—from staples such as peanut butter and cheese spread to additives such as vermouth. As a consequence, some industry sources were predicting in 1965 that the growth curve for food products would soon begin to resemble that of nonfood aerosols.

Reasons for aerosol usage.   According to a study by the Freon Products Division of du Pont, there were three primary reasons for the use of aerosol packaging: (1) increased product effectiveness, (2) greater user convenience, and (3) time savings. The study noted that not all successful applications exhibited all three advantages; even where effectiveness was not improved, convenience alone was often enough to stimulate sales.

Nevertheless, aerosol packaging was relatively expensive (see Exhibits 6 and 7). Some observers felt that cost would restrict the use of aerosol packaging for products with low profit margins.

Industry structure.   During World War II, the Bridgeport Brass Company produced most of the "bugbombs" used by the armed services. After the war, this company continued to make "bugbombs" which it sold through its regular sales force. Soon, however, Bridgeport, which had no product development activities, was forced out of the aerosol market by contract fillers, which carried on intensive product development programs. These contract fillers were small, regional companies which would purchase the cans from national firms such as American Can Company, the propellants from firms such as du Pont and the caps and valves from small companies like themselves. They would then assemble these components, including the product fill, which they usually manufactured, into the final aerosol product. The contract fillers would then sell the finished product to marketing firms, which resold to retailers under their own brands. By 1950, at least 50 firms met the contract filler definition.

As the demand for aerosols grew, two changes occurred in industry structure. First, the contract fillers became larger through both internal growth and acquisition of other contract fillers. Second, some national marketers began to erect their own filling facilities since they felt their volume now warranted such a move. Such a marketer was called a "captive filler."

By 1964, output of nonfood aerosols was about evenly divided between captive and contract fillers (see Exhibit 8). Most industry observers felt a definite trend toward captive filling had not yet emerged among national marketers, however. While firms such as Colgate, S. C. Johnson, Alberto-Culver, Johnson & Johnson, Mennen, and Gillette had established their own filling lines, firms such as Procter & Gamble and Breck still relied on contract fillers. Moreover, most of the firms that had established their own filling lines still relied on contract fillers to supplement their own production during peak sales periods.

The difficulty of deciding between captive vs. contract filling was partly responsible for the lack of a definite trend. The economics of the decision required the marketing company to consider not only the cost of filling equipment and personnel, but also distribution costs, inventory costs (since the contract filler usually kept part of the inventory), and research and development costs (since many contract fillers developed new product formulations for the marketers). In addition, the marketing company had to consider noneconomic factors such as the need for security in protecting the product formulation and the need for tight quality control.

One industry source (not ATI) agreed that the issue of captive vs. contract filling was complex. He estimated, however, that a yearly volume of 5 million units in a standard product might be an "average breakeven point" as far as the economics of the filling operation were involved. Although some companies used captive operations for as few as 1 million units a year, and others used contract fillers for annual volumes as high as 10 million, he felt that these companies were clear exceptions and were probably influenced by other-than-economic factors. He also thought that it was becoming easier for companies to set up their own filling operations, since the necessary equipment could readily be purchased, and an increasing number of people with experience in aerosol filling operations were becoming available.

Other industry observers felt that many marketers would not go captive because of the low profit margins on filling. They reasoned that such marketers would be far more interested in new marketing opportunities which promised high margins than in a production activity with a rapid rate of technological change. (For further discussion of the advantages of using a contract filler, see Exhibit 9.)

Contract fillers and their strategies.   Although the aerosol filling industry had grown tremendously, it had nevertheless become increasingly competitive during the mid-1960s as the 98 independent contract fillers fought for a large but limited supply of contracts. The intensity of competition was suggested by the fact that three contract fillers had been forced into bankruptcy in 1963, and Old Empire, Inc., of Clifton, New Jersey, one of the oldest and most respected names in aerosols, had also filed a bankruptcy petition.

On the other hand, several large companies entered the aerosol business through acquisitions. Borden's, for example, in 1963 and 1964 acquired Krylon, an aerosol paint manufacturer, and Aerosol Brands, a general contract filler. During the same period, Corn Products Company bought Peterson Filling in order to package its products in aerosol containers.

In an article in *Aerosol Age,* the industry trade journal, Mr. H. R. Shepherd, president of ATI, discussed the future role of the independent contract filler as follows:

> It is clear that in the future there will be only two types of contract fillers—first, the filler with national distribution and plants strategically distributed throughout the nation (or in several countries) which can adequately service a national or international marketing concern. The other type of successful contract filler will be the small filler, who can handle low volume runs of specialty products or products that are only beginning to be felt in the market-place.[1]

Vim Laboratories exemplified the latter type of company. One of the few publicly owned fillers, Vim had annual sales only slightly above $1 million. Custom filling represented part of its business, but the company's own specialty line, which included insecticides, paints, room deodorants, shaving cream, Christmas snow, insect repellent, sun tan lotion, and charcoal lighter, represented a significant portion of aerosol capacity.

George Barr & Company, which had been purchased by Pittsburgh Railways Company in 1962, was the second largest contract filler in the United States in 1965. Barr's 1962 sales had exceeded $15 million, but had not been reported separately since 1962. In May 1965, the company unveiled a new filling plant in Niles, Illinois, which was described as "the largest aerosol filling plant in the world." Barr's apparent strategy was to become a "packaging consultant." With this objective in mind, Pittsburgh Railways in 1963 and 1964 had acquired Advance Packaging Company, a filler of nonaerosol packages and Aero Valve Corporation, a manufacturer of caps and valves for aerosol containers.

Power-Pak, Inc., of Bridgeport, Connecticut, was a medium-sized contract filler. In 1962, Power-Pak formed agreements with three other contract fillers—one English, one Canadian, and one midwestern domes-

---

[1] H. R. Shepherd, "The Contract Filler's Role in Aerosol Product Development," *Aerosol Age,* December 1963, p. 48.

tic—under which Power-Pak licensed these companies to use some of Power-Pak's product formulations. Power-Pak also performed R&D activities for these firms for a fee. While Power-Pak did not see any direct increase in the sales of its own products, Mr. Edward Helfer, Power-Pak's president in 1962, felt that this arrangement might lead to a penetration in continental Europe, which was just beginning to experience an aerosol boom similar to that in the United States between 1955 and 1960.

Industry suppliers. The four principal components of an aerosol product—containers, propellants, caps and valves, and product fill—were supplied by diverse groups of companies.

The market for propellants was dominated by five large chemical companies: du Pont, Allied Chemical Corporation, Union Carbide, Pennsalt Chemicals Corporation, and Kaiser Aluminum & Chemical Corporation.

The market for aerosol containers was also dominated by large firms. Among the most important were Continental Can Company, Inc., American Can Company, Crown Cork & Seal Company, Inc., and National Can Corporation. Glass container manufacturers included Owens-Illinois Glass Company, Foster-Forbes Glass Company, and T. C. Wheaton Company.

Small companies, similar to many of the contract fillers, played an important part in the supply of caps and valves. The major supplier was Precision Valve Corporation, which had an estimated 50% of the market. The other half of the market was split among many suppliers.

The aerosol filler, contract or captive, usually produced the product fill. In the case of certain products, such as perfumes, however, the contract filler secured the product fill from the marketing company.

ATI HISTORY

Immediately after World War II, Mr. H. R. Shepherd joined the Bridgeport Brass Company as administrative assistant to the director of research. About a year later, he and three friends founded Connecticut Chemical Research Corporation. After eight years, Mr. Shepherd resigned to form his own company, Aerosol Techniques, Inc.

ATI was launched in 1955 with $20,000 capital invested by Mr. Shepherd, a $125,000 bank loan, and $600,000 in trade credit. Although contracts were obtained almost immediately to load hair sprays and colognes, ATI was $75,000 in the red after six months. At year's end, however, the company emerged with a modest profit of $5,000 on sales of $1.5 million. *Aerosol Age* reported as follows:

> During this stage of growth, Mr. Shepherd emphasized that the theme will be "give service—expand research—put profits into new equipment and technical development". . . . The company has started a research program with an eastern university on basic problems with aerosols. . . . A complete aerosol service center is a must for proper handling of customers in aerosol packaging, according to Mr. Shepherd.[2]

---
[2] *Aerosol Age*, July 1956, p. 21.

By 1960, sales had risen to $7.1 million and net profit to $101,000. Although hair sprays remained ATI's most important single product, the line had been expanded to include shaving creams, toothpaste, furniture polishes, and other items. In addition, R&D laboratories had been established. A continuing effort was being made to improve formulae for customers and to develop or adapt aerosol packaging to new products. Though product diversification and research had reduced ATI's dependence on a few major clients, three customers still accounted for almost 60% of sales in 1960.

Although ATI lost an account which contributed 13% of 1960 sales because the customer went captive, the addition of new products and growth of established lines pushed 1961 sales to a new high of $7.7 million. Early in 1961, ATI issued 130,000 shares to the public, representing a 30% interest in the company, at $4.00 per share. This financing helped to alleviate the financial pressures caused by the company's tremendous growth. Even though ATI had decided to retain all earnings and to conserve funds for working capital by leasing rather than purchasing facilities, creditors were supplying over three-fourths of the firm's invested funds in 1960. In October 1961, the stock was listed on the American Stock Exchange.

In 1962, ATI's spectacular growth trend was resumed as sales reached $10.8 million and net income climbed to $240,000. In addition, ATI established a subsidiary, Aeroceuticals, Inc., to produce and market an assortment of ethical drugs which company R&D had developed for aerosol containers. Major reasons for this move were the high growth rate (over 40% per year between 1957 and 1962) of pharmaceuticals and the relatively high gross margin on these products.

In 1963, ATI moved into first place in the contract filling business with sales of $21.3 million and profits of $583,000, partly as a result of the acquisition of two contract fillers: Western Filling Corporation in Los Angeles, California, and Continental Filling Corporation in Danville, Illinois.

When acquired, Western had shown a rapid growth similar to ATI's. Sales had doubled between 1960 and 1962 from $2.3 million to $4.7 million, while earnings had increased from $19,000 to $278,000. The Western acquisition was basically an exchange of stock.

Continental's sales had fluctuated in the four years prior to the acquisition, dropping from $9.6 million in 1960 to $6.9 million in 1962, but recovering somewhat in 1963. Profits had declined continuously during the period, however, from $118,000 in 1960 to $5,000 in 1962 and then to a $27,000 loss in 1963. Because of this somewhat weaker record, the Continental acquisition was a cash and deferred payment agreement, even though Continental's capacity was somewhat greater than Western's: 40 million vs. 35 million units annually.

To finance these acquisitions, ATI negotiated a $1 million loan with its New York bank, and in November 1964 offered 80,000 shares to the public at $18.00 per share.

In 1964, ATI acquired Armstrong Laboratories, Inc. of West Roxbury, Massachusetts, through an exchange of stock. Armstrong's sales had been $1.1 million in 1963, with profits of $52,000. Armstrong had already achieved a strong reputation as an aerosol producer specializing in pharmaceuticals and other close-tolerance filling operations. Armstrong had also opened a new building with advanced production and research facilities just prior to acquisition.

With this addition, ATI's sales increased to $34.6 million in 1964, with a net income of $920,000. This growth continued in 1965, with sales increasing to $47.0 million and profits to $1.2 million.

In December 1962 and again in December 1963, ATI declared 5% stock dividends.

ATI'S RECENT OPERATIONS

Product line. ATI's 1965 product line consisted of over 200 products manufactured for nearly 150 customers. The largest customer, however, accounted for over 45 million units, or nearly 17% of 1965 production. In addition, the top five customers accounted for about 50% of ATI's production, and the top 10 for slightly more than 75%.

By product class, ATI was concentrated in personal products, which represented nearly 65% of 1965 volume—hair sprays alone accounted for over 45%. Household products were next in importance representing about 28%. Most of this was starches, which accounted for 15%.

John Thomson, corporate director of sales, indicated that ATI's product line strategy was to reduce the company's dependence on personal products by placing more emphasis on household products and pharmaceuticals. Nevertheless, Mr. Thomson indicated that ATI planned to continue its outstanding record in hair sprays and personal deodorants.

According to Mr. Thomson, coatings, paints, and food products represented special cases for ATI. While he felt that the market for coatings and paints would not grow as fast as other product categories, he indicated that they might become more important for ATI. However, he also indicated that if ATI decided to enter the coating and paint field at all, it would probably market as well as manufacture these products. This move would represent a major change in ATI's present strategy of not marketing products to end-use consumers.

In Mr. Thomson's opinion, food products represented a far more promising field for ATI. Up to 1965, ATI had not devoted much effort to this area because of the technical problems encountered in propellants and caps and valves. However, Mr. Thomson indicated that ATI would increase its effort in this direction as the food aerosol market developed—perhaps three to seven years from now, he believed.

ATI was also studying the possibilities of aerosols for the industrial cleaning and sanitation markets, Mr. Thomson said.

Marketing. ATI's sales objective was a volume of $100 million in contract manufacturing by 1969. To reach this goal, the company planned to broaden its line, particularly in the household products area, and to concentrate its selling efforts on national marketers in the continental United States. In this sales push, ATI planned to rely heavily on what it considered its two distinctive competences: low distribution costs resulting from having plants located in the East, Midwest, and the West Coast; and a continuing flow of new and improved products resulting from its R&D.

Mr. Thomson felt that ATI would have to price more competitively if it expected to hold its large national accounts. However, he felt the new plant being erected at Milford would allow production economies which would keep ATI competitive for at least the next five years. In addition, Mr. Thomson felt that ATI might acquire or build a southern production facility which would permit lower prices because of reduced distribution costs.

In 1963, ATI started to develop a corporate marketing staff to coordinate sales activity and develop marketing plans. One of the staff's first jobs was to develop a yearly sales forecast. This was accomplished through account-by-account analyses by each ATI salesman, which were later combined at headquarters into a national sales forecast.

Throughout 1965, the corporate marketing staff was assisting ATI's salesmen with major presentations to national marketing companies. These presentations represented a relatively new development for the industry. They were made to old customers whom ATI hoped to retain by developing new products for them, and to prospective customers who were either existing or potential aerosol marketers. As a result of one of these presentations, ATI developed a complete program—product, package design, and advertising theme—for marketing an aerosol hair spray for the American Home Products Company. Even though American Home had never marketed a hair spray before, this new brand, Sudden Beauty, became one of the top four hair sprays in 1965.

At the end of 1965, ATI had two men on its corporate marketing staff, four divisional sales managers, and six field salesmen. In addition to helping make the major presentations, the salesmen served as a liaison between the customer's purchasing, research, and marketing groups and the ATI organization.

Research and development. In late 1965, ATI formed a new corporation called the Aerosol Techniques Research Center, Inc. This division was building a new research center in Milford, Connecticut, which would eventually be staffed by 15 to 25 people headed by Mr. Clarence Clapp, an ATI vice president formerly with Western Filling. At the same time, a new technical services department was formed under ATI vice president, Fred Presant, who had worked in the aerosol industry for 18 years. Technical services encompassed all the operating division's customer service, quality control, and product development laboratories. In Mr. Clapp's opinion, the new research center, combined with the technical services department, would give ATI the best research and product development activity among all contract fillers.

While the technical services department worked hand-in-hand with ATI's customers to improve product formulations, the research center was to be devoted solely to the development of new or improved products and new or improved technology in the aerosol field. According to Mr. Clapp,

> The direction of the research and development effort at the research center will be determined to a large degree by the market research department. Market research will be involved at both the initial and final stages of most projects. This is necessary because the ultimate dependence of our success rests with the consumer.

This policy implied that most projects chosen were expected to become commercially feasible within one to three years. Nevertheless, Mr. Clapp said that ATI would still have some commitment to "blue sky" projects, provided the financial commitments were not too heavy. He also indicated that ATI would seek technical assistance from its suppliers as much as possible, but, when necessary, would perform research in the areas of new containers, valves, and propellants. To help protect accomplishments, ATI planned to seek far more patents than in the past. When this was not possible, Mr. Clapp indicated that ATI would seek contractual agreements with its customers or utilize secrecy.

The contribution and importance of R&D to ATI's success up to 1965 is indicated by the company's record for new products and technical developments generated. These included the first personal deodorant, Right Guard; a patented water-based hair spray, which allowed cost savings of 10% to 30%; the first aerosol mouth freshener; the first dimethyl ether propellant system, which reduced costs because it was water-soluble; and the first aerosol barbecue sauce. In conjunction with a leading can company, ATI developed the first three-piece high-pressure container, which reduced costs since less propellant was required. ATI also developed new formulations which became leading products in their respective markets, e.g., Sudden Beauty hair spray, Dust and Wax furniture polish, Perform aerosol starch, and Fuller's oven cleaner. In addition, ATI had a complete cross-section of all types of aerosol products on the market in 1965, even though the company might not have been the original developer of some of these products.

Another indication of ATI's commitment to R&D was contained in Mr. Shepherd's exposition on "The Contract Filler's Role in Aerosol Product Development," which appeared in the December 1963 issue of *Aerosol Age:*

> In order to know of the future and to predict, within reasonable bounds, what we [the contract fillers] should be doing, we must understand the past and recognize the trends that are already discernible . . . we must understand what are the distinctive competences of the filler today and what these will be in the future. How should they be shaped and guided in order to continue the development of the aerosol industry? In the application of the resources at the disposal of the contract filler, how and when should these resources be allocated? How should they be developed? When I write of "resources," I mean things such as men, money and materials. I also mean the fund of knowledge and experience of the contract filler and new technological changes which shall come from the contract filler . . . I think we can expect to see a continual increase in the concentration of power in the hands of the marketing companies. We can expect to endure severe

conditions of excess capacity and price competition among fillers. Because of these increasing economic pressures on marketers and contract fillers, there will be an even greater need for creative, new product and marketing concepts. In order to continue to play a role in the development of this industry, the contract filler must now begin to use effectively those distinctive competences and resources which he has developed over the years. These distinctive competences are first *creativity* and the *ability to innovate technologically*. The second distinctive competence . . . is that of the many years of experience in the organizations of the members of this industry. The next resource is that of having capacity to manufacture a wide spectrum of aerosol products. Next, those contract fillers who have moved toward putting facilities up in strategic locations in this country and on the continent, have moved toward offering more complete servicing of both national and international markets in terms of distribution. Finally, one distinctive competence which is not universally held by contract fillers organizations is that of capably using new management techniques and tools.

Production.   Aerosol products were manufactured in two basic ways in 1965. The slower but more accurate method was called cold filling. In this method, the propellant and product fill were liquefied by refrigeration and "poured" into the containers in carefully measured amounts. The cap and valve were then inserted by hand and sealed by machine, after which the filled containers were passed through a hot water bath to test for pressure leaks. Finally, labels were applied and the product was packaged for storage or shipment. The more rapid method was called pressure filling. In this method, the cap and valve were inserted in the container and then sealed at the same time a vacuum was created in the container. Next the product fill and propellant were injected through the valve into the empty container by the application of extremely high pressure. The filled container was then labeled and packaged for storage or shipment. In 1965, filling speeds of 200 cans per minute were considered high for aerosol production. However, speeds of 100 cans per minute had been considered high in 1960. Mr. Donald Schoonmaker, ATI's eastern division production manager, indicated that filling speeds might double again by 1970.

At the end of 1965, ATI had four plants with 21 filling lines located across the United States so as to insure national distribution at minimal cost. About 50% of ATI's equipment was new and 50% was relatively old. However, Mr. Schoonmaker said ATI's production efficiency was equal to or better than that of other contract fillers. Mr. Schoonmaker also felt that ATI had extremely good quality control, which he thought most contract fillers would be hard pressed to match. At this time, ATI's annual production capacity was about 390 million units.

Table 3 indicates the location and number of filling lines for each of ATI's four plants.

In June 1965, ATI began an expansion program designed to raise capacity to 430 million units by the end of 1966. This $4.2 million program included (1) a new building in Milford, Connecticut, to house

Table 3

Location	Number of filling lines	Approximate annual production capacity (millions of units)	Warehouse space (thousands of square feet)
Bridgeport, Conn. (leased)	6	150	150
Los Angeles, Calif. (leased)	4	95	130
Danville, Ill. (owned)	6	100	100
West Roxbury, Mass. (leased)	5	45	30
Total	21	390	410

The Bridgeport facility, a converted piano factory, also contained the company's executive offices and research laboratories.

the company's main offices and eastern division plant, replacing the overcrowded Bridgeport factory and offices; (2) a new research center, also located at Milford; (3) acquisition of a new building and property in Danville, Illinois, to double the facilities of the company's Continental Filling division; (4) addition of a production line and new warehouse area in Los Angeles to increase the capacity of the Western Filling division; and (5) completion of a new aerosol pharmaceutical development and filling installation at Armstrong Laboratories in West Roxbury.

All facilities were designed to permit the installation of additional lines in the future. Expenditures required to bring capacity into line with future sales targets were estimated as follows:

Fiscal year	Target sales (millions of units)	Production capacity* (millions of units)	Capital expenditures to obtain additional capacity (thousands of dollars)
1967	330	467	$480
1968	400	497	490
1969	460	532	520

* Reserve capacity in excess of sales targets was required to handle emergency orders and seasonal fluctuations.

According to Mr. Schoonmaker, expansion would be aimed at meeting the needs of national marketers who had medium-volume, high-quality, high-margin products. He felt this policy would enable ATI to make better use of its distinctive competences in R&D instead of having to sell on a price basis as was necessary on mass produced standardized products.

Organization and control. In late 1965, ATI had four operating divisions in addition to the corporate staff and the research and technical services divisions. The name, location, and general managers of these divisions are listed in Table 4.

Table 4

Division	Location	General manager	Previous position of GM
Eastern division.........	Bridgeport, Conn.	John Kossak	Plant manager, General Foods, and operated own company
Western division.........	Los Angeles, Calif.	John Manara	President, Western Filling Company
Continental division......	Danville, Ill.	Chris Canaday	President, Continental Filling Company
Armstrong Laboratories division...............	West Roxbury, Mass.	Robert Armstrong, Jr.	President, Armstrong Laboratories

Each of these general managers was an ATI vice president. According to Mr. Rossetti, corporate treasurer, these general managers operated their divisions somewhat like independent entrepreneurs. For example, while the divisions sent monthly and quarterly profit reports to corporate headquarters, these reports were not standardized, and Mr. Rossetti said the divisional general managers were not evaluated on the basis of these reports. Nevertheless, Mr. Rossetti felt that the divisional general managers tried to maximize profits. The primary purpose of the reports was to enable the corporate staff to assist the divisional general managers by uncovering unfavorable performance trends.

In 1965, ATI did not employ a standard cost system or accumulate actual costs in such a way that it could estimate the relative efficiency of its different pieces of equipment or the relative profitability of its different products. While Mr. Rossetti indicated that such estimates might be desirable in the future, he felt it more important for ATI to keep up with rapidly expanding new product areas than to allocate its resources on the basis of estimated profitability.

In addition, since materials accounted for 85% of the total cost of finished products, Mr. Rossetti felt that costs could be effectively controlled by having efficient, modern equipment, by having careful quality control to minimize rejects and insure proper filling operations, and by purchasing high quality materials at competitive prices. In order to help control materials usage, ATI was installing an IBM 1401A computer at the end of 1965.

Financial situation. To finance new fixed assets and increase working capital, ATI sold 80,000 shares of common stock to the public in October 1965 at $22.00 a share. An additional $3.0 million was raised by the sale of 5½% 25-year secured notes of subsidiaries to an insurance company.

PROBLEMS AND ALTERNATIVES AT THE END OF 1965

An internal policy memorandum issued in December 1965 stated,

> . . . . ATI's position of leadership in the aerosol industry may not be sufficient to sustain ATI's objectives of $100 million in sales and 7% after taxes by 1969. This gap between our abilities and our goals has been brought about by factors underlying both the company's environment and the company's resources.

Environmental trends noted in this memorandum included the maturation of industry structure and aerosol technology, the increasingly heavy competition among contract fillers, the attendant threat to high-level profits, and the increasing power of the marketing companies. Mr. Shepherd commented as follows on these and other problems:

> Most of the problems ATI faces now—customers going captive and pressured profit margins—we faced 10 years ago and, in a sense, they're no more serious now than then. However, because of the trend toward competition on the basis of price, we are increasingly aware of the fact that ATI will have to become more formalistic and number-oriented—a prospect I would dislike *if* it saps creativity. Thus, if the only thing I can do is beat a competitor's price, I don't feel that I'm contributing much—and more to the point—I don't feel that ATI is contributing. Our historical excellence is in creating profits for our customers through the kind of innovation which helped us to develop Right Guard for Gillette and, more recently, miniatures, a development which was written up in the *Wall Street Journal*.[3]
>
> Again, this trend toward a more formalistic organization will have to be balanced with what I believe are my responsibilities to the people who make up our organization and its social and business interrelationships. Up until now our creativity has given us an opportunity to allow the people within our organization to find their own particular niche—even though this process takes time and in the short run uses up profits. However, in a really price competitive market there would be no time for slack, no time for learning, and no opportunity for personal change. I believe that, in the long run, such an atmosphere would be damaging to our organization and to the interests of the company. So it is for this reason, in addition to our natural desire to achieve economic success, that we are looking at other businesses where we can use the technical and organizational creativity that we have developed over the past ten years.
>
> This doesn't mean that we plan to de-emphasize the aerosol busi-

---

[3] "Marketing Miniatures: Now Products Come in One-Use Packages," *Wall Street Journal*, April 13, 1966:

> Make way for the teeny-weeny economy size.
>
> It contains one serving or application, and it's one of the hottest packaging concepts since the super-duper economy size. What's more, despite the increased cost per ounce the one-shot helping can prove to be a consumer's most economical buy.
>
>   *   *   *   *   *
>
> Many of the goods are sold in pressurized aerosol containers. Aerosol Techniques, Inc., for example, is about to start commercial production of a breath freshener in a small aerosol container—not one shot but much smaller than any previous models—and is testing small containers of an antiperspirant, a man's hair spray, and a nasal spray.

ness altogether. However, we are considering other businesses which we might enter to hedge against the threats we see in the aerosol business. Ten years from now I expect that the aerosol business might be like the can business today: efficient production, tight control, low margins, and no fun—except when creating new opportunities for new products through technical and marketing research.

In looking at other businesses, there are three things I consider important. First, we should get closer to the consumer, where price isn't the only reason for survival. This is where the real opportunity for product innovation lies. Second, the acquired company should have good management so that we can build on them, rather than being forced to decimate the company and start from scratch. Finally, I would like to have a "feel" for the business.

As a result of environmental trends and Mr. Shepherd's concern about the future nature of the aerosol business, considerable attention was being focused on the question of what economic opportunities were available to ATI.

Although the European aerosol market was expanding rapidly, ATI paid little attention to expanding its operations overseas. However, it was considering strategies that would allow continued success in the domestic aerosol business. At the end of 1965, it had three groups of Harvard Business School students working on projects related to forward or backward integration. One group was considering possible acquisitions of plastic cap and valve manufacturers; even though this industry appeared at first glance to suffer from strong price competition and from profit margins lower than for contract filling. Another student group was concerned about the future of the food aerosol business. The third was studying markets for other types of packaging services that ATI might provide.

Possible forward integration.   Some members of management felt that ATI should begin marketing products to the end-use consumer in order to get the higher profit margins associated with this business. There was, however, considerable concern lest such action cause ATI to lose some of its present customers, who would not want their supplier as a competitor. On the other hand, there had been little reaction from these same customers when ATI took Sudden Beauty hair spray to American Home Products, Inc., a company that had never been in the hair spray business, and essentially established AHP as one of the country's leading hair spray marketers. ATI's management also wondered whether ATI had the financial and managerial resources to market a consumer product nationally.

Diversification guidelines.   The major focus of ATI's attention, however, was directed toward diversification out of the aerosol business. According to the December policy memorandum,

> The need for an unconventional miracle is prompted by our objectives, by an assessment of the present economic progress of our aerosol business and by the question of whether ATI's strategy is viable for the next decade. . . . It is the contention of this paper that at least the following criteria must be met if a profitable diversification is to be achieved:

1. The company should promise a growth rate compatible with ATI's own rate of growth.
2. The company should promise a return on investment compatible with ATI's own ROI performance.
3. The company's management should not retard the growth of our own management structure.
4. The company should be a company to which ATI should be able to contribute synergetically so that there will exist the best possible opportunity for reaching the above listed financial criteria. In this context ATI's distinctive competences have been suggested as:

    a) Nationwide manufacturing and management facilities;
    b) A capacity to direct technological innovation toward supplying consumer and/or industrial needs;
    c) A strong series of relationships with the chemical industry; and
    d) A strong series of relationships with the financial community.

5. The company should be a company which has the capacity to contribute an additional distinctive competence to ATI. Examples of the kind of contribution we have in mind are:

    a) A sales force for the sale of (say) industrial specialty chemicals;
    b) A technological niche in a nonaerosol packaging service so that ATI can be in a position to develop an integrated system of packaging services backed by nationwide manufacturing facilities, a nationwide sales force, unique packaging machinery of our own design, and a research facility specializing in formulation chemistry related to personal, household, pharmaceutical, and food products.
    c) The ability to manufacture nonaerosol personal products—e.g., specialty soap, eye makeup, lipsticks, etc.

6. The size of the company should be such as to make possible a noticeable contribution to ATI's earnings per share after taking into account the potential effect of a synergetic relationship. In this regard the generation of an incremental 10¢ per share in earnings would be considered by ATI to be a noticeable financial contribution.

Such opportunities could lie in industries as diverse as microencapsulation and radiation as well as in consumer and/or industrial packaging and/or product services, but what is most important for us to develop is a sense for the future and a technological and marketing ability to meet this challenge within the framework of the financial criteria listed above and our own resources.

The Quality Products Company. At the beginning of 1966, Mr. Meyer was engaged in the evaluation of over 20 possible acquisitions in light of the above guidelines for diversification. He indicated that the guidelines did not adequately emphasize the desire of ATI's management for developing an end-consumer marketing activity. According to Mr. Meyer,

> ATI's management would like to reduce both the risks associated with being a one-product company and the risks associated with being solely a supplier to those companies which market a product to the end-consumer. While Mr. Shepherd would prefer to serve industrial end-customers, the real emphasis is to get closer to an end-use market

where ATI can best exploit its distinctive creative and innovative talents and yet not prejudice its relations with its existing customers. In this connection, it will be an interesting task to identify the "legitimate" path between customer loyalty and new opportunities in those end-use markets suited to our strengths.

Presently we're not sure whether we should acquire several small companies or one large one. Having a family of small companies is certainly a situation which we have learned to live with in a constructive and profitable way. It is also true that having several associated companies might help us to solve some management problems if it becomes necessary to move toward more centralized management of our aerosol operations, since these associated companies might then provide a constructive way to utilize the talents of those of our present divisional managers who are experienced and gifted entrepreneurs. On the other hand, a large acquisition might be the essential step necessary to help us build a reputation of excellence in a new field and this strategy might have substantial appeal to the entrepreneur who looks forward to corporate size as a means of at long last achieving the institution of a stable enterprise.

Basically then, no acquisition is too big or too small. Rather different, and, at first sight, perhaps conflicting, criteria must be used to judge each individual case. Meanwhile, we are trying to use the time we have to test the assumption that we have the brains and feelings necessary for growth into a different and changing environment with a different and changing organization.

The Quality Products Company[4] was one of the more promising acquisition prospects that Mr. Meyer was considering. Quality Products was a small company in the women's hand lotion business. During the fiscal year ended December 30, 1965, Quality earned about $92,000 on sales of $2.3 million which represented an increase of $28,000 in profits and $300,000 in sales from the 1964 fiscal year (see Exhibits 10 and 11).

Quality specialized in the manufacture of high-grade women's hand lotions, which it then sold to various prestige marketing companies who marketed the products under their own brands. Quality also manufactured hand lotion of normal quality, which it sold to various supermarkets on a private-brand basis. At the end of 1965, Quality was constructing a new plant in Philadelphia which would increase capacity from $2.5 million to $4.0 million and would make possible more efficient operations than the present three-building plant.

Quality's management felt that, as soon as the new plant had "shaken down," a minimum sales increase of $1.3 million could be expected on the basis of preliminary contacts it had made with potential customers. Quality's management also expected that demand for quality hand lotions would increase because of several trends: the increased wealth and general desire for luxury, the rapid growth of the fragrance market and the impact thereof on sales of higher priced hand lotions, and the public's increasing receptiveness to greater luxury in hand creams as a

---

[4] For reasons of security, ATI desired that the name of the company and the name of the industry be disguised. The basic characteristics of the company and of the industry (e.g., size, nature of competition, product-market characteristics, etc.) are not disguised, however.

result of mass advertising by the larger manufacturers who were improving their lower priced, mass-marketed hand creams.

Mr. Meyer indicated that the proposed acquisition was not without risk, however. His primary concern was that almost 50% of Quality's 1965 sales came from one customer, and that this percentage was expected to increase to 75% after the new factory was in operation. Mr. Meyer felt that with Quality producing nearly 30% of this customer's requirements, representing $3 million in sales to Quality, there was some risk the customer might decide to manufacture for himself. Nevertheless, given the willingness of ATI's management to live with this kind of risk, which was common in the packaging industry, Mr. Meyer felt that the decision to acquire Quality would rest on the cost of the deal and the degree to which ATI's resources could help Quality to grow and to minimize its vulnerability to the decisions of its major customer.

Mr. Meyer also indicated that if ATI acquired Quality, it would probably try to purchase the quality hand cream division of one of the large national manufacturers that was located in the Midwest, giving ATI national coverage of the quality hand cream business. He felt the chances of negotiating this purchase would be better than fifty-fifty, since the national manufacturer had not exhibited a deep interest in this division for over 15 years.

Exhibit 1

AEROSOL TECHNIQUES, INC.*

Balance Sheets for Years Ended September 30, 1960–1965
(dollars in thousands)

	1960	1961	1962	1963	1964	1965
Current assets						
Cash..............................	$ 60	$ 449	$ 290	$ 359	$ 1,067	$ 1,433
Accounts receivable—net.....	461	832	1,279	3,373	4,924	6,566
Inventories—lower cost						
or market....................	465	238	468	2,136	2,329	3,098
Prepaid expenses.............	15	15	16	103	185	185
Miscellaneous................	3	23	22	90	46	65
Total current assets....	$1,005	$1,557	$2,076	$6,061	$ 8,544	$11,348
Fixed assets						
Land........................	0	0	0	13	13	179
Buildings...................	0	0	0	362	365	880
Machinery and equipment.....	479	496	541	2,024	2,497	3,226
Other.......................	134	144	154	308	384	1,429†
	$ 613	$ 640	$ 695	$2,707	$ 3,260	$ 5,715
Less: accumulated deprecia-						
tion and amortization.....	175	240	307	1,377	1,556	1,805
Total fixed assets......	$ 438	$ 401	$ 388	$1,330	$ 1,704	$ 3,909
Other assets.................	19	18	24	155	75	125
	$1,462	$1,976	$2,488	$7,546	$10,322	$15,383
Current liabilities						
Notes payable...............	$ 0	$ 0	$ 0	$1,298	$ 1,500	$ 0
Accounts payable............	596	527	758	2,480	2,842	4,151
Federal and state taxes						
payable..................	89	164	238	564	695	886
Other.......................	179	209	200	388	396	1,318‡
Total current liabilities.	$ 864	$ 901	$1,196	$4,730	$ 5,434	$ 6,356
Long-term debt...............	217	98	34	241	200	3,152
Deferred federal taxes..........	36	43	47	53	55	60
Contingent deferred credit......	0	0	0	355	257	184
Stockholders' equity						
4% voting, cumulative,						
preferred.................	0	0	0	715	715	715
Common stock: 10¢ par value.	30	43	44	61	76	78
Capital in excess of par value..	20	20	20	20	20	20
Paid in surplus..............	0	421	456	131	2,083	2,179
Retained earnings............	295	450	691	1,240	1,480	2,639
Total stockholders' equity	$ 345	$ 934	$1,211	$2,167	$ 4,375	$ 5,631
	$1,462	$1,976	$2,488	$7,546	$10,322	$15,383

* Discrepancies may appear in totals as a result of rounding figures.
† Includes $934,000 for construction in progress.
‡ Includes $672,000 of current portion of long-term debt.
Source: ATI annual reports.

Exhibit 2

AEROSOL TECHNIQUES, INC.

Income Statements: 1960–1965*
(dollars in thousands)

	1960	1961	1962	1963	1964	1965
Net sales..................	$7,052	$7,734	$10,776	$21,327	$34,632	$46,975
Cost of goods sold, selling, administrative, and general exp......................	$6,835	$7,415	$10,302	$20,159	$33,079	$44,705
	$ 218	$ 319	$ 475	$ 1,169	$ 1,553	$ 2,270
Other income..............	10	12	24	66	222	36
	$ 228	$ 331	$ 498	$ 1,235	$ 1,775	$ 2,306
Other deductions...........	27	16	11	85	104	124
	$ 200	$ 315	$ 487	$ 1,150	$ 1,671	$ 2,182
Provision for federal income taxes....................	99	159	247	567	751	980
Net earnings...............	$ 101	$ 156	$ 240	$ 583	$ 920	$ 1,202
% Sales...................	1.4	2.2	2.2	2.7	2.7	2.6

* Discrepancies may appear in total as a result of rounding figures.
Source: Various ATI annual reports.

Exhibit 3

AEROSOL TECHNIQUES, INC.

Percentage Penetration of Aerosols as a Packaging Form in Various Market Segments: 1951–1964
(per cents of dollar volume)

	1951	1952	1953	1954	1955	1956	1957	1958	1959	1960	1961	1962	1963	1964
Insecticides............	30%	32%	37%	37%	39%	38%	39%	42%	47%	47%	47%	47%	48%	44%
Room deodorants........	0	0	40	44	58	56	67	73	82	79	85	89	91	91
Shave lathers..........	0	12	29	38	47	51	59	60	65	69	71	79	81	82
Colognes..............	0	0	0	13	33	45	48	51	57	58	62	64	66	64

Source: *Eighth Annual Aerosol Market Report, 1964*, prepared by Freon Products Division of du Pont. Data supplied to du Pont by *Drug Trade News*, New York, New York.

Exhibit 4

AEROSOL TECHNIQUES, INC.

Du Pont Company Estimate of Aerosol Production (Nonfood Products Only) (millions of units)

Category	Product													
PERSONAL PRODUCTS	SHAVE LATHER	27.3	47.0	53.1	51.0	59.3	65.0	75.0	79.1	84.7	94.8	97.6	102.6	108.1
	HAIR SPRAYS & DRESSINGS	16.1	34.5	55.8	83.4	95.6	112.1	88.7	120.9	152.5	245.6	294.0	314.0	337.0
	DENTAL CREAMS						23.0	11.8	5.8	3.1	3.1	3.0	3.0	3.2
	MEDICINALS & PHARMACEUTICALS	0.8	1.1	1.5	2.4	6.2	8.1	10.5	12.3	19.5	36.9	39.8	45.6	49.4
	COLOGNES & PERFUMES	0.1	3.0	7.0	8.8	18.6	30.0	37.9	43.1	54.7	55.1	60.4	66.2	69.2
	OTHER	3.8	4.4	7.2	7.7	7.1	9.6	12.9	18.7	18.5	36.9	38.5	47.1	52.8
	TOTAL	48.1	90.0	124.6	153.3	186.8	247.8	236.8	279.9	333.0	472.4	533.3	578.5	619.7
HOUSEHOLD PRODUCTS	INSECTICIDES	47.0	47.0	57.0	61.4	50.7	71.3	78.9	92.5	87.3	89.2	73.2	75.1	76.4
	ROOM DEODORANTS	17.3	21.3	33.1	38.4	44.6	62.8	62.9	78.1	86.3	99.0	118.5	126.4	131.6
	SNOW	8.9	7.1	6.8	8.9	9.0	9.8	9.5	10.5	8.6	9.5	10.5	12.5	13.5
	GLASS CLEANERS				8.0	11.2	6.6	24.2	22.2	26.0	31.0	47.3	52.3	54.3
	SHOE OR LEATHER DRESSINGS				1.5	4.3	7.7	14.1	16.6	7.3	4.7	8.9	11.1	13.0
	WAXES & POLISHES (ALL TYPES)							12.1	40.6	42.1	52.9	50.9	57.8	61.0
	STARCHES								20.6	50.5	65.4	86.9	99.0	107.3
	OTHER	2.3	3.1	8.2	16.4	8.3	11.6	25.4	10.5	15.7	18.6	11.8	13.2	14.8
	TOTAL	28.5	31.5	48.1	73.2	77.4	98.5	148.2	199.1	236.5	281.1	334.8	372.3	395.5
ALL OTHER PRODUCTS	COATINGS	13.0	13.1	14.7	22.5	43.0	50.0	63.2	77.1	95.6	110.3	137.9	158.4	174.5
	VETERINARIAN & PET PRODUCTS	0.3	0.5	1.0	1.5	2.3	3.3	4.3	6.3	8.3	7.1	7.6	8.7	9.4
	AUTOMOTIVE PRODUCTS											33.2	36.9	39.6
	MISCELLANEOUS PRODUCTS	3.1	5.9	10.3	13.3	15.0	14.3	30.2	42.2	52.8	44.7	23.6	21.4	19.7
	TOTAL	3.4	6.4	11.3	14.8	17.3	17.6	34.5	48.5	61.1	51.8	64.4	67.2	71.0
	GRAND TOTAL	140.0	188.0	255.7	325.2	375.2	485.2	561.6	697.1	813.5	1004.8	1140.1	1251.3	1334.8

INSECTICIDES include high pressure and low pressure products (including space, residual and moth proofers).
OTHER PERSONAL PRODUCTS include shampoos, sun tan preparations, personal deodorants, hand lotions, powders, depilatories, etc.
MISCELLANEOUS PRODUCTS include antistatic sprays, industrial applications, fire extinguishers, etc.
AUTOMOTIVE PRODUCTS included in Miscellaneous products prior to 1963.

Source: *Eighth Annual Aerosol Market Report 1964*, prepared by the Freon Products Division of du Pont, p. 24.

Exhibit 5

AEROSOL TECHNIQUES, INC.

Growth of the Food Aerosol Market

Year	Sales (millions of units)
1951	43
1952	50
1953	56
1954	60
1955	64
1956	69
1957	75
1958	80
1959	79
1960	59
1961	58
1962	63
1963	67
1964	75
1965	100

Source: *Eighth Annual Aerosol Market Report 1964*, prepared by the Freon Products Division of du Pont, p. 18.

Exhibit 6

AEROSOL TECHNIQUES, INC.

Cost Estimates for Various Aerosol Products

Product type	Starch[a]	Hair spray[b]	Shave cream[c]
Product fill	1.0¢	4.0¢	1.5¢
Propellant	0.3	12.0[d]	0.1
Can[e]	7.0	6.3	5.0
Valve	3.0	2.6	3.0
Cap	0.5	1.0[f]	0.5
Carton[g]	0.6	0.5	0.5
Direct labor	1.0	1.0	1.0
Overhead	1.5	1.5	1.5
Profit (maximum)	1.0	1.0	1.0
Factory price	15.9¢	29.9¢	14.1¢
Approximate retail price	39¢	$1.00–$1.20	$0.79 to $1.00
Approximate retail price of comparable product (non-aerosol)	19¢ for 12 oz.	none available	$1.00 for 10 oz.

[a] 16 oz. size, for laundry use.
[b] 12 oz. size, alcohol-base, "most name brands."
[c] 6 oz. size, "most name brands."
[d] Much more expensive than others shown because the product requires Freon as a propellant, which amounts to 70% of the weight of the contents. The propellants used in the other products shown are hydrocarbons, and are only 4% of the weight of the contents. Water-based hair sprays, with somewhat different characteristics, are available; these entail a lower propellant cost.
[e] Printed cans; no separate labels.
[f] More expensive only because usually fancier.
[g] Carton for a dozen cans.
Source: Estimates furnished by an industry source other than ATI. Estimates are for an established product with a volume per production run of about 25,000 units or more.

Exhibit 7

AEROSOL TECHNIQUES, INC.

Cost of a Typical Aerosol Food Product

Food Product: Pancake Mix

Cost	Per unit
Direct labor...............................	$0.04
Can (16 oz.)...............................	0.09
Gas (nitrous oxide)........................	0.005
Valve and release..........................	0.05
Product (pancake mix)......................	0.04
Overhead (interest and depreciation)*............................	0.01
Profit margin..............................	0.015
Cost to marketer before distribution charges.......................	$0.250

* Assumes an investment of $300,000 for a line that produces 9.6 million units a year for eight years with indirect labor and storage costs of $50,000 a year.
Source: Harvard Business School student reports conducted for ATI.

Exhibit 8

AEROSOL TECHNIQUES, INC.

ATI's Share of the Contract Filled and Total
Aerosol Filling Markets: 1963–1964

	Per cent of market contract filled		ATI share of contract market		ATI share of total market	
	1963	1964	1963	1964	1963	1964
Household products						
Room deodorants...........	36.9%	22.1%	7.1%	17.0%	2.6%	3.7%
Cleaners...................	64.1	62.0	34.8	31.0	22.3	18.9
Waxes and polishes........	18.9	22.1	28.9	23.5	5.5	5.2
Starch....................	82.9	84.0	26.7	25.0	22.2	21.0
Shoe and leather dressings....	86.9	96.1	1.3	3.9	1.1	3.8
Other.....................	69.4	82.0	21.5	5.7	14.9	4.7
Personal products						
Shave lather...............	23.0	37.0	7.1	1.6	1.6	.6
Hair spray.................	60.0	61.0	30.9	35.1	18.6	21.4
Medicinals and pharmaceuticals................	63.0	68.8	13.9	21.4	8.8	15.0
Colognes and perfumes......	51.0	38.1	15.9	31.0	8.1	12.0
Other.....................	36.1	38.9	29.3	3.2	10.5	1.3
Miscellaneous products						
Insecticides...............	34.0	31.0	54.4	30.5	18.5	9.5
Coatings..................	52.0	41.0	4.5	4.3	2.4	2.0
Vet and pet products.......	96.3	77.5	3.9	1.4	3.8	1.1
Automotive and industrial...	59.0	70.3	14.6	8.8	8.6	6.4
Other.....................	—	36.7	—	10.3	—	3.8
Total.....................	51.1%	50.4%	22.0%	21.9%	11.2%	11.1%

Source: ATI marketing statistics.

Exhibit 9

AEROSOL TECHNIQUES, INC.

Advantages of Using a Contract Packager

by

A. S. Pero

1. *Research & Development Advantages*

   a) Can draw from lab personnel already experienced in aerosols.
   b) Developments by fillers, either directly or in cooperation with other suppliers, are available promptly to marketers.
   c) Prevents added load being placed on marketers' lab facilities.
   d) Reduces marketers' outlay for research and development.

2. *Production Advantages*

   a) Can select latest and best equipment available for particular job required.
   b) Two or more products can be run simultaneously.
   c) Contract packagers offer facilities to cope with seasonal demands, or unexpected market fluctuations either of higher or lower volume than anticipated.
   d) Personnel of long, varied, and impartial experience available for quality control.
   e) Marketer can ask, and often gets, tighter specifications on his product.
   f) Supplier problems are handled by the filler.
   g) Can eliminate or minimize labor-management problems.

3. *Service Advantages*

   a) Marketer can warehouse both raw and finished materials, often at no charge, on filler's premises.
   b) Filler's trucking facilities can be used for drop shipments, emergency services, etc.
   c) Marketer can draw on know-how and information sometimes not available within his own organization.

4. *Economic Advantages*

   a) No money outlay for equipment and maintenance, plant building or expansion, or personnel and training of same.
   b) A contract packager is actually a co-op manufacturer who divides his labor, overhead, etc., among a wide group of customers and products.
   c) Working capital is conserved on material purchased by filler until product is completed.
   d) Material purchases are often less, due to filler's volume buying.
   e) Lowest costs on final product can be obtained through competitive bidding.
   f) Use of strategically located fillers can offer substantially lower shipping costs when products are to be nationally distributed.

How high a volume of product must an aerosol marketer be turning out before it pays him to consider doing his own filling?

Actually product volume is relatively unimportant in itself. More important is to seriously study the over-all advantages a good filler has to offer vs. the over-all advantages of the marketer doing his own work. Once this is determined, a further evaluation is needed on the aerosol product or products to be manufactured.

Is the product to be a low profit, highly competitive one? In this case a larger volume will be needed to justify the total expenditure involved. Or is the product a high profit one, in a noncompetitive line? In the latter, a lesser volume might justify doing one's own filling.

In general, a careful analysis of all factors involved by the marketer, in the light of his own capacities and business interests, should provide him with a satisfactory answer. A survey of the aerosol field today clearly indicates that most marketers have already decided it is to their advantage to have their aerosol lines produced by contract packagers. The aerosol filling industry is today so competitive that the margin above direct labor is small enough to discourage not only the marketer's equipment plan, but also new competitive contract packagers as well.

Source: Article by A. S. Pero of the Fluid Chemical Co., Newark, N.J., *Aerosol Age*, June 1957, p. 28

Exhibit 10

AEROSOL TECHNIQUES, INC.*

Quality Products Company
Income Statements
(dollars in thousands)

	1961	1962	1963	1964	9 months 1965
Income from sales..............	$1,258	$2,024	$1,890	$2,002	$1,744
Cost of sales..................	1,036	1,596	1,579	1,575	1,380
Gross profit....................	$ 222	$ 428	$ 311	$ 427	$ 364
Selling expenses...............	60	74	102	107	88
General and administrative......	60	72	91	109	81
Other.........................	3	2	9	7	7
Total deductions...............	$ 123	$ 148	$ 202	$ 222	$ 176
Income before officers' salaries, profit sharing and taxes........	$ 100	$ 280	$ 109	$ 205	$ 188
Officers' salaries...............	58	58	58	61	60
Profit sharing..................	16	24	23	30	—
Federal and state income taxes...	8	103	10	50	59
Net income....................	$ 17	$ 95	$ 19	$ 64	$ 69

* Discrepancies may appear in totals as a result of rounding figures.
Source: Quality Products annual reports.

Exhibit 11

AEROSOL TECHNIQUES, INC.*

Quality Products Company
Balance Sheet for Year Ending December 1965

Current assets

Cash.........................		$135
Treasury bonds................		2
Accounts receivable...........		193
Inventory....................		357
Other.......................		38
Total current assets......		$725

Fixed assets (net)

Machinery and equipment......		$122
Laboratory equipment.........		1
Furniture and fixtures..........		22
Leasehold improvements.......		34
Total fixed assets........		$179
Other assets....................		46
Total assets....................		$950

Current liabilities

Accounts payable and accrued expenses...................		$105
Notes payable to bank..........		225
Other........................		3
Taxes payable.................		72
Total current liabilities...		$406
Deferred tax credit..............		11

Stockholders' equity

Capital stock $25 par value......		$ 94
Capital surplus................		83
Retained earnings.............		356
Total stockholders' equity		$533
Total liabilities and stockholders' equity.......................		$950

* Discrepancies may appear in totals as a result of rounding figures.
Source: Quality Products 1965 annual report.

Head Ski Company, Inc.

THE HEAD SKI COMPANY, INC., of Timonium, Maryland, was formed in 1950 to sell metal skis which had been developed by Howard Head during three years of research. In the first year six employees turned out 300 pairs of skis. By the 1954–55 skiing season, output reached 8,000 pairs, and by 1965 it passed 133,000. Growth in dollar sales and profits was equally spectacular. When Head went public in 1960, sales were just over $2 million and profits just under $59,000. By 1965 sales were up to $8.6 million and profits to $393,713. In the next two years, volume continued upward, though growth was less dramatic. In the 53 weeks ended April 30, 1966, sales were $9.1 million and profits $264,389. For a like period ending April 29, 1967, sales were $11.0 million and profits $401,482. (For financial data, see Exhibit 1 pp. 46–48.)

THE INDUSTRY

Head was an enthusiastic participant in the growing market generated by leisure-time activities, of which skiing was one of the most dynamic segments. The industry association, Ski Industries America (SIA), estimated that skiing expenditures—including clothing, equipment, footwear, accessories, lift tickets, travel, entertainment, food and lodging—rose from $280 million in 1960 to $750 million in 1966–67. Gross sales were expected to reach $1.14 billion by 1969–70. This growth was attributed to both the rising number of skiers and greater per capita expenditures. In 1947 it was estimated that there were fewer than 10,000 active skiers in the United States. SIA estimated that there were 1.6 million in 1960, 3.5 million in 1966–67 and predicted 5 million for 1970. Another industry source estimated that the number of skiers was increasing by 20% a year.

As of 1966–67 the $750 million retail expenditures on skiing were estimated to be divided into $200 million going for ski equipment and

Exhibit 1

HEAD SKI COMPANY, INC.

Consolidated Balance Sheet, 1965–67

ASSETS

	As of April 24, 1965	As of April 30, 1966	As of April 29, 1967
Current assets			
Cash	$ 162,646	$ 233,330	$ 263,896
Short-term commercial paper receivable	1,200,000	800,000	1,200,000
Notes and accounts receivable—less reserve	334,503	174,127	242,632
Inventories—valued at lower of cost or market	2,815,042	3,522,235	3,102,069
Prepayments and miscellaneous receivables	207,279	223,864	402,879
Total current assets	$4,719,470	$4,953,556	$5,211,476
Fixed assets, at cost			
Building—pledged under mortgage	$1,014,738	$1,012,085	$1,010,149
Machinery and equipment	847,974	1,059,274	1,540,707
Other	147,336	213,692	715,089
	$2,010,048	$2,285,051	$3,265,945
Less accumulated depreciation	822,255	892,153	1,123,203
Total fixed assets	$1,187,793	$1,392,898	$2,142,742
Other assets			
Unamortized bond discount and expenses	$ 277,636	$ 263,564	$ 252,004
Cash surrender value of life insurance	103,117	120,589	133,568
Other	28,583	22,364	70,194
Total other assets	$ 409,336	$ 406,517	$ 455,766
Total assets	$6,316,599	$6,752,971	$7,809,984

LIABILITIES AND STOCKHOLDERS' EQUITY

	As of April 24, 1965	As of April 30, 1966	As of April 29, 1967
Current liabilities			
Accounts payable	$ 521,031	$ 299,040	$ 829,826
Current portion of long-term debt	20,600	21,000	23,100
Accrued expenses	451,062	413,865	549,720
Income taxes payable	39,102	299,452	333,514
Other	94,899	91,271	51,120
Total current liabilities	$1,126,694	$1,124,628	$1,787,280
Long-term debt			
Mortgage on building—5¾%, payable to 1978	$ 396,646	$ 376,036	$ 331,115
Convertible subordinated debentures	2,125,000	2,125,000	2,125,000
	$2,521,646	$2,501,036	$2,456,115
Less current portion	20,600	21,000	.....
Total long-term debt	$2,501,046	$2,480,036	$2,456,115
Commitments and contingent liabilities, stockholders' equity			
Common stock—par value 50¢ per share (authorized 2,000,000 shares; outstanding 1966, 915,202 shares; 1965, 882,840 shares adjusted for 2-for-1 stock split-up effective September 15, 1965)	$ 220,710	$ 457,601	$ 459,401
Paid-in capital	1,820,323	1,679,700	1,694,700
Retained earnings	647,826	1,011,006	1,412,488
Total stockholders' equity	$2,688,859	$3,148,307	$3,566,589
Total liabilities and stockholders' equity	$6,316,599	$6,752,971	$7,809,984

Consolidated Statement of Earnings

	52 Weeks ended* April 25, 1964	52 Weeks ended* April 24, 1965	53 Weeks ended* April 30, 1966	52 Weeks ended April 29, 1967
Net sales	$6,018,779	$8,600,392	$9,080,223	$11,048,072
Cost of sales	4,033,576	5,799,868	6,357,169	7,213,188
Gross profit	$1,985,203	$2,800,524	$2,723,054	$ 3,834,884
Expenses:				
Selling, administrative and general	$1,169,392	$1,697,659	$2,029,531	$ 2,756,939
Research and engineering	102,358	303,884	239,851	327,857
Total expenses	$1,271,750	$2,001,543	$2,269,382	$ 3,084,796
Income before income taxes and nonrecurring charges	$ 713,453	$ 798,981	$ 453,672	$ 750,088
Federal and state income taxes	367,542	392,515	221,034	348,606
Income before nonrecurring charges	$ 345,911	$ 406,466	$ 232,638	$ 401,482
Nonrecurring debt expense—after giving effect to income taxes		$ 63,678		.....
Net earnings	$ 345,911	$ 342,788	$ 232,638	$ 401,482
Net earnings as restated	376,788	393,713	264,389	401,482
Earnings per share before nonrecurring charges	$ 0.40	$ 0.51	$ 0.26	$ 0.44
Earnings per share after nonrecurring charges	$ 0.40	$ 0.43	$ 0.26	$ 0.44
Earnings per share as restated	$ 0.48	$ 0.49	$ 0.29	$ 0.44

Earnings per share are based on average shares outstanding of 904,237 in 1966 and 801,196 in 1965 after giving effect to the 2-for-1 stock split-up effective September 15, 1965, and the 3-for-1 stock split on July 7, 1964.

* Earnings restated April 29, 1967, to give effect to an adjustment in the lives of depreciable assets for federal income tax purposes.

(Statement is continued on next page.)

Exhibit 1—Concluded

	52 Weeks ended April 27, 1963	52 Weeks ended April 25, 1964	52 Weeks ended April 24, 1965	53 Weeks ended April 30, 1966	52 Weeks ended April 29, 1967
Net sales	$4,124,445	$6,018,779	$8,600,392	$9,080,223	$11,048,072
Net earnings	$ 191,511	$ 376,788	$ 393,713	$ 264,389	$ 401,482
Expenditures for plant and equipment	$ 272,154	$ 513,130	$ 558,865	$ 304,102	$ 1,027,854
Depreciation	$ 79,719	$ 132,497	$ 211,683	$ 238,161	$ 249,961
Working capital	$ 654,676	$1,525,015	$3,542,857	$3,828,928	$ 3,424,196
Plant and equipment and other assets, net	$ 701,875	$1,187,246	$1,745,839	$1,799,415	$ 2,598,508
Long-term debt	$ 287,245	$1,176,647	$2,501,046	$2,480,036	$ 2,456,115
Shareholders' equity	$1,069,306	$1,535,614	$2,787,650	$3,148,307	$ 3,566,589
Earnings per share	$ 0.25	$ 0.48	$ 0.49	$ 0.29	$ 0.44
Average shares outstanding	777,600	777,600	801,196	904,237	916,542

Average shares outstanding reflect the 2-for-1 stock split-up effective September 15, 1965, and 3-for-1 stock split on July 7, 1964.
Statistical data for the years 1963 to 1966, inclusive, have been adjusted to reflect retroactive adjustments.
Source: Company records.

ski wear, and $550 million going to the 1,200 ski areas and the transportation companies carrying skiers to their destinations. Ninety-eight manufacturers belonged to the SIA. *Skiing International Yearbook* for 1967 listed 85 brands of wooden skis available in 260 models, 49 brands of metal skis in 101 models, and 53 brands of fiberglass skis in 116 models. For each model there could be as many as 15 sizes. Many manufacturers made all three types of skis and some had multiple brands, but even so the industry was divided into many competing units.

The table which follows illustrates the division of the market by price and type:

Type	Number of brands of skis by price range		
	$0–$49.99	$50–$99.99	$100 and up
Wood.............................	69	27	3
(85 brands)			
Metal.........................	0	22	28
(49 brands)		(28 models)	(73 models)
Fiberglass.....................	0	24	39
(53 brands)		(35 models)	(81 models)

Source: *Skiing International Yearbook, 1967*, pp. 90–91. Copyright by Ziff-Davis Publishing Co.

Ski Business summed up an analysis of industry trends as follows:

> Imports of low-priced adult wood skis into the United States are skidding sharply.
>
> U.S. metal skis are gaining faster than any other category.
>
> The ski equipment and apparel market is experiencing an unusually broad and pronounced price and quality uptrend.
>
> Ski specialty shop business appears to be gaining faster than that of the much publicized department stores and general sporting goods outlets.
>
> The growth in the national skier population is probably decelerating and may already have reached a plateau.[1]

Supporting these statements of trends, *Ski Business* made some other observations.

> Foreign skis clearly lost in 1966 at the gain of domestic manufacturers. (The total of imported and domestic skis sold in the United States is believed to be running at over 900,000 pairs annually.) By conservative estimate, U.S. metal ski production in 1966 (for shipment to retail shops for the 1966–67 selling season) was up by at least 40,000 pairs from 1965. . . .
>
> But far more important than the domestic American ski gain (which will continue now that American fiberglass ski makers are entering the market) is the remarkable upward price shift. Thus while 10 per per cent fewer foreign skis entered the United States in 1966, the dollar value of all the skis imported actually rose by more than 10 per cent or $700,000. . . . Here was the real measure of growth of the ski market; it was not in numbers, but in dollars.

[1] John Fry, *Ski Business*, May–June 1967, p. 25.

The principal beneficiary of this remarkable upward shift in consumer preference for higher product quality is, of course, the ski specialty shop. The skier bent on purchasing $140 skis and $80 boots will tend to put his confidence in the experienced specialist retailer. The ski specialist shops themselves are almost overwhelmed by what is happening. Here's one retailer's comment: "Just two or three years ago, we were selling a complete binding for $15. Now skiers come into our shop and think nothing of spending $40 for a binding. . . ."

. . . Most of the department store chains and sporting goods shops contacted by *Ski Business* were also able to report increased business in 1966–67, but somehow the exuberant, expansionist talk seems to have evaporated among nonspecialty ski dealers. Montgomery Ward, for instance, says that ski equipment sales have not come up to company expectations. Ward's has specialized in low end merchandise for beginning and intermediate skiers. . . . Significantly, department stores or sporting goods shops which reported the largest sales increases tended to be those which strive hardest to cast their image in the ski specialist mold. . . .[2]

Ski imports for 1966 served both the low-priced and high-priced market. More than half the Japanese imports of 530,000 pairs of skis were thought to be children's skis which helped to explain the low valuation of the Japanese skis. This value of $6.84 a pair was the f.o.b. price at the door of the Japanese ski factory and does not include shipping, duty, importer's or retailer's margins.[3] *Ski Business* reported imports into the United States as follows:

1966 SKI IMPORTS INTO THE UNITED STATES
(by country of origin)

Country of origin	No. of pairs	Change: 1966 vs. 1965	$ Value	Average $* value per pair 1965	Average $* value per pair 1966
Canada............	7,091	+6,350	149,961	23	21.14
Sweden............	2,767	+1,131	22,386	9	8.09
Norway...........	1,125	−698	18,221	6	16.20
Finland...........	10,184	+5,411	98,275	9	9.65
Belgium...........	129	+129	6,327	. . .	49.05
France............	5,257	+2,828	265,018	49	50.41
West Germany.......	44,736	+9,959	1,010,354	18	22.58
Austria...........	72,536	−20,872	1,511,563	21	20.84
Switzerland........	2,835	+1,155	124,068	39	43.76
Italy.............	7,494	+351	195,723	14	26.12
Yugoslavia.........	22,540	+5,122	254,962	11	11.31
Japan.............	529,732	−89,632	3,625,639	5.54	6.84
Australia..........	2,307	+2,307	114,091	. . .	49.45
1965 total..........	785,746	. . .	$6,692,451	. . .	$8.52
1966 total..........	708,733	−77,013	$7,396,588	$8.52	$10.44

* The average value per pair of skis represents an f.o.b. plant price and does not include charges for shipping and handling, tariff, excise tax, or profit for trading company or wholesaler. Tariff on skis was 16⅔%.

Source: *Ski Business*, May–June 1967, p. 31.

2 Ibid.

3 Ibid.

In the high-price market segment, where skis retailed at $100 or more, the annual market was estimated by industry sources to be approximately 250,000 pairs of skis. Here estimates of the leading contenders according to these industry sources were:

Brand	Type	Estimated sales	Price range
Head (United States).............	Metal	125,000 pairs	$115.00–$175.00
Hart (United States).............	Metal	44,000 pairs	$ 99.50–$175.00
Kniessl (Austria)................	Epoxy	20,000 pairs	$150.00–$200.00
Yamaha (Japan)................	Epoxy	13,000 pairs	$ 79.00–$169.00
Fischer (Austria)................	Wood ⎫ Metal ⎬ Epoxy ⎭	13,000 pairs	$112.00–$189.00

Source: *Skiing International Yearbook, 1967*, pp. 90–91. Copyright by Ziff-Davis Publishing Co.

Fischer was believed to have $15–$18 million sales worldwide. Kniessl was believed to be about the same size as Head worldwide, but only about one-tenth Head's size in the United States. In addition Voit, the recreational products division of AMF, was entering the market with a fiberglass ski. Voit also manufactured water skis, a wide variety of aquatic equipment, and rubber products. AMF's total 1966 sales were $357 million. Recreational equipment accounted for approximately 20%, not including bowling equipment which accounted for an additional 22% of sales.

The skier's skill level was one determining factor in his choice of skis. (For those unfamiliar with the differences among skis designed for each group, a discussion of ski construction is included as Appendix A.) Of the 3.5 million active skiers, 17,000 were regarded as racers, another 75,000 were considered to be experts, and another 100,000 were classed as sufficiently skillful to be strong recreational skiers.

THE MARKET

Skiing was considered to be a sport which attracted the moderately well-to-do and those on the way up. This conception was borne out by the following market data:

A statistical study released early this year [1965] by the Department of Commerce disclosed that the American skier has a median age of 26.2 and a median annual income of $11,115. Moreover, it showed that about two-thirds of all skiers are college graduates.

How do these young, affluent and intelligent men and women spend their skiing dollars? At a typical resort, a person might spend each day $10 for accommodations, $10 for food, $5.00 for a lift ticket and $10 for renting everything needed to attack the slopes from pants and parka to skis, boots, poles and bindings. . . .

The initial purchases of a person determined to have his or her own good equipment and to look well while skiing could easily be about $200. For this amount, a skier could buy everything from winter underwear to goggles and perhaps even have a bit left over for a rum toddy in the ski lodge the first night of his trip.

For instance, ski boots cost from $20 to $150 and average $50 a pair. Skis range from $30 to $200 and poles from $5 to $35.

When it comes to apparel, costs vary considerably. Snow jackets or parkas might cost as little as $20 or as much as $1,000 for those made with fur. Many jackets are available, though, at about $30.

Stretch pants have an average price of about $20. Other apparel requirements for skiing include sweaters which retail from $10 to $50, winter underwear which costs about $5, and ski hats and caps which sell for $3 and up.[4]

There was an apparent fashionability to skiing. Fashion consciousness was apparent in the design of ski equipment, ski wear, and the influx of a new type of skier. Under the headline "The Nonskiers: They Flock to Ski Resorts For The Indoor Sports," *The Wall Street Journal* reported as follows:

Want to take up a rugged, outdoor sport?

Cross skiing off your list.

The sport has gone soft. Ski resorts now have all the comforts of home—if your home happens to have a plush bar, a heated swimming pool, a padded chair lift, boutiques and a built in baby sitter. . . . Skiing, in fact, has become almost an incidental activity at some ski resorts; indeed, some of the most enthusiastic patrons here at Squaw Valley and other resorts don't even know how to ski. They rarely venture outdoors.

So why do they come here? "Men, M-E-N. They're here in bunches, and so am I, baby," answers slinky, sloe-eyed Betty Reames as she selects a couch strategically placed midway between the fireplace and the bar. . . .

Squaw Valley houses half a dozen bars and restaurants and often has three different bands and a folksinger entertaining at the same time. Aspen, in Colorado, throws a mid-winter Mardi Gras. Sun Valley, in Idaho, has a shopping village that includes a two-floor bookstore and boutique selling miniskirts.

Life has also been made softer for those skiers who ski. . . . Also some resorts are making their chair lifts more comfortable by adding foam padding. But even that isn't enough for some softies. "What? Me ride the chair lift? Are you crazy? I'd freeze to death out in the open like that," says blond Wanda Peterson as she waits to ride up the mountain in an enclosed gondola car. She doesn't stand alone. The line of the gondola is 200 strong; the nearby chair lift, meanwhile, is all but empty. . . .

. . . for beginning skiers most resorts offer gentle, meticulously groomed inclines that make it almost impossible to fall. "We try to make it so that the person who has no muscle tone and little experience can't be fooled, can't make a mistake," says one resort operator. "Then we've got him. He's a new customer as well as a happy man."

Once he gets the hang of it—whether he's any good or not—the happy man starts spending lots of money, and that's what the resorts love.[5]

---

[4] *The New York Times,* December 12, 1965. © 1965 by The New York Times Company. Reprinted by permission.

[5] *The Wall Street Journal,* February 1967.

In line with the concern for style, some manufacturers of skiwear and ski equipment developed new colors and annual model changes to inspire annual obsolescence and fad purchases.

HEAD COMPANY HISTORY

Howard Head, chairman and founder of the company bearing his name, was the man responsible for the development of the first successful metal ski. Combining the experience of an aircraft designer with dedication to a sport which he enjoyed, he spent more than three years developing a ski which would not break, turned easily, and tracked correctly without shimmying and chattering. Others had tried to produce metal skis, but Head succeeded almost five years before his nearest competitors, Hart and Harry Holmberg, introduced the Hart metal skis. *Ski Magazine* described the reason behind Howard Head's success:

> . . . He was obsessed, to be sure, and being relatively unencumbered by stockholders, high overhead and strong yearnings for luxurious living, he was well braced for the long haul. . . .
>
> "I made changes only where I had to make them," he has said of the days when his skis were undergoing trial by fire. "When they broke, I made them stronger only where they broke. . . ."[6]

In 1960 Howard Head described the early years of his enterprise and the trials which surrounded it as follows:

> Twelve years ago I took six pairs of handmade metal skis to Stowe, Vermont, and asked the pros there to try them out. It had taken about a year to make those six pairs of skis. The design, based on engineering principles of aircraft construction, was radically different from any ever tried before. I thought it was sound but the pros weren't a bit surprised when all six pairs promptly broke to pieces. After all, others before me had tried to make metal skis and all they had proved was what everyone knew anyway—a ski had to be made of wood.
>
> That was in January 1948. Today about 60% of all high-grade skis sold in the United States are metal skis. The reasons for this revolution in ski manufacturing industry are simple. People like the way metal skis ski, they like their durability, and they like their easy maintenance. . . .
>
> Many small refinements and changes in design have been introduced through the years because of our continued testing and development program and to meet the advances in technique and changes in skiing conditions. But the basic structural design hasn't changed, which speaks well for the original concept.[7]

Mr. Head further indicated that his personal interest in technical problems played a major part in leading him to create his business:

> When I started out, I was a mechanical design engineer—the whole origin of the business was the feeling that it should be possible to build a a better ski. What started as an engineering puzzle ended as a business.
>
> I distinctly remember wondering at that time whether we would ever grow to the point where we would be making 5,000 pairs of skis a year.

---

6 *Ski Magazine,* January 1964.
7 "On Metal Skis" (manuscript by Howard Head, 1960).

Price-volume considerations exerted small influence over initial marketing policy. Mr. Head priced his first metal skis at $75 in spite of the fact that most skiers were using war surplus skis that cost $20, including bindings. Mr. Head discussed his early ideas on quality, costs, and prices as follows:

> The great disadvantage of all metal skis is simply their high price. This became apparent to us when we were pioneering the original metal ski and found it was going to cost a good bit more than a wood ski. We didn't let that stop us because we believed the striking advantages of a metal ski more than compensated for its high price. As it turned out, even with a higher initial price, Head Skis proved to cost less in the long run because they are so durable. . . .
>
> In the early days people had no way of knowing the skis would last so long that they actually ended up costing less than cheaper skis. They simply liked them enough to go ahead and buy them in spite of the price.[8]

Mr. Head found a market which was quite unexpected. In spite of the high price, Head skis appealed more to the average beginner or slightly better skier than to racers. Among skiers, Heads became known as "cheaters." This designation grew out of the skis' ability to make almost anyone look good. "They practically turned themselves." Soon the black plastic top of the Head ski became a ubiquitous status symbol on the slopes.

PRODUCT POLICY

The keynote of Mr. Head's product policy was quality. His fundamental belief was that the consumer should get all he pays for and pay for all he gets. The 17-year history of the company had seen considerable upgrading of the products. Several times in the past the company had called in particular models or production runs of skis which had been found to be defective. One executive commented that this had been done without hesitation, even when the company was in precarious financial condition.

Asked what set Head apart from its competition, Mr. Head replied as follows:

> I believe that it is a tradition of attention to detail which grew out of its entrepreneurial history. In every aspect we attempt to follow through. Service, dealer relations, product quality, style, advertising are all important and must be done in the best way we know how.
>
> We stress continued emphasis on quality of product and quality of operating philosophy. We pay meticulous attention to the individual relationships with dealers and the public.
>
> I have attempted to make creativity, imagination, and standards of perfection apply across the board. This was always our desire, and we only failed to live up to it when the business got too big for the existing staff. The philosophy remained constant, and now we have the people to live up to it.

---

[8] Ibid.

We get a return on this attention to detail. The feedback from success allows us to maintain the necessary staff to insure continuation of this philosophy.
We allow no sloppiness.

Head skis came in one color—black. There was no special trim to designate the model, only a modification in the color of the name "Head" embossed on the top of the ski and a change in the color of the case: red for some models, yellow or black for others. Although at one time a chrome top was considered, it was rejected because of the glare, and because it was difficult to see against the snow. In addition to these factors, one executive described black as being a conservative color which would go with anything. Howard Head explained that he "did not want to complicate the consumer's choice."

I deeply believe in sticking to function and letting style take care of itself. We have stuck so rigorously to our black color because it is honest and functional that it has become almost a trademark. While we constantly make minor improvements, we never make an important model change unless there is a performance reason for it. In other words, we skipped the principle of forced obsolescence, and we will continue to skip it.

This policy had been consciously chosen and maintained, in spite of competition which had introduced six or eight different colors and yearly color changes to keep up with fashion.

Apart from color and style, skis had to perform well on the slopes. There were three fundamental things which a ski had to do. It had to "track,"[9] "traverse,"[10] and "turn."[11] The need to perform these functions imposed certain constraints on ski design, and the necessity to both track and turn required some compromises in design. *Ski Magazine* lisited some of the characteristics which this balancing involved:

1. The tip must be pointed and turned up in a gradual curve to permit the ski to climb over obstacles without changing directions, to prevent it from diving beneath soft snow, and to help prevent the skis from crossing. (Splay)
2. The bottom should be flat and perfectly flush with its steel edges, except for a narrow groove extending the length of the ski which increases tracking stability.
3. The skis must be straight without warp or twist, each side must have the same curve to it, and the groove must be straight and in the middle.
4. The bottom surface must be slippery so that it will run smoothly.

---

[9] Track: If you point a ski down a slope and allow it to run freely, it should hold a straight course—over bumps and through hollows and on every type of snow surface.

[10] Traverse: A ski should be able to hold a straight line while moving diagonally across a slope over obstacles and various snow conditions.

[11] Turn: When a skier releases the edges of his skis, the skis must be capable of slipping sideways, and, when edged, they must bite into the snow evenly. (A skiing turn is nothing more than a slideslip carved into an arc by the controlled bite of the edges.)

5. To distribute the skier's weight over the length of the ski, a cambered or arched shape is necessary.
6. A ski must be flexible.
7. The shape or "sidecut" of the ski must be correlated to the flexibility of the ski and the torsional rigidity of the material used. A flexible ski will have difficulty holding if the sidecut is too straight, for the ends will barely touch the snow. Only a correct sidecut will tolerate a momentary twist of the skis, reducing the effect of edges just enough to allow smooth passage over bumps yet not enough to pull the ski out of line.
8. A sharp edge is needed to hold on hard surfaces.
9. For maximum stability, the skier must choose the proper length ski.[12]

Mr. Head found a proper combination of these elements for the recreation skier in his earliest metal ski. Designated the "Standard," this model underwent substantial improvement over its 17-year history. Until 1960, however, the goal of providing the best ski for experts eluded Head and other metal ski makers. Mr. Head said of this period, "During the early years at Head Ski, we were too busy making the best ski we could for the general public to spend much time developing a competition ski."

For experts, the basic complaint against metal skis was that they were too "soft" and tended to vibrate badly at racing speeds. This problem was substantially solved in 1960, when Head introduced its "Vector" model, to be followed in 1962 (and later entirely replaced) by the "Competition." In these skis, an imbedded layer of neoprene dampened vibrations and considerably improved performance. Whereas in 1960 most competitors in the Squaw Valley Olympics had stuck to their wooden skis, by the end of 1962 Head skis were in wide use, and they had carried 77 racers out of 141 to positions among the top six contenders at races conducted by the International Professional Ski Race Association in Canada and the United States. Also about half the skis used in the U.S. National Junior and Senior Championships that year were Heads.

By 1966 Head had established itself as an important factor in the ski racing world. Two Americans had set the world speed record—106.527 m.p.h.—on Head skis. In major international competition in 1966, one-third of all finishers in the top ten places at all events were on Head skis, and Head was the outstanding single manufacturer on the circuit with 18 gold medals, 15 silver medals, and 15 bronze medals.

The 1968 Head line included a ski for every type of skier from the unskilled beginner to the top professional racer. The line was described in Head's *Ski Handbook* as follows:

> . . . the most important design consideration is you—the type of skier you are and where you ski. That's why your dealer was able to offer you nine different models of Head Skis to choose from. You can be sure the model he helped you select was the optimum—for you.
>
> STANDARD—THE MOST FORGIVING SKI: For beginners of average size and athletic ability up to intermediates learning stem christies.

---

[12] *Skiing International Yearbook 1967*, pp. 62–63. Copyright by Ziff-Davis Publishing Co.

Also for the better, occasional skier who prefers an easy-going, lively, light-weight ski that practically turns for him.

The *Standard* is medium soft in flex overall for easy turning and responsiveness. Engineered side camber and relative overall width contribute to ease and slow-speed stability. Its light weight and torsional rigidity make traversing and other basic maneuvers simple. Thin taper in the tip allows the *Standard* to cut easily through the heaviest snow instead of ploughing.

Standard. $115. Thirteen sizes from 140 to 215 cm. Black top, sidewalls and bottom; white engraving.

MASTER—MORE OF A CHALLENGE: For the skier who has mastered the basic techniques and wants to begin driving the skis and attacking the slope. As lively as the *Standard,* this is also the ski for the heavier, more athletic beginner who wants more "beef" underfoot.

The *Master* is like the Standard in basic shape but thicker and heavier. The tip radius is longer for extra shock absorption. Slightly stiffer flex overall acts as a heavy-duty shock absorber over bumps.

Master. $135. Nine sizes from 175 through 215 cm. Black top and sidewalls; blue base and engraving.

THE FABULOUS 360—THE MOST VERSATILE SKI: Finest all-around ski ever made—for the skier beginning stem christies on through the expert class. Remarkable for its ease of turning as well as its steadiness and precision, the *360* is the serious skier's ski for attack or enjoyment on the slope, under any condition of snow or terrain.

With its smooth-arcing flex pattern, the *360* has the supple forebody of the other recreational skis, but is slightly stiffer at the tail. Its side camber is similar to that of the *Giant Slalom.* Narrower overall than the *Standard* or *Master.* Rubber damping in the lightweight top-skin unit makes the *360* a very responsive ski, allowing the expert to control his turns beautifully and set his edges precisely. Tip splay is designed to give easiest entrance through snow and to provide excellent shock absorption, particularly in heavily moguled areas.

The Fabulous 360. $155. Eleven sizes from 170 to 220 cm. Black top and sidewalls; yellow base and engraving.

SLALOM—THE HOT DOG: For the expert skier who likes to stay in the fall-line, slashing through quick short-radius turns on the steepest, iciest, slopes. The *Slalom* has been totally redesigned this year to fit the special needs of the expert recreational skier, who wants the lightest, fastest-reacting, and best ice-holding ski possible.

Slalom is Head's narrowest ski overall. And, thanks to the light-weight top-skin unit and core, it is also one of Head's lightest skis. Lightness and narrowness allow for carved or pivoted turns, reflex-fast changes in direction. Special engineered side camber and relative softness at the thin waist give the ultimate in "feel" and control on ice. Neoprene rubber gives the damping and torque necessary for a top-performance ice ski.

Slalom. $160. Five sizes from 190 to 210 cm. Black top and sidewalls. Racing red base and engraving.

DOWNHILL—BOMB!: Widest and heaviest Head ski, the *Downhill* is for the advanced skier—recreational or competitor—who wants to blast straight down the slope. It offers the ultimate in high-speed performance, tracking ability, and stability over bumps and moguls.

The long tip splay and supple forebody is the secret of the *Down-*

hill's exceptional speed advantage. It virtually planes over the surface of the slope. With its firm midsection and tail acting like the rudder of a hydroplane, the *Downhill* affords the skier utmost control coupled with great turning ability at slower speeds. Heavy duty topskin unit and added rubber damping contribute to the stability and high-speed "quietness" of the *Downhill*. This is the elite international-class racing ski, and experts have found it an excellent powder ski as well.

Downhill. $175. Seven sizes from 195 to 225 cm. Black top and sidewalls. Yellow base and engraving.

GIANT SLALOM—GRACE PLUS SPEED: The *"GS"* incorporates the best features of the *Downhill* and *Slalom* models. It offers the expert skier—recreational and/or competitor—the optimum in stable all-out speed skiing, combined with precise carving and holding ability in high-speed turns. It is another favorite on the international racing circuit.

The *Giant Slalom's* stability and precision come from a unique combination of sidecut and relatively stiff flex. The *"GS"* is similar to the *360* in overall dimensions, but has a stiffer flex pattern than the *360*, particularly underfoot. This gives the *"GS"* the versatility of the *360* but with greater control at high speeds. Tip splay is designed for maximum shock absorption and easy riding.

Giant Slalom. $165. Nine sizes from 175 to 215 cm. Black top and sidewalls. Yellow base and engraving.

YOUNGSTER'S COMPETITION—JUNIOR HOT DOG: Carrying the *Giant Slalom* engraving, this ski is designed for expert youngsters who want, and can handle, a faster, more demanding ski than the small size *Standard*. Similar in cut and performance characteristics to the *Giant Slalom*, but without the *"GS's"* neoprene damping, to provide the junior racer with easier turning ability.

Youngster's Competition. $120. Two sizes, 160 and 170 cm. Black top and sidewalls; yellow bottom and engraving.

SHORTSKI—FUN WITHOUT EFFORT: Not just a sawed-off *Standard,* but a totally different ski with totally different proportions. Very wide for its length, quite stiff overall, the *Shortski* is the only ski of its kind with an engineered side camber. Ideal for quick learning of the fundamentals of skiing. Also for the older or more casual skier who enjoys being on the slopes and wants the easiest-possible tracking and turning ski ever built.

Shortski. $115. Four sizes from 150 to 190 cm. Black top, sidewalls and bottom. White engraving.

DEEP POWDER—SHEER BUOYANCY ON THE SLOPES: Super soft flexibility and buggy-whip suppleness allow this specialized ski to float in powder, while maintaining easy turning plus full control and tracking ability on packed slopes.

The *Deep Powder* is very wide and soft overall, with a "hinge-like" effect in the forebody that enables it to glide through the deepest powder.

Deep Powder. $115. Five sizes from 195 to 215 cm. Black top, sidewalls and bottom. White engraving.

Head was constantly experimenting with new designs and introducing minor modifications to improve the performance and durability of its product. When asked about a major change in product construction, such as to the fiber-reinforced plastic type ski, Mr. Head gave the following reply:

We think that the metal sandwich construction is the best material. We do not see this situation changing in the foreseeable future. Certainly now the other exotic materials are not gaining ground. They lack the versatility of application of the metal sandwich ski. The epoxy or fiber reinforced plastic have low durability and don't have the wide performance range of our skis.

We believe that the advantage of the metal ski is that you can build in any performance characteristic which you desire. Naturally, we have a research department investigating other materials, but until a major improvement is found, we should stick to our basic material. We can always build the best ski for beginners, and we can adapt that ski to get the performance required by experts.

MARKETING POLICIES

Head's emphasis on quality extended beyond the product to the dealer and service network. The company sold through only a limited number of franchised dealers, who had satisfied management that "they know something about skis and skiing." Ten district sales managers were employed, who sold to about 900 dealers throughout the United States. Of these about 85% were ski specialty shops, 12% were large full-line sporting goods stores, and the remainder were full-line department stores (see Exhibit 2). Head skis were distributed in Europe through an exclusive distributor, Walter Haensli of Klosters, Switzerland. In 1964 he sold 19% of Head's output. This figure appeared to be declining gradually.

Exhibit 2

HEAD SKI COMPANY, INC.

Dealer Organization, 1962–67

(franchised dealers)

Year	Number at beginning	Newly franchised	Terminated or not renewed	Number at end
1962	390	105	41	454
1963	454	136	30	560
1964	560	167	57	670
1965	670	96	39	727
1966	727 (est.)	N.A.	N.A.	900
1967	900 (est.)	30	N.A.	—

N.A.—Not available.
Note: In addition the franchised dealers had approximately 300 branches which are not included in the above figures.
Source: Company records.

Head believed that a Head franchise was valuable to a dealer. Many large stores had wanted to sell Heads, but had been turned down. Saks Fifth Avenue had waited eight years before it was given a franchise. Mr. Head commented on dealer selection as follows:

Getting Saks Fifth Avenue as a dealer is consistent with our operating philosophy of expecting the same quality from our dealers as from ourselves.

Once they become a dealer, however, we get to know the people involved and work closely with them. Increasingly, we are recognizing the business value of providing more assistance and leadership to our dealers in helping them to do a better job for their customers.

Even a large, well-managed department store or sporting goods store may need help in the specialized area of skis. They may need help in display stock selection, or even personnel selection. We are increasingly concerned about the type of personnel who sell skis. There is a high degree of dependence on the salesman. He must be a good skier himself.

We have seen instances of two department stores of essentially identical quality in the same area where one store could sel¹ eight pairs of skis a year and the other three hundred simply because of a different degree of commitment to getting the right man to sell. Skis can only be sold by a floor salesman who can ski and who can sell from personal experience.

The company was committed to the belief that selling skis was an exacting business. The ski size had to be matched to the individual's height and body weight, flexibility had to be chosen correctly depending on use, and bindings had to be mounted properly.

Following up on the initial sale, Head offered extensive customer service. Dealers were expected to have service facilities for minor repairs and the factory had facilities for sharpening edges, rebuilding the plastic portion of the ski, and matching a single ski if the mate had been broken beyond repair. Even in the busiest part of the season, service time was kept under three weeks.

In March 1967, Mr. Harold Seigle, the newly appointed president and chief operating officer of Head, sent out a "management news bulletin" outlining Head's marketing philosophy:

Marketing Philosophy

1. Our current selective dealer organization is one of Head Ski Company's most valuable assets, next to the product itself.
2. Our continued sales growth will be based on a market-by-market approach aimed at increasing the effectiveness of our present dealers and by the very selective addition of new dealers wherever present dealers prove to be inadequate rather than by mass distribution and merchandising techniques.
3. Our future marketing efforts, particularly personal selling, advertising, merchandising, and sales promotion, will be geared to the specific needs of our dealers to sell all Head Ski products.
4. We want and will have the finest sales forces in the industry . . . who rely upon personal integrity, service, and hard work to do a professional selling job rather than inside deals and short cuts.
5. We feel that, next to quality products, strong personal selling at the manufacturer's level and the retail level is paramount to our continued success and tends to transcend other facets of marketing that contribute to the sale of merchandise.

Advertising was done on a selective basis. An outside source reported as follows:

The company invests about 2% of gross sales in advertising, split between the skiing magazines (50%) and *Sports Illustrated, The New Yorker,* and *Yachting*—"the same kind of people like to sail."

The most effective promotion, however, is probably the ski itself. Head is delighted at the growing demand for his skis in the rental market. "We sold 10,000 pairs—almost 10% of our business—for rental last year," he points out, "and everyone who rents those skis becomes a prospect."[13]

To aid in placing rental skis, Head gave an additional 12%–15% discount on skis which a dealer purchased for rental. Ski rental was seen as the best way to introduce a customer to the ease of skiing on Heads.

The Head Ski Company approach was a "soft sell." Unlike many sporting goods companies, Head did not rely on personal endorsements of famous skiers. According to one executive, it was impossible under American Amateur rules even to have posters featuring an amateur skier. Professional endorsements were probably ineffective anyway, since so many other sporting goods companies used them, and most of the public knew that such endorsements could be bought. Head tried to get actual news pictures of famous skiers or racers using Head skis and winning. To make certain that top skiers would use Head skis, the company did lend skis to racers for one year. Even this practice was expensive and had to be tightly controlled. A good skier might need upwards of nine pairs of skis a year, which would represent an expenditure of nearly $1,000. Head did feel this type of promotion yielded a secondary benefit of product development information which could not be overlooked.

Head had received many requests for a promotional film made in conjunction with United Airlines showing famous ski slopes. Head was mentioned in the title, at the end, and in a few identifiable spots in the body of the show. This film was used by ski clubs and other organizations to promote interest in the sport.

Other Head promotion came as a result of skiwear and resort advertisements. As *Sales Management* put it:

> So great is the worldwide prestige of Head skis that although Howard Head claims he makes no promotional tie-in deals, the ski buff can hadly miss seeing the familiar black skis in ads for anything from parkas to ski resorts. They're status symbols.[14]

PRODUCTION

Head skis were produced in three steps. The Detail Department made up the various components which were to go into the assembly, including the core, the nose piece, the tail piece, the top plastic, the top and bottom skins, the running surface, and the edges. The separate pieces were then taken to the Cavity Department, where they were assembled. Here, too, the various layers were laid into a mold and heated and bonded under controlled time, temperature, and pressure. At this point

[13] *Sales Management*, February 5, 1965.
[14] Ibid.

the skis were roughed out on a band saw. From that time on, all work was done on the skis as a pair. In the Finishing Department, the skis were ground to final form, buffed, polished, and engraved.

Manufacture involved a great deal of handwork, of which 70% was characterized as requiring a high degree of skill. The basic nature of the assembly process meant that operations did not lend themselves to mass production techniques.

In May 1967, Head completed the fifth addition to the plant since its construction in 1959. Prior to the new addition, the plant contained 105,668 square feet, of which 93,040 was devoted to manufacturing and warehouse facilities, and 12,628 to office space. Included were a cafeteria, locker rooms, and shower areas for the workers.

Howard Head commented on the difficulty of the manufacturing process and on the relationship between costs and price:

> [There are] approximately 250 different operations, involving a great number of specially developed machines, tools, and processes. None of the processes is standard. It all had to be developed more or less from scratch.
>
> Some of the special-purpose machines involved are those for routing the groove in the bottom aluminum, for attaching the steel edges, and for profiling the ski after it comes out of the presses. Also there are the bonding procedures which require an unusual degree of control of heat and pressure cycles.
>
> Supplementing all the special-purpose machines, we have learned to make rather unusual use of band saws. A good example of a demanding band-saw operation is the profiling of the plywood and plastic core elements. Since the stiffness of a ski at any point goes up as the square of the spacing between the top and bottom sheets—i.e., the core thickness—a normal band-saw tolerance of about 0.010″ would grossly affect our flexibility pattern and would be out of the question. However, by special adapters and guides, we are actually able to band saw these parts in high production at about ten seconds apiece to a tolerance of plus or minus 0.002″ over the entire contour.
>
> An example of effective but low cost equipment in our factory is the press used to laminate 3′ x 10′ sheets of plywood core material to their corresponding sheets of sidewall plastic. This operation requires a total load of some 90,000 pounds. By using a roof beam as the reaction point, the floor for a base, and three screw jacks for pressure, we are able to produce enough material for 600 pairs of skis at one shot with equipment costing a total of about $250.
>
> It's been our policy from the start to put absolute emphasis on quality of product. We never compromise on old material, nor reject a new one on the basis of cost. In principle, if better skis could be made out of sheet platinum, I suspect we would wind up with it. In other words it is our policy to make the best product we can regardless of cost and then price it accordingly to the trade.

Production at Head was on a three-shift basis throughout the year, with skis being made for inventory during the slow months. There were over 600 employees.

Six attempts had been made to unionize the plant, but all had been rejected, several times by three-to-one majorities. One warehouse employee with 12 years' seniority said, "It's a nice place to work. We don't need a union. If you have a problem, Mr. Head will listen to you."

All employees received automatic step raises based on seniority, as well as merit reviews and raises. In addition there was a profit-sharing trust plan which in the past had generally added 6%–7% to the employees' salaries. These funds became fully vested after three years.

Another important benefit in which exempt salaried employees participated was the year-end bonus plan. Under this plan, three groups received different bonus rates. For the lowest paid group, the rate was 3% if pretax profits on sales were under 2%, but 10%–11% if profits were 8%–12%. For the middle group, no bonus was paid if profits were 2% or below, but the rate was 20%–22% if profits ranged between 8% and 12%. For the top group rates were not disclosed, but it was indicated that their bonus plan was even more steeply peaked. For most of the past several years, the payoffs had been at or near the upper range.

FINANCE

The initial financing of Head Ski Company was $6,000 from Howard Head's personal funds. In 1953 Mr. Head sold 40% of the stock in the company for $60,000. This, together with retained earnings and normal bank debt, financed expansion until 1960 when common stock was issued. Additional financing was required to continue the rapid expansion, and in January 1965 a $3,527,500 package was sold, made up of 5½% convertible subordinated debentures in face amount of $2,125,-000, and 42,500 shares of common stock. Until the stock issue of 1965, Howard Head had owned 42.4% of the common stock, and the other directors and officers had owned 46.1%. At no time had there been any question about the commanding role of Howard Head when important decisions were made. Full conversion of the new issue would represent 17.1% ownership.

Expansion was viewed by many in the company as a defensive tactic. The belief was expressed that "if you do not grow as fast as the market will allow you to, you are taking substantial risk that someone else will come in and take that market away from you." In addition, the new funds provided capital for two diversifications started in 1966: The Head Ski and Sportswear Co., and the Head plastics division.

In spite of the drop in earnings growth, the stock market continued to evaluate Head's prospects at 29 to 60 times previous years' earnings. During the period January 1966 to July 1967, its stock sold in the range from 9⅜ to 17¾. As late as January 1965, however, the stock had sold at 22¾.

ORGANIZATION

As of June 1967, the Head Ski Company was organized along functional lines. Reporting to the president were the vice president for operations, the treasurer, and the directors of marketing, quality control, and the director of personnel. This organization pattern had been introduced by Mr. Harold Seigle when he was named chief operating officer on January 16, 1967 (see Exhibit 3).

Of the 26 men shown on the organization chart, 12 had been with Head one year or less. When asked about the potential difficulties of that situation, Mr. Head responded,

> I would only say that if you are to have a lot of new people, you must have one man in command who is an experienced and gifted professional at utilizing people. My job is to support and use that man.

Mr. Head reviewed the history of the organization which had led to the current structure as follows:

> I think that this is typical of the kind of business that starts solely from an entrepreneurial product basis, with no interest or skills in management or business in the original package. Such a business never stops to plan. The consuming interest is to build something new and to get acceptance. The entrepreneur has to pick up the rudiments of finance and organizational practices as he goes along. Any thought of planning comes later. Initially he is solely concerned with the problems of surviving and building. Also, if the business is at all successful, it is so successful that there is no real motivation to stop and obtain the sophisticated planning and people-management techniques. Such a business is fantastically efficient as long as it can survive. One man can make all of the important decisions. There is no pyramidal team structure.
>
> In our case this approach worked quite successfully until about 1955 when we sold 10,000 pairs of skis and reached the $500,000 sales level. The next five years from 1955 to 1960 saw a number of disorganized attempts to acquire and use a more conventional pyramidal organizational system. To put it succinctly, what was efficient at the $500,000 level was increasingly inefficient as we reached $1 million, then $2 million in sales. One man just couldn't handle it. I made too many mistakes. It was like trying to run an army with only a general and some sergeants. There were just no officers, to say nothing of an orderly chain of command.
>
> In 1960 came the first successful breakthrough, where I finally developed the ability to take on a general manager who later became an executive vice president. It was hard for me to learn to operate under this framework. The most striking thing missing from this period was a concept of people-management. I spent five years gradually learning not to either over- or under-delegate.
>
> Let me interject that the final motivation necessary to make a complete transition to an orderly company came because the company got into trouble in 1965–66. Even five years after the beginning of a team system, the company got into trouble, and this was the final prod which pushed me to go all the way. It is interesting that it took 12 years. Up until 1960 the company was totally under my direction. From 1960 to 1965 we stuttered between too much of my direction and not enough.
>
> The chief difficulty for me was to learn to lay down a statement of the results required and then stay out of details. The weakness was in finding a formula of specifying objectives, then giving freedom as long as the objectives were met.
>
> The appointment of Hal Seigle as president brought us a thoroughly sophisticated individual who can bring us the beginning of big business

Exhibit 3

HEAD SKI COMPANY, INC.
Organization Chart
(June 1967)

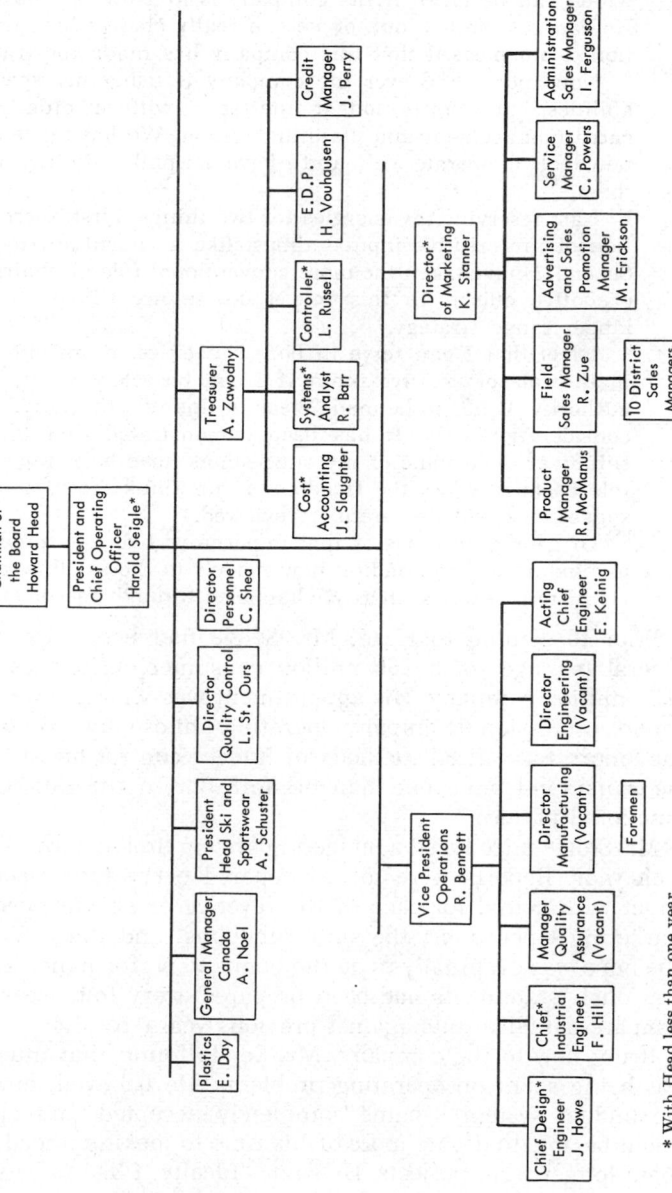

* With Head less than one year.
Source: Company records.

methods. On my part, this change has involved two things: first, my finally recognizing that I wanted this kind of organization; second, the selection of a man with proven professional management skills.

Unfortunately, with an entrepreneur, there are only two courses which can be taken if the company is to grow beyond a certain size. He can get the hell out, or he can really change his method of operation. I am pleased that this company has made the transition.

Now more than ever the company is using my special skills and abilities, but I am no longer interfering with an orderly and sophisticated management and planning system. We have given the company new tools to operate with, and I have not pulled the rug out from under them.

I am reserving my energies for two things. First, there is a continuation of my creative input—almost like a consultant to the company. Second, I have taken the more conventional role of chairman and chief executive officer. In this role I devote my efforts to planning and longer range strategy.

I feel that I can serve in both capacities. I can only be successful in the role of creative input if I can be solely a consultant without authority. It has to be made clear in this role that anything said is for consideration only. It has been demonstrated that this role is consultative, since some of my suggestions have been rejected. I like this role because I like the freedom. I can think freer, knowing that my suggestions will be carefully reviewed.

Of course, in areas of real importance like new product lines such as binding or boot, adding new models to the ski line, or acquisitions, etc., I must exert authority, channeled through the president.

Prior to coming to Head, Mr. Seigle had been vice president and general manager of a $50 million consumer electronics division of a $150 million company. His appointment was viewed as "contributing to a more professional company operating philosophy." He hoped to introduce more formalized methods of budget control and to "preside over the transition from a 'one man' organization to a traditionally conceived functional pattern."

Mr. Seigle introduced a budgeting system broken down into 13 periods each year. Reports were to be prepared every four weeks comparing target with actual for each of the revenue or expense centers, such as marketing, operations, the staff functions, and the three subsidiaries. The hope was eventually to tie the bonus to performance against budget. Previously statements had been prepared every four weeks, but only to compare actual results against previous years' results.

Being new to the company, Mr. Seigle found that much of his time was being spent on operating problems. He believed, however, that as the budget system became completely accepted and operational, he would be able to devote more of his time to looking ahead and worrying about longer term projects. He said: "Ideally, I like to be working six to eighteen months ahead of the organization. As a project gets within six months of actual operation, I will turn it over to the operating managers." He had hired a manager for corporate planning with whom he worked closely.

Under the previous organization from March 1966 until Mr. Seigle's appointment, Howard Head had presided directly over the various departments and marketing functions. There was no overall marketing director at that time. Even in the period from 1960 to 1966 when there was an executive vice president, Mr. Head indicated that he had concerned himself with the operating details of the business.

A VIEW TOWARD THE FUTURE

Head's first diversification was to ski poles. These were relatively simple to manufacture and were sold through existing channels. As with the skis, Head maintained the highest standards of quality and style. The poles were distinguished from competition by their black color and adoption of the tapered shape and extra light weight which at the time were unavailable on other high-priced, quality ski poles. Head's prices were well toward the upper end of the spectrum: $24.50, as compared with as little as $5 for some brands. Success in selling poles encouraged the company to look at other products it might add.

Two further steps taken were toward diversification in late 1966 when Head formed a plastics division and established a subsidiary, Head Ski and Sportswear, Inc.

The plastic division's activity centered on high molecular weight plastics. In March 1967 a press release was issued concerning this activity:

> Head Ski Co., Inc., has signed a license agreement with Phillips Petroleum Company . . . to use a new method developed by Phillips for extruding ultra-high molecular weight high density polyethylene into finished products. . . .
>
> Developmental equipment has been installed at the Head plant here and limited quantities of sheet have been extruded and tested in the running surface of Head skis with excellent results. . . . Production of ski base material is scheduled for this Spring. . . .
>
> In addition to its own running surface material, the Head plastics division has been developing special ultra-high molecular weight high density polyethylene compound to serve a variety of industrial applications. . . .
>
> Ultra-high molecular weight high density polyethylene is an extremely tough abrasion-resistant thermoplastic capable of replacing metal and metal alloys in many industrial areas. Compared with regular high density resins, the ultra-high molecular weight material has better stress-cracking resistance, better long-term stress life and less notch sensitivity.

The diversification into skiwear was considered by company executives to be the more important move. Howard Head talked about the logic of this new venture as follows:

> Skiwear is "equipment" first and fashion second. We are satisfied that our line of skiwear is better than anything done before. It represents the same degree of attention to detail which has characterized our hardware line.

The president of the new subsidiary, Alex Schuster, said:

> Many people thought that Head should stay in hardware such as poles, bindings, and wax. As I see it, however, by going into skiwear we are taking advantage of ready-made distribution and reputation.

There is no reason why the good will developed through the years can't be related to our endeavor.

This new market offers a greater potential and reward than the more hardware oriented areas. Any entry into a new market has difficulties. These can only be solved by doing things right and by measuring up to the Head standards. Having a Head label commits us to a standard of excellence.

Assuming that we live up to those standards, we shall be able to develop into a supplier in a small market but with formidable potential. We are creating a skill base for further diversification.

Our products are engineered, not designed. We are concerned with the engineered relationship among fabric, function, and fit. The engineering details are not always obvious, but they are related to functional demands. Emphasis is placed on function over fashion, yet there is definite beauty created out of concern for function. We are definitely in tune with fashion trends.

[See Exhibit 4 for examples of the new products.]

We will provide a complete skiing outfit—pants, parkas, sweaters, accessories, sox, and gloves. We will offer a total coordinated look.

Along with the design innovations, we shall offer innovations in packaging, display and promotion. We have to go beyond simply preparing the proper apparel.

Head Ski and Sportswear did both manufacturing and subcontracting. The products which had the highest engineering content were made in the Head plant. Sweaters, with less engineering, were contract-made to Head specifications by one of Europe's leading sweater manufacturers.

The collection was first shown to dealers in April 1967 and was scheduled for public release for the 1967–68 skiing season. Initial response by dealers and by the fashion press had been extremely encouraging. *Ski Business* reported:

HEAD'S UP.

. . . way up, in fact 194% ahead of planned volume on its premier line of skiwear.

Anyone who expected Howard Head's entry into the world of fashion to be presented in basic black was in for a surprise. Ironically the skiwear collection that blasted off with the hottest colors in the market is offered by a man who is totally color blind. . . .

On pants: The $55 pant was the big surprise. It was our top seller—way beyond expectations—and the basic $45 pant came in second in sales. Another surprise was the $70 foam waisted pant for which we only projected limited sales—it's a winner. . . .

On orders: Way beyond expectations. Ninety per cent of the orders are with ski shops and 10% with the department stores. Naturally we are committed to selling Head Ski dealers but it definitely is not obligatory.[15]

The sportswear subsidiary had been set up in a separate plant five miles from Head's Timonium headquarters. It was an autonomous operation with a separate sales force and profit responsibility. The initial premise was that the sportswear should be distributed through current

---

[15] *Ski Business*, May–June, 1967.

Exhibit 4

SAMPLES OF THE NEW HEAD SKIWEAR

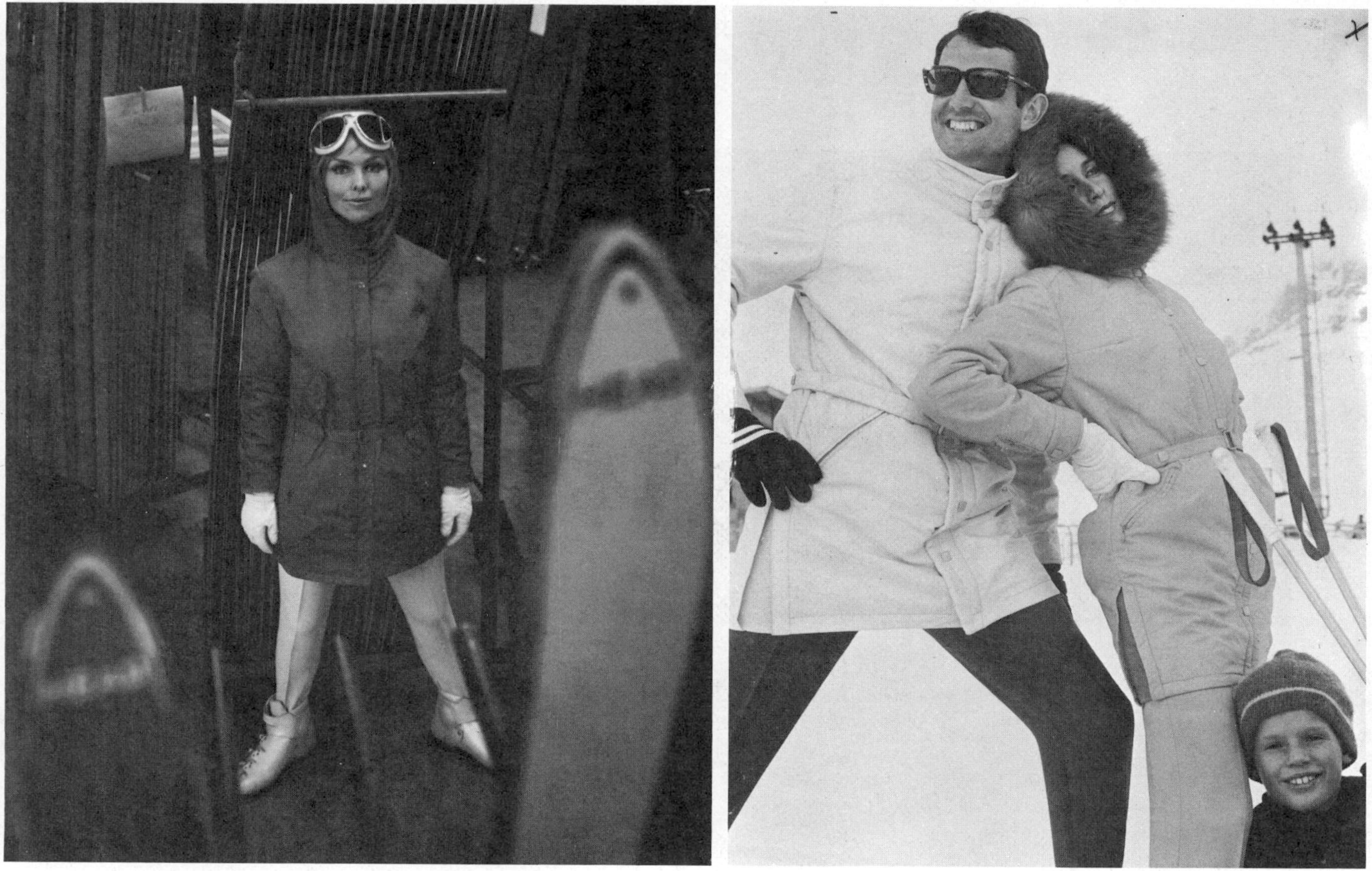

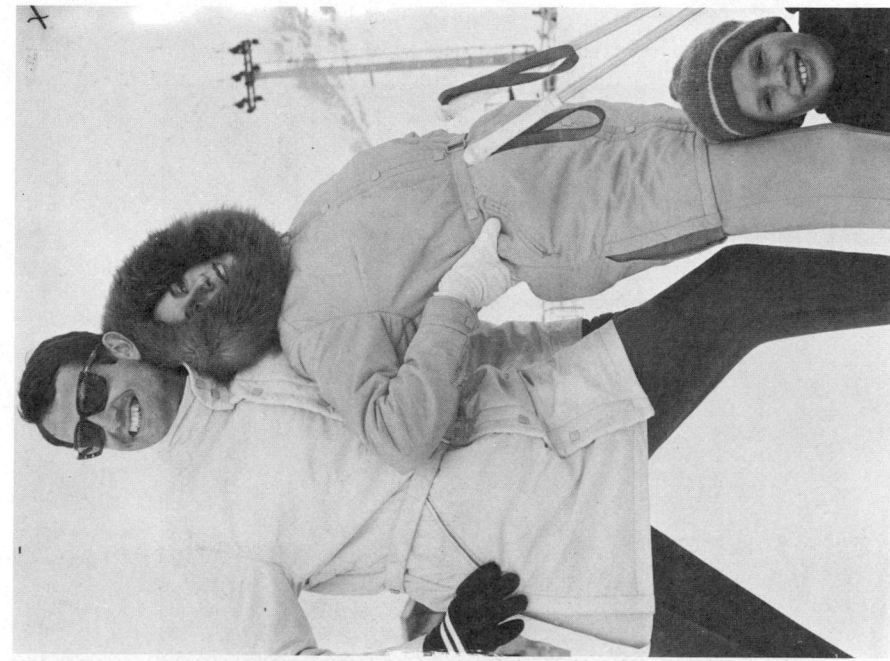

Exhibit 4—Continued
SAMPLES OF THE NEW HEAD SKIWEAR

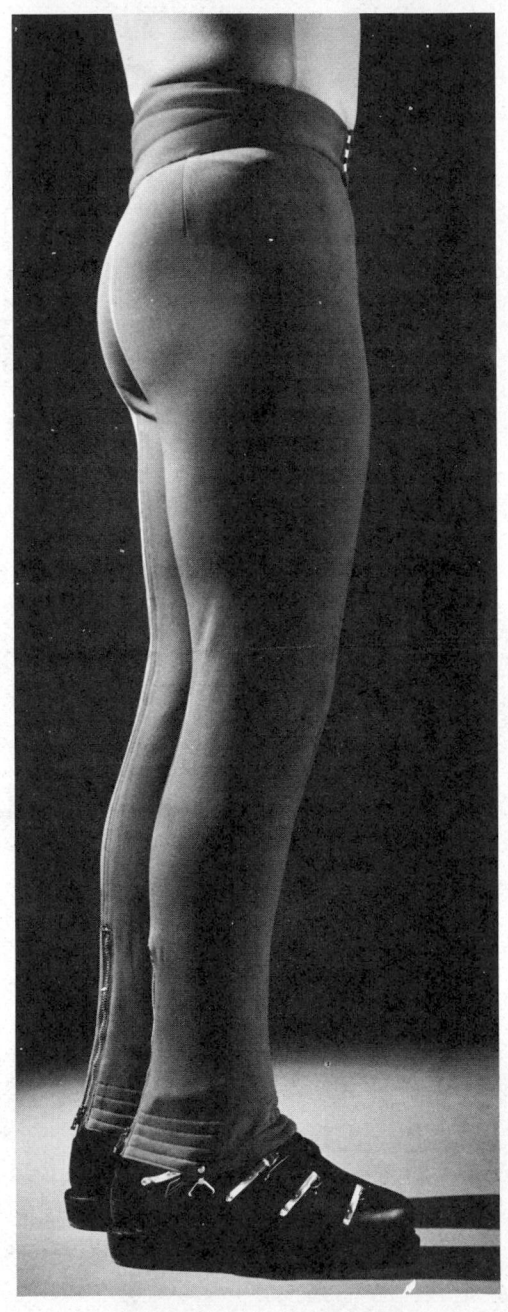

Head dealers, although according to Mr. Seigle the marketing decisions of the sportswear division would be made independently of decisions in the ski division. Although Head dealers were offered the Head sportswear line, it was not sold on an exclusive basis. Distribution would be directly from factory salesmen to the dealer. Within the company, the necessity for a separated and different type of sales force was acknowledged. As one executive phrased it, "I can't imagine our ski salesmen trying to push soft goods. Our salesmen got into the business first and foremost because they were excellent skiers." As with skis and poles, the product line was to be maintained at the high end of the spectrum in both quality and price.

When asked about future growth potential, Mr. Seigle replied that he believed Head would continue to grow rapidly in the future. He saw the potential of doubling the ski business in the next five years. Although he characterized the sportswear business as a "good calculated risk," he believed it offered the potential of expanding to $5 to $8 million per year. Beyond that he felt that Head might go in three possible directions. First, he believed that Head should once again explore the opportunities and risks of moving into the other price segments of the ski market, either under another brand or with a nonmetallic ski. Although he believed that by selling in a lower price range Head could sell 50,000 or more pairs of skis, the risks were also high. Second, he felt that Head should explore the opportunity in other related ski products, such as boots or bindings. Third, he felt that eventually Head should expand into other specialty sporting goods, preferably of a contraseasonal nature.

In looking to these new areas, Mr. Seigle had formulated a two-part product philosophy as follows:

> Any new product which Head will consider should:
> 1. Be consistent with the quality and prestige image of Head Skis.
> 2. Should entail one or more of the following characteristics:
>   a) High innovative content.
>   b) High engineering content.
>   c) High style appeal.
>   d) Be patentable.

> We will consider getting into new products through any of the normal methods such as internal product development, product acquisition, or corporate acquisition. If we are to move into a new area we definitely want to have a product edge. For example, if we were to manufacture a boot, we would want to be different. We would only seriously consider it if we had a definite product advantage such as if we were to develop a high quality plastic boot.

Howard Head, in speaking of the future, voiced the following hopes:

> I would like to see Head grow in an orderly fashion sufficient to maintain its present youth and resiliency. That would mean at least 20%–25% per year. This statement does not preclude the possibility that we might grow faster. We believe the ski business alone will grow 20%–25% per year. As our staff capabilities grow, we will probably branch into other areas.

As to our objectives for the next five years, I would say that the first corporate objective is to maintain healthy growth in the basic ski business. It is the taproot of all that is good in Head. Second, we must be certain that any new activity is carefully selected for a reasonable probability of developing a good profit and an image platform consistent with the past activity of Head.

APPENDIX A*

TYPES OF SKIS

ELEMENTS OF A WELL-DESIGNED SKI

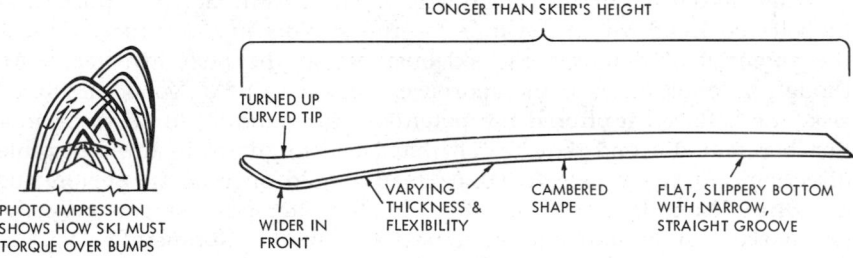

LONGER THAN SKIER'S HEIGHT

TURNED UP
CURVED TIP

PHOTO IMPRESSION
SHOWS HOW SKI MUST
TORQUE OVER BUMPS

WIDER IN
FRONT

VARYING
THICKNESS &
FLEXIBILITY

CAMBERED
SHAPE

FLAT, SLIPPERY BOTTOM
WITH NARROW,
STRAIGHT GROOVE

Wood skis

If you are on a tight budget, well-designed wood skis at low prices are available from domestic and foreign manufacturers. Wood is a bundle of tubular cellulose cells bound together in an elastic medium called lignin. The internal slippage of wood skis not only lets them torque over the bumps in traverse, but damps any tendency to vibrate or chatter on hard rough surfaces. There are wood skis for any snow, any speed, and they are fun to ski on. Their only problem is a lack of durability. Wood skis are fragile. Besides, as wood skis are used, the internal slippage of the fibers increases, and they lose their life.

In choosing a wood ski, it is probably wise to pay more than the minimum price. Multiple laminations of hickory or ash, a soft flex pattern, interlocking edges, polyethylene base, plastic top and sidewalls, tip and tail protectors are some of the features a beginner or intermedi-

WOOD SKI CROSS-SECTION

PROTECTIVE TOP EDGES   PROTECTIVE PLASTIC TOP

PLASTIC
SIDEWALL

STEEL EDGES   PLASTIC SOLE   MULTI-LAMINATED
WOOD CORE

---

* Source: *Skiing International Yearbook,* 1967, pp. 63–68. Copyright by Ziff-Davis Publishing Co.

ate should look for in a better wood ski. When you get past the $40 to $70 range, your own dealer's recommendations will be your best guarantee of value.

FRP skis

A few years ago there were only a handful of "epoxy" skis on the market, and skiers were eyeing them with mixed interest and distrust. Now the available models have multiplied almost unbelievably. New companies have been formed, and many of the established manufacturers have now brought out versions of their own. The plastic skis are still new enough for most skiers to be confused about their true nature —and with good reason, since there are so many types.

The word epoxy is part of the confusion. The true family resemblance of all the skis that are currently being lumped under that designation is the use of glass fibers locked into a plastic medium to create layers of great strength. The plastics engineers use the term fiber-reinforced plastic (FRP) to designate this type of structural solution. It is very strong.

The reinforcing layers used in these new designs derive their strength from the combined strength of millions of fine glass fibers or threads locked in the plastic layer. The potential strengths of materials in this family of structural plastics can exceed those of aluminum or steel. Unfortunately, there is no simple way to evaluate them or describe the materials actually in use. The wide variety of glass fibers, resins, and systems of molding and curing the fiber-reinforced layer produces a wide range of results. These can be evaluated only by laboratory tests or, finally, by actual in-service results.

FRP materials are being used for all sorts of sporting goods, industrial, and space-age applications. The strength-to-weight ratio is attractively high, and the possibility of creating new reinforced shapes by means of molding operations has proved to be attractive enough to encourage a great deal of experimentation. Skis seem to adapt to this structural technique.

Metal skis

In the search for more durable skis, the metal skis took over the quality market about a decade ago, and are widely accepted as ideal for both recreational skier and expert. Except for specialized racing uses, the wooden skis have been largely outmoded in the better ski market. Today, the fiber-reinforced plastic designs are the only challengers to the primacy of the metals.

Metal skis obtain their strength from aluminum sheets that are light in weight but very strong. The structure of a metal ski is somewhat like an "I" beam; when the ski is bent, the bottom sheet is stretched and the top sheet is compressed. The core material serves as the web—the vertical portion of the "I"—and must be attached to the top and bottom metal sheets securely enough to resist the shearing stress that occurs when the ski is bent.

Service potential of metal skis

The possibility of rebuilding and refinishing metal skis has been one of the key sales attractions of the metal ski in this country. So long as bonding remains intact, only the effects of wear and tear—rocks, skis banging together, rough treatment in transportation, etc.—limit the life of the skis. The possibility of having the plastic surfaces and edges, or even the structural members themselves, replaced has strong appeal for the skier investing well over $100 in his skis. The rebuilding potential also tends to keep the trade-in and used resale value of the skis higher, making it less expensive for the skier to move to higher performance or more recent models as his skiing ability—or his desire for something new—dictates. The American companies were the first to develop rebuilding techniques, but more recently European factories have been establishing service centers in the U.S.

METAL SKI CROSS-SECTIONS

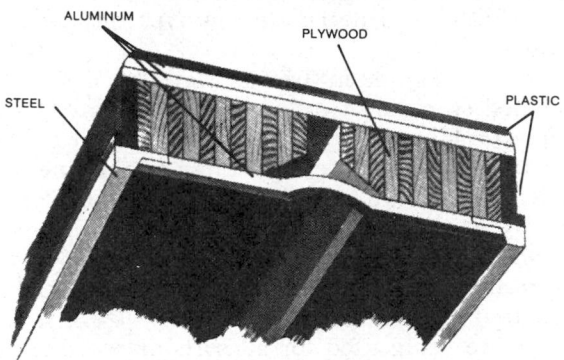

Northland Golden Jet—Cross-laminated fir plywood core with no filler in center, full-length bonded steel edge, aluminum sheets on both the top and the bottom.

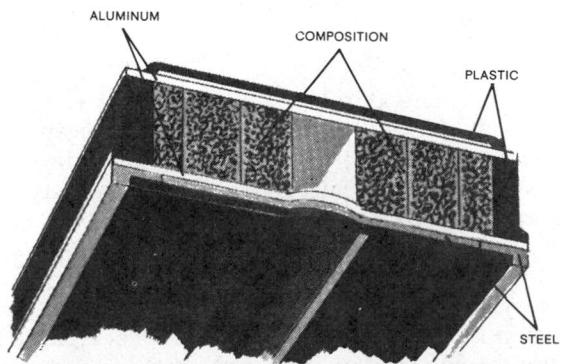

Hart Javelin—Grainless core of pressed particles, continuous full-length steel L edge welded to steel sheet, revealed aluminum top edge, phenolic plastic top.

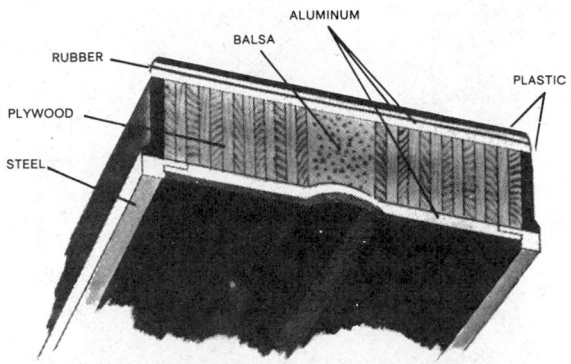

Head Competition—Cross-laminated fir plywood core, rubber damping layer on top of structure, full-length bonded steel L edge, high-density plastic base.

FRP CROSS-SECTIONS

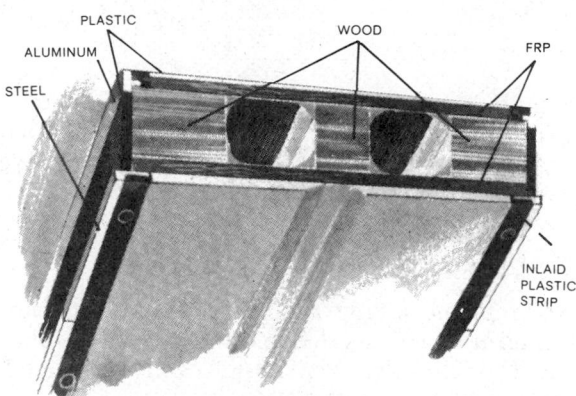

Kneissl White Star—Epoxy sandwich with interrupted wood core for lightness, sectional steel L edge screwed-in, aluminum top edge, two-color inlaid base.

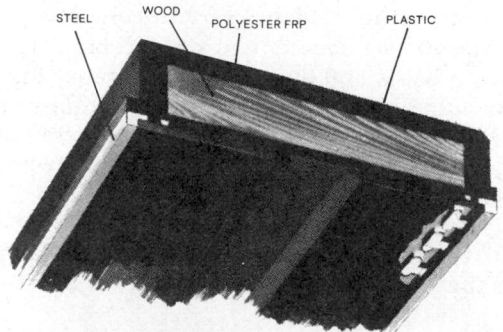

A&T K2—Vestigial core of pine, full wrap-around construction, bonded full-length L edge. ABS plastic top sheet. Bonded edges have tab construction for strength.

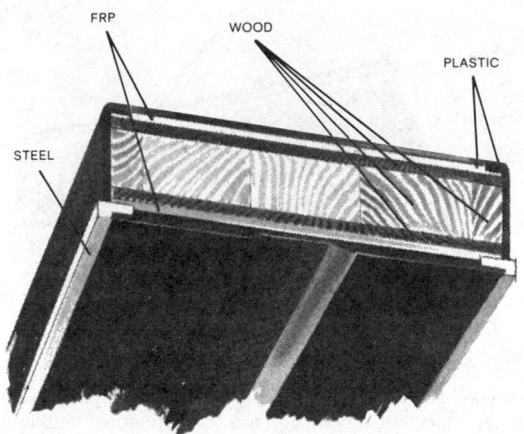

Yamaha Hi-Flex—FRP sandwich, hardwood core with grain running lengthwise, full-length bonded stainless steel L edges on bottom, with top edges of celluloid.

There are three basic elements of FRP construction: the plastic material or resin; the glass fibers themselves; and the method of combining, curing, and shaping the composite reinforcing layer. Variation of any of these three elements affects the characteristics of the end product.

Service potential of FRP skis

One of the problems facing the manufacturers of fiber-reinforced plastic skis has been how to service and rebuild them—once the normal wear and tear of skiing has taken its toll. Only the metal skis, it has seemed, could be refinished and rebuilt.

Though it is true that you cannot heat up an FRP ski, melt the glue, resand, recoat, and reconstruct it quite as easily as you can a metal ski, progress has been made in this direction during the past season. Several manufacturers have set up regional service centers.

What these various service centers can accomplish is considerable. They are replacing bases and edges. They are renewing and refinishing top surfaces. In some cases, the structural fiberglass members can be separated from the wood core and replaced, producing in effect a brand-new ski. The sum of all this is real benefit to the average skier, who is unwilling to discard a pair of skis every season or so. The gap between metal and FRP skis, as far as service potential is concerned, is being narrowed. You will find that the costs range over approximately the same spread as the metal skis and that guarantee provisions are similar.

The Saturday Evening Post

The real history is going to have to be written by a psychiatrist.[1]
—Cary Bok, grandson of the founder of Curtis Publishing Company.

ON THE AFTERNOON of January 9, 1969, standing before the glaring television lights at the Overseas Press Club in New York City, Martin Ackerman, Curtis Publishing Company's fourth president in six years, calmly read, "This is one of the saddest days of my life, a sad one for me, for our employees, officers, and directors; indeed, it is sad for the American public. Apparently there is just not the need for our product in today's scheme of living."[2] With Ackerman's announcement, Curtis officially ceased publication of *The Saturday Evening Post*.

The *Post*, which had been suffering from increasing costs and decreasing revenues for the past decade, had once been the most profitable magazine in the United States, considered both the pulse and maker of American opinion. The death of the *Post* had been predicted by denizens of Wall Street and Madison Avenue since its first financial troubles in the early 1960s. It is impossible, though, to isolate the plight of the *Post* from the plight of Curtis, a company whose assets included not only such national magazines as the *Post, Ladies' Home Journal,* and *Holiday,* but also paper mills in Pennsylvania, a sprawling printing plant outside Philadelphia (where every copy of every Curtis publication was printed), a circulation company, and extensive timberlands. During the years 1960–1969 inclusive, Curtis' operating revenues (net of commissions) declined from $192.8 million to $32.0 million, and the company sustained a cumulative loss of $67.6 million (Exhibit 1).

---

[1] Joseph Goulden, *The Curtis Caper* (New York: G. P. Putnam's Sons, 1965), p. 11.

[2] Otto Friedrich, *Decline and Fall* (New York: Harper and Row, 1970), p. 449.

HISTORY: 1897–1962

In 1897, Cyrus Curtis, the founder of Curtis Publishing Company, purchased a struggling journal put together for ten dollars a week by a newspaper man in his spare time. The journal, which Curtis bought for $1,000, consisted of a mailing list of 2,231 names, a wagon-load of battered type fonts, and a name, *The Saturday Evening Post.* At the time, Curtis was the publisher of the leading women's magazine in the nation, the *Ladies' Home Journal,* which he and his wife had built from scratch up to a circulation of 446,000 during the six-year period between 1883 and 1889. Referring to the *Post, Printers' Ink,* the printing trade journal, commented that the *Ladies' Home Journal* was a "wonderful property" but that Curtis was "blowing his profits on an impossible venture" with the purchase of this latest magazine.[3]

Curtis was undaunted, for he felt that just as the *Journal* had become a success by dealing with what was most important to the American woman, her home, the *Post* would become a success by dealing with what was important to men, "their fight for livelihood in the business world."[4]

The Lorimer *Post:* 1899–1936

For the first year under Curtis, the *Post* was edited by William Jordan, but Curtis soon became dissatisfied, and the editorship passed to George Horace Lorimer. The son of a famous Boston minister, Lorimer was considered one of the best newspaper men in Boston.

Lorimer immediately proceeded to alter the *Post,* changing it from a weekly newspaper into a magazine, and cutting the price from ten cents to five, thus making it less expensive than any competitive periodical. He also instituted a new procedure in American publishing, that of paying authors at the time their material was accepted for publication rather than when it was actually published.

> Lorimer knew exactly what he wanted to make out of the *Post.* It was to be a magazine without class, clique, or sectional editing, but intended for every adult in America's seventy-five million population. He meant to edit it for the whole United States. He set out to interpret America to itself, always readably, but constructively.
>
> As he settled into the job of interpretation, Lorimer sensed accurately the mood of the country at the beginning of the new century. People were weary of reading about problems, politics, radicalism, war, and even uplift. They wanted to read historical novels and dwell in the past, and Lorimer gave them covers showing Ben Franklin, Washington, and Independence Hall in appropriate poses, while inside he displayed the romances of the Rev. Cyrus Townsend Brady and Robert W. Chambers.
>
> Always the accent was heaviest on business. Charles R. Flint praised the benefits of the business combination; the mayors of San Francisco and Baltimore wrote jointly on the need for better business methods in

---

[3] Goulden, *The Curtis Caper,* p. 22.
[4] Ibid., p. 22.

civic administration; and Harvard's director of physical culture advised the businessman on home gymnastics.[5]

Lorimer himself contributed several articles related to business, which appeared in the *Post* as an unsigned serial entitled "Letters from a Self-made Merchant to His Son." An immediate success, this series was later published in book form and translated into "a dozen" foreign languages.

Lorimer must have hit some chord in the heart of the country, for the *Post*'s circulation increased from 33,000 in 1898 to 97,000 in the following year, and then to 182,000 in the year after that. Circulation reached half a million in 1903, a million in 1909, two million in 1913, and three million in 1927.

A propitious environment.   During the early 1900s fundamental changes were occurring in America. Mass production, transportation, and distribution were making America a nation rather than a collection of geographically contiguous regions. Curtis anticipated the need for a national magazine and adroitly applied the evolving principles of mass production and distribution to his publications.

Advertising revenue for the *Post* increased from $8,000 in 1898 to $160,000 in 1899 and then to more than $1 million in 1905, $3 million in 1909, and $5 million in 1910. By the end of the 1920s, advertising revenue was over $50 million and the *Post* collected almost 30 cents of every advertising dollar spent in magazines in the United States.

> The vehicle that the *Post* rode to tremendous financial success was the automobile. The *Post* carried its first auto ad, about a W. E. Roach horseless buggy, in an issue in March 1900. For the next two decades auto advertising expanded as rapidly as the industry; at one point it made up 25 per cent of the total volume.[6]

The zenith of this period of the *Post*'s history was the issue of December 1929, a virtual "paper monument" to Curtis and Lorimer.

> It contained 272 pages and weighed almost two pounds. Sixty forty-five ton presses rolled around the clock for three weeks to produce it, consuming 6,000,000 pounds of paper and 120,000 pounds of ink. The reading fare was enough to keep the average adult busy for more than 20 hours, *Post* editors estimated. And the issue—largest of any magazine in Curtis' history—put $1,512,000 from 214 national advertisers into Cyrus Curtis' money box. This grandiose effort was so mammoth in bulk that scrap dealers eagerly paid five cents to newstands for the paper alone.[7]

A series of blows.   With the end of the prosperity of the 1920s, *Post* advertising revenues decreased substantially. By 1932, issues of only 60 pages, a quarter of them filled with advertising, were commonplace.

Cyrus Curtis died in 1933 at the age of 83, leaving his daughter and two grandsons effective control of the company with 32% of the stock. Lorimer, retaining his position as editor of the *Post,* assumed the presidency. During the period between 1933 and 1936, the year of his re-

---

[5] John Tebbel, *George Horace Lorimer and The Saturday Evening Post* (New York: Doubleday and Company, Inc., 1948), pp. 23–26.

[6] Goulden, *The Curtis Caper,* pp. 25–26.

[7] Ibid., p. 32.

tirement, Lorimer increased advertising revenue from an $18 million low in 1933 to $26 million in 1936 in spite of the severe economic conditions and increased competition from Henry Luce's *Time* and *Life*. During this same period, Lorimer placed the editorial power of the *Post* behind an attempt to defeat Franklin D. Roosevelt in his reelection bid in 1936.

> Lorimer called the New Deal "a discredited European ideology"; he railed against "undesirable and unassimilable aliens"; and the *Post* declared: "We might just as well say that the world failed as the American business leadership failed."[8]

The election landslide for Roosevelt and his New Deal in 1936 was a humiliating blow to Lorimer and indicated "a fundamental, distinct shift of the *Post*'s role in American life. It would be accepted as entertainment, but not as a guide to life."[9]

Hand-picked successors: 1936–1962

Following Lorimer's retirement in 1936, Walter D. Fuller, Lorimer's hand-picked successor, was named chief executive officer of Curtis. Fuller, a man more conservative politically than Lorimer, had worked his way up in the organization from the accounting department as successively controller, corporate secretary, first vice president, and president, all while under the guidance of Curtis and Lorimer.

Fuller became chairman of the board for 1950–1957, and his protégé, Robert MacNeal, took over the position of president and chief executive officer. MacNeal had first attracted management attention during the 1920s by designing a folding machine that enabled the *Post* to print more than 200 pages, the previous limit.

> Even when he became president he would go into the machine shops and, at the risk of soiled white cuffs, talk about and help solve mechanical problems. In his coat pocket was a little leatherbound black notebook crammed with facts and statistics about Curtis and its multitude of subsidiary companies. The information—even including the names and addresses of directors—was typed on a "miniature Gothic" typewriter so more characters would fit onto a page. Why the notebook? MacNeal's superior in the scheduling division had carried a similar book way back in the 1920s. "He was the fount of all knowledge, so we had to have one, too," MacNeal explained.[10]

Corporate strategy. The corporate strategy under the guidance of Fuller and MacNeal was to build Curtis into a fully integrated magazine publishing company which grew its own trees, made its own paper, printed every issue of every magazine, and distributed the magazines through a circulation subsidiary. This was an arrangement that other publishers looked upon unfavorably, inasmuch as it tended to accentuate corporate losses in periods of economic decline, served as a

---

[8] Friedrich, *Decline and Fall,* p. 10.
[9] Goulden, *The Curtis Caper,* p. 45.
[10] Ibid., pp. 71–72.

drain on funds available for diversification, and tended to increase the size and complexity of corporate management.

Otto Friedrich, in *Decline and Fall,* discussed the Fuller and Mac-Neal years as follows:

> Fuller's presidency began during the difficult days of the Depression, when Curtis and many other companies tottered near bankruptcy, and the value of ideas may well have seemed less obvious than it does today. And then, during World War II, the shortage of supplies convinced many an executive of the value of hoarding and stockpiling. Whatever his reasons, Fuller held to his empire-building philosophy with an exceptional singleness of purpose. He could have bought the entire Columbia Broadcasting System for $3 million, but he declined the offer; a few years later, he declined a similar opportunity to buy the American Broadcasting Corporation. Television, radio, the growth in book publishing, the so-called "paperback revolution," the rise of suburban newspapers, the increasing need for school texts—Walter Deane Fuller had not been blessed with a gift for prophesying such developments. Instead, just after World War II, he bought a 108-acre site on the outskirts of Philadelphia, shipped in twenty new printing presses, and constructed the gigantic Sharon Hill printing plant. It was, in its day, the largest and best-equipped printing plant in the world. And as late as 1950, when Fuller finally passed on the presidency to his protégé, Robert A. MacNeal, Curtis reaffirmed its dedication to machinery by investing $20 million to become full owner of a paper company in which it already held a controlling interest.[11]

By 1960, the number of individuals actually employed in creating the Curtis magazines was miniscule compared to the number engaged in its manufacture:

> The editorial staff of the *Post* numbered about 125 people; the employees in the printing division numbered 2,600; the employees of the whole corporation numbered about 11,000. And in surveying the corporate assets, Curtis executives liked to boast that the company owned not just a few magazines but a $40 million printing plant, three large paper mills, 262,000 acres of timberland, and a circulation company that distributed 50-odd magazines through 100,000 outlets.[12]

Editorial strategy. In 1936, Lorimer's successor as editor of the *Post* was Wesley W. Stout. Like Fuller and MacNeal, Stout was hand-picked by Lorimer and was a conservative politically:

> In editorial outlook, Stout was every bit as conservative as Lorimer; the popular support given the New Deal by voters in 1936 goaded the *Post* into increasingly vicious attacks on the Administration. President Roosevelt never answered directly, but he showed several visitors a large envelope containing what he termed the "dirtiest" attacks published against the government. The bulk of them were from the *Post.* The magazine's editorials were a cacophony of ridicule directed against organized labor, social reform programs, social security, the Tennessee

---

[11] Friedrich, *Decline and Fall,* p. 15.
[12] Ibid., p. 15.

Valley Administration—in sum, just about anything attempted by FDR.[13]

Advertising revenue dropped $4 million during Stout's first year as editor, and at a stockholders' meeting in 1941 minority stockholders "denounced management's isolationism and called for the opening of *Post* pages to opposing points of view."[14] Stout's editorship of the *Post* came to an end in 1942 with what has been called "the biggest misunderstanding in Curtis editorial history."[15] Stout had published a three-article series on the American Jew, the last article of which was entitled "The Case Against the Jew." A furor erupted with cancellations of subscriptions and advertising, threats of a boycott, and destruction of *Posts* at newsstands. In May of 1942, the *Post* ran an editorial apologizing for the article, saying that Stout had believed

> . . . "a frank airing of the whole question would serve to clear the atmosphere in this country and perhaps help prevent anti-Semitism from gaining a foothold here." The *Post* expressed regret that the article had been "misunderstood."[16]

Discord between Editor Stout and President Fuller had been rumored for some time, and the controversy over the article and the *Post's* operating loss for the first quarter of 1942 precipitated Stout's resignation. The editorship of the *Post* then went to Ben Hibbs, a native of Kansas, who had been the editor of another Curtis magazine, *Country Gentleman*. Hibbs immediately began making major changes in the *Post*. He found the *Post's* editorial content resting on the same "glamour of business" product that Lorimer had developed decades earlier. Feeling that this product was dated, Hibbs broadened the *Post* by stressing that he considered to be the more enduring part of America— namely, life in country towns. But Hibbs also looked beyond middle America and recognized the Second World War as "the greatest news story of our time. Things were happening more exciting than what fiction writers could dream up."

> Hibbs and his lanky young managing editor, Bob Fuoss, reduced the emphasis on fiction and set out to cover World War II. The *Post* then had only one war correspondent, who was home on leave in New York. Hibbs recruited MacKinlay Kantor, Samuel Lubell, Edgar Snow, Richard Tregaskis, Demaree Bess. C. S. Forester wrote about the sinking of the *Scharnhorst*, Ambassador Joseph E. Davies wrote from Moscow about the Russian front, and Norman Rockwell painted his version of Roosevelt's slogan, the Four Freedoms. In this silver age, the money came and went at an unprecedented rate. Hibbs spent $175,000, a record for extravagance at that time, for *My Three Years with Eisenhower*, by the general's naval aide, Captain Harry C. Butcher. He spent another $125,000 for the memoirs of Casey Stengel, and $100,000 for a biography of General Douglas MacArthur. The last of these, which had been commissioned without any safeguard as to its quality, was

---

[13] Goulden, *The Curtis Caper*, p. 48.
[14] Ibid., p. 49.
[15] Ibid., p. 51.
[16] Ibid., p. 51.

never published, and Hibbs referred to it, in a private office memo-randum, as "my worst mistake in twenty years." At the same time, Hibbs willingly led the *Post* into a circulation war against *Life* and *Look*, and the *Post* bought its way up from 3.3 million to more than 6.5 million during his twenty-year regime. Advertising revenue rose just as spectacularly, from $23 million to $104 million a year.[17]

Losing the postwar race with competition. Under the continued guidance of Fuller as chairman, MacNeal as president, and Hibbs as editor of the *Post,* the 1950s proved to be difficult years. Although *Post* advertising revenue increased over the decade, the number of adver-tising pages per issue decreased. The circulation battles of the late 1950s between the *Post, Life,* and *Look* were a mixed blessing for Cur-tis. A two-year subscription to the *Post* cost the subscriber $7.95 and represented a liability to the *Post* of $20, the production and delivery costs. The larger circulation figures led to increased advertising rates, but these made it impossible for many of the small manufacturers, on whom the *Post* had depended for a substantial amount of its advertis-ing revenue, to continue advertising in the magazine. At the same time the *Post* was losing large corporation advertising to television, which in the years since World War II had built up advertising reve-nues twice those of magazines.

Market research studies continually eroded the effectiveness of the *Post* as an advertising medium. For example, *Life* underwrote a study which showed that each of its issues had a readership of 5.2 persons and that readership multiplied by circulation brought *Life* equal with radio and television in the numbers-game of media reach—a claim that the *Post* could not equal. *Life* then underwrote another study which indicated that the *Post* was a magazine bought for reading and not for looking; *Life* immediately turned this fact to its advantage by stressing to advertisers that the busy young housewife would not have time to read *Post* articles, so advertising in the *Post* would be less ef-fective than in a magazine bought for looking, such as *Life.*

Madison Avenue wanted to cover the younger segment of the con-sumer market (base age of 35, with the extra dollars to give discretion-ary buying power). In the late 'fifties, *Life*'s circulation included twice as many families in this category as the *Post*'s. Madison Avenue began to feel that the *Post* was not reaching the market "where the action was."

Life was also active during the 1950s building a power base with merchants. *Life* persuaded merchants to tag goods "as advertised in *Life,*" with the implication that *Life* put its editorial integrity behind the product.

> The retailers also received low-cost promotional material which a skilled young man would help convert into an attractive display, free of charge. The merchants, in turn, made their warm feelings toward *Life* felt all the way up the distribution line to top management at the manufacturer.[18]

---

[17] Friedrich, *Decline and Fall,* p. 12.
[18] Goulden, *The Curtis Caper,* p. 85.

The business recession of 1961 caused the number of advertising pages per *Post* issue to plummet even more. As the advertising pages decreased, the *Post* became thinner and thinner, and the professionals on Madison Avenue started placing even fewer ads in the *Post* as a result:

> "We're a bunch of sheep," David Ogilvy, of Ogilvy, Benson and Mather, said candidly. "One agency leaves a magazine, we all wonder why and follow. The magazine thins again, and more of us leave. Suddenly there's nothing left. No one wants his copy in a thin book."[19]

Curtis' profits declined during the 1950s from $6.2 million in 1950 to only $1.6 million in 1960. Although gross advertising revenue (including commissions) increased from $98.6 million to $151.8 million during the 10-year period, advertising pages decreased. Production and distribution expenses rose substantially over the same time, while selling and administrative expenses more than doubled, going from $27.7 million to $61.2 million.

The "new Post." Late in 1960, an administrative decision was made under President MacNeal that a "new *Post*" should be created with a "fashionable look" that would appeal to Madison Avenue, increase *Post* advertising revenue, and thus increase corporate profits. Editor Hibbs, on the other hand, felt that the *Post* was already hitting the American market:

> The *Post* was widely considered to be old and stodgy, edited by the old and stodgy to be read by the old and stodgy, and Ben Hibbs couldn't accept it. "The ad people were always hollering in my last year about the Norman Rockwell covers, that they were old-fashioned," he protested. "Heck, those were the *Post*'s most popular feature." And the books he kept buying kept becoming best sellers. "Dammit. We were hitting the American market," said Hibbs. "We had to be with that kind of record." And did someone say that *Post* fiction was unreal? "After all, the world is not entirely composed of hydrogen bombs, juvenile delinquency, race riots, mental institutions, heart disease and cancer," said Hibbs. "I can remember the time when people thought it was *fun to read*."[20]

The "new *Post*" was developed during 1961 and first appeared in September of that year. Six million dollars in advertising was sold for this issue, and its 148 pages created the thickest *Post* in years. Described as a "peculiar mixture of new and old,"[21] it featured a Norman Rockwell cover depicting the artist puzzling out a new *Post* cover; a new column entitled "Speaking Out," different print and layout styles; and articles ranging from the memoirs of Casey Stengel to an account of an American doctor in the jungles of Haiti. The response to the "new *Post*" was immediate.

> The look of the "new" *Post* infuriated its readers, and they wrote in to protest at a rate of ten thousand letters a week. "Idiotic . . . please

---

[19] Ibid., p. 95.
[20] Friedrich, *Decline and Fall*, p. 13.
[21] Ibid., p. 17.

change it back . . . Cancel my subscription. . . . I have been betrayed—and many others with me." As for Madison Avenue, for which the "new *Post*" had been created, it responded as it usually does to such efforts—with a shrug. "The mistake was," in the words of one cynical old *Post* editor, "that you forced them to read the magazine." Basically, the *Post* had announced change and then attempted to counterfeit change, and the increased advertising didn't last a month. Over the whole year, in fact, advertising plummeted from $104 million to $86 million. The *Post* consequently went into the red by $3 million, and Curtis by $4 million.[22]

Challenge and change: 1962

On March 29, 1962, President MacNeal announced Curtis' $4 million loss for the previous fiscal year, the first corporate loss since the company's inception in 1891. Apparently the loss would have been nearly $9 million except for a tax credit of $1 million and a nonrecurring profit of $3.5 million from the sale of securities.

Ten days earlier, the *Gallagher Report,* a Madison Avenue newsletter, had suggested that a major shake-up in Curtis' corporate leadership might be in the cards:

> THE CURTIS CRISIS. Major changes in Curtis Publishing management and ownership expected shortly. Financier Peter G. Treves has been quietly buying Curtis stock for more than a year. Has acquired sizable holdings.[23]

Apparently Curtis was an attractive target for corporate raiders. For one thing, the corporate assets were understated: 250,000 acres of timberland, for example, were valued at between $10–$15 per acre, while they were carried on the books at $3 per acre. Moreover, the company's stock was underpriced by the market, with the two issues of Curtis preferred selling well below their liquidation values.

In 1962, when Treves was buying into the company, effective operating control was in the hands of Curtis' heirs. A trust, to continue through the life of Curtis' daughter and her two sons, controlled 17.3% of the outstanding stock, and the Curtis heirs themselves owned 14.6%. With 32% of the Curtis stock, the heirs over the years had placed family friends and management sympathetic to the wishes of the family on the board of directors.

True, a minor change had occurred in the late 1950s, when minority stockholders complained that common stock dividends were too low ($.00 for 1933–1950 and $.20 from 1951–1956), and threatened a stockholder suit. As a result, President MacNeal had increased the size of the board and had dropped from it those Curtis executives who held ex-officio seats. The newly opened board seats went to investment and insurance interests. At the same time, however, effective working control of the company became vested in a newly created executive committee which included the same editors and executives who had

---

[22] Ibid., pp. 17–18.

[23] Matthew Culligan, *The Curtis Culligan Story* (New York: Crown Publishers, Inc., 1970), p. 30.

been removed from the board. Moreover, the men filling the newly opened board seats were sympathetic to the wishes of the heirs and thus were considered "family members" of the board.

In April 1962, Treves and Co. and J. R. Williston and Beane, the firms which had been purchasing Curtis stock, sent an cmissary to the Curtis Building. This was Milton Gould, a Philadelphia lawyer, who was to play a major role in Curtis' subsequent history. On this occasion, Gould requested an immediate appointment with MacNeal, and stated that the interests he represented wanted two seats on the Curtis board. Not knowing the extent of Treves' and Williston and Beane's ownership, the board agreed to enlarge the number of seats from 11 to 13, with the two new seats going to Gould and R. McLean Stewart, an investment banker. Asked why the directors did not fight the intrusion, Cary Bok, grandson of Cyrus Curtis and member of the board, replied as follows:

> "There are many reasons," Bok said one winter morning in 1964, during a rambling interview at his seaside home in Maine.
>
> "First of all, you never are assured of absolute control unless you have 51 per cent. We have only 32 per cent; we were unsure of what other people had.
>
> "Second, the Curtis board is elected with cumulative voting. The others could have pooled their votes and elected one director for sure; probably two, and possibly three."
>
> Third, Bok said, the company didn't relish the idea of a public proxy fight during a time of internal stress. First-quarter losses that year had already touched $4 million—more red ink than went on the books during all of 1961. Curtis management had more important things to do than scurry around the countryside soliciting proxies from widows and small-time investors. The Wall Street groups, on the other hand, specialized in just this type of scurrying. Had Curtis chosen to fight, there was at least a 50–50 chance that Curtis would have been licked. Management and the heirs feared this, because they didn't know any more about the investors' long-range intentions than they did of the investors' holdings.
>
> Additionally, Curtis by this time was so desperate for cash that it was ready to befriend anyone who came along and offered new ideas and fresh leadership. That spring it was forced to peddle two of its strongest sidelines to raise operating cash. Curtis sold part of its holdings in Bantam Books, Inc., and Treasure Books, Inc., to Grosset & Dunlap, Inc., for a $4.8 million profit. Both companies were returning a profit. But the need for immediate cash was overpowering and the book subsidiaries were something that could be conveniently cut from the empire.[24]

In an interview given shortly after he joined the Curtis board, Gould said that he had sought a directorship because the brokerage houses that had taken a substantial financial position in Curtis had become alarmed by the accelerated operating losses and by Curtis' inability to adapt to changing markets. "New and energetic management is

---

[24] Goulden, *The Curtis Caper*, pp. 123–124.

needed," he added.[25] (For a list of major changes in Curtis' direction during the 1960s, see Exhibit 2.)

"UNDER NEW MANAGEMENT": 1962–1969

In the early summer of 1962, MacNeal left for a trip to Europe, and during his absence, spurred by Gould, the board voted him out as president. Although it was decided to withhold the news from the press until his return, the news was leaked to *The Wall Street Journal* three hours after the meeting ended. An executive committee was formed to run the company until a new president could be found. Gould was named legal counsel to the executive committee.

The Culligan years: 1962–1968

Gould's personal choice for the presidency of Curtis was Matthew Culligan, an executive at Interpublic, an advertising conglomerate headed by Marion Harper. Previous to his employment at Interpublic, Culligan had been an executive vice president at NBC, where he had been credited with turning around the failing NBC Radio Network. Gould arranged a meeting between Culligan and the Curtis executive committee, which Culligan later described as follows:

> Gould conditioned the executive committee on my behalf, warning them that I was just about the final hope and softening them up for my salary demands and fringe benefits. He actually assigned one of his associates to write my contract for me![26]

Shortly after its meeting with Culligan, the executive committee named him president of Curtis. Culligan described his first week at the company as frantic. He raced between the editorial and sales offices in New York City and the corporate offices and the circulation, manufacturing, and paper companies in Pennsylvania. Marion Harper, Culligan's boss at Interpublic, got together the best "media brains" in his organization "to contribute the best cerebration and intuition to the problems at Curtis"[27] in order to help Culligan in his new position. Culligan described the resulting suggestions as follows:

> When the report was finished, Harper invited me to his office and gave me the benefit of the accumulated experience and judgment of a dozen of his best people. The report was fascinating. In essence, it said that Curtis could not survive in the form in which I had inherited it—with the same magazines, same circulations, same frequencies—under the economic conditions then prevailing at Curtis. The task force recommended that the *Post* go biweekly; that *Holiday* be sold to generate working capital; that *American Home* be folded into the *Ladies' Home Journal,* saving millions in subscription costs. The final recommendation was to get Curtis out of the paper and manufacturing business. I accepted the Harper report with overflowing gratitude and rushed back to Curtis as though I'd found the

---

[25] Ibid., p. 125.
[26] Culligan, *The Curtis Culligan Story,* p. 35.
[27] Ibid., p. 60.

Holy Grail. Calling in my inherited key men—Bob Gibbon, secretary of the executive board; Ford Robinson, head of Operations; Leon Marks, head of Manufacturing; G. B. McCombs, number two man in Circulation—I discussed the report with them. My soaring spirits plummeted as each of the Harper recommendations was shot down in flames, not because the ideas were faulty, but because of artificial, legal, or financial strictures that appeared to block every turn.[28]

Immediate tasks.   After assuming the presidency of Curtis, Culligan was faced with several immediate tasks. Curtis owed $22 million to four creditor banks that were expressing concern over Curtis' financial position. Culligan promised an extensive cost-reduction program, and the banks agreed to a 12-month extension of the loan with a commitment for an additional $4 million in working capital. One additional stipulation added to the agreement was that Culligan would attempt to remove a debt restriction from the Curtis bylaws, which required a two-thirds vote of the preferred stockholders before management could pledge any collateral for loans. This provision protected the preferred stockholders in the case of liquidation, but it also barred long-term loans. Up to this point in time, all Curtis debt had been short-term at higher interest rates. Culligan proposed the removal of the restriction to the preferred stockholders, who eventually voted down the change.

During the period he was negotiating with the banks, Culligan also busied himself with two other major problems at Curtis: the need for cost reductions, and the increasing loss of advertising. In a move that was to have serious repercussions, Culligan called in a former colleague, J. M. Clifford, who was suffering from political infighting at NBC, and made him executive vice president of finance and operations. Clifford ordered an immediate 20% cut throughout the entire Curtis structure:

> By mid-1963 enough rank and file deadwood was chopped out of Curtis—3,500 jobs in all—to lower the annual payroll by $13 million. Printing operations were streamlined; workmen disassembled the huge mechanical innards of the Curtis building and packed the presses off to Sharon Hill. Fixed expenses dropped by $15 to $18 million annually, meaning the *Post* and the other magazines had a lower break-even per issue. According to Curtis annual reports, selling, general, and administrative expenses in 1961 were $62.6 million; this was down to $58.2 million in 1962 and $44.9 million in 1963. Production and delivery expenses dropped from $116.3 million to $106.5 and $103.2 million in the same stages.[29]

With the internal organization left to Clifford, Culligan set out to do what he knew best, selling.

> Curtis was bleeding to death. Too much unnecessary expense and not enough advertising income would bury Curtis by January 1963, unless . . . .
>
> I was the "unless"; no one else was in a position to deliver. This statement is not intended to be boastful—the burden was actually on

[28] Ibid., pp. 60–61.
[29] Friedrich, *Decline and Fall*, p. 64.

my shoulders. No amount of promotion, advertising, or sales calls by others would suffice. So I followed my instinct and decided on an unprecedented personal sales effort. I determined to do what no other executive in United States business had ever done—call personally on the heads of America's two hundred leading corporations within six months.[30]

Culligan, noted for his travels by helicopter, and described as a "rambunctious figure whose black eye patch had become a trade-mark,"[31] began selling the presidents of the nation's largest companies on the *Post:*

> The new president set out on an orgy of salesmanship, with press agents keeping track of every move. It was said that he traveled 3,500 miles a week to sell ads. It was said that he flew to Detroit and made presentations to General Motors, Chrysler, and Lincoln-Mercury all in one day. It was said that he signed $30 million in new ads within his first month. "From late fall of 1962 through the spring of 1963," said Culligan, "I ran Curtis almost entirely by telephone, memo and crash personal meetings at airports, in cars roaring along turnpikes, in the Curtis plane (a sturdy old twin Beech), and even a helicopter, which I leased, to cut down the time wasted getting from New York to Philadelphia." He expressed his philosophy by saying, "I had two choices. I could have stayed in Philadelphia and listened to everybody's problems, or I could go out and start selling, and let the problems take care of themselves."[32]

Despite Culligan's selling efforts, advertising revenue of the *Post* continued to decrease, from $86 million in 1961 to $66 million in 1962 to $60 million in 1963. Curtis' losses, which had been $4 million in 1961, soared to $18.9 million in 1962, then decreased to $3.4 million in 1963, the first year for which Culligan was fully responsible. But part of the improvement was of an accounting nature. At the time of Culligan's takeover, Price Waterhouse, attempting to get Curtis' business, had suggested that Curtis change its accounting policies and handle subscription liabilities in the same manner as most other publishing firms. Following this advice, Curtis spread its subscription liabilities over the life of the subscriptions and thus decreased its losses for 1963 from $10 million to $3.4 million.

By mid-1963, Culligan was again faced with the problem of the short-term bank loans coming due. Assistance came in the form of Serge Semenenko, vice president of the First National Bank of Boston. Russian-born Semenenko was considered one of the "mystery men" of U.S. finance. His loans from the First for the period 1920–1950 "practically supported the United States film industry,"[33] and his list of corporate "saves" included Fairbanks, Whitney; The International Paper Company; the Hearst publishing empire, and the Kindall Company.

By August 17, which was the deadline on the short-term loans to

---

[30] Culligan, *The Curtis Culligan Story*, pp. 78–79.
[31] Friedrich, *Decline and Fall*, p. 4.
[32] Ibid., p. 64.
[33] Goulden, *The Curtis Caper*, p. 157.

Curtis in 1963, Culligan and Semenenko had agreed on a $35 million loan from six banks.

> Semenenko doesn't sign blank checks, however, and especially when they are for $35 million. From Curtis he elicited a pledge that all management decisions be "reasonably satisfactory" to him, as the designated agent of the banking syndicate. As a service fee Semenenko's bank got ¼ of one per cent of the loan ($87,500)—plus, of course, its interest, one per cent above the prime rate on its share of the total loan.
>
> There is conflicting testimony on just how active a role Semenenko took for himself in the day-to-day conduct of Curtis' affairs. One former executive maintains that Culligan "wouldn't push the elevator button without calling Serge." This is disputed, however, by Cary W. Bok. "All he asks is that he be kept informed of what's going on," Bok said recently. "So long as he is given complete information on what management is doing, he's satisfied." Bok had unconcealed admiration for Semenenko.
>
> "Were it not for Semenenko," he said, "Curtis would have been dead. . . . He is a quiet little genius who inspires confidence in everything he touches."[34]

Corporate infighting.   Although it appeared in early 1964, with the bank loans refinanced and a modest first-quarter profit for Curtis, that Culligan's major problems were over, internal problems were about to erupt that he had not anticipated. These problems were precipitated by Clay Blair, Jr., a Curtis executive who had aspired to Culligan's job, or, failing that, at least to the job which Culligan had given to Clifford.

Blair had come to Curtis in 1959 as assistant managing editor of the *Post* under managing editor Bill Sherrod, Blair's one-time supervisor at the Pentagon, when both had worked for *Time-Life*. When Fuoss, who had replaced Hibbs as editor in December 1961, resigned after four months, Sherrod became editor of the *Post*, with Blair moving up to managing editor. Back in 1962 Blair had been aware that Curtis was in financial trouble, that MacNeal would go, and that the result would be a void into which he might be able to move. In bidding for the presidency, Blair had hoped to gain some leverage from the fact that he was a personal friend of Admiral Lewis Strauss, formerly chairman of the Atomic Energy Commission, but currently a member of the New York brokerage firm which was providing the stimulus behind merger talks between Curtis and Doubleday & Company, book publishers. The Blair-Strauss friendship dated back to a time when Blair and his *Time-Life* colleague, James Shepley, had written a book praising Strauss' role in the development of the hydrogen bomb. What made the friendship relevant to Blair's ambitions was its implied ability to influence Doubleday.

At the same board meeting during which MacNeal had been fired, Blair had been elected vice president with unspecified responsibilities in the editorial offices of Curtis magazines. Asked by Gould what he

---

[34] Ibid., p. 163.

would do if elected president of Curtis, Blair had responded with a written report entitled "Tomorrow Morning Plan":

> Blair's recommendations were Draconian. For one, he recommended the liquidation of the *Ladies' Home Journal* and *American Home* which were losing several million dollars a year. He recommended selling the Curtis Building in Philadelphia, getting rid of the paper mills, tightening the Curtis Circulation Company, moving everything except printing and distribution to New York. For the *Post* he recommended a deliberate reduction in circulation from 6.5 to 5 million.[35]

Blair recounted that his "Tomorrow Morning Plan" had upset ex-president Fuller, who was still a power at Curtis as a member of the board and of its executive committee. Blair attributed his inability to attain the presidency of Curtis to Fuller's opposition:

> "Walter Fuller invited me privately to his office, a gloomy, oak-paneled room with a fireplace, on the fourth floor of the Curtis Building," Blair recalled. "It was Fuller who had integrated Curtis, bought the paper companies, built the Sharon Hill printing plant. Now he seemed disturbed that I wanted to divest them."[36]

After Culligan was chosen as president, Blair was placed in the newly created position of editorial director of all Curtis magazines, a position above that of his old boss and mentor, Sherrod. Blair related a conversation between Gould, Culligan, and himself on the day of Culligan's takeover:

> "Culligan," Gould said, "you're Mr. Outside." Then turning to me: "Blair," he said, "you're Mr. Inside." He paced the floor and puffed on a huge cigar. "Culligan, you bring in the advertising and straighten out the image of this company. Blair, you keep the books, fix the products, and deal with manufacturing and the rest of it." It was an eloquent proposition, and when he finished, Culligan and I took the deal, with Culligan pledging then that "no one will ever come between us." We shook hands all around.[37]

If Blair had believed that he would be "Mr. Inside," he was quickly disappointed, for Culligan in effect turned this position over to Clifford.

> The conflict between Clifford and Blair came quickly and inevitably. They fought over every one of the technical and financial problems that lie at the heart of corporate power. "During 1963, Clifford got a throttle hold on the company," Blair said later. "He took over circulation, manufacturing, and paper mills, then accounting, personnel, and legal. He brought in three obnoxious lieutenants: Maurice Poppei, controller; Gloria Swett, legal; Sidney Natkin, personnel. By summer, Clifford's control of money and people was so complete that nobody, including me, could hire or fire or give a raise or sign a check without his specific approval."[38]

---

35 Friedrich, *Decline and Fall*, p. 32.
36 Ibid., p. 33.
37 Ibid., pp. 33–34.
38 Ibid., p. 50.

By January 1964, Blair was refusing to permit any of Clifford's staff on the editorial floors of the Curtis Building in New York. Clifford retaliated by refusing any cooperation of the corporate operations and finance areas that he controlled. The conflict grew to include not only Blair, but most of the Curtis editors. Recognizing that action had to be taken, Culligan gave Clifford a $20,000 raise and removed him from his position as executive vice president of finance and operations. Culligan temporarily took over the duties of operations, which consisted mainly of manufacturing, and gave the financial responsibilities to Maurice Poppei, then treasurer.

Changing editorial policy.   At the same time he was fighting Clifford, Blair was also solidifying his control over the editorial pages of the Curtis magazines. Two months after becoming editorial director, Blair announced that he was taking over the editorship of the *Post* and that Sherrod would go to India to produce a story on Nehru with Norman Rockwell, the *Post* cover artist. Blair asserted his control over the other magazines by immediately firing the editor of the *Ladies' Home Journal* and three members of the *Journal's* art department.

As editor of the *Post*, Blair set out to change the magazine:

> Blair really needed only a few weeks, all in all, to change the entire magazine—not just what it published, photographic covers, investigations and exposés, fiction by celebrities, and raucous editorials, but the way it operated. Instead of letting editors putter along in their departmental specialties, he insisted on getting everyone involved in the continuous uproar. And at the end of these first few weeks, in January of 1963, he sent us all a memorandum: ". . . You are putting out one hell of a fine magazine. The articles are timely, full of significance and exclusivity. The . . . visual aspects have improved tremendously. . . . [Fiction] could be one of the great breakthroughs in magazine publishing. The final yardstick: We have about six lawsuits pending, meaning we are hitting them where it hurts, with solid, meaningful journalism."[39]

One of the lawsuits was to cost the Curtis Publishing Company over $1 million. The *Post* had published an exposé of an alleged football fix between the coaches Butts of Georgia and Bryant of Alabama. Even though Georgia's Attorney General concluded that the evidence "indicates that vital and important information was given about the Georgia team, and that it could have affected the outcome of the game and the margin of points scored,"[40] Butts won his libel suit, and the *Post* settled with Bryant out of court.

Building coalitions against Culligan.   During the days of corporate infighting and changing editorial policy, Blair was busy building coalitions against Culligan. He formed an Editorial Board consisting of the editors of the major Curtis magazines, with the idea "that it might serve as a political tool to offset the tremendous corporate political drives of Culligan and Clifford."[41] Blair also formed an alliance with

---

39 Ibid., p. 40.
40 Ibid., p. 461.
41 Ibid., p. 50.

Marvin Kantor, a former member of Williston and Beane, the brokerage firm that had helped to put Gould and Stewart on the Curtis board in 1962 (and, incidentally, a firm in which Culligan's father-in-law had once been a managing partner). Kantor had joined Curtis early in 1963 as a member of the board of directors and he had become chief executive assistant to Culligan in January 1964. Kantor stepped into the power vacuum created by the fight between Blair and Clifford:

> Within three months of his arrival at Curtis, Kantor had taken charge of editorial, advertising sales, manufacturing, and just about everything else that interested him. At this point, Culligan was doing his best to portray Curtis as a company that had been saved, a company that had already moved from paralyzing losses into a state of profit by the end of 1963. Once Kantor got access to the ledgers, however, he began expressing suspicions of Culligan's optimistic predictions. In March, Curtis neared the limits of its bank credit, and Kantor brought in some new cash by selling Curtis' one, halfhearted venture in book publishing, a one-third interest in Bantam Books, for $1.9 million. Culligan got the board to agree to new investments in Curtis' printing and paper plants, but Kantor, after looking into the plants, began arguing that they should be sold, just as Blair's group had said two years earlier. And when Kantor checked Culligan's advertising forecasts for the *Post*, he decided that they were going not up but down (in actual fact, *Post* ad revenues for the first six months of 1964 eventually proved to be 17 per cent lower than similar revenues for 1963). All in all, Kantor told Blair, Joe Culligan was leading Curtis not to salvation but to ruin. The company would again lose heavily during 1964, Kantor said—perhaps another $10 million. Blair was appalled.[42]

Blair and Kantor joined forces early in 1964 in an attempt to gain the presidency and control of Curtis. They presented findings of mismanagement to individual members of the board and rallied the editorial departments behind their bid. At one time, Blair and Kantor invited a dozen of the company's leading editors and publishing executives to Manero's steak house in Greenwich, Connecticut, to plot Culligan's overthrow. Largely at Kantor's insistence, Blair was elevated to the Curtis board in February 1964 replacing Stewart.

Culligan received a temporary reprieve from the Blair and Kantor onslaught in April 1964, when it was announced that Texas Gulf Sulphur had discovered major deposits of copper, zinc, and silver, valued at up to $2 billion, just 300 feet from 110,000 acres owned by a Canadian subsidiary of Curtis, the T. S. Woollings Company. Immediately Curtis stock rose from $6 to $19.25 per share.

Although the ore find promised a degree of financial solvency for Curtis, by Labor Day 1964 Curtis' losses for the year were predicted to be $7 million, and, in actuality, would reach $14 million. The company's working capital position was also dangerously close to the $27.5 million minimum level set by the banks. Given the discrepancy between Culligan's "turn around" predictions earlier in the year and the

---

42 Ibid., p. 76.

company's actual financial position, Blair and Kantor made their move, armed with a proposal for saving the company and with a letter signed by most of the editors asking that Culligan be stripped of his executive power.

Confrontation—An "ancient tribunal."   A confrontation took place between Blair, Kantor, and Culligan at an ensuing board meeting. Otto Friedrich, in *Decline and Fall,* discussed the composition of this tribunal at this time (Exhibit 3):

> Who, then, controlled the Curtis board of directors? Unlike many boards, which are acquiescent allies of the reigning management, the Curtis directors were divided into a number of factions, which not only were hostile to one another but scarcely even comprehended one another. The chairman was Joe Culligan, who counted on the support of his own appointees—Clifford and Poppei—but their loyalties were less than certain. Clifford, having been demoted from the Number Two position by Culligan, apparently believed that he himself would be a more efficient president than Culligan. Poppei's loyalties seemed to belong partly to Culligan, partly to Clifford, partly to the discipline of the accountant's profession. On the insurgent side, Blair spoke only for himself and the editors. Kantor had made himself an ally of Blair's but still had ties to the stock interests that had brought him to the board in the first place. The most ambiguous of all these new directors was Milton Gould, once the attorney for Kantor, once the discoverer of Culligan. Gould was also a partner in the law firm of Gallop, Climenko & Gould, and since the *Post* alone paid him more than $600,000 a year for legal expenses, Gould had a natural interest in this aspect of Curtis.
>
> Since none of the main antagonists could create a majority, their conflicts served as a kind of ballet staged for the amusement of the old board members, who represented a plurality of the stock, and who retained a veto over any attempts to save the corporation. Of these old board members, the basic group was known as "the family," which owned 32 per cent of all common stock and officially consisted of two people: Mary Louise Curtis Bok Zimbalist, then aged eighty-eight, the daughter of Cyrus H. K. Curtis, who occasionally was wheeled into critical board meetings by her Negro servants; and her son, Cary W. Bok, aged fifty-nine, who was in rather poor health but periodically came to Philadelphia, dressed in the old Khakis that he liked to wear at his country place in Maine. (There was another son, Curtis Bok, who might have helped to save the company, but that was not to be. Lorimer had denounced him a generation earlier as "that damned Bolshevik," and things were arranged so that Curtis Bok would never have a voice in the operation of the Curtis magazines. He went on to become a distinguished judge, and his son was recently made dean of the Harvard Law School.) As for Mrs. Zimbalist, let us remember her by a story told by a retired executive. Once a year, according to this chronicler, Mrs. Zimbalist would engage in exactly the same colloquy with Walter Deane Fuller, who was then president of the corporation. "She would very respectfully ask Mr. Fuller that her salary as a director be doubled. Very gravely he would reply that economic conditions were such that this could not be done. She would thank him and

sit down. Of course, her salary was only one dollar. But she and Mr. Fuller seemed to enjoy the byplay."

The rest of the old directors tended to support "the family," to the extent that they could determine what the family wanted, but Mrs. Zimbalist and her son rarely attended board meetings during these declining years—refusing either to sell the stocks they had held all their lives or to exercise the authority that these stocks gave them. The old directors were thus left to decide matters for themselves, and for this, they were of an age and distinction that would have done credit to the United States Senate. The most senior of them, of course, was Walter Deane Fuller, the tiny, bald gentleman of eighty-two, who had joined the accounting department of Curtis in 1908 and worked his way up to be president and board chairman for more than twenty-five years. Next came M. Albert Linton, seventy-seven, retired president of the Provident Life Insurance Company of Philadelphia and now chairman of the board's executive committee, assigned to deal with the accusations. Then there was Walter S. Franklin, aged eighty, retired president of the Pennsylvania Railroad; and Ellsworth Bunker, aged seventy, former president of the United Sugar Company, former U.S. Ambassador to India, former president of the American Red Cross; Moreau D. Brown, aged sixty-one, partner in the private banking firm of Brown Brothers, Harriman; Harry C. Mills, aged sixty-three, retired vice president of J. C. Penney; and Curtis Barkes, aged fifty-eight, executive vice president of United Air Lines.

Once the managerial civil war had broken out, it soon became apparent that this board, this ultimate court of appeals, knew relatively little about the Curtis Publishing Company and was quite bewildered by the problems that were being placed before it. More than half the directors were over sixty—"Why," someone asked Clemenceau, "are the presidents of France always octogenarians?" And Clemenceau replied: "Because we have run out of nonagenarians"—and most of them, except for the actual combatants, were weary of combat. Thus, when Blair and Culligan wanted to accuse each other of guilt for Curtis' condition, they had to carry their case before this ancient tribunal, which, in consenting to hear the arguments, denied that the ultimate guilt was its own.[43]

The result of the confrontation was the immediate dismissal of Blair and Kantor on October 30, 1964, and the eventual removal of Culligan from the presidency. Culligan's removal was announced after a meeting of several of the directors at Bok's apartment in Philadelphia. Culligan, not allowed to attend, found out a year later that Clifford and Poppei had threatened to resign if Culligan remained as president.

Rumors began to circulate as to who the next president of Curtis would be. Reportedly the job had been offered to Newton Minow, chairman of the FCC under Kennedy and to Ed Miller, publisher of McCall's, both of whom turned the position down. Miller commented on his reasons for rejecting the presidency of Curtis:

[43] Ibid., pp. 125–127. Reprinted from Decline and Fall by permission of Harper and Row. © 1969–1970 Otto Friedrich.

I came in ready to sign a contract that morning. The amount of money was almost embarrassing—$150,000 a year. But I had other conditions. One was that the banks guarantee a period of grace of twenty-four months, without anybody blowing the whistle, because no miracle would work in less than twenty-four months. Then the other element was John Kluge, the head of Metromedia. We talked to him about taking over the financial responsibilities, and Kluge loved the idea, but his bankers didn't see it in the same light. So that morning, I learned that neither of these conditions would be met, and I said, "To hell with it," and walked out.[44]

The Clifford presidency: 1964–1968

Apparently the board's difficulty in finding a new chief executive and the banks' increasing concern over Curtis' financial position created a situation into which Clifford could move. Clifford, supported by the second most senior board member, Linton, made a bid for the presidency and was accepted in December 1964.

Once in power, Clifford fired several editors, demanded that the magazines cut their budgets by 40%, appointed acting editor William Emerson editor of the *Post,* and changed the *Post* into a bi-weekly publication.

Worried about the $37.3 million that Curtis owed the banks, Clifford sold a paper mill in Pennsylvania for $10.3 million and used $8 million for debt reduction. He also negotiated $24 million in cash from Texas Gulf Sulphur for mining rights on Curtis' Canadian timberlands and utilized the money to pay off bank debts. During 1965, Curtis' assets decreased from $112.6 to $86.9 million with liabilities decreasing from $103 to $68.4 million. Curtis lost $3.4 million in 1965 and showed an operating profit of $347,000 in 1966, the first profit of the decade. Otto Friedrich described the method by which Clifford produced this profit:

The technique was simple. The conscientious employees worked hard at their jobs, because that was their nature, and then the supreme command ordered everyone to cut costs until the year's activities came out even on the balance sheets. This was not simply a matter of operating expenses. It was a philosophy of life. It was a perfect example, however, of the cost accountants' system of doing business—to cut, shrink, tighten, until we reached the theoretical goal of not producing anything at all. Or, as Emerson put it, "It's like being nibbled to death by ducks."[45]

The nibbling apparently would not save Curtis. The company recorded a loss of $4.8 million for 1967, which Clifford blamed on an advertising decline "due primarily to softened national economic conditions and costly strikes in key industries."[46] The company's cash position during this period became dangerously low:

As of the end of the year, current assets had declined by more than $6 million, liabilities had increased by more than $1 million, and

---

[44] Ibid., p. 172.
[45] Ibid., p. 270.
[46] Ibid., p. 307.

actual cash in hand had dropped from $10,102,000 at the start of 1967 to $425,000 at the start of 1968. Obviously, for a company that was operating on a budget of almost $130 million a year, a cash supply of $425,000 was virtually no cash at all.[47]

The low cash position necessitated a quick cash inflow. Clifford attempted to sell the old Curtis building in Philadelphia and offered CBS Curtis' magazines for $15 million provided CBS gave Curtis a printing and distribution contract. CBS reportedly was amazed, since they had just done a study on Curtis which indicated that the magazines alone would earn $10 million a year without the other Curtis overhead.

Ackerman takes over

Into this precarious financial position, with the banks reportedly pushing for a management change, stepped Martin Ackerman, who was quickly pressed into service as Curtis' next president. Aged 36, Ackerman, a former lawyer, was currently head of Perfect Film & Chemical Corporation, a conglomerate he had pushed from sales of $20 million in 1962 to $100 million in 1964 through a series of acquisitions.

Ackerman has related the origin of his interest in Curtis and also the events of a special meeting of the Curtis board in April 1968 that led to his entry into Curtis management:

> J. M. Clifford, then president of Curtis, reported a proposal which I had made under which Perfect Film & Chemical Corporation, which I headed, would arrange for a $5 million loan to Curtis. This loan was to be secured and guaranteed, and would give Perfect Film a chance to see whether the combinations of the activities of the two corporations made any sense. The proposal was discussed at length, along with a number of alternate proposals for obtaining the immediate capital needed by the company. Later in the afternoon, Milton Gould, a director, told the Board that I had informed him that the Perfect proposal was subject to withdrawal if not accepted then and there at the meeting. Accompanied by former governor Alfred Driscoll, another director, I was invited to attend the board meeting for about twenty minutes.
>
> After further discussion, my proposal was approved and I was elected a regular director, along with Eugene Mason, Perfect's attorney. Clifford was voted out of the presidency of Curtis and elected chairman of the Board of Directors. I was made president in his place.[48]

Ackerman began his presidency in April 1968 by arranging a two-month extension of all overdue bank loans and outlining a plan to save the *Post*. Ackerman announced that the *Post*'s circulation would be cut from 6.8 million to 3 million and that the *Post* would be promoted "as a magazine of class, not mass."[49]

In August 1968, Ackerman issued a report on the financial position at Curtis for the first half of 1968. A loss of $7 million on revenues of

---

[47] Ibid., pp. 307–308.

[48] Martin Ackerman, *The Curtis Affair* (Los Angeles: Nash Publishing, 1970), pp. 8–9.

[49] Friedrich, *Decline and Fall,* p. 328.

$58 million was reported, compared to a loss of $370,000 on revenues of $63 million for the first half of the previous year. He also disclosed that Curtis' bank loans of $13.2 million had been taken over by Perfect Film from the Semenenko group at an interest rate of one per cent above the prime rate with maturity on demand.

During his first six months at Curtis, while liquidating part of the Curtis empire, Ackerman also worked incessantly at the *Post* offices in New York, developing schemes to save the magazine, and attempting to write editorials and a column for it (much to the dismay of the editors). But with increased losses for 1968 becoming more evident, Ackerman moved out of the Curtis offices into a town house he had purchased. Friedrich describes the changes that ensued:

> An environment not only expresses a man's ambitions; it also changes his perspectives. The Ackerman who sat enthroned in the town house was not the same man who bustled in and out of offices on our editorial floor. Now, he received us only by appointment, negotiated through one of his two secretaries, and we appeared not as the managers of our own domain but as emissaries to his castle. And in the act of physical withdrawal from the Curtis building, he inevitably withdrew, to some extent, from his intense physical involvement in the day-to-day problems of the *Post*. This was quite understandable, too, for in six months of hard labor, his involvement had really accomplished relatively little. And so, as all executives like to fall back on the specialties that originally brought them their success, Ackerman in his town house began to revert to what he had been before he ever came to Curtis, a financier, a maneuverer of stocks and corporations, an expert at mergers and acquisitions, a banker and millionaire.[50]

As a financier and maneuverer of stocks and corporations, Ackerman reportedly was a master. For example, ostensibly to raise cash for Curtis, he sold the *Ladies' Home Journal* and *American Home* to Downe Communications, Inc., for 100,000 shares of Downe stock valued at $5.4 million, a price low enough to "evoke the image of a fire sale."[51] He later had Curtis turn the Downe stock over to Perfect Film for a $4.5 million reduction in the Curtis loans and then sold the stock privately through a Wall Street firm for $5 million.

> The same day that his sale of the Downe shares was disclosed, it was announced that Perfect Film was spending $9 million to buy from Gulf & Western two Desilu film studios in Culver City, California, the fourteen-acre Culver Studio and the twenty-nine-acre Culver Backlot, both of which were being used by Paramount and various television producers.[52]

But for all Ackerman's financial wizardry, by early 1969 he apparently had neither the ability nor the desire to save the *Post*. The predicted losses for the *Post* for 1969 were between $3.7 and $7 million, based on the trend of decreasing advertising revenue.

Utilizing this financial data as justification, Ackerman, who six

---

[50] Ibid., p. 416.
[51] Ibid., p. 417.
[52] Ibid., p. 417.

months before had stated that as long as he was at Curtis "there would not be a last issue of the *Post*,"[53] announced the end:

> No other decision is possible in view of the sizable predicted losses which continued publication would have generated. Quite simply, this is an example of a new management which could not reduce expenses nor generate sales and income fast enough to halt mounting losses. . . . Having refinanced the Saturday Evening Post Company with $15 million in new capital, I assured directors and stockholders of the company that regardless of my own personal feelings, if we could not return a profit we would have to shut down the *Post*.[54]

The reaction from the stockholders was immediate. Philip Kalodner, a young Philadelphia lawyer and representative of minority stockholders, filed suit against Ackerman for alleged illegal, oppressive, and fraudulent action that had wasted and misapplied more than $45 million of Curtis assets. The trustees of the Cyrus Curtis estate also began an assault against Ackerman:

> They, too, accused Ackerman of dissipating the Curtis assets, and they publicly demanded that he resign from the presidency by noon on the coming Saturday, February 8. They also demanded the resignations of his closest allies on the board of directors. The trustees were vague in their accusations, citing only "conflict of interest," but Cary Bok told a reporter who telephoned his home in Camden, Maine: "That company is in such a damn mess that it's time we got into it—don't you think?"[55]

POSTSCRIPT

At the next board meeting (March 1969), Ackerman resigned as president in favor of G. B. McCombs, who had recently been promoted to senior vice president, after being with Curtis since 1930. Kalodner, who held only 100 shares of stock, was named vice president, director, and a member of the executive committee "in return for agreement not to press his lawsuit against the company."[56]

McCombs lasted five weeks as president; the position then went to Kalodner after some stormy meetings of the board:

> The board itself, depleted by the latest resignations of Ackerman, Gould, and McCombs, now consisted of only six members (one of whom was serving as U.S. Ambassador to Saigon). Three of these had been allies of the departed Milton Gould, and they all favored a petition of bankruptcy. "But I spoke up against them," Kalodner said. "In fact, I filibustered against them." The board meeting went on for five hours, and then ended inconclusively. And the day after the crisis, Kalodner simply decreed himself to be, if not the president of Curtis, then "chief executive officer." Once again, Curtis was without a president.
>
> The deadlock lasted through most of April, and then, on April 24,

---

[53] *Newsweek*, May 20, 1968, p. 70.
[54] Friedrich, *Decline and Fall*, p. 449.
[55] Ibid., p. 466.
[56] Ibid., p. 469.

it was broken long enough for Kalodner, like yet another Roman emperor, to become president. In that capacity, he offered repeated invitations to the unhappy trustees to "join" him in salvaging the wreckage of the company, but the trustees had no intention of collaborating in Kalodner's presidency. Kalodner alone, therefore, had the responsibility of announcing that the Curtis operating loss during the Ackerman year of 1968 had been $18.3 million. He also had to admit that the Curtis contract to print the *Ladies' Home Journal* and *American Home* for Downe Communications would run out at the end of June. "The contract," said *The Wall Street Journal*, "is practically the only ongoing venture Curtis has left."[57]

Kalodner and the trustees spent the early weeks of May 1969 mailing rival proxy statements to the stockholders in anticipation of the May 21 stockholders' meeting. At the meeting the trustees won nine seats on the board of directors, and a representative of the trustees, Arthur Murphy, past president of *McCall's*, took over as president and chairman of the board. A short time later, Murphy dropped the presidency, and W. J. MacIntosh, a lawyer for the board, took over as acting chief executive officer.

In May of 1970, the trustees sold the 700,000 shares of Curtis stock they had controlled since 1933 to Beurt SerVaas, a self-made millionaire from the Mid-West, who took over control as president and principal stockholder of Curtis. SerVaas related his initial actions as head of the company as follows:

> "I came into this company to preside over its death, but instead I decided I could save it," he said. "I'm the first person since Cyrus Curtis himself who's been both the chief executive and the chief stockholder, and so I've had the kind of authority you have to have in order to make vital decisions."
>
> Throughout the summer and fall Mr. SerVaas proceeded to make a series of "vital decisions." He sold all the manufacturing companies that Curtis owned, including a printing plant and a paper mill, decreased the over-all size of its staff from 9,000 people to 100, and "reduced its voluminous debts to zero."
>
> It was the burden of these financial responsibilities that prevented the company from reaping profits, Mr. SerVaas explained.
>
> "Now we're no longer in manufacturing and real estate," he added, "we're just a little publishing company that puts out magazines, and for the first time in years we're no longer in the red."[58]

SerVaas has decided that the *Post* will return to publication as a "200 page quarterly directed toward the 'middle American.' "

> "Toward the end the *Post* became worldly and sophisticated and hard-nosed in an attempt to rejuvenate itself," Mr. SerVaas said, "but it failed, and what we intend to do now should make everyone happy. We're not going to print any more exposés or muckraking articles; we're going to concentrate on writing about those institutions and mores in contemporary America that are good for America."[59]

---

[57] Ibid., pp. 472–473.
[58] *The New York Times,* November 6, 1970.
[59] Ibid.

Exhibit 1

THE SATURDAY EVENING POST
Financial Highlights: 1960–1969
(dollars in millions)

Year	Operating revenues[a]	Operating profit[b]	Net profit	Stockholders' equity[c]	Current assets	Current liabilities	Total assets
1960	$192.8 (restated)	$ 3.5	$ 1.6	$ 49.7	$60.7	$23.3	$133.5
1961	178.4	(8.7)	(4.2)[d]	46.8[e]	56.7	24.5	135.5
1962	149.3	(21.0)	(18.9)[f]	27.9	55.6	41.9	127.8
1963	152.0	(1.4)	(3.4)	24.5	53.8	19.0	123.0
1964	139.4	(13.0)	(13.9)[g]	9.5	46.7	18.5	112.7
1965	122.7	(0.7)	(3.4)	20.5[h]	39.9	22.6	88.9
1966	128.8	2.0	0.3	21.5	44.4	24.6	94.6
1967	124.6	(3.2)	(4.8)	16.7	38.3	25.9	91.5
1968	98.7	(15.2)	(20.9)[i]	2.0[j]	16.7	19.8	43.6
1969	32.0	(10.7)	(19.4)[k]	(14.7)[l]	10.1	15.4	20.3

Note: Parentheses indicate deficit figures.

a Reflects advertising and circulation revenue (net of commissions), paper sales, and miscellaneous operations.

b After production and delivery expense, SGA, and depreciation, but before interest (ranging between $1.2 million and $2.7 million 1960–1968) and miscellaneous income and expenses.

c Includes prior preferred ($16.7 million), preferred ($2.4 million), common ($3.6 million), capital surplus (under $1 million) and undivided profits. As of December 31, 1969, arrears on preferred were $8.9 million.

d Reflects $3.5 million gain on sale of securities and $1.3 million tax credit.

e Reflects $1.7 million transferred to surplus from reserves.

f Reflects $3.8 million tax credit.

g Reflects $1.8 million profit on sale of securities.

h Reflects $14.3 million profit on sale of properties.

i Reflects $1.6 million loss on Saturday Evening Post, and $2.6 million net extraordinary charges (after $20 million provision for plant obsolescence and $1.5 million for future loss on home-office lease, partly offset by gains of $1.1 million on sale of property, $3.4 million on sale of circulation and subscription companies, $13.7 million on sale of Ladies' Home Journal and American Home, and $.7 million gain from reduction in Post circulation).

j Reflects $6.1 million recovery of pension plan funding.

k Reflects $8.3 million in net extraordinary charges associated with curtailment of operations.

l Reflects $2.7 million additional recovery of pension plan funding.

Sources: Curtis Publishing Company, Annual Reports, and Moody's Industrial Manual.

Exhibit 2

THE SATURDAY EVENING POST (R)
THE POWER STRUGGLE AT CURTIS—How They Rose and Fell

	1961	1962	1963	1964	1965	1966	1967	1968	1969
CHAIRMAN OF THE BOARD	Vacant since 1957			Mathew Culligan				Vacant	Thos Moses / Arthur Murphy
PRESIDENT	Robert MacNeal (since 1950)	Mathew Culligan				John Clifford		Martin Ackerman	Arthur Murphy
HEAD OF MAGAZINE DIVISION			Created in April 1963 / John Veronis	Marvin Kantor		Vacant		G. B. McCombs	DEATH OF THE POST
POST EDITOR	Ben Hibbs (since 1942)	Robert Sherrod	Clay Blair		Vacant	William Emerson			
NO. 2 POST EDITOR	Robert Fuoss (since 1942)		Davis Thomas*¹	Don Schanche* / William Emerson		Otto Friedrich			
NO. 3 POST EDITOR	Robert Sherrod (since 1955)	Clay Vacant / Clay Blair	Don Schanche*	William Emerson	Otto Friedrich	Don McKinney*			
TOP POST ADVERTISING EXECUTIVE	Peter Schruth* (since 1957)		C. L. MacNelly*	Vacant		Jess Ballew*		Stephen Kelly*	
MAIN EVENTS IN THE DECLINE AND FALL OF CURTIS	September 1961 Disastrous revamping of Post. December 1961 Curtis loses money for the first time.	July 1962 Blair hires new editors. September 1962 Post moves to New York.	March 1963 Butts article brings libel suits for $20 million. September 1963 Semenenko loans Curtis $35 million.	April 1964 Copper found under Curtis land. September 1964 Blair's rebels meet at Manero's. October 1964 Blair–Kantor dismissal.	January 1965 Post becomes a biweekly. October 1965 Clifford sells copper land for $24 million.	December 1966 Curtis manages a "mini-profit."	March 1967 Clifford purges Schanche. July 1967 Clifford purges Ballew.	April 1968 Ackerman arrives with $5 million.	January 1969 Ackerman kills Post. February 1969 Ackerman is sued. March 1969 Ackerman resigns.
FINANCIAL POSITION	LOSS $4 Million	LOSS $19 Million	LOSS $3.5 Million	LOSS $14 Million	LOSS $3.5 Million	PROFIT $347 Thousand	LOSS $5 Million	LOSS $18 Million	IN AUDIT

* Not mentioned in text.

Source: Otto Friedrich, *Decline and Fall* (New York, Harper & Row, Publishers, 1969), end papers.

Exhibit 3
THE SATURDAY EVENING POST (R)
The Curtis Board, 1964

(clockwise from Blair, nearest camera): John Clifford, Marvin Kantor, Walter Franklin, Harry Mills, M. Albert Linton, Mary Curtis Bok Zimbalist, Matthew Culligan, Gloria Swett, Cary Bok, Walter Fuller, Moreau Brown, Curtis Barkes, and Milton Gould.

BOOK ONE

*Determining
corporate strategy*

The concept of corporate strategy

WE come now to the idea of corporate strategy itself, the uses and limitations of the concept, the criteria that may be used to test the soundness and viability of a strategy, and the problems of evaluation that we may expect to encounter in considering strategic alternatives.

DEFINITION

Our use of the term corporate strategy comprises more than the usual military connotations of this term. For the military, strategy is most simply the positioning of armed forces on the battlefield to accomplish the defeat of the enemy. Less simply, it is the deployment of resources against an enemy in pursuit of goals prescribed by the leaders of the state. When we pass, as we must, from the military to the political sphere, strategy becomes the application of national resources to the accomplishment of national goals.

Our use of the term strategy extends its meaning still further to encompass the choice of goals, as well as the plans for attaining goals. The economist speaks often of strategy as the allocation of scarce resources; we intend more than the closely related selection of product-market relationships. For us strategy is the pattern of objectives, purposes, or goals and major policies and plans for achieving these goals, stated in such a way as to define what business the company is in or is to be in and the kind of company it is or is to be.

Because we are less concerned with exactness of language than we might be if development of theory were our first objective, we do not argue the question whether the term strategy should include the selection of goals or denote only the deployment of resources marshaled in pursuit of these goals. It is to us a matter of indifference. Little confusion results so long as we make clear what we are doing. In our experience, simplicity and convenience are served by combining the choice of goals and the formulation of major policy into one activity. The choice of goals and the formulation of policy cannot in any case be separate decisions. The Stanford Research Institute takes a different path when it equates strategy with the ways in which the firm, reacting to its environment, deploys its principal resources and marshals its main efforts in pursuit of its purpose. Alfred Chandler, in *Strategy and Structure*, takes the direction we favor when he called strategy, ". . . the determination of the basic long-term goals and objectives of an enterprise, and the adoption of courses of action and the allocation of resources necessary for carrying out these goals."[1]

A more important effort to subdivide the idea of strategy seeks to segregate those aspects that are enduring and unchanging over relatively long periods of time from those that are necessarily more responsive to changes in the marketplace and the pressures of other environmental forces. The strategic decision is concerned with the long-term development of the enterprise. The central character of a business organization and the individuality it has for its members and its various publics may, in the instance of mature and highly developed corporations, be determined with some clarity.

Thus the "personality" of firms like Polaroid, Xerox, Control Data, IBM, and General Motors clearly reflects aspects of company intent that are manifested only partially in such activities as research expenditures, choice of product line, and the recruitment and development of organization members. It would be likely to persist through substantial changes in the allocation of resources and in product policy, in part because the basic determinants of organization character would tend to prevent sharp discontinuity. The central character of *The New York Times* is likely to be unchanged, even if the services it offers are altered drastically in the direction of increased emphasis on its news service or on the development of other outlets for its news-processing capacity. In this view, the basic character of an enterprise and the core of its special competence would be considered separately from the manifestation of these long-range characteristics in changing product lines, markets, and policies designed to make activities profitable from year to year.

Our primary interest in isolating the need for strategic decision in concrete instances and in determining the most satisfactory pattern of goals and policies makes further refinement of definition or defense of our own preference of little importance. The student will wish to develop the definition presented here in directions which are useful to him. But before we proceed to clarification by application, we should comment on the terms in which strategy is usually expressed.

A complete summary statement of strategy will in fact say less about what the word means than it does about the company involved. First, it will define products in terms more functional than literal, saying what they do rather than what they are made of. At the same time, it will

---

[1] Alfred D. Chandler, Jr., *Strategy and Structure: Chapters in the History of the Industrial Enterprise* (Cambridge, Mass.: The M.I.T. Press, 1962), p. 13.

designate clearly the markets and market segments for which products are now or will be designed, and the channels through which these markets will be reached. The means by which the operation is to be financed will be specified, as will the emphasis to be placed on safety of capital versus income return. Finally, the size and kind of organization which is to be the medium of achievement will be described. It is, of course, more important than the identification of strategy capture the present and projected character of the organization than that it elaborate the categories of purpose just cited.

Thus of Continental Watchmakers Company,[2] a Swiss firm, we could say:

> It is Mr. Kellers' present plan to produce watches of the highest quality —in a price range between the hand-made ultra-exclusive level and Omega and Rolex. He aims to distribute his watches to all markets of the free world via exclusive wholesale agents and carefully chosen retailers, who are expected to convince customers of the particular value of the product. His growth of about 10% per year is not geared to demand but is deliberately restricted to the productivity of available skilled labor, and to his recognition of cyclical fluctuations in the industry. He aims to maintain within the rules of the industry a stable organization of highly skilled, fully trained workers and a management organization of some breadth, but he apparently wishes to retain personal direction over marketing and a close familiarity with the whole organization.

Companies seldom formulate and publish as complete a statement as we have just illustrated, usually because conscious planning is not carried far enough to achieve the agreement or clarification which publication presumes. These cases enable the student of Policy to do what the managements of the companies usually have not done. In the absence of explicit statements, the student may deduce from operations what the goals and policies are, on the assumption that all normal human behavior is purposeful. Careful examination of the behavior described in the cases will reveal what the strategy must be. At the same time, it is desirable not to infer a degree of conscious planning which does not in fact exist. The current strategy of a company may almost always be deduced from its behavior, but a strategy for a future of changed circumstance may not always be distinguishable from performance in the present.

Corporate strategy has two equally important aspects, interrelated in life but separated to the extent practicable in our study of the concept. The first of these is formulation; the second is implementation. Deciding what strategy should be is, at least ideally, a rational undertaking. Its principal subactivities include identifying opportunities and threats in the company's environment and attaching some estimate of risk to the discernible alternatives. Before a choice can be made, the company's strengths and weaknesses must be appraised. Its actual or potential capacity to take advantage of perceived market needs or to cope with

[2] See E. P. Learned, C. R. Christensen, and K. R. Andrews, *Problems of General Management—Business Policy* (Homewood, Ill.: Richard D. Irwin, Inc., 1961), p. 88.

attendant risks must be estimated as objectively as possible. The strategic alternative which results from a matching of opportunity and corporate capability at an acceptable level of risk is what we may call an *economic strategy*.

The process described thus far assumes that the strategist is analytically objective in estimating the relative capacity of his company and the opportunity he sees or anticipates in developing markets. The extent to which he wishes to undertake low or high risk presumably depends on his profit objective. The higher he sets the latter, the more willing he must be to assume a correspondingly high risk that the market opportunity he sees will not develop or that the corporate competence required to excel competition will not be forthcoming.

So far we have described the intellectual processes of ascertaining what a company *might do* in terms of environmental opportunity, of deciding what it *can do* in terms of ability and power, and of bringing these two considerations together in optimal equilibrium. The determination of strategy also requires consideration of what alternative is preferred by the chief executive and perhaps by his immediate associates as well, quite apart from economic considerations. Personal values, aspirations, and ideals do, and in our judgment quite properly should, influence the final choice of purposes. Thus what the executives of a company *want to do* must be brought into the strategic decision.

Finally, strategic choice has an ethical aspect—a fact much more dramatically illustrated in some industries than in others. Just as alternatives may be ordered in terms of the degree of risk that they entail, so may they be examined against the standards of responsibility that the strategist elects. Some alternatives may seem to the executive considering them more attractive than others when he public good or service to society is considered. What a company *should do* thus appears as a fourth element of the fateful decision we have called strategic.

The ability to identify the four components of strategy—(1) market opportunity, (2) corporate competence and resources, (3) personal values and aspirations, and (4) acknowledged obligations to segments of society other than the stockholders—is nothing compared to the art of reconciling their implications in a final choice of purpose. Taken by itself, each consideration might lead in a different direction.

For example, the manager of a radio station that is declining in ratings and income may decide that in his community the teen-age clientele is his best market, especially given the programming practices of competing stations. His program directors, announcers, and advertising salesmen are experienced, however, only in providing a mixture of news, music, and commercials addressed to the adult commuter-motorist, with housewife fare broadcast between rush hours. The manager may hate rock-and-roll music and commercials addressed to the skin problems of adolescents, and his staff may have no real rapport with younger listeners. He may believe that the franchise granted his station to make profit-making use of a publicly owned frequency as well as the policies of the Federal Communications Commission obligate him to some degree of public service more substantial than airing rock and roll.

Something will have to give before a unified strategy can be achieved out of this divergence. At first glance it appears that making a conventional rock-and-roll approach to teen-agers is out, unless personal taste and sense of responsibility are to be wholly ignored. Some innovations will be required to end the impasse—either a new approach to teen-age listeners or more successful programming for the audience preferred. A pioneering reconciliation is required, for the conventional alternatives in radio programming are inadequate for this problem. Furthermore, the balance finally struck must be adaptable to further changes in the community environment.

The implementation of strategy is comprised of a series of subactivities which are primarily administrative. Once purpose is determined, then the resources of a company must be mobilized to accomplish it. An organizational structure that is appropriate for the efficient performance of the required tasks must be made effective by information systems and relationships permitting coordination of subdivided activities. The organizational processes of performance measurement, compensation, management development—all of them enmeshed in systems of incentives and controls—must be directed toward the kind of behavior required by organizational purpose. The role of personal leadership is important and sometimes decisive in the accomplishment of strategy. Since effective implementation can make a sound strategic decision ineffective or a debatable choice thoroughly successful, it is as important to examine the processes of implementation as to weigh the advantages of the available strategic alternatives.

THE FUNCTIONS OF STRATEGY

It is relatively rare, although in substantial organizations less and less so, to encounter the conscious attention to strategy which our definition suggests is appropriate. The many reasons need not detain us now. At the moment, we should consider whether the advantages of a consciously considered strategy are worth the effort it obviously requires. Four considerations suggest an affirmative answer. These are the inadequacy of stating goals only in terms of maximum profit, the necessity of planning ahead in undertakings with long lead times, the need of influencing rather than merely responding to environmental change, and the utility of setting visible goals as an inspiration to organizational effort.

The age-old assertion that the only true purpose of business is profit is no substitute for a more detailed program. To specify how much profit in terms of "as much as possible" leaves unanswered questions about how it is to be made and whether any restraints are to be observed in the quest. The extent to which present profits will be forgone to prepare for larger profits at a later time is unspecified. The desirability of profit, like that of survival, good health, and growth, does not make it a magnetic pole establishing a directed course among many alternatives.

In an era of rapid change and intense interindustry and intereconomy competition, improvisation, however brilliant, cannot suffice as a company's sole weapon against the negative effects of change.

The range of activities planned in advance is generally wider than that determinable on the spur of the moment. Many moves, because they require long preparation, cannot be made at all without forward planning. When new product development requires years and a new distribution network may cost millions of dollars, purpose must necessarily be considered in detail well in advance of investment.

Colorful intuitive leadership may seem to render conscious planning unnecessary. For example, the elder Mr. Baker of Baker Metal and Foil[3] repeatedly confounded his subordinates by buying plants and equipment on the spur of the moment. He planned his moves in the solitude of his study during the early hours of the morning, and he doubtless reached a clear decision in his own mind about where he wanted to go. His vision was responsible for his company's status as a leader in its industry. But had he been able to articulate his goals, his associates—relieved of the frustration occasioned by continued chaos—could have more easily performed the financial planning to make them feasible. The forward look which Mr. Baker took in solitude did not in itself constitute the formulation of a coherent strategy that would permit his organization to know what he was up to and what was required of them.

Planned purpose can affect and change the character of future developments which otherwise might endanger even the healthiest organization. Reliance upon adaptation alone leaves the company at the mercy of the strongest currents. Innovation, and the creativity which supports it, can enable a company to carve out its own future rather than simply to depend on favorable circumstances. But such a course requires predetermination of what must be done. Thus at least one manufacturer of small radios and another of camera equipment, apparently about to be overwhelmed by Japanese imports, stemmed the tide and reversed a trend by a program comprising cost reduction, product restyling, and improved marketing, all of which took time and predetermined purpose to perfect.

From the point of view of implementation, the most important function of strategy is to serve as the focus of organizational effort, as the object of commitment, and as the source of constructive motivation and self-control in the organization itself. We shall have ample opportunity to see later that it is a common understanding of the goals to be served and a widespread acceptance of their importance, persisting through the inevitable distortions of individual and departmental needs, that are the soundest bases of cooperative action.

THE LIMITATIONS OF STRATEGY

These claims regarding the value of formulating a strategy are stated as ideas to be examined and tested, for the practice is not without its limitations. One objection sometimes voiced is that strategy involves planning, and that planning ahead poses serious obstacles. With increasing complexity and an accelerating rate of change, it grows more

---

[3] See G. A. Smith and C. R. Christensen, *Policy Formulation and Administration* (rev. ed.; Homewood, Ill.: Richard D. Irwin, Inc., 1955), p. 453.

and more difficult to predict the future in detail. Long-range plans cannot be detailed quantitatively with much confidence. Accuracy in forecasting is impossible. These complaints are not real limitations, however, for strategy does not require more knowledge of the future than we have. The extent to which a variety of alternatives is studied in advance reduces the possibility of surprise and permits the preparation of alternative plans for a range of possibilities. The more uncertain the future, in fact, the more necessary it is to contemplate what can happen and what is likely to happen and to assign probabilities to the imaginable possibilities.

A more serious limitation is that overdedication to plan may result in lost opportunity. The rise of research expenditures and the impossibility of knowing in advance what research will bring forth often lead opponents of planning to say with some justice that maintenance of flexibility to take advantage of unanticipated opportunity is more important than commitment to fixed plans over long time periods. One must admit at once that the determination of strategy must not be so rigid that unexpected opportunity cannot be considered. But it is possible to conceive of strategy as being firm and influential without its being cast in concrete. We shall ultimately be able to conceive of strategy as performing all that we ask of it without ever becoming finally solidified. To accommodate uncertainty and to preserve flexibility are not the easiest activities in the world, but a strategy formulated without regard for these necessities would indeed be folly. What is needed is the concept of a moving balance among the considerations on which strategy is based, the concept of a strategy that progressively evolves in the direction of improving the match between the company's resources and the opportunities in its environment. To design a strategy that is *optimal* is a challenge to insight and intelligence which simply lies beyond the capacity of many an effective operator. The skill required in the use of an idea may be a limitation to its usefulness.

A third set of limitations and problems which requires us to say at once that the concept of strategy is no panacea is the inevitability of conflict between corporate and departmental goals and between organizational and personal goals. We shall have more to say about these impediments to effective implementation at a later time. In the meantime we must accept as a fact of life that the most articulate, specific, and persuasive definition of strategy by the president of a company, ratified by the board of directors and promptly emulated by competitors, will never have the same meaning or appeal to all parts of the organization to which it is announced. To communicate a strategy requires as much trouble and time as to conceive it. To adhere to it wisely under the temptations posed by expediency is difficult. To adhere to it blindly when changing circumstance has made it obsolete is no more preferable than thoughtless opportunism. New opportunities, unexpected innovations, sudden emergencies, competitive pressures, and incomplete programming of action required by the strategy selected all constitute real problems in adhering to a plan once it has been made clear.

The limitations of the concept of strategy consist principally of the inherent difficulties of conceiving a viable pattern of goals and policies and implementing them wisely. Dealing with these limitations effectively means not abandoning the concept, but learning to use it successfully with reasonable perspective on what is possible. We cannot expect the concept of strategy to be a substitute for judgment or a shortcut to wisdom. It does not in itself point out the course of action to be taken in difficult situations. Nevertheless, it is the strategic decision to which judgment must be applied. Wisdom cannot be brought to a decision that is not recognized as needed. No consideration of the limitations of this idea invalidates the proposition that the essential business and character of an enterprise should be determined well in advance of shifting circumstances (which will otherwise become the determining factors), if the future of the corporation is to be kept to an appreciable extent within the control of its management.

CRITERIA FOR EVALUATION

The attempt to identify the actual or optimal strategy for a business firm raises at once the question of how the actual or proposed strategy is to be judged. How are we to know that one strategy is better than another in advance of validation by experience? As is already evident, no infallible indicators are available. A number of important questions can regularly be asked.[4] With practice they will lead to intuitive discriminations.

1. *Is the strategy identifiable and has it been made clear either in words or practice?*

The degree to which attention has been given to the strategic alternatives available to a company is likely to be basic to the soundness of its strategic decision. To cover in empty phrases ("our policy is planned profitable growth in any market we can serve well") an absence of analysis of opportunity or actual determination of corporate strength is worse than to remain silent, for it conveys the illusion of a commitment when none has been made. The unstated strategy cannot be tested or contested and is likely therefore to be weak. If it is implicit in the intuition of a strong leader, his organization is likely to be weak and the demands his strategy makes upon it are likely to remain unmet.

2. *Does the strategy exploit fully domestic and international environmental opportunity?*

An unqualified yes answer is likely to be rare even in the instance of global giants like General Motors. But the present and future dimensions of markets can be analyzed without forgetting the limited resources of the planning company in order to outline the requirements of balanced growth and the need for environmental information. The relation between market opportunity and organizational development is

---

[4] For an earlier statement of most of the criteria discussed here, see Seymour Tilles, "How to Evaluate Corporate Strategy," *Harvard Business Review*, July-August 1963, p 111.

a critical one in the design of future plans. Unless growth is incompatible with the resources of an organization or the aspirations of its management, it is likely that a strategy that does not purport to make full use of market opportunity will be weak also in other respects. Vulnerability to competition is increased by lack of interest in market share.

3. *Is the strategy consistent with corporate competence and resources, both present and projected?*

Although additional resources, both financial and managerial, are available to companies with genuine opportunity, the availability of each must be finally determined and programmed along a practicable time scale. The decision of the Wilkinson Sword Company to distribute stainless steel razor blades in the United States must have raised the question whether the company could in effect take yes for an answer from this market—that is, whether its productive capacity could be increased fast enough to fend off the countermoves of large competitors.

4. *Are the major provisions of the strategy and the program of major policies of which it is comprised internally consistent?*

A foolish consistency is the hobgoblin of little minds, and consistency of any kind is certainly not the first qualification of successful corporation presidents. Nonetheless, one advantage of making as specific a statement of strategy as is practicable is the resultant availability of a careful check on coherence, compatability, and synergy—the state in which the whole can be viewed as greater than the sum of its parts. For example, a manufacturer of chocolate candy who depends for two-thirds of his business upon wholesalers should not follow a policy of ignoring them or of dropping all support of their activities and all attention to their complaints. Similarly, two engineers who found a new firm expressly to do development work should not follow a policy of accepting orders that, though highly profitable, in effect turn their company into a large job shop, with the result that unanticipated financial and production problems take all the time that might have gone into development. An examination of any substantial firm will reveal at least some details in which policies pursued by different departments tend to go in different directions. Where inconsistency threatens concerted effort to achieve budgeted results within a planned time period, then consistency becomes a vital rather than merely an aesthetic problem.

5. *Is the chosen level of risk feasible in economic and personal terms?*

Strategies vary in the degree of risk willingly undertaken by their designers. For example, the Midway Foods Company,[5] in pursuit of its marketing strategy, deliberately courts disaster in production slow-downs and in erratic behavior of cocoa futures. But the choice is made knowingly and the return, if success is achieved, is likely to be correspondingly great. Temperamentally the president is willing to live

---

[5] See Learned, Christensen, and Andrews, *Problems of General Management*, p. 143.

under this pressure and presumably has recourse if disaster strikes. At the other extreme, a company may have such modest growth aspirations that the junior members of its management are unhappy. A more aggressive and ambitious company would be their choice. Although risk cannot always be assessed scientifically, the level at which it is set is, within limits, optional. The riskiness of any future plan should be compatible with the economic resources of the organization and the temperament of the managers concerned.

6. *Is the strategy appropriate to the personal values and aspirations of the key managers?*

Until we consider the relationship of personal values to the choice of strategy, it is not useful to dwell long upon this criterion. But, to cite an extreme case, the deliberate falsification of warehouse receipts to conceal the absence of soybean oil from the tanks which are supposed to contain it would not be an element of competitive strategy to which most of us would like to be committed. A strong attraction of leisure, to cite a less extreme example, is inconsistent with a strategy requiring all-out effort from the senior members of a company. Or if, for example, the president abhors conflict and competition, then it can be predicted that the hard-driven firm of an earlier day will have to change its strategy. Conflict between the personal preferences, aspirations, and goals of the key members of an organization and the plan for its future is a sign of danger and a harbinger of mediocre performance or failure.

7. *Is the strategy appropriate to the desired level of contribution to society?*

Closely allied to the value is the ethical criterion. As the professional obligations of business are acknowledged by an increasing number of senior managers, it grows more and more appropriate to ask whether the current strategy of a firm is as socially responsible as it might be. Although it can be argued that filing any economic need contributes to the social good, it is clear that a manufacturer of cigarettes might well consider diversification on grounds other than his fear of future legislation.

8. *Does the strategy constitute a clear stimulus to organizational effort and commitment?*

For organizations which aspire not merely to survive but to lead and to generate productive performance in a climate that will encourage the development of competence and the satisfaction of individual needs, the strategy selected should be examined for its inherent attractiveness to the organization. Some undertakings are inherently more likely to gain the commitment of able men of goodwill than others. Given the variety of human preferences, it is risky to illustrate this difference briefly. But currently a company that is vigorously expanding its overseas operations finds that several of its socially conscious young men exhibit more zeal in connection with its work in developing countries than in Europe. Generally speaking, the bolder the choice of goals and the wider the range of human needs they reflect, the more successfully they will appeal to the capable membership of a healthy and energetic organization.

9. *Are there early indications of the responsiveness of markets and market segments to the strategy?*

Results, no matter how long postponed by necessary preparations, are, of course, the most telling indicators of soundness, so long as they are read correctly at the proper time. A strategy may pass with flying colors all the tests so far proposed, and may be in internal consistency and uniqueness an admirable work of art. But if within a time period made reasonable by the company's resources and the original plan the strategy does not work, then it must be weak in some way that has escaped attention. Bad luck, faulty implementation, and competitive countermoves may be more to blame for unsatisfactory results than flaws in design, but the possibility of the latter should not be unduly discounted. Conceiving a strategy that will win the company a unique place in the business community, that will give it an enduring concept of itself, that will harmonize its diverse activities, and that will provide a fit between environmental opportunity and present or potential company strength is an extremely complicated task. We cannot expect simple tests of soundness to tell the whole story. But an analytical examination of any company's strategy against the several criteria here suggested will nonetheless give anyone concerned with making, proving, or contributing to corporate planning a good deal to think about.

PROBLEMS OF EVALUATION

The evaluation of strategy is as much an act of judgment as is the original conception, and may be as subject to error. The most common source of difficulty is the misevaluation of current results. When results are unsatisfactory, as we have just pointed out, a reexamination of strategy is called for. At the same time, outstandingly good current results are not necessarily evidence that the strategy is sound. For example, a candy manufacturer made more money from his newly established retail stores just after the war than from the rest of his operations, but these profits were poor evidence that he was doing what he should have been doing. With the end of sugar rationing and the return of a buyers' market, he went bankrupt. Extrapolation of present performance into the future, overoptimism and complacence, and underestimation of competitive response and of the time required to accommodate to changes in demand are often by-products of success. Usually high profits may blind the unwary manager to impending environmental change. His concern for the future can under no circumstances be safely suspended. Conversely, a high-risk strategy that has failed was not necessarily a mistake, so long as the risk was anticipated and the consequences of failure carefully calculated. In fact, a planning problem confronting a number of diversified companies today is how to encourage their divisions to undertake projects where failure can be afforded but where success, if it comes, will be attended by high profits not available in run-of-the-mill, low-risk activities.

Although the possibility of misinterpreting results is by far the commonest obstacle to accurate evaluation of strategy, the criteria previously outlined suggest immediately some additional difficulties. It is as easy to misevaluate corporate re sources and the financial requirements of a new move as to misread the environment for future opportunities. To be overresponsive to industry trends may be as dangerous as to ignore them. For example, if a manufacturer of jeweled-lever watches should switch his production to pinlever watches because of the success of Timex in the United States and the faster growth rate of inexpensive watches in other countries, his course would not necessarily be correct. The correspondence of the company's strategy with current environmental developments and an overreadiness to adapt may obscure the opportunity for a larger share of a declining market or for growth in profits without a parallel growth in total sales. The decision of American Motors not to follow trends toward big cars in the middle 1950s provides us with an opportunity to examine the strategic alternatives of adapting to, or running counter to, massive current trends in demand.

The intrinsic difficulty of determining and choosing among strategic alternatives leads many companies to do what the rest of the industry is doing rather than to make an independent determination of opportunity and resources. Sometimes the companies of an industry run like sheep all in one direction. The similarity among the strategies, at least in some periods of history, of insurance companies, banks, railroads, and airplane manufacturers may lead one to wonder whether strategic decisions were based upon industry convention or upon independent analysis. When the student examines the farm equipment industry he may wish to inquire whether the similarity of timing, decision, and reaction to competition constituted independent appraisals of each company's situation, or whether imitation took the place of independent decision. At any rate, the similarity of one company's strategy to that of its competitors does not constitute the assurance of soundness which it might at first suggest.

A strategy may manifest an all-too-clear correspondence with the personal values of the founder, owner, or chief executive. Like a correspondence with dominant trends and the startegic decisions of competitors, this may also be dysfunctional. For example, a personal preference for growth beyond all reasonable expectations may be given undue weight. It should be only one factor among several in any balanced consideration of what is involved in designing strategy. Too little attention to a corporation's actual competence for growth or diversification is the commonest error of all.

It is entirely possible that a strategy may reflect in an exaggerated fashion the values rather than the reasoned decisions of the responsible manager or managers and that imbalance may go undetected. That this may be the case is a reflection of the fact that the entire business community may be dominated by certain beliefs of which one should be wary. A critic of strategy must be at heart enough of a nonconformist to raise questions about generally accepted modes of thought and the conventional thinking which serves as a substitute for original analysis. The timid may not find it prudent to challenge publicly some of the ritual of policy formulation. But even for them it will serve the purposes of criticism to inquire privately into such sacred propositions as the one proclaiming that a company must grow or die.

Another canon of management that may engender questionable strategies is the idea that cash funds in excess of reasonable dividend requirements should be reinvested either in revitalization of a company's traditional activities or in mergers and acquisitions that will diversify products and services. Successful operations, a heretic might observe, sometimes bring riches to a company which lacks the capacity to re-employ them. Yet a decision to return to the owners large amounts of capital which the company does not have the competence or desire to put to work is an almost unheard-of development. It is therefore appropriate, particularly in the instance of very successful companies in older and stable industries, to inquire how far strategy reflects a simple desire to put all resources to work rather than a more valid appraisal of investment opportunity in relation to unique corporate strengths. We should not forget to consider an unfashionable, even if ultimately also an untenable alternative—namely, that to keep an already large world-wide corporation within reasonable bounds, a portion of the assets might well be returned to stockholders for investment in other enterprises.

The identification of opportunity and choice of purpose are such challenging intellectual activities that we should not be surprised to find that persistent problems attend the proper evaluation of strategy. But just as the criteria for evaluation are useful, even if not precise, so the dangers of misevaluation are less menacing if they are recognized. We have noted the inexactness of the concept of strategy, the limits to its usefulness in practice, the problems of making resolute determinations in the face of uncertainty, the necessity for judgment in the evaluation of the soundness of strategy, and the misevaluation into which human error may lead us. None of these alters the fact that a business enterprise guided by a clear sense of purpose rationally arrived at and emotionally ratified by commitment is more likely to have a successful outcome, in terms of profit and social good, than a company whose future is left to guesswork and chance. Conscious strategy does not preclude brilliance of improvisation or the welcome consequences of good fortune. Its cost is principally thought and hard work which, though often painful, are seldom fatal.

APPLICATION TO CASES

As the student attempts to apply the concept of strategy to the analysis of cases, he should try to keep in mind three questions:

1. What is the strategy of this company?
2. In the light of (a) the characteristics and developments of its environment and (b) its own strengths and weaknesses, is the strategy sound?
3. What recommendations for changed strategy might advantageously be made to the president?

Whatever other questions the student may be asked or may ask himself, he will wish constantly to order his study and structure his analysis of case information according to the need to *identify, evaluate,* and *recommend.*

By now the student has an idea, which discussion of the cases will greatly clarify, of what is meant by corporate strategy. He knows how it is derived and some of its uses and limitations. He has been given some criteria for evaluating the strategies he identifies and those he proposes. And he has been properly warned about errors of judgment which await the unwary.

The cases which immediately follow will permit the student to consider in the context of real situations what this text has been talking about. What contribution, if any, would the concept of strategy, mostly missing as a conscious formulation, have made to these companies? What strategic alternatives can be detected in the changing circumstances affecting their fortunes? Which ones would the student choose if he were responsible or were asked to advise? By the time these cases have been examined, the student will be ready to turn from the nature and uses of strategy to a study in sequence of its principal components —environmental opportunity, corporate capability, personal aspirations, and moral responsibility.

J. I. Case Company

J. I. CASE during its fiscal year ending October 1952 achieved a sales volume of $153.5 million resulting in a profit before taxes of $15.2 million. Gross assets on October 31, 1952, amounted to $174.4 million of which $128.5 million was financed internally. Debt financing contributed $27.6 million with the remaining $18.3 million coming from suppliers, tax liabilities, and other sources.

Nine years later, the 1961 fiscal year closed with sales of $128.7 million resulting in a net loss of $32.3 million. Gross assets on October 31, 1961, amounted to $234.7 million of which $81.5 million was financed internally. Debt financing contributed $127.4 million (not counting the obligations of Case's credit subsidiary) with the remaining $25.8 million coming from suppliers, tax liabilities, and other sources.

By the end of the nine-year period, J. I. Case's earned surplus had dropped by $80.6 million to a negative figure of $26.8 million. The following material, all drawn from published sources, bears on policies, policy implementation, and results achieved as three successive administrations wrestled during this period with the problem of working out a viable strategy for Case: (1) Mr. John T. Brown from 1953 to 1956, (2) Mr. Marc B. Rojtman (pronounced Roitman) from 1957 to 1959, and (3) Mr. William J. Grede during 1960 and 1961.

BACKGROUND

Stepping up from executive vice president to president of Case in mid-1953,[1] Mr. Brown assumed direction of a 111-year-old company. Its general offices (a careful reproduction of the Boston Public Library, with a roll-top desk and brass cuspidor in the president's office)[2] were

---

[1] Appendix A provides some background information on J. I. Case during the period 1945–1952.

[2] "The Rojtman's Tractor Race," *Fortune*, February 1958, p. 107.

121

at Racine, Wisconsin. Manufacturing operations were conducted in eight plants in five states. Some 4,000 dealers were served through 49 company-operated branches: 36 in the United States, 8 in Canada, and 5 in South America. Manufacturing facilities, expanded and modernized since World War II at a cumulative cost of some $30 million,[3] contained about eight million square feet—enough to support sales of over $300 million a year.[4] Except for a small volume of tractors for the industrial market ($3.2 million in 1953)[5] the company's whole peacetime business was in agricultural machinery.[6]

THE JOHN T. BROWN ADMINISTRATION

Policies.   In response to flagging sales and profits, Mr. Brown's policies included: (1) cutting costs; (2) increasing the sales effectiveness of dealers; (3) accelerating product development; and (4) remaining as financially liquid as possible.

Implementation.   To implement the policy of cutting costs, Mr. Brown's administration carried on a continuing program of reviewing expenses, installing new and improved machinery, and scrutinizing manufacturing methods. In 1956 it closed two plants and cut the number of domestic sales branches from 36 in 28 states to 28 in 24.

To implement the policy of improving the sales effectiveness of dealers, the Brown administration continued past programs of training dealers and modernizing branches; held the line on prices in 1954 in spite of cost increases; engaged in multimedia advertising in 1955 and 1956; and overhauled dealerships in 1956, making 345 additions or replacements.[7] The most important sales change, however, was increased use of company financing to carry dealers' inventories and a limited amount of farmers' paper. Reflecting an industry-wide trend, customers' accounts and notes receivable rose $26 million, or 70%, from 1952 through 1956. In the latter year, according to the Annual Report, the contract offered dealers was changed to increase their "opportunity and effectiveness in obtaining greater retail volume," while the contract offered farmers was changed to gear payments to the farm-income cycle.

To implement the policy of accelerated product development, which Mr. Brown, according to *Fortune*, saw as the most needed feature of his program, the company brought out three new tractors as well as new models of other machines and equipment. Reflecting an industry trend, the new tractors were relatively large: a five-plow diesel, "first with power steering" in August 1953; a "completely new four-plow model with more speeds, more usable power," and an engine adaptable to three types of fuel in February 1955, and a "revolutionary" three-plow model completed and marketed in 1956.[8] Other new models included grain

---

[3] J. I. Case, Annual Report, 1952, p. 5.

[4] *Implement & Tractor*, February 9, 1957, p. 76.

[5] J. I. Case, Prospectus, October 1958, p. 9.

[6] See Appendix B for some data on the farm equipment industry.

[7] Annual Reports.

[8] Annual Reports.

combines, hay balers, and a corn picker.[9] (After tractors and related equipment, these three lines made the greatest contribution to Case volume.)[10] Commenting on this development program, *Fortune* stated:

> Brown wanted to put more money into research. Like its competitors, Case was still producing prewar machines in 1946. Unlike its competitors, Case was not developing very much that was new. In 1949, its research budget was only $1 million, far less than 1 per cent of sales. Brown kept raising his research budget until, by 1956, it was $2,-500,000.[11]

To implement the policy of remaining as liquid as possible in spite of rising needs for working capital to use in the sales end of the business, an effort was made to limit short-term debt to its traditional function of meeting seasonal needs, and to reduce inventories mainly by holding production below sales. From a peak of $80.8 million in March 1953, inventories declined to $35.9 million at the end of fiscal 1956.[12]

Further attesting Mr. Brown's interest in staying liquid are the following figures for current ratios and net working capital:

	1952	1953	1954	1955	1956
Current ratio................	2.5	4.7	6.5	6.8	5.1
Net current assets (millions)................	$68.6	$88.2	$85.2	$84.5	$84.9

Source: Annual Reports.

Overall achievements and a new approach. Results for the Brown administration seesawed between profit and loss, with the cumulative four-year net after taxes falling to only $146,000, in contrast to almost $50 million during the previous four years. (For financial statements, see Exhibits 1 and 2.) Explaining these results, management stressed the need for continuing its "corrective action" and the impact of such unfavorable factors as the end of the postwar boom, poor crops and weather, political uncertainties about the farm program, shifts in foreign sales, and the downswing that carried net farm income from $14.3 billion in 1951 and 1952 to a low of $11.3 billion in 1955. When 1956 turned unprofitable despite the relatively good results achieved with the Brown program in the more depressed farm market of the previous year, management decided to try a new approach, even though still retaining faith in the long-run future of farm equipment as the only answer to the cost-price squeeze on farmers.[13]

The new approach was merger. According to *Fortune*, talks were under way for a time with two of Case's smaller full-line competitors, but what Mr. Brown really wanted was "a merger that would give him

---

[9] For pictures of these and other items, see Appendix C.

[10] Prospectus, 1952, p. 8; 1953, p. 6; 1956, p. 8.

[11] *Fortune*, p. 188.

[12] *Annual Report*, 1956.

[13] Annual Reports.

Exhibit 1

J. I. CASE COMPANY

Operating and Surplus Reconciliation Statements for Years Ending October 31, 1952–1961
(dollars in millions)

	1952	1953	1954	1955	1956	1957	1958	1959	1960	1961
Sales.										
Gross.	$153.5	$111.5	$92.4	$94.8	$87.1	$123.9	$177.9	$200.6	$111.5	$128.7
Net.										
Cost of goods sold.									111.1	117.7
Selling, general and administrative expense.									32.8	29.7
Total.	137.4	108.6	92.5	92.3	87.7	120.9	166.4	182.7	143.9	147.4
Operating profit or (loss).	$ 16.1	$ 2.8	$ (0.2)	$ 2.6	$ (0.6)	$ 3.0	$ 11.5	$ 17.9	$ (32.4)	$ (18.7)
Other income										
Discounts on purchases.	0.4	0.3	0.2	0.2	0.2	0.3	0.7			
Interest and financial charges earned.		0.2	0.3	0.4	0.6	1.1	1.9	1.3	1.7	1.3
Earnings, Case Credit Corp.								4.4	4.8	2.6
Miscellaneous.			0.2			0.4	0.2	0.2		
Other expenses										
Case Credit financial charges*							3.3	6.5	9.0	7.5
Interest paid.	1.4	1.7	1.5	1.4	1.7	2.8	3.0	4.3	5.6	7.2
Losses, French subsidiary.									6.0	1.2
Miscellaneous.				0.1						1.6
Income before taxes.	15.2	1.6	(1.0)	1.7	(1.6)	2.0	8.0	13.0	(46.4)	(32.3)
Taxes.	8.1	0.8	(0.5)	0.8	(0.6)	0.7	3.7	6.8	(6.6)	
Net profit.	$ 7.0	$ 0.8	$ (0.5)	$ 0.9	$ (1.0)	$ 1.3	$ 4.3	$ 6.2	$ (39.8)	$ (32.3)
Surplus, beginning.	39.4	40.8	36.4	34.1	34.1	32.7	45.9	49.1	54.1	13.1
Dividends										
Preferred.	0.6	0.6	0.6	0.8	0.4	1.0	1.2	1.2	1.2	
Common.	5.0	4.5	1.1							
Other charges.										7.6†
Special credits.						12.9†				
Surplus, ending.	$ 40.8	$ 36.4	$34.1	$34.1	$32.7	$ 45.9	$ 49.1	$ 54.1	$ 13.1	$ (26.8)

Note: (1) Consolidated figures, except for French subsidiaries and J. I. Case Credit Corporation. (2) Figures may fail to add because of rounding.
* Less interest received from Case Credit Corporation.
† Restoration of special reserves.
‡ Includes $2.95 million for taxes applicable to 1947–1954; $3.2 million for losses on plants, etc., and $1.4 million for additional loss on French subsidiaries.
Source: Annual Reports.

a growth product." A possibility that seemed to fill his need was the American Tractor Corporation, a small but fast expanding maker of crawler tractors for varied industrial and construction markets. Under the leadership of its founder and president, Mr. Marc B. Rojtman, ATC had grown from a volume of under $1 million in 1951 to over $10 million in 1956.[14] This success, in the face of competition from industry giants, seemed due in the main to Mr. Rojtman's flair for product development and merchandising. He had seen the advantages of putting out a crawler with a tank-type automatic transmission, had lured away a top engineer from Allis-Chalmers to work out the design, had been first with such a tractor on the market, and had exploited his position through a novel but dramatic promotional device, the "Tractorama," or tractor tug-of-war, in which the new transmission guaranteed that ATC would out-tug its competition.

Exhibit 2

J. I. CASE COMPANY

Balance Sheets as of October 31, Selected Years, 1952–1961
(dollars in millions)

ASSETS	1952	1956	1959	1960	1961
Current assets					
Cash..........................	$ 6.6	$ 5.2	$ 12.0	$ 13.2	$ 5.7
Accounts receivable					
Customers......................	37.7	63.9	33.8	20.7	19.6
Sundry........................	0.5	1.2	1.7	1.2	2.7
Reserve for doubtful accounts........	(0.5)	(0.7)	(0.5)	(1.0)	(1.5)
Claim for income tax refund.........	...	...	...	4.6	...
Prepaid expenses....................	...	...	1.5	1.3	0.7
Due from Case Credit Corporation....	...	...	13.4	4.7	...
Inventories.......................	70.1	35.9	56.7	65.9	59.0
Total current assets...........	$114.5	$105.6	$118.5	$110.6	$ 86.0
Investments and other assets					
American Tractor Corporation........	...	$ 1.0	...	...	...
Case Credit Corporation*...........	...	...	$ 44.9	$ 52.2	$ 53.4
French subsidiaries†..............	...	...	0.7	0.8	1.6
Deferred charges					
Engineering expense...............	...	...	4.1‡	...	...
Other.........................	$ 0.6	0.9	0.6	0.6	...
Miscellaneous.....................	0.2	0.3	1.4	2.5	2.8
	$ 0.8	$ 2.2	$ 51.8	$ 56.0	$ 57.7
Properties					
Land...........................	$ 2.3	$ 2.4	$ 2.3	$ 2.5	$ 2.1
Building and equipment..............	56.9	64.2	81.1	83.7	77.9
Less depreciation reserve............	27.1	35.4	43.3	45.4	44.7
Net........................	$ 32.0	$ 31.2	$ 40.0	$ 40.7	$ 35.3
Excess of cost of assets§..............	...	...	11.9	11.5	11.0
Total assets...................	$147.2	$138.9	$222.3	$218.9	$190.1

* At equity in underlying assets.
† At cost, 1959. Less reserves of $6.0 million in 1960 and $8.5 million in 1961.
‡ Charged to cost of goods sold in 1960, less related deferred income taxes.
§ Excess of acquisition cost over assigned value, American Tractor Corporation.

[14] J. I. Case, Prospectus, 1958, p. 9.

Exhibit 2—Continued

LIABILITIES	1952	1956	1959	1960	1961
Current liabilities					
Notes payable, banks	$ 27.6	$ 15.4	$ 36.8	$ 82.3	$ 85.1
Accounts payable	6.1	2.7	13.4	8.0	8.0
Accrued liabilities	4.3	1.8	4.8	5.1	5.0
Federal and other income taxes	8.0	0.8	3.7	0.4	3.4
Current portion, long-term debt	...	...	0.8	0.8	1.0
Due to Case Credit	...	...	...	...	3.7
Discounts, allowance, etc	...	...	...	3.2	5.6
Total current liabilities	$ 45.9	$ 20.7	$ 59.5	$ 99.9	$111.9
Deferred income tax	...	...	$ 2.4	...	...
Long-term debt					
Debentures due 1978	...	$ 25.0	$ 22.0	$ 21.0	$ 19.8
Subordinated debentures—due 1983	...	...	20.1	20.1	20.1
Mortgages payable	...	...	0.5	1.1	1.4
Total	...	$ 25.0	$ 42.6	$ 42.2	$ 41.3
Stockholders' equity					
7% cum. pf	$ 9.3	$ 9.3	$ 9.3	$ 9.3	$ 9.3
6½% cum. 2nd pf	...	...	8.4	8.4	8.4
Common	28.3	28.3	35.8	35.8	35.8
Capital in excess of par value	10.0	10.0	10.2	10.2	10.2
Special reserves	13.0	13.0	...	...	...
Surplus	39.7	32.7	54.1	13.1	(26.8)
	$101.3	$ 93.2	$117.8	$ 76.8	$ 36.9
Total liabilities	$147.2	$138.9	$222.3	$218.9	$190.1

Note: Figures may fail to add because of rounding.
Source: Annual Reports.

If ATC seemed to Case to offer growth prospects, Case, according to *Fortune,* offered ATC needed cash and space for manufacturing. Mr. Rojtman, therefore, responded favorably to Case feelers. Terms of merger were worked out, calling for exchange of stock, Case paying one-half share of common and one share of second preferred for each common share of ATC. At current market values, the price approximated $15 million, or $12.4 million more than ATC's book value. The excess was to be amortized over 20 years.

THE MARC B. ROJTMAN ADMINISTRATION: 1957–1959

Objective and policies. Following the merger, Mr. Rojtman became chief executive of the combined company, as had previously been agreed. His policies—outlined in a series of rapid-fire pronouncements and changes—were: (1) maximizing factory and dealer sales both at home and abroad; (2) enlarging emphasis on R.&D. "as the very foundation . . . of future growth and prosperity"; (3) increasing diversification; (4) relying on high volume to bring down costs in relation to income; and (5) utilizing debt to meet the capital needs of this program. Something of the tone and emphasis of the new administration emerged in an address made by Mr. Rojtman at the Case annual meeting shortly after he took office:

First and foremost . . . will come an aggressive sales program. Sales will take the No. 1 order of importance, and we will not rest until sales volume has filled all seven existing Case plants to maximum capacity [over $300 million]. . . .

Second . . . will be a strong emphasis on engineering and development of new products. . . . We will develop more products, more diversified products, and products that are technically well ahead of the industry. . . .

The third factor to be given major emphasis is the strengthening of the present worldwide network of over 3,500 Case dealers and factory-owned branches. . . .[15]

IMPLEMENTATION UNDER MR. ROJTMAN

Sales. To implement the policy of maximizing sales from the factory to dealers and from dealers to the field, Mr. Rojtman made a variety of moves, initiating most of them during his first year. His sales drive looked not only to the domestic market but also to markets abroad, and it involved many additions to field and home-office sales management for both the agricultural and industrial divisions.

One of Mr. Rojtman's earliest moves was setting up the J. I. Case Credit Corporation[16] (Exhibit 3) to provide sales financing facilities "equal to those offered by competing manufacturers."[17] Loans to farmers would be greatly increased, while existing aids for dealers would be both continued and expanded. Said a Prospectus issued the next year:

Case Credit also finances allied equipment of other manufacturers attached to or sold and used with company products as well as used units of any make when traded against the purchase of new Case equipment. . . . The company contemplates that either it or Case Credit may finance to a limited degree retail repair contracts involving Case parts, and also sales of shop equipment to company dealers.[18]

The increased scope of lending under Mr. Rojtman appears in the following figures:

NOTES AND CUSTOMERS' ACCOUNTS RECEIVABLE
(dollars in millions)

	1956	1957	1958	1959
J. I. Case Company	$63.9	$ 62.2	$ 37.1	$ 33.8
Case Credit Corporation				
Retail	. . .	23.7	83.9	100.7
Wholesale	. . .	20.6	61.4	112.8
Total	$63.9	$106.5	$182.4	$247.3

Source: Annual Reports; Prospectus, October 1958, p. 11.

[15] *Implement & Tractor*, February 9, 1957, p. 76.

[16] *Fortune*, p. 191, explained the reason for creating a separate subsidiary company to handle this business: "Lenders will balk when a manufacturing company like Case pushes its borrowing above 50% to 60% of net worth but they will loan a credit corporation 300% to 400% of its net worth."

[17] Prospectus, October 1958, p. 4.

[18] Ibid., p. 11.

Additional marketing moves aimed mainly at increasing factory sales to dealers included: (1) a campaign to sell agricultural dealers on carrying a "12-month line," i.e., one comprising not only seasonal farm equipment, but also Case light industrial equipment to "blanket" the requirements of the "home builder, remodeler, general purpose

Exhibit 3

J. I. CASE CREDIT CORPORATION
Statement of Financial Condition, 1959 and 1961
(dollars in millions)

ASSETS

	1959	1961
Cash..	$ 18.3	$ 8.7
Due from Case.................................	...	3.7
Notes receivable		
Wholesale......................................	112.8	74.1
Retail...	100.7	88.1
Unearned financial charges......................	(12.6)	(9.7)
Provision for losses............................	(2.0)	(4.4)
Total notes (net).........................	$198.9	$148.2
Other...	1.8	0.9
Total assets.............................	$219.1	$161.5

LIABILITIES AND CAPITAL

	1959	1961
Short-term notes payable.........................	$105.4	$ 33.7
Accounts payable................................	0.1	...
Due to Case....................................	13.4	...
Taxes..	2.0	0.1
Withheld from dealers...........................	3.3	3.9
Long-term notes		
Due 1964–1973.................................	25.0	} 70.0
Due 1965–1974.................................	25.0	
Total.....................................	$174.2	$108.1
Subordinated notes and equity		
Notes due Case................................	$ 22.0	$ 22.0
Capital stock...................................	20.0	25.0
Surplus.......................................	2.9	6.4
Total.....................................	$ 44.9	$ 53.4
Total liabilities and capital.................	$219.1	$161.5

INCOME AND ACCUMULATED EARNINGS

	1959	1961
Income from financing charges		
To Case wholesale notes.........................	$ 8.1	$ 8.8
From retail notes...............................	5.6	6.7
Other...	0.2	0.3
Total income.............................	$ 13.9	$ 15.8
Interest expense................................	$ 7.9	$ 8.4
Provision for possible losses......................	1.3	4.4
Other...	0.3	0.4
Total.....................................	$ 9.6	$ 13.2
Income before taxes.............................	$ 4.4	$ 2.6
Provision for, or in lieu of, taxes...................	2.4	1.4*
Net income.............................	$ 2.0	$ 1.2

* Paid to parent company, which had no tax liability because of losses.
Source: Annual Reports.

builder, sewer and waterworks contractor, landscaper, logger, and
. . . municipalities"; (2) a campaign to attract stronger dealers—although not increasing the total number—using the 12-month line as one
incentive, Case's stepped-up program of product development as another; and (3) a campaign to stimulate dealer enthusiasm through a
series of annual "World Premiers," where dealers could review new Case
equipment and place their orders for the coming year.

Owing to the interest they aroused, the yearly World Premiers merit
more attention. Four in all were held: at Phoenix, Arizona; Nassau, the
Bahamas; Bal Harbor, Florida; and in Hawaii. *Fortune* provides the
following description of the prototype at Phoenix:

> Last November and December the once staid J. I. Case . . . put on
> a million dollar extravaganza to dramatize its comeback in the farm-
> machinery business. . . . Amidst the blare of a fifteen-piece band,
> . . . Case unveiled sixty carloads of dazzling new equipment. . . .
> The first of over 3,000 guests who poured in to see the show were
> financial men. . . . Then came the farm-machinery dealers. Over a
> period of six weeks, 2,000 Case dealers and 700 more from competition
> were flown to Phoenix for a stay of three days.
>
> *   *   *   *   *
>
> . . . the whoop-de-do staged in Phoenix was pure Rojtman. . . .
> Farm machinery makers are conservative in their sales tactics. Nor-
> mally, new products are simply presented in catalogues by the sales-
> men when they call on dealers, or they are exhibited none to dramati-
> cally at a regional meeting. . . .[19]

Reviewing the results of the World Premiers, Case claimed that
dealers placed orders for over $150 million at Phoenix; over $200 million
at Nassau; over $218 million at Bal Harbor.[20] Besides producing orders,
the World Premiers reportedly also helped the company "in planning
orderly production," and the dealer "to receive needed seasonal merchandise according to a definite prearranged schedule."[21]

Marketing moves aimed mainly at increasing dealers' sales to farmers
included the following: (1) a greatly increased advertising budget—
reportedly over $2.5 million in 1958, and up to $2.9 million budgeted in
1959 for 1960;[22] (2) addition of novel promotional devices, including
movies of the World Premiers, tractor tugs-of-war, and a Case "service
and sales patrol" truck introduced in 1959 as a means for enabling
dealers to carry the Case story right to the customers' barn door; and
(3) assistance to dealers in meeting their new building requirements
through the Case Building Corporation established in 1959.

Moves designed to increase foreign sales included: (1) setting up
new European and Canadian export divisions under new managing
directors; (2) creating J. I. Case International S.A., under the recently
retired president of Massey-Harris Ferguson, Inc., in order to "gain
entry into some of the most lucrative overseas markets" by establishing

---

[19] *Fortune*, pp. 107, 191.

[20] Annual Report, 1957; *Implement & Tractor*, January 10, 1959, p. 36; *Business Week*, April 30, 1960, p. 57.

[21] Annual Report, 1958.

[22] *Implement & Tractor*, January 25, 1958, p. 28; *Business Week*, April 30, 1960. p. 57.

manufacturing operations abroad;[23] (3) buying a controlling interest in a French tractor manufacturer;[24] and (4) setting up a British subsidiary, "scheduled to begin operating in the construction, roadbuilding, and materials handling field in 1960."[25] In 1959, Case's net assets in foreign countries, "principally . . . current," peaked at a reported $29.8 million, while earnings of Case International S.A. were reportedly $826,000.[26]

Product development. To implement the policy of basing sales expansion on new products, Mr. Rojtman emphasized (1) automation; (2) more attention to styling and comfort; (3) increased size and equipment capacity; and (4) more rapid introduction of new products. Owing in part to the start in this direction made by Mr. Brown, Mr. Rojtman was able to push through several projects in 1957.[27] In the following year, he initiated a "four-year plan of new product development and diversification."[28]

The emphasis on automation was designed "to make the machine perform the big chores automatically, thus relieving the operator from excessive fatigue. . . ."[29] It was exemplified in the late 1957 introduction of the "Case-O-Matic Drive," a hydrostatic torque converter for use with conventional direct transmission. Pushed through by Mr. Rojtman in "eleven frantic months,"[30] the new drive, it was said, "matches power output with requirements; reduces jerking, gear shifting, and engine stalling; and increases 'pull power.' "[31] Introduced at first on only a few models, Case-O-Matic Drive, like power steering, was subsequently made available on other tractor series and self-propelled units.

The emphasis on styling was designed to bring "our farm tractors at a par with the luxury look of the modern car which the farmer is buying today."[32] It was exemplified by two-tone paint jobs and recessed headlights by mid-1957,[33] and in "new streamlined all-weather cabs" readied in 1959 for 1960.[34]

The emphasis on size was designed, in the agricultural line, to reflect the well-publicized trend toward larger farms, and was exemplified in the introduction of new farm tractor series with four, five, and five-six plow ratings for 1958; in the introduction of two new self-propelled

---

[23] Annual Report, 1957.

[24] Annual Report, 1958. A new president and manufacturing director were hired the next year from Remington-Rand of France; a new controller from General Motors of France.

[25] Annual Report, 1959.

[26] Ibid.

[27] *Fortune,* p. 188.

[28] Annual Report, 1958.

[29] *Implement & Tractor,* January 25, 1958, p. 25.

[30] *Fortune,* p. 108.

[31] Prospectus, October 1958, p. 8.

[32] *Implement & Tractor,* January 25, 1958, p. 25.

[33] *Fortune; Implement & Tractor,* January 25, 1958, p. 25.

[34] Annual Report, 1959.

grain combines claimed to have "the largest capacity in the industry"[35] for 1959; and in the introduction of a new two-row mounted corn picker for 1960, as well as other large implements and machines.

The emphasis on an increased flow of new products was exemplified in the new introductions made yearly at successive World Premiers— 32, for example, at Bal Harbor 1958–1959. According to *Business Week,* Mr. Rojtman "revamped 60% of Case's traditional line" in three years.[36]

While the agricultural product line was being thus overhauled, the industrial line was by no means left standing. Besides introducing new loaders, shovels, and backhoe loaders in a wider range of sizes, the company was working on a pull-type scraper in 1958, a self-propelled scraper in 1959, and on a new rubber-tired fork lift for heavy-duty materials handling.[37] Even larger models for many lines were planned for introduction after 1959, as indicated by the following figures:

Line	Top capacity of models in or nearing production	Top capacity of models planned
Crawler-tractor	100 hp.	135–150 hp.
Self-propelled scraper	6½ cu. yds.	21 cu. yds.
Rubber-tired fork lift	4,000 lbs.	8,000 lbs.
Four-wheel unit loader	2½ cu. yds.	"larger"
Crawler-tractor loader	2 cu. yds.	"larger"

Source: Annual Report for 1959, pp. 6–9.

Like the stepped-up program in marketing, the stepped-up program in development brought changes in structure and personnel. For the first time, control of R.&D. was taken out of the various plants, each of which had previously engineered its own products (to the detriment of family resemblance among them).[38] A new centralized engineering department was created under the direction of Mr. Theodore Haller, who had some years past been lured by Mr. Rojtman from Allis-Chalmers to ATC.[39] Into Mr. Haller's old job as head of crawler-tractor engineering went an outsider—the former chief of research and testing for Caterpillar Tractor Company.[40]

The extent of Mr. Rojtman's commitment to a policy of increased R.&D. is suggested by the report in *Business Week* that his administration laid out "about $28 million for engineering, new product development and tooling."[41] This contrasts with $12 million reported for the period 1950–1955.[42]

[35] Annual Report, 1958.
[36] *Business Week,* April 30, 1960, p. 57.
[37] Annual Reports.
[38] *Fortune,* p. 110.
[39] *Fortune,* p. 110.
[40] *Implement & Tractor,* November 2, 1957, p. 212.
[41] *Business Week,* April 30, 1960, p. 57.
[42] Annual Report, 1955.

Further diversification. Following its union with ATC, Case emerged as a diversified company serving agriculture, roadbuilding, and construction. Mr. Rojtman, however, had ambitions to enter other fields. Accordingly, by 1959, Case was in materials handling with two fork lifts and a tractor shovel; in commercial construction with Case Building Corporation; and in purchasing and selling small tools to farmers through a new Small Tools Division.

Costs. Mr. Rojtman indicated that his main approach to the problem of achieving a more favorable ratio of costs and income was one of spreading overhead through high volume:

> With minor capital expenditures . . . Case has the capacity to produce $335 million annual volume. The fundamental thing in my program was that the best way to make money for the company and its stockholders was to use that capacity.[43]

Bringing down unit costs through volume operation was also a key to one of Mr. Rojtman's plans for competing pricewise in the small (30–40 horsepower) tractor market with rising European imports. Believing that Case was losing sales to companies importing small tractors from affiliates abroad, Mr. Rojtman decided not only to try this game himself by purchasing a French subsidiary, but also to try making a competitive American tractor through exploiting techniques of mass production. To this end he equipped the Case Rock Island plant with high-production machines—many of them inexpensively converted to special purposes within his own shop—and planned through volume operation (20,000 units a year) to put out a U.S. tractor with a newly developed "Dynaclonic" diesel engine in the $2,700 price range, as compared with about $5,000 for the lowest listed current Case Diesel. Such a tractor was duly pictured in the next Case Annual Report, which described it as being "the first United States-manufactured small diesel tractor to compete pricewise with European imports." In contrast, the plan for a French import fizzled when it was found that the subsidiary's product was "inferior."[44]

Finance. For financing his program, Mr. Rojtman relied mainly on debt, which increased as follows:

	1956	*1959*	
	Case company	*Case company*	*Case credit*
		(dollars in millions)	
Short-term notes payable	$15.4	$36.8	$105.4
Current portion of long-term debt	. . .	0.8	. . .
Long-term debt	25.0	42.6	50.5
	$40.4	$80.2	$155.9

Source: Balance sheets.

[43] *Business Week*, April 30, 1960, p. 57.

[44] *Wall Street Journal*, July 2, 1959; *Implement & Tractor*, July 25, 1959, p. 80; *Automotive Industries*, February 15, 1959, p. 61; Annual Report, 1959.

Overall achievement under Mr. Rojtman. Helped by a good market in 1959, Case's net profits in three years under Mr. Rojtman totaled $11.8 million, compared with under $150,000 for four years under Mr. Brown. The value of Case common, which had hit a low of $11½ in 1956, climbed to $26⅝.

Back of the encouraging rise in profits was the fastest growth rate in the industry in terms of factory sales to dealers. Farm and industrial equipment both showed gains, as follows:

FACTORY SALES

	1956	1957	1959	Per cent increase 1956–1959
	(Dollars in millions)			
Agricultural	$83.8	$97.7	$137.6	+ 63
Industrial and utility	12.4*	26.1	63.0	+400

* Includes $2.3 million in industrial sales for Case, $10.1 million for ATC.
Source: Annual Reports; Prospectus, October 1958, p. 9.

Reporting on the effort to increase retail sales, Mr. Rojtman told stockholders that in 1957, "Agricultural sales to dealers showed an increase of over 15% and, significantly, retail sales by dealers increased by more than 20%."[45] For 1958 he told dealers that retail sales were up 57%.[46] Then in 1959, as was later revealed, dealers' sales were $174.9 million compared with factory sales of $200.6 million.[47]

Looking forward in 1959, Mr. Rojtman planned, by taking a bigger share of the market, to achieve his goal of capacity production—or sales of $335 million by 1964.[48]

THE WILLIAM J. GREDE ADMINISTRATION

In February 1960, Mr. Rojtman was replaced as president of Case by Mr. William J. Grede, previously head of Grede Foundries (a Case supplier), a Case board member since 1953, and a past ally of President Brown in pushing for more liberal development expenditures.[49]

Reason for the change, soon made clear at the Case annual meeting, was a fundamental divergence of objectives between Mr. Rojtman and the more conservative members of his board. As *Business Week* reported, "The farm-equipment maker's board thinks ex-President Rojtman was expanding too fast, making the company top-heavy on debt and inventory."[50] Causes of the board's financial jitters were summarized by *Forbes* as follows:

[45] Annual Report, 1957.
[46] From a statement by Mr. Rojtman at the Nassau World Premier, cited in *Implement & Tractor,* January 10, 1959, p. 36.
[47] Annual Report, 1960.
[48] *Business Week,* April 30, 1960, pp. 55, 57.
[49] *Fortune,* pp. 110, 188.
[50] *Business Week,* April 30, 1960, p. 54.

Out of the $502 million worth of sales that Case rang up between 1956 and 1960, only about $400 million . . . went into the hands of the ultimate customers. Most of the rest remained in dealers' inventory. Case, which had a rock-solid current ratio of 5 to 1 before Rojtman took over, was down to just 2 to 1 at the end of 1959. Its debt had risen from just $25 million to $216.8 million—counting obligations of its credit subsidiary. Total interest charges had climbed from just over $1.7 million to $12.2 million.[51]

Summing up, *Business Week* remarked, "The real question is whether Rojtman wheeled and dealed too much, or whether the company panicked too soon. . . . Now that Rojtman is out there is no way of knowing whether he could have succeeded."[52]

Objectives and policies under Mr. Grede.   Shortly after stepping into his new role, Mr. Grede explained Case's changed objectives at the stockholders' annual meeting. After pointing out that Mr. Rojtman had resigned because the new thinking of the board was a "complete reversal of all he had stood for," Mr. Grede went on to say that goals for the present would be reducing debt, inventory, and receivables, even though these measures would lead to a temporary cut in both sales and profits. Common stockholders were, however, assured that resumption of dividends (passed since 1955) would come about sooner than if expansion had gone on unchecked. In a more precise early statement of his target, reported by *Business Week*, Mr. Grede indicated that he aimed to cut at least $15 million out of inventory and $10 million out of receivables by the end of the year and to apply this $25 million to the bank debt.[53]

Mr. Grede's major policies, as inferred from his first Annual Report, might be summarized as follows: (1) shifting sales emphasis to the retail level to help work down dealers' inventories; (2) cutting back production below retail sales with the same purpose in mind; (3) slashing costs; yet (4) continuing to do some product development; and (5) attempting to work down short-term debt.

IMPLEMENTATION UNDER MR. GREDE

Sales.   Granting special allowances to move dealers' inventories, especially of noncurrent models, was a prominent feature of Case sales policy under Mr. Grede. Along with losses from the liquidation of receivables, this program cost $8.70 million in 1960 and $16.35 million in 1961, including reserves for 1962.

Other marketing measures described by Mr. Grede in his first Annual Report included establishing an overall marketing division and hiring a single marketing vice president in place of Mr. Rojtman's parallel sales organizations for industrial and agricultural lines, and setting up a program of market research. Speaking of these changes and of the shift in emphasis to retail sales, Mr. Grede remarked, "These are fresh

---

[51] *Forbes*, July 1, 1960, p. 23.
[52] *Business Week*, April 30, 1960, p. 54.
[53] Ibid.

concepts which are expected to increase the effectiveness of our product-development, production, and sales effort."[54]

Still other selling moves, as reported seriatim by the trade or business press, included a 1960 advertising program—much reduced, however, from Mr. Rojtman's $2.9 million budget; a special advertising campaign to scotch a rumor originating in Mr. Rojtman's day that Case was about to shift from independent dealers to direct selling; addition of accessory items (such as oil) to the line, reportedly in response to dealer and customer demand; limiting the already scheduled Hawaiian World Premier to dealers who had met stepped-up sales quotas, and eliminating World Premiers thereafter; revising the sales organization so that regional divisions followed major crop areas with the stated aim of improving service to dealers; and initiating an "aggressive promotional campaign" about mid-1961 "in an effort to maintain a proper balance between production, sales to dealers, and dealers' net sales."[55]

Reducing production. Besides emphasizing retail sales, Mr. Grede's two-pronged attack on dealer inventories included cutting factory production and shipments. Thus in 1960, with retail sales reportedly only $6 million off from the peak of 1959, factory production was cut $65 million and factory sales $74 million. (The resultant $9 million rise in factory inventory was explained as a deliberate move to make new equipment "available to our dealers in time for the selling season.")[56]

In 1961 factory sales and factory production were off again, by $17 and $24 million, respectively, and factory inventory also fell.

Results achieved under this program were a $39 million reduction in Case and Case Credit wholesale receivables in 1960, and a further decline of $14 million in 1961. This contrasted with an $89 million rise under Mr. Rojtman. "Unusual costs" were, however, attributed to the cut-back program—almost $30 million in 1960 alone (including the estimated effects of two plant strikes).[57]

Cutting costs. Early moves to cut costs, as reported by *Business Week*, included slashing more than $1 million from the advertising budget ("Grede says he came in too late to turn off the ad spigot entirely") and "eyeing" Case's parallel sales and service organizations for farm and industrial products with a view to consolidating these "as much as possible."[58] Still other steps were taken in 1961 when Case shut down two plants (the original ATC facility, and the unit converted to mass-produce small tractors in 1959); deactivated Case International S.A.; sold its assets in Argentina; dissolved the central engineering department, resorting instead to a liaison officer to coordinate engineering at the plants; and terminated the World Premiers.[59]

---

[54] Annual Report, 1960.

[55] *Business Week*, April 30, 1960, p. 54; *Implement & Tractor*, July 9, 1960, p. 24; October 10, 1960, p. 46; December 12, 1960, p. 79; March 15, 1961, p. 42; June 15, 1960, p. 50.

[56] Annual Report, 1960.

[57] Annual Reports.

[58] *Business Week*, April 30, 1960, p. 54.

[59] *Implement & Tractor*, March 15, 1961, p. 58; July 1, 1961, p. 55; July 7, 1961, p. 91.

Product development. While Mr. Grede promised to continue development, "recognizing its importance to the future of the company," he reduced its scale. Wrote *Forbes,* "Where Rojtman boasted of budgeting half his operating profits for engineering, Grede fired more than 100 engineers, according to some estimates."[60] New developments were not reported in detail, the 1960 Annual Report simply stating, "New products introduced are proving very popular."

By far the biggest news in the engineering area was the revelation in 1961 that the company had costs of $9.76 million for "reworking certain models of one product line,"[61] including a reserve $1.28 million for anticipated future costs in this connection.

Reducing short-term debt. In keeping with the goal of debt reduction, short-term bank loans to Case Credit were cut by $72 million by the end of October 1961, in part by means of placing a $20 million 15-year note with four institutional investors. The total short-term debt of the parent company, however, went not down but up—from $37 to $85 million—reflecting the fact that Case had to borrow under lines of credit from the banks to meet its working capital needs.

Overall results under Mr. Grede. The need to borrow for working capital reflected losses in the two years under Mr. Grede that totaled over $79 million. Not only was the earned surplus wiped out, but part of the common stock values as well, and Case was forced to seek extension of its bank loans in order to stay alive.

Explaining these results in its Annual Reports, the company ascribed the drop from a $13 million pretax profit in 1959 to a $46 million pretax loss in 1960 largely to "unusual costs" and "nonrecurring charges" of $59 million, while the loss of $32 million in 1961 was traced almost entirely to "costs attributable to inventories and receivables built up in prior years, their reduction in 1961, and the rework of certain models of our product line" (Exhibit 4). It was explicitly stated, however, that the 1961 tabulation of losses "was not intended to be construed as a listing of nonrecurring costs."

By the time the Annual Report for 1961 was published, some 91 bank creditors had decided to extend their loans to Case and thus allow the company "a three-year lease on life." As one senior lending officer explained, "We had no choice. We either had to give Case an extension or take responsibility for putting the company into bankruptcy." Lines of credit were rewritten under the terms that called for (1) a maximum loan figure of $140 million for Case and its credit subsidiary, with the maximum declining over a three-year period; (2) greatly scaled down interest rates; and (3) payment of additional compensation to the banks contingent upon profits until 1972. Nonfinancial conditions of the loan included, according to *Business Week,* a proviso that both Mr. Grede and Mr. Brown (then vice chairman of the board) should resign, thus making way for a new administration.[62]

---

[60] *Forbes,* October 1, 1961, p. 13.

[61] A tractor (*Wall Street Journal,* December 31, 1962).

[62] *Business Week,* January 6, 1962, p. 100.

Exhibit 4

J. I. CASE COMPANY

Explanation of Losses, 1960 and 1961

(dollars in millions)

1960 Operations Compared with 1959

Unusual costs attributable to reduced wholesale sales volume of $73,000,000 and reduced production level of $65,000,000 (including the estimated effects of strikes at Racine and Bettendorf plants)............................	$29.9
Nonrecurring charges:	
Increase in research and development expense, primarily as a result of change in accounting policy to write off such expense as incurred (before adjustment for related taxes on income)...................................	5.5
Other, principally special allowances to move dealer inventories and losses on liquidation of receivables..	8.7
Adjustment of carrying value of investment in French subsidiaries...........	6.0
Added costs during 1960 such as increases in interest and selling expenses.....	8.9
Difference in taxes on income, 1960/1959...............................	(13.0)
Difference in net profit, 1960/1959....................................	$46.0

1961 Operations

Losses incurred in collection of retail and wholesale receivables and provision for estimated future losses thereon...................................	$ 6.68
Scrapping of obsolete materials and provision for estimated obsolescence remaining in our inventories...	3.96
Cost of reworking certain products and provision for estimated future rework	9.76
Reductions in the retail selling price of goods (primarily noncurrent models) granted to dealers during 1961, and estimated reductions to be granted in 1962 applicable to products in dealers' inventories at October 31, 1961..........	9.67
	$30.07
Other..	2.27
Total..	$32.34

Source: Annual Reports.

CASE IN 1962

Following conclusion of the loan extension in 1961, Mr. Grede and Mr. Brown resigned, and the board, now chairmanned by Mr. Samuel B. Payne, a Morgan Stanley partner, began the search for a new president. Meanwhile, into the newly created post of executive vice president went Mr. J. C. Freeman, formerly vice president for domestic operations at Allis-Chalmers Corporation, who had joined Case in 1961.

Initial statements by these two leaders indicated that the banks had both a "plan" and an "action program" for Case. Mr. Payne stated that the plan put primary emphasis on debt repayment, but should make it possible to operate profitably. Profitable operations, he said, would enable the company to use a substantial amount of its tax loss carryforward to aid in the reduction of debt.

Included in the action program were moves designed to "streamline and strengthen" the still profitable J. I. Case Credit Corporation; to continue reducing inventories and receivables; and to effect plant consolidations which were expected to reduce overhead by $5 million or 43% when completed. Marketing emphasis would continue to be placed on retail sales.[63]

Reported actions of the new interim administration included sale of the Churubusco plant for about $1 million; an advertising campaign urging dealers to take a "new look" at Case on the grounds of its retail record and its combined farm-utility line; and a new promotional device—the dealer's open house with door prizes supplied in part by the company.[64]

At the end of the first quarter, sales and profits were down from 1961, but reportedly were better than original targets:

> . . . Sales to dealers were about 20% over those projected by the plan, and net loss was about 37% below anticipated. Retail sales by dealers to customers were encouraging, and were 21% above the plan.[65]

Shortly after this report was issued, Mr. Payne announced that the board had succeeded in its search for a new president—someone who would be "a man with a record of accomplishment in the farm machinery industry, someone who could promise something constructive and who could provide vigorous leadership for our new executive group."[66] This man was Mr. Merritt D. Hill, formerly a vice president of the Ford Motor Company and general manager of the Ford Implement and Tractor Division.

As had happened in previous administrations, the new president used the occasion of the annual stockholders' meeting in April for his first major public policy statement. The following account appeared in *Implement & Tractor:*

> My interest is only in the future. . . . I didn't take on this assignment with the idea of assisting in carrying out an orderly liquidation of the company. I came here to try and do a job which I am firmly convinced can be done.
>
> I accept no responsibility for what has taken place before I joined it. . . . On the other hand, I have assumed responsibility for correcting the problems which I find here. It is evident to me at this time that major changes in the organization structure here at the general offices are imperative and steps are being taken now to revamp it for the purpose of getting it properly set up to do a more effective and efficient job starting at the top.

Mr. Hill credited Freeman and other top-echelon personnel for their good work of the past few months, "which is now starting to show up on the financial statements of both Case and Case Credit Corporation":

> For example . . . real progress has been made in reducing inventory—most of the old products have been moved out of the distribution system. Warranty expense is down sharply this year. Accounts receivable from both wholesale and retail customers have been brought down to manageable proportions.

---

[63] *Implement & Tractor,* January 15, 1962, p. 107.

[64] *Implement & Tractor,* January 15, 1962, pp. 39, 44; March 1, 1962, p. 44; March 15, 1962, p. 43.

[65] *Implement & Tractor,* March 15, 1962, p. 48.

[66] *Implement & Tractor,* April 1, 1962, p. 14.

While confident of the industrial and utility market for Case, Hill was not as optimistic regarding farm machinery, stating, "The possibility of increasing our sales volume in the United States and Canadian markets is limited in view of the overall reductions in farm machinery volume during the past several years and the prospects for the future. United States tractor production has decreased by 60% (in units) in the past ten years, and other items of farm equipment in a similar ratio."

Hill concluded, "It is my job to put this Case machine together properly, making certain that the right men are in the right places and that they clearly understand their duties and responsibilities. These fundamentals and proper motivation will provide the kind of environment where men will want to do their best. From this combination will come a profitable organization."[67]

COMPETITION IN 1962

Serving the domestic farm equipment market in 1962 were 1,050 firms, of which only seven were full-line manufacturers; i.e., producers of both tractors and a complete line of equipment, attachments, and other agricultural machines. These seven companies reportedly shared some 65% of the total industry volume. (See Exhibit 5 for some financial data.) Another 12 to 15 long-line concerns produced specialized equipment that was widely marketed and comprised about 10% of the total. The balance of the manufacturers, all smaller companies, built specialty items sold locally.[68]

Included in the seven full-line manufacturers was one newcomer, the White Motor Company, which between 1960 and 1962 had acquired all the farm equipment business of three small full-line makers: the Oliver Corporation,[69] Cockshutt Farm Equipment, Ltd.,[70] and Motec Industries, Inc. (formerly named Minneapolis-Moline Company).[71] A spokesman for White indicated both the reasons leading his company to enter this business and certain main features of the strategy by which it meant to compete:

> Heavy farm machinery has a lot in common with trucks. . . . Also we wanted to move into a stable industry—one that involves essential income-producing, food-producing equipment that is the basis for our everyday living. We'll always have farms, and farmers will need machinery. We're counting on a replacement business in heavy tractors in which Oliver will increase its share. We're looking for an overall increase of about 15% in farm-equipment industry sales in the next

[67] *Implement & Tractor*, May 15, 1962, pp. 84, 85.

[68] Standard & Poor's *Industry Surveys: Machinery, Agricultural–Basic Analysis*, March 15, 1962, p. M-11.

[69] 1959 sales, $114.6 million; profits, 3% on sales during 1959 and same or lower during previous six years. White acquired Oliver assets producing $88 million in farm equipment sales.

[70] Certain assets, mainly fixed, of Cockshutt's farm equipment business were purchased by White for $8 million in 1962. White thereby expected to add about $25 million to its sales.

[71] Motec's farm equipment sales in 1962 amounted to approximately $50 million with the company about breaking even. The company's farm equipment assets and liabilities were purchased for $21 million at 60% of book value.

Exhibit 5

SALES AND PROFIT MARGINS, SELECTED COMPANIES, 1945–1961

Year	Allis-Chalmers		J. I. Case		Deere		International Harvester		Massey-Ferguson		Motec Industries	
	Sales*	Profit margin†	Sales*	Profit margin†	Sales*	Profit margin†	Sales*	Profit margin†	Sales*	Profit margin†	Sales*	Profit margin†
1945	98	10.6%	61	17.9%	47	13.2%	72	7.1%	82	5.9%	…	…
1946	32	def.	28	1.4	49	14.9	56	5.4	50	7.9	…	…
1947	71	5.2	60	12.8	72	16.2	86	10.1	59	11.5	110	15.8%
1948	110	8.9	114	14.7	105	17.2	109	9.3	94	15.0	111	16.0
1949	118	10.4	125	21.2	123	21.5	105	11.0	113	19.8	120	17.6
1950	116	14.5	107	23.3	114	24.5	109	13.9	116	23.4	138	16.5
1951	154	15.8	123	17.3	147	23.9	148	15.5	139	18.7	140	9.0
1952	173	12.8	115	13.8	130	18.8	139	10.8	159	13.2	160	6.4
1953	173	9.8	84	6.3	129	15.6	145	8.9	134	9.9	117	3.0
1954	166	11.8	74	4.0	100	16.8	115	8.6	237	6.4	110	4.7
1955	180	11.0	76	6.8	115	20.1	135	11.0	293	7.7	85	def.
1956	184	9.5	70	3.8	106	14.6	145	8.9	283	5.4	87	0.6
1957	180	8.8	99	6.0	132	18.8	137	9.5	311	3.6	81	3.7
1958	179	9.7	143	9.1	160	22.1	127	10.2	335	8.4	81	9.4
1959	182	10.0	161	11.4	185	21.5	199	14.0	379	9.6	75	8.3
1960	178	6.1	89	def.	159	10.5	195	11.0	391	9.3	88	6.6
1961	169	3.9	103	def.	173	16.7	186	10.0	414	8.8		
Average sales in 1947–49 base period, millions of dollars	$297.0		$124.6		$294.5		$865.2		$125.5		$ 66.0	

* Index form, 1947–1949 = 100.

† Operating income as a percentage of sales. Operating income is usually the balance left from sales after deducting operating costs, selling, general, and administrative expenses; local and state taxes; provision for bad debts and pensions; but before other income and before deducting depreciation charges, debt service charges if any, federal taxes, and any special reserves.

Source: Standard & Poor's *Industry Surveys: Machinery, Agricultural—Basic Analysis*, March 15, 1962, p. M-13.

five years and there's room for Oliver to pick up an increasing per cent as the market expands.

* * * * *

What's Sam White's formula? The main factor is dealer development. "We, along with others in this business, used to be concerned mainly with moving our production to dealers. We had a wholesale concept of sales. Now, we are mainly concerned with what happens at retail. We are embarked on a program of strengthening our ties with dealers and helping them to do a more efficient, profitable job of selling our line of equipment."

* * * * *

Sam White's second cardinal principle is prudent market management with an eagle eye on inventory. . . . The third point . . . is decentralized management for more effective use of executive talent.[72]

Of the remaining six full-line companies, three were heavily diversified (International Harvester, Allis-Chalmers, and Ford), while the three others were largely specializing in farm equipment (Deere, Massey-Ferguson, and J. I. Case). Highlights in the recent history of these six full-line companies were summarized by *Fortune* as follows during the summer of 1961:

Deere & Co. displaced International Harvester in 1958 as leader in U.S. sales. Nonetheless, to protect its competitive position, Deere felt obliged last year to invest $50 million for an entire new line of tractors and implements. President William A. Hewitt is also trying hard to expand sales of light industrial equipment ($40 million last year vs. total Deere sales of $468,500,000) and is committed to greater foreign expansion. A five-year-old investment in Germany may show a profit this year, and Deere will soon manufacture tractors in France.

International Harvester, no longer leader in the United States, is second to Toronto-based Massey-Ferguson outside North America. Its combined sales in all markets are still larger than those of any other farm-equipment company. Though Harvester's business traces its ancestry to McCormick's reaper, trucks and industrial equipment now dominate the company's sales and profit picture. Farm equipment last year made up only 35% of Harvester's $1.7 billion sales, continuing a long-term downward trend.

Massey-Ferguson, Ltd., leading in sales outside North America, is battling for third place in United States sales with Allis-Chalmers and Ford's Tractor & Implement Division. . . . The overseas market accounted for 58% of the company's $490-million sales last year.

Allis-Chalmers now does only about one-third of its business in the farm field. By far the largest share of total sales . . . is equipment for the electric-power industry, for mining and construction. A-C's sales to American farmers are declining while exports and sales from plants in Britain, France, and Australia gain.

Ford is much stronger in the farm market abroad than at home. . . . In the U.S., Ford's Tractor & Implement Division . . . nearly ran into disaster last year. Ford was handicapped by having no tractor to sell in the upper power ranges that American farmers now demand, also by a limited selection of implements. This year Ford introduced tractors in the 70-hp class, and its implement line is fatter.

[72] *Implement & Tractor,* January 15, 1962, pp. 82, 83.

J. I. Case is on the critical list. Last year the company lost $40 million, a deficit of $14.32 a share. Flamboyant sales tactics introduced by President Marc B. Rojtman (replaced in 1960) piled huge inventories on dealers' lots, which Case carried on credit. But final sales to farmers came nowhere near matching the factory sales to dealers. As a result, J. I. Case is now in debt $178 million to a group of 90 banks. The caretaker president, William J. Grede, former head of an iron-foundry company, says bravely, "We'll do our damndest to share in any increase in the market," but everyone else in the industry is watching with fascination to see if Case can stay alive.[73]

APPENDIX A

SUMMARY OF J. I. CASE OPERATIONS, 1945–1952

As World War II hostilities ended in 1945, about two-thirds of J. I. Case's sales were in farm machinery and one-third in special war materials, military tractors, and equipment. The 1945 Annual Report stated that "sales for the year were determined by production rather than by market demand. The demand exceeded the supply by a substantial volume." Even though peacetime reconversion of the manufacturing facilities was immediately started, shortages and controls on manpower, raw materials, and prices restricted sales.

Then, on December 26, 1945, a strike was called. (Some, but not all, of the farm equipment manufacturers were also affected by shorter strikes.) According to the 1946 Annual Report:

> In addition to the demand for company-wide bargaining, the UAW-CIO demanded a "closed shop," "irrevocable check-off of union dues, fines and assessments," "compulsory arbitration," "payment by the Company for union participants in the grievance machinery," "preferred seniority and other preferences for union officers." The acceptance of these confiscatory demands by the Company would have meant that the authority of the owners of the business over the conduct of its operations would have been transferred to the UAW-CIO.

Even though some of the Case plants never fully closed and others gradually resumed work, it took until March 10, 1947, for the strike to be formally settled for the major Racine plant. As a result, fiscal year 1946 closed with an operating loss. As to J. I. Case's dealer organization, the 1946 Annual Report stated:

> The Company expresses its sincere appreciation to the thousands of loyal dealers who, in spite of the shortage of certain machines and repair parts because of the strikes at Racine and Rockford plants, have carried on their sales and service programs in an efficient manner. They have cooperated fully with the Company in support of its efforts to retain the management of its business, rather than to permit control by union officials.

---

[73] George Bookman, "Farm Machinery Shifts Gears," *Fortune,* July 1961, pp. 130, 131.

Due to their steadfastness, the Company today faces the future with virtually an intact dealer organization capable of handling future sales and service.

With the strike being settled, Case sales increased rapidly. Yet the 1948 Annual Report stated that "the demand for Case farm machinery exceeded the available supply." To meet this demand the company since 1945 invested significantly in additional plants, equipment, and inventories, accomplishing simultaneously a factory modernization program. The heavy demand, with some minor cyclical variations, persisted so that the 1951 Annual Report commented: "The demand for farm machinery in 1952 should continue strong. Whether such demands can be met will depend largely upon the materials available and whether a balanced supply of materials can be obtained early enough to manufacture the machinery in time for seasonal use." At the same time working capital requirements, both for inventories and dealer credit, increased. In 1952, however, sales declined by 7.2%, due, according to the Annual Report, "principally to the drought . . . , a decline in sales in foreign countries . . . , and the inability to complete certain harvesting machines in time to meet the harvest season because of the strike in steel plants."

During the 1945–1952 period selling prices were mentioned yearly in the J. I. Case Annual Report. The following quote in 1950 is representative:

Selling prices follow costs. During the year costs of materials, wages, freight, taxes, and other important elements continued to rise. It is apparent that the inflationary pressure of these added costs will force prices still higher, and, furthermore, unless the inflationary trend is reversed, the results ultimately will be disastrous.

It is the established policy to keep selling prices as low as practicable, consistent with high quality products, and the cost of production and distribution, including taxes. This is the American way of raising living standards, and, further, it is recognized that this is desirable because high prices invariably restrict sales volume.

Reports issued by the Bureau of Labor Statistics show that the percentage of increase in farm machinery prices is relatively lower than on other products made from similar materials. This means that price increases have not kept pace with the increases in wages and other costs, and farmers for many years have had the benefit of such lower prices. This has been made possible only because of the larger volume of business done and improved methods of manufacture.

In contrast to selling prices and factory production, research and new product developments were not specifically mentioned in the Annual Reports from 1945 to 1952 with the exception of the following quote in 1945:

It has been a long established policy of the Company to carry on an extensive program of research and development work on machines for use on farms. It is no longer necessary to give attention to engineering of special war materials. It is therefore possible for the Company's staff of agricultural engineers to devote their entire time to its regular line of product. New items which have been developed and tested, and which are ready for production, include a nine-foot and a twelve-foot self-propelled combine, a forage harvester, and a small shop tractor for industrial use.

In 1953, however, the tune changed. The Annual Report mentioned that "engineering and development work on new products and on the improvement of other products was intensified during the year. It was the judgment of the Management that the cost of this increased program in engineering and development work was in the best long-term interest of the Company." Also, the 1953 Annual Report explained a $42 million sales decrease as follows:

> This large reduction in sales volume is very disappointing. In appraising its significance it should be pointed out that a large unfilled demand for farm equipment was built up during World War II when severe restrictions were placed on manufacturers. This accumulation of unfilled demand, stimulated by inflation and the Korean war development, resulted in a higher than normal demand for farm machinery which continued well into the year of 1952. Beginning in the latter part of 1952 the dealers and distributing organization were confronted with the complete return of a highly competitive market.

It was during this year that Mr. John T. Brown, who had joined J. I. Case as vice president on January 1, 1948 (formerly vice president of the Chain Belt Company for a number of years), became president.

Included below are some selected financial figures on J. I. Case for the 1945–1952 period.

J. I. CASE COMPANY

Income Statements and Balance Sheets, 1945–1952

(dollars in millions)

	1945	1946	1947	1948	1949	1950	1951	1952
Net sales	$79.6	$38.2	$75.3	$142.9	$156.4	$133.0	$154.1	$143.4
Cost of goods sold	62.5	38.9	62.0	114.3	114.7	93.3	116.3	112.1
Depreciation				2.5	3.0	3.2	3.3	3.6
Selling, general, and administrative expense	4.9		5.5	7.5	8.6	8.4	10.7	11.1
Operating profit (or loss)	12.3	(0.7)	7.8	18.1	29.6	27.8	23.2	16.1
Other income	0.3	0.3	0.3	0.4	0.4	0.3	0.5	0.5
Other expenses				0.1	0.1	0.2	0.4	1.4
Income before taxes	12.6	(0.4)	8.1	18.4	29.9	27.9	23.3	15.2
Taxes	9.5	[1.9]	3.2	8.0	12.3	12.8	13.5	8.2
Net profit	3.1	1.5	4.9	10.4	17.6	15.1	9.8	7.0
Surplus, beginning	10.0	9.7	8.9	12.0	18.1	28.5	38.7	39.4
Dividends								
Preferred	0.6	0.6	0.6	0.6	0.6	0.6	0.6	0.6
Common	1.7	1.6	1.2	1.5	1.7	4.3	4.7	5.0
Other charges (mostly appropriation to reserves)	1.0			2.0	4.9		3.8	
Surplus, ending	9.7	8.9	12.0	18.1	28.5	38.7	39.4	40.8
Cash and securities	$29.8	$ 8.4	$ 7.0	$ 7.0	$ 16.1	$ 10.0	$ 7.8	$ 6.6
Receivables (net)	4.3	1.3	2.4	4.2	2.3	20.8	30.3	37.7
Inventory	20.2	27.7	32.6	42.7	52.3	52.6	71.3	70.1
Gross fixed assets	26.0	29.2	37.7	44.4	48.3	50.1	54.1	59.2
Other assets	0.3	2.2	0.4	0.8	0.6	0.5	0.7	0.8
Total gross assets	$80.6	$68.8	$80.1	$ 99.1	$119.6	$134.0	$164.2	$174.4
Supplier, tax, and other credits	$16.1	$ 4.4	$11.4	$ 20.5	$ 23.2	$ 25.4	$ 31.0	$ 18.3
Debt							17.8	27.6
Equity (depreciation, reserves, retained earnings, and capital stock)	64.5	64.4	68.7	78.6	96.4	108.6	115.4	128.5
Total	$80.6	$68.8	$80.1	$ 99.1	$119.6	$134.0	$164.2	$174.4

Source: Annual Reports.

APPENDIX B

Charts 1–7

MAJOR TRENDS IN THE FARM MARKET

1. The cost/price squeeze on farmers

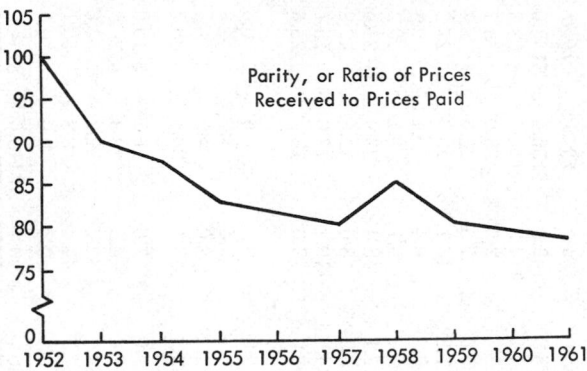

2. Fat and lean years in net farm income

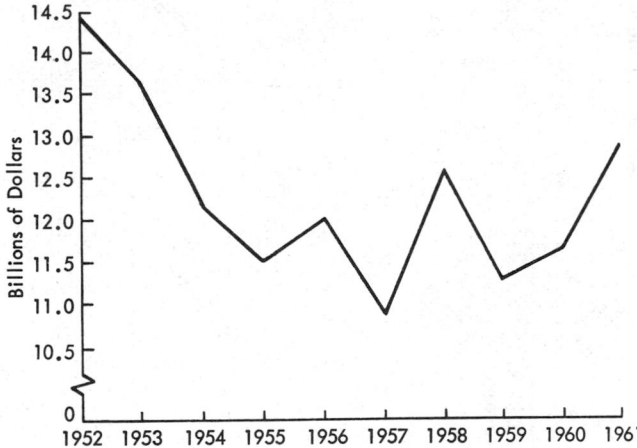

Charts 1–7—Continued

3. Fat and lean years in the farm equipment business
Index of Domestic Shipments
(1957–59 = 100)

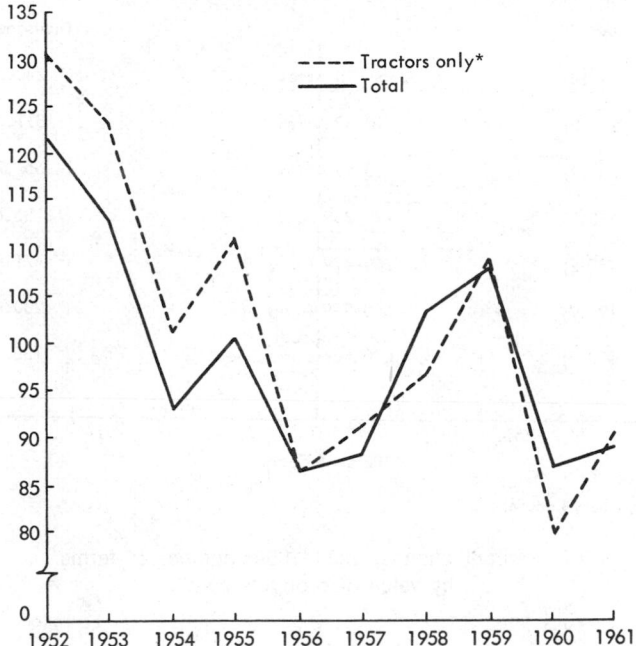

* Includes garden-type tractors and parts, excluded from Chart 7.

Source: Charts 1 and 2, U.S. Bureau of Census figures, cited *Statistical Abstract of the United States;* Chart 3, Farm Equipment Institute.

4. Percent change, 1954/1959: farms*

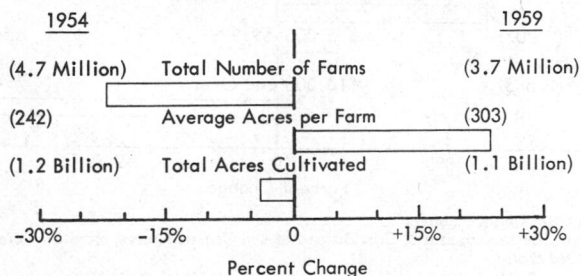

* Not adjusted for changes in the definition of a farm, which accounted for about two-thirds of the decline, mainly in the smallest size class.

Charts 1–7—Continued

5. Percent change, 1954/1959: number of farms by size class in acres*

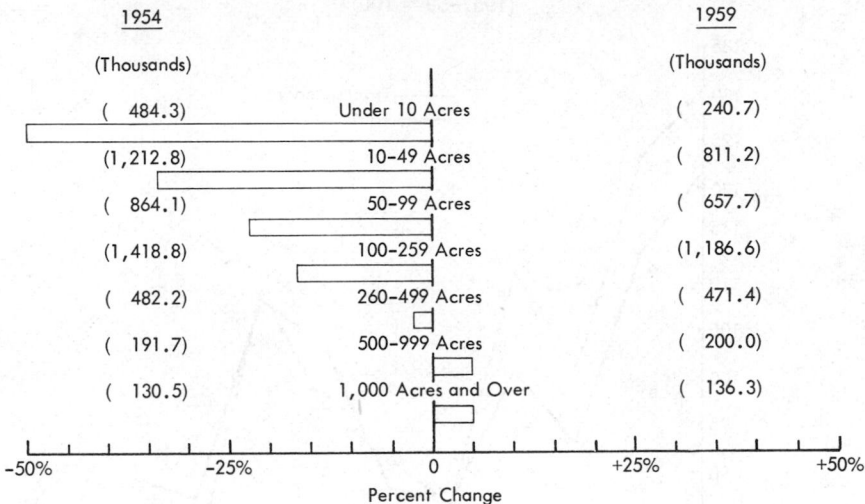

1954		1959
(Thousands)		(Thousands)
(484.3)	Under 10 Acres	(240.7)
(1,212.8)	10–49 Acres	(811.2)
(864.1)	50–99 Acres	(657.7)
(1,418.8)	100–259 Acres	(1,186.6)
(482.2)	260–499 Acres	(471.4)
(191.7)	500–999 Acres	(200.0)
(130.5)	1,000 Acres and Over	(136.3)

-50%   -25%   0   +25%   +50%

Percent Change

* See note, Chart 4 above.

6. Percent change, 1954/1959: number of farms by value of products sold*

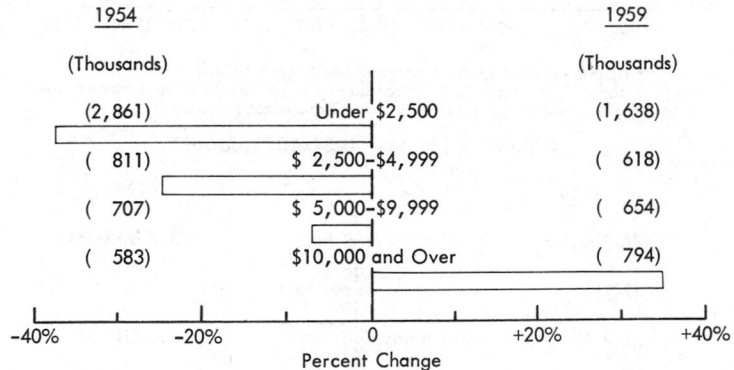

1954		1959
(Thousands)		(Thousands)
(2,861)	Under $2,500	(1,638)
(811)	$ 2,500–$4,999	(618)
(707)	$ 5,000–$9,999	(654)
(583)	$10,000 and Over	(794)

-40%   -20%   0   +20%   +40%

Percent Change

* See note, Chart 4 above.
Source: Charts 4, 5, and 6, U.S. Bureau of the Census figures, cited *Statistical Abstract of the United States.*

7. Percent change, 1953/1960 value of manufacturer's shipments for domestic farm use

1953 (Millions of Dollars)		1960 (Millions of Dollars)
(485.8)	Complete Tractors*	(290.7)
(908.7)	Other Machinery and Equipment (Inc. Parts)†	(919.6)
(103.1)	Planting, Seeding, Fertilizing	(90.8)
(73.0)	Harrows, Rollers, Stalk Cutters, Pulverizers	(79.2)
(59.3)	Plows, Listers	(57.5)
(248.0)	Harvesting Machinery	(295.0)
(179.1)	Haying Machinery	(123.1)
(22.8)	Farm Dairy Machinery and Equipment†	(18.6)
(31.4)	Sprayers, Dusters	(41.4)
(36.0)	Elevators, Blowers†	(27.1)
(51.7)	Cultivators, Weeders	(47.0)
(25.7)	Machines to Prepare Crops for Market or Use	(34.8)
(25.9)	Farm Poultry Equipment†	(25.9)
(14.9)	Barn Equipment†	(18.7)
(12.4)	Barnyard Equipment†	(24.8)
(25.2)	Farm Wagons, Trucks†	(35.5)

-100%   -75%   -50%   -25%   0   +25%   +50%   +75%   +100%

Percent Change

* Excludes garden tractors and tractor parts and accessories for domestic farm use valued as follows (dollars in millions):

	1960	1961
Garden tractors	$43,926	$ 51,920
Attachments (wheel and garden)	42,534	46,056
Parts (wheel and garden)	93,204	125,228

† Includes items not necessarily made by "full-line" producers.

Source: U.S. Bureau of the Census, "Tractors" and "Farm Machinery and Equipment," *Current Industrial Reports*.

APPENDIX C

WHEEL-TYPE TRACTORS, SELECTED PULL-TYPE, MOUNTED, AND SELF-PROPELLED FARM EQUIPMENT

CASE® the PLUS-POWERED Tractor Line
with DIESELS IN EVERY POWER CLASS
. . . revolutionary Dynaclonic, famous Powrcel engines

6 Power Sizes • 32 Models

| 430 3-Plow Tractor. 4-speed, 12-speed Tripl-Range, shuttle. Gasoline or Dynaclonic diesel. 3 models. | 530 3-4 Plow Tractor. Case-o-matic Drive, 4-speed, 12-speed, shuttle. Gas, LP-gas or Dynaclonic diesel. 4 models. | 630 4-Plow Tractor. Case-o-matic Drive, 4-speed, 12-speed, shuttle. Gasoline or Dynaclonic diesel. 5 models. | 730 5-Plow Tractor. Case-o-matic or 8-speed Dual-Range. Gas, LP-gas, Powrcel diesel. 5 models. | 830 5-6 Plow Tractor. Case-o-matic or 8-speed Dual-Range. Gas, LP-gas, Powrcel diesel. 6 models. | 930 6-Plow Tractor. 6 speeds. Powrcel diesel or LP-gas. Dual-Control hydraulics. Wide-swing drawbar. |

171 fuel, transmission and front-end options

A COMPLETE LINE OF CASE® PULL-TYPE EQUIPMENT

MOLDBOARD PLOWS	TANDEM DISKS	DRAWBAR CARRIER	ROTARY HOES

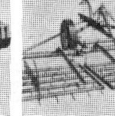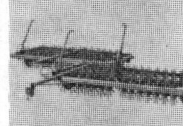

Case CH series plow is available with 3 to 5 bottoms, 14 and 16-inch sizes. Big 27x24-inch throat swallows heavy trash.

Case S series disk harrow is available in 7 to 17-foot sizes, with sealed anti-friction or steelite bearings. Transport wheels control depth.

The HD-100 hydraulic drawbar carrier handles from 3 to 7 spring tooth, spike tooth or rotary hoe sections . . . up to 42-foot working width.

WT wheel-type rotary hoe is available in 2, 4 and 6-row models . . . B trail-type in 7 to 42-foot widths . . . BE Eagle Hitch mounted in 7 to 10½-foot sizes.

PLANTERS	DRILLS	MOWERS	RAKES

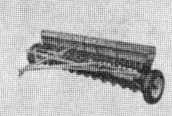

Pull-type corn planters are available in 4 and 6-row models. Attachments for pre-emergence weedicide, liquid or dry fertilizer.

D series plain grain drill is available in 6, 8, 10 and 12-foot sizes. Also fertilizer models, lister and plow press drills.

T-10 trail-type mower equipped with 7-foot cutter bar . . . also 5 or 6-foot. Easy hook-up to any tractor with standard PTO.

281 side delivery rake handles full 8-foot, 4-inch swath. Fast and gentle raking, short hay travel saves valuable leaves.

CONDITIONER	BALERS	FLAIL-TYPE CHOPPER	CHOPPER

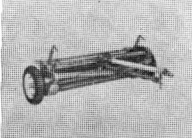

222 hay conditioner handles 7-foot swath. Saves leaves . . . speeds hay drying time 40 to 50%. Both crimps and crushes.

New Case 200 Sweep Feed baler. Twine-ties up to 10 tons per hour. Simple power train . . . fewer parts, less maintenance. Smooth, gentle baling . . . no surging.

Case 640 flail-type chopper cuts a 60-inch swath, 2½ to 6 inches high. Clips pastures . . . chops standing and windrowed crops, stalks and brush.

200 series forage harvester is available with 4 or 6-knife cutter wheel Three quick-change heads: row-crop, windrow pick-up, 60-inch cutter bar.

COMBINES	SPREADERS	MIXER-BLENDER	BUNK FEEDER

New Case 80 combine with 7-foot cut features straight-thru design. Big 32-bushel bin. Adjustable wheel spacing for row crops.

New 100, 115 and 135-bushel spreaders with exclusive V-belt drive, give 20% wider spread. Also 75 and 95-bushel ground-drive models.

Case-Helix auger unloader mixer-blender blends and transfers a ton of feed in 5 minutes . . . hauls up to 3 tons in one trip. 90 and 125-bushel.

Case-Helix power unloading wagon with bunk feeder has exclusive, self-cleaning Convey-o-matic floor. Unloads 6 to 7 tons in 2½ minutes.

JOB-MATCHED MOUNTED TOOLS

Your Case dealer has a complete line of front and rear-mounted tools, quickly attached and hydraulically controlled, for your Case 730 tractor. These include 4 and 6-row planters and cultivators, disk and moldboard plows, tandem and offset disk harrows, pickers and loaders, etc. — all designed to give your tractor greater versatility, quick maneuverability on many jobs.

PLANTERS...

Case 400-E series 4-row corn planters check row, hill drop and drill 36-42 inch rows. High speed valves assure accurate drop. Fertilizer attachment available.

CULTIVATORS

The 700 series cultivators include: 2-row to work 28-48 inch rows; 4-row for 28, 36, 38, 40 and 42-inch rows. Convenient drive-in attaching and detaching.

DISK PLOWS

Case 300 series disk plow is available in 2, 3 and 4-furrow sizes with 24-inch disks. Ideal for tough, heavy or sticky gumbo soils. Plows up to 16 acres a day.

Case 400 series reversible disk plow is available in 2 or 3-disk, 26 or 28-inch sizes. Designed for deep plowing (down to 14 inches) in irrigated areas — up to 10 acres a day. Leaves land level ... no ridges or furrows.

DISK HARROWS

Case SE and SEA disk harrows are available in 7, 8, or 9-foot widths. Sealed anti-friction or steelite bearings. Pivot action; adjustable gangs; heavy semi-rigid bolted frame.

PICKERS .. STRIPPERS

Case 426 2-row corn picker mounts easily. Exclusive forward gathering design gets more down ears. Long 48-inch picking rolls are adjustable from tractor seat. Picking points and elevator raise together for faster, safer turns.

Case 2-row cotton stripper harvests clean in storm-resistant, tight-locked varieties. Handles high yield irrigated cotton at normal speeds. Fits many tractors.

SUBSOILERS...

Case T-620 series subsoiler available in 1 and 2-point models. Tough steel points on strong narrow standards. Gauge wheels assure constant depth down to 22 inches.

LOADERS...

Case 190 series loaders with 10½ cubic foot capacity handle any loading job fast and easy. Sturdy, compact design ... 3,000-lb. break-out power. Lifts 9 feet. Manure fork, dirt or snow buckets available.

SCRAPERS...

Case-Danuser all-purpose blade available in 6 and 8-foot sizes. Ideal for barn or feed lot cleaning, ditching and backfilling, leveling and grading.

CASE. | SELF-PROPELLED WINDROWERS

CASE. | SELF-PROPELLED COMBINES

Courtesy J. I. Case Company.

American Motors Corporation I

AMERICAN MOTORS was formed on May 1, 1954, through the merger of two faltering automobile companies, Nash-Kelvinator Corporation and the Hudson Motor Car Company. Combined sales for the fiscal year ended September 30, 1954, showed unit sales off 42% from the preceding year of separate operations, and the combined statement of earnings showed a net loss of slightly more than $11,000,000 after receipt of a tax loss credit of $11,500,000, i.e., a total operating loss of more than $22,000,000 (see Exhibits 1 and 2).

In the three succeeding years sales volume declined about 25% and market share fell to less than 2%. Successive operating losses of $15,257,000; $32,362,000; and $11,035,000 forced the company to borrow heavily from various banks in order to maintain minimal working capital balances. Near the nadir of its fortunes, sometime financier Louis E. Wolfson began buying shares, and by early 1958 was believed to be within easy reach of a controlling interest in the company. In July 1957 one of his nominees joined the board of directors, and another in February 1958.

Then as the columnists began writing obituaries for the company, AMC made a spectacular comeback. By the end of 1960 unit sales had risen about 300% from their low, market share had more than tripled, the company had an operating profit of $105 million, and all bank indebtedness had been repaid. With its "compact" cars the company had become a leader in the low-price field, and the "Big Three" were taking preliminary steps toward following AMC's lead in making cars with a "unitized" body.

Commenting on the company's comeback, and on the public acceptance of compact cars, George Romney, AMC's chairman and president since 1954, noted that there was a long lead time between the development of a new basic concept, the acceptance of this concept by the organization, and finally its acceptance by the public.

153

Exhibit 1

AMERICAN MOTORS CORPORATION I
Consolidated Statements of Profit and Loss
(in thousands)

	1954		1955		1956		1957	
Sales..............	$416,845		$468,773		$429,074		$383,175	
Less: Excise taxes...	16,502		27,646		20,666		20,941	
Net sales..........	$400,343		$441,127		$408,407		$362,234	
Other income:								
Dividends from subsidiaries*....	$ 1,043		$ 2,900		$ 202		$ 133	
Interest on securities......	120							
Sundry income...	1,748	2,912	2,801	5,701	2,099	2,302	2,104	2,327
		$403,255		$446,828		$410,709		$364,472
Costs and expenses:								
Cost of product sold..........	$363,437		$395,950		$377,102		$323,009	
Depreciation (Plant), (Tools & dies)	6,342		5,307		5,033		5,088	
Cost of pensions..	4,267		5,278		6,272		3,127	
Selling, advertising & administration	48,339		54,100		50,508		41,004	
Refrigerator warranties.....	586		187		182		370	
Interest..........	2,202		2,119		2,502		1,842	
Sundry expenses..	740	425,913	541	462,085	969	442,571	973	375,507
Net profit or loss on operations.....		$ (22,658)		$ (15,257)		$ (32,362)		$ (11,035)
Credits on income tax...........		11,590		9,700		1,453		502
Nonrecurring income or (loss).......		....		....		10,662		(1,300)
Income tax........		....		....		....		
Net Income after Tax..........		$ (11,071)		$ (6,956)		$ (19,746)		$ (11,833)

* Changed in 1960 to reflect equity in subsidiaries rather than dividends received.
Note: Failure of figures to add is due to rounding.
Source: Annual Reports.

. . . it seems to require about seven years for a good idea to really catch on. It took seven years to develop the Rambler idea internally (1943–50)—and it wasn't sold internally at the end of seven years. Only three men in top management believed in the Rambler at that point.

It was just seven years—(1950–1957)—before the Rambler took hold publicly. It was in the Spring of 1957, just seven years after it was introduced, that Rambler's sales began to move up.[1]

Mr. Romney noted on other occasions that confidence in the Rambler had been anything but universal in the company up through 1956, thirteen years after the original experiments on a lightweight, compact car were begun. During this period, a handful of members of top management had built a strategy around this new idea, had merged two companies, closed factories, retired a number of key executives who were "big car minded," and borrowed to the limit of the company's capacity in order to put over this new concept. Perhaps most important of all, the company had discontinued its Nash and Hudson lines, and

---

[1] Report to Stockholders, February 7, 1962.

1958		1959		1960		1961		1962	
$502,788		$935,738		$1,139,508		$938,599		$1,135,190	
32,439		65,888		81,791		62,876		78,795	
$470,349		$869,849		$1,057,716		$875,723		$1,056,395	
$ 1,163		$ 1,567		$ 2,858		$ 1,009		$ 2,568	
2,413	3,577	5,040	6,607	5,574	8,433	3,556	4,565	6,475	8,944
	$473,926		$876,458		$1,066,849		$880,290		$1,065,439
$391,188		$684,198		$862,899		$726,529		$870,701	
4,787		4,717		7,239		10,608		9,744	
		11,933		10,892		18,041		19,876	
5,893		6,852		6,738		7,420		10,144	
42,896		62,543		72,003		67,101		81,731	
647		......		......		......		......	
993		390		300		210		120	
350	446,756	379	771,017	631	960,706	......	829,911	......	992,299
	$ 27,170		$105,441		$ 105,443		$ 50,378		$ 73,140
	515		......		......		......		......
	(1,600)		......		......		......		......
			45,100		57,200		26,800		38,900
	$ 26,085		$ 60,341		$ 48,243		$ 23,578		$ 34,240

had concentrated all its efforts on the remaining line, the Rambler. By 1957 the company had bet all of its chips on the next roll, the 1958 models, and Mr. Romney conceded to members of his organization that if they didn't bring the company into the black in 1958 the game was up.

As the company's fortunes improved during 1958, the strategy shifted to one of expansion in the compact field. But despite its rapidly increasing output, the company was unable to meet the total demand for its cars for almost a year. Then as the Big Three brought out directly competitive cars, company strategy shifted once again, as AMC sought to hold its share of market.

Mr. Romney frequently described AMC's strategy in terms of this seesaw between offense and defense, likening it to a sequence of "campaigns" where a campaign was a program of action stretching over a period of years. On one occasion he reviewed the campaigns following the founding of the company as follows:

> On many occasions I have discussed our program in terms of campaigns. Between 1954 and 1957 we won our "campaign for survival." Between 1957 and 1958 we won our "campaign opportunity" and since

Exhibit 2

AMERICAN MOTORS CORPORATION I

Consolidated Balance Sheets

(in thousands)

ASSETS	1954		1955		1956		1957	
Current Assets:								
Cash and government securities	$ 45,402		$37,859		$26,517		$22,600	
Accounts receivable (net)	19,996		20,925		23,624		23,788	
Due from subsidiaries	1,949		2,589		3,101		351	
Income tax refund due	16,853		9,683		......		......	
Inventories (net)	80,616		89,553		83,980		67,965	
Miscellaneous items	5,023	$169,841	4,078	$164,690	3,504	$140,728	3,300	$118,006
Investments in subsidiaries		13,957		12,888		7,355		8,563
Miscellaneous assets		774		6,741		3,524		3,467
Property, plant and equipment (net)		82,138		75,960		73,297		65,934
Total Assets		$266,711		$260,281		$224,905		$195,972
LIABILITIES AND NET WORTH								
Current Liabilities:								
Bank notes, and amount due on long-term debt	$ 31,200		$38,500		$36,000		$28,569	
Accounts payable	48,834		56,338		43,795		37,072	
Accrued expenses	2,212		2,251		2,172		2,731	
Warranties on refrigerators	4,729		4,096		3,491		2,886	
Income tax	......		......		......		......	
Miscellaneous	781	$ 87,756	1,097	$102,283	624	$ 86,084	504	$ 71,768
Long-term debt		16,000		14,000		14,569		13,000
Stockholders' Investment:								
Common stock	$ 28,352		$28,352		$28,352		$27,939	
Additional paid-in capital	27,136		27,136		27,136		26,334	
Retained earnings	107,465	162,954	88,509	143,998	68,763	124,251	56,930	111,204
Total Liabilities and Net Worth		$266,711		$260,281		$224,905		$195,972

Source: Annual Reports.

1959, as our competitors imitated Rambler, we have successfully faced their "campaign counterattack." We have shown those financial advisors and those who said we could not compete successfully with the Big Three head-on that they were wrong. We have demonstrated this by our success in competing with them head-on. We expect conclusively to win in this year [1962] by selling the largest number of Ramblers in our history despite all-out compact car competition. Next year we expect to resume the offensive with "campaign leadership." In the years ahead, we can expect to begin a long-range battle for the number one brand name position in the automobile industry in this country.

This case describes the automotive strategy of American Motors in relation to market conditions and the strategies of its major competitors in the American market. It omits the appliance business, in which AMC's Kelvinator division was a participant, and it also omits all but the briefest consideration of the foreign markets for automobiles. The case focuses on the seven-year period following the formation of American Motors, i.e., from 1954 to 1961. In particular, the case describes the competitive position of AMC at three points in time (1954, 1957,

1958		1959		1960		1961		1962	
$44,553		$ 60,041		$ 43,762		$ 69,752		$ 87,058	
28,757		33,177		38,856		36,239		45,579	
2,352		1,633		1,688		3,968		4,815	
......		......		......		......		......	
59,931		98,070		115,569		93,254		96,078	
3,010	$138,586	2,938	$195,861	3,938	$203,815	3,697	$206,913	3,916	$237,448
	10,603		24,428		33,416		34,635		40,946
	5,509		5,546		6,367		5,676		7,891
	51,484		58,617		94,792		85,731		88,789
	$206,184		$284,453		$338,392		$332,957		$375,076
$ 3,000		$ 3,000		$ 3,000		$ 4,000		0	
50,367		73,243		78,314		67,805		$ 86,998	
2,125		2,725		21,609		24,069		28,207	
2,669		2,570		......		......		......	
......		4,102		4,735		7,888		5,761	
508	$ 58,670	990	$ 86,631	3,442	$111,102	3,507	$107,207	4,654	$125,522
	10,000		7,000		4,000		......		......
$28,068		$ 29,694		$ 29,981		$ 30,096		$ 31,199	
26,429		34,052		34,518		34,866		44,772	
83,015	137,514	127,074	190,821	158,790	223,290	160,724	225,687	173,482	249,454
	$206,184		$284,453		$338,392		$332,957		$375,076

and 1961), and the AMC "campaign" strategy for dealing with each situation. In conclusion, it describes the situation in 1962 and poses the question of what "campaign leadership" might mean.

THE SITUATION IN 1954

As the postwar seller's market in automobiles changed to a buyer's market in 1953, the independents (Packard, Studebaker, Kaiser-Willys, Hudson, and Nash) began merger talks. Amid the varying combinations and deals, several considerations stood out.

First, the independents were producing too many body styles relative to the volume of cars for their unit costs to remain competitive with the big three. Packard, Nash, and Hudson together marketed only eight series of cars, yet required five basic body styles. In contrast, Ford made seven series from two basic body shells, while Chrysler made eleven series from four shells, and GM made fourteen from only four shells.[2] The difference in tooling costs thus gave the Big Three a sizable ad-

[2] Tom Mahoney, *The Story of George Romney* (New York: Harper & Bros., 1960).

vantage with each model change-over, and the greater volume of each model allowed the Big Three to spread the tooling costs over more cars. The advantage was thus twofold, and in a style-conscious market it was a compelling one.

Second, and less tangible, none of the independents could count on generating enough sales volume for their dealer organizations to keep the dealers profitable and strong. Declining dealer strength would lead to reduced service as well as reduced sales, and might sooner or later spell disaster. As a real buyer's market developed, and price wars developed, this would hasten the plight of the weak, "off-brand" dealer.

Thus the independents knew the days of "independent" operations were numbered. While various proposals were tried, the results were a merger between Hudson and Nash, and later a belated merger between Packard and Studebaker. In the aftermath of these mergers, three of the famous names in American automotive history disappeared. Nash and Hudson cars succumbed to the American Motors Rambler, and the Packard disappeared in favor of the Studebaker.

While the independents were working on their tooling and dealer problems, GM had returned to its strategy of the 1930's. It marketed progressively longer, lower, more powerful cars. Unlike the earlier era, however, Ford and Chrysler now followed suit. And as the 1954 model year got under way, Ford and Chevy were once more running neck and neck for leadership in total new car registrations.

In 1958 Mr. Romney, in discussing the background of these competitive developments, reviewed the industry's history as follows:[3]

> I think as further background we might review some of the basic changes that have taken place in the automobile market since the start of the industry. At the beginning, of course, a lot of companies went into the business. Then Ford emerged as the dominant factor as Henry Ford developed the concept of building a dependable piece of transportation within the reach of the mass market. He succeeded by 1921—his peak year—in securing 62% of total industry sales. In that year there were 88 companies manufacturing automobiles. At that time the Ford was a 100-inch wheelbase vehicle—in wheelbase, the same size as this Rambler American we have which is at the top end of the small-car field. From 100 inches, other makes went as high as 145 inches in wheelbase, 10 inches beyond anything on the market today. There was an assortment of vehicles in terms of size and engines and various components, and so on, of a very widespread character indeed.
>
> With the growth in American prosperity and with the growth that the Ford success helped to bring about, American car buyers began to indicate a desire for more than just bare transportation. General Motors excelled in its recognition of the change that was taking place in consumer preference. The result was that by 1927 they had succeeded in capturing about a third of the market, and Ford at that time still had a third. But a third of the market was not enough to permit Ford to operate profitably; so he shut down to convert over to the Model A in an effort to meet this new-type consumer demand.

---

[3] Tobé and Associates, *The Tobé Lectures in Retail Distribution, 1958–1959* (Boston, Mass.: Harvard Graduate School of Business Administration).

General Motors continued and adopted the basic philosophy that has dominated the automobile industry in the United States, from a product standpoint, until the last few years. As a matter of fact, you'd almost have to say it still dominates in terms of current product volume. But General Motors adopted the policy—clearly stated by their technical people and policy people—of building cars each year a little bit bigger, a little bit more stylish, for the purpose of progressive, dynamic obsolescence. That product philosophy, coupled with other contributions they made—because General Motors has made many very substantial and significant contributions to the concepts of large industrial management—made General Motors the largest industrial corporation in the world.

Ford never quite came back. Under Henry Ford, Sr., the company never really adopted the product philosophy of General Motors. But following World War II the new management, in an effort to recapture first place, literally jumped onto the General Motors bandwagon, and basically adopted the General Motors product philosophy.

Then five years ago, when there was a change in the Chrysler management, [1953–54] Chrysler did the same thing. By 1954, therefore, at the time of the formation of American Motors, you had the three dominant factors in the automobile industry all going down substantially the identical product road.

As a result of this philosophy of making their cars a little bigger and more powerful each year, they kept moving them up in size and reducing the degree of variation and distinction. The result was that they created a vacuum back of them in the market and they created a concentration of competition as between their own models, with effects that we're beginning to see.

American Motors set out to fill this vacuum. But it took several years to produce a car to fill the need, and still longer to convince the mass market that there was indeed something "below" the low-priced three. While working to develop the product and the market, the company very nearly succumbed to competitive pressures. Its strategy was one of fighting for survival.

CAMPAIGN SURVIVAL: 1954–57

American Motors' long-run objectives were to become a leading competitor in the automotive field. To accomplish this, the company was relying primarily on (1) its conception of the unfilled need in the American market, the need for a car between the big cars of the big three and the small cars imported from Europe; and (2) its belief that its concept of a "compact" car filled this need.

The evidence of need was supported by a survey of transportation habits which showed "that 85% of all [automobile] trips in the United States were 13 miles or less in length, and that the bulk of them were for essential purposes."[4] The automobile was not primarily a vehicle of transcontinental travel, nor one of pleasure cruising. It was becoming a part of everyday urban and suburban living. From this knowledge

---

[4] Mahoney, *The Story of George Romney*, p. 197.

sprang the conviction that there was a real market for a comfortable car with improved economy and maintenance which could be maneuvered easily, parked easily, and for which styling changes for change's sake might be avoided. It was this conception which lay behind the experimental development of the compact car.

In the design itself, the principles of aircraft engineering had been successfully applied by Nash-Kelvinator for almost a decade, permitting the company to make the car strong but light while at the same time preserving the riding comfort of which Americans are so fond. The resulting development was called a unitized or a single unit body, where the parts were welded together rather than being bolted to a strong, heavy frame, as was the universal practice in the United States at the time.

With this conception of a need and of a product to fill the need, American Motors faced the formidable task of devising a strategy which could (1) get the idea of this need across to the public, (2) gain the commitment of the organization to the product concept, and (3) keep the company from going under while management tried to get the first two steps accomplished. American Motors strategy in 1954–1957 was called a campaign for survival, since the short-run problems were so acute that long-range goals had to be tempered if the company was to survive. The strategy included the following major steps.

Product line. Effective with the consolidation of 1955 model production at Nash's Wisconsin facilities in December 1954, the product line was made up of three basic elements: the standard automobiles (with approximately a 116-inch wheelbase), the Rambler (some with 108-inch and some with 100-inch wheelbase), and the Metropolitan (with an 85-inch wheelbase). There were four models of the standard autos, two sold under the Hudson name (Hornet and Wasp) and two under the Nash name (Ambassador and Statesman). The Ramblers were sold under both brand names, giving the two surviving dealer organizations identical products to sell under different brand names. Sales of standard automobiles and Ramblers developed opposite trends over the first three years, as indicated by the following figures:

Year	Unit Total Sales	Hudson and Nash Standard	Hudson and Nash Rambler	Rambler as % of Total
1954	99,774	61,995	37,779	38%
1955	194,175	110,323	83,852	43
1956	104,189	25,023	79,166	77

Even more significant, however, was the fact that by 1955 sales of the 108-inch Ramblers were running four to one over the 100-inch model. It was on this basis that management decided to discontinue the 100-inch Rambler for 1956, and to concentrate on the larger model. But the problem of defining a clear product policy remained. The Hudson and Nash cars were just "above" the low-priced three in retail price, while the Ramblers were intended to be just below the low-priced—even though they were only slightly lower in price at this point. At any rate, the company did not market a car which was directly competitive in size and price with the low-priced three, but rather it straddled this market segment by being on both flanks. Was AMC going to compete with the low-priced three directly, or be above and below them, or just below them, or what?

Mr. Romney spoke on this question in September 1956, in a speech entitled "In League with the Future" at a meeting introducing the 1957 models:

> Sales of compact cars will continue to grow, but more big cars than compact cars will be sold during the transition period. For that reason American Motors has no plans to drop its big car program.
>
> American Motors is wedded to the program of supplying its dealers cars for each major segment of the future car market. For 1957 you have a big Nash or Hudson, the compact Rambler, and the small and increasingly popular Metropolitan. In 1958, Nash dealers will have an all new big car with the Nash name to sell and the Hudson dealers will have an all new big car with the Hudson name to sell.
>
> Our 1958 cars will be the first ones resulting from combined Nash and Hudson engineering. Our 1958 program will be the first one to basically reflect the new management's product philosophy.

Product styling.   In a speech to the dealer organization, Mr. Romney pointed out that company policy on automobile styling was being changed:

> We have changed the company's previous styling policy. Under the old policy, styling distinction was sought to the point of production designs with high controversial and sometimes unacceptable features. Looking ahead, American Motors cars will be styled in the basic advanced patterns of future cars with elements of distinction that are not so extreme as to be controversial. We should avoid styling controversy or pioneering because our cars themselves are basically advanced, distinct, and superior.

Marketing.   The marketing program faced the twofold task of selling the organization as well as the public:

> The biggest difficulty we had in the early marketing and merchandising of the Rambler concept was internal, not external. The biggest problem was to change the attitude of our own vice president in charge of sales and of our sales organization and of our dealers. As late as the spring of 1954, just following the merger—at a meeting of all the Nash zone managers—I asked how many of them thought the Rambler would ever become a bread-and-butter car for American Motors. There were only two out of twenty-three zone managers who thought that was even a remote possibility. Our vice president in charge of sales was insisting internally that what we had to have was a car directly competitive with the Chevrolet, Ford, and Plymouth. And our biggest dealers were taking the same position.
>
> *   *   *   *   *
>
> The first thing that happened after I succeeded to the presidency (in October of 1954) of the company was that I brought in a new man

(Roy Abernethy, now president of the corporation) to head up our sales effort who believed in this product approach. The second thing we did was to use the new model announcement meetings in the fall of 1954 to stress this theme with our dealers. The theme of my talk to our dealers across the country was "Get your sights up on the Rambler."

*   *   *   *   *

As a result of a lot of effort, we succeeded in convincing our dealer body that this product concept had merit in the market place. What convinced them as much as anything else that first year was that in the spring of 1954, the resale value of used Ramblers moved ahead of the resale value of Chevrolet, Ford, and Plymouth models. And it has remained above ever since. That was conclusive evidence that in one vital aspect of automotive marketing—namely, what the buyer can expect when he takes his car back in to buy a new car—we had a competitive advantage.

We also had public attitudes to deal with, as well as the internal attitudes. We were faced with a difficult public attitude created by the failure of all independent companies except two. And in the fall of 1954 somebody was giving us a mock burial almost every day in the press.

*   *   *   *   *

There was also a frozen big-car mentality in this country that had been built up almost from the beginning of the automobile industry, but particularly as the new product philosophy took over in the late 1920's.

Now how did we [try to] change that public attitude? Well, we went to work to tell the basic product advantage story of Rambler, and to tell it not only in terms of calling attention to the product specifically, but also by way of comparison. At that point people were not inclined to pay any attention to us. So we had to be dramatic, and we had to make people stop, look, and listen. And probably the biggest break we had was one day when I happened to read an article by an automotive editor, who talked about dinosaurs. And I said, "That's it, we're competing against gas-guzzling dinosaurs." And that stuck.[5]

Later Mr. Romney took to giving speeches where he used scale model dinosaurs as props. At a meeting of the National Parking Association in 1957 he led off as follows:

This fellow is called a Brontosaurus. He was about seventy feet long. . . . He weighed a good many tons. His fuel consumption was tremendous. His mouth was relatively so small that he had to spend all of his waking hours eating. This streamlined fellow here was called Dimetrodon and is considered a predecessor of the modern horse. One of his problems was he began developing a fin on his back to a point where it became larger and larger and finally upset his equilibrium.

This handsome model was known as Stegosaurus. He perhaps represented the highest development of the dinosaur in terms of useless, nonfunctional decorative treatment.[6]

*   *   *   *   *

---

[5] Tobé, *The Tobé Lectures in Retail Distribution, 1958–1959*, pp. 30, 34.
[6] Mahoney, *The Story of George Romney*, p. 21.

While moving with this concept of the competitors' "dinosaurs," American Motors also moved to change the way its own products were advertised and promoted. Mr. Romney pointed out that—

> We . . . changed our advertising policy, and that was a tough one. Boy, Madison Avenue has got fixed ideas. . . . It took us three years to get our advertising agency not only to agree that our policy should be different on advertising, but also to reach the point where they could reflect accurately our product story in ads that would command the attention of the American people.[7]

He went on to stress that American Motors advertising must henceforward meet standards such as the following:

> 1. American Motors copy must be as simple, informational, and factual as possible. Banish the superlatives . . . rule out conventional advertising language [and], use new language to the greatest extent possible.
> 2. Every advertisement must be centered on a dominant idea that is validated by a quality or feature in the product.[8]

Dealer organization. American Motors had a combined total of 2,800 Nash and Hudson dealers in 1954. In less than two years this had declined to 1,900, largely through dealer resignations. While the downward trend was reversed following the consolidation of the Nash and Hudson franchises, a weak distribution organization remained a key problem for the company. In 1956, with unit sales slipping almost 50% from the previous year, the company instituted a dealer bonus plan which credited the dealer with from $30 to $50 extra per car on all domestic sales. Over a two-year period, the plan cost the company more than $7 million, but it was credited with being instrumental in keeping the dealer organization together during these lean years.

Finance and control. At the time of the merger the company was losing about $2 million a month. On the one hand this called for drastic cost cutting, and on the other it called for a campaign to turn nonessential resources into cash so the company could carry forward long enough to give its compact car concept a chance to prove itself in the marketplace. Backing up this move meant betting the company's last chips on automobiles, just at a time when some of the most vocal stockholders were recommending the company bow out of the automotive field altogether.

In addition to securing a loan from an insurance company and increased credit from a group of banks, the company sold its Hudson body plant, its West Coast assembly plant, and its 60% interest in Ranco, Inc., a highly successful manufacturer of thermostatic controls for appliances. The three sales gave the company an additional $15 million in "chips" to put behind Rambler. Part of these funds was used to tool the company's own V-8 engine (introduced in March 1957) to replace the very expensive V-8 engine and transmission bought from Packard and used in the 1955 and 1956 models. Still, as 1956 progressed, it be-

---

[7] Tobé, *The Tobé Lectures in Retail Distribution, 1958–1959,* p. 34.
[8] Ibid.

came clear that more drastic measures were required. With working capital down almost 50% in two years, and only a few million dollars above the minimum required by bank loans, heroic cost cutting measures were taken.

In the management echelons, it meant selling the company airplanes, a new policy urging managers to take more modest hotel accommodations when traveling, and an "end to the two-hour lunches." The company resigned from the NAM, went through a systematic curtailment of magazine subscriptions, and to bring the point home to all concerned, Mr. Romney and other top executives took "voluntary" salary reductions up to 40%.

At lower levels, the company advertising agency was required to pay rent for its office space at the company headquarters. Company garages stopped giving free gas and service to executive cars.

> At one point, offices were cleaned only every other day, for a saving of forty thousand dollars a year. Another forty thousand dollars a year was deferred by delaying the customary gifts of watches or clocks to employees with thirty years of service. . . . Offices went unpainted, and sheet toilet paper replaced rolls.[9]

CONSOLIDATION

Besides the consolidation of production into the Nash plants and the sale of the Hudson facilities, American Motors was able to effect economies from utilizing common tooling for the 1955 models, and from running all of the 1956 models on the same assembly lines. Following consolidation, disposal of the surplus plants, and write-downs of $12 million of other Hudson facilities, the company entered the 1957 model year with an estimated break-even point at below 150,000 units. The 1956 annual report noted: "The primary automotive objective since the merger has been to reduce the automotive break-even point, and simultaneously, to develop new lines of cars needed to increase sales to profitable levels."

The significance of the consolidation is easily seen by comparing performance from 1955 through 1958:

Year	Unit Sales	Pretax Earnings
1955	194,000	$(16,700,000)
1956	104,000	(30,000,000)
1957	119,000	(11,000,000)
1958	189,000	26,000,000

By 1958 the break-even had been reduced to a point where a volume smaller than the one achieved in 1955 was adequate to generate a sizable pretax profit (American Motors Corporation was not able to fill all of its orders in 1958), and this even though 1955 had been a good year

---

[9] Mahoney, *The Story of George Romney*, p. 191.

in the industry, whereas 1958 was one of the worst in the postwar period. Survival was to be based in large measure on keeping the break-even low, and the low break-even was to be maintained by manufacturing only the bare essentials (motors, bodies, transmissions, and a few other items), by purchasing the remaining items from outside suppliers, and by maintaining a single assembly center. By the end of 1957 American Motors had become the least integrated manufacturer in the business, and had thereby helped prepare a flexible base from which to operate in the ups and downs of the auto business. So much for "campaign survival."

THE SITUATION IN THE FALL OF 1957

While American Motors was retrenching and proceeding largely unnoticed by others in the industry, a battle was shaping up in the medium-priced cars between General Motors and Ford. The battle came to a climax with the introduction of the 1958 models in the fall of 1957. As reported by *Fortune*,[10] the giants prepared for the clash in the following manner:

The Big Three were caught off base in the shifting markets of 1956 and 1957 because of some decision making back in 1954. That year, G.M.'s President Harlow Curtice and the high command at Chevrolet were disturbed by reports that Ford was planning to attack Chevrolet with a car "as big as Buick." It was to be ready for introduction in 1957.

Indeed, G.M. heard that Ford was committing itself to big cars in all its brands. Ford's Edsel division was being set up to swing across all price lines except at the very bottom and top of the market. This was as wide a market as Buick had carved out. The G.M. high command also knew that Ford was designing a bigger body shell for Mercury which would interchange with the larger Edsels, and that smaller Edsels would interchange with the big Ford.

What had happened was this: Ford had tested the lower end of the medium-price market with luxury-model Fords. It had found no resistance and raked in some nice profits. With this experience, and with the knowledge that consumer income was up sharply, Ford had every reason to believe that the markets of the future would favor the medium-price entries at the expense of the low-price cars. Also, Ford division officials were worried by the tremendous sales surge of Buick, which had recently pushed Plymouth out of third place. They believed that if the market continued to demand big cars, Buick might push the Ford for second place.

It seemed apparent to the bosses at Ford that the medium-price Mercury was no match for Buick. This meant that far too much of the burgeoning medium-price market would be captured by G.M., which had not only Buick in that arena but Pontiac, Olds, and the top end of Chevrolet. What to do? Fight Buick with Ford. How? By making Ford as big as a 1954 Buick.

By early 1955, G.M. knew that Ford had definitely committed itself to this strategy. Curtice and his officers also learned that Chrysler, with

---

[10] "Detroit Shoots the Works," *Fortune*, June 1959. Reproduced by permission.

no one division capable of achieving the savings that accrue to a factory that can make and sell a million units, had committed itself to one line of body shells for all of its cars. Watching their own labor costs mounting, G.M. officials reflected that one body shell for all their brands would save scores of millions of dollars. Late in 1955, G.M. decided on one big body shell for all its brands by 1958. It had to be big so that Chevrolet could meet the threat the big Ford would pose. And to hedge the bet on bigness, G.M. shortly put into motion plans for the compact Chevrolet that will be introduced this fall [1959], as related above, and Ford and Chrysler felt obliged to follow.

(While it takes eighteen months' to two years' lead time to make a major model change on a current car, it takes three years for a complete re-engineering job.)

Work had hardly been started on the big Chevrolet before G.M. statisticians pointed out that something odd was happening to Buick and Olds. Both had broken their records in 1955 (738,000 for Buick and 590,000 for Olds), but sales in the metropolitan areas had not kept pace with total sales. What could this mean? The big cities were normally the principal volume markets for these luxurious cars, for no other markets had enough upper-middle incomes. Evidently buyers outside the big cities had used three-year credit, which was widely available in 1955, to trade themselves up to Buicks and Oldsmobiles. This was apparently the reason for the 1955 increase in sales for these brands, for they were unable to hold their gains.

By the end of the first half of 1956, Buick and Olds were limping. Was the move to suburbia bad for Buick because more people needed two cars and couldn't afford two Buicks? Surveys showed that this might be one factor. Another factor might be the size of the new Buicks and Olds, which made them awkward to park in the cities. G.M. concluded that size and high prices were in some way at the root of Buick's and Olds' problem, so the company also put compact models for these two cars in work. And again Ford and Chrysler followed.

The figures show how radically the market changed between 1956 and 1957.

In 1956, 61 per cent of domestic sales were in the $1,800 to $2,300 range; the medium-price markets, which spread from $2,300 to $4,000, took about 35 per cent of the business; 4 per cent went to high-price cars. Buick had dropped back nearly 210,000 units to 529,000; and Olds, at 438,000, was off more than 150,000. This was the reverse of the sales pattern Ford had predicted for Buick—a fact that gave Ford, with the medium-priced Edsel poised for introduction the next year, something to ponder.

In 1957, when Ford began its fight against G.M. with big Fords, low-price cars tobogganed down from 61 per cent to a little under 20 per cent of the market. (The larger Fords were classed as medium-priced automobiles.) High-price cars went up to almost 6 per cent. Buick slid still further, to 395,000 units, Olds to 372,000, while the medium-price market soared to an astonishing 75 per cent. Imports more than doubled, to nearly 200,000 units—a figure that looked impressive for the first time. Ford trounced Chevrolet for the first time in a generation. Chrysler, which since 1953 had been on a feast-or-famine diet, did nicely with the Plymouth and its other lines. [See Exhibit 3.]

The sobering fact of the 1957 market was that the invasion of the

Exhibit 3

PER CENT OF INDUSTRY NEW CAR REGISTRATIONS BY MAKES
CALENDAR YEARS 1954–62

	1954	1955	1956	1957	1958	1959	1960	1961	1962
Chevrolet..........	25.6	22.9	26.3	24.3	26.6	23.5	25.8	27.2	29.9
Pontiac............	6.5	7.4	6.0	5.4	4.9	6.3	6.1	6.4	7.6
Oldsmobile.........	7.3	8.2	7.4	6.2	6.6	6.0	5.4	5.6	6.4
Buick.............	9.3	10.3	8.9	6.6	5.7	4.1	4.1	5.0	5.8
Cadillac..........	2.0	2.0	2.2	2.4	2.6	2.2	2.2	2.4	2.2
GM..............	50.7	50.8	50.8	44.9	46.4	42.1	43.6	46.6	51.9
Ford..............	25.3	21.9	23.1	25.0	22.1	24.4	21.6	22.7	21.2
Edsel.............	...	...	...	0.4	0.8	0.7	...	...	...
Mercury...........	4.9	5.2	4.6	4.4	2.9	2.6	4.7	5.3	4.6
Lincoln...........	0.7	0.5	0.7	0.6	0.6	0.5	0.3	0.5	0.5
Ford Motor Co.....	30.9	27.6	28.4	30.4	26.4	28.2	26.6	28.5	26.3
Plymouth..........	6.9	9.0	8.1	10.0	8.4	6.4	6.8	5.1	4.4
Dodge.............	2.8	4.0	3.7	4.3	2.9	2.8	5.4	3.9	3.4
De Soto...........	1.4	1.6	1.7	1.7	1.0	0.7	0.4	...	...
Chrysler..........	1.8	2.0	1.8	1.8	1.3	1.1	1.2	1.6	1.6
Imperial..........	...	0.2	0.2	0.5	0.3	0.3	0.2	0.2	0.2
Chrysler Corp......	12.9	16.8	15.5	18.3	13.9	11.3	14.0	10.8	9.6
Hudson............	0.6	0.3	0.2	0.1	...	...	...	...	...
Nash..............	0.9	0.6	0.5	0.2	...	...	...	...	...
Rambler...........	0.6	1.0	1.2	1.5	4.0	6.0	6.4	6.3	6.1
AM*..............	2.1	1.9	1.9	2.0	4.3	6.0	6.4	6.3	6.1
Studebaker.........	1.7	1.4	1.3	1.0	1.0	2.2	1.6	1.2	1.1
Packard...........	0.7	0.7	0.5	0.1	0.1	...	...	...	...
S-P..............	2.4	2.1	1.8	1.1	1.1	2.2	1.6	1.2	1.1
Crosley...........	...	...	...	...	...	...	...	...	...
Frazer............	...	...	...	...	...	...	...	...	...
Henry J...........	...	...	...	...	...	...	...	...	...
Kaiser............	0.4	0.2	...	...	...	...	...	...	...
Willys............	0.3	0.1	...	...	...	...	...	...	...
Others............	0.3	0.6	1.6	3.3	7.9	10.2	7.8	6.6	5.0
Industry..........	100.0	100.0	100.0	100.0	100.0	100.0	100.0	100.0	100.0

* Includes imported Metropolitan 1958 and prior years, but not 1959–62.
Source: *Ward's Automotive Yearbook, 1963*, p. 145. Reproduced by permission.

medium-price field by the former low-price three had murdered the old-timers in that market. Buick will never forget the slaughter of 1957, and neither will Ford, for in the process the big new 1957 Mercury lost business, and the brand-new Edsel fizzled in the market that wasn't there.

When 1958 and recession rolled around, G.M. offered a Chevrolet bigger than a Ford, as big, in fact, as a Cadillac.

It was the Cadillac-sized Chevrolet pitted against the almost as large Ford and Chrysler models which gave American Motors its opening for "campaign opportunity."

CAMPAIGN OPPORTUNITY

American Motors faced its crucial test just at the time when the medium-priced cars were being squeezed the hardest. Sales of Buick and Olds were declining, Edsel was unable to get rolling, and the medium-priced cars of American Motors—the Nash and Hudson lines—were declining sharply. Thus it was that in early 1957 a decision was made to stop production and to withdraw these lines from the market. American Motors made a historic decision to bet all of its chips on the Rambler, believing that the "Rambler concept" was the key to an opportunity. To back up its bet, the company took the following steps:

Product line. The Nash and Hudson lines were dropped after a stormy meeting of the board of directors, and two names of long-standing tradition disappeared from the market. The company made special allowances to dealers to help them move the last of these cars off the showroom floors.

Instead of introducing new Nash and Hudson models, as previously planned, the company introduced a 117-inch Ambassador by Rambler. By design this model used the same body shell as the 108-inch Rambler American, using largely the same dies and tooling as when the car had been discontinued in 1955.

When asked why American Motors had discontinued the 100-inch Rambler for almost three years and then revived it, Mr. Romney pointed out that the company had tried both the two-door 100-inch model and the four-door 108-inch model, and found that the latter had outsold the "more compact" model about four to one. He went on to point out that he believed there was a very good reason why the larger model had achieved greater acceptance:

> I think there's a very logical reason for that having happened. I once read that if you ever wanted to start a revolution—and after all, that's what we were trying to start in products—you should sell the basic idea with the least possible departure from existing forms. Now the 108-inch model was a smaller departure from the big-car concept in this country than the 100-inch model. And our figures indicated you could probably sell that size car, and break through the big-car mentality, quicker than you could with a 100-inch.
>
> Later the American public was not only accepting the compact car idea but also accepting the small car idea; and therefore we not only decided to have our Metropolitan model, which is an 85-inch small model, but also decided to bring back the 100-inch model because we were convinced that the small car idea had taken hold well enough to do that. And we brought it back in February of this year [1958], just the two-door model, and that two-door model is now second only to the Volkswagen in small car sales in America.[11]

Later that same day, asked why the 1958 Rambler had tail fins, Mr. Romney returned to the same theme, answering to the effect that "it's the basic idea that counts. If we have to use tail fins to get people to try compact cars, we'll use tail fins. Later on we will certainly be able

---

[11] Tobé, *The Tobé Lectures in Retail Distribution, 1958–1959*, p. 43.

to do away with them, and to build clean, simple, uncluttered cars."

Marketing. With the reintroduction of the 100-inch car, and with a restyled 108-inch car, 1958 was the "do or die" year for American Motors. In the fall of 1957:

> Romney felt constrained . . . to tell his deficit ridden [organization] that if the new year didn't see the corporation in the black, there could be a change in management. In consequence, 1958 [began] with Romney and every other executive who could grab a lapel, seize an ear, or clamber on a rostrum, hammering home the points that this was American Motors' year, this time the big three had gone too far, this was the moment when common sense in car buying could stretch the recession's "skimpy pay-checks."
>
> We resorted to something akin to shock treatment [one executive recalled], in an effort to shatter the prevailing myth that the greatest car values were to be found in products built by the Big Three.[12]

Not only did top executives take to the road selling and promoting,

> Celebrated cartoonists like William Steig, Whitney Darrow, and Chon Day were put to work on full page American Motors ads featuring . . . "Siegfried Slays the Dragon . . . Again" (he'd stabbed his fire breathing monster in the gas tank, after finding it unparkable and ungarageable). . . .[13]

With the "dinosaurs of the driveway" larger and longer than ever, the lampooning spread, and numerous cartoons appeared in magazines and newspapers all over the country. The spontaneous cartoons, plus the success of the Volkswagen, plus the persistent drumfire of American Motors, finally turned the tide.

> In March, Consumer Reports, a monthly buyer's guide, hit the stands with the news it had selected the Rambler Ambassador V-8 as the "consultant's choice," the one U.S. car that year which could "serve as the foundation for a hypothetical but eminently desirable automobile."
>
> In June, Ford became so alarmed over the success of American Motors propaganda that it devoted an entire advertising campaign to counter "talk about gas-guzzling monsters . . . claims of big car room with small car economy."
>
> In September, with . . . 26 million [in] profit (for the fiscal year just ended) George Romney announced he expected to sell 300,000 of his 1959 Ramblers, and to get 6 per cent [of the] market (vs. 4.4 per cent of 1958's).
>
> In October . . . sales were nearly triple those of October 1957.
>
> In December, the corporation started a $10 million expansion program that would permit an increase in Rambler capacity to 450,000 units by the end of 1959.[14] [See Exhibit 4.]

Dealer organization. Beginning early in 1957 the company was able to turn the tide in its dealer organization. Having slipped from 2,700 to about 1,900, the company lost 368 more, but was able to sign 741

[12] "Will Success Spoil American Motors?" *Fortune,* January 1959, p. 98. Reproduced by permission.
[13] Ibid.
[14] Ibid.

Exhibit 4

MARKET SHARES: 1953–62

Year	Imports	Independents	Big three
1953	0.5	9.0	90.5
1954	0.6	5.0	94.4
1955	0.8	4.0	95.2
1956	1.7	3.6	94.7
1957	3.4	3.0	93.6
1958	8.1	5.1	86.8
1959	10.2	8.3	81.5
1960	7.6	8.1	84.3
1961	6.5	7.7	85.8
1962	4.9	7.3	87.8

Source: *Ward's Automotive Yearbook, 1963*, p. 145. Reproduced by permission.

new ones to finish the year with 2,300. By September 1958 the number had reached 2,636. From this point on the effort was to upgrade the quality of the dealerships, and to see that the dealers earned enough to provide both the working capital and the incentives needed to provide good service for the cars being sold.

Finance and control.   The first fruits of operating in the black went for the repayment of bank debt. By September, the bank debt had been completely repaid, and working capital rose from less than $50 million the preceding year to $80 million. It was under these circumstances that the company appropriated $10 million to make provisions for a 50% increase in auto capacity, the $10 million going primarily for expanded assembly facilities. The company had reduced its break-even point to an estimated 125,000 units, and was in no mood to add the bricks and mortar necessary for a full-blown expansion of facilities. In addition, management could feel some satisfaction in the fact that though volume exceeded 1954, the number of salaried employees was only 50% as large as when the company had been formed.

THE SITUATION IN 1961

Strategies for 1959 differed little from those of 1958, as the Big Three played out their biggest, longest, most expensive models, appropriately adorned with the high watermark in fins and ornamentation. The serious business of new strategy formulation began to show up that fall, as four compacts were introduced in the 1960 product lines. The real punch came in the fall of 1960, however, as four more compacts were introduced in the 1961 lines, thus giving GM four and Chrysler and Ford two each. The competitive pressure generated by the proliferation of new models was particularly acute because the automobile market had, according to some estimates, settled down to being largely a replacement market, a market which fluctuated with purchasing power and grew with the population rather than one which expanded in reflection of rising living standards. The significance of this development was that if the overall market was no longer basically a growth market, then the flood of new models was competing for shares of a relatively stable pie. One could get a bigger share only if someone else got a smaller share. As *Fortune* remarked,[15]

> When the pie was getting bigger all the time, a manufacturer could accept a smaller slice and still come out ahead. Today, however, quite a different situation prevails. Automobile manufacturing in the U.S. has become primarily a replacement industry. The ratio of cars per person has changed only slightly since 1955; the car population itself stands at a whopping 61 million. Last year there was roughly one automobile for every three Americans, compared to one for five in 1945 and one for every seven in the middle Twenties. This does not mean thin pickings for Detroit from now on, but it does mean that in an average annual market of even 6,750,000 units between 1961 and 1965, a relatively small number will represent absolute growth. Some of the long-range forecasts: General Motors, most bullish of the Big Three, foresees a 3 per cent annual increase in new car sales, the trend line passing the seven-million mark in 1965. Ford's forecast is for a 2.8 per cent increase, a difference of some 80,000 cars in a seven-million car market.
>
> Those estimates show that the automobile manufacturer of 1961 has virtually given up the push for the bigger pie. Not very much can be done today about the total size of the market, summed up a Big Three economist this November. We measure success by per cent of penetration. Thus American Motors, Studebaker-Packard, and the imports are out to maintain, or better, their 17.4 per cent of the market (September registrations), three-fourths of which was wrung from G.M., Ford, and Chrysler between 1955 and 1960. As for the major manufacturers, G.M. with 42.7 per cent of the market is pressing to regain the 50.8 per cent it had in 1955; Ford at 26.9 per cent has set its sights on the 30.4 per cent of 1957; Chrysler's hope is to move its percentage from 12.9 to 20.

As far as Big Three strategies were concerned, *Fortune* had the following to say:

> The briefest summary of future strategies is this: Ford and Chrysler place prime emphasis on a generally lower-priced market, which includes the compacts, and Ford is strongly impressed by the "segmented" character of the over-all market. General Motors appears much less committed to the new emphasis on the bottom of the price range. It seems to be pulling for the standard-sized machine, and a rejuvenation of the middle-price brackets, with the compacts a fringe or supplemental market. With those very broad strategic patterns in mind, we can look more closely at the thinking of each company.
>
> At Ford, the central element is its concept of the new U.S. market. "The most important thing to remember about selling automobiles today," said the company's new president, Robert S. McNamara, in early December, "is that this isn't a single or homogeneous market. Ford's product strategy is based on a segmented market where different groups of consumers want different types of cars. We believe the general-pur-

---

[15] "Detroit Is Flying by the Seat of Its Pants," *Fortune*, January 1961. Reproduced by permission.

pose car will become a thing of the past; the expanding need is for specialized vehicles designed to fill a particular requirement."

In putting this concept into operation, Ford has undergone perhaps the most extensive transformation within the Big Three. The number of models it offered in the medium and high-price field was sharply cut, the Edsel being discontinued in 1960 and Lincoln's twelve models reduced to two for the 1961 market. At the same time Mercury was given six new models, raising its total to nineteen. These were heavily concentrated in the low-priced area; indeed, one of them was simply the Ford Galaxie, wearing the Mercury name plate and a slightly higher price tag. [See Exhibits 5 and 6.]

*   *   *   *   *

Ford's strategic posture, though committed to the compacts and to Mercury's new positioning in the low-price field, nevertheless preserves considerable flexibility. The company is acutely aware of the squeeze on profits that would occur should the proportion of compacts to standard-sized machines move from its present one-to-three ratio to parity or better. Any switch in public preference back to standard-sized machines, such as some of its executives now discern, will find Ford more than ready. What won't be altered is the impetus given interchangeability and cost control by a public in search of better but cheaper cars. Body stampings of the Continental and the Thunderbird are already interchangeable. So are those of the Falcon and the Comet, the latter being fundamentally a "stretched"—i.e., pieced-out amidships—version of the Falcon. Further economies of interchangeability can be expected to follow the centralizing of all car production under one manager, announced last November. Eventually there may be consolidations between the lines themselves.

. . . and as the two grand divisions come more and more to duplicate each other's products, their own consolidation into a single division may follow. Interestingly enough, where the divisions have in a sense been combined, with one dealer offering both the Falcon and the Comet, sales of each compact have showed marked improvement— a point that would gain force if the compacts took over more of the car market.

General Motors' over-all strategy, like that of Ford, recognizes the concept of a segmented market. This year in particular the variety of its 119 models—it was the only Big Three company to raise rather than lower the total—is the gauge of its efforts to offer something to virtually every segment. At the same time there are important differences in outlook and situation that differentiate G.M.'s strategy from Ford's, indeed from that of any other automobile manufacturer. To begin with, G.M.'s drop in total share of the market from 50.8 per cent in calendar 1955 to 42.1 per cent in 1959 came fundamentally from a decline of its middle-price makes. Chevrolet managed to do a little better than hold its own at 23 to 24 per cent, in part because G.M. permitted it to push up into the middle-priced market. But Buick declined steadily from 10.3 in 1955 to 4.1 in 1959, Oldsmobile slid from 8.2 to 6, Pontiac from 7.4 to 6.3. The actual unit volumes tell an even sadder story, Buick falling from 738,000 units to 246,000. On the other hand, Buick-Oldsmobile-Pontiac commanded 16.4 per cent of the 1959 market even after their slump and this made their representation in the middle-priced class five times more important than Ford's, more than triple Chrysler's. Thus the prime strategic question facing General

Exhibit 5
1961 MODEL PRICES

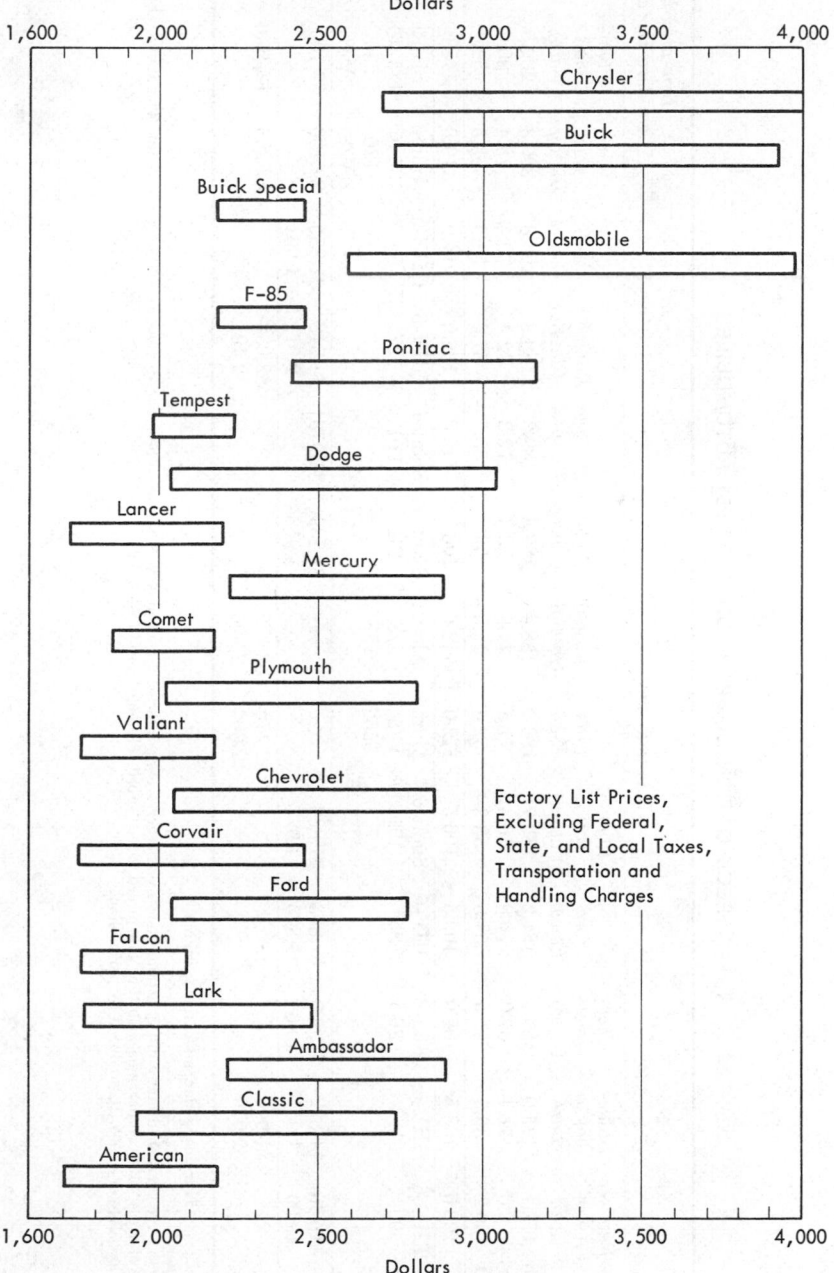

Ford and Chrysler, as the chart above reveals, are committed to the compacts and a generally lower-priced market; General Motors seems to be trying to husband its strength in Chevrolet, revitalize the middle-priced bracket, and give little play to the compacts.

Source: *Fortune*, January 1961. Reproduced with permission.

Exhibit 6

A.M.A. SPECIFICATION COMPARISON FOR 1961 AUTOMOBILES

	Compact cars											Low-priced standard-size cars		
	Rambler American	Studebaker Lark	Chevrolet Corvair	Ford Falcon	Plymouth Valiant	Olds F-85	Buick Special	Dodge Lancer	Pontiac Tempest	Rambler Classic	M-L Comet	Chevrolet Biscayne	Plymouth Savoy	Ford Fairlane
Overall length	173.1	175.0	180.0	181.2	183.7	188.2	188.4	188.8	189.3	189.8	194.8	209.3	209.5	209.9
width	70.0	71.4	67.0	70.6	70.4	71.5	71.3	72.3	72.2	72.4	70.4	78.4	80.0	79.9
height	56.2	56.5	51.5	54.5	53.3	52.6	52.5	53.3	53.5	57.3	54.5	55.5	54.4	55.0
Wheelbase	100.0	108.5	108.0	109.5	106.5	112.0	112.0	106.5	112.0	108.0	114.0	119.0	118.0	119.0
Engine type	LHD-6	OHV-6	Flat-6	OHV-6	Slant-6	Alum V/8	Alum V/8	Slant-6	Slant-4	OHV-6	OHV-6	Inline	Slant	Inline
horsepower	90	112	80	85	101	155	155	101	110	127	85	135 (6) 170 (V/8)	145 (6) 230 (V/8)	135 (6) 175 (V/8)
Price*	$1,730 1,809	$1,822 1,961	$1,800 1,860	$1,803 1,875	$1,838 1,927			$1,889 1,968	$1,975† 1,961	$1,918 2,071	$1,880 1,961	$2,106 2,106	$2,106 2,169	$2,105 2,213
Price: V/8 engine		$1,940 2,079				$2,175 2,300	$2,175 2,300			$2,038 2,191		$2,206	$2,169	$2,213

* Factory list price: four-door sedan, six-cylinder engine.

† Four-cylinder.

The Compacts have sharpened many old questions such as whether a car's interior dimensions would have to be reduced when overall length was cut. The above table provides answers to some of these, plus comparisons with the "low-priced three," Ford, Plymouth, and Chevrolet.

Source: *Fortune*, January 1961. Reproduced by permission.

Motors was how the company could move with the current trend toward cheaper, smaller cars at the least possible sacrifice of its B-O-P strength and profitability.

A partial answer was provided in the 1960 model year with the introduction of the Corvair by the Chevrolet Division. Nobody could reasonably conceive of Corvair's being a threat to B-O-P or to Chevrolet, either. For one thing, the car's rear engine—most radical engineering innovation since the Cord of 1934—made it an automotive novelty. Production of 250,000 did go higher than one might have expected of a novel machine making its way against no-nonsense competition in the economy field, but it merely emphasized the probability that G.M.'s strategy had been to get token participation in the compact-car market without injury to Chevrolet sales. Competitive figures tend to support this view. Ford Division production was off 1.6 per cent in the 1960 model year, while its Falcon volume reached a whopping 436,000 cars; conversely Chevrolet Division sales were up 11.7 per cent, with Corvair volume at only 250,000.

The complete tip-off on G.M.'s strategy came, however, with the introduction of its new small B-O-P cars in 1960. The Buick Special and the Olds F-85 extended B-O-P lines further down toward the low-price field, but a good $100 short of the most expensive Falcon, $17 short of the highest-priced Comet. Pontiac's Tempest alone touched the top of the Falcon range. Moreover, the term "compact" was sedulously avoided in describing them; they were billed as smaller versions of B-O-P cars. G.M.'s strategy, in essence, was to give the public what it wanted (i.e., smaller, cheaper, more economical cars) while at the same time trying to lead the buyers back to the standard-sized, middle-priced market, where G.M. still possessed so much competitive strength. Pointedly, G.M. refused to follow Ford's formula of concentrating on the lower-priced segments of the market with compacts and middle-priced cars at sharply reduced price tags. The G.M. strategy of going only part of the way down with the market was based on the hope that the "man who had always wanted an Oldsmobile" (or Buick or Pontiac) would buy one of the new less expensive models and eventually trade up in the line, to the rejuvenation of the middle-priced market. Chevrolet, in the meantime, would be expected to hold the fort in its own area. [See Exhibit 7.]

*   *   *   *   *

General Motors' power to implement its strategy is, of course, immense and it can be expected to use that power to the fullest. No fear of antitrust prosecution is likely to inhibit G.M.'s efforts to push its market percentages as high as they will go. Nor is it likely to pay much attention to the recent outcry against "planned obsolescence" in automobiles. For G.M. the cost of model changes is minimal: old body dies would wear out anyway after a couple of years' production at the huge volumes attained by G.M.; new dies with new designs can be had for little more than the cost of replacing the worn-out ones. Thus G.M. is attracted naturally to a two-year model cycle. By talking of such a cycle it may compel its competitors, most of whom would prefer a three-year cycle, to follow suit, even though a two-year cycle would often force them to discard dies that have not worn out simply because they lack G.M.'s high levels of production. G.M. initiative, in consequence, may force its competitors to bear model-change costs that G.M. itself will not bear.

Exhibit 7

MOTORS A LA MODE: THE STYLING RACE PICKS UP SPEED

While the horsepower race has petered out and the size race appears to be running backward, it is clear from the chart at right that the style race is hotter than ever. More models were offered by Detroit for 1961 than at any time in automotive history. G.M. alone spent $480 million for new tooling. Next year (1962) the pace is expected to slacken somewhat as the industry waits for its second wind. Ford will probably bring out a new standard-sized machine, to fit in between the Fairlane and the Comet. Chevrolet may follow suit with a smaller Chevy. Chrysler will likely strengthen its all-important low-price divisions with a new body for Plymouth and one for Dodge. But another big push for the industry is expected for 1963. Probabilities then are for three new G.M. cars (assigned to the Buick, Oldsmobile and Pontiac divisions and intended to compete against the Thunderbird) and a new Ford, a "subcompact," approximating the Volkswagen in size. Should Ford go ahead on its subcompact, G.M. stands ready to turn out a competitive car, built at its West German Opel plant. However some of the other companies might yearn for a three-year cycle, nobody can chance one so long as General Motors sticks to its two-year push.

Maker	Model	1949	1950	1951	1952	1953	1954	1955	1956	1957	1958	1959	1960	1961	1962	1963
	Chevrolet	B		M		B		B	M	M	B	B	M	B	M	B
	Corvette						C		B					M		M
	Corvair												C		M	C
	?															
	Pontiac	B				B		B	M	M	B	B	M	B	M	B
	Tempest													C		C
	?															
GENERAL MOTORS CORPORATION	Oldsmobile 88	B		B		M	B	M	M	B	M	B	M	B	M	B
	Super 88			B		M	B	M	M	B	M	B	M	B	M	M
	98				B		B	M	M	B	M	B	M	B	M	M
	F-85													C	M	B
	?															
	Buick Special Century	B		B		M	B	M	M	B	M	B	M	B	M	B
	Super Roadmaster	B		B		M	B	M	M	B	M	B	B	B	M	M
	Special												C	C		B
	?															
	Cadillac	M	B				B	M	M	B	M	B	M	B	M	C
	Ford	B			B			B		B	M	B	B	B	C	B
	Thunderbird							C		M	B	B	B	B	C	B
FORD MOTOR COMPANY	Falcon												C		M	C
	?															
	Mercury	B		M	B			B		B	M	B	M	B	M	B
	Comet												C		M	M
	Lincoln	B			B				B	M	B		M	B		
	Continental Mk. II								C							
	Edsel										C	B	B			
	Plymouth	B	M	M		B		B	M	B	C	M	B	M	B	M
	Valiant												C	B		M
	Dodge	B	M	M		B		B	M	B	B	M	B	M	B	M
CHRYSLER CORPORATION	Lancer													C		M
	De Soto	B	M	M		B		B	M	B		M	B	M		
	Chrysler	B	M	M		B		B	M	B		M	B	M	M	B
	Imperial			M		B		B	M	B		M	M	M	M	
	American															
AMERICAN MOTORS	Rambler								B		C	M	C	B	B	M
	Nash	B		M	B		M		M			M	B		B	M
	Studebaker	B	M	M	M	B			M			C	M	M		M

NEW CAR—C   NEW BODY—B   MAJOR CHANGE—M

Source: Fortune, 1961. Reproduced by permission.

The strategy of the remaining member of the Big Three, Chrysler, is focused on one overriding objective: remaining a member of the Big Three rather than joining American Motors and Studebaker-Packard in a Little Three. In calendar 1959, Chrysler's percentage of the market (in registrations) dropped to 11.3 per cent, the lowest level since 1930. Last year the company managed a significant gain; its percentage of the market rose to 14.4 for the first nine months, and it even turned in a third-quarter profit of $1,400,000, the first in that period since 1957.

The strategy employed was much like Ford's. Chrysler moved an increasing number of its entries down into the low-priced sector of the market, and put its main emphasis there. The Plymouth Division got a new compact, the Valiant. The Dodge Division models were concentrated in the lower-price areas, leaving only a single series of cars in the upper brackets. Then the destructive competition between Dodge dealers (who also handled Plymouth) and the Plymouth dealers themselves was mitigated by taking the Plymouth out of the Dodge agencies and replacing it with the new Dart, essentially a Plymouth under another name. With the Dart going very well indeed, Chrysler further strengthened Dodge dealership by giving them a new compact, the Lancer. This car was really a Valiant with slightly better upholstery, five inches added to trunk space, and a few dollars to the price tags, but it gave Chrysler two compacts to push. And push them it has. By mid-November, 34 per cent of Chrysler's 1961 model production was devoted to Valiant and Lancer. This performance was topped by the 39 per cent of Ford output going to its compacts, but way ahead of the 19 per cent of. G.M.'s smaller car volume. With its share of the market (registrations) rising, Chrysler had grounds for hoping that by the first quarter of this year it would be back to 15 per cent.

What Chrysler's strategy will be from here on out is not too difficult to foresee. It estimates that the compacts of all companies will take 33.4 per cent of the whole 1961 market, and that this figure will rise only slightly (34.7 per cent) in 1962. At the same time the company expects the Plymouth-Ford-Chevrolet-Dart sector to rise to 46 per cent this year and hold that percentage in 1962. Best bet is that Chrysler will make only minor changes in its compacts this coming September. With DeSoto discontinued, its fighting money will likely go into new bodies for Dodge and Plymouth, and even greater emphasis on the low end of the market.[16]

In summary, the counterattack by the Big Three included the following major steps. First, they reversed the trend toward longer, lower, more ornamented automobiles throughout their entire line. Second, they offered a greater variety of sizes, styles, and horsepower ratings, giving the public a much wider range of choice, particularly in the low-priced ranges. Third, they brought out eight new automobiles aimed specifically at the "compact" car market, the market where American Motors had been largely unopposed in 1958–59. Beyond this, their strategies appeared to diverge, with Ford and Chrysler appearing to bet that compacts were here to stay, while GM appeared to be betting that it could lead the public back up to larger cars in due time through its

---

[16] *Fortune,* January 1961.

Exhibit 8

1962 MODEL YEAR U.S. CAR PRODUCTION BY $100 PRICE GROUPS*
(entire model year)

$100 Price groups	Chevrolet	Chevy II	Corvair	Pontiac	Tempest	Oldsmobile	F-85	Buick	Special	Ford Galaxie	Fairlane	Falcon
$1,601–$1,700												
1,701– 1,800		11,457	16,245									64,2
1,801– 1,900		63,479	53,842								23,511	173,8
1,901– 2,000		168,044			52,903						65,282	31,5
2,001– 2,100	135,692	1,663	199,797		51,981				42,384		91,550	62,4
2,101– 2,200	72,195	40,467	3,716				15,983			26,114	99,804	55,2
2,201– 2,300	174,591	41,497	18,931		38,309		18,736		40,202	66,810	17,969	
2,301– 2,400	226,104			14,263			32,461		7,382	93,178		22,6
2,401– 2,500	430,298		13,491	68,620			6,864		36,874	288,126		4,2
2,501– 2,600	197,469			76,275			6,861	7,418	18,712	55,548		
2,601– 2,700	138,607					108,143	9,898	56,783	8,913	47,217		
2,701– 2,800	38,707			27,760		53,438	3,765	62,997		70,802		
2,801– 2,900	10,345			50,158		24,125				15,385		
2,901– 3,000				42,345		12,212		13,471		28,412		
3,001– 3,100				44,015		38,712		20,698				
3,101– 3,200				51,777		6,417		9,131		13,183		
3,201– 3,300				4,527				12,717				
3,301– 3,400						3,837						
3,401– 3,500												
3,501– 3,600						7,653		22,445				
3,601– 3,700	14,531					47,006		16,734				
3,701– 3,800						40,641						
3,801– 3,900								7,894				
3,901– 4,000						3,691		15,395				
4,001– 4,100												
4,101– 4,200												
4,201– 4,300						7,149						
4,301– 4,400												
4,401 & Over												
Totals	1,438,539	326,607	306,022	378,740	143,193	353,024	94,568	245,683	154,467	704,775	298,116	414,28

* Based on suggested factory list prices before excise tax, dealer handling charges and optional equipment installations. 1962 model prices include deduction of heater prices for General Motors Corp. and Ford Motor Co. car lines to put industry-wide prices on an equal basis with entire 1961 model year. Source: Ward's Statistical Dept.
Source: *Ward's Automotive Yearbook, 1963*, p. 22. Reproduced by permission.

"B-O-P" compacts, on the one hand, and through keeping its Corvair out of the styling race and thereby de-emphasizing it. Taken together, these strategies put the squeeze on American Motors, though at the same time they involved a significant change in industry competition. While attacking AMC (and each other) with their compacts, the Big Three were now playing on AMC's home ground, and they were advertising the values of compactness, economy, and durability—long the bywords at American Motors. The counterattack stood to help as well as hurt AMC.

FACING UP TO THE COUNTERATTACK: 1959–62

During the years 1959–62, American Motors reached and maintained about a 6% share of the market (Exhibit 8). Pretax profits reached a high of $105 million in 1959 and 1960, and then tapered off, owing in part to the rigors of immediate competition and in part to increasing outlays for automotive styling changes, including a significant redesign of the Rambler American for 1961. In facing the counterattack, then,

Thunderbird	Mercury Monterey	Meteor	Comet	Plymouth	Valiant	Dodge	Lancer	Chrysler	Cadillac Lincoln Imperial	Rambler	Studebaker	Total all cars Units	% of Total
.....	.....	.....	.....	.....	.....	.....	.....	.....	.....	29,948	.....	29,948	0.45
.....	.....	.....	.....	.....	21,803	.....	7,327	.....	.....	44,352	15,793	181,243	2.71
.....	.....	.....	62,491	.....	32,413	.....	16,775	.....	.....	62,071	23,897	512,345	7.66
.....	.....	.....	60,701	.....	47,967	.....	19,024	.....	.....	106,816	14,277	566,573	8.47
.....	.....	11,230	.....	47,682	34,303	35,457	14,140	.....	.....	5,521	3,115	736,931	11.02
.....	.....	30,603	29,128	27,885	8,867	13,648	2,699	.....	.....	76,793	9,599	512,757	7.67
.....	.....	21,524	10,667	21,344	.....	8,753	4,306	.....	.....	61,482	9,811	554,932	8.30
.....	641	5,695	.....	13,083	.....	19,138	.....	.....	.....	21,893	5,393	461,855	6.91
.....	5,328	.....	2,318	29,090	.....	27,743	.....	.....	.....	21,281	2,861	937,189	14.01
.....	26,435	.....	.....	14,115	.....	12,907	.....	.....	.....	4,379	1,149	420,268	6.28
.....	46,501	.....	.....	12,566	.....	21,963	.....	50,832	.....	6,401	.....	507,824	7.59
.....	8,932	.....	.....	2,410	.....	15,862	.....	10,313	.....	1,289	320	296,595	4.43
.....	15,085	.....	.....	3,959	.....	5,564	.....	7,705	.....	.....	8,467	140,793	2.11
.....	.....	.....	.....	.....	.....	3,933	.....	.....	.....	.....	.....	100,373	1.50
.....	.....	.....	.....	.....	.....	.....	.....	21,337	.....	.....	.....	124,762	1.87
.....	2,772	.....	.....	.....	.....	893	.....	3,319	.....	.....	.....	87,492	1.31
.....	.....	.....	.....	.....	.....	.....	.....	2,371	.....	.....	.....	19,615	0.29
.....	1,315	.....	.....	.....	.....	.....	.....	.....	.....	.....	.....	5,152	0.08
.....	.....	.....	.....	.....	.....	.....	.....	.....	.....	.....	.....	.....	...
.....	.....	.....	.....	.....	.....	.....	.....	1,786	.....	.....	.....	31,884	0.48
.....	.....	.....	.....	.....	.....	.....	.....	.....	.....	.....	.....	78,271	1.17
57,845	.....	.....	.....	.....	.....	.....	.....	12,083	.....	.....	.....	52,724	0.79
10,282	.....	.....	.....	.....	.....	.....	.....	6,638	.....	.....	.....	72,377	1.08
.....	.....	.....	.....	.....	.....	.....	.....	.....	.....	.....	.....	29,368	0.44
.....	.....	.....	.....	.....	.....	.....	.....	.....	.....	.....	.....	.....	...
.....	.....	.....	.....	.....	.....	.....	.....	.....	.....	.....	.....	7,149	0.11
8,457	.....	.....	.....	.....	.....	.....	.....	781	.....	.....	.....	9,238	0.14
1,427	.....	.....	.....	.....	.....	.....	.....	1,374	206,238	.....	.....	209,039	3.13
78,011	107,009	69,052	165,305	172,134	145,353	165,861	64,271	118,539	206,238	442,226	94,682	6,686,697	100.0

the company had a profitable operation with a relatively stable market share, i.e., a much stronger position than in the days of the "campaign for survival."

Product line.   The American Motors product line consisted of the 117-inch Ambassador, the 108-inch Rambler Classic, the 100-inch Rambler American, and the 85-inch Metropolitan, with the two larger models accounting for approximately 70% of sales, the American about 20%, and the Metropolitan about 5%.

Forbes,[17] in discussing the product line, made the following observations:

> The product that American sends to compete in the market place shows interesting similarities to the facilities that bore it. As a car, the Rambler could be described as a sound whole made up of frequently improvised parts. Most Ramblers, for example, are powered with a basically old-fashioned six-cylinder engine first designed in the 1930's. (There is also a quite modern V-8 that is used on one Rambler

---

[17] "Can George Do It Again?" *Forbes*, August 1, 1961. Reproduced by permission.

Classic line and on the larger Rambler Ambassador.) However, in typical Rambler fashion this engine was converted in 1956 from L-head to valve-in-head design for use on most Ramblers, and in addition is now being offered with an ultra-modern aluminum cylinder block.

Nevertheless, management believed that continued successful participation in "economy runs" by this engine contributed significantly to Rambler's reputation for economy and quality.

To continue with *Forbes:*

> Yet the Rambler has consistently had elements of solid and often unique worth. Its unit-body-and-frame construction is miles ahead of the traditional technique followed on U.S. cars, although all the new compacts have come over to Rambler's side. Its ceramic-coated muffler promises to remedy at last an almost scandalous piece of automotive misdesign; its dip-coating of the entire body shows how to prevent the moth-eaten appearance around the bottom that marks so many five-year-olds and up among U.S. cars; and Rambler bodies now get the benefit of a water spray test that should at least keep them from leaking when brand new, as many U.S. cars do.

Given this combination of homemade improvisations plus specific technological leads over major competitors, American Motors' timing of introducing new models was of particular interest. On several occasions the company employed what has been called a "Notre Dame" strategy, a strategy of introducing major model changes one year after its competitors. *Forbes* illustrated this in the case of the Rambler Classic, the company's bread-and-butter model:

> This quiet, almost sedate vehicle plays a crucial part in American Motors strategy. The company feels that to date it has had practically no direct competition for its major product, the 108-inch wheelbase Rambler Classic that Romney describes as a "family-sized compact." For the two leading competitive compacts are nearer in size to the 100-inch wheelbase Rambler American (an "economy compact," in Romney lingo). But within the next few months (fall 1961) both Ford and Chevy will introduce brand new lines, slightly larger than the Falcon and Corvair, that will meet the Rambler Classic head-on.
>
> Romney expects to take on this new competition with only slightly face-lifted versions of the present Ramblers, praying that the car's general reputation will carry it through. Meantime, however, he is preparing new 1963 models whose tooling alone will cost considerably more than this year's entire $20 million–$25 million capital outlay for tooling, expansion, plant modernization and whatnot. American's future will hinge on how much ground (if any) it must give in the fiscal year just ahead, and how much it gains back as a result of its 1963 counterattack.
>
> Thus Romney displays a strategy of timing not unlike that Notre

Dame once used in football, namely, employing the second team to take the initial shock before putting the first team in.

The second team was aided, however, by across-the-board price cuts. Thus the company advertised that every single model had been reduced in price for 1962. The following fall, when the new Classic and Ambassador models were introduced, prices were raised some $30 to $50 per car. Meanwhile, American Motors was able to maintain its market share in 1962, choosing to do this at the expense of substantially lowered profits for that year. As the 1963 models were introduced and the price increases became effective, profits improved sharply, up 30% from the preceding year.

Mr. Romney explained this strategy to the AMC shareholders in the following way: ". . . we sharply increased product value without a corresponding increase in prices in 1962 models. This was a very calculated decision because we thought it was more important to increase our penetration of the market—more important in terms of the interests of stockholders and others associated with this company—than to make maximum current profits our primary objective."[18]

Marketing. With acceptance of the compact car idea, AMC advertising and promotion focused increasingly on specific product features, such as the unit-body construction, deep-dip rust prevention, and the ceramic muffler. The company also took the lead in extending the warranty on its automobiles, a move which spread rapidly, and led competitors to extend 90-day warranties up to five years in some cases. Longevity had become a selling point—a development which would have seemed unthinkable only a few years previously.

Dealer organization. Having rebuilt its dealer organization during the previous campaign adroitly captained by the aggressive Roy Abernethy, who succeeded George Romney in 1962 as president of the corporation, the company now attempted to maintain existing numbers and to strengthen individual dealerships. To implement this, the company once again resorted to granting extra discounts to dealers when the going got tough. Thus as the United States slid into a recession in 1961, the company sales and profits slipped, but at the same time dealer discounts were increased $30–$40 per car, causing corporate profits to slide still more. By paying an extra $6 to $8 million in dealer commissions (while operating profits dropped from 105 to 50 millions), the company was able to report a net loss in dealers of 1.3% in the first six months of 1961 while its competitors reported losses as follows:[19]

```
G.M..................................... 1.0%
Ford.................................... 1.7
Chrysler................................ 4.3
Studebaker-Packard..................... 7.9
```

---

[18] Report to Stockholders, February 7, 1962.

[19] *Forbes,* August 1, 1961, p. 17.

This left the company's dealer strength relatively unimpaired, though AMC's dealer organization was still weaker than those of its major competitors. *Forbes* noted that AMC's dealers

> were outnumbered six-to-one by G.M.'s dealers and nearly three-to-one by Ford's and Chrysler's. But old sales boss Abernethy has some factors working for him, too. The rapidly increasing number of Ramblers on the road—now close to 2 million—means an equally rapid increase in the parts-and-service business that provides the dealer's bread and butter. And Rambler leads all U.S. cars except Cadillac in owner loyalty, as measured by the percentage of Rambler owners who become repeat buyers. The latest score: 67%. Thus American has the distinction of being the only carmaker that is increasing its dealer corps, though its map is not still without blank spots.

Finance and control.   In 1961 the company became the only U.S. automobile manufacturer to be completely free of long-term debt. The company maintained, however, a standing line of credit of approximately $50 million which it could call upon in an emergency.

The company's elimination of all debt had been accompanied by an expansion of capacity to an estimated 600,000 cars per year. To accomplish the debt reduction and the expansion of output at the same time, the company had maintained its policy of not integrating its operation to include any but the essential elements. Thus, capacity was doubled from 300,000 to 600,000 at an estimated investment of about $30 million, mere peanuts compared to the outlay for a comparable expansion of an integrated operation.

> That American could get so much additional capacity at this relatively small cost is partly because of the company's style of play and partly because of a fortunate break. The style of play refers to American's preference for making maximum use of its suppliers' investment rather than pouring its own money into integrated facilities. If G.M. were given an index number of 100 on an "integration scale," then Ford would rank perhaps a little above 100 (with its steel and glass plants more than offsetting certain other components that Ford does not make) and American Motors probably at about 70. Thus new capacity will obviously cost American less per unit (the degree of integration remaining unchanged) than its two biggest competitors.
>
> The lucky break was the sudden availability in Kenosha, Wisconsin cheek by jowl with American's main plant, of a 2-million square-foot plant where Simmons once made metal beds. The Simmons plant was quite capable of being converted into the building of Rambler bodies, one of American's worst bottlenecks. Precisely this was done, at an annual rental cost (with options to buy) of only $450,000. And while it took nearly $15 million to equip it for production, the company still

got by with a fraction of the capital cost it would have taken to build a new facility from scratch.[20]

Corresponding to this lack of integration, the company was estimated to have a smaller profit margin per car than GM or Ford, but a higher return on the capital invested, as below:

1960 RESULTS*

| | Pretax Profits | | Capital Employed per Vehicle Produced | Return on Capital before Income Taxes |
	Per Vehicle Produced	As a % of Auto Sales		
General Motors	$400	16%	$1,000	40%
Ford	240	15	825	29
American	200	11	400	50

* In American's case the fiscal year ends September 30; for the other two it ends December 31.

All figures are *Forbes'* estimates. In each case they represent earnings and capital employed in the auto business on a worldwide basis. Non-automotive activities have been screened out. In GM's case, GMAC earnings and capital are included in automotive results.[21]

With this approach, the company was able to maintain a low break-even point even with its sharply expanded scale of operations. Thus *Forbes* estimated the break-even in 1961 to be 150,000 units, up only slightly from 1959 despite the increase in productive capacity from 300,000 to 600,000 units. On the other hand, one American Motors executive noted that with this approach the company was not able to attain significant economies of scale in the 400,000–600,000-car range. Unit costs were about the same over the entire range. Strategy remained essentially unchanged, then, with the company placing heavy emphasis on safety (via a low break-even) at the expense of the opportunities for rising profits per unit from integrated operations (with their attendant fixed costs).

    Production. As for the strength of American's production sinews, the company's car output takes place in two Kenosha, Wis., plants and a third in Milwaukee, 40-odd miles away. Little about any of the plants represents a production man's dream of efficiency. For example, the very thought of trucking Rambler bodies from the Milwaukee body plant to Kenosha for assembly, at a $5 cost per car, would flabbergast the average factory boss. But American's production heads are hardened to the practice. They insist that in view of the huge capital

---

[20] Ibid., p. 16.
[21] Ibid.

costs that would be involved it would not prove economical to move the Milwaukee operation to Kenosha. They take much the same view toward the frequent multi-story sections in America's plants: conveyor belts simply run upstairs and down, in fine disregard of auto industry dogma that only single-story plants make sense.

All of American's auto production operations have an air of artful and thrifty improvisation, as though new equipment is added only when absolutely essential, or when it is a leadpipe cinch to pay back its cost in a matter of months. Thus, fine, new automated tools operate side by side with virtual clunkers—a practice perhaps necessary for a company in American's spot, but one that always carries the danger of falling too far behind.

American also contravenes industry—or at least Big Three—practice by crowding all its auto output into one Wisconsin area, instead of seeking a calculated scatter of component and assembly plants across the country. In fact, measured in unit output American's Kenosha assembly plant is the industry's largest, outranking even Ford's River Rouge.

Romney explains: "In 1948, we made a study which showed that a volume of 200,000 cars assembled on the West Coast yielded a saving of $60 per unit, which justified the use of east and west coast plants. However, a 1958 study, assuming a volume of 400,000 cars, showed that freight rates on components vs. completed vehicles had changed so much in the meantime that a West Coast assembly plant meant a penalty of $59 per car." American is, therefore, quite content with its current concentration—though its executives readily grant that it might not pay other companies to change their own established patterns.[22]

Labor relations. In keeping with its strategy of maintaining a low break-even for safety in bad years at the expense of possible economies and profits in good years, the company negotiated an unusual labor contract in 1961. Called a "progress sharing" agreement, the contract provided for profit sharing in lieu of a certain portion of the straight hourly increase granted by the Big Three.

Mr. Romney explained the concepts involved in the 1961 agreement as follows:

> While much has been written about this historic Progress Sharing labor agreement, which we negotiated with the UAW last summer, we find continuing public interest in this subject. Since my written report to you on the agreement, all of our nonrepresented salaried employees also are now participating in this program.
>
> The management of your company is convinced that the progress sharing approach—founded on the principle of sharing progress equitably among employees, stockholders, consumers, dealers and suppliers—will make it possible to expand our sales, increase our earnings and substantially benefit our stockholders. If you had been

---

[22] Ibid.

familiar with the internal operation of the company, you would realize that this dedication to progress sharing has been as fundamental in this company's growth as has the pioneering of the compact Rambler.

Let me tell you why this contract with the union is important:

First, in the initial paragraph of our new union contract, it is recognized by the union as well as the management that for employees to enjoy high wages and good working conditions, they must make progress *and it must be shared with customers*. In other words, our contract repudiates the idea that you can turn over to workers, or workers and stockholders, *all* of the progress—and still make progress. It's premised on the concept that if you're going to make progress, you must share that progress with the customer. This is sound. Without progress sharing, the American economy would not be what it is today. But this was a unique principle to write into our labor contract in face of national policies that are of an opposite character.

Second, our unique contract with the UAW is designed specifically to meet the needs and opportunities of American Motors. It is not a pattern settlement imposed on us—it was our idea—nor a pattern settlement to be imposed on others. We weren't trying to say what others ought to have. Flexibility and freedom of action and choice are great principles. It is based on the opportunities of American Motors and the needs of American Motors.

Third, the fixed-cost increases are *lower* for American Motors than for any other automobile company. In other words, while the employee benefit increases which all the companies have provided for in their labor contracts are generally similar, their method of financing is not the same. All the benefit increases granted by the Big Three represent fixed-cost increases. Virtually all the increased benefits granted under our contract will come out of profits, and therefore our fixed-cost increases are *lower* than those of our major competitors. And "if there ain't no profits, there ain't no sharing." It's just that simple.

Fourth, a large share of our cost increases is placed on a variable basis—subject to actual earnings. This is a distinct advantage to us because the determinations are to be made after the facts instead of before the facts are known. This permits more realistic forecasting, sounder fiscal approaches and greater mutuality of interest in progress.

While the "Progress Sharing Agreement" has been described previously as "unusual," consideration of this plan must include the entire 1961 labor agreement of which the plan was only a portion. Additional considerations in the contract affecting such matters as paid time not worked, seniority benefits, and production standards resulted in tangible savings of several millions per year, and intangible, but nonetheless significant benefits, which have improved the company's competitive position.

THE SITUATION AT THE END OF 1962

In its 1962 Annual Report, American Motors described its competitive position in part as follows:

Setting a new Rambler world-wide record, wholesale sales of Rambler cars in the U.S. and foreign markets increased to 478,132 units. This was a 24.2% gain over the 1961 fiscal period.

With several new entries attracted to the compact car segment of the U.S. car market in 1962, Rambler experienced the most vigorous onslaught to date on its domestic market position [see table]. Our strengthened distribution and dealer organization, however, demonstrated full capability for meeting the competitive challenge. Rambler U.S. wholesale sales increased 18.5% over the previous fiscal year.

Year	U.S. only	Outside U.S.	Total
1961	366,384	18,445	384,829
1962	434,486	43,646	478,132

Rambler's percentage of U.S. industry registration was 6.7%, virtually unchanged from the previous year.

* * * * *

Advertising and selling expense increased during the fiscal year as Rambler made a successful bid for larger volume. Additional customer benefits were provided by the extension of warranty terms.

The building of a stronger distribution system to meet the requirements of a growing business is a continuing activity. To provide better service to dealers and retail customers, we added a new automotive zone office in Newark, N.J., and a new parts warehouse at Queens, L.I., during the fiscal year. Additional parts warehouses have since been opened in Houston and San Francisco. We also expanded our financial program of assisting the development of Rambler franchises in important markets.

A net of ninety-six new Rambler dealers was franchised in the U.S. during the fiscal year, bringing our total automotive dealer count as of September 30 to 3,076 dealers.

Increased strength of our Rambler dealers is reflected in their aggregate net worth of $216,714,000 currently which compares to $100,877,000 in 1957.

* * * * *

In line with our policy of making changes only when they truly benefit the customer, American Motors introduced major engineering and structural improvements in the 1963 Classic and Ambassador models which permitted wholly restyled cars.

An advanced method of unit construction, which contributes greater strength, solidity, precision and quality to Rambler bodies, made feasible the attractive new styling of the 1963 models. The new Rambler car body was designed to use curved glass side windows with doors that curve into the roof. This feature is available only on a few expensive U.S. cars. Combined with these exterior appearance changes is a new development in power transfer—the Tri-Poised engine mount—which provides a quieter Rambler ride at all speeds.

The Rambler American line has been broadened and enhanced with the addition of new hardtop models. A new Twin-Stick floor shift transmission with overdrive is available as optional equipment on the top line of all series. U.S. prices were maintained at the same level as a year ago on fifteen of the 1963 models, were reduced on two models and increased modestly on 12 models.

Rambler remains the leader in the segment of the U.S. market that continues to be the fastest growing. We believe the compact car will take an ever greater share of total car sales in the 1963 calendar year. The factors that have contributed to Rambler's rapid growth are accelerating: the dispersal of population to suburban areas, the dependence of more and more people upon the motor car for personal mobility, and the traffic congestion, parking problems and other trends arising from increasing urbanization.

Cars that are more practical and convenient to use, while equally comfortable and attractive, are in the ascendency in the American market. Rambler's present and future product programs are well timed and ideally adapted to those strong trends in customer preference.

American Motors also launched major moves overseas during 1962. The annual report noted, for instance, that the company's overseas investment increased fivefold during the year. Continuing, the report had this to say about AMC's international operations:

More Rambler cars are appearing throughout the world.

American Motors now accounts for 18% of shipments of new cars from the United States. Sales of these cars, plus Ramblers produced by foreign plants, increased 136% over unit sales in the prior year.

American Motors of Canada is developing a firm position in the Canadian market. The subsidiary recorded a 75% gain in sales, reaching a level of 19,000 units, and substantially increased its percentage of industry registrations over the previous year. Our Canadian automobile manufacturing plant has under construction at Brampton, Ontario a new addition which will enlarge its work space by two-thirds. The new building is scheduled to be completed in the March quarter. The cost of this expansion will be paid for out of the subsidiary's earnings.

Rambler is now the best selling car of American origin in Latin America. Production of Rambler cars has been under way since January 1962 in Argentina. Despite political unrest in that nation, the output of our cars by Industries Kaiser Argentina S.A. is at a highly satisfactory rate. Rambler is now taking 40% of U.S. car sales in that country.

Rambler assembly for distribution in Common Market countries commenced in March 1962 in the Renault plant at Haren, Belgium. Since then a steady monthly step-up in Rambler output has been achieved, and further growth is indicated as Rambler gains the benefit of added distribution through Renault's wide network of dealers.

In sum, then, American Motors was maintaining its domestic position and expanding abroad. With the introduction of restyled Ambassadors and Classics for 1963, it was hoping to move ahead in the domestic market as well.

Reviewing these events in February 1962, Mr. Romney noted that the company had successfully weathered "campaign counterattack." Looking to 1963, he stated that "next year we expect to resume the offensive with 'campaign leadership.' In the years ahead, we expect to begin a long-range battle for the number-one brand-name position in the automobile industry in this country."

American Motors Corporation II

"The rule is, jam to-morrow, and jam yesterday—but never jam *today.*"

"It *must* come sometime to 'jam today,' " Alice objected.

"No, it can't," said the Queen. "It's jam every *other* day: to-day isn't any *other* day, you know."—Lewis Carroll in *Through the Looking-glass and What Alice Found There*

ON NOVEMBER 17, 1971, Roy D. Chapin, Jr.,[1] Chairman, and William V. Luneburg, President of American Motors Corporation (AMC), announced that earnings for the year ended September 30, 1971, were $10.2 million on sales of $1.2 billion, and that these results "reflect substantial improvements in every major sector of the company's business and demonstrate that we are making good progress in developing opportunities . . . available to the company as a result of expansion and acquisition." Thus ended a five-year period during which AMC's new leaders had brought about dramatic changes in the strategic course of the company.

Mr. Chapin and Mr. Luneburg had been appointed to their present positions in January 1967 in an atmosphere of crisis. In the four previous years, unit sales had fallen 37% and market share from over 6% to under 3%. Cumulative pretax losses (Exhibit 1) had forced the company to borrow heavily (Exhibit 2) in order to maintain minimum working capital. Near the nadir of company fortunes, financier Robert B. Evans had acquired 200,000 shares of AMC stock at about 40% below book value. By mid-1966 he had been elected chairman of the

---

[1] Coming to AMC at its inception, Mr. Chapin had moved from assistant treasurer to treasurer and then to executive vice president of the Automotive Division. He had previously worked since 1938 in production and engineering at the predecessor Hudson Motor Company, of which his father had been a founder and a long-term president.

board, and soon he was instrumental in bringing about the appointment of Mr. Chapin, in whose favor he soon resigned.[2]

New leadership, however, proved unable to reverse the tide during the remainder of fiscal 1967. Sales showed dollar volume off 42% from the all-time high of 1963, and earnings showed a net loss of slightly less than $76 million after including a $9 million charge due to discontinued operations; thus, the total operating loss was about $67 million. Market penetration, too, continued to fall (Exhibits 3 and 4).

Then, as columnists again began writing obituaries for the company, AMC began a four-year recovery. By the end of 1971 the company had refinanced its debt, introduced five new cars, checked a decline in unit sales, consummated a major acquisition, and, with the exception of fiscal 1970 when acquisition and strike-related losses topped $56 million, had made a small operating profit every year.

This case describes in a broad manner the course of strategic happenings at AMC as they evolved over the period 1962–1972. It begins where *American Motors Corporation I* leaves off, touches on the disastrous events of the mid-1960s, focuses briefly on the short-run survival actions taken by management in 1967, and then considers the strategic steps taken during 1968–1970 with the aim of ensuring a profitable future for the corporation. The case then shifts to a more detailed description of the situation as it stood in 1971. In particular, it considers the automotive market in the early 1970s, the status of the industry and competition at that time, and the place of American Motors in that context. The case concludes with a brief discussion of some of the major alternative courses of action open for AMC as the company moved into the 1970s.

HISTORY

"Campaign opportunity": "Out Detroiting Detroit" (1962–1966)

> He had brought a large map representing the sea,
> Without the least vestige of land:
> And the crew were much pleased when they found it to be
> A map they could all understand. [Lewis Carroll in *The Hunting of the Snark. Fit the Second.*]

On November 30, 1962, Mr. Roy Abernathy had been appointed President and chief executive of American Motors. For several months previous to his official elevation he had been at the helm, relieving the former President, George Romney, who had been successful in campaigning for the governorship of Michigan. The optimism and heady enthusiasm which characterized the early years of the Abernathy administration are reflected in this excerpt from the 1962 *Annual Report:*

---

[2] Late in 1971, Mr. Evans was still on the board and headed the finance committee. By April, when he sold a block of 48,500 shares, his holdings had been reduced to 10,000 shares. This action left Mr. Chapin, with 25,180 shares, the largest individual stockholder. On announcing his sale, Mr. Evans said that it should not be regarded as indicating his view of AMC's future.

Without borrowing, and in fact, while paying off a $89,600,000 debt, we have put $161,000,000 into plant modernization and expansion during the past few years and paid our stockholders $71,600,000 since the resumption of divided payments in January 1959.

Our 1962 net earnings represent 15.2% on stockholder investment. Profit margins were improved through higher volumes and greater operating economies in 1962. . . .

The strengthening of our engineering and research organizations has become a vital part of our program to build for the future. Larger expenditures for forward planning than ever before were authorized in the 1962 fiscal year.[3]

This optimism appeared warranted by results in model year 1963 (see Exhibit 3).[4] However, as sales began to slacken late in the year, restyling was ordered for 1964, and major changes were announced for the 1965 model year. These were explained to stockholders as follows:

To some extent buyers continue to identify Rambler primarily with conservative design and economy in a period of increased customer interest in extra options, luxury features and higher performance. Rambler has been moving with this trend and the lag in identity should be amply corrected by the 1965 models, which represent the most sweeping changes in our history. While maintaining the basic virtues that established Rambler popularity, all three Rambler lines are now dramatically in the three divisions of the most active segment of the automobile market.[5]

Unfortunately, the "lag in identity" persisted. Profits fell substantially in 1965, then gave way to losses. Unit sales plummeted in 1964, while market share, too, took a steep dip. Mr. Luneburg, in looking back over what he called the company's "Cinderella period" and the "rude awakening" that followed, offered this analysis of AMC's decline:

There are various reasons why this happened; it is not simply that the Big 3 got into the compact field and provided their usual tough competition.

In fact, with the benefit of hindsight, it can be seen that American Motors in large measure brought the fall upon itself, that there were no immutable business laws which foredoomed the company because of its smaller size.

Competition was a factor, of course. It always is. The introduction in 1961 and 1962 of models like the Buick Special, Pontiac Tempest, Oldsmobile F-85, Dodge Lancer (later the Dart), Ford Fairlane and Chevy II was bound to cost American Motors some share of market.

Yet, the company compounded the effects of this competition by failing to broaden its horizons in order to serve changing buyer requirements. The Rambler had won a large following. It was lost when the strict economy theme began to lose effectiveness in the market place and the company had no alternatives to offer.

The increasing popularity of hardtop models was the first sign of

---

[3] AMC *Annual Report,* 1962, p. 10.

[4] The industry model year ends August 30th, and AMC's fiscal year, September 30th. Hence fiscal and model years roughly correspond, both ending some three months ahead of the calendar year.

[5] AMC *Annual Report,* 1964, p. 3.

change. The new market opportunity was to be the lower priced sporty car.

The opportunity was first exploited—and with a bang—by Ford and the Mustang.

GM and Chrysler also missed the boat on this but American Motors was the last to respond—and the effect of this delay was devastating.

The company had planned all-new Rebels and Ambassadors for 1967 on the competitive four-year cycle of all-new sheet metal; unwilling to forego this change on models representing 70 per cent of volume at that time, and unable to simultaneously finance a new sporty car, the company elected to postpone a sporty car entry until 1968. By then, the damage had been done.

Non-competitive purchasing costs were another part of the Achilles' heel. These costs require careful attention when you are considerably less integrated than competition, as is true with American Motors. In the early 1960s, the company was taking a severe beating in this respect.

As a result, by 1964, the company was being bled to death by excessive costs, even though it was still in the black.

To illustrate just what this meant, the 1960 net earnings of $48 million would have been nearly double that if the company had been meeting levels of manufacturing and purchasing efficiency we achieved after 1967.

[However] . . . I want to emphasize one important plus factor which emerged from the ashes of the mid-sixties. A heavy capital expenditure program during these years had given the company highly modern plant facilities, particularly for manufacture of engines and axles.

In January 1967 when Roy Chapin and I were given top management responsibility, this was a valuable, tangible asset on which we could build.

Of course, a lot of people in and out of the auto industry said there wasn't anything worth building on. American Motors was being written off once and for all.[6]

Newsweek exemplified the gloomy predictions widely made by the press when it identified the problems inherited by AMC's new leadership as follows:

> . . . a flabby dispirited management, a product solid enough, but styled with about as much flair as corrective shoes, and a public image that melted down to one unshakable label: loser. [Said Mr. Chapin] "We were driving with one foot on the accelerator and one foot on the brake. We didn't know where the hell we were."[7]

"Campaign survival" revisited (1967)

> "Take some more tea," the March Hare said to Alice, very earnestly.
> "I've had nothing yet," Alice replied in an offended tone: "so I can't take more."
> "You mean you can't take *less,* said the Hatter: "it's very easy to

---

[6] W. V. Luneburg, unpublished speech presented to the Harvard Business School Club of Milwaukee, April 30, 1970.

[7] "The Turnaround at AMC," *Newsweek,* February 12, 1968, p. 80.

take *more* than nothing." [Lewis Carroll in *Alice's Adventures in Wonderland.*]

Mr. Chapin set the tone for the new administration before the stockholders in early 1967:

> We plan to direct ourselves more specifically to those areas of the market where we can be fully effective. We will use our resources where they count. We are not going to attempt to be all things to all people, but to concentrate on those areas of consumer needs we can meet better than anyone else.
>
> We believe the "shotgun" approach to the general market is not for us, but instead we should take a rifle approach to specific segments of it. The spectacular success of the Rambler was largely due to an attack on a single unfulfilled part of the market.
>
> Today we intend to pick up the rifle again, although not in pursuit of one quarry but several, and provide a new freedom of choice.[8]

Mr. Luneburg, chief operating officer, was the one to whom Mr. Chapin handed the rifle—and the axe; Mr. Luneburg described the actions taken as follows:

> . . . We knew what the problems were—immediate and longer range. We weren't ready to throw in the towel by any means. We felt that the foundation for a successful, profitable future was there, and that if a smaller company was fleet afoot and smart enough to place its bets selectively, then it could be a growing, competitive member in an industry of giants.
>
> The inherent economic disadvantages of scale could be counterbalanced by advantages that a smaller company can have in reaching decisions quickly, in mobility of action and in freedom from some burdensome administrative expenses.
>
> There were problems early in 1967 which demanded immediate attention, and which accounted for much of our time for several months. Nevertheless, we began planning beyond them, establishing objectives, programs and timetables through 1972. Whatever happened in the short run, we had to prove ourselves in the market place in the long run.
>
> Of the immediate problems, five were paramount.
>
> 1. The company was virtually out of cash and an immediate supplemental bank loan of $20 million was essential—to be negotiated with a disconsolate banking group that in February 1966, had already anteed up a $25 million supplement to their basic credit line of $50 million. The new $20 million supplement was negotiated within two weeks. This $20 million raised the total loan to $95 million, a top-heavy indebtedness. Therefore, as the "quid pro quo" for obtaining these additional funds, it was necessary to sell Redisco, our finance subsidiary. This was a profitable, independent operation, engaged in wholesale financing for white goods, radio and TV, musical instruments, boats, etc. However, because it performed virtually no auto sales financing, its sale in May 1967, had little effect on American Motors' basic business.
>
> 2. Car inventories—company-owned and dealer-owned—had reached

[8] *Report to the Stockholders of American Motors Corporation at the Annual Meeting,* February 1, 1967, pp. 4, 5.

unmanageable levels. The solution to this glut took five months—it could only be accomplished by an intermittent series of plant shutdowns beginning in January 1967.

3. Sales of the Rambler American series had stagnated and inventories were burdensome. A dramatic merchandising move was concocted post-haste and implemented in February. This consisted of dropping the price tag on the American to a position midway between the VW and the competitive smaller U.S. compacts. This was accomplished through an actual price cut to the dealers and by also trimming the dealer discount from 21% to 17%. The move was successful from the outset, and by April the American was in short supply.

4. Administrative and commercial expense levels were too high in relation to the sagging sales volume. In February, a vigorous cost reduction program was initiated in this area that trimmed $15 million in cost on an annualized basis.

Manufacturing and purchasing costs were also trimmed, but much had already been accomplished in these areas previously. We were reasonably competitive on materials; cost and manufacturing efficiency was beginning to approach the most effective levels in the industry.

5. Perhaps most importantly, our public image had deteriorated— the press was pessimistic, the financial community had by and large written us off, and there was a widespread doubt among at least the sophisticated sectors of the car buying public as to the continuity of the company. We held numerous formal and informal meetings with the press, bankers, investment firms, government officials, etc. The response was gratifying. The press became more friendly and encouraging, the financial community adopted a more positive attitude, and for the first time in years investment funds began buying American Motors stock and in important quantities. While the seriousness of the company's continuing problems was recognized in all quarters, the external world began to accord us a good chance to put our house in order.

With the immediate fires put out, we could put in place the pieces of a corporate growth plan—a definition of a way of life in the auto industry for American Motors.

We had the mistakes of the past to guide us, combined with a vision of the future.

We didn't use rose-colored glasses. We didn't foresee a Cinderella story for the company—a dramatic rise from the brink of disaster. We based our plan on the reality of moving ahead in carefully planned increments, with the first steps building a foundation for succeeding steps. We felt that our reason for being, which would enable us not just to survive but to grow, lay in bringing a different and refreshing approach to the auto market—in picking our spots and then being innovative and aggressive.

We had established the internal organization and operating controls necessary to enable us to operate profitably at volume we could reasonably hope to achieve in the short-run. We had plugged the dike to stop the flow of heavy losses.

As a result, between 1967 and 1968, we achieved a turnaround of more than $70 million in our automotive operations and moved into the black with net earnings of $4.8 million. We followed this up with another profitable year in 1969. Volume was up in both of these years from the low point of 237,000 units in 1967, but not dramatically. At cost levels anywhere near what they had been, we could not have realized a profit.[9]

"The New American Motors" (1968–1970)

"A slow sort of a country," said the Queen. "Now here, you see, it takes all the running you can do, to keep in the same place. If you want to get somewhere else, you must run at least twice as fast as that!" [Lewis Carroll in *Through the Looking-glass and What Alice Found There*]

As indicated by Mr. Luneburg, once the "immediate fires" were put out, AMC sought to find "a way of life" in the auto industry that would lead not just to survival but to growth. Somewhat more specifically, Mr. Luneburg identified a need for "bringing a refreshing approach to the market" and "picking our spots" in which to compete. What these moves could and would involve in practice emerged over the next few years as AMC's new leadership revised promotion, tinkered with cars already in the pipeline, and shaped its "new generation" of cars. In addition, AMC's leadership saw and seized a chance to supplement these pre-planned moves by an acquisition late in 1969, when Kaiser Industries, Inc., decided that it wanted to sell its remaining foothold in the auto business, namely, Kaiser Jeep.

Changing the approach to the market. To implement a changed marketing approach, a concerted effort was mounted to move AMC away from Mr. Abernathy's emphasis on size and luxury and to establish a "youthful image" for the company. Thus the sporty new Javelin car, the design of which had been ordered by Chairman Evans in 1966, was rushed to market in time for the 1968 model year. Mary Wells and her Wells, Rich, Greene advertising agency were charged with promoting the car with a series of highly unorthodox advertisements aimed at capturing the imagination of "young minded" buyers. By the end of the 1968 model year, Javelin had boosted AMC sales by 56,000 units and was reaching a buyer some 15 years younger than the average 1967 buyer.

In addition AMC entered the automobile racing field with the Javelin, and in the spring of 1968 brought out a new car more precisely adapted to this purpose. This was the AMX, which was billed as the first American sports car with prices starting under $3,300. A high-powered, two-seater fastback that had been raced already while still in the prototype stage, the AMX aimed at maintaining the sporty momentum generated by the Javelin. It was not as well received, however, and was discontinued after two years.

As a final symbol of the break with the past, the Rambler name was dropped in favor of American Motors. Thus, the compact Rambler American became simply the American. Likewise, the Rambler Ambassador, the luxury intermediate, became the Ambassador. The intermediate Rambler Rebel was renamed Matador.

Changing the product line. Besides a new approach to the market that involved promotion and product adaptation, AMC undertook a product

---

[9] Luneburg, unpublished speech, April 30, 1970.

development program that, starting in model year 1970, would "change the product line from one end to the other" by 1972. Promising the press "a new car every six months," AMC set its sights on a sales target of 500,000 units by 1975.

The initial outcome of this new product program was an all-new compact called the Hornet. Introduced in the fall of 1969 on the heels of Ford's similarly sized Maverick, this was the first of AMC's "new generation of cars," and replaced the American. Named for its Hudson rather than its Nash (Rambler) progenitors, the Hornet was billed as "the little rich car" because of the variety of versions and options it offered while still selling in the "import" range of $2,000. Introduction of the Hornet was marred by two unforeseen developments, however. First, Ford set the price of Maverick lower than had been expected; to compete, AMC had to set the Hornet price lower than had been planned. Second, in mid-October, the crucial peak of the new model year, AMC was struck by the UAW. The strike exceeded five weeks, and during that time Hornet lost much unrecoverable momentum. AMC has estimated the costs stemming from that strike at $23 million and 36,000 vehicles.

Although Hornet cost $45 million to develop (Ford's Maverick cost $71 million), it provided AMC with "derivative capability" for up to six new cars. Derivative capability referred to the fact that the tooling was designed with considerable flexibility so that very different bodies could be produced without major capital expenditure.

The first of these derived cars, christened the Gremlin, was a shortened version of the Hornet, and cost only $6 million to tool. More important, the Gremlin achieved the distinction of being the first U.S. car in the "subcompact" size class. This class, in turn, had one key objective—namely, to stem the tide of foreign imports, which all domestic makers agreed was the greatest of their common problems. Introduced in March 1970, six months before Ford's subcompact Pinto and GM's Vega, the Gremlin was snapped up by minicar buyers, but still did not achieve the volume expected of it in light of its exclusive position. AMC's marketing vice president felt that "AMC 'blew' its opportunity because it didn't get its own dealers to improve their facilities and increase their marketing efforts in exchange for their share of the new 'hot' merchandise."[10]

The third car in the Hornet series was the Sportabout. Introduced in the fall of 1970, it was designed to fill the so-called "small-wagon gap" that had existed since the Hornet replaced the American in 1969. Industry observers attributed this deficiency to a lack of cash and management time needed to pursue more than one design simultaneously. (Exhibit 6 is a Wells, Rich, Greene advertisement designed to convey the thrust of the company's new product policy.)

Acquiring Kaiser Jeep.   A third major move toward rebuilding AMC came in November 1969, when AMC took advantage of an opportunity to acquire Kaiser Jeep Corporation. In a 1970 interview, Mr. Chapin ex-

---

[10] Lawrence G. O'Donnell in *The Wall Street Journal,* July 9, 1971.

plained how AMC raised the money for the purchase and what the acquisition meant to AMC:

> I'll admit that part of these funds came from the liquidation of assets. We sold Kelvinator [appliance division], giving us the finances and the organizational capability to take on Kaiser Jeep. But this vehicle company will be a hell of a lot more important to us.
>
> As you may realize, we've decided to concentrate on the transportation industry—almost everything from roller skates to air-planes. Broadly speaking, we're interested in big-ticket consumer durables. We've looked at snowmobiles, all-terrain vehicles, motorcycles, farm equipment, garden tractors, etc.[11]

The Jeep, a car of World War II fame, had been originated by Willys-Overland, a company founded in 1903 and already 50 years old when purchased by the Henry J. Kaiser interests. A colorful "tycoon" in his own right, Kaiser had amassed a vast cement and shipbuilding empire during the war. Afterwards, having added steel, chemicals, and primary aluminum production to his stable of industries, he was ready to try automobiles. Although sales flourished during the era of pent-up demand, they plummeted thereafter. Tombstones added to the automotive graveyard by Kaiser are inscribed with such names as Willys, Kaiser-Frazer, Jeepster, the Henry J., and Allstate (marketed by Sears). Henry J. Kaiser's son and successor Edgar, carried the surviving line of Jeeps and utility vehicles overseas, where one of the company's main affiliates in joint-venturing these foreign moves was AMC. Thus began a 10-year relationship that led up to the 1969 acquisition. Furthermore, Kaiser Industries was rumored to be anxious to dispose of its automotive operations in order to concentrate on other activities that were beginning to show signs of sagging sales and earnings.

Terms of the sale were $10 million in cash, $9.5 million in 8½% five-year notes, and 5.5 million shares of AMC common. Since the transaction was accomplished by the "purchase method," AMC assumed all the assets and all the liabilities of Kaiser Jeep, including $45 million in working capital. Issuance of the stock boosted the number of AMC shares outstanding to over 25 million and gave Kaiser Industries 22% of AMC's common stock. In addition, two Kaiser representatives were given seats on the AMC board.

In April 1970, Mr. Luneburg outlined the plans underway to assimilate Jeep and improve its profitability:

> First, there are some basic truths about the job of putting two large organizations together: (1) it is costly; (2) it takes time; (3) it enables the new owner to do some things the former owner couldn't do or wasn't interested in doing. Of course, the changes also generate some inevitable unsettling influences.
>
> We see the opportunity for substantial cost reductions and for economies of scale, in manufacturing, purchasing, administrative costs, and other areas. The results of these actions will begin to appear

[11] Joseph M. Callahan, "The Face of Management at AMC," *Automotive Industries,* April 1, 1970, p. 42.

this year [1970]—but most of the resulting profit improvements will be realized next year and the following year.

In addition to examining sales costs and conducting a thorough study of the dealer organizations, market by market, we are looking closely at the Jeep product line.

Jeep commercial products are sound, well-known and respected; but there is a clear need to do some leading, innovating and more aggressive merchandising in order to take advantage of these strengths, and to meet the intense competition in the fast-growing recreational vehicle market. We are putting together a completely new product planning organization, which has begun to assess both present Jeep products and possibilities for product lines that do not exist today.

We believe we have some ideas and skills in the product area that can be applied effectively in the recreational vehicle field. Now we have a chance to prove it. We will bring to Jeep products the same kind of innovative product development we have underway in passenger cars.

The same is true in distribution. Improvements here are a key element for Jeep as they are for American Motors. We are now developing plans for strengthening and upgrading Jeep dealerships.

We believe Jeep's government business should hold up well for some time. It consists principally of 2½ and 5 ton trucks for the military. The backlog of contracts is about $500 million, after reductions reflecting lower defense requirements. Thus, we aren't in a position where we have to expect cancellations, although there could be some, of course.

We are operating Jeep's government business as a separate division of the corporation. We have designated it the General Products Division, reflecting our objective to expand into non-governmental areas.

I have concentrated on the domestic market in these remarks because it is domestically where we must prove ourselves. However, our international operations are, to say the least, a significant part of the picture.

Jeep will accelerate our progress overseas. We are well positioned in a number of markets with considerable potential. With the broader product line, we are better equipped to take advantage of opportunities which arise.

American Motors products are manufactured or assembled in 12 nations outside the U.S. and we are represented by distributors and dealers in 111 foreign countries. To this Jeep adds assembly and manufacturing facilities in 30 nations.

The close cooperation which has existed between Jeep and American Motors in international markets for a number of years is an obvious advantage in putting the organizations together.[12]

Mr. Luneburg's assessment of the situation contrasted sharply with that of a *Dun's* writer who commented as follows:

[AMC] got a company that has been on the skids since 1964. A decade ago, Jeep had the domestic 4-wheel-drive vehicle market all to itself. But since then, International Harvester, Ford and General Motors have entered the field and Jeep's share has dwindled to 28%.[13] Even

---

[12] Luneburg, unpublished speech, April 30, 1970.

[13] The figure cited here is larger than the 20% claimed in AMC's *Annual Report* for 1970, p. 4.

worse, the prospectus issued by Kaiser Industries at the time of the merger stated: "Kaiser Jeep's management believes that its commercial business [37% of sales] has not been profitable since 1964."

No line in a prospectus was ever truer. In the first nine months of 1969, Jeep's commercial business incurred a pretax loss of $6.4 million. And the margins on Jeep's business for the military, which had kept the company out of the red in the past, became so thin that in the first quarter of 1970 the newly acquired company added $1.3 million to American's pretax loss of $14 million. Color Roy Chapin's face red.

Asked why he was willing to spend so much money for another company also knee-deep in trouble, Chapin rips off the answer: "We can't remain just a little carmaker. We're in the transportation business, and it's about time we took advantage of our accumulated knowledge."

What Chapin means is that with only 3% of the domestic auto market, American is on a weak footing when it has to fight against its giant competitors. By branching into recreational vehicles, trucks and military vehicles, Chapin believes that American will have a cushion to soften the impact of getting squeezed by General Motors, Chrysler and Ford.

But was Jeep the right move? Chapin thinks he can pull it off. "Sure, Jeep gives us only an entry into the recreation market, and just a small toehold in the truck market," he admits. "But we have a pretty good understanding of these areas, enough so we can put two and two together and get five. This not only means we'll have to manage Jeep's business better, but we'll also have to run some aspects of our own business better."

To achieve his goal of making Jeep profitable, Chapin eventually plans to come up with some new Jeep products. As a partial explanation for its recent poor showing, he points to the fact that Jeep has not introduced a new vehicle since 1967, nor did it attempt to sell commercially the trucks it now makes for the U.S. Post Office.

However, for the immediate future, Chapin hopes he can turn Jeep into a more profitable company by trimming costs to the bone, just as he did when he first took control of American. "Jeep's added volume gives us more leverage in dealing with suppliers," he says. "And there are many overlapping functions that can be combined into one slightly larger operation. That's a savings of millions of dollars a year."

Granted Chapin can save a buck here and a buck there by eliminating such things as corporate planes (Jeep had to get rid of its corporate jet) and combining administrative functions. The real question, however, is whether he can afford to spend money on new jeeps and on the development of a dealer network tuned to the truck and recreational markets.[14]

Retrospective, 1967–1970. By the start of fiscal 1971, management had taken major steps to reposition AMC in the marketplace and restore it to health. Except for strike-torn 1970, operations had turned the profit corner, and even 1970 had been a success in terms of dollar volume, with the company rejoining The Billion Dollar Club for the first year since 1964. Messrs. Chapin and Luneburg sought to put these results in perspective in reviewing the then current picture for the press:

[14] "Chapin's Folly?" *Dun's Review,* May 1970, p. 63.

The setbacks of 1970 did not alter the objectives toward which our growth program is directed and they should not be allowed to obscure the fact that we completed two major steps in our growth plan during the year—the acquisition of Jeep Corporation and the bringing to market of an entirely new passenger car line incorporating the most expensive product changes in the company's history.

We expect to resume in fiscal 1971 the growth pattern established in 1968 and 1969. The company is currently operating profitably and we anticipate reporting a profit for the first quarter, ending Dec. 31.

In combination with an intensified marketing effort, we have reduced operating cost in a number of areas not essential to short-term growth. In addition, the industry price structure in 1971 reflects more realistically the kind of cost pressure everyone has been facing.[15]

THE INDUSTRY IN 1971

The automotive market

The market in which American Motors competed in 1971 was vastly different from what it had been 10 years earlier. New trends included changing buyer motives, fewer basic style changes but more proliferation of models, a small-car boom, increased government regulation, rising costs, continued domestic competition, and more foreign inroads on the U.S. market.

Buyer motives. Reviewing auto prospects in 1971, *Fortune* emphasized the decline of the car as a status symbol; the rising number of two-car families in which one car was simply a convenience, although the other might be bought to fill some specialized need; the consequent demand for a larger variety of cheaper models; and the start of such adverse trends as the public's association of cars with pollution and of Detroit-made cars with costly bills for repairs.[16] One industry executive was reported as being "remarkably candid about the distressing results of a recently completed study of people that he describes as on 'the leading edge of opinion'—younger, better educated than the norm, with higher-status jobs and above-average incomes.

" 'There was a significant negative attitude—a pro-foreign, anti-Detroit syndrome,' he says. 'Mercedes was the ultimate, although these people might never have had one. People believed that we make too many changes for change's sake—nonfunctional changes. There was a credibility gap. People don't believe our advertising. It has almost done more harm than good.' "[17]

Model proliferation. The proliferation of models in the 1960s could be attributed to the increasing importance attached by auto makers to studies that pointed out the potential segmentation in the automotive market. Whereas the late 1950s had witnessed only the most elementary

---

[15] *The Wall Street Journal,* November 17, 1970.

[16] Dan Cordtz, "Autos: A Dangerous Stretch Ahead," *Fortune,* April 1971, p. 67 ff. (This *Fortune* summary acknowledged its indebtedness to a recent study titled *Aspirations and Affluence* by Dr. George Katonah of the University of Michigan Survey Research Center.)

[17] Ibid., p. 71.

segmentation, primarily by price, the 1970s were to see the market divided up on a variety of dimensions. For example, the low-price buyer in the 1950s simply made his choice from among Chevrolet, Ford, or Plymouth; by 1970 such a buyer had not only to select among domestic vs. foreign makes; he had further to decide what size of car he wanted; whether it would be for sporty, family, or recreational use; what degree of economy he preferred; and, finally, what choice he would make from among a host of models and options. In fact, Exhibit 5 shows 45 different lines of domestic cars for 1970, more than double the number of a decade before. Furthermore, within each line, models had proliferated to the point where this number peaked at 375 in 1970:

NUMBER OF DOMESTIC AUTO MODELS

Year	AMC	Chrysler	Ford	GM	Total
1970	23	123	88	141	375
1971	21	101	85	134	341
1972	15	81	75	125	296

Source: *Automotive News* (1971 Almanac Issue), p. 64, and Standard & Poor's *Trade and Securities, Industry Surveys*, "Autos—Auto Parts, Current Analysis," December 9, 1971, p. A123.

Small-car boom. In the 1960s, consumer taste in cars by size and price class underwent a series of upheavals (Exhibit 7A). Thus, in 1961 small cars of subcompact size or less peaked at the expense of cars in the standard-and-up categories, only to be outpaced in turn by two "sportier" classes of cars—namely, "specialties" and "intermediates." By 1968, however, these classes had reached their highest penetration, while small cars were embarked on a second spurt of growth. Since about half of these small cars were imports, all U.S. makers except Chrysler opted to fight this foreign "threat" by producing minicars of their own. By 1971, it was still too early to tell what the long-term impact of this move would be, but at least one result was clear: when U.S. small cars were added to imports, the total came to more than one-third of the market without even counting small "specialty" cars:

SALES BREAKDOWN OF CARS BY SIZE-CLASS
(percent)

Year	Sub-compacts	Compacts	Imports	Small Car Total	Special-ties	Inter-mediates	Standards
1970	1.65	13.94	14.73	30.32	10.84	20.94	37.96
1971	7.42	12.07	15.15	34.64	8.65	18.07	38.72

Note: Col. 4 = Cols. 1–3 combined; specialties include small and more luxurious subtypes; standards include standard, medium, and luxury cars.
Source: *Automotive Industries*, February 21, 1972, p. 1.

Regulation. With the rise of popular interest in consumerism and ecology, the automotive industry of the 1970s was facing new and stringent regulation to assure both cleaner and safer cars. Thus, the Clean Air Act of 1970 demanded that automotive emissions of carbon

monoxide and hydrocarbons be reduced 90% below their 1970 levels by
the 1975 model year. To help defray the costs, the federal government
had appropriated almost $100 million to experiment with new power
sources: e.g., the German Wankel rotary engine (on which GM had
spent $50 million to secure production rights), the gas-turbine engine,
the steam engine, and battery-powered cars. According to industry
sources, however, none of these devices could be developed to meet the
target date in time. A more hopeful approach was the improvement of
the present combustion engine, but this too was seen as doubtful. In
the first quarter of 1972, members of the U.S. auto industry were continuing a concerted campaign to get the emissions target modified.

The industry and its regulators were similarly locked in combat over
safety requirements. At issue here was the role of the so-called "passive
restraint," i.e., one that would operate independently of human action
or inaction. Government was demanding passive restraints to protect
car occupants from serious injury in a head-on collision at 30 mph by
1973, and at even higher speeds thereafter. To achieve the first objective, car ignition might be made dependent on the previous locking of
the seat belt, and this approach was being pushed by Ford. To achieve
the second objective, however, the only potential device in prospect was
the highly controversial air-bag. According to the industry, the air-bag
was far from perfected and could be dangerous in and of itself. Industry critics in contrast argued that safety and anti-pollution development was not being pushed as fast as possible.

Besides health and safety legislation, there was also pressure for
legislation setting standards on auto-damage resistance and repair-
ability. The federal agency charged with passenger safety had begun
to extend its mandate to cover damage to the vehicle itself, and some
legislation applying to bumpers had been proposed in Congress. With
auto-damage claims rising rapidly, the insurance industry was pressing
hard on this point.

Cost escalation.   One impact of all these new regulations would
clearly be higher costs of manufacture. In April 1971, AMC's Chapin
told *Fortune* that regulations already in sight could add $600 to the
price of any car.[18] This would be regardless of size, make, etc. Thus,
safety and clean-up costs, plus an annual inflation factor widely estimated at about 5%, spelled a steady rise in car costs.

With the public expected to resist price escalation, Detroit was looking for places to squeeze money out of its total expenses. One obvious
way was to cut what *Fortune* called the "vast" outlays for "wheels-up"
and/or annual restyling.[19] This goal might be accomplished either by
lengthening the basic body cycle or by making the changes themselves
less striking. By 1971, at least the first approach was being followed.
Thus, the two-year cycle of basic model changes started by GM in the

---

[18] Cordtz, ibid., p. 135.

[19] Ibid., p. 146. In 1970, for example, the Big Three reportedly spent $1,874 mil-
lion for the special "tools, dies, jigs, and fixtures" required to tool up for new models. See Standard & Poor's *Trade and Securities: Industry Surveys,* "Autos—Auto
Parts, Basic Analysis," July 15, 1971, p. A146.

1950s was definitely a thing of the past, and even the more recent three-year cycle was to be replaced by cycles of four, five, or even six years. In particular, makers had announced that they would keep their newly introduced small cars unchanged in style for as long as five years.[20] In line with this trend, the year just coming up—1972—would see very few basic changes since these would be limited to full-size Chryslers and intermediate and luxury Fords.[21]

Industry analysts pointed out that risks might be involved in lengthening the styling cycle, provided past assumptions held true that "newness" helped to generate basic demand. In answer, some executives argued that proliferation of models was an alternative way of meeting this need and of filling dealer showrooms with plenty of variety.[22]

Competition.   If regulation posed a relatively new problem for the auto industry, competition posed an old one. Knocking out old and new entrants alike, it had pared domestic contenders to four, all at least in the billion dollar size class.[23] Undisputed leader of the group was GM with sales of $28 billion in 1971 and a market penetration normally around 52%. Ford, Chrysler, and AMC trailed GM, but kept the same relative order in spite of fluctuations in their yearly market shares that might be substantial, especially in the case of third-ranked Chrysler. More volatile than over-all standings were market shares and even rankings for the divisional profit centers that produced and/or sold the three-to-five makes of cars marketed by each of the Big Three. In the volume sweepstakes, sales success was important to all, since either an upswing or a downswing in production was accompanied by a much bigger swing in profits. This relationship, though often complicated by other factors, shows up in the following industry figures:

CHANGES IN YEAR-TO-YEAR PRODUCTION AND PROFITS
FOR PASSENGER CARS
(percent)

Change	1966/1965	1967/1966	1968/1967	1969/1968	1970/1969
Production	− 8	−14	+19	− 6	−20.3
Profit	−15	−23	+33	−11	−58.1*

* Reflects strike losses at General Motors.
Source: Standard & Poor's *Trade and Securities: Industry Surveys*, "Autos-Auto Parts, Basic Analysis," July 15, 1971, p. A147.

During and after the later 1960s, all makers suffered some erosion of their margins as the market moved toward smaller cars with lower per unit dollar profit and lower associated demand for high-margin

---

[20] Ibid., and *Business Week,* June 12, 1971, p. 27.

[21] Standard & Poor's, *Trade and Securities: Industry Surveys,* "Current Analysis," December 9, 1971, p. A123.

[22] Cordtz, "Autos: A Dangerous Stretch Ahead."

[23] In spite of its absolute size, AMC's relative size led it to be classified as a "Small Business" in 1966, thus making the company eligible for special consideration in the sale of government fleets.

optional equipment (Exhibit 7B). This profit erosion was in addition to such downswings as might be caused by a poor year for sales or by strikes. Major strikes over contract terms typically hit the larger companies in turn, and could be both lengthy and expensive. For example, G.M. lost over $200 million in the last half of 1970 when the United Auto Workers waged a "pattern-setting" 10-week strike against it. Even so, G.M. did not have an unprofitable year, and had not had one since World War II. Over the same period, Ford dipped into the red once; Chrysler twice; and AMC seven times since its founding in 1954.

As indicated by Exhibit 8 on selected financial and other comparative industry data, 1970 was a particularly difficult year. Besides the strike setback to GM, both Chrysler and AMC suffered losses, with AMC also hurt by a strike and Chrysler by a mix of factors, including a failure to follow market trends:

> Chrysler's problems became serious in early 1969 when it geared production to the large-model automobile when demand was swinging to smaller cars. Shriveling overall car demand, high interest costs and an overseas loss of $7.6 million brought the company's already low-profitability problems to a head in 1970.[24]

Besides competing with one another, the four U.S. producers all had at least some makes and lines of car that competed directly with foreign imports. By 1971, the steady rise in these had become not only an economic but also a political issue, and the U.S. government took several major steps to give more protection to the domestic market: (1) a three-phase war against inflation was begun on August 19, with Phase No. 1 being a three-month temporary price and wage freeze; (2) the tariff on imported cars was temporarily raised from 3.5% to 10%; (3) when the tariff was readjusted down again, the dollar was devalued at the same time by being allowed to float—a move expected to make imports more expensive. Besides these steps, which would help domestic competitors only, the government moved to help sales for the whole car market by repealing the federal excise tax (7% of wholesale, or about 5% of retail).[25]

However competitive the U.S. auto industry might seem to some or all of its domestic members, the relative strength of GM had not passed unnoted by social critics. Over a long span of years, 18 antitrust actions had been brought against it, and in 1970 consumer champion Ralph Nader was campaigning for a ceiling on market shares. Against this backdrop, G.M. was moving to forestall forced breakup by making it more difficult. Thus, abandoning the widely copied structure which past managements had helped to pioneer, the company had started in 1968 to centralize assembly for all its cars, with assembly to be followed by production. If and when completed, these moves would make GM's structure more like that of rivals Ford and Chrysler. Instead of being

---

[24] Smith, Barney & Co., Inc., Research Service, "The Automotive Industry," February 8, 1972, p. 8. (Chrysler was the only maker with no domestic minicar of its own. In 1970 and 1971, it sought to compensate for this lack by importing Colts and Crickets from Japan and England.)

[25] "Detroit Gets Its Chance to Shine," *Business Week*, August 21, 1971, p. 66.

almost separate companies, their car divisions were essentially market-ing profit centers.[26]

AMC's POSITION IN 1971

To meet the competition that lay ahead in 1972, AMC would be moving forward from the foundation already laid. As earlier noted, at this point in time management claimed "good progress in developing opportunities available . . . as a result of . . . acquisition," plus a record of "substantial improvements in every major sector of the com-pany's business."[27]

Product/market posture

Product lines. On the issue of the length of its line, as *The Wall Street Journal* pointed out, AMC had some outside critics, to whom its spokesmen offered a "stout defense":

> Many marketing men in Detroit believe that the company is floun-dering in the midst of the current small car boom because it has elected to continue selling many sizes of cars rather than reverting to its successful one-car formula of the late 1950s. . . . "AMC's big mis-take was to toss aside the idea of one car. . . ," says one official of a rival company. "The cost of proliferation has killed them. . . ." But Mr. Chapin stoutly defends AMC's basic multi-car strategy. . . . After careful study AMC's management concluded it couldn't get the mini-mum volume it needs to turn a profit unless it stays in three basic markets—small cars, sporty cars, and intermediates.[28]

Although the model lineup for 1972 would be cut back from 21 to 15, and styling changes (if made at all) would be limited to ornamen-tation and grilles, AMC remained committed to several different lines and sizes of cars. As Mr. Chapin put it, "The basic game plan was to hit the bottom end of the market strong, but to stay with the next biggest segment of it (the intermediates) without any major capital expenditures." Elaborating further on AMC's official reasoning, the *Journal* noted, among other points, that the company expected that some of the customers attracted to the showroom by small cars could be traded up to the larger lines with higher margins.

In pursuit of the above product strategy, AMC was offering a minicar (the Gremlin), a general-purpose small car (the Hornet) including a small wagon (the Hornet Sportabout), a small sporty car (the Javelin), and two intermediates (the Matador and the Ambassador). At the bottom of this line, Gremlin was priced between Ford's Pinto and GM's Vega but was heavier and had a larger engine. At the top of the line, six models of Ambassador competed with several different makes of the Big Three. Ambassador's promotion emphasized the amount of luxury equipment carried as standard—even to air-conditioning. (For ad-

[26] "G.M. Moves to Centralize All Operations," *Automotive News,* September 20, 1971, p. 1 ff.

[27] Company press release and *The Wall Street Journal,* November 18, 1971.

[28] *The Wall Street Journal,* July 9, 1971.

ditional data on AMC's lines and for sales by line, see Exhibits 3, 5, and 9.)

Besides its several lines and models of cars, AMC offered a variety of Jeeps to the recreational and utility vehicle markets. In common with others in the industry, AMC expected this market to boom from its 1970 level of about 140,000 units. In fact, AMC's forecast was for a growth of 600% during the decade of the 1970s.[29] Military and post-office vehicles, also added to the line through the acquisition of Kaiser Jeep, completed the AMC offerings going into 1972.

Price. In pricing its models for 1972 (Exhibit 9), AMC held off until the Big Three had spoken, then said increases would be "competitive." Industry plans were all upset, however, when the Federal Government imposed a three-month price freeze just at model introduction time. Although manufacturers could seek relief if they could show their products had been upgraded, the Big Three started the model year by selling 1972 cars at 1971 prices. About a month into the freeze, however, AMC got a special permit for an increase said to average about 1.0%. After the freeze, when car manufacturers started to apply at varying dates for varying raises, analysts concluded that it might be some time before prices for 1972 became definitely established.[30]

Dealers. In the three years ending 1971, AMC suffered some attrition of its dealers, in line with well-established industry trends that were forcing marginal outlets out of business:

NUMBER OF PASSENGER CAR DEALERS

Year-End	AMC	Chrysler	Ford	GM	Total
1969...............	2,371	6,038	6,864	12,520	27,793
1970...............	2,256	5,688	6,697	12,240	26,881
1971...............	2,025	5,485	6,666	12,125	26,301

Source: *Automotive News* (1971 Almanac Issue), p. 64, and *Automotive News*, January 1, 1972, p. 1.

Of the 2,025 dealers in the AMC group at the end of 1971, most were independent, and most sold only AMC cars, in line with common industry practice. AMC had equity in some of its dealers, however (the book value of which was estimated at about $10–$15 million). More unusual was the number of "intercorporate duals," or dealerships selling AMC cars along with those of some other maker (mostly GM's). Of 680 such outlets in the industry, AMC used 665.

Besides its passenger-car dealer corps, in 1970 AMC also had 1,621 Jeep dealerships to handle its four-wheel drive vehicles. Of these, 389 handled both Jeeps and passenger cars, but most of the other Jeep dealers were too small. In any event, such a combination of lines was still uncommon in the industry.

---

[29] AMC, *A Corporate Profile* (1970).

[30] *The Wall Street Journal,* August 11, August 21, September 24, and November 18, 1971.

Although AMC had no subsidiary engaged in financing either customer car purchases or dealer inventories, some AMC dealers were receiving the latter type of help in 1971 from GM. This program had been started at the time when AMC was rebuilding its strength after the strike which had crippled production just as the 1970 model year was getting under way in 1969.

Seeing distribution as one of their major problems, AMC's leaders had hopes of building up their dealerships in both numbers and strength. In a 1970 speech Mr. Luneburg outlined the company's future plans as follows:

> In order that we can take full advantage of our aggressive product plans, the building of a larger and stronger dealer organization capable of handling volume of 500,000 units a year is of prime importance. Lack of over-all dealer strength has been our biggest weakness—and we have launched a multi-pronged attack on the problem.
>
> Our first objective is to close about 900 open market areas across the nation. Longer range over the next five years, we are aiming at a level of about 3,000 dealerships for our passenger cars—approximately 700 more than the low point reached in 1968.
>
> We now have a full-time dealer development activity, whose assignment is to upgrade existing dealerships and locate and sign new dealer prospects.
>
> The corporate identity program we have underway is closely related to dealer development, since it is designed to bring the corporation and the dealer organization together under one banner. Our objective for this year is to install new signage,[31] utilizing our corporate symbol, at key dealerships throughout the country.[32]

Besides aiming at more and stronger dealers, AMC aimed at improved locations. Unlike its sales, much of its dealer strength was concentrated in rural areas, and urban areas accounted for many of the "open dealerships" that Mr. Luneburg had in mind to fill.

As for AMC's unit sales per dealer, this figure stood at 114 in 1971. Over-all company totals were as follows:

NEW CAR SALES PER DEALER

	AMC	Chrysler	Ford	GM	Average
1969	104	233	332	351	307
1970	109	230	338	268	269
1971	114	240	343	361	320

Source: *Automotive News* (Almanac Issues), 1971, p. 14, and 1972, p. 59.

Warranties. Starting with its 1972 model year, AMC would use as a major sales tool a new warranty program covering all parts except tires.

---

[31] The 1971 *Annual Report* noted that "key dealers who account for about 70 per cent of domestic volume now have the new American Motors identification" (the "A" mark). Nonetheless, in 1971 many dealerships still displayed the old neon "Rambler" signs, even though there had been no Ramblers for several years.

[32] Luneburg, April 30 speech to Harvard Business School Club of Milwaukee.

Called the Buyer Protection Plan, it was described by Mr. Chapin as much the strongest plan currently offered by the industry, and also as "the most significant corporate commitment our company has ever made." The provisions of the plan and Mr. Chapin's explanation of how it would help AMC were summarized as follows by *The Wall Street Journal:*

> The new plan has five elements. The key parts of the program are the expanded guarantee and the promise of the free loan of a car to customers whose cars are being held for repairs overnight. In addition it includes beefed-up quality control at the factory, improved dealer preparation of cars and the establishment of a toll-free customer-complaint hot line to Detroit.
>
> The new AMC guarantee differs from the company's past warranties, officials said, in that it is expanded to cover many parts of the car that traditionally have been excluded from warranty coverage. Such parts include spark plugs, windshield wipers, radios, batteries, brake linings and front-end alignment.
>
> Mr. Chapin said the plan would have "a vast influence on the future of our company," and added, "We're playing for very high stakes." He predicted that "it will result in substantial increases in our sales volume in years to come" and that it would be "a strong weapon in getting new dealers."[33]

In response to questions, company officials declined to estimate either the sales gains or the financial "stakes" involved in the move. Reminded that the industry as a whole had drawn back from the 5-year-or-50,000-mile warranty introduced by Chrysler in 1963 to a uniform 1-year-or-12,000-mile standard, and that consumers reportedly were dissatisfied with warranties and auto repairs in general, "Mr. Chapin conceded that a lack of faith by consumers in past warranty programs would provide a major credibility obstacle in selling the Buyer Protection Plan to the public. 'There have been a lot of unfortunate experiences.' he said."[34]

Promotion. As for other car makers, promotion for AMC was a relatively heavy expense. Since the following figures exclude some media, they understate the actual total:

ADVERTISING EXPENDITURES, SIX MEDIA TOTAL,* 1970, 1971
(dollars in millions)

Year	AMC	Chrysler	Ford	GM
1970				
Company...............	$14.8	$36.6	$59.0	$ 74.2
Dealers................	1.1	9.5	9.4	13.1
1971				
Company...............	14.1	37.1	69.0	101.4
Dealers...............	1.1	12.8	12.9	21.0

* Includes magazines, newspaper supplements, network and spot TV, network radio, and outdoor advertising.
Source: *National Advertising Investments*, 1970 and 1971 Annuals.

---

[33] *The Wall Street Journal,* August 11, 1971.
[34] Ibid.

For 1972, AMC planned a switch from the somewhat "off-beat" advertising themes exemplified by Exhibit 5. Main emphasis was to be placed on the new Buyer Protection Plan outlined in AMC's warranties.

Engineering and research. According to AMC's 1971 *Annual Report,* "Engineering effort in fiscal 1971 was concentrated on meeting consumer requirements for improved quality and reliability." "Based on a rating of AM cars against items that are important to consumers . . . 17 areas of function and design were singled out for improvement" and "more than 100 engineering changes were made in the 1972 passenger car lines." "In support of the Buyer Protection Plan, the resources of design, engineering, manufacturing, marketing, and purchasing were concentrated on eliminating potential product problems." "The number of passenger car models for 1972 was reduced from 21 to 15, thus permitting greater concentration on manufacturing and assembly details."

As for the mandatory engineering effort that would enable AMC to comply with the law on safety and emission controls, AMC's *Annual Report* indicated only that "company engineers devoted considerable . . . time and resources" to this. Meanwhile, AMC had quietly turned to General Motors for help. In both 1970 and 1971 the Justice Department had grudgingly approved a joint GM-AMC pact whereby GM would provide technical assistance on this problem. In commenting on the 1971 appeal for approval, one observer argued that "AMC is, in effect, contending that without GM's help, it won't be able to meet federal anti-smog standards. And, AMC says that if it's thus unable to maintain its competitive position, its 'very survival would be in jeopardy.' "[35]

Manufacturing

Production. In 1971 American Motors' manufacturing policy continued to be aimed at providing facilities which were integrated to the greatest possible extent. Although less integrated than the Big Three, AMC produced all or some of its own forgings, castings, stampings, standard transmissions, engines, bodies, axles, differentials, torque tubes, injection-molded plastic, and trim. This was enough to give AMC a substantial ratio of labor costs to sales, although reportedly not as high as for other U.S. auto makers:

PURCHASES AND LABOR COSTS AS A PERCENT OF SALES, 1970

	AMC	*Chrysler*	*Ford*	*GM*
Purchases/sales	N.A.	63.4	57.3	50.0
Labor costs/sales	22.0	30.0	25.0 (1971)	34.0 (1971)

Source: Standard & Poor's Corporation, *Trade and Securities, Industry Surveys,* "Autos—Auto Parts, Basic Analysis," July 15, 1971, pp. A141, A142, and *The Value Line,* April 14, 1972, pp. 129–133.

---

[35] *The Wall Street Journal,* May 26, 1971, p. 4. (Justice Department approval was necessary because of a 1969 consent decree which forbade cooperative arrangements among car manufacturers.)

Over the five years through 1971, sales per employee almost doubled at AMC, as average employment fell from 23,700 in 1967 to 16,900 in 1969, then rose as a result of the Jeep acquisition to approximately its starting level.

Facilities. Manufacturing locations were varied, as attested by the following table.

Activity	Line	Location
Manufacture, assembly..........	Passenger cars	Brampton, Ont., Kenosha and Milwaukee, Wis.
Manufacture, assembly..........	Jeeps	Toledo, Ohio
Manufacture, assembly..........	General (military) Products	Indianapolis, Mishawaka, and South Bend, Ind.
Manufacturing..................	Parts	Evart, Mich., Evansville, Ind., Sarina and Stratford, Ont.

Source: AMC *Annual Reports.*

The Toledo facility producing Jeeps, as well as AMC's main assembly plant at Kenosha, were characterized as "antiquated," but for Kenosha at least AMC denied the implication that "old" meant "inefficient." Of the other plants, those at South Bend were characterized as modern and efficient.[36] In line with this over-all plant picture, consolidation and streamlining were identified as major production objectives, and several moves were made in 1971 with these goals in mind. Over the three most recent years, relative investment in plant, property, and equipment had moved as follows in the industry:

RELATIVE INVESTMENT IN PLANT, PROPERTY, AND EQUIPMENT*
(dollars in millions)

Year	AMC	Chrysler	Ford	GM
1969.............	$47	$375	$534	$1,044
1970.............	41	174	564	1,134
1971.............	27	114	609	1,013

* Except for AMC, excludes additions for special tools and dies. AMC includes tools and die additions less disposals.
Source: Annual Reports.

Labor relations. While wages rose at an effective compound rate of 6% from 1967 to 1971, in the latter year AMC obtained some concessions from the UAW. Whereas the contract which emerged from the strike late in calendar 1969 was due to expire in 1970, the union agreed to work until a new contract could be reached. Moreover, as signed in April 1971, this new pact would cover four years, or one year longer than normal: while the rest of the industry would renegotiate in 1973,

[36] "AMC: The Rush to Put Strong Points Together," *Automotive News,* April 17, 1972, p. 15, and "AMC Makes Its Size Pay Off," *Iron Age,* September 17, 1970, p. 50 ff.

AMC would do so in 1974. Most important, although AMC would have to meet the current industry level of wages, the company was given a one-year lag on the package of other benefits.[37]

Break-even.   AMC was often asked to indicate its break-even point in units. Executives usually turned aside this question, but early in 1972 Mr. Chapin was quoted as putting it at 260,000 cars. Indicating that his short-term sales goal was 300,000 units, Mr. Chapin added, "Profitability shoots up when you go from where you break the nut." According to the marketing vice president, once the break-even point was passed, AMC "turned a profit of $600 a car."[38]

Finance

As earlier noted, getting finances "under control" was a "major challenge" when Messrs. Chapin and Luneburg took over in January 1967, and AMC "almost didn't know how its next payroll would be met" (Exhibit 1). Financial moves included selling off Redisco, AMC's consumer credit operation, and selling Kelvinator, AMC's subsidiary making white goods. Although resulting in book losses, these successive sales added $28.5 million to working capital in 1967 and provided $45 million for working capital and other purposes in 1968. In addition, AMC initiated steps in 1967 that led to the passage of special tax legislation whereby its tax-loss carryback was extended to five years from the then prevailing legal period. (In return the company agreed to forfeit $27 million of tax-loss carryforward, which would have reduced taxes on future earnings by approximately $14 million.) This arrangement resulted in a special tax credit of $19.2 million in 1968 (see Exhibit 2).

Owing partly to these moves, partly to restored profitability, and partly to the fact that arrangements were already well under way to increase capital by $35 million through the private placement of 20-year notes, the end of calendar 1968 found AMC free of short-term indebtedness to banks, and this condition obtained again at the end of fiscal 1969. In drawing attention to this point, management reminded stockholders that early in troubled 1967, short-term debt had stood at $95 million—or $20 million more than the line of credit with which Messrs. Chapin and Luneburg had started their regime a few months earlier.

Another chapter in AMC's financing began in fiscal 1970, which saw both the acquisition of Jeep and an operating loss of $56.2 million. The impact of Jeep was mixed: it increased the year's loss and committed AMC to a $10 million debt repayable in five equal installments, but it also added $44.7 million to AMC's working capital, and it gave AMC a subsidiary that could obtain short-term loans from banks at a point in time when the parent company found itself unable to borrow under its own $25 million line of credit owing to "restrictive covenants."

Although AMC was able to arrange a new $15 million line of credit early in 1971 (shortly after its former line expired), the terms again

[37] *The Wall Street Journal,* April 14, 1971.
[38] *Automotive News,* op. cit., p. 37.

proved onerous. For example, they included a requirement that AMC delay one of the payments owed on its five-year debt to Kaiser for Jeep. Partly for this reason, AMC allowed the line to lapse from what a spokesman called "benign neglect," after the peak seasonal need. Accordingly, both in 1970 and in 1971, the short-term debt appearing on AMC's year-end balance sheet (Exhibit 2) was debt of the Jeep subsidiary. In 1970 this was Jeep Corporation; in 1971 it was the separate AM General Corporation, formed to handle Jeep's government business. The debt was secured by both receivables and inventory (over $50 million in both years), and the terms were 0.5% above prime in 1970 and 1.0% above in 1971.

Besides affecting AMC's borrowings, restrictive covenants also affected its dividend policies. Under terms of its short-term and/or long-term loans, AMC had paid no dividends since 1966, in contrast with an industry average of 60%–70% of earnings. AMC's stock price record also differed from industry norms (Exhibit 8), with its 1971 high and low being respectively $9 and $5⅞.

Looking forward, AMC pointed out that future profits would be protected by various reserves:

> At September 30, 1971, the Company's financial statements do not reflect possible future tax benefits of approximately $53,000,000, of which $30,000,000 results from loss carryforwards available to offset tax liabilities of future years and $23,000,000 relates to established product warranty and other reserves which are not deductible for tax purposes until payments are made.[39]

Progress with the Jeep acquisition

When Mr. Chapin in November 1971 claimed "good progress" with acquisitions, he was in effect claiming good progress with Jeep. Although Jeep brought with it a 1968 sales level of $477 million, some 600,000 U.S. registered vehicles on the road, and enough foreign activity to more than double AMC's overseas operations, it was losing money when acquired and it contributed to AMC's losses during troubled 1970. Jeep's red ink, however, flowed only from its civilian lines; as a producer of military and post-office vehicles, the company was "consistently a profit-making low bidder."[40]

How far AMC succeeded in turning Jeep's civilian business around by the end of fiscal 1971 was not clear from published information, since this made no mention of profit. Some specific progress was reported, however: namely, the incorporation of AMC engines in all Jeep models, including optional V-8s for all; a reversal of the trend toward declining market share; and an increase of 9% in overseas unit sales and of more than 21% in domestic unit sales. Future plans included "a long-range product development program based on detailed studies of what four-wheel drive vehicle buyers want," but AMC said Jeep would not add any two-wheel drive models to compete with those that Har-

---

[39] AMC *Annual Report,* 1971, p. 22 (Note F).
[40] AMC *Annual Report,* 1970, p. 5.

vester and GM were selling at a price differential of about $500.[41]

Company reports on Jeep's government business during 1971 emphasized the winning of three large contracts (one army and two post office) totaling $189 million. In another 1971 move, rights were obtained from Flyer Industries of Canada to build and sell diesel and electric city transport busses. Meanwhile, sales were up 6% to $261 million and backlogs held almost steady (down less than 7% to $340 million). To this official news, press reports added that the Army had canceled a 1968 contract with GM in order to study a similar truck that could be bought more cheaply from Jeep ($81 million vs. $113 million), after some reworking to meet all major specifications.[42]

By early 1971, Jeep Corporation's government business had been concentrated in a new subsidiary, AM General Corporation, and this, according to the Annual Report, had made "important contributions" to net. Analysts perusing AMC's 10K Report discovered even more precise information: while special government vehicle sales accounted for about 21% of AMC's revenues, they accounted for about 88% of its 1971 pretax profit.[43]

THE FUTURE OF AMERICAN MOTORS

As American Motors entered the 1972 model year, what the future would bring was the subject of much speculation. Although committed to a policy of internal growth and expansion, Mr. Chapin did not dismiss the possibility of a radical change in plans. His thinking, as recorded in a published interview, went as follows:

> Mr. Chapin, candidly discussing the prospects, holds out two possibilities. One is more large acquisitions, like the Jeep take-over, which would deemphasize AMC's dependence on passenger car sales. He says "there might" be more such acquisitions in fields related to car making —companies in the $50 million range—although currently AMC is working on only "a couple of small acquisitions." Such acquisitions would presumably help AMC's profits, although so far Jeep's contribution has been marginal.
>
> Another possibility is a big merger. Mr. Chapin says there have been "evidences of interest" from other companies but "nothing tangible." He scoffs at recurring speculation that International Harvester might be a merger partner, saying the talk stems from the fact that the president of International Harvester "is my brother-in-law." He rates as "interesting" rumors that White Motors might be interested in American Motors now that Semon (Bunkie) Knudsen, former president of Ford, is chairman. But Mr. Chapin says he assumes that Mr. Knudsen has "got a few things to do" at financially troubled White before he could put White into the merger market. (Mr. Knudsen says White isn't talking to AMC or anybody else at present.)

[41] "Truck Operations Bolster AMC Bid," Automotive Industries, April 12, 1972, p. 29.

[42] The Wall Street Journal, June 4, 1971. (At year's end, the sequel remained unreported.)

[43] The Wall Street Journal, March 22, 1972.

Mr. Chapin explains the various rumors linking AMC to a foreign auto maker this way: "If you are going to be a world auto company, you're not going to be that unless you are something big in the U.S. car market, the biggest single auto market in the world. Obviously, the way to get established in this market in a big way is right here," meaning a deal with American Motors. He adds, however, that he doesn't know that any foreign company has such a plan. "And I am not going to spend a lot of time worrying about it."

Such a take-over could provide a foreign auto maker with a major distribution network in the U.S.; AMC has 2,200 dealers, 1,000 more than any importer. By investing in AMC, a foreign manufacturer would keep its profits in the U.S. and curb some of the mounting criticism of auto importers as aggravators of the balance-of-payments problem.

Mr. Chapin makes it clear that his main criterion in evaluating any merger or take-over by another company is the survival of AMC as a car maker. "I'm not interested in AMC becoming part of somebody else for the purposes of liquidating American Motors, because I believe there is a very real place for us," he says. He views Edgar Kaiser, chairman of Kaiser Industries, as an ally. Kaiser Industries got a 22% interest in AMC in exchange for its Jeep operations, making it AMC's biggest shareholder by far. Its block could be the key to any merger plan. Mr. Chapin says Mr. Kaiser "has a basic interest and concern in the automobile business, and he wants to see American Motors become a really successful company."[44]

Blue sky interviews aside, this joint statement by Chapin and Luneburg left little doubt as to the nature of their intentions as the company moved into 1972:

In many respects, American Motors is now better positioned to capitalize on growth opportunities than ever before. Our products are positioned in the segments of the automotive market showing greatest expansion. We have a significant position in the rapidly growing recreational-utility vehicle market and have become an increasingly important supplier of vehicles to the government. Most importantly, the Buyer Protection Plan is an innovative step which gives American Motors a leadership position in providing car buyers with what they want and have a right to expect—protection against costs or inconveniences resulting from mistakes which are the manufacturer's fault and the manufacturer's responsibility.[45]

[44] *The Wall Street Journal,* July 9, 1971.

[45] Joint statement issued in conjunction with the announcement of fiscal 1971 results, November 20, 1971.

Exhibit 1

AMERICAN MOTORS CORPORATION II*

Income Statements 1962–1971

Year ending September 30

(in thousands of dollars)

	1962	1963	1964	1965	1966	1967	1968	1969	1970	1971
Net sales	$1,056,395	$1,132,356	$1,095,362	$990,619	$870,449	$651,215	$761,069	$737,449	$1,089,787	$1,232,558
Earnings (loss) of unconsolidated subsidiaries	2,569	5,308	1,686	833	(872)	5,056	5,012	11,005	8,429	7,865
Other income	6,476	6,823	6,482	6,108	6,812	—	—	—	—	—
	1,065,440	1,144,487	1,103,529	997,560	876,389	656,272	766,082	748,454	1,098,216	1,240,423
Cost of products sold	870,702	942,056	903,252	835,034	737,334	574,076	623,450	603,021	967,868	1,046,031
Selling, advertising and administrative	81,851	88,018	100,820	101,655	106,608	76,639	74,953	91,382	121,942	124,998
Amortization of tools and dies	19,827	19,277	32,920	28,318	32,321	36,525	28,630	23,893	30,606	22,354
Depreciation and amortization of plant and equipment	9,775	10,709	13,333	15,293	15,199	13,141	11,035	10,335	12,709	13,774
Cost of pensions for employees	10,145	9,870	8,587	9,198	13,369	11,033	11,182	10,650	15,386	16,521
Interest	—	—	—	570	2,319	4,802	3,361	2,195	5,946	5,568
Equity in net loss of unconsolidated subsidiaries	—	—	135	137	156	5,714	2,166	—	—	—
	992,299	1,069,930	1,059,046	990,205	907,307	721,930	754,776	741,476	1,154,457	1,229,246
Earnings (loss) before taxes	73,141	74,557	44,483	7,356	(30,918)	(65,659)	11,305	6,978	(56,241)	11,177
Taxes (credit)	38,900	36,750	18,256	2,150	(15,200)	1,110	6,515	2,050	—	5,650
Net earnings (loss) from operations	34,241	37,807	26,227	5,206	(15,718)	(66,769)	4,790	4,928	(56,241)	5,527
Loss from discontinued appliance operations	—	—	—	—	—	3,601	1,808	—	—	—
Net earnings of unconsolidated subsidiaries sold	—	—	—	—	—	156	329	—	—	—
Net earnings (loss) before extraordinary items	34,241	37,807	26,227	5,206	(15,718)	(70,526)	3,312	4,928	(56,241)	5,527
Tax credit†	—	—	—	—	3,070	—	19,200	—	—	4,650
(Loss) on sale of Redisco, Inc.	—	—	—	—	—	(5,289)	—	—	—	—
Net (loss) on sale and discontinuance of appliance operations	—	—	—	—	—	—	(10,750)	—	—	—
Net earnings (loss)	34,241	37,807	26,227	5,206	(12,648)	(75,815)	11,762	4,928	(56,241)	10,177

* Discrepancies may appear in totals because of rounding figures.

† The 1966 and 1968 items represent special tax credits, applicable only to AMC, authorized by Acts of Congress. The 1971 item is a tax credit arising from operating loss carry-forward.

Source: American Motors Corporation *Annual Reports*, 1962–1971.

Exhibit 2

AMERICAN MOTORS CORPORATION II*

Balance Sheets 1962–1971
Year ending September 30
(in thousands of dollars)

ASSETS	1962	1963	1964	1965	1966	1967	1968	1969	1970	1971
Cash	$ 45,942	$ 47,631	$ 34,779	$ 29,382	$ 17,158	$ 11,741	$ 7,835	$ 7,602	$ 10,732	$ 18,239
Marketable securities (approximately market)	41,116	47,751	15,986	6,491	3,099	8,998	50,995	61,703	11,427	—
Accounts receivable (net)	50,395	53,172	65,336	69,439	68,309	64,277	71,536	56,527	106,213	122,518
Inventories—at lower of cost (FIFO) or market	96,078	127,360	136,757	151,239	135,563	122,413	93,794	107,539	202,286	172,340
Prepaid expenses	3,916	4,078	5,335	8,774	7,237	3,785	2,518	3,385	4,933	6,345
Refundable taxes†					22,569	9,753				4,550
Anticipated tax benefits‡					10,861					
Total current assets	237,448	279,992	258,193	265,324	264,796	220,967	226,678	236,756	335,591	323,992
Capital in unconsolidated subsidiaries	40,947	46,680	38,099	41,563	44,923	9,820	5,195	8,475	12,395	11,524
Miscellaneous advances and investments	4,323	7,465	7,771	9,279	9,551	9,257	10,743	12,306	20,575	21,458
Idle plant and equipment held for sale	3,565									
Anticipated future tax benefits					3,155					
Total investments and other assets	48,839	54,145	45,870	50,842	57,630	19,076	15,937	20,781	32,970	32,982
Land	2,939	3,007	3,793	4,375	4,370	4,348	4,043	4,592	6,859	6,718
Buildings and improvements	43,263	47,447	55,987	57,998	59,426	59,106	50,469	53,236	96,346	100,304
Machinery and equipment (including tools and dies)	121,448	142,155	179,509	189,189	209,986	199,998	164,651	181,214	226,809	222,834
Total property, plant and equipment	167,650	192,608	239,289	251,562	273,782	263,451	219,162	239,042	330,014	329,856
Less accumulated depreciation	78,861	86,373	102,414	110,726	122,689	125,815	112,731	119,799	161,818	170,648
Total property, plant and equipment	88,789	106,235	136,874	140,836	151,092	137,636	106,431	119,243	168,196	159,208
Unamortized debt expense								8,225	7,651	7,020
Goodwill arising from acquisitions									2,210	2,210
Total Assets	$375,076	$440,373	$440,937	$457,002	$473,518	$377,680	$349,046	$385,005	$546,810	$525,412

LIABILITIES	1962	1963	1964	1965	1966	1967	1968	1969	1970	1971
Notes payable	$ —	$ —	$ 2,707	$ 52,040	$ 73,176	$ 65,730	$ 23,000	$ —	$ 29,759	$ 25,248
Accounts payable	74,564	90,081	94,307	85,034	92,503	81,840	84,417	92,814	169,099	148,396
Employee compensation due	12,436	13,927	14,532	10,789	8,126	6,450	4,587	6,781	13,323	14,436
Accrued expenses	28,207	30,017	31,650	30,337	31,798	29,219	34,623	28,902	38,141	34,914
Taxes on income	5,761	27,100	9,594	2,797	3,372	2,718	3,197	5,711	5,669	5,278
Current portion of long-term debt	—	—	—	—	—	—	—	—	3,361	5,308
Total current liabilities	120,968	161,125	152,791	180,998	208,975	185,956	149,825	134,208	259,352	233,580
Long-term debt§	4,654	6,145	6,450	5,681	7,940	10,899	8,652	35,000	44,998	42,969
Other liabilities—noncurrent‖	—	—	—	—	—	—	—	11,792	38,845	34,846
Total other liabilities	4,654	6,145	6,450	5,681	7,940	10,889	8,652	46,792	83,843	77,815
Minority interest—Kelvinator of Canada	—	—	2,978	3,074	2,002	2,029	—	—	—	—
Paid-in capital	75,972	80,597	81,838	81,846	81,846	81,854	81,868	90,368	146,034	146,451
Retained earnings	173,482	192,507	196,881	185,404	172,756	96,941	108,702	113,630	57,389	67,566
Total stockholders' investment	249,454	273,103	278,718	267,249	254,601	178,796	190,570	204,005	203,423	214,017
Total Liabilities	$375,076	$440,373	$440,938	$457,002	$473,518	$377,680	$349,046	$385,005	$546,618	$525,412

* Discrepancies may appear in totals because of rounding figures.

† The 1966 and 1967 items are the result of changes in the method of accounting for accrued income taxes. The 1971 item represents federal excise taxes refunded to retail purchasers in anticipation of Government legislation enacted December 10, 1971, repealing the excise tax on passenger cars.

‡ Maximum amount of credit arising from operating loss carryback under the then applicable law. Supplemented in 1968 with an additional $19.2 million by special legislation extending the carryback period.

§ In 1969, $35 million 20-year, subordinated convertible 6% notes were issued, repayable starting 1978. In 1970, $10 million 5-year, 8½% notes were issued in connection with the Kaiser Jeep acquisition, repayable in equal annual installments.

‖ Other liabilities include miscellaneous notes and mortgages, extended product warranty reserves, residual obligations arising from the sale of the appliance operation, and the long-term obligations assumed in connection with acquisitions.

Source: American Motors *Annual Reports*, 1962–1971.

Exhibit 3

AMERICAN MOTORS CORPORATION

AMC passenger car registrations by line, 1962–1971

Model	1962	1963	1964	1965	1966	1967	1968	1969	1970	1971
American	114,583	109,241	146,147	93,069	75,843	67,799	84,208	60,970	84,000	—
Hornet								27,506	39,701	67,052
Gremlin										70,096
Classic/Rebel/Matador	273,725	289,199	204,413	169,826	116,498	97,439	67,102	51,062	45,186	44,239
Ambassador	34,796	29,906	28,852	58,424	67,657	59,644	61,142	59,957	56,033	38,593
Marlin				3,350	5,714	2,733				
Javelin						10,270	40,414	34,096	25,672	22,705
AMX							6,480	6,346	3,735	453
Total AMC	423,104	428,346	379,412	324,669	265,712	237,885	259,346	239,937	254,327	243,138
Total U.S.*	6,938,663	7,556,717	8,065,150	9,313,912	9,008,488	8,357,421	9,403,862	9,446,524	8,388,204	9,729,109
AMC shares (%)	6.10	5.67	4.70	3.48	2.95	2.84	2.76	2.54	3.03	2.50

* Includes foreign and miscellaneous domestic.

Source: *Automotive News (Almanac Issue)*, 1963–1971, and *Automotive News*, February 21, 1972, p. 1.

Exhibit 4

AMERICAN MOTORS CORPORATION II

Percentage of car makes to total U.S. registrations, 1962–1971

	1962	1963	1964	1965	1966	1967	1968	1969	1970	1971
Buick	5.77	6.01	5.96	6.53	6.32	6.76	6.67	7.17	5.88	6.52
Cadillac	2.18	2.11	1.88	2.04	2.18	2.51	2.18	2.58	1.97	2.58
Chevrolet	29.95	28.61	26.35	26.03	23.97	23.68	21.91	21.81	19.89	22.35
Oldsmobile	6.35	6.28	6.36	6.54	6.44	6.60	6.64	6.81	5.51	6.80
Pontiac	7.62	8.03	8.53	8.93	9.22	9.98	9.33	8.42	6.49	6.92
GM TOTAL	51.87	51.04	49.08	50.07	48.13	49.53	46.73	46.79	39.74	45.17
Ford	21.21	20.63	21.69	21.45	22.11	18.20	19.17	19.91	22.04	19.50
Lincoln	0.45	0.42	0.46	0.46	0.55	0.42	0.61	0.62	0.67	0.68
Mercury	4.64	3.82	3.86	3.56	3.42	3.53	3.91	3.73	3.70	3.37
FORD TOTAL	26.30	24.87	26.01	25.47	26.08	22.15	23.69	24.26	26.41	23.55
Chrysler	1.64	1.51	1.70	2.18	2.56	2.47	2.35	2.24	1.82	1.59
Dodge	3.43	5.02	5.74	5.60	6.03	5.89	6.18	5.70	6.01	5.29
Imperial	0.20	0.20	0.26	0.18	0.16	0.19	0.17	0.20	0.13	0.12
Plymouth	4.34	5.64	6.11	6.71	6.64	7.50	7.55	6.98	8.13	6.72
CHRYSLER TOTAL	9.61	12.37	13.81	14.67	15.39	16.05	16.25	15.12	16.09	13.72
STUDEBAKER	1.12	0.85	0.32	0.13	—	—	—	—	—	—
AMERICAN MOTORS	6.10	5.67	4.70	3.48	2.95	2.84	2.76	2.54	3.03	2.50
IMPORTS & MISC. U.S.	5.00	5.20	6.08	6.18	7.45	9.43	10.57	11.29	14.73	15.15
GRAND TOTAL—U.S. (100%)	6,938,863	7,556,717	8,065,150	9,313,912	9,008,488	8,357,421	9,403,862	9,446,524	8,388,204	9,729,109

Source: *Automotive News* (1971 Almanac Issue), p. 20; and *Automotive News*, February 21, 1972, p. 1.

Exhibit 5

AMERICAN MOTORS CORPORATION II

Entire 1970 model year U.S. car production by $100 price groups

$100 Price Groups	Under $1901	$1901 -2000	$2001 -2100	$2101 -2200	$2201 -2300	$2301 -2400	$2401 -2500	$2501 -2600	$2601 -2700	$2701 -2800	$2801 -2900	$2901 -3000	$3001 -3100	$3101 -3200
Gremlin	25,300	—	—	—	—	—	—	—	—	—	—	—	—	—
Hornet	26,640	12,348	22,630	5,306	—	—	—	—	—	—	—	—	—	—
Rebel	—	—	—	—	—	—	15,762	15,706	7,260	—	1,966	5,055	—	—
Javelin/AMX	—	—	—	—	—	—	—	4,147	5,220	19,587	—	—	—	4,116
Ambassador	—	—	—	—	—	—	—	—	—	—	9,565	—	—	—
Total AMC	51,940	12,348	22,630	5,306	—	—	15,762	19,853	12,480	19,587	11,531	5,055	—	4,116
Maverick	210,885	—	—	—	—	—	—	—	—	—	—	—	—	—
Falcon	—	—	—	—	22,460	28,058	9,879	1,752	3,882	6,453	—	—	—	—
Torino/Fairlane	—	—	—	—	—	—	12,435	62,577	59,571	23,149	30,907	64,470	11,614	8,569
Mustang	—	—	—	—	—	—	—	22,762	105,741	791	14,019	6,444	40,970	191,130
Reg. Ford	—	—	—	—	—	—	—	6,651	34,023	38,154	655	254,406	116,564	—
Thunderbird	—	—	—	—	—	—	—	—	—	—	—	—	—	—
Total Ford	210,885	—	—	—	22,460	28,058	22,314	93,742	203,217	68,547	45,581	325,320	169,148	199,699
Montego/Cyclone	—	—	—	—	—	—	11,904	24,666	30,957	73	11,651	8,444	11,879	2,668
Cougar	—	—	—	—	—	—	—	—	—	—	—	49,479	—	—
Monterey/Marquis	—	—	—	—	—	—	—	—	—	—	—	—	24,980	14,391
Total Mercury	—	—	—	—	—	—	11,904	24,666	30,957	73	11,651	57,923	36,859	17,059
Continental	—	—	—	—	—	—	—	—	—	—	—	—	—	—
Mark III	—	—	—	—	—	—	—	—	—	—	—	—	—	—
Total Lincoln	—	—	—	—	—	—	—	—	—	—	—	—	—	—
Total Ford Motor Co.	210,885	—	—	—	22,460	28,058	34,218	118,408	234,174	68,620	57,232	383,243	206,007	216,758
Nova	—	—	118,797	158,646	29,837	—	—	—	—	—	—	—	—	—
Chevelle	—	—	—	—	—	7,547	19,299	52,183	315,389	8,409	7,572	5,503	13,496	6,642
Camaro	—	—	—	—	—	—	—	12,578	112,321	—	—	—	—	—
Reg. Chevrolet	—	—	—	—	—	—	—	12,289	8,976	89,938	6,534	409,587	198,799	37,824
Monte Carlo	—	—	—	—	—	—	—	—	—	—	—	145,975	—	—
Corvette	—	—	—	—	—	—	—	—	—	—	—	—	—	—
Total Chevrolet	—	—	118,797	158,646	29,837	7,547	19,299	77,050	436,686	98,347	14,106	561,065	212,295	44,466
Tempest/Lemans	—	—	—	—	—	—	6,822	15,412	20,388	57,872	57,418	9,893	37,828	63
Firebird	—	—	—	—	—	—	—	—	3,134	15,740	—	—	18,961	7,700
Reg. Pontiac	—	—	—	—	—	—	—	—	—	—	←	65,382	77,207	—
Grand Prix	—	—	—	—	—	—	—	—	—	—	—	—	—	—
Total Pontiac	—	—	—	—	—	—	6,822	15,412	23,522	73,612	57,418	75,275	133,996	7,771
F-85/Cutlass	—	—	—	—	—	—	2,836	—	10,658	134,732	77,736	—	12,535	33,749
Reg. Oldsmobile	—	—	—	—	—	—	—	—	—	—	—	—	—	—
Toronado	—	—	—	—	—	—	—	—	—	—	—	—	—	—
Total Oldsmobile	—	—	—	—	—	—	2,836	—	10,658	134,732	77,736	—	12,535	33,749
Skylark	—	—	—	—	—	—	—	6,602	25,453	101,184	25,793	36,367	29,606	—
Reg. Buick	—	—	—	—	—	—	—	—	—	—	—	—	—	—
Riviera	—	—	—	—	—	—	—	—	—	—	—	—	—	—
Total Buick	—	—	—	—	—	—	—	6,602	25,453	101,184	25,793	36,367	29,606	—
Cadillac	—	—	—	—	—	—	—	—	—	—	—	—	—	—
Eldorado	—	—	—	—	—	—	—	—	—	—	—	—	—	—
Total Cadillac	—	—	—	—	—	—	—	—	—	—	—	—	—	—
Total GM Corp.	—	—	118,797	158,646	29,837	7,547	28,957	99,064	496,319	407,875	175,053	672,707	388,432	85,986
Duster/Valiant	—	—	134,173	81,400	3,867	—	22,117	—	—	—	—	—	—	—
Belvedere/Satellite	—	—	—	—	—	—	9,992	16,670	55,101	26,159	32,003	4,826	4,101	1,979
Barracuda	—	—	—	—	—	—	—	6,156	19,495	237	8,196	20,200	580	—
Fury	—	—	—	—	—	—	—	—	3,157	28,369	47,016	71,862	62,766	25,932
Total Plymouth	—	—	134,173	81,400	3,867	—	32,109	22,826	77,753	54,765	87,215	96,888	67,447	27,911
Dart/Swinger	—	—	—	—	—	110,996	48,632	15,584	16,774	—	—	—	—	—
Coronet	—	—	—	—	—	—	1,593	9,301	9,662	55,791	27,361	4,100	3,885	5,429
Challenger	—	—	—	—	—	—	—	—	10,614	42,723	375	6,618	17,653	—
Charger	—	—	—	—	—	—	—	—	—	—	250	39,181	—	—
Polara/Monaco	—	—	—	—	—	—	—	—	—	—	—	—	49,574	7,511
Total Dodge	—	—	—	—	—	110,996	50,225	24,885	37,050	98,514	27,986	49,899	71,112	12,940
Chrysler	—	—	—	—	—	—	—	—	—	—	—	—	—	—
Imperial	—	—	—	—	—	—	—	—	—	—	—	—	—	—
Total Chrysler Corp.	—	—	134,173	81,400	3,867	110,996	82,334	47,711	114,803	153,279	115,202	146,787	138,559	40,851
Total U.S. Cars	262,825	12,348	275,600	245,352	56,164	146,601	161,271	285,036	857,776	649,361	359,017	1,207,792	732,998	347,711
Percent of Total	3.37%	0.16%	3.53%	3.14%	0.72%	1.88%	2.07%	3.65%	10.99%	8.32%	4.60%	15.47%	9.39%	4.46%

Source: *Ward's Automotive Yearbook*, 1971, p. 33.

$3201-3300	$3301-3400	$3401-3500	$3501-3600	$3601-3700	$3701-3800	$3801-3900	$3901-4000	$4001-4100	$4101-4200	$4201-4300	$4301-4400	Above $4400	Car Total	$100 Price Groups
—	—	—	—	—	—	—	—	—	—	—	—	—	25,300	Gremlin
—	—	—	—	—	—	—	—	—	—	—	—	—	66,924	Hornet
1,936	—	—	—	—	—	—	—	—	—	—	—	—	47,685	Rebel
—	—	—	—	—	—	—	—	—	—	—	—	—	33,070	Javelin/AMX
13	8,437	27,942	—	8,270	—	5,714	—	—	—	—	—	—	59,941	Ambassador
1,949	8,437	27,942	—	8,270	—	5,714	—	—	—	—	—	—	232,920	Total AMC
—	—	—	—	—	—	—	—	—	—	—	—	—	210,885	Maverick
—	—	—	—	—	—	—	—	—	—	—	—	—	72,484	Falcon
—	—	—	—	—	—	—	—	—	—	—	—	—	273,292	Torino/Fairlane
—	—	—	—	—	—	—	—	—	—	—	—	—	190,727	Mustang
44,602	21,333	—	35,100	63,338	—	—	—	—	—	—	—	—	805,956	Reg. Ford
—	—	—	—	—	—	—	—	—	—	—	—	50,364	50,364	Thunderbird
44,602	21,333	—	35,100	63,338	—	—	—	—	—	—	—	50,364	1,603,708	Total Ford
20,887	—	1,997	1,631	—	—	—	—	—	—	—	—	—	103,873	Montego/Cyclone
—	—	—	—	—	—	—	—	—	—	—	—	—	72,363	Cougar
7,662	1,357	3,432	3,507	959	12,177	11,013	19,330	14,213	6,053	10,006	—	—	129,080	Monterey/Marquis
28,549	1,357	5,429	5,138	959	12,177	11,013	19,330	14,213	6,053	10,006	—	—	305,316	Total Mercury
—	—	—	—	—	—	—	—	—	—	—	—	37,695	37,695	Continental
—	—	—	—	—	—	—	—	—	—	—	—	21,432	21,432	Mark III
—	—	—	—	—	—	—	—	—	—	—	—	59,127	59,127	Total Lincoln
73,151	22,690	5,429	40,238	64,297	12,177	11,013	19,330	14,213	6,053	10,006	—	109,491	1,968,151	Total Ford Motor Co.
—	—	—	—	—	—	—	—	—	—	—	—	—	307,280	Nova
2,220	—	—	—	—	—	—	—	—	—	—	—	—	438,260	Chevelle
—	—	—	—	—	—	—	—	—	—	—	—	—	124,899	Camaro
45,855	31,328	—	15,498	22,051	—	—	—	—	—	—	—	—	978,679	Reg. Chevrolet
—	—	—	—	—	—	—	—	—	—	—	—	—	145,975	Monte Carlo
—	—	—	—	—	—	—	—	—	—	—	—	17,316	17,316	Corvette
48,075	31,328	—	15,498	22,051	—	—	—	—	—	—	—	17,316	2,012,409	Total Chevrolet
7,543	—	—	—	—	—	—	—	3,196	—	—	—	—	213,239	Tempest/LeMans
—	—	—	—	—	—	—	—	—	—	—	—	—	48,739	Firebird
—	3,686	33,504	17,826	27,220	44,241	3,537	4,861	5,629	7,033	—	—	—	290,126	Reg. Pontiac
—	—	—	—	—	—	65,750	—	—	—	—	—	—	65,750	Grand Prix
7,543	3,686	33,504	17,826	27,220	44,241	69,287	4,861	8,825	7,033	—	—	—	617,854	Total Pontiac
—	2,933	11,758	23,336	—	—	—	—	—	—	—	—	—	310,273	F-85/Cutlass
47,067	33,017	62,422	16,149	31,527	—	13,249	—	—	9,092	14,098	21,111	51,543	299,275	Reg. Oldsmobile
—	—	—	—	—	—	—	—	—	—	—	—	2,393	2,393	Toronado
47,067	35,950	74,180	39,485	31,527	—	13,249	—	—	9,092	14,098	21,111	53,936	611,941	Total Oldsmobile
1,416	—	—	—	—	—	—	—	—	—	—	—	—	226,421	Skylark
49,567	87,140	43,863	13,511	6,541	—	33,798	18,123	—	24,593	14,338	40,111	71,159	402,744	Reg. Buick
—	—	—	—	—	—	—	—	—	—	—	—	37,336	37,336	Riviera
50,983	87,140	43,863	13,511	6,541	—	33,798	18,123	—	24,593	14,338	40,111	108,495	666,501	Total Buick
—	—	—	—	—	—	—	—	—	—	—	—	214,903	214,903	Cadillac
—	—	—	—	—	—	—	—	—	—	—	—	23,842	23,842	Eldorado
—	—	—	—	—	—	—	—	—	—	—	—	238,745	238,745	Total Cadillac
253,668	158,104	151,547	86,320	87,339	44,241	116,334	22,984	8,825	40,718	28,436	61,222	418,492	4,147,450	Total GM Corp.
—	—	—	—	—	—	—	—	—	—	—	—	—	241,557	Duster/Valiant
2,161	7,748	—	—	—	—	—	—	—	—	—	—	—	160,736	Belvedere/Satellite
635	—	—	—	—	—	—	—	—	—	—	—	—	55,499	Barracuda
2,041	14,384	3,864	8,400	—	—	—	—	—	—	—	—	—	267,797	Fury
4,837	22,132	3,864	8,400	—	—	—	—	—	—	—	—	—	725,589	Total Plymouth
—	—	—	—	—	—	—	—	—	—	—	—	—	191,986	Dart/Swinger
1,779	2,319	—	296	—	—	—	—	—	—	—	—	—	121,516	Coronet
3,979	1,070	—	—	—	—	—	—	—	—	—	—	—	83,032	Challenger
—	—	10,337	—	—	—	—	—	—	—	—	—	—	49,768	Charger
2,663	4,651	18,615	3,663	—	—	2,212	2,935	—	—	—	—	—	91,824	Polara/Monaco
8,421	8,040	28,952	3,959	—	—	2,212	2,935	—	—	—	—	—	538,126	Total Dodge
38,780	21,660	31,215	17,509	1,128	—	—	10,084	9,846	—	1,077	14,306	35,172	180,777	Chrysler
—	—	—	—	—	—	—	—	—	—	—	—	11,816	11,816	Imperial
52,038	51,832	64,031	29,868	1,128	—	2,212	13,019	9,846	—	1,077	14,306	46,988	1,456,308	Total Chrysler Corp.
380,806	241,063	248,949	156,426	161,034	56,418	135,273	55,333	32,884	46,771	39,519	75,528	574,971	7,804,829	Total U.S. Cars
4.88%	3.09%	3.19%	2.00%	2.06%	0.72%	1.73%	0.71%	0.42%	0.60%	0.51%	0.97%	7.37%	100.00%	Percent of Total

Exhibit 6

AMERICAN MOTORS CORPORATION II

The new American Motors.

A couple of years ago we decided to do things differently.

Now the difference is showing up in our cars.

Last April, we introduced America's first small economy car, the Gremlin, and sold every one we made. This year, even with competition, it's still the most fun to drive. Mainly because it comes with more standard horsepower than Vega or Pinto.

We thought women had struggled with big clumsy wagons long enough. So we made a different kind of car this year: the Sportabout. It has all the advantages of a station wagon, yet it's styled along the lines of a sporty car.

Then it seemed to us that Mustang, Camaro, and 'Cuda were looking pretty much alike. So we went all out to make our new Javelin the hairiest looking car on the road, even at the risk of scaring some of you off.

But we didn't stop with these cars. We made our compact Hornet a better buy than the Maverick. The features on our Matador make the other intermediates look stingy. And our Ambassador is the only car line in America with standard air-conditioning and automatic transmission.

If all this sounds like we're trying to turn the auto industry around, maybe we are.

We figure if we make big changes, we'll get bigger.

If you had to compete with GM, Ford and Chrysler what would you do?

▼▌American Motors

Source: *Automotive News* (1971 Almanac Issue), p. 141. (Agency: Wells, Rich, Greene, Inc.)

Exhibit 7

AMERICAN MOTORS CORPORATION II

A. Composition of automobile sales by size class, U.S.
market, 1960–1970

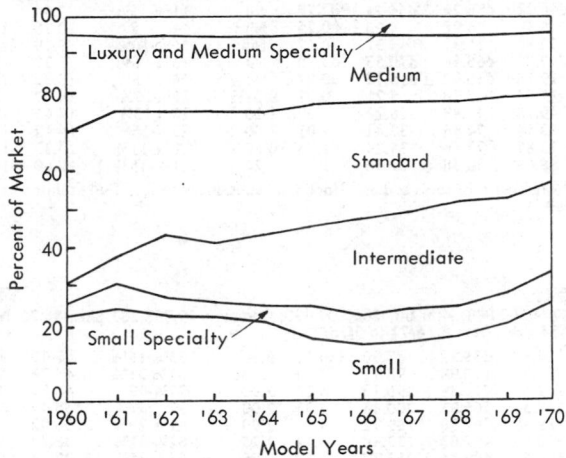

Source: Adapted from Dan Cordtz, "Autos—A Hazardous Stretch
Ahead," *Fortune*, April 1971, p. 70

B. Percent of factory installed equipment, overall by company and for lowest
priced company line, U.S. production, 1970

Company	Automatic trans- mission	V-8 engine†	Power steering	Power drum brakes	Air condi- tioning
AMC					
Overall.....................	75.0	22.8	51.9	22.5	34.4
Gremlin*....................	44.7	—	11.5	3.0	9.5
Chrysler					
Overall.....................	89.2	60.9	80.0	24.7	50.8
Valiant*....................	75.9	27.5	42.7	1.6	18.8
Ford					
Overall.....................	90.3	56.3	79.4	1.0	56.3
Maverick*...................	65.4	—	7.1	—	18.9
GM					
Overall.....................	93.5	62.5	91.3	24.3	66.5
Chevy Nova*................	75.1	31.4	50.1	2.4	14.3
Total industry...............	91.3	59.3	85.0	18.1	60.1

* Lowest priced company line. (See Exhibit 5.)
† Standard. (For the industry as a whole, optional installations of V-8s added another 29%, so that
6-cylinder cars accounted for only 11.6% of the total.)
Source: *Ward's Automotive Yearbook*, 1971, pp. 37–38.

Exhibit 8

AMERICAN MOTORS CORPORATION II

Comparative company analysis

[3] AMERICAN MOTORS CORP. **YEARS TO SEPT. 30**

Funded Debt: $44,998,000; Cap. Stk. 25,380,000 Shs., $1.66⅔ Par.

	Net Sales (Millions $)	*Oper. Inc. (Millions $)	Net Bef. Taxes (Millions $)	Net Income (Millions $)	Common $ Per Share: Earns.	Common $ Per Share: Divs.	Common $ Per Share: Price Range (Calendar Yrs.)	Book Value	Net Wkg. Cap. (Mil. $)	Curr. Ratio Assets to Liabs.
1970....	1,089.8	[2]d46.02	d56.24	d56.24	[4]d2.28	Nil	11⅝- 5½	7.64	76.2	1.3-1
1969....	737.4	8.51	6.98	4.93	[4]0.26	Nil	14 - 8	10.26	102.5	1.8-1
1968....	761.1	22.86	11.31	3.31	0.17	Nil	16¼-10¼	9.99	77.9	1.5-1
1967....	651.2	d47.06	d65.66	d70.53	d3.70	Nil	15⅞- 6⅝	9.38	35.0	1.2-1
1966....	870.4	d19.18	d30.92	d15.72	d0.82	Nil	14 - 6¼	13.35	55.8	1.3-1
1965....	990.6	15.84	7.36	5.21	0.27	0.87½	15⅛- 7¼	14.02	84.3	1.5-1
1964....	1,095.4	49.78	44.48	26.23	1.38	1.15	18⅜-13½	14.62	105.4	1.7-1
1963....	1,132.4	73.14	74.56	37.81	2.01	1.00	23 -16	14.42	118.9	1.7-1
1962....	1,056.4	73.87	73.14	34.24	1.85	[1]0.80	18⅜-11⅞	13.33	116.5	2.0-1
1961....	875.7	56.63	50.38	23.58	1.31	1.20	21¼ -16⅜	12.50	103.1	2.0-1

[1] Plus 2% in stk. [2] Aft. amort. of tools & dies. [3] Incl. Can. subs. after 1963. [4] Fully diluted earns. were, d$2.28 in 1970 & $0.26 in 1969.

[1] CHRYSLER CORP. **YEARS TO DEC. 31**

Funded Debt: $774,500,000; Min. Int. $80,200,000; Common 49,858,287 Shs., $6.25 Par. (Warrants to buy 1,800,000 shrs. at $34 a shr. from 8/16/71 to 5/15/76.)

1970...	6,999.7	[2]216.4	d35.52	d7.60	[3]d0.16	0.60	35¾-16⅛	42.40	618.8	1.4-1
1969...	7,052.2	372.0	186.94	98.97	2.09	2.00	57⅞-31⅝	43.84	585.8	1.4-1
1968...	7,445.3	749.8	611.34	290.73	6.23	2.00	72¾-48	42.81	782.4	1.5-1
1967...	6,213.4	518.5	366.91	200.43	4.35	2.00	57 -31¼	38.44	539.2	1.4-1
1966...	5,649.5	489.9	367.90	189.22	4.16	2.00	61⅝-29¾	36.02	445.1	1.4-1
1965...	5,299.9	552.1	452.03	233.38	5.44	1.25	62¼-41⅝	33.78	542.9	1.6-1
1964...	4,287.3	474.6	409.35	213.77	5.50	0.96	65¼-36¼	27.17	407.1	1.5-1
1963...	3,505.3	382.2	329.81	161.60	4.23	0.42	48 -17¼	22.41	576.4	1.7-1
1962...	2,377.6	186.9	134.91	65.43	1.74	0.24	18 - 9¼	20.47	569.0	2.3-1
1961...	2,127.3	94.2	21.44	11.14	0.30	0.24	13⅞- 8⅞	19.00	506.4	2.3-1

[1] Co. & wholly-owned subs. in 1962 & pr. yrs.; Co., wholly-owned & majority-owned subs thereafter. [2] Aft. amort. for spec. tools in all yrs. [3] Based on avge. shs. in all yrs. Per shr figs. adj. for two 2-for-1 splits in 1963 & 4% stk. div. in 1964.

[2] FORD MOTOR CO. **YEARS TO DEC. 31**

Funded Debt: $528,500,000; Min. Int., $103,700,000. [1] Cl. A Stk., 23,394,642 Shs., $2.50 Par: [3] Class B stk., 12,167,583 Shs., $2.50 Par; Com., 73,820,138 Shs., $2.50 Par.

1970...	14,979.9	1,428.4	1,006.2	515.7	4.77	2.40	56½-37⅛	47.57	1,083.0	1.3-1
1969...	14,755.6	1,495.2	1,115.1	546.5	5.03	2.40	54 -40	45.22	1,107.7	1.4-1
1968...	14,075.1	1,645.0	1,291.3	626.6	5.73	2.40	60¼-48	42.62	1,134.3	1.4-1
1967...	10,516.0	494.5	133.5	84.1	0.77	2.40	55½-39½	39.32	868.4	1.4-1
1966...	12,240.0	[1]465.4	1,166.8	621.0	5.63	2.40	57½-38½	40.97	1,438.3	1.6-1
1965...	11,536.8	1,549.9	1,305.3	703.0	6.32	2.10	62⅞-50⅛	37.88	1,473.7	1.6-1
1964...	9,670.8	1,228.3	992.1	505.6	4.56	2.00	62¼-48⅞	33.85	1,173.7	1.6-1
1963...	8,742.5	1,261.1	1,026.3	488.5	4.42	1.80	59 -42	31.22	1,198.2	1.7-1
1962...	8,089.6	1,235.4	1,003.7	480.7	4.36	1.80	58 -36⅛	28.54	1,107.4	1.7-1
1961...	6,709.4	1,029.0	816.6	409.6	3.72	1.50	58¾-31⅞	25.97	947.9	1.6-1

[1] All owned by Ford Foundation. [2] Consol. incl. all subs. except finance & insur. & domestic dealership subs. aft. 1959. [3] All held by Ford family and interests. Per shr. data adj. for 2-for-1 split in 1962.

*Before depreciation. d–Deficit.

[2] GENERAL MOTORS CORP. **YEARS TO DEC. 31**

Funded Debt: $280,236,400; Pfd., 1,000,000 Shs., $3.75 Cum., No Par; 1,835,644 Shs., $5.00 Cum., No Par; Com., 286,072,720 Shs., $1.66 Par.

1970...	18,752	[1]1,473.0	778.0	609.0	2.09	3.40	81⅝-59½	33.39	3,010.5	1.9-1
1969...	24,295	4,067.0	3,454.0	1,711.0	5.95	4.30	83⅝-65½	34.64	4,352.0	2.3-1
1968...	22,755	4,123.7	3,524.8	1,731.9	6.02	4.30	89⅞-72⅝	32.96	4,230.3	2.4-1
1967...	20,026	3,612.7	3,013.4	1,627.3	5.66	3.80	89⅜-67½	31.17	4,006.4	2.4-1
1966...	20,209	3,770.5	3,270.8	1,793.4	6.24	4.55	108¼-65⅝	29.27	3,606.0	2.5-1
1965...	20,734	4,482.5	4,091.6	2,125.6	7.41	5.25	113¾-91¼	27.47	3,684.9	2.7-1
1964...	16,997	3,615.3	3,283.7	1,734.8	6.05	4.45	102⅝-77¼	25.22	3,651.0	3.0-1
1963...	16,495	3,698.6	3,353.9	1,591.8	5.56	4.00	91⅜-57⅞	23.53	3,727.4	3.3-1
1962...	14,640	3,171.6	2,934.5	1,459.1	[3]5.10	3.00	59⅝-44½	21.81	3,528.0	3.2-1
1961...	11,396	2,065.4	1,768.0	892.8	3.11	2.50	58 -40⅝	19.69	3,058.6	3.1-1

[1] Before deprec., but after deducting amortization for spec. tools & empl. bonus, in all yrs. [2] Consol.; incl. all subs. engaged in mfg. or wholesale marketing opers.; does not incl. G.M. Acceptance Corp. & Yellow Mfg. Acceptance or their subs. [3] Incl. non-recur. inc. of $0.27 a sh.

Source: Standard & Poor's Corporation, *Trade and Securities, Industry Reports*, "Autos-Auto Parts, Basic Analysis," July 15, 1970, pp. A-152, A-157. Reproduced with permission.

Exhibit 8—Continued

Sales Record

(1957–59 = 100)

	AUTOMOBILE				
	American Motors	Chrysler	Ford Motor	Ford Canada	General Motors
1970	192	251	295	276	177
1969	130	253	290	274	230
1968	134	267	277	264	215
1967	115	223	204	224	189
1966	153	202	241	213	191
1965	175	190	227	211	196
1964	178	154	190	187	160
1963	200	126	172	158	156
1962	186	85	159	137	138
1961	154	76	132	108	108
Average Sales in 1957-59 Base Period, In Millions of Dollars					
	567.4	2,791	5,085	490.1	10,581
Year Ends:	Sept.	Dec.	Dec.	Dec.	Dec.

Net Income

(1957–59 = 100)

	AUTOMOBILES				
	American Motors	Chrysler	Ford Motor	Ford Canada	General Motors
1970........	def.	def.	180	328	78
1969........	20	330	190	341	218
1968........	13	1,081	218	237	221
1967........	def.	745	29	149	208
1966........	def.	703	216	79	229
1965........	21	868	245	73	271
1964........	106	795	176	35	221
1963........	153	601	170	110	203
1962........	138	243	167	161	186
1961........	95	41	143	49	114
Average Net Income In 1957-59 Base Period, In Millions of Dollars.					
	24.77	26.90	287.2	21.20	783.40
Yr. Ends:	Sept.	Dec.	Dec.	Dec.	Dec.

Net Income

(as a percentage of sales)

	AUTOMOBILES				
	American Motors	Chrysler	Ford Motor	Ford Canada	General Motors
1970...	def.	def.	3.4	5.1	0.3
1969...	0.6	1.3	3.7	5.4	7.0
1968...	0.4	3.9	4.5	3.9	7.6
1967...	def.	3.2	0.8	2.9	8.1
1966...	def.	3.3	5.1	1.6	8.9
1965...	0.5	4.4	6.1	1.5	10.2
1964...	2.6	5.0	5.2	0.8	10.2
1963...	3.3	4.6	5.6	3.0	9.7
1962...	3.2	2.8	5.9	5.1	10.0
1961...	2.7	0.5	6.1	2.0	7.8

Exhibit 9

AMERICAN MOTORS CORPORATION II

Summary of AMC passenger cars and Jeep commercial vehicles, 1972 model year

	WHEEL BASE (inches)	LENGTH (inches)	HORSE POWER RANGE	BASE PRICE RANGE	MODELS	REMARKS
GREMLIN	96	161.2	100–150	1971 $1,899–$1,999 1972 $1,999	1	Subcompact Class Introduced March 1970 Shortened version of Hornet 2–Door Sedan Six
HORNET SPORTABOUT	108.0	179.3	100–175	1971 $2,174–$2,663 1972 $2,199–$2,587	3	Compact Class Introduced August 1969 Replaced Rambler American Wagon, 2–Door, 4–Door Sedan Sixes
JAVELIN	110.0	191.8	100–255	1971 $2,879–$3,432 1972 $2,807–$3,109	2	Small Specialty Class (Sporty) Introduced Fall 1967 2–Door Hardtops Six and Eight

Exhibit 9—Continued

	WHEEL BASE (inches)	LENGTH (inches)	HORSE POWER RANGE	BASE PRICE RANGE	MODELS	REMARKS
MATADOR	118.0	Sedans 206.0 Wagons 205.0	100–255	1971 $2,720–$3,163 1972 $2,784–$3,140	3	Intermediate Class New Tooling 1967 (Originally named Rambler Classic, then Rebel, then Matador) 4-Door Sedan, Wagon 2-Door Hardtop Sixes
AMBASSADOR	122.0	Sedans 211.1 Wagons 209.7		1971 $3,616–$4,430 1972 $3,885–$4,437	6	Termed Intermediate by AMC (Competes in Standard Class) New Tooling 1967 4-Door Sedans, Wagons 2-Door Hardtops Eights
JEEP	84.0 104.0		100–150	1971 $2,886–$2,986 1972 $2,955–$3,171	2	Standard Utility Vehicle (Derived from World War II Model) Six or Eight

Exhibit 9—Concluded

	WHEEL BASE (inches)	LENGTH (inches)	HORSE POWER RANGE	BASE PRICE RANGE	MODELS	REMARKS
JEEP COMMANDO	104.0		100–150	1971 $3,197–$3,297 1972 $3,257–$3,534	1	Introduced 1967 (Last New Jeep Vehicle) Originally Named Jeepster Six or Eight
JEEP TRUCK	120–132		110–175	1971 $3,251–$4,218 1972 $3,328–$4,262	2	Half and Three-Fourths Ton Weights (Most Expensive Model) Adapted for Camper
JEEP WAGONEER	110.0		110–175		1	

Source: AMC, 1972 Auto show news material and Automotive News (Almanac Issues), 1971, pp. 50, 88; 1972, pp. 38, 80.

The company and its environment: Relating opportunities and resources

DETERMINATION of a suitable strategy for a company begins in identifying the opportunities and risks in its environment. This text is concerned with the identification of a range of strategic alternatives, the narrowing of this range by recognizing the constraints imposed by corporate capability, and the determination of one or more economic strategies at acceptable levels of risk. We shall examine the complexity and variety of the environmental forces which must be considered and the problems in accurately assessing company strengths and weaknesses. Economic strategy will be viewed as the match between qualification and opportunity which relates a firm to its environment. We shall attempt in passing to categorize the kinds of economic strategies that result from the combination of internal capability and external market needs, and to relate these categories to the normal course of corporate development.

THE NATURE OF THE COMPANY'S ENVIRONMENT

The environment of a company in business, like that of any other organic entity, is the pattern of all the external conditions and influences that affect its life and development. The environmental influences relevant to strategic decision operate in industry, business community, city, country, and world. They are technological, economic, social, and political in kind. Technological developments are, of course, among the most far-reaching and fastest unfolding. They include the discoveries of science, the impact of related product development, and the progress of automation. We see in technical progress a continually accelerating rate of change—with new developments piling up before the implications of yesterday's changes can be assimilated. Industries hitherto protected from obsolescence by stable technologies or by the need for huge capital investment become vulnerable to new processes or to cross-

229

industry competition. Science gives the impetus to change not only in technology but also in all the other aspects of business activity.

Economic influences include the extension of the Industrial Revolution to the underdeveloped countries of the world, which has in turn created a vast expansion of demand and an unprecedented upward surge in standards of living. Other major economic trends that affect a company's potential markets are the internationalization of competition, the increased importance of the large corporation, and new interrelationships between private and public sectors of the economy and between privately owned and state-owned enterprises. Social developments include such influential forces as the increasingly insistent quest for equality by minority groups, the changing patterns of work and leisure, the Americanization of taste and culture throughout the world, the urbanization of fully industrialized countries, and the changing composition of an increasing world population. Political forces important to the business firm include the relation between communist and noncommunist countries, the regulation of business by government, the impact of changing legislation and administrative law, the attitude of courts, and the impact of national planning on private corporate planning.

Because so much of what is changing in the world affects the markets for a company's present products, the prospects for future products, and the success of product and market choices, it is, of course, impossible for us to describe or even to know for all business the relevant characteristics of today's world, to say nothing of tomorrow's. We know that a firm—itself a system—is bound in a variety of interrelationships to other larger systems that comprise its economic, technological, social, and political environment. We may conclude that the changes taking place in these larger systems bode both good and ill for the firm. Change threatens all established strategies and requires the businessman to be alert to the possibility that the opportunity he has seized will expire. At the same time, change brings new opportunity for the application of developed expertness and new market needs which entrepreneurial energy may seek to satisfy. No matter how secure a company's position, obsolescence of strategy is a continuous threat. At the same time, new opportunities are emerging everywhere as relative affluence puts unprecedented discretionary income into the hands of consumers in developing countries, and as rising income introduces underdeveloped countries to material conveniences.

If environmental developments are destroying and creating business opportunities, advance notice of this fact in specific instances is essential to intelligent planning. Fortunately, the fundamental characteristics of any industry can be determined and the requirements of success can be identified and their implications noted, so that responsive action can be taken. The behavior of competitors, for example, is impossible to conceal completely. It can be appraised for the influence it will have and for the assumptions about the future by which it seems to be determined. The identification of new opportunity or of impending threat therefore depends upon knowing what kind of information is relevant.

Surveillance of developments becomes more practicable once the critical elements to look for have been determined.

IDENTIFICATION OF OPPORTUNITIES AND RISKS

It follows then, despite the staggering difficulty of foreseeing what is to come or even of recognizing what is already at work in the total environment of business, that some means must be found for organizing systematic intelligence about the changing nature of those forces that most vitally affect a given industry and company. For the man who cannot know everything and whose firm may never reach the size of the global giants, a few simple questions kept constantly in mind will serve to highlight changing opportunity and risk. For the student of cases, who is conveniently presented with the most important information needing interpretation, these questions will lead in short order to an estimate of opportunities and dangers in the present and predictable company setting.

1. *What are the essential economic and technical characteristics of the industry in which the company participates?*

Whether these are in flux or not, they may define the restrictions and opportunities confronting the individual company, and will certainly suggest strategy for it. For example, knowledge that the cement industry requires high investment in plant, proximity to a certain combination of raw materials, a relatively small labor force, and enormous fuel and transportation costs, suggests where to look for new plant sites and what will constitute competitive advantage and disadvantage. The nature of this product may suggest for a given company the wisdom of developing efficient pipeline and truck transportation and cheap energy sources rather than engaging in extensive research to achieve product differentiation or aggressive price competition to increase market share.

2. *What trends suggesting future change in economic and technical characteristics are apparent?*

Changes in demand for the product of one industry in competition with the products of another, and changes in the product itself, occurring as a result of research and development, affect the chance for growth. For example, the glass container industry's development of strong, light, disposable bottles recouped part of the market loss by glass to the metal container. The need for the glass industry to engage in this development effort was made apparent by the observable success of the metal beer can. Similarly the easy-opening metal container suggested the need for an easily removable bottle cap. The physical characteristics of any product can be examined against the master trend toward simplicity, convenience, and serviceability in consumer goods and against competitive innovations.

3. *What is the nature of competition both within the industry and across industries?*

A small rubber company in an industry led by Uniroyal, Goodyear, Goodrich, and Firestone, will not, under the economic condition of overcapacity, elect to provide the automobile business with original tires for new cars. The structure of competition, quite apart from the resources of the firm, may suggest that a relatively small firm should seek out a niche of relatively small attraction to the majors, and concentrate its powers on that limited segment of the market.

Present and developing competition usually extends, of course, beyond the industry in which a company finds itself. For example, the competition for the cement industry from producers of asphalt road-building materials is as important as that from other cement producers.

4. *What are the requirements for success in competition in the company's industry?*

In every industry some critical tasks must be performed particularly well to ensure survival. In the ladies' belt and handbag business style and design are critical, but so (less obviously) are relationships with department store buyers. In the computer business, a sales force able to diagnose customer requirements for information systems, to design a suitable system, and to equip a customer to use it, is more important than the circuitry of the hardware.

Although the question of what tasks are most critical may be chiefly useful as a means of identifying risks or possible causes of failure, it may also suggest opportunity. Imagination in perceiving new requirements for success under changing conditions, when production-oriented competitors have not done so, can give a company a leadership position. For example, opportunity for a local radio station and the strategy it needed to follow changed sharply with the rise of television, and those who first diagnosed the new requirements paid much less for stations than is now necessary.

5. *Given the technical, economic, social, and political developments that most directly apply, what is the range of strategy available to any company in this industry?*

The force of this question will become obvious when we look at the drug industry. The speed and direction of pharmaceutical research, the structure of the industry, the characteristics of worldwide demand, the different and changing ideas about how adequate medical care should be made available to the world's population, the concern about price, and the nature of government regulation suggest some constraints within which a range of opportunity is still vividly clear. Similarly, in a more stable industry, there is always a choice. To determine its limits, an examination of environmental characteristics and developments is essential.

OPPORTUNITY AS A DETERMINANT OF STRATEGY

Awareness of the environment is necessarily a continuing requirement for informed choice of purposes, not a special project to be undertaken only when warning of change becomes deafening. Planned exploitation of changing opportunity ordinarily follows an orderly course which both permits and provides increasing awareness of areas to which a company's capabilities may be profitably extended. For a typical company, which is governed by the determination that after a dividend adequate to maintain stockholder confidence profits will be reinvested, the search for opportunity appears to take a variety of forms. First, within its domestic market, a company will try to increase its volume, to expand the market, and to increase its market share. This step does not require a changed strategy but a more intensive implementation. Policies regarding quality, service, price, promotion, and sales management will be shaped in detail to reflect extensive knowledge of a relatively specialized area of business. In response to detailed awareness of market need, the product will appear in a variety of forms and will proliferate into a family of related items, like a full range of small motors or a series of breakfast foods. The opportunity for growth stems from increase of demand, and competitive success is measured by increased market share.

If the original strategy proves workable in its original sphere, the growing company will typically move next into new geographical areas, either within a large domestic market like the United States or overseas. The product-market combinations remain the same. Macroeconomic and political developments have opened the world to companies not confined by law to their domestic markets. The American firm no longer limits its search for opportunity to the continental United States. The growth of free trade, the relative stability of East-West relations, the appearance of the management contract as an opportunity for free enterprise in socialist economies, and the development abroad of consumer purchasing power means a marked geographical expansion of opportunity. The consequence is that the strategist's interests and information must henceforth be global in extent. Geographical expansion of the sphere of the original strategy thus introduces the problem of systematizing intelligence to which we have already alluded.

A growing company that has successfully extended its activities to wider geographic areas is thereafter likely to enlarge its operations and the scope of its strategy by reaching forward toward the ultimate consumer or backward to the sources of supply. Vertical integration is logically the next step, since the firm's knowledge of its environment will naturally focus its attention on opportunities in those areas that are most closely related to original activities. Furthermore, geographical expansion may well involve acquisitions and mergers of firms that are integrated in varying degrees. The growth of the oil industry is a classic example of both geographical expansion and vertical integration.

Once a company has successfully come to terms with its original milieu, has expanded its market geographically, and has extended the range of the related functions it performs in its markets, then it is likely to seek still further growth by diversifying its product line horizontally. Product diversification of this type imposes the most severe requirements, since it calls for knowledge of present situations and future possibilities in industries where the company has no prior experience to guide it.

Theoretically, then, the course of growth finally spans the full range of business activity for any firm not limited by special legislation. The identification of opportunity in the context of risk is simplest in the instance of the manufacturer of a single product sold within a clearly defined geographical area to meet a known demand. As geographical coverage is extended, or more stages are added in the making of a product, or the product becomes a line of related products via vertical integration, more attention to a more complex pattern of environmental forces is required. For example, the proprietor of a small engineering company specializing in electromechanical devices—unless he wishes to grow greatly—need not concern himself with anything besides meeting the demand for his highly specialized products and making sure that, whatever happens, enough demand remains to sustain his company. He need spend on the state of the world less time than the few minutes he devotes every hour to overseeing his entire production operation. The chief executive of General Electric, on the other hand, would be hard put to it to identify any significant political, social, economic, or technological development in the world that did not have some influence on the future strategic opportunity of his company.

The multiplication of strategic alternatives which accompanies the progress of a single enterprise along the course just sketched presents, finally, problems which escape solution. The more one finds out what might be done, the harder it is to make the final choice. The demonstrated existence of an opportunity is not an adequate basis for the decision to seek it out. Before we pass to the other factors that must be considered, two consequences of the development pattern we have described should be clearly defined. They will be of great importance for a growing company in pondering its proper decision.

First, the sheer number of alternatives which will be disclosed by a well-directed scrutiny of world markets constitutes an embarrassment of riches. Some large firms, slow to make the decision to become multinational, seem now to have Klondike fever on a global scale. Those who refuse to go everywhere at once do not find choice easy. For example, the McGraw-Hill Book Company has the good fortune to have an economic opportunity of enormous proportions for its future expansion. Its distinctive strategy of furnishing technical and scientific information to particular groups previously identified as having a special need for these data is obviously applicable to all countries of the world where education is transforming the life of the people and technical progress is nurturing a growing need for more information. The problem for McGraw-Hill is not where opportunity exists for expansion overseas—it is everywhere—but which opportunity to pursue first. This choice begins in the determination of potential return, and though it does not end there, the ranking of alternatives in order of their economic significance is probably the first step.

The objective assessment of opportunity is difficult because of the unreliability of statistical information in developing countries and the hazards of predicting the political, social, and technical developments in a given area. But with the assignment of sufficient analytical brainpower to the task, a degree of order can be imposed upon the range of alternatives available. The investment in this activity is preferable to opening up operations in all countries at once on the grounds that some will succeed, or to acquiring any business that foreign nationals decide to sell to Americans at what their local competitors consider an outrageous price.

The diversified company has another problem different from that of trying to make the best choice among many. If it has divisionalized its operations and strategies, as sooner or later in the course of diversification it must, then divisional opportunities come into competition with each other.

The corporate management will wish to invest profits not distributed to stockholders in those opportunities that will produce the greatest return to the corporation, and, if need be, management will be willing to let an individual division decline if its future looks less attractive than that of others. The division will wish to protect its own market position, ward off adverse developments, prolong its own existence, and provide for its own growth. The division manager, who is not rewarded for failures, will program projects of safe but usually not dramatic prospects. The claims regarding projected return on investment, which are submitted in all honesty as the divisional estimate of future opportunity, can be assumed to be biased by the division's regard for its own interest and the manager's awareness of measurement.

The corporate management cannot be expected to be able to make independent judgments about all the proposals for growth which are submitted by all the divisions. On the other hand, all divisions cannot be given their heads, if the corporation's needs for present profit are to be met and if funds for reinvestment are limited. In a decentralized organization, it is inappropriate to centralize planning. In any case, the greatest knowledge about the opportunities for a given technology and set of markets should be found at the divisional level.[1]

The strategic dilemma of a conglomerate world enterprise is one that may not have a satisfactory solution. When the range of what must be known exceeds the capacity—as these days it soon does—of a single mind, and when the range of a company's activities spans many industries and technologies, the problems of formulating a coherent strategy get out of hand. If the identification of opportunity results in its being pursued without regard for any consideration other than return on investment, then total performance is apt, in the long run, to become at best mediocre.

We have said that the identification of opportunities and risks in the environment of a company committed to growth will lead it to increase its volume in a given market, to develop products related to its original product, to expand geographically, to integrate vertically, and ultimately to diversify its product line. From the point of view of maintaining control of strategy, the critical step is diversification away from the company's original business. Guided by a strategic concept of the nature of the enterprise and the unity of its businesses, a company may successfully enter fields that appear to be different but are fundamentally related. Guided only by the entrepreneurial estimate of attractive return on investment or by the opportunistic impulse to embark on a new venture, the large diversified enterprise may find itself unable to compete effectively with more specialized firms which are better

---

[1] See Norman Berg: "Strategic Planning in Conglomerate Companies," *Harvard Business Review,* May–June 1965.

able to know what they should do. Though it may be equal to capitalizing on the present opportunity, it may not be able to solve the problem of resource allocation posed by future requirements.

To decide which is the best among several opportunities identified by informed examination is a task that requires more than economic analysis. If the difficulties inherent in following through on new undertakings in a swiftly changing world are to remain manageable, then some criterion for choice besides the opportunity for profit must be observed. Economic opportunity abounds, but not the ability to capture it. For example, a company jaded by shrinking margins may be tempted by the fortunes to be made in land development in Australia. But the fact that there is much money to be made in a new field or in a strong growth industry does not mean that a company with abilities developed in an unrelated field is going to make it. We must turn now to the critical factors which for an individual company make one good opportunity better than another.

DETERMINING CORPORATE COMPETENCE AND RESOURCES

The first step in validating a tentative choice among several opportunities is to determine whether the organization has the capacity to prosecute it successfully. The capability of an organization is its demonstrated and potential ability to accomplish, against the opposition of circumstance or competition, whatever it sets out to do. Every organization has actual and potential strengths and weaknesses. Since it is prudent in formulating strategy to extend or maximize the one and contain or minimize the other, it is important to try to determine what they are and to distinguish one from the other.

The strengths of a company which constitute a resource for growth and diversification accrue primarily through experience in making and marketing a product line. They inhere as well in (1) the developing strengths and weaknesses of the individuals comprising the organization, (2) the degree to which individual capability is effectively applied to the common task, and (3) the quality of coordination of individual and group effort.

The experience gained through successful execution of a strategy centered upon one goal may unexpectedly develop capabilities which could be applied to different ends. Whether they should be so applied is another question. For example, a manufacturer of salt can strengthen his competitive position by offering his customers salt-dispensing equipment. If, in the course of making engineering improvements in this equipment, a new solenoid principle is perfected that has application to many industrial switching problems, should this patentable and marketable innovation be exploited? The answer would turn not only on whether economic analysis of the opportunity shows this to be a durable and profitable possibility, but also on whether the organization can muster the financial, manufacturing, and marketing strength to exploit the discovery. The former question is likely to have a more positive answer than the latter. In this connection, it seems important to remember that individual and unsupported flashes of strength are not as dependable as the gradually accumulated product- and market-related fruits of experience.

Even where competence to exploit an opportunity is nurtured by experience in related fields, the level of that competence may be too low for any great reliance to be placed upon it. Thus a chain of children's clothing stores might well acquire the administrative, merchandising, buying, and selling skills that would permit it to add departments in women's wear. Similarly, a sales force effective in distributing typewriters may gain proficiency in selling office machinery and supplies. But even here it would be well to ask what distinctive ability these companies could bring to the retailing of soft goods or office equipment to attract customers away from competitors.

The "distinctive competence"[2] of an organization is more than what it can do; it is what it can do particularly well. Thus a hapless manufacturer of chocolate candy who finally lost his chain of candy stores was not really a surpassingly efficient retailer of candy. He just thought he was. His real skill lay in production, in his ability to design special machinery to permit quality production at low cost. The proper application of his real strengths would probably have confined him to manufacturing for wholesalers and supermarket chains.

To identify the less obvious or by-product strengths of an organization, which may well be transferable to some more profitable new opportunity, one might well begin by examining the organization's current product line and by defining the functions it serves in its markets. Almost any important consumer product has functions which are related to others into which a qualified company might move. The typewriter, for example, is more than the simple machine for mechanizing handwriting that it appears to be when looked at only from the point of view of its designer and manufacturer. If closely analyzed from the point of view of the potential user, the typewriter will be found to contribute to a broad range of information processing functions. Any one of these might suggest an area to be exploited by a typewriter manufacturer. Thus the definition of product that would lead to identification of transferable skills must obviously be expressed in terms of the market needs it may fill rather than the engineering specifications to which it conforms.

Besides looking at the uses or functions to which his present product line contributes, the would-be diversifier might profitably identify the skills that underlie whatever success he has achieved. A watch manufacturer, for example, must have design and engineering skills, and he could apply these to other small precision products. It might be more likely, however, that success in this competitive industry turns less on design and engineering (obvious requirements, whose incidence is widespread) than on special skills in international marketing (a more subtle need, and a capability that seems relatively rare in the watch industry). Perhaps, then, merchandising skill could provide a basis for

---

[2] This phrase is used by Philip Selznick, *Leadership in Administration* (Evanston Ill.: Row, Peterson & Co., 1957), p. 42.

diversification by a successful manufacturer of watches. If so, it is again something quite different from the physical characteristics of a product that provides the clue a company should follow in seeking new areas for growth.

The insight required to perceive in the humdrum qualifications of an organization efficient at performing its long-accustomed tasks the essential strength to justify new ventures does not come naturally. Its cultivation can probably be helped by recognition of the need for analysis. In any case, we should look beyond the company's capacity to invent new products. Product leadership is not possible for a majority of companies, so it is fortunate that patentable new products are not the only major highway to new opportunities. Other avenues include new marketing services, new methods of distribution, new values in quality-price combinations, and creative merchandising. The effort to find or to create a competence that is truly distinctive may hold the real key to a company's success or even to its future development. For example, the ability of a cement manufacturer (to spare the candy manufacturer this time) to run a truck fleet more effectively than his competitors may constitute one of his principal competitive strengths in selling an undifferentiated product. Similarly, the ability of Crown Cork and Seal to provide prompt delivery on specialty containers sets this company apart from its larger competitors whose forte is to provide standard cans at lower prices. Unless Crown's skill in giving fast service on nonstandard items proves limited to specialty containers, it might be extended to other products and activities—for instance to fast service on equipment breakdowns. But even if the company never leaves the container industry, there are many additional markets overseas in which it can employ its inconspicuous but highly valuable abilities.

The way, then, to narrow the range of alternatives is to match opportunity to competence, once each has been accurately identified and its future significance estimated. It is this combination which establishes a company's economic mission and its relationship to its environment. The match is designed to minimize organizational weakness and to maximize strength. In any case, risk attends it. And when opportunity seems to outrun present distinctive competence, the willingness to gamble that the latter can be built up to the required level is almost indispensable to a strategy that challenges the organization and the people in it.

Before we leave the creative act of putting together a company's unique internal capability and evolving opportunity in the external world, we should note that—aside from distinctive competence—the principal resources found in any company are money and people—technical and managerial people. At this stage of economic development, money seems less a problem than technical competence, and the latter much less critical than managerial ability. In reading the cases that follow, by all means look carefully at the financial records of each company and take note of its success and its problems. Look also at the apparent managerial capacity and, without underestimating it, do not assume that it can rise to any occasion. The recent vigorous diversification of American industry is marked by hundreds of instances in which a company strong in one endeavor lacked the ability to manage an enterprise requiring different skills. The right to make handsome profits over a long time period must be earned. Opportunism without competence is a garden path. Where it leads cannot be predicted, but in any case it is beyond the confines of a sober essay in praise of predetermined purpose.

Besides equating an appraisal of market opportunity and organizational capability, the decision to make and market a particular product or service should be accompanied by an identification of the nature of the business and the kind of company management desires. Such a guiding concept is a product of many considerations, including the management's personal values. As such, this concept will change more slowly than other aspects of the organization, and it will give coherence to all the various company activities. For example, a president who is determined to make his firm into a worldwide producer and fabricator of a basic metal, through policies differentiating it from the industry leader, will not be distracted by excess capacity in developed markets, low metal prices, and cutthroat competition in certain markets. Such a firm should not be sidetracked into acquiring, for example, the Pepsi Cola franchise in Africa, even if this business promised to yield a good profit. (That such a firm should have an experimental division exploring off-shoot technology is, however, entirely appropriate.)

In each company, the way in which distinctive competence, organizational resources, and organizational values are combined is unique. Differences among companies are as numerous as differences among individuals. The combinations of opportunity to which distinctive competences, resources, and values may be applied are equally extensive. Generalizing about how to make an effective match is less rewarding than working at it. The effort is a highly stimulating and challenging exercise. The outcome will be unique for each case and each situation, but each achievement of a viable economic strategy will leave the student of strategy better prepared to take part in real-life strategic decisions.

APPLICATION TO CASES

The student could profitably bring to the cases he studies not only the questions suggested earlier, but the following as well:

> What really is our product? What functions does it serve? To what additional functions might it be extended or adapted?
>
> What is happening to the market for our products? Is it expanding or contracting? Why?
>
> What are our company's major strengths and weaknesses? From what source do these arise?
>
> What is our strategy? Is the combination of product and market an optimum economic strategy? Is the central nature of our business clear enough to provide us with a criterion for product diversification?

What, if any, better combinations of market opportunities and distinctive competence can our company effect, within a range of reasonable risk?

These questions will prove helpful throughout the course in the task of designing an economic strategy. However, they are never wholly sufficient, for the strategic decision is never wholly economic in character.

Heuer-Leonidas*

"A TOUGH YEAR, 1971!" commented Jack Heuer, 38 years old, President of Heuer-Leonidas, and greatgrandson of the original founder of the company. "I sometimes had the feeling that we no longer controlled our destiny. It was discouraging to see our sales shrink. But we have a new line of products for 1972, and electronics should really begin to move. We'll be back on the track in '72. I'd rather forget 1971. We just might have a good year ahead of us."

The year 1971 had been a bad one for the company, located in Bienne, Switzerland. Consolidated sales were off 8.6% from the previous year, and consolidated profit was down 44%. Even so, the final figures were somewhat better than had been feared as the year progressed.[1] The 1971 performance of the company contrasted sharply with steady increases in sales and profits recorded by the company in recent years. Heuer-Leonidas had a reputation as Switzerland's fast-growing, dominant producer of stopwatches and other specialized time-keeping instruments for the measurement of short time intervals. For example, sales of the parent company in 1970 were up 18% from 1969, attaining 17.9 million Swiss francs[2] for a 10-year growth rate in excess of 20% per year. Consolidated sales, which included the sales figures of its U.S. and U.K. sales subsidiaries as well as Sportex S.A., a recently-purchased manufacturer of inexpensive stopwatches, were up 30% to 22.4 million francs. The initial public issue of Heuer-Leonidas common stock had added over 3 million francs for further expansion of the company's operations.

---

* Copyright 1972 by l'Institut pour l'Etude des Méthodes de Direction de l'Entreprise (IMEDE), Lausanne, Switzerland. Reprinted by permission.

[1] By comparison, the value of exports by the Swiss watch industry increased 1.1% world-wide, despite a setback of 6.3% in exports to the U.S.

[2] Sfr.4.32 = U.S. $1.00 in 1970 and earlier. In 1971, monetary fluctuations saw the franc at an average of Sfr.4.00 = $1.00, increasing to about Sfr.3.85 = $1.00 by the end of the year.

BACKGROUND

The original company was founded in 1860 by Edouard Heuer, who soon began specializing in the manufacture of stopwatches[3] and chronographs.[4] Technological leadership in the field was not long in coming; in 1867, Edouard Heuer Company obtained one of the first patents for stemwound pocket watches, thus making obsolete the keywound watch. The company's collection of pocket chronographs—put into production in 1882—won a silver medal at the 1889 World's Fair in Paris.

Over the next 50 years distribution, using the Heuer name, was expanded until it became world wide. Family control continued. World War II severely disrupted exports of Heuer products. Unlike ordinary watches, stopwatches and chronographs were considered war material by the surrounding Axis powers, who only permitted their exports with a great deal of difficulty. As a result, Heuer was forced to concentrate on improving its distribution to the Swiss market. (As late as 1971, 14% of Heuer sales were derived from Switzerland, against 3% for the watch industry as a whole.) Distribution after the war expanded rapidly to match the post-war boom in the sale of chronographs. Chronographs became the mark of the physically-fit, dashing Army or Air Force veteran in Switzerland, but by 1949 the boom fizzled, and Heuer sales dropped dramatically.

To utilize unused capacity, company management added a line of self-winding wrist watches, sold primarily to American customers under private label. Sales in this market fluctuated wildly, and proved quite unsatisfactory for the company. In 1958 the family called on Jack Heuer to examine the strategic position of the company. "I had just completed my education as an electrical engineer with a Masters in production engineering," recalled Jack Heuer, "and although I had wanted to enter the consulting profession, I agreed to spend a year working with the family business, to examine the operating strategy and take a look at the organization of operations" (Exhibit 1).

Jack Heuer recommended a curtailment of watch production and return to specialization in the domain of short time measurement. In 1971, Jack said, "It is such a nice niche for our company—it gives us a basis on which to compete. As a watch producer, we would be just another one of 600 or so Swiss companies, never able to establish a reputation or brand name." The family prevailed upon Jack to stay on as company President, and in 1962 he purchased a majority interest in Ed. Heuer Co. from the family, and effective control of total company operations passed into his hands. Sales in that year were 2.3 million francs. By 1970, the company had grown as indicated by Exhibits 2, 3, and 4. (Exhibit 5 gives the 1971 organization chart, and

---

[3] Stopwatch: a watch for short time measurements with no time-of-day reading.

[4] Chronograph: a watch with an independent mechanism permitting measurement of short time intervals on a continuous or interrupted basis. In effect, a combination of a normal watch or wristwatch and a stopwatch.

Exhibit 6 gives background information on the 1971 management group).

MARKETING

Exhibit 7 depicts typical products and retail price ranges for the traditional Heuer-Leonidas stopwatches and wrist chronographs. Their particular characteristics are as follows:

The Heuer line

The jeweled-lever "Heuer" stopwatch is produced for 1/5th, 1/10th, and 1/100th of a second applications, in six basic configurations or functions." The number of stopwatch combinations is further increased by the addition of special dial faces, which permit the "tailoring" of the stopwatch to specific uses. Heuer, for example, has a line of stopwatches for parachutists, waterskiers, referees, rowers, yacht enthusiasts, photographers, TV program directors, nurses, etc. In all, the number of "Heuer" stopwatch models exceed 100. Sales of these models in 1971 were down about 10% from the previous year, reaching almost 90,000 units or 27% of sales.

"Heuer wrist chronographs are offered in self-winding ("automatic") and non-self-winding versions, the self-winding having been introduced in 1969 after an extensive developmental effort with Breitling, another chronograph manufacturer. The automatic wrist chronograph offers a 31-day calendar and stopwatch movement that records elapsed times of either 30 minutes or 12 hours; the non-automatic comes with or without date, and also records elapsed times of either 30 minutes or 12 hours, depending on the model. A summary of "Heuer" wrist chronograph basic models is shown below:

| "Heuer" wrist chronograph | Year of latest model | Records elapsed times up to: | | 31-day calendar | Switzerland retail price range (Sfr.) |
		30 min.	12 hrs.		
Automatic	1969		X	X	550–700*
Automatic	1971	X		X	390–490
Non-automatic	1970		X		350–400
Non-automatic	1970	X		X	220–300
Non-automatic (fibreglass case)	1971	X			195

* Does not include solid 18 k. gold model retailing for Sfr.1,400.

The company sold about 35,000 wrist chronographs in 1971 (1970—50,000), of which 35% were the automatic version. Wrist chronographs represented about 30% of H-L's sales in 1971.

"Heuer" pocket chronographs and dashboard instruments were relatively minor product lines, representing about 5% of sales for the last few years.

The Leonidas line

By 1959, the expansion of commercial activities in Europe and the U.S. had begun to exert pressure on the productive capacity of Heuer. That year the company produced 1,400 wrist chronographs and about 24,000 jeweled-lever[5] stopwatches. By 1963, production was 5,000 and 44,000 units, respectively. Unfortunately, expansion of the factory in Bienne was not deemed feasible.

However, Heuer had recently entered into a joint venture with Leonidas Watch Factory, Ltd., of St. Imier, for the development and production of a special stopwatch. Leonidas, a family-owned business of approximately the same size as Heuer, produced a line of wrist chronographs, jeweled-lever stopwatches, and inexpensive Roskopf[6] stopwatches. A merger seemed to be in the best interests of both companies and after a period of difficult negotiations, it was completed at the beginning of 1964.

Production was reallocated between the two factories, the total number of models of chronographs and stopwatches was reduced, and the company put into effect the brand-name policy that continues today: the use of "Heuer" on all wrist chronographs and jeweled-lever stopwatches, and "Leonidas" on all pin-lever products.

In the "Leonidas" line are the following products:

"Leonidas" pin-lever, 7 jewel stopwatch has been a staple item in the Heuer-Leonidas product line since the merger, with a peak sales volume of 44,500 units in 1967. Unit sales declined significantly to 12,000 units in 1971, however; the result, no doubt, of the success of the "Trackmaster" stopwatch (below).

"Leonidas" Trackmaster, introduced in 1968, is a stopwatch utilizing a simple, mass-produced movement in a brightly-colored plastic case. Unit sales reached 108,000 in the first year; by 1970, sales peaked at above 190,000 units, declining to 168,000 units by the end of 1971. Despite the decline, Trackmaster continues to provide a substantial proportion of sales, representing close to 18% in 1971.

"Easy Rider" wrist chronograph, also a Leonidas product, was introduced in December, 1971, as the world's first Roskopf wrist chronograph, recording elapsed times of up to 15 minutes. The colored fibreglass case and low price were both expected to prove attractive to the youth market. Heuer-Leonidas was anticipating a success with "Easy Rider" that would rival the figures of "Trackmaster."

---

[5] Jeweled-lever: the classical Swiss movement uses an escapement mechanism equipped with jewels to protect the lever from wear (see illustration). In addition, a number of other jewels are provided at points of high friction to serve as bearings.

[6] Roskopf: The Roskopf movement is a simpler and less accurate watch movement, using considerably fewer parts than the classical jeweled-lever movement. Few, if any, jewels are used. The escapement mechanism uses two steel pins instead of jewels. Often called *pin-lever* movement.

The Sportex line

Finally, the 10 "Sportex" models, similar to the traditional "Leonidas" stopwatches in design, but somewhat lower in price, added 75,000 units to the Heuer-Leonidas totals for 1971. The Sportex Company at Arogno had been purchased in 1970 and continues to be operated separately from the Heuer-Leonidas operation.

Distribution

Between 70% and 80% of Heuer-Leonidas' sales were made through the wholesale trade, with the remainder sold direct to large customers under private label. Ordinarily, the private label sales were below 25%, but a large Sears, Roebuck order in 1970 for the Trackmaster boosted this percentage above 30%. By the end of 1971, however, the private label sales were back down to 25%.

Independent wholesalers in 96 countries carried Heuer-Leonidas products on an exclusive basis, reselling to the jewelry trade and other outlets for a margin that averaged between 25% and 35%. The wholesalers carried other watch and jewelry products as well, using a salesforce averaging 1–5 men to visit the retail outlets.

The retail outlets could be of one type, as in Switzerland, where 100% of the wholesalers' sales were to jewelry stores; or highly varied, as in the U.S., where less than 30% of sales were to jewelry stores—the rest being divided among sports stores, laboratory suppliers, government agencies, auto accessory stores, and the like. Retailers typically took a 40–50% margin on sales.

Heuer-Leonidas encouraged retail variety, and worked to increase the importance of its products to the wholesaler. Wide differences existed in this area; for example, H-L products were less than 5% of the Portugese wholesalers' sales in 1970, while in Switzerland H-L products represented over 75% of the Swiss wholesalers' volume.

Geographically, North America and Western Europe dominated as the two significant markets for stopwatches and wrist chronographs. One of Jack Heuer's first moves to increase company sales had come in 1959 as a serious effort to penetrate the U.S. market for stopwatches and chronographs. Heuer invested an initial sum of Sfr.200,000 to create Heuer Time Corporation, a U.S. sales subsidiary, in New York.

HTC began operations in 1959 with a director/salesman, secretary, watch repairman, and warehouse man. The subsidiary's goal was a 20% share of Swiss exports of stopwatches and chronographs to the U.S.— the same export share enjoyed by Heuer in Western Europe. Between 1959 and 1963, Jack Heuer spent two-thirds of his time in the U.S. overseeing the subsidiary's operations.

Following the successful increase in sales in the United States—sales had reached U.S.$675,000 or Sfr.2.9 million by the end of 1967, about ⅓ of Heuer-Leonidas' total sales—the Board of Directors approved the establishment of a sales subsidiary in the U.K., in London. The cost of setting up Heuer-Time Limited was 78,000 francs, plus working capital of Sfr.300–400,000; first year operations in 1968 produced a sales volume of £41,000 (Sfr.430,000). (See Exhibit 8.)

Compared to the watch industry, H-L was relatively absent in the less-developed countries, but most industry observers reasoned that the market for stopwatches and chronographs was virtually limited to economically advanced countries.

	Percent of Sales			
	Heuer-Leonidas		Swiss Watch Industry	
Market	1971	1970	1971	1970
U.S., Canada...................	35	43	18	20
Switzerland....................	14	11	3	3
Other Western European.........	33	28	34	34
Rest of the world...............	18	18	45	43
Total....................	100%	100%	100%	100%

Walter Hunsperger, the H-L sales manager, and Jack Heuer considered the distribution network as one of the company's major strengths. According to Mr. Hunsperger:

> Our distributors have been doing a great job for us over the years. We feel that they are extremely loyal and act as if they are a part of the H-L organization rather than independent businessmen. They help us every year, particularly in the preparation of our sales budget by indicating how their markets look in every product segment. I don't think many watch manufacturers enjoy this type of cooperation.

JACK HEUER: We have always encouraged our distributors to innovate in their sales of Heuer products by prospecting unusual retail outlets: auto and boat accessory shops, hospital and laboratory suppliers, sports stores, etc. Their response to this has been very encouraging—their sales increase, they are less tied to the traditional jewelry trade, and they start to think in true marketing terms.

We, of course, benefit as well—once a distributor has opened up a new channel, we can think in terms of new products to fill the channel. Having traditional products in boating stores encourages us to develop specialized products for the boating enthusiast, and so forth. This need not be limited to watch-type products—we are beginning to think in very nontraditional ways about potential products.

One of the major concerns of the distribution system was retailer motivation: how to motivate the retailer to push Heuer products more aggressively. Jack Heuer discussed the basic problem:

> This has always been a tough issue. The average jeweler understands watches, but he is afraid of stopwatches and chronographs because the movements are complicated. He may feel inadequate to give advice to a potential customer on what product to buy—explaining the differences between products and prices, for example—or he may be worried about the quality of our repair services and fear the consequences if a product sold on his recommendation breaks down.

We try to develop materials to educate the jeweler to our products, and we continually strive to upgrade our after-sales repair service, but the jeweler remains timid. The only time he really seems to push our products is when he is loaded down with an inventory of Heuer products. This requires an extensive distributor effort and is not without a number of risks.

Private label sales

H-L's private label business—representing on average one-quarter of yearly sales—involved sales of pin-lever stopwatches directly to a few major clients, thus bypassing the wholesaler and the system of traditional margins. Each private label customer could represent as little as 1% or as much as 12% of sales, depending on the year. Sears, Roebuck and Co., the huge U.S. retailing chain, went from 2% of sales in 1969 to 12% in 1970 on Trackmaster orders, only to fall back to 5% in 1971.

Five to ten private label customers were served in any given year, falling among the company's twenty most important customers (which included Heuer Time and Electronics Corp. as number 1 and Heuer Time Limited as number 5). The percentage of private label business was monitored closely by Jack Heuer and Walter Hunsperger to gauge the risk profile of the company and the strength of the branded products in the marketplace.

Publicity

The company had increased the overall level of publicity expenditures since the merger with Leonidas in 1964. Advertising at that time was slightly over 3% of sales, but recent expenditures had more typically been in the range of 6%. The bulk of the increase went to general company-wide publicity; in 1964, about 25% of the advertising budget was spent for general publicity, the rest being used for wholesaler advertising support. By 1970, 45% of the budget was being used for general publicity, although this percentage was reduced in half in 1971. Wholesaler publicity support nevertheless increased from over 500,000 francs to 600,000 francs from 1970 to 1971.

The general publicity focused on improving public awareness of the brand name and logo "HEUER," which was associated with sporting themes—particularly in the domain of auto racing. Two well-known European racing drivers, Jo Siffert and Clay Regazzoni, were sponsored by the company, their cars displaying the logo during races. Heuer point-of-display posters carried the pictures of Siffert and Regazzoni with their cars, and the theme was extended to the "Easy Rider" wrist chronograph, which featured a blue display of four Easy-Rider chronographs and a bright red Formula 1 racing car.

The company received an unexpected boost to its publicity efforts when the American movie actor Steve McQueen decided to wear a prominent Heuer patch on his racing coverall in the recent film *The 24 Hours of Le Mans*. The point-of-display publicity for the film showed McQueen and the patch clearly, and millions of round self-adhering stickers of McQueen were distributed world-wide by the film producers to promote the film; these, too, displayed the Heuer patch clearly below McQueen's right shoulder.

The theme of auto racing was not without its risks. Jo Siffert was killed in a fiery crash in England in late 1971, raising editorial concern about the morality and safety of auto racing. The company nevertheless decided to continue this campaign, but cautiously and only after a year-by-year review of the policy. To avoid the risk of sponsoring only individual drivers, though, Heuer decided to sponsor several factory car teams as well. Beginning in 1972, the factory cars of Ferrari, BRM Formula 1, and Lola would all carry the Heuer logo. Clay Regazzoni, Jacky Ickx, and Ronnie Peterson, all of whom were Ferrari team drivers, would be the individual drivers sponsored by the company.

Competition for world markets

The competition among stopwatch and chronograph manufacturers was considered by Heuer-Leonidas to be less severe than the competition among world watch manufacturers. In jeweled-lever stopwatches, fifteen companies (ten Swiss) competed for the world market. Besides Heuer-Leonidas, the major well-known names for these products were Omega (Swiss) and Hanhart (German).

Eleven companies (ten Swiss) produced Roskopf stopwatches of a competing nature, while in wrist chronographs, over fifty companies were involved. Among these latter companies, however, only six marketed an automatic wrist chronograph: Heuer, Seiko (Japan), Zenith-Movado, Breitling, Hamilton, and Kelek.[7] Omega, Bulova, and Zodiac were expected to begin marketing automatic wrist chronographs in 1972.[8] The Swiss competitors sold automatic wrist chronographs at prices equivalent to those of Heuer; Seiko, on the other hand, sold its chronographs at prices approximately 40–50% below the Heuer prices.

World production statistics were not available for these particular products. To measure relative market share, Heuer-Leonidas and other Swiss manufacturers utilized Swiss export statistics to compute the percentage of Swiss exports enjoyed by the company. Heuer-Leonidas saw its overall export share increase from 15.9% in 1966 to 27.3% in 1971, although not all products shared equally in this growth.

While little was known about the purchaser of any particular H-L product, the company had conducted a mail survey of 475 purchasers in 1970. This study indicated that the average purchaser was likely to be over 30 years of age, in middle or top management, who bought the product for fun or sports usage. The company planned to retain the services of a marketing research firm in 1972 to determine the consumer profile of the potential "Easy Rider" purchaser.

PRODUCTION

As was the case with most Swiss watch manufacturers, Heuer-Leonidas was an assembler of its products rather than a fully-integrated

---

[7] Of these companies, all except Seiko and Zenith-Movado used the automatic movement developed jointly by Heuer and Breitling in 1969.

[8] Bulova and Zodiac would use the Heuer/Breitling movement.

manufacturer. The basic parts that went into the complete stopwatch or chronograph were purchased from Swiss companies that specialized in the production of watch parts. The parts suppliers were highly specialized, each of them usually producing only a few specific parts for the watch assembly. Major parts and sources of supply for Heuer-Leonidas were as follows:

1. *Unassembled movements ("ébauches" in French).* The plates, bridges, mainspring, barrel drum, wheels, gear train, direct and indirect drive mechanism for the hands—the major parts of the watch —were purchased principally from *Ebauches S.A.,* which supplied movements to the entire (non-integrated) industry. The specialized movements required for stopwatches and non-automatic chronographs were produced by specialized subsidiaries in the Ebauches holding group. The movement for the automatic chronograph, by contrast, was purchased from a non-Ebauches company that produced the movement exclusively for Heuer-Leonidas, Breitling, and a list of clients approved by the two companies.

2. *Hairsprings, balances, escapement mechanisms.* The "regulating" mechanisms that released the energy of the mainspring at a controlled rate—were purchased from specialized companies in the *ASUAG* holding trust (Allgemeine Schweizerische Uhrenindustrie Aktiengesellschaft).

3. *Jewels, faces, hands, cases, bracelets, etc.* These accessories were purchased from parts manufacturers that formed a part of the *UBAH* holding group (Union des Branches Annexes de l'Horlogerie)

Ebauches S.A., ASUAG, and UBAH had a virtual monopoly on the production of parts for Swiss watch assemblers. Only the few fully-integrated manufacturers (Rolex, SSIH [Omega and Tissot], *et al.*) had an alternate source of supply. This constraint made the parts purchasing decisions extremely important for Heuer-Leonidas, both from the standpoint of cost (raw materials represented about 70% of the manufacturing cost of H-L products) and scheduling.

In addition to supplying the unassembled movements for H-L products, Ebauches S.A. also undertook the development work on new products, either at its own initiative or at the specific request of Heuer. Since practically every watch innovation required a unique movement, due to changes in the shape, size or operating characteristics of the product, Ebauches occupied a position of central importance.

When the new product idea was generated by the company, the three basic issues to be discussed with Ebauches concerned *design, delivery,* and *cost* (including tooling expenditures). Other watch companies could be brought in on the design to spread the tooling expenditures, if the company so desired.

When the product idea was generated by Ebauches design engineers, as was the case with the Trackmaster and Easy Rider movements, the additional issue of *exclusivity* was added to the previous three. Whether the new movement would be sold to the company on an exclusive basis or made available to the entire watch industry was an issue to be negotiated by Ebauches and the company.

In Heuer-Leonidas' case, exclusivity was granted on the Trackmaster, based on H-L's participation in the idea and design and the company's perceived ability to develop sales of high volumes. The "Easy Rider" movement, on the other hand, was sold to Heuer on an exclusive basis for six months only; after this period, it would be sold to any interested customer. Jack Heuer described the negotiation process as follows:

> I can't even describe how tough the discussions can be. They can't be delegated to anyone; Ebauches won't talk to anyone but the man in charge. The results of the negotiations are absolutely critical to the success of a company; if you want exclusivity, or if you are pushing for certain delivery deadlines, you have to be as tough and confident as Ebauches. The talks are friendly—we've all been in this business a number of years—but behind the friendliness a very serious game is being played.

Delivery problems with the "Easy Rider" had been a concern of 1971. With only six months of exclusivity, Jack Heuer wanted to be assured of strong Christmas sales. The company worked closely with Ébauches S.A. on technical problems that developed with the movement, hoping to speed up final delivery. Despite these efforts, a delay in delivery of the movement permitted the company to assemble only 8,000 Easy Riders by the end of the year, barely in time to display the product in jewelry store windows by Christmas.

Assembly operations

The fabrication of stopwatches and wrist chronographs was conducted by the Technical Department under the direction of Mr. André Meylan. Mr. Meylan's other responsibilities entailed the purchasing of materials and coordination of new product development with Ébauches S.A. and other suppliers.

The factories at St. Imier and Bienne were organized by product assembly responsibilities, with product sections headed by experienced watchmakers who reported directly to Mr. Meylan. Under these section heads were the factory workers, who assembled, tested, adjusted, and packed the products for storage and shipment.

Each worker performed a limited number of operations on each piece, working in front of an individual, revolving worktable equipped with tools, testing equipment, and lighting. Each worker was licensed to work in the watch industry and was classified according to his proficiency and professional knowledge in the field. Simple assembly operations were performed by the lowest level licensee, while the delicate testing and final calibration operations were performed only by Master watchmakers.

H-L had worked during the past few years to reduce the complexity of assembly to permit greater utilization of lower-level licensees. "Watchmaking has always been a family tradition," stated Mr. Meylan, "but fewer and fewer sons are following their fathers into the trade. The supply of high-level watchmakers is dwindling every year. This is why a product like Trackmaster becomes so important to us: it has a simple movement that can be assembled on an assembly-line basis by relatively unskilled workers. We simply have to reduce our skilled labor input."

The present system of revolving worktables was installed in 1966. A measurable result was a reduction in the direct labor percentage of the cost of the final product:

	Direct product costs	
	1971	1965
Labor	17.5%	22.5%
Materials	71.0%	66.0%
Production overhead	11.5%	11.5%

In this same period of time, the sales per employee increased from Sfr.40,700 to Sfr.89,260. "We've had some real productivity increases during the past five years," stated Mr. Meylan. "But I don't know how much further we can go."

Heuer-Leonidas employed a total of about 255 persons, including overseas subsidiaries.

ELECTRONICS DIVERSIFICATION

Two major factors led the company towards the development of an electronic product line in 1965. The first was the growing competitiveness of amateur and professional sports, particularly skiing, which began to demand greater precision in timing to differentiate among competitors at the finish line. Precisions of $\frac{1}{10}$th of a second were used until the early 1960's, but tie finishes occurred so frequently that $\frac{1}{100}$th of a second precision was becoming a necessity.

Another influence was the direct relationship that existed with the Austrian ski team through the promotional efforts of the Heuer agent for Austria. In 1964, the agent donated a wrist chronograph to each member of the Olympic ski team as a goodwill gesture. In the relationship that subsequently developed, some members of the ski team pointed out the deficiencies in the present timing equipment and helped to define the hardware requirements for a line of up-to-date ski timers.

Heuer Electronics Corporation

One such device—an electro-mechanical actuator for a standard $\frac{1}{100}$th of a second stopwatch—was designed and produced in Switzerland. The other proposed timers appeared to be beyond the electronic state-of-the-art in Europe. As a result, the company turned to the U.S. and in 1965 located three "moonlighting" engineers from an electronics company who agreed to design and produce the required timing devices, which would have an accuracy of $\frac{1}{1000}$th of a second.

In 1966, the engineers incorporated as Heuer Electronics Corporation (HEC), with Heuer-Leonidas retaining 51% of the voting shares and 30% of the capital. In 1970, following an agreement whereby H-L relinquished majority control, Heuer Electronics Corporation forfeited the "Heuer" portion of its name, becoming "Electrodata Concepts, Inc."

The Electronics Division

The Electronics Division in Bienne was formed in 1968 when Christian Nitschke, a young German electrical engineer, was hired to sell the products being produced by Heuer Electronics Corporation. Mr. Nitschke had helped to finance his university degree by timing automobile races and designing equipment to be used for this function. Before long, he came into contact with Jack Heuer, who proposed that Nitschke head an Electronics Division for Heuer-Leonidas.

The products at Nitschke's disposal were the electro-mechanical stopwatch actuator "STARTOMAT," and the electronic $\frac{1}{1000}$th of a second "BCD Timer" produced by HEC. In addition, HEC had recently completed work on a $\frac{1}{1000}$th of a second timer that *printed*, rather than merely displayed its results: the "Centigraph" timer.

The sales effort for these products was difficult to formalize, since it was not entirely clear where to make direct sales calls. The regular H-L wholesalers were encouraged to keep their "ears to the ground" and pass on any potential sales leads; Nitschke followed up on the leads himself and sent out a large number of direct mailing brochures explaining the line of Heuer electronic timers.

Electronic product development

While the sales effort was developing, the company increased its product development activity in this division for industrial and sports applications. Two industrial products were developed:

IC Tester, a production-line test device that tested integrated circuits. Developed by ECI in the U.S. Price: about Sfr.7,500.

Data Printer, an output device for digital instruments. The printer was designed for use in industrial, laboratory and field applications, where it would accept the outputs of counters, voltmeters, process control devices, or small computers and provide a printed record of the data and its time of occurrence. Developed by the Electronic Division in Switzerland. Price: between Sfr.4,000 and 5,000.

The sports developmental effort, which involved only the Electronics Division, concerned the design of a complete, portable system for automobile timing, using as a base the previously-developed Centigraph printing timer and a series of photocell actuators. Several automobile racing teams were contacted about the developmental effort, and Ferrari was sufficiently interested to request a timing system that would permit "pit" crews to time Ferrari and competitive cars. The basic objective was to reduce the number of personnel required to time the race crews by hand.

Traditional hand timing, though relatively accurate, was costly in terms of personnel. One timer with three stopwatches could check only one car, and the results he obtained were incomplete, since they had to be checked against the results of other timers.

Nitschke and his design engineer spent four–five months timing automobile races to determine the basic needs of the timing crews. Out of this effort grew the Centigraph Le Mans, a timing system that permitted one timer to check 10 cars simultaneously.

The Le Mans installation was a small computer about the size of a desk adding machine that gave the time of day or elapsed time from the start of the race. It also printed the car and lap numbers, the time between cars, the lap time, and the length of pit stops for each car. The Centigraph operator punched a button representing the car number as the car crossed the photo cell actuator, and the Centigraph would do the rest: perform the calculations, store the data, and print all the information in one line of print.

The Le Mans version was the most sophisticated product in the complete Centigraph product line. Less sophisticated versions were available for amateur automobile racing clubs, and a variation of the system was produced for manufacturers' car testing tracks:

Model	Use	Approximate price (Sfr.)
Centigraph Standard	Amateur racing clubs	10,000–20,000
Centigraph Le Mans	Professional pit crews	27,000
Centigraph Car Test	Manufacturers' test tracks	30,000 and up

Special accessories: electric eyes, digital display boards, etc., added to the basic price of the models.

"Our interest was in developing salable equipment for amateur and professional groups," explained Chris Nitschke. "We had no interest in the expensive, single-event timing situations performed by Omega and Longines. We think we're plugging an important gap. The real problem is in reaching the market."

Efforts in 1970 were directed towards identifying potential customers. Rolf Gasser, the Sales Manager employed by the division, put together a list of amateur automobile clubs and racing associations to be contacted by mail. In the meantime, leads from the field continued to be forwarded from wholesalers and interested parties.

The company was also looking forward to active involvement in ski racing. The expected development of the professional skiing association with professional-size purses appeared to make this a potentially exciting market.

Electronics results

Electronic sales increased from about Sfr.350,000 in 1969 to 650,000 in 1970 and 710,000 in 1971. Nevertheless, actual results were disappointing when compared to Jack Heuer's expectations when the division was formed:

> We put together a 5-year financial plan in 1969 for the period 1970–1974. I must say we were pleased when Electronics made its 1970 forecasted sales figure. But we were overly optimistic in 1969; we thought

Electronics would hit a minimum of Sfr.1.85 million in 1971 and Sfr.4.65 million by 1974. We'll have to lower our sights a bit. We'll also have to work harder to sell the products we have and spend less of our time in development until they begin to move.

FINANCE AND CONTROL

The most significant event in the company's recent financial history was the initial public offering of Heuer-Leonidas common stock in 1970, which offered 4,000 shares (Sfr.250 par value) for Sfr.925 per share. According to the prospectus:

> The new funds will be used to intensify research and development in the electronics sector, in view of a diversification in this direction. They will also permit the company to purchase land for the construction of a factory, and to enlarge the distribution organization by the foundation of new sales subsidiaries and the strengthening of those already in existence.

The public offering was rather unique in Switzerland, since only one other watch company—Girard-Perregaux—had ever taken this step, despite the fact that the industry association had long been advising "concentration and capital" as two remedies for the weaknesses of the Swiss watch industry.

Heuer's capital needs became apparent following the preparation of the five-year financial plan in 1969. The company anticipated doubling its sales by 1974, which would have severely strained its liquidity. "We had the choice of slowing down growth or finding new capital," declared Jack Heuer. "For a while we considered going public in the U.S. with our U.S. sales subsidiary—everyone was making a killing on the N.Y.S.E. with new issues during 1968—but the market began its long slide, and I'm just as glad we changed our mind."

The financing of sales subsidiaries by the parent company was an important funds use during recent years, particularly in the U.S. Heuer-Leonidas' direct investment in HTEC mounted to Sfr.500,000[9] in share capital and about Sfr.400,000 in long-term loans. In addition, accounts receivable from HTEC averaged about Sfr.2.5 million. The U.S. practice of granting extensive credit to retail jewelers ("dating" plans) made collection periods long—123 days for HTEC—and this burden was inevitably carried by the parent company.

Funds from the public offering were used in part to purchase the factory and some extra land at St. Imier, thus permitting future expansion but changing the company's long-standing practice of renting its facilities. The planned creation of a German sales subsidiary was delayed.

Despite the increase in the number of shares, Jack Heuer continued as the majority shareholder in the voting stock of the company. He discussed the effect of going public in the following way:

---

[9] Book value of the investment in 1971, net of a substantial amount of additional investment that had been written off directly against income during the past 10 years.

A number of things have changed for me since the public issue. Before, if we had a good end-of-year, it was good for the family and we all felt happy; now, my responsibilities have been expanded and we have a *moral* obligation to perform. We *owe* it to our shareholders, who invested because they had faith in our ability to grow.

Another fact of going public is that we have to consolidate our accounts for financial reporting purposes. This makes us focus more attention on the performance of our overseas subsidiaries than was the case in the past. If they mismanage their inventories or fail to produce sales and profits, our financial statements will tell the unhappy story. This causes me and my Board a great deal of concern, and I must admit it is a consequence of going public that we hadn't really considered before the offering.

Exhibit 3 shows the company's consolidated income statements for the years 1969–1971.

The company had practiced a policy of paying a 15% dividend on the par value of its stock. In 1971, the dividend was reduced to 12%, with Sfr.360,000 being paid out on the share capital of Sfr.3 million.

Management control

Budgeting and financial control of operations were monitored by Mr. Willy Monnier, the company's controller, who became a part of Heuer-Leonidas in 1964 following the merger. Mr. Monnier described his role as follows:

The last few years have been a bit hectic, particularly with the public issue and the need to consolidate accounts for the first time. With that period behind us, however, we can get back to the business of focusing on the performance of our current operations.

Like most watch companies, we have always been able to know our production costs and control them within fairly precise limits. Watchmaking has always been fairly production-oriented, which means production cost conscious.

This company is a bit different, though, in that the management—except for Mr. Meylan—is so marketing oriented. The fact that we control production costs is taken for granted; for the rest, growth in sales seems to be the center of attention. You'll never know how crushed Mr. Heuer was when we didn't increase our sales in 1971. For my part, though, I'd be a bit happier if the word "profit" was used more frequently.

I feel my job is to prod everyone to think more about profits. The U.S. subsidiary is a case in point. Sales have been growing rapidly (Exhibit 8), but where are the profits? Growth is fine, but when the return on investment is below average, what have we gained?

Mr. Heuer is becoming more conscious of this problem. So is the Board of Directors. Perhaps the 1971 experience was really a gift in disguise.

The company budgeted on a yearly basis, using sales estimates supplied by wholesalers in January as the basis for projections. The budget covered the period January–December, but as a rule the final document was not completed until late February. "I have discussed this problem with Mr. Hunsperger," stated Mr. Monnier, "but he doesn't think we can get the wholesalers' sales estimates any earlier. I wish something could be done, though."

Mr. Monnier regularly prepared a number of reports for Jack Heuer and the Board of Directors, focusing attention on sales, profits, accounts receivable, and inventory levels. In addition, Mr. Monnier worked closely with the controllers of the overseas subsidiaries in an effort to improve reporting, collection of accounts receivable, and inventory management.

Board of Directors

The Board of Directors grew in size and importance since the Leonidas merger and the public offering. Previous to 1964, the Board and management of the company were one and the same, but the two above events— and particularly the public offering—saw the Board begin to play a more independent role.

The backgrounds of the Board members are given in Exhibit 9.

A smaller Executive Committee of the Board was established in 1969 to prepare the bulk of the work requiring Board decisions. Composed of Jack Heuer, Dr. W. Ryser, and Thüring von Erlach, the Committee met formally once each month but kept in contact informally on a more frequent basis.

According to Mr. von Erlach, an occasional lack of information increased the difficulty that the Board otherwise incurred in executing its responsibilities:

> We're quite dependent on the information we get from Jack in order to make our decisions. Sometimes the information is complete, but at other times we're a bit left in the dark. This doesn't make it easy when it comes to criticizing Jack or the other managers. Jack is a great guy, but you have to watch him: he's quick, and he's sometimes ready to say that "everything is under control" when we have the feeling that it may be otherwise.

LOOKING AHEAD

The management team had a formal opportunity to discuss the company's management and strategy during a 2½-day seminar held during 1971. The discussions treated new product development in the watch and electronic sectors, opportunities and resources for expansion, and the particular strengths and weaknesses of the various departments.

Out of the discussions came a new draft of the company's objectives, which included the following:

1. Our primary objective remains to continue as one of the world's leading specialists in the domain of short time measurement, and to continue to develop our specialty. The pursuit of this goal, however, should not become a detriment to the rational utilization of our resources.
2. This implies for our product policy:
    a) A sustained effort in the development of our current program of traditional stopwatches;

b) The accelerated development of our diversification into the electronic measurement of short time intervals;

c) Diversification into the sector of measurement instruments, if we master its technology;

d) Improvement of the utilization of our existing distribution channels by increasing our product range.

Jack Heuer felt justified in being optimistic about the future, despite the setback of 1971:

> We lost a bit of faith in ourselves in 1971, but we learned some valuable lessons. One of them is profit-consciousness. Mr. Monnier has been trying to teach that lesson for a number of years, but 1971 put some teeth into his arguments. We are taking a harder look at the profitability of our operations, particularly in the U.S., where strong measures need to be taken.
>
> As for the future, we are well-placed to succeed. The capacity of our management has yet to be tested. We could manage a Sfr.50 million business with our current management—we have the flexibility and the market orientation, and we work together well. I know my deficiencies, but I have good men backing me up in every area. Our strengths and weaknesses mesh like teeth on a gear.
>
> We expect results from new products. We can exploit our flexibility in distribution. In addition, our flexible attitude towards distribution permits us to change with the times.
>
> European distribution is changing, and I think we'll see mass merchandising on a grand scale. Sears will move to Europe. Intersport (a multinational distributor of sports equipment) is growing and will bypass the wholesalers who think only in terms of national boundaries.
>
> We've come a long way since 1958, and I'm pleased with our progress. Now we're solidly in electronics, and I think we can develop some unusual products that will create real growth. We're publicly-owned, and we have a responsibility to create and manage our growth. We won't let the shareholders down.

Exhibit 1
HEUER-LEONIDAS
Organization in 1958

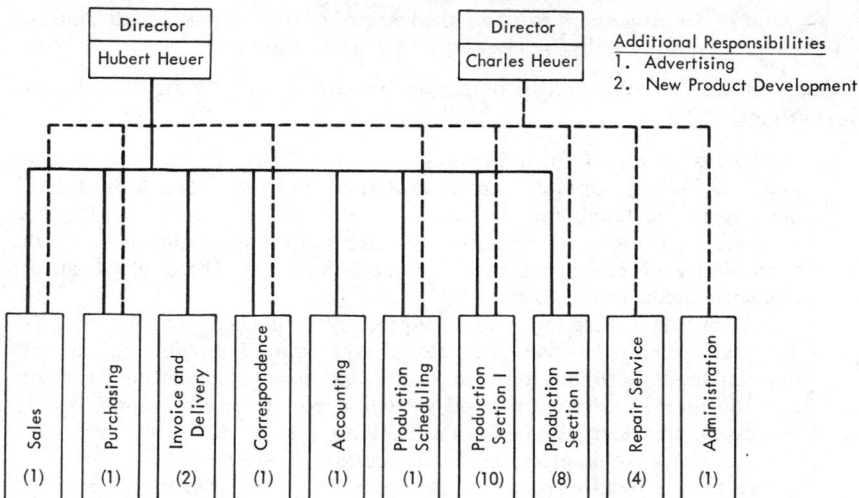

Notes: 1.   The two directors, each holding 50% of the outstanding shares, compose the Board of Directors and General Assembly of shareholders.
2.   The figures in parentheses indicate the number of persons in each department.
Source: Company records.

Exhibit 2

HEUER-LEONIDAS

Operating History 1966–1971 (unconsolidated)
(in Swiss francs)

	1971	1970	1969	1968	1967	1966
Sales	16,601,945	17,993,035	15,267,314	11,392,724	8,460,785	7,339,824
Less Discount	486,561	556,343	504,191	350,708	262,311	233,643
Net Sales	16,115,384	17,436,692	14,763,123	11,042,015	8,198,474	7,106,181
Cost of Goods Sold	11,117,945	12,592,265	11,172,866	8,413,852	6,225,479	5,599,861
Gross Margin	4,997,439	4,844,427	3,590,257	2,628,163	1,972,995	1,506,320
Sales, General, Administrative Expenses	3,452,478	3,705,096	2,899,821	1,997,134	1,544,676	1,124,352
Amortization	873,640	273,096	224,328	275,770	185,675	95,463
Profit from operations	671,321	866,235	466,108	355,259	242,645	286,505
Extraordinary Income	31,062	74,332	26,163	—	—	—
Less Allocation to Reserves	25,000	50,000	40,000	50,000	30,000	90,000
Profit before tax	677,383	890,658	452,271	305,259	212,645	196,505
Tax	209,977	114,218	111,126	77,729	76,395	20,243
Net Profit	467,406	776,440	341,144	227,530	136,250	176,262

Note: Figures may fail to add because of rounding.

Exhibit 3

HEUER-LEONIDAS

Consolidated Income Statements, 1969–1971
(in thousands of francs)

	1971	1970	1969
Sales	19,302	22,397	17,223
Less discount	539	567	463
Net sales	18,762	21,830	16,761
Cost of goods sold	12,207	14,948	11,615
Gross margin	6,555	6,882	5,146
Sales, General, Administrative	5,268	5,685	4,429
Amortization	304	344	228
Profit from operations	983	852	488
Extraordinary income	6	104	29
Extraordinary expenses	271	56	93
Profit before tax	718	900	425
Tax	293	159	119
Net profit	424	740	305

Note: Figures may fail to add because of rounding.

Exhibit 4

HEUER-LEONIDAS

Balance Sheets, 1966–1971 (unconsolidated)
(before allocation of profits to reserves and dividends)
(in Swiss francs)

ASSETS	1971	1970	1969	1968	1967	1966
Current assets						
Cash	19,686	43,031	22,612	19,016	21,264	64,753
Accounts receivable	5,977,070	5,653,176	3,232,451	1,976,712	1,516,559	1,171,865
Inventories*	4,000,000	4,500,000	2,600,000	1,600,000	1,300,000	900,000
Prepaid expenses & deferred charges	52,342	18,936	30,314	—	—	—
Total Current Assets	10,049,098	10,215,143	5,885,377	3,595,728	2,837,823	2,136,618
Fixed assets						
Cars	2	1	1	1	1	1
Tools & machinery	2	2	2	2	2	2
Furniture & equipment	150,001	200,001	2	2	2	1
Building	440,000	445,000	—	—	—	—
Other assets						
Investments	604,001	1,374,000	618,000	588,000	528,000	202,807
Other	12,000	12,000	12,000	12,000	12,000	12,000
Total Assets	11,255,103	12,246,147	6,515,382	4,195,733	3,377,828	2,351,429
LIABILITIES + CAPITAL						
Current liabilities						
Accounts payable	808,755	1,283,169	1,713,155	1,407,294	839,119	672,509
Notes payable	2,707,946	3,031,147	1,412,279	876,044	623,956	—
Accrued expenses	234,654	155,489	19,459	10,500	141,087	167,405
Total Current Liabilities	3,751,355	4,469,805	3,144,893	2,293,838	1,604,163	839,914
Other liabilities						
Loans	635,000	550,000	250,000	685,000	688,800	682,400
Stockholders capital						
Capital stock	3,000,000	3,000,000	2,000,000	555,000	555,000	370,000
Paid-in capital + reserves	3,361,000	3,417,413	750,700	405,000	371,000	330,000
Open reserves from previous retained earnings	40,342	32,489	28,645	29,365	22,615	5,452
Carry forward net profit (before distribution)	467,406	776,440	341,144	227,530	136,250	123,663
Total Liabilities and Capital	11,255,103	12,246,147	6,515,382	4,195,733	3,377,828	2,351,429
Dividends Paid (based on par value of capital stock)	12%	15%	15%	15%	15%	15%

* Inventories were valued conservatively for book purposes. Accounting practices permitted a direct write-down of up to 35% of the gross inventory value. The gross inventory figures for 1966–1971 were as follows: 1971—5,396,000; 1970—6,418,445; 1969—4,365,391; 1968—2,488,837; 1967—1,811,590; 1966—1,423,175.

Exhibit 5

HEUER-LEONIDAS

1971 Organization Structure

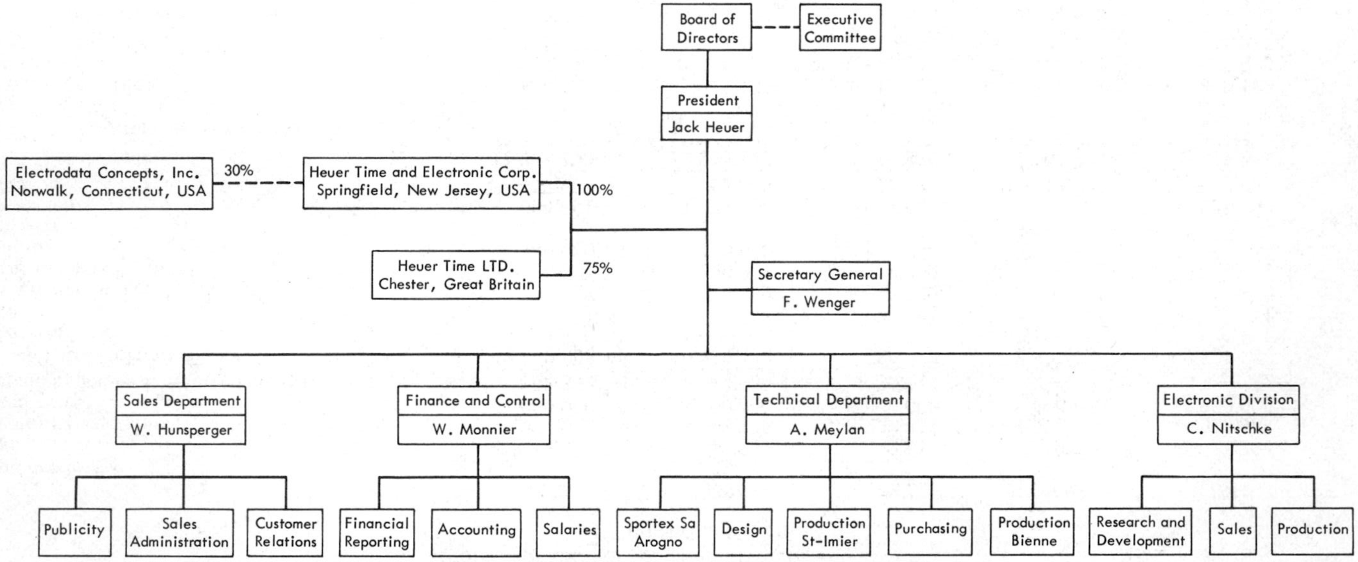

Exhibit 6

HEUER-LEONIDAS

Backgrounds of H-L Managers, 1971

Jack W. Heuer, President, age 39. Swiss Federal Institute of Technology, Zurich. Formerly Executive Vice-President, Heuer Time Corporation, 1959–1963. President, Heuer-Leonidas, 1965-present. With Heuer-Leonidas for past 12 years. Major outside interests: skiing, golf, sports in general.

Frédéric Wenger, Secretary-General, age 34. University of Berne. Formerly legal advisor, Touring Club, Genève. With H-L for 2 years. Major interests: skiing, tennis, horseback riding.

Walter Hunsperger, Sales Director, age 43. Previously Sales Manager, Fabrique Ebel S.A. With H-L for 7 years. Major interests: sports.

Willy Gad Monnier, Finance Director, age 40. Previously with Leonidas Ltd. as Chief Accountant. With H-L for 10 years. Major interests: sports and gastronomy.

André Meylan, Technical Director, age 44. Formerly Chief of Development, Felsa S. A., a subsidiary of Ebauches S.A. With H-L for 6 years. Major interest: photography.

Christian Nitschke, Manager of Electronics Division, age 37. Technical University of Stuttgart, Georgia Institute of Technology (U.S.), University of Freiburg. Formerly Research Assistant, Arnold-Bergstraesser-Institut, University of Freiburg. With H-L for 3 years. Major interest: social change in industrial and underdeveloped countries.

Exhibit 7

HEUER-LEONIDAS

Typical Products in the "Heuer" Line

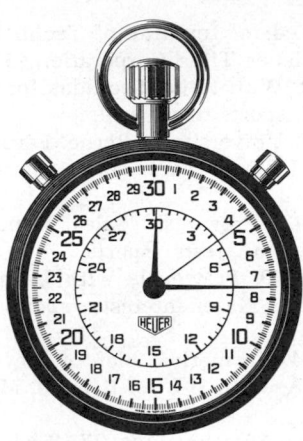

Stopwatch
Jeweled-lever, 7–15 jewels
100 + models
Sfr.100.— to 250.—

Dashboard Instrument
Jeweled-lever, 7–15 jewels
11 models
Sfr.195.— to 500.—

Non-automatic Wrist
    Chronograph
Jeweled-lever, 17 jewels
40 + models
Sfr.195.— to 400.—

Pocket Chronograph
Jeweled-lever, 17 jewels
8 models
Sfr.300.— to 750.—

Automatic Wrist Chrono-
    graph
Jeweled-lever, 17 jewels
11 models
Sfr.390.— to 700.—

All prices refer to approximate Swiss retail prices.

Exhibit 8

HEUER-LEONIDAS

Performance of Overseas Sales Subsidiaries

HEUER TIME & ELECTRONICS CORP. (U.S.)

Year	Sales ($)	% H-L Sales	Profits ($)	Remarks
1959	$ 867	—	$(9,632)	
1960	70,336	12%	(35,724)	
1961	100,456	24%	(20,753)	
1962	141,357	26%	(24,931)	
1963	176,145	27%	(1,633)	Manager fired; new manager.
1964	229,672	19%	4,158	
1965	425,600	28%	30,299	
1966	461,095	27%	21,649	
1967	677,481	34%	6,774	
1968	777,364	29%	(28,497)	Theft of $25,000 in merchandise.
1969	1,045,885	29%	(29,753)	
1970	1,179,914	28%	(64,301)	Manager fired; new manager.
1971	952,841	22%	(154,458)	Exchange loss of $51,000. Manager fired in early 72.

HEUER TIME LTD. (U.K.)

Year	Sales (£)	% H-L Sales	Profits (£)	Remarks
1968	£41,051	4%	(£721)	Devaluation loss of £1,893.
1969	85,918	6%	732	
1970	120,155	7%	(296)	
1971	132,457	8%	576	Devaluation loss of £3,000.

Exhibit 9

HEUER-LEONIDAS

Composition of the Board of Directors

* *Dr. W. Ryser, Chairman,* age 46. Lawyer; Vice-President of Fiduciaire Générale; professor of tax law, University of Berne; member of the Board of several Swiss companies and Guyerzeller Zurmont Bank in Zürich. Chairman and member of H-L board since 1968.

* *Jack W. Heuer, President,* age 39.

Charles E. Heuer, Member, age 75. Former president of Heuer-Leonidas, and father of Jack Heuer.

Hubert B. Heuer, Member, age 70. Former president of Heuer-Leonidas, and brother of Charles E. Heuer.

Charles Jeanneret, Member, former Chairman, age 79. Former owner of Leonidas S.A. and Sportex S.A. Owner of Berna Watch Company. On H-L Board since 1964.

Dominique de Charrière, Member, age 47. Mechanical engineer; sales manager of Maillefer S.A. Son-in-law of Charles Heuer. Member since 1968.

* *Thüring von Erlach, Member,* age 38. Lawyer; secretary to general manager of Galenica S.A. Son-in-law of Hubert Heuer. Member since 1968.

Dr. Jean Michel Junod, Member, age 52. Physician, surgeon, heart specialist, and writer. Adoptive son of Charles Jeanneret. Member since 1968.

* Members of Executive Committee.

Prelude Corporation

IN JUNE 1972, Prelude Corporation could look back on 12 years of pioneering in the newly developed offshore segment of the Northern Lobster fishing industry. (See Appendix.) Having accounted for 16% of the offshore poundage landed in 1971, this Massachusetts company ranked as the largest single lobster producer in North America. Mr. Joseph S. Gaziano, president since 1969, looked forward to a still more dominant position and, in the long run, to further vertical integration beyond what he had already introduced:

> Basically, we're trying to revolutionize the lobster industry by applying management and technology to what has been an 18th century cottage industry heretofore. Other companies have become giants by restructuring such commodity businesses as crab, tuna, avocados, celery and chicken; we want to become the Procter & Gamble of the lobster business. Until we opened up the offshore resource there was no way to bring about this revolution, but now the chance is there. Furthermore, the technology and money required to fish offshore are so great that the little guy can't make out; the risks are too great. The fishing industry now is just like the automobile industry was 60 years ago; 100 companies are going to come and go, but we'll be the General Motors.
>
> We have toyed with the idea of establishing a restaurant chain featuring the Prelude lobster, similar to Black Angus or Red Coach [local chains which offer only a small selection of beef as their fare], but have never really gotten serious about it. We find we have enough to manage now. The Deep Deep and Wickford distribution systems, which we purchased in the past fiscal year, have given us some vertical integration.

As Mr. Gaziano voiced these expectations, Prelude hopefully saw itself as starting to recover from a recent precipitous and unexplained decline in its per trip catch (Exhibit 1). This decline had plunged the company back into the red for the fiscal year ending in April (Exhibit 2) and had raised the specter of depletion of the offshore lobster population by pollution or over-fishing. Mr. Gaziano viewed these possibilities as bleak, but discounted them:

> The vessels we have are especially designed and constructed for our lobster gear and couldn't be used for any other purpose without costly refitting. I suppose we could go south into the Caribbean for crawfish or go after finfish that are amenable to the long line techniques. We could even use the vessels for research, laying cables, or as oil-survey ships. Practically speaking, if someone said tomorrow that we couldn't sell lobsters due to mercury content or some other reason, I guess we would be forced to close the doors. However, I foresee this risk as minimal. Certainly it is possible but there are no studies or indications that this is at all a likely occurrence.[1]

HISTORY

Prelude's predecessor company had been organized in 1960 to develop techniques for deep-sea lobster fishing. Its founder was an ordained minister, the Reverend William D. Whipple, and its name reflected Mrs. Whipple's profession—music. In the course of raising money for a company that was never in the black until 1971, Rev. Whipple had incorporated in 1966 and had arranged a private placement of 140,000 shares (58% of the total). This brought in $350,000, which was supplemented by debt. Late in 1968, when Rev. Whipple felt ready to start commercial operations, prospects for growth plus creditor pressure led to additional financing (Exhibit 3), some of it completed before the ending of the go-go market in 1969:

Date	Financing	Amount
February 1969	250,000 common shares at $8.50	$2,125,000 gross
September 1969*	10% senior notes (John Hancock Insurance Co.)	500,000
September 1969	40,000 rights at $6.75 (John Hancock)	270,000
June 1970	50,000 common shares at $3.00 (private placement)	150,000

* This financing became necessary when an expected government subsidy for fishing fleets failed to materialize.

Also during 1969, Mr. Whipple agreed to bring in Mr. Gaziano as president, and to have him put together a professional management team. The purchase of two 101-foot trawlers for $1,585,000 completed Prelude's make-ready, and the year ending April 30, 1971, brought operating earnings of $273,000 from a lobster catch of 1.1 million pounds.

---

[1] In support of his belief that depletion of the resource was unlikely, Mr. Gaziano employed a widely used argument—namely, that the average weight of offshore lobsters caught was holding steady at about 2½ pounds (with a range of 1–11 pounds or more), a fact taken to indicate that the more mature lobsters were not being fished at a rate higher than their natural replacement.

Spurred by this success, Prelude purchased two more ships of 96 ft. and 125 ft. for $1,118,000 and acquired two nearby subsidiaries in the lobster distribution business. The latter were the Wickford Shellfish Company and the distribution segment of Deep Deep Ocean Products; these would, it was hoped, reduce price fluctuations and raise margins by reducing Prelude's dependence on independent wholesalers. In the three fiscal years prior to their purchase, Wickford had had two nominal profits and one nominal loss. Deep Deep had suffered significant losses, but these were laid by management chiefly to Deep Deep's operation of three ships[2] which Prelude did not buy—although it agreed to market their catch. Prelude saw both firms as competently managed, but beset by inability to raise enough capital to finance their rapidly expanding sales:

	1969	1970	1971	1972
		(dollars in thousands)		
Wickford (years ending February 28)....	—	$ 870	$1,000	$1,600
Deep Deep (years ending December 31)...	$950	1,623	1,414	—

Both Prelude's new ships (which began fishing in July 1971 and January 1972) and its acquisitions (effected in December and January) led to additional financing:

Date	Financing	Amount
April 1971.......	Two ships mortgages consolidated at 1% above prime	$1,200,000
December 1971...	Paid 17,500 common shares, valued at $7.00,*	122,000
	for Wickford, plus cash	170,000
January 1972.....	Paid 22,845 common shares valued at $7.00 for Deep Deep distribution, plus assumption of certain liabilities	—

* According to the terms of sale, if the former owner should sell his stock at less than $6.50 a share, the company would pay the difference.

Still another episode in Prelude's history deserves mention because of the worldwide attention it received. In the spring of 1971, Prelude became the focus of a well-publicized international incident involving the United States and Russia. Early in the year, ships of the Russian commercial fishing fleet had caused the loss of more than $70,000 of Prelude's gear by dragging fishing nets over the bottom on which Prelude's traps were resting, clearly marked by buoys and radar reflectors. Such fixed gear had legal right-of-way, so Mr. Gaziano not only sued the Russian Government for $177,000 in actual damages plus $266,000 in punitive damages, but also caused a Soviet merchant ship to be attached in San Francisco. The actual out-of-court settlement was for only $89,000, but it was hailed as a precedent in commercial relations between the two countries.

[2] By June 1972, one of these ships had been sold.

PRELUDE IN 1972

In mid-1972, Prelude was organized primarily along functional lines, with departments for operations, engineering, research, and finance and administration. Distribution functions were divided among the Deep Deep and Wickford subsidiaries (Exhibits 4, 5).

Operations

Fishing. Fishing operations and the logistics involved in landing and distributing the lobster catch were under the direction of Robert E. (Gene) White, age 33, vice president, operations. Prelude's four ships operated year-round on a two-week cycle, 10 days fishing and 4 days in port for unloading and resupply. Each ship carried a crew of 10: captain, mate, engineer, cook, and six deckhands. After a 12-hour steam to the offshore lobster grounds, the crew would begin "hauling pots" 12 hours a day. (See Appendix.) When the lobsters were brought up and removed from the pots, their claws would be pegged with a red plastic peg which displayed the Prelude brand, and then they would be stored in the hold. The empty trap would be rebaited and stacked until the line was ready to be payed out again for another three days of fishing.

Whether the trawl was relaid where it had been or in another location was a decision made by the captain, depending very much on how the catch was running. In any event, the captain was charged with bringing in as many pounds of lobster as possible on each trip, an amount which could vary tremendously. Although Prelude's ships averaged about 20,000 pounds per trip, the results of a single trip could range from 4,000 to 40,000 pounds. (An indication of the variation in the size of the catch can be obtained from Exhibit 1.) In Mr. Gaziano's words:

> The biggest problem in the production process is the variability in the size of the catch. It is not like a manufacturing business. The size of the catch is uncertain. There is no proven way of forecasting where the lobsters will be on a given day. Mating habits, weather, etc., are some of the many variables which determine the size of the catch. Black magic is used by the captains to find lobsters. Presently, it is an art, not a science. Actually it is on a trial and error basis. If one canyon is not producing, the skipper moves to another location.

Work force. Along with dispatching and supplying the vessels, Mr. White was responsible for staffing both the ships and Prelude's truck fleet and storage facility. These operations used 50 people who were engaged in manning the ships or moving lobster. Because Prelude was located in Westport Point, these workers were nonunion. In nearby New Bedford, where the larger portion of the fishing industry was located, unions were a predominant force. Unlike most others in the fishing industry, who were required by the union to pay their crews a straight percentage of the catch, Prelude paid a base salary plus a sum of 20 cents a pound on everything over 25,000 pounds, to be divided among the crew on a pro rata basis. Mr. White commented on some of the problems with people:

The fisherman is an independent worker. He is always in demand and has a job waiting at his beck and call. His reputation stays with him, although references are not easy to evaluate. Since there is "always a ship leaving" he does not hesitate to tell his boss to "get screwed" if he is unhappy about something. How do you get a reference on somebody who has told his last three bosses to "get screwed?" So we end up hiring them and taking a chance based on their informal reputation which I get from my sources in the industry. We spin our wheels on quite a few. We attempt to hire experienced fishermen but 20% of our crews are bank tellers and "potato farmers" who want to try something more exciting and more financially rewarding. We start the experienced fisherman at $225 per week and the layman at $150. If the latter pans out after two or three trips he goes to $225 also.

The cook is one of the most important men on the ship. If I get a bad cook morale goes to hell. Most ship cooks are drunks—it is just a question of whether they are good drunks or bad drunks. I try to have at least one crewman on each ship to have welding expertise. This avoids having to return to shore to make minor repairs. Engineers are hard to get—their education allows them to earn good money on shore and avoid the hard sea duty. Lobstering is a hard and demanding job. Guys over 40 break up after several trips.

Logistics.   Since the inlet leading to Prelude's headquarters in Westport Point was not deep enough for the draft of the four ships, the company rented 225 feet of pier space at the State Pier in Fall River, about 15 miles away. Here the vessels tied up for unloading, maintenance, and resupply. The company owned and maintained a fleet of refrigerated trucks with which to transport the catch. After a returning ship had docked, the mesh baskets of pegged lobsters were lifted out of the hold and into these trucks. If the catch had already been sold, the truck, driven by a member of the shore crew, began its delivery rounds immediately.

If there was an excess, however, or if it was desired to hold the catch for better prices, then the truck would make the 20-minute run to Westport Point, where the lobsters would be transferred to the Prelude holding tank. This tank, built during 1968 and 1969 at a cost of $250,000, was capable of holding 125,000 pounds of lobster in seawater cooled to 42° F. The tank was designed around an experimental system aimed at reducing handling costs by keeping the lobster in mesh baskets aboard ship and stacking these baskets in the storage tank. The system had not worked out well in practice, however, since one dead lobster could cause the loss of 10% to 15% of its tankmates within a 24-hour period. As a result, the baskets had to be hauled out and culled regularly. Prelude management felt that if they did expand their holding capacity it would be with conventional three-tier tanks which, even though they required more space and lobster handling, could be culled more efficiently and could be built for only $1 per pound of storage capacity. Security measures, both at the holding tank and on the trucks, were important since lobster was a readily marketable commodity at any roadside stand.

Engineering

Engineering activities at Prelude were under the direction of Howard W. Gifford, age 37, vice president, engineering. These activities included the maintenance and procurement of vessels and equipment as well as the development of gear, etc.

Maintenance.   With each ship representing an investment of over $500,000 and subject to continual stress at sea, maintenance was an important and continual activity. This work was carried out by a seven-person maintenance department located at the pier in Fall River. Available there were complete facilities for the welding and machining necessary to overhaul and repair a ship's engines, life-support equipment, and trap-handling gear. Additionally this crew performed periodic preventative maintenance on the holding tank at Westport Point. This life-support system was particularly important since its failure, if full, would result in the loss of 125,000 pounds of lobster. Mr. Gifford was responsible for the hiring and firing of the maintenance personnel. Also, even though the ship's engineers were under the operational command of Mr. White, Mr. Gifford was responsible for their technical direction.

Purchase of ships and gear.   Mr. Gifford was responsible for evaluating potential vessels for use as fishing platforms; writing the specifications for their conversion; and initiating, supervising and approving their fitting out. In all these activities Mr. Gifford worked closely with Rev. Whipple in improving designs. Mr. Gifford also spent considerable time working with manufacturers' representatives on developing improved refrigeration technology for the life-support systems. The corrosive nature of the seawater coupled with the lobster's sensitivity to trace amounts of certain metals which were traditionally used for refrigeration systems made this a difficult area.

Research

Rev. Whipple, age 41, held the title of director of research. Since 1958 he had devoted a major portion of his time to commercial fishing and to developing a number of improvements and innovations in its equipment. Among these were a hydraulic power block and various rigging and hauling devices related to high-speed handling of deep-water lobster trapping systems.[3] Rev. Whipple was constantly evaluating the operational design of the ship's fishing gear and experimenting with ways to improve it. A qualified captain himself, Rev. Whipple would often take a ship out when a captain was sick or missing for some reason. In any case, he was generally at sea whenever there was a new idea to be tried out, a frequent occurrence.

In an effort to enhance their knowledge about the habits of the lobster, Prelude's management had recently hired a marine biologist. Mr. Gaziano remarked regarding research on the "product":

> We knew a lot about management and lobster fishing when we
> started, but we didn't know a damn thing about the lobster. We hired

---

[3] Although the company held design patents on certain of these mechanisms, management stated that the patents were no protection against competitors using similar but not identical equipment.

Jerry [a marine biologist] to give us some expertise in this area. He started with the task of accumulating all the data he could find on the lobster. It turned out nobody really knows a heck of a lot about them. He has three current projects. One is to set up a lobster rearing facility downstairs [corporate headquarters] and see what we can learn from that. The second project is to help us figure out what to do with the crabs we catch in our traps along with the lobsters. They are highly perishable and only bring 25 cents per pound. There is not much market for them, but, since we haul them in from the sea in quantities equal to or greater than the lobsters, we would like to exploit the resource. And lastly, we've chartered a little research sub. Jerry's going to spend five days on the bottom seeing what really goes on down there. It's going to cost us $25,000 but we will have information that no one else has.

Marketing

Prior to the acquisition of Wickford and Deep Deep late in fiscal 1971, Prelude sold most of its catch directly to wholesale lobster dealers in large lots, usually an entire shipload. As a result, the number of transactions was limited, and Mr. Gaziano was able to handle the telephone negotiations himself. He commented on the bargaining process as follows:

> The distributor knows when you have a large catch. He may say, "You have 30,000 pounds—well, we don't really want any today," and thereby drive down the price. Even with our large holding capacity we have been caught in this situation. There are no long-term, fixed-price contracts. It is cutthroat haggling to a great degree. We are really in the commodity trading business—buy and then sell at a profit; there is very little value added.

With the acquisition of Wickford and Deep Deep, each of which owned a variety of trucks and sorting tanks of 50,000 pounds capacity, marketing arrangements had changed. The original plan was for the two acquisitions combined to handle some three-fourths of Prelude's catch, although, in line with the intent to treat all three entities as profit centers, each could sell or buy where it got the best price. In the event, the Wickford and Deep Deep acquisitions happened to coincide with the precipitous drop in lobster catches, so all of Prelude's lobsters were sold "inside" during the first half of 1972.

Wickford, located in North Kingston, R.I., had brought Prelude a business in live lobsters (about 70% of sales) and in other types of seafood, including other shellfish and frozen-fish products. It distributed in various ways: thus, it had a combined retail seafood store and restaurant located in its home town, which accounted for 30% of its sales; it had a mail-order business in prepackaged clam and lobster dinners; and it operated a wholesale business in a market area that extended along the Eastern Seaboard south to Pennsylvania. Customers were restaurants and small dealers, whom it reached by making four delivery runs a week, locally, and to Pennsylvania, Connecticut, New York, and New Jersey.

Deep Deep, located in Boston, Mass., brought Prelude a business that consisted of distributing lobsters to dealers and restaurants in New England, New York, the Midwest, West, and South, the latter three markets being served by air shipments. Deep Deep's major accounts, however, were wholesalers serving restaurants in New York City. Shipments to these accounts had to be made by common carrier, since Prelude's nonunion drivers could not gain safe access to the city's highly organized Fulton Fish market.

Critical to selling all accounts of both companies was knowing who wanted to buy what, where, when, and at what offered price. "Contacts" were a marketer's paramount asset in the lobster trade. Prelude's management believed that Mr. John P. McGeough, former owner of Wickford, and Mr. Robert D. Usen, founder and ex-president of Deep Deep, were highly qualified in this regard, basing this opinion partly on a three-week cross-country trip that the financial vice president had made with Mr. Usen prior to the Deep Deep acquisition.

Both Messrs. Usen and McGeough had agreed to follow their companies into Prelude, where they continued to serve as presidents of the two subsidiaries. Here the compensation of each would be based primarily on the total profit of his unit. Although the decline in the lobster catch had prevented a full-scale testing of the two companies' performance, Prelude management indicated that their expectations had been largely fulfilled to date.

Besides bringing in Mr. Usen and Mr. McGeough, Mr. Gaziano had staffed marketing with a new sales manager, hired in November 1971. This was Mr. Duncan Scott, who had been on the road since his arrival, "cold calling" potential new distributor and restaurant accounts, and visiting old ones. Any business Mr. Scott turned up was referred to either Wickford or Deep Deep.

In still another marketing move in the spring of 1971, $15,000 had been invested in advertising on two Boston radio stations, WBZ and WHDH. This advertising was aimed at raising the ultimate consumer's awareness of Prelude's offshore lobster. Mr. Gaziano outlined the rationale behind this program:

> We are trying to establish brand identification for the Prelude lobster. We want people to ask for Prelude lobster—not just lobster— similar to the Chiquita Banana strategy. Towards this end we have used radio advertising and promotional devices in the form of handouts and red plastic lobster pegs with the Prelude name etched on them. The handouts are put in our lobster shipping boxes and Scott leaves them wherever he goes. We plan to start direct mailings. But our radio advertising was ill-timed in that we didn't follow up soon enough with sales calls and our catches were not large enough to satisfy the demand we created.

Finance and administration

Mr. John A. Jensen, age 33, was in charge of the financial affairs of the company. In the past he had been responsible for shepherding the financial transactions required to raise needed capital. Mr. Jensen kept close tabs on the day-to-day state of affairs, maintaining an eight-week

cash flow projection which he revised weekly, monitoring the daily transactions of the subsidiaries, and monitoring accounts receivable. (Restaurants and their suppliers were notoriously slow payers.)

His most current concern was centered around providing the funds
needed to finance the two new ships which were planned for 1973.
Exhibit 6 shows the projected income statement assuming the two new
ships were added. The cost of the two vessels was estimated at $1.3
million of which all but $300,000 could be mortgaged. Additionally, Mr.
Jensen and Mr. Gaziano were concerned about the impact of interest
charges on net income, interest being the main component of the fairly
substantial figure carried in the operating statement as "other" income
and expense (Exhibits 2 and 6). They felt that they needed a reduction
in short-term debt of between $200,000 and $450,000 to "clean up" their
balance sheet and reduce interest charges.

The company's underwriter had prepared a prospectus proposing a
private placement of 100,000 to 150,000 shares of stock at $5 per share
in order to secure the needed funds. Unfortunately, the release of the
prospectus in March 1972 coincided with the drop in the catch and the
issue had had to be withdrawn.

THE OUTLOOK FOR THE FUTURE

By the summer of 1972, Prelude had weathered the downturn of fishing catches which had so far occurred that year. The company's boats
had been able to bring in enough lobster to meet its $190,000 per month
cash flow breakeven (including the subsidiaries). Breakeven costs were
divided as follows:

Vessel operations	$120,000	SGA	$23,000
Selling	42,000	Taxes, interest	13,000

In terms of breakeven per trip, this monthly $190,000 (which ex-
cluded depreciation of about $25,000), worked out to about $22,000.
The breakeven catch in pounds varied, of course, with the price attainable in the market. In the spring of 1972 it ran about 8,000 pounds a
trip, since the wholesale price of "select" lobster had risen to more than
$3.00 per pound during some of this period.

Although the lobster catch had recently risen (Exhibit 1), no one
knew when or whether it would return to normal. On the one hand,
industry optimists argued that the scarce condition was only a transient
event and that there were still "plenty of lobsters out there for everybody."
On the other hand, industry pessimists, championed by Federal Fishery
officials, raised doubts about the long-term viability of the resource, and
were calling for some form of management to sustain the yields.

Competition

Even under "managed" conditions, Prelude's leaders expected the
company to survive if not to prosper—barring total disappearance of the

offshore lobster. They felt that they had the staying power to outlast the one-boat competitors who had come in on a shoestring, and, further, that they had an edge of experience and success which would enable them to outdistance the newer and better capitalized multi-boat competitors. Chief among these had been Deep Deep; Mr. Usen had had three new boats fishing out of Boston since 1968, but had not been able to make them pay. He was presently operating two of these boats under a separate company, but selling his catch at market price to Prelude and attempting to dispose of the fleet. A second established competitor, MATCO, which fished five boats off the Virginia Coast, was also reported to be in financial trouble, having been dragged under by its allegedly over-extended parent, Marine International Corporation. Although three other firms were putting three to five boats each out to sea, Mr. Gaziano was not particularly worried about the threat they presented. He summed up his feelings as follows:

> This is going to be one hell of an interesting summer [1972]. We're going to have some new boats out there, each backed by some rich Johnny who is fascinated by the sex-appeal of lobstering. They're going to find out the hard way how much it really costs to pot fish offshore. We have got a real shakeout coming.

In management's eyes a more real threat was that Prelude itself would be "taken over" by a larger company. Although there were no blocks of stock large enough to make for an easy takeover, the depressed state of Prelude's stock made a tender bid not unlikely.[4] For example, Mr. Jensen had heard a speech in which a spokesman for a West Coast seafood firm with 1971 sales of $25 million had stated:

> We are, then, a seafood company. And we want to remain a seafood company. The potential in utilizing the rich harvest of the sea is enough to keep any company of our size busy for as long into the future as we care to look.
> Already we are expanding from a solid base in the Pacific salmon industry into a much broader segment of the total spectrum of Alaskan and Northwestern fisheries. But we do not see ourselves as confined to Alaska and the Pacific Northwest. Rather we are interested in fisheries virtually anywhere on the globe if we can find a way to enter them in a sound and profitable manner. And, yes, we are constantly looking for acquisitions which could expand and complement our activities in the seafood industry.[5]

---

[4] In June 1972, the bid price of Prelude's stock was in the range of $2¼–$3. Five brokers made an over-the-counter market in the 530,000 shares outstanding. Of these, Rev. Whipple held 92,400; a prominent Boston family, 70,000; Mr. Usen, 22,845, and Mr. McGeough, 17,500. The balance of the holdings were widely fragmented, with no individual or institution owning more than 15,000 shares. No other officer or employee held more than a few thousand shares, although this group as a whole held qualified options granted at prices of $6.50 to $9.00 on 53,500 shares.

[5] Larry M. Kaner, Vice President, Whitney-Fidalgo Seafoods, Inc. Speech to Boston Security Analysts, February 9, 1971.

Expansion and diversification

With the acquisition of Wickford and Deep Deep, Prelude had achieved integration all the way through to the consumer, and management was considering expanding this chain in several ways. One way would be to develop more restaurant/lobster stores similar to the one in Wickford, R.I. Another way would be to enlarge on the branding program already underway. One California firm, Foster Farms, Inc., had been very successful with branding its fresh chickens and placing them in supermarkets.

A third alternative entailed broadening the product base by marketing other types of seafood that could be purchased outside and then resold through the company's distribution system. Flounder, trout, clams, oysters were among the types of gourmet seafood products bought by restaurants in much the same way as lobster was.

Processing and marketing crab meat was another possibility, but somewhat remote. Canning crab meat required a multi-million dollar investment in centrifuging equipment and a continuous supply of crab meat. Although Prelude did catch a lot of crabs, they could not be stored together with lobsters, and, furthermore, the catch was sporadic. There was, however, a minority small business company in New Bedford, Mass., which was using government funds to develop a crab processing plant, and Prelude was watching this development with interest.

Nor were Mr. Gaziano's interests entirely confined to seafood. Previously the company had looked at the possibility of acquiring a manufacturer of small boats, but had been beaten out by the CML Group, Inc. In any event, Mr. Gaziano did feel that any future expansion or acquisition efforts should be seaward-oriented, once the present difficulties were resolved.

Exhibit 1

PRELUDE CORPORATION

Average Monthly Company Landings per Trip as Percent of Fiscal 1971 Average

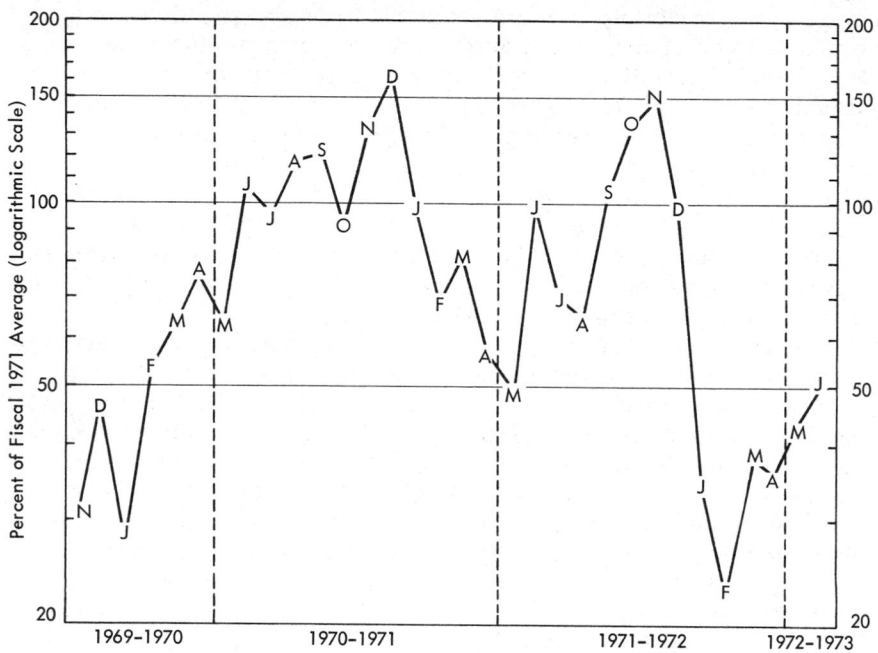

Source: Company records.

Exhibit 2

Statement of Operations and Accumulated Deficit, 1967–1972

(dollars in thousands)

	Year ended April 30					
	1967	1968	1969	1970	1971	1972 (Consolidated)*
Net sales	$128	$176	$152	$ 371	$1,511	$ 3,064
Costs and expenses:						
Cost of vessel operations	$108	$161	$225	$ 445	$ 832	$ 1,175
Cost of purchased seafood	—	—	—	—	—	1,062
Depreciation	22	23	21	68	135	253
Selling, general and administrative†	53	90	193	249	271	565
	$183	$274	$439	$ 762	$1,238	$ 3,055
Income (loss) from operations	$(55)	$(98)	$(287)	$(391)	$ 273	$ 9
Other income (expense)	—	(1)	(69)	(21)	(107)	(157)
Income (loss) before income taxes and extraordinary items	$(55)	$(99)	$(356)	$(412)	$ 166	$(148)
Provision for income taxes	—	—	—	—	84	—
Income (loss) before extraordinary items	$(55)	$(99)	$(356)	$(412)	$ 82	$(148)
Extraordinary items:						
Write-down of vessels	—	—	—	(133)	—	—
Credit arising from carryforward of operating losses	—	—	—	—	72	—
Net income (loss)	$(55)	$(99)	$(356)	$(545)	$ 154	$(148)
Accumulated deficit at beginning of year	—	(55)	(154)	(510)	1,055	(901)
Accumulated deficit at end of year	$(55)	$(154)	$(510)	$(1,055)	$(901)	$(1,049)
Income (loss) per share of common stock assuming full dilution	$(.23)	$(.41)	$(1.25)	$(1.15)	$ .28	$(.27)
Shares assumed outstanding	240	240	285	474	550	550

* Includes the results of subsidiary operations from Nov. 1, 1971 on.
† Includes all operating costs incurred after landing such as vehicle operations, salaries of delivery and restaurant personnel, and tank maintenance as well as executive salaries and general overhead.
Source: Company records.

Exhibit 3

PRELUDE CORPORATION

Balance Sheet

(dollars in thousands)

	April 30	
ASSETS	1971	1972 (Consolidated)
Current assets:		
Cash and marketable securities......................	$ 460	$ 253
Accounts receivable................................	22	243
Lobster and seafood inventories......................	13	62
Trapping supplies..................................	158	323
Prepaid expenses...................................	55	108
Total current assets.........................	$ 708	$ 989
Fixed assets..	$2,743	$3,471
Less—accumulated depreciation......................	189	420
	$2,554	$3,051
Goodwill...	—	315
Total assets...............................	$3,262	$4,355
LIABILITIES AND STOCKHOLDERS' EQUITY		
Current liabilities:		
Notes payable......................................	$ —	$ 350
Current portion of long-term debt...................	79	270
Accounts payable..................................	107	257
Accrued taxes and expenses........................	46	75
Total current liabilities......................	$ 232	$ 952
Long-term debt.....................................	$1,616	$1,857
Stockholders' equity:		
Common stock		
Authorized—1,100,000 shares		
Issued and outstanding—569,985 shares in 1972,		
530,000 shares in 1971..........................	$ 265	$ 285
Additional paid-in capital.........................	2,065	2,325
Accumulated deficit...............................	(901)	(1,049)
	$1,429	$1,561
Less—6,200 treasury shares......................	15	15
	$1,414	$1,546
Total liabilities..............................	$3,262	$4,355

Source: Company records.

Exhibit 4

PRELUDE CORPORATION

Organization Chart

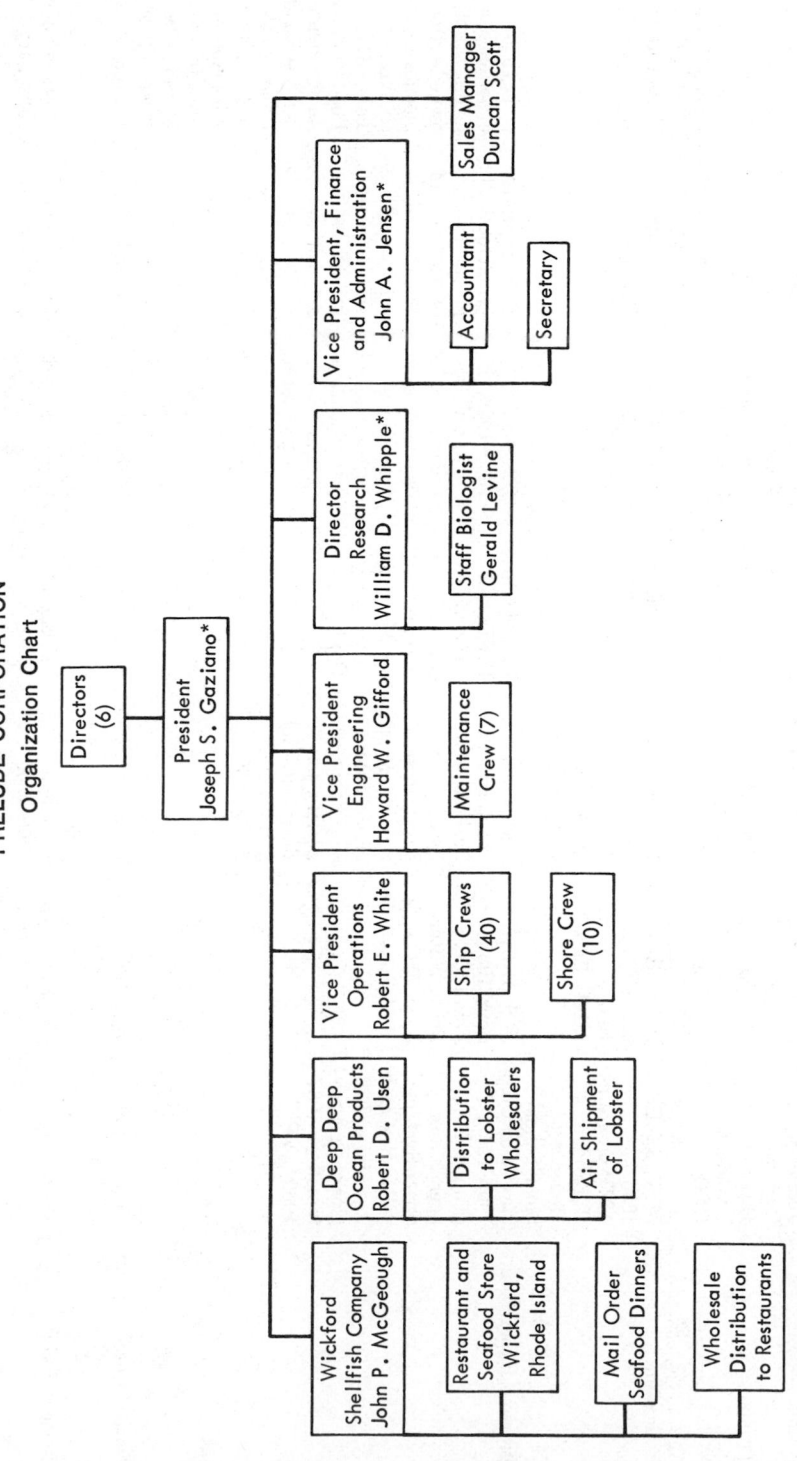

* Indicates director of corporation.
( ) Indicates number of personnel involved.
Source: Company records.

Exhibit 5

PRELUDE CORPORATION

Personal Data on Officers and Management Personnel

Name	Joseph S. Gaziano	John A. Jensen	W. D. Whipple	Howard W. Gifford	Robert E. White	John P. McGeough	Robert D. Usen
Title(s)	Director President CEO	Director VP Finance & Administration	Director Director of Research	Vice President Engineering	Vice President Operations	President, Wickford Shellfish Co., Inc.	President, Deep Ocean Products, Inc.
Age	36	33	41	37	33	31	42
Education	MIT, B.S.E.E., 1956 AMP programs: Harbridge House Sloan School	Babson Institute BS/BA, 1962 MBA, 1963	Princeton, BA, 1953, Boston Univ. School of Theology, STB cum laude, 1958	New Bedford Institute of Technology, B.S.	U.S. Navy Nuclear Sub School.	Providence College, BS, 1962	Tufts University, BA
Previous Experience	Raytheon Co., 1962–1967, rising to Manager, Major Space Systems. Allied Research Associates, Engineering & Systems Div. 1967–1969, VP & GM.	U.S. Army, Sept. 1963–Feb. 1964. Price, Waterhouse & Co., 1964–June 1968.	Owner of a charter yacht business, 1954–1958. Inventor and innovator in the area of fishing equipment, especially for deep-water lobster fishing, 1958–1959.	Electric Boat Division of General Dynamics, rising to supervisor in the Mechanical Engineering Dept.	U.S. Navy, 1960–1969, rising to 1/C Engineman. Held technical assignments, including mechanical inspection, systems and machinery testing.	Former professional football player. Increased sales of Wickford almost tenfold in the five years prior to its acquisition.	Over 15 years experience in several family-owned seafood businesses, including the Tabby Cat Food Company. As president, Mr. Usen had expanded this to $25 million sales volume prior to its sale. Founded Deep Deep in 1968.
Date of Entry	January 1969 Exec. VP	June 1968	Founded predecessor company, 1960.	May 1969	March 1969	December 1971	January 1972
Office(s) Held	President	VP, June 1970 Director, Sept. 1971	President, 1960–1969	VP, Sept. 1971	Vice President	President of subsidiary	President of subsidiary

Note: The three outside directors were: Chester A. Barrett, Chairman, Merchants National Bank of New Bedford; Joshua M. Berman, Partner, Goodwin, Proctor and Hoar; Robert F. Goldhamer, Vice President and Vice Chairman of the Executive Committee, Kidder, Peabody and Co.

Source: Company data.

Exhibit 6

PRELUDE CORPORATION
Projected Statement of Operations
(dollars in thousands)

| | For years ending April 30 | | |
	Actual 1972	Projected 1973	Projected 1974
Sales*			
Prelude......................................	$ n.a.	$2,656	$3,990
Wickford†....................................	n.a.	1,250	1,360
Deep Deep†.................................	n.a.	850	840
Total...................................	$3,064	$4,756	$6,190
Costs and expenses			
Vessel operations............................	$1,175	$1,464	$2,246
Purchases....................................	1,062	1,420	1,416
Depreciation.................................	253	312	362
S, G & A.....................................	565	780	1,084
Total...................................	$3,055	$3,976	$5,108
Operating income (loss)......................	9	780	1,082
Other income (expense)‡......................	(157)	(123)	(180)
Income (loss) before taxes....................	$ (148)	$ 657	$ 902
Provision for income taxes....................	—	338	464
Income (loss) before extraordinary credit...........	$ (148)	$ 319	$ 438
Extraordinary credit from operating loss carryforward................................	—	272	347
Net income...................................	$ (148)	$ 591	$ 785

* Assumes that fishing conditions parallel those of May 1970–January 1972; that two new ships for a total of six begin fishing in fiscal 1974; that sales of the subsidiaries continue at mid-1972 levels; and that Prelude receives a price per pound of $1.33, with 25% of its sales to outsiders.

† Assumes that the subsidiaries will handle 75% of sales reported by the parent.

‡ Primarily interest expense.

Sources and Uses of Funds
(dollars in thousands)

| | For years ending April 30 | |
	1973	1974
Uses of funds:		
Increase in fixed assets (new vessels)..................	$ 300	$ —
Increase in current assets (32% of sales)..............	531	460
Reduction in note payable.........................	350	—
Reduction in long-term debt.......................	370	270
Total Uses of Funds...........................	$1,551	$ 730
Sources of funds:		
Increase in accounts payable (11% of sales)............	$ 191	$ 157
Net operating income.............................	319	438
Anticipated operating loss carryforward...............	272	347
Depreciation......................................	312	362
Total sources of funds.........................	$1,094	$1,304
Funds needed (surplus).............................	$ 457	$ (574)

Source: Company records.

APPENDIX

THE LOBSTER INDUSTRY

Having graced the Pilgrims' first Thanksgiving, the Northern Lobster remained a U.S. gourmet delicacy, demand for which was growing abroad. Supply had not kept pace, however, even though the U.S. market drew 80%–90% of the Canada-landed catch, thereby roughly doubling poundage available for domestic consumption and export. From a 1960 peak of 73.2 million pounds live weight, supply had dropped to 56.5 million pounds in 1967, but rose again thereafter, partly owing to the success of new techniques of offshore fishing:

TOTAL U.S. SUPPLIES OF NORTHERN LOBSTER, LIVE WEIGHT IN MILLIONS OF POUNDS

	1968	1969	1970	1971
U.S. landed............	32.6	33.8	34.2	33.3
Imports*..............	31.3	31.6	30.2	34.5
Total†............	63.9	65.4	64.3	67.9

Note: Figures may fail to add because of rounding.
* Converted to live weight equivalent.
† Includes exports (about 1% in 1968, and growing).
Source: National Marine Fisheries Service.

Shortage had sent prices rising even faster than general inflation, and in 1971 the 33.3 million-pound, U.S.-landed catch brought fishermen $35.1 million in sales, making lobsters the second most valuable single species (after Gulf shrimp) in the $643 million fishing industry.

The resource

The Northern Lobster inhabited the chilly waters of the North Atlantic from Newfoundland to North Carolina. Two populations had been observed, one in the shallow water from Canada's Maritimes south to New Jersey, the other further out, usually in the deep, cold canyons of the continental shelf from Massachusetts to the Carolinas. During the spring and fall the latter population migrated, and weights and numbers for "legal sized" (legally fishable) lobsters in the two populations were as follows:

Population	Total weight (millions of pounds)	Annual replenishment (millions of pounds)	Number (millions)	Average weight (pounds)
Inshore..........	25–31	15–20 Est.	20–25	1¼
Offshore.........	100–120	25 Est.	25–30	4

Besides fluctuating from year to year, lobster catch rates were seasonal, being lowest in the winter when lobsters and fishermen were least active, and highest in October and May. Since demand was highest in midsummer (shore-dinner time) prices rose then, giving dealers a motive to buy and hold lobsters in enclosed tidal pools until values increased.

Harvesting the resource

Inshore fishing. Inshore and offshore lobster fishing differed in technique, the inshore method being much the same in the 1970s as in the 1840s. A 30-foot boat, manned by its owner and a relative, could manage 300–800 lathe traps or "pots," sinking each at depths of less than 30 fathoms, and hauling it up with a power winch to empty, bait, and toss overboard again.

By 1971 some 8,000 individuals were engaged in inshore lobster fishing, and a million pots were being used. Fishing was so intensive that government sources estimated that 90% of the legal-sized inshore lobster population was caught every year. Of this total, some 70% was delivered to ports in Maine. Optimum investment for entering this trade was estimated at $8,000–$10,000, but anyone could enter who had a few used traps, an outboard motorboat, and a license.

Offshore fishing. Only after World War II were feasible methods devised for fishing the offshore lobster population, and only in the late 1950s did the industry start significant growth. By 1968, two techniques were being used: trawling, and potting on long lines.

Trawling involved scooping up migrating lobsters from the offshore flats by dragging weighted nets along the bottom. With the government pointing the way on methods, catches rose quickly, fluctuating around 5.5 million pounds a year in 1965–1971, but ranging between 3.9 million in 1966 and 7.1 million in 1970.

Attractive features of offshore trawling included the absence of competition from Canada and Maine (where it was illegal to land the catch), relatively modest manning requirements compared with other types of fishing, and the low investment needed to equip a boat for switching back and forth from ground fish to lobsters. Increasingly unattractive features included overcrowding, loss of expensive gear when nets were dragged across the rising number of offshore pots, and injuries to the catch which might render 50%–70% of it unsalable. Thus, government sources believed that this industry segment would level off at 100–130 boats.

Offshore lobster potting started with experiments to develop gear for trapping lobsters in the deep canyons of the continental shelf, where government researchers reported a year-round abundance. Prominent among the first experimenters was Prelude's Rev. Whipple, who finally settled on a method that entailed a mile-long line, buoyed and anchored at each end, to which 50–75 weighted traps were attached by four-foot wires. Keys to his system were gear strong enough to haul the heavy line, and also a special clip to permit the automatic attachment and detachment of the traps as the ship steamed along.

In 1970 this technique proved its worth when Prelude landed nearly all of the 1.5 million pounds attributed to offshore potting in the first statistics to segregate this figure. In 1971 the offshore potting catch rose to 2.3 million pounds, but this was shared by a growing number of competitors, lured in part by Prelude's success. By mid-1972, 92 vessels were fishing 50,000 offshore pots, nearly half of which had come into service during the previous six months.

Such an influx brought technical problems. These included loss of gear when one's boat line was laid across another's, or when the lines were cut by boats pursuing fin-fish. Crowding, too, was a problem in the canyons, with the result that some pot lines had been set upon the flats, where they ruined the offshore trawlers' nets and motivated trawlers to retaliate.

Costs varied widely for putting a vessel into offshore lobster potting, some vessels having been converted from dragging to potting for as little as $50,000, whereas Prelude's fourth ship came to almost $600,000, including both cost of the hull and conversion.

Regulation

Lobstering was a regulated trade, the regulations being set by the states, the Federal Government, and international conventions. Thus, to protect the resource, all states except North Carolina and Virginia set a minimum size for a landable lobster, and most states forbade the harvesting of egg-bearing females. To protect the consumer, the Federal Government required all lobsters to be alive when sold, and forbade U.S. ships to process them at sea. To govern fishing rights, nations had agreed not to fish within 12 miles of one another's coasts, and most had signed an international convention establishing a court-enforced code of conduct for vessels.

One clause in this code, of special interest to lobstermen, gave right of way to "fixed" equipment such as pot lines. This requirement tended, however, to be ignored by ships in "hot pursuit" of finfish, particularly, lobstermen believed, by foreign ships. In any event, losses were frequent and significant: one incident alone could damage or destroy several trap lines costing about $7,000 each and thereby put a one-boat operation out of business. Lobstermen vociferously complained, but the U.S. Coast Guard lacked enough patrol boats for adequate policing. New England congressmen, however, had been persuaded to sponsor a bill to reimburse fishermen for cumulative gear losses of about $500,000.

In other future plans, the Federal Government was pressing the states to enact uniform and more stringent laws for resource protection within the three-mile limit, which was the area of state jurisdiction. To protect the resource further out, the Federal Government might take several steps, from imposing a federal license requirement to extending the 12-mile limit to a highly controversial 200 miles. What fishermen favored was bringing foreign as well as domestic deep-sea lobstermen under federal control, an objective that could be accomplished by officially declaring lobsters to be "creatures of the shelf" as opposed to "free-swimming" fish.

How urgent it might be to take protective action on the offshore resource was not clear. Reported removal of 14 million pounds[1] by all

---

[1] In 1972, U.S. offshore trawling and potting reported 5.7 million and 2.3 million pounds; foreign lobstermen about 5 million, and U.S. ground-fish fishermen about 1 million.

takers was well below the 25 million pounds a year that government biologists estimated could be removed without depleting the resource, but no one knew how many pounds were being taken out unreported or how many were being maimed and killed through fishing operations. One highly placed official admitted, "It would not be at all unreasonable to speculate that as much as 25 million pounds might be being removed."

Handling and transport

Unlike inshore lobstermen, offshore lobstermen making 10-day runs required refrigerated tanks to hold their catch, not just barrels and some seaweed for moisture. Once delivered to the dock, most lobsters again went into holding: perhaps for a few days in a dockside "car" or floating tank, then for a few months in a "pound" or tidal pool, and then for a few more days in a dealer's sorting and culling tank. In total, cars, pounds, and dealers' tanks in the Northeast could accommodate an estimated 7 million pounds.

With the advent of refrigeration and lightweight packing containers, shipments by rail or truck posed no problem, and shipment by air could carry Northern lobsters to far-distant points.

Over the years, consumers had come to expect their lobsters live. Weak and dying lobsters could be culled and cooked, then canned and frozen, but despite high prices these operations barely recovered their costs, so dealers pressed suppliers for a high-quality catch.

Aquaculture

Although worked on for some time, techniques to supplement lobster fishing by "farming" remained undeveloped in 1972. Progress had been made, however, especially on the biological side: lobsters had been got to breed in captivity, and experiments had been started to breed selectively for fast growth, bright color, two crusher claws, and high meat content. Already, lobsters had been grown to one-pound size in two years compared with six years in the wild. And lobsters had been grown to half-pound size in six to seven months, with tails bigger than any commercially available shrimp.

The big problem lay with engineering the life-support system. Depending on investment in development and plant, the start of commercial operations was put at two to five years away by the best known authority in lobster hatchery.

Marketing the resource

Channels. As indicated by solid lines on the diagram (on p. 288), lobsters typically moved from the fishermen's barrel or tank to a local buyer with a lobster car or so, who then sold to a large dealer operating a lobster pound. From thence, the lobsters passed to a primary wholesaler, who sold to a retail outlet—most likely to a restaurant, since about 80% of all lobsters reached the consumer that way. Lobsters could pass to the retailer in several alternate ways, however, as indicated by dotted lines. These could either add or eliminate a step.

Price. As indicated by the price data on the diagram, prices more

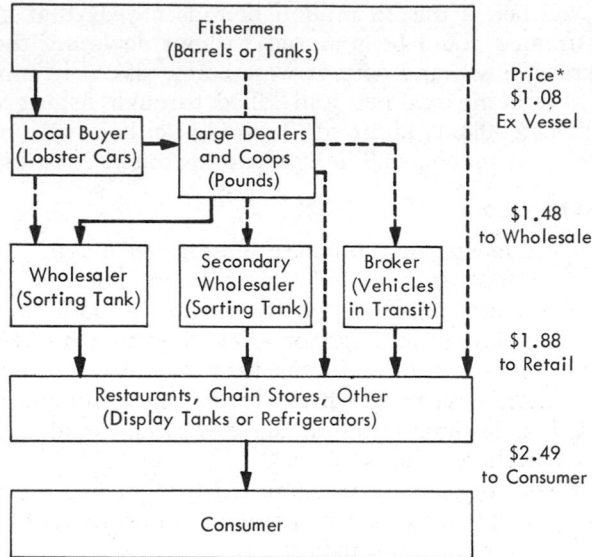

* Casewriter's estimate, typical 1971 prices per pound.

than doubled between the fisherman and the consumer, with retailers (largely restaurants) accounting for the biggest rise. The estimated price figures shown conceal wide seasonal variations, as well as variations for different weights of lobsters, and a steep, year-to-year uptrend:

LIVE WEIGHT WHOLESALE PRICES
PER POUND, FULTON FISH MARKET, NEW YORK CITY

	"Chix" 1⅛ lbs.	"Quarters" 1¼ lbs.	"Duces" 2 lbs.
1970			
High....................	$1.85	$1.88	$1.89
Low....................	1.24	1.34	1.36
1971			
High....................	2.06	2.14	2.66
Low....................	1.45	1.46	1.47

Source: National Marine Fisheries Service, *Shellfish Situation and Outlook, Annual Review, 1971.*

Two major market segments combined to yield these aggregate statistics. Restaurants and fancy seafood stores, which favored "select" (1½–2½ pound lobsters) had a relatively constant demand, so that prices sometimes reached astronomical levels. Supermarkets and volume restaurants had a price-sensitive demand and tended to drop out

WEIGHTED AVERAGE ANNUAL PRICE PAID
TO MAINE FISHERMEN

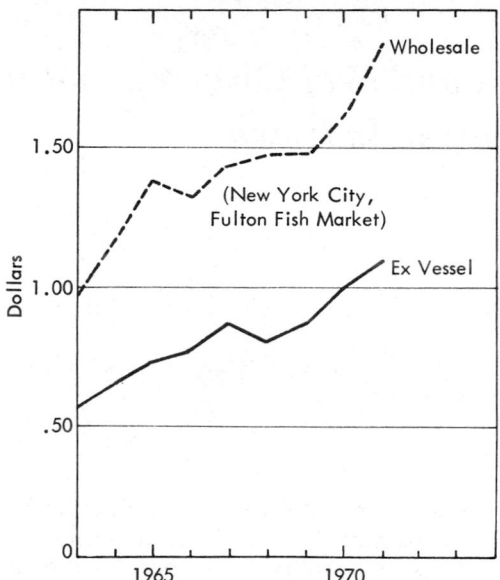

of the picture when prices went above a certain level. When prices were low, however, chains tended to buy for promotions, thus helping to stabilize the market.

Competition among distributors. Companies of varying types and sizes were engaged in lobster distribution, and they competed fiercely to handle the limited supply on a price basis favorable to themselves.

Two of the largest entities in the business were J. Hook and Bay State, both of Boston, who together handled an estimated 30 million pounds a year. Despite their size, they might find themselves outbid by "small lotters," who were able to sell crate lots in Europe for twice what their large competitors were getting from a high-volume restaurant account.

Hook and Bay State operated quite differently, thus illustrating the wide variety of ways that entities in lobster distribution could be linked together or combined. Bay State specialized in furnishing the restaurant trade with sorted lobster at a stable year-round price, which might be above or below the current market. While it had preferred to confine itself to a wholesale function, it had recently been forced to enter the dealer function of running a pound in order to secure its sources of supply. In contrast, Hook maintained only a skeleton staff year-round, but geared up when the market was good to provide tremendous quantities of case lots of unsorted lobsters to secondary wholesalers. Hook also brokered a large volume to chains.

Crown Cork and Seal Company and the Metal Container Industry

IN 1963, the Crown Cork and Seal Company, a major producer of metal cans and crowns with sales of $205 million, had experienced the largest growth in sales and profitability since 1958 of any company in the metal container industry. Unlike most other can manufacturers, Crown had not diversified into packaging fields outside of metal containers in response to increasing competitive pressures. Instead it narrowed its product line, concentrating upon supplying the fast-growing aerosol market and the expanding market for canned beer. Crown had also invested extensively in international facilities, particularly in underdeveloped countries, anticipating a tremendous growth in the overseas demand for metal containers.

Company executives believed the international markets, as living standards increased, would be the major source of future expansion. According to Mr. John F. Connelly, President and Chairman of Crown Cork and Seal, "We have been moving as fast as we can into the international field, building plants in all underdeveloped countries. Presently we are only producing crowns in most of these facilities as nobody is canning in these areas as yet. But when they do start canning, we need only to add a body-maker and a seamer in order to produce cans.

Mr. Connelly planned for Crown's domestic operations to be the stable base from which the company would expand internationally. Connelly's approach to doing business represented a considerable contrast both to the policies of his predecessors at Crown and to the strategies adopted by his principal competitors. The problem he faced in 1963 is still perplexing today, how to develop a base of stable domestic earnings in a highly competitive mature industry.

The following pages describe the nature and structure of the metal container industry, the crisis facing Connelly in 1957, the pattern of operations and strategy that evolved from this crisis, the outlook for the future, and the situation as of February 1964.

THE METAL CONTAINER INDUSTRY

The metal container industry produced metal cans, crowns (bottle caps) and closures (screw caps, bottle lids) for over 135 industries that use these products to hold or seal an almost endless variety of consumer and industrial goods. During the 1950s a number of metal container manufacturers experienced declining profit margins and loss of market share because of increasing competitive and technical pressures from within and outside the industry.

In 1963, two firms dominated the metal container industry: the American Can Company and the Continental Can Company. Of the 48 billion cans produced in 1963, 34 billion were manufactured by these giant corporations. Another 5 billion cans were manufactured by the Crown Cork and Seal Company and the National Can Company, both companies having an annual sales volume of over $100 million. In 1963, Crown Cork and the Bond Division of the Continental Can Company also produced approximately 70% of the 313 million gross of crowns used. In all, there are about 100 companies in the industry.

The 48 billion cans produced in 1963 had an estimated shipment value of $2.3 billion. The primary users of metal containers have been the food and beer industries, the two industries utilizing almost 80% of all metal cans produced (see Exhibit 1A). In the five years from 1960 to 1964 the soft-drink bottler also became an important user. In addition to consuming annually approximately 70% of all metal crowns produced, bottlers used over 2 billion cans in 1963, an increase of 500% from 1958.

Despite the over-all growth, however, the industry faced a number of challenging problems. This industry description focuses on: (1) new competitive pressures that have confronted the industry from 1955–1964; (2) the effect of these pressures on the industry; and (3) the strategic responses of the major companies in the industry to these pressures. Additional information as to economic and technological characteristics of the industry is provided in an Appendix.

New pressures

While industry executives were confident that the "tin can is not on its way out," major strategic questions arose during the 1953–1963 decade that stemmed from efforts to assess the long-term effects on the industry of:

1. changes in the basic concept of a container—termed by many the "packaging revolution."
2. the rapid acceleration in packaging technology.
3. the increased threat of self-manufacture.

The "packaging revolution"

Perhaps the trend of greatest long-run significance to the industry is the increasing number of functions the "container" is being asked to perform. Originally the container was designed solely to hold, protect, and preserve its contents. Then someone decided that a container,

Exhibit 1

CROWN CORK AND SEAL COMPANY

A. Shipments of Metal Cans by Product Packed Expressed in Terms of Thousands of Base Boxes* of Metal Consumed in Their Manufacture

	1955	1956	1957	1958	1959	1960	1961	1962	1963
Total shipments	98,024	105,107	101,702	103,818	108,162	105,166	109,358	114,956	109,707
For sale	85,477	89,928	87,667	89,180	93,993	89,917	89,656	93,764	88,739
For own use	12,547	15,179	14,035	14,638	14,169	15,249	19,702	21,192	21,192
Type of metal									
Steel							n.a.	112,714	107,350
Aluminum							n.a.	1,792	2,356
Food cans, total	61,773	66,884	62,046	64,054	65,060	65,073	66,164	68,618	
Fruits & vegetables (including juice)	31,764	34,899	31,980	34,236	33,684	32,984	34,805	37,081	
Evaporated and condensed Milk	6,138	6,150	5,425	5,175	5,085	4,883	4,737	4,393	
Other dairy products	1,034	1,083	889	728	636	510	519	582	
Fish and seafood	2,535	2,588	2,636	2,843	2,657	2,850	2,898	3,082	
Lard and shortening	2,580	2,394	2,248	2,383	2,324	1,986	2,256	2,356	
Meat (including poultry)	2,919	3,825	3,047	2,951	3,190	3,203	3,460	3,483	
Coffee	4,000	4,213	4,286	4,452	4,707	4,567	4,846	4,846	
All other food cans	10,803	11,732	11,584	11,286	12,777	14,090	12,643	12,795	
Nonfood cans, total	36,251	38,223	38,278	39,764	43,102	40,093	43,194	45,888	
Oil, open top—1 qt. and 5 qt.	6,778	6,778	6,230	6,338	6,811	5,715	6,026	6,304	
Beer cans	14,919	15,806	16,305	16,902	18,563	17,776	17,522	18,150	
Pet food	3,485	4,034	4,154	4,154	4,332	4,486	4,475	4,654	
All other nonfood cans	11,069	11,605	12,370	12,370	13,386	12,116	15,171	16,780	

* A base box is a measure of metal use.

B. Comparative Growth of Population, Gross National Product, and Can Shipments (1953 = 100)

	1953	1954	1955	1956	1957	1958	1959	1960	1961	1962
Population (millions)	100.0	101.8	102.9	103.9	105.0	106.1	107.22	108.36	109.5	110.7
Gross national product (billions)	100.0	99.5	108.7	114.2	120.9	121.1	131.9	137.4	141.9	151.8
Can shipments (000's of base boxes)	100.0	100.1	110.0	117.8	112.0	112.9	121.8	117.6	122.0	128.2

Source: U.S. Department of Commerce—Bureau of the Census.

imaginatively labelled, could also provide a strong point-of-purchase reminder of the consumer's need for the "product inside." So the container was redesigned to add more utility and appeal to the product by means of devices ranging from recipes printed on the outside to easy-dispensing spouts. The result has been that during the 10 years from 1954–1963, this redesigning in combination with advances in methods of product preservation and packaging technology, has reduced the importance of the preservation function of the container relative to its sales function. The container, or rather the "package," and the "product inside" have become increasingly one unit in their selective appeal to the consumer, and, to a lesser extent, in creating primary demand, e.g., aerosol dispensed whipped cream.

Some authorities have attributed the preoccupation with packaging in the United States to radical changes in merchandising patterns. The package now functions as the salesman. Also, with the rapid advances in manufacturing technology, products tend to be of increasingly high quality and often little product differentiation can be achieved by "just more quality." In addition, there has been a rapid growth in the use of private labels, and this has tended to make brand names a somewhat less important influence on sales. All these factors, packaging experts argue, put a burden on products to speak for themselves. As one authority concluded:

> These days you had better have an easier-to-open beer can [and] an easier-opening cereal carton or you are out of business.[1]

"Extras" on consumer goods have taken many forms, for example, plastic bottles for hair preparations, aerosol containers which spurt products ranging from mustard to touch-up paint, miniature beer kegs that provide tap beer in the family refrigerator, and self-opening or "pop-top" metal cans. Extras on industrial packages have been added to increase the usability and convenience of handling, both for the distributor and the ultimate customer, e.g., color coded packages to facilitate inventory maintenance and the use of polystyrene foam instead of shredded paper as packing material to obtain lighter and more compact containers.

The tremendous growth in the sale of packaging materials since 1940 reflects, in part, the increasing recognition given by manufacturers to the role of packaging in selling their products. In 1940, shipments of packaging materials totaled slightly over $2 billion. By 1958, these shipments had growth to about $10 billion. In 1963, shipments of packaging materials amounted to $13 billion (55% of the total expenditure for packaging activity), an increase of 650% since 1940. During the same period two general economic indicators, Gross National Product and Consumer Expenditures for Nondurables, increased 550% and 234%, respectively.

A major reason behind the growth of the packaging industry has

---

[1] Carmon M. Elliot, Jr., Manager of Package Design, Eastman Kodak Co., as quoted in Leon Morse, "The Swing to Service," *Dun's Review & Modern Industry*, November 1963, p. 133.

been the shift to packaging for products previously sold in "containers." For example, starch in the aerosol dispensing form was introduced in 1960 and in 1963 accounted for over 25% of consumer starch purchases. Similar shifts were experienced with other household products such as room deodorants, car waxes, and furniture polishes. Estimated to be increasing at an annual rate of over 12%, sales of nonfood aerosol units in 1963 were over 1 billion units—18 times the number sold in the first year after the commercial aerosol container was introduced in 1948. Recent technological developments have also introduced food items to aerosol dispensing.

The aluminum top easy-opening can was heralded as the first significant innovation in the beer industry since the introduction of the can. This was quickly followed by the "pull-tab" top developed by Alcoa, providing still another example of the impact of imaginative packaging. Pull-top cans, introduced in the spring of 1963, accounted for 40% of the beer cans sold in 1963. Beer company executives predicted this figure would climb to 75% by the fall of 1964.

The evolution of the packaging concept has posed major, strategic issues for the metal container industry. This is an industry that grew up converting steel into shapes designed to achieve a high level of product preservation (over 55% of the cans produced in 1963 packaged food) and one which has had little or no contact with the ultimate buyer generating and responding to the new trends.

The rapid acceleration in packaging technology

The original characteristics that promoted the use of the tin can and the crown in the early 1900's still make them well suited to certain food and beverage packaging jobs. These qualities are: (1) immunity to handling abuse, (2) ability to resist great heat and pressure, allowing pasteurization in the package, (3) preservation of a sterile condition for long periods, (4) lightness compared to the contents, (5) amenability to fabrication into differing sizes, and (6) low cost, allowing destruction after use. However, recent advances in packaging technology have challenged the future competitive strength of these characteristics.

The integration of packaging into the production process. As the distinction between the product and its container has become increasingly blurred, product manufacturers, pushed by the machinery companies who design custom packaging systems, have moved toward carrying out a greater number of container conversion functions in their own plants. The development "that may ultimately prove to have the most far-reaching impact on the [package-supplying] industry is the production of the container by the customer himself, with only the basic packaging material being supplied by the 'container manufacturer.' Packaging Corporation of America has a system which allows carton making as well as filling by frozen food packers all at once; the company only delivers the rolled stock to the customer rather than the finished container as is the usual case now."[2]

---

[2] "Container Makers Grow with the Economy," *Financial World*, May 29, 1963, p. 7.

Reduced container requirements. The technical requirements of the can and crown have been, for the most part, a function of high-speed manufacturing and the *need* for a perfect seal to preserve (1) sanitation, (2) container strength and (3) the flavoring or coloring of the contents. But for some products, these characteristics have been relatively unimportant, e.g., a container for wrapped candy in contrast to aerosol dispensed whipped cream. The packaging of the candy, termed an easy application by trade experts, has not required a coated or sealed container nor one able to withstand pressure, all in contrast to the whipped cream dispenser.

Packagers who have made heavy use of tin cans have been experimenting with new production processes and product designs that, among other things, reduce the structural demands placed on the container. The beer industry is a prime example of this trend. Brewers, who used 20% of the cans produced in 1963, have been experimenting with changes in the basic pasteurizing process. Traditionally, beer has been pasteurized in the bottle or can. But lately, brewers have been experimenting with pasteurization in bulk. If successful, the techniques would reduce the need for strong containers.

New methods of food preservation. The development of better methods of product preservation has been a major goal of food processors. Since the early 1950's, despite the short shelf-life of frozen foods, their relatively high cost due to slow processing methods, and the sometimes poor quality, the fastest growth in food consumption has been in foods preserved by freezing rather than by canning (see Exhibit 2).

Exhibit 2

CROWN CORK AND SEAL COMPANY

Consumption of Fruits and Vegetables in Pounds Per Capita, (1953–1962)

	Vegetables			Fruit		
	Fresh	*Canned*	*Frozen*	*Fresh*	*Canned*	*Frozen*
1962............	99.4	45.0	10.5	90.9	35.2	10.9
1961............	104.3	44.6	10.0	92.1	35.3	8.9
1960............	106.0	44.5	9.8	97.5	34.5	9.1
1959............	102.9	44.8	8.9	100.9	33.9	8.8
1957............	104.6	43.9	7.5	99.5	35.6	9.0
1955............	104.6	43.5	6.6	101.6	35.5	8.7
1953............	108.6	43.3	5.4	111.3	34.0	7.1

Source: U.S. Department of Commerce.

To overcome the problems of quality, shelf-life, and production time, a technique called freeze drying has been developed. Products processed by this method can be stored at room temperature for long periods. Reportedly the technique has been improved to the point where food quality closely approximates that of fresh items.

Although the commercial use of freeze drying has thus far been limited, trade experts anticipate that the improved quality combined with handling and transportation economies (in contrast to canned foods) will greatly increase the number of applications.

New packaging materials. Expenditures for packaging materials (excluding value added by filling, labelling, and sealing) accounted for almost 35% of total U.S. expenditures for packaging during 1963. Of the estimated $13 billion spent on materials, $2.6 billion was spent on metal materials, 80% of which was used in the fabrication of metal cans. Steel has been virtually the sole metallic raw material used by the metal container industry. Next to automobiles and construction, the industry has been the third largest consumer of steel in the country. During the last decade, however, aluminum, and to a lesser extent fibre-foil and plastic, have increasingly entered traditional tinplate markets.

Discussing the growing competitive strength of aluminum, one author stated: [3]

> Steel has been the master of the can makers' fate for so long that both American and Continental seemed to find it [the competitive strength of aluminum] hard to recognize when it came along. In discussing aluminum, too many can executives had been tending to talk problems, not potential. Aluminum was commonly more costly than steel; it could not resist the same pressures. Changes would have to be made in production lines before aluminum could be run through. . . . The aluminum industry, led by Reynolds Steel Co., claims it had to shoulder its way directly to the can buyer to overcome can company inertia.

Although still a relatively small factor in the metal container field in 1963 (see Exhibit 1A) aluminum has made sizeable inroads in the container market for motor oil and frozen concentrates, products that are shipped long distances and are not packed under pressure. Reflecting these inroads, the use of tinplate containers in 1963 dropped 5% from 1962, while the use of aluminum containers rose 20% despite a curtailed demand for citrus containers.

The use of aluminum for beer can ends, spurred by the introduction of the self-opening top developed by Alcoa, has become another major market for this metal. Both Reynolds and Alcoa, furthermore, have built can plants to hasten the acceptance of an all-aluminum container in the beer industry. Reynolds also has built plants in Florida to supply aluminum cans to the citrus packers.

The principal appeal of aluminum has been its light weight, particularly when transportation costs have been an important factor in total cost. Aluminum experts argue, however, that the aluminum can is also (1) a better looking container than its tin counterpart, (2) cheaper to lithograph as the brushed aluminum plate serves as a base color, and (3) capable of sharper lithographing. In addition they point out that brewers have long agreed that aluminum is "more friendly to beer," reducing the problem of flavoring, a major concern of both the brewing and soft drink industries. If the aluminum executives' confidence that the beer industry can be converted to use of aluminum is

---

[3] "The Fight for ⁹⁄₁₀ of a Cent," *Fortune* magazine, April 1961, p. 157.

Exhibit 3

CROWN CORK AND SEAL COMPANY

The Aluminum Can Market

	Total potential annual market (millions of cans)	Aluminum cans produced (millions of cans)			Penetration % of total		
		1961	1962	1963*	1961	1962	e-1963
Frozen Juice Concentrate.........	1,750	900	1,000	1,400	51	57	80
Motor Oil.............	1,700	300	350†	800†	18	21	47
Aerosol...............	1,000	25	30	45	2	3	5
Beer Cans.............	9,000	40	60	120	0.5	0.7	1
Beer Lids (on tinplate beer cans) .	9,000	25	600	3,000	0.3	7	40

* Estimated.
† Includes foil-fibre cans.
Source: Reynolds Metals Company as quoted in *Standard and Poor's Industry Survey.*

confirmed, domestic brewers would be the aluminum industry's biggest market. Exhibit 3 gives one company's estimate of the potential market for the aluminum can.

Aluminum has made further inroads in traditional tinplate markets as a component of the new fibre-foil containers. Packaging experts point to the fibre-foil container as an example of the great potential of composite materials. Developed jointly by the R. C. Can Company and Anaconda Aluminum in 1962 for the motor oil market, the composite can accounted for an estimated 55% of the 2 billion motor oil cans sold in 1963 and 10% of total can production.

> Cans made of fibre-foil are also making a strong bid for other metal container markets. Citrus juice may be next. Coca-Cola's Minute Maid Division reportedly has converted already to fibre-foil. . . . If, as it is believed, the can can be made strong enough for beer and vacuum packaged coffee, for example, their potential market may be as large as 15 billion units, or a third of the 45 billion cans currently sold. . . .
>
> The potential of the new type container is deemed so great that other major companies have invaded the market. These include Container Corporation, Crown Zellerbach, Seal-Right-Oswego Falls and Stone Container. . . .[4]

A strong appeal of the composite can, as with the aluminum can, has been its low weight. Generally the composite has run about 20% lighter than its "thin-tin" counterparts but slightly heavier than the all-aluminum container. But in addition to the advantages accruing from lighter weight, the composite can reportedly costs about 15% less to manufacture than either type of all-metal can.

Despite these advantages, many industry experts expect some of the recent gains of the composite can to be of short duration. The motor oil market is a case in point. In late 1963, blow-molded plastic containers, following developments that gave them significant econo-

---

[4] *Financial World,* May 29, 1963, p. 7.

mies over the metal and composite containers available, were introduced in one-quart sizes by major oil companies. In the last few years blow-molded plastic containers also packaged the major portion of liquid detergent sold, which as late as 1958 had been packaged solely in glass or metal. A recent article in *Printer's Ink* magazine reported that blow-molded plastic containers strong enough to serve as aerosol dispensers had been developed. While the plastic aerosol is more expensive than its metal aerosol counterpart, its proponents point out that the plastic aerosol can be fabricated into a variety of hitherto "impossible" can shapes.[5]

Perhaps the greatest long-term significance of the influx of new materials will be that can companies will have to contend with the research and marketing strength of such giant, integrated companies as Du Pont, Dow Chemical, Weyerhaeuser Timber, Reynolds, and Alcoa. The forward integration of major material suppliers into the metal container industry has economic repercussions for the can manufacturer. In late 1963, for instance, Reynolds & Alcoa announced price increases in the sheet aluminum stock sold to can makers, but neither were reported to have increased the price of their own aluminum cans.

The threat of self-manufacture

The threat of customers manufacturing containers for their own use has hung over the metal container industry since World War II. For years the Campbell Soup Company has been the third largest manufacturer of cans in the country.

While only one large user of metal containers, Libby, McNeil & Libby, has converted to manufacturing its own cans since 1955, other packagers, smaller than the giant food packers but users of billions of cans annually, have been giving serious consideration to self-manufacture.

Effects of pressures on the metal container industry

The primary effects on the industry during the 1950s of the three principal pressures described in the first section of this note were the loss of minor market shares, and the narrowing of profit margins in traditional product lines.

Loss of market share

In 1957, the president of American Can estimated that his company was losing over $70 million annually in sales because of self-manufacture.

Department of Commerce figures indicate that from 1950 to 1960, self-manufacturers increased their share of the metal container market from 11% to 15%.

During the same period, packagers of motor oil and citrus concentrates, users of 4 billion cans a year moved rapidly away from the tin can, switching first to aluminum and then to fibre-foil containers. By 1960, the tin can's share of these markets had declined 50%.

While statistics on the packaging industry are characterized by many

___
[5] *Printer's Ink,* April 24, 1964, p. 19.

Exhibit 4

CROWN CORK AND SEAL COMPANY
Growth in the Production of Plastic and Metal Containers 1953–1962
(1957–1959 = 100)

	1953	1954	1955	1956	1957	1958	1959	1960	1961	1962	1965*	1970*	1975*
Plastic.....	50.1	49.0	64.6	74.4	82.9	91.9	125.8	134.7	156.0	189.5	263	437	720
Metal......	100.3	90.2	98.3	98.8	101.5	92.9	105.3	107.6	106.5	117.1	128	150	175

* Projected.
Source: Federal Reserve Board Index of Industrial Production. Projections adapted from forecast of *Printer's Ink* magazine, August 30, 1963, p. 315.

gaps, Exhibit 4 illustrates the decline in the growth rate of tin cans in contrast to "never" packaging materials.

Narrowing of profit margins in traditional product lines

From 1956 to 1960, the average net income (before nonrecurring items) of the major producers of metal containers fell from 4.7% of net sales to 3.3%. One contributing factor was that steelmakers since 1954 had raised their prices five times, totaling a 15.2% increase. During this same period can makers raised their prices six times for a 19% increase, but in 1959 on the initiative of American Can the industry reduced its prices by 8%. In 1960, price increases had not offset rising raw material costs to the can makers, let alone increases in labor costs.

Reflecting the pressure of rising material and labor costs and the threat of self-manufacture, the margin on the typical packer's can (65% of independent can sales in 1960 were packer cans) declined to the point where in 1960 on a price of 2½¢ per can approximately 1.6¢ went to the tinplate producer. The remainder had to cover fabrication costs, the cost of coating and sealing compounds, and the cost of packing and shipping the can.

An executive of one can company, in summarizing his feelings about the difficulties his company was experiencing in adjusting to declining margins throughout the industry, commented: "Sometimes I think the only way out of this is to sell out to U.S. Steel, or to buy General Foods."[6]

The response of the metal container industry

In responding to the events of the 1950s, the four major companies reacted in one or more of the following ways: product diversification, increased customer service, heavy investment in research, closer co-operation with the steel industry, movement abroad, and product specialization. Exhibit 5 provides data on the four major competitors.

Product diversification

During the last decade three of the four major companies in the industry have adopted some form of diversification. In each case the move to diversify was an effort to (1) gain opportunities in packaging

---

[6] As quoted in *Fortune* magazine, "The Fight for ⁹⁄₁₀ of a Cent," April 1957.

Exhibit 5

CROWN CORK AND SEAL COMPANY

Summary Financial Figures—Four Major Can Manufacturers
(in millions)

	1954	1955	1956	1957	1958	1959	1960	1961	1962	1963
American Can										
Sales	652.4	714.8	771.6	1,000.6	1,037.0	1,107.4	1,059.0	1,093.3	1,180.5	1,149.4
Profit Margin*	11.5	12.2	11.7	12.7	12.9	11.8	11.8	13.6	13.0	12.3
Continental Can										
Sales	616.2	666.3	1,010.3	1,046.3	1,080.4	1,146.5	1,117.0	1,153.3	1,182.9	1,154.0
Profit Margin*	8.4	9.5	11.4	10.5	10.7	9.8	8.7	10.6	11.4	11.5
Crown Cork and Seal										
Sales	111.4	113.0	115.1	114.9	116.3	123.2	121.2	177.0†	190.2	205.4
Profit Margin*	6.1	5.7	3.5	3.7	5.5	6.7	8.1	12.8	13.4	13.2
National Can										
Sales	41.1	70.9	81.5	88.4	100.7	101.8	109.5	114.8	121.8	126.6
Profit Margin*	4.4	6.7	9.1	7.2	6.9	5.0	5.6	7.5	7.1	7.6

* Operating profit margin before interest, taxes and depreciation.
† Crown Cork & Seal merged with International subsidiary.
Source: Adapted from reports by the *Value Line*.

areas growing more rapidly than the metal containers sector, and (2) to reduce vulnerability to competition from new packaging materials.

The American Can Company and the Continental Can Company moved from being can manufacturers to become "diversified suppliers of packaging."[7] Both companies manufacture products to supply almost any form of packaging desired. Whereas metal containers used to account for over 75% of Continental's volume, they comprised only 50% in 1963. American's reliance on metal can sales dropped from 80% in 1955 to slightly over 60% in 1963.

"These two firms have diversified to the point where they are important factors in papers, plastics, and glass products. . . . With their integrated paper-making facilities, they are in a good position to serve the needs of any customer who prefers foil-fibre containers. . . ."[8]

National Can, the third largest producer of metal containers, moved into the production of plastic containers, purchasing a small plastic firm in 1963. The company also invested heavily in fibre-foil machinery.

Increased customer service

As competition from new material suppliers and the interest of packagers in self-manufacture intensified, all four companies moved to expand the services they offered their customers. American Can, for example, provided customers with market studies of pet food consumption, and of seasonal and demographic influences on the consumption of citrus fruits, beer, and frozen bakery goods. Another service increasingly offered by the four companies has been help in new product planning and development, material handling advice, and assistance in production layout and design. American Can and Continental Can and to a lesser extent Crown Cork and National Can have established special service organizations to work with manufacturers on a large variety of technical and marketing problems. By broadening the scope of the peripheral services offered to their customers, the companies hoped to increase the economic reliance of the packager upon the industry.

Heavy investment in research

It is estimated that during the early 60s, packaging suppliers were spending over $150 million annually on research to upgrade materials and machinery.[9] Both Continental Can and American Can spent an estimated 1.5% of their annual gross sales on research.

In 1963, the Continental Technical Research Center in Chicago occupied several buildings, employed over 1,000 people, and was reported to be the largest and most comprehensive packaging research and development center in the United States. A principal focus of the center's efforts has been the testing and evaluation of all types of materials and production processes for the creation of new packages. In

---

[7] "Price Trends Favor Can Makers," *Financial World,* August 22, 1962, p. 14.

[8] "Container Makers Grow with Economy," *Financial World,* May 29, 1963, p. 7.

[9] "The Packaging Push, Aerosols to Flip Tops," *The Wall Street Journal,* April 9, 1963, p. 23.

1962, Continental reported that it had budgeted over $20 million for research during the 1963 fiscal year.

In 1963, American announced the start of construction on a research center at Princeton, New Jersey. The company's annual report of that year stated that the center would give major attention to "basic research in such areas as solid state physics and electro-chemical phenomena, as a potential source of new products."

In addition to searching for new applications for existing containers and competitive uses of new materials, the can companies also have concentrated upon cutting their manufacturing costs. One way was to increase the speed at which cans were manufactured. As recently as 1958, typical production speeds rarely exceeded 400 cans/minute. In 1963 the most modern machinery produced certain types of cans as fast as 1,500/minute.

New methods of decorating the can have also appeared. "Electrostatic printing," a process designed to improve printing on irregular surfaces, is expected to make feasible the use of containers with more unusual shapes and surfaces. These types of containers have had limited use because of labeling difficulties. The process, unlike present methods, requires no contact with the material to be printed.[10]

Closer cooperation with the steel industry

Because the metal container industry has bought over $2 billion a year in tinplate, the threat of the technological obsolescence of the tin can created a strong response from the steel industry. One such development has been a new lighter weight "skinny" tinplate, resulting from double rolling the conventional gauge of tinplate.

> Until they [steelmakers] were faced with aluminum's claim based on lightness, the steelmakers had traditionally solved canners' problems by sheer bulk with heavier cans than need be. But . . . by cold-working the metal by a second pass through the rolling mill . . . the rolling mill . . . they could cut the cost of freight for the material, the can, and the ultimate product.
>   . . . With all their new special equipment, tinplate makers can continue reducing the gauge of their material as far as can makers find it safe and convenient to go. . . .[11]

The economic stake of the steel industry in the future of the can companies, many can company executives believed, would be a significant factor in the ability, particularly of the non-giants, to adjust effectively to new competitive pressures. As an executive of one of the smaller companies put it: "A week doesn't go by that we are not working with some steel company on a new development . . . we won't lose this market to the aluminum and paper companies as they [the steel companies] have the resources to do fantastic things with steel."

Recently the United States Steel Corporation announced the introduction of a new steel foil designed to be used with composite con-

---

[10] "American Can Acquires Rights to New Process for Printing on Packages," *The Wall Street Journal*, November 7, 1963.

[11] "Thin Tin Gets Rolling," *Business Week*, May 11, 1963.

tainers. Steel manufacturers have also been testing an assortment of cans to be used as cooking utensils and serving dishes.

> U.S. Steel [has] tested bulk cheese in a decorated reclosable tin can, which doubles both as an original container and as a table server. The company has no plans to enter the consumer packaging field; it devised the new containers as a stimulus for tinplate, a company spokesman says.[12]

Movement abroad

As margins in traditional markets narrowed in the United States under the increasing competitive pressures, some can companies established manufacturing facilities overseas, not only in Europe but also in Latin America, Africa, and the Far East. The purpose was to get into a position to profit from the rising standard of living of overseas countries. There was a need for inexpensive food preservation in many countries and needed demand for convenient food packaging was increasing in the more advanced foreign countries. Crown Cork and Seal, for example, established or expanded plants in 17 foreign countries from 1958 to 1964, becoming the largest potential overseas producer of tin cans in the short space of six years.

Product specialization

The Crown Cork and Seal Company, nearly bankrupt in 1957, in large measure because of poor operating procedures, had not expanded outside the metal container field by the end of 1963. Instead, it specialized in the aerosol field, becoming the largest producer of steel aerosol containers. Following the strategy of concentrating upon the development of this container, while downgrading product lines (such as packer cans) most vulnerable to self-manufacture, Crown Cork enjoyed the highest profit margins of the four leaders in the industry. The remainder of this case focuses on the development of Crown strategy.

CROWN CORK AND SEAL COMPANY

The crisis

In 1956, Crown reported earnings of $381,000 on domestic sales of $115 million, not enough to cover payment of $550,000 in preferred dividends. The steady downward trend in operating profits during the early 1950s, in part a result of the elaborate line and staff organization and the increasingly costly research and development programs maintained, also stemmed from the company's very large and geographically concentrated production facilities (see Exhibits 6 and 7). For example, in 1954 Crown had built a plant in Leeds, Alabama, transferring a major portion of its crown production there in order to be near the Birmingham steel mills. In Philadelphia the company operated one of the largest can plants in the world, concentrating over 80% of its can production under on roof on 55 can lines. (Although industry execu-

---

[12] "The Packaging Push, Aerosols to Flip Tops," *The Wall Street Journal,* April 9, 1963, p. 23.

Exhibit 6

CROWN CORK AND SEAL COMPANY

Organization

(February 1957)

Division	*Plant locations*
Crown & Closure....................	Baltimore, Maryland
	Detroit, Michigan
	Leeds, Alabama
	St. Louis, Missouri
Can..............................	Philadelphia, Pennsylvania
	Erie Avenue Plant
	Ashton Road Plant
	Baltimore, Maryland
	Chicago, Illinois
	Bartow, Florida
	Orlando, Florida
Machinery........................	Baltimore, Maryland
Western..........................	San Francisco, California
	Los Angeles, California

tives did not agree on the optimum number of lines for a can plant, most concluded that anything over 20 lines tended to be unwieldy and uneconomical.) In both cases the plants were located hundreds of miles from the markets needed to utilize the huge capacity of these facilities.

Except for the investment in the new Leeds plant in 1954, less than $1 million was invested in updating and replacing the machinery used in all locations between 1950 and 1957.

In the spring of 1957 after Crown reported a loss of $600,000 in its first quarter of operations, the Bankers Trust Company of New York withdrew its line of credit and asked for repayment of the $2½ million currently being extended. At a special meeting of the board of directors, Mr. John F. Connelly, Chairman and a substantial stockholder of the company (estimated at 24% in 1964) was named president.

Domestic operations since 1957

When Mr. Connelly assumed the presidency of Crown Cork, the company was on the verge of bankruptcy. In addition to the $2½ million loan called by Bankers Trust, there were $4½ million of short-term notes due by the end of 1957. In his first annual message to the stockholders, Mr. Connelly described his task as "halting, reversing and rebuilding [the company's] status with the stockholder and customer alike," a task he saw as "appalling" in the spring of 1957.

> Management was extremely discouraged. Sales were diminishing as reports were freely circulated among our customers that we were in difficulty. The complaints of stockholders were numerous and violent. . . . Six and one-half million dollars were owed to the banks and it was thought that an additional $7 million would be needed to get us through the seasonal peak of our business.

Exhibit 7

CROWN CORK & SEAL COMPANY
Manufacturing Facilities
Domestic Plants

1955

Location	Products
Baltimore, Maryland	Machinery, crowns, closures, cans
Bartow, Florida	Cans
Chicago, Illinois	Cans
Leeds, Alabama	Crowns and cans
Los Angeles, California	Cans
Orlando, Florida	Cans
Philadelphia	Cans
San Francisco, California	Cans
St. Louis, Missouri	Crowns, closures

1962

Atlanta, Georgia	Cans, crowns and closures
Baltimore, Maryland	Machinery, crowns, closures
Bartow, Florida	Cans
Chicago, Illinois	Crowns and cans
Dallas, Texas	Cans
Ft. Worth, Texas	Cans
Orlando, Florida	Cans and crowns
Philadelphia	Cans and crowns
San Francisco, California	Cans, crowns and closures
Spartanburg, North Carolina	Cans and crowns
St. Louis, Missouri	Cans, crowns and closures
Winchester, Virginia	Cans and closures

Foreign plants

Antwerp, Belgium	Crowns, closures and machinery
Rio de Janeiro, Brazil	Crowns
Sao Paulo, Brazil	Crowns
Toronto, Canada	Cans and crowns
Montreal, Canada	Crowns
London, England	Crowns
Paris, France	Crowns
Tredegar, Wales	Crowns
Milan, Italy	Crowns
Mexico City, Mexico	Crowns
Casablanca, Morocco	Crowns
Rotterdam, The Netherlands	Crowns
Lima, Peru	Crowns
Lisbon, Portugal	Cork rods, discs, etc.
Salisbury, Southern Rhodesia	Crowns
Johannesburg, South Africa	Crowns
Port Elizabeth, South Africa	Crowns

As a result of these conditions, Mr. Connelly instituted severe changes in the company's pattern of operations in an effort to survive the crisis of 1957 and rebuild the company into a stronger long-term competitor. These changes, initiated over a period of two or three years were:

1. An extensive reorganization of the management and financial structures.

2. The modernization and geographical diversification of product facilities.
3. Product specialization.
4. Emphasis on customer service.

The management reorganization. Shortly after he became president, Mr. Connelly moved the company's headquarters from Baltimore to Philadelphia and started to eliminate the complicated divisional structure, an outgrowth of the previous management's efforts to improve the company's earnings position. The old structure had consisted of four major operating divisions: the Crown and Closure Division, the Can Division, the Machinery Division, and the Western Division (see Exhibit 6). A fifth division had existed, but in December of 1955 this [the Specialty] division, whose main plant was in St. Louis, was merged with the Crown and Closure Division "in the interests of economy."

The 1955 Annual Report had commented on the rationale behind the institution of the divisional organization and the increased overhead it brought about:

> In 1953 the company began to adapt a headquarters and operating division type of organization such as has been employed successfully by a larger number of American industrial corporations. The three former principal subsidiaries became divisions of the company and the Baltimore operations were established as two separate divisions in addition to the headquarters staff.

From 1957 to 1959, Mr. Connelly consolidated the management structure, reducing sharply the overhead. By 1959, Crown's employment had been reduced by 1,647 people or 24% of its labor force. As one executive carefully put it: "We also lost the services of 11 or so vice presidents." In addition, the central research and development facility was disbanded. Within two years, overhead was reduced from over $11 million to $5 million. In the 1957 and 1958 Annual Reports, Mr. Connelly described these changes:

> A few years ago, the company introduced an elaborate and costly line and staff type of organization. Aside from its cost and other disadvantages, it was incompatible with the size of our business. This type of organization has been largely eliminated and changed to one of greater simplicity, flexibility, and effectiveness. We consolidated three independent divisional product selling groups into one integrated sales organization. [In addition] a careful review of all classes of personnel accomplished by year end [1957] a reduction of 968 employees. These reductions were unrelated to business activity in that they largely comprised excess and nonessential personnel. In headquarters alone, which in the past has been severely criticized, there was a reduction of 80 people to approximately one-half of its original size. . . .
> Elimination of this divisional staff-type of organization and the institution of straight-line operating management in our various manufacturing plants [has given] us better and more direct control over our operations.

While the company did not maintain an organization chart in 1963 ("we would spend all our time just trying to keep it up-to-date"), Exhibit 8 reflects how one might have looked.

Exhibit 8

CROWN CORK AND SEAL COMPANY

Organization

(February 1964)

Chairman and President
John F. Connelly

Vice President of
Manufacturing
Mr. Luviano

Vice President of
Sales
Mr. Siebert

Vice President
and Treasurer
Mr. Blair
(Director)

— Domestic Plant Managers

— Quality Control

— Traffic

— Manager—Manufacturing

— Director of Research

— Purchasing

— Industrial Relations

— 7 Regional Managers

— 5 Product Line Managers

— Vice President
  Southeast Region

— General Manager
  Machinery Division

— Assistant Treasurer

— Controller

— Credit Manager

In addition to the drastic reorganization and reduction of executive positions undergone since 1957, Crown also experienced a considerable turnover in top-level personnel. Mr. Siebert, Mr. Luviano, and the controller had been in their present positions less than two months as of February 1964. These gentlemen were the third group of executives to occupy these positions since 1958. The rapid turnover of top-level personnel reflected, in part, Mr. Connelly's strong belief as to (1) the importance of an immediate and measurable contribution from his subordinates and (2) the company not being a "training ground or retirement home" for executives.

As part of the company's reorganization, Mr. Connelly discarded divisional accounting practices at the same time he eliminated the divisional line and staff concept. Except for one accountant maintained at each plant location, all accounting and cost control was performed at the corporate level, the corporate accounting section occupying one-half the space used by the headquarters group.

According to Mr. Connelly, "When we took over this place, it was completely demoralized. So we started talking profits, a $10,000 saving would improve earnings 1 cent a share, a $1,000 saving $\frac{1}{10}$ and so forth. We went to all our plants and did this, stressing that the company's future and that of the individual manager would depend solely on his profit performance not on whether he was related to someone at corporate headquarters."

Whereas in 1956 each plant manager had had his own accounting-control section and was responsible for all costs controllable at the plant level, in 1963 the control function was centralized; also, each plant manager had been made totally responsible for plant profitability, including any allocated costs (all company overhead, estimated at 5% of sales, was allocated to the plant level). As explained by Mr. Blair, Vice President and Treasurer, the cost and profit consciousness of the plant managers had expanded to all aspects of company operations when they were made responsible for al costs. "The manager is even responsible for the profits on each product manufactured in his plant." The plant manager's compensation was not tied directly to profit performance. But as Mr. Blair pointed out, "He is certainly rewarded on the basis of that figure."

Financial reorganization.   Reductions in personnel and inventory levels moved Crown past the 1957 crisis with the banks. Since that time the company had reduced the cash drain of its capital structure by purchasing or redeeming a major portion of the outstanding preferred and preference stock. By so doing, the company reduced required dividend payments by over $600,000. Crown also purchased and retired about 1.2 million shares of common stock (after giving effect to a four to one stock split in 1963). The company also repurchased its plants, which had been sold on a leaseback arrangement during the late 1940s.

In 1963, Crown, through the sale of 400,000 shares of common stock and the issuance of $30 million in convertible debentures, raised $42 million. It used this to refund all existing long-term indebtedness, substantially reducing its interest expense. Mr. Blair believed this last change in the company's capital structure had corrected all the financial errors that had carried over from the pre-1958 period (see Exhibits 9 and 10).

Modernization and diversification of facilities.   In 1957, the bulk of the company's products were produced in three locations (Baltimore, Leeds, and Philadelphia). Because of this concentration, high transportation costs had, in effect, eliminated Crown as a factor in many market areas. An additional limitation had been imposed by the fact that the company's 13 plants typically produced only one classification of products (see Exhibit 7). Consequently, the new management sought to introduce greater "flexibility" to their production capacity by expanding the number of geographical areas that could be served profitably. Crown, from 1958 to 1963, spent almost $82 million in relocation expenses and on new facilities, a sum representing over one-half its total plant investment as of 1963.

In Baltimore, the company's crown and closure manufacturing facilities, occupying over 50 multistoried buildings, were vacated, much of the obsolete equipment being sold. New facilities occupying three single-storied buildings replaced the former ones. The company's electrolytic tin mill in Baltimore also was sold, in 1958.

The company's gigantic can plant in Philadelphia was vacated and set up as rental property. Its can lines were relocated to existing plants in order to expand their capacity and to convert them from single to multiproduct facilities. In 1959, the Leeds, Alabama, plant was vacated, its crown lines being transferred to a new plant constructed in Atlanta. In 1960, a plant was opened in Winchester, Virginia, to manufacture packer cans for the apple packing industry in the Shenandoah Valley region. A plant to manufacture cans and crowns was purchased in Dallas. This plant was to be a temporary facility until a new plant could be constructed in Texas. Crown manufacturing equipment was added to the Chicago can plant. Can lines were installed in the St. Louis crown and closure plant. In 1963, the company was constructing can plants in Fort Worth, Texas, and Spartanburg, South Carolina. Aerosol can lines were installed in the Atlanta, Chicago, and San Francisco plants and aerosol capacity was being expanded in Philadelphia and Baltimore.

Crown management believed that, because of this extensive investment in new facilities, its domestic equipment was the most technically advanced in the industry. Mr. Blair thought it was unlikely that any other major can producer could claim 60% of its total investment as being new within the last five years. To this factor, Mr. Blair attributed much of Crown's recent ability to maintain the highest operating margins in the industry.

In November 1963, Crown announced the purchase of the Mundet Corporation, a producer of polystyrene and specialty cork insulation materials and gaskets made of composition cork and rubber. The company also produced metal bottle caps and had a small plastics operation. By early 1964, Crown had sold the insulation and plastics portions of the business, recovering almost its entire initial investment. Crown also discontinued the manufacture of insulating materials. As explained by Mr. Connelly, "We are primarily interested in obtaining the Mundet crown plant which is ideally located to service the New York Metropolitan Area. The plant is being expanded to include can-forming lines." Previously, New York customers had been serviced from the Philadelphia plant at a substantial transportation expense to the company. Mr. Connelly estimated that savings in trucking expense alone would exceed $300,000 a year.

Product specialization. In 1963 Crown derived about 50% of its sales from the production of cans and metal containers, about 43% from crowns, and the balance from bottling and packaging machinery. Domestically, cans accounted for over 65% of the total volume and almost 40% of profits. Although the profit margin on crowns was typically higher than those on cans and closures the percentages were also generally representative of the importance of any one product group to net earnings.

The breakdown of total volume by the individual product groups had remained relatively constant since 1960. Within the container group,

Exhibit 9

CROWN CORK AND SEAL COMPANY (A)

Comparative Statement of Profit and Loss for the Fiscal Years
1954–1963, 1961–1963 Consolidated

	1963		1962		1961*		1960	
Sales								
Products sold....................	$205,396	100.0%	$190,178	100.0%	$176,992	100.0%	$121,211	100.0%
Interest, royalties and other income...	908	0.4	505	0.3	874	0.5	804	0.6
Dividend from Crown International...							700	0.6
	$206,304	100.4%	$190,683	100.3%	$177,866	100.5%	$122,715	101.2%
Costs and expenses								
Costs of products sold excluding depreciation....................	163,033	79.3	150,093	78.9	139,071	78.6	101,931	84.1
Selling and administration..........	15,033	7.4	14,694	7.7	15,311	8.7	9,488	7.8
Depreciation.....................	6,039	3.0	4,908	2.6	4,627	2.6	2,513	2.1
Interest.........................	2,636	1.2	1,579	0.8	1,252	0.7	1,225	1.0
Nonrecurring expense covering relocation of operating facilities, etc......	1,505	0.7	1,820	1.0	2,517	1.4	1,826	1.5
	$188,246	91.6	$173,094	91.0	$162,778	92.0	$116,983	96.5
Profits from operations...............	$ 18,058	8.8	$ 17,589	9.3	$ 15,088	8.5	$ 5,732	4.7
Estimated taxes on income...........	7,250	3.5	8,081	4.3	7,625	4.3	2,325	1.9
Net profits........................	$ 10,808	5.3	$ 9,508	5.0	$ 7,463	4.2	$ 3,407	2.8
Pro forma combined summary of earnings reflecting terms of 1961 merger								
Net sales.							$168,866	100.0%
Cost of product sold excluding depreciation.....................							135,276	80.2
Depreciation.....................							3,828	2.3
Selling and administrative expenses...							15,972	0.5
Interest.........................							1,298	0.9
Income tax......................							5,491	3.2
Net income......................							$ 6,392	3.8

however, Crown had concentrated upon producing cans for "hard-to-hold" products such as beer, soft drinks, and whipped cream that needed high strength or sensitivity protection from their containers and/or utilized convenience features such as aerosol dispensing or a "tear-top" lid. Specializing in these types of high-margin applications, the company had dropped over $20 million in low margin or breakeven applications since 1957; the percentage of "packer" cans in Crown's total volume declined greatly relative to the other three major manufacturers.

According to Mr. Siebert, Sales Vice President, the specialization in difficult applications, particularly beer and aerosol containers, had reduced the threat of self-manufacture to the company. Part of the reasoning behind the decision not to produce the fibre-foil container for the oil industry was a case in point. Despite its several million-dollar stake in the motor oil can business, Crown having captured 50% of this market by introducing the first aluminum one-quart oil can in 1958, management had decided not to produce the composite can. Their reasoning was:

1. There is a better and quicker return in the beer and carbonated beverage industries.
2. That the economies of the paper can are such as to give the paper companies a significant cost advantage.
3. That because (a) the technology is simple, and (b) the petroleum

1959		1958		1957		1956		1955		1954	
$123,191	100.0%	$116,348	100.0%	$115,923	100.0%	$115,098	100.0%	$112,954	100.0%	$110.064	100.0%
339	0.3	559	0.5	237	0.2	188	0.1	499	0.4	190	6.2
600	0.5	500	0.4	500	0.4	400	0.4	400	0.4	400	0.4
$124,130	100.8%	$117,407	100.9%	$116,660	100.6%	$115,736	100.5%	$113,583	100.8%	$110.654	106.6%
104,251	84.6	96,922	83.3	98,278	84.8	95,803	83.3	92,430	81.8	90,449	82.2
10,636	8.6	13,074	11.2	13,337	11.5	15,280	13.3	14,042	12.4	13,598	12.4
2,087	1.7	2,381	2.1	2,494	2.1	2,577	2.2	2,672	2.4	2,723	2.5
955	0.8	677	0.6	894	0.8	1,150	1.0	1,030	0.9	1,160	1.0
2,033	1.7	1,203	1.0	637	0.5	440	0.4	448	0.4	112	0.1
$119,962	97.4	$114,257	98.2	$115,640	99.7	$115,250	100.1	$110,622	97.9	$108,042	98.2
$ 4,168	3.4	$ 3,150	2.7	$ 1,020	0.9	$ 486	0.4	$ 3,230	2.9	$ 2,612	2.4
1,525	1.2	1,213	1.0	266	0.2	105	0.1	1,406	1.3	1,196	1.1
$ 2,643	2.2	$ 1,937	1.7	$ 754	0.7	$ 381	0.3	$ 1,824	1.6	$ 1,416	1.3
$171,012	100.0%	$161,733	100.0%	$158,668	100.0	$153,578	100.0%	n.a.		n.a.	
137,162	80.4	130,183	80.6	129,260	81.5	123,541	80.4				
3,395	2.2	3,706	2.4	3,787	2.4	3,669	2.4				
16,745	9.8	17,694	10.9	17,597	11.2	19,001	12.3				
1,104	0.8	896	0.7	1,115	0.7	1,342	0.9				
5,076	3.2	3,801	2.5	3,165	2.1	3,024	2.0				
$ 5,831	3.6	$ 4,739	2.9	$ 3,232		$ 3,173	2.0	n.a.		n.a.	

* Crown Cork and Seal merged with Crown International in 1961.

industry is very standardized, the paper can lends itself to self-manufacture, nor could the price be low enough to prevent it.

4. If necessary, the company could always make the container as they already made spiral paper tubing in which to ship can ends. In addition, the "Dacro" bottle cap utilizes a paper-foil composite material.

5. Finally, the composite can appeared to be only a stage as some oil companies were already experimenting with plastic containers.

By the end of 1963, the company had lost over $8 million in sales to the composite oil can.

One manager described the concentration on producing cans of high ability as:

> A result of the way we think the industry is going. Easy applications are already taken care of. To expand the use of the can, and particularly the aerosol, greater demands are being made of the "can as a package."

One measure of the reliance upon difficult and demanding can applications was that aerosol sales, in 1963, accounted for 20% of total company sales, and sales to the beer industry 50% of total volume. The emphasis on the beer can was also in part an outgrowth of a belief that

Exhibit 10

CROWN CORK AND SEAL COMPANY (A)

Balance Sheets for Fiscal Years 1954–1963, 1961–1963 Consolidated
(dollars in thousands)

	1963	1962	1961	1960	1959	1958	1957	1956	1955*	1954*
Current assets										
Cash	$ 6,235	$ 5,831	$ 5,343	$ 2,204	$ 2,587	$ 1,905	$ 1,677	$ 3,030	$ 2,786	$ 4,064
Government securities	1,735	913	527				2,179†			
Receivables	30,199	25,387	23,729	15,775	15,286	15,781	14,962	12,919	11,743	9,705
Inventories										
Finished goods	33,349	27,206	25,011	16,251	16,013	13,417	16,582	19,319	17,845	17,625
Work-in-process	14,168	11,644	10,275	3,416	6,039	10,068	10,062	14,133	14,036	13,384
Prepaid expenses	3,539	2,397	1,463	513	593	479	610	817	776	771
	$ 89,225	$ 73,378	$ 66,348	$38,159	$40,518	$41,650	$46,072	$50,218	$49,318†	$45,676†
Current liabilities										
Notes payable	$ 31,344	$ 21,635	$ 5,190	$ 1,875	$10,000			$ 7,700	$ 3,200	$ 5,700
Accounts payable	21,017	20,597	14,956	8,887	10,620	$ 8,205	$ 8,005	7,494	7,575	4,644
Customer deposits				213	291	160	268	212	213	180
Provision for income tax	2,722	2,926	4,679	2,056	1,529	2,038	749	172	1,280	1,211
	$ 55,083	$ 45,158	$ 24,825	$13,031	$22,440	$10,403	$ 9,022	$15,578	$12,268	$11,736
Working capital	$ 34,142	$ 28,220	$ 41,523	$25,128	$18,078	$31,247	$37,050	$34,640	$35,050	$33,940
Investment in Crown International Corporation			13,215	13,215	1,460	1,460	1,460	1,460	1,460	1,460
Investment in Crown Financial Corporation	750	750								

Plant and Equipment

Buildings	51,889	42,005	35,119	17,834	14,310	12,231	16,924	16,875	16,751	16,724
Machinery equipment	95,666	77,486	65,621	49,158	40,675	36,030	44,855	45,490	45,018	45,994
Construction in progress	7,667	5,102	3,387	1,446	7,372	3,744	1,007	1,111	1,306	1,543
Loss: Depreciation	(59,899)	(48,719)	(45,004)	(26,339)	(24,717)	(24,258)	(32,464)	(31,167)	(29,468)	(28,899)
Land	4,563	4,000	3,131	1,694	1,383	1,706	1,615	1,720	1,744	1,515
Patents, less amortization	332	382	616	312	329	350	368	536§	393	382
	$100,218	$ 80,256	$ 62,870	$44,105	$39,352	$29,803	$32,305	$34,582	$35,744	$37,258
Total assets less current liabilities	$135,110	$109,226	$104,393	$82,448	$58,890	$62,510	$70,815	$70,682	$72,293	$72,702
Preferred stock	$ 5,007	$ 5,624	$ 6,279	$ 7,269	$ 7,269	$ 7,875	$11,475	$12,375	$12,375	$12,375
Convertible stock			9,917							
Common stock	11,527	10,642	2,699	2,448	2,423	2,655	3,019	3,019	3,019	3,019
Paid-in surplus	11,274		2,036	9,793	9,656	10,420	11,059	10,705	10,705	10,705
Earned surplus	61,157	54,724	55,609	40,717	25,878	25,702	25,936	24,383	24,794	24,003
	$ 88,965	$ 70,990	$ 77,540	$60,229	$45,226	$46,652	$51,489	$50,482	$50,893	$50,102
Minority shareholders' equity in subsidiaries	8,320	7,871	7,639							
Long-term debt	30,676	25,454	17,654	21,125	13,000	15,400	19,000	20,200	21,400	22,600
Deferred income taxes	7,149	4,911	1,560	1,094	664	458	326			
	$135,110	$109,226	$104,393	$82,448	$58,890	$62,510	$70,815	$70,682	$72,293	$72,702

* Discrepancies in total figures due to rounding.
† Claims for prior years' federal income and excise profits taxes.
‡ Adjusted to reflect cash surrender value of life insurance, $132,000 and $126,000, respectively.
§ Listed as Other Assets in 1956 Annual Report.
‖ Since January of 1963.

the crown market was stagnating as beverages were being packed increasingly in cans.

Strong customer service. Believing that (1) there was little technical difference in product quality throughout the industry, all manufacturers having the ability to produce a high-quality can; and (2) the company with the strategically located and available line capacity would have a competitive advantage; Crown executives viewed their greatest competitive strength and challenge to be the provision of a very high level of customer service. Mr. Connelly and Mr. Blair believed this to be the advantage of "operating the company as a small business —we are only as big as our local plant." Messrs. Connelly, Luviano, and Siebert estimated they spent at least half of their time traveling in order "to stay close to the business and informed." Mr. Connelly explained that he gave a major portion of his time to sales, and handling accounts. "I insist on personally hearing about all complaints and problems. I may not know the answer but I will show concern and see that an answer is obtained very quickly." The deep involvement of the top corporate officers in the operations of the company reflected, according to Mr. Blair, "the key aspects of the can industry: the fact that nobody stores cans, and customers want them in a hurry and on time. As far as we are concerned, fast answers get customers."

As part of the policy of providing the fastest possible service, Crown tried to avoid the necessity of changeovers on its lines preferring to invest in additional equipment. As explained by one manager:

> Our thinking has been to have the equipment and then go out and sell it. We believe the cost of 90% machine utilization and warehousing to be prohibitive. Also changing machine setups is a slow and inefficient process. Therefore we have had a heavy investment in additional lines which are maintained in a setup condition and can be gotten rolling in 15 or 20 minutes.

A major objective of the reorganization in 1957–1959 had been to increase the service capacity of the sales force by consolidating the sales organization. Dividing the sales force geographically rather than by product, each salesman was given account responsibility for all products. This consolidation was thought to provide customers with a service unique in the industry, a single contact for crowns, cans, closures and machinery.

According to company executives, however, the most important aspect of Crown's emphasis on service was not its ability to deliver quickly, but rather the ability of the Crown sales force and its technical department to solve customer problems. For example, to the bottler this often meant a complete study of his markets, their growth potential, his distribution methods; for the food packer, a study of his most effective plant layout or technical help on a sanitation problem; for the aerosol packager, the redesign of a dust cap, or help with a production problem resulting from faulty valve mechanisms; and so forth.

Both the manufacturing engineering group and the research and development section devoted a large portion of their time to customer's production process and product development problems, respectively. Dr. Cliffcorn, Director of Crown Research, estimated that over 60% of his section's time was spent on test-packing new products.

A heavy service orientation was reflected in all aspects of the company's research program. As explained by Dr. Cliffcorn:

> Our problem isn't basic research. Our research activities are directed primarily to technical problems. For example, the greatest problem facing the packaging industry is the determination of the true requirement of the container. We are using materials today that five years ago everybody said wouldn't do. We just get more out of it, but also we re-evaluate the true demands placed upon the container.
>
> Basically, we are looking for new uses for cans and new uses for existing shapes. For instance, I have been trying to interest the sales department in the extruded metal can—perhaps for dog food—so I have had some made up and sent to interested friends. As soon as we learn what they want we will make 1,000 of them within a week—timing is crucial around here.

Mr. Luviano, Vice President of Manufacturing, believed there was often a great deal of value in being second to implement a new idea thereby learning from the mistakes of the first.

> There is a tremendous asset inherent in being second, especially in the face of the ever-changing state of flux you find in this industry. You try to let others take the risks and make the mistakes as the big discoveries often flop initially due to something unforeseen in the original analysis. But somebody else, learning from the innovator's heartaches, prospers by refinement. For example, the "spot" insert used in a beer crown is 0.0018 inches thick. Now what determined that? Not brains, nobody envisioned that a 0.0018 inch thickness would be just what was needed, but rather experience; the trial and error of building upon, and learning from, your own and other people's mistakes and problems.

Mr. Blair felt that Crown's lack of interest in not "becoming enamored with all the frills of an R&D section of high class, ivory towered scientists getting little use out of such expenses," was a significant factor behind its recent success.

> Certainly in the electronics industry high class research is needed but this is a much different "being" than the can industry. Too many people have been sucked in on this and have lost a great deal of money. In fact, at one time even Crown made this mistake but we have recovered from these errors.

According to Mr. Connelly, Crown limited its pioneering.

> We are not truly pioneers. Our philosophy is not to spend a great deal of money for basic research. However, we do have tremendous skills in die forming and metal fabrication, and we can move to adapt to the customer's needs faster than anyone else in the industry.

Mr. Luviano believed that Crown's introduction of the tear-top lid reflected another aspect of the company's service policy. "When we developed our first tear-top lids we made them available to all our customers at the same time rather than committing ourselves to giving preferential treatment to one of the large national brewers as did Continental."

With the exception of Mr. Blair, Mr. Connelly and all of his vice presidents were ex-sales executives. Mr. Connelly said this was indicative of the importance he attached to an "aggressive sales-minded" organization. Aggressiveness was emphasized by Mr. Siebert. While he admitted that personal relationships were important selling factors in the industry, Crown salesmen were evaluated on the basis of new business produced, all of the company's products being sold directly to customers by 100 technically-trained salesmen.

In addition to the direct-line sales organization, five product sales managers also reported to Mr. Siebert. Their primary responsibility was the development of new product applications and the maintenance of customer service within their respective product lines or industries. These industries and lines were: (1) the brewing industry, (2) the soft drink industry, (3) fabricated aerosol cans, (4) drawn aerosol cans, and (5) packer and general-line cans. The manager of fabricated aerosol containers described his job as:

> A combination of titles—sales and product development. On the development side—new applications, and ideas. The problem is to put more and different products into the can. If I see a future in any idea, I work it out with R&D and quality control to test its feasibility. If there is enough volume to justify tooling costs, I will go to the supplier and develop his interests. We don't do basic development, but we will work with supplier to provide specs and answer technical questions. The basic thing is to sell him on an idea to increase his market and then to work with him to develop it.

To the soft drink industry and to a lesser extent with the brewing industry, Crown Cork was the only company in the country which could supply all of the packager's needs from the filling equipment to the cans and/or the crowns needed to seal the bottles. The machinery division supplied 60% of all the filling equipment used in the soft drink industry and 90% in the brewing industry. The company's ability to offer a unique range of services, i.e., cans, crowns, machinery, to major beverage packers, had often provided an entryway for new crown and can business.

March 1962

In his stockholder message of March 1962, Mr. Connelly concluded that the rebuilding and sharpening of Crown Cork's domestic operations had been more than accomplished.

> In 1957, your present management accepted the challenge to rebuild your company. At that time we planned a very ambitious five-year program, the goal of which was to produce additional profits of $1 per share each year.
> We have exceeded this goal so it is only natural to ask about the future.

We still feel that we have hardly scratched the surface of our potential. We have built a splendid organization full of enthusiasm— one that is now ready to take on a new challenge. We are confidently planning for the years 1962–1967, expecting equal or even more dramatic performance than the past five years.

Admittedly long-range prognostication is risky but the groundwork has been laid so solidly that again we are setting goals to add a minimum of $1.00[13] per share profit in each of these years. We consider this goal very realistic and will determinedly do everything within our power to accomplish this objective.

The expansion of production capacity and its breaking up into smaller and more dispersed units, along with a strong service orientation, all introduced to correct conditions which had helped to precipitate the 1957 crisis, had become, according to company executives, the "solid groundwork" on which the effort to accomplish this objective would be based. International expansion was to be the principal means.

International expansion

Following its policy of selling in selected geographical markets, and locating plant facilities as near as possible to large customers, Crown, in 1960, had established a program to build plants in overseas locations. The objective was to be closer to what was anticipated would be the major growth areas for metal cans in the next 20 years. In 1928, Mr. McManus had organized an International Company as a subsidiary to manage the production and sale of crowns overseas. In 1961, the two companies were merged. The merger's proxy statement listed four primary objectives:

1. Corporate structure will be a simplified and a single management will be able to better coordinate and integrate the operation of the domestic and international business.
2. The foreign subsidiaries will become more closely identified with Seal and with each other by working directly with Seal rather than through an intermediary company.
3. Seal and International presently hope to eliminate the risk inherent in the substantial reliance of International's subsidiaries on a single product (crowns) by adding new products when market conditions are suitable in certain countries. The merger will simplify efforts to this end by enabling Seal to provide directly to the subsidiaries the necessary experience and management.
4. The merger will result in a reduction of administrative expense.

By the end of 1963, Crown was operating 21 plants outside the United States: seven in Europe, five in South America, two in Canada, one in Mexico, one in the Far East and five in Africa. Several additional building sites had been selected in Africa for construction within the next five years.

Crown's policy was to create a wholly-owned subsidiary operated by

---

[13] In 1963 this goal was restated to read $0.25 per share due to a 4 to 1 stock split.

the nationals in each country. The corporate headquarters assisted but did not get directly involved in the development of the organization, nor the production facilities. For instance, in Nigeria, the British subsidiary had played the major role in developing the facilities because they had a long-standing understanding of the key social, political and educational aspects involved. "Then we don't get involved in the personnel problems of family moving, fringe benefits, local tax problems, tax laws, and so forth."

In the 1963 Annual Report, Mr. Connelly commented on the development of the international side of the business.

> Our associate companies are very well established locally and well guided by experienced, competent managements, nearly all being nationals of the countries where we are located.
>
> It is impossible to place a value on our international business since the rights we have to operate in these countries, some on a pioneer basis, could not be obtained today.
>
> Our profits and sales in the United States will continue to grow each year and growth in the international market is unlimited.

According to Mr. Blair, the company did not worry about expropriation as "our country diversification greatly reduces this risk. In addition, if we didn't believe in the people and their basic goodwill, we would not have any business being there at all."

The outlook for the future

Assessing the probable effect new materials would have on the company, both Mr. Luviano and Mr. Siebert stated that the company had no present plans to become involved in composite containers or to expand its use of aluminum beyond its current commitment to aluminum ends for beverage cans and the production of aluminum cans for citrus packers at its Bartow, Florida plant. As to plastics both executives pointed out that the company was familiar with the technical problems of plastic fabrication, having been one of two developers of the plastic-lined crown, which in 1963 accounted for 20% of the industry's domestic crown sales. In addition Crown recently had acquired two small plastic moulding companies in England. Both men believed the company would probably become involved with new materials as their acceptance became "a fact." In the meantime Crown didn't plan "to pioneer."

Mr. Luviano questioned the wisdom of investing huge sums of money in a container "that next year may be obsolete. Our belief is that the aluminum and paper composite is still an interim package—one which just holds the product and costs less. We can't afford to work on the same thing. Ideally, you would like to anticipate our competitors, but if you're caught off guard you try to come up with something better."

Commenting on the possibility of further integration by major suppliers and customers, Mr. Siebert, Vice President of Sales, thought the steel industry would not become involved in can manufacturing as "we (can manufacturers) are their biggest single profit factor right now."

As to the possibility of major breweries producing their own cans, Mr. Siebert believed the beer can was "so far too technical" for self-manufacture to be a meaningful threat.

Mr. Blair, Vice President and Treasurer, believed that Crown's future sources of growth would be twofold: that which would come from (1) an increase in the general consumption of cans as consumer income rose, particularly in overseas markets; and (2) attacking the 75% market share held by Continental and American.

> I think the basic tin can has been put to nearly every use there is so I don't feel new uses offer our greatest potential. Rather, if we can get 20% to 40% of all new (geographic) areas we enter, we have a great growth potential in contrast to American and Continental. This is where better service comes in and if you're a customer with a gripe you will always be able to immediately reach John Connelly. (Crown maintained an open-phone policy for all its executives.)

According to Mr. Connelly the important dimension of the company's future growth would be international development.

> Right now we are premature but this has been necessary in order for Crown to become established in these areas. In 20 years, I hope whoever is running this company will look back and comment on the vision of an early decision to introduce can-making in underdeveloped countries.

February of 1964.   In 1963, Crown's operating margins declined for the second year in a row. In late 1963 and early 1964, Mr. Connelly made major personnel changes in the operations area of the company replacing (1) the manager of the company's largest can plant ($50 million in annual sales), and (2) the vice president of operations, the latter's job being filled by Mr. Luviano, the new vice president of manufacturing.

According to Mr. Connelly, the ex-vice president of operations' inability to control operating variances had brought about his replacement. Mr. Luviano's predecessor had sought to control manufacturing operations by maintaining strong functional responsibility at the corporate level. Discussing the changes he planned to institute Mr. Luviano stated:

> I'm a great believer in responsibility at the plant level. Consequently I plan to remove all authority from the corporate level people, making their function that of giving assistance to the plant managers. Then if the plant managers can't do the job—we will get someone who can.

As to the objective established in 1962 of adding $0.25 per share per year in earnings, 1963 fell short of this goal. In his 1963 message to the stockholders, Mr. Connelly commented:

> While 1963 produced the highest sales and profits of our history, we in management are far from being satisfied with these results for we feel we could and should have done better.

Mr. Connelly, however, was able to report earnings of $2.03 per share compared with 1962's figure of $1.83, the latter being computed on the basis of 400,000 fewer shares of stock outstanding.

APPENDIX

A BRIEF DISCUSSION OF THE ECONOMICS AND HISTORY OF THE METAL CONTAINER INDUSTRY

The problem for the can companies of responding profitably to environmental change has historically been influenced by two major industry characteristics:

1. The high capital investment required for a manufacturing facility, and
2. Marketing and distribution practices.

The evolution of the structure of the metal container industry represents the efforts of companies and the federal regulatory agencies to cope with these two phenomena.

The production of metal containers is a highly mechanized and expensive operation in which direct labor represents a small part of the final price. (See Exhibit A1.)

The capital costs of installing a "line" (the equipment required for making cans) have been extensive. For example, a line to run beer cans costs from $750,000 to $1 million. The basic machinery or body forming equipment costs approximately $500,000 per can line and lithography and coating equipment require an additional $300,000 and $225,000, respectively. One lithography and coating line typically feeds three or four forming lines, most can plants having a minimum of 12 to 15 forming lines. A complete line for beer might cost $1.5 million. It might have the capacity to produce more than 100 million cans in a year.

The large capital investment coupled with high cost of changeover has placed can plants in the difficult position of trying to maintain a high level of line utilization while minimizing setup costs. Consequently, volume discounts are often given for quantities in excess of 700,000 cans in order to obtain long runs.

Because of the high level of facility investment, it has been natural for can manufacturers to seek customers with large volumes. The standardized needs of brewers and packers were ideal. In fact a single large packet might easily absorb the output of more than one plant. Brewers and food packers have been the major can industry customers taking over 75% of annual can production.

Because certain customers were so desirable, and because idle plant was so expensive, competition had a tendency to be severe. Efforts to avoid this competition led to two of the most important antitrust cases in United States history. The American Can Company was a classic trust formed to eliminate cut-throat competition among can manufacturers through merger. Prosecuted in 1913 under the Sherman Act and

Exhibit A1

CROWN CORK AND SEAL COMPANY

1962 Value Added by Manufacture

	No. employees	Production workers	Man-hours (in millions)	Wages (in millions)	Value added (in millions)	Cost of materials (in millions)	Value of shipments (in millions)
All manufacturing establishments.	16,777,734	12,138,758	24,306.0	$59,176.0	$179,322	$221,404	$399,327
Fabricated metal product.	1,085,000	834,090	1,724.0	4,287.0	11,115	11,217	22,298
Metal cans.	53,069	46,018	99.0	305.4	772	1,339	2,112
Rubber and plastics.	397,958	313,590	636.0	1,585.0	4,313	4,255	8,516
Stone, clay, glass.	573,926	464,619	944.0	2,281.0	6,600	6,600	11,537

convicted in 1916, the public spirited behavior commended by the judge in his decision not to dismember American, provided the quiet climate in which Continental was able to grow.

During the 1920s and 30s, both American and Continental used their resources to develop faster closing machinery for their cans. This machinery, covered by patents, was only made available to customers who would buy American or Continental cans as well on five- and ten-year contracts. Thus through patent protected positions in closing machinery, American and Continental continued to dominate the container business. The Justice Department's suit begun in 1946 and concluded in 1956, brought such "tie-in" contracts under the scope of the antitrust laws.

Pricing and distribution practices

Pricing.   Where the manufacturers have been unable to respond to market conditions with new or differentiated products, price competition has been severe. For example, in the fall of 1963, Continental Can announced plans to raise prices on aluminum beer can ends, motor oil can ends, citrus cans, and miscellaneous other products. The company gave recent increases by aluminum companies in the price of aluminum sheet as the reason for the increases in keeping with its "policy of adjusting can prices to reflect changes in plate costs."[1] Because other can manufacturers, particularly American, did not announce similar increases, Continental was unable to maintain the new prices. Customers sometimes "punish" such attempts at increasing prices by reducing the offender's share of the business.

The competitive situation has also been aggravated by the trends noted in the earlier description of the industry. Also, faced with rising costs, the can manufacturers have not wanted to provide, by raising prices, further inducement for large can users to set up their own can plants. Also, rising prices would weaken the competitive position of tin cans in relation to plastics, aluminum, and glass containers.

Distribution.   Because cans are relatively bulky items, transportation costs have been a major consideration in setting distribution policies. Various estimates have placed the radius of economical distribution for a plant at between 150 and 300 miles, depending upon the size and weight of the cans.

A critical determinant of transportation costs is the weight/volume relationship, the cost climbing rapidly with an increase in can size and/ or weight. A major advantage of aluminum and composite cans has been their low weight/volume ratio relative to the standard tinplate can.

The high cost of transportation has led can companies to operate many plants (American and Continental manufacture cans in over 100 domestic locations). Usually a plant is located next door to or down the street from its major customer. Because of this, the manufacturer who has lost a large account has been in a difficult position.

---

[1] "Continental Can Planning Some Increases," *The Wall Street Journal*, October 17, 1963, p. 26.

Note on the Major Home Appliance Industry

In 1970, the major home appliance industry, including refrigerators, freezers, ranges, disposals, dishwashers, clothes washers and dryers, and room air conditioners, shipped 28.2 million units with a retail value slightly in excess of $6 billion. This represented an 82% increase in units and a 62% increase in dollar sales over 1961. It was believed that the 1970s promised even greater growth.

These shipments in 1970 represented a unit volume over three times as great as the automobile industry though less than one fifth the dollar value. Compared to the four automobile manufacturers, there were more than 60 appliance manufacturers. But seven of these firms accounted for 75% of the volume. (See Exhibits 1 and 2.)

While during the decade of the 1960s, the automobile industry suffered increasing public criticism for its failure to produce a better and less expensive product to meet consumer needs, the appliance industry (often referred to as the white goods industry)[1] produced greatly improved appliances whose average price declined 10% in the span of the same decade. (See Exhibits 4, 5, and 6.)

Prior to World War II, most appliance manufacturers produced a limited line of appliances developed from the original products of their companies. General Electric started a refrigerator business, Maytag made washers, and Hotpoint produced electric ranges. The lines broadened but not until after World War II did manufacturers recognize the demand for a full line of products. Expansion continued in the decade following the war.

After 1955, however, the industry experienced overcapacity, concentration through mergers and acquisitions among the manufacturers (see Exhibit 7), and a proliferation of brands, both national and pri-

---

[1] The term white goods stemmed from the original color of these products and was used to distinguish them from other appliances like televisions, stereos, and radios which were referred to as brown goods.

vate. There was some feeling in the industry that home appliances were destined to become commodities sold on price alone and that then the Japanese might well become a dominant industry force. Others felt that certain peculiar industry forces, such as the giant vertically integrated retailers (e.g., Sears Roebuck), would lead to the development of a unique structure. Finally, there were those who felt that entirely new products and revolutionary changes in existing products would drastically alter the industry.

If the structure of the industry was changing, so was the business competed for (see Exhibits 4 and 5). Several products experienced very high rates of growth during the 1960s. For example, room air conditioner sales almost quadrupled, dishwasher sales more than tripled and clothes dryers sales more than doubled. Even products in highly saturated markets like refrigerators and ranges (99% of wired homes had refrigerators and ranges) were selling about 50% more units by 1970. At the same time, the individual products themselves were changing. New features were added and the capacity of appliances increased (witness the trend toward larger refrigerators and air conditioners). Product reliability also increased.

With this brief scanning of industry history and trends as background, the remainder of this note examines white goods and their manufacturers, major industry trends, and industry performance, and considers possible future trends.

THE INDUSTRY: ITS PRODUCTS AND ECONOMICS

In 1970, there were two basic ways to classify the products of the appliance industry—by customer use and by technology. Looking first at customer use, appliances were sold for the kitchen—refrigerators, freezers, ranges, dishwashers, and disposals; for the home laundry— washers and dryers; and for room air conditioning. Technologically, appliances could be categorized as: water bearing—dishwashers, disposals, clothes washers, and some dryers; refrigerating—refrigerators, freezers, and room air conditioners; and heating—ranges. A number of part-line producers had diversified by filling out a line of products along one or both of these classifications (see Exhibit 1).

Appliances were manufactured on specialized high capacity assembly lines. Typically, a single factory would produce several models of a single product (e.g., side-by-side and top mount refrigerators) or for some companies a product category. The assembly lines in these factories were not generally convertible for use in manufacturing other product categories. An efficient plant's capacity would range from 100,000 air conditioners a year to 500,000 ranges, refrigerators, and dishwashers. One engineer estimated that production costs for refrigerators, ranges, and dishwashers might be 10% higher for a plant half the optimal size and 20%–40% higher for a plant a fifth the optimal size (see Exhibit 8).

The cost of a production facility that operated at minimum efficient scale (MES) for a full product line was estimated by an industry source to be around $500 million. The cost of a single-product plant at MES for dishwashers was estimated to be $50 million, while the cost of a single-product plant for refrigerators, freezers, clothes washers, clothes dryers, or ranges was estimated to be somewhat more than $50 million.

Even with capacity of the minimum efficient size, a firm might refrain from totally integrated manufacturing. Indeed, appliance companies often chose to buy components such as compressors and motors since these could be purchased from a number of large and efficient competing firms. Having a plant larger than the minimum efficient size resulted in economies in maintenance, quality control, inventory, and management. These had to be weighed against the increased transportation costs associated with the larger geographic area necessary to support the larger plant.

Economic analysis helps in understanding the manufacturer's problem. The industry in 1971 comprised a number of stages—product design, manufacturing, sales, distribution, and post-sale service. There were economies of scale at each stage. The significant economies of scale affecting the choice of plant size were in manufacturing and distribution (i.e., shipping). It was generally recognized in the industry that a manufacturer could reduce his transportation costs an estimated 8% to 10% by shipping full carloads. A full-line producer could fill a carload with a number of kinds of appliances, and hence could ship full carloads to those retailers who would never buy a full carload of one appliance. By placing all his production facilities in one location the full-line producer could exploit these economies of scale in shipping.

On the other hand, a single production location increased the total shipping distance in comparison with shipping distances expected for geographically dispersed production facilities. Hence, the manufacturer faced a dilemma. It appeared to the casewriter that economies of scale in production were more important than the cost savings from geographical diversity. G.E., for example, did not build at a new location until they felt that they could no longer lower costs by expanding a given facility.

Turning to sales cost, other economies of scale could be realized in selling the full line. Most appliance purchasers—both retail and contract— bought more than one type of appliance. Hence the additional time it took a salesman to sell more than one appliance was small in comparison with the time he spent traveling and waiting to see a buyer. Estimating the magnitude of this economy of scale is difficult. Tappan, a part-line manufacturer with dollar sales one eighth of G.E.'s, estimated that its sales costs per unit were twice those of G.E. Hence, this economy appears to be significant.

Economies of scale also existed in product development. Volume supported a higher R&D budget at lower unit cost. Since the materials technology was similar for the various white goods there were also economies of scale in being a multiple-product producer. But, R&D could be contracted from firms outside the industry. Firms in the industry tended to view economies of scale in R&D as the least important in terms of gaining a competitive advantage.

There were economies of scale, as well, in providing service once the appliance was sold and installed in the home. Large full-time manufacturers like G.E. and national retailers like Sears sold a sufficient number of appliances in most areas to allow them to provide their own service. Since servicemen serviced all white goods there were economies of scale to be derived from a full line as well as from high volume of any single product. Other firms in the industry that did not have as great a volume as Sears and G.E. relied heavily on franchised service agents who serviced several brands. Industry sources believed that owning the service facility did not reduce cost significantly, but did allow a greater control over service quality, which could in the long run improve the owner's brand image.

Finally, there was a different kind of economic power which had proved important: buying clout. High-volume national retailers (e.g., Sears, Penneys) were able to exact price concessions from manufacturers, which tended to shift cost savings derived from scale economies of production and shipping from the manufacturer to the retailer. Retail muscle, then, could operate to deny to the manufacturer some of the advantage of scale economies.

MANUFACTURERS' LINES AND SOURCING

There were seven full-line manufacturers in 1971. However, many of the specialist producers (e.g., Tappan) would "source"—buy from another manufacturer—appliances that they did not manufacture in order to broaden their lines. Even a full-line producer like G.E. sourced certain products during a period when it was considering whether to mass-produce them. Examples include gas ranges or small apartment-sized washers and dryers. At the retail level, some national chain retailers sourced their entire line and sold under their own brand name. Sears led in this practice, buying most of its appliances from Whirlpool, Design and Manufacturing, and Roper. Other national chain retailers were moving in this direction. In 1966 Penneys introduced its Penncrest appliances made by G.E.

APPLIANCE BRANDS

Brands such as Kenmore, Coldspot, Penncrest, etc., were national brands but they were *retail* national brands as opposed to *manufacturers'* national brands. They were the only brand carried by a given chain of stores. Still other retailers sourced a product for use as "bottom-of-the-line" brands to be sold primarily on a low-price basis. Jordan Marsh's (Allied Stores) Ambassador washer and dryer, produced by Westinghouse, was an example of this practice. These private brands were not available nationally and were carried along with other brands. The retailer carrying private brands usually did not advertise them heavily or require that they be designed to their specifications. Some appliance manufacturers, e.g., White Consolidated, specialized in producing for this market segment, and most manufacturers were engaged in it to some extent. (See Exhibit 9.)

These three types of brands—manufacturers, retail, and private—also differed significantly in feature content. A feature is an extra, added to the basic appliance unit. The self-cleaning oven, the microwave oven, and thermostatic controlled burner were features available on the basic range. Traditionally, new features were introduced at the "top-of-the-line" with a high price. Then, over time, as other new features were added and competitors copied them, the price on older features fell until eventually they became standard equipment. In fact, the product line of a manufacturer was defined in terms of feature content, the appliances with more and newer features being higher in the line. All national manufacturers followed this policy. Sears, however, made no attempt to introduce new features, but instead copied the last year's "top-of-the-line" features and sold them at "middle-of-the-line" prices. Private brands had low feature content and hence usually were competitive with the "bottom-of-the-line" of the national brands.

MARKET SHARE

In terms of market share, the industry leaders were in the full-line national brand category. By 1969, the four leading brand groups—Sears (Kenmore-Coldspot), G.E. (G.E.-Hotpoint), Whirlpool, and Frigidaire —enjoyed 71% of the washer market, 65% of the dryer market, 42% of the range market, 63% of the refrigerator market, and 65% of the dishwasher market. (See Exhibits 2 and 3 for market shares.) Sears was the leader in most product categories. Since Whirlpool produced many products for Sears, Whirlpool was by far the largest manufacturer after G.E. In spite of the impressive production capacity of G.E. and Whirlpool, even essentially single-product manufacturers like Maytag, Hobart (KitchenAid), and Tappan had increased their market share during the 1960s.

Of all the major producers, only Frigidaire was losing market share in 1971. Frigidaire, one of the oldest and most identifiable brands, had a unique problem. Being a division of GM its labor contract was negotiated by the UAW at the corporate level even though the division had an IUE union. Other manufacturers in the industry had IUE contracts set at considerably lower hourly wages. (The difference was in excess of $1 per hour lower.) The result was a cost disadvantage that severely threatened Frigidaire's future. (See Exhibit 10.)

APPROACHES OF COMPETITORS

Competitors in the appliance industry followed a variety of basic approaches, the diversity of which was unusual for American industry. More unusual still is the fact that firms as different in basic approach as Sears, Tappan, and G.E. were all successful. This section describes in some detail the approaches followed by a selected group of competitors in the white goods industry. General Electric, Westinghouse, and

General Motors represent the full-line manufacturers; D&M and Tappan, the part-line producers; Sears and Penneys, the large national retailers; and Raytheon, the high technology approach to appliance manufacturing.

General Electric (G.E.).   G.E. entered the appliance field in 1918 with the acquisition of Hotpoint. Hotpoint, which produced and marketed irons and ranges, operated as a separate division and constituted G.E.'s sole effort at that time in the appliance field. Hotpoint's business grew rapidly through the 1920s. In the 1930s, with the advent of the electric refrigerator, G.E. introduced its own appliance brand. Gradually during the 1930s and after the war, the G.E. and Hotpoint lines expanded independently and began to compete with one another. Independent development continued through the 1950s under G.E.'s decentralized organization structure, although the two appliance divisions were formally merged in 1952.

In the 1950s, G.E. adopted a policy of building capacity ahead of demand. Construction of the vast Louisville manufacturing facility was the result. The goal seemed to be to achieve high market share and attendant scale manufacturing economies. Low unit production costs thus attained later gave G.E. a distinct competitive advantage in the increasingly price-sensitive appliance industry. This advantage was not shared as fully by the Hotpoint line which maintained separate and more modest production facilities into the 1960s.

In the 1960s, development of the appliance business took a back seat at G.E. to three new capital-intensive businesses: computers, breeder reactors, and heavy jet aircraft engines. The 1960s did, however, see the merger of Hotpoint and G.E. production facilities in 1965.

As G.E. entered the 1970s, the appliance business again moved to the forefront as a potential money maker in the wake of disappointments and even some outright failures in the three glamour businesses of the 1960s. Organizationally, G.E. integrated Hotpoint and G.E. appliance lines into one centrally coordinated appliance group. This merely gave official recognition to the informal working arrangements which had been followed since the merger of production facilities in 1965. In 1973, the company was considering another large investment in production capacity to maintain its cost advantage and protect its market share in the appliance field.

In the 1970s, G.E.'s basic approach appeared to be aimed at achieving high-volume, low-cost production coupled with extensive retail marketing coverage through multiple branding. The G.E. brand was marketed primarily through traditional, higher margin channels. Hotpoint also penetrated the national retail brand market (and increased production volume) by manufacturing appliances for Penney's Penncrest line.

In addition, G.E. pursued a regular program of product innovation and placed engineering emphasis on product reliability. Since these two qualities were associated in the customers' eyes with technical competence and quality, G.E.'s approach here was designed to establish and maintain a favorable brand image.

The other major thrust of G.E.'s appliance strategy was in the new construction segment of the appliance market. Here the G.E. brand and reputation for innovation were a tremendous asset in competition for the business of home builders. Manufacturing and distribution muscle also helped in fighting for share in this highly price-sensitive market. With no competition from Sears both the G.E. and Hotpoint brands achieved important market positions.

Westinghouse.   Westinghouse entered the appliance field in the 1920s and like G.E. gradually became a national full-line appliance manufacturer. From World War II through the better part of the 1960s, Westinghouse held its own as a full-line producer and marketer of home appliances. However, Westinghouse did not achieve the same low level of production costs as G.E. and signs of discontent appeared in Westinghouse's appliance business. For one thing, the Consumer Products Division lost money in 1971—a record year for Westinghouse as a whole. As a result, management adopted an attitude of retrenchment toward its traditional business. Cost cutting became the watchword.

Westinghouse seemed to be coasting with the traditional appliance business while it shifted emphasis to new concepts. The theme of the new approach was Homecology—improving the quality of life in the home. To this end, Westinghouse created new appliance products (e.g., the room air cleaner, the tap water purifier) and introduced new appliance systems to replace, in time, part of the market for the older appliance units. Examples of the new systems were home security systems and interior subsystems for industrial housing—including prepackaged kitchens, bathrooms, and central air conditioning apparatus. To gain better control of the flow of systems containing appliances to the ultimate buyer, Westinghouse constructed the first of what might become a series of plants for factory production of modular housing units.

Design and Manufacturing (D&M).   In the late 1950s, D&M management perceived that the major dishwasher producers (G.E. and Hobart) were not willing to supply the national retailers with dishwashers. D&M elected to fill this market niche by producing only dishwashers for the private brand market of the national retailers—especially Sears. By restricting production to dishwashers in a market segment with just two other producers, D&M was able to develop sufficient volume to manufacture efficiently and at very competitive cost. Low cost, in turn, enabled D&M to supply Sears and thus build volume. At the same time, D&M was able to establish attractive profit margins on sales to those customers who could be made to pay higher prices than Sears could negotiate. Thus D&M was very successful in the market niche in which it operates.

Tappan.   Tappan has been in the stove business since the 1880s, first with wood and coal burning stoves and later with gas fueled ranges. By 1946, Tappan was a leading producer of gas ranges with 8% of a market with 140 competitors.

Though Tappan continued to grow in the decades of the 1950s and 1960s, it found itself with problems to surmount in the seventies. It was at a cost disadvantage with respect to full-line producers and at a disadvantage in penetrating retail channels because large retailers preferred to carry a full line of a given brand. To deal with these problems, Tappan introduced major feature innovations to induce large retailers to carry its line, and went after private brand and mobile home business to build volume and thereby lower production costs.

For the longer term, Tappan was also developing major new products (e.g., unit kitchen, gas air conditioners) as well as a new channel of distribution—the Tappan Home Center, to sell the unit kitchen concept.

Sears.   Founded in 1895 as a catalog operation, it was not until 1925 that Sears began to move into direct retail selling. From the beginning, home appliances were a mainstay of Sears' retail operations. These operations expanded through the 1920s and 1930s. But it was after the war that Sears' current approach began to take shape. In the late 1940s, Sears dropped the idea—which it had toyed with since the 1920s—of integrating backward into appliance production. Instead, Sears began to use its rapidly expanding retail volume to advantage in negotiating low-cost production arrangements with appliance manufacturers.

At the same time, Sears began to adopt distinctive brand names under which to sell its appliances nationally (e.g., "Coldspot" and "Kenmore"), thereby creating the concept of a retail national brand.

Since the late 1940s, Sears had attempted to establish the fullest possible control over retail sales. Sears continued to use the buying clout derived from its high volume of retail sales to exact near-cost selling prices from manufacturers. Volume buying permitted Sears' suppliers to produce appliances at a price to Sears less than the production cost of all but the most efficient manufacturers. Thus Sears had firm control over the cost of appliances it retails.

Sears took advantage of low cost in two ways. First, in advertising it played up the low prices of the lower end-of-the-line products. This attracted customers to Sears stores. Then, Sears used its sales force—also fully within Sears' control—to trade customers up to the higher price models on which Sears realized handsome profit margins, especially handsome in view of Sears' low unit cost throughout the range of appliance models.

Sears tailored its product line to the trade-up strategy by positioning products at convenient price increments throughout the possible range of sales prices. Indeed, Sears was first to establish and exploit the idea of a retail price point spectrum.

Penneys.   Since 1963 Penneys had adopted a policy of head-on competition. Penneys added large ticket items, especially appliances, to new full-time stores. It followed an aggressive building program, matching Sears store for store. In 1970, Penneys was the second largest national retailer with 240 stores carrying appliances compared with Sears' 827.

On the supply side, Penneys, like Sears, was having its private brand appliances manufactured outside the company umbrella. G.E. manufactured the Penncrest appliance line, an arrangement that enabled Penneys and G.E. to cooperate in competing with Sears.

Raytheon. Though founded in 1928, Raytheon did not enter the appliance field until 1965, when it acquired Amana, an old-line refrigerator and air-conditioning manufacturer. Raytheon followed that acquisition with another in 1967 when it acquired Caloric Corporation, a manufacturer of gas ranges and other kitchen appliances.

Raytheon was an example of a high technology company which, by expanding into the appliance field, began to introduce radically new technologies to the industry. For example, by 1971 Raytheon had gained a significant share of the new microwave oven market—a market which it pioneered.

Other new products in the offing included a home trash compactor (introduced in 1971), compact refrigerators and freezers made possible by improved insulation technology, quiet air conditioners which took advantage of the noise engineering competence which Raytheon had gained from the defense industry, and an electric ignition gas range which eliminated the pilot light.

Raytheon's approach to the appliance business was designed to create new markets or capture a share of existing markets by catching current manufacturers off guard with new technology.

THE MARKET FOR WHITE GOODS

The diversity of the markets for which these very different firms competed was just as great as the variations, unusual for industry, in the firms themselves. This section examines the characteristics of the market segments in which white goods were sold in 1970 and estimates the possibilities for future growth in these segments.

White goods were sold to two entirely different sets of buyers—retail merchants and construction firms of various types for installation in dwelling units prior to purchase. The former is called the "retail market" segment, while the latter is referred to as the "contract market" segment. Since the basic characteristics of these two market segments, as well as their growth rates in the past and projections for the future, were quite different, they will be considered separately.

The contract market. The contract segment of the market had grown in importance since World War II. It accounted for over 70% of the unit sales of built-in ranges, under counter dishwashers, and disposals. In total, contract sales accounted for around 28% of all appliance unit sales in 1970 according to study. The future of contract sales appeared even brighter.

Contract sales were related directly to new housing starts.[2] In the 1960s housing starts held at a low level, but in the 1970s they were expected to rise dramatically in the wake of a sharp expected rise in the rate of new family starts. Housing starts during 1966–71 had totaled 8,000,000. The 1971–75 projection of 12,000,000 represented a 50% increase. If this jump actually occurred, and assuming an average of three appliances installed in a new home prior to purchase, the contract market segment was expected to capture 34% of total appliance unit

---

[2] These forecasts are from a study made by one appliance manufacturer, as is the data on housing starts. Other companies differed somewhat in their estimates.

sales. According to econometric projections of retail demand growth (based on the age configuration of present appliances in 1971 and projections of disposable income), this growth in contract sales represented 50% of forecast growth in total appliance unit sales. Growth in total unit sales of appliances for 1971–75 was forecast at 30%. Looking at the decade to 1980, G.E. forecast a 91% increase in industry dollar sales on an increase of 74% in units shipped. Given these projections, and assuming the same average dollar price per unit in both the retail and contract segments,[3] contract dollar sales would account for 60% of the growth in total appliance dollar sales and have 42% of the total dollar market by 1980. Other estimates forecast contract sales to be as high as 50% of the total dollar market by 1980.

The nature of new housing starts was also undergoing a fundamental change. In 1963, apartments accounted for approximately 25% of total new starts.[4] By early 1971, apartments were accounting for approximately 50% of housing starts. Because many young families wanted to live in or near a large city and because the cost of home ownership was rising, many in the industry believed that the apartment share of the market would continue to increase. The impact of this trend was twofold. The number and types of appliances furnished in single-family dwelling units, apartments and mobile homes, were different in each case. (See Exhibit 11.) The differences were greatest in refrigerators, clothes washers and dryers, and perhaps, unit air conditioners (though here no data are available). With refrigerators and unit air conditioners, the trend toward apartment living implied increased sales for the contract segment since these were provided in many apartments but few homes. With home laundry, the impact of the trend was harder to anticipate. If coin-operated laundromat equipment, often placed in the basement by the builder, gained acceptance, it could mean slower growth since one machine would serve several families. On the other hand, if mini-washers and dryers, designed to fit into small apartments, gained consumer acceptance, rapid growth could result. These, however, were sold through retail channels.

The second impact of the trend toward apartment living was to increase the average number of appliances purchased by a given builder since each apartment would require appliances. With this larger volume, more builders would buy directly from the manufacturer.

Manufacturers sold appliances to the contract segment both directly to the large builders and indirectly through local builder suppliers. Direct sales to construction firms and mobile home manufacturers were made by corporate salesmen for most of the full-line companies and to a limited extent by independent distributors for the smaller manufacturers. These direct sales accounted for 80% of the contract sales and it was thought that the trend toward apartment living could increase their importance.[5] To understand the approaches various manufactur-

---

[3] The implications of this assumption are explored later in the subsection entitled "The Retail Market."

[4] See footnote 2.

[5] Industry estimate.

ers took to these direct sales, the needs of the builder must be considered.

Appliances were crucial in selling homes even though they made up a small percentage of total home costs (10% or less). In the industry it was generally believed that the consumer did not have the knowledge to evaluate objectively the quality of the dwelling unit. On the other hand, it was thought that he did have opinions as to the quality of various brands of appliances and that he associated this judgment with the quality of the dwelling unit. It was believed, therefore, that appliance brand image was crucial in selling to builders. In fact, because of the perceived importance of brand image, builders seldom bought private brands.

Builders, however, were very cost conscious. They typically bought the middle and lower end of the product line. By buying all the appliances from one manufacturer they could save on transportation costs and also establish the leverage to demand and obtain a lower price. Finally, when a dwelling unit was ready for the appliance, it was crucial that the appliance be there. If it was not, the builder had to hold the completed dwelling in inventory. The interest cost could be substantial. By maintaining a relationship with one manufacturer, the builder could put on pressure for timely delivery.

The major companies in the contract market segment in 1970 were G.E. (G.E. and Hotpoint brands), Whirlpool, Frigidaire, Tappan (sourcing products not manufactured) and Westinghouse.[6] Whether Sears could compete in this market was one of the most interesting questions facing the industry. Sears had yet to make any significant inroad, though it appeared to be planning an attack. Many in the industry thought that Sears' brand image and lack of experience in the contract market would preclude the success it experienced in the retail market segment. Yet given the past success of Sears, few were willing to deny the significance of the Sears threat. By 1973, there were clear indications that Sears would attempt to enter this market segment.

All of the major companies active in the contract market sold full lines. Some manufacturers provided kitchen designing services to large builders and all were able to advise builders how to match the quality of the appliance to the price and quality of the dwelling unit. The market traditionally was highly price competitive because each builder could play the manufacturers off against one another. The larger construction firms—with substantial buying power—were able to negotiate lower prices on the same principle that Sears used at the retail level.

For selling the finished unit it was crucial to have highly trained salesmen who could convince the builder of the merits of the particular brand. Delivery also was important, and the major manufacturers gave close attention to logistics.

The major manufacturers differed only slightly in their approach to the market—Westinghouse favored large-scale land and community

---

[6] No data were available on market share in the contract segment as opposed to the retail segment. In general, these five companies were viewed by industry experts as enjoying the bulk of the contract market.

developments; Tappan sold cabinets as well as appliances. Hotpoint had its own home centers in markets where there were no builder suppliers. G.E. and Westinghouse enjoyed one advantage over other manufacturers in the contract segment. Having a diverse product line of electrical goods, certain divisions frequently received builder contracts for wiring, for heavy electrical equipment, and so on. This gave other areas of the company, like the appliance group, early information as to future construction. It also gave G.E. and Westinghouse a chance to sell a larger package of goods to the builders. But this was not a great advantage. Price, brand image, and delivery were believed to be the three dominant factors in the contract market segment.

There were, however, some signs that the basic nature of the contract market might change. Two of the most likely changes were the evolution of the "core-kitchen" and the development of a systematic kitchen remodeling business. The core-kitchen was a prefabricated kitchen including all kitchen appliances, cabinets, and counters. It could be installed as a single unit in the home. The core-kitchen reduced the amount of relatively expensive on-site craft labor. In 1970, Tappan already had begun to produce these core-kitchens on an experimental basis. Two factors inhibited the growth of the core-kitchen: labor union resistance and the need to ship more "kitchen-cores" than most builders could use, in order to reduce transportation costs.

While the development of the core-kitchen would not change the traditional channels of distribution in the contract market since it would still be sold to builders, the development of the remodeling business might well bring substantial change. One industry expert estimated that there were 5 million kitchens in existence that needed complete remodeling—new appliances, cabinets, and counters. Traditionally small builders and, to a lesser extent, Sears had serviced this market. Most manufacturers agreed that lack of a major marketing effort and generally poor service had limited the exploitation of this market segment. By 1973, however, Sears had begun to consider the remodeling market more seriously. Its most recent catalog featured several pages on the home center concept. Tappan was exploring another more comprehensive approach to this market segment. This was based on setting up Tappan home centers that displayed six or more model kitchens, provided a kitchen design service, and installed the new kitchen. This approach was predicated on the assumption that customers needed to see what could be done by remodeling and also needed a guarantee that the job could be done in a few days. Tappan felt that most small builders could supply neither of these services and hence new channels had to be developed.

The retail market. While total dollar sales were expected to increase 91% by 1980 and retail dollar sales were expected to increase 52% during the same period, retail as a share of total dollar sales was expected to drop from 72% in 1970 to 58% by 1980.[7] The faster growth of the contract market meant that the absolute growth of the retail segment represented a declining share of the total market.

---

[7] Industry estimate.

The conclusion was a tentative one, however, for two reasons. First, since total unit sales were expected to increase only 74% by 1980 (compared with 91% for dollar sales), the analysis reflected a belief that average prices per unit would rise over the decade of the 1970s. This could happen in one of two ways: (1) The average price per unit could increase, or (2) customers could be traded up more frequently to expensive products. The first of these possibilities contradicted the 1960s experience of declining average appliance prices. The second possibility was plausible only for customers in the retail segment because of the extreme price sensitivity of builders in the contract segment. However, prices in the contract segment had tended to be lower on the average than in the retail segment. There was, therefore, uncertainty surrounding the forecasted price increase.

WHOLESALE DISTRIBUTION CHANNELS

Retail sales in 1970 were made through distributors, either company-owned or independent. National retailers, like Sears, had complete control over distribution since they bought directly from manufacturers and did the retailing themselves. Manufacturers sold their products to retailers through both independent and owned distributors. G.E. led in sales through owned distribution. All of Hotpoint's sales and 90% to 95% of G.E.'s brand sales were made through company-owned distribution.[8] Frigidaire was second, with roughly 60% through owned distribution in 1970, down from 80% in the mid-1960s.

Most large full-line manufacturers had sufficient sales in large metropolitan areas to operate their own distribution network efficiently. Except for the very largest manufacturers, it was not efficient to own distribution in low-volume areas. Most part-line and single-product manufacturers were at an absolute disadvantage since they could not utilize their salesmen efficiently or ship full truckloads of their products to retailers. Hence, they were forced into accepting higher distribution costs or using private distributors. They were forced, as well, to accept higher sales costs.

Ownership of distribution channels was important to both manufacturers and retailers because whoever owned the distribution channels would have substantial influence over the retailer. Three degrees of control were observed, depending on who owned the distribution channels.

National retail brands like Sears had complete control since manufacturers sold directly to Sears and Sears controlled wholesale distribution as well as retail selling. They could set retail price and control sales presentations and advertising. They could also control inventory directly.

Single-product manufacturers like Maytag and Hobart exemplified a second degree of control. They sold and shipped directly to carefully selected retailers (often exclusively franchised) and maintained close communication with these retailers. Their retail strategy was one of

---

[8] Industry estimate.

intensive coverage. Though they could not set retail price or inventory levels, they did have considerable influence over both. These manufacturers concentrated on the high-price/high-quality end of the line. The choice of retailers to maintain or enhance this image was believed to be crucial. The effort they placed on dealer relationships was of key importance.

A third degree of control was obtained by manufacturers which owned distribution. This allowed the manufacturer to choose his retailers, set the wholesale price and determine advertising allowances. For the large multiproduct manufacturers, however, the close relationship with individual retailers obtained by Maytag and Hobart was impossible. They not only sold to a much larger number of retailers, but they also sold to retailers that carried several brands of each product. Direct shipment from the factory to many retailers was impossible because of their strategy of extensive coverage. They did, however, ship direct to very large retailers.

The most indirect control was obtained through selling to independent distributors. This method of selling precluded direct control by the manufacturer over wholesale price and choice of retail outlets. Private distributors posed a threat to national brand manufacturers since they could sell anywhere to anyone and had strong incentives to do so. For example, independent distributors could sell to builders and hence could create problems in the contract market segment for companies that sold to this segment directly.

RETAIL MARKETING STRATEGIES

The choice of the desired degree of control depended to a large extent on the choice of marketing strategy. Though all the firms in the industry were selling very similar products, there was considerable difference in their marketing approach. One way of distinguishing between these approaches was to classify their marketing strategies as "pull" or "push."

A pull strategy was characterized by national advertising, leadership in product innovation (i.e., introducing more and better new features than any other manufacturer), selective choice of local dealers with the best reputations, and development of a very good service network. Pull brands such as G.E., Frigidaire, Westinghouse, Maytag, Hobart, Caloric, and Amana followed various mixtures of these methods. The full-line producers tended to depend more on national advertising and less on careful dealer choice and close dealer relationship than did the single-product manufacturers. On the other hand, the full-line producers owned as much of their distribution as possible. Product innovation was important not only because it temporarily differentiated the manufacturer's product from the others, but also because consumers associated continued innovation with high quality.[9] Studies at G.E. had shown that innovation was directly related to brand image. The pur-

---

[9] Industry experience had been that new product features were usually copied by other manufacturers in 12 to 18 months.

pose of the pull strategy was to get the customer to make the decision as to the brand he would buy before he entered the store. Hence, "switching" him to another brand in the store would be difficult for a salesman.

A push strategy attempted to encourage switching in the store. Here, it was important to have a unique product—a brand not readily available elsewhere or a feature or model no other store in the area carried. To encourage switching, push brands usually had higher retail margins and higher local advertising allowances. Private brands fell into this category. Carried by selected stores in a single retail area, they were low price but not necessarily low margin. Leading push brands were Philco-Ford, Fedders-Norge, Hotpoint, and White Consolidated.

The national retail brands like Sears were neither push nor pull but rather a hybrid. Sears pulled customers into the store with its store name and heavily advertised sales on low-price/low-feature items. Sears' salesmen then attempted to "sell the customers up" to higher featured, higher priced products. The service contract offered by Sears was used to distinguish it from other brands, as was the fact that only Sears stores carried the brand. Sears could pursue this strategy because it controlled retail price, sold only through its own stores, and trained and motivated its salesmen to "sell up" with strong commission incentives.

BRAND LOYALTY

Each of these strategies was designed to get sales volume in an industry with high brand loyalty. One survey showed that 70% of appliance owners would strongly consider buying the same brand that they now owned. (See Exhibit 12.) Yet, this brand loyalty did not appear to be the result of heavy advertising. For example, in 1971 G.E. spent $3,300,000 on national advertising, Tappan spent $106,000, and Maytag spent $562,000.[10] This is less than 1% of sales for each of these companies. All companies did, however, give retailers an advertising allowance based on sales, which was to be spent on local newspaper advertising.

Firms in the industry had different views on the causes of brand loyalty. Some firms thought it resulted from their continuing production of a reliable product over a long period of time, others felt that it was the result of leadership in product innovation, while still others indicated that loyalty was decreasing as consumers had more experience with the product and as the products in general became more reliable. No executive interviewed suggested that national advertising was a major factor in generating brand loyalty.

RETAIL CHANNELS OF DISTRIBUTION

The various approaches to marketing and distributing appliances must be considered in light of the changes in channels of distribution.

---

[10] Leading National Advertiser, Inc., *National Advertising Investment.*

The channels of distribution were changing rapidly during the 1960s. The small appliance retailer carrying a limited number of brands and models of appliances lost volume relative to the large chain appliance dealers and discount stores. (See Exhibit 13.) Sears, Penneys, Montgomery Ward, and other national chains grew in importance. These stores carried predominantly retail national brands.

Also, large regional chain stores specializing in appliances developed during the 1960s—Lechmere in Massachusetts and Polk Brothers in Illinois, for example. In the early 1960s, these regional chain stores sold national manufacturers' brands as well as private brands. According to one industry executive, the strategy of some of these stores was to switch customers to their private brands and eventually develop their own retail brand. Such stores found, however, that to induce such a switch they had to price their private brands so low as to make little money. They soon discovered that their strength lay in generating traffic and underselling competition on the basis of the operating efficiencies gained from high volume. These lessons learned, by the end of the 1960s virtually all of the mass merchandisers were concentrating on national manufacturers' brands, and these stores were rapidly gaining strength as the primary outlet for national manufacturers' brands. The "discounters" attempted to limit the number of brands and models that they carried in order to reduce inventory and gain maximum savings from volume buying. Hence, they tended to buy predominantly from full-line manufacturers.

The growth of the giant discounters did not affect all appliance products in the same way. Room air conditioners were more often sold through department stores and other small outlets like radio and TV shops than were kitchen and home laundry appliances. Room air conditioners (RAC) were referred to as impulse goods in the industry. On the first hot day of summer sales skyrocketed. Consumers tended to go to the closest store to buy air conditioners since they wanted their house cooled immediately. In aggregate data, such as that shown in Exhibit 13, the rapid growth in RAC sales during the 1960s tended to mask the trend toward chain and discount stores as preferred channels for retail sales of the rest of the appliances.

FOREIGN COMPETITION

Along with changing markets and channels of distribution, another problem facing manufacturers of white goods was the threat of foreign competition. In 1966, 309,000 refrigerators were imported. By 1970, refrigerator imports had tripled in volume to 935,000 with a retail value of $58 million.[11] Though refrigerator imports were primarily small units often used for home bars, offices, or recreational vehicles the increase was still significant. It represented slightly less than 20% of the units sold in 1970 but, because of the lower price, less than 5% of dollar sales. Foreign competition also was making inroads on other

---

[11] *Merchandising Week,* February 22, 1971, p. 34.

appliances—again primarily with small-sized units like counter top microwave ovens. Most imports were small-sized appliances because these were the type typically used abroad. Exports to the U.S. market represented incremental volume for Japanese and Italian manufacturers. As per capita income rose, especially in Japan, it was thought that larger appliances might become more common. In that event the United States could expect a similar influx of larger appliances in the future.

The role of the United States as an incremental market stemmed from the need for economies of scale in production. Industry experts considered it doubtful that a foreign competitor could gain a large enough market share in the United States to justify producing for the United States alone. If, however, he could sell the goods in his own country as well, he could gain the size to compete in the United States.

PATTERNS OF INDUSTRY PERFORMANCE

Price and growth. The white goods industry had been characterized by high growth in unit volume, price erosion in a time of general inflation and rapid product innovation. The 82% increase in units shipped during the 1960s was matched by only a 62% rise in dollar sales. But to truly appreciate the 10% drop in retail prices during the 1960s, one has to consider that average product size increased. Feature content and reliability also improved. (See Exhibit 16.) At the same time as wholesale and retail prices were falling, production costs were increasing by up to 40% for labor, metalworking, machinery, and nonferrous metal. (See Exhibit 6.) This price-cost squeeze put tremendous pressure on the manufacturers not only to produce existing products more efficiently, but also to redesign the products to achieve lower manufacturing costs. Since the price of an average service call according to G.E. was rising dramatically toward $20,[12] manufacturers were also under continual pressure to improve reliability while cutting costs. This pressure came because appliances carried a one-year warranty period. One result of this effort to produce a more reliable product was that service calls made during the warranty period had fallen 60% on dryers and 75% on washers during the decade of the 1960s. (See Exhibit 14.)

Innovations. As noted, the price cost squeeze had not suppressed innovation in the industry. To the contrary, Exhibit 15 shows that many innovations took place in the highly saturated products—in particular washers, ranges, and refrigerators. A major innovation on one of these highly saturated products tended to differentiate the product from that of the competitors and speed up replacement demand—i.e., innovation induced consumers to buy a new appliance before the old one was worn out (see Exhibit 16). A successful innovation could expand total market size as well as market share. For less saturated products experiencing high growth, the impact of innovations on the growth of total sales was less significant.

---

[12] Service calls were labor intensive and hence the cost tended to rise faster than in appliances where capital could be substituted for labor.

Innovations came from several sources. A number originated from changes in contiguous industries such as food processing or synthetic fabrics. For example, the side-by-side refrigerator had its origin in the growing use of frozen food and the resulting need for more freezer space. The mini-basket on washers was designed to handle small loads of delicate synthetic fabrics previously requiring hand washing.

Other innovations resulted from attempts to cut manufacturing cost. For example "foamed-in-place" insulation was cheaper than regular insulation and equally effective, but it dramatically reduced the wall width of refrigerators as well. The plastic case developed for room air conditioners was less expensive and lighter than metal, and did not rust. But, the bulk of major innovations listed in Exhibit 15 were the result of an explicit effort to fit the appliance better to the needs of the consumer. For example, the self-cleaning oven was developed because consumers disliked the messy job of cleaning the oven. An ice dispenser on the outside of the refrigerator door made it easier to get ice and eliminated the primary reason for opening the freezer door.

Profits. Financial performance varied considerably for the firms involved in the industry. One industry expert estimated that return on assets averaged 6% to 8% for the industry as a whole. Though it was impossible to obtain financial data on most of the major competitors, Exhibits 17 and 18 give financial data on a number of firms in the industry. Maytag was generally accepted as the industry leader in terms of return on assets and sales. In sharp contrast Admiral Corporation was only one tenth as profitable In commenting on the industry leaders, one executive stated that G.E. and Sears were well above the industry average in terms of profitability while Frigidaire and Westinghouse were below average.

SOME CONJECTURES AS TO THE FUTURE

Speculation as to the future of any industry is difficult at best, but there were several threats to the industry in 1971 that warrant consideration. If the industry doubled in volume during the 1970s, as suggested by the predictions previously discussed, there would need to be a marked increase in capacity. But the primary source of growth would be new family formation. If the population growth rate stabilized, the decade of the 1980s and 1990s could see substantial overcapacity. In an industry where price stability had been an ongoing problem, the results of this overcapacity could be disastrous.

Another threat to the industry was continuation of the price-cost squeeze. This squeeze could result in elimination of the new product development effort and turn the industry into a commodity industry. Becoming a commodity industry not only would adversely affect the consumer, but would also increase the threat of foreign competition since production efficiency would be the major ingredient of success.

The industry was also susceptible to revolutionary new technologies. There was little to guarantee that the majority of traditional competitors would be able to adapt to such radical changes. Raytheon entered the industry in the mid-1960s through the acquisition of Amana and Caloric in order to apply the technologies they had developed for the aerospace and other high technology industries. By 1971, Raytheon had gained a significant share of the microwave oven market. Corning had also entered the market to utilize its superior knowledge of glass and had introduced the glass surface range. The threat of such companies could not be ignored, especially in light of the rising pressure on high technology firms to diversify out of the aerospace and defense industries.

Finally, increasing control of the industry by a few large manufacturers coupled with a rising tide of consumerism enhanced the possibility of government intervention. Government intervention might take the form of legal action to limit the market share of large firms or, as was more likely, it could take the form of a bar on future acquisitions. Finally, there was the possibility that legislation similar to the Automotive Safety Act might be passed for appliances.

Exhibit 1

NOTE ON THE MAJOR HOME APPLIANCE INDUSTRY
Product Lines of Appliance Producers
(January 1, 1971)

Name	Dishwashers	Disposals	Air conditioners (unit)	Ranges	Refrigerators	Home laundry
Full-Line Producers						
Fedders Corp.	x		x	x	x	x
General Electric (G.E. & Hotpoint)	x	x	x	x	x	x
General Motors (Frigidaire Division)	x	x	x	x	x	x
Westinghouse	x	x	x	x	x	x
Whirlpool	x	x	x	x	x	x
White Consolidated (Gibson, Hupp, Franklin, and Kelvinator Div.)	x	x	x	x	x	x
Raytheon (Amana, Caloric Division)	x	x	x	x	x	x
Part-Line Producers						
Admiral Corp.			x	x	x	
Malleable Iron Range Co.	x			x	x	
Modern Maid, Inc.	x			x		
Mullins Mfg.	x	x		x		
Norris Industries, Inc.	x			x		
Ford (Philco Division)			x	x	x	x
Rangaire Co.	x		x	x	x	
Tappan Co.	x	x		x		
Waste King Corp.	x	x		x		
King Refo Co.			x		x	
Maytag Co.	x	x				x
Hobart Mfg.	x	x				
Republic Co.	x		x	x		
Single-Product Producers						
Athens Stove Works				x		
Autocrat Co.				x		
Boston Stove Co.				x		
Brown Stove Works, Inc.				x		
Columbus Stove Co.				x		
Cory Corp.				x		
Crown Stove Works				x		
Eagle Range Mfg.				x		
Gray and Dudley				x		
Hardwick Stove Co.				x		
Hedges Mfg.				x		
Hill Shaw Co.				x		
Knox Stove Works				x		
Magic Chef				x		
Peerless Enamald Products				x		
Corning Co.				x		
Phillips and Buttorf Co.				x		
Prizer Painter Stove Works, Inc.				x		
Roper Co. (Sears Subsidiary)				x		

Exhibit 1—Continued

Name	Dishwashers	Disposals	Air conditioners (unit)	Ranges	Refrigerators	Home laundry
Sunral Stove Co.						
(Division of Glenwood Range Co.)...				x		
Wolf Range Co.....................				x		
Hager, Inc.........................					x	
Herrick Refrigerator Co..............						
(Division of Diebold, Inc.)..........					x	
Nor-Lake, Inc......................					x	
Victory Metal Mfg. Co..............					x	
Blackstone Corp.....................						x
Centrex Corp.......................						x
Ero Industries, Inc.................						x
Hoover............................						x
Midwest Metal Stamping Co..........						x
Design & Manufacture, Inc...........	x					
Day and Night Mfg. Co..............			x			
National Union Electronics Corp.......			x			
Addison Products Co.................			x			
Albion Division (McGraw-Edison).....			x			
Carrier Corp.......................			x			
Heat Controler, Inc.................			x			
International Heater Co..............			x			
York (Division of Borg-Warner).......			x			
Residential Air Conditioning						
(Division of American Standard)....			x			
Emerson Radio and Phonograph Co....			x			
Tran Co...........................			x			

Source: *Standard and Poor's Directory, Moody's Industrial Manual.*

Exhibit 2

NOTE ON THE MAJOR HOME APPLIANCE INDUSTRY
Market Share, Percentage of Units Shipped
Home Laundry

	Automatic washers		
	1954	*1964*	*1969*
Sears.................................	8%	18%	34%
G.E...................................	8	11	13
Maytag................................	8	11	10
Whirlpool.............................	10	9	12
Frigidaire............................	8	8	9
Westinghouse..........................	n.a.	n.a.	3
Hotpoint..............................	n.a.	n.a.	3
All other.............................	58	43	16
Total.................................	100%	100%	100%

	Dryers		
	1954	*1964*	*1969*
Sears.................................	17%	35%	33%
G.E...................................	6	8	11
Whirlpool.............................	9	8	12
Maytag................................	2	9	9
Frigidaire............................	9	8	6
Hotpoint..............................	n.a.	n.a.	3
Westinghouse..........................	n.a.	n.a.	3
All other.............................	57	32	23
Total.................................	100%	100%	100%

Kitchen Appliances

	Ranges—gas and electric		
	1954	*1964*	*1969*
Sears.................................	9%	18%	17%
G.E...................................	7	9	11
Magic Chef............................	5	6	13
Tappan................................	7	6	12
Frigidaire............................	7	9	8
Westinghouse..........................	n.a.	n.a.	3
Whirlpool.............................	n.a.	2	2
Roper.................................	n.a.	n.a.	2
Hotpoint..............................	5	4	4
All other.............................	60	46	25
Total.................................	100%	100%	100%

Exhibit 2—Continued

	Refrigerators		
	1954	*1964*	*1969*
Sears................................	8%	18%	20%
G.E..................................	19	15	15
Frigidaire...........................	19	18	15
Hotpoint............................	7	6	6
Whirlpool...........................	n.a.	6	7
Admiral.............................	n.a.	n.a.	5
Kelvinator..........................	n.a.	n.a.	5
Westinghouse........................	n.a.	n.a.	7
All other............................	47	37	20
Total...............................	100%	100%	100%

	Home freezers	
	1954	*1964*
Sears...............................	13%	27%
G.E.................................	7	6
Frigidaire...........................	5	5
Whirlpool...........................	n.a.	4
Montgomery Ward....................	n.a.	7
All other............................	75	51
Total...............................	100%	100%

	Dishwashers		
	1954	*1964*	*1969*
Sears...............................	8%	18%	21%
G.E.................................	38	30	23
Hobart..............................	11	10	20
Whirlpool...........................	n.a.	10	5
Frigidaire...........................	12	7	10
Hotpoint............................	n.a.	n.a.	6
Westinghouse........................	n.a.	n.a.	5
All other............................	31	25	8
Total...............................	100%	100%	100%

	Room air conditioners	
	1954	*1964*
Sears...............................	6%	19%
Frigidaire...........................	10	4
G.E.................................	8	12
Whirlpool...........................	4	6
Fedders.............................	4	11
All other............................	68	48
Total...............................	100%	100%

Source: Estimates by casewriter based on industry research.

Exhibit 3

NOTE ON THE MAJOR HOME APPLIANCE INDUSTRY
Summary of Exhibit 2 for the Year 1969

	Share of market (percent) in 1969							
Company	*Dish-washers*	*Dis-posals*	*Freezers*	*Room A.C.*	*Ranges*	*Refrig-erators*	*Washers*	*Dryers*
Sears............	21	↑	27	↑	17	20	34	33
G.E.............	23	1969 Data not Avail-able	6	1969 Data not Avail-able	11	15	13	11
Hotpoint.........	6		?		4	6	3	3
Frigidaire........	10		5		8	15	9	6
Whirlpool........	5		4		3	7	12	12
Tappan..........	?		?		12	?	?	?
Westinghouse.....	5		?		8	7	3	8
Maytag..........	—	↓	—	↓	—	—	10	9
Total Market in Units for 1970 (000,000).......	2.1	2.0	1.4	5.9	4.5	5.3	4.1	3.0

Source: Derived from Exhibits 1, 2, and 4.

Exhibit 4

NOTE ON THE MAJOR HOME APPLIANCE INDUSTRY
Sales, Price, and Growth Data, 1961–1970
Home Laundry

	Clothes washers					
	(1)	*(2)*	*(3)*	*(4)*	*(5)*	*(6)*
	Total washer sales units (000)	*Total washer sales dollars (000)*	*Average price (2) ÷ (1)*	*Average growth in units (%)*	*Auto-matic units as % of total units*	*Satura-tion* (%)*
1961.............	3,444	$ 881,585	$256		79%	85.4%
1962.............	3,795	887,675	234	10%	80	85.7
1963.............	4,030	936,632	233	6	88	86.2
1964.............	4,190	981,006	234	4	85	86.5
1965.............	4,430	1,013,885	229	6	85	86.9
1966.............	4,446	1,018,134	235	—	88	87.4
1967.............	4,323	1,016,860	235	(3)	90	88.2
1968.............	4,482	1,074,296	240	4	92	89.3
1969.............	4,379	1,045,823	239	(2)	93	90.8
1970.............	4,094	957,316	237	(6)	95	91.9

Average life span, 10 years
Replacement sales as percent of total, 50%–75%

* As a percentage of wired living units as of January 1 of each year.

Exhibit 4—Continued

	Clothes dryers						
	Total dryer sales units (000)	Total dryer sales dollars (000)	Average price gas dryer	Average price electric dryer	Gas units as % of total units	Growth in total units	Satura-tion (%)
1961..........	1,236	$245,278	$215	$189	36%		19.6%
1962..........	1,420	275,745	212	185	34	15%	21.1
1963..........	1,599	303,972	208	181	34	13	22.9
1964..........	1,826	319,900	185	170	35	14	23.5
1965..........	2,098	366,600	184	170	34	15	24.2
1966..........	2,360	422,440	190	174	32	12	26.4
1967..........	2,648	474,523	195	172	31	12	30.5
1968..........	2,862	520,122	197	175	31	8	34.6
1969..........	3,022	547,241	200	173	30	6	38.8
1970..........	2,981	525,089	194	169	29	(1)	40.3

Average product life, 12 years
Replacement sales as percent of total sales, 30%–44%

Kitchen Appliances

	Refrigerators				
	Unit sales (000)	Dollar sales (000)	Average price	Growth in units (%)	Saturation (%)
1961............	3,480	$1,026,600	$295		98.2%
1962............	3,775	1,083,425	283	8%	98.3
1963............	4,125	1,146,750	274	9	99.0
1964............	4,545	1,172,610	258	10	99.1
1965............	4,430	1,281,800	260	8	99.3
1966............	4,974	1,328,058	267	1	99.5
1967............	4,713	1,286,649	273	(5)	99.6
1968............	5,151	1,442,280	280	9	99.7
1969............	5,296	1,466,992	277	3	99.8
1970............	5,286	1,448,364	274	—	99.8

Average product life, 15 years
Replacement sales as percent of total, 67%–70%

Exhibit 4—Continued

	Dishwashers						
	Total sales units (000)	*Total sales dollars (000)*	*Price of portable dishwashers*	*Price of undercounter dishwashers*	*Portable units as % of total units (%)*	*Average growth in total units (%)*	*Saturation (%)*
1961...........	620	$155,000	$236	$259	39%		7.1%
1962...........	720	174,260	212	259	36	16%	7.9
1963...........	880	211,285	212	255	35	22	8.9
1964...........	1,050	231,600	180	240	32	19	9.0
1965...........	1,260	276,060	188	236	35	20	11.8
1966...........	1,528	330,048	184	234	36	21	13.5
1967...........	1,585	337,640	185	230	38	4	15.7
1968...........	1,961	432,432	195	234	35	24	18.1
1969...........	2,118	474,646	193	239	32	8	20.8
1970...........	2,116	465,904	191	234	32	—	23.7

Average product life, 10 years
Replacement sales as percent of total, 24%–29%

	Ranges							
	Total sales units (000)	*Total sales dollars (000)*	*Average price gas*	*Average price electric*	*Gas units as % of total units (%)*	*Growth in units (%)*	*Gas saturation (%)*	*Electric saturation (%)*
1961..........	3,360	$ 680,275	$150	$266	54%		62.5%	37.3%
1962..........	3,656	746,311	158	259	54	9%	61.3	38.5
1963..........	3,942	866,531	187	256	53	8	60.8	39.0
1964..........	4,135	831,839	186	218	52	5	59.8	40.1
1965..........	4,331	880,772	192	216	52	5	58.4	41.4
1966..........	4,192	867,820	193	222	52	(3)	57.4	42.4
1967..........	4,033	836,745	195	221	53	(4)	54.3	44.6
1968..........	4,592	1,001,863	207	230	50	14	52.8	47.0
1969..........	4,814	1,071,716	215	230	51	5	49.9	49.9
1970..........	4,519	1,005,528	216	229	48	(6)	47.2	52.7

Average product life, 16 years
Replacement sales as percent of total, 61%–70%

Exhibit 4—Continued

Disposals

	Disposal sales units (000)	Disposal sales dollars (000)	Average price	Average growth in units (%)	Satura-tion (%)
1961...............	800	$ 63,960	$80		10.5%
1962...............	890	66,750	75	11%	11.5
1963...............	1,090	79,570	73	22	12.5
1964...............	1,300	78,000	60	19	13.4
1965...............	1,360	81,600	60	5	13.5
1966...............	1,410	84,600	60	4	13.6
1967...............	1,357	81,420	60	(4)	15.9
1968...............	1,738	104,280	60	28	18.0
1969...............	1,943	126,295	65	12	20.5
1970...............	1,976	128,440	65	2	22.9

Average product life, 9 years
Replacement sales as percent of total, 24%–29%

Freezers

	Total sales units (000)	Total sales dollars (000)	Average price	Average growth in units (%)	Satura-tion (%)
1961...............	1,050	$293.205	$279		23.4%
1962...............	1,670	283,790	265	2%	24.7
1963...............	1,090	277,320	254	2	25.6
1964...............	1,110	261,525	236	2	26.4
1965...............	1,160	271,485	234	5	26.7
1966...............	1,100	255,658	232	(6)	27.2
1967...............	1,100	256,290	233	—	27.5
1968...............	1,125	262,677	234	2	27.7
1969...............	1,195	272,450	228	6	28.5
1970...............	1,359	302,173	222	14	29.6

Average product life, 18 years
Replacement sales as percent of total, 45%

Exhibit 4—Concluded

	Room air conditioners				
	Total sales units (000)	Total sales dollars (000)	Average price	Average growth in units (%)	Satura- tion (%)
1961..............	1,500	$ 388,500	$251		15.1%
1962..............	1,580	410,000	260	5%	17.0
1963..............	1,580	490,140	252	23	18.8
1964..............	2,755	592,325	215	42	19.4
1965..............	2,945	624,390	212	14	20.2
1966..............	3,345	699,105	209	14	24.2
1967..............	4,129	867,090	210	23	27.9
1968..............	4,026	845,460	210	(2)	30.7
1969..............	5,459	1,119,095	205	36	33.5
1970..............	5,887	1,206,835	205	8	31.7

Average product life, Not Available
Replacement sales as percent of total, Not Available

Source: *Merchandising Week*, February 22, 1971. Reproduced with permission.

Exhibit 5

NOTE ON THE MAJOR HOME APPLIANCE INDUSTRY
Summary of Exhibit 4 for 1961 and 1970

	1970		1961	
Item	Units (000)	Dollars (000)	Units (000)	Dollars (000)
Washers....................	4,049	$ 957,316	3,444	$ 881,585
Dryers.....................	2,981	525,089	1,236	245,278
Refrigerators..............	5,286	1,448,364	3,480	1,026,600
Dishwashers...............	2,116	469,904	620	155,000
Ranges....................	4,519	1,005,528	3,360	680,275
Disposals..................	1,976	128,440	800	63,960
Freezers...................	1,359	302,173	1,050	293,205
Room Air Conditioners.......	5,887	1,206,835	1,500	388,500
Total.....................	28,173	$6,043,649	15,490	$3,734,403

Source: Derived from Exhibit 4.

Exhibit 6

NOTE ON THE MAJOR HOME APPLIANCE INDUSTRY
Major Appliance Price Index and
Significant Cost Indices (1957–1959 = 100)

	Major appliance	Paint	Steel	Nonferrous metal	Metalwork machinery	Straight hourly wages*
1960	94.2	100.7	102.0	103.6	105.5	107.9
1961	93.1	103.6	101.8	100.9	107.0	110.0
1962	89.0	103.8	101.8	97.7	110.0	114.7
1963	87.8	105.1	103.8	101.0	110.0	116.8
1964	82.0	104.8	103.4	113.4	114.2	116.3
1965	82.0	105.9	103.3	117.2	118.9	118.8
1966	83.0	108.0	104.3	121.0	126.3	120.7
1967	83.0	112.2	107.0	123.7	125.8	129.5
1968	84.7	115.9	109.1	123.5	130.5	135.6
1969	83.0	120.3	116.4	150.1	138.0	145.8
1970	82.5	123.3	123.5	141.1	142.5	—

* At a major appliance manufacturer.
Source: U.S. Department of Labor (except column 1, which was derived from Exhibit 4).

Exhibit 7

NOTE ON THE MAJOR HOME APPLIANCE INDUSTRY

Industry Mergers and Acquisitions

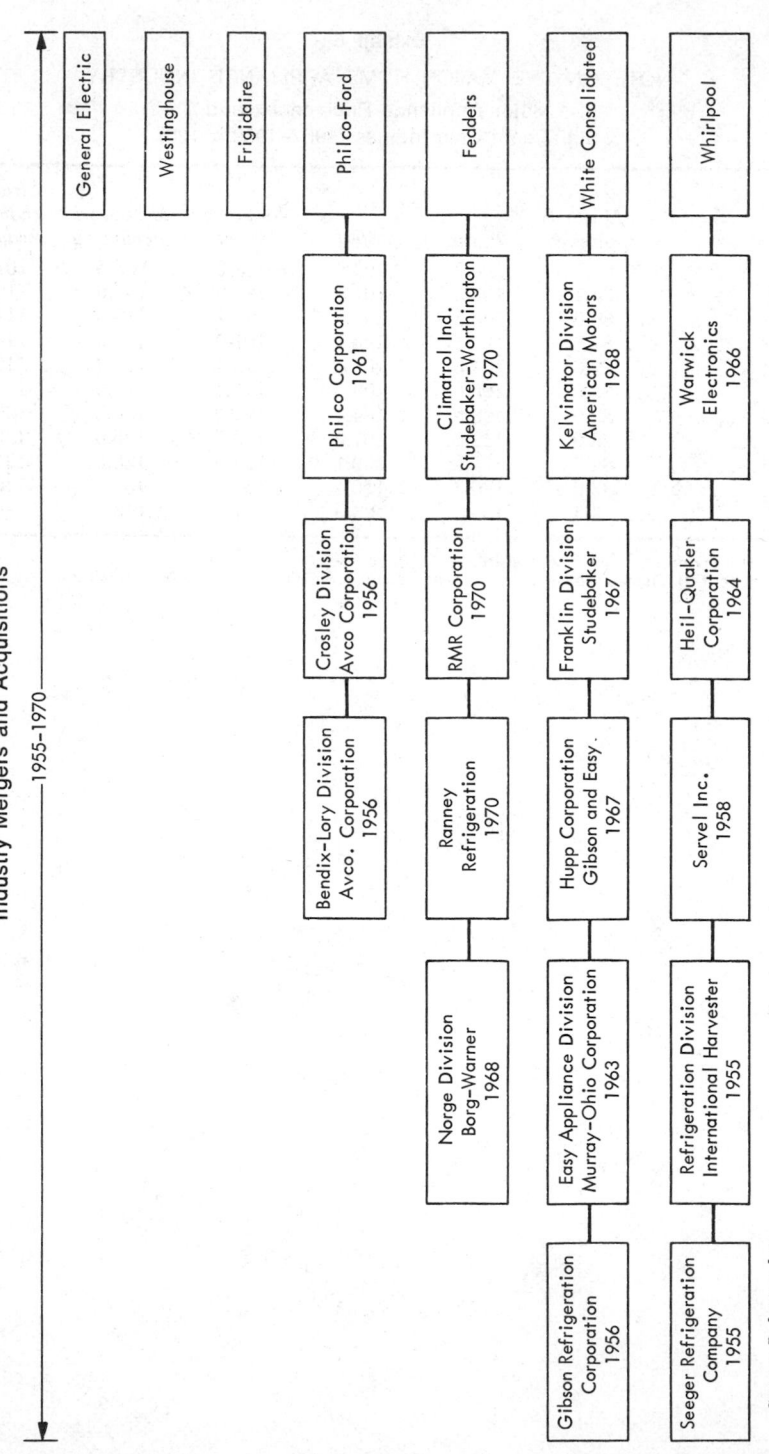

Source: Industry data.

Exhibit 8

NOTE ON THE MAJOR HOME APPLIANCE INDUSTRY
Average Variable Cost Curve for Dishwashers, Home Laundry, Ranges, and Refrigerators

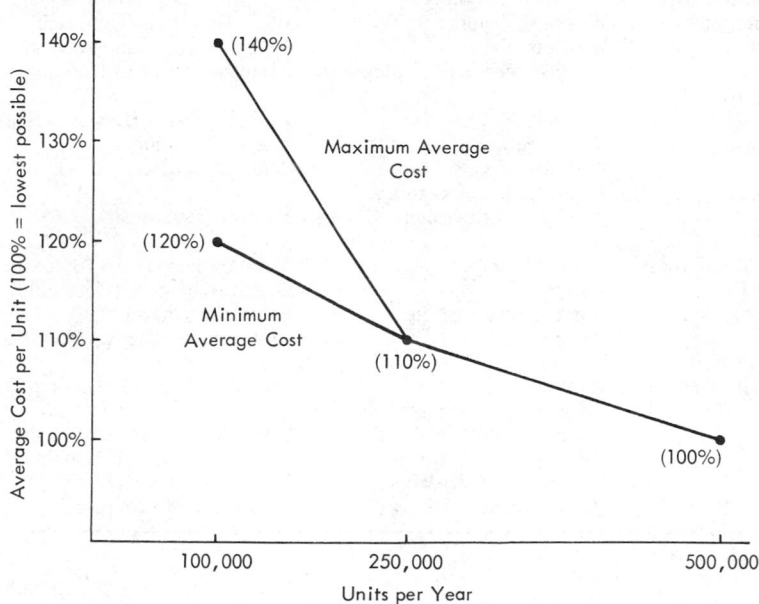

Source: One industry engineer's estimate. (Please note that this exhibit is a very rough estimate of the kind of variable cost relationship that might be expected. It is offered to illustrate the form this relationship could take and is in no way intended to represent a definite consensus of industry experience.)

Exhibit 9

NOTE ON THE MAJOR HOME APPLIANCE INDUSTRY
Selected Manufacturers and Retailers of Private Brand Appliances

Manufacturer	*Product*	*Retailer (brand name)*
Westinghouse......	Washers, dryers	B. F. Goodrich (Goodrich)
	Washers, dryers	Allied Stores (Ambassador)
	Ranges, refrigerators, freezers	Montgomery Ward (Signature)
Kelvinator		
(White Cons.)...	Washers, dryers	E. J. Korvette (Leonard-Korvain)
Whirlpool........	Refrigerators, freezers	Sears (Coldspot)
	Washers, dryers	Sears (Kenmore)
G.E..............	Refrigerators, freezers,	
	ranges, dishwashers, dryers	Pennys (Penncrest)
Borg-Warner		
(Fedders-Norge).	Washers, dryers	Montgomery Ward (Signature)
Magic Chef.......	Ranges	Gamble-Skogmo (Coranado)
Roper...........	Ranges, dishwashers	Sears (Kenmore)
Tappan..........	Ranges	Montgomery Ward (Signature)
Franklin Div.		
(White Cons.)...	Washers	Associated Merchandising Corp.
"	Refrigerators, freezers,	
	washers, dishwashers	Gamble-Skogmo (Coranado)
"	Refrigerators, freezers	B. F. Goodrich (Whiteking)
"	Refrigerators, freezers	W. T. Grant (Bradford)
"	Refrigerators, freezers	Western Auto (Wizard)

Source: Industry data.

Exhibit 10

NOTE ON THE MAJOR HOME APPLIANCE INDUSTRY

GM's Frigidaire Slates Layoff of 1,152 Workers In Dayton Area Friday

By a WALL STREET JOURNAL *Staff Reporter*

DAYTON, Ohio—The Frigidaire division of General Motors Corp. said it plans to lay off 1,152 employes on Friday, and Harold W. Campbell, a GM vice president and general manager of the division, said "our competitive problem is very serious, and we have been hard at work to find a solution."

Mr. Campbell issued the statement after a series of "state of the company" meetings with employes, which have been conducted for several weeks.

The division has undergone a series of layoffs in recent months. It had about 11,400 union workers prior to the most recent layoff announcement, down from around 15,000 in early 1970.

In seeking to solve the division's problems, Mr. Campbell said, "We have investigated having another manufacturer build our appliances. We have investigated the possibility of plants located in areas outside of Dayton. We have talked with one of the largest manufacturers in Japan, concerning the possibility of building our appliances. These investigations haven't been resolved at this time and no decisions have been made."

He said Frigidaire is "restructuring our organization in many areas to meet this challenge. Also, we are working to eliminate certain of our practices in the plants, and we are working to increase our productivity."

In explaining the company's situation, Mr. Campbell said "Frigidaire has been disadvantaged for some time because it's hourly-rate employes in the appliance end of the business are receiving the much higher rates paid in the automotive industry as compared to employes in the appliance business generally."

Mr. Campbell's statement said Edward Cole, GM's president, during a recent trip to Dayton, had "reflected the confidence General Motors has in the future growth of the appliances business. The appliance business, industry wide, is good. The projected growth is very good." Other competitors, Mr. Campbell said, appear to be expanding facilities and employment.

Source: *The Wall Street Journal*, June 15, 1971. Reproduced with permission.

Exhibit 11

NOTE ON THE MAJOR HOME APPLIANCE INDUSTRY
Appliances in New Housing
(1970)

	Percent of Units Containing Appliance on Occupancy			Percent of product sold to new housing*
	Single family (homes)	5-Family and over (apartments)	Mobile homes	
Ranges.............................	96	99	100	38
Refrigerators......................	15	96	100	21
Dishwashers.......................	60	58	6	42
Disposals..........................	65	65	1	53
Clothes washers...................	3	3	20	3
Clothes dryers.....................	3	3	15	3
Commercial washers (coin-operated).................	—	10	—	n.a.
Commercial dryers (coin-operated).................	—	5	—	n.a.

* Includes homes and apartments but not mobile homes. Mobile homes have thus far represented a negligible percentage of the appliance market.
Source: *The Major Appliance Industry*, Oppenheimer & Co., 1971, N.Y.

Exhibit 12

NOTE ON THE MAJOR HOME APPLIANCE INDUSTRY
Survey of Appliance Owners' Brand Loyalty
Question: If you were going to get a new appliance, do you think it would be the same brand or a different brand, or don't you know?

Appliance	Would buy same brand again	Would not	Don't know
Electric refrigerator......................	67.4%	14.8%	17.8%
Electric range............................	63.1	17.9	19.0
Gas range................................	51.3	23.7	25.0
Dishwasher..............................	81.3	5.1	13.6
Clothes washer...........................	74.3	12.3	13.4
Electric clothes dryer....................	75.4	12.1	12.5
Gas clothes dryer........................	81.1	9.0	9.9
Room air conditioner.....................	70.6	8.7	20.7
Disposal.................................	67.1	19.2	13.7
Average for all appliances................	70.1	13.6	16.3

Source: *Look, National Appliance Survey, 1963.*

Exhibit 13

NOTE ON THE MAJOR HOME APPLIANCE INDUSTRY

Channels of Distribution

Retail Outlets

	1967			1963		
	Number of outlets	Sales (millions)	Market share	Number of outlets	Sales (millions)	Market share
Total....................	22,872	$3,529.4	100.0%	19,522	$2,300.8	100.0%
Appliance dealers...........	15,044	1,747.5	49.5	13,663	1,245.3	54.1
Department stores, chain stores, and discount stores..................	3,877	1,496.4	42.4	2,444	935.3	40.7
Radio and TV stores........	3,951	285.5	8.1	3,415	120.2	5.2

Appliance Dealers

	1967		1963	
Number of stores	% of stores	% of sales	% of stores	% of sales
Single stores..............	73.0	63.9	75.7	67.1
Chains				
2–5 stores..............	5.8	12.3	7.5	12.2
6–25 stores.............	4.1	8.6	4.3	8.9
25+ stores.............	17.1	15.2	14.7	11.8

Source: *Home Furnishing Daily.*

Exhibit 14

NOTE ON THE MAJOR HOME APPLIANCE INDUSTRY
Index of Trends in Service Requirements of
Home Laundry Equipment
(based on number of valid warranty service calls per year)

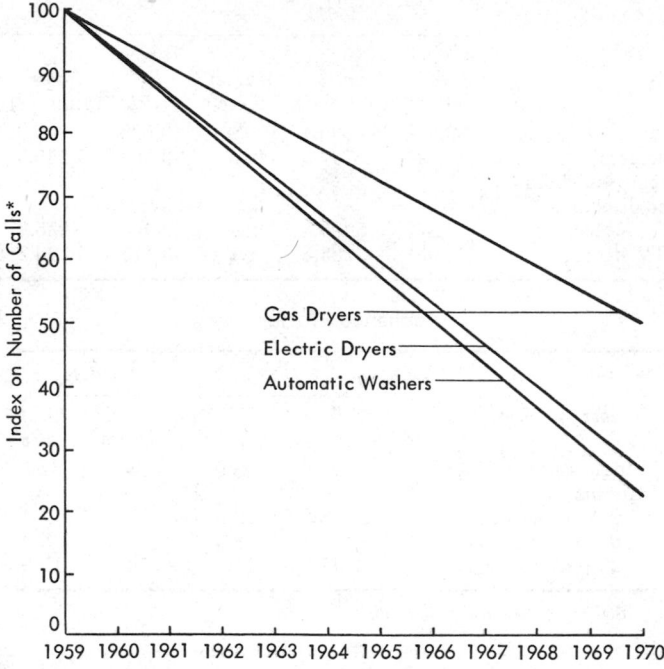

* 1959 = 100
Source: Association of Home Appliance Manufacturers.

Exhibit 15

NOTE ON THE MAJOR HOME APPLIANCE INDUSTRY
Appliance Industry Innovations
(1960–1970)

1. WASHERS:
   Mini-basket—washer within a washer—G.E.
   Large capacity—increased from 8–10 lbs. to 18–20 lbs.
   Solid state controls—Hotpoint
   Mini-washer and mini-dryer—Maytag
   Over/under "skinny mini" washer and dryer—Frigidaire

2. RANGES:
   Self-cleaning pyrolytic oven—G.E.
   Double oven over/under configuration—G.E. Americana
   Electronic oven—Tappan
   Countertop electronic oven—Amana "Radarange"
   Self-cleaning combinal electronic/conventional oven—G.E.
   Catalytic oven cleaning—Norge
   Glass-top surface unit—Corning

3. DISHWASHERS:
   Convertible dishwasher (free standing or built in)

4. DISPOSERS:
   Stainless steel disposer with lifetime warranty on water bearing parts—G.E.

5. REFRIGERATORS:
   36″ SXS refrigerator—Admiral
   Foamed-in-place insulation—G.E.
   Custom ice and water dispenser—G.E.
   Compact refrigerators and freezers (Ignis/Delmonico—Italy)

6. ROOM AIR CONDITIONERS:
   "Portable" air conditioner—Westinghouse
   Zoneline—40″ air conditioner—G.E.
   Non-rusting lexan plastic case—G.E.
   Carry-Cool portable air conditioner—G.E.

7. NEW PRODUCTS:
   Waste compactor—Whirlpool

Note: Precise dates on which these innovations were introduced were not readily available in trade publications nor had they been documented by the industry.
Source: Industry data.

Exhibit 16

NOTE ON THE MAJOR HOME APPLIANCE INDUSTRY

Refrigerator Models, 1952 and 1969

1952   1969

   Comparably priced (about $299 at retail) refrigerators of 1952 (left) and 1969 (right) demonstrate product engineering concentration on consumer value. Differences include 8.2 versus 16.6 cu.ft. capacity, one door versus separate freezer and refrigerator doors, manual versus automatic defrosting, white versus improved styling in a choice of three colors or white. Newer model also provides easier access to foods including the door storage shelves and more specialized storage drawers and compartments. Individual temperature controls, versus one in the 1952 model, provide independent compartment control. The 1969 freezer compartment can maintain zero, which the 1952 compartment could not achieve. An automatic icemaker can be installed, before or after refrigerator purchase, as an option on the 1969 unit. The back of the new appliance is free of coils for cleanliness, flush-to-wall installation. Roll-out wheels provide for cleaning beneath the 1969 unit. Some added benefits: more efficient and higher-capacity compressor; acrylic finish for increased corrosion protection and longer-lasting beauty.

   Source: *Appliance*, January 1970.

NOTE ON THE MAJOR HOME APPLIANCE INDUSTRY

Financial Data for Selected Corporations

	1970	1969	1968	1967	1966	1965	1964	1963	1962	1961
Whirlpool*										
Sales ($)	1,196,845,000	1,153,530,000	1,019,408,000	773,717,000	704,816,000	630,745,000	590,777,000	538,704,000	465,257,000	436,865,000
Profits (A.T.) ($)	35,619,000	45,943,000	36,223,000	33,272,000	36,219,000	35,860,000	29,327,000	24,294,000	18,643,000	13,500,000
Assets ($)	549,794,000	573,929,000	499,599,000	401,196,000	343,816,000	282,711,000	252,669,000	199,695,000	212,309,000	222,683,000
Return on assets (%)	6.5	8.0	7.2	8.3	10.5	12.7	11.6	11.4	8.8	6.1
Profits as a percentage of sales (%)	3.0	4.0	3.6	4.3	5.2	5.7	5.0	4.5	4.0	3.1
Ten-year average return on assets (%)	9.1									
Ten-year average profits/sales (%)	4.2									
Maytag										
Sales ($)	173,685,326	166,302,646	157,335,028	139,873,132	131,285,920	120,769,510	124,399,018	117,249,231	111,150,457	107,405,254
Profits (A.T.) ($)	22,713,675	21,614,231	22,600,000	17,275,000	16,044,974	15,157,350	16,185,379	14,007,100	12,731,516	12,092,821
Assets ($)	106,389,969	99,909,888	89,681,961	88,386,561	85,701,356	81,147,454	80,263,290	76,272,971	71,770,922	69,189,968
Return on assets (%)	21.4	21.6	25.2	19.5	18.7	18.7	20.2	18.4	17.7	17.5
Profits as a percentage of sales (%)	13.1	13.0	14.4	12.4	12.2	12.6	13.0	12.0	11.4	11.3
Ten-year average return on assets (%)	19.9									
Ten-year average profits/sales (%)	12.5									
Admiral†										
Sales ($)	368,532,957	354,393,567	377,013,813	380,941,526	414,644,696	306,903,967	238,014,520	216,146,661	201,505,441	193,548,438
Profits (A.T.) ($)	(16,103,313)	1,492,449	494,430	(3,770,061)	10,016,963	653,146	4,042,474	3,024,532	1,965,501	2,915,265
Assets ($)	228,879,013	200,197,798	262,883,820	214,140,762	201,613,083	144,276,516	120,251,473	115,252,878	113,819,757	110,649,688
Return on assets (%)	(7.0)	.8	.5	(1.8)	5.0	.5	3.4	2.6	1.7	2.6
Profits as a percentage of sales (%)	(4.4)	.4	1.3	(1.0)	2.4	.2	1.7	1.4	1.0	1.5
Ten-year average return on assets (%)	1.7									
Ten-year average profits/sales (%)	.4									
Fedders										
Sales ($)	295,812,000	264,341,000	134,964,000‡	88,872,000	62,345,000	63,685,000§	56,827,000	51,165,000	60,550,526	59,316,003
Profits (A.T.) ($)	15,561,000	12,080,000	6,345,000‡	4,342,000	1,182,000	3,395,000§	3,150,000	1,689,000	2,511,344	3,508,221
Assets ($)	194,488,000	161,503,000	129,050,000‡	61,477,000	57,614,000	58,268,000§	46,367,000	49,271,000	49,528,421	38,943,867
Return on assets (%)	8.0	7.5	4.9	7.1	2.0	5.8§	6.8	3.4	5.1	9.0
Profits as a percentage of sales (%)	5.3	4.6	4.7	4.9	1.9	5.3	5.5	3.3	4.2	5.9
Ten-year average return on assets (%)	6.0									
Ten-year average profits/sales (%)	4.6									
Hobart Corp.										
Sales ($)	212,022,000	201,016,000	172,305,000	156,031,000	142,101,000	123,055,000	104,208,000	92,829,000	85,050,000	77,006,000
Profits (A.T.) ($)	11,389,000	13,102,000	11,684,000	11,678,000	12,290,000	10,334,000	7,386,000	6,527,000	6,665,000	5,752,000
Assets ($)	175,224,000	162,328,000	141,110,000	121,904,000	105,463,000	83,715,000	73,478,000	68,352,000	63,238,000	58,290,000
Return on assets (%)	6.5	8.1	8.3	9.6	11.7	12.3	10.0	9.6	10.5	9.8
Profits as a percentage of sales (%)	5.4	6.5	6.8	7.5	8.6	8.4	7.1	7.0	7.8	7.5
Ten-year average return on assets (%)	9.6									
Ten-year average profits/sales (%)	7.3									
Tappan Company										
Sales ($)	313,892,000	133,878,000	124,209,000	95,746,000	97,175,000	93,755,000	85,775,000	76,975,000	72,994,000	71,465,000
Profits (A.T.) ($)	2,231,000	3,441,000	3,970,000	1,005,000	1,105,000	2,640,000	2,860,000	2,845,000	2,803,000	5,019,000
Assets ($)	80,129,000	76,833,000	60,340,000	52,376,000	50,626,000	48,047,000	41,098,000	36,090,000	33,286,000	30,456,000
Return on assets (%)	2.8	4.5	5.3	1.9	2.8	2.8	8.3	8.1	8.4	8.6
Profits as a percentage of sales (%)	1.7	2.6	2.6	1.0	1.5	1.5	3.6	3.8	3.8	3.7
Ten-year average return on assets (%)	5.9									
Ten-year average profits/sales (%)	2.8									

* Sales include nonwhite goods (estimated less than 10 percent of sales).
† Includes brown goods.
‡ Purchased Norge.
§ Diversified into other white goods besides room air conditioners.
Source: Corporate Financial Reports.

Exhibit 18. NOTE ON THE MAJOR HOME APPLIANCE INDUSTRY

Financial Data on Corporations*

(dollars in millions)

	1970	1969	1968	1967	1966	1965	1964	1963	1962	1961
Sears										
Sales ($)	9,262.0	8,863.0	8,198.0	7,330.0	6,805.0	6,390.0	5,740.0	5,116.0	4,603.0	4,268.0
Profits (A.T.) ($)	464.0	441.0	418.0	382.0	377.0	354.0	330.0	282.0	253.0	243.0
Assets (approx.) ($)	5,000.0	4,600.0	4,300.0	3,900.0	3,800.0	2,400.0	3,000.0	2,500.0	2,200.0	2,000.0
Return on assets (%)	9.3	9.6	9.7	9.8	9.9	10.4	11.0	11.3	11.5	12.1
Profits as % of sales	5.0	5.0	5.1	5.2	5.5	5.5	5.7	5.5	5.5	5.7
Ten yr. avg. ROA (%)	10.5									
Ten yr. avg. profits/sales (%)	5.4									
G.E.										
Sales ($)	8,726.7	8,448.0	8,381.6	7,741.2	7,177.3	6,213.6	5,319.2	5,177.0	4,986.1	4,666.6
Profits (A.T.) ($)	328.5	278.0	357.1	361.4	338.9	355.1	219.6	272.2	256.5	238.4
Assets (approx.) ($)	3,000.0	2,800.0	2,400.0	2,100.0	1,850.0	1,500.0	1,300.0	1,200.0	1,350.0	1,250.0
Return on assets (%)	11.0	10.0	14.8	17.2	18.3	23.6	16.8	22.6	19.0	19.0
Profits as % of sales	3.8	3.3	4.3	4.7	4.7	5.7	4.1	5.3	5.1	5.1
Ten yr. avg. ROA (%)	17.2									
Ten yr. avg. profits/sales (%)	4.6									
Penneys										
Sales ($)	4,150.9	3,828.5	3,379.2	2,927.0	2,702.8	2,407.9	2,155.1	1,834.3	1,701.3	1,553.5
Profits (A.T.) ($)	114.1	114.3	111.5	94.3	82.4	80.7	69.2	55.3	54.8	51.7
Assets (approx.) ($)	1,627.1	1,394.5	1,207.3	953.9	847.0	744.8	667.4	611.0	537.0	447.0
Return on assets (%)	7.0	8.2	9.2	9.8	9.7	10.8	10.4	9.0	10.2	10.8
Profits as % of sales	2.7	3.0	3.3	3.2	3.0	3.4	3.2	3.0	3.2	3.3
Ten yr. avg. ROA (%)	9.5									
Ten yr. avg. profits/sales (%)	3.1									
Montgomery Ward† (MARCOR Inc.)										
Sales ($)	2,227.0	2,155.0	1,986.0	1,879.0	1,894.0	1,748.0	1,697.0	1,500.0	1,425.0	1,326.0
Profits (A.T.) ($)	35.2	43.8	23.3	17.4	16.5	24.0	21.9	21.0	20.4	15.9
Assets (approx.) ($)	893.0	833.0	Not Reported	1,187.0	1,177.0	1,147.0	986.0	790.0	624.0	572.0
Return on assets (%)	3.9	5.3	"	1.4	1.4	2.1	2.2	2.7	3.3	2.8
Profits as % of sales	1.5	2.2	1.7	0.9	0.87	1.3	1.3	1.4	1.4	1.2
Ten-year ROA (%)	2.8									
Ten-average profits/sales (%)	1.4									

* These four companies include three major retailers and one diversified industrial company. The data reported is for the full product line of each company, not just their appliance sales.

† After 1967, data is just for Montgomery Ward Division of MARCOR.

Source: Corporate Financial Reports.

Association of Home Appliance Manufacturers

"THE CRUCIAL task I face is one of both leading and serving at the same time," commented Mr. Guenther Baumgart, President of the Association of Home Appliance Manufacturers (AHAM).[1] "A trade association exists to serve its members. Traditionally this meant a passive role for trade association administrators. However, with the growing complexity of industry generally and ours in particular, an increasing scope of activities is required. Rather than existing purely to arrange meetings and take minutes, an association's professional staff now is required to also develop policy recommendations to the members, and work with them to arrive at wise decisions as to what positions the industry should take on an almost limitless range of issues. I have to make sure that this increased role AHAM plays in policy formulation is backed by our members—because if there is reluctance or hanging back in any significant measure, we will lose our effectiveness!"

In discussing AHAM's role Mr. Herb Phillips, Technical Director, stated:

> In today's society any industry as conspicuous as the major home appliance industry is continually faced with the threat of government regulation. The only way to avoid governmental regulation is to move faster than the government. The alternative to government regulation, in my opinion, is judicious self-regulation. AHAM will play an increasingly active role in this area.

To provide leadership in this area while maintaining the satisfaction of the members was felt by many of AHAM's staff to be the key challenge

[1] AHAM is a manufacturers' trade association to which belong the producers of major home appliances such as room air conditioners, refrigerators, freezers, dishwashers, disposers, ranges, dehumidifiers, humidifiers, and home laundry equipment and the producers of portable appliances such as electric fry pans, toasters, blenders, hand irons, etc. This case, however, will focus on the AHAM's role in the Major Home Appliance Industry which in 1971 represented the bulk of AHAM's activities.

of the 1970s. It would certainly increase the complexity of what Mr. Baumgart described as his "crucial task."

The remainder of this case will describe the functions of AHAM as they existed in December 1971. Before describing these functions a brief history of AHAM and a description of its organization will be presented in order to provide context for examining AHAM's functions.

AHAM'S HISTORY

The twentieth century saw the development of the first mechanical home appliance—the clothes washer. By 1915, a number of manufacturers of clothes washers formed the Washing Machine Manufacturers Association (WMMA). One purpose of this association was to educate customers to the need for and use of the clothes washer. (See Exhibit 1 for example of early publication.) WMMA was headed by an executive secretary who implemented the decisions made by its members.

By the mid-1920s, other major appliances particularly refrigerators were coming into their own. The manufacturers of these products formed the consumer products section of the National Electrical Manufacturers Association (NEMA). NEMA was organized similarly to WMMA and was headed by William Donald, a man highly respected by the industry.

By 1954, WMMA had been renamed the American Home Laundry Manufacturers Association (AHLMA) including manufacturers of clothes washers, dryers, and ironers. In 1954, a study of AHLMA was done by Booz-Allen and Hamilton. The study recommended that AHLMA be reorganized and headed by a president. The study argued that AHLMA needed professional management to serve its members effectively. The thrust of this change was to allow the president of AHLMA more power in recommending to the board of directors, made up of manufacturers, the policies that AHLMA should adopt.

Shortly after the recommendations of the Booz-Allen report were adopted, Mr. Guenther Baumgart became president of AHLMA. Under his direction AHLMA's membership rose to include all the manufacturers in the industry. AHLMA developed a statistics department that was the model for the current AHAM department. A promotional program was undertaken with a central theme that was used throughout the country, yet cost the AHLMA very little because AHLMA convinced retailers and other groups to use the program to promote their own interests. For example, an electric utility would advertise, "Waltz through wash day with an *electric* dryer."

AHLMA started a conference attended by home economists from colleges, universities, the government, and various consumer groups which provided a great deal of information as to the care and use of home laundry products. AHLMA also developed a program to develop standards for its products similar to those of AHAM described later. Throughout the late 1950s and early 1960s, the activities of AHLMA expanded. Parallel with their expansion, and critical to its success, AHLMA received growing support from its members.

In sharp contrast the consumer products group of NEMA was experiencing increasing dissatisfaction by its members. The fact that NEMA's increasing budget was spent primarily on promotional activities aroused total dissatisfaction. The solution to the appliance manufacturers' problems was divorce from NEMA and marriage to ALHMA.

In 1967, AHAM was formed by merging the consumer products group in NEMA with AHLMA. Membership in AHAM was open to manufacturers of both major and portable home appliances. The merger was led by several leading manufacturers including Whirlpool, Westinghouse, and Kelvinator. Guenther Baumgart was asked to take the presidency and bring his staff members from AHLMA into key positions in AHAM.

One AHAM executive made the following comments about AHLMA and AHAM:

> The move to the professional management concept in the mid-1950s was crucial in developing an effective trade association. The change in itself, however, didn't guarantee an effective association. The association became effective by gradually developing the confidence of its members. This confidence allowed the staff a larger policy role.
>
> Even now if we fail to serve our members we could lose this confidence and our effectiveness. A trade association at best is very fragile. Guenther's ability as a manager has undoubtedly been responsible for AHAM's growth and effectiveness. He knows and understands the members and is a diplomat of the highest order.

ORGANIZATION

In 1971, AHAM was headed by a board of directors elected by the members. (See Exhibit 2 for organizational chart.) All actions taken by AHAM had to be approved by this board. Reporting to this board were two separate groups—AHAM's various program committees made up of industry members, and AHAM's president and professional staff. Over 500 individuals from member firms served on the program committees, while AHAM's professional staff consisted of a dozen professionals and about 20 support personnel.

The professional staff was organized in parallel with the various program committees. The staff provided support services for these committees and was responsible for administering AHAM's activities. In discussing his staff Guenther Baumgart commented:

> It is crucial to the success of AHAM to have a staff of comparable competence to its industry counterparts. Without this level of competence it would be impossible to gain and hold the confidence of our members necessary to do the job we have undertaken.
>
> We try to pay at least as well as industry for executives of comparable ability. We also offer a broader challenge in some respects because all our professional staff members are required to fill several functions. Besides functional competence, our staff needs general management skill to gain the cooperation of the various committees they work with. Given that those committees are staffed by volunteers from many companies this is often a formidable challenge.

Commenting on the role of AHAM's staff, one of AHAM's executives said:

To be effective we have had to understand our members' needs. But at the same time we spend a lot more time than our members in dealing with the government and consumers groups. Hence, we often have different information and occasionally different opinions as to what should be done.

When these differences arise, our role is to provide information to our members. By giving them this information, we can affect their decisions.

It gets to be frustrating when you know something should be done and can't get the members to do it. But, at that point you have got to remember who you are. We would lose our effectiveness if we felt superior to our members.

The frustrations, however, are fairly limited. Our members are very intelligent and if we have a valid point we can almost always get them to move.

Administering AHAM's functions and channeling information were generally considered to be the two key functions of AHAM's professional staff.

AHAM'S FUNCTIONS

In 1971 AHAM served six basic functions:

1. It served as the industry's spokesman with the government.
2. It developed standards.
3. It certified products.
4. It collected and distributed industry data.
5. It participated in various consumer education and consumer affairs programs.
6. It served its members in a number of other specific ways.

These six functions were handled by the various program committees and the parallel staff function. The remainder of this paper will look at each of these functions in detail.

Government spokesman

In its role as the industry spokesman in dealing with the government, AHAM employed the Washington law firm of Lee, Toomey and Kent to aid in representing them before Congress and regulatory agencies, as well as for the purposes of general counsel. Under the 1971 laws, AHAM did not have a registered lobbyist, although it served many of the functions of a lobbyist.

AHAM's Government Committee (See Exhibit 2) was responsible for keeping informed on pending government legislation at the federal, state, and local level and making recommendations to the board as to the position AHAM should take. After board approval, Mr. Lamb (a partner in Lee, Toomey and Kent), Mr. Baumgart, or other staff members would present these positions to the various government agencies. If possible, members also participated in making the presentations.

With the rising trend of consumerism exemplified by the passage of auto safety legislation, this role of AHAM was becoming increasingly important. Where AHAM had traditionally testified before congressional committees on taxes, labor relations, freight rates and other such areas, it was now presenting evidence in the areas of product safety, and guarantees and warrantees to congressional committees, the Department of Health, Education and Welfare, and the National Commission on Product Safety. (See Exhibit 3 for an excerpt of Guenther Baumgart's testimony before the National Commission on Product Safety.)

Commenting on AHAM's role vis-à-vis the government, William Comstock, Director of Public Affairs, stated:

> Presenting one statement as the industry position rather than having each individual manufacturing firm present a statement to the government not only is less expensive for our members but improves their credibility with the government.
>
> The statements we make to the government are drafted in the program committees that deal with the specific area in question. Hence, the government committee has to keep the program committees informed as to the issues the government is considering.

By serving as the industry spokesman, AHAM not only provided a valuable service for its members, but it also provided information that stimulated the program committees to deal with issues crucial to the industry's future.

Standards

A second function of AHAM was developing standards. There were two basic types of standards—safety standards and product standards. Safety standards specified what the minimum level of product safety was for a number of aspects of the product (e.g., wiring) and a method for testing to determine whether this level was achieved. Product standards specified certain performance dimensions of the appliance (e.g., how much soil a washer removed from clothes) and a method for testing that would yield a measure of this aspect of performance. Product standards, however, unlike safety standards did not set a minimum acceptable level of performance.

This difference between the two types of standards stemmed from a basic difference in the rationale for setting them. Safety standards were developed to protect the consumer from an unsafe product. Product standards were set to allow manufacturers to compare their products with those of their competitors' products, and to provide consumers with comparable information about all brands.

In the area of safety standards AHAM did not develop its own standards, but rather made recommendations to the Underwriters Laboratory (UL) and occasionally to the American Gas Association as to what AHAM felt the standards should be. Though AHAM only made recommendations to UL, AHAM was one of UL's prime sources of standards information. The two groups worked closely together. Commenting on the safety standards, Guenther Baumgart remarked:

> It is necessary to have strong safety standards. The reason for this is that consumers don't have the knowledge to evaluate what is a safe

product. No salesman has the time to educate all his customers to what is or is not a safe product and why.

For example, as a group we decided that the box on a refrigerator should be grounded to prevent it from becoming electrically charged. This was not a simple problem. It turned out each piece had to be grounded separately. This added $8 to $10 to the production cost of a refrigerator or maybe $20 at retail. It would be very difficult for any salesman to explain why the third prong cost $20. Unless everybody complied, no one could do it. We recommended to UL that they require our method of grounding. They did.

UL standards are all voluntary. But many state and local governments require UL certification; beyond that, many retailers will not carry products without the UL seal. Hence all manufacturers comply with UL standards. [See Exhibit 4 for the listing of UL appliance standards.]

Handled through an independent testing organization all manufacturers in effect have the same rules for safety. Thus safety is not sacrified for unwise cost economies and price competition.

Recommendations to UL came from the engineering committee (see Exhibit 2). In commenting on the process by which recommendations were arrived at Mr. Herb Phillips, Technical Director, stated:

We continually monitor all the accident data and government reports so as to be able to move quickly. We also are looking on our own for new standards. It is my opinion that appliances are continually improving along the safety dimension.

Safety is the first item on every engineering agenda. Thus, we are almost continually making recommendations to UL.

Product standards for each appliance were developed by AHAM, but were submitted to the American National Standards Institute (ANSI) for certification as national standards. It was generally agreed by AHAM management that ANSI's status guaranteed that the standards covered aspects of performance crucial to consumer satisfaction. A product might have six to twelve standards that applied to it.

In talking about product standards, Herb Phillips commented:

I can't imagine what the industry would be like without product standards. There are so many conceivable measures of product performance that without some guidelines it would be very difficult for a manufacturer to evaluate his product. I feel product standards have positively contributed to improving the quality of appliances.

When asked why all manufacturers were not required to publish how their product fared on each standard, Herb Phillips commented:

We have no power to compel our members to comply. We could certify those products that complied as we already do for some products [see following section] but this would be too expensive in general and not worth the added price which consumers would have to pay.

We are trying to develop a fact list that each manufacturer would publish. This would be voluntary, but if we can work out a good one our members will comply. This list would contain information stemming from our standards program.

Standards of all types were worked out by the engineering committee. (See Exhibit 2.) "By working out their differences in open discussion, I feel we get good standards that everyone can live with and do at a meaningful level," commented Guenther Baumgart. "I would hate to see the government get involved in formulating standards. It doesn't have the engineering expertise and would have great difficulty in formulating standards that were scientifically sound and fair to all producers."

Besides safety and product standards, AHAM also developed guidelines for fair advertising practices, warranties, and service. (See Exhibit 5 for example.) These guidelines were voluntary and were basically a code defining what "honest statements" were. Though these guidelines were voluntary Guenther Baumgart stated, "when it comes to my attention that a guideline has been violated, 99% of the time upon notifying the offender he corrects the situation. In my opinion our voluntary guidelines are virtually always followed."

Product certification

"The product certification program arose from the need for some products for a guarantee of the statements made by manufacturers as to crucial product characteristics," stated Guenther Baumgart. "The first product to be certified was the room air conditioner (RAC). In the early 1950s the RAC was advertised in terms of horsepower, BTUs, Watts, room-size cooled, tons, and other characteristics. It was impossible for consumers to compare most products. Also where products were comparable manufacturers were forced into a position where claims were of doubtful validity and confusingly stated." One industry executive explained the reason for this phenomenon as follows, "If one manufacturer lied, what could the rest do. For example, if one manufacturer sold a 5,000 BTU RAC for $140 and his competitors found out that it was only 4,000 BTU RAC, they had little recourse other than to lower the capacity of their product." In describing the situation, Guenther Baumgart stated, "Consumers were dissatisfied; the FTC was investigating and the whole industry was being hurt because a lot of people wouldn't buy any RAC."

Through the trade association, it was agreed after lengthy discussion that the crucial measures of performance were Watts, Amps, and BTUs. A program was set up whereby an independent laboratory tested a sample of all the RACs produced by firms in the program to see if the claims made were correct. The association published a directory quarterly listing the results of the tests. Each RAC produced by a participating member was given a sticker certifying that the statements made to these three characteristics were correct as stated in the directory.

Participation in the program was voluntary. One industry executive commented to the casewriter, "Participation may be voluntary, but try selling a noncertified product to a retailer." There were no known RACs sold in the U.S. that are not AHAM certified.

Besides RACs, refrigerators were certified as to cubic feet and dehumidifiers were certified as to pints of water removed per day. In all cases the cost of certifying was covered by selling the certification stickers to the manufacturers. Seals for RACs cost 5¢, for RACs that also heated 15¢, for dehumidifiers 4¢, and refrigerators 1.6¢. The total cost of the certification program was $400,000. In comparison the budget for the rest of AHAM's functions raised by dues was a little less than $1.2 million.

Industry data

AHAM, like most trade associations, collected data from its members, aggregated it and distributed summary totals to its members for individual products. AHAM collected both shipment and inventory data at both the factory (manufacturer) and distributor levels for a broad range of products. This data was collected and distributed weekly for most products; however, on some a monthly time cycle was used. Once a month AHAM also collected and issued distributor sales data by county for the entire U.S. for most products. In some instances geographic data was collected for broader areas such as trading areas.

Data was collected and distributed quarterly for a broad range of product feature characteristics and price classifications (e.g., manufacturer's price classifications; size classifications such as BTU output for room air conditioners, cubic capacity of refrigerators and chest and upright freezers, width and type of range configurations; feature characteristics such as automatic icemakers, freezer location and defrosting systems for refrigerators, the number of speeds for automatic washers, and shipments by various color classifications). Also, twice a year members were asked to estimate industry sales: once for the next two years and once for the next five years. A complete array and the median forecasts were then distributed. Finally, twice a year data was collected on the service incidence for several products. The array of all participants and a weighted average level was reported.

In discussing the use of this data, Paul Roman, Director of Marketing and Economics, stated:

> AHAM data is used in a myriad of ways by participants and to some extent its use and value to a participant is determined by the imagination and ingenuity of those who receive it.
>
> The data enables a manufacturer to judge his own performance in relation to the industry and properly used assists in planning business and marketing strategies. The geographic data is useful in defining sales territories, in establishing sales goals and in evaluating the performance and effectiveness of the distributor organization and the total sales effort. The product characteristics data is useful in analyzing the model and feature offerings embodied within the product line of an individual manufacturer and is extremely valuable in product planning. Overall the historical trend data and forecasts assist in both short term and long range company planning. Without question this activity is one of AHAM's most useful services to our members.

As in all areas of AHAM, extreme care was taken to comply with the legal restrictions placed on trade associations. In the area of data collection the law prevented collection and distribution of data that would aid firms in fixing prices.

Consumer education and consumer affairs

AHAM carried on a myriad of activities relating to educating the public—ranging from an annual national educational conference to dissemination of teaching materials to advertising campaigns on safety.

The Home Appliance Conference was a yearly conference sponsored by AHAM. The conference was attended by home economists from colleges and universities, government agencies, consumer publications and consumer groups. Attendance was between 800 and 1,000. The purpose of the conference was to educate home economists and through them consumers as to the selection, care and use of appliances. Along with the conference, AHAM provided at cost a number of teaching aids to be used in the classroom. In discussing this program Guenther Baumgart commented, "the more consumers know about appliances and how to use them, the more likely they are to buy an appliance and be satisfied with it. We feel that by educating consumers we do more than if we undertook promotional campaigns for the various products. We leave the latter up to the companies."

In all, AHAM published and offered to the educational community over 100 different books, pamphlets, slidefilms, tape cassettes, etc. During 1971 it received over 68,000 requests for its materials and distributed over 14,000,000 copies or pieces. Most of the orders were from educational institutions.

It also published a number of periodicals including a monthly newsletter about industry activities concerning educators, a quarterly bibliography of magazine articles about appliances and a semi-annual bibliography of educational aids available from industry.

Perhaps its most visible effect to the general public was its advertising campaign warning of child entrapment and suffocation in abandoned refrigerators. Several times a year radio and television materials were distributed to all broadcast outlets. At the same time millions of copies of a six-page leaflet explaining how to avoid entrapment were distributed through public health organizations. The leaflet was also placed by manufacturers in each new refrigerator produced.

In the area of consumer affairs one of AHAM's most visible efforts was participation along with the Gas Appliance Manufacturers Association and the American Retail Federation in establishing and funding the Major Appliance Consumer Action Panel (MACAP). MACAP, however was an autonomous panel staffed by experts with no industry ties. With the exception of the chairman, Dr. Virginia Carter, panel members were compensated only for the expenses they incurred. (See Exhibit 6 for list of members).

MACAP was chartered to resolve consumer complaints which hadn't been solved at the local level or by the manufacturer. Manufacturers agreed to usually accept the decision of MACAP as to the way the complaints should be resolved but they were not bound to. MACAP was also empowered to make broad studies of industry practices and make recommendations to the government and the industry as well as directly to consumers where MACAP felt changes were necessary.

MACAP since its founding had reviewed over 3,800 complaints. Of these 3,164 had been resolved with the consumer satisfied with the resolution in 3,022 cases and unsatisfied in 142 cases. In only 267 cases did MACAP actually consider the complaint, however. The other 2,837 cases were resolved directly by the manufacturer when they were notified—at the top management level—that MACAP had received a complaint. Where MACAP considered the complaint they found the complaint justified in over 60% of the cases and recommended that the company involved take specific action. Compliance with the recommendations was virtually 100%.

MACAP at its second meeting decided to undertake studies of warranties, point of purchase information as well as service availability, cost, and quality. The results of the warranty study and MACAP's recommendations were presented to the manufacturers and the Interstate and Foreign Commerce Committee of the House of Representatives. MACAP recommended legislation as to the minimum standards for warranties, clear disclosure of warranty terms and remedies for nonperformance of contractual agreements. The other studies were in progress.

In commenting on MACAP Bill Comstock stated:

> With the shift to mass merchandisers from small owner-managed stores an old outlet for complaints is dwindling. Consumers are increasingly complaining to manufacturers rather than retailers. MACAP is one attempt to help manufacturers equitably handle this problem. Also, its studies provide the industry with valuable information as to areas where action should be taken.

It was generally felt that MACAP's role in the industry would increase as it became better publicized.

Member service

Though all the activities of AHAM were aimed at serving its members, AHAM also engaged in several activities beyond those previously described. Two further areas where AHAM served its members were in areas of industrial relations and transportation.

In the area of industrial relations AHAM collected data on wages, benefits, premium pay practices, and general wage information for blue collar workers. Data was also collected on salaries and incentive compensation for a selected group of exempt supervisory and management positions. This data was summarized and then redistributed to the participating members. The data was used by the members in contract negotiations and executive compensation. AHAM also administered a program whereby published labor contracts were exchanged.

Along with this statistical program AHAM on occasion held seminars dealing with industrial relations problems. In these seminars managers met to discuss a wide range of problems and how they had solved them. The topics of these seminars ranged from social responsibility issues like training the hard-core unemployed and job discrimination to general problems of labor relations.

The traffic committee had been one of AHAM's most active. It monitored proposed changes in transportation rates and regulations which affected the industry and negotiated with the involved carriers and regulatory agencies. This also included presentations before rate making bureaus and the submission of information to the Interstate Commerce Commission in support of industry positions which were arrived at by the members. This activity was broadened in scope to include transportation packaging and damage in response to mounting economic pressure. Given the importance of transportation costs and quality to the industry, this was viewed by the members as a key function. The committee also worked with other groups such as the Association of American Railroads in establishing and publishing procedures for proper handling and loading appliances for shipment.

In discussing AHAM, its members, and the industry, Guenther Baumgart stated:

> The appliance industry has grown rapidly over the last two decades. Prices have fallen continually, product quality has increased as well as reliability. This performance has been the result of strong competition. Yet in this highly competitive environment manufacturers have been able to work together to solve common problems. Their top managements have had the imagination and farsight to develop the kinds of programs AHAM conducts and the social consciousness to take a responsible position in the best interests of both consumers and manufacturers. Without this cooperation it would have been difficult if not impossible to have achieved good association performance especially in the areas like product safety, product certification, and consumer education.
>
> In the decade of the 1970s and beyond with the increasing role that will be played by the government and consumer groups, trade associations like AHAM will be of crucial importance in dealing with the critical problems facing our society.

Exhibit 1

ASSOCIATION OF HOME APPLIANCE MANUFACTURERS

Laundering
At Home

BULLETIN ONE

Removal of Stains

This series consists of six Bulletins:

Bulletin 1—Removal of Stains.
Bulletin 2—Supplies for the Home Laundry.
Bulletin 3—Washing Cottons and Linens.
  Washing Woolens and Silks.
Bulletin 4—Washing Machines.
Bulletin 5—Ironing.
Bulletin 6—The Equipped Home Laundry.

Issued by

The American Washing Machine Manufacturers' Association

Chicago · Illinois

Copyright 1921

Exhibit 2

ASSOCIATION OF HOME APPLIANCE MANUFACTURERS

AHAM Organization Chart

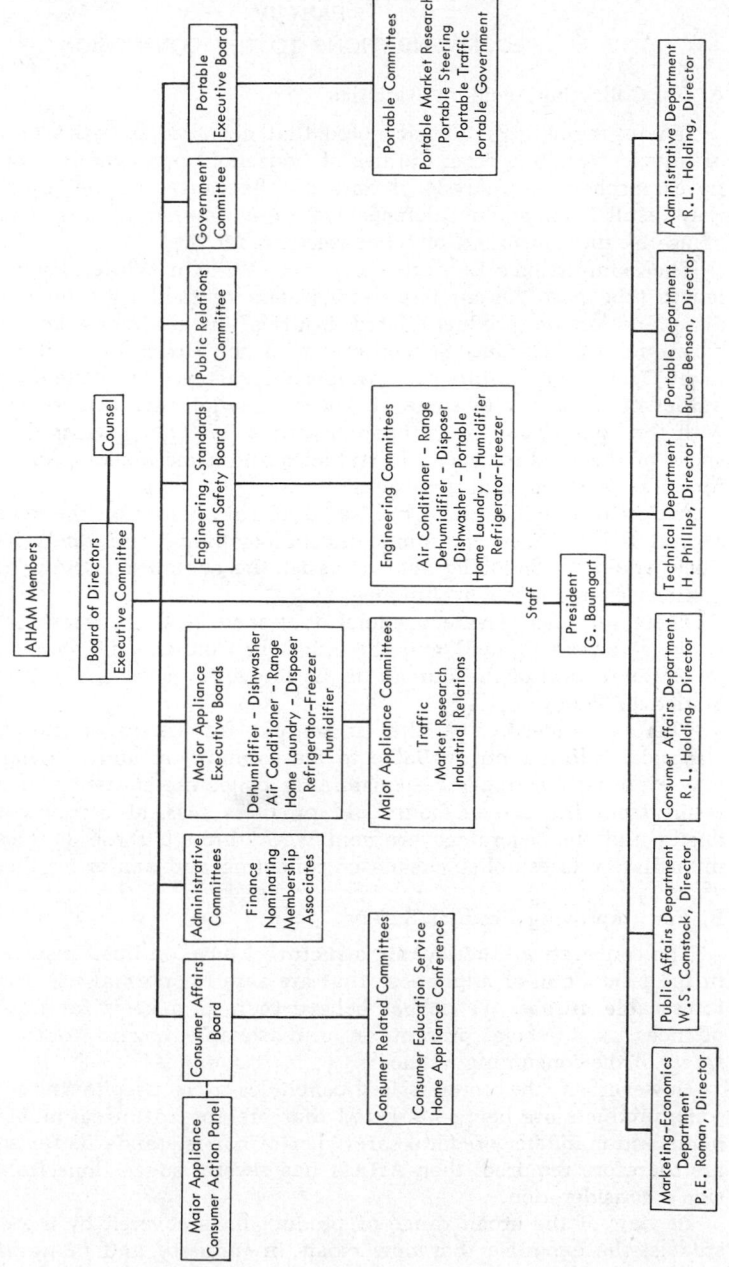

Exhibit 3

ASSOCIATION OF HOME APPLIANCE MANUFACTURERS

PART IV

RECOMMENDATIONS TO THE COMMISSION

A. For Collecting Accident Statistics

It now seems generally accepted that accurate statistics on the number of injuries resulting from the use of household products are not available— no comprehensive analysis of data on the causes of the injuries, whether they result from product defects, from environmental causes, from manner of use by the consumer, or other relevant factors.

The commission's Executive Director, William White, discussed at some length "the need for an improved system of data collection, analysis and dissemination on product-related injuries" in testimony before the Intergovernmental Relations Subcommittee of the House Committee on Government Operations on June 26. Attached to his printed statement were summaries of testimony of some 18 witnesses who have discussed the problem with the commission in its open hearings. Without dissent these witnesses spoke of the need for accurate statistics and some made specific suggestions for collecting and analyzing data.

AHAM need not repeat what has been said before on the need. There are several federal agencies competent in compiling and analyzing statistics. They would no doubt be able to assist the commission with concrete suggestions on statistical techniques.

There are also private agencies that may be of assistance, such as the National Safety Council and the Advisory Council on Federal Reports, set up at the request of the Bureau of the Budget to assist the Bureau's Office of Statistical Policy.

There is, indeed, a wealth of sources for advice on the gathering of statistical information available to the commission and to whatever agency may eventually be made responsible for collecting statistics on injuries that result from the use of household products. AHAM recommends that industry and the federal government work through these sources and begin immediately to establish means of collecting and analyzing these statistics.

B. For Improving Product Safety

The cooperative, interlocking structure I have outlined results, we believe, in the production of appliances that are safe for normal use and reasonably foreseeable misuse. We do not believe there is a basis for finding that appliances as a whole 'present an unreasonable hazard to the health and safety of the consuming public.'

However, if the commission concludes that despite industry's efforts, some products are being marketed that present an unreasonable risk in the home and mandatory federal safety performance standards for such products are therefore required, then AHAM has several suggestions for the commission's consideration.

In view of the broad range of product lines covered by the commission's studies, the expertise that now exists in industry and in nationally recognized standards-setting organizations should be fully utilized in the initiation or development of standards. In our judgment this would represent a wise use of the country's available resources. Coupled with this an appropriate agency of the federal government should be given the authority to:

Exhibit 3—Continued

1. Pass judgment on the adequacy of existing safety performance standards.
2. Promulgate and enforce the safety performance standards found to be adequate, and
3. Upon a finding of need for a new or revised safety performance standard, call upon industry or a nationally recognized standard-setting organization to develop and submit such a standard.

Further in our judgment the authorized agency should be required before finalization of such a standard to observe the requirements of the Administrative Procedure Act; that is, notice opportunity for filing written comments and where warranted, public hearings. Changes or revisions in a safety performance standard should be developed and promulgated after observance of the same procedures.

A safety performance standard for household products would be defined as setting a level of safety performance for the products to which it applies and establishing the means for determining whether the product meets such requirements.

It is important, we think, that such performance safety standards once adopted for a product apply to all such products sold in the United States whether manufactured there or imported; that they take precedence over any state or local safety standards covering the same products and that they be enforced by government. AHAM would favor an enforcement pattern which would permit the enforcing authority to delegate testing authority to independent testing laboratories or state or local agencies.

I recognize that these suggestions are but a broad sketch of a pattern and that many details are missing. However, on behalf of AHAM I am prepared to offer the assistance of our counsel and staff to work with the commission and its staff if the commission feels our suggestions have merit.

Source: Statement by Guenther Baumgart, President, Association of Home Appliance Manufacturers on October 1, 1969, before the National Commission on Product Safety.

Exhibit 4

ASSOCIATION OF HOME APPLIANCE MANUFACTURERS

PART III

REVIEW OF SAFETY STANDARDS FOR
SELECTED HOME APPLIANCES

The safety standards followed by manufacturers of home appliances are those of Underwriters' Laboratories for electrically powered appliances and for the electrically operated components of gas-powered appliances. Standards of the American Gas Association are followed in the manufacture of other parts of gas-powered appliances. (Only one of these, gas clothes dryers, is among the products under AHAM's jurisdiction.) Manufacturers of home appliances must also follow the safety standards of the National Electrical Code, the National Plumbing Code, and other applicable local building codes. In addition, many manufacturers incorporate safety devices of their own into their appliances, but these are not standards since by definition a standard is a level established by authority, custom, or general consent to be followed by an industry.

Most safety standards for home appliances are performance standards,

Exhibit 4—Continued

rather than design standards. That is, they set levels of performance which should prevent hazards, such as current leakage, fire, access to moveable parts, in the normal use of the product. The design of a product to assure the maintenance of the levels of performance is left to the manufacturer, though often the same or similar designs are used by the manufacturers.

Testing for compliance of a finished product is done by the manufacturers through their quality control programs, after a prototype or one of the first of a model to come from the production line has been tested by Underwriters' Laboratories or by the American Gas Association. These procedures have been described in other parts of the statement filed on behalf of the Association of Home Appliance Manufacturers, and in statements by representatives of UL and AGA.

Each of Underwriters' Laboratories' safety standards, the most comprehensive group of safety standards for home appliances, is made up of numbered paragraphs. The paragraphs state the requirements for the component parts of an appliance or for different aspects of its operation that can present a hazard if not properly manufactured or controlled. Many of the requirements deal with generic problems and are included in all or most of the standards. Other requirements are made necessary by distinctive components or modes of operation for a particular product, and are included only in the standard for that product.

The requirements of the latest editions of ten safety standards that govern the manufacture of twelve home appliance lines have been tabulated to show those that deal with problems common to all the twelve appliances, and those that deal with the distinctive problems of each appliance line.

Exhibit 4—Continued

UNDERWRITERS' LABORATORIES SAFETY STANDARDS
FOR SELECTED HOME APPLIANCES

Requirements Common to Most Standards	UL 73 — Motor Operated Appliances	UL 560 — Dryers	UL 560 — Washers	UL 560 — Combination	UL 250 — Refrigerators—Freezers	UL 484 — Room Air Conditioners	UL 749 — Dishwashers	UL 430 — Disposers	UL 499 — Electric Heating Appliances	UL 858 — Electric Ranges	141 — Electric Flatirons	UL 859 — Hair Dryers
Scope	✓	✓	✓	✓	✓	✓	✓	✓	✓	✓	✓	✓
Construction												
Frame and Enclosure	✓	✓	✓	✓	✓	✓	✓	✓	✓	✓	✓	✓
Mechanical Assembly	✓	✓	✓	✓	✓	✓	✓	✓	✓	✓	✓	✓
Corrosion Protection	✓	✓	✓	✓	✓	✓	✓	✓	✓	✓	✓	✓
Supply Connections												
Cord-Connected Appliances												
Cords and Plugs	✓	✓	✓	✓	✓	✓	✓	✓	✓	✓	✓	✓
Strain Relief	✓	✓	✓	✓	✓	✓	✓	✓	✓	✓	✓	✓
Bushings	✓	✓	✓	✓	✓	✓	✓	✓	✓			
Permanently Connected Appliances												
Wiring Terminals	✓	✓	✓	✓	✓	✓	✓	✓	✓	✓		
Live Metal Parts	✓	✓	✓	✓	✓	✓	✓	✓	✓	✓	✓	✓
Heating Elements		✓	✓	✓	✓	✓	✓	✓	✓	✓	✓	✓
Wiring Methods (Internal Wiring)	✓	✓	✓	✓	✓	✓	✓	✓	✓	✓	✓	✓
Insulating Material												
Electrical	✓	✓	✓	✓	✓	✓	✓	✓	✓	✓	✓	✓
Thermal		✓		✓			✓		✓	✓	✓	
Automatic Temperature Controls		✓		✓		✓			✓	✓	✓	✓
Motors												
Overcurrent Protection	✓	✓	✓	✓	✓	✓	✓	✓	✓	✓		✓
Overload Protection		✓	✓	✓	✓	✓	✓	✓	✓	✓		
Switches and Controllers	✓	✓	✓	✓	✓	✓	✓	✓	✓	✓	✓	✓
Capacitors	✓	✓	✓	✓	✓	✓	✓	✓		✓		
Lampholders	✓	✓	✓	✓	✓			✓	✓	✓	✓	✓
Receptacles	✓	✓	✓	✓				✓	✓	✓		✓
Spacings	✓	✓	✓	✓	✓	✓	✓	✓	✓	✓	✓	✓
Grounding	✓	✓	✓	✓	✓	✓	✓	✓		✓		✓
Flooding of Live Metal Parts		✓	✓	✓	✓	✓	✓			✓	✓	
Performance												
Power Input	✓	✓	✓	✓	✓	✓	✓	✓	✓	✓	✓	✓
Starting Current	✓	✓	✓	✓		✓	✓					
Dielectric Withstand	✓	✓	✓	✓	✓	✓	✓	✓	✓	✓	✓	✓
Insulation Resistance	✓	✓	✓	✓	✓	✓	✓	✓	✓		✓	✓
Temperature	✓	✓	✓	✓	✓	✓	✓	✓	✓	✓	✓	✓
Ratings and Markings	✓	✓	✓	✓	✓	✓	✓	✓	✓	✓	✓	✓

Source: Statement by Guenther Baumgart, President, Association of Home Appliance Manufacturers on October 1, 1969, before the National Commission on Product Safety.

Exhibit 5

ASSOCIATION OF HOME APPLIANCE MANUFACTURERS
AHAM Recommended Guidelines on
CONTENT OF WARRANTIES

A. A guarantee or warranty should clearly set forth:
1. The name and address of the warrantor or other identification adequate to locate the warrantor.
2. To whom the warranty is extended.
3. The product or parts thereof covered.
4. The specific time for which the product or parts thereof are covered.
5. In case of a claim under the warranty:
   a) Exactly what the warrantor will do and at whose expense.
   b) Exactly what the owner must do and at whose expense.
B. All language should be clear, concise, and simple.
C. All exceptions or exclusions which are considered as conditions to maintaining the warranty in force should be set forth with the same degree of prominence.
D. The printing should be clear, well-spaced and easy to read rapidly. "Small print" items should be avoided.
E. Care should be taken to make sure that a heading or title used in connection with a warranty does not mislead the customer as to the nature and extent of the warranty coverage actually provided.

Approved by AHAM's Board of Directors January 31, 1969.

Exhibit 6

ASSOCIATION OF HOME APPLIANCE MANUFACTURERS
Major Appliance
Consumer Action Panel

Dr. Virginia F. Cutler, Department Chairman, Family Economics and Home Management, Brigham Young University.
Dr. Elsie Fetterman, Family Economics Specialist, University of Connecticut.
Mrs. Virginia Habeeb.
Miss Dianne McKaig, Executive Director, Michigan Consumers Council.
Dr. Aurelia Toyer Miller, Director, Bureau of Research and Program Resources, National Board YWCA.
Dr. Beatrice Paolucci, Professor, Department of Family Ecology, College of Human Ecology, Michigan State University.
Dr. Mary Purchase, Associate Professor, Department of Design and Environmental Analysis, New York State College of Human Ecology, Cornell University.
Mr. Frederick Waddel, Director of Education and Research, Credit Counseling Centers, Inc.

Source: *MACAP Progress Report.*

Sears, Roebuck and Company: Appliances*

BEGINNING after World War II, Sears, Roebuck and Company had steadily expanded its share of the White Goods market. (See Exhibits 1 and 2.) In 1970 more appliances were sold carrying the Sears brands of Kenmore and Coldspot than any other brand. Sears' 827 retail stores were well positioned to exploit the pre-1970 appliance markets. The decade of the 1970s, however, brought with it the first major threats to Sears' supremacy in the White Goods industry. A fat 72% of appliance sales in the United States were in the retail segment of the market. In contrast, the bulk of the growth in the appliance industry was expected to be in the contract segment.[1] In fact, contract sales were forecast to account for roughly 50% of the market by 1980.[2]

The growth of contract sales was one of two significant phenomena Sears would have to contend with over the decade of the 1970s. The other is the growing threat of meaningful direct competition from J. C. Penney, among others at the retail level.

Currently, Sears' share of the appliance market was due almost entirely to retail sales. And Sears' appliance strategy had thus far been directed to the retail segment. But if Sears was to maintain its appliance market share over the next decade without entering the contract market, it would have to increase its share of the retail segment by about 14 share percentage points during that time (see Exhibit 3).[3] Given grow-

---

* This case is based entirely on published information and statements about Sears made to the casewriter by individuals knowledgeable in the field. Sears in no way participated in its preparation.

[1] The term "contract segment" is shorthand for sales to construction firms for installation in dwelling units prior to occupancy.

[2] The casewriter could find no detailed information on contract sales or projections in either public or private sources. It should be noted, however, that other estimates of the share of the market in 1980 which would be accounted for by contract sales ranged as low as 42% (see *Note on Major Home Appliance Industry*, p. 332).

[3] This represents a rate of increase of 1.4 share percentage points per year, but a rate of increase over Sears' existing share of 4% per year (44% over 10 years).

ing retail competition from Penneys and others (including energetic competition for appliance sales), many industry experts believed this could be difficult even for Sears. By this line of thought, Sears would have to consider making a major effort in the contract segment to maintain or expand its share of the appliance market. Alternatively, Sears could opt to compensate for declining appliance share by putting strategic emphasis on other areas of its business which held out greater promise of growth. In any event, the changes occurring in the appliance business raise serious questions about Sears' current appliance strategy.

This case briefly examines Sears' history, including the evolution of Sears' retail strategy and organization. Next, it focuses on what appears to have been Sears' appliance strategy; it examines Sears' various functional policies and their relationship to Sears' appliance strategy. Then the case describes recent changes in the nature of Sears' competition. Finally, it explores the implications for Sears of its changing environment.

SEARS' HISTORY

Richard Warren Sears entered the mail-order business in 1886 with the founding of the Sears Watch Company. The watch industry at this time was engaged in a fierce attempt to maintain price. By buying discontinued lines (often encouraging the company to continue production of them) and by buying the stock of bankrupt companies, Sears put itself in a position to undercut prices. This advantage, enhanced by the low overhead of a mail-order business relative to the small retail jewelers, and high volume, allowed Sears to sell profitably for just slightly more than the retail jewelers' costs.

In 1895 Richard Sears, then in partnership with Alvah Roebuck, a watch repairman, was joined by Julius Rosenwald and Aaron E. Nusbaum. These two men brought with them the capital and executive ability necessary for the profitable exploitation of the rural American market. "In his semiannual catalogue, Sears offered the American farmer a wide variety of goods and, because he purchased in large quantities and often directly from the manufacturer, offered them at a lower price than did the local merchants and storekeepers."[4]

Between 1895 and 1925 the Sears company grew at a very rapid rate. A highly centralized, functional operation was developed in Chicago to handle purchasing, sales promotion, and distribution. This centralized organization allowed the company to take advantage of the economies of mass purchasing and also allowed for tighter inventory control.

"In 1925, Sears initiated a strategy that quickly put an excessive strain on Sears' top management."[5] The new component of strategy was entry into direct retail selling. General Robert E. Wood, the president of Sears and an avid reader of the *Statistical Abstract of the United States,*

[4] Alfred D. Chandler, *Strategy and Structure* (Cambridge, Mass.: The M.I.T. Press, 1962), p. 226.
[5] Ibid., p. 233.

had identified the trend toward urbanization in the United States. General Wood thought that the shifting market required direct retail selling if Sears was to continue to grow.

Wood approached the retail market with a three-pronged attack based (1) on store location (locating on the fringes of urban areas with populations over 100,000), (2) on the character of the stores (concentrating on hard goods like hardware, guns, tools, and consumer durables like major home appliances), and (3) on mass purchasing and limited backward integration into the production of these goods. The importance of durables in this strategy led Sears toward "basic buying." "The merchandising departments [at Sears] began to design their own products, determine the best location for production in relation to the market and supplies, and then to go to a manufacturer in a given area with these specifications and negotiate a contract."[6] To guarantee supply Sears also purchased common shares (often a controlling interest) of its suppliers of these "big ticket items."

Sears' new strategy placed increasing pressure on its centralized organization. Throughout the 1920s and 1930s a new form of organization developed (see Exhibit 4). The merchandising functions (e.g., purchasing, designing, and advertising) were controlled at the corporate level. While the retail operations were each organized into profit-center territories, each store manager had considerable autonomy as to his actions. If he wanted, he could even do his own purchasing. He had available to him, however, the merchandising support of the home office. Needless to say, almost all stores took complete advantage of these services.

The three-pronged strategy developed by General Wood and the organization that evolved to implement that strategy continued to serve Sears up to 1970. It is important to note that sales of appliances played an important role in this strategy. By 1965, $1 billion of Sears' $6 billion revenues were White and Brown Goods.[7] Two major strategic changes did occur at Sears between 1945 and 1970 that directly affected appliance sales, and these are discussed below.

Brand name

Sears had since its very beginning sold its products (including White Goods) under a variety of names. As the number of products Sears carried increased, the number of names escalated. Also, with the advent of Fair Trade Laws, Sears' ability to set its own prices appeared to be in question. In order to avoid fair trade difficulties, in 1945 Sears reduced the list of its brands to less than 50 and stressed the importance of having a unique product. Dating from this move are "Coldspot" refrigerators and freezers, and "Kenmore" washing machines and ranges. These two brands replace more than 15 names associated with various lines and models of appliances.

---

[6] Ibid., p. 236.
[7] *Mart Magazine,* July 11, 1965, p. 95.

The growth of Sears' appliance business made the two brands widely known. Still, by 1970 Sears' appliances were carrying the phrase "by Sears" in addition to the Kenmore or Coldspot label. Industry observers suggested that Sears was strongly considering dropping the Kenmore and Coldspot and selling under the single brand name of "Sears."

THE DECLINE OF VERTICAL INTEGRATION

A second major change in strategy during the postwar period was the move away from factory ownership. At the outset in 1925 the appliance industry was highly fragmented with many regional privately owned producers. To guarantee a steady source of supply, part ownership was important to Sears—especially since Sears could often increase the efficiency of the controlled operation. But with the growing concentration of the appliance industry after World War II, the increasing complexity of the product and production process, and Sears' rapidly increasing retail volume, backward integration became less attractive. The investment and management required were a distraction. Moreover, others were doing the manufacturing job well.

To understand the decreasing attractiveness of backward integration for Sears, it is important to look at Sears' relationship with its suppliers. With the scale required for economic production rising to 500,000 units for many White Goods, Sears could not purchase from small regional companies and remain cost competitive. Forced into buying from national manufacturers, Sears faced a critical problem because the large, efficient national producers viewed Sears as a competitor. Even so for any given product, Sears' volume was so large that it permitted any one of the smaller national producers to achieve the economies of scale in production.

Furthermore, it was to Sears' advantage to have its suppliers sell their own national brand because it forced the manufacturer to keep up on new product development. Though Sears could design its own products, it did not have the engineering capability necessary for continual development of new features or imitation of competitors. Since Sears needed a product with competitive features, it was essential that Sears' suppliers have strong product development capability. Finally, in this postwar environment Sears no longer had the production expertise to improve the efficiency of its large, sophisticated suppliers.

Sears' response was to develop strong ties with Whirlpool (home laundry and refrigerator/freezers), Design and Manufacture (dishwashers), and Roper (ranges) but to avoid ownership. Of these three companies, Sears had a controlling interest only in Roper and this position was reduced from 76% to 59% by the sale of 300,000 shares of Roper stock in 1965. One observer commented that "The mutual dependency between these suppliers and Sears allows Sears to buy at a low price while allowing the suppliers a fair profit, especially when the cost savings on their other sales are considered. And then," he said, "the [Sears] organization takes over."

SEARS' APPLIANCE ORGANIZATION

Two segments of the Sears' organization were of crucial importance to its appliance business—the retail merchandising office at the corporate level and the department managers' office at the store level. This section of the case examines these two activities in detail.

Merchandising office (corporate level)

In their study of Sears, Corey and Star noted that "The largest Parent Department was the Merchandising Department, which was responsible for the development, procurement, and promotion of all merchandise sold in Sears' stores or catalogs."[8] Reporting to the merchandising vice president were 51 national merchandising managers, each with responsibility for a given group of products. In appliances, four national merchandisers were responsible for, respectively, home laundry; freezers, air conditioners, and dehumidifiers; refrigerators; and kitchens (including ranges, disposers, and dishwashers).

"Reporting to each National Merchandiser Manager was a Retail Sales Manager, a Catalog Sales Manager, a Merchandise Controller and from six to 25 buyers."[9] Since catalog sales were not significant for major appliances, the two key positions were the buyer and retail sales manager. The buyer was responsible for everything having to do with his product. He determined the source of the product, the purchase price, product design, product research and development, retail pricing, service and, most important of all, sales and profit. The retail merchandising office was responsible for advertising, promotion, placement within the store, and so on.

The merchandising manager and his staff, however, had no power to compel the retail stores to make use of any of their services or, for that matter, even their products. In fact, the stores typically followed the policies set by the buyers. In these circumstances one of the prime functions of the retail merchandising office was to keep in close touch with the stores to make sure that friction did not develop between store operations and the buyer.

Sears was organized so that each buyer was a profit center, with responsibility for the sales and profits of his products in all of the retail stores and the catalog. He took this responsibility very seriously and was encouraged to do so by an aggressive reward system. One industry observer in close contact with Sears described the buyer compensation scheme as follows:

> Each buyer receives a bonus that can work out to be greater than his salary. It is based entirely on his annual sales and margin growth. Buyers can become very wealthy, *if* they can keep growth up along both of these dimensions. The last thing a buyer wants is to get

---

[8] E. Raymond Corey and Steven H. Star, *Organization Strategy* (Boston: Division of Research, Graduate School of Business Administration, Harvard University, 1971).

[9] Ibid., p. 301.

stuck with a lot of inventory at the end of the year since getting rid of this inventory would reduce his profit margin. That could kill his bonus and endanger his job.

Department manager's office (store level)

At the retail end of the chain, each retail store in the Sears' operation was also a profit center. Reporting to the store manager were department heads responsible for various product groups within the store. These department heads, with the store manager's approval, had the power to set product policy for that store. Usually they followed the buyers' guidelines. As the buyers were evaluated on the basis of the profits these divisions earned, it was reasonable to conclude that they had strong incentives to develop a product policy that would maximize the division head's profits and bonus. Indeed, it is not surprising that there was a good deal of cooperation between department heads and buyers.

These evaluations were reflected in compensation. At the retail store level, from the manager down to the salesman, a bonus based on profits was a large part of total compensation. Many in the industry felt that the heavy bonuses available to Sears' salesmen were crucial to Sears' success in the appliance field.

SEARS' APPLIANCE STRATEGY

Because of the overall importance of big ticket items as traffic builders, Sears' *appliance* strategy cannot be separated from Sears' *corporate* strategy. In turn, the facts that Sears had entered the retail market early, had located its stores in what would rapidly become prime shopping areas, and not least of all, that the name "Sears" was associated with low price and high quality by many consumers, certainly affected Sears' strategy. Sears' appliance strategy was characterized as a focused approach to retailing through merchandising. In order to get the sales and profit growth expected from appliances, Sears' buyers concentrated on two things—generating traffic, that is, getting customers into their stores, and selling the middle and top of their line. Sears got traffic by heavily advertising their low-priced/low-featured appliances, by maintaining consistent quality and providing good service, and by taking advantage of the natural traffic a Sears' store generates. However, once the customer was in the store, every effort was made to sell him up the line. Salesmen were trained and heavily rewarded for doing this, and individual product lines were designed and priced to make it easier.

The Sears' strategy was based on volume. The higher the volume, the lower the price Sears could get from its suppliers and the lower Sears' distribution costs. The latter cost reduction was based on the savings achieved from shipping full carloads both to regional warehouses and to the larger Sears stores. This saving could be as much as 8% to 10% of the freight cost. In fact, volume was important to Sears' entire appliance strategy. Volume determined *cost* and margins. The higher Sears' volume, the stronger the competitive position Sears achieved vis-à-vis its competitors—particularly "the National-Full-Line-Manufacturers."

To achieve such volume, Sears placed emphasis on product development, pricing, advertising, sales training, and service. These policies will be described in detail below.

Product development

A Sears' national merchandising manager for home laundry described product development as follows:[10]

> In structuring our product line we pay close attention to the selling strategy used in the stores. We begin with the top-of-the-line, the very best product we can make with all the most advanced features. We then build a low-priced machine, of the same quality as the top-of-the-line but with fewer features.

One industry expert with considerable knowledge as to Sears' operations elaborated on this statement:

> To understand Sears' product development policy you have to understand the dilemma facing the buyer. To stay competitive Sears needs to have the really hot new features. But every time the buyer changes the line he increases the production costs. Production costs fall the longer a given model is produced—partly because efficiency increases and partly because fixed costs associated with the line can be written off against a larger volume.
> The buyer could keep adding models to the top-of-the-line, but this hurts him in two ways. The more the volume is spread across a larger number of models, the higher the cost for each model. Second, the larger the number of models, the higher the inventory costs.
> Given this environment, you can bet that buyers want to make as few changes as possible. By and large Sears doesn't introduce any major new features—the risk is too great. They copy the really hot new features (i.e., those that sold well) of their competitors and that is about all they do.

The above observation that Sears' top-of-the-line products had fewer features than some national manufacturers' brands seemed to be true in 1972. For example, the GE Americana series range had features such as burners with thermostatic controls and ovens thermostatically controlled by a meat thermometer. These features were not available on the Sears' top-of-the-line. Sears had, however, followed GE by introducing a self-cleaning oven, Tappan by introducing an "over-under" range, and Admiral by introducing an automatic ice maker. These features were viewed by the industry as crucial selling points on ranges and refrigerators.

Sears' pricing policy

In describing Sears' pricing policy, the National Merchandising Manager for Home Laundry stated:[11]

---

[10] Ibid., p. 302.

[11] Ibid.

After we have established the top-of-the-line and the bottom-of-the-line (our opening price point) we ask, "How many models do we need to fill the gap?" On the one hand, each price point must give the consumer real benefits as compared to the price point below it. On the other hand, the jump between price points must not be so great that the consumer will not be willing to move up. And we do not want to have too many price points, since every increase in stock-keeping units increases inventories. On automatic washing machines we have six basic retail price points: $119, $149, $169, $189, $219, and $239. Approximately 60% of our sales are between $189 and $219.

There were two key aspects to the pricing policy described above. First, the "bottom-of-the-line" price was set to be as low or lower than any of Sears' competitors. This was important for attracting the customer into the store. The second crucial aspect was the use of a limited number of carefully spaced "pricing points"—each point associated with a separate feature. This was necessary to facilitate the trade-up.

In talking about Sears' pricing policy, one expert on Sears stated, "The beauty of the pricing policy is that it makes selling up a cinch. Given that margins on Sears' appliances rise faster than price, selling up is crucial to Sears' financial success."

Sears' advertising policy

"Our advertising covers various models but usually emphasizes the lower price machines," stated the National Merchandising Manager for Home Laundry.[12] Besides heavily advertising the bottom-of-the-line, Sears frequently ran heavily advertised sales. A study done by an appliance dealer in Chattanooga, Tennessee, showed that in one year Sears ran 18 sales on their low-priced freezer, 10 sales on their low-priced electric range, 7 sales on their low-priced washer and 6 sales on their low-priced refrigerator.[13] The vast majority of Sears' regular and sale advertisements for appliances were full-page ads in local newspapers. Sears ran at least one full-page ad a week in each area and often one a day during sales.[14]

Given that the bulk of Sears' sales were not in these low-priced range appliances (e.g., as stated before 60% of washer sales were in the $189–$219 range), there could be little doubt that the rationale for Sears' advertising was to get customers into the stores so that they could be traded up to more expensive models by the salesman.

Sales training

The appliance strategy and each of the functional policies described above were predicated on the Sears' salesman's ability to sell the customer up. Because the "sell-up" was crucial to Sears' success, Sears made a strong effort to train its salesmen in "the art of selling up."

The cornerstone of this training was the Sears' salesman's handbook. This document explained why selling up was important and how the

[12] Ibid.
[13] *Mart Magazine*, July 11, 1965, p. 59.
[14] *The Story of Sears* (Fairchild Publications, Inc., N.Y., 1961), p. 61.

salesman should go about doing it. (See Exhibit 5 for examples of training material.) Each Sears' salesman was required to read this book and pass an examination on its contents. One of the key jobs of a department supervisor was to work continually with his salesmen to develop this skill.

Beyond education, Sears structured its commissions and other incentive programs to reward salesmen for selling up. Finally, since department supervisors were rewarded heavily on the basis of department profits, they had strong incentives to work with the salesmen to develop this selling-up skill.

Sears' service policy

Prior to the late 1960s, service represented Sears' clearest competitive advantage—only Sears offered a service contract backed up by its own servicemen. While other manufacturers were forced to rely on franchised service operations, Sears could undertake its own service because of its high volume, especially in home laundry (the highest service call product). Just as important, the ability to locate service facilities in or near its stores allowed Sears' store managers to supervise the service operation. Finally, Sears had always serviced its own products, and this extensive experience permitted Sears to develop a superior service capability early in the development of the appliance industry.

Sears' suppliers, however, were responsible for breakdowns during the warranty period. This motivated Sears' suppliers to design as reliable a product as possible as well as one that was easily serviceable. This policy also led Sears' suppliers to train Sears' servicemen so as to minimize the cost of service during the warranty period.

The competitive advantage Sears derived from providing its own service was beginning to erode by 1970. GE was developing factory service outlets in most metropolitan areas with a population over 100,000. Even a part-line producer like Tappan was beginning to supply its own service in major metropolitan areas. Still, only a high-volume, full-line manufacturer like GE had sufficient service volume to compete effectively with Sears.

COMPETITION

While in the past Montgomery Ward had been thought of as Sears' closest retail competition, a new and much more energetic competitor began to emerge in the 1960s. That competitor was J. C. Penney, which by 1970 had become the second largest retailer in the United States.

Exhibit 6 shows that Penneys has been growing more rapidly than Sears in both sales and profits over the past 10 years.

Exhibit 7, which compares retail store construction for Sears and Penneys, gives part of the reason why. Since 1963 Penneys has been committed to a "full-line department store"[15] strategy. All of its new stores since then have been full line. And Penneys has been growing, store for

---

[15] Full-line stores carry hard goods like appliances while the older soft-line stores did not.

store, with Sears during that time. Indeed, in the last two years reported, Penneys had actually been adding substantially more stores than Sears.

Thus, since 1963 Pennys has apparently been implementing a new strategy of head-on retail competition with Sears. Exhibit 6 shows that this new strategy has been very effective for Penneys. It is clear that Sears must worry not only about Penneys in the future, but also about other large retailers (e.g., Montgomery Ward), who may well be tempted by Penney's success to take on the giant themselves.

And if this were not enough, Penneys is tied in with GE, Sears' largest competitor in the appliance market. GE has contracted to sell appliances to Penneys for resale under the Penneys name. This alliance between the largest national full-line appliance manufacturer and the second largest retailer could be a source of trouble for Sears' appliance business in the future. At the least, such an arrangement will help both GE and Penneys make inroads on Sears' current volume advantage.

THE FUTURE

As the 1970s unfolded two clear threats to Sears' appliance strategy began to emerge from the changing environment of the appliance industry.

First, since Sears' strategy now emphasized retail sales, the growing importance of builder (i.e., nonretail) sales meant that Sears could lose market share to its competitors who were better positioned to exploit the contract segment. A loss of market share to major competitors could erode Sears' relative cost advantage—which was volume sensitive.

This threat was especially great if Sears' suppliers were unable to attack the builder market successfully—because then suppliers' volume would drop and with the decline would come loss of scale economies. On the other hand, if Sears' suppliers did penetrate this market segment, Sears' business would not be as important to them. Hence, Sears would lose some of its buying power.

The second threat took the form of strong and growing competition to Sears at the retail merchandising level. Strong competition from retailers like J. C. Penney meant it was unlikely that Sears could count on dramatic increases in retail market share to make up for the declining magnitude of this segment in the total appliance market. Indeed, the competition might even make headway into Sears' current share of the retail segment. In either event, Sears would have to plan to move into the contract business to hedge the growing threats to its retail share.

Loss of market share would not only put pressure on Sears' cost advantage, it might also result in the loss of Sears' service advantage. GE was already establishing factory service outlets in major metropolitan areas. If other competitors grew to GE's size (in appliance sales share), they could also start their own service operations.

Despite these changes in the environment, Sears' management did not appear to be directing a large part of its attention to the appliance business. Indications were that the primary changes in Sears' strategy went in the opposite direction—placing heavier relative emphasis on soft goods. Indeed, a *Business Week* article[16] tended to confirm this conclusion. It indicated Sears had a new strategy to maintain growth despite bigness. The strategy called for broadening Sears' entire market and diversifying its growth. To accomplish this as the company approaches saturation of its traditional middle-class market, Sears planned to aim for the low- and high-income segments of the market which it previously eschewed. Soft goods, especially clothing, were expected to lead the way.

There were signs, however, that Sears had also begun to consider the contract appliance market. In fact, the 1972 Sears catalog featured several pages on the home center concept. This concept could attract business from the rehabilitation market but without further elaboration was unlikely to attract the business of builders of new dwelling units who, for example, expected volume discounts.

In this environment, Sears faced the future. The final strategy its management adopted vis-à-vis the contract market would clearly have far-reaching effects for Sears as well as for the industry.

---

[16] "How Giant Sears Grows and Grows," *Business Week,* December 16, 1972.

Exhibit 1

SEARS, ROEBUCK AND COMPANY: APPLIANCES
Results for the Year (all products)

	1961	1962	1963	1964	1965	1966	1967	1968	1969	1970
Net sales (millions)	$4,268	$4,603	$5,116	$5,740	$6,390	$6,805	$7,330	$8,198	$8,863	$9,262
Net income (millions)	243	253	282	330	354	377	382	418	441	464
Long-term debt (millions)	475	475	475	451	439	427	403	483	455	630
Shareholders' equity at year end (book value) (millions)	1,860	1,994	2,152	2,339	2,531	2,732	2,939	3,173	3,440	3,708
Return on average shareholder's equity (percent)	13.6	13.1	13.6	14.7	14.5	14.3	13.5	13.7	13.3	13.1
Earnings per share (dollars)	1.61	1.67	1.86	2.17	2.32	2.47	2.50	2.73	2.87	3.01
Retail stores (excluding foreign stores): Number of	747	748	761	777	786	801	809	818	826	827
Store space (gross sq. ft. in millions)	52	53	56	61	65	71	76	80	83	86
Catalog, retail and telephone sales offices and independent catalog merchants	994	1,009	1,112	1,216	1,449	1,653	1,731	1,934	2,131	2,310

Source: 1971 *Corporate Annual Report.*

Exhibit 2

SEARS, ROEBUCK AND COMPANY:
APPLIANCES

(unit sales in thousands)

	1964	1969
Clothes washers.............	745	1,420
Clothes dryers...............	639	997
Refrigerators................	818	1,059
Ranges......................	744	818
Dishwashers.................	189	445
Room air conditioners........	523	1,037*
Total units.................	3,658	5,776
Sears growth 60%		
Industry growth 35%		

* Assuming same market share in 1969 as 1964.
Source: Exhibits 2 and 4 in the *Note on the Major Home Appliance Industry.*

Exhibit 3

SEARS, ROEBUCK AND COMPANY: APPLIANCES
Market Segment Analysis for Sears
U.S. Appliance Sales

	Retail	Contract
1970	72%	28%
1980 (est.)	50%	50%

Sears Share of Market—1969 Data

	Dishwashers	Freezers	Ranges	Refrigerators	Washers	Dryers	Air conditioners
Percentage of units	21	27*	17	20	34	33	19*
No. of units (000)	445	322	818	1,059	1,420	997	1,037
Average dollar value per unit†	220 (est.)	228	222	277	239	190 (est.)	205
Estimated dollar sales ($000)	93,500	73,500	182,000	294,000	348,000	190,000	213,000

Calculation of Sears' 1969 Share of Total Appliance Market

	Sears	Total	Sears %
Unit sales (000)	6,098	26,283	23.3
Dollar sales (000,000)	1,394†	5,998	23.3†

Analysis of Sears' Appliance Market Share for 1980

Question: Assuming Sears' appliance sales in 1969 were all retail sales, and assuming the changing mix in retail and contract segments by 1980, what percentage of retail sales will Sears need in 1980 to keep its 23.3 percent share of the total market?

x = Total appliance market

y = Sears' percent of retail segment

1969

$.233\ x = y(.72)x$

$y = 32.3\%$

1980

$.233\ x = y(.5)x$

$y = 46.5\%$

Conclusions:

Sears will need to increase its share of the retail market by 44 percent (14.2 share points) over the decade to 1980 to retain the same 23.3 percent share of the total appliance market solely with retail sales. This represents a compounded growth rate of about 4 percent per year.

* 1964 S.O.M.

† Sears probably sold greater than the average dollar amount per unit, given its trade-up policy, so these numbers are undoubtedly low.

Source: Basic data from Exhibits 2 and 4 of the *Note on the Major Home Appliance Industry*.

Exhibit 4

SEARS, ROEBUCK AND COMPANY: APPLIANCES

Corporate Organization Chart, 1967

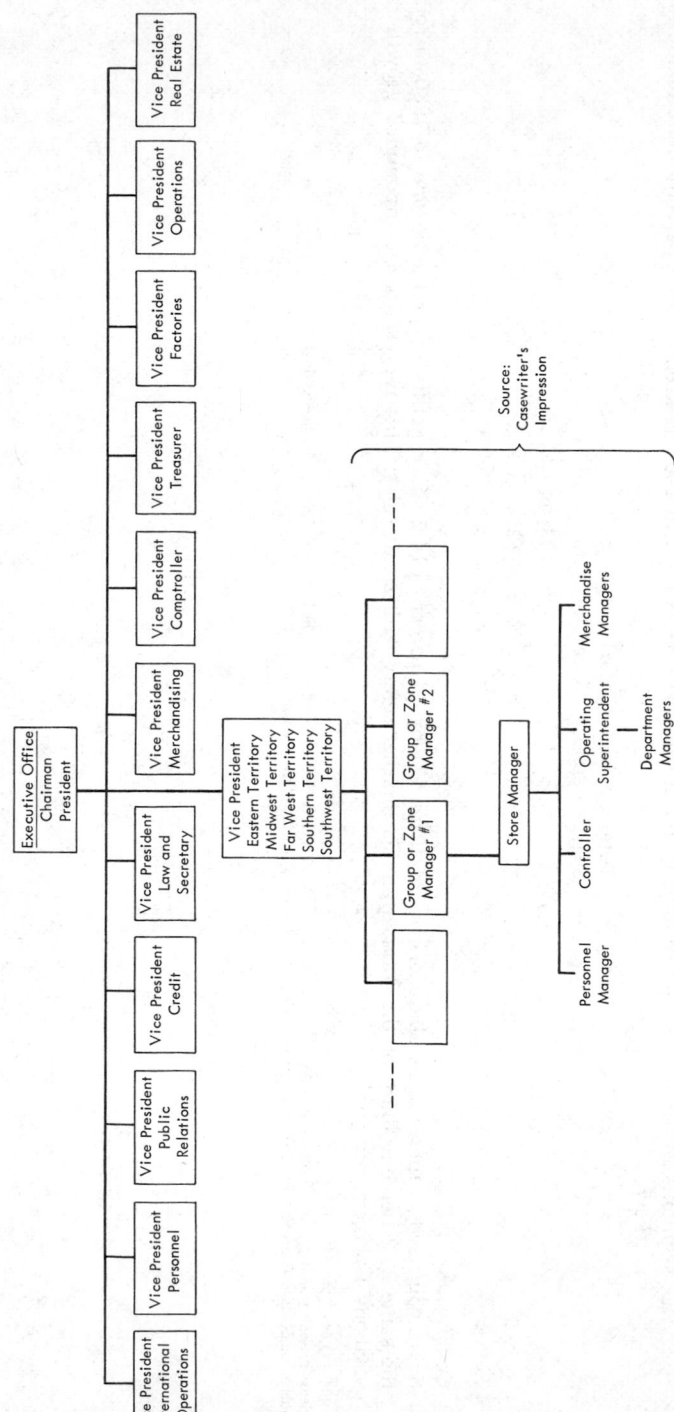

Source: E. Raymond Corey and Steven H. Star, *Organization Strategy: A Marketing Approach* (Boston: Division of Research, Graduate School of Business Administration, Harvard University, 1971), p. 319.

Exhibit 5

SEARS, ROEBUCK AND COMPANY: APPLIANCES
A Page from *Sears Sales Handbook*

Platoon System for Division 26

Division 26 has four lines of merchandise: automatic washers, automatic dryers, and the Kenmore Combination automatic washer and dryer, complete in a single unit, and wringer washers.

All the division's merchandise is divided into three "platoons," or selling groups, based on the price and quality of the items.

Although the 1st, 2nd, and 3rd platoons correspond roughly to Sears' "good-better-best" classifications, the platoon system goes further than just grouping. For example, the function of Platoon 1 is to advertise; of Platoon 2, to trade up to and through; of Platoon 3, to sell in depth. It's important to note that each platoon includes a complete assortment. Platoon 1 has a good representation of each item in the division for the customer who buys strictly on price. So Sears can state honestly in their advertising that we will not be undersold by any legitimate competition, including discount houses.

Platoon 2 merchandise satisfies the needs of the customer who is willing to pay a little more to get more features or better quality. More important, Platoon 2 is the logical place to begin trading up to Sears' top-quality lines, the third platoon.

Platoon 3 is the top of each of the division's lines. It's the group that offers the most in quality and features. And it makes the most profit for you and Sears. Merchandise in the third platoon is responsible for the tremendous success of the Kenmore home-laundry lines. Although this de luxe, top-quality line is usually sold successfully through the use of the first two platoons, many customers who are attracted by Platoon 1 prices can be traded up directly to Platoon 3. Some may be sold Platoon 3 merchandise without trading up at all.

The system should be regarded as flexible, and its most effective use is largely a matter of the skill and judgment of the salesman. In order to develop this skill and judgment, the salesman must know his merchandise.

Kenmore Automatic Washers

The automatic washer line, the largest in Division 26, accounts for about 64 percent of national sales. The line offers a dependable washer that is durable, completely automatic, and will add style and beauty to the basement, laundry, or kitchen. Twelve-pound automatic washer cabinets are available in acrylic or all-over porcelain. All models come in white although the Lady Kenmore models are also available in pink, yellow, shaded copper and aqua. The 24-inch models are available in white acrylic finish only. All Kenmore automatic washers (except 24-inch models) are available with Suds-Saver. Washers offer 2-speed washing, self-cleaning filters, water temperature selections, porcelain tops, lighted dials, plus many other work-and-time saving features.

Source: A page from the *Sears Sales Handbook* as it appeared in *Mart Magazine*, July 11, 1965, p. 48.

Exhibit 6

SEARS, ROEBUCK AND COMPANY: APPLIANCES

Comparison of Selected Retail Competitors

($000,000)

	1970	1969	1968	1967	1966	1965	1964	1963	1962	1961
Sears										
Sales	9,262	8,863	8,198	7,330	6,805	6,390	5,740	5,116	4,603	4,268
Profits (A.T.)	464	441	418	382	377	354	330	282	253	243
Assets (approx.)	5,000	4,600	4,300	3,900	3,800	3,400	3,000	2,500	2,200	2,000
Return on assets (%)	9.3	9.6	9.7	9.8	9.9	10.4	11.0	11.3	11.5	12.1
Profits as % of sales	5.0	5.0	5.1	5.2	5.5	5.5	5.7	5.5	5.5	5.7
Ten-year ROA (%)	10.5									
Ten-year average profits/sales (%)	5.4									
Penneys										
Sales	4,150.9	3,828.5	3,379.2	2,927.0	2,702.8	2,407.9	2,155.1	1,834.3	1,701.3	1,553.5
Profits (A.T.)	114.1	114.3	111.5	94.3	82.4	80.7	69.2	55.3	54.8	51.7
Assets (as reported)	1,627.1	1,394.5	1,207.3	953.9	847.0	744.8	667.4	61.1	53.7	47.7
Return on assets (%)	7.0	8.2	9.2	9.8	9.7	10.8	10.4	9.0	10.2	10.8
Profit as % of sales	2.7	3.0	3.3	3.2	3.0	3.4	3.2	3.0	3.2	3.3
Ten-year ROA (%)	9.5									
Ten-year average profits/sales (%)	3.1									
Montgomery Ward (MARCOR Inc.)										
Sales	2,227.0	2,155.0	1,986.0	1,879.0	1,894.0	1,748.0	1,697.0	1,500.0	1,425.0	1,326.0
Profits (A.T.)	35.2	43.8	34.3	17.4	16.5	24.0	21.9	21.0	20.4	15.9
Assets (approx.)	893.0	833.0	†	1,187.0	1,177.0	1,147.0	986.0	790.0	624.0	572.0
Return on assets (%)	3.9	5.3	†	1.4	1.4	2.1	2.2	2.7	3.3	2.8
Profits as % of sales	1.5	2.2	1.7	0.9	0.87	1.3	1.3	1.4	1.4	1.2
Ten-year ROA (%)	2.8									
Ten-year average profits/sales (%)	1.4									

* After 1967, data are for Montgomery Ward Division of MARCOR.
† Not reported.
Source: Annual Reports for each company.

Exhibit 7

SEARS, ROEBUCK AND COMPANY: APPLIANCES
Competitive Analysis: Sears and J. C. Penney

A. Store Data

	Total stores		Millions of sq. ft. (gross)		Total stores carrying appliances*		New stores carrying appliances†		Old stores dropped	
	Sears	Penneys	Sears	Penneys	Sears	Penneys	Sears	Penneys	Sears‡	Penneys§
1970	827	1,647	86	70.0	827	240	24	32	6	31
1969	826	1,646	83	64.9	826	208	27	32	5	36
1968	818	1,652	80	60.8	818	176	32	32	8	41
1967	809	1,658	76	55.5	809	141	32	34	11	31
1966	801	1,656	71	50.3	801	108	46	24	11	34
1965	786	1,664	65	46.5	786	82	38	32	9	37
1964	777	1,671	61	43.4	777	52	41	16	7	23
1963	761	1,678	56	41.4	761	36	25	8	1	—

B. Investment in New and Improved Facilities‖ (millions)

	Sears	Penneys
1970	$292	$267
1969	235	214
1968	169	214
1967	186	173
1966	224	122

* Generally these are full-line or hard-line stores.
† Includes new markets as well as relocations of old stores (new additions for both Sears and Penneys are full-line stores).
‡ Smaller hard line.
§ Soft line.
‖ Includes amounts invested by landlords in improvements.
Source: Annual reports for each company.

Design and Manufacturing
Corporation

"MY biggest problem is to develop the management capability of Design and Manufacturing Corporation (D&M) so that we can continue to fashion a better product at a lower cost," stated Mr. Samuel Regenstrief, president of D&M. "Our success over the last twelve years has been based on accomplishing these two tasks and I see no reason for any change in the future."

This case will examine the history of D&M and its present strategy. It will then describe D&M's organization and functional policies. Finally, it will explore the threats and opportunities D&M's management see in the future.

HISTORY OF THE DESIGN AND MANUFACTURING CORPORATION

In the late 1950s Mr. Samuel Regenstrief undertook a study of the dishwasher market. The study concluded:

1. The dishwasher market had high growth potential.
2. The industry was dominated by GE, which sold a very high-priced dishwasher.
3. No manufacturer existed with the capacity to supply the national retail brand companies (like Sears) and manufacturers of other appliances with dishwashers to be sold under their brands.

Mr. Regenstrief was committed to the report. In commenting on it he stated:

> It was clear to me that the dishwasher market was going to take off. The dishwasher accomplished a chore most families disliked and gave the housewife more free time. It also was beneficial from a health standpoint since very hot water could be used.
> I also felt that the national retailers offered a very attractive market. Originally manufacturers were creating the need for a specific brand of appliance. The "Frigidaire refrigeration" and "G.E. range"

were examples of this. But as consumers came into closer contact with a wider range of appliances and appliances became more uniform in quality, the need that was being created was the need for the appliance. Value became key. National retailers gave the most value per dollar. In my opinion their success will continue because they are catering to the needs of today's consumers—the need for value.

There was another more philosophical reason for my interest in dishwashers. Home appliances like dishwashers improve the quality of life. I feel that the social problems that face this country arise from the great divergence in the quality of life. In the late 1950s dishwashers were too expensive to be purchased by any but the rich. This in my opinion contributed to the divergence in the quality of life.

Yet the only measure of performance available to a businessman is profits. The dishwasher business offered a unique opportunity. By going into it with the intention of mass producing appliances and selling to national retailers and other manufacturers, I would make a profit only by continually lowering my production costs. Dishwasher prices would fall and dishwashers would quickly become available to any consumer that wanted one. Hence, by concentrating on profits I could make a positive contribution to society.

In 1959 Mr. Regenstrief left an executive position at Philco and purchased the Appliance Division of Avco located in Connersville, Indiana. A former Avco executive described this Avco Division and its problems as follows:

The Appliance Division of Avco in 1959 was producing dishwashers, other major appliances, sinks, and cabinets. After World War II, like most major manufacturers of appliances, it had broadened its line. However, the division was having trouble getting retail distribution because of the extreme competition within the industry. It was furthermore in direct competition with other divisions of Avco also manufacturing and selling their own brands of appliances.

With regard to dishwashers the Avco Division had a quality product. In the middle 1940s we began work on the dishwasher. By 1959 we had a competitive product and the capacity to be a major competitor in the market. "All" we lacked was sales!

By 1958 the Appliance Division was incurring substantial and consistent losses. We had considerable excess capacity. For example we made only 50,000 dishwashers and we could have made several times that with the existing plant and equipment. Given the drain other Avco divisions were placing on Avco's resources and management, Avco decided to sell the division.

A D&M executive described the purchase of the Avco Division as follows:

The Avco Division had a good production facility and a good dishwasher. What it lacked was a viable approach to the market. In simple terms, it lacked management.

The Avco Division was precisely what Sam was looking for. Its book value was low because the plant was almost fully written off. It was also incurring heavy losses. Hence, Sam could afford to buy it and Avco could afford to sell it. Sam had the management capability to turn it around and turn it around he did.

In commenting on the past 12 years Mr. Regenstrief stated:

> When I acquired the Avco Division it had a core of good engineering and production talent as well as the physical plant. With this as a base, we got rid of everything but the dishwasher, sink, and cabinet business. The latter two we kept until the mid-sixties before dropping them because of their contribution to overhead. This contribution helped in the early days.
>
> Starting with less than 100 employees and sales of 60,000 units we have grown to a position of being the largest producer of dishwashers in the world with over 25% of the U.S. market. Our sales go to a leading national retailer and to 12 manufacturers. We now have in excess of 1,600 employees.
>
> Prices have fallen over the last 12 years. We have, however, at the same time reduced costs considerably, but our margin has also decreased. [See Exhibit 1 for financial data.] Total profits have definitely increased.

An executive employed by a competitor, in commenting on D&M's performance, said, "D&M is privately held so I don't have any numbers, but based on what I do know I can safely state D&M's financial and growth performance is exceptional for this or any other industry."

D&M'S STRATEGY

In commenting on D&M's strategy Mr. Regenstrief stated:

> Our basic approach hasn't really changed over the last 12 years. We are in business to make as high profits as possible by fashioning and manufacturing a quality dishwasher and selling it to national retailers and other manufacturers. To succeed we have to have a product of competitive quality and a low cost position in the industry.
>
> The reason that the low cost position is crucial is that we can succeed only if we can sell a product for less than our customer can make it or buy it elsewhere. Our maximum margin is determined entirely by our production efficiency relative to our customers, our present competitors and our future competitors.
>
> Given the importance of cost to this approach, I have been concerned with getting volume up and costs down since day one. We needed volume to have the operating efficiencies necessary for low cost. But we also need the most efficient product facility possible. As a result, we often scrap a piece of machinery a year or two after we buy it, if we can replace it with a better machine.
>
> The whole reason for starting D&M was that I felt that we could get the volume to make the strategy work. G.E. was skimming the cream off the market and no one was around to do what I wanted to do. The market had obvious growth potential. By getting it first and getting the volume, we could have a natural advantage.
>
> Things have changed in the last 12 years. G.E., for example, is now willing to slug it out on a cost basis where volume is involved. But we have the volume and the efficiency now to play this game profitably. No one can match our production costs today.

In summarizing D&M's strategy, one executive said: "Sam knew precisely what segment of the market he was going after; he hit it at exactly the right time; and he has set up a tightly run organization to take full advantage of these opportunities."

D&M'S ORGANIZATION

In describing the organization he had developed at D&M, Mr. Regenstrief stated:

> I could draw you an organization chart with vice presidents in charge of production, engineering, new product development, etc., on it, but it would be meaningless. We have a very informal operation here. Each of my executives has a general area of responsibility but there are no empires here. If I see that production costs are out of line for a given day, I don't call up Bud Kaufman, my production vice president. I call the foreman responsible and find out why. If his explanation doesn't suit me or it happens again, then I talk to Bud.
>
> When I or any of my executives see a problem, they deal with it. We can't afford the time or the money to go through formal channels. Everyone knows that's the way things work around here and accepts it.
>
> My general approach is to keep the corporate overhead as low as possible. I want the best possible managers, but as few as possible. The same is true with our data collection. I want to know exactly what is going on in as few numbers as possible.
>
> Red tape would kill this organization. It would raise our costs and slow us down. We have to be ready to turn on a dime and this takes a lean, flexible organization not a fat, rigid one.

In discussing compensation, Mr. Regenstrief stated:

> Our executives are rewarded heavily on the basis of corporate performance. Bonuses in a good year may be greater than salary. We carry this philosophy down to the worker level. A worker may earn 25% of his salary in bonus during a good year. Since our basic wage is competitive with other manufacturers, this means that we are among the highest paying firms in the industry.
>
> We do this not out of a sense of altruism but rather to guarantee that we get maximum effort out of everyone.

In talking about D&M, Mr. Glenn "Bud" Kaufman, vice president in charge of production, made the following comments.

> There is no "red tape" at D&M. We each deal with the problems we see. This goes all the way down to the worker. If he is going to run out of parts it is his responsibility to get them—not just tell his foreman.
>
> I guess this is what I like about D&M. The hours are long. I get here at 6:15 A.M. and leave after 6:00 P.M. Last year there might have been three Saturdays I didn't work. But the pay is good and I can see the results of the work I do. I couldn't stand to work in a big company where everything has to get approved by five different people.

Throughout the company, the casewriter observed a strong commitment to getting cost down and volume up by whatever means were necessary. Cutting across functional lines in this endeavor appeared to be the rule rather than the exception.

FUNCTIONAL POLICIES

D&M's strategy was predicated on strengths in several key functional areas—particularly production, sales, finance, new product development, and quality control and service. This section will look at D&M's policies in each of these key areas.

Production policy

Bud Kaufman commented on D&M's production policy as follows:

> Our approach to production is based on two concepts—simplicity and standardization. We want to produce the least complicated product possible because it will be cheaper to make and more reliable. At the same time we strive to get as many standardized parts as possible for each model. Since we sell several different models to 13 different customers, it is crucial that we get as much standardization as possible in the parts. This allows us longer production runs and lower costs.
>
> We are continually installing new, more efficient equipment. The age of the equipment we replace is not important. We are continually looking for the best way to make the product. We have a subsidiary company that specializes in machinery and equipment and automation with the aim in mind of reducing material usage, improving the quality, and offering the latest in automation. I feel this is a tribute to our production leadership.
>
> Another factor that contributes to our efficiency is ingenuity. For example, what is now our main plant used to be made up of several buildings. We realized that we could speed the flow up if we had all these operations in one building. But we couldn't afford to shut down to build a new plant. Sam and an architect figured out the solution—build the new plant over the existing buildings and then tear them out. They got the plant we needed without slowing production.

Throughout the company the casewriter observed a strong concern with daily volume and cost in relation to schedule. Meeting or bettering this schedule was the prime concern of almost everyone at D&M.

Sales policy

In commenting on sales Mr. Regenstrief said:

> I handle sales. The crucial three factors in each contract are price, volume, and design specification. These are obviously related.
>
> In setting the price I start with a margin I am trying to achieve for our total sales. But with regard to each of 13 companies I set the price based on what they could produce it for and/or what it will take to keep them in business. Hence, I have to consider the companies' volume and their marketing and distribution costs. I want to supply as many companies as possible but only if each of them can give me the volume I need.
>
> With regard to design I give more leeway to the companies with higher volume. I occasionally will give a new company more leeway than their volume deserves to get them established in the market. But if the volume doesn't come I won't carry them. In the long run custom designing for a customer has to be justified by volume. If I didn't follow this philosophy our costs would go sky-high.

In support of this approach to sales all inventory was carried at direct cost. Mr. Regenstrief explained the reason as follows: "Given our approach to the industry what I need to know is the direct cost. The product doesn't make us any money until it is sold regardless of what we inventory it at."

Financial policy

D&M was privately held with 97% of the stock owned by members of the company. Mr. Regenstrief owned the vast majority of this stock. One D&M director described the effect of this as follows:

> Since the company is privately held, Sam doesn't have to worry about earnings per share. The result of this is that he can scrap equipment and take a capital loss without worrying about the short-term impact on profits. In my opinion this freedom has contributed strongly to D&M's present strong position.

D&M had no substantial long-term debt at the time of the case. The rapid expansion in output, and hence plant and equipment, throughout the 1960s was financed almost entirely out of current profits. As one D&M executive described it, "After the first couple of years, the capital needed for expansion didn't really make much of a dent in current profits."

New product development

"Our basic philosophy in this area is to maintain D&M's position in the industry by helping our customers maintain theirs," said Dr. Harold DeGroff, vice president of new product development and professor of business policy at Purdue University. "We basically work in three areas—new features, environmental acceptance (e.g., noise and safety), and new processes. The first area is handled by our engineering staff at Connersville while the second two areas are handled at a facility we built in Lafayette, Indiana, near Purdue University.

In commenting on the feature aspect of product development, Dr. DeGroff stated:

> To understand our approach you have to understand the needs of our customers. The large national retailer we sell to needs a product of competitive quality that he can sell at a low price. He is particularly concerned with having unique features, and he also needs to have those successful features that his competitors have.
>
> With the rest of our customers, dishwashers serve the purpose of broadening their product line. They need the dishwasher especially for the builder market, and this market is highly competitive.

In commenting on the environmental acceptance and process segments of the operation Dr. DeGroff stated:

> These two operations are located in Lafayette because they draw heavily on Purdue for part-time consultants. We work in these two areas to protect ourselves. In areas like noise and safety we are continually faced with the threat of new standards or tightening of old standards. We have to be ready to respond.

In the area of new processes, we are faced with the threat of a whole new way to clean dishes. We are periodically working on ultra-sonics and other approaches to protect ourselves from being out of business should one of these new technologies come to market.

The reason for using part-time help is not because it is cheaper— I am not entirely sure that it is. Rather we can get people with highly specialized skills to deal with each problem. These people are experts in their respective area and hence minimize the chance that we will overlook something.

It was generally agreed at D&M that the chief thrust of their product development was defensive. However, having a good defense resulted in occasional innovations. Finally, D&M occasionally introduced a new feature or product (e.g., the counter top dishwasher) where they felt that there could be considerable demand and being first would be a strong advantage.

Service and quality control

Though D&M did not service the appliances they sold, they were responsible for service incurred during the warranty period. As a result of this responsibility D&M was greatly concerned with quality control.

D&M's approach to quality control was twofold. First, they were continually concerned with designing as simple a product as possible. They felt that a simple product would be less likely to break down and would be cheaper to service if it did. Second, they had a rigid inspection system throughout the production operation, and they are continually going through a "customer acceptance" check where the product is thoroughly tested to assure that the day's production meets the rigid quality necessary.

Since D&M was responsible for repairs incurred during warranty, they also engaged in training their customers' service personnel. The rationale for this was to minimize the service expense for any given breakdown by improving the efficiency of the customers' field service staff.

In commenting on the problem of quality control, Mr. Lee Burke, executive vice president, stated:

We are becoming more and more concerned about improving the reliability of our product. The reason for this increasing concern is that repair costs are rising very rapidly. This rise in cost stems from the fact that repair work is highly labor intensive and labor costs are rising quickly. Hence, it is cheaper to handle as much as possible of the problem in the factory.

D&M'S FUTURE

In commenting on the future Mr. Regenstrief stated:

The future looks good. Only 25% of the U.S. homes have dishwashers. This means that there is considerable growth potential for the product. If anything, the market share of national retailers will expand because they offer the greatest value. Hence, I see no reason to expect our growth to slow.

Of course I am concerned about competition. A lot of companies would like to take our business away from us. To do that they would need our volume. The only way they could get it is if they introduced a significantly better product and could match our costs. Since we are continually improving our product I doubt if anyone could do this. But it is certainly something we are always looking at. It is one reason we stay lean and flexible. We must be able to move quickly to match any major changes in the product.

Another D&M executive described what he viewed as D&M's biggest threat as follows:

I doubt if any company could take our market away from us. What I see as the biggest problem is making sure that someone in our organization will be able to carry on as a replacement for Sam. Sam is in his early 60s. He is without a doubt the most creative, energetic, dynamic person I have ever known. He built D&M and runs it with superb skill.

It was in this environment that D&M faced the future. The plans for 1972 showed no decrease in D&M's sales or profit growth.

Exhibit 1

DESIGN AND MANUFACTURING CORPORATION
Unit Volume, Dollar Sales, and Margin Growth
(1961 = 100%)

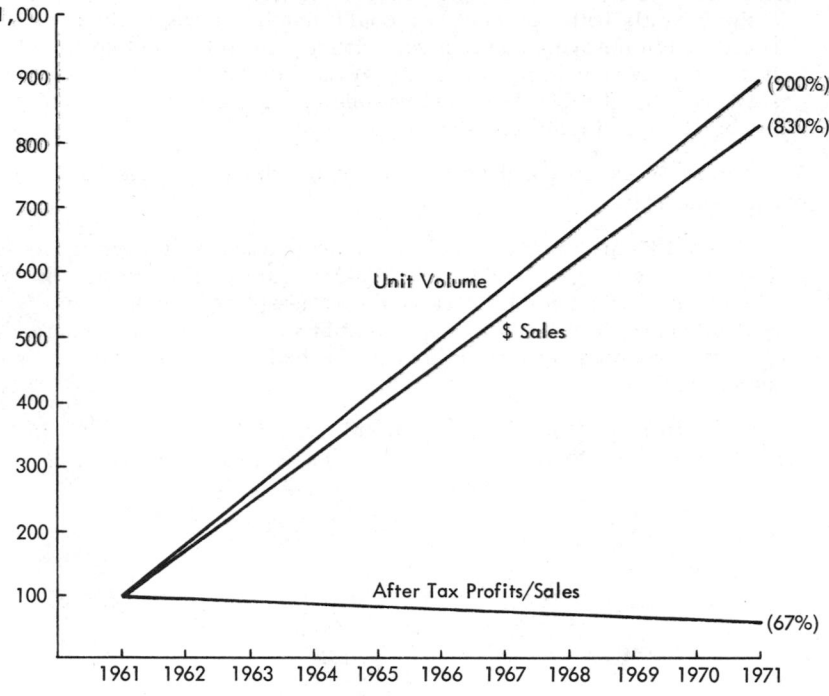

Tappan Company (A)

"My biggest problem is the competition, especially the giants like GE, Frigidaire, and Whirlpool," commented Mr. W. "Dick" Tappan, president of the Tappan Co. "The appliance industry is a numbers game and we're a pretty small number. The critical problems facing me as president are how do we survive now, and how do we get to a big number in the future. Certainly one option is to sell out, but frankly I, and most of our executives, wouldn't like the loss of freedom. Hence, we want to make it and make it as an independent."

HISTORY

The Eclipse Stove Co. was founded in 1881 as a partnership by W. J. Tappan, W. A. Gorby, and H. M. Lewis. They produced and sold cast-iron ranges both coal and wood burning. When Mr. Tappan married the "favorite" niece of Mr. Gorby who had provided the financial backing, Mr. Lewis was bought out and the name was changed in 1921 to the Tappan Stove Co. Its location was in Mansfield, Ohio, and W. J. Tappan was president. The name was changed again in 1957 to the Tappan Co. The presidency of Tappan Co. has continued to be filled by Tappans with W. R. Tappan assuming the presidency in 1962 upon the retirement of his uncle, Alan P. Tappan.

The twentieth century saw the Tappan Co. move from wood and coal burning ranges to gas-fueled ranges. Tappan built the first porcelain enamel range and the first insulated range. By 1946, out of 140 competitors Tappan was a leading producer of gas ranges with about 8% of the market.

Since 1946, the company has continued to grow. Two major sources have been increased market share in the growing range market and new products deriving primarily from acquisitions. Though the rationale for diversification was the low growth potential of the highly saturated range market and the marketing advantages arising from offering a broader range of kitchen products, development of the gas range business, and Tappan's diversification will be described separately.

RANGE BUSINESS

Between 1946 and 1950, three major decisions were made concerning the Tappan range business. First, realizing the growing importance of electric ranges (see Exhibit 1), Tappan designed and produced its first electric range. Also during this time Tappan began experimentation with microwave cooking, obtaining a license for the basic technology from Raytheon. The rationale for entry into microwave cooking was twofold. First, Tappan felt that this quick cooking method would eventually revolutionize the range industry. Second, Tappan was still thought of by consumers and more importantly by retailers as a gas range company. By having the most advanced product on the market it was hoped that Tappan's credibility as a producer of electric ranges would be improved. Tappan introduced the first electronic range in 1954. Though Tappan continued its efforts in microwave cooking, it did not become the success envisioned and efforts were slowed in 1970.

The second major decision was to build a large modern gas range plant in Murray, Kentucky. This 285,000-square-foot plant was designed to be one of the most efficient facilities in the country. It was located near the population center of the United States and in a region that appeared to have low labor costs. Labor trouble developed almost from the start, however, and the construction of a federal atomic energy plant nearby accentuated the problem. Plagued by strikes, the plant was almost closed down at one point and not until the mid-1950s did it become profitable. By 1970, however, the plant, now expanded, had capacity to produce 340,000 ranges per year and was Tappan's most efficient range plant. (See Exhibit 2.)

The third major decision was to acquire O'Keefe and Merrit, a leading West Coast manufacturer of branded gas ranges. (See Exhibit 3 for financial data.) Dick Tappan described the reasons for the move:

> The West Coast at this time [late 1940s] was a different market. Ranges sold on the West Coast had more chrome and different features, like built-in griddles, from those sold elsewhere. Also there was a substantial freight disadvantage for eastern manufacturers competing with local companies. We felt the fastest and best way to get into this market was by acquiring one of the best producers of gas ranges on the West Coast. O'Keefe and Merrit (O&M) fit this plan well.
>
> Unfortunately, 1950, the year we acquired O&M was their best year ever. Since we have maintained the O&M brand, O&M has also posed a management problem to us. They often find themselves in direct competition with the Tappan brand and since O&M is a separate profit center, friction has often developed between the Tappan and O&M divisions.

By 1970 the O&M division had the capacity to produce 200,000 ranges per year.

Though these three decisions increased the breadth of the range line and production capacity, the basic strategy for competing in the range market remained unchanged from that followed prior to 1946. One Tappan executive described this strategy as follows:

> We sold a high quality range with the newest features to retailers and contractors under the Tappan and O'Keefe and Merrit brands.

Basic changes in the appliance industry, however, led to a reexamination of this strategy by the mid-1960s.

"The growing power of large full-line manufacturers with the retailers,[1] the increasing sales of private and national retail brands, and the increasing importance of electric range sales where we were still at a disadvantage because of our late entry led us to consider new markets for ranges," stated Mr. Dick Tappan. Tappan chose to enter the private brand market by selling to Montgomery Ward on a contractual basis and selling ranges to Admiral from whom Tappan purchased refrigerators.[2] Tappan also went after the mobile home market, which was primarily gas. By 1970, these new markets (private brand and mobile home) accounted for 30% of the Tappan division sales and more than one third of Tappan's ranges went to these markets. The basic strategy for Tappan brand products in the traditional markets remained unchanged.

HISTORY OF DIVERSIFICATION

In 1956, Tappan sold only ranges. By 1970, about 35% of the Tappan corporate sales were outside the range market. The first move toward product diversification came with the introduction of the Tappan dishwasher in 1957. Tappan manufactured this dishwasher with reversing spray arms[3] at its Mansfield plant. According to Mr. Dick Tappan, "The rationale for entering the dishwasher business was simple. We were selling a lot of gas ranges to builders. Up until 1957, the range was just about all that was built in by the builder. But with the increasing popularity of the dishwasher more and more of these were being built in. Selling dishwashers strengthened our position in the builder market and was profitable in and of itself."

The next major move toward product diversification came with the acquisition of the Crystal Disposal Co. (1963) and the Whirlaway Disposer Co. (1964) both producers of electric food waste disposers. (See

---

[1] Large retailers relied more heavily on the full-line manufacturers—partly because these full-line manufacturers could reduce shipping and inventory costs and partly because to get the volume necessary to run a high-volume retail outlet the retailers had to carry the major brands. Single product producers found it increasingly difficult during the 1960s to get retail floor space.

[2] In 1971, the company's largest single customer, Montgomery Ward, accounted for approximately 10% of sales. A majority of Ward's gas and electric range sales were supplied by Tappan under an agreement that extended to December 31, 1973. The company also sold trash compactors and portable electronic air cleaners to Montgomery Ward.

[3] By developing spray arms that reversed, Tappan increased the cleaning performance of their dishwashers in comparison with the existing machines on the market at that time.

Exhibit 3 for Tappan's expenditures on each of its acquisitions.) These two acquisitions were merged into the Anaheim Manufacturing Co. and a new 52,000-square-foot facility was built to house it. Anaheim produced disposers to be sold under the Tappan, O'Keefe and Merrit, Whirlaway, and private brands. Anaheim set a pattern of multiple branding that was followed in future acquisitions. The Tappan and O'Keefe and Merrit brand disposers were transferred at the market price to the respective range divisions to be distributed. The Whirlaway brand was sold by Anaheim salesmen as were the private brands.

The Anaheim division pioneered in private brand selling of disposers by designing a disposer that could be assembled on one assembly line with the individual features any private brand wanted. This flexibility in production made Anaheim the low-cost producer of disposers in the country. Anaheim had capacity to make 1,000,000 disposers a year.

The next step in the diversification program was Tappan's acquisition in 1964 of Nautilus Industries of Freeland, Pennsylvania. Nautilus was the nation's largest producer of nonduct ventilating fans and hoods for bathrooms and kitchens. As with Anaheim, Nautilus sold under the Nautilus brand and also produced Tappan brand products sold through the Tappan division. Transfer pricing was not as easy for Nautilus products as there was not a readily usable market price. The Nautilus products were transferred at standard cost plus a markup.

Tappan acquired Kemper Brothers Cabinet in 1965 and in 1969 acquired Quaker Maid, the "Cadillac" of the kitchen cabinet industry. Tappan also built a 150,000-square-foot cabinet plant in Williamsport, Pa., to make Kemper and Tappan cabinets. The rationale for going into kitchen and bathroom cabinets was stated by Mr. Dick Tappan, as follows:

> Kitchen cabinets are the single most expensive item in a kitchen. Traditionally they have been made by carpenters in small shops. The market is still highly fragmented and is wide open for economies arising from mass production. Plants, however, will have to be limited in size because the market is regional in nature due to the high cost of shipping cabinets. Shipping boxes by air a long distance is prohibitively expensive.
>
> By getting into the market early and by growing rapidly to become the industry leader, we hope to establish Tappan in this industry. We now have a full range of cabinets in terms of price levels and sell under the Kemper, Quaker Maid, and Tappan brands.

Unlike the Anaheim and Nautilus divisions, the cabinet division, though selling cabinets under the Tappan brand, sold only through their own division's salesmen. Commenting on this Mr. Dick Tappan said, "Appliance salesmen just don't know how to sell cabinets. We tried getting them to sell Tappan cabinets and it was a failure."

Tappan had made various efforts to expand internationally during the 1950s and 1960s. Two major efforts had been made by setting up a Canadian subsidiary and a joint venture with Singer in Europe. Both of these had failed. Though it still had small international investments, by 1970 Tappan relied on licensing agreements as its primary source of income from foreign markets.

ORGANIZATIONAL HISTORY

Tappan had been functionally organized up until 1950. Later each of the acquired divisions was set up as an independent operating unit with the president of Tappan Co. also president of the Tappan division. By 1965, severe problems with this form of organization were developing. Mr. Dick Tappan commented as follows:

> I was trying to run the company while I was head of the Tappan division. I just couldn't do both as we got to be larger. Inventory was getting out of hand across the whole company and profits were dismal. In 1966 we set up a small corporate staff with division presidents reporting to it.

By 1970, the formal organization was as shown in Exhibit 4. Each division was a profit center. Division presidents received a bonus based half on their division's profits and half on corporate profits. This bonus might range as high as equal to their salary.

Besides the change in formal organization, other fundamental changes in the Tappan organization were initiated during the 1960s to improve corporate performance. Two areas where these changes were most dramatic were in corporate planning and inventory control.

"In 1963 Tappan was a marketing company," commented Mr. Walter Gummere, executive vice president. "Major decisions such as product design and wholesale price were made on the basis of the sales that would be generated." The result of this approach was a proliferation of models as each regional sales manager pushed for the design and price that would fit his needs. Salesmen also tended to order large numbers of potential "hot items" in order to be able to guarantee delivery. The result was a rapid increase in inventory.

Along with the change in formal organization, Tappan implemented a formal planning system—called Blueprint Planning. Mr. Gummere described this change as follows.

> We didn't change overnight. We worked steadily to get our division executives to think in terms of profits—first in terms of total division profits and eventually down to profit for each model. The planning system allows us to communicate with the divisions. They tell us what we can expect one year out and in general for the next five years. We tell them what we need. Then we work out a detailed plan for the next year for each division.

By 1970, formal planning was in full operation at Tappan.

In the mid-1960s Tappan also hired an outside consulting firm to do a large systems analysis of the Tappan Co. with a view toward gaining a tighter control over inventory. By 1970, a new inventory control system and production scheduling system were under way. During 1971, inventory was reduced by $5 million in the face of more than a 10 percent increase in sales. Complaints as to late delivery also dropped drastically. The results of these two programs were described by Mr. Gummere as follows, "Tappan is still a marketing-oriented company, but we have moved so as to take advantage of our marketing skills rather than being led by them."

PERFORMANCE

The 1960s saw Tappan's sales almost double, rising from $71.5 million to $131.9 million. But during 1966–1970 return on assets and on equity fell considerably from the 1961–65 level. (See Exhibit 5.) Commenting on the low profits, Mr. Dick Tappan noted:

> There were several reasons for this downturn. First the company was getting out of control. Second, about half of our sales go to builders. The last half of the 1960s was very bad for the construction industry—especially 1967. In 1967 we bought market share by cutting our prices and profits fell off. The reorganization and other steps to get the company back under control didn't take effect until 1968. They did improve overall operations, but 1970 was another bad year for housing starts.

The upturn in the economy in 1971 led to record third-quarter profits for Tappan.

Tappan was still primarily a range producer in 1970. In 1969, 67% of corporate sales were ranges, 12% were cabinets, 5% were hoods and fans, 5% were disposers, 6% were dishwashers, 3% were refrigerators, and 2% were from foreign operations and other sources. The bulk of profits, however, came from ranges and disposers. The casewriter estimated that these two products contributed 90% of total corporate profits. Cabinets (Kemper and Quaker Maid), dishwashers, and refrigerators were estimated to contribute 10%. The Williamsport cabinet facility ran at a loss, as did the Nautilus division.

Tappan had increased its market share in the range industry steadily through the decades of the 1930s, 1940s, and 1950s up to about 10% of the total market. From 1960 through 1968, Tappan's market share fluctuated but drifted downward. Then the addition of private brand business and gas ranges for mobile homes reversed the trend, as Tappan's market share rose dramatically to 13% of the total market.[4] Tappan Co. had about 17% of the gas market and 9% of the electric market in 1970 as compared with 10% and 6%, respectively in 1965.[5] The casewriter estimated that Tappan had about 15% of the disposal market and about 4% of the dishwasher market in 1970.

PRODUCT-MARKET STRATEGY—1971

The two major problems facing the Tappan Company as described earlier by Mr. Dick Tappan—short-run survival and long-run success—provide a basis for analyzing Tappan's history and its present strategy. One Tappan executive explained the reason for dual strategies as follows:

---

[4] According to industry sources, mobile home production in 1971 was 491,700 units, up from 217,300 in 1966. Tappan's share of the market increased from approximately 11% to 40% and represented 19% of total net sales of ranges.

[5] Tappan's profitable growth occurred during a period of rapid increase in concentration—especially in the gas range market. In 1946, there were 140 producers of gas ranges as compared with about a dozen in 1970.

We can't beat the GEs at their own game. If we followed the traditional approach to the industry we would either be driven out of
business or become a supplier of private brand goods. We would lose
our key resource—the Tappan name. Hence, the key is to come up
with new products and new approaches to existing products. But this
takes time and hence we have to concentrate on profitable survival in
the short-run as well as long-run success.

In this section the short-run and long-run product-market strategies of
Tappan will be described. The next section will look at the key functional policies of Tappan. The last section will look at the internal and
external threats to the success of these strategies.

The short-run strategy

Mr. Tappan commented:

One of the biggest problems we face is keeping our products on the
retail floor. Full-line producers use the power of their line and sales
incentives like "trips"[6] to push us off the floor. The loss of retail floor
space means not only lost retail sales but less opportunity to build
brand image. Brand image is built at the retail level, but is crucial to
the builder market.

A second major disadvantage when compared to the full-line producers is higher sales costs and somewhat higher production costs.
A GE salesman might sell $1 million worth of appliances compared
with less than half that for a Tappan salesman. On the production
side the Mansfield and O'Keefe and Merrit facilities are higher cost
plants than some of the newer plants in the industry.

Tappan's short-run strategy was designed to attempt to offset these
weaknesses. "To get into the retail outlets we have to have a product
with unique features," stated Mr. Tappan. "We have to give the retailer
something no one else has—something he can sell."

Some of the recent examples of these features for Tappan were the
"Pan-O-Matic" (see Exhibit 6), the smooth top range (one that did not
require special utensils), and the gallery warming shelf.

On the cost reduction side Tappan made several efforts to improve its
cost competitiveness. Mr. Tappan commented, "The private brand
business and mobile home business are low margin business but high
turnover. They not only are profitable because of the high turnover and
low sales costs, but absorb a large chunk of overhead that helps reduce
the cost of other Tappan ranges." Tappan had also attempted to reduce
the number of models and standardize the chassis for ranges to reduce
production costs. The latter effort had been highly successful.

"By selling unique highly featured products we have been able to
command a retail price premium that has more than compensated for
our cost disadvantage," stated Mr. Tappan. "The builder market is
easier for us since the big companies like GE didn't sell gas ranges until

---

[6] Many appliance firms, especially full-line producers, gave retail salesmen bonuses like trips to Europe or Mexico in return for selling more than a certain number of various types of their appliances.

very recently. We have been able to get a lot of business because of our high brand image and selling both gas and electric ranges."

Dishwashers presented a different short-run problem. Tappan had developed a dishwasher in 1957 that was unique. It gained considerable acceptance in the builder trade and sold 60,000 units in 1970. But these were all undercounter units. To get production costs down to make dishwashers meet the corporate objectives for profitability Tappan had to increase volume drastically. Tappan couldn't source dishwashers because of their unique design.

To get the volume needed for production economies Tappan had to go after the portable dishwasher market dominated by Sears, GE, and Hobart. The problem was that the existing product even if produced in higher volume would be too expensive to sell in the portable market. A good competitively priced portable dishwasher would strengthen Tappan's position in the retail market as well as increase dollar sales per salesman. A new dishwasher design was needed and much of Tappan's short-run success in this market would be based on its design.

Another problem that faced Tappan Co. was the strong tendency of its divisions—especially the Tappan and O&M divisions—to concentrate sales efforts on the products they produced because they could make higher division profits. The divisions often gave their salesmen a higher percent commission on their own products. Added to this was the desire of the O&M division to not make Tappan ranges even though they could set longer production runs and lower costs. Here the reason was that they would have to give up to the Tappan division the production of the higher price/higher featured ranges. It was felt by many corporate executives that an integral part of the survival strategy would be a new form of organization and control system that would solve these problems.

One final short-run problem facing Tappan was improving the profitability of current nonrange operations. This was especially urgent for the Williamsport cabinet plant and the Nautilus division. It was felt that the Williamsport plant would improve as Tappan developed a more efficient marketing operation for cabinets. At the time of the case Williamsport was operating well below 50% of its capacity and hence costs were well above the break-even point. The Nautilus division, however, posed a more serious problem because its Nautilus brand image was poor. This was compounded by the fact that the Tappan division was not as interested in selling Nautilus products under the Tappan brand. The hope for Nautilus rested with the development of new products which will be discussed later and cost reduction from tighter management.

In terms of the long-run cost reduction the systems study undertaken in the late 1960s was felt to offer great promise in reducing inventory and lengthening production runs. A new plant under construction in Ontario, Ohio, near Mansfield with eventual capacity for 500,000 ranges was described by one manufacturing executive "as guaranteeing our long-term cost position." The plant was being built in stages starting with a 300,000-square-foot distribution center already completed.

Then the assembly, paint, and metal fabrication sections would be built in that order. This method would allow the subcontracting of the incompleted sections to outside firms as well as other Tappan plants. In this way the plant could upon completion operate at full capacity of 250,000 units. Then it could be expanded to 500,000 units. Another advantage of this method was that if demand for ranges fell off, the plant construction could be slowed down.

The long-run success strategy

If the short-run survival strategy was to be based on improving Tappan's operations and profitability in traditional markets, "the long-run success strategy was," as Mr. Tappan described it, "based on new approaches to the appliance industry and new products while continuing to hold Tappan's position in traditional markets." The rationale for this strategy was the limited growth potential in the traditional appliance market where GE and other large manufacturers were dominant and would remain so even if Tappan's short-run strategy was a success.

Though Tappan was interested in new products and approaches, it limited its search to the "core of the home"—the kitchen, the heating/air-conditioning system, and bathroom. Mr. Tappan explained the rationale for this as follows:

> The core of the home makes up about 35% of the construction cost of a home or apartment. We feel that concentrating on this core offers the best chance for long-run success for several reasons.
>
> First, a home that is heated and cooled by electricity is unlikely to be hooked up for gas. With the advent of electric air-conditioning peak demand for electricity moved from the winter to the summer in many areas. Given that electric utilities are highly capital intensive, they responded by lowering their rates in the winter, making electric heat more attractive than gas. The result was that an incremental number of new homes are heated by electricity and hence not hooked up for gas.
>
> This phenomenon has been partially responsible for the decline in gas cooking. If we could develop an efficient gas air-conditioner we could get gas into more homes. This development not only offers a large market for heating/air-conditioning units but it would increase the sale of gas ranges where we are still the strongest.
>
> A second reason for considering the core of the home as our market is that it presents the opportunity for new approaches to the industry. By viewing the kitchen as our product rather than individual appliances we pioneered in developing the kitchen wall [see Exhibit 7]. The kitchen wall contains all the kitchen appliances and cabinets. It can be assembled in the factory and shipped completed to the builder. This means that much relatively expensive construction labor can be eliminated.
>
> There are two major problems with the kitchen wall. First, the construction unions are opposed to it. However, the need for lower cost housing is so great that the unions in many areas are already giving in. The second disadvantage is that to get the cost down these units have to be shipped nine to the truckload. Not many builders com-

plete nine units at a time. This means that the unit must be kept in inventory. This is not only expensive, but increases the probability that they will be damaged.

But if we build a bathroom on the back of the wall and put in a heating and air-conditioning unit we can put two into a truckload rather than nine. There are a lot of builders that finish two units at a time.

A third advantage to viewing the core unit as our market stems from the remodeling business. There are 40 million dwelling units that need a new core. With the rising cost of housing many people will turn to remodeling rather than buying a new house. But the remodeling business is highly fragmented and no one does a very good job of meeting the customer needs.

We are approaching this market segment with the Tappan Home Center [see Exhibit 8]. The Home Center will have six to thirteen model kitchens and several model bathrooms in it. It will have the facilities to custom design a kitchen, install it via reliable subcontractors, and finance it through channels we have set up.

The Home Center will be set up as a franchise limiting our capital commitment to it. It will display and sell our full line of cabinets and appliances. It will pay its subcontractors a premium over the going price in return for a guarantee that they will meet all scheduled commitments. Hence, a kitchen will have to be torn up for only a couple of days rather than several weeks as often happens now.

The problem with the Home Centers to date has been finding and training people to run them. It is important that a Home Center should develop a good reputation in its area, which means that it has to be run well. We are moving slowly opening up a few a year for the time being. People trained in one then can go out and start new ones. We hope to be able to expand more rapidly in the future.

We are also moving into new products for the home. We have designed and are ready to market what we feel is the best compactor on the market. We have a new electrostatic air cleaner and are working on many other new products. [See Exhibit 9.] But again these pertain to the core of the home.

Though the above describes the basis for much of Tappan's growth in the future, it was agreed by most Tappan executives that the existing business would contribute to the success and that businesses like Montgomery Ward and mobile homes would someday provide a substantial market for these new products just as they did now for traditional appliances.

Mr. Tappan commented on research and development possibilities:

We don't have the money or the talent to undertake research and development on a lot of these sophisticated products. We really scramble a lot to get the money and the talent. For example, we made a presentation to the American Gas Association and explained why it would benefit them to fund our research on a low-cost gas air-conditioning/heating unit. We got a substantial sum from them to do this research. We often go directly to companies that are doing research that we might be able to use. We went to Thermo-Electron when we heard about their work in heating and cooling. We worked out an agreement with them so that we got the rights to the commercial applications of their research. We exchanged some of our stock for 5% of their stock which in and of itself turned out to be a pretty good deal.

Tappan was engaged in joint projects with a large number of companies and organizations like Thermo-Electron, AGA, Rheem, Owens-Illinois, Pittsburgh Plate Glass, Honeywell, Philco-Ford, and others (see Exhibit 9). One Tappan executive commenting on this stated, "Dick Tappan's greatest contribution in the long run may well be his ability to get other companies to develop new products for us often while also providing the money."

FUNCTIONAL POLICIES

The short- and long-run product strategies described in the preceding section were dependent for their success on the various functional policies—particularly finance, new product development, manufacturing, and sales and service. In this section each of these policies will be discussed and the next section will consider the potential threat from the environment.

Financial Policy

"The financial criteria for investment are that they make 5%, net of tax, on sales and 15% return on gross investment," said Mr. Lorin Ellison, vice president and controller. "These are what we view as reasonable corporate goals and not the result of an elaborate financial analysis. Acquisitions are judged on their short-term impact on earnings per share and how the product fits in."

Commenting on capital budgeting and control, Mr. Ellison stated:

> We don't go in for highly sophisticated financial analysis of investment projects. We look at whether they meet the objectives and at the pay back. Until recently we approved almost all the requests. But, the capital spending of $9 million in 1969 and 1970 created a cash drain. Hence we placed a $2.5 million year limit on capital expenditures for 1971. However, the expenditures for 1972 and beyond will be substantially greater. This may mean that we have to consider individual expenditures more closely.
>
> Big expenditures that relate to the long-run success of the company are occasionally made on the basis of "gut feel." We won't undertake them if they are considerably below our stated corporate objectives for investments or acquisitions, but they don't necessarily have to meet our short-run financial objectives.

Mr. Walter Gummere explained the reason for this "gut feel" approach:

> Often you just don't have time to do an elaborate analysis—especially in acquisitions where other firms are interested. It is also true that in some situations where the long-run success of the company is at stake short-run profitability may be outweighed by the long-term impact.

It was generally felt by Tappan executives that the flexibility allowed by this "gut feel" approach was crucial to Tappan's success.

In further commenting on the nature of capital budgeting, Mr. Ellison stated:

> We have become slightly more sophisticated over the last several years. We track investment projects via an internal audit so that we can judge whether they meet the estimates. We also have developed a more formalized planning system.
>
> The impetus for these changes has come partly from our rapid growth and diversification which requires more formal control. The impetus has also come partly from new members on the board who want this information.
>
> We will become more formal in the future as we need to be, but this change will be an evolutionary one, not a revolutionary one.

New product development policy

New product development and product innovation were of crucial importance to both Tappan's short- and long-run strategies. Mr. Chuck Lair, corporate manager of product development, described Tappan's activities as follows:

> For a long time we were a pretty small company. Most of our innovations came internally. The "Fabulous 400," the first over-under double oven range was developed internally in the late 1950s. That one innovation nearly doubled our sales in one year. It was copied by Frigidaire about a year later and we lost a legal suit protecting our design. Most innovations follow this pattern of being copied within a year or two.
>
> Most product innovations still come internally. We read all the scientific literature, our salesmen make suggestions, our design engineers make suggestions, and we get 600 to 700 calls a year from independent inventors. I circulate a letter periodically to the divisions listing potential new products and innovations. Often divisions don't have the man-hours to undertake development of these suggestions, but sometimes they do.
>
> For example, after Whirlpool introduced the compactor, I asked our divisions if any of them would be interested in developing one. Anaheim had two engineers with some free time. In six months they designed and tested a compactor that was more efficient and easier to use than Whirlpool's. We got it on the market in less than one year after we first thought about it. One of our largest competitors with a huge engineering staff wants to license it.
>
> Of course, we often don't have the man-hours to undertake major innovations. Here we go to independent design outfits to get the work done. For example, Ford has a lot of design engineers that are idle because Ford has cut back in its automobile design efforts. We approached Ford with a proposal to design a new product for us. It was in their interest to keep their men employed. We got some of their best men working on it—talent we couldn't afford to keep.
>
> Where innovations require basic research, we work almost entirely through our suppliers and outside companies. We can't afford basic research. But by not doing it ourselves we often can get a number of firms to do the development and, what's more, pick up the bill for it.

We get a lot of opinions and get to choose from a lot of different ideas. If we did it ourselves we would get locked in to one idea early in the development process. We have used this approach for projects like the smooth-top ranges and self-cleaning oven. In both cases we feel we have developed a better product than the introducer of the innovation. [Corning and GE, respectively.]

For entirely new products like the new gas heater and air-conditioner and others, we work entirely through outsiders. But here again they pick up a large chunk of the bill as do agencies like AGA.

Our total R&D budget runs between $1 million and $2 million a year. In addition we get half this much typically from outside sources —like our suppliers, AGA, and many others. You have to sell a lot of ranges to net over half a million dollars. Not only that but by using our approach we avoid a lot of overhead in high-priced talent.

Commenting on the disadvantages of using outside design and research, Mr. Lair stated:

There are some disadvantages. Occasionally you get locked into a project that limits you elsewhere. When working on the smooth-top range we guaranteed one firm that in return for their design we would introduce a gas smooth-top before an electric. It took us two years to get to the point that we could cost out their design and find that it was too expensive. That hurt us.

Suppliers occasionally make promises they can't keep because it turns out that they can't develop a product they thought they could. If we had our own talent we would be in a better position to judge their problems and evaluate their statements.

But I feel that the flexibility we get by shopping around offsets these disadvantages even ignoring the money we save.

Describing his job, Mr. Lair remarked:

I guess to be good at my job you have to be a carnival man—you have got to be able to sell dreams both outside and inside the organization. On the other hand you have to be pragmatic because you are dealing with engineers. If an engineer had been in charge of producing the first wheel he would still be trying to make it rounder and we would still be walking. You have to be able to say it's good enough, let's make it.

One football fan made the following statement that summarized Tappan's product development strategy as follows, "If you can't afford the best front line in football, it pays to have a quarterback who can scramble."

Manufacturing policy

One Tappan manufacturing manager said:

Marketing is the tail that wags the dog at Tappan. However, things have changed somewhat in the last few years. The company has limited the number of models and given us longer guaranteed orders (eight weeks instead of four). Because of this we have been able to standardize the chassis for the range and have cut production costs. Also, the longer orders allow longer production runs again reducing costs.

Commenting on the potential for future cost reduction one manufacturing executive said:

> The biggest opportunity for cost reduction will come from the new plant. It will have longer production lines which will reduce handling. It will have newer equipment in some areas. But most important it will give us the space to build a lot of components we are now sourcing. I think that we can make 20% to 30% return on investment by making some of these.

Commenting on the practice of redesigning products so as to cut cost, Mr. Lair stated:

> We don't do much of this in general—especially for ranges where we have a lot of volume. Where we do this is with something like the dishwasher. To go into the portable market we have to cut costs. We told our design engineers—design a dishwasher such that if we double our volume its costs will be let's say 75% of present cost.

Other ideas of cost cutting came from the production engineers, foremen and workers. When driving out to the Mansfield plant, the casewriter noted another car was parked in Mr. Dick Tappan's space. Mr. Tappan explained that each month one employee was given this for his cost-cutting suggestion. Other competitions of this nature netted cost reductions of about $1 million per year.

The location, size, and age of the company's principal facilities are set forth in Exhibit 2.

Sales distribution and service policy

Tappan had about 200 salesmen with about 120 of these in the Tappan division. These salesmen sold to retailers, large builders, and independent builder distributors. Until 1970, these salesmen were paid on straight commission and averaged about $14,000 per year. As was stated earlier in the case, commissions were often higher for products their divisions produced. One major change being undertaken at the time of the case was to switch salesmen to a base salary, plus commission and a bonus. The commission structure would not favor any division's products. The bonus would be based on whether the salesman sold the mix of products and models set out by the company. It was hoped that this method would get salesmen to sell products and particular models of these products that were most profitable to the company.

Tappan did no national television advertising because it was prohibitively expensive. But Tappan did provide prizes for give-away shows like "Queen for a Day." "This provides us with a lot of cheap publicity," stated Mr. Tappan. "It also gets to a large segment of our potential customers. Each show stresses the Tappan name and one feature. We get more out of this than magazine and co-op newspaper advertising where we spend a lot."

Distribution was also changing. Tappan had originally shipped to 60 private warehouses. The systems study suggested that Tappan set up its own central and regional warehouses. Tappan was in the process of implementing this suggestion, having completed construction of a central warehouse and planning of a dozen regional warehouses. "We still don't know what is in some of those old warehouses. With our new system we can get a computer printout that will tell us where everything is at any point in time," commented Mr. Tappan.

Tappan had factory service outlets in six cities. "We just don't have the volume to support factory service in any but the largest cities. We do, however, train in our factory the servicemen that we franchise. We are at a disadvantage here when compared with the giants. But we work on getting our franchised agents to do a good job."

THREATS FOR FUTURE SUCCESS

Mr. Dick Tappan commented on possible threats to success:

> Certainly one threat would be that none of our new products come to fruition, but given the number of projects and talent of people working on them as well as the need for them this is highly unlikely.
>
> The Japanese are a big threat. As appliances become more sophisticated and higher value in terms of physical volume the Japanese will be in a better position. They already have come out with a countertop microwave oven for $100 less than the American model. But the best way to prevent the Japanese from taking over the market is to develop more and better new products. If you stand still, you're dead. We have, also, sent a number of our men to Japan to look for opportunities for sourcing components and get a feel for what they are doing.

"Labor troubles could be a problem," Mr. Tappan said. "My dad was great with our employees, but I am more interested in new products. I could get us into trouble."

The casewriter noted, however, while walking through the plant at Mansfield that Mr. Tappan knew and was known by most of the employees. One worker stopped him and showed him a part that Tappan made in Mansfield and shipped to O&M where it was reworked and then shipped back to Mansfield. Later in the day, this situation was corrected. Another worker had a short discussion with him about the possibility of acquiring a favorite bird dog of Dick's. (The offer was refused.) Throughout the plant and the company first names were used and a very informal atmosphere prevailed.

Mr. Tappan summarized his problem as follows:

> The Tappan Co. is changing rapidly—it is growing and moving into new markets. These changes present managerial problems in terms of organization and other types. But to succeed we have to keep flexible and be ready to move. We can't become inflexible by over-reacting to our problems. We have to steer a delicate middle course if we are to become a big number in this numbers game.

Exhibit 1

TAPPAN COMPANY
Ratio of Gas to Electric Ranges Sales,
1934–67

Year	Ratio of gas ranges to electric ranges manufactured
1934	6.9
1935	5.1
1936	4.6
1937	3.5
1938	3.6
1939	4.5
1940	3.4
1941	3.1
1942	n.a.*
1943	n.a.*
1944	n.a.*
1945	n.a.*
1946	3.9
1947	2.0
1948	1.9
1949	1.9
1950	1.6
1951	1.6
1952	2.0
1953	1.7
1954	1.5
1955	1.4
1956	1.4
1957	1.4
1958	1.4
1959	1.2
1960	1.2
1961	1.2
1962	1.2
1963	1.1
1964	1.1
1965	1.0
1966	1.0
1967	1.1

* War year.
Source: Tappan Company records.

Exhibit 2

TAPPAN COMPANY

Property

The following table sets forth the location, size and age of the Company's principal facilities (all of which are owned by the Company), and the principal products or use of each:

Location	Approximate square feet (000) floor space	Original construction	Last major addition	Principal products or use
Mansfield, Ohio............	414	1875	1971	Gas, electric and electronic ranges, dishwashers
Ontario, Ohio..............	365	1970	1972	Warehouse for appliance products and data processing center
Elyria, Ohio...............	895	1900	1970	Air conditioning and heating products
Cleveland, Ohio............	70	1928	1954	Engineering laboratory for air conditioning division
Murray, Kentucky...........	420	1946	1970	Gas and electric ranges
Los Angeles, California.......	416	1933	1971	Gas and electric ranges, dishwashers
Richmond, Indiana..........	500	1909	1957	Kitchen cabinets and bathroom vanities
Anaheim, California..........	60	1970	1970	Food waste disposers
Leesport, Pennsylvania.......	200	1961	1968	Kitchen cabinets
Williamsport, Pennsylvania...	150	1969	1969	Kitchen cabinets

In addition, the company leases a 160,000-square-foot plant in Freeland, Pennsylvania, which presently is operated by the Nautilus Division.

Source: Prospectus, the Tappan Company, June 6, 1972.

Exhibit 3

TAPPAN COMPANY
Acquisitions

Name	Year acquired	Method of payment	Value ($)	Accounting treatment
O'Keefe & Merrit	1950	a) Cash b) 2-year notes c) Stock	a) $3,044,437 b) 200,000 c) 2,025,024* Total $5,269,461	Purchase
Tappan-Gurney†	1954–1968	Cash	1,609,000	Purchase
Crystal	1963	Stock	100,000*	Purchase
Hedland (Whirl-a-way).......	1964	Cash	2,556,000	Purchase
Nautilus............	1965	Stock	1,400,000*	Pooling
Kemper............	1965	Stock	5,039,663*	Pooling
Quaker Maid........	1969	a) Stock b) Cash	a) $5,825,000* b) 200,000 Total $6,025,000	Pooling/ Purchase

* Estimated value of stock at time of acquisition.
† Canadian operation.

Exhibit 4

TAPPAN COMPANY

Organization Chart, March 1, 1971

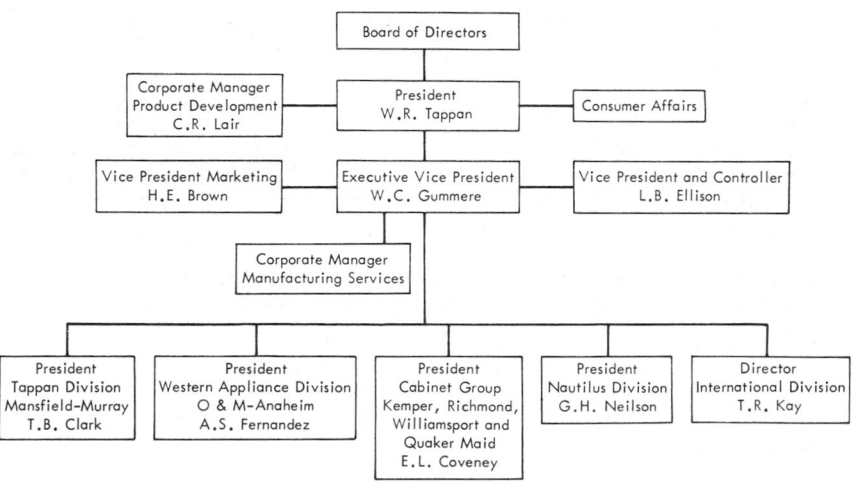

Source: Tappan Company, *Annual Report*, 1970.

Exhibit 5

TAPPAN COMPANY
Financial Data, 1961–70
(000s omitted)

	1970	1969	1968	1967	1966	1965	1964	1963	1962	1961
Financial results										
Sales	$131,892	$133,878	$124,209	$95,746	$97,175	$93,755	$85,775	$76,975	$72,994	$71,465
Earnings before federal income taxes	4,306	7,041	7,154	1,984	2,547	6,046	6,190	5,770	5,453	5,019
Federal income taxes	2,075	3,600	3,970	1,005	1,105	2,640	2,860	2,845	2,650	2,405
Net earnings	2,231	3,441	3,184	979	1,442	3,406	3,330	2,925	2,803	2,614
Depreciation provisions	1,688	1,266	1,058	1,104	1,176	1,134	1,066	975	922	987
Capital expenditures, net of disposals	4,833	4,531	1,235	755	1,156	1,461	1,384	1,703	78	1,039
Common stock*										
Average number of shares outstanding	2,477,434	2,457,610	2,448,208	2,427,883	2,415,908	2,421,063	2,417,639	2,411,790	2,399,477	2,375,557
Earnings per share:										
Primary	$ 0.90	$ 1.40	$ 1.30	$ 0.40	$ 0.60	$ 1.41	$ 1.38	$ 1.21	$ 1.17	$ 1.10
Fully diluted	$ 0.89	$ 1.31	—	—	—	—	—	—	—	—
Dividends per share	$ 0.40	$ 0.40	$ 0.40	$ 0.475	$ 0.70	$ 0.85	$ 0.80	$ 0.75	$ 0.75	$ 0.75
Book value per share	$14.81	$14.31	$13.29	$12.33	$12.40	$12.42	$11.80	$11.00	$10.33	$ 9.34
Financial condition										
Working capital	$ 42,635	$ 45,259	$ 32,631	$ 23,006	$ 24,458	$ 24,938	$ 18,159	$ 18,422	$ 17,090	$ 14,019
Current ratio	3.31	3.81	3.04	2.39	2.53	2.93	2.44	2.95	3.03	2.54
Net plant	13,938	10,730	7,464	7,862	8,190	8,210	7,883	7,564	6,819	7,663
Total assets	80,129	76,833	60,340	52,376	50,626	48,047	41,098	36,090	33,286	30,456
Long-term debt	24,991	25,319	11,668	4,500	4,750	5,000	—	—	—	—
Shareholders' equity	36,694	35,435	32,639	30,183	29,864	30,107	28,503	26,599	24,846	22,341
Return on assets†	2.8%	4.5%	5.3%	1.9%	2.8%	8.3%	8.1%	8.1%	8.4%	8.6%
Return on equity†	6.1%	9.7%	12.2%	3.2%	4.8%	11.3%	11.7%	11.0%	11.3%	11.7%
Debt/equity ratio†	0.68	0.71	0.36	0.15	0.16	0.17	0	0	0	0
Profit/sales ratio†	1.7	2.6	2.6	1.0	1.5	3.6	3.9	3.8	3.8	3.7

* Prior years have been restated for a two-for-one stock split in 1969 and a 2 percent stock dividend in 1963.
† Computed from above data.
Source: Tappan Company, *Annual Report*, 1970.

Exhibit 6

TAPPAN COMPANY

Pan-O-Matic Range

Source: *Appliance Manufacturer*, December 1970.

Exhibit 7. TAPPAN COMPANY
Kitchen Wall

Integral Kitchen Satisfies Industrialized Building Needs

Tappan's innovative ability is vividly exemplified in the "kitchen wall module" which it developed for the Dept. of Housing and Urban Development's "Operation Breakthrough" program. Designed to cut on-site kitchen installation costs, the module combines the kitchen wall, appliances, cabinets, electrical wiring and plumbing into a single, factory-assembled unit. The concept allows two men to install a complete kitchen in less than an hour.

Practically everything needed for the module is made by Tappan's divisions. If the concept is broadly accepted by builders, the module could become Tappan's most profitable product in the future.

Two HUD contract winners —Aluminum Co. of America and Republic Steel Corp.—are planning to use the modules in their industrialized building concepts. A number of other HUD selectees are also working with Tappan on the use of the modules.

"The Government wants to build homes as fast and as economically as possible," Robert M. Lamb, Jr., kitchen systems administrator, explains. "Pre-fab construction may be the answer because it eliminates expensive on-site labor and the weather factor. It will also assure better uniformity of construction.

"Before the concept can move, however, the Government must resolve certain issues on building codes. Some plan will also have to be created to integrate the building trade unions and builders into the program, rather than eliminate them."

To date, about 50 of the kitchen modules have been made at the Mansfield plant for evaluation by various builders. The modules will be assembled at the Ontario plant when it is completed.

"If there is a big demand for kitchen walls, we will probably have to assemble them at various locations throughout the country because of the shipping problems," Lamb concludes. "We could wind up making them at our distribution centers."

The factory-built "kitchen module" is trucked to a home site and hoisted in place. The unit is supported by a stress wall of 1⅛-in.-thick sheets of U.S. Plywood's "Novoply" compressed particle board. To this wall are attached the kitchen storage cabinets, range, sink, dishwasher, refrigerator and other appliances, along with the necessary water piping and electrical wiring.

Source: *Appliance Manufacturer,* December 1970.

Exhibit 8

TAPPAN COMPANY

Tappan Home Center

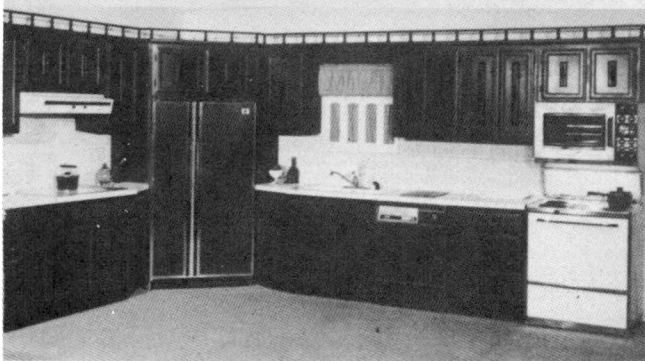

HOME CENTERS— Showcase for Remodelers

A nationwide network of franchised remodeling centers is being set up by Tappan. Primary purpose of the Home Centers is to provide a permanent location for remodelers and homeowners to obtain professional assistance in planning remodeling projects.

Illustrated on this page is the Mansfield, Ohio, Tappan Home Center which the Tappan Div. will use as a training center for other home center franchisees. The Mansfield unit will also function as a remodeling center locally.

Within the Home Center are a number of "designer kitchens" which are intended to serve as a guide for remodeling jobs. Naturally Tappan appliances and cabinets are used throughout.

Adjacent to the Mansfield Home Center is a home furnishings store. This retail outlet is intended to serve as a source of supply for items not showcased within the Home Center itself.

The company is not planning to expand the Home Center concept too quickly, since a great amount of investigation and training will be involved before Home Center franchisees are selected.

Source: *Appliance Manufacturer*, December 1970.

Exhibit 9

TAPPAN COMPANY

New Products under Development

'Firsts' for the Future

COMPACT HEAT EXCHANGER. An improved gas warm air furnace that is only one-third the size of conventional furnaces. The unit is based on a modular design. Each module has an output of 40,000 btuh. The furnace, which can be made in upflow, downflow or counterflow models, was developed by Thermo-Electron under the sponsorship of Tappan, Rheem and the American Gas Assn.

TOTAL GAS COMFORT SYSTEM. The unique system combines a Freon vapor generator with a Rankine cycle engine that drives the compressor of a mechanical refrigeration system. The generator provides high-pressure vapor for the engine in the cooling mode and also serves as the heat source. Thermo Electron is researching the system under the joint sponsorship of Tappan, Rheem and A.G.A.

SMOOTH-TOP RANGE. Four infra-red burners will heat cooking areas of a thermo-resistant glass top to over 1000 F for direct radiant heating of utensils. Tooling for the range is complete, and it will go into production shortly. The unit was developed by Tappan. The glass top was developed by Owens-Illinois and will be made by Pittsburgh Plate Glass.

SAFETY CONTROL PANEL. Designed to increase home safety, the panel could combine solid-state devices that sense odors to turn on and off an air purification system; signal when air filters are clogged; detect gas leaks and electrical failures; and combine burglar and fire alarms. Research on the panel has been completed by Honeywell. Tappan plans to use it on future range lines.

THERMIONIC GENERATOR. A method of generating electricity from heat with no moving parts. The generator could be placed in a furnace exhaust duct to make electricity to power the blower drive motor. The concept is being vigorously pursued by Thermo Electron, but no real breakthrough has yet been made.

FURNACE/WATER HEATER COMBINATION. A low-cost unit that will be compact enough for use in mobile homes. It has just one burner which is sized to provide instantaneous hot water and heat. Thermo Electron is developing the unique boiler under a program sponsored by Tappan, Rheem and A.G.A.

AIR PURIFIER. A low-cost unit which could be portable or added to a furnace, air conditioner or range hood to effi-ciently remove dirt and smoke from the air. Tappan has funded money for research on electrostatic air purification to Honeywell, Gourdine, Thermo Electron and its own engineers.

"COOL" OVEN. Heat from a gas burner will be forced through the oven. The heat movement is expected to cut cooking time in half and greatly reduce oven temperatures. The cool operation may permit the use of plastic for the range side panels. Tappan is researching this forced-convection oven itself.

"MINI" DISPOSER. About half the size of conventional disposers, the unit provides more storage space under the sink. The product, which has been under development at the Anaheim division for three years, also mounts flush against the sink drain to eliminate mounting ring and collar.

Source: *Appliance Manufacturer*, December 1970.

The company and its strategists: Relating economic strategy and personal values

Thus far the situations we have examined have required us to decide whether a concept of purpose and a sense of direction would sufficiently strengthen a company's position in changing circumstances to be worth the effort. We have attempted to examine the concept of strategy in order to understand and use it in our appraisal of company situations and in our quasi-managerial decisions. We have seen the relationship between the obsolescence of strategy and the decline of company fortunes. We have also seen how results are affected by clear versus unclear conceptions of the nature of the company's product or its market segments, and by internally consistent versus inconsistent departmental policies and programs of action.

STRATEGY AS PROTECTION OF PREFERENCE

Until now, our interest has been focused on an impersonal analysis of environmental information and decisions taken in response to it. True, we have noted in passing the contributions made to the formulation or execution of strategy by forceful personalities. But we have tried in the main to perfect a purely *economic* strategy—one that, in our judgment, constituted the most suitable combination of the company's strengths and its opportunities, no matter who might be the chief executive or what might be his aims in life.

We turn now to a series of cases which will provoke discussion of the relationship between a sensible economic strategy on the one hand and the personal values of those who design strategy on the other. We shall see at once that executives in charge of company destinies do not look exclusively at what a company might do and can do. Sometimes— in apparent disregard of at least the second of these considerations— they seem heavily influenced by what they personally *want* to do.

If we think back far enough, the strategies we recommended for the companies already considered probably reflect what *we* would have wanted to do had we been in charge of these companies. We tell ourselves (perhaps as part of the tendency to rationalize) that our personal inclinations harmonize with the optimum combination of economic opportunity and company strengths. For professional managers, especially in large companies, this convergence of what appears to be a sound economic strategy and personal desire is often likely to be quite genuine. But for certain entrepreneurial types, whose energy and personal drive far outweigh their formal training and self-awareness, the direction in which they want to go is not necessarily the direction which a logical appraisal suggests. Such disparity appears most frequently perhaps in small privately held concerns, or in companies built by successful and self-confident owner-managers. However, the phenomenon we are discussing may appear in any company.

Our problem now can be very simply stated. In examining the alternatives available to a company, we must henceforth take into consideration the preferences of the chief executive—and also those of other key managers—who must either contribute to or assent to the strategy if it is to be effective. Thus, besides trying to cope with the divergence between the chief executive's desire and the strategic choice which seems most defensible, we shall be confronted with the conflict among several sets of managerial personal values which must not only be reconciled with an economic strategy but also with each other.

The cases that follow were gathered and are presented to you as empirical evidence that the personal desires, aspirations, and needs of the senior managers of a company actually *do* play an influential role in the determination of strategy. We ourselves would argue also that they probably *should*—at least within the broad limits imposed by the managers' fiduciary responsibility to the owners and perhaps to other nonmanagement groups.[1] The conflict which often arises between what general managers want to do and what the dictates of economic strategy suggest they ought to do is best not denied or ruled out of order. It should be accepted as a matter of course. Then, to the extent practicable, the divergent implications of the elements of a strategic decision should be reconciled.

As you read the cases in this section of the book, apply to them the reasoning you have used thus far. In addition, note the impact of the personal desires of the chief executive upon the nature of the company and the principal characteristics of the strategy. Instead of rejecting such an intrusion of personal values into the formulation of strategy as unwarranted, try to recognize, in your recommendations for improved strategy, the need to meet the most important demands of the senior managers. In the study of human relations, you have no doubt recommended on occasion that the personal needs of the hourly worker be taken seriously and be at least partially satisfied as a means to securing the productive effort for which wages are paid. It should, then, come

---

[1] See p. 578, "The Company and Its Societal Responsibilities: Relating Corporate Strategy and Moral Values."

as no surprise that the president of the corporation also arrives at his desk with his own needs and values—to say nothing of his relatively greater power to see that they are taken into account.

It becomes our mission now to attempt a reconciliation of economic strategy and the observed personal preferences of the executives of the company. The information in the cases will enable us to determine what these preferences are. After determining what strategies appear economically appropriate and what set of goals and policies we ourselves prefer, we must then examine this set to see how it might be amended to accommodate the values of the managers in the cases. This order of priority reflects the fact that it is not our *principal* function to conceive of strategies that will be *acceptable* to management. As students of Policy, we need to be able to design sound strategies more than we need to be able to sell these strategies door-to-door throughout the executive offices. The latter job, however, is not to be ignored. It is a part of the overall task for anyone who wants his ideas to be effective.

Knowing that personal values (often unexpressed and unclear) influence strategic choices and produce results different from what might be called the optimal economic strategy, we can now see why strategic proposals stemming from different unstated values come into conflict and why such conflict cannot be reconciled by talking in terms of environmental data and their match with corporate resources.

At first glance it seems futile to attempt to reconcile a strategic alternative dictated by personal preference with other alternatives oriented toward capitalizing on opportunity to the greatest possible extent. In actuality, however, the additional complication poses fewer difficulties than at' first appear. The analysis of opportunity and the appraisal of resources themselves often lead in different directions. To compose three, rather than two, divergent sets of considerations into a single pattern may increase the complexity of the task, but the integrating process is still the same. We can look for the dominant or immovable consideration and treat the others as constraints; we can probe the elements in conflict for the possibility of reinterpretation or adjustment. We are not building a wall of irregular stones so much as balancing a mobile of elements, the motion of which is adjustable to the motion of the entire mobile. As we have seen, external developments can be affected by company action and company resources, and internal competence can be developed.

MODIFICATION OF VALUES

The question whether values can be changed is somewhat less clear. A value, for our purposes, is a "conception, explicit or implicit, distinctive of an individual or characteristic of a group, of the *desirable* which influences the selection of available modes, means, and ends of action."[2]

---

[2] William D. Guth and Renato Tagiuri, "Personal Values and Corporate Strategy," *Harvard Business Review*, September–October 1965, pp. 123–32. The definition is quoted from Florence R. Kluckhohn *et al.*, *Variations in Value Orientation* (Evanston, Ill.: Row, Peterson and Company, 1961).

Guth and Tagiuri emphasize that values are *concepts* of the desirable, not the "things, conditions, or ideas judged desirable as a result of applying the values to specific situations." Acquired early in life as the result of the "interplay of what he learned from those who reared him, and of his particular individuality and 'times,'"[3] a person's basic values are a relatively stable feature of his personality, although they may change somewhat with his level of knowledge and analytical skill.

Nonetheless, the preference attached to ends in concrete circumstances is not beyond influence. The physicist in a representative research company, who in his reflection of the values of pure science is opposed to commercial production, might withdraw his objection if he sees that his freedom to pursue his own projects can be better sustained by profits from operations than from government research contracts. Furthermore, his departure from the university and his present membership in the firm reflect some economic values and interest in profit for its own sake. He will retain the value orientation of the scientist, but may assent in this instance to the strategic alternative conceived in the value orientation of the businessman. At any rate, to presuppose that he would not do so is a common but futile approach to the value problem.

Guth and Tagiuri report some very interesting research which indicates that we may, in our use of stereotypes, ascribe much stronger value commitments to others than is justified. They report the results of a questionnaire regarding six basically different value orientations[4] that was administered to 178 R.&D. executives, 157 scientists, and 653 managers; despite differences among these groups that might be assumed to exist, all three showed relatively high theoretical, economic, and political value orientations, and relatively low aesthetic, religious, and social values. Indeed, all three groups put theoretical values first.

A second finding of this study indicates that R.&D. executives see the scientist and the manager as exhibiting greater value differences than is actually the case. Thus the scientist is viewed as much more dominantly theoretical than he actually is, the manager as much more dominantly economic and political. The latter's theoretical and religious orientation is seriously underestimated.

From these findings, two implications follow that merit particular

---

[3] Guth and Tagiuri, "Personal Values and Corporate Strategy," p. 4.

[4] These are the six types identified by Edward Spranger, who classifies all individuals as falling into one or another of the following:

1. *The Theoretical* (dominant intellectual interest in an empirical, critical, rational approach to systematic knowledge).
2. *The Economic* (orientation toward practical affairs, the production and consumption of goods, the uses and creation of wealth).
3. *The Aesthetic* (chief interest in the artistic, in form, symmetry, harmony, in experience for its own sake).
4. *The Social* (primary value the love of people and warmth of human relationships).
5. *The Political* (orientation toward power, influence, and recognition).
6. *The Religious* (mystical orientation toward unity and the creation of satisfying and meaningful relationship to the universe).

emphasis at this point. First, the manager is much more "theoretically" oriented than the stereotype of the American businessman would indicate (but not, we would assert, more than his duties require). Second, values for these different groups may be easier to reconcile with each other and with requirements for a sound economic strategy than might at first be anticipated. Although one value orientation may be dominant in an individual and color his judgment of where opportunity lies and of what his company has power to achieve, other values are present, and effective appeal can be made to these by persons who want to influence the course of strategy. Sometimes, also, an appeal can be successful if it can show that a chosen strategy threatens the value it was designed to serve. For example, the extreme resistance of Mississippi and Alabama to integration, by evoking vigorous federal action, wound up pushing civil rights faster and further in these areas than would otherwise have been the case.

AWARENESS OF VALUES

Your interest in the role of value in strategic formulations should not be confined to assessing the influence of other people's values. Despite the well-known problems of introspection, we can probably do more to understand the relation of our own values to our choice of purpose than we can to change the values of others. Awareness that our own preference for an alternative opposed by another stems from values as much as from rational estimates of economic opportunity may have important consequences. First, it may make us more tolerant and less indignant when we perceive this relationship between recommendations and values in the formulations of others. Second, it will force us to consider how important it really is to us to maintain a particular value in making a particular decision. Third, it may give us insight to identify our bias and thus pave the way for a more objective assessment of all the strategic alternatives that are available. These consequences of self-examination will not end conflict, but they will at least prevent its unnecessary prolongation.

The object of this course of study is not to endow us with the ability to persuade others to accept the strategic recommendations we consider best: it is to acquire insight into the problems of determining purpose and skill in the process of resolving them. For students of Policy not yet in executive positions (as well as those who are), the chance presents itself now to assess their own personal opportunities, strengths and weaknesses, and basic values by means of the procedures outlined here. For a personal strategy, analytically considered and consciously developed, may be as useful to an individual as a corporate strategy is to a business institution. An effort, conducted by each individual, to formulate his personal purpose might well acompany the effort, made by the group within the classroom, to design purposes for various corporations. The problems encountered here may temper your criticism of the executives in the cases. If, more importantly, the encounter leads to a clarification of the purposes you seek, the values you hold, and alternatives available to you, the attempt to make personal use of the concept of strategy will prove extremely worthwhile.

As you consider the cases which follow, we have urged you, first to complete the same kind of analysis you have previously undertaken to determine an economic strategy and to test it against the criteria which by now you habitually use. But look to see to what extent the strategy you have formulated corresponds to or comes into conflict with the values of the president or executives whose acceptance of the strategy is necessary to its implementation. So far as you can, try to identify the values that are implicit in your own decision. As you look at the gap between the strategy which follows from your values and that which would be appropriate to the values of the chief executive of the case, look to see whether the difference is fundamental or superficial. Then look to see how the strategy you believe best matches opportunity and resources can be adapted to accommodate the values of those who will implement it. Reconciliation of the three principal determinants of strategy which we have so far considered is often possible by adjustment of any or all of the determinants.

You should not warp your strategy to the detriment of the company's future in order to adjust it to personal values. On the other hand, you should not expect to be able to impose an unwelcome pattern of purposes and policies on the people in charge of a corporation. Strategy is a human construction; it must be responsive to human needs. It must ultimately inspire commitment. It must stir an organization to successful striving against competition. Somebody has to have his heart in it.

Multi-Products, Inc.

"THE average young fellow today has no concept of how to beat a competitor and how to squeeze money out of every dollar," Richard B. Haws, president of Multi-Products, Inc., of Los Angeles, California, said in February 1959 to Bertram Stace, an old friend and stockholder. "It's not really their fault—they've just had lousy training over the past 20–30 years, as far as the acceptance of responsibility and of being held accountable for the stewardship of a job is concerned. If we ever begin to have a depression as we did back in 1929 to 1931, God knows how the industries of this country would suffer. Just look at the way they waste money. . . ."

MR. HAWS'S CAREER, 1902–56

"I was born in 1902, the son of poor parents," Mr. Haws continued. "One day when I was a small boy I was sitting in our hometown drugstore and the wealthy owner of a pottery (his son lost all of it) came in and sat down beside me. He talked to the druggist and then he turned to me and said, 'No use talking to you, you'll never have any money.' I will never forget those words. I don't resent them—they were the greatest driving force in my life. If they've been before my eyes once, they've been before them five million times."

Picking up his office copy of *Who's Who*, Mr. Haws showed Mr. Stace that he had attended college for three years, worked as a salesman in a local business for another five, and then moved to New York in 1929 to sell for the Lawton Machinery Company. "We were living in a nice apartment and had all our money in the market when the crash came. I went to our landlord and asked him to let me break the lease, but he pointed out that he needed money more than ever now and refused. I went home to think about it and then returned and pleaded with him to let us move to one of his cheaper apartments. Finally he agreed. He

438

moved us the next day and that night brought up a new lease for me to sign. I looked him in the eye and said, 'Oh, no. When you moved us out of that first apartment, you broke the lease. We're moving out of here tomorrow.' That's the sort of sharp thinking—in that case born out of financial necessity—that young fellows don't seem to use today. They certainly don't learn it in business schools."

Mr. Haws thought his Lawton Machine Company days had been an invaluable experience. "Young fellows today are soft—they don't believe me when I tell them that my wife often would wait for my phone call in the late afternoon to see if I'd sold a machine. If so, I'd have enough money for her to buy food for supper! Those were the days when we were ashamed to admit we had lost an order. We were paid straight commission; anyone could ask for a raise but all you got was 'Go out and sell some more machines.' I remember the sales manager used to say, 'Any salesman can come in, push the desk in my lap and call me a S.O.B. as long as he produces—but he'd better keep on producing.'

"When I was with Lawton, I met a young statistician whose head was full of ideals and up in the clouds, but he was dead broke. I suggested he sell machines until he found another job. I showed him the sales pitch and sent him off with a machine under his arm. The next day he was back saying he couldn't take it. I told him anybody could sell machines and if he couldn't he had no guts. He stuck with it two months until he got another statistical job. You've got to have guts and imagination to get someplace. A friend of mine who was president of a large company put it this way, 'If I have a guy around me who hasn't been in jail, I have a weak man!'

"It was during my time with Lawton that I realized I wanted a nice house, expensive car, fine clothes—the things that money can buy. I decided then and there I had the ants in my pants to want excitement and to get all or nothing. If you know what you want and what you can afford, it's pretty easy to set up a program for yourself. I've tried to get others to do the same, but they don't. It's pretty difficult for a young man or a student because he's not had the business experience to see what you can get out of life, and what money will buy. But then, even older men don't do it. Take my associate Joel Dennis. He's happy to earn about $15 an hour, save up for a new expensive camera, throw on a $47 suit of clothes that doesn't fit properly, and just lead that sort of life. Maybe he's happy, but he doesn't have the ants in his pants I do. . . ."

Mr. Haws told his friends that he decided he didn't aspire to be a Lawton sales manager, but rather wanted a "show of my own" and was willing to pay for the necessary experience. He had left his $18,000 Lawton job to work first for a large company as a $6,000-a-year procedures man and later for a medium-sized company as a financial officer. During his stay with the second company he was given warrants and stock. When he left he had about 27,500 shares which had cost him some $12,000; by 1959 these shares were worth over $1 million. In 1953 he became president of a small manufacturing company, and four years later he was asked to head Multi-Products, Inc.

MULTI-PRODUCTS, INC., 1946–56

Mr. Haws's friend, Mr. Stace, was a stockholder in Multi-Products, Inc., and knew something about its early history from published records. The company was founded by Earle M. Cave in January 1946 to make a consumer item. By 1951 the company had lost some $500,000 on five years' sales of $625,000 and Mr. Cave started a new line. During the next two years Multi-Products expanded into two related and one unrelated lines through acquiring three small companies. The company's 1954 statements showed a net profit of about $290,000 on $5.7 million sales, a net worth of $3.3 million, and an accumulated deficit of $80,000; however, the auditors "were unable to form an opinion as to the overall results of operation" because management had decided to defer certain expenses totaling $375,000.

The next year, Mr. Stace recalled, the company ran into difficulties. The June 1955 quarterly report showed a six months' profit of about $60,000 on about $2.7 million sales, but when the annual report came out there were losses of about $3.6 million on $6 million sales.

Early in 1956 the company underwent litigation. Mr. Stace recalled the basic issues were whether the net income for the period ending June 30, 1955, were overstated and both income statement and balance sheet invalid and whether at the time the quarterly report was issued management knew the company was operating at a loss. The testimony showed that four entries, labeled "management adjustments" by the disapproving controller, had turned a $300,000 March quarter loss into a $60,000 profit before the statement was forwarded to the company's banks. The court ruled that the June profit had been overstated by almost $1 million owing to improper deferment of certain expenses, calculation of the cost of goods sold on the basis of cost formulae rather than by using the cost system, and failure to establish reserves for anticipated losses.

In court Mr. Cave said that accounting, especially details such as divisional operating data or cost entries, was beyond his "purview of operation," interest, or knowledge. He stated that he relied completely on the judgment of Mr. Bangs, vice president of finance, on all accounting matters, and on the auditors on all financial questions pertaining to the company statements. He said that in general "it was not my custom to have any contact whatsoever with the people at the working level, such as Mr. Land or Mr. Heyden (assistant controllers). If I had identified myself at any time with the minutiae between the juniors below any of the vice presidents, then I would have been totally unable to have kept my proper purview of the overall operation of the company and longer term planning of the company. I stayed expressly away from all matters which fell totally below the vice presidential levels." He said the first time he had "any conception" of the losses was when the new auditors showed him the 1955 financial statements in February 1956 after his return from a vacation. Besides, over $2 million was due to auditors' adjustments.

Both Mr. Cave and the Multi-Products, Inc., counsel stressed that investors bought the company's stock on the basis of its potential long-term growth, not the statements, and so it would not have materially mattered one iota if the six months' statement ending March had shown a profit or a small loss. According to published reports, Mr. Cave never owned over 2% of Multi-Products, Inc., stock and did not speculate.

After losing $4 million on $5.9 million sales in 1956, the firm faced financial disaster. Only selling a large block of shares at $2 a share to an investment fund in January 1957 avoided bankruptcy. (Mr. Stace ruefully recalled that the stock back in 1952 had sold for $42 a share.) New directors and a new management, including Mr. Haws, were brought in, and the division making products unrelated to the other lines was sold.

MULTI-PRODUCTS, INC., UNDER MR. HAWS'S MANAGEMENT, 1957–59

Mr. Haws explained to Mr. Stace that since coming to Multi-Products, Inc., he had concentrated on three areas: organization, acquisitions, and employee motivation and compensation.

Organization. "For about the first month after I joined Multi-Products, Inc., I just watched operations and got the feel of the situation," Mr. Haws said. "Then I went to work on our organization. There were 51 people in the accounting department. I called in the head of the department and told him to move the people into another room. He protested there was only room for 12 there and I said, 'That's right, by tomorrow you'll only have 12 people in your department.' I also called in the head of the merchandising department and showed him a new room with space for three people and the secretary. He had to reduce his staff from 11. Quality control had seven people and a secretary. I told the superintendent he would have two people including himself to do all the scheduling, the expediting and control. The department heads said this was impossible. I said, 'All right. I will stay after five o'clock tonight and want you to come in and tell me if you're man enough for the job or else resign.'

"Actually, volume has grown much better than I anticipated, and we still have only 12 people in the accounting department. Goes to show there were a lot of people sitting around on their hands doing nothing. You know, a partially employed person is the most ineffectual person in the business; he is inaccurate, lazy, and—worst of all—keeps other people from working.

"About March I took the department heads to dinner at the hotel. I told them what I was trying to do, put up a sales and profit chart, and said, "We'll start work at 8:15 in the morning, and not 8:45 or whenever you seem to feel like wandering in.' The treasurer broke in with, 'Let's take a vote on it.' I said, 'Fine, but if anyone votes against the proposal, I'll accept his resignation.' There was no vote.

"After the meeting the treasurer said, 'You certainly got off easy.' I replied, 'No, I had to listen to you. That's enough anguish for one evening. I don't have enough cash on me, so come in tomorrow morning and you can get your check.' I fired him right there; he was 45 years old but as yet he had not learned that organization conduct was more important than personal convenience."

In reorganizing the company, Mr. Haws said he decided whom to let go almost on a replacement basis. "Who cares about accountants, salesmen, shop foremen, or treasurers? But purchasing agents, merchandisers, and engineers are rather important to you. You have to know where to start a fight and where not to. You must move slowly because you have not possession of all the facts. . . ."

Acquisitions and new business.   The company needed to generate sufficient new business to utilize the large loss carry-forward generated since December 31, 1955. "The fundamental reason for our being in business is to utilize the tax losses," Mr. Haws explained. During 1957 he revamped the product line, acquired two small companies making similar products, and reduced the size of the loss to about $470,000 on sales of $3.7 million. By June 1958 the company showed earnings of $75,000 on sales of about $2 million, but much faster profit generation was needed. Mr. Haws started to diversify.

The first acquisition was the Seward Company which was obtained through an exchange of stock in July 1958. Shortly before, Seward had invested in a relatively large amount of new fixed assets. By changing the write-off period from three years to ten, Multi-Products maximized the immediate profit and thus effectively deferred the tax loss carry-forward beyond its normal expiration date. The extra profit was recorded as deferred income on the statements and was included in income for tax purposes only. By February 1959 Multi-Products had protected almost $1 million of its tax loss.

The other two unrelated businesses were bought in October 1958 and January 1959 on an "incentive" basis. Mr. Haws explained, "The man who owned the first one foresaw estate problems and wanted to sell the business for $1.5 million, its asset value. I said I would offer him $2 million if I could have it my own way with less than 30% down. I paid him $500,000 and picked up $400,000 of the company's cash the next day. In order to make up the $1 million balance of his original $1.5 million asking price, he will receive two thirds of the after-tax profit without limit of time. Obviously, if there are never any profits, he will never get any more than the down payment already made. Over the next five years, if his two-thirds share of the profits generate more than the $1.5 million asking price, he gets his excess up to the full $2 million offer. The business is currently producing after tax profits of $40,000 a month. I was talking to the seller the other day about cutting out his fancy profit-sharing ideas, Cadillacs, hotel suites, and other perquisites, and he said he wouldn't work so hard without them. I replied, 'You scare me to death! You've only got $500,000 for your company so far and that's *all* you get if you don't produce profits.' I paid $25,000 down for the second business, which had $280,000 in cash, and made a similar incentive arrangement for the rest of the sales price.

"In other words, I am giving these men an incentive to continue to produce profits and thus am much more sophisticated than others using similar formulas. Some are good at this sort of thing. They pay an inflated cost above the company's net worth as a *contractual* obligation, which puts ether on the balance sheet as goodwill or some other evasive term, and they have to amortize the ether over a stipulated period on their operating statement, which adversely affects profits and gives their stockholders an untrue picture of earnings. On the other hand, I give the seller the full purchase price above asset value *only* if he earns it.

"I can't understand acquiring a company to add to your losses. Men who contractually overpay must be either awfully young or look too far into the future. Look at this article in today's *Wall Street Journal*[1] about Mr. Zeckendorf's company. Real estate is the safest investment in an inflationary economy and Webb & Knapp's assets have grown from $7 million in 1945 to $210 million in 1957, yet it lost money last year; the common stockholders have never received a dividend, and the preferred is $60 in arrears. When that happens, something is really wrong! Anytime you increase assets, your return on investment should increase proportionately. There's no point in getting big just for bigness' sake. Under my incentive system, we know the management of the purchased company will work hard to show a profit and not allow earnings to show a decreased return on investment."

Employee motivation and compensation.   "The problem that really concerns me the most is turning young men into cost- and profit-conscious executives, who are worried about getting sales, controlling costs, setting profitable prices, and spending the company's money. I put a young man in charge of a division. He'd go out and buy some steel. If it were too brittle, would he tell the purchasing department to send it back? Heavens no! He'd just put it in inventory! Same with capital equipment. He'd buy some machinery, and if it didn't work, he'd put it to one side and forget about it, and not even try to get salvage value out of it. Another division head was losing $120,000 but was very indignant when I called him into the office to hear what he was going to do about it because he thought we could just borrow money from a bank. I said, 'You've got 60 days to turn this situation around. I've got no place in the company for a loser.'

"I've got another fellow who came in and said, 'It has been just 14 months since my last raise.' I said, 'What do you want to talk about?' He replied, 'my raise.' And I said, 'The length of time has no relation as to whether you get a raise or not.' I added that he was reviewed a few months ago, at which time he told me about how many letters he wrote but didn't tell me what business he had brought into the house and the profit that he had earned. He replied, 'I worked hard,' and I said, 'I don't know about that. We've got working rules that you start work at 8:15; you're here at 8:30 or 8:45, and during the baseball season you're at the ball park. Sure, I know that you tell the secretaries that you are calling on a customer, but I just happen to know that you were at the baseball game. You come back tomorrow and tell me how much busi-

[1] *The Wall Street Journal*, February 9, 1959, p. 1.

ness you have brought in, and how much profit you have made for the company, and whether you are earning the salary you have.'

"Engineers are far too loyal to what they call their 'professional ethics.' A company may have a contract to do something, but the engineer will see that he could do it just that much better. The customer didn't ask for it, the specifications didn't ask for it, and if we do it, we won't be able to make a profit or deliver on time. But because of this professional idealism, the engineer goes ahead and does it anyway, with the result that we lose money, the customer is mad because we are late, and perhaps it doesn't work any better than it would have anyway.

"All the other professions—doctors, lawyers, teachers—except the engineer have to collect their bills. Ninety-nine per cent of the latter are living off somebody else's money. If you ask them what have they contributed to earn their money, they get insulted. And if I suggested I wasn't going to pay them unless they contributed to the company, they'd quit. It's never seemed to dawn on some of them that they have to earn their keep.

"Dr. Collins is an example. I noticed that he had more and more unexcused absences and was coming in at 9:00 or 10:00 A.M. and leaving at 3:00 P.M. so I inquired around and learned he was discussing setting up his own company. I called him in the next day and said, 'Let's let our hair down. I'm not going to have this sloppy behavior.' He said, 'You never said anything about my working Saturdays and Sundays when we set up that new division,' to which I replied, 'No, I didn't say anything about my doing it either, but that's why we pay you a good salary. When are you going to leave?' He asked me when I wanted him to and got the reply, 'Tomorrow.' He said, 'I'd hoped you'd let me stay around until I get my company going. Anyway, my time ought to be my own.' And I said, 'O.K. fine, I'll give you a check tomorrow and you'll have all the free time you want.' You know, he's got a wife, two kids, is buying a home, but doesn't recognize the security he owes his family judging by the way he treated his job. His company never got off the ground and now he's broke and looking for a job. I'd like to help him, but my responsibility ended when he transferred his loyalties.

"Expense accounts and perquisites are another problem. Some fellows never put a limit on their hotel bill, so of course they get the most expensive room in the house. I just stopped three executives from leaving in the company plane at 3:00 P.M. instead of 5:00 P.M. They just wanted to get to their destination in time for supper; they hadn't thought that their salaries cost the company $55 an hour, or $110. Another young fellow came in here and said the company should give him a country club membership for entertaining customers. I said, 'No. You may be entertaining five customers now, but soon it will be fifteen people because in fact the company would be paying for your wife's and kids' weekends at the club.'

"You find this lack of cost-consciousness at all levels of the organization. Take those three girls out there, who are executive secretaries and assistants and are paid from $450 to $550 per month. I told them, 'I have a fetish against coffee breaks, which I think are the doom of

American industry. Just get a few people around a coffee machine, and I'll bet three out of five of them will have something to gripe about. You are being paid enough money to know that this really does cost money. I don't want coffee drunk at the desk, but if you want to drink coffee, you can check in and out on a time clock and be paid an ordinary clerical salary.' I also asked them to exert their influence on the other girls to try and stop this coffee break business.

"About a week later I went past the coffee machine and found one of the three girls there talking to another secretary. She asked me if I would like a cup of coffee and I said I couldn't afford it. She said, 'Oh, I would be glad to spend the 10 cents.' And I said, 'That's not the point. The company can't afford the time.' So I put in an order to cut her salary $50 per month. That brought all three girls into my office, saying it was a very unfair thing to do. I said, 'I wasn't unfair. Here's a girl who violated an order that I had given. . . .' I then pointed out that I am not running a charitable organization, but running a business, and I can't allow any individuals to destroy the organization. So she has $50 less a month.

"In short I guess people don't realize—and perhaps I didn't either when I was an employee—that you buy manpower the same way you buy productive machinery. You must get a return for your investment.

"We have constant reviews and checks to be sure we're getting a return. Those with an annual salary of $6,000 or less get a semiannual review, while those over $6,000 get an annual one. If the supervisor doesn't recommend a raise, the man has 90 days to correct the faults found. If he does not correct them, he is out. Of course, when I let a man go, the supervisors often come in and really squawk; however, they are more careful the next time when writing their appraisals.

"There are several ways I check on the supervisors' evaluations. I sometimes call in a supervisor and make up fictitious stories about how I never saw so-and-so at work, or how I always see him coming in at 9:00 o'clock in the morning. Then I ask him if he is afraid to put a complete evaluation on somebody. Then I start in on another man. I make him defend all his recommendations. Sometimes they just plain collapse—the supervisors can't really defend their recommendations. They have to have a really good look at what each man does and not just say the whole department has done well. Also, I'll pick out three or four cards sent to me by the personnel department on people coming up for review, and I'll walk around their departments in the morning and at 4:45 in the evening. You can really get an idea of how hard a person works by doing that a couple of times for three or four days. You pick up enough information to justify your comments, and my objections to the supervisors often hit near enough home."

Future plans.   Mr. Haws's long-term objective for the company was to utilize the tax loss carry-forward through more diversification, but he told Mr. Stace that his personal objective was to leave Multi-Products, Inc., after another year or so. "I've really worked myself out of a job; I don't do a darn thing except read *The Wall Street Journal* and look for new acquisitions." His contract, which he—but not the company—

could cancel, was up in 1961; his salary was about $35,000 with a $17,500 a year consulting fee guarantee for five years after leaving the company, and he had 60,000 of the 113,000 outstanding warrants at $2 a share. The stock was selling for $9 a share in February 1959.

In summing up his career, Mr. Haws felt he had learned to take calculated risks and win, but that young men with whom he worked did not do so. "If I ever had $5,000 in the bank, I'd be mad because it is not earning me a penny. When I am 60 or 65, I don't want to be a total dependent on somebody else, as nine-tenths of these people are destined to be. I offered 5,000 shares of the company at $2 apiece to one young man, and he said, 'I'll let you know in a while. I've got to think it over.' I said, 'I'll give you ten seconds to decide and those ten seconds have just passed, and the offer is off.' Heavens, a young man should have jumped at a chance like that!"

Ing. C. Olivetti & C., S.p.A.(A-1)

THE OLIVETTI STORY: TOCCO OLIVETTI

In 1966, Ing. C. Olivetti & C., S.p.A., was one of the world's leading producers of typewriters, calculators, and other business machines. Olivetti was listed by official Italian government sources as the sixth largest industrial company in Italy. Olivetti was number 103 on *Fortune*'s list of 200 largest industrial companies outside of the United States. Olivetti's U.S. subsidiary, Olivetti Underwood, ranked as number 483 on *Fortune*'s list of the 500 largest industrial companies in the United States.

The Olivetti Company in 1965 comprised 28 associated companies, in as many countries, each with its own commercial distribution network; 108 general agents operating in 117 countries; 18 industrial plants, of which 9 were in Italy and 9 abroad; and 54,000 employees, of which 25,000 were in Italy and 29,000 abroad.

Olivetti's consolidated sales of 281 billion lire in 1965 (approximately $450 million) were divided 20% in Italy and 80% abroad, while manufacturing output was divided 75% in Italy and 25% abroad.

Financial statements for 1965 showed Olivetti earning net profits after taxes equal to 4.0% of sales, and equal to 8.2% of shareholders' capital stock.

The worldwide Olivetti organization was managed from headquarters in Ivrea, a small town in the foothills of the Alps in northern Italy. It was here that Camillo Olivetti founded the company in 1908. Under Camillo Olivetti, and later his son Adriano, the company broadened its line of products from typewriters into office furniture and filing cabinets in 1931, teleprinters for teletype communication in 1937, adding machines in 1940, calculators in 1946, bookkeeping machines in 1951, and electronic computers in 1960.

Exhibit 1 contains summary information on Olivetti earnings, as-

Exhibit 1

ING. C. OLIVETTI & C., S.p.A.

Statement of Financial Situation

(the table below shows the financial position from the year ended March 31, 1957, to the year ended December 31, 1965.)

(million lire)

	31-III-57	31-III-58	31-III-59	31-XII-59	31-XII-60	31-XII-61	31-XII-62	31-XII-63	31-XII-64	31-XII-65
ASSETS										
Buildings	6.419,5	7.149,5	7.789,3	8.199,4	9.081,7	10.777,9	15.741,8	19.889,0	20.931,9	20.669,5
Plant and equipment	7.197,6	9.099,8	10.637,2	11.401,5	12.726,8	15.212,7	20.518,3	24.524,8	25.406,6	24.530,7
EDP equipment	...	...	...	...	...	1.430,0	3.282,4	7.132,4	10.512,4	820,0
Inventories	4.935,5	5.324,2	4.453,6	5.290,8	7.066,9	10.867,8	14.919,4	21.781,1	20.865,2	13.326,0
Cash, banks, securities	1.789,1	1.957,2	1.486,5	1.797,9	1.859,7	2.114,1	3.707,3	3.757,3	2.270,9	3.760,7
Investments in subsidiaries	3.187,9	4.555,9	7.029,7	11.888,4	26.740,8	33.228,3	38.034,8	25.615,8	45.422,6	50.257,4
Accounts receivable, notes receivable	9.270,9	10.437,5	10.988,1	11.497,0	14.447,9	24.293,0	32.344,2	39.508,5	37.365,9	38.715,9
Due from subsidiaries	6.585,7	9.217,5	10.034,0	14.440,8	24.159,1	33.037,2	50.845,9	56.387,3	41.901,3	46.321,3
Uncalled capital, unpaid share premiums	...	...	...	...	...	...	7.079,6	...	...	...
Unamortized expenses	...	...	...	114,2	79,7	169,4	1.995,6	1.560,9	1.145,0	729,1
Total	39.386,2	47.741,6	53.018,4	64.630,0	96.162,6	131.130,4	188.469,3	200.157,1	205.821,8	199.151,6
LIABILITIES										
Capital stock	7.800,0	10.800,0	13.500,0	13.500,0	25.000,0	40.000,0	60.000,0	60.000,0	60.000,0	60.000,0
Reserves: ordinary	126,9	152,2	181,7	216,9	260,0	460,6	8.000,0	873,2	873,2	876,8
Reserves: extraordinary	2.531,1	1.726,1	1.133,1	2.272,5	1.624,6	799,7	1.074,8	1.000,0	1.000,0	1.066,8
Reserves: premiums on shares	...	...	...	...	...	12.500,0	17.962,3	...	...	...
Accumulated depreciation: Industrial buildings	498,8	665,8	863,6	1.373,0	1.945,9	2.581,7	2.944,0	3.537,9	5.951,2	7.877,7
Accumulated depreciation: Machinery and special equipment	4.013,0	5.654,5	7.370,8	8.467,7	9.656,1	10.965,6	11.760,2	13.395,3	17.063,7	19.435,5

Accumulated depreciation:

	31-III-57	31-III-58	31-III-59	31-XII-59	31-XII-60	31-XII-61	31-XII-62	31-XII-63	31-XII-64	31-XII-65
EDP equipment	3.094,4	3.690,3	4.439,2	5.246,5	6.807,1	314,6	644,5	1.519,3	4.578,3	568,5
Retirement fund						9.069,6	12.446,0	16.263,5	19.455,9	21.127,9
Social activities and welfare fund						140,8	193,2	300,9	300,9	200,9
Debentures	5.246,5	8.188,0	8.125,3	11.010,6	10.887,9	10.637,2	35.368,9	35.081,8	34.655,3	34.074,9
Swiss loan	2.190,0	2.190,0	2.190,0	2.190,0	2.190,0	2.190,0	2.190,0	2.190,0	2.190,0	2.190,0
Accrued liabilities	1.588,9	1.813,6	2.062,6	2.012,6	2.373,8	2.589,3	3.232,4	4.316,7	4.540,6	6.588,9
Due to subsidiaries	13,9	60,0		223,7		163,0	160,5	5.335,5	2.436,2	359,0
Accounts payable	1.297,2	966,9	1.324,6	2.428,1	4.285,2	2.777,9	6.188,5	12.989,9	7.216,3	6.688,0
Due to banks	4.799,3	4.624,1	4.560,6	6.063,8	12.544,6	15.517,6	7.396,5	20.258,5	16.629,6	5.848,0
Mortgage loans	1.947,4	2.930,4	2.407,4	2.152,1	1.802,0	1.967,8	1.596,7	1.318,0	1.099,5	864,9
Notes payable				2.200,0	2.300,0				4.000,0	
Miscellaneous liabilities	3.733,5	3.689,3	4.155,8	4.633,6	10.249,1	13.651,5	12.109,4	21.776,6	23.759,4	26.459,3
Net profit	505,3	590,4	703,7	862,6	4.012,6	4.803,5	5.201,4		71,7	4.924,5
Total	39.386,2	47.741,6	53.018,4	64.630,0	96.162,6	131.130,4	188.469,3	200.157,1	205.821,8	199.151,6

Income Statement

(the table below shows the income statement from the year ended March 31, 1957, to the year ended December 31, 1965.)

	31-III-57	31-III-58	31-III-59	31-XII-59	31-XII-60	31-XII-61	31-XII-62	31-XII-63	31-XII-64	31-XII-65
	(million lire)					(million lire)				
EXPENSES										
General expenses	6.986,9	9.428,2	11.565,4	9.156,8	15.222,8	19.474,9	24.049,6	32.400,9	30.658,7	28.343,3
Taxes	1.362,0	1.112,1	1.262,9	879,8	1.584,2	2.362,7	3.068,3	4.643,4	2.028,4	3.014,2
Depreciation	1.445,5	1.865,6	2.073,1	1.735,5	2.042,2	2.497,0	1.887,6	3.350,3	9.543,8	6.016,4
Retirement fund	718,2	702,2	748,9	806,2	1.560,6	2.262,6	3.373,5	3.678,2	3.192,4	4.124,4
Extraordinary reserves	750,0	1.100,0	520,0	700,0						
Net profit	505,3	590,4	703,7	862,6	4.012,6	4.803,5	5.201,4		71,7	4.924,5
Total	11.767,9	14.798,0	16.874,0	14.140,9	24.422,4	31.400,7	37.580,4	44.072,8	45.495,0	46.422,8
REVENUE										
Gross profit	11.692,5	14.733,4	16.800,4	14.063,8	24.282,1	31.283,5	37.422,3	43.921,4	45.270,6	46.188,5
Other income	75,4	65,1	73,6	77,1	140,3	117,2	158,1	151,4	224,4	234,3
Total	11.767,9	14.798,5	16.874,0	14.140,9	24.422,4	31.400,7	37.580,4	44.072,8	45.495,0	46.422,8

Source: Company records.

sets, and liabilities, for the years 1957–65. Exhibit 2 presents a detailed income statement and balance sheet taken from Olivetti's annual report for 1965.

Exhibit 3 shows pictures of several Olivetti products: the Lettera 32, the Praxis 48, the Tekne 3, the Electrosumma 20, the Divisumma 24, and the Programma 101. (See pages 454–456.)

Exhibit 4 shows pictures of the Olivetti home office building and two factories in Italy. (See pages 457–458.)

Exhibit 5 shows pictures of the Olivetti employee health center, employee housing and employee cafeteria in Ivrea. (See pages 458–459.)

In 1962, Olivetti published a booklet titled: *Olivetti, a Contemporary Image of Style and Industry*, which contained a history of the company, emphasizing the evolution of its philosophy of management. Excerpts from this booklet follow:

A small factory at the foot of the Alps

The Olivetti typewriter factory, later incorporated as Ing. C. Olivetti & C., S.p.A., began operations in 1908 at Ivrea, a pleasant little town in Piedmont, at the foot of the Alps. The social climate in which the firm was born had scarcely felt the impact of the Industrial Revolution, but the idea of Progress and a general belief that hard work and practical enterprise would produce a radiant future were in the air. In Italy, professional technicians were growing in number, and in public esteem were beginning to rank with philosophers, scientists and artists. Prominent among them were the new captains of industry. In this group, the name of Olivetti has a particular resonance, for Camillo Olivetti, the founder of the company, stood out among other industrial pioneers in background, original character and in the conscious ideals that gave his enterprise a special significance.

Camillo Olivetti did not exactly fit the old romantic stereotype of the self-made man who works his way up from the bottom. He came from a moderately prosperous small-town family. His father farmed and dealt in real estate in the Canavese district of northern Piedmont, which lies between the Valle d'Aosta and the Po River. Camillo took his degree in electrical engineering under the celebrated scientist, Galileo Ferraris, at the Turin Polytechnic, and then spent two years in California as assistant to Ferraris when he held the chair of electrical engineering at Stanford University. Subsequently Camillo established the first plant in Italy for electrical measurement instruments, the C.G.S. factory. When he was almost 40, he decided to leave C.G.S., which had been set up in Milan, to return to his native region.

By history and geography, the Canavese district has a distinct regional character. In 1907 its center, Ivrea, was like an overgrown village, living mainly by handicrafts and trade with the farmers of the fertile surrounding countryside. The sleepy small town, agreeably situated between the River Dora and the foothills, was dominated by its ancient past and its great four-towered medieval castle. Certainly it did not seem to be the most suitable setting for the revolutionary ventures of an engineer who had been living in the great world of the United States and Milan, and who now intended to start making a machine for which nobody appeared to feel the need.

While in other countries typewriters were already coming into general use, in Italy they were still regarded with distrust. Little had changed in the half century since the Novara lawyer, Giuseppe Ravizza, invented the "clerk's clavichord." The first practical example of a device for mechanical writing, the invention met with a general indifference that embittered Ravizza's life. But Camillo Olivetti set about carrying out his own project in a spirit very different from that of Ravizza's visionary and essentially dilettante approach. His experience in the United States had shown him that it was inevitable for mass production to replace artisan ingenuity in the field he was entering.

In Turin, the nearest big city, the largest Italian automobile plant— Fiat—had been operating for ten years and employed fifty workers. Camillo Olivetti started industrial production of typewriters with some 20 men, headed by Domenico Burzio, a former blacksmith who had worked with him for many years. The factory was a plain red-brick building covering about 500 square yards. It still stands in Ivrea, dwarfed by the huge Olivetti plants that have since grown up beside it.

The modest factory, which housed the firm's first Browne and Sharpe automatic lathes and its first milling machines, also served as a school for the largely untrained staff. Two years went into training and experiment before the first typewriter, the model M1, could be put into production, and it was only in 1911 after being shown to the public at the Turin Exhibition, that the M1 started on its way to success. In the same year it received official sanction, winning the Ministry of the Navy's competition for an order of 100 machines, and a little more than a year later another official order was received from the government postal system. "From that moment," Camillo Olivetti later wrote, "began the truly marvelous progress of our industry." Between that moment and today, more than half a century after Olivetti started as an unlikely challenge to the giants of the industry established in America and abroad, the company has earned an international position of the first rank. Ivrea is still the headquarters and home of the company, but it would now be hard to find much trace of the old home's original handicraft atmosphere. The antiquated Piedmontese town has become part of the history of modern industry, and the Ivrea of today has grown along with the company, whose presence has influenced the environment materially and morally.

Camillo Olivetti's democratic ideals were dramatically put to the test right after the First World War when throughout Italy the relations between labor and capital were violently strained. To back up their demands the workers occupied the factories, and it was then that the unusual relations between management and labor that had been established with the founding of the company proved to be based on far-sighted moral views and not on mere paternalistic makeshifts. Camillo's evident good faith convinced the union leaders that the workers' interests would be met, without the need for agitation, by a man whose expressed ideal in operating the plant was "a state of things in which the greater share of the fruits of labor go to those who have labored usefully."

Camillo Olivetti owed his forcefulness as an industrialist to moral attitudes of this sort, which had a particular allure at a time when such views were considered highly unconventional. As an ethical capitalist, he felt it his duty to criticize the inadequacies that weakened the system. He never had any doubts about the worker's right to share in the profits, and it was on this basis that he understood

Exhibit 2

ING. C. OLIVETTI & C., S.p.A.

Income Statement for the Year Ended December 31, 1965

INCOME

Sales........................	Lit.	121,920,483,423
Miscellaneous income........	Lit.	234,278,232
Total........................	Lit.	122,154,761,655

EXPENDITURE

Beginning inventory 31–12–1964......			Lit.	20,865,231,783
Transfer to Olivetti Bull........			Lit.	−3,868,674,449
Net beginning inventory........			Lit.	16,996,557,334
Purchases........			Lit.	26,034,091,817
Work done and related costs........			Lit.	60,415,342,031
Cost of production and administration........			Lit.	13,658,227,175
Financial liabilities:				
Interest, costs, and bank charges.........	Lit.	2,269,309,821		
Interest on loans........	Lit.	141,325,011		
Interest on debentures........	Lit.	2,010,723,385		
			Lit.	4,421,358,217
Tax liabilities........			Lit.	3,014,247,876
Depreciation of fixed assets:				
Ordinary........	Lit.	2,728,441,335		
Extraordinary........	Lit.	3,287,944,077		
			Lit.	6,016,385,412
Less:				
Ending inventory........			Lit.	13,325,991,919
Net profit........			Lit.	4,924,543,712
Total........			Lit.	122,154,761,655

Balance Sheet for the Year Ended December 31, 1965

ASSETS

		31-12-1965
1. Fixed assets:		
Residential buildings	Lit.	1,344,884,948
Industrial buildings	Lit.	19,345,589,007
Machinery and specific equipment	Lit.	15,340,680,072
General plant	Lit.	8,163,452,211
Electronic equipment	Lit.	820,000,000
Furnaces	Lit.	468,609,405
Motor vehicles	Lit.	557,954,815
Patents and furniture	Lit.	1
	Lit.	46,041,170,459
2. Inventories	Lit.	13,325,991,919
3. Current bank a/cs and cash:		
Cash	Lit.	637,726,552
Banks	Lit.	2,186,569,029
	Lit.	2,824,295,581
4. Other current assets:		
Government bonds and security deposits	Lit.	936,464,014
Investments in subsidiaries	Lit.	50,257,426,367
	Lit.	51,193,890,381
5. Accounts receivable:		
Customers	Lit.	32,007,231,823
Subsidiaries	Lit.	46,321,293,777
Notes outstanding	Lit.	6,708,628,417
	Lit.	85,037,154,017
6. Unamortised expenses	Lit.	729,129,312
Total assets	Lit.	199,151,631,669
7. Contra items:		
Directors' deposits	Lit.	2,600,000
Securities	Lit.	455,088,772
Guarantees	Lit.	27,601,022,343
	Lit.	28,058,711,115
Total	Lit.	227,210,342,784

LIABILITIES

		31-12-1965
1. Capital stock:		
Common stock	Lit.	36,000,000,000
Preferred stock	Lit.	24,000,000,000
	Lit.	60,000,000,000
2. Reserves:		
Ordinary	Lit.	876,823,416
Extraordinary	Lit.	600,000,000
Reinvestment in South Italy	Lit.	400,000,000
	Lit.	1,876,823,416
3. Accumulated depreciation:		
Ordinary depreciation	Lit.	16,705,056,290
Extraordinary depreciation	Lit.	11,176,697,285
	Lit.	27,881,753,575
4. Retirement fund	Lit.	21,127,944,115
5. Social services and activities fund	Lit.	200,843,573
6. Accrued liabilities	Lit.	6,588,894,395
7. Funded liabilities:		
Debentures	Lit.	34,074,865,000
Swiss loan	Lit.	2,190,000,000
	Lit.	36,264,865,000
8. Debts:		
To banks	Lit.	5,847,966,870
Guaranteed	Lit.	864,951,428
Notes receivable guaranteed	Lit.	—
To suppliers	Lit.	6,688,007,855
To subsidiaries	Lit.	358,958,843
Miscellaneous	Lit.	26,459,321,155
	Lit.	40,219,206,151
9. Net profit	Lit.	4,924,543,712
10. Profits brought down	Lit.	66,757,732
Total liabilities	Lit.	199,151,631,669
11. Contra items:		
Directors' deposits	Lit.	2,600,000
Securities	Lit.	455,088,772
Guarantees	Lit.	27,601,022,343
	Lit.	28,058,711,115
Total	Lit.	227,210,342,784

Source: Company records.

Exhibit 3
OLIVETTI PRODUCTS
Lettera 32—Portable Typewriter

Praxis 48—Compact Electric Typewriter

Exhibit 3—Continued

Tekne 3—Electric Typewriter

Electrosumma 20—Electric Adding Machine

Exhibit 3—Concluded

Divisumma 24—Printing Calculator

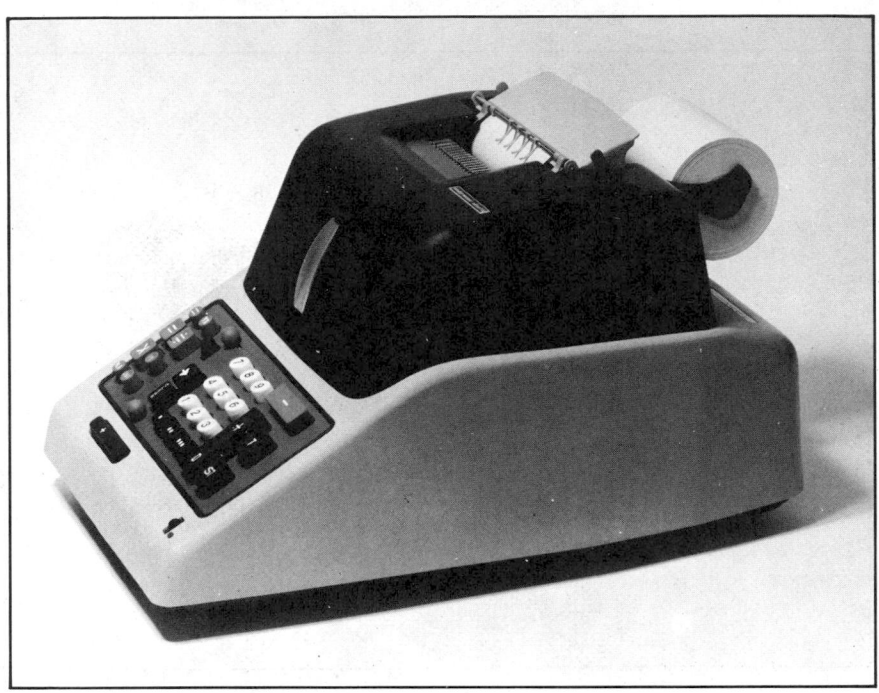

Programma 101—Desk Top Computer

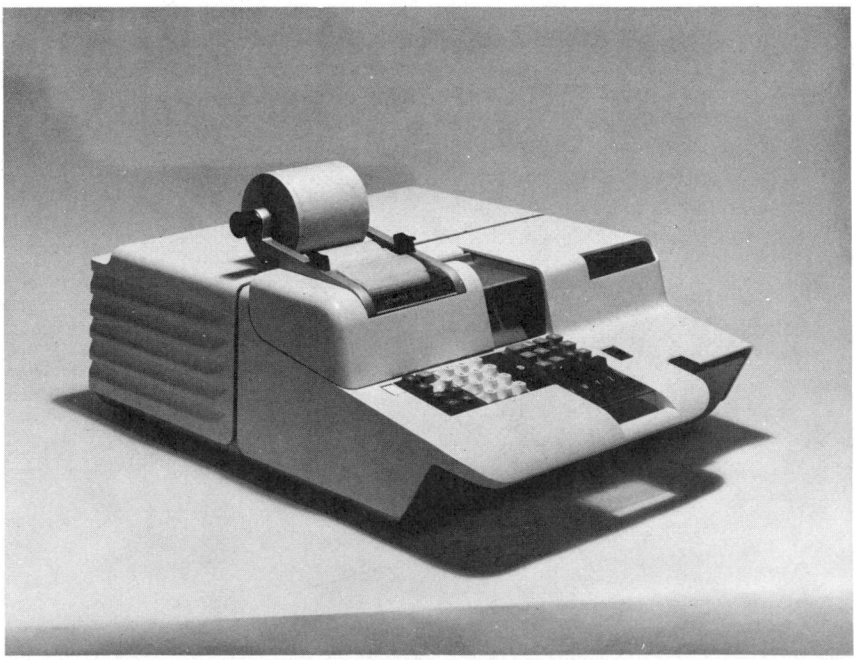

Exhibit 4

OLIVETTI COMPANY HEADQUARTERS AND TWO FACTORIES
IN ITALY

Company Headquarters in Ivrea, Italy

Typewriter Factory in Scarmagno, Italy

Exhibit 4—Concluded

Adding Machine Factory in Pozzuoli, Italy

Exhibit 5

OLIVETTI EMPLOYEE HEALTH CENTER, EMPLOYEE
CAFETERIA, AND EMPLOYEE HOUSING, IN IVERA, ITALY

Employee Health Center, Ivrea, Italy

Employee Cafeteria, Ivrea, Italy

Exhibit 5—Concluded
Employee Housing, Ivrea, Italy

cooperation between the classes, a conciliation whose ethical premise he found in religious inspiration. He wrote: " 'Forgive us our debts as we forgive our debtors,' goes an ancient prayer to which all believers can subscribe. We do not ask for total forgiveness, for this would require that all men have the Christian spirit one hundred per cent— and this is too much to ask. But if men had fifty per cent of this spirit, it might then be possible to insist that the interest rate on capital be low enough so that even the working man can develop his capacities. As is often the case, following moral law in this instance would also have an immediate practical value."

New approaches to techniques and organization

For the Ivrea factory the period between the two World Wars marked the end of the handwork and pioneering phase. To survive in a market dominated by experienced foreign competitors, Olivetti had to face problems which more firmly established concerns in other fields had already solved. A new typewriter, the M20, was brought out in Italy in 1920 and immediately afterward was shown at the Brussels International Fair. In 1922 a new corporation, the Olivetti Foundry, was established; in 1924, the O.M.O. (Officina Meccanica Olivetti) machine-tools plant. In that year the company employed 400 workers and typewriter production reached the rate of 4,000 a year. By 1926 the number of workers had risen to 500 and production to 8,000. The rhythm of expansion, reflecting the inner dynamics of the firm, was intense and continuous. The growing number of employees made the old, almost patriarchal, type of management obsolete. The first industrial revolution of the pioneers like Camillo Olivetti was about to be superseded by the second, that of the managers. In 1925 and 1926 Adriano Olivetti, at the request of his father, Camillo, traveled in the United States to study American production methods. On his return to Ivrea he applied the ideas acquired on his visits to American factories to the reorganization of the Olivetti plants and the creation of new cadres of trained young personnel. Thanks to these systematic innovations, by 1929 production soared to 13,000 annually, without any increase in the labor force.

The company was accordingly in a good position to face the great depression of 1930 and 1931. The lowered costs of production made it possible to initiate a bold expansion campaign by building up the Italian sales organization, opening new branches in the main cities and staffing them with additional sales personnel. The first associated company abroad, the S.A. Hispano Olivetti was established at Barcelona in 1929, and the next year Olivetti Belge, the Belgian associate, was founded. A new product, the M40 typewriter, was brought out and subsequently held the market successfully for many years. Other products were planned, such as the Olivetti portable and the Synthesis horizontal card files. Along with production and sales, human relations within the company were transformed. Social insurance and assistance provisions were broadened; new work-time study methods were adopted; and new psychological and esthetic criteria were applied in advertising.

Adriano's innovations added impetus to the heritage of Camillo's experience and moral force, and he was gradually given full responsibility for running the firm. By 1933, the year in which Adriano Olivetti became director general of the company, the battle to survive the world depression had been won.

A specific meaning underlying the Olivetti story was becoming apparent. The replacement of manual by mechanical writing and calculating, and the creation of machines for rationalizing office work in business and industry were the motive force of an enterprise inspired by a responsible view of the economic, social and cultural implications of labor and industrial life. In this respect, the impress of Adriano Olivetti's personality was tangibly evident in the company's achievements, whether in organizing the social services, planning a new factory in terms of economic and social development, opening another line of production, studying the design of a new product, balancing form and function in an industrial building, or in drafting effective advertising copy.

The Olivetti style

When Olivetti celebrated its 25th anniversary, in 1933, the reorganization begun in 1927 had revamped every aspect of the company's life. Production amounted to 15,000 office machines and 9,000 portables. The company employed 870 people. In Italy, the sales network included 13 branches and 79 concessionaries, and abroad Olivetti was actively represented in dozens of countries.

In succeeding years, the line of products was extended and elaborated. Studies for the construction of adding machines began in 1934. The semistandard Studio 44 was brought out in 1935. Plans for a teleprinter got under way in 1936 and the year following, it went into production. The first planer milling machine, designed by Camillo Olivetti, was produced by the O.M.O. plant in 1938.

The years between 1938 and 1942 saw the construction of the group of buildings for the new I.C.O. plant, whose long facade in reinforced concrete and glass still stands out among successive enlargements as a bold and functional architectural solution. At Massa, in Tuscany, the Olivetti Synthesis company began production of filing cabinets, card files and metal office furniture. The first permanent summer camp for employees' children was inaugurated at Champoluc, a mountain area near Ivrea. In 1938 Adriano Olivetti succeeded his father as president of the company, a position he held, except for brief interruptions, until his death in 1960. For 22 years the history of the Ivrea plant and the biography of its president make a single story. Adriano Olivetti set a perhaps unique example of how full and coherent a part industry can play in the social and cultural life of the community.

A personal religious inclination, which he owed in part to his father's influence, was fused in him with a responsible sensitivity to contemporary values. Adriano Olivetti was aware of the spiritual impoverishment and the moral corruption that the superficial acquisition of the means of "civilization" visit on society and the standards proper to Western culture, but he considered them errors in the system which could be corrected. This was his outstanding trait as a modern industrialist, thinker and reformer. He considered material progress as an essential factor in human redemption. He did not view science as a destroyer of tradition, fundamental values and the feeling for the absolute that goes with religious morality. On the contrary, he identified the course of science with that of truth, its conquests with a con-

tinuous verging toward freedom from suffering. The background for
his philosophy lies in various sources, ranging from his personal interpretation of the contemporary French Catholic trend represented by
Mounier, Weil and Maritain, to his familiarity with American developments in the social sciences. But they are united in a single theme
running through everything he accomplished: the reconciliation of material and spiritual values. It is a motivating idea which he formulated
in a book published just after the War, *L'Ordine politico delle communita* (*The Political Order of the Communities*), and which recurs in
his most disparate activities. Thus it underlies his work in industrial
organization, town planning, social services, political campaigning,
adult education, sociology, technical and scientific research, the visual
arts, publishing and public administration. His interest was centered
not so much on the industrial enterprise considered as an end in itself,
as on the human and physical environment in which it operates. Even
the most specifically technical and organizational problems were studied by him from this point of view. Whatever he gave his attention to
achieved a firm balance between the growing industrial power of his
company and the world around it. This approach led him to an intense
interest in town planning, considered not merely as a means of pragmatic and esthetic improvement, but as a positive factor in group living
and social progress. The idea of organically reconstructing city and
territory by planning at local and regional levels was in his view of the
world innate and necessary. He saw everything in terms of how best
the individual could live with his neighbors in a given environment,
and of democratic social organization "on the scale of man." His enthusiasm for town planning was an integral part of his interest in
social assistance methods, the use of free time, and the administration
of community life to permit the most effective individual expression.

The future historian of 20th-century Italian life will find that at the
beginning of all the studies and work in town planning during the last
several decades is Adriano Olivetti's master plan for the Valle d'Aosta,
which was published in 1937. Going beyond municipal limits, it was
the first attempt at regional planning. Moreover it was the first time, at
least in Italy, that a public leader considered town and regional planning an essential field of study in building a modern country. The creation of the social services and housing settlements in Ivrea and the
model village of La Martella, near Matera, in one of the worst of southern Italy's depressed areas, are only two of the important examples of
Adriano Olivetti's work as a social thinker and organizer. Town planning, understood as the science of community living, is necessarily also
concerned with architecture. Adriano's passion for industrial architecture was closely connected with his philosophy, hence with the need he
acutely felt to improve living conditions by means of specific programs
and actual constructions. The form of a building interested him, but he
was even more concerned with its purpose. Radically different in approach from the pure esthete, he aimed to promote the construction of
buildings, whether for habitation, work, study, research or recreation,
that would correspond to people's needs, be satisfying esthetically and
above all embody the feeling of community life. This particular concept is one of the most salient traits in his personality as a modern
humanist. His outstanding merit, as George Friedmann recently put it,
is that of "having succeeded in bringing together mechanized industry

and the new form of beauty that has appeared on our horizon—the beauty of technical civilization."

In his vision, factories built "on the scale of man" would produce a continual stream of products designed for man. The desirability of devoting special attention to product design had been emphasized by Camillo Olivetti from the very beginning of the Ivrea factory. At that time he wrote, "A machine should not be a gewgaw for the living room, ornate and in questionable taste. It should have an appearance that is serious and elegant at the same time."

His son echoed these words in more contemporary terms when he summed up the principles of Olivetti design: "The design of every product stands out for its clarity, unity and logic. The office machine designs are pleasing but not oversmooth, rational but not inhuman, discreet but not banal."

With respect to Olivetti design, a few years ago an American writer quoted an observation by Schiller which might well apply to the achievements promoted by Adriano Olivetti: "One of culture's most important tasks is that of subjecting man to the influence of form even in his merely physical life, and to make his life esthetic by introducing the norm of the beautiful wherever possible, for only from esthetic conditions and not from physical conditions can moral life develop." If the "norm of the beautiful" is an essential condition for a fuller life, this same norm is an indispensable influence on man's will and psychology, making him aware of his powers of mind, imagination and fantasy. In the light of this reasoning, advertising must be seen as a means of stimulating and developing the moral and esthetic values inherent in human nature. Believing this, Adriano Olivetti contributed to his company's advertising the standards determined by his close involvement with current cultural developments and his lively feeling for the forms of contemporary art. He had no faith in the hard sell. The company produced quality products and its advertising would have to meet the same high standards. Planned and maintained on the level of art, Olivetti advertising does not aim at quick impact, but at fresh and personal expression having a long-term effect in depth. These principles have themselves become "the company's true hallmark, standing for a firm founded on modern technology, efficiency, honesty, elegance and human welfare."

The close bond between technology and the forms of publicity, and the influence of functional architecture and modern geometric design on the company's products, graphic work and printing, have created a unified image embracing numerous activities that complement each other. Each achievement is identifiable as expressing the company's "style," in the broadest sense of the term.

Olivetti, a world enterprise

This complex but unified image is the creation of Adriano Olivetti and the many technicians, industrial designers, graphic artists, architects, painters, writers and social scientists he enlisted to work closely with him. The image took its present form mainly during the last several decades, in step with Olivetti's development on a world scale. Before the war the company had already begun to attract intellectuals and artists. The war years created a hiatus. Camillo Olivetti died toward the end of the sinister period when the triumph of extremist nationalism, racism, and the forces of destruction saw the wreck of the values and ideals for which he had worked, and in which he believed religiously. Adriano Olivetti, obliged to go into exile in Switzerland, was able there to develop and then publish his political and social ideas, in his book *L'Ordine politico delle communita,* which served as a point of departure for his activities on his return to Italy after the liberation. By 1945, the factory was employing more than 4,000 people. Besides typewriters, the company was producing adding machines, calculators and tele-printers. A new plant was built in Turin to supplement the production capacity of those in Ivrea. The factory at Massa, which had been partially destroyed during the hostilities, was rebuilt. Between 1948 and 1954 the entire range of products was redesigned. Four new typewriter models and three calculators were produced. Increased production called for the reorganization of the distribution network not only in Italy and the few countries where the company was represented before the war, but all over the world. The last ten years were marked by the unprecedented growth of what today is the largest manufacturer of office machines in Europe.

Adriano Olivetti's theories in politics, social service, town planning and esthetics presupposed a forward-looking policy of expansion in production and sales, for only the physical expansion of the enterprise could provide daily proof of the validity of his "revolutionary" approach.

In his personality, thinker and reformer, farsighted organizer and dynamic promoter complemented each other without conflict. Underlying his thought was the conviction that organized production is part and parcel of contemporary culture. He refused to follow what he called "the tragic march toward efficiency and profit," in the materialist sense, but was dominated by the idea of directing every effort toward ideal ends. In 1958 he wrote: "Labor has to participate in the aims of the factory, I realized when I started working. This realization implied the answer to some of the fundamental questions of my life, questions dramatically repeated in moments of doubt and uncertainty, questions profoundly decisive for the faith they presuppose and the obligations they denote: Can industry have aims? Are these aims simply to be found in the index of profits, or is there not also an ideal, a destiny and vocation in the life of the factory?"

The program of technical and organizational improvements initiated some 30 years ago in the Ivrea plants has been continuously carried forward, with the same objectives, up to the present day. At the end of 1951, after completion of the postwar reorganization, the labor force numbered 5,000 and clerical and managerial personnel, 1,000. By 1956 the total number of employees, including those in the Italian and foreign sales organizations, was 16,000. In 1959 there were 25,000 employees, while production reached 735,000 unit equivalents of a standard typewriter. The year following, production rose to 1,035,000, and in 1961 to 1,390,000 units. The number of Olivetti employees in 1961 was about 39,000. In the same year the Underwood Corporation (whose connections with Olivetti will be discussed below) had about 12,000 employees. New divisions had been added in recent years to the Ivrea plant constructed between 1938 and 1942. In line with the main building and connected with it by an overhead passage, a series of new plants houses various production facilities. Behind these, a large building for the company school and cafeteria has been erected. Nearby, the

Study and Experiment Center, inaugurated in 1955, is used by specialists engaged in designing new machines and working out new production methods. Opposite, on the same street, stand the social services and cultural center and the library, which are the concrete expression of the particular human climate that distinguishes the organization.

The development of the company and its increasingly broad economic influence on the region centering on Ivrea, suggested the desirability of a progressive decentralization program. Accordingly, a teleprinter plant was set up at San Lorenzo; the new machine-tools factory was constructed at S. Bernardo; and other small plants and workshops for the production of accessory equipment were similarly decentralized. Also in Piedmont, the Algié plant was purchased in 1955 for the mass production of portables; and in Lombardy the more recent electronic research laboratory was constructed at Borgolombardo, near Milan. Finally, there is the Pozzuoli factory, near Naples, which not only raises Olivetti's production capacity, but also contributes to the needed industrialization of southern Italy and has helped to raise the living standard of a depressed area. Other factories were constructed abroad. Most extensive of the foreign plants is that of the Hispano Olivetti company, in Barcelona, where production and assembly shops are laid out around an office building, dining hall, sports fields and swimming pool. Also in operation abroad are the factories of British Olivetti in Glasgow, Olivetti Argentina in Buenos Aires, Olivetti Industrial in Sao Paulo, Brazil (the last two recently constructed), and of Olivetti Africa in Johannesburg.

The list of Olivetti products today ranges from typewriters to office furniture, from teleprinters to machine tools, from calculators to accounting machines, and from data-processing equipment to electronic computers. Sales have been developed as dynamically as production. Thirty-nine branches and two hundred and fifty exclusive distributors make up the commercial network in Italy. Abroad, a group of 22 companies associated with Olivetti have created their own sales organizations, either patterned on the Italian system or based, where more suitable, on local conditions. The Olivetti associated companies are located in Argentina, Australia, Austria, Belgium, Brazil, Canada, Colombia, Denmark, France, Germany, Great Britain, Japan, Mexico, Peru, Portugal, Spain, the United States, Sweden, Switzerland, South Africa, and Venezuela.

The last years of Adriano Olivetti's life saw the achievement of projects that had been on the company's program for some time, as well as the opening of highly interesting new prospects. In 1958 when Olivetti celebrated its 50th anniversary, new products, new factories, new sales organizations were carrying the image of a vital contemporary enterprise all over the globe. Olivetti's advanced level of technology and organization allowed it to compete successfully in all the main foreign markets, and production was now predominantly devoted to export. Consequently, every move to reduce tariff barriers and customs obstacles created new possibilities for Olivetti sales abroad. In fact, the measures already adopted toward trade liberalization and European economic integration have confirmed this by stepping up the rhythm of exports, and justify particularly favorable prospects for the future as the common market treaties are progressively implemented.

Another factor promising further notable development for Olivetti is the agreement that was signed at the end of 1959 with Underwood, the famous American office machine company. Under the terms of this agreement for close cooperation, Olivetti became the majority shareholder in the American company. Mr. Ugo Galassi of Olivetti, still in charge of the Italian Sales Organization, took over as President of the new American Allied Company. Underwood, operating an extensive sales network in the United States, needed other competitive products to offer along with models produced in its American factories. Following the merger, Underwood filled this need with machines constructed by Olivetti, especially in the calculator and accounting machine line. Similar relations were established between Olivetti and Underwood Ltd. of Toronto to cover distribution in Canada.

The Underwood deal was the last large-scale operation conceived and carried out by Adriano Olivetti. On February 27, 1960, he died on a train traveling near Aglié. He was at the height of his dynamic career at the service of his company and the country, and the many-sided enterprise he summed up and represented was progressing as he had intended. A few months before his death he wrote: "Time is flying. Things are on the move. We cannot stop to rummage among the old formulas and institutions of the past. We now stand before the new. In easier times we may and should improve the social institutions of the past, but we would still be looking backward if these improvements were to be only technical. It is necessary to go beyond that, to see whether within the limits of a given economy and a changing society these forms and institutions can be modified or replaced by new solutions inspired by new principles."

The secret of the achievement connected with the name of Olivetti lies in this moral impetus which has vitalized the company from its pioneering period to the present day. The company's world importance was not achieved fortuitously. Besides the ability of its labor staff and management, it owes a great part of its success to the broad ideas of Adriano Olivetti, and of those who are continuing his work. In 1960, Giuseppe Pero, who entered the firm in 1920 as one of the first associates of Camillo Olivetti, became president of the company. In the present as in the past, his dedication to the company has been a central factor in its development.

In little more than half a century, the Italian, then the European public, and now the whole world have seen this company project a constantly varied but fundamentally unified series of ideas, forms and colors which make up its theme and visual image. If the result has been the creation of a distinctive style, a recognizable "face," it is thanks to what lies behind this face: a spirit whose aim is to unify this variety for a specific objective. And the objective has been to make a moral and cultural as well as a practical contribution to the life of our times.[1]

Tocco Olivetti: the Olivetti touch

From the time Adriano Olivetti joined Olivetti he had concerned himself with the development of a unified approach to both the internal and external world of his company. Ricardo Musatti, who was director

---

[1] *Olivetti, a Contemporary Image of Style and Industry* (published by the Olivetti Company, 1962).

of the advertising and press department for Olivetti in 1962, expressed Adriano Olivetti's underlying philosophy.

> Two fundamental ideas inspired the thought and action of Adriano Olivetti. First, the conviction that industry in view of its great influence in the contemporary world, ought to have a code of ethics and a system of objectives going beyond the purely economic sphere which in any case it has long overlapped. Second, the conviction that present-day mass civilization, more dynamic and richer in technical and scientific resources than any period in the past, should make every effort to achieve the "kingdom of Vocations," a human society organized so that every man may give the best in him by expressing himself most fully and constructively.[2]

Horizon wrote of the roots of the Olivetti style.

> In the late twenties, the Olivetti Company reflected the state of Italian industrial design, which had got off to a lively start and then fallen back into eclectic, perfunctory and sentimental habits. But by 1930, the philosophy of the Weimer Bauhaus group began to filter into Italy, just at the time when its influence in Germany was being undermined by the Nazis. The philosophy of this school was congenial to Olivetti's temper. It combined high technical skill with the purest aesthetic ideas. Besides, as one of his assistants has put it, "Olivetti's force is that he has always wanted to be in the vanguard." The Weimer school brought together workers in all the arts: the architects Mies van der Rohe and Gropius; the painters Klee and Kandinsky; designers such as Herbert Bayer and Moholy-Nagy. In the early thirties, the painter Xanty Schawinsky, who had spent four fruitful years at the Bauhaus, came to work for Olivetti. Soon one could sense the direction the new Olivetti style was taking. The stern austerity of the Bauhaus was somewhat softened and made more poetic by the Italian atmosphere, but here was the same formidable use of photography, the brilliant play of type, and the disdain for irrelevant frippery which marked the Bauhaus style. By 1938, Olivetti had recruited an extraordinary team of designers who were to transform his wishes into reality in a series of startling posters, striking exhibition displays, and subtly conceived booklets.
>
> Discussing the role which [Adriano] Olivetti himself played in creating the company style, Pintori [one of the designers who played an important role in developing Olivetti advertising] recently remarked: "At the beginning, he was intimately involved with everything we did, . . . He not only chose the men who did the work, but he gave suggestions and criticisms of the finished work down to the last detail. Particularly with the architects, he was constantly involved in the job—but with us too. He is a man teeming with intuition. He has a style and although he may not be able to fabricate it in any special way he knows how to communicate its sense and then to judge its results.[3]

The Olivetti style became known inside and outside the company as the *"Tocco Olivetti,"* or the "Olivetti Touch." While the Olivetti touch, according to company executives, had influenced virtually every aspect

---

[2] Ibid.

[3] "Olivetti: A Man and a Style," by Kermit Lansner (November 1959, *Horizon*). © 1959 by American Heritage Publishing Co., Inc. Reprinted by permission.

of the company's operations, it was most visible in the areas of advertising, product design, company architectures, and social services.

Advertising

Advertising was the first area in which *tocco Olivetti* came to be expressed. Adriano Olivetti's first job in 1928 with the Olivetti Company was advertising director, and he continued to supervise this area actively until his death in 1960.

The approach which Adriano Olivetti took to advertising set the company apart radically from its competition.

> The innovation it [the Olivetti Company] introduced in Italian advertising was based on the refusal to conform to the so-called public taste. The refusal did not stem from the desire to be in the vanguard at any cost, but from the conviction that public taste does not exist: like fashions it is not created by masses of people but by individual personalities whose example is accepted and then becomes general habit. To convey the idea of special quality requires stimulating the average taste by means of unconventional forms and language. In this connection Olivetti advertising put less emphasis on the product than on the service it offered and its message of modernity and progress.[4]

The underlying philosophy was, "We do not stupefy the customer with the sound of our advertising voice, or use it as an instrument of aggression against him. We do not evoke vast materialistic instincts or sexual urges. We are not tied to the salesman's fleeting problems." Another early member of the advertising staff is quoted as saying, "We know the rules of advertising so that we can disobey them. For us advertising is like soap for the spirit, clean and virtuous." Dr. Musatti put it this way:

> Olivetti has always insisted that we must present the ideal of a mechanical culture, that we must give the idea that the machine, the typewriter, is the last word in modern culture. Do you remember one of Pintori's most famous posters? On the left was an inkwell with an old fashioned pen. In the inkwell was a beautiful rose. To the right there was nothing but the words Olivetti Studio 42. The pen belongs to romantic past, the typewriter is of the world today.[5]

Industrial design

Camillo Olivetti had had an appreciation for the importance of the aesthetic in machine design, but his tastes had called for a revolution against the traditional "ornate gewgaws." He had approached design from the functionalist point of view, arguing that anything which did not have a place in the mechanical functioning of a machine was unnecessary. This approach had been contrary to the standards of his contemporaries who still reflected the love for "gingerbread," of the early 1900's. Dr. Musatti said of this period:

---

[4] Ibid.

[5] "Olivetti: Elegant and Tough," *Fortune,* September 1960, pp. 137 ff.

The problem of the relations between useful object and aesthetic form has existed from the earliest times, and has always found a contemporary solution. The triumph of the Machine Age and the somewhat misunderstood principle of functionalism led to the debasement of the aesthetic value of tools and utensils, which at other times had been the object of elaborate handworks.[6]

Adriano Olivetti, however, approached the problem differently from his father. He said: "The design of every product stands out for its clarity, unity and logic. The office machine designs are pleasing, but not over-smooth, rational but not inhuman, discreet but not banal." Starting in 1930, Adriano Olivetti had tried to make this concept of industrial design a reality in the Olivetti products. He had met some resistance from his father who still could not see the reasoning behind the great concern and expense for the aesthetic. It was reported that there had been some heated discussions about the necessity of redesign for aesthetic reasons but Adriano Olivetti persisted.

The height of Olivetti advances in product design stemmed from the work of Marcello Nizzoli. Marcello Nizzolo, when a young painter and advertising artist had been encouraged by Adriano Olivetti to become a product designer and then an architect. Destined to become world-famous as an industrial designer Nizzolo over the years had been responsible for the industrial design of many Olivetti machines including the Lexikon 80, Lettera 22, the Studio 44, the 82 Diaspron typewriters and the Divisumma, Tetractys and Audit calculating and accounting machines. Olivetti won several international prizes for the design of these products. The Lettera 22 was selected in a worldwide poll conducted by Illinois Institute of Technology as first among the ten best examples of contemporary industrial design. It has been exhibited at the Metropolitan Museum of Art.

The evolution in product design has proceeded around two basic themes since 1940. The first theme, expressed in the calculating machines, was that of a six-sided solid parallelogram with rounded corners. The second major theme was the "fluid ovoid" form expressed in the typewriters. Variety in relation to these themes was introduced through keyboard design, which was directed at relating the required key positions to cubic, cylindrical and rectangular overtones. Color, too, was a tool which was widely employed.

In later typewriters, Olivetti exhibited a trend away from the fluidity for which it had become stylistically famous. As other manufacturers followed by rounding corners and making graceful sweeps of metallic form, the Olivetti style turned to intersecting planes, oblique angles, and sharply contrasting colors. The Praxis 48 and the Olivetti Tekne epitomize the concept of sharp linearity in both form and color.

The importance of design in Olivetti's history can perhaps be measured by one executive's comment: "With Adriano, you always knew when you had to consult him. Any question of product design had to be personally approved." Even in 1966, the men in research and de-

---

[6] *Notes Towards the History of a Factory* (published by the Olivetti Company, 1958).

velopment admit that they made compromises to get the required product characteristics within an aesthetically pleasing package. One executive, looking toward the future said, "Clearly, Olivetti no longer has a position as a leader. Others have become aware of the importance of that which Olivetti pioneered." Olivetti executives often attested to the fact that in 1966, Thomas J. Watson, Jr., president of IBM Corporation, paid tribute to Olivetti's pioneering understanding of the importance of industrial design. While accepting the Tiffany Award for "Encouragement of American Design," he said:

> I'd like to take credit for all of the things you've seen as coming out of my own head . . . actually they came from a company called Olivetti, which hasn't had the success in the business field lately that it really deserves, but Adriano Olivetti, an Italian, many, many years ago decided that it was with a theme of excellence, through color, through interiors, through design and through products, and particularly through buildings, that he could establish his company as a worldwide symbol. And he did. . . . And some of us in IBM thought perhaps we could do it too, so I wanted to pay my respects to his leadership. He's now gone.

Architecture

Architecture was another important concern of Adriano Olivetti. The earliest Olivetti factory built in Ivrea had been patterned after the original Underwood plant in Hartford, Connecticut. It was done in the red brick style common in New England. Planning expansion of facilities immediately preceding and following World War II, however, Adriano Olivetti decided to apply principles of modern functional design when enlarging the factory building. His idea was the creation of a unified environment which would allow the buildings and the workers to fit harmoniously with the environment. In this regard, Dr. Zorzi, director of advertising, in 1966 said, "Architecture and the role of man in an urban society were the two great passions of Adriano Olivetti, and in building his factories he was able to serve them both. He disliked the idea that work should be solely a source of income for the worker, a necessary evil which should be endured in order to gain material recompense. He hoped that by introducing 'the norm of the beautiful' into the workers' surroundings, some of the drudgery might be eliminated."

In making his selection of architects, Adriano Olivetti reportedly did not rely upon a single school of design. Again according to Dr. Zorzi, "He believed in intelligence. He chose young men, 25 to 30 years old, in whom he had confidence and gave them the commission." By the time of his death he knew most of the great architects of Europe, some of whom were in his debt for having been given their first chance.

The example which was often cited as the culmination of the effect of *tocco Olivetti* on the company's architecture was the factory at Pozzuoli (see Exhibit 4). This factory allowed Olivetti to show his concern for both architecture and social responsibility. In 1952, when Olivetti decided to build the plant in Pozzuoli, in the economically underdeveloped South, the town was very poor. It was located about 20 kilometers north of Naples on the Gulf of Baia. The inhabitants had never done factory work, and were largely dependent upon agriculture and tourism. Adriano Olivetti decided to build the factory, without particular government encouragement, except for a limited fiscal advantage.[7] "He was making a pilot experiment in a depressed area. . . . He chose a poor town with little employment, yet not so poor as to be crushed. His aim was to found a productive enterprise in the presumably inefficient South and to lure other industry into the area if it were successful."[8]

Adriano Olivetti appointed Mr. Cosenza, an avowed communist, as his architect for the Pozzuoli factory. Both men felt that there would have to be a transition from the unfettered agrarian life which the people of Pozzuoli were used to leading to the regimented existence of a factory population. The architect described his concept as follows: "I wanted to make the factory less like a prison. You can't change the fact that it is a prison, but I wanted to make it as different from the old-fashioned factory as I could. I know Olivetti feels the same way." *Horizon* described the factory as follows:

> From Via Domitiana, which passes the main facade, the building might be taken for an elegant resort hotel or a sanatorium in the modern style. For there in the background are the heights of Mount Campiglione, and stretching before the factory is the Gulf of Baia with Capri and Ischia visible in the distance when the day is clear. Cosenza has created a plant which is unique in its sense of freedom and elegance. From every bench and point of the assembly line there is a view of the outdoors. Light pours in with all its Mediterranean clarity and abundance. Spotted here and there among the low buildings which are joined together in a coherent whole are ponds caught in free form concrete walls. Landscaping encloses the entire industrial bulk and reunites it with nature. . . .
>
> So splendid is the whole establishment that there is a wry truth to the remark which the director of the plant made as he summed up the effect of the factory on the people of Pozzuoli: "For those who haven't found employment here, the factory is like Kafka's castle. It is a kind of Paradise where the lucky ones have gained entrance."[9] (See Exhibit 4.)

As *Fortune*[10] declared, "the *tocco Olivetti* included turning aesthetics into profit." The Pozzuoli plant was a good example. Judged on an output per man-hour basis, productivity in the plant was as good as, if not better than, in the plants in the more industrial North, according to company executives.

The architectural design of the most recent building, a large structure erected in Ivrea to house the firm's headquarters, has been a matter of controversy. (For a photograph of this building see Exhibit 4.) One executive spoke somewhat disparagingly about it saying that it was a

---

[7] There was some tax advantage; for ten years no tax on income was required.

[8] K. Lansner, "Olivetti: A Man and a Style."

[9] Ibid.

[10] *Fortune*, "Olivetti: Elegant and Tough," September 1960.

"$5,000,000 hostage to the Canavese region." Another made the comment: "If Adriano saw this, he would go to Tanganyika and start over. It is so out of place in the Canavese countryside." Several executives pointed out that the new building disrupted many of the more informal patterns of communication which had existed prior to 1963. With its long corridors and enclosed offices, these executives reported that informal contact with other executives was less frequent than it had been previously. Also some executives wondered about the appropriateness of having the headquarters of a large international corporation in a remote provincial town like Ivrea.

Social services

From the beginning of the Olivetti Company, there has been a strong concern for the well-being of the workers. Camillo Olivetti had been a humanist as well as an industrialist. Adriano Olivetti in *Notes Towards the History of a Factory*, described the social services of the early period.

> My father before me guided the workshop with an eye to intelligence, but listening also to the wisdom of the heart. In those days they took on at the plant all the youths who had a reputation in the parish of being capable, hard workers. They used to set aside at least one hour a day for the employee who wanted a job for his wife or sister-in-law, or who needed a loan to buy furniture or pay off a debt; the employee who felt underrated by his section chief or wanted a transfer for reasons of health or a leave for a period of convalescence. For all of them, whenever possible, a remedy or a solution was found.
>
> This personal touch, introduced by men of heart, was inevitably lost as the factory became larger. My father understood this long before I did. . . . My father created a fund. This fund served to guarantee social security to the employee above and beyond the limited amount provided by Italian law. Thus, no one was forced to go into debt in order to pay for his father's or sister's funeral. No one had to forego a last farewell to his mother who might be dying in a distant place. Mothers were furnished with beds, mattresses, coats, shoes for their children; and no one remained without wood in the winter. Orphans and widows received ample assistance; and no convalescent was ever forced to return to work before he was able.
>
> In the process of reorganizing these services, I came to understand the intimate relationship between health assistance and social assistance. I realized how insensitive to such problems are those who have never had to face them, or those concerned only with the objectives of efficiency or profit.[11]

In order to "establish a responsible administration with some guarantee of stability and to develop higher standards of scientific objectivity" Olivetti set up the Labor Management Council to run the Olivetti social services. The charter of that group said: "The Olivetti Social Services place joint responsibility on workers and management. Each employee, by his work, contributes to the life of the company and so to the life of the organizations created within it, and is therefore entitled to assistance without any question of charity arising. Likewise, all workers have

---

[11] *Notes Towards the History of a Factory.*

an equal right to social service benefits; each case is judged on its merits and by criteria as objective as possible which are subject to constant study and revision."

Adriano Olivetti said of the work in social services: "If the material and moral aims of our work are upheld, one day this factory will be an integral part of a new and authentic civilization directed toward a freer, happier and more conscious development of the human individual." In 1966 the company estimated it spent 2,700 million lire for social services. In addition the by-laws of the company state: "Once 8.5% [of the par value of the shares] has been assigned to both preferred and common shares and before any other appropriation that may be resolved by the general meeting, a sum equal to 4% of the net profit of the financial year shall, provided there are sufficient funds, be deducted from the residue and placed at the disposal of the board of directors, which with a view to supplementing the company's ordinary expenditure on social services and activities shall assign said sum to boards, institutions or organizations situated in the areas where the company's main factories are located and having as their object the development of education and technical and scientific research."

Dr. Volponi, the director of social services at Olivetti, explained: "We consider the social services as an important part of the system. Everyone working in the company has a right to these services, and the process of determining who gets what is public knowledge. At present we have a cafeteria; a complete health clinic, including medical services for dependents; library facilities with over 150,000 volumes; vacation houses in the mountains and on the seashore; recreational facilities of varied natures; employee housing [see Exhibit 5]; transport facilities to get workers from their homes to work; and a cultural center."

One executive explained the reasoning behind the extensive social services: "The Italian government was far behind in accepting its responsibilities toward its citizens. The money which it took in was used inefficiently and the recipients of state largess often got too little too late. Perhaps this explains some of the traditional Italian attitude towards taxes." Illustrating the early concern of the Olivetti Company for employee welfare were the maternity benefits. Long before paid maternity leaves were required by law, Olivetti was granting time off with pay. In 1966 an expectant mother was given nine and a half months off with full pay—three months before the baby was born, and six and a half months after. This contrasted with the national allowance of five and a half months at 80% pay. All medical care for both mother and child were taken care of by the company.

The company had long advocated an enriched cultural life for its employees. It sponsored concerts, plays, debates, and any other form of activity which the employee council requested, with the objective of "making life to the measure of man."

Dr. Volponi explained how the programs were controlled:

> The Consiglio di Gestione is structured in such a way to secure a balanced representation of the interests of both employees and management. It includes:

A president, who is nominated by the company's chairman of the board;

Ten elected members (four are elected by factory employees and four by office employees through a two-stage election process; one by both factory and office employees, one by executives);

Eight appointed members, nominated by the company's chairman of the board (chosen among experts in the field of health, recreation, dietetics, sociology, etc.).

Elected members are entitled to be away from the job for the time required in performing their functions within the Consiglio di Gestione without any loss of pay.

This committee is a survivor of many which were set up in Italy after the war. The others died out because of pressure from managements and from Communist unions which preferred to have a complete spilt between management and the workers. I think that our committee at Olivetti survived because we gave it practical day-to-day problems to deal with. They had weekly meetings to apply the more general schemes which they developed to the particular case.

When asked about the future direction in which the social services of Olivetti might go, Dr. Volponi replied:

The main reason that Olivetti social services are so large is that the gap between public social services and those which were required was so large. Now there is a trend to control the general amount of special services which we offer since the public services are improving. We will no longer duplicate that which the country is doing. For example, there is now a national kindergarten, so the meaning of our kindergarten is reduced. We hope we can remain advanced over the other companies and over the state services. Certainly I don't see a rapid expansion, but as the state takes over functions which we served previously, we will be using our ingenuity to give better service. The amount we spend is practically a part of an unwritten contract. It is my job to help make sure the money is wisely spent.

The most important feature for the workers is the participation in and free discussion of the content of the social services. They get to work with the whole picture. It is a process of civic education. Olivetti social services have kept alive some important social awareness. In this sense we have helped to preserve some of the traditional features of the environment so as not to have just a uniform Olivetti suburb.

The effect of *tocco Olivetti* had been profound in years past. An article in *Fortune* magazine, September 1960, characterized the Olivetti spirit as being "elegant but tough." Most members of management felt a deep commitment to an attempt to continue with this distinctive corporate style. They recognized the large role which Adriano Olivetti had in formulating and spreading the style, and the knowledge of its existence was valuable to them. As one young executive said: *"Tocco Olivetti* meant that I was working for something which was more than an economic institution. As an Italian I am proud of our cultural heritage, and the spirit of Olivetti, *tocco Olivetti,* is a form of its expression. It is the humanist approach to capitalism."

Ing. C. Olivetti & C., S.p.A.(A-2)

DURING the period 1958–1963 unconsolidated sales of the Olivetti Company rose from 40,045.5 million lire to 121,687.7 million lire, or by about 204%. Personnel increased from 24,974 in 1958 to 56,536 in 1963. The book value of property, plant, and equipment, net of depreciation, rose from 9,105.3 million lire to 33,093.7 million during the same period.

The extraordinary growth experienced by the company during the late 1950s and early 1960s was financed through retained earnings and through debt. Debentures amounting to 33,190 million lire were issued during the period 1958–1963 and bank overdrafts were increased by more than 15 billion lire.

Among the reasons for the company's extraordinary growth was the acquisition of working control of the Underwood Corporation in the autumn of 1959. The Underwood Corporation, a U.S. typewriter manufacturer long-established but on the verge of bankruptcy in the late 1950s, proved to be the key to the large opening up of the U.S. market to Olivetti. During the early 1950s, Olivetti's representation in the United States (through the Olivetti Corporation of America) had been restricted to exclusive sales agents in the principal cities. In 1950, only 1.7% of company sales volume was achieved in the United States; by 1966, 21.5% was realized in the American market.

The Underwood acquisition, however, had a serious impact on the financial structure of the Olivetti Company. An investment of almost $100 million—an amount far in excess of anticipations—was required before Underwood was placed on a firm, profitable footing. In addition, substantial increases in the Olivetti Company's inventories took place, partly as a result of overoptimistic predictions about the immediate achievement of sales results in the United States, and partly as a natural result of providing stocks of Olivetti products to the former Underwood dealers. Compounding these difficulties was the Italian recession which in the early 1960s, cut substantially into the company's sales at home. (See the Appendix for a description of the Italian environment.)

At about the time that the Underwood acquisition was being undertaken, the Olivetti Company was becoming seriously involved in first developing and then distributing a line of computers and peripheral equipment. Even by 1963, computers did not represent a large part of Olivetti's sales—about 5%—but the computer program provided a substantial drain on company funds.

Extraordinary growth in sales of the company's basic product lines, acquisition of the Underwood Corporation, and the attempt to enter the computer field all contributed to a difficult financial situation clearly in evidence by mid-1963.

These events were described in an article in the September 12, 1964, issue of *Business Week* as follows:

Business Abroad: "Why GE is joining Olivetti"

It took a long time. Since last February, Olivetti has been dickering with General Electric about control of its capital-draining computer division. But not until last week were the final details ironed out and the deal signed.

The two companies plan to form a jointly owned subsidiary to be called Olivetti-General Electric, in which GE will hold controlling interest, reportedly 60%. [It actually turned out to be 75%.] GE will pay an unspecified amount of cash—estimated to run well over $20 million —to Olivetti for its computer operations. GE also will supply the bulk of the capital over the next few years for expansion of the new company. . . .

New life. For Olivetti, the present deal with GE is very important. It lops off an operation that helped put the company into a tight financial squeeze. GE's cash payment, plus the fact that Olivetti's subsidiary —Underwood—has gone into the black for the first time since the Italian company took it over, will pump new life into Olivetti's shaky finances.

Instead of cash, Olivetti will throw the bulk of its electronics division into the new Olivetti-GE. This includes three plants, a spanking new electronics research laboratory at Rho (near Milan), its three basic computer models—the Elea series—with most of their peripheral equipment, and the company's electronics sales organization.

Olivetti still is keeping one foot in electronics, however. It will continue producing its electronic accounting and billing machines, along with the rest of its equipment for mechanical integration. It also hangs on to its automatic production data collector, and numerical control equipment for machine tools. It plans to bring out additional products, including a desk computer.

I. *Luxury product*

Computers never did represent a large part of Olivetti's sales. Last year they probably accounted for no more than 5% of total consolidated sales of $422.7 million (but perhaps 25% if important peripheral equipment is included). The computer operation absorbed a disproportionate amount of money. According to one company source, Olivetti has invested "not less than $30 million to $50 million" in the electronics field. The total sum is probably a great deal more, and most of it went into the computer operation.

"Sales," as in most computer operations, were actually almost entirely rentals, so that each computer sold meant more capital tied up. At the end of last year, Olivetti listed on its balance sheet $11.4 million as the value of the computers rented out. The computer business was a luxury Olivetti couldn't afford.

Three models. Olivetti's venture into computers goes back to 1954, when it launched a computer research project. In 1959—about two years after IBM entered the Italian computer market—Olivetti brought out its first computer, the Elea 9003, which falls into the range of the IBM 7070. Two years later, Olivetti introduced its second model, the 6001, which was designed primarily for scientific work, then modified for commercial use. Finally, late last year, Olivetti added the smaller 4001, a relatively low-cost machine.

To complement its computers, Olivetti had to sell peripheral equipment made by other companies until it could develop its own, which took it until 1962. It never did manage to make its own punch-card system; instead it acted as exclusive sales agent in Italy for a system developed by Machines Bull.

Stiff competition for the Italian market also complicated Olivetti's computer efforts. Today, nine companies vie for a share of the Italian market, and this number could double in the next four years.

Limited range. Olivetti's basic problem was that it simply wasn't big enough to play the computer game. While the money it poured into research and development was a heavy stake for Olivetti, it was peanuts compared to the sums laid out by the American giants.

As a result, the company's technology was weak. While its competitors were bringing out third-generation computers, Olivetti's whole line was limited in range and basically a modification of the computer it first developed.

In the eyes of Milan financial men, the GE deal marks a turning point in Olivetti's fortunes. With world competition on the upswing and Italy's economy anything but healthy, Olivetti's rehabilitation won't be easy, even after the computer amputation. But at least the operation has staunched the flow of capital away from further development of its basic lines, which have made Olivetti the biggest European office machine producer and one of the world's largest makers of calculating machines.

II. *Family affair*

The late Adriano Olivetti was the man largely responsible both for building Olivetti up to its glittering stature and, ironically, for pushing it into its financial crisis. . . .

Adriano was the eldest of Camillo's six children, each of whom got an equal share of the 60% of the company's stock that Camillo had held.

Despite the fact that he controlled no more stock than any of his five brothers and sisters, Adriano held full command of the company because of his age and personality.

Buildup. Under Adriano's hand, Olivetti flourished. The company already had branched out from its original typewriter business when it brought out a line of office furniture in 1930. In 1937, it started making teleprinter equipment that, since it has a monopoly in Italy, still provides a comfortable source of profit. Three years later, Olivetti sold its first adding machine.

Then came a series of achievements that helped bring Olivetti to the head of its field. In 1948, the company brought out its Lexikon 80 and Divisumma 14, the world's first printing-calculating machines and, in 1956, the first automatic printing calculators, the Divisumma 24 and then Tetractys. Along the way, Olivetti moved into electric typewriters, bookkeeping and billing machines, office filing systems, machine tools, and the variety of by-products of its electronics work.

Even today Olivetti accounts for more than a fifth of world typewriter production, almost a third of world calculator output, over 40% of world calculator exports.

Last straw.   To reach this position, Adriano set Olivetti spinning through a period of almost feverish growth, especially after World War II. For the Italian operation alone, sales shot up from $64.1 million to $194.7 million from the fiscal year ending Mar. 31, 1958, to Dec. 31, 1963.

Abroad, Olivetti complemented its massive export growth with heavy investments, building or buying plants in Scotland, Spain, Argentina, Brazil, Mexico, Colombia, South Africa, the United States, and Canada. This expansion, along with the heavy development costs and—above all—Adriano's plunge into computers, blotted up an enormous amount of black ink.

Adriano's last big move—buying control of Underwood Corporation in 1959—pushed the company and the Olivetti family to the wall. Underwood was old and sick. Olivetti had to replace its machinery almost entirely and revamp its sales organization. It took more than four years to put Underwood into the black. For the record, Olivetti claims the Underwood venture has cost it a total of about $48 million. Actually, insiders say, it cost a good deal more.

Hard times.   Under the strain of these investments, Olivetti's debts snowballed. Between 1958 and the end of 1963, long-term debt rose from $21.3 million to $66.6 million. More ominously, bank debts shot up from $7.6 million to $32.5 million.

Even in the best of times, Olivetti would have been hard pressed to finance its investments out of its own coffers. As it was, times were getting harder. Rising labor costs bit into profits; competition on the home market increased, while the market itself grew less buoyant as the Italian economic miracle faded.

More important, the situation grew bleaker in Olivetti's export market, which accounts for about 70% of the sales of its Italian plants. Olivetti had based a good deal of its expansion on the expectation that the Common Market would absorb its increased output. But sales didn't rise as fast as expected. Economic crises in Argentina and Brazil in 1962 also hurt badly.

The company entered 1964 with substantial overcapacity and warehouses full of unsold products.

Setting the stage.   As if these problems weren't enough, the Olivetti company was afflicted with the squabbling of the Olivetti family. When Adriano died in 1960, the family named long-time company man Giuseppe Pero to run it.

Pero's death last November finally set the stage for the deal that has now been made. The family was unable to agree on a successor.

Adriano's son, Roberto, was its most active member in the company, but he couldn't influence his older relatives. Olivetti lurched into its financial crisis with no one at the helm.

With money tight and the company headless, the banks balked at extending Olivetti's loans. Moreover, the family had cornered itself into its own financial crisis. The company's mounting debts and reinvested profits had not been enough to finance expansion, so its capitalization had been increased from $17.2 million in 1958 to $96 million in 1962.

Unwilling to give up control of the company to outsiders, and afraid to let one branch of the family get more shares than another, the six family branches subscribed most of the capitalization increases themselves, and boosted their total control of voting stock from 60% to 72%. To raise the money, they borrowed from banks, putting up their stock as security. But as the value of Olivetti's stock plummeted with the whole Italian stock market, the banks began pressing the family to put its financial house in order.

III. *Band of angels*

This spring, the family finally faced the inevitable. In May, it agreed to sell almost half of its stock (at well below market value) to a group that is providing the money and management to put Olivetti back on the track. This group consists of the government-controlled bank Mediobanca (government-controlled medium-term credit institution), Istituto Mobiliare Italiano (IMI), the government-controlled credit institution, Fiat, Pirelli, and LaCentrale, a Milan *holding company*.[1] (private)

The consortium has put up the money to consolidate Olivetti's short-term debts. It also has overhauled the company's management. The prestigious Bruno Visentini, long-time adviser to the Olivetti family, vice-president of IRI, the powerful government holding company that controls Mediobanca, and the man who engineered the family sell-off, moved into the presidency. . . .

Although a sell-off of the computer division was brewing for a long time, it was the new controlling group that pushed through the GE deal. With the computer business lopped off, glutted warehouses cleared by cuts in work hours and a sell-off of inventory, and with Underwood finally in the black, Olivetti's prospects are much brighter now than a few months ago.[2]

EVENTS AS REPORTED IN OLIVETTI ANNUAL REPORTS

The 1964 Olivetti Annual Report described the agreement with General Electric Company as follows:

Activities in the electronic sector. In the electronic sector, we have to place on record before all else the agreement we have reached with the General Electric Company of New York. On the basis of this agreement, the Olivetti Electronics Division and the Olivetti Bull Company are to continue their activities in design, production and distribu-

---

[1] The respective shares of the deal amounted to approximately 50% each for the government-controlled institutions (Mediobanca and IMI) and the private companies (Fiat, Pirelli, LaCentrale).

[2] Quoted from p. 140 of the September 12, 1964, issue of *Business Week* by special permission. Copyrighted © 1964 by McGraw-Hill, Inc.

tion of electronic computers and of other equipment for data processing, and associated research activities, in a company in which General Electric will have a 75% stock holding and to which it will contribute the financial means required for subsequent development.

The agreement, ensuring full employment for workers and the future workers and technicians brought together and trained by Olivetti, foresees further gradual increases in activities in the sector with matching development of research, production and distribution. In addition the opportunity will be presented to offer products in all Common Market countries, the rest of Europe and in the world as a whole, and will offer Italian users, on the other hand, an increasingly wide and complementary range of equipment of high technical and functional quality.

It must be remembered that right from the beginning this activity—initially pioneered by nature and later established in the industrial and commercial fields—was deliberately confined to the Italian market. In fact, the huge financial commitment, arising necessarily from the system of establishing computer centers rather than that of selling outright, rapidly came to such an amount in this field as to necessitate a limitation on installations, with a consequent ceiling to the volume of output, and hence ever greater difficulties in amortizing the costs of overheads and research. To this had to be added the huge burden of scientific and technical research and the expense of the organization of sales and technical assistance to cover which, apart from any other consideration, expansion abroad would have been essential while being impossible from the point of view of finance and organization by ourselves alone.

The agreement with General Electric permits our company to reappraise what it has accomplished in this field, to remain in the field of large and medium computers, even if with no more than a minority interest, and at the same time—since our company will continue to produce independently machines which are based increasingly on the use of electronic techniques and components—to benefit from a wider scientific and technical experience for those products which it is our task to develop.

Contrary to the rumors which had circulated, it was found that the basic structure of the company was sound. Olivetti used only one-fifth of the line of credit which had been established for it by the intervening consortium. In terms of dollars this amounted to a little more than 6 millions on an asset base of over 300 millions. The Underwood operation, which had been cited as one of the major financial drains on the company, began to earn a profit in March 1964, only 10 months after the new management group moved in.

By the end of 1965, the crisis had passed. It was clear to all in management that there was no danger of imminent collapse. The 1965 Annual Report opened with the following statement concerning the improvement in Olivetti's position:

To the Stockholders:

In our last report, we described to you the comparatively difficult circumstances of 1964. In that year, at the lowest point of a recession which involved the whole Italian economy, and which, following a period of exceptional expansion, afflicted in particular the capital goods market, our Company had to give effect to a series of measures aimed at:

a) relieving itself of the heavy financial burden represented by research and production in the field of medium and large electronic computers;

b) allowing a process of financial and business reorganization of our subsidiaries in Italy and abroad and, in particular, undertaking the thorough consolidation of Underwood's position;

c) intensifying our efforts to contain production costs as necessitated by the continuous increase in the cost of labor on the one hand, and by the sharpened competition on world markets on the other;

d) laying the foundations for bringing our products up to date as demanded by the increasingly rapid evolution of the office equipment market. In this market a number of our competitors have strengthened their structure or have been merged into larger groups. Likewise in this market the pace of technical progress imposes an increasingly rapid rate of renewal of traditional products. In this setting, our company had to prepare the instruments in its traditional policy of technical excellence, to anticipate the future evolution in the development of demand in new and complex fields requiring increasingly refined technology.

A year ago we explained the agreements reached and the measures taken for these purposes, and noted the practical beginning during 1964 of the work of reorganization which, as we announced, was to be developed and extended over successive years. We cannot yet say that we have covered the greater part of the course we set for ourselves. Above all with respect to the development of products for new and future fields, we have to face up to growing efforts in research, experimentation and design. But we have certainly taken several important steps forward in the process of renewal and diversification of our traditional product ranges (typewriters and calculating machines).

The first favorable evidence of our efforts is represented by business and financial results. To be explicit, in 1965 there was definitely an improvement in our company's financial position. Also, in spite of further pressure on the costs of many of the factors of production and distribution and the contraction of turnover in Italy due to the persistence of general economic difficulties in the country, the accounts show favorable developments in our business. Consequently, after two years of sacrifices suffered by the stockholders, it is with satisfaction that we propose to resume payment of a dividend. We also inform you that the liquidity position of our company (and in general terms of the group as a whole) permits us to look forward with sufficient peace of mind to the demands imposed by forthcoming burdensome corporate plans.

APPENDIX

SOME NOTES ON ITALY

In 1966 Olivetti was the sixth largest company in Italy. The five larger companies were Fiat, a producer of automobiles, tractors, aircraft and engines with sales in 1965 of $1.5 billion; Finsider, producer of iron and steel with sales of $979 million; ENI, a government-owned producer of petroleum products, engines, textiles and machinery with sales of $938 million; Pirelli Group, a producer of rubber products with sales of $739 million; and Edison Group, a producer of chemicals and synthetic fibers with sales of $732 million, which—with government encouragement—merged with Montecatini, a producer of chemicals and minerals with sales of $581 million in mid-1966.

Postwar economic achievements and problems

During 1948–1961, Italy achieved one of the highest and best sustained economic growth rates in the world and became a strong and solvent international competitor. Starting in 1962, however, the country suffered from a reduction in the rate of expansion from which it began visibly emerging in late 1964. Rates of yearly increase in gross national product at 1963 prices were as follows for the period from 1952 to 1965:

1952	+4.3%	1959	+6.4%
1953	+7.6	1960	+6.2
1954	+3.9	1961	+7.8
1955	+6.4	1962	+6.2
1956	+4.5	1963	+5.5
1957	+5.3	1964	+2.7
1958	+4.9	1965	+3.4

Source: *Main Statistical Data of Italy*, Istituto per gli Studi di Economia (ISE), Milan, 24–26 May, 1966.

In 1965 the country's population of 52 million attained a per capita income of $802. The comparable figure for 1938 was $365; for 1951, $467; and for 1959, $645.

This economic achievement, however, was not equally shared throughout the country. The part of Italy north of Rome was very prosperous and technically advanced, while the southern part, called the Mezzogiorno, was impoverished and still largely agrarian. This dualism in the Italian economy contributed significantly to the problem of unemployment and underemployment which had long plagued Italy, even during its boom years. With a total labor force of approximately 21.5 million, unemployment was estimated by one source at 721,000, and underemployment (workers who were working less than 33 hours a week) at 520,000, or in total about 6%.

Mostly as a result of the great boom of the late 1950's, the country faced an inflation in the early 1960s. Wholesale price indices, on a base of 1953, increased from 99 in 1951 to 110.4 in 1965; retail prices took an even sharper rise from 117.8 in 1951 to 145.8 in 1965. In consequence, the current balance of payments turned more sharply negative, and the net short-term reserve position deteriorated. Beginning in 1963, government action was initiated to bring the rapid expansion of money and credit under control. By mid-1964 the balance-of-payments deficit had been abolished, and the economy showed signs of stabilizing.

Whether or not the government had overreacted, thus causing a greater than necessary decrease in the growth rate, was a subject still being debated by some Italian executives.

Foreign trade in 1938, 1951, and 1965 in millions of lire at 1965 prices was as follows:

	1938	*1951*	*1965*
Import of goods.............	737,968	1,559,691	4,592,000
Export of goods.............	575,675	1,336,879	4,492,500
Trade balance..............	−162,293	−222,812	−99,500

Source: *Main Statistical Data of Italy*, ISE, Milan, 24–26 May, 1966.

Gross national product in billions of lire at 1963 prices in 1951 was 15,370; in 1965, it was 32,084.

The mixed economy

In 1966 the Italian government had direct and complete control over tobacco manufacture, matches, salt processing, iodine, railroads, telephones, electric power, and hydrocarbon exploration and development. In addition, it controlled several large holding companies, which in turn controlled a broad variety of enterprises.

Istituto per la Ricostruzione Industriale (IRI), the largest of the holding companies, controlled, according to one estimate, approximately one-fourth of total national industrial investment in 1965. The IRI, established in 1933, controlled more than 140 companies in industry and public utility.

> IRI companies produce 94% of the nation's pig iron and 58% of its steel, and are represented in nearly all branches of engineering; IRI shipyards account for 80% of the nation's shipbuilding capacity, and IRI ships account for 65% of Italian mixed passenger-and-cargo tonnage and for 8% of dry cargo tonnage; IRI's airline stands in the front rank of the world's air companies in international services. IRI is responsible for all Italy's urban telephone services and for the bulk of short-distance trunk lines, for Italian broadcasting and television, and for the construction and management, during 30 years, of a network of more than 2,200 km. of toll motorways, of which some 1,000 km. were in service at the end of 1964.[1]

Other state-owned and operated activities were described by a February 1966 *Business International* report on Italy as follows:

> Ente Nazionale Idrocarburi (ENI), created in 1953, operates worldwide in oil, natural gas and petroleum products, and pipelines. ENI's corporate structure controls 100% of the country's oil output, 15% of oil refining, and 97% of methane gas output. In three 50-50 ventures in the South with the state financing company Breda, ENI manufactures plate glass, railroad equipment, and electro-technical apparatus—

---

[1] IRI, *Salient Aspects of Business in 1964*, p. 3.

in some cases in direct competition with private Italian and foreign firms. . . .

Ente Nazionale per l'Energia Elettrica (ENEL) was formed in 1962 to take over 80% of power production and all distribution. Private power companies are compensated with obligations which will be redeemed over a 10-year period. Private power production is only allowed for use within a company, not for outside sale.

Ente Minerario Siciliano (EMS) was created in 1962 for the promotion of mineral development and manufacturing deriving from minerals in Sicily. It was to be capitalized at $35 million, with authority for five-fold expansion. EMS will have first option on exploration permits. If a private firm gets a license and makes a strike, EMS has an option to acquire 25% of the exploiting firm. If firms that held permits at the beginning of 1963 make strikes, EMS has first claim on 51% of any companies set up for exploitation, except in the case of firms such as ENI, Montecatini, and Edison, which are already exploiting their funds.

Most commercial banks (in addition to those owned by IRI) and the majority of medium- and long-term credit banks are owned and controlled in part by the Government. About 80% of Italy's credit activities are under direct or indirect control of the Government.[2]

The government

In 1966 Italy was governed by a "center-left" coalition of Christian Democrats, Democratic Socialists, Nenni Socialists, and Republicans, which together represented 60.3% of the popular vote. The remaining percentage of the popular vote went to the Communists (about 25%), and to two very small extreme right-wing groups, the Liberals and Neo-Fascists.

In the postwar years, it had been the Christian Democrats who were the leaders of the coalition. This group comprised big-business conservatives, moderate reformers and welfarists, and some leftist planners favoring government control and private operation of industry. (It had the support of the Roman Catholic Church, which at certain times had threatened excommunication to Catholics who voted for the Communists.) The Democratic Socialists, as their name implied, favored the mixed economy, with state intervention through ownership. The Republicans also favored the mixed economy but did not claim Marxist heritage. The Nenni, or old-line Socialists, favored state ownership of industry, but in addition had traditionally leaned toward the Marxist concepts of proletarian revolution. Until 1957 the Nenni Socialists had formed a coalition with the Communists. In 1963 they joined the existing coalition of Christian Democrats, Democratic Socialists, and Republicans. Efforts were under way to merge the Democratic Socialists and the Nenni Socialists, a move which would further strengthen the coalition, but which would increase the relative power of the Christian Democrats.[3]

---

[2] Reprinted from the chapter on Italy, dated February 1966, *Investing, Licensing & Trading Conditions Abroad*, a monthly updated reference service, published by Business International Corporation, New York.

[3] The Nenni Socialists and the Democratic Socialists merged on October 31, 1966.

The private business community reportedly was shaken by the nationalization of the electric power industry in 1962, the introduction of a withholding tax on dividends in 1962, and the imposition of tight monetary and credit moves to check inflation in 1963–64. To some big-business conservatives, these moves illustrated the growing power of the Socialists in the management of the affairs of the country. On the other hand, some analysts pointed out that an even greater problem was the fact that a coalition government was inherently unstable and therefore incapable of providing any firm and consistent direction.

The five-year economic development program, 1965–69

On January 29, 1965, the Italian Cabinet approved an economic development program for the five years 1965–69. This program, the first of its kind in postwar Italian history, was developed on the basis of an evaluation of the present situation, which led to the identification of the problems to be solved, to the establishment of objectives or targets to be achieved, to the development of policies to be pursued and the instruments to be used, and to identification of the cost of the action planned. The objectives of the program and the policies to be pursued in the industrial sector of the country are presented below:

> The targets of the scheme approved by the Italian Cabinet on January 29th of this year may be compared with the general objects of the government's economic policy announced by Prime Minister Moro in his programmatic declarations to Parliament on December 12, 1963.
> These objects, to which the present Moro government made explicit reference when presenting itself to Parliament on July 30, 1964, were at that time expressed by the Prime Minister in the following words:
> > It is our common conviction that problems connected with government action cannot be tackled singly and occasionally, but must be viewed within the general framework and in compliance with definite priorities regarding importance and urgence; in relation, that is to say, to a policy of economic planning making it possible, provided there is an adequate expansion of income—and this is an indispensable condition—to redress the existing area, branch and distributional imbalances and remove the major shortcomings in our country's social facilities.
> The scheme for the 1965–69 five-year plan submitted to CNEL[4] translates these general objects into the following terms:
> (1) Full employment of the labour forces (by 1969 open unemployment should be reduced to a level not exceeding 1.5%–1.6% of the labour forces, as compared with 2.7% in 1964);
> (2) Narrowing of the gap between argicultural and non-agricultural incomes to be achieved essentially by increasing the gross product of agriculture (at an average annual rate of 2.8%–2.9%) and by reducing agricultural underemployment by 750,000 units over the five-year period considered;
> (3) Localization in Southern Italy of 40–45% of the new jobs in non-agricultural branches, as compared with 25% in the five years 1959–63;

---

[4] Consiglio Nazionale dell'Economia e del Lavoro.

(4) Raising the level of social uses of income (housing, education, social security, scientific research, transportation, etc.) to 27%–27.5% of the available domestic resources as compared with 24% in the five years 1959–63.

An essential feature of development, as described in the scheme, is the rate of growth of the national income, assumed to be equal to a yearly average of 5% taking into account on the one hand prospective increases in employment and productivity, and on the other hand the volume of resources to be allocated to various uses—investments, social objectives and consumption—during the five years considered.

Policies in Industry—In laying down the general lines of industrial policy the programme is based on the following development assumptions:

increase of the added value in industry at the average annual rate of 7%, this being the mean between 6%–6.1% for Central and Northern Italy and 11.5%–12% for Southern Italy;

development of employment at an average annual rate of 2.4% (Center North 2.0%; South 4.2%);

expansion of productivity at the rate of 4.3% a year (Center North 4.0%; South 7%–7.5%).

The above-mentioned developments should be made possible by a volume of gross investments amounting to about 11,300 billion lire, of which 4,000 billions are in Southern Italy.

In the field of industry, the intervention policy aims at creating the conditions required for the attainment of these targets. The scheme does not make forecasts or fix production targets for each branch of industry, but supplies lines of guidance for the development of the three basic branches: power sources, steel and chemistry.

The scheme also considers the general lines of intervention by public and government-controlled enterprises in the coming five years. All together these enterprises should absorb 4,700–4,900 billions of lire of investments, of which 3,400–3,500 in industrial branches.

The scheme also establishes the priorities to be respected by public action for the purpose of improving the efficiency of industry: improvement of external economies through the attainment of targets in the field of social expenditure and territorial readjustments; the financing of technological research and development; the reorganization and strengthening of financial and fiscal incentives for the purpose of reorganizing and rationalizing the less efficient branches (giving priority to investments in the textile industry, the machine tool industry, the agricultural food industry and shipbuilding). Fiscal and financial incentives and forms of technical aid should also be provided for the rationalization and development of small industries and handicraft concerns.

As far as the financing of industry is concerned, the requirements of the planning policy are essentially those of ensuring an adequate flow of funds in forms providing greater stability as regards the financial management of enterprises. In this connection a better organization of medium-term industrial credit is expected as well as an expansion of the financing of small and medium enterprises through the acquisition of minority shareholdings not involving entrepreneurial responsibilities.

The scheme provides, moreover, for the protection of free competition as well as for the adoption of policies designed to prevent dumping by foreign enterprises.

Lastly, public action will aim at promoting exports, particularly by strengthening the system of credit facilities and export credit insurance.

This policy is linked with the necessity of maintaining a high rate of increase for exports in order that a balance of current items may be achieved before the end of the five years.[5]

---

[5] "The Five-Year Economic Programme (1965–1969)," Giovanni Pieraccini, Budget Minister, *Review of Economic Conditions in Italy, Banco di Roma,* Vol. XIX, No. 2, March 1965, Rome.

A Note on the Manufacture and Distribution of Portland Cement in the United Kingdom*

CEMENT MANUFACTURE

PORTLAND CEMENT was developed from an invention of a laborer in Leeds, England, in 1824. It was called "portland" cement because the concrete made from it resembled the well-known Portland building stone in color and texture. Its manufacture is today a major world industry. World consumption has risen from 81 million tons in 1938 to 315 million in 1960 and is still rising.

Cement itself is manufactured from a closely controlled mixture of calcium carbonate, alumina, and silica. Calcium carbonate is found in various forms of limestone fairly liberally throughout the world. To be suitable for the manufacture of cement, the calcium carbonate content of the limestone must be relatively free from impurity. Soft chalk, which is very high in calcium carbonate, is found uniquely on either side of the English Channel toward the southern part of the North Sea. Chalk is easier to process than hard limestone, and its availability accounts, in part, for the fact that nearly half of British production is located in southeastern England.

Alumina is found in some forms of clay or shale. A relatively small amount of sand supplies the silica requirements.

From 3,000 to 3,600 pounds of raw materials are required to make a ton of cement. These are quarried with large diesel or electric-power shovels and conveyed to the works, which is normally placed nearby. There they are crushed and ground to a fine powder, and—in what is known as the "wet process"—mixed in strictly controlled proportions with water to form cement slurry. (Slurry normally contains about 40%

---

* Much of the material included in this description was taken, with permission, from a paper, "The Manufacture and Distribution of Cement," prepared by the Chairman of The Rugby Portland Cement Company Lt., Rugby, England.

Copyright 1964 by l'Institut pour l'Etude des Méthodes de Direction l'Entreprise (IMEDE), Lausanne, Switzerland. Reprinted by permission.

water by weight.) The liquid state of the mixture is necessary to facilitate a perfectly homogeneous mixture of the raw materials and to permit rapid adjustment of the proportions by merely adding materials which quickly become uniformly dispersed throughout the liquid.

The slurry, when chemically correct, is fed to the kiln, which in a modern works is a large steel cylinder from 300 to 500 feet in length and 9 to 14 feet in diameter. It rotates at the rate of approximately once every 45 seconds, on a slightly inclined axis. The slurry is fed in at the higher end.

Near the lower end of the kiln is the burning zone, where fuel is injected into the kiln and fired to produce a temperature of about 2,500°F. Pulverized coal is the usual fuel in Britain, but oil and natural gas are used in other countries where these fuels are readily available. The water in the slurry is driven off as steam, together with the carbon dioxide content of the calcium carbonate and minor quantities of other gases. The remaining materials are fluxed in the intense heat and leave the kiln in the form of pea-sized nodules called "cement clinker." The chemical part of the process, completed at this point, is closely controlled throughout by chemists who test the raw materials, the coal, and the slurry every hour, day and night.

Thereafter, the process is largely mechanical. The cement clinker is ground in large water-cooled mills to a predetermined fineness, and a small amount of calcium sulphate, or gypsum, is added, in order to control the "setting time" of the resultant powder, now finished cement.

As it leaves the mills, the cement is weighed automatically and then pumped through pipes by compressed air to the large concrete silos in which it is stored. It remains in storage until it is withdrawn by mechanical means to the packing plant, where it is packed into paper sacks, which are automatically filled, sealed, weighed, and delivered by means of conveyors to the truck, the rail car, or the ship. It may be withdrawn from the silos into special bulk trucks which deliver it unpacked.

THE USES OF CEMENT

Cement is used as the binding agent in concrete and in mortar. Concrete, one of the world's primary construction materials, is composed of cement, sand, aggregate (clean gravel and stones), and water. Cement reacts chemically with the water and hardens, within a few hours after mixing, binding the sand and gravel particles in a solid mass. Concrete can be used without reinforcing (as in highway pavements, which contain only wire matting for temperature stresses), or it can be used with steel reinforcement, as in buildings and bridges.

THE STRUCTURE OF THE INDUSTRY IN THE
UNITED KINGDOM, 1960

The cement industry in the United Kingdom consists of six financially independent groups, all of which have been members of the Cement Makers' Federation since its establishment in 1934.

The three largest interests held, in 1960, about 88% of the home market and have provided much of the leadership within the Federation. Associated Portland Cement Manufacturers Limited is considerably the largest company, with about 62% of the United Kingdom market. The Tunnel Group and The Rugby Portland Cement Company Limited have each about 14% of the United Kingdom market. Practically all the United Kingdom export trade is conducted by these three makers, which are also the only companies having manufacturing subsidiaries abroad.

The Federation regulates the internal affairs of the industry and arranges an interchange of technical information and industry-wide statistics. By far its most important function, however, is establishing the basis of selling prices and conditions of sale, in order, it is asserted, that the costs of distribution—which average nearly 20% of delivered cost of cement—can be controlled. Membership is voluntary, and voting power is proportionate, although not directly, to the previous year's home deliveries. Approval of any proposal, however, requires the concurrence of at least four of the nine members. The Federation has no control over the production of any manufacturer, nor is it concerned with the export trade.

The British cement industry also maintains a large research and promotional organization, the Cement and Concrete Association, part of whose function is to increase the use and uses of concrete. Cement itself has no substitute; however, it is used only to form concrete, which is in competition with steel, brick, stone, tile, timber, and many other materials.

The industry also organizes its conduct of labor relations. For more than 35 years it has operated a National Joint Industrial Council at which industry-wide wage rates and working conditions are set. The industry has never had a national strike or lockout. Holidays with pay and profit-sharing plans were features of the industry for many years before World War II.

POSTWAR GROWTH OF THE INDUSTRY

The postwar progress made by the industry is shown in Exhibit 1.

THE ECONOMICS OF THE INDUSTRY

Siting of the plant.   It is considered a matter of prime importance that cement plants be located as close as possible to raw material deposits. Adequate water supplies, fuel, and electricity and access to road, rail, and water transport must also be available. Thorough technical investigation is required, since both the physical and chemical properties of the raw materials will influence the design of many of the factory components.

Costs of production.   The manufacture of cement is a highly mechanized process and employs comparatively little labor. The capital investment is among the highest for any industry; it equals almost £20,000

Exhibit 1

U.K. CEMENT DELIVERIES

(000 tons)

	Home	Export	Total
1939............	7,587	665	8,252
1946............	5,479	1,095	6,574
1951............	8,144	1,974	10,118
1952............	9,147	2,055	11,202
1953............	9,335	1,917	11,252
1954............	10,079	1,769	11,848
1955............	10,759	1,766	12,525
1956............	11,275	1.600	12,875
1957............	10,709	1,382	12,091
1958............	10,675	1,145	11,820
1959............	11,683	1,088	12,771
1960............	12,463	1,000	13,463
1961............	13,800	800	14,600
1962............	13,768	315	14,083
1963............	13,715	251	13,966
1964............	16,545	258	16,803

per man employed, which is over six times what it was before the War. Depreciation is therefore a heavy charge, and will become progressively heavier as prewar plants are replaced.

Coal is the largest individual item in the cost of production. It takes approximately 800 pounds of coal, including the coal used to generate electricity, to make a ton of cement.

In general, industry production costs are distributed as follows:

	Percent
Coal and power...	45–50
Direct labor..	10–15
Consumable equipment.......................................	9–12
Depreciation (installed cost).................................	9–12
Indirect factory labor and other overheads (supervision, testing, maintenance, cost accounting, etc.).........................	15–20
Manufacture cost...	100

Average haulage..	20–30 of M.C.
Sales expense..	5– 8 of M.C.
General administrative overhead.........................	10–15 of M.C.

Profit margins are not disclosed. It has been asserted that current prices allow profits only because the manufacturers are still using, in part, equipment installed in the late 1930s. As greater proportions of new, more expensive plant installations are brought into use, prices may rise to cover increased depreciation charges.

Leaders of the British cement industry have repeatedly stated that manufacture of cement in the United Kingdom has for years been conducted with the highest efficiency and one of the lowest unit costs of any producing country in the world.

Distribution. The distribution of cement to the site where it will be used is a more technical and complicated problem than at first sight appears, for it is not the cost of production at the place where the cement is made but the cost at the site where it will be used that is important. The geographical distribution of demand, which in itself varies quite considerably from year to year (and can be materially distorted at different times by large airport programs, road works, reservoirs, and similar forms of construction using large quantities of cement), is not coincident with the geographical distribution of the works.

Many companies in the industry maintain a fleet of trucks for road delivery. Little bagged cement goes by rail, owing to the costs of double-handling. Delivery in bulk (in special vehicles both by road and rail) has rapidly increased in recent years and now accounts for nearly 60% of the home trade.

PRICING AND THE ROLE OF THE CEMENT MAKERS FEDERATION

The manufacturers feel that a joint policy of distribution and price can avoid the severe price competition which, in the early 1930s, created difficulties for both producers and users. For example, a works near to a large consuming area might be able to supply only one third of the demand in that area, leaving the remaining two thirds to come from a much greater distance. If there were not a coordinated price policy, it has been said, a builder taking his supplies from the nearer works would pay one price, while his competitor would have to pay a higher price for cement coming from a more distant works. This would assertedly lead to endless complications in bidding for construction projects.

The Federation's price arrangements, therefore, have the following objectives:[1]

1. To sell and distribute cement throughout the country in the most efficient and economical manner commensurate with the interests of the country as a whole, of the users of cement, and of the manufacturers—in particular by:
    a) Encouraging the delivery in any particular area from the nearest works, with the object of avoiding unnecessary and wasteful haulage.
    b) Eliminating depots (except where these perform useful functions) and delivering straight from works to construction sites.
    c) Providing a stable system of prices which takes into account the high proportion of the cost of transport in the price of cement and avoids disproportionate price differentials which would otherwise arise between various parts of the U.K.
2. To provide a price system giving sufficient stability to enable manufacturers individually and collectively to plan production in advance efficiently and economically, and individually to undertake the heavy expenditure required to meet increasing demand for cement.

---

[1] Summarized from a policy statement of the Federation.

3. To ensure during any temporary shortage of cement that prices remain at a reasonable level.
4. To eliminate unnecessary and expensive advertising.
5. To provide for standard forms of packages, bulk delivery, and the like.
6. To arrange, for the convenience of both manufacturers and buyers, standard conditions of supply and forms of quotation and contract.
7. To facilitate joint research and exchange of information to improve the standard and the potential utility of cement.

To achieve these aims, the Federation's present system provides for the same delivered price at the same point of delivery for all brands of cement, irrespective of the works from which the cement may come.

There are 48 cement works in the U.K. (Cement works very near one another usually have the same base price.) There are 37 base prices, one for each location where cement is manufactured. These base prices are nearly the same at every factory, although there are slight variations made for the type of raw materials used and the delivered price of fuel to the works. For the former, for instance, plants using chalk as their source of calcium carbonate have base prices about 5% lower than those using limestone, since all limestone crushing and grinding expenses are eliminated. In 1961, the base factory price (delivered within five miles of plant) of ordinary portland cement ranged from 111/6d. to 127/6d. per ton.

Radiating from each works is a series of concentric circles at four- or five-mile intervals, the circles from any particular works continuing until they meet the circles radiating from another works. The delivered price within each of these circles increases by 1/6d. for each of the first six circles and by 1/- for each subsequent circle (see Exhibit 2).

These price increments do not, in fact, cover actual transportation costs; therefore, manufacturers allow 10–15% of the base price plus the zone price increments for covering haulage costs. As a result, between 20 and 30 miles from a producing unit is considered the "break-even" haulage distance, below which haulage costs are less than the allowance in the base price plus the incremental price increases, and above which the converse is true. The more efficiently a producer can operate his truck fleet, the greater will be his break-even haulage distance.

The pricing scheme means that every buyer at a particular point will pay exactly the same price for his cement. It also means that there is every inducement for a manufacturer to save transport costs by selling as much of his production as possible within the circles controlled by his own works. The further he delivers cement from his own works, the more likely he is to run into the circles controlled by another works, where the price he will receive will begin to decrease. The Federation asserts that the effect of this arrangement is to save as much as possible of the heavy transport costs and so maintain throughout the country, on the average, a lower level of prices than would otherwise be the case.

There exist standard merchant discounts. Retail building material

Exhibit 2

ILLUSTRATION OF THE FEDERATION'S PRICING AGREEMENT

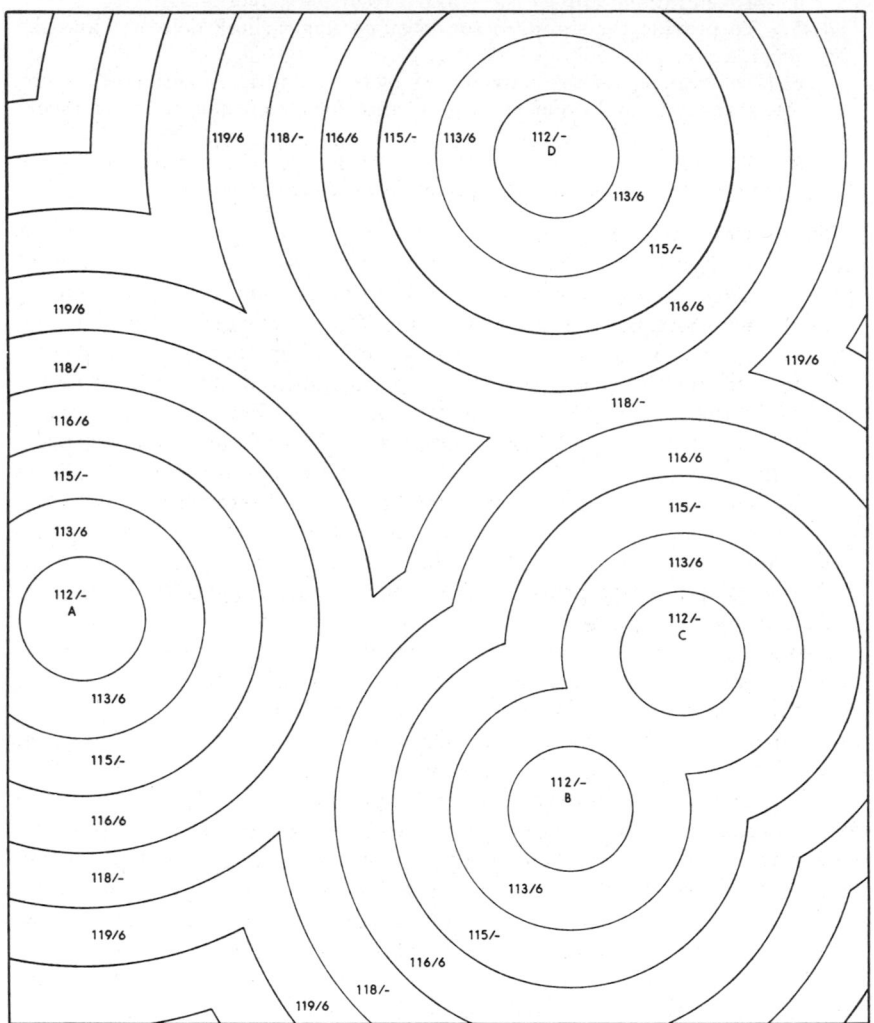

Sales price in shillings and pence per ton shown for each four- or five-mile zone.

suppliers are entitled to a merchant's discount, but they in turn must sell cement at the same prices, in the particular zones, which apply to the manufacturers. Thus a buyer pays the same price whether he buys from a manufacturer or a merchant. Merchants play a major role in supplying small orders, since the minimum order normally accepted by a manufacturer is six tons. A relatively small percentage of industry sales is made directly to merchants for their own accounts, but much more cement is delivered to the customer "on site" at a merchant's order.

THE RESTRICTIVE TRADE PRACTICES ACT

In 1956 England passed the Restrictive Trade Practices Act, which required that all trade agreements be registered with the Registrar of the Restrictive Practices Court. These agreements subsequently had to be justified before the court, which would decide whether they were contrary to the public interest. On March 16, 1961, the Restrictive Practices Court handed down its decision: it upheld the Federation's price agreements with only minor modifications.

In essence, the Federation argued that, because of its price-fixing agreement, U.K. cement manufacturers could operate with more certainty of profit than under free competition. Because of this greater security, they were willing to accept a lower return on investment and thus could sell cement appreciably lower than if prices had not been fixed.

Experts on both sides agreed that, in order to attract new capital into the industry, a net return on investment of at least 15% would have to be available. The Federation proved that, in order to yield such a return, a new cement plant would have to price its cement at least 25 shillings per ton higher than the current average price. It also established that Federation members were earning, on the average, less than 10% return on investment. The court therefore concluded that, had the price-fixing arrangement not existed, the price of cement would have been "significantly" higher, and the public would have suffered accordingly. Thus the court upheld the main price-fixing clause. It found that the industry was efficient and had acted with a sense of responsibility.

The presiding judge was concerned only that the price-fixing agreement should be as honorably administered in the future as had been true in the past. Thus he requested, and the Federation agreed, that if at any future date the Registrar should wish to determine whether prices were still being kept at a fair level, the Federation would cooperate fully by making cost and price data available for inspection.

The Federation's practice of giving quantity discounts based on total annual purchases from *all* Federation members was disallowed by the judge, on the grounds that it did not reflect true economies from volume sales.

The court also scrutinized, and upheld with one exception, minor agreements regarding terms of sale. In summing up his decision, Mr. Justice Diplock remarked:

> In the result, therefore, the Respondents have satisfied us that the main price-fixing conditions, other than those providing for general rebates to large users and large merchants, are not contrary to the public interest, and that the ancillary restrictions, other than that relating to the prohibition upon the quotations and contracts for the supply of cement for periods exceeding twelve months, are also not contrary to the public interest.[2]

---

[2] *Judgment in the Restrictive Practices Court on an agreement between Members of the Cement Makers' Federation,* printed by the Cement and Concrete Association, 1961.

In commenting on the court's decision, Sir Halford Reddish observed:

> I am not being wise after the event if I say that the judgement accorded closely with our expectations, for we were confident throughout that a detailed examination of our arrangements would show conclusively that they were in the public interest, and the cement makers were not alone in their satisfaction with the outcome of the case. Over four thousand buyers of cement sent us replies to a questionnaire before the hearing: something like 97 percent of them were strongly in favour of a continuation of the present system."[3]

[3] *Investors Chronicle,* March 24, 1961.

The Rugby Portland Cement Company Limited (A)*

HISTORY, GROWTH, AND ORGANIZATION

THE RUGBY COMPANY began producing lime in the early 19th century at a works near Rugby, England. Cement manufacture under the company's "Crown Cement" trade-mark began at the works in the 1820s, and thereafter became its principal product. In 1925 the company, which hitherto had been a partnership, became a private limited company with a share capital of £100,000 owned by descendants of the previous partners. In 1929 Mr. (now Sir)[1] Halford Reddish, then a young chartered accountant with a consulting practice, joined the board, which previously had comprised only representatives of the two descendant branches of the original owners. Four years later, upon the death of the general manager, Sir Halford Reddish became managing director, and shortly afterwards, chairman.

At that time, the cement industry was in the middle of a deep depression. Prices were at a very unprofitable level. In spite of this crisis, Sir Halford decided to expand and modernize the company's production facilities. Contrary to previous industry tradition, he also decided to operate the plant 52 weeks per year, thus ensuring steady employment for the workers. Despite the depression and the difficulties of selling the increased output, a profit was realized at the end of the first year of the new management. A second manufacturing site was obtained when a nearby company went into receivership. Erection of a new factory at the second site, plus the modernization and expansion of the Rugby works, required substantial fresh capital. In 1935 the company became a public company with its shares quoted on The London Stock Exchange, and additional capital of £140,000 was introduced. Later, additional equity capital was raised by occasional "rights" issues.

* Copyright 1973 by L'Institut pour l'Etude des Méthodes de Direction de l'Entreprise (IMEDE), Lausanne, Switzerland. Reprinted by permission.
[1] In early 1958, Her Majesty Queen Elizabeth II knighted Mr. Halford Reddish for his public services.

Rugby also acquired substantial chalk-bearing lands near Dunstable (about 48 miles to the south of its Warwickshire plants) from which high calcium carbonate chalk was railed daily to its Warwickshire plants.

By the mid-1930s Rugby was already the second largest cement company in the United Kingdom. (For an operations flow chart, see Exhibit 1.)

In 1936 Rugby acquired a third site and erected its Rochester works. In 1939 another company was purchased and its facilities were combined with those at Rochester. In 1945 Rugby acquired still another company, and, although its production facilities were closed, Rugby used its brand name and distribution organization.

Many major additions were made to these three facilities in the period after World War II, and during the 1960s Rugby made three additional acquisitions that expanded its U.K. operations, not only in cement, but also in another industry serving the building materials field.

Thus, in 1962 Rugby acquired the entire share capital of Eastwoods Cement Limited (owning three cement plants in the United Kingdom) and in 1963 the entire share capital of Chinnor Industries Limited (owning one cement plant in the United Kingdom). In 1968 Rugby acquired the entire share capital of The Rom River Company Limited, designers, fabricators and fixing subcontractors of steel reinforcement.

During the immediate postwar years, export trade was very profitable, with unit margins several times those of the home-market sales. The proportion of Rugby's deliveries accounted for by exports reached a maximum in 1951 and 1952 at about 43%. In 1961, however, Sir Halford Reddish said that in recent years export sales had become almost marginal because of the increased competition (much of it subsidized) from non-British manufacturers and the growth of cement industries in areas formerly importing cement. Rugby had itself established overseas subsidiaries, and had built manufacturing plants in Trinidad and Western Australia. The former started production in 1954, the latter in 1955. Both units were able to underprice existing imports by a substantial margin, and these facilities made useful contributions to Rugby's consolidated profits.

With a rapidly developing local market plus export trade in the Eastern Caribbean, the Trinidad factory had to be extended within less than five years of starting its operation. In 1963 the capacity of the Australian plant had to be doubled. By 1971 its capacity had been raised to one million tons per annum.

In highlighting Rugby's growth, Sir Halford spoke as follows in 1971:

> In 1946 our total share and loan capital and reserves were £1,671,-551. By 1970 they had grown to £56,220,048, and if we substituted current values in place of the book values of the assets, they would amount to at least £25 million more.
>
> In 1946 our pretax profit was £135,664; in 1970, £7,111,867.
>
> For 1946 we paid out in dividends on the Ordinary shares £40,625. For 1970 dividends on the Ordinary and Participating (non-voting) shares amounted to £2,448,000.

We now have 27,942 shareholders compared with 2,877 twenty-five years ago.

Additional capital introduced from 1st January 1933 to 31st December 1971 amounted to £60,370,867. Here is how the money has been found:

Shareholders have subscribed for shares (including premiums and loan stock)	£28,982,500
Profits have been left in the company	28,836,245
Others have contributed (by minority interests, or loans to, subsidy companies)	1,863,285
From Investment Grants	688,837
Total	£60,370,867

Net profit before taxes rose from less than £4,000 in 1933 to over £9 million in 1971. Postwar growth produced 26 years of successively record group profits, 1946–1971 (see Exhibits 2–4). By 1972 the Stock Exchange value of the company's equity capital was approximately £120 million.

In 1971 the nine company works and their annual capacities in tons were as shown in Table 1.

Table 1

COMPANY WORKS AND CAPACITIES

United Kingdom		Overseas	
Southam	540,000	Trinidad	390,000
Rochester*	400,000	Western Australia	1,000,000
Rugby	600,000	Total	1,390,000
Barrington	500,000		
Ferriby*	350,000	Grand Total	4,140,000
Lewes	80,000		
Chinnor	280,000		
Total	2,750,000		

* The Rochester and Ferriby plants were in the process of being doubled in 1972.

The company also continued to work its extensive chalk quarries near Dunstable, some 48 miles from Rugby.

At the end of 1971, Rugby had about 3,900 employees in its seven U.K. factories and subsidiaries, its overseas operations, and its headquarters at Rugby, England. The head office was organized into nine departments: engineering, production, transportation, sales (home and export), finance and accounting, legal, secretarial, property management, and computer. Above these departments was a small control and coordination group, called the administration department. This group, consisting mostly of assistants to top management, directed and coordinated the activities of the functional departments and served as the intermediate link between subsidiary companies. The subsidiaries addressed all inquiries and reports to Sir Halford Reddish, who was the chairman of each, and to the headquarters staff departments.

The board of directors comprised eight members: four "outside" (non-executive) directors, and four full-time executive directors. For over 30 years Sir Halford Reddish, as chairman and managing director, had as his deputy Mr. R. L. Evans, who passed away in 1968. Sir Halford and Mr. Evans had worked closely with each other, attempting to attain an interchangeability of talents. Sir Halford played a leading role in all major policy decisions, and was particularly concerned with financial management and public relations. Mr. Evans' background was also in accounting; as second in command, he in effect had headed the administration department.

In 1972 the executive directors were Sir Halford Reddish, chairman and chief executive; Mr. Maurice Jenkins, managing director; Mr. R. J. Morgan, and Mr. R. H. Yeatman. The last three had been with the company for many years before appointed to the board. Mr. Jenkins had moved up from assistant managing director after Mr. Evans' death. Mr. Morgan, also a chartered accountant, was particularly concerned with accounting and taxation matters and with financial administration. Mr. Yeatman, for many years general sales manager, was still primarily concerned with sales.

Sir Halford, who served on the boards of five other corporations and on a number of semi-public councils, spent the greater part of each week in London. His days in Rugby included the weekend, and he normally met with the other executive directors on Sunday morning to discuss current operations and problems, and also to engage in planning for up to "two or three balance sheets ahead."

REASONS FOR GROWTH

Sir Halford believed that the company's growth and profitability were attributable to several interrelated factors. But overriding them all, he insisted, was the human element—good human relations. These he defined simply as a recognition of the essential human dignity of the individual:

> The efficiency, the good name, the prestige, the progress of any business depend in the final analysis, not on the magnificence of its plant, not on the splendor of its offices, but on the spirit of the human beings who are working together in that business and whose lives are bound up with its success.
> The most valuable asset in any company's balance sheet is one written in invisible ink. It reads something like this: "The loyalty, the efficiency, the capacity for work of all employed by the company, their pride in the job and in the company's achievements, and their joy in having a part in those achievements."

Besides good human relations, Sir Halford identified five other factors as critical to his company's success:

1. *Emphasis on operating efficiency* was considered one of the most

important of these factors. Sir Halford said that the key to lower unit costs when producing with expensive, continuous-process equipment was keeping the plant operating as close to full capacity as possible and minimizing every element of operating and overhead costs. Therefore, avoiding down-time, improving efficiency of men and machines, and achieving fuel and power economies were all-important. To accomplish these ends, Rugby employed an elaborate monthly cost-reporting system which facilitated pinpointing the items of excessive costs. The factory managers were held responsible for costs under their control, and the chief engineer and production manager and their staffs were continually watching fuel and power costs and working on means of increasing machine efficiency. Excess overtime, costly repairs, stores usage, and factory staff costs were other items which attracted the attention of the central cost control department. One manager said, "We continually work on the weakest point reflected by the cost analyses."

The company's research on improvement of its manufacturing process produced several cost savings. One major outcome of such research was the development of a "wetting" agent for the slurry. Without affecting the chemical properties of the finished product, this agent produced the same "liquidity" and thus the same mixing and handling properties in a slurry containing only 35% water contrasted with 41% previously required. The smaller amount of water to vaporize meant appreciable fuel savings.

Another recent development was the installation of a pipeline from the chalk quarries near Dunstable to the two Warwickshire plants, through which a chalk slurry was pumped a total distance of some 57 miles. This became a possibility when a Pipeline Act came into force in 1962. The Rugby company received the first authorization granted under this Act.

Worker efficiency was also a matter of continuous attention. Because of the expensive equipment and the need to operate without stoppages, misconduct on the job, unexcused absences, and excessive tardiness were considered grounds for release. Such strictness was necessary because, for example, a kiln burner[2] could, through 10 minutes' neglect, permit many thousands of pounds' worth of damage to the equipment. Sir Halford said that his insistence that all employees "play the game according to the rules of the organization" was not only necessary for efficiency but was also a matter of loyalty. "But," he added, "I hold firmly to the view that loyalty should be a two-way traffic. If the head of a business expects a man to be loyal to him, then I say that that man has every right to expect that same loyalty from the head of the business. And I am sure that without discipline there can be no real happiness or success in any organization."

Finally, emphasis was placed on clerical and procedural efficiency. Sir Halford said that greater use of mechanical accounting and invoicing, and continuous analysis and improvement of office procedures had slightly reduced the head office staff in the past few years. Periodic

---

[2] The kiln burner was the worker in charge of operating one or more kilns.

evaluation of the forms and paper-work systems was conducted to eliminate the unnecessary. "We have even had our competitor friends," he
said, "come to look over our reporting and accounting systems. They
are amazed by the fact that we get our data faster than they do with a
proportionately smaller clerical staff."

2. *An effective sales organization* was said to be the second contributing factor to growth and profits. Manufacturing savings effected by
maintaining peak production were attainable only as long as the output
could be sold. The general sales manager remarked, "Since the industry
sells on a common price arrangement, you don't sell cement by selling
cheaper than the next man. You sell on delivery service, good will,
product quality, and on contact with the customer. We like to think that
we rate very high on all these counts. Selling cement is very much of a
team effort, and we have a fine organization here." Under the general
sales manager were an export manager and five area sales managers.
Depending upon the circumstances, each area manager controlled a
number of salesmen, ranging from seven in the Midlands to three in the
South West. There were in all 28 salesmen, all of whom worked from
their homes. The greatest concentration of salesmen was in the London
area where three were located. The salesmen were paid entirely by salary.

3. *Overseas manufacture and other subsidiary activities* were a third
factor to which credit was given for much of the company's growth and
its increased profits in the past few years. Rugby was continually conducting site investigations and negotiations in search of new overseas
opportunities for expansion.

4. *"Efficient" transportation of the U.K. cement sales* was another
reason given for Rugby's growth and profitability. Rugby's fleet had
grown from 52 trucks in 1946 to 394 in 1971 (102 flat-bed trucks, 12
bulk tippers and 280 pressurized bulk wagons),[3] and extra trucks were
hired in the peak construction season. Rugby was proud of the efficiency
of its fleet, the operating costs of which remained below the transportation allowance in the delivered price. At one time the fleet averaged less
than 7% delays for repairs, less than 10% nonoperating idleness, and
6% on-the-job delays. The requirements of the Transport Act of 1968
had, however, increased the delays for repairs. Company officials believed that their truck fleet was one of the most efficient in the industry.
The major reason for this efficiency, the directors believed, was the
highly centralized scheduling of truck dispatches. Each day the central
transportation department, working with the sales department, prepared
schedules of the following day's dispatches of all trucks from each of the
works. Scheduling attempted to maximize the number of deliveries by
each truck and to make as uniform as possible the work-load at the packing and loading plants.

5. *A company-wide philosophy of teamwork* was seen by Sir Halford
and the other directors as the most important reason for the company's

---

[3] Flat-bed trucks carried cement in bags; pressurized bulk wagons carried loose
cement in large tanks which were slightly pressurized to remove the cement at the
delivery site; bulk tippers were fully enclosed dump trucks which carried loose
cement.

success. Teamwork had been achieved, they believed, through the chairman's human relations philosophy and through the application of profit-sharing and employee-shareholding plans. Rugby had no "personnel" department; development of teamwork was the job of managers at all levels within the firm. The impersonal term "personnel" and the word "welfare," with its connotation of charity, were banned from the Rugby vocabulary.

During the course of his career, Sir Halford had developed a philosophy of business as a team effort. A concrete expression of this philosophy was his introduction at Rugby of employee-shareholding and profit-sharing plans. Commenting on the relationship between his philosophy and these plans, he said:

> I am convinced that no scheme of profit-sharing or employee-shareholding can succeed unless it is built on a firm foundation of confidence within the business and of real *esprit de corps*—a strong feeling on the part of all employees of pride in the company and its achievements. The good will of those working together in an industrial enterprise cannot be purchased for cash—of that I am sure. A scheme which is put in with the primary object of buying good will is almost certainly doomed to failure from the start. It may indeed not only do no good but man even do positive harm by creating suspicion, however ill-founded.[4]

Teamwork, seen as commendable in any organization, was held to be doubly important in the cement industry where production in large units of continuous-process plant made it impossible to associate individual effort with specific product output. Mutual confidence was felt to be the basic ingredient of teamwork: on the part of the board, this meant confidence that all employees would put forth a fair day's work, would operate and maintain the plant intelligently, and would follow the leadership of the company; on the part of the employees, it meant confidence in the capability and integrity of the directors and a conviction that discipline "which was as fair as it was firm" would be maintained.

Leadership, in Sir Halford's view, was primarily setting an example. "You lead from in front," he said, "not from behind. It is saying, 'Come on,' not 'Go on.'"

ESPRIT DE CORPS AND COMPANY POLICIES

The following paragraphs summarize the policies singled out by Sir Halford as making the most important contribution to the sense of *esprit de corps* within Rugby.

1. *Personal contact between top executives and operating people all over the world* was relatively frequent. Sir Halford visited the Trinidad and Australia plants at least once a year, and someone from the central headquarters staff visited them, on an average, every two or three months. At home, Sir Halford not only delivered his annual message to

---

[4] Quotation from "This Is Industrial Partnership," a pamphlet written by Sir Halford in 1955 to explain his philosophy and the profit-sharing and employee-shareholding schemes of Rugby.

his "fellow-workers," but he always personally made presentations which were given to men with 25 years' service and again after 50 years' service. Such presentations were made in the presence of the recipients' colleagues, and Sir Halford usually gave a brief review of the recent progress of the company.

2. *Annual messages from Sir Halford to his "fellow employees"* described recent developments within the company, and emphasized the cooperative roles played by employees and shareholders. On these occasions, Sir Halford frequently discussed the importance of profits. The following example is from his message on operations for 1951:

> I want now to say something about profits, because a lot of nonsense has been talked about profits in the last few years, often by politicians of all parties who have never been in industry and have no practical knowledge of industry.
>
> You and I know that profits are the reward and the measure of economy and efficiency, and are essential to the maintenance and expansion of a business. They are, in fact, the real and only bulwark behind our wages and salaries, for if this company ceases to make profits it can only be a comparatively short time before you and I are out.
>
> Let us recognize that it is up to every one of us in this team to go all-out all the time, to give of our best, to maintain and increase our production with economy and efficiency, and in turn, the profits of the company: first—and note that I put this first—because it is the job we are paid to do, and it is only common honesty to our shareholders to do it; and secondly in our own interest to safeguard our jobs for the future.

3. *A "Works Committee" at each plant* functioned as another instrument of teamwork. Composed of the works manager, the works engineer, the safety officer, and five representatives elected from the factory work force, the committee met without exception each month with a senior member of the headquarters staff in attendance. The committee discussed matters of particular interest to the works concerned, and considered suggestions for operational improvements. The head office staff took this opportunity to clarify and discuss newly announced changes in policy and other company developments, such as the annual financial statements.

Toward the end of 1961, an IMEDE[5] researcher had the opportunity to attend a Works Committee meeting at the Rochester Works. The late Mr. R. L. Evans was the head-office representative in attendance. The committee chiefly discussed matters of plant safety and amenities for the workers, such as a sink and hand towels for workers at a remote plant location. The Rochester Works manager said that this meeting was typical, especially insofar as it was primarily concerned with safety and working conditions. The researcher was impressed at the free and easy manner in which the workers entered into the discussions. Mr. Evans explained in great detail some minor points of company policy

---

[5] The *Institut pour l'Etude des Méthodes de Direction de l'Entreprise,* Lausanne, Switzerland.

on tardiness and vacation time. He commented that the worker representatives occasionally brought up very minor points in the committee. "I think," he added, "that some men do this just to show that they are on their toes and doing a good job for their fellow-workers. The result is that the committee functions very well, and in a very good spirit."

4. *Layoffs, and even decisions about layoffs*, were treated as a matter of top consideration. Thus, no one but Sir Halford had the authority to release people during slack periods. He had in fact never authorized a layoff. For instance, the rail strike in 1955 almost closed the Rochester factory as coal reserves ran low.[6] As the shutdown date approached, Sir Halford announced that no one would be laid off, but that (*a*) some men would have to take their vacations during the shutdown; and (*b*) everyone would have to agree to do any job given him (at his usual pay rate) during the shutdown.

5. *Low employee turnover* had long been the rule at Rugby. One executive commented on the fact that the turnover of weekly paid workers was low, as follows:

> If we set aside employees with less than two years of service, our average worker has been here about 13 years. We do find that some new employees, especially young men, are not prepared for the demanding work in a cement plant, and such men leave, usually within 12 months. Thus, new employees should not fairly be included in our average turnover figure.
>
> Incidentally, taking total annual wages and bonuses as an indicator, the cement industry ranks in the top half-dozen British industries in terms of earnings.

6. *Early and adequate communication* was regarded as important by Sir Halford, who summarized his views on this key policy as follows:

> If there is to be a lively interest and pride in the company and its doing, then it is necessary that all employees be kept informed as far as possible about what is going on.
>
>   *   *   *   *   *   *
>
> We try as far as we can to ensure that everyone has an opportunity of reading on the company's notice boards a few hours *before* it appears in the newspapers any release issued to the Press. We do not think it right that a man should learn from the newspapers something which he could quite properly have heard at first hand within the company.
>
> And all Press comments on the company are posted on all our notice boards as soon as they appear.[7]

Sir Halford held strongly to the view that, to be effective, leadership must embrace an adequate system of communication—and communication in the widest sense of the term. "Example," he said, "is in itself one facet of communication."

Besides all the above-listed means of building teamwork, other means

---

[6] Last-minute settlement of the rail strike saved Rugby Cement from its contemplated shutdown.

[7] Quotations from "This Is Industrial Partnership."

of interest to Sir Halford included well-designed profit-sharing or share-holding schemes. To be effective, Sir Halford believed these must have two necessary features. First, they must be tailored to suit the circumstances of the company and the outlook, philosophy, and intent of its leader. Second, the schemes must be simple.

THE PROFIT-SHARING SCHEME

Sir Halford said that the Rugby profit-sharing scheme, inaugurated in 1935, was designed to emphasize two things:

a) that the efforts of the employees are the efforts of a team—that we are all working to one end; and
b) the essential partnership which exists between the ordinary shareholders and the employees.[8]

In speeches to both shareholders and workers, Sir Halford referred to the partnership between capital and employees. He said that capital was nothing more than the "labor of yesterday—the production of yesterday which was surplus to the consumption of yesterday."

Fundamental to the partnership was the following bargain:

> . . . the labor of today is guaranteed payment for its services and the profit is calculated only after the remuneration of that labor has been paid. Capital, therefore, takes the risk and in return takes such profit (or loss) as arises after the labor of today has been paid in full.
>
> But to my mind this difference in the basis of their respective remuneration in no way destroys the conception of industrial enterprise as essentially a partnership between the labor of yesterday (capital) and the labor of today. Nor is it destroyed if the "bargain" is varied slightly by guaranteeing the greater part of labor's remuneration irrespective of profit or loss and by making an additional but smaller part of it dependent on the results of the enterprise as a whole.[9]

The Employees' Profit-Sharing scheme provided for an annual bonus in excess of industry-negotiated wages or contracted salary for all Rugby wage earners and staff. Basic points of the scheme are summarized below:[10]

1. To qualify for the profit-sharing bonus, an hourly or salaried employee must have completed, on December 31, 12 months' unbroken service to the satisfaction of the directors. An employee who joined the company after January 1 but not later than July 1 would for that year qualify for one-half of the bonus he would have received if he had completed one year of service.

2. For the purpose of calculating the bonus, each qualified employee was treated as if he held a certain number of Ordinary shares in the company. A staff employee's "notional shares" were related to his annual salary. An hourly worker's shares varied in proportion to his length of service up to 40 years.

---

[8] Ibid.
[9] Ibid.
[10] This explanation summarizes only the major aspects.

3. The bonus was calculated at the full rate per share of the gross dividend declared and paid to the Ordinary shareholders for the financial year in question, and was paid immediately after the annual general meeting. For example, in 1971 the Ordinary dividend declared was 3.75 pence per share. Thus a worker with five years' service holding 1,315 notional shares, would receive a bonus of (1,315 × 3.75p) or £49.31.

4. Certified sickness or compulsory National Service were ignored in calculating the number of years of unbroken service.

5. Any employee who left or was under notice to leave prior to the date of payment forfeited his bonus.

6. The scheme conferred no rights in respect of any capital distribution other than those declared as dividends on the Ordinary shares of the company out of profits.

7. The scheme was subject to modification or withdrawal at any time at the discretion of the directors.

Sir Halford emphasized that the bonus was not automatic. In a very small number of cases each year, bonuses were withheld completely or in part because service was not "to the satisfaction of the directors." If a man's record for the year was questionable, including several unexplained tardinesses, for instance, it was submitted, without name, to the Works Committee of the factory. In all cases, the directors had abided by the committee's recommendation. Sir Halford said that withholding the bonus was not so much a penalty to the slack worker as it was a necessary act of fairness to those who gave 100% service during the year. Summarizing, Sir Halford said:

> I believe that this is important: the bonus must be something that is earned—not something which becomes a right. I also feel that the link with the Ordinary shareholders' dividend is fundamental: if the dividend per share goes up, so does the bonus; if the dividend is reduced, the bonus falls too—which is as it should be.

THE "A" SHARE SCHEME[11]

After World War II, Sir Halford saw two factors that made the profit-sharing scheme inadequate for emphasizing the partnership between capital and labor. He felt that the twin virtues of hard work and thrift no longer assured a man of personal savings for his old age—*taxation* restricted savings and *inflation* devalued them. Unlike the Ordinary shareholder's income, which flowed from an asset whose market value reflected both the company's prosperity and inflationary pressures, the employee's profit-sharing bonus was not reflected in a realizable capital asset. Thus he did not have a "hedge" against inflation.

To supply this need, Sir Halford presented his "A" share plan, in late 1954, for approval by the Ordinary shareholders. He said that the scheme was designed to do three things:[12]

---

[11] In 1966 the "A" shares were re-named Participating (non-voting) shares.

[12] This explanation of the "A" share plan is summarized from "This Is Industrial Partnership."

To give practical form to the unity of interest which I have always held to exist between the Ordinary shareholders and the employees; to give a return to the Ordinary shareholders on profits "ploughed back" in the past; and to give to every full-time employee the opportunity to have in his hands a capital asset readily realizable on death or retirement. It was received enthusiastically by shareholders and employees alike.

One million "A" shares with a par value of one shilling each were created with the following conditions attached to them:

1. Starting with 1955, in any fiscal year for which (a) pretax net profits were not less than £900,000, and (b) the gross amount distributed as dividend to the Ordinary shareholders was not less than £300,000, the holders of the "A" shares would be entitled to an amount of £70,000 plus 20% of any excess of the said net profits over £900,000 (see Exhibit 5). However, (i) the amount attributable to the "A" shares would not exceed 12½% of the net profits; and (ii) in the event of the issue of additional Ordinary share capital by the company after 31st December 1954 (otherwise than by the way of a capitalization of reserves or undistributed profits), the said figure of £900,000 would be increased by a sum equal to 6% of the proceeds or other consideration received by the company.[13]

2. Any amount attributable to the "A" shares as ascertained under (1) above would be distributed as dividend or carried forward in the books of the company to the credit of the "A" shares for subsequent distribution, as the directors might decide.

3. The holders of "A" shares would have no voting rights.

4. In a winding-up, the "A" shares would participate only insofar as the amount of their paid-in capital value and the "A" share credit carried forward on the company books, but would have no further participation in assets.

5. No further "A" shares would be created without the sanction of an extraordinary resolution passed by the holders of the "A" shares.[14]

Half of the "A" shares were offered to the Ordinary shareholders at par and half to the employees.

"*All* full-time employees of the company were included: this was not a get-rich-quick exercise for the favored few," said Sir Halford.

Allocation to the employees was effected by dividing all employees into groups according to remuneration, responsibility, and status within the company; length of service was not a factor. Those in the first group (which included most factory production workers) were offered 250 shares; other groups were offered 500, 750, 1,000, 1,500, 2,000 shares, and so on. After some years, when these one shilling "A" shares were quoted at over £6 on the Stock Exchange, the allocation of shares to newcomers was proportionately reduced. Over 95% of Rugby's employees had exercised their option and purchased the "A" shares.

---

[13] Because additional equity was introduced after 1954, the "A" shares began participating at a net profit of £1,748,190 for 1972.

[14] After January 1964, the number of "A" shares was increased, however, by a "scrip" issue of five new shares for each one held. See "The 'A' Share Scrip Expansion," below.

Sir Halford was particularly concerned about two aspects of the scheme. About the first, he wrote as follows:

> I was anxious that there should be no element of a "gift" from one partner (the holders of the Ordinary shares) to the other (the employees), and that the equity owned by the Ordinary shares should be unimpaired. I was convinced that the holders of the Ordinary shares could have no legitimate cause for complaint if the profits were so substantially increased in the future and some comparatively small part of the increase went to the employees as a reward for their efforts.
>
> The "A" shares should be worth no more than was paid for them when issued, so that the employees could feel that whatever increased value accrued thereafter was due to their teamwork, with, I do not forget, nor do I allow them to forget, the capital provided by their partners in the enterprise.[15]

Both this reason and tax considerations [16] dictated that the minimum profit level at which the "A" shares would start participating (originally £900,000) should be well above the profit levels when the "A" shares were issued.

The second aspect of the scheme that was of concern to Sir Halford was that the main object would continue to be assuring employees a capital sum on death or retirement. Sir Halford foresaw that the "A" shares might have some speculative attraction to the general public, and he did not want the employees to be tempted into selling and thus depriving themselves of retirement or death benefits from the plan. He also felt that anyone leaving the firm should be required to sell his shares back at par, thus enabling newcomers to participate. To accomplish these ends, Sir Halford designated that the shares allocated to the employees were to be held on their behalf by an entity called Staff Nominees Limited. This would be accountable to the employees for dividends declared, and it would be authorized to act on their behalf in all matters relating to the "A" shares.

The following conditions applied:

1. Initially, whenever an employee moved upward to a new group, he would be given the opportunity to buy his allocation of shares at par. Failing to do so, he would not be given a subsequent opportunity.
2. "A" shares could be sold by the employee at any time at par to Staff Nominees Limited, and must be sold whenever he left the company.
3. An employee's shares could be sold at market value[17] *only* in the event of the employee's death while in the service of the company, or upon his reaching age 65 (55 for women).
4. Any dividend declared on the "A" shares would be paid immediately to the employee.

The "A" share scrip expansion. After the original "A" share distribution, 50,000 shares remained unallocated. These were held by RPC

---

[15] Quotation from "This Is Industrial Partnership."

[16] See "The Taxation Aspect," below.

[17] Market price was established by quotation on The London Stock Exchange of the "A" shares allotted originally at par to the Ordinary shareholders.

Benevolent Fund Ltd. (a company formed for the aim indicated by its title) pending their issue to newcomers. The directors felt that this block of shares, plus those which Staff Nominees Limited bought back at par from departing employees, would be sufficient to offer shares to new and promoted employees for the foreseeable future. Thus, no expansion in the number of "A" shares was originally contemplated.

In December 1963, however, the company's Articles of Association were amended, giving power to the "A" shareholders to capitalize from time to time any part of the profits allocated to the "A" shares in the past but remaining undistributed, and therefore to increase the number of "A" shares for this purpose. The "A" shareholders agreed to capitalize £250,000 of the net amount standing to the credit of the "A" shares by a scrip issue of five new shares for each one held. The effect was to amend the market price of the "A" shares, which had by then reached over £9, to around 30 shillings. By this action, the marketability of the shares was increased. In 1971 a second scrip expansion brought the par value of the "A" shares from £300,000 to £360,000.

The taxation aspect.   For the company, the profit-sharing bonus was considered a wage bonus and therefore a before-tax expense. The "A" share dividends, however, were similar to Ordinary dividends, being paid out of after-tax profits.

For the employees, the profit-sharing bonus was taxed as ordinary wage or salary income. Taxation of the employees in connection with "A" share distribution was a most difficult problem and one on which Sir Halford spent many hours in consultation with the Board of Inland Revenue.

The law held that if, at the time of issue, the value of the shares was greater than the amount the employees paid for them, the difference was taxable as a "benefit" arising from employment. The Rugby "A" share sale to its employees, however, had two characteristics which affected any ruling under this law:

1. "A" shares were not quoted on the market until two months after issue; thus it was a matter of discussion whether at time of issue they were worth more than the par value paid for them.
2. Employees were not free to sell their shares at market price except on retirement or death.

Final agreement with the Inland Revenue was reached, putting the assessed value of the "A" shares at the time of issue slightly above par.

Tax assessment for shares issued subsequently to newcomers or to promoted employees required a different arrangement with the Inland Revenue, since by that time a market value had been established. Final agreement resulted in considering a variable fraction of the difference between current market value and par value as taxable income. The fraction varied inversely with the length of time between the recipient's age and the date when he would reach age 65, and be able to realize the market price of the "A" shares. For instance, a 25-year-old newcomer receiving 500 "A" shares would have to consider as income, for income tax purposes, only 10% of the difference between market value and the price

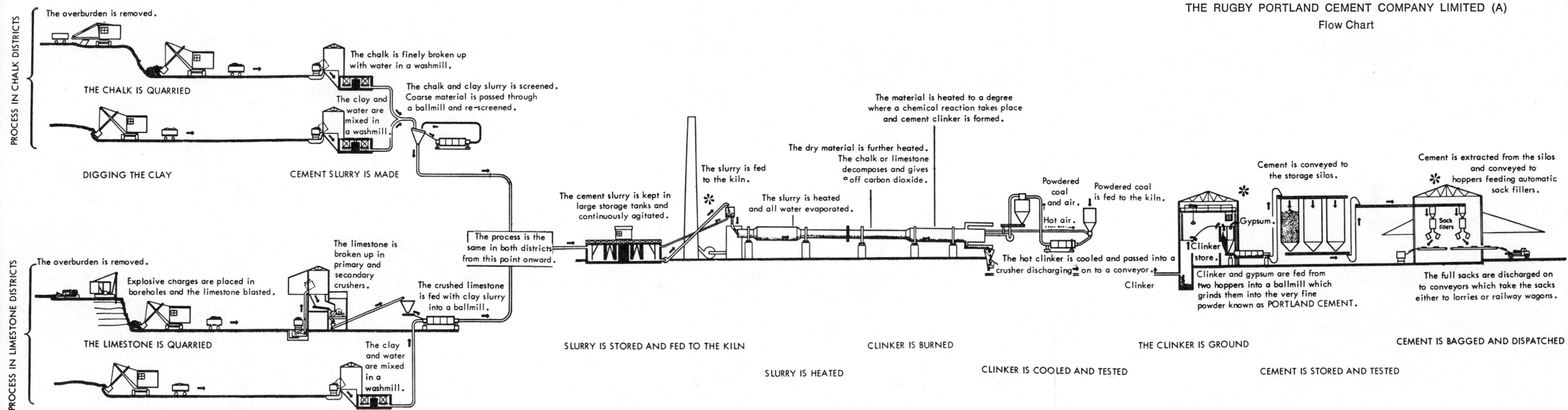

Exhibit 1

THE RUGBY PORTLAND CEMENT COMPANY LIMITED (A)

Flow Chart

PROCESS IN CHALK DISTRICTS

The overburden is removed.

THE CHALK IS QUARRIED

The chalk is finely broken up with water in a washmill.

The chalk and clay slurry is screened. Coarse material is passed through a ballmill and re-screened.

DIGGING THE CLAY

The clay and water are mixed in a washmill.

CEMENT SLURRY IS MADE

The material is heated to a degree where a chemical reaction takes place and cement clinker is formed.

The dry material is further heated. The chalk or limestone decomposes and gives off carbon dioxide.

The slurry is fed to the kiln.

The slurry is heated and all water evaporated.

The cement slurry is kept in large storage tanks and continuously agitated.

The process is the same in both districts from this point onward.

Powdered coal and air.

Powdered coal is fed to the kiln.

Hot air.

Cement is conveyed to the storage silos.

Cement is extracted from the silos and conveyed to hoppers feeding automatic sack fillers.

The hot clinker is cooled and passed into a crusher discharging on to a conveyor.

Clinker

Gypsum.

Clinker store.

Clinker and gypsum are fed from two hoppers into a ballmill which grinds them into the very fine powder known as PORTLAND CEMENT.

Sack fillers

The full sacks are discharged on to conveyors which take the sacks either to lorries or railway wagons.

PROCESS IN LIMESTONE DISTRICTS

The overburden is removed.

Explosive charges are placed in boreholes and the limestone blasted.

The limestone is broken up in primary and secondary crushers.

The crushed limestone is fed with clay slurry into a ballmill.

THE LIMESTONE IS QUARRIED

The clay and water are mixed in a washmill.

DIGGING THE CLAY

CEMENT SLURRY IS MADE

SLURRY IS STORED AND FED TO THE KILN

SLURRY IS HEATED

CLINKER IS BURNED

CLINKER IS COOLED AND TESTED

THE CLINKER IS GROUND

CEMENT IS STORED AND TESTED

CEMENT IS BAGGED AND DISPATCHED

* Electrostatic precipitators and other dust arresting devices are installed at these points on most cement works.

paid (one shilling per share), because he could not realize the market value for 40 years. On the other hand, a 50-year-old man receiving 500 "A" shares would have to consider 42½% of the difference as taxable income, because he was much closer to realizing the gain. (All dividends received by employees on their "A" shares up to retirement age were treated, for tax purposes, as "earned" income and therefore were subject to the earned income allowance.)

Results.   In his message to his fellow-workers in the company following the 1958 operations, Sir Halford spoke about the "A" share plan as follows:

> . . . Quite often a man will say to me: "This 'A' share scheme of yours—tell me, has it increased production?" and I reply: "I haven't the slightest idea, but I shouldn't think so." So he says, "But surely that was the object. It's an incentive scheme, isn't it?" "On the contrary," I tell him, "I have always insisted that it should *not* be called an incentive scheme, because that to my mind would imply that we in Rugby Cement were not already doing our best, were not doing our duty in return for our wages and salaries. And that I will not have."
>
> What our "A" share scheme does is to give to the employees the opportunity to build up capital available on retirement or on earlier death, and to promote the feeling that we are all one team working on the same end in partnership with our shareholders. The value of the "A" shares depends in the long run on the success of our efforts in making profits. And don't overlook the fact that half the "A" shares were issued, also at par, to the holders of our Ordinary shares. They very rightly benefit too, as they have seen these one shilling shares change hands on the Stock Exchange at prices up to 42 shillings.[18]
>
> Apart from the capital aspect, the holding of "A" shares by the employees of the company, and also, of course, our "profit-sharing" schemes, give some reward for successful endeavor—which is surely right.

---

[18] In January 1964, prior to the scrip issue referred to above, the "A" shares were quoted on the Stock Exchange at up to the equivalent of 186 shillings per share.

Exhibit 2

THE RUGBY PORTLAND CEMENT COMPANY LIMITED (A)

Consolidated Balance Sheet Statements,
Selected Years, as of December 31
(in thousands of pounds)

	1946	1956	1961	1966	1967	1968	1969	1970	1971
ASSETS									
Current assets	576	4,521	8,226	14,581	17,560	22,875	27,592	30,550	31,592
Fixed assets (as valued, or at cost, less sales)	1,673	8,613	11,258	24,989	30,571	37,916	40,890	45,332	50,349
Less accumulated depreciation	436	1,969	3,930	7,589	8,876	10,328	13,119	15,064	17,129
Net fixed assets	1,237	6,644	7,328	17,400	21,695	27,588	27,771	30,268	33,217
Investment in subsidiary companies (nonconsolidated)	209	—	—	—	—	—	—	—	—
Premiums on acquisition of shares in subsidiary companies			—	4,226	4,226	7,424	7,424	7,424	7,424
Total assets	2,022	11,165	15,554	36,207	43,481	57887	62,787	68,242	72,233
LIABILITIES AND NET WORTH									
Current liabilities	367	1,759	1,328	4,138	5,134	5,898	6,073	7,945	10,410
Bank overdraft	—	—	—	2,126	4,382	961	2,490	3,085	1,343
Debt capital:									
4% debenture	420	—	—	—	—	—	—	—	—
Mortgage and unsecured loans	—	1,980	2,268	608	1,130	1,035	940	846	751
6% unsecured loan stock, 1993/98	—	—	—	—	—	12,000	12,000	12,000	12,000
7¾% unsecured loan stock, 1993/98	—	—	—	—	—	—	500	500	500
Total debt	420	1,980	2,268	608	1,130	13,035	13,440	13,346	13,251
Share capital:									
4% and 6% Preference shares*	325	825	825	1,000	1,000	1,000	—	—	—
Ordinary shares 5s. Od. par	325	1,500	2,000	10,000	12,000	13,200	13,200	13,200	15,400
"A" shares ls. Od. par†	—	50	50	300	300	300	300	300	360
Capital reserve	325	1,358	2,002	3,728	5,667	7,066	7,403	7,458	5,483

	1	2	3	4	5	6	7	8	9
Revenue reserves:									
General reserve‡	100	1,750	—	—	—	—	—	—	—
Taxation equalization account§	—	—	—	1,137	—	—	—	—	—
Investment Grants suspense account	—	—	—	—	39	413	1,001	847	689
Reserve for future taxation‖	—	320	1,373	380	594	790	1,140	1,163	1,023
Reserve for Ordinary and "A" share dividend payments¶	—	230	383	1,575	1,575	1,515	1,873	2,448	3,210
Undistributed profit	161	275	4,520	10,671	10,972	12,964	15,006	17,459	19,997
Total capital and reserves	1,236	6,308	11,153	28,791	32,147	37,248	39,923	42,875	46,117
Minority interests	—	1,117	805	544	688	745	861	991	1,112
Total liabilities and net worth	2,022	11,165	15,554	36,207	43,481	57,887	62,787	68,242	72,233
Net working capital	210	2,762	6,898	8,317	8,044	16,016	19,029	19,520	19,839
Equity debt ratio	2.9/1	3.2/1	4.9/1	47.4/1	28.4/1	2.9/1	3.0/1	3.2/1	3.5/1

Note: Some figures may fail to add because of rounding.
* Cancelled on December 31, 1969. Loan stock substituted.
† Name changed to Participating Non-Voting (PNV) shares in 1966.
‡ Merged with undistributed profit in 1958.
§ Transferred to undistributed profit in 1967.
‖ From 1966 onward, this reserve applied only to overseas taxes.
¶ Net in 1946–1961; gross for remaining years on the chart.
Source: Company records.

Exhibit 3

THE RUGBY PORTLAND CEMENT COMPANY LIMITED (A)

Consolidated Profit and Loss Account, Selected Years
(in thousands of pounds)

	1946	%	1956	%	1961	%	1966	%	1967	%	1968	%	1969	%	1970	%	1971	%
Consolidated trading profits	213		1,369		2,465		4,895		5,067		6,423		7,844		8,902		10,687	
Other income	—		65		105		103		170		157		241		284		402	
Less depreciation	79		340		550		1,070		1,276		1,415		2,166		2,074		2,083	
Net profit before taxes	134	100	1,093	100	2,020	100	3,928	100	4,561	100	5,165	100	5,919	100	7,112	100	9,006	100
Taxation—Profits tax/corporation tax	39		109		174		510		370		276		273		667		1,717	
Income tax/overseas tax*			255		602		393		733		912		1,170		1,305		1,247	
Total taxes	39	29	364	33	776	38	903	23	1,103	24	1,188	23	1,443	25	1,972	28	2,964	33
Net profit after taxes	95		729		1,244		3,025		3,458		3,977		4,476		5,140		6,042	
Minority interests	—		—		—		—		152	4	142	3	210	4	239	3	234	2
Preference dividends†	12	9	23	2	24	1	50	1	50	1	50	1	50	1				
Ordinary dividends†	22	16	194	18	306	15	1,200	31	1,200	26	1,380	27	1,650	28	1,848	26	2,310	26
"A" share dividends‡	—		36	3	77	4	375	10	375	8	413	8	525	8	600	9	900	10
Retained in business	61	46	477	44	837	42	1,400	35	1,681	37	1,992	38	2,041	34	2,453	34	2,598	29
Ordinary dividend per share (gross)	7½d		1½d		1½d		7.2d		0d		6.6d		7½d		8.4d		3.75p§	
Capital distribution per share (gross)	3d		—		—		—		—		—		—		—		—	
"A" share dividend per share (gross)	—		⅓d		⅔d		1s.3d		1s.3d		1s.4½d		1s.9d		2s.0d		12.50p	
Net profit before taxes as return on total capital and reserves	10.85%		17.30%		18.11%		13.64%		14.19%		13.87%		14.83%		16.66%		19.53%	
Gross Ordinary dividend as return on capital equity employed, i.e., Ordinary shares plus disclosed reserves (less reserves credited to "A" shares)	4.36%		6.36%		5.06%		4.47%		4.00%		3.95%		4.29%		4.49%		5.22%	

* Profits tax and corporation tax were the estimated liability for the year ending with the statement. Income tax was the estimated liability for the subsequent two-year period. This procedure gave rise to the reserve for future income tax in the balance sheet. The estimated income tax for the future period was put into this reserve, and at the end of each year, the actual tax liability for the year was withdrawn from the reserve and put into current liabilities, from which the actual remittance was made.

† Net 1946–1961; gross for remaining years on chart.

‡ Changed to Participating (Non-Voting) shares in 1966.

§ After Britain went on a metric monetary system, the number of pence per pound changed from 240d to 100p.

Source: Company records.

Exhibit 4

THE RUGBY PORTLAND CEMENT COMPANY LIMITED (A)
Indices of Deliveries, Profit, and Net Worth, Selected Years
(base: 1946 = 100)

Year	Deliveries*	Capital†	Profits
1946....................	100	100	100
1956....................	307	510	816
1961....................	388	902	1,507
1966....................	729	2,329	2.931
1967....................	766	2,601	3,404
1968....................	845	3,014	3,854
1969....................	851	3,230	4,417
1970....................	859	3,469	5,307
1971....................	946	3,731	6,723

* These are total group deliveries, in tons, and as an index basing point.
† "Capital" here equals total equity capital, including reserves.
From 1947 through 1971, the capital account was affected by the following transactions:

Year	Amount	Transaction
1947........	£1,000,000	Sale of new Common shares (£500,000) and new preference shares (£500,000).
1953........	500,000	Sale of new Common shares.
1954........	1,050,000	Sale of new Common shares (£1,000,000) and of "A" shares (£50,000).
1959........	1,075,000	Sale of new Common shares.
1962........	n. a.	Rights issue of 2 million Ordinary shares, and payments of 2 million Ordinary and 175,000 preference shares to shareholders of the acquired Eastwoods Company.
1963........	—	Ordinary shares split three for two; "A" shares split five for one.
1966........	—	Ordinary shares split four for three.
1967........	—	Ordinary shares split six for five.
1968........	n. a.	Rights issue of 4,800,000 Ordinary shares on the basis of two new for twenty old.
1971........	—	"A" shares split six for five.

Source: Company records.

Exhibit 5

THE RUGBY PORTLAND CEMENT COMPANY LIMITED (A)

Summary of Earnings and Gross Dividend Payments

Selected Years

(in thousands of pounds)

	1956	1961	1963	1964	1965	1966	1967	1968	1969	1970	1971
Profit before tax............	1,093	2,020	2,656	3,311	3,664	3,928	4,561	5,165	5,919	7,112	9,006
Gross Ordinary dividend........	338	500	938	1,125	1,125	1,200	1,200	1,380	1,650	1,848	2,310
Gross payable to "A" shares......	109	252	287	414	458	491	540	613	696	836	1,074
Actual "A" share dividend......	63	125	187	300	388	375	375	413	525	600	900
Difference carried forward as "A" share credit.......................	46	127	100	114	120	116	165	200	171	236	174
Cumulative "A" share credit*......	91	493	316†	430	550	666	831	1,031	1,202	1,438	1,514‡

* The "A" share (later PNV share) credit was contained in the undistributed profit account in the balance sheet. The directors considered this credit as a "dividend equalization reserve" to supply "A" dividends if they were not earned according to the formula (i.e., if pretax profits were below £1,568,190 from 1964 to 1967; £1,618,846 for 1968; and £1,748,190 from 1969 onwards).

† After deducting £408,163, the gross equivalent amount of the scrip issue of £250,000.

‡ After deducting £97,959, the gross equivalent of a scrip issue of £60,000.

Source: Company records.

The Rugby Portland Cement
Company Limited (B)*

LATE IN 1961, an IMEDE research team decided to attempt to expand the Rugby Portland Cement case by adding information on the ways in which various employees of the company viewed their jobs. To this purpose, an IMEDE researcher toured each of the company's three cement works in England; he also conducted interviews with a number of hourly paid workers and with a substantial number of middle- and top-management executives. This case includes excerpts from some of these interviews, as well as some of the researcher's impressions of what he saw.

VIEWS OF SOME RUGBY WORKMEN

Rugby's management was very cooperative in helping the researcher to interview some of the workmen. Although, in theory, it would have been useful to interview a rather large number of workers selected at random, this was not practicable for certain reasons:

1. There were limitations on the research time available for these interviews.
2. There was a chance that some men, if chosen at random, might:
    a)   Not be able to articulate their views;
    b)   Be less than wholly frank;
    c)   Be unable to leave their work posts at the desired time.

Accordingly, Mr. R. L. Evans, deputy managing director, and Mr. Baker, works manager of the Rugby works, selected from the Rugby work force four workers who, they thought, would be articulate, honest, and as representative as possible of the general sentiments of the entire Rugby

* Copyright 1964 by l'Institut pour l'Etude des Méthodes de Direction de l'Entreprise (IMEDE), Lausanne, Switzerland. Reprinted by permission.

worker group. The researcher interviewed the four men separately, in an office at the Rugby plant; nobody else was present during the interviews. The names of the four men interviewed have been disguised.

Interview with Mr. Ryan

Mr. Evans and Mr. Baker, in arranging the interviews, mentioned that Mr. Ryan should provide a highly entertaining and useful interview, that he was outspoken and highly articulate. Mr. Ryan, who had been working for the company since 1956, was an Irishman; he appeared to be about 40 years old. He worked in the transport department of the company as a truck driver and had been a member of the Rugby works committee for some time. The researcher asked each of the four men only one question to begin: What did the man think about working for the company, what were the bad points and the good points? Mr. Ryan began:

> Well, I might tell you I'm an old union man, been a sort of union agitator all my working life. Before I came here I never held a job longer than eighteen months. I've been here almost six years now, and I can tell you this, I'm going to stay here the rest of my life. And, mind you, I got a lot less to gain by staying here than most of the men. I have no A-shares, because you know you only get one chance to buy them A-shares, and when I had to buy them, I didn't have the money because my wife just had to have an operation. So now for the rest of my life I got to work here knowing that I'll never have no A-shares, and I think this is unfair, and I keep fighting to get me shares, and maybe I will and maybe I won't, but I'll stay on here no matter what.
>
> And another thing is I'm a very bad timekeeper—sometimes it's my fault, and sometimes it was because I had to take my wife to the doctor and so I'd come in late, and so for three straight years I lost my profit-sharing bonus on account of being late so much. [Mr. Ryan had actually lost his bonus in two nonconsecutive years, management reported.] So you can see what I mean when I tell you that I got much less to gain by working here than the other men.
>
> But even though there's lots of little things could be done, this is a wonderful place to work, and that's the Lord's own truth. I'm not saying anything to you I wouldn't say right to the Chairman's face if he asked me—I'm not a man to say what he doesn't mean.
>
> You got to remember this: It's no good coming down to a cement works if you don't want to work hard. But they pay you good, and the main thing is, you always get treated fair. If you got a complaint, you can take it as high as you want, right up to the Chairman himself, but it's no good complaining unless you give 'em the facts. That's what they want to see: facts.
>
> Another thing you ought to write down is this: In this company, I'm just as good as anybody, as good as the Chairman or Mr. Evans—that's what you won't get anywhere else. We all know this here, and we know you've got to work as a team. And I'll tell you this, I know the Chairman would let me buy my A-shares if he could, but you see he's got to be fair to the other workers too. But I do think that you get punished awful hard for being late. [Mr. Ryan's profit-sharing bonus would have amounted, in those years when he lost it, to about £30. His weekly wages were about £15.]

Over in Coventry, you know [about 15 miles away], in the car and airplane factories a man can make £30 a week, while here he'll only make about £15, but we get the £15 for 52 weeks of the year, plus the profit-sharing, the A-shares, and lots of other benefits. The company buys up lots of clothes for us, so we can get them cheaper. I once compared what I earned in a year with a friend of mine who works in Coventry for £29 a week, and you know what? I came out £48 ahead of him for the year, because those fellows are always getting laid off.

And let me tell you this: You'd never get a better firm to work for, no matter where you went; there isn't another company like this, at least none I've ever heard about.

You know, when I tell you we work hard here, you've got to remember that the Chairman doesn't ask us to do anything he doesn't do himself. You know, he works 18 hours a day, and when he come down sick recently and had to have that operation, his doctors told him to take it easy, and so he did—he only worked ten hours a day.

[Mr. Ryan then gave the researcher a very detailed description of what was involved in his truck driving. He stressed that the equipment was the best obtainable, that the company paid much more attention to driver safety than to delivering a maximum daily tonnage of cement, that scrupulous care was taken, at great expense, to be certain that the customer received all the cement he had been billed for.]

You see my truck out there? That truck, it's brand new, and it cost £10,000, and they expect me to take care of it like if it was my own, and I do. [The truck in fact cost slightly over £3,500.] And I know I've got 42 hours a week guaranteed, and more hours on weekends if I want to make extra money, and that's a hell of a nice thing for a truck driver. And as soon as I've driven 11 hours in a single day, even if I didn't get home with the truck by the time my 11 hours was up, the company would send out another lorry with two drivers to drive me and my truck home, that's how careful they are about the 11-hour rule. And you see them fine overalls we drivers got, and them jackets? Mr. Reddish, I believe, bought them for us out of his own pocket. That's just the kind of man he is. [In fact he didn't; they are provided by the company.]

I told you I used to be a union man, but I tell you this, if a union came in here now, it would hurt the workers—they'd get less pay, they couldn't touch anything they weren't supposed to. That's the kind of a union man I am today.

In summing up, and this is God's own truth, I think Sir Halford Reddish ought to be England's Prime Minister, and Mr. Evans ought to be the Secretary for Foreign Affairs.

Interview with Mr. Mason

Mr. Mason was a foreman in the "raw plant," where the slurry was made. He had been working for the company about 14 years and appeared to be about 50. He began:

Well, wherever I went, I don't think I could better myself, that's what I'd say. The Chairman puts us in the picture about what's going on; he has more of a fatherly concern for us, I think. I've known the Chairman 30 years, and if he says a thing he means it. He's put in some wonderful plans for the men, he has. For example, when my father died, we got about £1,000 for his A-shares, and this was a big help, because I've got a sister who isn't very well, and this money pays for her. From the workman's point of view, if you want it, I find that they're very, very satisfied. I've got 30-odd men working for me, and I get all the points of view, so to speak, and I think I can say that they're all happy to be working here. Now, of course, there's some men as will always find something to complain about, you're going to have that anywhere, but in the main I think that the men like working here very much.

You're an American, so I'll put it in American: Damn it all, we're on to a good thing here and we know it.

I've got a brother, a son, and two brothers-in-law working here, and my father before he died. They all came to work here before I did. Now do you think they'd have come if this wasn't a good place to work?

I do believe honestly, and I'm not handing you any bull, that we couldn't better ourselves. And you've got to remember this: Sir Halford will give any of his men a proper hearing any time. And what's astonishing is that as the firm gets larger, the company seems to give us more attention, when you'd think it'd be the other way around.

Now you take your average Englishman, he's the biggest grumbler in the world, about anything at all. But you won't find much grumbling here. You'd have to kick them out to get the men here to leave.

Interview with Mr. Toot

Mr. Toot, who appeared to be about 50, had been with Rugby about seven years. The researcher received the distinct impression that Mr. Toot was temperamentally a sort of cynic who only grudgingly would admit that a workman's life could be decent, although this impression was formed on the basis of very little evidence. Mr. Toot began:

Taken all around, I should say that this is a very good place to work. A workman here knows that he can go as high as he likes, if he has the ability. You get fair treatment here. I suppose that work here is 80% satisfactory. For the other 20%, it's hard to say what the objections might be. But one thing is, when a man first came to work here, he didnt get enough participation in the bonus system [the profit-sharing scheme], but they've changed that now.

If a man's willing to do an honest day's work, he'll generally be satisfied here. I suppose I could say this: The longer a man's been here, the more he wants to stay.

Now, you get some fellows, especially young ones, come in and they can't stick the work; it's too heavy or too hard for them. They usually leave, if they're this type, in 12–18 months. If a man sticks it a year or a year and a half, he'll probably stay here until he's through working.

This is a long-term policy job, so to say. It's good if you're thinking about your old age, because the company really takes care of you after you retire. I don't suppose you know this, but all the company's pensioners [retired workers] get a ton of coal from the Chairman at Christmas. There's a Christmas party for the pensioners. And men like Mr. Evans and Mr. Baker visit the pensioners very regularly. The company doesn't just forget you when you've stopped working for them—they take care of you.

I suppose when I think of it, it's hard to say what kind of objections, you might say, a man could have to working here, if he's not just a casual laborer who doesn't care about doing an honest day's work, if he doesn't care about doing a good job. This is a good place to work.

Interview with Mr. Forster

Mr. Forster had been working for Rugby for 48 years, and he worked in the quarry. He talked rather little, much less than the previous three men.

> Well, I've been working here all my life, and that's a fact. It's hard work, and no doubt about it, but it's a wonderful company to work for. I was here, you know, when Sir Halford took over, and it was wonderful when he did. He promised us steady work, and we've had it ever since. Some of your casual lads, now, who come here looking for an easy day's work and high pay, they don't stay; but a real man, a man who doesn't mind work, he'll be happier here than anywhere else I've ever heard of.

RANDOM IMPRESSIONS OF THE RESEARCHER

In the course of his tour of the three different works, the researcher spent a great deal of time with Mr. R. L. Evans, who toured each plant with him, and with the works managers. The researcher was especially struck by two facts. First, Mr. Evans and the works managers appeared to know a great deal about the background of every company employee. The researcher was, while walking through the plant, introduced to one worker who had been a chef in Wyoming some years ago. Another worker was pointed out as having been (he was now 72) a good rugby player in his youth. These and similar details were forthcoming quite frequently from Mr. Evans or the works managers. Second, the workers all said "Hello" to Mr. Evans as he passed through the plant, and Mr. Evans would chat with them about their families and how things were going.

Another impression, although a difficult one to justify with explicit evidence, was that the various managers were more than superficially concerned with their workers and their lives. Words and phrases which often recurred in the four days of conversation included: "fair treatment," "decent work for a man," "take care of our men," "expect them to work as part of a team." All individuals interviewed referred to themselves as being part of a single team; they did so either implicitly or explicitly.

Raadgevend Bureau Ir. B. W. Berenschot N.V. (A)

IN 1938 B. Willem Berenschot, a young Dutch engineer, joined with seven engineering colleagues and founded one of the first management consulting firms in the Netherlands. By 1972 Raadgevend Bureau Berenschot N.V. had grown to comprise 250 professional personnel and employed over 400 people in total. The firm operated out of four offices—Utrecht and Hengelo, the Netherlands; Brussels, Belgium; and White Plains, New York. With approximately $9 million in billings, it was the largest management consultant in Holland, and held about a 30% share of the Dutch consulting market.

In the summer of 1972, the Berenschot company was faced with its first potential operating loss in almost a decade along with a worsening financial situation (see Exhibits 1 and 2). To increase profitability, management was exploring two areas for further expansion. First, since most of its billings were within Holland, international expansion was considered by some executives to be a necessity. Second, with a large portion of its billings concentrated in production, personnel, and systems work, management felt a need to diversify the firm's "product line" and offer more consulting with a top management emphasis.

The six men who constituted the Executive Board of Berenschot (see Exhibit 3) realized that decisions in these two areas could have significant impact on the firm's future. Thus, they were trying to appraise the organizational, personnel, and operating ramifications of the various alternatives being considered. Also, the additional managerial stresses of a large organization, first felt in the late 1960s, had caused many people in the firm to question seriously a traditional growth policy. The firm had experienced steady increases in revenue and personnel (see Exhibit 4) and continued growth had always been taken for granted.

522

Data about Berenschot is presented in a series of four cases. Berenschot (A) contains background on the European consulting business and a history of the firm up to 1972. Berenschot (A1) explores the internal situation in Berenschot in 1972. Berenschot (B) deals specifically with the question of international expansion and details the firm's past international activity and management arguments for and against internationalization. Berenschot (C) deals with the issue of product line diversification and explores the firm's experience in top management consulting and the alternatives for expanding into this area.

MANAGEMENT CONSULTING IN EUROPE

Management consulting in Europe had a relatively short history and the market in most countries was dominated by a local firm. Reflecting the outlook of their clients, most firms emphasized production work until the 1960s and had little international activity.

Exhibit 5 lists the major consultancies operating in Europe and the location of their offices and the size of their staffs. These thirteen firms employed about three-fourths of the management consultants working in Europe.[1] The analysis provided below focuses first on Holland and its consulting firms, then on the other countries and firms of western and southern Europe, and finally on the most significant recent event in European management consulting—the "invasion" of American consulting firms beginning in the late 1950s.

Holland

From its beginning, Berenschot had always been the largest and most important consulting firm in the Netherlands. Its share of the 90 million guilder Dutch consulting market was approximately 30% in 1972, but at the height of its dominance in the 1950s, the share was much greater. A newer firm—Bakkenist, Spits & Co.—held an estimated 11% of the market, while the established firm of Bosboom held about 8%. The rest of the Dutch consulting market was split among 30 or so firms—including 6 American and 5 English—operating in the Netherlands. The main Dutch consulting firms are described in Exhibits 6 and 7.

Berenschot's dominance was perhaps more substantial than its 30% market share indicated. A 1970 article on European consulting in the French business periodical *Entreprise* described the competitive situation in the Netherlands: "The Netherlands market offers opportunities to others only to the degree that a local firm, Berenschot, permits. . . .

---

[1] Three remarks are in order, however, before Exhibit 5 and the textual analysis can be understood. First, because of competitive pressures and because many firms are privately held, data about the consulting business is scarce and the best available is dated. Second, for obvious reasons of publicity many firms inflate the numbers of their professional staff by including lower level technicians. Finally, a direct quantitative comparison between firms is often unfair because of the nature of the work done. For example, American top management consultants are often not comparable to production experts from a typical European firm, yet both are often called consultants.

By its dedication and with its effective staff, it dominates by 'head and shoulders' the Dutch market."[2]

Berenschot's management, however, was somewhat more reserved about the firm's competitive position. Piet Koppen, the Chairman of the Executive Board, commented:

> Within Holland, competition in the management consulting market has become much more intense. There are a few large firms with general practices—such as Bosboom and Bakkenist—that offer us competition in several areas. The most recent successes, however, have been among several smaller firms which have specialized in areas such as building construction where Berenschot has traditionally been strong.

Western and southern Europe

Great Britain.　The United Kingdom had probably the longest history of management consulting and four of the top six European firms were English, as were approximately half of the 6,000 consultants practicing in Europe.

The largest firm in Great Britain was P.A. Management Consultants, founded in 1943, and owned by a foundation. P.A. expanded dramatically into the international arena during the 1960s. In addition to 550 consultants in the United Kingdom, it had 150 in continental Europe and 175 in Australia. Other important English firms were A.I.C., P.E. Consulting Group, and Urwick Orr & Partners. These firms, together with P.A. and 15 others, shared about 70% of the English consulting market.[3]

France.　Management consulting in France was a relatively new phenomenon. The largest firm in Europe, Metra International, had its beginning in Paris in 1958. Perhaps part of the difficulty with consulting in France was the nature of French management, as was well described in a *Fortune* article on consulting in Europe: "For French managers to admit that anyone from the outside could know better than they what was good for them required a radical change in their outlook. The cream of the French managerial class, both in business and government, has been highly inbred, self-conscious, and arrogant for centuries."[4] In addition to Metra, which had grown dramatically outside of France by acquisitions and joint ventures, the French had one other major firm—Groupe Cegos-Idet—and several smaller organizations. Among the better known of these are Cie Générale d'Organisation, Cofror, Groupe Bossard, and Vidal.

West Germany.　The traditional German propensity for efficiency and precision had created a market for consulting with a narrow emphasis. Kienbaum, with about 175 consultants, was the largest German firm. Kienbaum had traditionally worked in production and personnel, and

---

[2] Claude Riviere, "Consultants: ruée sur l'Europe," *Entreprise,* October 3, 1970, pp. 4–5.

[3] Ibid., p. 2.

[4] Robert C. Albrook, "Europe's Lush Market for Advice—American Preferred," *Fortune,* July 1969, p. 181.

while recently seeking to offer more services to top management, had attempted little international expansion. Behind Kienbaum the main firms were all non-German. P.A. Management Consultants, A. T. Kearney, McKinsey,[5] and Booz, Allen & Hamilton all had large German operations.

Italy. One of the European consulting markets with good growth potential was Italy. Because of the autocratic family tradition of Italian industry and the penchant of successful Italian consulting firms for breaking up into smaller firms, there were very few national firms of any significance in Italy. In the late 1960s, however, the Italian market began to expand. Several foreign consultancies had established operations there or had bought small local firms. McKinsey, A. T. Kearney, The Boston Consulting Group, and Urwick were reputedly the most successful non-Italian firms operating in Italy.

The American firms

The beginnings of the American involvement in European management consulting were described in the *Fortune* article:

> The first American consultant to make a business trip to Europe must have felt somewhat like the first man to drill an oil well in Kuwait. The situation could hardly have been more promising. American companies were scoring some marvelous successes in the late 1950s, and everywhere the model of business success was an American model. American management advice became a hot commodity. And for many clients, American advice continues to seem like the best buy, even though it is usually more expensive than the services offered by European consultants.
>
> As they have moved abroad, U.S. consultants have become conduits for American managerial concepts, especially those related to big markets. They have introduced ideas such as the profit center, executive-development programs, marketing strategies, the decentralization and pinpointing of executive responsibilities, and long-range corporate planning, employing the latest techniques of mathematical analysis. Most of these ideas were not unknown in Europe, of course. But they gained a good deal of credence when they were introduced by a confident bunch of American advisors, who had some firsthand experience in carrying them out.[6]

In 1972, over seventy American consulting firms operated in Europe. The most successful firm—McKinsey & Company—had begun operating in London in 1959. McKinsey quickly accumulated a roster of blue-chip British clients such as Royal Dutch/Shell, British Petroleum, The B.B.C., and the Bank of England. Almost all of the firm's work in Europe had been with top management, and the standard engagement involved a reorganization and redefinition of management's role and duties. The firm's name had practically acquired generic characteristics in England

---

[5] For an example of McKinsey's activity in West Germany, see *Dynamit-Nobel A.G.*, copyright 1969 by l'Institut pour l'Etude des Méthodes de Direction de l'Entreprise (IMEDE), Lausanne, Switzerland. Reproduced by permission for use at the Harvard Business School. Case #BP 926.

[6] Europe's Lush Market for Advice—American Preferred," p. 127.

where the phrase "doing a McKinsey" had become commonplace. Various periodicals had also coined terms such as the "McKinsey phenomenon" and the "McKinsey complex" to describe the enormous impact the firm had on the European consulting scene.

Other American consultants, quick to note McKinsey's success, began to establish operations in Europe—Arthur D. Little, a firm with extensive research facilities in Cambridge, Massachusetts; Booz, Allen & Hamilton, the largest consulting firm in the world; and A. T. Kearney, emphasizing transportation and distribution. Other leading U.S. consultants with permanent European operations were: Wofac (a division of Science Management Corporation) with a practice emphasizing production and systems work; H. B. Maynard & Company, Inc.; Cresap, McCormick, and Paget, Inc.; The Boston Consulting Group; Lester B. Knight & Associates, Inc.; and several large accounting firms with consulting divisions.

Surprisingly, the greatest impact the Americans had on European consulting was not the business taken from the national firms. Even though the American firms charged up to 50% more in fees, they were estimated by *Fortune* to have held only 10–15% of the $200 million European management consulting market.

Instead, American presence in European consulting had a philosophical effect. The American firms, particularly McKinsey, had redefined management consulting in Europe. Throughout the 1940s and 1950s European consultants were small, provincial organizations dealing primarily with industrial engineering and production work. The idea of operating internationally and advising top management was relatively unheard of until the 1960s. According to the *Fortune* article: ". . . the English firms acknowledge privately that McKinsey's success has been good for them. It has roused greater interest in consulting and has emboldened British consultants, accustomed to an essentially 'shop floor' practice, to raise their sights."[7] In addition to this redefinition of management consulting, U.S. firms had generated a great deal of publicity that benefited both them and their European counterparts and had forced the European firms to become more competitive.

Like many other European firms, Berenschot had not felt much direct competition from American firms because of its concentration in Holland and the differences in the type of consulting done and size of the clients served by each. Still, most people in Berenschot were painfully aware that McKinsey had received huge fees for work done at some of the major organizations in the Netherlands—Royal Dutch/Shell, Unilever, Akzo, Amro Bank, the Dutch University System, and many others. However, for several of these studies Berenschot had obtained follow-up engagements to help clients implement or modify McKinsey's recommendations. Professor Driesser, an advisor to the Executive Board, reflected what seemed to be the thinking of many in the firm:

> The Americans have either the only knowledge of international business or else, and I think this is more appropriate, they have the

---

[7] Ibid., p. 180.

image that they have the only knowledge. But, there is also a matter of face involved. I would rather lose business to the Americans than to another European firm. In many cases losing business is inevitable since governments and other politically sensitive organizations will give work to an American firm rather than to a local firm. As long as the Americans confine themselves to the top of an international or giant organization, they don't compete directly with us, and don't hurt us as much.

HISTORY OF BERENSCHOT

Throughout its history, Berenschot had responded to and capitalized on governmental and industrial activity in Europe and the Netherlands. Since the firm's development and tradition was closely related to these events, background on Berenschot is organized into three phases—1938 to 1945, 1945 to the early 1960s, and the early 1960s to the present.

Phase I: 1938–1945

In 1938, B. W. Berenschot was a senior partner in a small Dutch firm of consulting engineers. Founded in 1925 by Mr. Berenschot and J. M. Louwerse, this firm had grown to 16 employees before a philosophical difference developed between the founders. Mr. Berenschot felt that further growth was necessary to foster specialization and support research, while Mr. Louwerse was satisfied with his small firm. Unable to resolve their differences, the two agreed to part ways and on November 1, 1938, the B. W. Berenschot Company was begun with seven industrial engineers as the first employees and offices in Amsterdam and Hengelo, the Netherlands.

Mr. Berenschot soon put his philosophy of specialization into practice and hired two economists and a psychologist—the first nonengineers in the firm. The psychologist, Drs.[8] Joe da Silva, who in 1972 served as an advisor to the Executive Board, described the founder's philosophy of consulting:

> According to B. W. Berenschot, the man who wanted to be a management consultant could not be a "jack-of-all-trades" since the field was already too big and the demands were far too complicated. So he decided to specialize in branches of industry and functional area. From a practical point of view, this would only be possible with a large organization.
>
> The limited knowledge available and the complexity of the problems demanded something further—research. Research costs money and must be risked before there is any chance of return. This again is only possible with a large unit. Specialization and research have indeed formed the main theme during our development to a large company.

On May 10, 1940, the Germans invaded the Netherlands and World War II began. Not interested in productivity-increasing activities for the

---

[8] Drs. is a Dutch academic title roughly equal to the American Master's degree. Ir. is a title at the same level except that it signifies a technical or scientific specialization. Dr. is a title roughly equal to a Ph.D. and is used for any field.

German controlled industry and confident that the war would eventually
end, Berenschot began to develop expertise in other areas. The first attempt to specialize by industry was in 1940 when a building engineer
was hired to develop modern management techniques and procedures
for coordination in home building. Courses in supervisor training,
standard costing techniques, and participation in an industrial psychology center were also added between 1940 and 1945. By the end of the
war the firm had built up a significant expertise in personnel and industrial psychology to add to its already strong base in production and
industrial engineering.

In addition to forcing an expansion in Berenschot's services, Drs.
da Silva described a unifying effect that the occupation had on the firm:

> At the end of 1944 there was hardly any apparent scope for our
> profession. In some ways there was lots of scope, however, as under
> wartime conditions the word "organizing" had taken on a new mean-
> ing. Gradually, and then later with a sudden shock, our eastern col-
> leagues realized that we, in the western part of the country, were
> really hungry. The feats of their comradeship deserve to be written in
> gold as large-scale food collecting expeditions were organized.
>
> Well-planned with every possible illegal transport, even hidden in
> German army trains, our eastern colleagues succeeded in sending
> food to the west of Holland. In the severe winter of 1944 some of our
> men, laden with sacks of potatoes and a bicycle, jumped out of a train
> and brought food, life, and hope to us in the west. During these times,
> human bonds were created that have been crucial to the staying to-
> gether of so many for so long in the firm.

Phase II: 1945 to the early 1960s

After 1945 there was widespread acceptance of the services the firm
had added during the occupation, particularly in home building and
supervisor training. Still, Dutch industry was expanding rapidly and the
demand for trained personnel exceeded the supply. Berenschot responded
by locating a Swiss industrial psychologist, Paul Silberer, who had developed a method of operator training. Drs. da Silva described this effort:

> Within a group from Berenschot, Silberer's system was further de-
> veloped and has since become well known and applied throughout
> industry as accelerated training. To be able to train unskilled labor
> within weeks or months to a skilled level was, especially after the
> war, vital to get the wheels of our dilapidated industry turning again.
> Hundreds of assignments were carried out. Training courses were
> set up and introduced for just about every known semiskilled and
> skilled job. But even more, for thousands of young people these
> courses offered a quick and unthought-of way up.

The acceptance of accelerated training by Berenschot's clients provided an impetus for growth. From the original twenty employees who
struggled together during World War II, the firm grew to one hundred
by 1949. This expansion caused some to worry about growth in Berenschot for the first time. Drs. da Silva reflected on this and earlier times in
the firm:

The announcement that Berenschot had founded a pension fund, made at the Annual Meeting in 1952, was greeted by prolonged, enthusiastic cheering. However, there were also a few present who felt a strange sadness and something of a farewell to the romantic pioneering age. Berenschot had now become a true company with a pension fund.

How young we were when we each wanted to become a management consultant and joined Berenschot. What drove us? The charm of pioneering, perhaps, but hardly any conscious idealism. There was no time for that—we were busy doing time studies.

The postwar period also found Berenschot undertaking foreign assignments for the first time. Accelerated training was the basic export for assignments in Europe and several developing countries. In 1951 the firm carried out its first training engagement in the United States. Until the 1960s, however, international work was to remain a very small part of the firm's total billings, and was almost exclusively concentrated in training assignments.

In addition to the above developments, the period from 1945 to the early 1960s was highlighted by two general conditions that significantly affected the development and policies of Berenschot. First, the postwar industrial expansion in the Netherlands created a large demand for the services of management consultants. A second major condition was that in Holland, as in all of Europe, business was primarily concerned with industrial production and there was little attention given to marketing. Professor Driesser described this period:

> All of Europe was building an industry from nothing and anything that could be produced could be sold. Berenschot thus offered production, personnel and other services that had to do with the making of a product since the selling was easy. During this time, we were not really management consultants but industrial engineers.
>
> Also, prices and wages in the Netherlands were tightly controlled by the government after the war. Wage increases would only be granted if accompanied by higher productivity, so Berenschot was often hired for productivity improvement. We actually performed sort of an audit function for the government by monitoring wage increases.

These two conditions—industrial expansion and an emphasis on production—encouraged the development of three policies and characteristics in Berenschot that were still in existence in 1972:

Transfer of knowledge. A trend encouraged by the firm was that many clients eventually developed the capabilities to do things that they had often hired Berenschot for. Drs. da Silva described the evolution and reasons for this policy:

> A decision was made to develop a training course for work study men for our clients. From the very beginning of our profession, work study had consumed a substantial amount of the man hours spent by the management consultant. So the training of work study men for our clients became the first indication of a policy which, today more than ever, has become accepted. The policy is that whenever possible

we must transfer our knowledge to our clients. Only then is there a healthy guarantee of our work being continued and followed up within the clients after we have left.

Consulting "products."   After the war and through the 1950s, Berenschot's approach to management consulting acquired a product rather than a personal emphasis. The firm performed specific studies in a limited number of areas—primarily production and personnel. Berenschot became known for accelerated training, plant start-up, time and motion studies, etc., rather than for specific people within the firm. It sold a technique to a client that could be performed by many different consultants. Jan Verschoor, a board member with specific responsibilities in 1972 for product development, described the firm's approach:

> The consulting business can be placed on a spectrum. At one end is the old style where people are well versed in a technique such as psychological testing or time study. The other extreme is personal, general consulting where an individual is what a client buys and not a technique. Berenschot has been on the lower end of this spectrum and we have few people at the upper end.

Implementation.   Since Berenschot often dealt with a client on the work-floor level where tangible results of recommendations were evident, the firm became heavily involved in implementation. Drs. da Silva characterized Berenschot's operations:

> The consultant gains his most valuable experience through a kind of implementation feedback. It definitely makes him more modest. Here he learns what did work and what did not. When utilizing these nose-to-the-grindstone experiences, he is developing his own professional wisdom: "God give us the peace of mind to accept the things we cannot change, the courage to change the things we can, and the wisdom to know the difference."
>
> It is, we believe, this basic philosophy, perhaps the philosophy of the "work horse," which is to a great extent responsible for the growth and prosperity of Berenschot. Although full credit is given, of course, to the creative, imaginative, synthesizing part of the consultant's job, the truth is learned only by sheer implementation. And Berenschot's reputation is largely identified with getting things done.[9]

Phase III: Early 1960s to 1972

The transition from Phase II to Phase III of Berenschot's development took place over a period of several years. Three events highlighted this:

The death of Berenschot.   B. W. Berenschot, the firm's founder and guiding force, died suddenly in January 1964. Professor Driesser described this event:

> Mr. Berenschot was almost a de Gaulle type of leader and before his death this firm was a one-man show. Several others were second in command, but a very distant second. When he died, a different situation developed as everybody of any importance became involved in

---

[9] "A Dutch Consultant Goes Worldwide," Columbia University *Journal of World Business,* July 1970, pp. 48–49.

management. This was a confusing time, but we were luckily protected by the economic boom in Holland. Business was easy to get and we survived our lack of management skills and focus.

The Common Market.   The European Common Market was established in 1958. Since the Netherlands was one of the original six members, new international markets were opened to Berenschot's clients. This increased emphasis on internationalization was accompanied by a change from the traditional focus of European business on industrial production. Industry began to become increasingly aware of marketing and many of the American marketing and management techniques.

The economy of the Netherlands.   The Dutch economy was gradually decontrolled beginning in 1960. Throughout the 1960s, the remaining controls were much less stringent than in the 1945–1960 period. Thus, much of Berenschot's work of Phase II, where productivity increases were needed to gain wage increases, was not as much in demand.

Any of the above could have seriously affected the health and growth of Berenschot. However, the firm weathered these changes very well as staff size more than doubled and billings, partially spurred by inflation, increased fivefold in the 1960s. In addition to the continuation of the postwar industrial boom that created a demand within Holland for the standard Berenschot expertise, there were two other major factors that contributed to the firm's success:

New products.   Several new services were added to the Berenschot repertoire. A marketing group that was started in 1950 gained many assignments in the 1960s helping Dutch firms to learn about and operate in the Common Market. In 1960 Berenschot entered into a joint venture with John Diebold for electronic data processing work. A technique for faster plant start-ups was developed in 1962 and was well received, especially in the United States. These and other advances broadened the product line, and enabled the firm to compete in areas outside of its traditional specializations. Exhibit 8 gives details of the broadening of the firm's services from 1960 to 1971.

In 1972 research was being done on three new products that many people in the firm felt had possibilities of becoming major sources of revenue in the future. "Urbanics" was a technique that employed computers for modeling the long-range planning process in regional governments. "The Management of Innovation" was a technique being developed by Peter Veen, a young industrial psychologist. This was an attempt to help organizations identify and manage not just change or expansion—as Berenschot had long done with accelerated training and plant start-ups—but actual innovation. "Director Training" was a response to a 1971 Dutch law that made outside directors more responsible for the policy and results of their organizations. Berenschot was developing a program to teach directors their responsibility under the law and to equip them with the managerial skills necessary to meet this responsibility.

New markets.   Several new markets were discovered by Berenschot in the 1960s (see Exhibit 8). The firm's work during Phases I and II was almost exclusively for private industry within Holland. In 1964 B. W.

Berenschot's secretary, W. Smit, began to develop the nonprofit market. He was very successful and by 1972, 24% of the firm's billings were derived from business with various parts of Dutch government. Also in 1964 the first study in the health care market was made. By 1972 a separate health care division existed and it had billings of almost three million guilders to the health care market. Financial institutions were first served by Berenschot in 1967, and by 1972 the firm had captured a large segment of the consulting market for Dutch banks, brokerage houses, and insurance companies. Finally, although Berenschot had had international work since after World War II, the 1960s saw several developments take place in this market. These are described in detail in the (B) case.

Exhibit 8 gives an idea of the size of Berenschot's industrial clients in 1972. In many instances, the firm had dealt with clients for years on a continuing basis for not just specific engagements, but also for ongoing advice given by a Berenschot consultant. Exhibit 9 lists details of the largest assignments carried out by Berenschot in 1971 and 1972. The average engagement in 1971 was 40,000 guilders.

One of the main concerns that had arisen in Berenschot in the early 1970s was growth. Piet Koppen commented on the growth question:

> I think we have grown too fast. Before Mr. Berenschot's death, I personally recruited every consultant we hired and I critically evaluated the requests of our department heads for more people. When I became chairman, I could not do this any more and the job was delegated. For several years afterwards, when the market was rising, we hired to fill our immediate needs. In 1969, for example, we added almost fifty people and could not adequately absorb that many.
>
> Our plans are to decrease our size gradually. We now have ten people less than at the end of 1971 and the goal is to reduce by twenty more in the next year. This is just a total decrease as we will still be working on quality improvement and trying to bring good people into the firm.

Jan Verschoor analyzed the firm's growth from a historical standpoint and related this to the financial problems of 1972:

> After the war, there were two pressures that contributed to our growth. Government legislation required every industrial organization that wanted to raise wages—and there was much pressure from unions to do so—to justify wage increases with productivity gains. This created a tremendous market for the services of consultants in productivity improvement, cost control and efficiency work. The second reason for our growth was the belief of Mr. Berenschot that a large firm was essential. This also was the source of many of our problems today. We added people during this period that had narrow skills. When the government eased up on productivity requirements, the market for these people began to shrink.

The downturn in billings and earnings for 1972 had been foremost on management's mind for quite some time. Indeed, one of the Board members described the situation early in the summer as one of "panic."

Willem van der Scheer, who directed operations for the firm, commented on the recent difficulties:

> Our profits are down this year for two reasons. The political situation in the Netherlands is currently very uncertain. This has directly affected the government practice, where billings are down by about 2 million guilders this year. It has affected other divisions also. For example, building in Holland is 50% financed by the government and so our building practice has suffered.
>
> A second reason is that the nature of the markets has changed. From 1950 to the late 1960s, most of the work was of the work-floor type. Now, however, with the large French and German companies selling their products in Holland, Dutch companies need more advice in areas such as marketing and corporate strategy and Berenschot has not the people to deal with these areas. This reason has especially affected our industrial divisions.

Exhibit 1

RAADGEVEND BUREAU IR. B. W. BERENSCHOT N.V. (A)

Income Statements
(thousands of Dutch guilders*)

	1960	1961	1962	1963	1964	1965	1966	1967	1968	1969	1970	1971	(6 months) 1972
Gross billings	4,481	4,866	5,949	6,956	9,710	12,181	13,480	14,196	16,564	19,360	24,286	27,956	12,857
Expenses:													
Salaries	2,900	3,348	3,904	4,541	5,907	6,784	7,850	8,978	10,012	12,213	15,211	18,025	8,478
Travel	400	586	725	802	1,043	1,169	1,391	1,474	1,714	1,839	2,022	2,292	1,114
Rents	120	195	210	230	320	341	390	408	475	605	657	925	677
Other costs	613	927	847	1,017	1,615	2,190	2,036	2,080	2,089	2,635	3,732	4,831	2,351
	4,033	5,056	5,686	6,590	8,885	10,484	11,667	12,940	14,290	17,292	21,622	26,073	12,620
Profit before taxes	448	(190)	263	366	825	1,697	1,813	1,256	2,274	2,068	2,664	1,883	237
Income taxes	152	(54)	119	157	290	460	371	394	638	449	591	358	110
Net income	296	(136)	144	209	535	1,237	1,442	862	1,636	1,619	2,073	1,525	127
Growth in billings† (1960 = index of 1.0)	1.00	1.08	1.32	1.54	2.15	2.70	3.00	3.15	3.70	4.30	5.40	6.24	5.74
Net income as a % of gross billings	6%	-3%	2%	3%	5%	10%	11%	6%	10%	8%	8%	6%	1%

* One guilder equals approximately 32¢. Results are for calendar years.
† Annual inflation in the Netherlands from 1960 to 1971 has been 8%. Thus, a base of 100 in 1960 would be at 233 in 1971 without any real growth.
Source: Company records.

Exhibit 2

RAADGEVEND BUREAU IR. B. W. BERENSCHOT N.V. (A)

Balance Sheets—December 31
(thousands of Dutch guilders*)

ASSETS	1963	1969	1971
Cash	795	2,647	1,300
Marketable securities	524	814	840
Accounts receivable—clients	1,251	4,728	6,900
Accounts receivable—personnel	404	1,066	1,100
Prepaid expenses	96	282	1,200
Total current assets	3,070	9,537	11,400
Fixed assets	1,133	1,277	2,420
Investments in joint ventures	—	1,220	2,060
Intangible assets	—	—	200
	4,203	12,034	16,020

LIABILITIES AND EQUITY	1963	1969	1971
Accounts payable	919	1,579	2,660
Salaries and bonuses	804	2,557	2,250
Pensions payable	842	999	1,400
Prepaid billings	335	1,177	1,500
Total current liabilities	2,900	6,312	7,810
Deferred taxes	590	2,126	3,170
Other long-term liabilities	238	705	1,160
Retained surplus	475	2,891	3,880
	4,203	12,034	16,020

* One guilder equals approximately 32¢.
Source: Company records.

Exhibit 3

RAADGEVEND BUREAU IR. B. W. BERENSCHOT N.V. (A)

Members of the Executive Board

Piet L. Koppen
Age: 58   Years with firm: 19
Education: Naval Academy

Willem A. van der Scheer
Age: 49   Years with firm: 25
Education: B.S.—Mech. Eng.

Jan Verschoor
Age: 51   Years with firm: 22
Education: B.S.—Chem. Eng.

Peter L. M. Van Berkel
Age: 47   Years with firm: 11
Education: M.S.—Technical Univ.

Mauk L. G. J. D. Dolleman
Age: 45   Years with firm: 10
Education: M.A.—Economics

Wim Smit
Age: 48   Years with firm: 23
Education: B.A.—Behavioral Sciences

Exhibit 3—Continued

Advisors to the Executive Board and Division Directors

Advisors to the Executive Board

Drs. Joe da Silva
Age: 61   Years with firm: 32
Education: M.A.—Chem. & Industrial Psy-
chology

Prof. Marco P. Gans
Age: 49   Years with firm: 1
Education: M.B.A., Ph.D.—Finance

Prof. Joop M. F. Driesser
Age: 56   Years with firm: 27
Education: M.S.—Technical Univ.

Division Directors

Theo J. Steenbergen
Age: 46   Years with firm: 6
Education: M.B.A.

Gelein Meijer
Age: 41   Years with firm: 17
Education: B.S.—Elec. Eng.

Exhibit 3—Continued

Division Directors

Hendrik K. J. Melessen
Age: 47   Years with firm: 23
Education: M.S.—Mech. Eng.

Dirk Langelaar
Age: 59   Years with firm: 5
Education: M.A.—Industrial Psy.

Exhibit 4

RAADGEVEND BUREAU IR. B. W. BERENSCHOT N.V. (A)
Growth in Personnel, 1938–1971

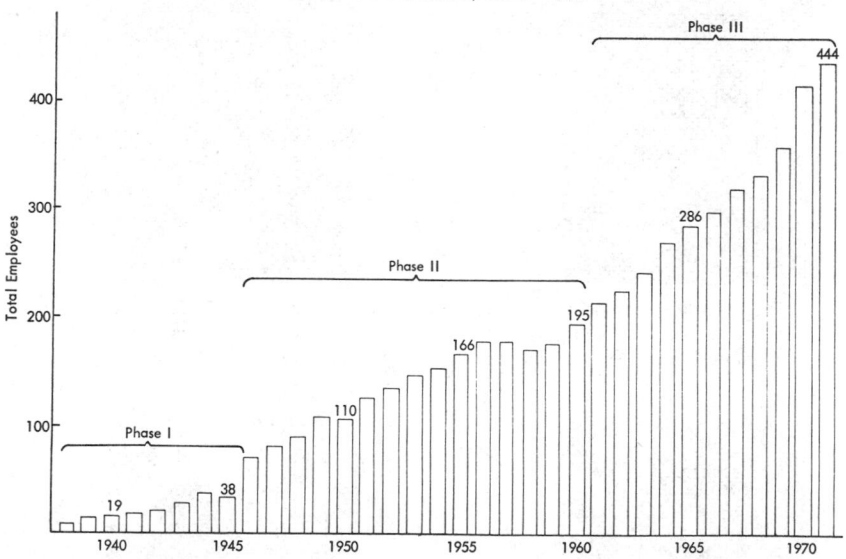

Note: Professional, fee-earning consultants have always equaled 60% of employees.
Source: Company records.

Exhibit 5

RAADGEVEND BUREAU IR. B. W. BERENSCHOT N.V. (A)
European Management Consultants

Firm and headquarters	*Offices*		*Professional staff in Europe**
1. Metra International Paris, France	Paris Rome London Madrid Milan Vienna	Brussels Frankfurt Geneva Montreal New York	1,000
2. P.A. Management Consultants London, England	U.K. (12) Scandinavia (5) Paris Frankfurt	Madrid Milan Athens Brussels	750
3. Assoc. Ind. Consultants London, England	London		700
4. Cegos Puteaux, France	Paris Brussels Madrid	Milan New York	400
5. P.E. Consulting Group London, England	U.K.		400
6. Urwick Orr & Partners, Ltd. London, England	U.K. (17) Amsterdam	Brussels Dusseldorf	325
7. Berenschot Utrecht, The Netherlands	Hengelo Brussels White Plains		250
8. Kienbaum Gummersbach, West Germany	Dusseldorf Vienna		250
9. WOFAC (Science Management Corporation) Morristown, New Jersey	Brussels Frankfurt London Milan Paris		200
10. McKinsey & Company New York, New York	Amsterdam Dusseldorf London Milan Paris Zurich		185
11. Booz, Allen & Hamilton Chicago, Illinois	Amsterdam Brussels Dusseldorf London		110
12. A. T. Kearney Chicago, Illinois	Brussels Dusseldorf Milan Paris London Birmingham		70
13. Arthur D. Little Cambridge, Massachusetts	Athens Brussels London Paris Zurich		70

* Axel Krause, "What Consultants Do and How They Do It," *International Management*, April 1969, p. 24; and Casewriter's research, Harvard Business School.

Exhibit 6

RAADGEVEND BUREAU IR. B. W. BERENSCHOT N.V. (A)
Major Dutch Management Consulting Firms

Firm & head office	Other offices	Professional staff		1970 billings (millions of guilders)	% of revenues.		Fees charged (guilders)
		Total	With degrees*		Private industry	Public clients	
1. Adviesbureau voor Bedrijfsorganisatie AUB Utrecht	Brussels Paramaribo	45	21	3	80	20	300–900/man day
2. Bakkenist Spits & Co. Amsterdam	Basel Zurich	110	60	10	70	30	300–1,000/man day
3. Bureau Berenschot Utrecht	Brussels Hengelo White Plains	240	150	25	70	30	300–1,000/man day
4. Bureau Bosboom & Hegener Amsterdam	Zurich	80	46	7.5	60	40	400–1,050/day
5. Van der Bunt & Co. Amsterdam	Copenhagen Louvain (Bel.)	30	7	3	90	10	45–125/hour
6. Bijleveld Consulting Leiden	Aschaffenburg (Ger.)	22	11	2.5	80	20	120/hour
7. Krekel v.d. Woerd, Wonterse Rotterdam	London Geneva California	18	18	1.3	65	35	400–1,300/day
8. Bureau Twijnstra Deventer	—	38	25	5	N.A.	N.A.	350–1,100/day
9. Dr. M. G. Ydo Amsterdam	—	50	25	3.5	80	20	300–1,000/day

* At least a Master's degree equivalent.
Source: "Nederlandse Bedrijfs-Adviseurs Gebukt Onder McKinsey-Complex," *FEM*, April 1971, pp. 20–21.

Exhibit 7

RAADGEVEND BUREAU IR. B. W. BERENSCHOT N.V. (A)

Major Foreign Consulting Firms Operating in Holland

Firm & location of Dutch office	Country of origin	Professional staff*		1970 billings worldwide (millions of guilders)	% of revenues*		Fees charged* (in guilders)
		Total	With degrees		Private industry	Public clients	
1. Associated Industrial Consultants Amsterdam..........	United Kingdom	15	11	50	75	25	3,500–4,000/man week
2. Booz, Allen & Hamilton Amsterdam..........	United States	12	12	220	100	0	540–2,160/man day
3. McKinsey & Co. Amsterdam..........	United States	32	32	100	85	15	360–2,700/man day
4. P.A. Management Consultants Amsterdam..........	United Kingdom	12	9	90	100	0	4,500/man week
5. Urwick International Amsterdam..........	United Kingdom	12	12	50	100	0	1,000–2,000/man day

* All figures are for Dutch operations unless otherwise indicated.
Source: "Nederlandse Bedrijfs-Adviseurs Gebukt Onder McKinsey-Complex," *FEM*, April 1971, pp. 20–21.

Exhibit 8

RAADGEVEND BUREAU IR. B. W. BERENSCHOT N.V. (A)

Billings Analysis and Client Information

Billings by area of study	*1960*	*1971*
General and overall surveys.........................	15%	23%
Production and planning............................	60	33
Marketing..	5	3
Personnel..	15	20
Data processing...................................	5	5
Regional planning.................................	—	10
Other..	—	6
	100%	100%
Billings by industries served		
Textiles & clothing................................	35%	11%
Metal and heavy industry..........................	20	10
Chemical and process industry......................	20	11
Construction and building..........................	25	5
Financial institutions..............................	—	16
Health care.......................................	—	10
Government.......................................	—	24
Other..	—	13
	100%	100%

Client Information, 1972

Number of employees in company	*% of firms in all of Holland*	*% of Berenschot's clients*	*% of clients for all Dutch consulting firms*
1–49..................	68	} 10	18.8
50–99..................	16		
100–199................	8	30	} 36.0
200–499................	5	25	
500–999................	2	20	21.6
Over 1,000..............	1	15	23.6
	100	100	100

Source: Company estimates and The Association of Management Consultants (Holland).

Exhibit 9

RAADGEVEND BUREAU IR. B. W. BERENSCHOT N.V. (A)

Details of Large Berenschot Assignments, 1971 and 1972

Dutch governmental units	Assignment	Fee (000 guilders)
Social Economic Council	Simplification of social security system	2,000
Netherlands Railways	Service and operations improvement	1,000
Ministry of Health	Control system	800
	Construction control for three hospitals	800
Province of North Brabant	Study workings of office equipment	500
University of Utrecht	Construction control for a dental clinic	500
City of Utrecht	City planning	300
City of Rotterdam	Study of water management and wharfs	270
Ministry of Defense	Increase of volunteers for armed forces	300
	Merger program	260
Space Planning Agency	City planning	240
Dutch Private Enterprises		
Trucking company	Organization and classification study	780
	Organization study and acquisition search	300
Savings bank	Organization, classification, and marketing study	275
Wood and furniture company	Importing study	330
Machinery firm	Study of machinery building in the chemical industry	250
Food company	Information systems study	200
Shipbuilder	Study of the yacht and boat building industry	200
Clothing company	Policy, planning and marketing study	200
Building company	Executive search and management education	158
Bank	Decentralization study	150
Conglomerate	Reorganization and cost reduction study	150

Raadgevend Bureau Ir. B.W. Berenschot N.V. (A-1)

AN UNDERSTANDING and appreciation of Berenschot's internal situation in 1972 can best be obtained by examining the firm's structure and operations in five areas—organization, management, ownership, personnel, and organizational climate.

ORGANIZATION

By the late 1960s, B. W. Berenschot's founding belief in specialization had been realized in his firm. There were seventeen separate departments: twelve "trade" departments serving specific industries and industry groups and five "functional" departments for marketing, industrial psychology, control, corporate strategy, and management information systems. The primary emphasis was on trade specialization and the largest number of consultants had industry rather than functional responsibility.

In the fall of 1971, the firm underwent a reorganization and the seventeen departments were merged into five divisions of relatively equal size. Only two of the functional groups retained a separate identity while the other three were split into the various divisions. Piet Koppen, the chairman of the Executive Board, described the reasons for this move:

> In our latest reorganization we retreated somewhat from the specialization favored by B. W. Berenschot. The main reason was that we felt we did not have enough managerial talent to run all the separate departments. So we picked our five best managers and organized into five divisions that were logical groupings of the industries we served.
>
> Our organizational structure now is better than in the past when we had 17 separate departments, but I don't think it is the optimum. We now have a situation where the division director is rather strong

544

as a position and since we are organized by industries, there is little functional emphasis or identification possible in areas such as marketing.

The 1972 Berenschot organization is shown in Exhibit 1. The five divisions and their main functions were:

Division 1—Financial institutions and data processing. This division's primary market was in Dutch financial institutions. Dr. Th. J. Steenbergen estimated that his division had captured 30% of the consulting market for banks, 30% for insurance companies, 50% for brokerage firms, and 80% of the consulting work of the Dutch Social Security System. The data processing group retained its functional identity after the reorganization and served clients from all five divisions.

Division 2—Manufacturing and construction. This division served three main industrial groups—metal, wood, and building and construction—which accounted for 85% of the division's revenues. Since several of these industries had long been served by the firm, the division had a heavy emphasis on production and personnel work.

Division 3—Process and service industries. With 22% of the firm's billings in 1971, this division had the second largest volume in Berenschot. It consisted of five industry groups—agriculture and food, paper and printing, chemical and mining, transportation and services, and textiles. As with Division 2, billings in this divison were mainly in production studies.

Division 4—Health care and industrial psychology. The division's billings were about equally split between a group serving the health care market and a functional group—industrial psychology—that performed all types of personnel work and served clients from all divisions. In the health care market half the work was in planning and starting up new hospitals. The remainder was split between productivity studies, organizational studies, and regional planning for governmental bodies.

Division 5—Government. This division was the largest in Berenschot (24% of billings) and dealt with all levels of Dutch government. The primary emphasis was on regional planning, but there was also a large amount of work in some of the traditional Berenschot fields.

Within each division, there were four levels for the professional consulting staff:

Division director. These five men spent the largest portion of their time managing their divisions. They planned budgets, monitored studies and financial results, directed the utilization of personnel, marketed the firm and its services, and guided the professional development of their consultants. In addition, since they had once been full-time consultants, most of them spent some portion of their time in consulting work. One division director commented on this split in his time: "I still consult because I like it, and because there can be no such thing as a full-time manager in a consulting firm. Only a consultant can direct other consultants."

Willem van der Sheer, who headed all operations in the firm, expressed a similar opinion:

For operational management in a consulting firm, professional experience is necessary. This is why the division directors and I must actually consult with clients. Remember our business is one of relations with clients and I mean more than just an occasional sherry. We need actual professional contact. Holland is a small country and contacts are how we do business.

Consulting group head.   These eight men assisted the division directors by taking responsibility for a specific industry or industry group. They directed consulting engagements in their particular industries and attempted to stay abreast of any new developments in their sectors. Like the division directors, they also did a good deal of active consulting.

Project leader.   Operations in Berenschot centered around the 35 project leaders. Each project leader had specific client responsibilities. When a client indicated a problem or an area for a possible Berenschot engagement, the project leader carried out an initial survey, defined the scope of the issue, and estimated the cost. If a commitment was made by a client, the project leader, in consultation with the division director, assembled a team of consultants for the engagement, drew up a budget, and undertook active management of the project.

Consultant.   The consultants spent the greatest part of their time working for clients on consulting engagements. Of the 141 people in this category, 56 were classified as senior consultants. This position was only attainable after six years with the firm and was a requisite for any further advancement in Berenschot.

Exhibit 2 gives a picture of the professional personnel in Berenschot. While predominantly Dutch, the firm had quite a degree of divergence in ages, longevity, salary, and educational background.

MANAGEMENT

An analysis of management at Berenschot can best be undertaken by looking at the managerial structure, process, and succession.

Management structure.   Until 1947 there was no formal management structure in the firm as the founder, B. W. Berenschot, was president and exercised control over all operations. In 1947 the first managerial group was established. Drs. Joe da Silva described this occasion and subsequent developments in management structure:

In 1947 B. W. Berenschot chose eight of his original employees and created the Executive Board. This group met monthly to discuss the problems of the company, but Mr. Berenschot was still Mr. Berenschot and he generally used these meetings to convince us of his ideas. The group gradually grew and by the early 1960s consisted of sixteen people. Not desiring further growth, B. W. Berenschot set up two boards in 1962. A new Executive Board of eight people was formed that again consisted mainly of the original employees in the firm. The entire sixteen of the old Executive Board were then placed on a Policy Board which met far less often and was finally done away with in 1970.

One policy we instituted in 1970 was that membership on the

Executive Board would only be allowed until a person reached sixty years of age. I was one of the first affected by this rule and retired from the Board in 1971. We feel this policy opens up room for younger people in the firm, and also frees the senior people from management responsibility so they can return to professional work with clients.

The Executive Board, as a body, dealt with both broad policy issues and specific managerial questions. Exhibit 3 gives details of subjects considered at several recent board meetings. In addition to operating as a group, each of the six board members had specific individual responsibilities. These responsibilities in 1972 were:

Piet Koppen—Chairman—Chaired the Board meetings, handled financial and legal affairs, directed overall operations.
W. A. van der Scheer—Directed operations for the five divisions and all supporting services.
Drs. Mauk Dolleman—Directed personnel and staff recruitment, training, and development.
Jan Verschoor—Coordinated all professional development. Directed some international operations.
Ir. Peter Van Berkel—Formulated policy in international affairs.
W. Smit—Formulated policy for nonprofit consulting and served temporarily as director of Division 5.

Management process.   While the role of the board and its members was somewhat explicit, decision making in the firm was not so well-defined. Piet Koppen commented on this:

Just before his death, Mr. Berenschot asked me to become the managerial coordinator of the firm when he left. I was rather surprised since I had never been a consultant and I asked him where I would get my authority. He answered that it should come from a practice of common decision making by the Board members. Only in such an environment could one man act as a leader.

During the past eight years, this tradition of a collegial body with a consensus of decision making has been maintained for questions of policy. The Executive Board does act as a group and I have only one vote out of six. Still, we never vote anyway since we must agree on all decisions.

During the last few months, however, in the execution of policy I have found it necessary to work closely with the operations director, Mr. van der Scheer. Together we act as the top management team from an operational standpoint.

The managerial style appropriate to Berenschot is complex. I was a naval officer for several years, but I am not military minded. In this firm one could not function as a strong disciplinarian—there is too much independence to do so.

The five division managers operated quite independently of the board, both by design and necessity. They drew up yearly operating budgets and once these were approved by the board, were allowed autonomy not only in operations but in such areas as educational development. A division director commented on his relations with the board: "I have good personal relations with the board members but operate my division as I see fit. The financial results of this division are impressive and unless I miss my budget, they don't interfere or object. My method of operation is necessary since the board does not dictate a clear policy." Another division director had similar thoughts. "I have always followed the policy to act in internal activities as if there were not any policies from the top. If I need a policy decision, I ask for it."

Some of the younger consultants in the firm even questioned the entire Berenschot management structure. One of them commented:

> With Mr. Berenschot, at least a consultant ran the firm. Now we have a board of self-appointed, full-time administrators and the consultants are just their machines. Since we have no ownership, I would like to see a temporary management structure where consultants would be elected by their colleagues to run the firm for three years. This would prevent the isolation between management and the consultants that we now have.

Management succession. Piet Koppen commented on his role as the first leader of the firm and what he thought his successor should be like:

> I have been the first and only chairman of the Executive Board of this company since Mr. Berenschot's death. My perception of my role has been to ensure the firm's survival and to keep the group together. I think I have been successful at these activities. Since 1964 only one man has left to start his own consultancy. I have not, however, attempted to win new markets for the firm or to lead the development of new products. I have never actually been a consultant and so have confined myself to the job of management.
>
> I am now 58 and we have a policy that one must leave the Board at the age of 60. In general, I agree with that policy. So, for the past few years, the question of my successor has been a big concern of mine. This is a difficult problem. Should the person be a consultant or at least have a consultant's background? Should he be someone from the inside or should he be a well-known outsider? I am convinced of one thing, however—the next chairman should have a broader role than I have had.

Willem van der Scheer also thought that the next chairman needed broader skills:

> The next chairman of Berenschot must have the ability to determine strategy for the entire firm. He must be able to see what is going on in the market. This is the primary need. It would also be nice if he had connections in the government and in the Common Market Commission, but this is not so important.

OWNERSHIP

Until 1958 B. W. Berenschot was the sole owner of Berenschot and Company, an unincorporated sole proprietorship. In 1958 he incorporated his firm to limit his personal liability, an unprecedented move in Holland. After incorporation he retained all of the stock, but in the early 1960s began to become concerned about the future of his firm after he left. Drs. da Silva described this concern and what happened because of it:

> B. W. Berenschot thought that at his retirement—this type of man never thinks he will die—the continuity of his firm had first priority. Unsure of what his wife and children would do if they were to inherit the firm, and wanting the advantages of the company to go to the employees, he created a foundation and gave it all of the company's stock. This foundation is perpetual and pays no dividends. All of the income is either retained as a reserve for difficult times or expansion or else is returned to the employees in pensions and bonuses.
>
> There are seven trustees of the foundation. Three are from the Executive Board; three are outsiders; and one is Berenschot's son. These people meet quarterly to primarily decide on distribution of income from the firm. They generally accept the recommendation of the Executive Board.

This ownership—or really nonownership—situation was highly regarded among almost all employees in the firm. Piet Koppen commented on it:

> I am very content and see few problems with our ownership system. One must understand that there is a trend in the Netherlands toward income equalization. I do not see this as totally desirable. If it goes too far, there is no motivation, but I think it is wrong for a few people to make a great deal of money. If I made 500,000 guilders I would find it difficult to lead others who made much less.
>
> The compensation of the division directors or the board is not related to the yearly budget. I think this is important since I don't believe in money as the only carrot you can keep before people's noses. In this firm, freedom, independence and the job satisfaction are the main motivators.

Cees Limborgh, of the personnel department, had a similar opinion:

> We have no problems with our ownership situation. Everyone here is really a part owner in the firm since the employees receive all of the distributed earnings. In effect, everyone works for himself and the only group that is interested in the earnings of Berenschot are the employees. The traditional type of ownership, which I shall characterize as stockholders outside of the firm with a disproportionate interest in power and profit, has lately been under criticism in Holland.

One of the consulting group heads echoed this opinion: "Our lack of ownership doesn't bother me since I know that all of the profits are for the employees. We also have the added benefits of no ownership pressures and complete independence from outsiders."

Some people, however, discerned difficulties with the foundation ownership. A few of the younger consultants thought that individual motivation was less in Berenschot than they envisioned it to be in other firms where partnership or ownership and the attendent wealth was a possibility. Others thought that the foundation structure was essentially fair, but would be better with some modification. Drs. Mauk Dolleman, a member of the Executive Board, ventured his opinion:

The ownership situation is good at Berenschot, but we actually work for continuity and fair pay. In a way, one could say we are a nonprofit organization and to the government this might be a positive point. However, in the industrial world, where a consultant is expected to help increase profits, a consultant should be profit-oriented himself. In summary, I would say that Berenschot is a profit-minded organization tempered by our professional standards and ownership situation.

PERSONNEL

An analysis of Berenschot's personnel policies and practices requires examination of selection, training, evaluation, and separation.

Employee selection.   With few exceptions, Berenschot always hired graduates of Dutch universities. Half of the professional staff held at least a degree equal to the American Master's degree in engineering, economics or psychology—the traditional academic disciplines in Berenschot—with the other half holding a Bachelor's degree or less. Cees Limborgh commented on one of the deficiencies he saw in the firm's hiring policies:

> In our approach to consulting, you must not only deal with the highest levels in an organization but also with middle management and lower employees. This is the case especially in projects involving implementation where, in my opinion, a consultant cannot bring only his academic viewpoint. This is why I would like to hire more people with work experience than we now do. 20% of our new consultants have experience and I think 50% would be better.

The firm had not often had to recruit actively for new employees. Direct application to Berenschot by university graduates or referrals from Dutch professors had been the main sources for new consultants. Berenschot had always been high on the list of potential employers for most graduates and in one recent year 600 applications were received for 20 positions.

In 1970 Berenschot began an experiment by hiring three young MBAs from American graduate schools of business—one from MIT and two from Columbia University. While no final appraisal of the MBA experience could be definitively made, most people were satisfied with the results obtained so far. Dr. Steenbergen, an MBA from Harvard in whose division all three MBAs were working, commented on his experience with them: "I find the MBAs to be very useful. They are more practical from the beginning of their careers, but the Dutch university graduates eventually catch up."

Drs. W. Zonneveld, a project leader in Division 4 who had spent three years working at the White Plains office, was in charge of recruiting MBAs at American business schools. He described the process he went through in hiring them:

> Before I start recruiting, I determine exactly what needs we have for MBAs. I talk with Mauk Dolleman and with the division director who wants the MBAs. I appraise the division's personnel, clients, and type

of business to make sure the MBA will fit into the division. Of course, with the Americans the Dutch language and social system present problems at first, but these can be overcome.

This changing emphasis in personnel selection had caused a problem of personnel differentiation to arise. This was a relatively new phenomenon and disturbed many people in Berenschot. For the first twenty or so years of its existence, the firm had employed consultants with similar backgrounds. While this homogeneity was still predominant in 1972, some differentiation was definitely noticeable. Exhibit 4 is an analysis of two divisions that had different consulting practices and consequently had personnel with different backgrounds. The consultants of Division 1, which emphasized top management work, were younger, more educated and had less longevity than those of Division 3, where most of the work was concentrated in personnel and production. Drs. Dolleman was concerned with this problem but was not sure how to deal with it:

> We must be careful not to let an elite group build up within the firm. Such a situation would create problems of compensation, age, and promotion that we have not had to face in the past. Still, if we want to keep good people we must allow them to develop and they must be given interesting assignments. Perhaps, then, some differentiation is inevitable.

Personnel problems such as the above were causing the management process in Berenschot to become both more complex and less standardized. W. Smit, the director of Division 5, commented on the problems he experienced within his division:

> I have the greatest diversification of disciplines—lawyers, architects, and town planners, in addition to the typical Berenschot backgrounds of engineering, economics, and psychology. The coordination of such diverse people is difficult at times. Also, many young people have joined this division in the last two years. They have come from universities where they have participated in decision making and they expect the same in Berenschot. Finally, several older consultants have been transferred to this division. Since much of our original government work was of the "work floor" variety, I thought they could be used here. However, our focus has rapidly changed to more sophisticated studies such as long-range planning, and governmental structure and decision making and these people are becoming obsolete. All of these problems force me to spend more time than I would like on managing my division.

Personnel training. In 1955 Berenschot began a training program for all new consultants. Drs. da Silva described the beginning of this program and the reason for its existence:

> In 1955 we received a rather unusual request from the president of a prominent business to train a young, newly engaged, promising executive for a period of one year within our company. A most stimulating request and since then, a well-organized training program has

become an institution in Berenschot and has been further developed in recent years.

A training program is especially necessary in our firm since management, as a field of study, is not widely taught in Holland or in Europe. Thus, the beginning management consultant usually has an academic background in engineering, economics, or psychology and when he becomes a member of a consulting group, he must receive extensive business training.

By the 1960s the firm had an established, nine-month training program that all new consultants were assigned to. Drs. Dolleman, who had responsibility for training, described the situation in 1972:

> For years we had a standard program of nine months for all new consultants regardless of their background. We taught techniques of time study, personnel evaluation and other Berenschot specialties. However, as people with different backgrounds were brought into the firm, and others were pulled out of training early to begin working, the program began to disintegrate. We are now changing it to make the training more flexible for different people.

Personnel evaluation.   In 1972 Berenschot instituted a new evaluation system. Each consultant was evaluated yearly on a seven-page form that contained sections on professional ability, client and colleague relationships, selling skills, managerial and leadership potential, ability to plan and work within a budget, and language skills. Prior to 1972 department managers were required to review their employees, but in some departments little was actually done. Cees Limborgh described the development of the new system:

> For years we advised our clients on employee evaluation and never did it in a professional way ourselves. We now evaluate employees once a year. The division director does the first evaluation and it is sent to the personnel department for screening. Then the division director, Drs. Dolleman, and I sit down to review the evaluation. We try to assess the present quality of the consultants individually and as a group, and also draw up a plan for development and recruitment. Any follow-up after this meeting is the responsibility of the division director although the personnel department will check up and give support.
>
> The new evaluation system is more professional than in the past, but I expect that we will move to a system where a consultant is reviewed after every engagement of certain importance. I would also like a more intensive yearly evaluation with respect to career-planning which can result in courses and seminars, job or divisional rotation, promotion inside Berenschot or advice to leave the firm.

Personnel separation.   B. W. Berenschot had a paternalistic attitude toward his employees and while he was living, there were very few involuntary separations from the firm. His attitude, together with a high degree of employee satisfaction, led to historical turnover rates of less than 5% a year.

Mr. Berenschot's opinion prevailed long after his death. However, in 1972 when the new evaluation system was established, consultants were asked to leave the firm for the first time. Most members of management considered this to be a painful experience when it was done for the first time, but generally expected the practice to continue in the future as critical evaluation became more commonplace.

There was still a concern on the part of everyone for older employees. This group, estimated at from fifteen to thirty consultants, had skills that were becoming obsolete, received high salaries because of their longevity, and were considered because of their age as not retrainable. Ordinarily, they would be separated from the firm for economic reasons, but no one in Berenschot expressed such a desire. Management felt a responsibility to these consultants (indeed many of them had once trained some of the present managers) and would make efforts to ease their separation from the firm.

Drs. Dolleman summarized the changes in personnel policies in the firm:

> The entire personnel function is undergoing change at Berenschot. This was started when we modified our hiring philosophy and no longer guaranteed a new person five years of employment. This change then forced us to evaluate consultants more critically and we began the new evaluation system. Our training program has also been affected and is now being modified. Finally, the more professional evaluation system has led to separations from the firm. This year there were about twelve people whom we let go and this practice will continue.

THE ORGANIZATIONAL CLIMATE AT BERENSCHOT

The traditionally low turnover of employees at Berenschot was a function not only of the paternalistic attitudes of the founder, but also of the high degree of employee satisfaction. Good compensation, liberal benefits, the status of a consultancy, little pressure, and the ownership situation all contributed to this satisfaction. Cees Limborgh described his feelings about the firm:

> Relations between employees—even between the chairman and the youngest kitchen girl—are excellent. We have very little status difference. Everyone has a great deal of flexibility and freedom to do things. Since most consultants work on more than one project at a time, they also plan their own schedules. All of these factors make Berenschot a fine place to work and create a high demand for our jobs.

This *esprit de corps* had become institutionalized in two ways at Berenschot. Since 1961, the firm held an annual meeting for all employees and their families. This gathering was a unique event in Holland when it was first established. At the meeting the chairman discussed the past year's financial results and disclosed the distribution of income. In addition to giving a brief summary of the firm's accomplishments, future plans and activities were revealed.

A second institution was the establishment in 1971 of an employee council—the Bureauraad. Such a body was required for all organizations of over one hundred employees by a 1970 law. However, Berenschot's management claimed that the firm had gone much further than the law required. The council consisted of fifteen members—nine consultants and six nonconsultants—elected by all of the employees. The council's function was to hear employee grievances, discuss working conditions, and in general review company policy and indicate areas of concern to the employees and then attempt to promote further discussion. It had no absolute power to decide matters or veto Executive Board actions except in areas such as pension benefits. But if a disagreement arose, it was usually settled between the two groups.

The organizational climate in Berenschot was well summed up by Joe da Silva:

> The task of describing the atmosphere in our firm could probably be better performed by someone who has come from the outside. After all, I have been associated with Berenschot for over thirty years. Nevertheless, people who come into the firm are surprised at the atmosphere here. Most feel that it is one they have never encountered before in any organization.
>
> In our firm everybody finds it natural to work very hard because everyone else does. We have an atmosphere of friendship, of being willing to help each other and if necessary, to comfort each other. Above all, our leaders strive to be human, to be considerate, and maybe even to tolerate things that would not be tolerated in industry.
>
> This atmosphere of collaboration, of hard but wonderful work, of the greatest possible freedom all stems from our founder, Mr. Berenschot, and his initial colleagues who laid the unshakable foundation for this firm. After more than thirty years, the atmosphere in our firm still deserves praise.

Exhibit 1

RAADGEVEND BUREAU IR. B. W. BERENSCHOT N.V. (A-1)

Organization Chart, 1972

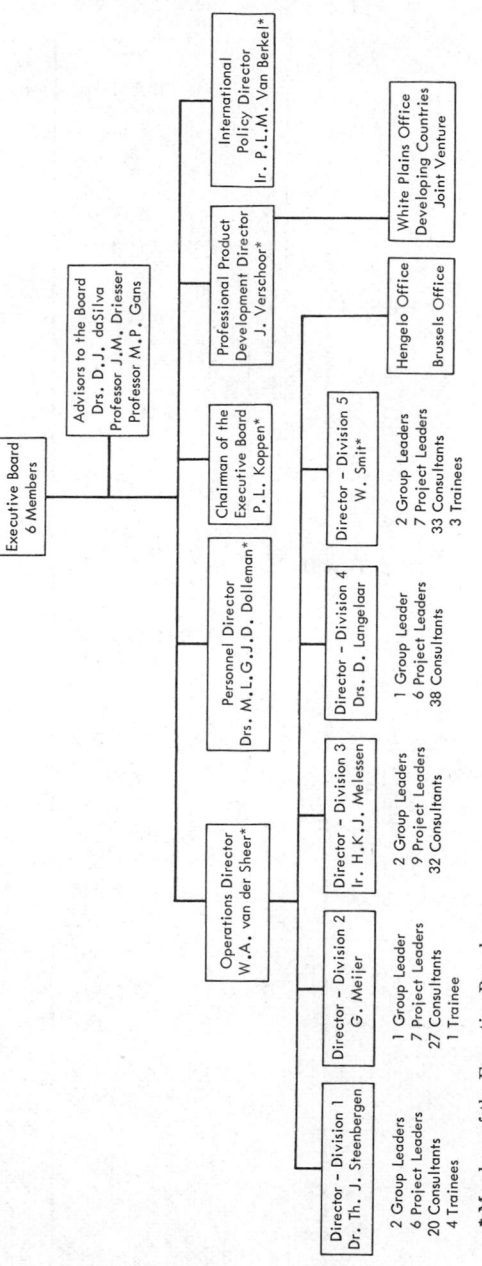

* Members of the Executive Board.
Source: Casewriter's analysis.

Exhibit 2

RAADGEVEND BUREAU IR. B. W. BERENSCHOT N.V. (A-1)

Personnel Data for Professional Employees

Organizational level	Number	Salary data (guilders)*		Ages		Nationality		Education					Years with Berenschot N.V.	
								Master's or doctorate degree				Bachelor's degree or lower		
		Average	Range	Average	Range	Dutch	Other	Engineer	Economist	Psychologist	Other		Average	Range
Division Head	5	65,000	55,000–77,000	48	41–59	5	—	1	1	1	—	2	14	5–23
Consulting Group Head	8	56,100	36,000–66,000	47	35–55	8	—	4	—	—	—	4	20	12–25
Project Leader	35	45,600	34,000–62,000	43	30–55	34	1	5	6	4	3	17	10	1–26
Senior Consultant	56	39,000	28,000–50,000	46	30–62	53	3	20	8	5	1	22	12	1–37
Consultant	85	23,500	15,000–33,000	33	25–53	79	6	25	13	11	9	27	4	1–26
Trainee	8	22,700	12,000–27,000	29	24–40	6	2	1	2	2	1	2	0	0–1
Totals for firm	197†	31,000	12,000–77,000	39	24–62	185	12	56	30	23	14	74	8	0–37

* 1 U.S. dollar = 3.15 Dutch guilders. 1 guilder = 32¢.

† Does not include data for consultants assigned to joint ventures.

Source: Company records.

Exhibit 3

RAADGEVEND BUREAU IR. B. W. BERENSCHOT N.V. (A-1)

Agendas of Executive Board Meetings

January 19, 1972 from 9:45 to 17:00

To be decided: 1. Social policy regarding employee housing problems caused by the move to Utrecht.

To be discussed: 1. Possibilities of cooperating with a Belgian consulting group.
2. A new evaluation system for consultants.
3. Priorities for 1972.
4. Internal research fund.
5. Subjects for future agendas.

March 15, 1972 from 9:45 to 12:30

To be discussed: 1. A possible merger with another Dutch consulting firm.

May 3, 1972 from 9:45 to 12:30

To be decided: 1. A cost-benefit analysis of the Documentation Department.
2. Procedures for handling and controlling invoices.
3. The winner of the Berenschot contest for the best student thesis.
4. Procedures for handling assignments.

May 17, 1972 from 9:45 to 17:00

To be decided: 1. Budgeting of costs.
To be discussed: 1. Entering the educational market.
2. The European consortium.

Source: Company records.

Exhibit 4

RAADGEVEND BUREAU IR. B. W. BERENSCHOT N.V. (A-1)

Personnel Comparison—Divisions 1 and 3

	Division 1	Division 3
Total professional staff	32	44
Average age	37.9	40.5
Nationality:		
Dutch	29	43
Non-Dutch	3	1
	32	44
Educational background:		
Master's degree or higher—engineering	5	13
economics	10	5
other	6	2
Total master's degree or higher	21	20
Bachelor's degree or lower	11	24
	32	44
Average years with Berenschot	4.8	10.1

Source: Company records and casewriter's analysis.

Raadgevend Bureau Ir. B.W. Berenschot N.V. (B)

BY THE SUMMER OF 1972 the headquarters of Raadgevend Bureau Berenschot N.V., the largest management consultancy in the Netherlands, had become solidly established in a new location. For 33 years the firm had operated out of the rambling, ancient Centraal Railroad Station in Amsterdam, a city often referred to as the "Venice of the North." In late 1971 Berenschot had begun relocating to a new office building on the outskirts of Utrecht—an old, industrial city of 300,000 people located on a flat plain in west-central Holland.

Secure in their new environment, the Executive Board of Berenschot in June of 1972 was confronted with a report written by one of its members—Ir. Peter L. M. van Berkel. Mr. van Berkel had been associated with the firm since 1962 as the manager of a joint venture between Berenschot and an American computer software firm. In 1971 he was given the responsibility for formulating a policy in the international area and the report being considered by the Executive Board was the culmination of his efforts. In it he argued quite vigorously and persuasively for further international expansion by Berenschot.

Mr. van Berkel knew that some members of the board were hesitant about certain kinds of international activities. Others, such as Jan Verschoor who was in charge of part of Berenschot's international operations, were concerned about what they considered to be an excessive concentration of business in the Netherlands—88% of total billings in 1971 (see Exhibit 1)—and were in favor of immediate moves toward further internationalization.

This case deals specifically with the issue of international expansion. Details of Berenschot's past and present international activities are first presented, and then the arguments for and against internationalization are explored. Finally, a detailed proposal from Peter van Berkel's report, included as Appendix A, is examined.

INTERNATIONAL ACTIVITY AT BERENSCHOT

As reported in the (A) case, Berenschot's first international work consisted of accelerated training projects in Spain and Scandinavia. These engagements, beginning in 1948 and continuing through the 1950s, were handled from the firm's offices in the Netherlands. Drs. da Silva described the first international work and subsequent developments:

> The first foreign assignment was for accelerated training of spinners and weavers in Sweden. This proved to be the beginning of many training assignments abroad which have steadily increased over the years. Such assignments represent a tremendous opportunity for our consultants to obtain international experience. Through these activities Berenschot has become well known abroad, which is of great value in our relationship and cooperation with consultants in other countries.

In addition to foreign assignments handled from the Dutch offices, Berenschot had employed three different vehicles for international work —foreign offices, a consortium, and a joint venture.

Foreign offices

Hengelo, the Netherlands. The Hengelo office was established at the beginning of the Berenschot organization on November 1, 1938. Drs. da Silva described the origins:

> The Hengelo office was opened right from the start, together with our Amsterdam office. Some of the firm's very first assignments were in the textile industry located in the Hengelo region. Also, Mr. Berenschot was born and lived in this area. After the Amsterdam office grew, and when far more consultants operated from there, we joked that while Amsterdam was the headquarters, Hengelo was the residence because the "King" was living there.

Being close to the German border, this office gradually built up a small German practice, particularly in the heavily industrialized Ruhr Valley. Concentration was on cost reduction and training assignments in the textile, garment, and paper industries. In 1972 four consultants were permanently assigned to this office and occasionally other consultants were drawn from the main office in Utrecht. Jan Verschoor commented on the future of the firm's German practice:

> The market that seems most promising for Berenschot is Germany. German business is being confronted with more changes than ever before. The solid, arrogant German managers are discovering that their traditional practice of passing technical skills from one generation to another is not enough. They are shedding their Prussian nature and becoming more open to outside advice.
> So, the opportunity exists in Germany, but we have to decide how to capture it. There are only a few substantial German firms, but the English and the Americans are well established there. We must simply find the holes in the market that Berenschot can fill.

White Plains, New York. In 1952 Berenschot became the first European consultant to open an office in the United States. In a 1970 interview Drs. da Silva described the reasons behind the move:

> In 1952 when the company consisted of around 125 people B. Willem Berenschot challenged the company to "cast water into the Thames." He wanted to send two men to build up a consulting nucleus in the United States, the most advanced industrial society of the world. Let's be honest. He did not get unanimous support. Many considered it sheer vanity and a waste of money.
>
> But B. Willem Berenschot knew what he wanted. He argued: Look, there is only one country in the world where we can see our future— in the United States and nowhere else, management is using methods which will eventually be accepted, adapted, and applied on this side of the ocean. So, if we want to be ahead of our clients, as well as leaders in our profession, we have to be operating at the source.[1]
>
> We now state with pride that since 1952 we may count amongst our American clients such concerns as General Electric, Johns Manville, Owens Corning Fiber Glass, Raytheon Company, *New York Times* and to name the very first—Builders Iron Foundry.

During the 1950s, under the leadership of Jan Verschoor, the White Plains office did mainly assignments in accelerated training. In 1962 a new Berenschot specialty called plant start-up was created and was well received in the U.S. Drs. da Silva explained the origin of this technique:

> Johns Manville, an important and progressive American client, initiated plant start-ups at Berenschot with the request "can you help us to get the manpower and machinery as quickly as possible into production in a new factory ready for occupation." It led to the setting up of a big recruitment, selection and training project. All kinds of workers including foremen, supervisors, and specialists had to be trained.
>
> A stage, normally arrived at after months, was reached as a result of our work in weeks—a highly important factor in a competitive environment. Advice on lay-out has been added as well as coordination of the whole project, including the actual construction.

White Plains gained many engagements in training and start-ups and specialized in what became known as "the management of expansion." The office grew rapidly, and by the late 1960s had a staff of 15 consultants and billings of over half a million dollars. However, the recession of 1969 affected capital investment and thus demand for the Berenschot services decreased. By 1972 the White Plains office had a permanent staff of only three consultants and billings were at a break-even level.

There had been much discussion in late 1971 and early 1972 about closing the White Plains office. Peter van Berkel commented on this:

> Few of our original motives for opening the White Plains office exist today. Transportation and communication have improved to the

---

[1] "A Dutch Consultant Goes Worldwide," Columbia University, *Journal of World Business,* July 1970, p. 51.

point where we don't need the "listening post" to learn American management methods. I can go from Amsterdam to Dallas with no trouble at all and most of our consultants would be quite comfortable operating in America. Also, we don't need to earn a hard currency like we did in 1952 since the guilder is stronger than the dollar today.

Several European firms, Kienbaum for example, are in the process of establishing American offices to aid European companies that are beginning operations in the States. We cannot benefit from this, however, since most Dutch firms have been in America for decades.

We have debated time and again the decision to close White Plains and have not yet resolved the issue. There were times when the U.S. office was very profitable but today it is only self-sufficient and we could better use the personnel back in Holland or in the developing countries. We have to decide how much having White Plains on our letterhead is really worth.

Jan Verschoor also expressed his thoughts on the future of the White Plains office:

We are asking many questions now about the products, markets, and personnel in White Plains. Several of our consultants don't see enough value in American management practices to justify an office in the U.S., but I do. Underlying all of my thinking, however, is a feeling that the office must be at least self-sufficient to remain in existence.

We are also considering combinations with some American firms. One of the Big Eight accounting firms, for example, has proposed a venture involving our work in plant start-ups. Whatever moves we finally make, they will have to be made by the end of 1972.

Brussels, Belgium. In 1961 Berenschot started an office in Brussels by hiring an established Belgian management consultant as managing director and sending several consultants to work for him. Drs. da Silva described the reasons for beginning a Belgian office and the subsequent developments:

Expansion to Belgium seemed natural. It was geographically close, the language was similar to Dutch, and there were few management consulting firms in Belgium at the time. Brussels also seemed to offer a huge potential market. It was the headquarters of several large American corporations and many international organizations such as NATO and the EEC.

We made a few mistakes in our Belgian venture. I think we did not appreciate how parochial the Belgians were nor did we realize the importance of being tied into a banking relationship which is something we did not want to do.[2] Even though we went there like children, we learned some valuable lessons. Most importantly, we learned that the director of a foreign operation is the crucial factor.

The Brussels office in 1972 was the responsibility of the division directors and had billings of approximately one million guilders.

---

[2] In Belgium, the Société Générale, a large banking group, controls or influences a major portion of the country's industry. Other banks are similarly important, if less predominant.

Consortium of consultants

In 1966 Berenschot entered into a consortium with two other management consulting firms—Carlberg, the main Swedish firm, and Planus, a small French firm. The consortium, appropriately named the BerCa-Plan, was started to gain international assignments that the member firms could not get on their own. The mid-1960s was a period when many European companies were expanding across national boundaries and since neither Berenschot, Carlberg, nor Planus had extensive international operations, they were not gaining much of the consulting business associated with this expansion.

An office was established in Paris, a French engineer was hired as the managing director, and Jan Verschoor was appointed chairman of the consortium's board. Each of the three firms contributed consultants to the BerCaPlan with Berenschot having at most five people working in this undertaking at one time. The consortium was able to gain eight assignments in international work.

The BerCaPlan lasted only one year as Berenschot's partners ran into difficulties. Carlberg was acquired by P.A. Management Consultants, the English firm, and Planus was merged into Vidal, a larger French firm. However, when it existed there were also internal problems in the consortium. Drs. da Silva described these:

> We experienced some minor problems in having three different nationalities working together, but these were expected. A more fundamental problem was the allocation of business between the individual partners and the BerCaPlan. Like always, the French were the difficult ones. One example was an assignment discovered by Berenschot relating to the building of the Brussels subway system. We had construction experience, but since Planus had done work in subways before, we gave the engagement to the BerCaPlan. When a similar situation arose, Planus would not reciprocate.

Developing countries joint venture

In 1967 Berenschot entered into a joint venture with Bosboom, the second largest firm in Holland, to concentrate on work in developing countries. Jan Verschoor described the beginnings of this venture:

> Our interest in developing countries originated when a Dutch union leader came to Berenschot in 1965 and proposed working together. He died, but we retained our enthusiasm for the possibilities of such a project and decided to wait for the right man to come along. In 1967 Dr. A. P. G. Poyck came to us in response to an unrelated advertisement. He had a broad international background and many contacts in the financing institutions for developing countries, so we made him the manager of our joint venture. We joined with Bosboom so that we might have a larger pool of consultants to draw from to do this work.

Dr. Poyck was very successful in getting business and by 1972 the joint venture had billings of over four million guilders and there were 25 consultants permanently assigned to this activity. Exhibit 2 gives details of some of the engagements carried out between 1967 and 1972. Of these assignments, the largest was the Congo water transportation project which accounted for about 75% of the joint ventures' total billings from 1969 to 1971.

The work in third world countries was viewed with mixed feelings by people in Berenschot. Jan Verschoor summarized the advantages and disadvantages of these projects:

> The third world assignments are quite difficult. Often the financing institution—the World Bank or the Asian Development Bank, for example—is separate from the country we are working for and so we have to deal with political problems between them. These assignments are less profitable, more unpredictable, and the clients are more critical than in our regular work. Also, further difficulty arises since our joint venture can only provide managerial expertise, so we often have to join with other technical consultants. For example, on our airport projects we must team up with a firm of airport consulting engineers.
>
> Why do we do this work? It is interesting and younger consultants like it. More importantly, it gives us expertise in the third world where many of our clients are expanding and enables us to learn new skills.

RATIONALE FOR FURTHER INTERNATIONALIZATION

There was widespread agreement within Berenschot that more international activity was desirable. As can be seen by Exhibit 1, the firm had traditionally been heavily concentrated in the Netherlands. A trend toward expansion that started in the early 1960s reached a culmination in 1966 when 18% of billings were outside Holland. This trend was reversed, however, as the Belgian and White Plains offices became less significant. By 1971 only 12% of billings were in international work and one-third of this was from the Congo River project of the developing countries joint venture.

While most people in Berenschot felt strongly in favor of international expansion, some members of management had doubts about both the necessity and possibility of further internationalization. Thus, both the arguments for and against expansion will be explored.

Reasons for international expansion

With a dominant position within Holland, Berenschot could not expect continued growth in its domestic market at the same rate as during the 1960s. The international area provided many more opportunities for growth—the dramatic thirty-fivefold increase in third world billings, for example—and for this reason expansion was supported by many in the firm. Piet Koppen estimated that the Dutch consulting market, which was one of the most saturated in the world, would grow at a rate of 10% in the coming years compared to the widely projected rate of 20% a year for the European market as a whole.

A second reason for internationalization was not one of growth as much as preservation of Berenschot's current position. Jan Verschoor expressed this idea succinctly:

> The reason for internationalization is to follow the home market clients. The choice of a consultant is not always a rational decision. Once it is made and an allegiance is formed, a client wants to maintain

an established relationship wherever possible. However, if a consultant cannot provide service—and Berenschot cannot on some international problems—the client will select a new consultant. Most clients will not be satisfied with just Dutch answers any more.

Peter van Berkel had similar thoughts:

We must be prepared to serve international clients in an international manner. We usually work at a middle level in an organization and this, together with our emphasis on implementation, means that we must have a local presence when a client wants work outside of Holland. Also, if we want more top management consulting we must be international. The decision makers in many companies are outside of Holland and our consulting competition has quite an international reputation.

Besides further growth and preservation of existing clients, Mr. van Berkel presented other reasons for international expansion. Dependency on the economy of one country would be decreased. Although the Netherlands had been in a continuous economic boom since after World War II, there were signs in 1972 that this might be leveling off and any change would definitely affect Berenschot. From the personnel standpoint, a broader international base would help the firm recruit better consultants and would offer more opportunities for advancement and fulfillment.

Mr. van Berkel also considered Berenschot to be in a unique position to expand internationally as the firm had many international strengths:

First of all, we are Dutch and this means that we are politically harmless. The heads of many international organizations have often been Dutchmen because of this fact. Also, no other firm in Europe has the linguistic capabilities of Berenschot. Almost all of our consultants speak Dutch, English, and German, and 20% speak French.

Our extensive experience with governmental work and our familiarity with large companies such as Shell, Unilever, and Phillips definitely give us an international focus. A Frenchman or a German travels with his culture, but the Dutchman is more cosmopolitan and open to the environment around him. Other nationalities can travel to America and come back having learned nothing, but not the Dutch.

Reasons against international expansion

Few people in Berenschot argued explicitly against international expansion, but several members of management had reservations. Except for the developing countries joint venture, the firm's past activity had only been moderately successful and the losses incurred had made some people hesitant about making such commitments again. Drs. da Silva expressed this opinion: "Most of the Board members are not absolutely against international expansion, but are not sure what it will bring us. They will back it if the financial risks are not too great."

Peter van Berkel, the author of the report on international expansion, hoped that the Executive Board would reach a decision soon. He knew that the European Common Market Commission was looking for a consortium of consulting firms to do studies in preparation for the expansion of the EEC to ten members. With this thought in mind, he had been able to line up four possible partners for a consortium—a large English firm, the largest German firm, a medium-sized French firm and a small Italian firm. He hoped that this combination would begin by doing studies for the EEC and then could eventually move up to international work for the clients of the four members. Excerpts from his report on this consortium are presented in Appendix A.

Mr. van Berkel was aware of the hesitancy of some of the board members toward another consortium. He had thus argued for consideration of other vehicles for international expansion and felt that some action was essential in the near future:

> If Berenschot stays as it is, it will in ten years be just a small, wealthy, provincial Dutch firm. What we want and what we need is to be an international consulting firm. The game is changing. It is now an international game and we must change to play it.

Exhibit 1

RAADGEVEND BUREAU IR. B. W. BERENSCHOT N.V. (B)

Billings Analysis

	1960	1961	1962	1963	1964	1965	1966	1967	1968	1969	1970	1971
*Growth in billings (index)**												
Holland (1960 = 100)	100	111	138	160	222	270	290	310	360	430	530	630
Europe (1960 = 100)	100	149	200	440	600	980	980	710	890	1010	1260	990
U.S.A. (1960 = 100)	100	82	83	90	116	174	253	260	300	142	120	105
Developing countries (1967 = 100)	—	—	—	—	—	—	—	100	670	1840	3900	3500
Total (1960 = 100)	100	108	132	154	215	270	300	315	370	430	540	624
Percentage breakdown of billings												
Holland	85%	88%	89%	87%	87%	84%	82%	84%	83%	86%	84%	88%
Europe	2	3	3	6	6	8	7	5	5	5	5	4
U.S.A.	13	9	8	7	7	8	11	10	10	4	3	2
Developing countries	0	0	0	0	0	0	0	1	2	5	8	6
Total billings	100%	100%	100%	100%	100%	100%	100%	100%	100%	100%	100%	100%

* Annual inflation in the Netherlands from 1960 to 1971 had been 8%. Thus, a base of 100 in 1960 would be at 233 in 1971 without any real growth.
Source: Company records.

Exhibit 2

RAADGEVEND BUREAU IR. B. W. BERENSCHOT N.V. (B)

Examples of Developing Countries Assignments for
Berenschot-Bosboom N.V.

Economic Infra-Structure

Thailand —Design of a coordinating and planning organization for the building of a new port in Bangkok.

Zaire —For The World Bank and the Zaire government, a study of the port and river transportation system of Zaire.

Korea —Design and implementation of a new structure and systems for the highway ministry.

Congo —Rehabilitation of the entire transportation system on the Congo River.

Nigeria —Design of a National Airport Authority.

Nicaragua—A feasibility study on the canalization of the Rio San Juan.

Peru —Improved costing procedures in the government-owned iron and steel industry.

Productive Investments

Colombia —Design of an organization to administer the returning of reclaimed land to farmers.

Morocco —Analysis of the existing structure of the Ministry of Agriculture.

Ghana —Assistance in the starting up of a cotton mill.

Technical Assistance

Tanzania —Management surveys in the paper industry.

Yemen —Textile factory improvements.

Cameroon —Training assignment in small industry.

Romania —Introduction of computers in the metal and chemical industries.

Poland —Improvement of management systems in the Polish Management Institute.

Banking Institutions

Indonesia —An improvement program for the Indonesian Rural Credit System.

Nigeria —A study for the Dutch Overseas Development Authority.

Mali —Appraisal of agricultural credit needs for an expanded rice program.

Algeria —Modernization and expansion of the National Savings System.

Source: Company records.

APPENDIX A

EXCERPTS FROM PETER VAN BERKEL'S REPORT ON A CONSULTING CONSORTIUM

Introduction

At the suggestion of officials of the European Economic Commission, the five consulting firms—AVA in Paris, France; Berenschot in Utrecht, Netherlands; Kienbaum in Gummersbach, Germany; P.E. Consulting Group Limited in London; and Studio Organizzazione Aziendale in Torino, Italy—have prepared plans to set up a consortium of consultants that would be independent of banks, industrial groups, or governments. Such a group would be capable of performing studies for the commission on transfrontier industrial cooperation and offering all services to bring about multinational mergers between industries and to coach them to healthy and successful new enterprises. Officials of the Commission have indicated willingness to discuss assignments for studies and to provide easy access to information needed to determine markets for a consortium.

Purpose of the consortium

The initial, though not the principal, purpose of the consortium would be to provide a comprehensive consulting service to the European Economic Commission, the European Development Bank, and any other appropriate body within the community organization. The initial effort in staffing and marketing strategy will be directed toward establishing a reputation for ability and integrity with the Commission.

However, the market offered at present by the European Commission is too limited to serve as the sole financial basis for the consortium. The Commission spends an estimated 500 million Belgian Francs[1] on consultancy, but much of this goes for engineering work and to ex-EEC officials who act as free-lance consultants. Also, we could not hope for our consortium to be the sole vehicle utilized by the Commission for general consulting work.

For this reason, the consortium must seek a wider market. In addition to providing an information service to all members of the consortium relating to the activities, intentions, and strategies of the Commission and to European industry in general, the consortium would act as a main contractor for assignments where partner companies:

Felt they lacked the total competence to perform.
Felt they lacked the necessary multinational staff.
Felt a conflict of interest might arise.
Felt that the consortium approach would be more likely to obtain an assignment than on their own.

Business for which these criteria apply is usually found in the field of multinational mergers. To acquire this type of business is the primary purpose of the consortium. A good reputation with the Commission, established by activities as mentioned above, would give the consortium easy access to information and together with other indirect support from the Commission would give the consortium an enviable position from which to attract commercial clients.

A market for the consortium is probably assured since it seems that the European Economic Commission is about to undertake a number of measures to facilitate transnational industrial regrouping within the member nations. Among these measures are the establishment of a Bureau de Mariage and an extension of the role of the European Investment Bank. With a few exceptions, up to now the mergers in in-

---

[1] About $12,500,000.

dustry and in the financial world have taken place mainly within each of the member countries. In the majority of cases, where transnational actions took place, these actions were more of the nature of take-overs than mergers.

As an example of future opportunities, European insurance companies, observing their markets decreasing by rapidly growing government-controlled social security systems, are looking for alternative opportunities. One of the reasons for them not to start this type of activity is that they lack knowledge about opportunities and procedures that the consortium may be able to provide.

From a competitive standpoint, there are at present a number of activities in the transnational merger field. There is the International Merger Service (assisted by Booz, Allen & Hamilton) formed by a number of banks in Europe, often with American ties. As there is a good chance that a company, intending to use the services of this group, is banking with a bank nonmember of the group, their market is limited. There are further a number of small consulting groups such as Interfinanz in Dusseldorf and L. St. James in Brussels, that can give financial and legal advice for transnational mergers, but cannot offer the extensive coaching needed in the post-merger situation in order to realize rapidly the merger's advantages.

Consortium organization and partner relations

The consortium staff will primarily consist of a director-general and a secretary. The director-general will report to a board with representatives of the consortium partners as directors. His reporting should be so frequent, timely, and complete that the board needs to meet at most four times a year.

Within each member firm, a contact person must be appointed who will assist the director-general by:

Providing inside information concerning industry structure and problems in the relevant area.
Assisting in formulating a proposal.
Accompanying the consortium director-general to meetings with prospective clients.
Attending joint meetings with the experts of other partner-companies together with prospective clients in order to formulate together the terms of reference for an assignment.

There is often uncertainty about the commitments a man in the position of consortium director-general can make. When a partner has made a commitment in regard to a particular consultant, it is expected that it would be honored. Also, it is recommended that all commitments be in written form and that a consortium partner receives a copy of a proposal to a client every time the proposal contains names of consultants of this partner.

One of the most significant potential problems will be establishing the dividing lines between each partner-firm's own international operations and the consortium. No problems would be expected when consortium operations would be limited to EEC studies, work for which would take place by each partner in his nation, and to assignments which partners choose to bring under the consortium's control voluntarily, provided they are of a multinational nature. As a guideline it must be agreed that post-merger top management consultancy is a consortium activity, whereas every well-defined local job will be performed by the local partner.

Operating procedures

Arranged chronologically, procedures for a typical engagement would be as follows:

1. The director-general will be in regular contact with all appropriate departments and agencies of the Commission.
2. The director-general will identify possible assignment opportunities and will take discussions to the stage where technical input is required. He will not normally conclude the sale of an assignment without reference to professional staff of the members.
3. All assignments will become the responsibility of a project leader supplied by one of the partners.
4. It will be necessary for the project leader to be selected at an early stage so that he can participate with the director-general in negotiations with a client.
5. As soon as a possible assignment has been identified, the director-general will notify the appropriate partners, with a request to nominate a project leader.
6. Project leaders will be chosen according to the following criteria:

   Capability and technical ability.
   Availability.
   Nationality (e.g., different from the clients).
   Language capability.
   Geographical distance from the client.

7. The project leader will participate in negotiations and in the preparation of the proposal. The form of the proposal and its content will be the responsibility of the project leader, but the director-general's view, particularly in regard to the fee quotation, must be taken into account.
8. If there is significant knowledge in the consultants of one or more partner-companies and these people are not available for assignments, the consortium director-general may propose a Steering Committee composed of these experts who will then advise the active consultants on the job. The addition of such experts to a proposal will increase the consortium's credibility and make the gaining of assignments easier.
9. In order to facilitate the work of the consortium director-general, each contact person will provide him with all information that can be useful in formulating proposals.
10. Although selling will be the most important task of the director-

general, clients will probably desire to maintain contact with him during an assignment. However, this contact must be limited, and if possible should be taken over by a project leader. The project leader represents the consortium with respect to the client during the assignment.

11. Consultants for an assignment will, as a rule, be obtained from the consortium partners in whose territory the assignment is carried out and will be selected by the project leader.

12. It will be necessary to audit all assignments of greater than a certain fee.

Financial matters

The cost of staff, accommodation and other expenses will vary mainly with the amount that has to be paid to the director-general. A reasonable total amount to budget for would be 1,500,000 Belgian Francs. The fixed costs would be divided *equally* between the partners as it is assumed that there are five equal partners right from the beginning. As the risks are equal, it is logical that the consortium director-general will try, in the long run, to distribute the work evenly. However, in the short run, this must not keep the consortium director-general from forming the best possible team for a proposed task.

For assignments, partner-firms will bill the consortium at 90% of normal fee rates for consultants. The consortium will then bill clients directly.

An initial goal would be to have a minimum income of 15–20 million Belgian Francs within two years from the EEC. This would mean capturing about 3% of the Commission's total consulting work.

CONSORTIUM PARTNERS

Firm and head office	Other offices	Age of the firm	Estimated* total billings	Estimated* professional staff	Nature of practice	Character of the firm
1. Kienbaum Beratungen Gummersbach, Germany	In Germany: Dusseldorf Bonn Frankfurt Stuttgart Munich Outside Germany: Vienna São Paolo	Founded 1945	$5,000,000	175	General Management Personnel Production Marketing Finance Data Processing	One-man ownership (Mr. G. Kienbaum) with all the usual accompanying characteristics. Largest firm in Germany
2. Groupe AVA (Andre Vidal & Ass.) Paris, France	In Belgium: Brussels In Africa: Abidjan	Founded 1945	$3,000,000	120	General Management Personnel Data Processing	Ownership 35% by own personnel, 65% by at least 7 French industries and banks. Not the largest firm in France, but closest to the Berenschot philosophy
3. P.E. Consulting Group London, U.K.	In U.K.: 9 regional offices Outside U.K.: Dublin Copenhagen Paris Milan Sydney Johannesburg	Founded 1934	$9,000,000	250	General Management Production Personnel Marketing Data Processing Engineering Physical Distribution	Trust structure. Board of Management with 9 members. 4th largest consulting firm in U.K.; suffered from recent recession, went through complete restructuring
4. Studio Organizzaazione Aziendale Torino, Italy	none	Founded 1956	$ 500,000	12	General Management Production Plant Start-up Work Study	Partner ownership. Small, but of good professional level

* Figures are disguised.

Raadgevend Bureau Ir. B.W.
Berenschot N.V. (C)

In late 1971 Jan Verschoor, a member of the Executive Board of Raadgevend Bureau Berenschot N.V., the largest management consultancy in the Netherlands, was given responsibility for professional product development in the firm. In June of 1972, he reflected on the Berenschot product line and the future directions he hoped it would take:

> As I said before, the consulting business can be placed on a spectrum. At one end is the old style where people are well versed in a technique such as psychological testing or time study. The other extreme is personal, general consulting where the individual is what the client wants, not the technique. In between these two lies what I consider a product—a contemporary problem in a particular area of business for which we have a general answer. Berenschot has been on the lower end of this spectrum and is moving to the middle, but we have few people at the upper end.
>
> * * * * *
>
> Earlier this year we asked our division directors to analyze and describe the product-market matrix for their division. While the general conclusion was that there had been a shift in direction from our traditional concentration in the past, Berenschot still had two weaknesses in its product line. We are not strong outside of the factory wall or with top management. These are the directions we must move in and the need is as great in this area as it is for international expansion. Dutch business is becoming more sophisticated and we must also or we will lose clients.

In the summer of 1972 the management of Raadgevend Bureau Berenschot N.V., was struggling with the question of diversifying the firm's services. While significant strides had been made away from a long-standing consulting practice in the areas of production and personnel, there were still many people who desired further diversification. This group, which included a large number of the younger consultants, wanted a greater emphasis on general management and strategic consulting of the type that McKinsey & Co. had made famous in Europe. Others, including some of the members of senior management, were more reserved about the need and the possibility of Berenschot successfully competing for business in the top management area.

This case will explore the issue of diversification in Berenschot by first describing the firm's experience in the top management area up to 1972, and then looking at some of the alternatives for further expansion into this kind of work. Finally, the concepts of top management consulting held by several members of Berenschot's Executive Board will be presented.

TOP MANAGEMENT CONSULTING AT BERENSCHOT

Advising and working with upper management levels of its clients had long been a practice at Berenschot. Even the most routine production work was generally initiated by, and a final report made to, top management. As for dealing directly with general management, a small practice had always existed in organizational work. Drs. da Silva described this effort at a meeting held in 1961 to review Berenschot's progress in top management consulting:

> For a week about twenty Brenschot consultants met in a typical Dutch countryside hotel with Professor Juran of New York University to exchange ideas and experiences on top management structure. In this seminar we came to realize how far we had all travelled in organizational work and how much practical experience Brenschot had gained in this area through a variety of assignments. Indeed, several small groups within the firm had for some years been studying the development of theories of organization.

In addition to such general organizational work, upper management consulting took several other directions in Berenschot beginning in the 1950s and continuing into the 1960s.

In the late 1950s, a method for integrated diagnosis of a company was developed. This technique, which became known as survey work, involved a group of specialists from different functional areas as well as an industry specialist and was designed to give an overall analysis of a firm. These studies were almost always performed for senior management or the board of directors and had consistently accounted for about 10% of Berenschot's total billings.

In 1967, a distinguished Dutch economics professor joined Berenschot and together with three other consultants organized a group to do research and gain assignments in corporate strategy. Drs. da Silva described this experience and the reasons for its ultimate failure:

> The corporate strategy group consisted of four brilliant people who were to do research and be at the disposal of the commercial departments for work on consulting projects. The group failed to make any significant contribution and lasted only about two years. I suppose the reason for failure lies partly with the firm and partly with the individuals. Our department heads felt that there was sufficient expertise

in their departments to handle top management work and resented the existence of a special group exclusively for such assignments. On the other hand, the corporate strategy group did not develop any specific consulting products, and did not aggressively attempt to penetrate any markets. They seemed content to just theorize in an academic sort of way.

Of the five main divisions, only the financial institutions division had a definite emphasis on top management work. In 1972, 40% of the billings of Division 1 were concentrated in top management and survey work. Dr. T. J. Steenbergen, the division director, commented on his division:

> When I first started with Berenschot in 1967, the firm had neither reputation nor experience in dealing with financial institutions. Thus, the first contacts involved utilization of our standard production techniques and some data processing. This way we got our foot in the door and gradually we moved up to organization studies and began to deal with some of the concerns of general management. I would like to see this trend continue and even hope someday to be able to do mergers and acquisition work for a fee. This, of course, is now forbidden by the professional society rules.

But not all of the division directors were as committed as Dr. Steenbergen to top management consulting. Ir. Melessen of Division 3 had definite opinions about limits on this type of work and about what he considered to be a desirable product mix for his division.

> About 10% of my sales are now in the top management and special studies area. While much of this work is quite interesting, I would not like to see it account for more than 20% of the division's total billings. I have a large number of people in this division and we must retain our standard work to keep them employed. Also, I have always contended that a consultant needed knowledge of the basic areas such as marketing and production before he could work with top management.
>
> Any future developments in my product line will be guided by a six-point statement of product policy that I have developed:
>
> 1. A product must fulfill a client's need.
> 2. We must choose products that will generate further business with a client.
> 3. A product must provide for an adequate volume of business to support the firm.
> 4. A product must be specific enough to be labeled.
> 5. A product must be standard enough to be repeated with several clients. We want no one-time studies.
> 6. Our products must yield tangible measures of accomplishment—more sales, lower costs, higher productivity, or higher ROI.
>
> I think there are some interesting directions that our development work can move toward and still be within the above guidelines. For example, there are definite trends in European society—threats to our economic system, movement to central planning, tougher unions, broader participation in decision making—that Berenschot should recognize and respond to by developing specific consulting products. Better forecasting techniques is one example.

ALTERNATIVES FOR DIVERSIFICATION

There were several possible alternatives for Berenschot to choose from in its quest for more work in the top management area. Jan Verschoor described the options he was considering and also some of the feelings he had about the firm's present strengths and how these related to his decision:

> Some of the possibilities here are similar to those for international expansion. We could acquire or enter into a joint venture with another consulting firm that had top management expertise. Unfortunately, there are not a large number of such firms available.
>
> The other options are essentially internal. We could take our best consultants and organize them into a separate unit to concentrate solely on top management work. This unit could even be set up as a subsidiary company and thus would not be closely tied to the rest of the firm. The main difficulty with this choice is that it creates resentment among others in the firm who feel shut out of the top management area. Another internal alternative is to modify our recruiting efforts and attempt to hire more people—such as MBAs perhaps—that could deal with top management work. This obviously is a long-term alternative.
>
> No matter what choice or choices we make, we should recognize and build on the already existing strengths of Berenschot. We have always stressed our complete systems approach to consulting and have developed an operational reputation for being able to actually put our ideas to work. We also have a good deal of experience in dealing with the bottom and middle levels of an organization that is invaluable in understanding and operating with the upper levels. One could, however, also argue that these strengths are actually limitations and that they have created a reputation and image for Berenschot that we cannot break away from.

CONCEPTS OF TOP MANAGEMENT CONSULTING

When asked for their definitions of consulting to top management, the following responses were received from members of the Executive Board:

> Piet Koppen, Chairman:
>
> My definition of top management consulting is that it involves solving the difficult problems that top management is concerned with. Many people limit their conception of this type of work to just organizational structure, but it is actually much broader.
>
> To be good at this type of work, a young person should often start out at the plant floor level. This gives an appreciation for working under conditions where the results of recommendations are immediately apparent. It is also an important experience since it teaches the consultant how the workers in a firm and their bosses think.
>
> Willem van der Scheer, Director of Operations:
>
> My conception of top management consulting depends on the type of client. For the huge firms, like Shell, a systems approach—à la McKinsey—is necessary. But there are only 20 or 30 such firms in Holland. For the 3,000–5,000 companies that are the market for

Berenschot, personal relations with the top management is the crucial aspect.

Jan Verschoor, Professional Product Development Director:

Top management consulting must be concerned with the decision-making process of the manager and usually involves decisions as to what type of business the company is to be in. The consultant can either participate directly in the decision making, can prepare the decisions for the manager to make, or can help the top manager implement his decisions.

There is, however, no standard concept of top management consulting either in this firm or among our clients. For middle-sized companies—and this is where the volume lies since consulting for Shell represents honor and not volume—I think we can deal adequately with the technical concerns of top management—information systems, for example. Where we have problems is in helping them deal better with their environment—in understanding and being sensitive to outside influences.

The company and its societal responsibilities: Relating corporate strategy and moral values

WE come at last to the fourth and final component of strategy—the moral aspects of choice. In our consideration of strategic alternatives, we have so far moved from what the strategist *might* and *can* do to what he *wants* to do; we now move to what he *ought* to do—from the point of view of society and his own inner standards of right and wrong. Ethics, like preference, may be considered a question of value. To some the suggestion that an orderly and analytical process of strategy determination must find its way through the tangle of ethics is repugnant. Proponents of this view find it sufficient if business lives up to its legal obligations: obeys the antitrust acts, keeps honest expense accounts, and pays its bills and taxes. Beyond this point, they argue, we cannot and should not prescribe codes of conduct or standards of responsibility. Nor should we imply that the choice among alternatives should be influenced by the judgment that one is morally superior to another.

THE MORAL ASPECT OF STRATEGIC CHOICE

While fully aware of the problems involved, we contend that the businessman must examine the impact on the public good of the policy alternatives he is free to elect and implement. We are not impressed by the argument that it is difficult to distinguish in what way one strategic choice is morally superior to another. The study of comparative ethics reveals that every known human society has been governed by codes of conduct. Despite numerous tragic interruptions, these codes have progressively tended to embody a more comprehensive concept of the public good and a fuller recognition of social rights and duties. This progress—which presumably continues, at least in slow motion, within most democratic societies today—has not been achieved in the absence of any consensus as to what, in the confrontation of responsibility with self-aggrandizement, separates right from wrong.

578

Thus in the professional sector of the business community, away from the back alleys of self-interest and used car lots, it is quite often possible to distinguish legal but shabby behavior from that of a higher ethical quality. One who manipulates the letter of an agreement to his own advantage can be told from the person willing to observe its spirit. The exploiter of human relationships for narrow ends reveals himself, and the quality of an individual's personal purposes can be readily deduced from his behavior.

We are concerned here, however, with the ethics of strategic choice, not with the morality of personal behavior. The ethics of strategy often involves a conflict of obligations. For example, the cigarette industry has an obligation to tobacco farmers, workers, and stockholders on the one hand, and to the consuming public on the other. Similarly, the pharmaceutical manufacturer is caught between the need for safety and the need for speed in exploiting a new drug. Anyone in genuine doubt about the ethical quality of a strategic alternative will find plenty of advice available as to which is on the side of the angels (although advice may differ from different quarters when legitimate claims are in competition). Formal and informal associations of businessmen and corporations themselves develop observable norms of conduct which influence the behavior of their members in matters where law and regulation do not apply. On the average these norms are rising in response to the expectations of the total society that men free to choose between meaner and better purposes will choose the better. It may, even so, be hard to get a good decision, but it is not difficult to locate in any range of alternatives the issues to ponder.

RELEVANCE OF THE PUBLIC GOOD

Explicit attention to questions of the responsibility of business to society is criticized by those who argue that uninhibited pursuit of self-interest is in the long-range interest of society. Classical economic theory postulates that in atomized markets, perfect competition produces not only the optimum allocation of economic resources but also optimum satisfaction of the general interest. But classical economic theory is only partially applicable in practice. Instead of transitory small firms in perfect competition, we have permanent organizations of great size, power, and influence. Instead of a free market, we have a mixed economy, with different industries operating under varying degrees of public regulation and control.

The alternative to still greater intervention by the state in the economic sphere is for businessmen to exhibit a clear and lively sense of public obligation. Indeed, the emergence of the doctrine of social responsibility is the principal justification for leaving corporation power unchecked.[1] And large segments of our society—government, organized labor, organized religion, and educational institutions—are gradually

---

[1] The argument for limiting corporate power by new controls is stated by Carl Kaysen, "The Corporation: How Much Power? What Scope?" In Edward S. Mason, *The Corporation in Modern Society* (Cambridge, Mass.: Harvard University Press, 1960).

raising the standards of performance which they expect business to meet. The expectation that business will behave not only legally but with due regard for the rights of competitors, customers, and the general public grows daily more determined. Supposed as well as real abuses are sufficient to put businessmen on the defensive. Their critics are an articulate group, with easy access to the ears of legislators. In the press and in congressional hearings, some critics will inflate alleged instances of business irregularities with an unscrupulousness that would put the Robber Barons to shame.

The strategist who is sensitive to these aspects of the business environment soon concludes that there are two reasons for examining the impact of his policy choices upon the public good. The first is his professional concern for legality, fairness, and decency—his professional contempt for returns improperly or unfairly secured. The second is the threat of regulation that will be forthcoming if business behavior does not meet the standards applied to it by society. Men of conscience will be concerned with their public responsibilities because they choose to be. Other men will be concerned because they must be.

With confidence men and embezzlers, we have no problem of policy. When their alleged fraud is proved, they go to jail. But if the Stock Exchange ignores the association, however innocent, of one of its members with a scandal, the Securities and Exchange Commission would be quick to apply both its regulatory and its persuasive powers. If the National Associations of Broadcasters did not have its so-called Voluntary Code to govern programming, the recurrent aspirations of the Federal Communications Commission to impose new restrictions on telecasters would long since have had more tangible effects. Though to many observers the broadcasting code seems more honored in the breach than the observance, its inadequacy does not alter the conclusion that voluntary industrywide agreements to restrain competitive practices in the public interest are a potent deterrent to additional legislation and could be an impetus to more responsible practice. This code might usefully be broadened, in response to newly evident needs, to check dramatized violence.

You will find that most instructors in Business Policy will not presume to prescribe what is right in detailed codes. They will ask, however, that you take into account the impact on society of your strategic choices and plans. They will remind you that the business firm, as an organic entity meaningfully related to its environment, must be as adaptive to demands for responsible behavior as for economic service. At the same time the opportunity remains to shape public attitudes and expectations in much more effective presentations of the inherent difficulty in business of satisfying all the conflicting claims made upon it.

CONFLICT OF RESPONSIBILITIES

Once it is established that the firm must take into account the legitimate interests of other segments of society, the problem is far from solved. Rather, the already complex process of formulating a strategy capable of balancing economic opportunity, corporate resources, and personal and organizational aspirations is complicated now by an additional dimension. Furthermore, though right and wrong may be easy to determine in cases where all good lies on one side and all harm on the other, in other cases obligation to society may lead in several different directions. In some of these instances, determination of the proper course of action from the point of view of contribution to the public good is virtually impossible. The basic problem is the variety of interests which must be harmonized, the range of insistent and sometimes shrill definitions of right and justice, and the conflict among legitimate claims.

The professional manager of a large, publicly held corporation is clearly in some sense responsible to the owners of his business, to its employees, to its suppliers and customers, and even to his competitors —since he owes it to them to compete "fairly." He is also responsible in some ways to certain institutions, including the local government and community, the national government and community, and the fraternity of businessmen with which he identifies himself. It is clear at once that if the interests of any one of these groups are pursued exclusively, the interests of the others will suffer. It is clear also that the stockholder interest, which was once thought to be dominant, is no longer of unchallenged primacy. Indeed, in the publicly held corporation, it is not even particularly insistent. Conventions as to what constitutes a fair dividend in relation to market price are fairly well observed. When return does not meet the individual needs of an investor, his recourse is to make other investment choices. Conventions governing the extent to which other interests must be considered exist but are less clearly defined. Often the executive finds himself in situations in which it is impossible to reconcile the legitimate claims of everyone concerned. For example, there is frequently a need to move an obsolescent plant from a town that is economically dependent upon its payroll. Once such a problem has been allowed to arise, it is almost impossible to solve it without damage to some interests.

You will find, therefore, that the cases and issues presented in this section—and the similar issues which you will encounter in your business life—are even less susceptible to predetermined answers than some of the other problems we have encountered. But wrestling with the problem and debating the solutions proffered by your associates can have a result that will be of immense value to each individual. That is, it can help you to develop your own values and personal philosophy and to clarify the standards of moral and ethical behavior which you yourself will elect to live by. The consideration of strategic alternatives will thenceforth be simplified for you, since you will very quickly rule out alternatives which require action that you consider improper. Similarly, within the corporation, the range of strategic alternatives that must be evaluated is reduced to more manageable scope if the chief executive will make a clear pronouncement indicating what broad limits are imposed by social and ethical considerations. Acting responsibly thus becomes one of the shared goals of the corporation.

The philosophy that you develop must be a personal achievement, reflecting personal goals and purposes, the level of culture to which heredity and education have brought you, and the degree to which your personal purposes are other than self-centered. Breadth of perception must be allied to breadth of purpose before either is effective. The increasing professionalization of business management, which is in part consequent upon the recognition of obligations that go beyond the short-run financial interests of the corporation and the individual, provides stronger and stronger support to those who look beyond their own goals to those of the society of which they are important and influential members.

But events of 1966–68 have greatly accelerated the participation by business in the social problems of our time. Corporate involvement in public issues is increasing on two fronts—educational activities as contribution to community development and entrepreneurial ventures in undeveloped areas or needed services that are expected to produce some profit for the service rendered. The entry of firms like General Electric, Time, Inc., Raytheon, Litton Industries, and Xerox into education, the efforts of U.S. Gypsum, Aerojet, Lockheed, Ford, and of innumerable individual business leaders in the National Alliance of Businessmen to rehabilitate housing, establish factories and training facilities in the ghettos, and to provide training and jobs for hard-core unemployed reflect a genuine and widespread recognition of obligation. The profits which may ultimately attend this enterprise will not be large. In any case they are clearly less the likely reward than the satisfaction that accompanies effective contribution to problems hitherto intractable to individual or governmental attention.

Under an acceptance of responsibility to society accelerated by the idealism of our youth, public inquiry into racism and injustice, and violence in the cities, business and society are redefining the proper role of industry. It is now expected that corporate power and management skill should be applied in areas like education, social justice, and the rehabilitation of cities and regions. These are the problems left unattended by medicine, law, the church, and the schools. They are complex enough to be worthy of the highest technical, professional, and organizational skills that business executives can muster.

CORPORATE RESPONSIBILITY AND INDIVIDUAL SELF-EXPRESSION

We have thus far been concerned with the question of the firm's responsibility to those segments of society which its activity affects. An increasingly important problem is the firm's responsibility to insiders. This problem concerns the relative freedom of members of the firm to express views on public issues, even though these views may bring criticism upon the organization. It is at best difficult to balance the freedom of the individual and the consequences of his participation in public affairs against the interests of the corporation. The difficulty is increased if the attitudes of management, which instinctively are overprotective of the corporation, are harsh and restrictive. Short-run embarrassments and limited criticism from offended groups—even perhaps a threatened boycott—may be a small price to pay for the continued productivity within the corporation of men whose interests are deep enough and broad enough to cause them to take stands on public issues. The degree to which an organization is efficient, productive, creative, and capable of development is dependent in large part on the maintenance of a climate in which the individual does not feel suppressed, and in which a kind of freedom (analogous to that which the corporation enjoys in a free-enterprise society) is permitted as a matter of course. Overregulation of the individual by corporate policy is no more appropriate internally than overregulation of the corporation by government. On the other hand, personal responsibility is as appropriate to individual liberty as corporate responsibility is to corporate freedom.

The complexities of successfully integrating public responsibility into corporate strategy are great, but not insuperable. Conflicting responsibilities can be ordered in the same way as conflicting personal values, never perfectly, but often workably. Just as no one individual can achieve all he wants, so no corporation can satisfy all the demands made upon it by the special interest groups of society. If his concept of what constitutes the greatest good is clear, the executive who chooses his course accordingly can in good conscience withstand the abuses of those who demand a different course. So long as he does not make his decision in deliberate disregard of his responsibilities to the system which gives him power, he may not be much hurt.

The scandals of price fixing in the electrical equipment industry, conflicts of interest in Washington, and the personal interests of some corporation presidents in companies serving their firms as suppliers have all suggested that a code of conduct for executives should be formalized. It would alert insensitive men who thought they were doing no real wrong to their responsibilities. To supplement the negative and sometimes contradictory prohibitions of the law and to cover borderline cases of conflict of interest, our colleague, Robert W. Austin, has suggested a simple code as follows:

1. The professional business manager affirms that he will place the interest of the business for which he works before his own private business.
2. The professional business manager affirms that he will place his duty to society above his duty to his company and above his private interest.
3. The professional business manager affirms that he has a duty to reveal the facts in any situation where (a) his private interests are involved with those of his company, or (b) where the interests of his company are involved with those of the society in which it operates.
4. The professional business manager affirms that when business managers follow this code of conduct, the profit motive is the best incentive for the development of a sound, expanding, and dynamic economy.[2]

[2] Robert W. Austin, "Code of Conduct for Executives," *Harvard Business Review,* September–October 1961, pp. 53–61.

This code is intended to govern behavior rather than strategic choice, but the first two affirmations it calls for are unequivocal guides to policy. Such a code would have considerable impact on the scope of business-men's effort to achieve a reconciliation or combination among economic strategy, their personal values, and their societal responsibilities. Clarification of personal, corporate, and national purpose is essential before the relevant interests are known and the proper priority of duty determined. Explicit, perhaps sequential, attention to all these categories of purpose will disentangle many an otherwise hopeless confusion.

THE PROBLEM OF FINAL CHOICE

We have now before us the major determinants of strategy. The cases studied so far have required consideration of what the strategy of the firm is and what, in your judgment, it ought to be. Concerned so far with the problem of formulating a viable strategy rather than implementing it, you have become familiar with the principal aspects of formulation—namely, (1) appraisal of present and foreseeable opportunity and risk in the company's environment, (2) assessment of the firm's unique combination of present and potential corporate resources or competences, (3) determination of the noneconomic personal and organizational preferences to be satisfied, (4) identification and acceptance of the social responsibilities of the firm. The strategic decision is one than can be reached only after all these factors have been considered and the action implications of each assessed.

In your efforts to analyze the cases, you have experienced much more of the problem of the strategist than can be described on paper. When you have relinquished your original idea as to what a company's strategy should be in favor of a more imaginative one, you have seen that the formulation process has an essential creative aspect. In your effort to differentiate your thinking about an individual firm from the conventional thinking of its industry, you have looked for new opportunities and for new applications of corporate competence. You have learned how to define a product in terms of its present and potential functions rather than of its physical properties. You have probably learned a good deal about how to assess the special competence of a firm from its past accomplishments, and how to identify management's values and aspirations. You may have gained some ability to rank preferences in order of their strength—your own among others.

The problem implicit in striking a balance between the company's apparent opportunity and its evident competence, between your own personal values and concepts of responsibility and those of the company's actual management, is not an easy one. It is not solved either by your familiarity with the basic concepts expounded in this text or by the practice which your case discussions have so far provided. The concepts we have been discussing will help you to prepare to make a decision, but they will not determine your decision for you. Whenever choice is compounded of rational analysis which can have more than one outcome, of aspiration and desire which can run the whole range of human ambition, and of a sense of responsibility which changes the appeal of alternatives, it cannot be reduced to quantitative approaches or to the exactness which management science can apply to narrower questions. A man contemplating strategic decision must be willing to make it without the guidance of decision rules. He must have confidence in his own judgment, which will have been deepened and seasoned by repeated analysis of similar questions. He must be aware that more than one decision is possible and that he is not seeking the single right answer. He can take encouragement from the fact that the manner in which an organization implements the chosen program can help to validate the original decision. For example, the wisdom of deciding to expand from national to international operations may depend on the quality of the implementing action taken.

Some of the most difficult choices confronting a company are those which must be made among several alternatives that appear equally attractive and also equally desirable. Thus a large land-development company with a very large income could move cash into virtually any activity it wished. But since its special competence was essentially non-transferable to other activities requiring large amounts of capital, and since the expansion of land development seemed unwise, the company was faced by an embarrassment of riches. Once the analysis of opportunity has produced an inconveniently large number of possibilities, any firm has difficulty in deciding what it wants to do and how the new activities will be related to the old.

In situations where opportunity is approximately equal and economic promise is offered by a wide range of activities, the problem of making a choice can perhaps be resolved if reference is made to the essential character of the company and to the kind of company the executives wish to run. The study of alternatives from this point of view will sooner or later reveal the greater attractiveness of some choices over others. Economic analysis and calculations of return on investment, though of course essential, may not crucially determine the outcome. Rather, the logjam of decision can only be broken by a frank exploration of executive aspirations regarding future development, including perhaps the president's own wishes with respect to the kind of institution he prefers to head, carried on as part of a free and untrammeled investigation of what human needs in what parts of the world the organization would find satisfaction in serving. The fiction that return on investment alone will point the way ignores the values implicit in the calculations and the contribution which an enthusiastic commitment to new projects can make. The rational examination of alternatives and the determination of purpose are among the most important and most neglected of all human activities. The final decision, which should be made as deliberately as possible after a deliberate consideration of the issues we have attempted to separate, is an act of will and desire as much as of intellect.

A Note on the U.S. Prescription Drug Industry—Part I

CONTINUING the upsurge that started with the advent of antbiotics, establishments in the drug industry grew faster than the all-manufacturing average in 1963–1970. Key role in this achievement had to be played by pharmaceuticals (medications manufactured in dosage form), since it was much the largest of three subindustries classified in drugs. The others were biologicals (mainly plasmas and vaccines) and bulk medicinal chemicals and botanicals:

SHIPMENTS OF MANUFACTURING ESTABLISHMENTS BY INDUSTRY*

(dollars in millions)

Class of establishment (based on primary product)	1963	1970	Change
All manufacturing..................	$420,973.0	$630,710.5	+49.8%
Drugs............................	3,715.9	6,792.8	82.8
Pharmaceuticals................	3,314.3	6,027.8	81.9
Biologicals.....................	95.7	236.7	147.3
Bulk medicinals, etc.............	305.8	528.3	72.8

* U.S. Bureau of the Census, *Census of Manufactures*, 1967, Vol. 1, pp. 29, 35, and "General Statistics for Industry Groups and Industries," *Annual Survey of Manufactures*, 1970, pp. 4, 12 (Washington, D.C.: U.S. Government Printing Office, 1971 and 1972).

Growth in pharmaceuticals was in turn mostly due to one of two component product types—namely, "ethical" pharmaceuticals. Although most ethicals were available only on prescription, any pharmaceutical was classed as an ethical if it was promoted only to members of the medical profession. If promoted to the general public, a pharmaceutical was classed as a "proprietary" and it was available "over-the-counter."

Shipment data for these two product types, as gathered from establishments classified in pharmaceuticals or elsewhere, were as follows in 1963–1970:

ALL-INDUSTRY SHIPMENTS OF PHARMACEUTICALS BY TYPE*

(dollars in millions)

Type of pharmaceutical	1963	1970	Change
Ethical (domestic)	$2,054.9	$3,781.3	+84.0%
Proprietary (domestic)	836.2	1,344.2	60.8
Unclassified (export)	102.0	150.2	47.3
	$2,993.1	$5,275.7	76.2

* U.S. Bureau of the Census, "Pharmaceutical Preparations, Except Biologicals," *Current Industrial Reports 1963, 1970* (Washington, D.C.: U.S. Government Printing Office, 1964 and 1971).

Even stronger than the sales growth record for drugs was the profit record. Often in the lead, drugs were outperformed by few other industries, although top honors for the post-tax profit on sales might go to petroleum refining, while leadership in post-tax profit on net worth might pass in some quarters to motor vehicles and equipment or, more rarely, to instruments and related products:

Range of Quarterly Post-Tax Earnings, 1957–1970*

	Profit on sales	Profit on stockholders' investment
All manufacturing	3.4%– 5.9%	6.8%–14.7%
Drugs	9.1 –11.7	14.7 –22.0

* U.S. Federal Trade Commission and U.S. Securities and Exchange Commission, *Quarterly Financial Reports for Manufacturing Corporations* (Washington, D.C.: U.S. Government Printing Office, 1958–1971), Tables 2 and 4.

In keeping with this growth and profit record, drug finances were strong (Exhibit 1), and several drug companies had made their way into *Fortune*'s 500 (Exhibit 2). Although many of these firms were diversified (Exhibit 2) and published no financial results covering drug operations only, such data were available for 1958 (Exhibit 3) and confirm the impression of a very profitable industry indeed.

DRUGS AND PHARMACEUTICAL PRODUCTS

Drugs are single chemical entities, having, or supposed to have, a positive therapeutic effect. Partly because much the same effect may be attached to a whole family of entities that differ only slightly in molecular structure, the number of drugs is very large—about 7,000 in

588   Business policy: Text and cases

mid-1967.[1] Each drug has a single scientific name, known as its generic name.

A single drug or possibly a combination of drugs may be incorporated into anywhere from one pharmaceutical product to hundreds, the number depending on whether the drug is patented or not and on how many different companies are interested in serving as sources of supply. When made and/or sold by many different sources, the drug may acquire many different names in addition to its generic name, since each supplier has the option of coining a distinctive brand name for it (although he must also cite the generic name). Still more variety is introduced when the pharmaceutical is made in different strengths and dosage forms.

The therapeutic effect of a drug, or the body system it acts upon, provides a basis for classification. Thus, pharmaceuticals for human use are grouped by the Census Bureau into eight major (five-digit) classes (Exhibit 4) and 145 (seven-digit) subclasses.[2] These differ widely in volume and growth rate, reflecting such factors as the relative incidence of disease, breakthroughs in research, the size of the class in the base year, changes in acceptance by the medical profession, or, in a few cases (particularly vitamins, antibiotics, or steroid hormones used for arthritis), price weakness based on oversupply.

Numerous as drugs and pharmaceutical products are, relatively few at any one time enjoy a large commercial success. As for drugs, only 51 of them accounted for "at least two-thirds" of the total value of ethicals sold in 1958, according to the findings of the first big Congressional drug investigation—that conducted by the late Senator Estes Kefauver (D., Tenn.).[3] As for pharmaceuticals, the top 200 sellers normally account for about two-thirds of all new prescriptions filled,[4] according to a normally confidential Audit conducted for members of the industry each year. Further information derived from the Audit for 1965 was revealed by a second big Congressional investigation—that conducted in 1967–1970 by Senator Gaylord Nelson (D., Wis.).[5] This revealed that 188 of the top 200 sellers were brand-name (or single-source) products, versus only 12 identified in the prescriptions by their generic names.[6] Furthermore (Exhibit 5), the strongest selling product in a group might well have 30% of the market and the three strongest products 50%, even though the number of competing products might be 50 to 80 or more.

---

[1] U.S. Senate Subcommittee on Monopoly of the Select Committee on Small Business, *Competitive Problems in the Drug Industry, Hearings*, Part 4, p. 1222. These Hearings were held 1967–1970 (90,91 Cong.), and are hereafter referred to as the Nelson Hearings, for their Chairman, Senator Gaylord Nelson.

[2] U.S. Bureau of the Census, *Pharmaceutical Preparations*.

[3] U.S. Senate Subcommittee on Antitrust and Monopoly of the Committee on the Judiciary, *Report on Administered Prices, Drugs* (87 Cong.). This report (Washington, D.C.: U.S. Government Printing Office, 1961) emerged from Hearings held in 1959–1960 (86 Cong.). These sources are hereafter referred to as the Kefauver Report and Hearings, for their Chairman, Senator Estes Kefauver.

[4] *Drug & Cosmetic Industry*, June 1969, p. 58.

[5] See footnote 1, above.

[6] Nelson Hearings, Pt. 4, p. 1424.

Even if a product is fortunate enough to achieve a large market share, its market position may decline abruptly. In explaining drug industry economics to Congress and the public, industry spokesmen stress the rapid displacement of old drugs by new. To document the rapid pace of change, the industry commissioned two special studies from the consulting firm of Arthur D. Little. In an often cited passage, the earlier of these reports summarized its findings by saying that in 1960 nearly 70% of pharmaceutical sales were accounted for by products introduced within the past 10 years.[7] The second study, which painted the picture as of 1965, was less comprehensive than the first, but still covered 17 product subclasses which accounted for 58% of dollar sales. Within these classes, 185 out of 213 leading products, or 55% had been introduced since 1956.[8]

INDUSTRY STRUCTURE

Number of producers

No one knows exactly how many companies make pharmaceuticals. According to the Bureau of the Census, there were 791 in 1967, but in that same year more than 2,000 were registered with the Federal Drug Administration (FDA) as producing pharmaceuticals for human use. This number, moreover, did not include suppliers who were simply "repackers" of drugs they bought in bulk from others.[9] Nor did it include suppliers whose business was only intrastate. According to a spokesman for the Pharmaceutical Manufacturers Association (PMA), there were "literally thousands" of companies in the latter category that did not have to register with the FDA.[10]

Opinion differs as to whether pharmaceuticals should be regarded as a concentrated industry or not. According to Census data the top 20 firms accounted for some 70% of sales from 1958 through 1967 (Exhibit 6). Yet, as industry sources often emphasized, no single company accounted for more than 7% of the total U.S. retail and hospital market.[11] As a PMA spokesman put it, "This low degree of concentration is approached by very few other manufacturing industries of comparable size."[12]

Number of competitors

Since drugs do not compete across the board but only with alternative remedies, it is meaningful to look not only at the total number of makers, but also at the number of makers and/or sellers for each of the major classes of drugs. According to the PMA, in 1967 not one among

---

[7] Standard & Poor's Corporation, "Drugs, Cosmetics, Basic Analysis," *Trade and Securities,* December 13, 1962, p. D–10.

[8] Nelson Hearings, Pt. 5, p. 1786.

[9] Ibid., Pt. 2, p. 772.

[10] Ibid., Pt. 4, pp. 1412, 1413.

[11] Nelson Hearings, Pt. 6, p. 2297; PMA *Year Book,* 1968–1969, p. 105. 1969–1970, p. 85.

[12] Nelson Hearings, Pt. 4, p. 1416.

11 major classes of pharmaceuticals for human use had in it fewer than 14 representatives from among the PMA's 63 top members. And every category accounting for as much as 3% of industry sales had 42 or more of these firms represented.[13]

Still another way used by some analysts to measure competition is to look at the number of producers and/or sellers of an individual drug. The previously mentioned Kefauver study gathered such data on the 51 drugs found to account for "at least two-thirds" of ethical sales in 1958. As for producers, 27 of the 51 drugs had only one; 8 had two; 10 had three, and none had over seven.[14] As for sellers, these were more numerous in some but not all cases. Thus, 18 of the 51 drugs had only one seller; three had two to four, four had five to 14, but the rest had at least 44 and nine had at least 100.[15]

Patents, licensing, and competition

The reason why some high-volume drugs have few sellers and even fewer makers lies in the patent and license situation. Unlike many European countries, the United States grants full patent protection on drugs, including both "product" and "process" patents, the former being more iron-clad since they are more difficult to evade.[16] In addition, owing to a landmark court decision, drugs are not bound by the usual U.S. rule that products found in nature are nonpatentable.[17]

Normally, a patent lasts 17 years, but, according to the majority report of the Kefauver Committee, drug companies have found a way to extend this normal period "far longer" by means of "judicious spacing of improvement patents over the years, or making slight changes in the drug's molecular structure, allegedly increasing its potency, efficacy, or safety."[18]

Although a patent grants a legal monopoly position, not all patented drugs are produced and sold on an exclusive basis. For a variety of reasons, the patent holder may license other makers and/or sellers. These reasons include "virtually simultaneous discovery, a *quid pro quo* arrangement . . . , or the desire to profit from sales made by a firm with a larger distribution organization."[19] The first is the most compelling reason, since near-simultaneous discovery might lead to a patent interference suit which would bar exclusivity for any firm until the case was settled.[20]

While licensing means sharing, the impact of this can be modified by licensing only a few other sellers, and by inserting a restrictive clause that prohibits the licensee from selling the drug in bulk to others. A thornier problem of licensing is the possibility of "running afoul" of

---

[13] PMA, *Year Book*, 1968, p. 105.
[14] Kefauver Report, p. 68.
[15] Kefauver Hearings, Pt. 19, p. 10825.
[16] Kefauver Report, p. 105.
[17] Nelson Hearings, Pt. 5, p. 2118.
[18] Kefauver Report, p. 141.
[19] Ibid., p. 143.
[20] Ibid., pp. 152–154, and Nelson Hearings, Pt. 5, p. 1877.

antitrust restrictions, since the patent holder may be accused of "trying to secure observance of his price."[21] Few legal cases have arisen on this basis, but the most celebrated involved five makers of broad-spectrum antibiotics in both civil and criminal suits. These remained unsettled in 1972, despite 12–14 years of litigation and a joint company offer to pay $120 million to customers filing tripe-damage suits in the wake of an unfavorable lower court decision.[22]

Company dependence on single categories and products

Where a company has a very strong position in a single drug class, subclass, or drug, it might, as a corollary, have a very heavy dependence on it. Thus, the PMA revealed that in 1965 half its members with sales above $5 million depended on a single major product class for more than half of their revenues.[23] Even some firms in *Fortune*'s 500 depended heavily on one drug or subclass. For example, Smith Kline & French owed most of its growth to potent tranquilizers; Searle, to "the pill."

When companies rely for a large part of their sales on a narrow range of products, they may be reluctant to publicize this fact. Nevertheless, some case histories have found their way into the business press:

> In 1950, because a research gamble paid off, Merck captured the entire market for [corticosteroids]; sales jumped from $94 million in 1950 to $160 million in 1953. But in 1954, competitive steroid drugs entered the market, and Merck's sales dipped to $145 million. By 1958, . . . only the advent of other new drugs kept the sales curve rising.
>
> In 1950, too, Parke, Davis introduced the first broad-spectrum antibiotic under the trade name Chloromycetin; in one year, sales climbed $35 million. However, before the company could recover its development costs, patients began reporting unfavorable reactions to the new drug and doctors turned away from it. In two years, sales fell $28 million and profits nearly $10 million before confidence in the drug was [temporarily] restored.
>
> In a different field, Lilly had put a heap of money into research on tissue culture. When the Salk polio vaccine came along, Lilly was in the best position to fill demand. Sales went from $141 million in 1955 to $200 million in 1957, profits from $16 million to $32 million. Then the rush demand evaporated; in 1958, sales dropped to $180 million and profits to $23.7 million.[24]
>
> *   *   *   *   *
>
> Actually, even the wildest optimist couldn't have expected Searle to maintain its annual growth rate . . . indefinitely. Searle was the first drugmaker to introduce an oral contraceptive, Enovid; and, until 1963 . . . it had the market to itself. This was the reason for its fantastic growth [from $36.9 million in 1960 to $86.5 million in 1964]. Now [1966] Searle must compete with J & J and five others.[25]

---

[21] Kefauver Report, p. 141.
[22] *The Wall Street Journal*, April 23, 1971 and July 3, 1972.
[23] Nelson Hearings, Pt. 6, p. 2303.
[24] *Business Week*, December 10, 1960, p. 150.
[25] *Forbes*, October 1, 1966, p. 28.

Integration

Although large pharmaceutical firms might be heavily dependent on a single drug class or drug, they were at least represented in other categories, and many were also represented in other segments of the drug industry. Thus, by 1967 establishments classified under pharmaceuticals accounted for 24% of all shipments of medicinal chemicals and 38% of all shipments of biologicals.[26]

Integration of firms in pharmaceuticals and firms in medicinal chemicals proceeded apace after World War II, since it provided the former with access to wonder-drug capability and the latter with a means of getting wonder drugs to market without selling to a host of small repackers whose competition might break the price. This happened in the case of some early wonder drugs, and the experience reportedly exerted a strong shaping force on the future structure of the drug industry.[27]

Exit, merger, and new entries

In view of sales and profit trends for pharmaceuticals, it is perhaps surprising that the number of companies fell instead of rising after 1958 (Exhibit 6). This trend suggests several possible causes: poor performance by marginal firms, mergers, and barriers to entry. Poor marginal performance is borne out by income tax data. Thus, of 1,265 corporate returns filed in 1967 by the drug industry as a whole, 579 showed no net income on an insignificant volume of receipts.[28]

Mergers, too, have shrunk the industry. Out of the relatively few drug firms with assets of $10 million or more, 14 were acquired in 1948–1970.[29] At least three of the industry's majors owe their growth importantly to mergers.[30] Thus, when two of the largest firms[31] paired up in 1970 to create a billion-dollar company with 5% to 6% of the market, the action was sufficient to touch off a politically sensitive FTC suit for divestment, plus a major public study of the drug merger movement.[32]

Barriers to entry can best be assessed after moving on to look at drug company functions. Meanwhile, it can be said that most outsiders entering drugs have chosen the acquisition route, and that some who elected to break in on their own have not so far reported great success. Included in the latter category were McKesson & Robbins and du Pont. M & R (now Foremost-McKesson) started making pharmaceuticals in 1961, after being the biggest drug wholesaler for years. Since its products were to be low-priced generics, and since its market emphasis

---

[26] U.S. Bureau of the Census, *Census of Manufactures,* 1967, Vol. II, Pt. II, pp. 28C–10, 28C–11.

[27] Nelson Hearings, Pt. 5, pp. 2115–2120, 1916, 1978–81.

[28] U.S. Internal Revenue Service, *Statistics of Income, 1967: Corporate Income Tax Returns* (Washington, D.C.: U.S. Government Printing Office, 1971), p. 12.

[29] U.S. Federal Trade Commission, *Large Mergers in Manufacturing and Mining 1948–1970* (Washington, D.C.: U.S. Government Printing Office, 1971), pp. 16–65.

[30] American Home Products, Pfizer, and Warner-Lambert.

[31] Warner-Lambert and Parke, Davis.

[32] *The Wall Street Journal,* November 13, 1970 and November 27, 1970.

soon got shifted to South America, M & R was not in the same league as the brand-name firms using its distribution service. Their reaction was hostile, nonetheless, especially after M & R announced a U.S. version of a high-volume antibiotic made by the five brand-name producers who were being sued for patent fraud and collusive pricing. One of the five retaliated by cutting off supplies to M & R, and another sued M & R for patent infringement. Suits and countersuits were later settled,[33] but of its drug business M & R said little. Pharmaceuticals, "detailed" by mail, numbered 149 by 1964. The line was pared in 1970, but total drug distribution was up some 60% over 1963.[34]

Publicity from du Pont was even less. This company entered drugs to exploit existing R & D capacity, and its initial aim was to achieve "chemical control of viral diseases." Its first product fizzled, however, and in 1969 du Pont purchased an established pharmaceutical concern[35] to help "guide" future research and marketing efforts in drugs.[36]

TWO INDUSTRIES

With 50 top firms accounting for 90% of shipments and at least 740 dividing the remaining 10% (Exhibit 7), not all makers of pharmaceuticals conducted their business alike. Wide variations existed in the way firms handled R & D, production, and marketing, to say nothing of opportunities abroad or possible diversification. Under these circumstances, larger firms and their spokesmen in the PMA argued that ethical pharmaceuticals ought to be regarded as two industries, not one. Based on the salient difference between them, these might be called the "brand-name" and the "generic" industries. According to the president of the PMA, "It is not an exaggeration to say that much of the misunderstanding that exists with respect to the drug industry arises from the failure to distinguish between these different types of manufacturers."[37]

Research and development

Research by pharmaceutical firms ranges from none at all through duplication of existing drugs up to molecular modification and beyond to the creation of compounds that are wholly new.

Most companies, including all outside the PMA, fall into the "little or no research" contingent.[38] Even inside the trade association, only 77 of 136 members reported making R & D expenditures in 1965, and of

[33] *Forbes*, October 15, 1964, p. 26; *The Wall Street Journal*, January 19, 1969 and April 25, 1969.

[34] McKesson & Robbins, Annual Reports, 1963 (unpaged); 1964, p. 15. Foremost-McKesson, Annual Report 1970, pp. 11, 30.

[35] Endo Laboratories, with assets of about $21 million. The price was approximately $73 million in stock.

[36] E. I. du Pont de Nemours, Annual Reports, 1964–1971; *The Wall Street Journal*, October 12, 1968; *The New York Times*, October 9, 1969, and U.S. Federal Trade Commission, op. cit., p. 58.

[37] Nelson Hearings, Pt. 4, pp. 1415, 1416.

[38] U.S. Department of Health, Education and Welfare, Task Force on Prescription Drugs, *Second Interim Report,* cited Nelson Hearings, Pt. 9, p. 3771.

these the largest 52 accounted for 98.9% and the largest 13 for 66.9%.[39] By 1970, a somewhat shrunken PMA had only 70 members which reported their R & D expenses.[40]

Although made by relatively few companies, global R & D expenditures by U.S. based pharmaceutical firms were large and fast-growing: $616 million in 1970, up from only $105 million in 1956 (Exhibit 7). For reporting PMA members, domestic R & D totaled $558.6 million, of which 62% was for development, 25% was for applied research, and 13% was for basic research (down from 17.9% in 1967).[41] Individual company expenditures ranged up to 11% of sales for Syntex and to $70.5 million for Merck (Exhibit 7).

Defining pharmaceutical R & D the PMA stated that it included "any scientific or technical activity that could result in a new drug."[42] A more detailed definition itemized the work required to discover or synthesize a new compound, to determine its possible medical impact, and to test its various effects *in vitro*, on animals, and finally, with FDA permission, on humans. Also included in R & D was the cost of producing test quantities.[43]

Defining R & D less broadly than the PMA, government agencies or investigators might knock a few percentage points off the industry's claimed allocation. Nevertheless, all parties agreed that the drug industry spent a higher portion of its own money on R & D than any other.[44]

The results of pharmaceutical R & D show up in new drug introductions, especially in new single chemical entities. These averaged 43.6 a year from 1958 thruogh 1962, but only 16.8 in the next nine years (Exhibit 8). This decline reflected both tougher scientific problems and tougher government requirements for putting a new drug on the market.

When the trend in R & D results is compared with the trend in R & D expenditures, it is clear that costs are high and going up. As one industry witness put it, "Certain trends are alarming. New chemical entities marketed per $100 million of R & D expenditure, for 1959 through 1966, were 32, 22, 21, 11, 6, 6, 7, and 3, respectively. They may rise again to 6 or 8 . . . but more than 6 or 8 are needed."[45]

Besides being costly, drug research, according to the PMA, is both risky and time consuming:

> Only one out of about 6,000 compounds tested by drug companies turns out to be a marketable product, and even then it can reach the market only after years of animal and clinical testing. In addition, a

[39] Nelson Hearings, Pt. 4, p. 2329.

[40] PMA *Year Book,* 1970–1971, p. 83.

[41] PMA *Year Book,* 1967–1968, p. 112, and *Year Book,* 1970–1971, p. 86.

[42] Nelson Hearings, Pt. 6, p. 2350.

[43] Ibid., Pt. 2, pp. 628, 629.

[44] U.S. HEW Task Force on Prescription Drugs, *Final Report* (Washington, D.C.: U.S. Government Printing Office, *GPO,* 1969), p. 7.

[45] Nelson Hearings, Pt. 5, p. 1740.

competitor's new or improved product for treatment of the same disease can appear at any moment to overshadow or make obsolete a profitable product perfected at great cost.[46]

By 1969, getting a new drug to market was alleged to take from five to seven years and to cost $2.5–$4.5 million, counting from the point at which "a compound from a research program demonstrates an interesting spectrum of biological activity."[47]

If U.S. drug firms have so far been willing to spend increasing sums on R & D in spite of rising costs, risks, and delays, the two basic reasons, according to the PMA, have been profits and strong patent protection. These are said to have given the nation "the most dynamic and the most innovative" drug industry in the world. This verdict is supported by pointing to the record of new drug introductions: out of 823 new single chemical entities introduced from 1940 through 1966, 503 originated here, all but 13% from private firms.[48]

Those who take a less euphoric view of U.S. R & D achievements once sought to moderate its claims by pointing to the number of important wonder drugs developed in Europe, without the impetus of strong product patents.[49] More recently, critics of drug R & D have shifted their attention to other issues. For example, how many new single chemical entities represent fresh breakthroughs versus mere molecular modifications? How many molecular modifications represent real improvements versus mere change? And how many drugs, especially older ones, support their therapeutic claims with evidence derived from a sophisticated research design rather than, say, doctors' testimonials? Opinion differs, but statements are not lacking that "most" of the evidence is unfavorable.[50]

Production

Production by firms in pharmaceuticals might range from none at all in the case of sellers buying materials to be bottled or tableted on a contract basis, through the "repacking" of drugs bought from others, to production of chemicals, vehicles, and coatings and their combination into finished pharmaceutical products.

As suggested by the fact that most drugs had more sellers than makers, even large companies might be dependent on outside sources for a large proportion of their drugs. For example, among the 15 major

---

[46] Joseph D. Cooper (Ed.), *The Economics of Drug Innovation* (Washington, D.C.: The American University Center for the Study of Private Enterprise, 1970), pp. 116, 117.

[47] Nelson Hearings, Pt. 4, p. 1420. See also Raymond A. Bauer and M. G. Field, "Ironic Contrast: U.S. and USSR Drug Industries," *Harvard Business Review*, September–October 1962, pp. 89–97.

[48] Kefauver Report, pp. 114–126 and 320–333.

[49] For example, two of the highest-volume potent tranquilizers, one of the most important sedatives, and the leading oral anti-diabetic.

[50] Kefauver Report, pp. 126–132; U.S. HEW Task Force on Prescription Drugs, *Final Report*, p. 8; Nelson Hearings, Pt. 5, pp. 1863–1873, 1911–1917, 1961, 1962, 2078–2091, 2113–2120.

pharmaceutical concerns that handled one or more of the 51 high-volume drugs which were featured in the Kefauver study, only six firms produced half as many of these drugs as they sold. Five firms produced a third as many; one firm sold 20 while producing only one.[51] Notwithstanding the extent to which even large firms purchased a chief ingredient outside, "value added by manufacture" was exceptionally high in this industry, however: from 1958 through 1970 it ranged from 73% to 80%.[52]

The grinding and mixing, tableting and coating or bottling procedures required to turn bulk medicinals into pharmaceuticals were said to be relatively low-cost and simple. Testifying in 1967, one economist spoke of "the simple technology of most finished dosage forms, the low operating costs of these processes, and the modest capital requirements for such facilities." Even if a pharmaceutical company was integrated backward into making at least some of its own bulk medicinals, this same economist, writing in 1962, declared that investment requirements were small and economies of scale insignificant.[53]

Both an asset breakdown for the drug industry (Exhibit 1) and drug production costs were consistent with this view. The latter averaged only 32% of sales in 1958 (Exhibit 3) and perhaps 35% in 1968.[54] Direct factory costs might be considerably lower still. By using bulk-powder price quotations and contract tableting and bottling charges, the Kefauver investigators found that in 1958 or 1959 these costs (except royalties, if any) might be as low as 10% of the price at which some products were sold to wholesalers.[55]

Quality control.   Even if relatively simple to produce, drugs and pharmaceuticals run such risks as contamination by dirt or other drugs, deviant potency, and mislabeling. Accordingly, leading pharmaceutical firms emphasize the money spent on quality control: in 1965 PMA members with sales above $1 million averaged 2.4% of sales for this purpose, the peak being 7.5%.[56] In 1969 all PMA members spent a total of $120.8 million and employed the full-time equivalent of 8,950 people on quality control.[57]

One large producer, claiming that it made 808 checks on a single product, added through its spokesman, "I cannot conceive that everyone in the business has the extensive standards and practices that we have."[58] The implication here that smaller, weaker makers concentrating

[51] Kefauver Report, pp. 67, 68.

[52] U.S. Bureau of the Census, "Industry Profiles," *Annual Survey of Manufactures,* 1970, p. 118.

[53] Nelson Hearings, Pt. 5, p. 1952.

[54] U.S. HEW Task Force on Prescription Drugs, *The Drug Makers and the Drug Distributors* (Washington, D.C.: U.S. Government Printing Office, 1968), p. 14. The estimates for 1968 were not for drug operations only, but covered 17 diversified and specialized firms. Other estimated costs were marketing and G & A, 35%; R & D, 6.5%; taxes, 10% and profit, 13.5%.

[55] Kefauver Report, pp. 15–25.

[56] Nelson Hearings, Pt. 6, pp. 2311, 2312.

[57] PMA *Year Book* 1969–1970, p. 89.

[58] Nelson Hearings, Pt. 3, p. 989.

on generic-name drugs might be neglecting quality control was widely and explicitly repeated. This charge was also hotly denied, not just by the producers that were the target of it, but also by large buyers of generics, some elements in pharmacy and medicine, and politicians anxious to see the drug industry grow more competitive and its products cheaper.

As one way to settle this disagreement over relative quality control, disputants have tried to use evidence available from the FDA, namely, its annual record of drug recalls and a special study of drug potency, published in 1966. Generic makers were delighted when the latter unearthed a higher portion of violations in the brand-name samples tested than in their own: 8.8% to 7.8%. Fighting back, major companies called the design of the study into question and successfully challenged some of its results. After months of dispute, the then Commissioner of the FDA, Dr. James L. Goddard, said that while he still stood behind the potency study, it had not been presented as "statistically significant" or "representative of the market place."[59]

Summing up on the quality issue in 1967, Commissioner Goddard said that "the drug industry—large companies as well as small—has much to do before we can conclude that the drug supply is what the nation deserves." Pointing to a rising number of drug recalls, he said these indicated "two basic problems:" first, that not all drugs on the market were of the "highest quality," and second, that the FDA itself was not "properly tooled up to monitor the drug supply." He hoped that continued work with the industry on official "Standards of Good Manufacturing Practice" would help with the first of these problems, and that a new automated testing facility would help with the second.[60] In any event, recalls continued to rise, after as well as before this speech:

Numbers of Drug Recalls*

1965	340	1969	709
1967	651	1970	927

* U.S. HEW *Annual Report*, 1970 (Washington, D.C.: U.S. Government Printing Office, 1971), pp. 273, 274.

Equivalence. Amid disputes evoked by their long-standing claim to more reliable quality control, large innovative firms in the 1960s initiated a new campaign designed to show that they made pharmaceuticals more carefully than their smaller rivals. This time they argued that off-brands and generics might not be "equivalent" to established versions of the selfsame drug in their therapeutic effect, even though the "me-too" version might conform to all official specifications and pass all standard tests for purity and safety. Elaborating, a brand-name spokesman said that standards might permit at least some variations in such factors as vehicle, coating, or grain-size, and that these might alter absorption of the drug into the patient's system. Also, standard

[59] Ibid., Pt. 2, pp. 475–486; 792–794.
[60] Ibid., pp. 791–796.

tests might not be designed to reveal such factors as pill-to-pill variation in strength, or possibly even subtle differences in molecular structure.[61]

Because these charges were aired, early on, in the *Reader's Digest*, and because the examples by which they were supported failed to stand up upon analysis, they earned the brand-name faction much ill will. This came from all its usual critics, plus those elements in pharmacy whose perogative it was to design official tests and standards for drugs. By 1969, however, some two dozen drugs had been found where nonequivalence really was a problem, one of these a high-volume antibiotic. Thus, after a "decade of debate" the brand-name faction could point with pride to statements supporting its point of view in the influential *Journal of the American Medical Association* (JAMA).[62] And the Final Report of the government Task Force studying prescription drugs for oldsters did not deny the problem altogether, though calling it "grossly exaggerated as a major hazard to public health."[63] The FDA agreed to test for nonequivalence on a selective basis, but said this program might take five years.[64]

MARKETING

Marketing in ethical pharmaceuticals ranges from sending a catalog and order blank to pharmacists,[65] up through elaborate programs designed to build a franchise, not just with middlemen but still more with doctors. In this connection, it should be noted that a doctor's prescription dictates not only what drug his patient will get, but also what brand or version of that drug. This result is achieved by antisubstitution laws in 49 states, most of them passed 1954–1959.[66]

Elements in the marketing mix, nearly all of them controversial, include company policies on brand names, budgets, detail men or salesmen, advertising and other promotion, service activities, geographic coverage, distribution channels, retailer relations, and price.

Brand names

While even large companies sell some common drugs as generics, the majors pursue a brand-name strategy, particularly though not exclusively for high-volume items and "specialties" with patent or license protection. Brand names have been called the "crux of the marketing system."[67] A financial service tells why:

> . . . Once the trade-named product has won wide acceptance by physicians, it is difficult to supplant. Thus, it may stubbornly hold its market

[61] Nelson Hearings, Pt. 6, pp. 2229–2239.

[62] PMA, *Brands, Generics, Prices and Quality: The Prescribing Debate After a Decade* (Washington, D.C.: PMA, 1971), pp. 96, 97.

[63] U.S. HEW Task Force on Prescription Drugs, *Final Report*, p. 31.

[64] PMA, op. cit., p. 41.

[65] Bernard G. Keller, Jr. and M. C. Smith (eds.), *Pharmaceutical Marketing* (Baltimore: The Williams and Wilkins Co., 1969), p. 144.

[66] Ibid.

[67] Standard & Poor's Corporation, "Drugs, Medical Care, and Cosmetics, Basic Analysis," *Trade and Securities*, May 8, 1969, p. D–12.

share, despite subsequent development of more advanced competitive products or increased competition following expiration of the patent.[68]

Under these circumstances, expiration of a patent on a brand-name drug poses a problem to any supplier, large as well as small, planning to enter the newly opened market. Should he try to promote a Johnny-come-lately brand name of his own, or try to devise some other way to sell? With patents expiring on hundreds of early postwar wonder drugs starting in the later 1960s, this was not an academic question. Accordingly, the news spread quickly when one of the middle-ranking majors pioneered a new product-market approach, namely, the so-called "branded generic," priced about 25% below its major brand-name competition:

> The move to branded generics was led by Smith, Kline & French, a major drug house, which has had difficulty in recent years in coming up with significant new entities. To counter this lack . . . the company launched a line of eight well-known generic drugs under the *SK-Line* brand name . . . . Other drug companies . . . have marketed branded generics recently and the trend is likely to widen.[69]

The introduction of branded generics was believed to be at least one factor in a growing trend toward generic prescribing. From 6.4% of all new prescriptions in 1966, this rose to about 9.0% in 1969 and 1970.[70] Although it was too early to predict, some analysts believed this trend would level off at about 10%.[71] In any event, generic prescriptions were not a true measure of generic sales. As pointed out in a 1967 Congressional hearing, the druggist tends to fill generic prescriptions with a brand-name drug in about half the cases.[72]

Marketing budgets and expenditures

For large companies with high-volume sales of brand-name specialties, marketing costs run high: almost 25% of sales was the average for 22 major sellers in 1958, and 15%–35% of sales was the range for major sellers volunteering data 10 years later.[73] (It should be noted that only the first of these figures is based on drug operations only, and that even this covers proprietary drugs as well as ethicals. Proprietaries drive the figure up, inasmuch as their marketing costs are unlikely to run under 35%.)[74]

Since ethical drugs are, or should be, necessities of life, questions have been raised from both a social and a business point of view as to

---

[68] Ibid., p. D–10.

[69] Standard & Poor's Corporation, "Health Care, Drugs and Cosmetics, Basic Analysis," *Trade and Securities*, June 24, 1971, p. H–14.

[70] PMA, op. cit., p. 9.

[71] Standard & Poor's, op. cit., p. H–14.

[72] U.S. Senate, Subcommittee on Antitrust and Monopoly of the Committee on the Judiciary, *The Medical Restraint of Trade Act, Hearings*, Pt. 1, p. 494, 90 Cong. (Washington, D.C.: U.S. Government Printing Office, 1967.)

[73] U.S. HEW Task Force on Prescription Drugs, op. cit., p. 9.

[74] *Drug & Cosmetic Industry*, June 1968, pp. 51, 52.

why they should cost so much to sell. These questions demand a look at how the marketing budget is spent.

Detail men.   By far the largest single marketing cost for ethical drugs is the cost of detail men, or missionary salesmen. Of these, the industry reportedly had about 20,000 by 1967[75]—a figure still cited in 1969.[76] At an estimated average annual outlay of some $16,500 each for salary, expenses, recruitment, and training, detail men in the latter year cost the industry some $330 million, according to one consultant's figures.[77] Their services included calling on druggists and dispensaries, and, above all, calling on doctors with news of their company's specialty drugs. This activity, the industry asserted, served not only a promotional but also an educational function. This contention was borne out by a number of studies (1954–1966), which showed that up to 65% of doctors cited detail men as their major single source of new drug information.[78]

Whether detail men would play as large a role in the future as in the past might depend on trends, not only in the drug industry itself, but also in delivery of medical care. Owing to the fast rising costs[79] of care and to the rising work-load on doctors, some analysts predicted that the independent solo physicians would increasingly give way to group practice and to medical care delivered on an out-patient basis by hospital dispensaries, factory medical offices, etc. Within this context, was it a meaningful straw-in-the-wind when late in 1970 Smith Kline & French (the same company that shortly pioneered brand-name generics), reduced its detail force by 18%, in the wake of a general cost-cutting program?[80]

Advertising, etc.   Besides detail men, major ethical companies use many promotional methods: direct mail, free product samples to doctors, displays and hospitality at conventions, symposiums and research grants, gifts of equipment to graduating medical students (recently returned by some recipients), and advertising in medical journals. Some 200 of the latter were in circulation in 1969, "most" of them distributed free and thus dependent on advertising income. Of this, the drug industry provided an estimated $120 million.[81]

Next to drug products themselves, advertising is one of the most regulated aspects of the drug industry, and has been since the passage of the Drug Act Amendments of 1962. In the wake of the "thalidomide disaster"[82] the President of the United States himself asked Congress to

[75] Nelson Hearings, Pt. 9, p. 3782.

[76] U.S. HEW Task Force on Prescription Drugs, op. cit., p. 10.

[77] *Drug & Cosmetic Industry*, October 1971, p. 43.

[78] Kefauver Report, p. 190; Nelson Hearings, Pt. 11, p. 4346.

[79] U.S. Bureau of the Census, *Statistical Abstract of the United States*, 1971, p. 339. From 1963 to 1970, the consumer's price index for medical care rose from 85.6 to 120.6 compared with a rise from 91.7 to 116.3 for the index as a whole (1967 = 100).

[80] *The Wall Street Journal*, January 22, 1970 and October 26, 1970.

[81] *Drug & Cosmetic Industry*, October 1971, p. 42.

[82] Sold in many countries under numerous trade names, thalidomide sleeping pills were later held responsible for thousands of crippling fetal abnormalities. Resisting heavy pressure from the U.S. licensee (and some pressure from her own superiors), Dr. Frances Kelsey of the FDA had refused to clear the drug for the

make sure that "promotional material tells the full story about the drug—its possible bad effects as well as the good—and the whole truth about its therapeutic usefulness.[83] This was enough to tip the scales against the industry's plea that labeling,[84] not advertising, was the only proper place for negative comment. Accordingly, since 1963 drug advertisements have been scanned by the FDA with an eye to seeing that they balance the message on claims, if any, with data on side effects and contraindications. No use other than those approved by the FDA can be implied for the drug, and the generic name has to be mentioned in letters at least half as large as the trade name.[85]

Although the FDA had only 10 men to police advertising, agency spokesmen said in 1967 and 1968 that its quality seemed to be improving.[86] To secure compliance, the agency could resort to sanctions. Thus, it could demand correction of misleading statements through a "Dear Doctor" letter to each of the nation's some 300,000 practicing physicians, or through the more novel and recent approach of insisting on a "remedial ad." The ultimate sanctions were forcible seizure of a mislabeled drug and the threat of criminal prosecution.[87]

Despite the control to which it was subjected, drug advertising was seen as effective, even as sometimes too effective. Thus, critics blamed promotion in part for alleged over-prescribing. "I will have to stick my neck out here," said one clinical pharmacist testifying in 1967, "but I would say that out of every $10 spent on drugs, $6 are unnecessarily spent."[88] Critics also blamed promotion when sales of relatively dangerous drugs bounced back after a scare and reached a volume that could only indicate their use, or misuse, for trivial diseases. For this, of course, doctors had to bear the major onus. In the words of the Task Force, "Very few practicing physicians seem inclined to voice any question of their competency in this field of therapeutic judgments," yet this competency was "a matter of serious concern to leading clinicians, scientists, and medical educators."[89]

Coverage and service

Service in the drug industry might include developing and stocking drugs for rare diseases; supplying small, inaccessible markets; or producing specialties in low- as well as high-volume dosage forms and strengths. One large company testified as follows on service as an element in competition:

U.S. market. Even so, under then-existing regulations, the licensee had been able to distribute "investigational" supplies of the pill to some 1,200 U.S. doctors.

[83] Nelson Hearings, Pt. 9, pp. 3557–3563; Pt. 11, p. 4324. U.S. House of Representatives Subcommittee on Intergovernmental Relations of the Committee on Government Operations, *Drug Safety, Hearings*, Pt. 5, pp. 1995–2004. These hearings were held 1964–1966 (88, 89 Cong.) and are hereafter referred to as the Fountain Hearings, for their Chairman, Representative L. H. Fountain.

[84] Labeling, or descriptive package inserts, had to accompany every package of the drug—at least as far as the corner drug store.

[85] Ibid.

[86] Nelson Hearings, Pt. 8, p. 750.

[87] Ibid., and *Time*, September 25, 1972, p. 50.

[88] Nelson Hearings, Pt. 2, pp. 838–841.

[89] U.S. HEW Task Force on Prescription Drugs, *Final Report*, p. 22.

Lilly places its broad line of products within the reach of patients everywhere in the United States. The company strives to have its products stocked in all of the more than 50,000 retail pharmacies and 9,000 hospitals scattered throughout the country. Several hundred wholesale drug distributors are utilized to provide complete regional depots for speedy delivery to point of need.

* * * * *

Furthermore, constant attention is given by Lilly salesmen to assuring that stocks of Lilly products in wholesale houses, neighborhood pharmacies, and hospitals are adequate. This, of course, involves a system for replacement of any Lilly products that are damaged or outdated. Incidentally, last year the value of merchandise returned to us was $7.5 million. . . .

Leading pharmaceutical companies provide such full distribution service, but there are many firms that elect not to do so.[90]

Channels and retailer relations

In distributing drugs, manufacturers have a choice of wholesaling or selling direct. Whereas in 1954 wholesalers did 59% of the business,[91] they had slipped to 47.8% by 1964 and to 46.9% by 1970.[92] In 1967 the largest manufacturers used wholesalers for just under 40% of their sales; other groups for 50% to 70% (Exhibit 9).

Besides wholesalers, factory sales went mainly to retailers (29.0% in 1970), private hospitals (13.6%) and governments (7.9%). Dispensing physicians, repackers and others made up the small remainder of the market (2.6%), although physicians were a controversial outlet that the smallest makers regarded as well worth fighting to hold.

Counting what retailers bought from producers plus what they bought from wholesalers, retailers handled some 70% of ethical pharmaceutical volume.[93] Among retailers, drugstores were the dominant force, their share of this particular line having been but little eroded by such outlets as department stores, discounters, mail-order houses, or others:

BREAKDOWN OF CONSUMER SPENDING ON PHARMACEUTICALS
IN RETAIL OUTLETS*

	Drug store sales to total store sales		Share of drug store gross	
	1963	1970	1963	1970
Prescriptions	97%	90%	28.90%	34.88%
Packaged Medications	65	65	13.96	12.99

* "Annual Consumer Expenditure Studies," *Drug Trade News,* 1971.

[90] Nelson Hearings, Pt. 3, pp. 996, 997.
[91] Foremost-McKesson, *Annual Report,* 1972, p. 8.
[92] PMA *Year Book,* 1965–1966, p. 180; 1970–1971, p. 80.
[93] U.S. Bureau of the Census, *Census of Business* 1963, Vol. IV, Pt. I, Table 1, p. 4–1; 1967, Vol. III, Table 1, p. 4–1. Assumes about 85% of sales through merchant wholesalers and merchandise agents and brokers pass to retail stores, an estimate in line with *Census of Business* figures for 1967.

With prescriptions accounting for a large and growing share of drug store sales, druggists had fought, and fought successfully, to protect this business through special legislation. Thus (1), only a registered pharmacist could dispense prescription drugs—even though the growth of ready-packaged products had reduced his drug-compounding function from "most" pharmaceuticals to only 5%.[94] Also (2), from the start of state and federal fair-trade laws in 1931 to their widespread erosion by 1959,[95] no affected retailer could legally sell branded drugs for less than the maker's authorized price. In addition (3), many states were persuaded to pass laws forbidding druggists to advertise or post prescription prices. This prohibition came to be a prime target of reformers. Its deadening effect on retail competition was confirmed by several surveys, including one for the AMA in 1967. This showed that charges for identical prescriptions varied from one drug store to another by at least 100% and by as much as 1,200%.[96]

Successful as druggists had been in getting protective legislation, they had not been so successful in persuading the producers to modify some of their distasteful practices. These included selling to hospitals at "substantially" lower prices than to stores; supplying doctors with numerous free samples; selling to dispensing physicians at a discount; complicating druggists' inventory problems by multiplying drugs, brands, and dosage forms; and supporting (at least briefly) the proposal to eliminate state laws against publishing prescription prices.

Based on so many causes of ill will, the American Pharmaceutical Association (APhA) proved willing, in the words of the PMA, to throw the brand-name "industry" to the "Congressional wolves."[97] Not only did the APhA air druggists' grievances to Congress, it also came out in favor of low-priced generic-name prescribing. In a related move, the druggist would protect his own net income by switching from a mark-up to a fixed professional fee. About $2.00 per prescription would, it was figured in 1966, enable the druggist with an "average" volume to earn just as much one way as the other.[98] Contemplating this new pricing plan, which several groups in pharmacy were said to favor, a spokesman for the APhA predicted that the "brand name era" was coming to an end in prescription drugs and that the pharmacist "would have no regrets."[99]

Under this attack, the PMA was conciliatory. Not so some outside observers. These were quick to point to the druggists' contribution to high drug prices. They also pointed out that the druggists' own future looked more cloudy in some crystal balls than that of the major drug

---

[94] Nelson Hearings, Pt. 9, p. 3800.

[95] Clair Wilcox, *Public Policy Toward Business* (2d Ed., Homewood, Ill.: Richard D. Irwin, Inc., 1966), pp. 379, 380. Druggists were, in fact, the spearhead of the "fair-trade" drive. Not only did the National Association of Retail Druggists (NARDA) help to push these laws through 41 state legislatures, it also drafted the wording of the model statute on which more than half of these laws were based.

[96] *Advertising Age*, November 20, 1967, p. 16.

[97] Nelson Hearings, Pt. 4, p. 1277.

[98] Ibid., p. 1298.

[99] Ibid., pp. 1290–1293.

manufacturers. This point raised a storm when made in an impolitic statement by the FDA's Commissioner Goddard:

> Suggesting that within about 20 years prescription drugs will probably be dispensed primarily in medical centers and in doctors' offices, [Goddard] concluded with a slight exaggeration: "I would say that the corner drugstore should be closed down."
>
> First to respond was the NARDA, a potent lobbying force with 40,000 members which immediately called for the Commissioner's resignation. . . .
>
> Long ago [however] many drug marketing and packaging experts suggested that the extension of hospital drug dispensing for more and more patients, the trend toward "third party" payments of prescription prices, and the possibility of medical centers and even doctors' offices routinely dispensing drugs all are inevitable. If these factors are related to the rising percentage of proprietary sales in supermarkets and discount stores, the slightly overstated Goddard conclusion becomes undeniable. Unless the drugstore quickly "catches up" to the latter third of the 20th Century . . . the soothsayers may have the last laugh.[100]

Price

Widely as the brand-name and the generic "industries" differed in most aspects of marketing, their most publicized difference was in price. On a given drug, the listed wholesale price of the leading brand was often two to four times as high as the lowest generic-name price, and was sometimes twenty times as high or even higher.[101] Except on "drugs of choice" protected by a patent or license, however, the listed price might be misleading. According to the previously cited Task Force, listed prices are mostly maximums. "They serve merely as an umbrella beneath which actual prices are set by quantity discounts, hospital discounts, government discounts, two-for-the-price-of-one deals, rebates, and other special arrangements."[102]

Besides pricing high when conditions allowed it, brand-name makers were seen as following other controversial policies on price, such as pricing high for a quick return on their newest drugs, and pricing drugs made or sold abroad at much less than the U.S. price in some markets. At the time of the Kefauver investigation, evidence was brought forward that brand-name makers had also (1) maintained some prices unchanged for several years, (2) engaged in price leadership and followership, and (3) posted the same effective price on different drugs designed to treat the same disease. At the time of the Nelson investigation about a decade later, these three charges were not repeated. Senator Nelson rather focused on how and why one established seller of a drug could keep the price on his brand high when other, equally well-known sellers were offering their brands at a fraction of this price.

Contemplating not so much drug price policies as drug price trends, the PMA voiced pride in the fact that drugs were among the few com-

---

[100] *Drug & Cosmetic Industry*, February 2, 1968, p. 27.

[101] Richard Burak, *The New Handbook of Prescription Drugs* (New York: Ballantine Books, Inc., 1970), pp. 285–323. *Drug Topics Red Book* (annual).

[102] U.S. HEW Task Force on Prescription Drugs, *Final Report*, p. 11.

modities on which consumer prices were going down, according to the Bureau of Labor Statistics (BLS). Critics acknowledged this decline, but retorted that the BLS, in the interest of continuity, tracked mainly older drugs, on which falling prices flowed from waning market interest. To measure price trends on whatever drugs were currently selling, critics called attention to an index that reflected annual average prescription prices:

PRICE INDICES (1961 = 100)[103]

	1963	1970
BLS consumer price index, prescription subsection............	93.8	104.3
Lilly Digest, average prescription charge.....................	89.9	124.9

Confronted by such figures, the industry could still reply that the biggest cost of illness was hospital and doctor's charges, plus days lost from work. Insofar as they cut down the length and severity of an illness, drugs were a plus for the patient's pocketbook.

REGULATION

In spite of criticism leveled at competitive practices in drugs, regulation of the industry was little oriented toward economic goals, but rather toward health and safety. The first federal law in this area, passed in 1906, prohibited only misbranding and adulteration. Decades later, four stronger laws were passed, each in the wake of a major disaster. Thus, 100 deaths from a "sulfa elixir" led to passage of the Food, Drug, and Cosmetic Act of 1938. The tragedy of thalidomide preceded the Drug Act Amendments of 1962, and spreading drug addiction led to the Drug Abuse Control Amendments of 1965 and 1970.

Dominating all other laws in importance was the Act passed in 1962. According to the then-Commissioner of the FDA, Mr. George P. Larrick, this Act not only gave the FDA more teeth but plugged 10 "loopholes" in existing law, as follows:

(1) The producer of a new drug did not [previously] have to establish that his drug would be effective, as well as safe, for its intended uses.

(2) We were forced to work against deadlines of 60 and 180 days to prevent the automatic approval of the new drug.

(3) There was no provision requiring regular record keeping and reporting of clinical and other experience, good or bad, with the new drugs.

(4) We could not remove a new drug from the market unless we could prove that it was unsafe; it was not enough to show that new developments had drawn the question of its safety sharply into issue.

(5) There were inadequate controls over the distribution and use of investigational drugs, as the thalidomide episode clearly showed.

---

[103] Eli Lilly & Co., Lilly Digest, 1971, p. 25.

(6) Prescription drug advertising, at an estimated expenditure of a quarter of a billion dollars per year—$1,000 for each physician in the United States—was virtually unregulated.

(7) Trade names were being used without proper relationship to generic names, with resulting confusion to the profession.[104]

(8) The quality of "old drugs" was not assured, as it was with the "new drugs."

(9) Only five of the classes of antibiotic drugs—used to treat life-threatening infections—were subject to routine batch testing and certification by our laboratories.

(10) And factory inspection authority was so limited as to seriously handicap our operations.[105]

Although some of these provisions were supported by liberal drug companies,[106] disputes multiplied as the FDA moved into implementation. For example, as the advertising rules were being developed, the PMA, backed by the AMA, unsuccessfully challenged the agency's right to review any portion of an ad except for a special boxed-in section which supplied the mandatory "balance" in the message.[107]

Many additional conflicts resulted from the "efficacy review" of older drugs required by the Act and applied in the case of those introduced during 1938–1962.[108] One PMA suit would have nullified this provision altogether on the grounds that all existing drugs had a right to the protection of a "grandfather clause," not just those predating 1938. Another suit would have kept the FDA from demanding to see the research studies on which drug efficacy claims were based, and another would have overruled the FDA's contention that "doctors' testimonials" and "market acceptance" did not qualify as "substantial evidence" of effectiveness, since the Act specified that such evidence must be based on "well-controlled clinical investigation." When a major court decision[109] ruled against the industry view, the PMA unsuccessfully sued to force the FDA to hold a separate, time-consuming hearing on each drug charged with ineffectiveness before its removal from the market could be ordered.[110]

---

[104] Among the changes made by the Act, only (7) and (10) aimed directly at economic goals, their objective being to make doctors both more aware of and more confident in generics.

[105] Fountain Hearings, Pt. 1, pp. 22, 23.

[106] Led by Merck and Lilly, this faction prevailed on the PMA not to oppose the Act in its entirety.

[107] Richard Harris, *The Real Voice* (New York: Macmillan Co., 1964), pp. 142–144; Fountain Hearings, Pt. 5, pp. 1995–2004.

[108] *The Wall Street Journal*, February 18, 1971, and May 3, 1971. More than 2,800 prescription and over-the-counter drugs were involved in this review, which took almost three years (1966–1969) and was conducted for the FDA by expert panels under the joint auspices of the National Academy of Science and the National Research Council (NAS-NRC).

[109] This case involved Upjohn's Panalba, a "top 200" combination antibiotic with a volume of about $30 million. This product was "regularly prescribed" by about 23,000 doctors, many of them active in its defense.

[110] U.S. HEW, *Annual Report*, 1970, pp. 248–250.

Besides its efforts on behalf of drugs classed as "ineffective," the PMA sought with more success to help the much larger numbers classed as only "possibly" or "probably" effective.[111] Like most of the "ineffective" category, many of these were "fixed combinations."[112] As such, they were under a cloud because their active ingredients could not be "tailored" to each patient's needs. Yet combinations were commercially important: they made up about 50% of all products on the market in 1971, and 40% of the top 200. Under these conditions, the industry was much relieved when the FDA, reversing an earlier stand, dropped its demand for further studies of the "probably" effective group. And even on the "possibly" effective group, the evidence requirements were reduced in the wake of some political pressure exerted by the industry with the aid of doctors.[113] Summing up late in 1971, a spokesman for the PMA said, "We won the fight on combination drugs. The final guidelines were quite reasonable."[114]

Looking ahead at this same time, another spokesman for the PMA said the industry was not worried about new legislative curbs. Seen as "far reaching" but "unlikely to pass" was the bill introduced by Senator Nelson, in the wake of his four-year hearings. Key provisions called for (1) the strengthening of rules on labeling and certification; (2) the transfer of drug testing from private hands to a national center,[115] on the grounds that testing was poorly policed by the FDA and too often poorly controlled; (3) the compilation of a drug compendium that would, unlike the one in widest use, give doctors information on price, and (4) the compilation of a list of "recommended" drugs that could be used to restrict reimbursement for oldsters' medications—if and when Medicare should be expanded to cover out-patient drugs.[116]

Given the trend toward third-party payment of medical expenses, the brand-name faction in the drug industry feared that this last widely backed idea might prove a long-lived threat to high-priced products competing with generic, me-too versions. Another feared idea that kept resurfacing was that of compulsory licensing for drugs still under patent protection.

---

[111] Of 2,752 prescription drugs in the study, 1,137 were rated "effective"; 341 "probably effective"; 699 "possibly effective"; 245 "ineffective"; and 330 "effective but." In mid-1971, the FDA roused industry ire by insisting that these ratings be included in both drug labeling and advertising.

[112] Only 45 combination drugs out of some 1,200 reviewed were placed in the "effective" category.

[113] The "tempering" of the FDA's demands was announced by the agency to the House Commerce Committee, newly come to the field of drug investigation and friendly to the industry. Feeling infringed upon and upstaged, long-time industry critics on the House Committee of Government Operations then scheduled hearings on the FDA for alleged lax control of drug advertising and lax policing of the ban on cyclamates.

[114] *The Wall Street Journal*, April 30, May 3, May 5, May 27, 1971; *The New York Times*, June 8, 1971; *The National Journal*, November 12, 1971, p. 2455.

[115] The impetus was a *Times* exposé, "Prison Drug and Plasma Project Leaves Fatal Trail."

[116] *National Journal*, loc. cit.; *The New York Times*, July 29, 30, August 13, 1969.

DIVERSIFICATION AND FOREIGN OPERATIONS

Whereas small companies in drugs might be only local with a narrow product line, large ones tended to be both international and diversified (Exhibit 2). By 1968, leading companies made a fifth to a third of their sales abroad, while an early entrant (Pfizer) made almost half. Favorite diversifications at home, apart from the three drug sub-industries, were cosmetics, food and household products, hospital supplies, chemicals, and laboratory services.[117]

Interestingly, these outside activities did not escape Congressional attention, even when they lay beyond Congressional control. Congress wanted to know whether drugs were more profitable than other lines, and also whether the rules of the drug game differed according to where it was played. Besides trying to get at the facts, Congress wanted to raise the question of how any differences were justified.

PROSPECTS

As a glamor industry, drugs were closely watched by Wall Street. Despite their strong relative showing, their absolute showing was drifting down:

RANGE OF QUARTERLY PRETAX PROFIT ON DRUGS*

Year	Profit on sales	Profit on stock-holders' investment
1963	18.4%–21.5%	29.3%–36.1%
1967	17.3 –19.7	31.6 –35.9
1971	16.1 –17.5	30.0 –32.9

* U.S. FTC and SEC, *Quarterly Financial Reports.*

Looking back, analysts could find several explanations for this trend. Looking ahead, they expected percentages to slip further, but saw the drop as limited by rising demand. True, a threat might possibly be posed by critics who had long bombarded the public with claims that drugs must be lower-priced and safer.[118] But how far would this goal get translated into action? Judging from their forecasts, drug-stock analysts, at any rate, predicted no climactic change.

[117] *The New York Times*, July 7, 1968.
[118] See "A Note on the U.S. Prescription Drug Industry—Part II," (p. 615).

Exhibit 1

A NOTE ON THE U.S. PRESCRIPTION DRUG INDUSTRY—PART I

Financial Statements in Ratio Form, Fourth Quarter, 1971

	All manufacturing	*Drugs*
INCOME		
Net sales	100.0%	100.0%
Cost, expenses	92.8	82.7
Net operating profit	7.2	17.3
Other income (expenses)	(0.3)	0.2
Federal income tax	2.8	7.2
Net profit	4.1	10.3
ASSETS		
Cash, U.S. Government securities	5.9	12.2
Receivables (net)	17.1	19.9
Inventories	22.1	22.8
Other current assets	3.7	3.5
Total current assets	48.9	58.4
Property, plant, equipment (net)	39.9	32.8
Other noncurrent assets	11.3	8.9
Total assets	100.0	100.0
LIABILITIES AND STOCKHOLDERS' INCOME†		
Total current liabilities	24.1	23.9
Long-term debt	18.3	9.1
Other noncurrent liabilities	4.2	3.2
Total liabilities	46.5	36.2
Stockholders' equity	53.5	63.8
Total	100.0	100.0

Note: Failure of columns to add is due to rounding.

* In terms of profit, the fourth was the second-best quarter for both all manufacturing and drugs.

† Ratio of equity to debt, 2.25 for all manufacturing; 4.23 for drugs.

Source: U.S. Federal Trade Commission and U.S. Federal Securities and Exchange Commission, *Quarterly Financial Report for Manufacturing Corporations.*

Exhibit 2

A NOTE ON THE U.S. PRESCRIPTION DRUG INDUSTRY—PART I
U.S.* Pharmaceutical Companies in FORTUNE's Top 500 Industrials, 1971
(dollars in millions)

1971 rank	Company	Sales	Net income	Net income/ sales	Net income/ stockholders' equity	Average annual growth, compounded 1961–1971	Drug sales/ total sales	Foreign sales/total sales
252	Abbott Laboratories	$ 458.1	$ 23.4	5.1%	8.7%	5.41%	37%	32%
83	American Home Products	1,429.3	160.0	11.2	26.7	10.83	52	25
419	Baxter Laboratories	242.1	18.2	7.5	10.8	19.44	41	25
118	Bristol-Myers	1,066.4	75.8	7.1	17.8	14.73	27	15
113	Johnson & Johnson	1,140.5	101.8	8.9	16.4	19.36	20	31
172	Eli Lilly	723.4	96.1	13.3	18.7	14.71	66 (human use)	31
151	Merck & Co.	828.5	127.2	15.3	24.4	15.27	90	40
344	Miles Laboratories	321.8	4.9	1.5	4.6	(3.80)	74 (incl. nutritionals)	23
317	Morton-Norwich	345.6	21.8	6.3	11.6	7.88	25	22
133	Pfizer, Inc.	951.5	90.6	9.5	15.1	8.69	49	49
276	Richardson-Merrell	408.5	29.8	7.3	12.3	5.91	87	42
265	Schering-Plough	436.8	59.2	13.5	21.5	13.98	66	39
301	Smith Kline & French	357.2	44.9	12.6	21.5	5.26	63	24
150	Squibb	830.2	63.5	7.6	14.7	6.12	41 (ethicals)	—
195	Sterling Drug	652.4	63.1	9.7	18.8	9.39	62	37
264	Upjohn	438.4	39.8	9.1	13.5	5.18	66	34
90	Warner-Lambert	1,346.1	108.1	8.0	14.5	9.83	41 (ethicals)	37
	Industry medians:							
	Pharmaceuticals	—	—	9.1	15.1		62	
	All industries	—	—	3.8	9.1			

* Also active in the U.S. pharmaceutical market were three of the top 300 non-U.S. based industrials: Ciba-Geigy (ranking No. 41 in sales, with $1.8 billion); Hoffman-LaRoche (No. 59 with $1.4 billion); and Sandoz (No. 120 with $.7 billion). All three were Swiss; the first and third were substantially diversified.

Source: *Fortune*, May 1972, pp. 188–209 and 222–224; August 1972, pp. 154–158 and 162; *The Value Line Investment Survey*, August 4, 1972, pp. 542–577.

Exhibit 3

A NOTE ON THE U.S. PRESCRIPTION DRUG INDUSTRY—PART I

Percentage Breakdown of the Sales Dollar* for 22 Drug Companies
(drug operations only,† 1958)

Companies Which Have Appeared Before the Subcommittee on Antitrust and Monopoly

	American Cyanamid (Lederle)	American Home (Wyeth, Ayerst)	Bristol Labora- tories	Carter Products	Ciba	Eli Lilly	Merck	Pfizer	Parke, Davis	Schering	S.K.F.	Upjohn
Net profit	15.6	14.7	.9	20.4	12.7	13.3	12.9	10.5	16.0	15.9	17.2	13.7
Taxes	16.2	15.9	6.5	23.4	12.9	13.8	12.8	5.7	15.3	13.4	20.0	14.4
Selling	25.4	24.0	32.3	27.8	33.9	18.1	18.1	26.7	25.2	32.7	19.5	20.9
General and administrative	10.2	14.9	18.0	6.5	7.4	10.5	10.2	7.1	6.1	8.8	10.9	16.6
Research	6.4	3.2	13.7	2.7	13.9‡	8.8	8.0	4.9	4.8	8.2	8.9	8.8
Cost of goods	26.2	27.3	19.6	19.2	19.2	35.4	38.0	45.1	32.6	20.9	23.5	25.6
Total	100.0	100.0	100.0	100.0	100.0	99.9	100.0	100.0	100.0	99.9	100.0	100.0

Companies Which Have Not Appeared Before the Subcommittee

	Abbott	Hoffmann- La Roche	Mead Johnson	Norwich	Olin Mathieson (Squibb)	Searle	Sterling	U.S. Vitamin	Vick	Warner- Lambert	22 Companies
Net profit	11.0	8.7	11.3	11.6	6.8	21.3	10.1	12.2	10.4	13.4	13.0
Taxes	10.1	9.4	12.6	12.0	7.1	21.9	9.6	10.9	10.9	14.4	12.8
Selling	28.4	17.4	29.4	40.5	19.7	19.4	36.7	33.7	25.3	26.3	24.8
General and administrative	10.0	30.0§	14.9	6.6	17.2	7.4	8.3	8.0	7.2	11.8	10.9
Research	5.6	6.9	5.7	4.4	5.4	12.2	3.2	5.1	3.7	5.2	6.3
Cost of goods	34.8	27.5‖	26.1	24.8	43.7	17.8	32.0	30.1	42.4	28.8	32.1
Total	99.9	99.9	100.0	99.9	100.0	100.0	99.9	100.0	99.9	99.9	99.9

Note: Since 1958, Bristol Laboratories has become Bristol-Myers; Carter Products, Carter-Wallace; Ciba, Ciba-Geigy; Schering, Schering-Plough; Norwich, Morton-Norwich; and Vick, Richardson-Merrell. Mead-Johnson, U.S. Vitamin, and Parke-Davis have been acquired, respectively, by Bristol-Myers, Revlon, and Warner-Lambert. Squibb has been spun off and merged with Beechnut Life Savers, Inc., the survivor being renamed Squibb Corporation. A contemplated merger of Abbott and Searle failed to go through.

* Includes royalties and other income.
† Includes ethicals and proprietaries.
‡ Includes expenditures in Switzerland.
§ Includes some amounts which should be carried as "Cost of goods."
‖ Too low, since some items in "general and administrative" should be here.

Source: Reports by drug companies to the Senate Subcommittees of Antitrust and Monopoly of the Committee on the Judiciary, *Report on Administered Prices, Drugs*, 87th Cong., 1st Sess. (1961), p. 31. (The Kefauver Report.)

Exhibit 4

A NOTE ON THE U.S. PRESCRIPTION DRUG INDUSTRY—PART I

Domestic Shipments of Ethical Pharmaceutical Preparations
(Except Biologicals) by Major Category
(dollars in millions)

	1963	1970†	Change
Total domestic shipments........................	$2,055	$3,781	84.0%
For human use,* affecting:			
Neoplasms, endocrine system, metabolic diseases....	262	501	91.2
Central nervous system, sense organs..............	485	1,054	117.3
Cardiovascular system..........................	145	306	111.0
Respiratory system.............................	153	248	62.1
Digestive or genito-urinary system................	283	478	68.9
Skin..	64	117	82.8
Vitamins, nutrients, hematinics..................	206	328	59.2
Parasitic and infective diseases...................	398	663	66.6
For veterinary use................................	53	86	62.3
Not otherwise classified...........................	6	1	(83.3)

* The PMA classification of drugs for human use included 11 subclasses: the eight listed here, plus biologicals, diagnostic agents, and "other."
† Preliminary.
Source: U.S. Bureau of the Census, "Pharmaceutical Preparations, Except Biologicals," *Current Industrial Reports* (annual).

Exhibit 5

A NOTE ON THE U.S. PRESCRIPTION DRUG INDUSTRY—PART I

Market Share Data for Leading Products in 17 out of 137 Product Groupings
Accounting for Approximately 58% of 1965 Prescription Dollar Volume

Product grouping	Number of products in audit	Market share		Share of prescriptions taken by products introduced since 1956
		Top product	Top three products	
Nonnarcotic analgesics........	182	30.0%	49.6%	Over 50%
Nonsteroidal antiarthritics....	48	19.7	52.3	" 44
Antibiotics, broad and medium spectrum..................	84	15.2	30.6	" 40
Antibiotics, penicillins........	89	20.9	50.5	" 43
Antihistamines..............	62	24.0	57.3	" 8
Antiobesity—amphetamines...	80+	20.3	50.3	At least 29
Ataraxics (tranquilizers)*.....	56	30.1	55.3	Over 50
Rauwolfia—diuretic combinations....................	Not given	19.5	53.5	" 100
Coronary vasodilators........	68	22.1	53.5	Over 40
Diabetic therapy, other than insulin....................	8	72.8	93.2	" 100
Diuretics....................	43	24.2	49.1	Nearly 100
Hormones, corticoids........	125	11.9	33.5	Over 60
Corticoids with anti-infectives..	101	12.1	33.3	At least 45
Oral muscle relaxants.........	47	10.5	29.5	" " 58
Psychostimulants............	36	30.2	60.9	" " 66
Sedatives—barbiturate.......	78	16.2	47.6	Not Over 25
Sulfonamides...............	173	24.7	49.4	At least 32

* Excludes tranquilizers for hospital use only.
Source: Derived from an Arthur D. Little study for the PMA of market data in the National Prescription Audit for 1965. Cited Nelson *Hearings*, Part 5, pp. 1785–1805.

Exhibit 6

A NOTE ON THE U.S. PRESCRIPTION DRUG INDUSTRY—PART I

Concentration in Pharmaceuticals

Year	Number of companies	Value of company shipments (millions)	Percent of shipments accounted for by			
			4 largest companies	8 largest companies	20 largest companies	50 largest companies
1954	1,128	$1,643.1	25	44	68	N.A.
1958	1,064	2,533.4	27	45	73	87
1963	944	3,314.3	22	38	72	89
1967	791	4,696.4	24	40	73	90

Note: For 1969, PMA data showed 68.9% of U.S. sales made by 17 companies with sales of $100 million and up, and 18.4% of sales made by companies with sales of $30 to $100 million.
Source: U.S. Bureau of the Census, *Census of Manufactures*, and PMA *Year Book*, 1969–1970, p. 88.

Exhibit 7

A NOTE ON THE U.S. PRESCRIPTION DRUG INDUSTRY—PART I

Global Research and Development Expenditures
of U.S. Based Pharmaceutical Firms
(dollars in millions)

Year	Expenditures	Percent of global sales
1954	$ 78†	5
1958	170†	7
1963	282	6
1967	448	9
1968	485	9
1969	549	9
1970*	616	9

* Preliminary.
† The 1954 and 1958 percentages relate to dosage-form global sales only. The rest of the percentages relate to dosage form plus bulk global sales.

1971 research expenditures
of leading companies

Company	Expenditure	Percent of sales
Abbott	$28.8	6
Baxter	12.5	5
Bristol-Myers	40.0	4
Johnson & Johnson	46.7	4
Lilly	67.5	9
Merck	70.5	8
Morton-Norwich	9.7	3
Pfizer	37.2	4
*Richardson-Merrell	18.0	4
Schering-Plough	25.1	6
Smith Kline & French	35.1	10
†Syntex	11.6	11
Upjohn	45.3	10

* Fiscal year ended June 20.
† Fiscal year ended July 21.

Source: Industry data from PMA *Year Book* 1969–1970, p. 101. Company data from Annual Reports, assembled by Standard & Poor's Corporation, "Health Care, Drugs and Cosmetics, Basic Analysis," *Trade and Securities*, June 24, 1971, p. H–14.

Exhibit 8

A NOTE ON THE U.S. PRESCRIPTION DRUG INDUSTRY—PART I

Pharmaceutical Specialities Introduced in the United States

Period	Number of firms	New single chemicals*	Combination products	Duplicative single products
1953–1957 (avg.)	117	42	261	85
1958–1962 (avg.)	112	45	205	53
1963–1967 (avg.)	67	19	84	28
1968	48	14	51	36
1969	48	11	34	26
1970	60	16	42	52
1971	46	14	30	50

* Includes new salts.
Note: Figures for 1962–1968 are revised.
Source: Paul de Haen in *Drug & Cosmetic Industry*, March 1968, p. 46, and in Standard & Poor's Corporation, "Health Care, Drugs and Cosmetics, Basic Analysis," *Trade and Securities*, June 24, 1971, p. H-14.

Exhibit 9

A NOTE ON THE U.S. PRESCRIPTION DRUG INDUSTRY—PART I

A. Breakdown of Manufacturers' Domestic Sales of Dosage Form Ethicals for Human Use, 1970

Customer class	Percent of total sales
Wholesalers	46.9
Retailers	29.0
Private hospitals	13.6
State and local government hospitals	3.9
Federal government (hospitals and other)	4.0
Practitioners	1.6
Manufacturers, repackagers, and other	1.0
Total	100.0

B. Percentage Distribution of Sales by Size of Firm, 1967

Customer class	Over $100 million	$30–$100 million	$5–$30 million	Under $5 million	Average all firms
Wholesalers	39.2	61.1	70.4	49.8	47.8
Retailers	37.3	13.7	13.5	24.6	29.3
Non-federal hospitals	16.8	18.9	9.1	5.2	15.9
Federal government	4.6	5.3	3.1	1.0	4.5
Practitioners	1.4	0.8	1.5	16.1	1.7
Other	0.7	0.2	2.4	3.3	0.8

Source: *PMA Yearbook*, 1968, p. 106; 1970–1971, p. 80.

A Note on the U.S. Prescription Drug Industry—Part II

LATE in 1959, having investigated what he called "administered prices" in steel, automobiles, and bread, the late Senator Estes Kefauver of the Senate Subcommittee of Antitrust and Monopoly turned his attention to a much smaller industry and one hitherto little studied, namely, drugs. Headline-capturing testimony soon fueled demands for stiffer regulation, and amendments to the existing Drug Act were shortly on their way through Congress—the first major overhaul in this area since 1938. More hearings followed, and from the thousands of pages of testimony taken at that time, critics distilled a serious indictment—to wit, that members of the drug industry, especially large makers of "ethical" drugs, were not adequately discharging their responsibilities to the public.

The essence of this criticism is captured in the following paragraph by Professor Seymour Harris of Harvard:

> Many are concerned that an industry which comes close to being a public utility achieves the highest profits in relation to sales and investment of any industry; is highly concentrated in its control of the market; reveals serious monopolistic trends; increases the cost to consumers by differentiating the product at a dizzy pace, with the differentiated product usually similar to or identical with existing products; and greatly inflates the cost through record expenditures on selling. The competition among companies to overwhelm the doctors by repetitious and often misleading advertising, and a failure to give as much publicity to the bad side effects as to the immediate beneficial effects, are unfortunate. Thus competition forces even highly moral firms to become less ethical in their behavior. In the drug industry the relation of labor to total costs is minimal; and like the soap and tobacco industries, using similar selling techniques, their relation of labor to value added is a minimum—selling expenditures and profits are the large items in gross receipts.
> The cost of drugs is too high. I say this, though I am aware that the

research contributions of the industry are important and that the lives saved, the suffering averted, and the acceleration of recoveries are worth more than the $4 billion spent on drugs. But the cost could be substantially less.[1]

Even after passage of the Drug Act Amendments of 1962, the drug industry continued to be the target for further investigation. In a long series of congressional hearings, the most protracted has been that conducted by Senator Gaylord Nelson on competitive problems of the drug industry. These hearings started in 1968 and did not end until 1970. Senator Nelson gave the industry a new opportunity—or, more accurately, a new challenge—to defend its strategy before the public.

How effectively the industry responded—and how valid its arguments were—can to some extent be judged from the following excerpts from testimony offered by industry spokesmen. Among the witnesses, some were officers in large drug companies, while others were officers in, or were experts selected by, the Pharmaceutical Manufacturers' Association (PMA), a group whose 136 member firms reportedly accounted for 95% of the industry's domestic ethical sales.

Owing to limitations of space, the excerpts presented here are less than complete and thus admittedly may be less than fair.[2] Even so, they convey some "feel" for the kind of confrontation that can take place at congressional hearings, as well as some idea of the major arguments advanced by drug industry critics and defenders.

Like the original testimony, the excerpts spill over from one topic to another. The arguments, however, can be scissored up and arranged around a few big issues:

1. Price, cost, quality, and service relationships for branded and generic drugs.
2. Alleged "control of the market" by a relatively few large firms, and the role of patents and promotion in market control.
3. Drug safety, drug efficacy, and the veracity of drug advertising.
4. The direction of research.
5. Risk in relation to profit.

PRICE, COST, QUALITY, AND SERVICE RELATIONSHIPS FOR BRANDED AND GENERIC DRUGS

Price differentials—brand name and generic drugs (Lilly's "Seconal" versus generic sodium secobarbitals)

Knowing that the brand name—generic price differential was a main ground of attack on the brand name segment of the drug industry, Mr.

---

[1] Cited in Hearings of the U.S. Subcommittee on Monopoly of the Select Committee on Small Business, *Competitive Problems in the Drug Industry* (Washington, D.C.: U.S. Government Printing Office, 1968), p. 1813. Chaired by Senator Gaylord Nelson (D–Wis.), these hearings will be referred to hereafter as the Nelson *Hearings.*

[2] To avoid wearying the reader's eye, only major gaps in the testimony cited have been indicated explicitly.

Henry F. DeBoest, vice president for corporate affairs at Lilly, came prepared to argue that the differential had been overstated:

MR. DEBOEST: It has been stated that there is a great difference in the price which the patient pays for Lilly's brand of sodium secobarbital— Seconal Sodium—and the price of sodium secobarbital marketed by other companies. It has been stated that Lilly charges the pharmacist $18.30 for 1,000 100-mg. capsules of its trademarked product, while another sodium secobarbital product can be purchased for as little as $4.50. It has also been stated that the customer's price would be about $30.50 for Seconal Sodium and $7.50 for the other sodium secobarbital product.

This is not the case. In the first place, Lilly does not sell Seconal Sodium directly to the retail pharmacist at $18.30 but to the wholesale distributor at $15.24; he in turn, sells to the pharmacist.

Much more important, the consumer does not pay four times as much for Seconal Sodium as for the least expensive generic sodium secobarbital. What the consumer actually pays for the Lilly product is only a fraction of a cent more per capsule for assurance of a good night's sleep.

The average retail prescription price in the 12 months ending June 30, 1967, was 6.8 cents per capsule for Seconal Sodium, as compared with 6.3 cents per capsule for generic sodium secobarbital. This information is from the Gosselin National Prescription Audit. The audit shows that, for the average prescription of 28 capsules, an average of $1.89 was charged for Seconal Sodium, 100 mg., while a prescription for sodium secobarbital cost the patient $1.77. Thus, the price differential, 12 cents per prescription, is not four times as great for Seconal Sodium as for the generic sodium secobarbital but only one-half of 1 cent per capsule.

SENATOR NELSON: Let me interrupt there. This was a survey of the retail market, was it not?

MR. DEBOEST: Yes, sir.

SENATOR NELSON: So there is no way for the Gosselin National Prescription Audit survey to determine whether or not the prescription they [the buyer] got was actually the generic product, was there?

MR. DEBOEST: Well, sir, every product on the American market today bears a generic name, accompanying, in certain instances, brand names; and if it was ordered generically, we would assume that it was filled generically.

SENATOR NELSON: This is the point I would like to make right here. That is an assumption for which there is no support or justification. As you know, under the law the drug companies have gone to more than 40 states and gotten a law passed which provides that if the doctor prescribes a brand name drug, the pharmacist may not substitute the generic equivalent, even if the generic equivalent is manufactured by Eli Lilly, or Merck & Co., or Schering. You just cannot substitute.

On the other hand, if the doctor writes a generic name, the pharmacist does not have to fill the prescription with a generic. He can substitute any brand name he wants. What happens time after time after time is that when the generic prescription is written, it is filled with a brand name, probably because the pharmacist is not carrying the generic. He is carrying the brand name which is the one the doctors most often prescribe. So one of the great faults of the surveys that are brought up to prove a point such as this is that the prescription is often not filled with a generic. The druggist simply does not carry it.[3]

---

[3] Nelson *Hearings*, Pt. 3, pp. 965, 966.

Service differentials—brand name and generic drugs (Schering's "Meticorten" versus generic prednisones)

Rather than seeking to minimize brand name—generic price differentials, many industry witnesses attempted to prove that they were justified. Such was the case with Mr. W. H. Conzen, president of Schering:

MR. CONZEN: In your letter to me, you asked that I discuss pricing policies and practices of our brand of prednisone. You said that "striking differences in prices of prednisone among various manufacturers" had been referred to in recent testimony before your subcommittee.[4]

Before I address myself to your specific question, I think it would be helpful if I explained some of the magnitudes involved to establish the relative significance of what we are discussing.

In the first place, the domestic ethical pharmaceutical industry is estimated to have a volume of about $3 billion at the manufacturers' level. The sales volume of all corticosteroid tablets totals approximately $40 million; this not only includes prednisone, but all other corticosteroid tablets. The estimated volume of prednisone tablets is $3 million. Consequently, this product represents one-tenth of 1 percent of this country's total ethical pharmaceutical market.

Nevertheless, those who require this medication have every reason to ask why Meticorten tablets should cost more than products which contain the same active substance available from other companies at much lower prices.

The answer lies in the basic difference in the nature of the functions and services performed by Schering Corp. in our economy, as contrasted with those performed by distributors of generic prednisone. Schering Corp. and the generic distributor operate in such different ways as to be engaged in totally different businesses.

Let me explain what I mean by "different kinds of businesses." Schering Corp. is fully equipped and fully staffed with highly skilled research scientists to discover and to develop new drugs, to produce them under the most rigid standards of good manufacturing procedures and quality control, to disseminate promptly throughout the scientific and professional world full and complete information about such new drug discoveries, to make available a wide range of dosage forms to meet all physician needs, to market them widely in all parts of the free world, and to continue to service its discoveries for the medical profession.

How completely different is the business carried on by the large majority of the distributors of generic prednisone.

For the most part, they are essentially distribution operations; in fact, many of them have the finished product manufactured for them. These companies do not develop new drugs. They do not have the scientific staffs nor the facilities to develop them. They do no animal testing or clinical investigation. Usually generic distributors do not work for years to gain Government approval.

They do not introduce new drugs. They lack the personnel and skill necessary to communicate to doctors all that needs to be communicated to them about the indications for the drug, the dosage regimen, the methods of application, the side effects and precautions, and so on. They cannot answer

---

[4] Prednisone, mainly an antiarthritic. Schering's brand was Meticorten.

questions about the drug's use in individual cases or provide other services to the doctor. They do not supply samples liberally or provide special formulations of the drug to use in treatment of eyes, ears or other organs, or special strengths for treatment of children, the elderly or other groups. These markets are usually too small and specialized. They limit quality control activities to legal requirements. They do not, in short, encounter the major burden of costs necessary to develop and launch a new drug successfully and prove its worth.

Without these activities, generic distributors contribute little to medical progress.

On the other hand, after someone else has developed a drug and after someone else has incurred the costs of introducing it properly, so that it gains widespread usage, they are able to copy it as soon as copying is legal. When the active ingredient is well known and highly regarded, they take advantage of this to sell it cheaply, in quantity, and frequently on a mail order basis. They concentrate on the one or two forms in widest use and on types of users easiest to reach. Sometimes such companies concentrate on Government bids only and operate in such a way as to minimize investment in facilities and personnel. Their entire business is built upon the pioneering work of others. Their appeal is based solely on their contention that their cheaper versions have the same active ingredient.

In fact, this is what happened in the marketing of prednisone.

When all is said and done, it was Schering's research which discovered prednisone, Schering's development which gave that product to the world and to the medical community, Schering's marketing and distribution which made it known and used throughout the world, Schering's activities which broadened its usefulness, and Schering's licensing which made it available from so many distributors. Without all this, there would not be today any generic prednisone at all.

The "striking differences" in price you referred to are the inevitable consequence of these contrasts. In my judgment, they are fully justified. At generic-level prices, we cannot have new discoveries. At generic-level prices we will stifle research and the development of new medicines, and soon we will have neither the new drugs nor the generics.

* * * * *

The application of this pricing policy has not resulted in excessive profits. Over the past 5 years, Schering has averaged a return on investment which is slightly below the median for the industry, and certainly not out of line with the risks and competitive situation with which it is faced.

Nevertheless, I should not leave you with the impression that we are unaware or unmindful of the continued critical attacks in these hearings and in the press.

We are not callous to the difficulties which our older citizens face because, due to their limited, fixed incomes, and often chronic illnesses, medical costs, including drugs, are high. They need to be helped, and governmental and voluntary programs are doing just that.

It will serve our society poorly if, in seeking to resolve these difficulties, we limit the ability of our creative pharmaceutical industry to serve the professions and the public through the discovery of new drugs.

Thank you, Senator Nelson.

SENATOR NELSON: Thank you very much, Mr. Conzen.[5]

[5] Nelson *Hearings,* Pt. 2, pp. 622–636.

Price-quality relationships and brand-to-brand price differentials (Schering's "Meticorten")

As soon as Schering's President Conzen finished his general statement on the brand-generic price differential, Senator Nelson began to question him, and from the questions posed the reasons for the Senator's special interest in a drug with such low volume as prednisone appeared.

SENATOR NELSON: You state that you think Meticorten is the best [prednisone] product, and I am sure as the president of Schering Corp. and knowing its operation you believe that.

Now, I refer to the Medical Letter of June 2, 1967. As you know, the Medical Letter is a very highly esteemed professional publication. The Medical Letter asked the Fitelson Lab in New York to test 22 brands of prednisone, some generic and some brand name products. In the Medical Letter they state [of prednisones] that from their consultants, pharmacologists, clinical physicians, they can find no differences or variations in formulations that are causing any problems in the treatment of patients. What I am asking is does the Schering Corp. have any double-blind clinical test to prove that the therapeutic efficacy of its prednisone is better than any other one of the 22 prednisones listed in the Medical Letter?

MR. CONZEN: No, sir. . . . I cannot comment on the findings of these scientists, pharmacologists, chemists, and physicians. All I can testify to is to the quality and efficacy of our own brand.

SENATOR NELSON: The Chair, of course, won't argue with that. I am sure it is of very high quality, one that ranks with all the other 22 as meeting USP standards.[6] But the Medical Letter is so concerned about the great price spread that they suggest the desirability of prescribing by generic name. Are you suggesting that the Medical Letter is not qualified to make a judgment about this, after the tests they have made and the consultations they have made with distinguished clinicians and pharmacologists around the country?

MR. CONZEN: Sure they are, but I have not seen any clinical evidence conducted by the Medical Letter or anybody else to prove that other brands of prednisone are therapeutically, in patients, more or less or equally effective.[7]

SENATOR NELSON: What we are really concluding here is that there is no clinical evidence to prove that any one of these 22 is any better or any less effective, including Schering's?

MR. CONZEN: That is right.

SENATOR NELSON: Isn't that correct?

MR. CONZEN: Yes.

SENATOR NELSON: Then, the doctor who is prescribing [your] drug for $17.90, when Merck has one available for $2.20 and Upjohn for $2.25, is simply charging his patient a lot of dollars for a drug on which there is no proof that it is any better than these that are available at a cheaper price; isn't that correct?[8]

MR. CONZEN: No; I differ.

---

[6] The National Formulary (NF) and the U.S. Pharmacopia (USP) provide "official" standards of potency, purity, etc. for drugs.

[7] The reference here is to a persistent debate over the "therapeutic" equivalence of chemically equivalent drugs, particularly brand names and generics.

[8] Merck and Upjohn—brand-name companies larger than Schering.

SENATOR NELSON: Then we get back to where we started. What is the proof?

MR. CONZEN: The proof is the abundant experience of a practicing physician of the results which he has achieved in his patients.

SENATOR NELSON: I don't want to put words in your mouth, but what you are really saying is that whatever doctors prescribe the most provides a satisfactory scientific judgment of what is best?

MR. CONZEN: I would agree with this.

SENATOR NELSON: Are you suggesting, then, that when the Defense Supply Agency purchased 1,000 prednisone tablets on a bid basis, at $4.94—the DSA is supplying Walter Reed, where Presidents, Congressmen, and generals are treated, and Bethesda, and the soldiers overseas—are you suggesting that when they buy Upjohn's tablets at $4.94 on a competitive bid, that they are buying a drug that is not equivalent in its therapeutic value to Schering's?

MR. CONZEN: Therapeutically it is not proven that they are equivalent, but I do not suggest that they are buying inferior drugs for their patients.

SENATOR NELSON: What is there about Meticorten that makes it worth $170-1,000 when the Government is buying it for $4.53, New York City is buying it for $4.58–1,000, the Government is buying it in various bids for $4.52 to $4.94? What distinguishes Meticorten which should justify this price differential is what I am trying to get at.

MR. CONZEN: Several points. One, the overwhelming clinical evidence as to the efficacy of our brand which is unmatched by any other brand or make of prednisone.

Second, our continuing research and the contributions which the sale of Meticorten makes to enable us to continue to compete in this business as a research-oriented company, which strives for innovation, and plays its part in bringing benefits to the public which, in terms of health and anything else, are unsurpassed anywhere in the world.

SENATOR NELSON: But doesn't Upjohn do research and U.S. Vitamin do research?

MR. CONZEN: Certainly. They do it on other drugs. And our share of the Meticorten market supports our over-all research.

SENATOR NELSON: You are basing your statement on the overwhelming selection by individual physicians in prescribing Meticorten in the retail market around the country, is that correct?

MR. CONZEN: Yes.

SENATOR NELSON: Do you think the judgment of an individual practicing physician is better than the judgment of all the combined doctors, surgeons, physicians, pharmacologists, in Walter Reed Hospital who have an opportunity in a clinical situation to observe the value of the drug prednisone that they are using? Do you think the individual doctor's judgment is better than that of a fine hospital in New York or Walter Reed?

MR. CONZEN: I would say that the practicing physician who is faced with a particular case history of illness in a particular patient uses his own best judgment, based on his experience with the drug and his diagnosis and his prognosis, and that this will be, I hope, always the overriding consideration of the practicing physician.

SENATOR NELSON: I would agree that that is exactly what the practicing physician does, but that does not answer my question.

*   *   *   *   *

Now, Merck reduced the price of its prednisone called Deltral in January of this year from about $17.90 to $2.25 per 100. How come you haven't gone down to meet the competition?

MR. CONZEN: I think the answer [is] that Merck, to my knowledge, does not sell prednisone to any significant degree, so it is no longer an important factor in the market.

SENATOR NELSON: I think that is exactly correct. I think that is the reason. There is no competition on the retail market. This demonstrates what I have been trying to say all along. The one thing known on the market is Meticorten and Merck can reduce its price to a nickel, and no doctor is going to prescribe it because he does not know that Merck, or any of the other producers, meet the Medical Letter's standards or USP standards. The dominant name on the market is Meticorten; isn't that the case?

MR. CONZEN: I would say that with 130 different manufacturers' products of prednisone available on the market, there are few items in today's armamentarium which have more competition.

SENATOR NELSON: If the physician does not know about comparable products—and it is said that he does not—then you have no competition.

MR. CONZEN: Senator Nelson, I would submit that—

SENATOR NELSON: I think you have done an excellent job. I am not critical of you. If I were running your company and could make my product dominant on the market, and that is the rules of the game, I certainly would do it. I am not saying there is anything wrong with that from the standpoint of your company ethically or anything else. I have some concern about the way the system works, but I do not have any criticism for you and your success in convincing the doctors that Meticorten is the one they ought to buy. I am not critical of that at all.

MR. CONZEN: But I would like to submit that first of all Meticorten is not the leading seller in the prednisone field. If you think in terms of units, actual tablets prescribed and taken by the patient, Meticorten amounts to approximately 5 percent, and 95 percent of the rest of the market is handled by other brands.

SENATOR NELSON: And yet, through your sales, you represent one-third of the total of the $3 million market, is that correct?

MR. CONZEN: That is right; but I also believe that it would be hard to find a practicing and prescribing physician in this country who is not aware of the fact that prednisone is available at much lower prices than Meticorten.

SENATOR NELSON: We have had testimony, as you probably know, from very distinguished professors, pharmacologists and doctors who assert quite flatly that it is impossible for a practicing physician, busy as he is, to keep up with the names of the various drugs, to say nothing about prices. I have a suspicion that there is a substantial element of truth in their claims. But that is my feelings. I might be wrong and we will find out in the course of these hearings.[9]

Price-cost relationships and drug store—institutional price differentials (Parke, Davis' prednisone prices)

In questioning Schering about its Meticorten brand of prednisone, Senator Nelson was unable to measure price against the yardstick of costs because Mr. Conzen, like several of the other company witnesses, produced no cost figures bearing on this one drug out of the many the company produced. This gap in the data was plugged, at least crudely, by getting cost figures from another supplier, Parke, Davis & Co.

---

[9] Nelson *Hearings*, Pt. 2, pp. 637–654.

Of equal if not greater importance in the Parke, Davis testimony was the illustration it provided of the price differentials between the drug-store and the institutional market. Though Parke, Davis' price through retail channels was $17.88 (almost the same as Schering's), its actual realized price was only $1.36—the explanation being that Parke, Davis had been unsuccessful in breaking into the retail market and nearly all its volume in prednisone (under $30,000 in 1966) came from lower-priced sales to institutions.

Spokesman for Parke, Davis in the following exchange was President Harold H. W. Burrows.

MR. BURROWS: You have asked for our costs and I am obliged to say that because of the very small amount of business we have done, it is not practical to determine our costs with any great degree of accuracy. As best we can figure, the bare manufacturing cost of this item in 1966, including the purchase price of the raw material, was about 50 cents out of the average selling price of $1.36, or 37 percent of the selling price. This does not include any allocation for such [costs] as research, general overhead, handling, distribution, inventory carrying costs, and administrative expenses.

Actually, we may not in fact have achieved any profit on the small volume of prednisone sales which we made.

SENATOR NELSON: Do you have any evidence that in selling at $1.36 for 100 tablets, that the company did in fact sustain a loss in the production of and sale of this item?

MR. BURROWS: I don't think that I could prove that the company actually incurred a loss. However, as an exercise, if we prorated our unallocated ex-penses in the United States such as our general and administrative ex-penses; our selling expenses—and I will leave out advertising from the selling expense group because we did no advertising on this product; our excess of actual production costs over standard costs; a percentage factor for research; and if we add these prorations to our 50-cent base standard cost of manufacturing, we come out about even-steven. These added charges also would include the royalties paid on the product sold,[10] cash discounts allowed on sales and the like that were involved in this particular product.

SENATOR NELSON: Do I understand you to say that if you took into con-sideration all factors of cost—

MR. BURROWS: As we incurred them in the United States and related them to this average U.S. selling price of $1.36.

SENATOR NELSON: That you think you would have about broken even, is that correct?

MR. BURROWS: About broken even. Obviously, we are not in the business of breaking even.

*   *   *   *   *

In sum, our [$17.88 retail] U.S. catalog price has no real significance because sales are virtually nonexistent to or through the retail drug trade. Further, our average sale price of $1.36 per 100 tablets in the United States during 1966 is competitive with other suppliers in this country and also is lower than our prices for the same product abroad.

SENATOR JAVITS:[11] Senator Nelson, may I ask one question? Mr. Burrows, here you say, "Our U.S. catalog price has no real significance because sales are virtually nonexistent to or through the retail drug trade." Yet with this

---

[10] A 6% royalty was paid by Parke, Davis to Schering, which was the patent holder on prednisone.

[11] Senator Javits (R–N.Y.) ex officio member of the Nelson Subcommittee.

catalog price I suppose there are a few [buyers] really being victimized. It gives a completely false impression to the whole business, with your catalog [12] times your actual average sales price. As a merchandising proposition, isn't this bound to cause tremendous difficulty with the retail druggist unless it is corrected throughout the whole pharmaceutical industry?

MR. BURROWS: I don't think it is as simple as that. First, I think the the doctor, if he elects to prescribe a Parke, Davis product, should have the right to prescribe a Parke, Davis product. I don't find fault with the price of $17.88 per 100 tablets at which this item is included in our catalog. I find fault with the fact that we leave it in the catalog when this is not the kind of business that we should be pursuing.

We made an attempt at that business. We didn't succeed. We should have directed our attention to other more promising fields, and let this one drop. That should have been our alternative, and I think that it would have been prudent on our part if we had taken the product out of our list entirely. That we neglected to do, and it is the neglect that bothers me, rather than our price.

Our sales policy has to be such as, hopefully, to produce an economic climate in which we will be inspired and encouraged to spend money for research. Somebody has to spend money for research if the health and well being of this country and of the world is going to be advanced. Perhaps some people might advocate the Government as a substitute. For myself, I would prefer to place reliance on private enterprise.

SENATOR JAVITS: Mr. Burrows, I too would prefer to place the emphasis on private enterprise, which I think is more productive, but I think private enterprise must also meet public interest standards. That is the purpose of our hearing, and I am very pleased that you are cooperating, as are the other witnesses.

I would like to ask you this question because I think it is very pertinent. Based upon the practices of your industry, is it, in your judgment, necessary to price an item at 10 or 12 times the price at which it is sold to city, county, State and Federal agencies, in sales to the retail druggist, in order to deal with the manifold costs, including reasonable profit? It seems to me that would be way, way out of line. But you tell us. Is it necessary, in terms of your business?

MR. BURROWS: It is necessary to charge somebody. Let me put your question somewhat in reverse. If Parke, Davis, for our 1966 year, had reduced our prices by 20½ per cent, we would not have made any money. That is the maximum margin that we are talking about, assuming that we maintain our present level of research expense and the like.

SENATOR JAVITS: Mr. Burrows, I apologize for interrupting, sir, but it seems to me that, even accepting your explanation, the internal structural difference seems unduly lopsided to the retail druggist.

Is it essential in the structure of your business that there be this lopsided relationship? Isn't the retail druggist, and, therefore, the retail buyer, being asked to pay far too much of these costs, and an equitable share not being assessed, as it were, upon other buyers, to wit, city, county, State and Federal agencies? That is my question.

MR. BURROWS: I don't know that I can provide an answer for that. I have to assume that we used our best judgment under the circumstances. It is conceivable that for one reason or another we wanted the Parke, Davis label represented in these institutions. We knew from previous experience what the bid prices were liable to be, and if we wantd to have our name represented we knew that we would have to bid at or near the past prices in order to accomplish that end.[12]

Cost, price, quality relationships and price differentials in different markets (Ciba's "Serpasil" brand of reserpine)

Besides discussing reserpine with a spokesman from Lilly, which had 5% of the retail sales at a list price of $10.95 per 1,000 tablets, Senator Nelson questioned a spokesman for Ciba Corporation, which had about one-third of the "new prescription" market at a retail price to druggists of $39.50.

Company spokesman in the following excerpts is Mr. Charles T. Silloway, president of Ciba's U.S. subsidiary.

SENATOR NELSON: Since you asserted that your drug is better than all the rest, can you show us results of any double blind clinical tests to prove that it is better than APC's, for example, which sold to New York City at half as much as you bid? Your argument does not mean anything.[13] That is all. I am not being unfriendly to you. I am just being honest with you. I do not believe in glossing things over. The argument does not amount to a hill of beans any more than Schering's argument that its brand of prednisone is [better] because more doctors prescribe it. Of course more doctors prescribe it. That is the only brand they know. That is the reason more doctors prescribe Serpasil. Why should a doctor prescribe your reserpine if there is reserpine on the market that is selling to New York City for $3? You will agree, won't you, that New York City sets a high standard for the drugs they purchase?

MR. SILLOWAY: I do not. At this point I am not quite familiar with what they do.

SENATOR NELSON: According to the testimony before our committee as to what they do, that is the case.

*   *   *   *   *

Let me ask you this because I cannot understand this pricing. In November 1964 you bid to DSA[14] $6.95 for 1,000 tablets, 0.25 milligram. Your price to the druggist for 1,000 tablets was $39.50. Then in May of 1966, 2 years later, you bid $7.15 to DSA for 1,000 tablets. The druggist price stayed at $39.50. Then in November of 1966, just a few months after your $7.15 price you dropped to $3.95 to DSA for a thousand tablets but the price to the druggist stayed at $39.50. You have cut your price almost in half to DSA, but the druggist has paid $39.50 all the time. How do you explain the disparity between what the pharmacist has to pay for this product and what is offered on a competitive bid to DSA?

MR. SILLOWAY: In the first place, I would like to be sure we are [not] talking apples and pears, Senator. I don't think those comparisons are legitimate, either.

SENATOR NELSON: You don't?

MR. SILLOWAY: I would like to get that $39.50 out of the pattern, because

---

[12] Nelson *Hearings*, Pt. 2, pp. 604–612.

[13] The argument had been that, since instances had been observed where "slight changes in the formulation" of a drug "had doubled the blood levels and halved the therapeutically effective dose," there was "no such thing as a generic equivalent unless proven by adequate experimental data."

[14] DSA, Defense Services Administration.

it is always compared with a purchase of many thousands of tablets. We have a published price available to the average pharmacy of five times 5,000, which brings it down to $28.75.

SENATOR NELSON: All we did is take the prices from the Red Book.[15] We used your figure. . . . Well, all right.

MR. SILLOWAY: And let me address myself to these recent $3.95 transactions. Let me explain what happened. The Department of Defense suddenly found that the tablets they had purchased of generic reserpine failed to meet the requirements and withdrew the stocks from all the hospitals over the country. They suddenly required eleven million tablets, and there was no one else who had the inventory who could supply them, and they pled with us to provide them as a matter of patriotism, at the most favorable price we could, and this was substantially above the price of the material which they had had to withdraw.

SENATOR NELSON: That is an interesting commentary on the economics of the situation. It proves you are the only ones who could supply it, so you could charge five, six, and seven times as much as other previously successful bidders.

MR. SILLOWAY: Well, perfectly obvious, Senator, if we did not have to do research, if we did not have to have our products in distribution, if we did not have to have our products properly labeled, which these other products, incidentally, are not, if we did not have to contribute these values, we could sell at very low prices, too. But to take out of context the kind of business we are doing and equate it [with generics] in this way simply is comparing apples and pears.

SENATOR NELSON: Nobody is objecting to a reasonable profit. I certainly do not. I want to see you make a fine profit. Companies have to make a profit to survive. But you are saying here that the reason you have to charge this higher price is that you do research. There are several issues that we are going to have to raise that somehow just do not fit that argument, such as why you sell reserpine for a lower price in foreign countries than you do here. The research was done in Switzerland and you sell the drug at one-third the U.S. price in Switzerland.

We have a whole list of bids here to New York City, one-seventh, some of them one-tenth of what yours are. Now, let's take some brand name companies. Here is Parke, Davis. They sell their reserpine under the name Serfin, charge the druggist $33.96. Now, I suppose they give some discount as you do. Parke, Davis did not do any research on this drug. You justify your high price on the grounds that you did all the research. Parke, Davis is charging almost as much as you are and they did not do an ounce of research. You licensed them. They did not have to do anything, and they charge $33.96. Upjohn with Reserpoid charges $33.58. Lilly with Sandril sells at $15.75.[16] Here are three very distinguished companies. Your justification is that you had to do a lot of research. Do you have any idea why they should charge $33, when these other little companies are charging $2 and $3?

MR. SILLOWAY: I can only speculate, Senator, on their economics. I know that the economics of Lilly and Parke, Davis and Upjohn are not dissimilar to ours, and if we did not have to label our products properly, if we did not have to provide proper—

---

[15] *Drug Topics Red Book*, a published source of list prices for drugs sold to drugstores.

[16] Actually $10.95. See Nelson *Hearings*, Pt. 3, p. 973.

SENATOR NELSON: Who does not have to label their products properly?

MR. SILLOWAY: Many of these [200 odd generic reserpines] are inadequately labeled, as I indicated in my opening statement.

SENATOR NELSON: Maybe you did not mean it this way, but I understood you to say that they were not required to meet adequate labeling standards. Everybody must meet those.

MR. SILLOWAY: In our particular case, reserpine has been characterized as an old drug by the Food and Drug Administration. Therefore, they are not required—people who come in after the drug has been declared an old drug apparently are not required to maintain FDA-approved labeling. The only reserpine insert[17] which the FDA, under its current laws and regulations, is reviewing is ours. Of the 36 package inserts that we studied of generic reserpine, the dosage for maintenance therapy in hypertension, the leading indication, in 16 was up to four times higher than the FDA-approved package insert we have. Six listed no side effects at all. We have details on this.

SENATOR NELSON: I think that is very valuable information, and it certainly is shocking information. I had no notion that some companies go on the market with a drug that may have very dangerous side effects under certain circumstances and do not accurately describe the drug or fail to name the side effects or describe proper dosage. Why doesn't the law cover that?

*   *   *   *   *

SENATOR NELSON: The next question that occurs to me is, why the differential in cost for the actual input?

The drug was isolated in 1952 in Switzerland. Using the Red Book price as a common denominator, how do you explain that for 100 0.25-milligram tablets in the United States you charge $4.50, while in Rome, where there is no patent allowed, your price is $1.25. In Berne, Switzerland, where there are no drug [product] patents, you charge $1.25, Vienna $1.56, London $1.19, Bonn $1.05, Rio $1.60.

Research was done in Switzerland by the Swiss corporation, Ciba. Can you explain to me why Ciba charges four times as much in the United States for Serpasil as in Bern, and more than four times as much as Ciba charges in Bonn? I don't understand it. The research was done in Switzerland.

You argue that you have to pay for research. Well, why should the American citizens pay for research for the benefit of the people in Switzerland or Rome or Bonn? There is a vast differential between the [price] of the drug in these places and in the United States.

MR. SILLOWAY: Senator, I read in a press release last night that you would ask me this question today, but I did not read in the press release my answer.

SENATOR NELSON: You hadn't given it to us, I guess.

MR. SILLOWAY: I would like to give it the best I can.

SENATOR NELSON: All right.

MR. SILLOWAY: In the first place, and of overwhelming importance, there is no material made here which is sold in these foreign markets. There is no international traffic in Serpasil. They are made and formulated locally.

Now, just as an exercise, we applied an index of manufacturing wages paid in each of these countries to those prices. Instead of coming out with

---

[17] The package insert which accompanies the drug gives labeling information—i.e., dosage, warnings, etc.

a 3- or 4-to-1 ratio, we came out with a ratio of more like 4 to 3. There is a difference to be sure, but again I remind you that each of these markets are entirely independent, and there are many other commodities [for] which prices differ because of the differing economics. For example, a completely related statistic, the cost of the hospital room per day in Washington, D.C., according to the State Department index, this year is $38; in Bonn it is $13.

SENATOR NELSON: What does that have to do with the question here?

MR. SILLOWAY: Well, my only point is that the local circumstances may produce economics that are as different from ours as the hospital comparison. You pay $40 in Washington and you pay $13 in Bonn.

SENATOR NELSON: I have never been much of a businessman, but let me advise your company of something. If you can make Serpasil in Bonn and sell it for $1.05 a hundred versus $4.50 here, why don't you just make it there and import it into the United States and make yourself a whale of a profit? Why don't you take that up at the next board of directors meeting?

SENATOR SCOTT:[18] And please note that the chairman of the subcommittee has recommended a certain degree of unemployment for American workingmen in so doing.

SENATOR NELSON: I will accept the unemployment figure for the benefit of the consumer. What I am saying to you is that I don't believe it, to be blunt with you.

I don't believe that any company that produces these tablets for one-fourth or one-fifth of the cost wouldn't bring them into the United States. I think you could fly it in and charge half as much as you are now charging in the United States.

Now, let's skip to another country where the labor costs are very small. In Mexico City, 1,000 tablets cost $30, so you have $39.50 in the United States, $15.20 in Rome, $11.09 in Berne, $15.60 in Vienna, $11.20 in London, $10.53 in Bonn, $16 in Rio, and $30 in Mexico City. Now, what are the economic factors in Mexico which account for this?

MR. SILLOWAY: Senator, the economic factors in each country have got to be evaluated independently, and I am not familiar with the complex of problems that result in this determination of price, and I simply would remind you that taking a figure like this out of context, out of the context of our total operation is not appropriate. But if we were making as much profit as . . . this seems to imply, we would be in a very much better position than we are today. But I can tell you that, considered in the context of our total operation, our company, our pharmaceutical company, had a profit on sales last year of 8.6 per cent. In the first half of 1967, because the research has not been very productive, a figure of 4.4 percent—

SENATOR NELSON: What was your profit based on net worth?

MR. SILLOWAY: We have no comparable figure, sir, since we are a conglomerate corporation and it is impossible to segregate those assets and debt appropriately. I must say that our directors are unhappy with the 4.4 per cent for the first half of 1967.

* * * * *

SENATOR NELSON: I must say, frankly, I am puzzled by the answers. Every company which has been here that sells overseas, whether their product is manufactured here or abroad, charges a higher price in the United States than in any other country. We have cases of companies who manufacture a product in the United States and then sell it in Bonn cheaper than they do in the United States. . . . Now, how do you explain that?

---

[18] Senator Hugh Scott (R-Pa.), minority member of the Nelson Subcommittee.

MR. SILLOWAY: I can't explain any other company's activities, Senator.

SENATOR NELSON: No, but I think the honest fact is that the present policies of the pharmaceutical manufacturing companies are absolutely inexplicable. They aren't understandable in terms of the testimony given by the companies who have tried to explain the policy. I suspect that the answer is competition.

SENATOR SCOTT: Senator Nelson, may I just say for the record that I think the comparative prices in foreign countries and in the United States is a completely worthless document unless it shows in the same comparison the labor cost, the production cost, any process or product development cost, and the amount of research, and I think it is an exercise in oratory rather than in investigation to attack any company, and I realize in saying it that some columnist will say I am over here to protect the company and therefore I have a disclaimer: I have no stock in the company, and no interest in the company.

I do have a great interest in the balance in the hearings, and I think that we ought not to be throwing around figures on percentages for the benefit of our audience, unless the figures are valid by the comparative costs, or by the cost of research, or by the amount of taxes involved.

I hope the Senator doesn't mind my making that observation.

*　*　*　*　*

SENATOR NELSON: Now, with reference to Senator Scott's engaging suggestion, I draw the inference that I am taking unfair advantage of the pharmaceutical manufacturing companies.

SENATOR SCOTT: I don't think you are taking any unfair advantage, Senator Nelson, other than that which exists from the fact that you and I are behind this end of the table and the witness is behind that one, which always puts the witness at a little disadvantage. That is all I meant.

SENATOR NELSON: If I had their public relations fellows and their researchers, I would take that side and clobber this side any time. I have one economist and one very fine young lady research assistant, and the industry has more research resources than the whole Congress.

SENATOR SCOTT: The thing is, Senator Nelson, we have that inestimable thing, dateline Washington.

SENATOR NELSON: I think the industry can defend itself. They are defending it all over my State right now. I can't afford the TV and radio time, letters, and other activities that they are sponsoring out there. I can't even keep up with them. So I am not worrying too much about them defending themselves at all. I am not trying to put them on the defensive.

Let's get to the matter of labor cost for a moment. The point is always raised that the labor cost is higher in the United States than in other countries.

Will you clarify something for the whole Congress? Would you mind having your auditors do a cost accounting, and give it to us? You would do a great favor to the Congress and increase the credibility of your justification for the price differential you charge if you could come in here showing a differential in cost. I give you that challenge. The day you have the figures, the day you are prepared to bring [them] before this committee, you will have the whole show to yourself. If the cost justifies the charge, fine, the argument is over. Is that fair enough? Are you willing to do that?

MR. SILLOWAY: I am not sure that I can do that, sir, but I will accept your charge.[19]

---

[19] This information was not supplied to the committee.

SENATOR NELSON: Why do you consider the element of the wages paid in a country as a measure of what you ought to charge for the product? [That] pricing policy seems to depend on what the traffic will bear. Even if you don't call it that, I do. To consider the wages, income, standard of living as factors in your pricing is all right. It is a free world. You can do it. But I think the public ought to understand that.

MR. SILLOWAY: Isn't that a factor in the pricing of any commodity, Senator? It seems to me so.

SENATOR NELSON: Can you buy a Ford automobile in Rome cheaper than you buy it here?

MR. SILLOWAY: I don't know.

SENATOR NELSON: I don't think so.

*   *   *   *   *

Do you know what the production costs are per 1,000 or 5,000 tablets for your reserpine, Serpasil, made by Ciba USA?

MR. SILLOWAY: We have data which is not very significant because it is so difficult to isolate one product out of the context of the whole company. I have already provided the total costs for our Serpasil. I indicated that our average realized price per quarter milligram tablet for Serpasil in 1966 was approximately 3.4 cents.[20] Our total costs associated with this were 2.6 cents leaving 0.8 cent profit for a quarter-milligram tablet to the best of our ability to allocate the indirect expenses which are such an enormous part of the kind of business we are in.

SENATOR NELSON: That figure puzzles me. If it costs 2.6 cents per tablet, that means $26 a thousand.

MR. SILLOWAY: Pretty good mathematics.

SENATOR NELSON: Yes. The mathematics I do not understand is how you sell it to the Defense Supply Agency for $3.95. Is it that you make a profit because you sell such a big volume?

MR. SILLOWAY: Certainly, sir, this is an average figure, and the transaction that occurs in a bottle of 100, as a single transaction, has got a completely different economic background than a transaction for 1 million tablets. I am quite sure we did not make any money at that $3.95.

SENATOR NELSON: Other companies who are in this for profit underbid you substantially and I assume they make a profit.

MR. SILLOWAY: They can do that because they do not provide the same kind of values we do, sir.

SENATOR NELSON: But quite frankly I cannot understand how you can claim that it costs 2.6 cents per tablet, or $26 a thousand to produce it.

You have to be assigning one cost to this $26 figure and quite another cost to the $3.95 figure. It either costs you a certain amount to make a tablet or it does not.

Under your bid to Defense Supply, if it costs $26 per 1,000 you are losing $22.05 a thousand. It does not add up to me. I understand the argument that if you sell a big volume you can reduce the price, but that much of a reduction is too much. Your figure of 2.6 cents just cannot represent the cost of production per tablet, if you are selling 1,000 tablets for $3.95.

SENATOR NELSON: I have another question which I will also ask of the Veterans' Administration and the Defense Supply Agency. There is a peculiarity about the pricing of Serpasil which involves the Veterans' Ad-

---

[20] Average realized price on sales to wholesalers, drugstores, institutions, and other customers.

ministration and the Defense Supply Agency. Your offer to the Veterans' Administration for 1,000 0.25 milligram tablets of Serpasil since 1963 has risen from $1.10 to $7.19, while at the same time your price to the DSA has dropped from $6.95 to $3.95. So to one agency the price has gone up more than six times, and to another it has been cut to almost half. Can you explain that?

Mr. Silloway: Well, I think that I would prefer to pass on that. The 1966 transaction with the DSA was a unique transaction in which they were in a jam, and they needed the material immediately. We did the best we could to help them. We quoted such a price and I promise you we will not quote such again.

Senator Nelson: Well, we have a figure here for April 1967, a bid of $3.95 to DSA for 1,000 0.25 milligram tablets. We have a 1967 bid to the VA of $7.19.

Mr. Silloway: We will not bid $3.95 again, I can assure you.

Senator Nelson: This is 1967.

Mr. Silloway: I say we will not do it again.

Senator Nelson: I did not want to talk you into raising the price to the DSA, but rather to drop the one to the VA. Can you think of anything we have not covered that I might ask?

Mr. Silloway: If I could, I do not know whether I should tell you.

Senator Nelson: You have been a very fine witness. All the questioning is intended to be friendly and your answers have been very friendly. We have enjoyed it so much we hope that you will like to come back again.

Mr. Silloway: Thank you, Senator Nelson. I am not sure that my pleasure in returning will be as much.

Senator Nelson: Thank you very much. You have been a very gracious witness, your testimony has been very valuable, and we know that you do represent a highly reputable corporation. We are glad to have you here, and, as I said, we will be glad to have you back any time. Thank you.

Mr. Silloway: Thank you, Senator Nelson.[21]

CONTROL OF THE MARKET

Besides charging that drug prices were unreasonably high, the Kefauver *Report* also charged that prices were "administered," as evidenced by price leadership, price followership, and long-term price inflexibility. Explaining how administered prices were maintained, the *Report* pointed to three key factors: patents, intensive promotion, and company success in getting physicians to write their prescriptions in terms of brand names rather than generic names.

Although the industry was no longer being charged with "administered" prices at the Nelson hearings seven years later, it was still being charged with prices that were "too high"—especially for some customer classes. Under these conditions, industry spokesmen came prepared to argue in defense of the existing patent and promotional systems.

The role of patents (PMA)

The role of patents came up in the course of testimony presented on price trends by the PMA. The Association's witness on this occasion was

---

[21] Nelson *Hearings,* Pt. 3, pp. 908–942.

an academician, Dr. John M. Firestone of the City College of New York, designer of a pharmaceutical price index commissioned by the PMA.

SENATOR NELSON: Let me ask you a question. [In your written testimony] your sentence is, "When drug products were classified by their patent status, patented products showed a [price] decline of 24.8 percent [1949–1966]— while the nonpatented products had risen by 1.1 percent in this same period." So you are saying that during the course of this period from 1949 to 1966, prices for drugs that were still under patent declined 24.8 percent?

DR. FIRESTONE: Yes, sir. The interesting thing is [that] when you have the most competition, when the products are not covered by patents, you have rising prices instead of falling prices.

SENATOR NELSON: Where what?

DR. FIRESTONE: Where you have no patent protection and you have the greatest degree of competition, prices do not fall.

SENATOR NELSON: But do your statistics show that when the patent goes off and a number of other firms go into the marketplace, the price of the product drops?

DR. FIRESTONE: It does not.

SENATOR NELSON: It does not drop?

DR. FIRESTONE: Yes, sir.

SENATOR NELSON: If that is the case I wonder if it does not prove something that I have suspected all along and that many people have asserted.

There is no competition in the marketplace; that is why the price did not drop. In other words, once the drug has 17 years of patent protection behind it and the doctors in the country know only that particular drug, they continue to prescribe it despite the fact that in the marketplace there may be a comparable drug for a half, a fifth, a 10th, or even a 20th of the price, which indicates something peculiar about the pricing structure.[22]

The role of promotion (Lilly)

The smaller the role of patents in drug pricing, the greater the role which critics were likely to ascribe to promotion. That selling costs for drugs ran relatively high had been established by the Kefauver study: $580 million for 22 companies in 1958, or 24.8% of sales, based on subpoenaed financial data for company drug operations only. Ever since this finding, drug makers had faced the charge that their selling costs were "too high" and the further charge that their $200 million corps of "detail men" (or representatives calling on doctors) were much more influential than reliable, considered as a source of doctors' information.

A chance to combat both these charges fell to Vice President DeBoest of Lilly, at a time when leadership of the questioning passed temporarily from Senator Nelson to a minority member of his group, Senator Mark O. Hatfield (R-Ore.).

SENATOR HATFIELD: What about the sales representatives of the various pharmaceutical houses? We are told that the physician's judgment is greatly influenced by the sales pitch made by the representatives of such pharmaceutical houses. We have also been told that the sales representatives

---

[22] Nelson Hearings, Pt. 5, pp. 1696, 1697.

have limited technical background, limited educational background in many instances, and here is the physician listening to a sales pitch for a product and making some determinations and the basis of his evaluation is much influenced by such people. Now tell me a little bit about these people.

MR. DeBOEST: Well, there has been much use of the word "brainwashing" in recent weeks. The inference has been made many times that the pharmaceutical representative has brainwashed the physician.

In the first place, in knowing over the years many hundreds of physicians, I think this is an insult to his clinical integrity. I know of no more dedicated body of people in the world than the practicing physician. He guards his clinical judgment very zealously.

It is true that the pharmaceutical representatives do call. Many of them call in a service capacity as well as a selling capacity. I don't mean to give the impression that the pharmaceutical institutions, in calling on physicians, regard themselves as eleemosynary institutions. They don't. They are in business for a profit, to the mutual benefit of the American public. In our own case, we have, roughly, a thousand salesmen, 91 percent of whom either have degrees in pharmacy or scientific degrees in another discipline. Not only that, after receiving their bachelor's degrees and coming with us, they are very thoroughly trained, and this is not being trained by tub-thumping sales managers. It is by the physicians we have, the pharmacologists, the chemists, who make an honest and very determined effort to teach these people things that can be of benefit to the practicing physician.

SENATOR HATFIELD: I understand further that we have had testimony that the physician is making some of his evaluation based upon the deluge of advertising and promotion on the part of the pharmaceutical houses rather than upon technical and professional basis. We have heard, I think, the figure used that the pharmaceutical houses have spent some $600 to $800 million last year in promoting their products.[23]

MR. DeBOEST: This figure has been handled, I believe, somewhat loosely by certain people. The figure, so far as I can determine, for the pharmaceutical industry is roughly $600 million for marketing. Now, marketing embraces many, many elements other than the mere factor of advertising or promotion.

Now, marketing embraces distribution as well as selling and promotion; so if we were to remove, again so far as I can determine, the actual distribution cost, the physical cost of getting material to wholesalers and that sort of thing, you can take off $100 million. That leaves us $500 million for 200,000 physicians.

There are roughly 150 promoting companies in the United States. So we take the $500 million and allocate that per doctor, and the amount per doctor per company is $16 per year.

Now, for this $16 in our case the representative makes his calls on the physician. We pay for the advertising cost. We call on the hospitals with all of the service to our line that is involved. We call on the drugstores to see that they have the proper things, if they are not out of date, if they are not stored properly, if they have to be returned; this is all taken care of. We see that the wholesaler has adequate stocks against need. This is the full marketing package. This is not just four-color ads at the rate of about $600 million a year.

---

[23] The $800 million figure had been given to the Committee by Dr. James L. Goddard, Commissioner of the FDA.

Now you asked about Seconal.[24]

SENATOR HATFIELD: I just used that as an example.

MR. DEBOEST: Well, in the last 10 years our expenditure for advertising Seconal per physician has been $1.75. That is 17½ cents a year per doctor for the horrendous rate of promotion which is being talked about.

May I just bring out an example or two of the type of thing that we do? I suppose this would be called severe brainwashing. It is a book, "The Evaluation of Liver Function in Clinical Practice." We collected in one volume much of the current modern knowledge and bound it, as you see, and presented it to the physician for his library. This is one of our types of promotion.

We try to handle samples in a very sensible fashion. If the physician is interested in a drug and would like to try the drug, we see that he has adequate samples, but we are not interested in covering his desk in order that somebody [else] coming along won't have a place to put some more.

SENATOR HATFIELD: Do you consider the general surgeon is not a general ignoramus, not knowing what he has been prescribing, which has been the general impression left to this committee by some of our previous witnesses?

MR. DEBOEST: In my experience, Senator, the American practicing physician is anything but an ignoramus in any area.

SENATOR HATFIELD: I have no further questions.[25]

The "special problem" of detail men

Of all the means of drug promotion, the army of detail men (20,000 of them by 1967) was reportedly the most influential. From the point of view of the Kefauver critics, detail men posed a "special problem" because their statements, being oral and made in the privacy of the doctor's office, were bound to be more difficult to regulate than printed advertising in journals, etc.

That detail men might pose a "special problem" not just for the FDA but for company top management as well is suggested by the following excerpt. Sent anonymously to the Nelson Subcommittee, it formed a part of a series of middle-management directives from a regional sales office to the field. The disclosure proved most embarrassing to the leadership of the firm involved, not only because of the "hard sell" tactic depicted, but also because admitted side effects were played down and some of the therapeutic claims suggested had not yet been accepted by the FDA. Though top management repudiated the directives as inconsistent with official policy, they were widely cited and excerpted.

> Bulletin No. 93, July 28, 1965
> To: All Western District Sales Associates.
> From: [26]
> Subject: Profit Improvement Promotional Program "——,"[27] August, 1965.
>
>   All reports indicate that this one is a Real Winner. Obviously, "——" sales greatly Exceed all initial sales forecasts. New revised

---

[24] See above, p. 617.

[25] Nelson *Hearings,* Pt. 3. pp. 976–980.

[26] Name withheld.

[27] The name of the drug withheld.

projections are being developed. My guess is that our original objective will be tripled. The best way to beat this—or any other objective—is to continue to sell H—out of "——."

Since "——" is known to convey effective relief from the pain and inflammation of [the] most difficult lesions and to do this with an extended margin of safety, it is obvious that "——" will work in that whole host of rheumatic crocks and cruds which every General Practitioner, Internist, and Orthopedic Surgeon sees everyday in his practice.

"——" is anti-inflammatory. "——" is analgesic. "——" breaks up the pain—thus increasing joint mobility. Yet, "——" is a unique, new chemical entity which affords an extended margin of safety in the long-term management of arthritic disorders.

Run scared! Get a sense of urgency into every presentation. When you do, you will convince the physician that—

Whenever the problem is oppressive joint pain associated with heat, redness, tenderness, and swelling. . . .

When the muscles around an inflamed joint are in spasm causing a limitation in motion. . . .

Whether the tentative diagnosis is osteoarthritis of the hip, gout, rheumatoid arthritis, rheumatoid spondylitis, or just plain musculoskeletal aches and stiffness. . . .

For short-term use in acute conditions or long-term use in chronic conditions. . . .

"——" will afford relief to 3 out of 4 patients effectively. . . .

With an extended margin of safety . . . probably with fewer tablets . . . and, therefore, at less cost . . . with less dosage adjustment . . . and, therefore, fewer problems for both the physician and the patient than any other currently available product.

You've told this story now, probably 130 times. The physician, however, has heard it only once. So, go back and tell it again and again and again and again, until it is indelibly impressed in his mind and he starts—and continues—to prescribe "——."

Let's go![28]

SUBSTANTIVE ISSUES OF SAFETY, EFFICACY, AND RESPONSIBLE ADVERTISING

Apart from any question as to whether drug advertising is "too influential," there is a question as to whether some of it may also be "misleading." In the following exchange, Senator Nelson raises this issue with respect to Chloromycetin, Parke, Davis & Co.'s largest selling drug (worldwide sales of $70 million in 1966).

The Parke, Davis spokesman, Dr. Leslie M. Lueck, was the company director of quality control. Advertising issues were not among the matters this witness had come prepared to discuss. Rather, his appointed role had been to convey to the Nelson Subcommittee some news which comment in the press described as a "godsend" for the industry and a "bombshell" for its critics. This news was to the effect that generic counterparts of Chloromycetin—a drug on which the patent

---

[28] Nelson *Hearings*, Pt. 8, pp. 3481–3517, especially pp. 3495–3497.

had recently run out—had been decisively proven to be not "equivalent" to the original in their therapeutic effect. It was after presenting this prepared testimony that Dr. Lueck was called on to discuss advertising.

SENATOR NELSON: Now, Doctor, I understand that your product, Chloromycetin, has been responsible for deaths resulting from bone marrow disorders, is that correct?

DR. LUECK: I do not know in what frame of reference you are phrasing the question. If you mean Chloromycetin and all chloramphenicol products [these] have required statements on the labeling that include warnings and side effects.

SENATOR NELSON: Maybe you did not understand the question. I said I understand that your product, Chloromycetin, has been responsible for deaths from bone marrow disorders. Is that correct or incorrect?

DR. LUECK: I do not know in what reference you are phrasing that question. I know that Chloromycetin, the Parke, Davis brand of chloramphenicol—

SENATOR NELSON: Has never resulted in any deaths?

DR. LUECK: No, I did not say that.

SENATOR NELSON: Maybe I did not put the question correctly. Some people have died from the administration of Chloromycetin, I understand. Will you tell me what you know about that?

DR. LUECK: I understand that Chloromycetin has been alleged to be related to or associated with some serious side effects, some serious reactions. Those things are related and detailed in considerable length in the package information, in the labeling, Mr. Chairman.

SENATOR NELSON: You say you understand. You really are not sure that any deaths have resulted from this drug?

DR. LUECK: I think there have been instances where some reactions can be related to the use of Chloromycetin.

SENATOR NELSON: Have you ever read the warning that your company now belatedly puts in its advertising for this drug? Here is an ad from the *Journal of the American Medical Association,* February 20, 1967:

"Warning: Serious and even fatal blood dyscrasias-aplastic anemia, hypoplastic anemia—"

And so forth—

are known to occur after the administration of chloramphenicol. Were you aware of that?

DR. LUECK: Yes, sir.

SENATOR NELSON: That was my question Doctor: Do you know of any cases of fatal side effects occurring after the administration of Chloromycetin?

DR. LUECK: I was attempting to respond to your question by referring to this warning statement in the labeling, which is precisely identical to that in the advertising. I am sorry if I misled you.

SENATOR NELSON: You did not mislead me. You are aware, then, that deaths have occurred in this case?

DR. LUECK: Absolutely.

*   *   *   *   *

Now, Mr. Chairman, let us look at the potential dangers of chloramphenicol in true perspective; in other words, comparing it to other anti-infective agents or other antibiotics. Let us take a look at disabling and death-dealing reactions that may occur with the other antibiotics. The last significant and over-all review of severe reactions to antibiotics was communicated to the medical literature by personnel of the FDA in 1957. These authors brought out the fact that penicillin was found to produce the greatest number and the most severe reactions of all antibiotics presently available.

MR. GORDON:[29]   This was when?

DR. LUECK: 1957.

MR. GORDON: Are you aware of the fact, however, that the risk [of chloramphenicol] at that time was considered to be considerably less than it is today? For example, I think the risk at that time was considered to be one in 800,000. A recent report to the California State Assembly and Senate by the California Medical Association and the State Department of Public Health, has revealed that the risk, on the basis of an average dose of 7.5 grams, is 1 in 24,000.

DR. LUECK: Mr. Gordon, with your permission, I will finish my brief review of the 1957 FDA publication. Then I would go on to the California report.

MR. GORDON: But isn't it correct that considerably more is known today about the effects of chloramphenicol than was known, say, 12 or 13 years ago? Is that not correct?

DR. LUECK: I do not know that we have a higher incidence of side effects now than we had in 1957. I will treat that subject in a moment, Mr. Gordon.

MR. GORDON: Could you answer my question, Doctor?

DR. LUECK: I am sorry.

MR. GORDON: I asked the question: Is it not correct that we know considerably more today about the side effects and dangers of chloramphenicol than we did say 12 or 13 years ago when that particular report was written?

DR. LUECK: No, sir; I do not believe we do.

MR. GORDON: You do not believe we know any more today than we did at that time?

DR. LUECK: I do not believe we know any more.

SENATOR NELSON: I would like to ask you a question about something that puzzles me.

You were aware of serious blood dyscrasias, even fatal blood dyscrasias 10 years ago. [Yet] your ad in 1960, an ad in the *Antibiotics and Chemotherapy* magazine, was a one-page ad that we will submit for the record.

There is nothing here that would scare anybody. Your claim was for a potent therapeutic agent and because certain blood dyscrasias had been associated with its administration, you simply said that the drug should not be used indiscriminately.

How do you explain that you knew how serious these effects could be 10 years ago, and yet in 1960 you were running an ad that did not call this sharply to the attention of the doctor, but then suddenly, 7 years later, you are running this [February 20, 1967] ad?[30]

DR. LUECK: Mr. Chairman, I would like to comment that since 1952, every ad, every advertisement that has appeared on Chloromycetin, has first been reviewed with the Food and Drug Administration before that ad was ever submitted for publication in any journal.

SENATOR NELSON: I am prepared to indict the FDA along with your company for that.

DR. LUECK: This was the opinion, the combined opinion, apparently, of the experts in Parke, Davis, the experts in the Food and Drug Administra-

---

[29] Mr. Gordon, staff economist to the Subcommittee.

[30] As described above, p. 366.

tion, that adequate warning was included in those ads and in the labeling at any given time. We have diligently worked with the Food and Drug Administration and disseminated the information to the best of our ability on any changes or improvements in that labeling through the years. And to carry the message to the physician, Mr. Chairman, each and every time.

SENATOR NELSON: Do you really mean to tell me, Doctor, that you think the first [1960] ad says the same thing as the second [1967] ad? Do you really mean to say that?

DR. LUECK: I am not saying that they say the same thing.

SENATOR NELSON: Do they give the same warning?

DR. LUECK: Yes; I think they give the essential warning.

SENATOR NELSON: Let's read it again. I think that this is preposterous.

MR. CUTLER.[31]   Mr. Chairman, I hope I will not sound impertinent, but may I ask what this has to do with the evidence Dr. Lueck has submitted with regard to therapeutic differences among brands?

SENATOR NELSON: I can give you several answers, but I will give you one that ought to satisfy you. If quality control is important, and I think it is as important as you say it is in the production of drugs for the marketplace, quality control of advertising is just as important.

It does not do any good to have good quality control so the drug will do exactly what you expect it to do and then be outright dishonest about what it will do. I think quality control in advertising is as important as quality control in the production of a drug. That is exactly what I am getting at.

Now, I will read the two ads again. I will let the public judge this one. You tell me if they both tell the doctor the same thing, and I am going to ask the doctors who testify what their opinion is. . . .

DR. LUECK: The second warning is an exact duplicate of the package insert and, in my opinion, would be considered a stronger warning, Mr. Chairman.

SENATOR NELSON: I bless you for that.

DR. LUECK: Mr. Chairman, I think our advertising of all our products has been much in keeping with the order of the day and regulatory requirements appropriate to advertising the product.

SENATOR NELSON: Well, my questions have been directed at the proposition that the evidence was available several years ago that there were some major serious side effects, and that the ads did not indicate it. For example, there had already been known deaths—I think that is indisputable—by 1954.

The National Research Council in 1952 made statements that certain cases of serious blood dyscrasias had been associated with chloramphenicol —that was 1952—and still an ad in the *General Practitioner*, in March 1954, did not mention this fact.

How do you explain that, even 2 years after the National Research Council's statement, there is no warning at all in the ad?

DR. LUECK: Mr. Chairman, I would like to point out that the warnings and so forth on Chloromycetin were introduced into the official labeling and were delivered to practicing physicians by Parke, Davis and Co., following the first report from the National Research Council.

SENATOR NELSON: What information was disseminated at that time, sir?

DR. LUECK: The National Research Council report of 1952, plus the conclusions that the Food and Drug Administration arrived at as a result of that report.

---

[31] Mr. Cutler, special council, PMA.

SENATOR NELSON: I will go back to that in a moment. But now that you mention the [NRC] report, are you aware of what notice Parke, Davis sent to its detail men at that time?

DR. LUECK: Am I aware of what, Mr. Chairman?

SENATOR NELSON: What information on that point was sent to the detail men from Parke, Davis at that time?

DR. LUECK: No; I would not be specifically advised on that. Mr. Chairman, I would like to state a detail man would have the official labels with him and leave them when he talked to the physician.

MR. GORDON: Dr. Lueck, I just tried to read it. You need a magnifying glass to read it. I could not read it.

SENATOR NELSON: The real point is, even though the detail man may have had the insert—whether or not he gives it to the doctor, I do not know—but the instruction was to say that this study by the specialists of the National Research Council "resulted in unqualified sanction of continued use of Chloromycetin for all conditions for which it has been previously used."

I hope I am not misinterpreting this Kefauver report,[32] but the National Research Council said that certain cases of serious blood dyscrasia had been associated with chloramphenicol. In the instructions to the detail man, Parke, Davis did not say anything about that. They said the report resulted in an unqualified sanction of use of the drug.

Do you think it is natural for the detail man to start emphasizing problems when the company has told him something else?

DR. LUECK: I do not think that the company told him something else.

Along with [the instructions] was this labeling that the doctor should read, which carried the warnings and which carried the uses and the recommended dosage, Mr. Chairman. This is official labeling. We do not want our detail men to paraphrase this. This is physician language and he must make the decision; the physician.

SENATOR NELSON: Well, I am well aware of that. But the companies have testified repeatedly here that one of the responsibilities of the detail man is to be well informed and inform the doctor about what the drug is, how it is to be used, and all benefits and risks involved in the use of the drug so the doctor will be well informed. Yet what was set out to the detail man in this case did not say that at all.

DR. LUECK: Our detail men, I will repeat again, Mr. Chairman, have instructions to leave with the physicians the official package insert that is current at that time. That is the document on which the physician must make his judgment.

SENATOR NELSON: I might say that, even with my brand new glasses, I have to concentrate very hard to read the warning on the insert.

DR. LUECK: I would like to comment on that. I personally have changed that. That was the package insert that was current in 1961. This is the one that is current today.

SENATOR NELSON: Can you read that more easily?

MR. CUTLER: Yes.

SENATOR NELSON: All right. Just a couple more points on these ads before I conclude.

I was just about to refer to the ad of February 20, 1967, the ad that I

[32] The Kefauver *Report,* source of Senator Nelson's information, devoted five pages to this incident.

spoke of before. Is it the intent of the company henceforth to publish this kind of [serious] warning in all of its ads?

DR. LUECK: Yes, sir. When the ad includes indications for usage, Mr. Chairman, and dosage schedules, we will include the full warning statements, all the side effects, and so forth.[33]

SENATOR NELSON: Then take the [1961] ad I just gave you. You would not run that 1961 ad again, then?

DR. LUECK: No, sir; we would not run that 1961 ad.

SENATOR NELSON: You do not think that it is adequate?

DR. LUECK: No, sir; it does not meet the present requirements.

SENATOR NELSON: Do you think these present requirements, in view of the history of this product, are justifiable?

DR. LUECK: Yes; I think they are. I think they are very adequate.

SENATOR NELSON: Now, let me ask you another question. I have here an ad from the *British Medical Journal* of February 11, 1967. That British ad does not have any warning in it at all. (Reads the text.) No warning at all in that ad. How do you explain that?

DR. LUECK: Mr. Chairman, is that the complete ad?

SENATOR NELSON: Yes; do you not have a copy of it?

DR. LUECK: I only have one page. I did not know if that was the complete ad or not.

SENATOR NELSON: Yes; I will show you the journal.

DR. LUECK: I would like to comment that the warning requirements on Chloromycetin are different in practically every country of the world. Parke, Davis & Co., has always met all the requirements, the legal requirements of whatever country we distributed our products in and we have met the necessity of the medical profession in that country. These ads, so far as I know, met all of those requirements.

SENATOR NELSON: Well, the effect of the drug is the same on people in other countries as it is here; is it not?

DR. LUECK: Largely.

SENATOR NELSON: Do you know of some differentiation?

DR. LUECK: Yes; there are some minor differentiations, but for the sake of this discussion, let us say they are the same.

MR. CUTLER: Mr. Chairman, I think you will find that the point you are developing is true of every single ad in this magazine, which is a distinguished magazine of the British Medical Society and I assume it meets all of what they consider to be appropriate requirements.

SENATOR NELSON: I have not questioned whether or not it met their requirements. I have assumed that. There is a very serious moral question involved that ought to be brought up. It sure shocks me. What the witness says is we will meet the standards of the country where the drug is sold. That means, of course, there is not a single underdeveloped country in the world that has any defense against the exploitation of their people for profit by an American corporation who does not warn them of the serious, mighty serious, possibly fatal consequences here. So you mean to testify that your company will stand on the proposition that we will send drugs to all the underdeveloped countries in the world and since they do not have any standards, we will fool them all we can and make a great big profit and never tell the doctors that there is a risk of serious blood dyscrasias. Is that what you are telling the committee?

---

[33] Under the Drug Act Amendments of 1962, advertisements giving use and dosage data had to provide a balanced view of side effects and contraindications.

MR. CUTLER: No, sir. I think you know that, sir. This is a British Medical Society. The British doctors are sophisticated doctors, just as sophisticated as the doctors in this country. This meets all their requirements. This is, of course, only a small part of the information that goes to a British doctor.

SENATOR NELSON: That is not the testimony.

MR. CUTLER: You are indicting every drug company in Great Britain and the United States.

SENATOR NELSON: Any company, drug company or any other kind of company, that would do that, I would be pleased to indict on moral grounds. I think they ought to be indicted on moral grounds. I do not understand what standard of ethics would govern a great industry of this country that would find it satisfactory to finally, under compulsion in this country, warn the public and warn the doctors about serious blood dyscrasias and then cavalierly advertise in another country without telling those people about the risks. I should think you people would not be able to sleep.

MR. CUTLER: Mr. Chairman, I think you are reaching awfully far to criticize a witness and a company that brought you some evidence that you have been asking for, for months, about therapeutic equivalency of various drugs. It so happens that the pharmaceutical industry, as you know, has believed that advertisements of drugs are not the primary source of information on which the doctor relies. In 1962, this issue was fought out in this Congress and it was decided by the Congress that all advertisements should contain brief summaries, warnings, of complications and side effects, and the FDA was given power to regulate in that area. These companies have done their very best to live up to that law, the need for which they did not agree with at the time. They have observed that law, and you are digging back to 1952, some 15 years ago, to whip this company which brought you some evidence.

I must object to that, Mr. Chairman, most respectfully.

This witness did not come to testify about advertising. Neither you nor Mr. Gordon said anything to him in advance to indicate you intended to question him about advertising. If you want to query Parke, Davis about its advertising, give them notice and they will produce a witness to reply to you.

SENATOR NELSON: We intend to ask questions about the whole spectrum of issues related to the drug industry as we have of every other witness who has come here. You are the first one to complain and you have not yet been a witness. I can't predict every question we will think of as various issues arise. But if you think this is unfair, as I say, you can notify my office as to when Parke, Davis wants to go through these ads with us and we will pick out a time very soon for Parke, Davis to bring their advertising people. Let them talk about the morality of this ad.

But it shocks me that you do not even blush when you defend a company advertising drugs in another country without the warning required here when the reason it is required in this country is because the ad without the warning does mislead doctors, it does cause people to prescribe a dangerous drug for illnesses that are not serious. That is why the ad is run with the warning. And you know it and everybody else knew it, too.

I would like an answer to that. If this is the standard of ethics by which the industry operates, I tell you, you fellows are in for some sad trouble. I do not think this country will stand for it.

I do not have any more questions of this witness.

Thank you, Dr. Lueck.[34]

---

[34] Nelson *Hearings*, Pt. 6, pp. 2167–2173, 2221–2225.

THE DIRECTION OF RESEARCH

Criticism of its medical performance put the drug industry in a particularly sensitive spot. It has been the industry's failings in the medical area rather than in the economic area that have, in the past, brought on both criticism and more stringent regulation. Although the most "sensational" problems in the medical area are those that have to do with drug side effects and company reluctance to acknowledge these,[35] another much emphasized issue has been how far economic rather than scientific objectives dominate the direction of research.

In the following excerpt, the industry's position is briefly outlined by Mr. Stetler, president of the PMA.

MR. STETLER: The pharmaceutical industry as we know it today is very young—less than 30 years old. Within these three decades, we have seen the emergence of a variety of new drugs that have all but revolutionized the practice of medicine—sulfonamides and antibiotics, cardiovascular preparations and antidepressants, vitamins, hormones, and tranquilizers—an impressive array of drug products that have virtually wiped out some killing diseases, have shortened the length of the average stay in hospitals, have reduced the space requirements of mental institutions, and have been a boon to doctors everywhere in the practice of their calling.

From 1940 to 1966, an amazing total of 823 new single chemical entity drugs were introduced as prescription drugs in the United States. I think this compilation is significant, for it shows that the United States originated 502 of the 823 new weapons against disease and suffering. . . . Of the 502, the laboratories of American manufacturers were responsible for 87%.

SENATOR NELSON: May I interrupt for a moment? You mentioned 823 new weapons against disease. Were they all brand-new entities that treated some disease in a different way, or were they drugs that went on the market although there was already a drug available to treat the disease?

MR. STETLER: Well, I am sure they varied. They are single chemical entities. Some of them replace a drug on the market for the reason probably that it was a more effective product for that particular disease. But [the 823 figure] does not include combinations or mixtures. They are really the new single entities, innovative type of drugs.

SENATOR NELSON: Is there any claim by the industry that in each one of these 823 cases the new chemical entity was a better and more effective drug to treat a particular condition than the ones already in existence?

MR. STETLER: No; that is not the claim. The point is merely that each drug is effective for the claims made.

As you know, under the Food and Drug Act, that agency does not look at relative effectiveness. It looks at safety and effectiveness. So that there obviously are drugs on the market that—all or several of which—treat a particular disease.

SENATOR NELSON: You are aware that there are distinguished people in the field of pharmacology who state that a considerable amount of research is done simply to find molecular manipulations of other drugs. These modifications, which do the same thing as the original drugs, can get their own trade names, when in fact they are not necessary, and do not do anything other drugs do not do. You are aware of that assertion, are you not?

MR. STETLER: Very definitely. . . .

SENATOR NELSON: We have had testimony, as you know, that there have been fruitful results from what is sometimes called molecular manipulation and modification. On the other hand, we have had testimony that there is a considerable amount of research which is really aiming at getting another combination of molecules which is not more effective than a drug that is already on the market. But the new version can be identified with a brand name, and then promoted.

MR. STETLER: Of course, the mere existence of multiple drugs on the market that have a similar effect is not necessarily bad. I suppose if we were to outlaw that, we would eliminate a lot of very healthy competition. So that there is an economic and a medical aspect to this question, both of which are complex.

SENATOR NELSON: I have not suggested that it be outlawed. But I think there ought to be come attempt to understand this.[36]

RISK/RETURN RELATIONSHIP IN DRUGS

The issue of whether high returns in the drug industry were or were not warranted by abnormally high risks was viewed by both industry and government as a technical economic question to be entrusted to "expert" witnesses rather than to businessmen or politicians.

The essential disagreement between the two sides pertained to the definition of risk. Spokesmen for the industry contended that risk should be defined as "the dispersion of individual companies' rates of return about their industry's average rate of return for a given year." Based on this definition, which was said to measure "uncertainty" of return for the "prospective investor," drugs emerged as the fourth most risky industry among 59 included in a statistical study covering a 15-year period.

Commenting on this conclusion, a government witness first briefly questioned its "fit" with the high P/E ratio accorded by the market to drug stocks. Then, turning to the definition of risk selected by the industry spokesman, he said that its "chief conceptual shortcoming" was its failure to tell "anything about the probability of incurring losses." Using this measure, he said, "An industry may be defined as risky even though all firms in it earn excessively high profits." Conversely, "This measure may define an industry as having very low risk even though all firms are making little or no profit."[37] As for the industry's 15-year study, "We must alway be skeptical of simple statistical associations among complicated economic phenomena." " 'Garbage in, garbage out is a sound approach, even to the most elegantly computerized simulation.' "[38]

---

[36] Nelson *Hearings*, Pt. 4, pp. 1350–1352.
[37] Nelson *Hearings*, Pt. 5, pp. 1638–1861.
[38] Ibid.

Xerox Corporation

ON SEPTEMBER 8, 1971, Mr. C. Peter McColough, then president and chief executive officer of the Xerox Corporation, announced an experimental Social Service Leave Program to begin in January 1972. The program provided an opportunity for approximately 20 Xerox employees in the United States to take up to a one-year leave of absence, with full pay and benefits, and devote the time to working with a social service organization of their choice. They were also guaranteed the same or an equivalent job with the same pay, responsibilities, status and opportunity for advancement upon return to the company.

In announcing the program to Xerox employees, Mr. McColough spoke of corporate and individual commitment and what the program represented for each:

> Xerox has always had a basic philosophy that we should be involved as a corporation in the problems of our society. We've encouraged our people to be involved. Social Service Leave is a logical extension of our commitment. We are determined to put something back into society.
>
> Many of our people share our commitment. But on a part-time basis, there is only so much they can do. A lot of them would like to really sink their teeth into a problem full time. We'll give them a chance to do this during the prime of their working careers, when they're best able to do it. They won't have to wait until they retire.
>
> Many of our best people would not be here today if Xerox stood only for profits.
>
> In the future, our conduct as corporate citizens will be even more important—if that's possible—as we try to recruit the best young people available. As a result of programs like the Social Service Leave, we think that the bright young people will be more apt to join us than some other big company.

By January, Mr. McColough and others in top management were beginning to evaluate the program to determine whether it ought to be continued and, if so, whether the scope, policies and procedures underlying it were appropriate. As far as they could determine, it had been favorably received both inside and outside the company. Several overseas affiliates had evidenced an interest in a program of their own, usually to be operated under somewhat different policies. Moreover, it had so far been implemented according to plan and without serious mishap. On the other hand, a number of unforeseen organizational problems had already been encountered and the difficult tasks of responding to the needs of the men and women on leave and replacing them in equivalent career opportunities remained ahead.

The evaluation was accompanied by a degree of urgency. There was a general feeling among those closely involved in planning the program that the best time from the employees' standpoint to begin a social leave was in September, which, if adopted, would advance the announcement of a 1972–73 program to April or May.

XEROX HISTORY

In 1971 Xerox had sales of $1.94 billion and profits of $212.6 million, placing it among the largest fifty-five industrial corporations in the *Fortune* 500. Growth had been spectacular since 1959 when sales were $33.3 million and profits $2.1 million. In fact, from 1960 to 1970, earnings per share increased at a compound rate of 47.3% per year, highest on the *Fortune* list.

The primary source of growth for Xerox had come through the commercial development of an electrostatic-photographic copying process later known as xerography. Formed in 1906 in Rochester, New York, as the Haloid Corporation by Joseph R. Wilson and three associates to process and sell sensitized photographic paper, the company had struggled through the depression and emerged from the war years with sales in 1946 of $6,750,000 and profits of $101,000. That year Joseph C. Wilson succeeded his father as president. Confronted by increasing competition and decreasing margins in traditional product lines, the younger Mr. Wilson was eager to develop new products but lacked the resources to support a significant research effort. At this time the Battelle Institute, a non-profit research organization, had been seeking industrial support for the development of a copying process patented by Chester Carlson in 1940 and since 1944 supported by the Institute. Although numerous corporations, including Kodak, IBM and RCA, had turned the invitation down, Mr. Wilson in 1947 agreed to acquire from Battelle certain licensing rights in return for future royalty payments and an annual contribution of $25,000. A short time later Xerox renegotiated the arrangement and became the sole licensing agency for all patents in the xerography field.

Xerox invested heavily in research during the next years, greatly expanding its patent position, and yielding a series of specialized applications for xerography which by the mid-1950's contributed over half of the company's revenues. From 1953 to 1960 over $70 million was poured into research, slightly more than half of it contributed by outside debt and equity financing. It was not, however, until 1960 and the introduction of the 914, the first fully automatic dry copier in the office equipment industry, that this investment really began to pay off.

On the strength of the 914, sales nearly tripled from 1960 to 1962 as Xerox became the leader in the copier field. The company sought to expand that position by aggressively broadening its product line to include desk top copiers and high-speed machines with expanded reproduction capabilities. As machine speeds increased and reproduction quality improved, the traditional distinction between the copying and duplicating fields became blurred. The pace of development and marketing efforts in office copiers and duplicators was intense as the partial list of product introductions below suggests:

Year	Product	Feature
1960............	914	Basic console model (400 copies per hour)
1963............	813	Desk top model (330 copies per hour)
1965............	2400	Copier-duplicator (2,400 copies per hour)
1966............	720	Expanded version of 914 (720 copies per hour)
1967............	660	Expanded version of 813 (660 copies per hour)
1968............	3600	Expanded version of 2400 (3,600 copies per hour)
1969............	7000	Duplicator, expanded capabilities (3,600 copies per hour)
1971............	4000	Small console, expanded capabilities (2,000 copies per hour)

By 1971, Xerox was estimated in the business press to have 65% to 80% of the office copier market in the United States. The company's record had encouraged competition from such large firms as Eastman Kodak, Minnesota Mining, Litton, Singer, and Sperry Rand and a variety of smaller ones. A recent entrant was IBM which in April 1970 introduced a machine having much in common with the Xerox model 720. *Financial World*,[1] noting that some 70% of commercial and government establishments already contained a copier, was among those predicting increasing competition in the future. Nevertheless, Xerox 1971 revenues from copiers and rentals in the United States increased 12% over the previous year, with steady improvement relative to 1970 throughout the year.

In 1956, Xerox formed a joint venture with the Rank organization of London to manufacture and sell xerographic products in world markets, a relationship which in 1961 also led to the formation of a second joint venture between Rank-Xerox and Fuji Photo Film Co., Fuji-Xerox, directed specifically at markets in the Far East. Revenues overseas also increased dramatically after the introduction of the 914. Then in 1969 Xerox purchased the 51st percent of Rank-Xerox and renegotiated certain royalty provisions in exchange for stock valued at $20 million.

During the 1970s, Xerox sought participation in several new fields. First, in 1963 Electro Optical Systems (EOS), an aerospace company involved in laser technology, solar power conversion and space reconnaissance, was acquired to gain entry into the high technology, government financed, R & D business. Then, beginning in 1964 and con-

---

[1] "Copiers: Competition Heating Up," *Financial World*, May 6, 1970, p. 6 ff.

cluding in 1968 with the acquisition of a prominent textbook publisher, Ginn & Co., Xerox assembled an education group producing a wide range of materials and information services. Finally, in 1969 in exchange for approximately $1 billion in stock, the company acquired Scientific Data Systems, a mainframe computer manufacturer with revenues of $100 million, about 70% of it derived from scientific and engineering applications.

These new ventures had not, as yet, produced a record approaching that in office copiers. Cutbacks and reallocations in government programs had seriously affected the aerospace business and dampened the growth in spending for education. The computer group, renamed Xerox Data Systems (XDS) had been subject to similar pressures and, in part due to more conservative accounting policies, had been operating at a loss. Revenues from computer products were off about 20% in 1971 and management indicated that losses were expected to continue through 1973.

A breakdown of revenues by product line was reported as follows:

	1969	1970	1971
Business products	56%	58%	56%
International operations	27	30	34
Computer products	8	5	3
Educational materials and information services	6	6	6
Government sponsored research and military products	3	1	1
	100%	100%	100%

Profits after taxes from international operations were $72 million in 1970 and $92 million in 1971 or 38% and 43%, respectively, of the corporate total. A financial summary is provided in Exhibit 1.

Xerox had a publicly stated goal of achieving continuing growth of 20% per year in earnings per share with a return on stockholder investment of 20%. This target was generally perceived in the organization to be a very demanding one. In 1971 Mr. McColough indicated that growth would be guided by two broad policies, the first directed toward industry leadership in the information industry and the second toward becoming a "great multinational company."

> We think that our field of interest is the business of supplying knowledge and information on a worldwide basis. It seems to me that this will be the fastest growing business in the world in the 1970s. The demand for knowledge and information in every country of the world is increasing geometrically each year. There seems to be no limit to where we can go in that field if we apply ourselves to it in the right way. . . . I think in the middle 70s, you will see us bring [computer and imaging capabilities] together in combination to offer new services that will be very important to our business worldwide.
>
> *   *   *   *   *
>
> One of our major objectives for the 1970s clearly has to be to make Xerox a great multinational company. Multinational. Not inter-

national. In the 1960s, as we spread our wings from the United States into the rest of the world through various partnerships we became an international company in the sense that we operated in many parts of the world.

But in the 1970s we must become a multinational company. Among other things a multinational company must provide opportunities for all its people regardless of what country they come from. The young person who joins the company today—whether in Milan or Sao Paulo or New York City—should have an equal opportunity to take my job in the future.

*   *   *   *   *

We must also put great emphasis in the 1970s on having manufacturing operations in many locations. We have to realize that if we are going to be large in the major countries of the world, we are going to have to contribute to those countries. We can't simply go in with products manufactured somewhere else; we must put something back in.

ORGANIZATIONAL STRUCTURE

Managing the company's growth constituted a formidable challenge for the Xerox organization. The number of employees grew from 9,000 in 1960 to 63,000 in 1971, about 25,000 of them overseas. Moreover, by the late 1970s this total was expected to more than double again. The average employee in the United States was estimated to be less than 30 years old and about a third of them had been with the company less than three years. Xerox had entered the 1960s with a functional organization but over the next decade changes at all levels were frequent as the company moved toward a divisionalized structure. The consequences of growth for individual managers were described by one personnel executive in the Business Products Group (BPG), which alone had 33,000 employees:

> Xerox has the ability to make organization changes quickly. In BPG going from $100 million to $1.2 billion in ten years has meant that just by staying in the same job, a manager's responsibilities increase dramatically. One of the rewards of my work is seeing people literally grow. Of course, some don't and we have had to move them down or aside. We no longer have employment contracts with our top managers but instead give them a six-month turnaround time should we decide to part ways.

Rapid growth had also prompted the company to seek managers for high-level positions from outside the company. Mr. Archie McCardell (45), president, who joined Xerox in 1966 from Ford[2] where he had held various jobs in the finance and control area, commented:

> We have grown so fast that there has not been time for enough managers to come up through the ranks. We have brought in a num-

---

[2] Other senior executives coming to Xerox from other companies since 1967 included Dr. Jacob Goldman (Sr. V.P., R & D) and Mr. James O'Neill (Gr. V.P., BPG) from Ford, Mr. Joseph Flavin (Ex. V.P.) and Mr. William Glavin (Gr. V.P., XDS) from IBM, and Mr. Robert Haigh (Gr. V.P., Education Group) from Standard Oil (Ohio).

ber of outsiders at high levels and will probably continue to do so for another two or three years. With the pressures on our organization, getting sufficient attention devoted to management development has been a continuing source of concern for us.

In 1969, Xerox announced plans to relocate the corporate offices in Connecticut. On an interim basis, pending construction of a new office building in Greenwich, headquarters were moved to the neighboring town of Stamford, Connecticut.

In December 1971, a major rearrangement at the corporate level was announced to align the organization with the company's strategy for the 1970s. The announcement, although planned for some time, took place several weeks after the unexpected death of Mr. Wilson. Mr. McColough, who came to Xerox in 1954, rose through sales to executive vice president in 1962, president in 1966, and chief executive officer in 1968, became chairman. Mr. McCardell, executive vice president since 1968, became president and chief operating officer. All U.S. operations in computers, copying/duplicating, education and aerospace were assigned to Mr. Raymond Hay (43), who formerly was responsible for BPG and for a short time overseas activities as well. Mr. Joseph Flavin (43), formerly senior vice president for planning and finance and then briefly in charge of XDS, was made responsible for international operations. The new organization is shown in Exhibit 2.

CORPORATE RESPONSIBILITY

Xerox management believed that the company was a social as well as an economic institution and had responsibilities to society beyond economic performance. Mr. Wilson articulated this attitude in a 1964 speech:

> The corporation cannot refuse to take a stand on public issues of major concern; failure to act is to throw its weight on the side of the status quo, and the public interprets it that way.
> Inevitably the corporation is involved in economic, social and political dynamics whether it wills or not, and to ignore the noneconomic consequences of business decisions is to invite outside intervention. . . .

There was a general feeling in the company that Mr. McColough's commitment to this point of view was also very strong.

The company had been involved in a number of programs which related to this social concern. In 1968 Xerox participated with local community organizations in Rochester in the founding of FIGHTON, Inc., a manufacturing company owned and managed by Blacks in the inner city, and continued to be a major customer for its products and a consultant to its management. Investments and deposits had also been made in minority-owned banks. Internally Xerox had instituted a minority hiring and development program that had substantially increased the number of minority employees. A pollution abatement control committee had also been formed to monitor the company's activities in that area.

The company had been active in sharing sponsorship of TV events of educational or cultural significance, among the recent programs being the "Civilisation" series and Sesame Street. In addition, charitable contributions of about $5.0 million were made during 1971, up from $4.4 million in 1970 and $3.7 million in 1969. The majority of the funds went to educational institutions; other recipients included Community Chests and United Funds in locations having Xerox facilities and a wide variety of civic, legal, health and urban affairs organizations. Asked in 1969 whether contributions should be cut back, 90.2% of the stockholders, representing 96.9% of the shares, voted "no."

THE SOCIAL SERVICE LEAVE PROGRAM— CONCEPTION AND DESIGN

In August 1970, Mr. McCardell and Mr. James Wainger took the night flight from New York to Los Angeles. Mr. Wainger, who originally joined Xerox in 1960 but left the company from 1966 to 1969 to teach and write plays, had been made director of personnel two months earlier.[3] The conversation turned to how Xerox might be more responsive to social and employee needs in the 1970s. Mr. McCardell suggested that the company consider making some of its people available to work on problems of their choosing. By the time the wheels touched in Los Angeles, a leave program had been outlined in some detail.

Upon his return, Mr. Wainger discussed the idea briefly with Mr. Sanford Kaplan, his immediate superior at the time, and Mr. Mc-Colough, receiving in each case enthusiastic support. He then described the program in a memorandum sent to corporate executives (see Exhibit 3).

Mr. McColough suggested one modification almost immediately: that the evaluation committee be composed of lower level Xerox employees rather than a prestigious outside board. He commented:

> Xerox is a very young company. Our average age is less than 30 and we will be hiring tens of thousands of young people in the next few years. Large corporations inevitably tend to be dictatorial which runs counter to the needs of many young people. They would like to have a voice in policy and not have to wait until late in their careers. This committee is the first of a number of things that will involve our employees in either decision or advisory roles.
>
> I also believe that such a committee can do a better job of evaluating projects. Its members are probably more in tune with the needs that those applying for leave are hoping to satisfy. This procedure will erase any tinge that the committee is there to serve our [top management's] interests.

While the remainder of the top management group was positive about the leave program, there was some feeling that the fall of 1970 was not the appropriate time to initiate it. A soft economy in the latter

---

[3] Mr. Wainger recalled that his assignment had come as a surprise; "I told Peter [McColough] I had no experience in personnel, but he said what he was looking for was someone with a sense for the company in a society in evolution." He was elected vice president in 1971.

half of the year was putting pressure on operating budgets which in turn was forcing "modest" layoffs at headquarters and in Rochester. As one manager put it, "the psychology didn't set right—to be laying off and at the same time doing this." Mr. McColough decided to delay the announcement of the program.

Mr. Wainger began to reactivate the program the following spring. It was June, however, before the interview with Mr. McColough which was to appear in the brochure describing it could be arranged. Then with summer vacations approaching and the desire to "do the brochure right," the announcement date was put off until September.

In the meantime, Mr. Wainger set in motion a procedure for selecting members of the Evaluation Committee. He first contacted the top personnel executive in each division and asked them to identify people in their units who were relatively young, had some background in social service activities, possessed an "intellectual and emotional affinity for social issues," and were not members of top management. He then reviewed the list with Mr. Robert Schneider, assistant to the president and formerly manager of corporate contributions, and selected from it those that appeared most appropriate, keeping in mind the desire for a representative group in terms of operating unit, race, background and sex. The two men, individually, then visited these people in the field. Offers to join the committee were extended to and accepted on the spot by the first five interviewed. Messrs. Wainger and Schneider, as the two "old men," rounded out the committee shown in Exhibit 4.

The final ground rules for administering the program were also worked out for inclusion in the brochure. Xerox employees in the United States with three or more years of service were to be eligible for leave. No restrictions were to be placed on the type of projects acceptable except that they be legal, nonpartisan and under the sponsorship of an existing nonprofit organization of some kind. In addition to describing how they proposed to spend their time, applicants were to have the written acceptance of the sponsoring agency. It was Mr. McCardell's original idea that to help insure the commitment of applicants to projects, the company should play no part in matching people and opportunities.

Applications were to be submitted directly to the Evaluation Committee; employee names, however, were not to be available to the committee during their deliberations. Employees would not be asked to seek permission to apply nor were their superiors to be consulted at any time in the selection process. The brochure also noted that, "It's possible that in a rare case a person selected may be so essential in his work at Xerox that he cannot be released. If that should happen, the burden of proof will be on the manager and the final decision will be made by Peter McColough."

Mr. McColough commented on the reasons behind avoiding an "up the line" approval procedure:

> I do not want Social Service Leave to be looked upon in the organization as a reward for good performance. Nor do I want it, speaking pragmatically, to be a device for managers to get rid of people they

don't want. There are other ways of doing these things, and this program should not be used as a substitute. I also do not want managers to be able to block someone from seeking leave. I would say O.K. to a manager who is emphatic about not losing a subordinate, but I could not do it lightly. Finally, putting the decision in the hands of an independent committee removes the inference that we have our own pet projects. I am able to tell agencies who call me directly that the choice is not mine.

Mr. Wainger added some further thoughts on the organization of the program:

Having a multi-level approval process—God, doesn't that sound like jargon!—would dilute the corporate commitment to the project. This is *Xerox* doing something and not the units themselves, and the judgments should be those of the corporation. I favor functionalizing not decentralizing responsibility for an activity such as this.

A bottoms-up approach, I'm afraid, would introduce a lot of extraneous judgments in this case which would cut the heart out of the program. Worst of all, approval would be based on their [operation managers] view of the value of a project. That view could be influenced by administrative convenience—can't let a good subordinate go and so forth. That's especially serious when it comes to salesmen because so often those skills are what are most needed by social service agencies. We've gone to great lengths to involve on the committee the right people with right values to judge applications.

While the employees were on leave, their salaries, including a normal increase, were to be paid from a corporate account and not charged to the operating units. The aggregate cost was estimated at about $600,000.

ANNOUNCEMENT AND REACTION

On September 9, every Xerox employee in the United States was mailed a letter from Mr. McColough, the illustrated brochure and an application form (reproduced as Exhibit 5) which together described the program, the Evaluation Committee and the procedures for applying. Thus, everyone in the company, with the exception of those few corporate executives who had been directly involved, was apprised of the program at the same time. Although he did not like the idea of a press release, Mr. Wainger had one issued to avoid the confusion and conflicting stories that he felt might reach the media from such a large mailing.

The outside reaction was "overwhelming." Newspapers all over the country carried stories about the Social Service Leave, a television network inquired if a special feature might be made of it, and numerous radio stations and magazine reporters called for interviews. Mr. Wainger spoke for many in the corporation when he said:

I felt embarrassed about the attention this has received and did what I could to draw back from it. After all, the program is a very modest, experimental expression of our concern. Naturally, the publicity is good for our image, but that's not the reason we did it.

Several hundred social agencies have also called and we have had to send them a letter saying it's up to the employees, not us.

Within the organization, the response was described by one manager as that of "quiet admiration—a feeling that the company is really putting money and people behind its words."

From his vantage point, Mr. McColough said:

> The response I have had from the organization has all been favorable. In this case, that should not be surprising, of course, since it was clearly my decision and had already been done. I am sure, on the other hand, that had the expense gone into the operating budgets, there would have been some opposition.

There being no further policy matters to attend to, for the time being, Mr. Wainger's office settled down to wait until November 1, the deadline for applications.

APPLICATIONS

There was little conversation in the organization during September and October about social leave. Mr. Douglas Reid, manager of personnel operations at BPG, received a few phone calls from applicants in need of information which he referred to Mr. Wainger's office and on one occasion from a manager in support of a subordinate's project. However, the period was an active one for those assembling proposals. Mrs. Frayda Cooper, an editor at Ginn and eventually among those selected for leave, recalled her experience:

> I had lunch with Mr. Baker's[4] secretary on September 9 and she told me about the Social Leave Program. It perked my interest. For some time I have wanted to work with the aged. That night I talked about it with my son who encouraged me to try. When the brochure came a few days later I had mixed reactions; the committee didn't look very old—would they be interested in a program for the elderly? On the other hand, this field wasn't mentioned among the examples it provided —maybe if the committee tried to pick people in different areas, others wouldn't have thought of this one. Anyway, I decided to go ahead.
>
> I didn't talk about my plans in the company. The executive editor knew I was applying because I borrowed his brochure to write the proposal, having given mine away and being unable to find another one. Of course, out of courtesy, I had earlier told my immediate superior. I didn't have the sense that a lot of people around me were applying but with 25,000 people eligible, there were bound to be a lot.

In the next three weeks, Mrs. Cooper talked during lunch hours and Saturdays with a variety of people in government and social agencies and at Brandeis University about the problems of the elderly and her interests and background. These discussions resulted in a letter of support, including a budget of $17,000 for various expenses, and a four-page work plan from the Massachusetts Department of Community Affairs, which Mrs. Cooper appended to her handwritten application form. Since a manuscript had recently been accepted by Ginn con-

---

[4] Mr. Baker was president of Ginn.

ditional upon her availability to edit it, she advanced the starting date in the leave proposal to April 1972.

Another successful applicant was Mr. Irving Bell, a salesman with Xerox Graphic Services. Referring to these weeks he said:

> I found out about the program by reading the AP story in the newspaper. I was interested—said to myself, "Now that's a good idea!" I have a few rich friends and they never get a year to do their thing. I started to think about my background and where I'd fit; I wanted to contribute more than the ordinary person working at night.
>
> This was right after Attica.[5] I have some friends who talked with me about the prisons in Massachusetts and that got me thinking. A few years ago I had taught at a technical school, but unfortunately teaching was a luxury I couldn't afford then. Nevertheless, it was very gratifying. It seemed to me that someone who wanted to teach in penal institutions could give a little dignity and a pride of accomplishment to some people who really need it.
>
> It was a lonely time, but working on this was such a personal thing. I thought my program was pretty good—I used to dream about it. I brought my plans up a little at home, but never mentioned them to my boss. Maybe I was hedging my risk—in case I didn't get it. I figured there would be an application from everyone who was eligible.

A few applications were received in Mr. Wainger's office in the first two weeks, but then the flow virtually stopped. By mid-October only 30 were in hand. However, the number began to increase rapidly during the last week; the total rose to 96 by Friday, October 28 and to 197 by November 1, including all those postmarked before midnight. Another 20 or so were postmarked after the deadline and were regretfully disqualified. Each application was given a quick review by the legal department to assess whether the project and agency involved was politically nonpartisan and legal. None was eliminated.

EVALUATION AND SELECTION

On November 1 the Evaluation Committee was convened at Xerox headquarters in Stamford. Since, with the exception of the two corporate managers, the committee members did not know one another, Mr. Wainger invited them to his house for dinner the night before to help them become acquainted with one another. The next morning, the group met with Mr. McCardell who told them that the corporation was not going to give them instructions on who or what should be selected and that it was their responsibility to set standards to govern their choices.

The committee then read a dozen proposals and with this common background set about developing the evaluation process. After considerable discussion seven criteria evolved:

1. Social impact
2. Ability (of applicant to fulfill proposal)
3. Commitments (of both individual and agency)

---

[5] There had been a violent end to a prison revolt at Attica State Prison in New York State in September 1971.

4. Innovativeness
5. Multiplier effect
6. Continuity of program (after volunteer leaves)
7. Realism

An eighth one—favorable or unfavorable impact on the corporation—was explicitly raised and set aside as not in the spirit of the Social Leave Program. The committee then agreed that each member should study each proposal and grade it high, medium, or low. After a batch of 25 or 30 had been read, the committee would then stop and compare notes before going on.

Mr. Wainger described the tenor of the ensuing deliberations in these terms:

> The discussions were very democratic. There was surprisingly little ego involved. Although I acted as chairman to keep the book,[6] I consciously avoided dominating the discussion. In most cases there was a consensus on the low end. If there was wide disagreement, we would stop and talk it through, which often led to changes in opinions. As a result, some applications went quickly while others occupied us for two hours.
>
> After we had been through most of the proposals, it became clear that some of them were bubbling up as clear winners—seven in fact. We listed these by area of concern. Then someone said that they were all similar in that they exhibited a high intellectual content and were global in scope—proposals to set up programs or work on an institutional level. On the other hand, many of those we had given low evaluations to were one-on-one type projects. Someone else noted that all the pictures in the brochure showed people helping people in a very direct way. Was narrow bad? Was that what we had encouraged? The debate lasted a while and eventually resulted in a decision to go back and re-evaluate some of those we had rated poorly.

The committee labored with an increasing sense of cohesiveness from 9:00 A.M. until dinnertime from Monday to Thursday and concluded in the midafternoon Friday. As the week progressed, the committee identified 38 proposals in 17 areas of social concern to be given special attention. A conscious attempt was made to spread the final choices across these areas of concern (15 were eventually included). In addition, a less explicit effort was made to use the salary information requested on the application to insure that a balanced cross-section of levels in the organization was represented.

Ultimately 21 employees were selected, 2 of them requesting six-month leaves. Included in the group were three women and eighteen men. Their ages ranged from 26 to 60 and lengths of service at Xerox from 3 to 10 years. Four had monthly salaries of less than $850 while one had a monthly salary in excess of $4,000. Thirteen were employed in BPG with the remainder spread among other line and staff groups. People and projects are described in Exhibit 6. Another five employees were named as alternates, with any substitutions to be made in the

[6] The only record of the meeting was kept on a flip chart; one page devoted to criteria, two more to areas of social concern and employee proposals and two to an analysis of those selected by age, salary level and operating unit.

same field if possible. The alternates were not to be notified and remained identified by number only.

Before the committee adjourned, Mr. McCardell met with them again. He asked the group, "If you had another 10 places, could you recommend individuals to fill them with equal enthusiasm?" The group said, "No." He then asked, "Are there five among the ones you have selected that you consider marginal?" Again the group said, "No."

That afternoon registered, special delivery letters of acceptance were sent to each of the winners. With the letter was a plane ticket and an invitation to attend a meeting at the Westchester Country Club near Stamford the following Friday and Saturday morning. The purposes of the meeting were to provide the participants with an opportunity to understand the policies to govern them while on leave, to share backgrounds, to meet members of the Evaluation Committee and to receive some advance counseling on the stresses and frustrations many of them were likely to encounter as they left the structured life of a large corporation. They were told to keep their selection in confidence until after the meeting, though it was anticipated that they might have to tell their managers in order to explain their two-day absence.

All 21 attended the meeting. Mr. McColough and Mr. McCardell mingled with the group and addressed them briefly on Friday. In addition to a considerable amount of time for informal conversation, the schedule included group meetings in which each participant described his program, and others in which an industrial psychologist and a "down to earth" urban consultant discussed potential problems. Company public relations officials also discussed how to handle press inquiries.

Mr. Wainger commented later on the relationship between Xerox and those on leave that he had stressed with them.

> I could have thought of a long list of dos and don'ts but didn't want to get into that. Basically I told them that they were still Xerox employees and we wanted them back and that we would try to help them personally if they needed it. While they are away no reports will be required or evaluations made. Members of the Evaluation Committee will visit each person at least twice to see how the program is working and we have asked for a report from the volunteer at the end of the year.
>
> There are bound to be situations we haven't anticipated. For instance, what happens if one of our people gets into legal difficulties in the course of his work? It's the agency's responsibility to back him up, but we'll do all we can to help. Or the Massachusetts Correctional Agency asks our man teaching in their prisons if Xerox will interview inmates for jobs when they are released. In such cases I told them to call me. The relationship between Xerox and the agency is a corporate matter. My suspicion is that we won't start lots of little programs to suit agencies. We have several major on-going ones initiated from the corporate level and new ones will come in the same way.

By Saturday noon, the mood was described by one man as "euphoric." Another said, "It was beautiful—the most moving experience of my life." Still another remarked, "I could sense a sigh of relief from the committee after they had been with us for a little while. By the end, we had been transformed from a bunch of individuals into a group with common bonds and a sense of purpose."

SEPARATION

Prior to the meeting at the Westchester Country Club, Mr. Wainger reviewed the list for anyone he felt might be considered indispensable, Although Mr. John Teem, Director of the Technical Staff in R & D would be difficult to replace and Mr. William Gable was a senior executive at XDS, he anticipated no major problems securing their release. Then on November 18 he sent a letter to each manager having a subordinate chosen for leave, formally announcing the selection and forcefully reminding the manager of Mr. McColough's guarantee of the same or an equivalent job for the employee after the leave. One of these letters is reproduced in Exhibit 7.

The employees were greeted with applause and admiration, although as one account representative related, it was not always universal:

> It's funny how people react. The first thing my boss said when I told him I was going to Stamford for two days was, "Who's going to look after your accounts?" Perhaps I'm expecting too much. After all, he has needs and losing his best producer won't help.
> And the other night one of those who wasn't selected called me at 11 o'clock and said that he understood the Evaluation Committee had a tough job, but he couldn't see why they had picked my project rather than his. He had been with Xerox a lot longer than me and had really gone to a lot of work in putting his proposal together; it even included a letter from the governor.
> But the response I've gotten from others, especially my clients, has more than made up for it. They have a lot of respect for Xerox. It makes me glad I'm working here.

While Mr. McColough received no petitions claiming indispensability, a number of situations were uncovered during the next several weeks which reflected the complexity of administering the Social Service Leave Program and foreshadowed the problems to be encountered reinstating those on leave in the organization.

In one instance, a manager was to have received a substantial increase in the scope of his job two days after he was notified of his selection by the Evaluation Committee. He had not known about the impending promotion prior to accepting the leave.

In another case, one of the people chosen was to have been laid off. He was a specialist, very well thought of in his division, for whom no work was available because of government spending cutbacks. The company had tried for some time to relocate him in some other unit but had been unsuccessful. In fact, while the Evaluation Committee was meeting, the lay-off request was waiting on Mr. Wainger's desk for his approval.[7] Along with the others, however, he had been guaranteed an equivalent career opportunity when he returned.

A more difficult variation of the above situation also arose. A rela-

---

[7] Xerox maintained the policy that before an employee with eight or more years of service could be released, permission had to be granted by either Mr. McColough or Mr. Wainger.

tively senior man selected for leave was in the process of being terminated because his performance did not measure up to the standards set by the manager of his department, and other departments were reluctant to pick him up. He had accepted this fact and informally agreed during the fall to use the next six months to relocate. The department manager indicated that he was not aware of the social leave application until about the time the news broke.

A final case was described by Mr. Reid:

> I got a call one day in December from a branch manager. That was unusual in itself since he was calling three or four levels up the line. He said one of his area sales managers had been selected for leave. He didn't have a replacement and regional management told him that with the budgets cut to the bone there wasn't $5,000 to cover the relocation costs associated with moving somene else in. They then suggested that he put the sales planning manager into the ASM slot. The branch manager said that meant he would end up covering for the sales planning manager.
>
> I didn't like the sound of it so I called the regional personnel manager. It finally came out that they were interested in getting the branch manager more involved in sales planning and saw this as a good way of doing it. I told him that wasn't in the spirit of the program and some way of getting a replacement had to be found.
>
> A later discussion with the branch manager revealed that there was a good salesman there who could be made ASM. The branch manager was reluctant to do this because it would mean demoting him when the old ASM returned. I suggested that he could be moved to an ASM job elsewhere, but apparently he can't move for personal reasons for two years.

Mr. Wainger indicated that he had been informed that non-budgeted relocation expense might be involved. Rather than providing the money from corporate funds, however, he decided to leave it as a proper operating unit responsibility.

CONSIDERATIONS FOR THE FUTURE

In addition to worrying through the problems of specific individuals, corporate executives were concerned about how to measure the success of the Social Service Leave Program. Mr. McCardell noted four conditions he felt were important:

1. The careers of people who have gone on leave do not suffer,
2. They have a sense of accomplishment in their year away,
3. They have a broadened perspective on the job and outside, and
4. The social agencies say their efforts have been useful.

Difficulties which he and others quickly acknowledged with such evaluation criteria were the lack of clear factual evidence and the long time span over which benefits were likely to occur.

Of more immediate concern were the number who returned to Xerox and the company's ability to reinstate them satisfactorily. A loss rate of 50% was generally viewed at corporate headquarters as "disappointing" and highly unlikely; 20% was thought by several to be "an acceptable price to pay" though again higher than expected. Mr. McCardell commented on reinstatement:

> This is probably the biggest problem we face, but with only 20 we
> can take a personal interest. That's why Peter's name was on the
> letters to the employees' supervisors. Of course, letters have been writ-
> ten before which have gone unheeded. A chief executive can't rule by
> fiat. We'll have to wait and see.

Aside from evaluation, several policy questions were raised at various
levels in the organization. The first involved accounting for the costs;
should they be allocated to the operating units or retained in a corporate
account similar to that for charitable contributions? If the former were
chosen, how far down in the organization should charges be allocated?
Some difference of opinion existed among corporate officers though an
immediate choice was not deemed necessary. Mr. Wainger indicated,
however, that if the program grew, as he hoped it would, pressure
would mount for doing away with a large, easily identifiable corporate
budget item.

The second question related to the selection procedure. A senior
manager in BPG put it this way:

> Had I been doing this, I would have put in more feedback from the
> organization and made it less a corporate-individual deal. That way we
> could have ironed out a lot of the administrative problems beforehand.
> A study of who goes on leave might be useful too. Are we encouraging
> the right type of people to work here? Are the ones who do this mar-
> ginal? At this level—only 21 people—it isn't so bad, but if it gets any
> larger, I think we'll have some problems.

While most corporate executives favored direct employee access to the
Evaluation Committee in the United States, for the reasons noted
earlier, the issue was not as clear overseas. Mr. McColough described
his dilemma:

> Just after the Social Service Leave Program was announced, I was
> in Europe talking with our people there. They were enthusiastic about
> it but asked why they weren't included. Aside from saying it was ex-
> perimental, I told them this is the way we get into trouble. If we
> limit it to the United States, it's favoritism and if we spread our
> program worldwide, it's applying United States solutions to foreign
> problems. I told them if you want it, you must *ask* for it.

Inquiries had been received from a number of overseas subsidiaries including those in Holland, New Zealand and Canada. In most instances
the subsidiary leaned in the direction of an "up-the-line" selection and
approval process. However, in January the nature and scope of overseas
participation remained undefined.

As the month drew to a close, the management group considered
again the direction of the Social Service Leave Program. Mr. Mc-
Colough's original charge had been expressed in the following way:

> Granting twenty people a leave isn't much for a company as large
> as Xerox. There are certain to be problems which can't be anticipated
> with precision beforehand. However, if we dwell on the problems, we
> will end up doing nothing. So, let's be cautious, but let's do it.

He now shared the task of interpreting that charge in light of the
events of the previous four months.

Exhibit 1

XEROX CORPORATION

Ten-Year Statistical Comparisons

	1971'	1970'	1969'
Yardsticks of Progress			
Net Income Per Common Share	$ 2.71	$ 2.40	$ 2.08
Dividends Declared Per Share	$ .80	$ .65	$ .58⅓
Operations (Dollars in thousands)			
Total Operating Revenues	$1,961,449	$1,718,587	$1,482,895
Rentals, Service and Royalties	1,563,805	1,343,252	1,094,794
Net Sales	397,644	375,335	388,101
Payroll (Excluding Benefits)	590,744	514,172	419,888
Depreciation of Rental Equipment	245,164	200,189	183,187
Depreciation of Buildings and Equipment	38,999	36,149	29,888
Amortization[3]	20,070	21,406	17,449
Expenditures for Research and Development	104,137	97,524	83,682
Income Before Income Taxes	471,081	432,938	389,722
Income Taxes	217,600	211,800	204,500
Outside Shareholders' Interests	40,871	33,447	23,854
Equity in Net Earnings of Rank Xerox Limited	—	—	—
Net Income	212,610	187,691	161,368
Dividends Declared	62,834	50,935	43,969
Financial Position (Dollars in thousands)			
Cash and Marketable Securities	$ 197,921	$ 148,982	$ 56,836
Net Trade Receivables	347,768	326,623	311,997
Inventories	226,597	222,001	172,747
Current Assets	916,731	825,416	649,011
Rental Equipment and Related Inventories at Cost	1,633,207	1,345,303	1,104,506
Accumulated Depreciation of Rental Equipment	872,283	714,833	577,832
Land, Buildings and Equipment at Cost	541,817	431,624	352,951
Accumulated Depreciation of Buildings and Equipment	172,383	144,339	116,056
Total Assets	2,156,094	1,857,325	1,531,271
Current Liabilities	532,806	457,571	391,257
Long-Term Debt (Including Current Portion)	482,731	429,690	319,407
Shareholders' Equity	1,051,767	892,500	738,455
Additions to Rental Equipment and Related Inventories[4]	382,792	312,580	279,519
Additions to Land, Buildings and Equipment[4]	121,498	88,869	75,890
General and Ratios			
Average Common Shares Outstanding During Year	78,533,533	78,315,911	77,445,464
Shareholders at Year End	143,554	146,534	129,944
Employees at Year End	66,728	59,862	54,882
Income Before Income Taxes to Total Operating Revenues	24.0%	25.2%	26.3%
Net Income to Average Shareholders' Equity	21.9%	23.0%	24.1%
Current Ratio	1.7	1.8	1.7
Long-Term Debt to Total Capitalization[5]	29.4%	30.5%	28.3%

1968[1]	1967[2]	1966[2]	1965[2]	1964	1963	1962
$ 1.68	$ 1.42	$ 1.20	$ .92	$ .68	$ .39	$ .24
$ .50	$ .40	$ .30¾	$ .20	$ .14¼	$ .08⅓	$ .04⅔
$1,224,352	$ 983,064	$752,508	$548,795	$317,840	$176,036	$115,220
896,673	673,548	477,954	327,814	184,157	114,077	65,847
327,679	309,516	274,554	220,981	133,683	61,959	49,373
336,602	289,009	223,855	160,725	93,921	55,112	36,653
175,692	135,975	97,221	69,110	37,295	20,236	12,454
26,747	23,779	18,519	12,637	7,243	4,338	3,267
12,304	8,437	6,026	5,439	3,695	3,070	1,570
59,888	50,806	53,329	38,170	24,050	14,609	8,547
309,096	226,500	182,113	138,872	86,800	50,423	30,779
164,020	108,576	86,490	68,199	44,598	27,850	16,801
16,126	11,540	8,923	4,984	–	–	–
–	–	–	–	1,523	428	(84)
128,950	106,384	86,700	65,689	43,725	23,001	13,894
34,363	28,555	21,996	14,698	10,788	4,895	2,688
$ 66,022	$ 70,670	$ 59,508	$ 26,289	$ 10,622	$ 6,933	$ 6,322
244,838	197,650	150,810	93,982	40,847	25,233	16,284
146,871	128,303	102,116	70,633	35,531	14,300	8,672
554,530	460,904	362,204	232,255	109,678	59,327	37,412
905,180	734,708	562,480	383,044	197,408	114,517	70,868
458,350	307,482	216,972	147,272	76,512	41,565	21,760
281,285	244,964	201,546	143,833	81,317	48,219	35,798
90,360	68,414	49,212	33,124	21,080	10,980	8,222
1,268,489	1,155,274	933,991	647,359	356,142	215,801	138,917
372,942	286,496	195,613	161,013	62,774	41,982	29,310
298,904	357,888	379,870	228,622	102,982	54,028	41,258
601,003	474,155	326,254	229,104	154,770	85,235	48,686
193,303	213,169	214,058	147,061	84,802	45,401	30,929
35,424	43,323	54,117	40,152	21,148	12,828	9,163
76,565,650	75,039,803	72,467,603	71,705,645	63,897,723	59,134,557	58,263,831
91,712	87,659	89,060	73,217	62,195	26,375	14,925
45,142	40,639	33,595	24,239	12,728	7,918	5,297
25.2%	23.0%	24.2%	25.3%	27.3%	28.6%	26.7%
24.0%	26.6%	31.2%	34.2%	36.4%	34.4%	33.4%
1.5	1.6	1.9	1.4	1.7	1.4	1.3
31.1%	40.8%	50.9%	47.4%	40.0%	38.8%	45.9%

[1] The data include the accounts of Xerox Data Systems and of Rank Xerox Limited for its fiscal year ended October 31.
[2] The data include the accounts of Xerox Data Systems and of Rank Xerox Limited for its fiscal year ended in June.
[3] Amortization of deferred research and development, patents, licenses and other intangible assets.
[4] Additions prior to 1969 shown net of disposals.
[5] Total capitalization defined as the sum of long-term debt (including current portion), outside shareholders' interests in net assets of subsidiaries, and shareholders' equity. Common share data adjusted to reflect change of each common share into five common shares effective December 17, 1963, and the distribution of two additional common shares for each common share held at May 16, 1969.

Exhibit 2

XEROX CORPORATION

Organization Chart

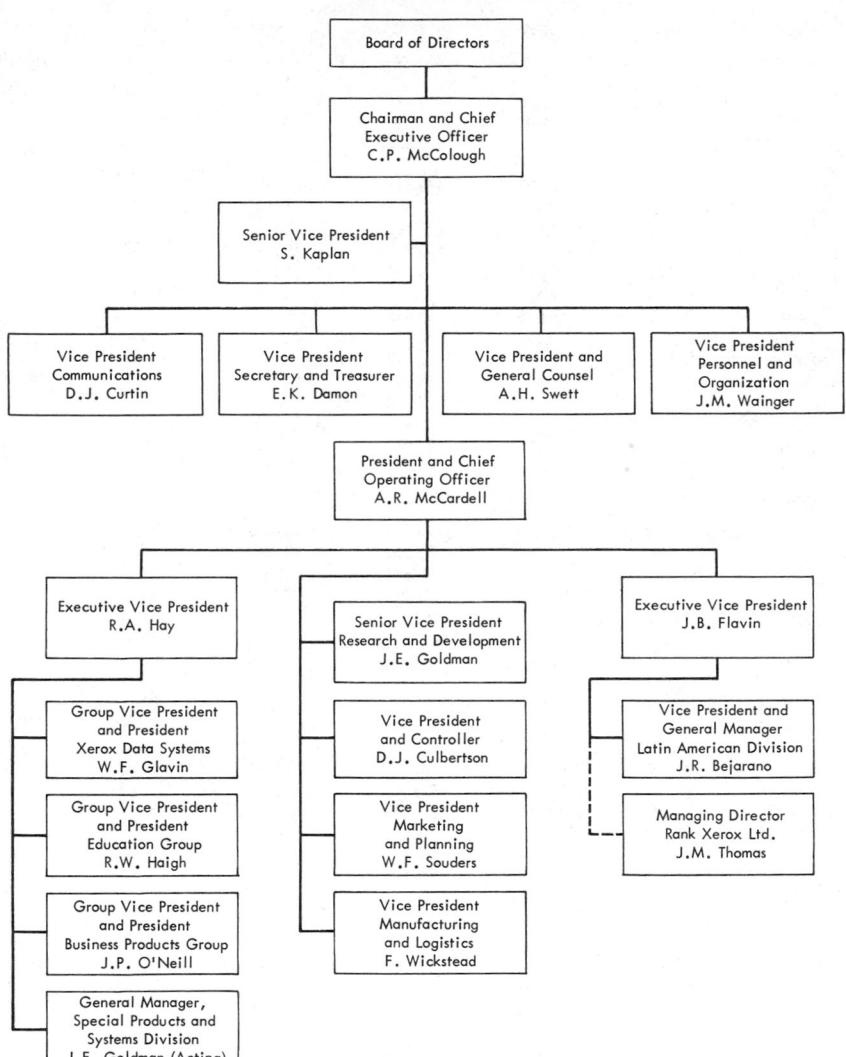

Exhibit 3

XEROX CORPORATION
Memorandum to Corporate Executives

To	See Distribution	Date	August 7, 1970
From	J. M. Wainger	Location	HR 2
Subject	Xerox Social Action	Organization	Corporate Personnel

We have decided to institute, as promptly as possible, a program for Xerox employees which we think will have substantial positive impact internally and externally, both now and for our future.

We will offer to twenty Xerox employees, regardless of level in the Corporation, (though excluding all of you) the opportunity to work for a year out of Xerox in some position that has high social value. As examples, the jobs might be with some community organization attacking urban problems, or some Federal Government agency, or a school, etc.

We plan to use the following approach. Through appropriate Xerox communications media, we will publicize the program and ask all those employees who are interested to submit a short description of the project they wish to work on and their reasons for choosing it. As part of their submission, they must include assurance that they have agreement from the prospective employer to take them on if they are freed up. We hope to receive many submissions.

All of these submissions will be screened by an impartial, outside board of prestigious men who will choose the twenty they consider to be most worthy according to the social criteria we've established.

The twenty selected employees will then be given a year to work at their chosen task. We assume they will return to Xerox at the end of that time, though no guarantee can be exacted. We will require that the projects they select be in or near their present communities. In other words, this program should not carry with it relocation subsidies for attractive long-range trips to such places as Los Angeles, Washington or Hawaii.

Xerox will maintain the employees' total compensation at the rate prevailing at the time they left Xerox by paying them the difference between whatever they receive from their outside job and their then Xerox salary.

We need to set up our outside screening board as soon as possible. I need your help. Would you please submit to me as soon as possible the names of one or more people you deem suitable to serve. The names you submit should be of people you feel fairly confident you can "deliver" if asked to contact them directly. I anticipate a board of perhaps five men, disparate in background but uniform quality.

I recognize that there are problems inherent in this program, and I'm sure you do too. However the results will more than justify taking the problems on. We will benefit and, by leading, we will influence.

You will, of course, be apprised of the details of the program as it is shaped up.

May I have your nominees for the selection board as soon as possible.

JMW/sd

Distribution:	D. J. Curtin	A. R. McCardell
	J. B. Flavin	C. P. McColough
	J. E. Goldman	J. W. Rutledge
	S. Kaplan	J. C. Wilson

EUGENE R. ALLEN, director of international operations of the Xerox Education Group in Stamford, joined XEG in 1970 following three years as director of urban education at Litton Industries. Allen, 37, was born in Sacramento, Calif.

ROBERT M. FLEGAL, 29, is a scientist in the computer science laboratory at the Palo Alto Research Center. He served in the Peace Corps in Ghana for two years. He is a native of Salt Lake City, Utah. He joined Xerox in 1970.

ERROL L. FORKNER, 29, a commercial analyst in the product management department of Xerox Data Systems in El Segundo, is working for an MA in computer sciences at UCLA. He came to XDS in 1969 after three years with IBM.

JANET L. KNIGHTON is an educational and training specialist in the Business Products Group in Webster. Before joining Xerox in 1970, she had been assistant director of the adult department of the Rochester YWCA.

ROBERT M. SCHNEIDER, assistant to the president of Xerox in Stamford, was manager of corporate contributions for three years before assuming his present post in 1969. A native of Passaic, N.J., he is 40 years old.

ROLAND A. STENTA, 31, is national accounts manager of the Philadelphia branch of BPG, following work in personnel and sales. Born in Brooklyn, he joined Xerox in 1968, from the Office of Economic Opportunity in Washington.

JAMES M. WAINGER is corporate vice president, personnel and organization, in Stamford. He joined Xerox in 1960, but left from 1966 to 1969 to teach English in high school and write plays. He's 44, and a graduate of Harvard Law.

Exhibit 5

XEROX CORPORATION

Application

XEROX SOCIAL SERVICE LEAVE APPLICATION

To be returned to:

Evaluation Board,
Social Service Leave Program
Xerox Corporation
Stamford, Connecticut 06904

My name: _____
       (print)   first   middle   last

Home address: _____

Phone: _____
              home   Xerox

Xerox Group/Division: _____ Location: _____

Present Position: _____ Employee Number: _____ Date Hired: _____

| don't write here | Application No : |

- -

| don't write here | Application No : |

In one sentence, what I want to do is: _____

_____

Time desired: _____ Dates desired: _____

This is the organization I'll work with: _____
                                                     name

_____
   address   department   name & function of person I would report to

Phone: _____ Acceptance Letter attached ☐   Salary, if any, I'll receive from the organization: _____

These are the details of the program I want to work on: (goals, history, scope, program, people affected, other workers involved, nature of activities, budget — *very specific description, please,* that will help us understand the project; attach any literature or reports or clippings that will help)

_____

_____

_____

_____

_____

My specific work will be: (what skill, what function, what tasks, what aims — or programmed results, if these can be stated in advance)

_____

_____

_____

_____

_____

_____

_____

Exhibit 5—Continued

I am specially qualified to do this by: (cite specific experience, training, skills, prior involvement, personal history — or just gnawing desire)

_____

_____

This is why I want to work on this project and this is what I hope to accomplish:

_____

_____

_____

_____

_____

My present monthly salary is: $ _____

Circle Highest Grade Completed:

High School	College	Graduate
9 - 10 - 11 - 12	13 - 14 - 15 - 16	17 - 18 - 19 - 20 - 21 - 22

College or University Attended	Degree Awarded	Major Subject
_____	_____	_____
_____	_____	_____
_____	_____	_____
_____	_____	_____

Please use as many extra sheets as you need to answer the questions fully.

Exhibit 6

XEROX CORPORATION
1972 Recipients

Name & Xerox job	Age	Years with Xerox	Project	Agency
Joel N. Axelrod / Business Products Group / Group Program Manager	39	5	Develop and implement techniques for evaluating training programs funded under the Drug Abuse Act	U.S. Office of Education
Oswaldo Aymat / Xerox Reproduction Center / Quality Control Supervisor	35	11	Counsel and guide Puerto Rican college students with the objective of reducing the high drop-out rate.	Aspira of New York
James E. Bales / Business Products Group / Technical Representative	35	10	Manage the development of a literacy program	Greater Little Rock Literacy Council
Irving C. Bell / Xerox Reproduction Center / Sales Representative	43	4	Teach mathematics to inmates in two prisons and instruct them in building trade skills	Massachusetts Department of Correction
Robert P. Britton / Business Products Group / Technical Representative	29	6	Set and teach an entry level course in electro-mechanical job skills for unskilled and unemployables	Opportunities Industrialization Center
Frank V. Cliff, Jr. / Business Products Group / Account Executive	43	9	Work with minority businessmen	Economic Development Corporation of Greater Detroit
Mrs. Frayda F. Cooper / Ginn and Company / Elementary Mathematics Editor	47	4	Organize an experimental program to provide services to the aged in a multi-town area where no such service is now available	Massachusetts Department of Community Affairs
Robert B. Cost / Business Products Group / Account Representative	26	5	Teach and counsel in a drug rehabilitation center service high school age children from New York City	Pius XII School
Joe A. Duardo / Electro-Optical Systems / Physicist	40	9	Counsel hard-core youth in a Mexican-American area	Abraham Lincoln High School
William Cable / Xerox Data Systems / Vice President	43	3	Assist low-income families in black neighborhoods in achieving home ownership	Protestant Community Services
James P. Herget / Business Products Group / A Regional Marketing Manager	27	4	As the agency's director of marketing, guide and assist minority-owned businesses in developing their marketing capability	Interracial Council for Business Opportunity of Greater Washington

Exhibit 6—Continued

Name & Xerox job	Age	Years with Xerox	Project	Agency
Robert S. Huddleston Business Products Group Technical Representative	44	9	Expand the work of an agency devoted to assisting former convicts in their return to life in their communities	The Seventh Step Foundation Topeka, Kansas
Paul S. Israel Business Products Group Area Sales Manager	38	8	Direct an effort to build a model classroom for teaching mentally retarded preschoolers	The Arizona Preschool for Retarded Children
Mrs. Esther E. Kapuschat Business Products Group Staff Nurse	60	7	Serve as director of nursing in an interdenominational crippled children's hospital	The Holy Land Christian Mission, Kansas City, Missouri
Kenneth R. Lane American Education Publications Special Education Department Editor	41	3	Establish an in-service training program leading to accreditation of house-parents in residential schools for the deaf	Conference of Executives of American Schools for the Deaf, White Plains, New York
Frederick Lightfoot Business Products Group Multiple Drill Operator	36	3	Work as a community organizer in central city area	Action for a Better Community Rochester, New York
Raymond E. Poehlein Business Products Group Development Engineering Manager	33	5	Help develop physical science curriculum and teach in a secondary school for Aglala Sioux Indians	Red Cloud Indian School
Lionel E. Reim Business Products Group A Regional Marketing Manager	28	3	Serve as business manager for an on-going coffeehouse and medical clinic for youth	General Conference of Seventh Day Adventists
Michael I. Slade Corporate Research Physicist	30	5	Provide research and develop information bulletins on ecology problems (transportation and water)	Rochester Committee for Scientific Information
John M. Teem Corporate Research and Development Director of Technical Staff	46	13	Develop and teach a science curriculum in an experimental "school without walls"	Alpha Learnings Community School
Mrs. Jean G. Williams Business Products Group Programmer	26	4	Tutor and counsel minority college and pre-college students to reduce dropout rate	Project Equal Opportunity University of Colorado

Exhibit 6—Concluded

Recapitulation

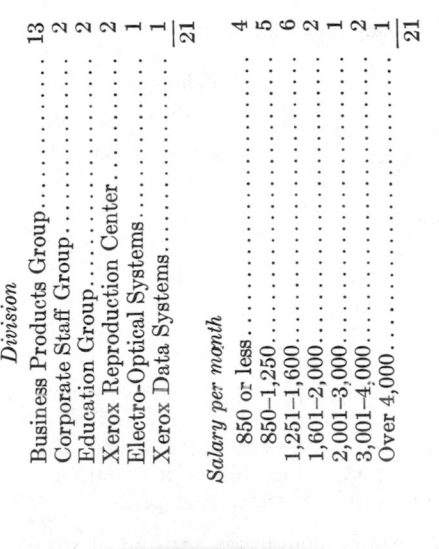

Division

Business Products Group.............. 13
Corporate Staff Group................. 2
Education Group....................... 2
Xerox Reproduction Center............ 2
Electro-Optical Systems............... 1
Xerox Data Systems................... 1
                                     ——
                                      21

Salary per month

850 or less........................... 4
850–1,250............................ 5
1,251–1,600.......................... 6
1,601–2,000.......................... 2
2,001–3,000.......................... 1
3,001–4,000.......................... 2
Over 4,000........................... 1
                                     ——
                                      21

Exhibit 7

XEROX CORPORATION

Memorandum to Supervisors

November 18, 1971

Dr. J. E. Goldman
Xerox Corporation
Corporate Headquarters
Stamford, Connecticut 06904

Dear Jack:

John M. Teem, who is employed in your organization, has been selected to receive a Xerox Social Service Leave. Based on his application, he will be engaged full time away from the company for the next year on a voluntary social program of real value. Xerox is proud of the commitment of this employee, and I'm sure you share that pride.

As you know, Peter McColough has assured all employees that those who are chosen for Leaves are *guaranteed* that on their return they will return to their former job or one of equal pay, responsibility, status and opportunity for advancement. Peter and I will review each returning employee's job placement to make certain that this guarantee is fully honored.

Therefore, as you plan for the carrying on of John's work, I'm sure you'll want to keep in mind this essential provision of the Social Service Leave policy. If the job of the person going on leave is one of many jobs of the same type, I'd expect no special provisions need be made at this time.

If, however, the job is relatively unique, I suggest that you give consideration to designating any replacement as "acting." Certain jobs may even lend themselves to developmental use, permitting the rotation of several people in them during the period of the Social Service Leave.

I'm asking relevant Personnel Departments to monitor and approve the method used to fill each job vacated, and I'm requesting, too, that Personnel Departments inform me of the action taken to fill each job vacated by an employee going on Leave.

Sincerely,

James M. Wainger
Vice President
Personnel & Organization

JMW/sd
cc: C. P. McColough
    A. R. McCardell
    G. F. Wajda

BOOK TWO

Implementing corporate strategy

The accomplishment of purpose: Organizational structure and relationships

WE must now turn our attention to the concepts and skills essential to the implementation of strategy. The life of action requires more than analytical intelligence. It is not enough to have an idea and be able to evaluate its worth. Persons with responsibility for the achievement of goals, the accomplishment of results, and the solution of problems, finally know the worth of a strategy when its utility is demonstrated. Furthermore, a unique corporate strategy determined in relation to a concrete situation is never complete, even as a formulation, until it is embodied in the organizational activities which reveal its soundness and begin to affect its nature.

INTERDEPENDENCE OF FORMULATION AND IMPLEMENTATION

It is convenient from the point of view of orderly study to divide a consideration of corporate strategy, as we have divided it, into aspects of formulation and implementation and to note, for example, the requirement of the former for analytical and conceptual ability and of the latter for administrative skill. But in real life the processes of formulation and implementation are intertwined. Feedback from operations gives notice of changing environmental factors to which strategy should be adjusted. The formulation of strategy is not finished when implementation begins. A business organization is always changing in response to its own makeup and past development. Similarly, it should be changing in response to changes in the larger systems in which it moves, and in response to its success or failure in affecting its environment. For the sake of orderly presentation, we have arranged the cases so that henceforth the data will require us to focus less on what the strategy should be than on ways to make it effective in action and to alter it as required. We are taking forward with us, however, all our previous interests. We shall continue to examine each firm's strategy aganist the criteria we have developed in order to practice the skills we have gained and to verify the decisions made by the executives of the company.

We have already seen that the determination of strategy has four subactivities: the examination of the environment for opportunity and risk, the systematic assessment of corporate strengths and weaknesses, the identification and weighting of personal values, and the clarification of public responsibilities. Implementation may also be thought of as having important subactivities. In very broad terms, these are the design of organizational structure and relationships and the effective administration of organizational processes affecting behavior. The development of effective personal leadership, crucial to success in achieving planned results, has already been discussed in the first section of this text.

In deciding on strategy, the general manager must force his mind to range over the whole vast territory of the technological, social, economic, and political systems which provide opportunity for his company or threaten its continued existence. When he turns his attention to carrying out the strategy tentatively determined, he addresses himself within the limitations of his knowledge, to all the techniques and skills of administration. To deal with so wide a range of activity, he needs a simple and flexible approach to the aspects of organized activity which he must take into account. By considering the relationships between strategy and organizational structure, strategy and organizational processes, and strategy and personal leadership styles, the student should be able to span a territory crowded with ideas without losing sight of the purpose which he seeks in crossing it.

Each of the implementing subactivities constitutes in itself a special world in which many people are doing research, developing knowledge, and asserting the importance of their work over that of other specialists. Thus the nature of organization, about which every general manager must make some assumptions, is the subject of a richly entangled array of ideas upon which one could spend a lifetime. The design of information systems—particularly at a time when the speed and capacity of the computer fascinates the processors of information—appears to require long study, an esoteric language, and even rearrangement of organizational activities for the sake of information processing. Similarly, performance appraisal, motivation and incentive systems, control systems, and systems of executive recruitment and development all have their armies of theoretical and empirical proponents, each one fully equipped with manuals, code books, rules, and techniques.

It will, of course, be impossible for us to consider in detail the knowledge and theory which have been developed during the course of a half century of researches in administration. It will be assumed that your own experience has introduced you to the major schools of thought contending in the developing administrative disciplines, and that where necessary, the knowledge you have will be supplemented by further study. Just as the general manager must be able to draw upon the skills of special staffs in leading his company, so he must be able to draw upon these special studies in effecting his own combination of organizational design and organizational practices. The simple prescription we wish to add here is that *the corporate strategy must be made to dominate the design of organizational structure and processes.* That is, the principal criterion for all decisions on organizational structure and behavior should be their relevance to the achievement of the organizational purpose, not their conformity to the dictates of special disciplines.

Thus the theses we suggest for your consideration are first that conscious strategy can be consciously implemented through skills primarily administrative in nature. Second, the chief determinant of organizational structure and the processes by which tasks are assigned and performance motivated, rewarded, and controlled should be *the strategy of the firm,* not the history of the company, its position in its industry, the specialized background of its executives, the principles of organization as developed in textbooks, the recommendations of consultants, or the conviction that one form of organization is intrinsically better than another.

The successful implementation of strategy requires that the general manager shape to the peculiar needs of his strategy the formal structure of his organization, its informal relationships, and the processes of motivation and control which provide incentives and measure results. He must bring about the commitment to organizational aims and policies of properly qualified individuals and groups to whom portions of the total task have been assigned. He must ensure not only that goals are clear and purposes are understood, but also that individuals are developing in terms of capacity and achievement and are reaping proper rewards in terms of compensation and personal satisfactions. Above all, he must do what he can to ensure that departmental interests, interdepartmental rivalries, and the machinery of measurement and evaluation do not deflect energy from organizational purpose into harmful or irrelevant activity.

To clarify our approach to the problem of adapting the concepts and findings of special disciplines to the requirements of policy, we list here 12 aspects of implementation which may serve as a convenient map of the territory to be traversed. It should be remembered that cases you will analyze have not been researched or written to prove these propositions. The list is designed only to make it possible for you to use your own specialized knowledge and adapt it, within limits imposed by your own characteristic attitudes toward risk and responsibility, to strategic requirements.

1. Once strategy is tentatively or finally set, the key tasks to be performed and kinds of decisions required must be identified.

2. Once the size of operations exceeds the capacity of one man, responsibility for accomplishing key tasks and making decisions must be assigned to individuals or groups. The division of labor must permit efficient performance of subtasks and must be accompanied by some hierarchical allocation of authority to insure achievement.

3. Formal provisions for the coordination of activities thus separated must be made in various ways, e.g., through a hierarchy of supervision, project and committee organizations, task forces, and other *ad hoc* units. The prescribed activities of these formally constituted bodies are not intended to preclude spontaneous voluntary coordination.

4. Information systems adequate for coordinating divided functions (i.e., for letting those performing part of the task know what they must know of the rest, and for letting those in supervisory positions know what is happening so that next steps may be taken) must be designed and installed.

5. The tasks to be performed should be arranged in a time sequence comprising a program of action or a schedule of targets. So that long-range planning may not be neglected, this activity should probably be entrusted to a special staff unit. Its influence may be enhanced by attaching it to the president's office, its usefulness by having it work in close cooperation with the line. While long-range plans may be couched in relatively general terms, shorter range plans will often take the form of relatively detailed budgets. These can meet the need for the establishment of standards against which future performance can be judged.

6. Actual performance, as quantitatively reported in information systems and qualitatively estimated through observation by supervisors and the judgment of customers, should be compared to budgeted performance and to standards in order to test achievement, budgeting processes, and the adequacy of the standards themselves.

7. Individuals and groups of individuals must be recruited and assigned to essential tasks in accordance with the specialized or supervisory skills which they possess or can develop. At the same time, the assignment of tasks may well be adjusted to the nature of available skills.

8. Individual performance, evaluated both quantitatively and qualitatively, should be subjected to influences (constituting a pattern of incentives) which will help to make it effective in accomplishing organizational goals.

9. Since individual motives are complex and multiple, incentives for achievement should range from those that are universally appealing —such as adequate compensation and an organizational climate favorable to the simultaneous satisfaction of individual and organizational purposes—to specialized forms of recognition, financial or nonfinancial, designed to fit individual needs and unusual accomplishments.

10. In addition to financial and nonfinancial incentives and rewards to motivate individuals to voluntary achievement, a system of constraints, controls, and penalties must be devised to contain nonfunctional activity and to enforce standards. Controls, like incentives, are both formal and informal. Effective control requires both quantitative and nonquantitative information which must always be used together.

11. Provision for the continuing development of requisite technical and managerial skills is a high-priority requirement. The development of individuals must take place chiefly within the milieu of their assigned responsibilities. This on-the-job development should be supplemented by intermittent formal instruction and study.

12. Dynamic personal leadership is necessary for continued growth and improved achievement in any organization. Leadership may be expressed in many styles, but it must be expressed in some perceptible

style. This style must be natural and also consistent with the requirements imposed upon the organization by its strategy and membership.

The general manager is principally concerned with determining and monitoring the adequacy of strategy, with adapting the firm to changes in its environment, and with securing and developing the people needed to carry out the strategy or to help with its constructive revision. The manager must also ensure that the processes which encourage and constrain individual performance and personal development are consistent with human and strategic needs. In large part, therefore, his leadership consists of achieving commitments to strategy via clarification and dramatization of its requirements and value.

We shall return to each of these considerations, looking first at some general relationships between strategy and organizational structure. We shall look also at the need for specialization of tasks, the coordination of divided responsibility and design of effective information systems.

STRATEGY AND ORGANIZATIONAL STRUCTURE

It is at once apparent that the accomplishment of strategic purpose requires organization. If a consciously formulated strategy is to be effective, organizational development should be planned rather than left to evolve by itself. So long as a company is small enough for a single individual to direct both planning for the future and current operations, questions of organizational structure remain unimportant. Thus the one-man organization encounters no real organizational problem until the proprietor's quick walks through the plant, his wife's bookkeeping, and his sales agent's marketing activities are no longer adequate to growing volume. When the magnitude of operations increases, then departmentalization—usually into such clusters of activities as manufacturing, production, and finance—begins to appear. Most functional organizations ultimately encounter size problems again. With geographical dispersion, product complexity, and increased volume of sales, coordination must be accomplished somewhere besides at the top. We then find multiunit organizations with coordinating responsibility delegated to divisions, subsidiaries, profit centers, and the like. The difficulty of designing an organizational structure is basically consequent upon and proportionate to the *diversity* and *size* of the undertaking.[1]

The subject of organization is the most extensive and complex of all the subtopics of implementation. It has at various times attracted the interest of economists, sociologists, psychologists, political scientists, philosophers, and, in a curiously restricted way, of creative writers as well. These have contributed to the field a variety of theoretical formulations and empirical investigations. The policy maker will probably find himself unable to subscribe wholeheartedly to the precepts of any one school of thought or to the particulars of any one model of the firm. Indeed, established theories of the firm are inadequate for general manage-

---

[1] A model of corporate development has been described by Professor Bruce R. Scott of the Harvard Business School faculty in his unpublished paper, "A Stages Model of Corporate Development," January 1968.

ment purposes. The impact of most organizational studies, from the point of view of the eclectic practitioner looking for counsel rather than confusion, has been to undermine confidence in other studies. The activities of present-day social science have in particular badly damaged the precepts of classical scientific management. Progress in the reconciliation of divergent insights into the nature of organization, however, can be expected in due course.

Regardless of disputes about theory among scholars, the executive in, say, a company that has reached some complexity, knows three things. The tasks essential to accomplishing his purposes must in some way be subdivided; they must be assigned, if possible, to individuals whose skills are appropriately specialized; and tasks that have been subdivided must ultimately be reintegrated into a unified whole. The manager knows also that once he lets performance out of his own hands, and once no one in the organization is performing the total task, information about what the left hand is doing must be made available to the right. Otherwise problems and risks cannot be detected and dealt with.

SUBDIVISION OF TASK RESPONSIBILITY

In every industry conventional ways of dividing task by function have developed to the extent that the training of individuals skilled in these functions perpetuates organizational arrangements. But identification of the tasks *should* be made in terms of a company's distinctive purposes and unique strategy, not by following industry convention. True, the fact that every manufacturing firm procures and processes raw materials and sells and delivers finished products means that at least production and sales and probably procurement and distribution will always be critical functional areas which must be assigned to specialized organizational units. But these basic uniformities which cut across company and industry lines provide the individual firm with little useful guidance on the issues it finds so perplexing, namely, how much weight to assign to which function, or how to adapt nearly universal structural arrangements to its own particular needs.

A manufacturer who plans to perform services for the government under cost-plus-fixed-fee contracts, to cite a very limited example, feels less need for a fully developed cost control system and cost-related incentives than one whose contracts are governed by a fixed price. To illustrate more broadly the way in which strategic choice determines the relative importance of tasks, consider the manufacturer of a line of industrial products who decides to diversify in view of declining opportunity in his original field. Product improvement and the engineering organization responsible for it become less vital than the search for new products, either internally or through acquisition. But if the latter task is not recognized as crucial, then it is unlikely to be assigned to any individual or unit, but will rather be considered as an additional duty for many. Under the latter circumstances, accomplishment may well be impaired.

Once the key tasks have been identified (or the identification customary in the industry has been ratified as proper for the individual firm), then responsibility for accomplishing these tasks must be assigned to individuals and groups. In addition to a rational principle for separating tasks from one another, the need will soon become apparent for some scale of relative importance among activities to be established.

Distribution of formal authority among those to whom tasks have been assigned is essential for the effective control of operations, the development of individual skills, the distribution of rewards, and for other organizational processes to which we shall soon give attention. The extent to which individuals, once assigned a task, need to be supervised and controlled is the subject of voluminous argument which, temporarily at least, must leave the general practitioner aware that too much control and too little are equally ineffective and that, as usual, he is the man who must strike the balance.

The division of labor is thus accompanied by the specialization of task and the distribution of authority, with the relative importance of tasks as defined by strategy marked by status. The rational principle by which tasks are specialized and authority delegated may be separation by functions, by product or product lines, by geographical or regional subdivision, by customer and market, or by type of production equipment or processes. The intermixture of these principles in multiunit organizations has resulted in many hybrid types of formal structure which we need not investigate. The principal requirement is that the basis for division should be relatively consistent, easily understood, and conducive to the grouping of like activities. Above all, the formal pattern should have visible relationship to corporate purpose, should fix responsibility in such a way as not to preclude teamwork, and should provide for the solution of problems as close to the point of action as possible. Structure should not be any more restrictive than necessary of the satisfaction of individual needs or of the inevitable emergence of informal organization. The design should also allow for more complex structure as the organization grows in size.

As you consider the need to create, build, and develop an organizational structure for the firms in the cases you will study shortly, you will wish to avoid choosing a *typical* pattern of organization on the grounds that it is "typical" or "generally sound." Any preference you may have for divisional versus functional organizations, for decentralized rather than centralized questions, for a "flat" rather than a "steep" or many-stepped hierarchy, should be set aside until you have identified the activities made essential by the strategy, the skills available for their performance, and the needs and values of the individuals involved. The plan you devise should ignore neither the history of the company nor that of its industry, for in ongoing organizations formal structure may not be abruptly changed without great cost. Any new plan that you devise for gradual implementation should be as economical as is consistent with the requirements for technical skill, proper support for principal functions, and reserve capacity for further growth. The degree of centralization and decentralization that you prescribe should not turn on your personal preference, and presumably will vary from one activity to another. Strategic requirements as well as the abilities and experience of company executives should determine the extent to which responsibility for decisions should tend toward the center or toward the field. In a consumer credit company, for example, freedom to extend credit to doubtful risks can really be allowed only to relatively experienced branch managers though company strategy may prescribe it for all.

That so little need be said about the nature of the formal organization, and so much must be determined by the particulars of each individual situation, should not be taken as evidence that formal organization does not matter—a conclusion implied by some students of organizational behavior. On the contrary, progress in a growing organization is impossible without substrategies for organizational development. Restructuring the organization becomes a goal in itself to be worked toward over a period of years—perhaps without the interim publication of the ultimate design.

But though it is impractical, except in cases of harsh emergency, to make sweeping organizational changes with little preparation and upon short notice, this is not to say that no major role is played by structure, by clear and logical subdivisions of task, or by an openly acknowledged hierarchy of authority, status, and prestige—all serving as the conscious embodiment of strategy and the harbinger of growth to come. As you check the relation between strategy and structure, whether in your study of cases or in your business experience, ask yourself always the policy questions: Is the strategy sound and clear? If goals are clear, have the tasks required been clearly identified and assessed for their relative importance? If key activities are known, have they been assigned to people with the requisite training, experience, and staff support they will need? The answers to these questions do not carry one very far along the road toward successful strategy implementation, but they provide a convenient starting point from which the rest of the trip can be made.

COORDINATION OF DIVIDED RESPONSIBILITY

As soon as a task is divided, some formal provision must be made for coordination. In baseball, the park outside the diamond is subdivided into left, center, and right fields, and a man is assigned to each. But if there is no procedure for handling a ball hit halfway between any two areas, the formal division of labor will help only the opposing team. Most important work of organizations requires cooperation among the departmental specialists to whom a portion of the total task has been allocated. Many forces are at work to make coordination so essential that it cannot be left to chance. For example, the flow of work from one station to another and from one administrative jurisdiction to another creates problems of scheduling and timing, of accommodating departmental needs, and of overall supervision lest departmental needs become more influential than organizational goals.

As soon as a second individual joins the first one in an organization, he brings with him his own goals, and these must be served, at least to a minimal degree, by the activity required of him in service to the organization. As soon as a group of such individuals, different in personal needs but similar in technical competence and point of view is established to perform a given function, then departmental goals may attract more loyalty than the overall goals of the organization. To keep individual purposes and needs as well as departmental substrategies consistent with corporate strategy is a considerable undertaking. It is a major top-management responsibility in all organizations, regardless of the apparent degree of commitment and willingness to cooperate in the common cause.

The different needs of individuals and the distinctive goals of functional specialties mean that, at best, the organization's total strategy is understood differently and valued for different reasons by different parts of the organization. Some formal or informal means for resolving these differences is important. Where the climate is right, specialists will be aware of the relative validity of organizational and departmental needs and of the bias inevitable in any loyalty to expertise.

Formal organization provides for the coordination of divided responsibility through the hierarchy of supervision, through the establishment and use of committees, and through the project form of organization (which, like temporary task forces, can be superimposed upon a functional or divisional organization). The wider the sphere of any supervisor's jurisdiction, the more time he is likely to need to bring into balance aspects of organized life which would otherwise influence performance toward the wrong goals. The true function of a committee—and were this role more widely understood and effectively played, committees would be less frequently maligned—is to bring to the exploration and solution of interdepartmental problems both the specialist and generalist abilities of its members. The need for formal committees would be largely obviated in an ideal organization, where each member was conscious of the impact of his own proposals, plans, and decisions upon the interests of others. To the extent that an individual manager seeks out advice and approval from those whose interests must be balanced with his, he performs in face-to-face encounters the essential coordination which is sometimes formalized in a committee structure.

Coordination can play a more creative role than merely composing differences. It is the quality of the way in which subdivided functions and interests are resynthesized that often distinguishes one organization from another in terms of results. The reintegration of the parts into the whole, when what is at stake is the execution of corporate strategy, is what creates a whole that is greater than the sum of its parts. Rivalry between competing subunits or individuals—if monitored to keep it *constructive* rivalry—can exhibit creative characteristics. It can be the source of a new solution to a problem, one that transcends earlier proposals that reflected only the rival unit's parochial concerns. The ability to handle the coordinating function in a way that brings about a new synthesis among competing interests, a synthesis in harmony with the special competence of the total organization, is the administrator's most subtle and creative contribution to the successful functioning of an organization.

EFFECTIVE DESIGN OF INFORMATION SYSTEMS

If corporate strategy is to be effectively implemented, there must be organizational arrangements to provide members with the information they will need to perform their tasks and relate their work to that of others. Information flows inward from the environment to all organizational levels; within the company it should move both down and up. In view of the bulk of information moving upward, it must be reduced to manageable compass as it nears the top. This condensation can be accomplished only by having data synthesized at lower levels, so that part of what moves upward is interpretation rather than fact. To achieve synthesis without introducing distortion or bias or serious omission is a formidable problem to which management must remain alert. Well handled, the information system brings to the attention of those who have authority to act not the vast mass of routine data processed by the total system, but the significant red-flag items that warn of outcomes contrary to expectations. A well-designed information system is thus the key to "management by exception." This in turn is one key to the prevailing problem of the overburdened executive.

In the gathering and transmitting of information, accounting and control departments play a major task. One obstacle to effective performance here is devotion to specialty and procedure for its own sake, as accountants look more to their forms than to larger purposes. The Internal Revenue Service, the Securities and Exchange Commission, the Census Bureau, and the Justice Department, all with requirements which must be met, impose uniformities on the ways in which information is collected and analyzed. But nothing in the conventions of accounting, the regulations of the government, or the rapidly advancing mathematical approaches to problem solving in any way prevents the generation and distribution within an organization of the kind of information management finds most useful.

Now, with the speed of the computer, data can be made available early enough to do some good. We shall have much more to say about the uses of information when we turn to the organizational processes that determine individual behavior. It is important to note that the generation of data is not an end in itself. Its function should be to permit individuals who necessarily perform only one of the many tasks required by the organizational mission to know what they need to know in order to perform their functions in balance with all others, and to gain that overview of total operations which will inform and guide the decisions they have discretion to make. Designing the flow of information is just as important as choosing a principle of subdivision in outlining organizational structure. Information is often the starting point in trying to determine how the organization should be changed. It is a way to monitor the continuing adequacy of strategy and to warn when change is necessary.

The Solartron Electronic Group, Ltd. (A)*

ORGANIZATION, OBJECTIVES, AND PRODUCT PLANNING

"I DO NOT THINK we could have expanded as we have if it had not been for forward planning" said Mr. John Bolton, chairman and managing director of The Solartron Electronic Group Limited, in November 1958. "Nor would I have the same degree of confidence in our future as I do if we were not continuing to plan ahead."

The Solartron Electronic Group and its subsidiary companies, with headquarters in Thames Ditton, Surrey, England, designed and manufactured two main types of electronic equipment: (1) A range of approximately 80 laboratory and other precision test instruments ranging in price from £50 to £700, such as oscilloscopes, power supplies, amplifiers, and servo test equipment. In the year ending June 30, 1958, such instruments comprised 66% of total company sales and 69.9% of total company deliveries. (2) A variety of "systems engineered" products with higher unit prices, which were broadly defined as electronic systems designed to perform a series of operations comprising a definable task. In a majority of cases these systems were designed, constructed, installed, and serviced by Solartron for customers relatively unfamiliar with electronic equipment. They comprised single products or families of products, each one of which was so chosen that it could constitute an important field of activity for companies in the Solartron group. They included:

> a) *An electronic reading machine* designed to read digits 0 to 9, eight alphabetical letters, and four accounting symbols at speeds up to 300 characters per second. The first production model of this machine had been sold to Boots Chemists (a chain of pharmacies) at a price of £223,000 and was scheduled for delivery in November 1959. It was to be used in connection with a digital computer to analyse daily the

* Copyright 1959 by l'Institut pour l'Etude des Méthodes de Direction de l'Enterprise (IMEDE), Lausanne, Switzerland. Reprinted by permission.

sales registered on tapes from approximately 2,000 cash registers. During the 1958–59 year, six additional orders from large firms were expected to bring total sales to seven.

b) *Radar simulator devices* designed to reproduce the radar image of aircraft or missiles, operating singly or in formation, for defense planning and training purposes. By November 1958, £400,000 of orders, varying from £60,000 to £180,000 per system, had been received from defense and military authorities of European countries including Germany, Italy, and Sweden.

c) *High-speed electronic checkweighers* designed to checkweigh packaged products at an accuracy of ±0.2% as the filled packages moved on a production line at a speed of up to 120 per minute; to deflect and count underweight and overweight packages; and to signal continuously to the packing mechanism any correction required to keep the delivered weight constantly correct. Thirty-two production units at £1,500 each were planned for 1958–59, for sale largely to food and other consumer goods manufacturers.

d) *An X-ray spectrometer* designed to provide an automatic, non-destructive method for the quantitative analysis of crystalline materials, such as metals and chemicals. Six units at approximately £10,000 each were planned for 1958–59, for sale to scientific and engineering organizations.

e) *Cybernetic teaching machines* designed to teach punch-card operators the manual skills needed for punch-card preparation by giving a series of exercises, evaluating progress and mistakes, and automatically varying the speed of the exercise while concentrating on those parts in which errors were made. This machine was the first of a planned series of inductive logic computing devices. Ten to 12 units at £500 each were planned for 1958–59, for sale to companies employing punch-card equipment.

f) *A range of analogue computer "building blocks"* from which a custom-built analogue computer could be assembled, designed chiefly for use in solving complex mathematical problems.

Solartron also performed precision engineering and design and development work on a contract basis, and sold electronic equipment made by other firms through its domestic and foreign sales organizations.

Exhibit 1 shows actual and forecast sales by product group and company. Exhibit 2 shows the companies of the Solartron group, their dates of incorporation, deliveries in the fiscal year ending June 30, 1958, and principal products or functions. Exhibits 3 and 4 present the Group's consolidated balance sheets and profit and loss statements for recent years, with forecasts through June 1963. Exhibit 5 shows operating profits and losses of the various subsidiary companies for the nine months ended March 31, 1958. The table at the bottom of page 685 indicates the rate of Solartron's growth from 1950 through mid-1958.

Organization

In November 1958 Solartron included The Solartron Electronic Group Ltd. (the parent company), eight domestic, and three overseas subsidiaries. The parent company was owned largely by members of management and their families. A number of employees were also shareholders. From 1951 to 1958 a majority of the common shares had been held by Mr. Bolton. After December 1958, holdings were distributed as follows:

	Percent
Mr. Bolton	40
Other managers, employees, and families	40
Outside shareholders	20

Solartron's senior executive group was the eight-man Group board of directors which met monthly and included two men for each of the following major functions: general management (including personnel administration), production, and finance, and one each for marketing and research and development. The average age of these men in November 1958 was 38 years. As indicated in the company letterhead, they held the degrees shown below, and most of them held executive positions in Solartron's subsidiary companies:

~ J. E. Bolton, D.S.C.,[1]/M.A. (Cantab.), M.B.A. (Harvard), Member British Institute of Management (M.B.I.M.), chairman and Group managing director, and temporarily chairman of Solartron Industrial Controls Ltd., and Solartron Radar Simulators Ltd.

~ L. B. Copestick, Associate Member Institute of Electronics (A.M. Inst. E.), Associate Member British Institute of Radio Engineers (A.M. Brit. I.R.E.), chairman and managing director, Solartron Engineering Ltd.

~ J. E. Crosse, chairman and managing director, Solartron Engineering Ltd.

~ R. A. Henderson, director of Robert Benson Lonsdale, Merchant Bankers.[2]

~ Eric E. Jones, Member Sales Managers Association (M.S.M.A.), Group marketing director, managing director of Solartron-Rheem Ltd.

~ E. R. T. Ponsford, chairman and managing director, Solartron Laboratory Instruments Ltd.

STATISTICS INDICATIVE OF SOLARTRON GROWTH

(years ending June 30)

	1950	*1951*	*1952*	*1953*	*1954*	*1955*	*1956*	*1957*	*1958*
Personnel	18	22	66	110	240	400	550	600	830
Floor space (sq. ft. 000)	4	4	6	8	30	35	65	70	85
Assets (£000)	8	12	34	74	226	420	654	902	1,344
Deliveries (£000)	13	20	34	90	152	399	758	1,005	1,434
Exports (£000)					10	20	80	186	335
Development write-off (£000) (specific products)						24	38	76	72
Net profits after taxes and development write-off (£000)*		1	1	3	5	4	12	6	23
Nonspecific development expenditure (£000)†					10	25	50	75	120

* Includes retained profit plus sundry appropriations (see Exhibit 3).
† Written off in overheads—e.g., market research, planning new factories, etc.

---

[1] Distinguished Service Cross (war decoration).
[2] An investment banking firm.

Exhibit 1

SCHEDULE OF DELIVERIES 1954–55 TO 1957–58 AND TARGETS THROUGH 1962–63*

(in £000's)

Product group	Actual				Possible targets for next five years				
	1954–55	1955–56	1956–57	1957–58	1958–59	1959–60	1960–61	1961–62	1962–63
Solartron Laboratory Instruments Ltd.:									
Standard instruments	£300	£589	£ 741	£ 945	£1,400	£2,000	£2,750	£3,500	£4,500
Government and outside contracts	42	63	37	57	60	100	150	250	250
Solartron Engineering Ltd.:									
Government and outside contracts	35	87	115	96	60	100	125	150	200
Solartron Research & Development Ltd.:									
Government and outside contracts	5	10	44	75	100	100	125	125	150
Data processing	...	...	...	32	130	250	300	400	500
Radar Simulators Ltd.	...	...	6	111	250	400	500	600	750
Solartron Industrial Controls Ltd.	...	...	6	12	60	150	250	300	350
Solartron Electronic Business Machines Ltd.	...	...	2	10	50	200	300	400	500
Solartron Electronic Group Ltd.:									
Merchanting and sundries	16	9	54	96	140	200	250	275	300
Total deliveries	£398	£758	£1,005	£1,434	£2,250	£3,500	£4,750	£6,000	£7,500
Export content included in above figures	£ 20	£ 80	£ 186	£ 335	£ 600	£1,000	£1,500	£2,250	£3,500
Total orders	400	800	1,250	1,900	2,750	4,000	5,500	7,000	8,500
Total personnel at year-end	400	550	600	830	1,250	1,750	2,250	2,750	3,500

* It was apparent in March 1959 that it would probably be necessary to extend the 1962–63 targets to 1963–64, that is, to spread the five-year program over six years. Figures for 1959–60 through 1962–63 are "maximum" targets.

Source: Company records.

Exhibit 2

COMPANIES OF THE SOLARTRON ELECTRONIC GROUP LTD.

(Subsidiaries wholly owned except otherwise indicated)

Companies in United Kingdom	Date of incorporation	Personnel strength in Nov. 1958	External deliveries in year ending June 30, 1958 (000)	1957–58 deliveries as a percentage of total	Functions
Solartron Laboratory Instruments Ltd. (SLI)	1948	375	£1,002	69.9	Manufactured approximately 80 standard laboratory and precision instruments at Thames Ditton plant in production lots of batch size (0–50 per month). Sales were made largely to scientific and engineering organizations in the U.K. through a sales force of approximately 20 technical service representatives.
Solartron Engineering Ltd. (SE)	1951	194	£ 96	6.7	Supplied the mechanical engineering requirements of the individual companies within the Group. Also undertook a selected amount of outside work to ensure competitiveness and to utilize fully its capacity. Located at recently built Farnborough plant.
Solartron Electronic Group Ltd. (parent company)	1954	280	£ 96	6.7	General management and staff activities, merchanting, and sundries.
Solartron Research and Development Ltd. (SR.&D.)	1954	144	£ 107	7.5	Performed outside contract R.&D. work; all research and development on standard electronic instruments; plus a portion of the work on "systems engineered" products (chiefly data handling and analogue computers). Also produced prototypes and initial production runs of instruments and other equipment (such as magnetic data tape recorder). Located in Dorking, Surrey.

Exhibit 2—Continued

Company	Year	Employees	Sales (£)	%	Function
Solartron Electronic Business Machines Ltd. (SEBM)	1955	20	£10	0.7	One of three "development" companies at the Farnborough plant. Responsible for developing, manufacturing, and marketing (in cooperation with Group commercial department) electronic business machines primarily for office use. Principal product in 1958 was the reading machine.
Industrial Automation Developments Ltd. (jointly owned with Scribbans-Kemp Ltd.)	1956	...	...	...	Responsible for developing under contract hydraulic programmed actuator for industrial packaging use. Work actually being carried out by SIC.
Solartron Industrial Controls Ltd. (SIC)	1956	29	£12	0.8	Responsible for developing, manufacturing, and marketing industrial controls* under "quasi-consulting assignments." Principal products checkweigher, X-ray spectrometer, and punch-card teaching machine.
Solartron Radar Simulators Ltd. (RS)	1957	58	£111	7.7	Responsible for developing, manufacturing, and marketing radar simulator devices for defense and training purposes. Principal product aircraft simulator sold to NATO countries.
Solartron Rheem Ltd. (jointly owned with Rheem Co. of New York)	1958	...	...	...	Responsible for developing products of joint interest to Solartron and Rheem.
Total		1,100	£1,434†	100†	

Overseas subsidiaries

Solartron Inc. (Associated Company in U.S.A.)	1956	6
Solartron SRL (Italy)	1957	3
Solartron GMBH (West Germany)	1958	12

Associated companies in India, France, and Sweden, and a subsidiary in Holland were in process of formation.

* An industrial control was broadly defined as a device to improve the quality of an industrial process by sensing some property of the product, processing the data thus obtained, and actuating the controls of the plant or machine involved to achieve a desired end. The variety of sensing effects that might be used ranged from simple weighing to spectroscopic examination by X-ray.

† Includes £335 or 23.4% exports.

Source: Company records.

Exhibit 3

OUTLINE PROFIT AND LOSS ACCOUNTS FOR THE YEARS ENDED JUNE 30, 1955–58 AND TARGETS THROUGH 1962–63

(in £000's)

	Actual				Possible targets for next five years				
	1954–55	*1955–56*	*1956–57*	*1957–58*	*1958–59*	*1959–60*	*1960–61**	*1961–62**	*1962–63**
Deliveries	£398	£758	£1,005	£1,434	£2,250	£3,500	£4,750	£6,000	£7,500
Less: Direct labor	75	119	141	192	270	420	560	720	900
Materials	134	226	289	468	750	1,180	1,590	2,000	2,500
Gross margin on deliveries	£189	£413	£ 575	£ 774	£1,230	£1,900	£2,600	£3,280	£4,100
Add: Overheads in development and W.I.P. increase	30	60	60	48	70	100	100	100	100
Gross margin on trading	£219	£473	£ 635	£ 822	£1,300	£2,000	£2,700	£3,380	£4,200
Less: Manufacturing overheads	105	214	258	356	480	730	950	1,150	1,400
Administration overheads	20	50	63	66	90	120	160	200	250
Commercial overheads	53	123	197	226	320	480	620	720	900
	£178	£387	£ 518	£ 648	£ 890	£1,330	£1,730	£2,070	£2,550
Net profit before development write-off	41	86	117	174	410	670	970	1,310	1,650
Development write-off (specific products)	24	38	76	72	125	175	225	300	400
Net profit before appropriations	£ 17	£ 48	£ 41	£ 102	£ 285	£ 495	£ 745	£1,010	£1,250
Loan interest	5	6	16	29	30	32	32	32	32
Preferred dividends (gross)	4	15	15	16	18	18	18	18	18
Ordinary dividends (gross)	...	...	...	...	22	44	88	132	220
Sundry appropriations	4	...	...	2	...	...	...	...	...
Taxation	4	15	4	34	120	220	320	433	517
Retained profits	...	£ 12	£ 6	£ 21	£ 95	£ 181	£ 287	£ 395	£ 463

* See note, Exhibit 1.

Source: Company records.

Exhibit 4

THE SOLARTRON ELECTRONIC GROUP LTD.
Balance Sheets as of June 30
(in £000's)

ASSETS	Actual				Forecast				
	1955	1956	1957	1958	1959	1960	1961	1962	1963
Cash at bank	£ 77	£ 1	£ 3	£ 7	£ 5	…	…	£ 175	£ 283
Trade and sundry debtors	99	154	259	400	475	£ 750	£1,000	1,200	1,500
Stock-in-hand and materials, etc.	85	89	121	158	200	270	350	450	560
Finished instruments	29	96	105	118	150	180	200	225	250
W.I.P. production	59	62	72	233	270	350	440	540	650
W.I.P. development	40	72	103	90	75	50	25	…	…
Associated companies	…	…	…	109	150	150	175	200	225
Total current assets	£389	£474	£663	£1,115	£1,325	£1,750	£2,190	£2,790	£3,468
Freehold land and buildings	40	74	118	88	96	100	110	120	130
Improvements to leasehold factories	2	3	5	7	75	100	125	150	175
Equipment, plant, and machinery	22	36	35	46	125	175	225	275	325
Furniture, fixtures, and fittings	11	26	31	34	80	110	130	160	200
Motor vehicles	13	23	33	37	17	15	20	20	25
Goodwill	18	18	17	17	17	…	…	…	…
Total fixed assets	£106	£180	£239	£ 229	£ 410	£ 500	£ 610	£ 725	£ 855
Total assets	495	654	902	1,344	1,735	2,250	2,800	3,515	4,323

LIABILITIES

Bank overdraft	£ 75	£139	£173	£ 58	£ 118	£ 77	£ 20	...	...
Progress payments	...	...	21	109	75	...	...	...	...
Trade and sundry creditors	104	117	166	410	410	600	700	800	900
Higher purchase commitments	10	18	18	18	40	75	70	65	60
Current taxation	8	18	21	30	20	150	260	375	505
Total current liabilities	£197	£292	£399	£ 625	£ 663	£ 902	£1,050	£1,240	£1,465
Future tax	£ 6	£ 18	£ 20	£ 51	£ 150	£ 260	£ 375	£ 505	£ 625
Unsecured loans	53	85	218	364	365	350	350	350	350
6% preferred shares (£1 each)	97	100	100	100	100	100	100	100	100
7½% preferred shares (£1 each)	95	100	100	100	100	100	100	100	100
Ordinary shares (10/each)	47	47	47	47	220	220	220	220	220
Retained profit and reserves	...	12	18	57	137	318	605	1,000	1,463
Total liabilities	£495	£654	£902	£1,344	£1,735	£2,250	£2,800	£3,515	£4,323
Note: Monthly sales volume	£ 55	£ 70	£125	£ 200	£ 250	£ 400	£ 500	£ 600	£ 750

Source: Company records.

Exhibit 5

SUBSIDIARIES AND GROUP ABRIDGED MANUFACTURING, TRADING, AND PROFIT AND LOSS ACCOUNTS FOR THE NINE MONTHS ENDED MARCH 31, 1958

Subsidiaries	SLI	SE	SR.&D.	SEBM	SIC	RS	Total
Sales	£365,996	£221,473	£114,389	£9,798	...	£15,226	£726,882
Increase/decrease in W.I.P.	64,775	(5,850)	30,589	4,667	£30,874	...	125,055
Net output	£430,771	£215,623	£144,978	£14,465	£30,874	£15,226	£851,937
Materials consumed	272,995	75,189	60,977	2,596	16,964	4,069	432,790
Direct wages	47,318	38,507	29,213	5,275	6,182	4,959	131,454
Manufacturing overheads	99,145	79,302	39,028	10,713	13,326	6,157	247,671
Works cost	£419,458	£192,998	£129,218	£18,584	£36,472	£15,185	£811,915
Net profit (loss) of subsidiaries	£11,313	£22,625	£15,760	£(4,119)	£(5,598)	£41	£40,022

Holding company

	SEG	
Sales	£917,756	
Cost of sales	636,742	
Gross profit	£281,014	
Commercial overheads	£157,779	
Administration overheads	46,412	
Net profit of holding company	£76,823	

	Total
Net profit of holding company	76,823
Combined net profit	£116,845
Appropriations:	
Interest (gross)	21,734
Preferred dividend (gross)	10,103
Total	£31,837
Profit before development write-off, taxation, and participating dividend	£85,008

Source: Company records.

~ Bowman Scott, M.B.E.,[3] M.B.A. (Harvard), B.Sc. (Eng.), Associate City and Guilds Institute (A.C.G.I.), Associate Member Institute of Electrical Engineers (A.M.I.E.E.), Group personnel director, and managing director of Solartron Electronic Business Machines Ltd.

~ J. L. E. Smith, M.A., director of Coutts & Co., Bankers,[4] and chairman of Solartron Industrial Automation Developments Ltd.

The purpose of board meetings was described as follows in a memorandum written by Mr. Bolton to explain and defend his practice (once criticized by the outside members) of allowing board meetings to "wander away" from a strict interpretation of the agenda:

> . . . they are not, in these days, intended for transmission of information because this can be done effectively via detailed management data in the form of monthly reports. . . .
>
> It seems to me that [their] main purpose lies in the area of creative discussion in order to achieve not only a better understanding of each other but also of the human and technical factors which govern the job we are doing. These factors of course change almost continuously. This in my view is how an effective and flexible policy (whether it be at board level or at research level) is rough hewn from the range of opinions which a balanced team should have. As you may have seen, I usually endeavour to bring out something controversial so that at least one member of the board will get hot under the collar about it. If we can each of us do this without fear then I think we are creating a very powerful team relationship which will ensure that we are approaching the various new problems which we shall continuously face in a coordinated and constructive way. . . .

In addition to the general management functions performed by the board, the parent company also provided a number of services to the Solartron companies, including purchasing, personnel, commercial activity (such as overseas selling), publicity, secretarial, accounting, and internal consulting (Group productivity services department).

The boards of directors of some of the subsidiary companies did not actually meet; management responsibility rested with the managing directors and other senior executives concerned.

Company objectives

A number of Solartron's objectives had been stated explicitly in recent years, either in the firm's Annual Reports, in other written documents, or orally by company executives. These statements have been quoted or paraphrased below:

For the long run. Expansion into rapidly growing sections of the electronics industry as fast as "balanced attention" to the various factors of production would allow, taking into consideration (1) rate of development of the existing staff; (2) rate of integration of new personnel; (3) rate of development of the company's markets; (4) pace of R.&D. activity, as influenced by human and financial considerations.

---

[3] Member of Order of British Empire (war decoration).

[4] A commercial bank.

For the next five to ten years. (1) Achieving more intensive effort in the major fields already chosen, in order to build "strong, viable, subsidiary units in those areas." There were to be fewer radically new products developed than in recent years, and emphasis was to be placed instead on perfecting and increasing the applications of equipment already developed. (2) Increasing export sales of Solartron products in order to broaden the company's customer base and spread development costs over an increased number of production units. (3) Making more effective use of the relatively large organizational structure created for the purpose of preparing for future expansion.

With respect to people. "Our emergent philosophy of life lays great stress not only on the importance of the individual as a person, but on the essential need to devise a 'permissive' system in which individual initiative is nurtured and encouraged to make its maximum possible contribution to the whole. . . . We recognize that in selecting a team of potentially outstanding young men and women at all levels and in training them to carry increasing responsibility, the natural corollary is that they should want to make a personal contribution to decisions affecting their particular working group or company's future, in an atmosphere which is as free as possible of status barriers and prejudice. Furthermore, that they should want to know that those who demonstrate outstanding qualities of leadership and judgment can progress to Board level." In line with this objective the following policies had been adopted:

a) Whenever possible, promotions to senior positions were made from within the organization. The principal exceptions to this rule were senior specialists such as Mr. Christopher Bailey, designer of the reading machine, and Mr. George Sanders, head of the Group productivity services department.

b) To the extent possible, managers at all levels of the company were given the opportunity to discharge their responsibilities as they thought best within the broad framework of agreed-upon objectives. In this regard, Mr. Gordon Bates, who was leaving Solartron to do management consulting in the consumer marketing field, said that he and many of his colleagues felt themselves to be "part of an experiment in British industry." He contrasted Solartron with a number of older, larger firms that he and his friends had worked for, saying, "The standard form in many of these firms is to treat the younger men like useless appendages during the first 15 years or so, and then gradually let them in on one aspect of operations. Here the form is to give man a little more than he thinks he can handle as soon as possible."

c) To encourage personnel to increase their potential, fees for suitable training courses and conferences were paid by the company, while "Training within Industry" classes were held during working hours. There was also a library of technical and management books.

d) An attempt was made to keep executives throughout the company informed on current developments. In this regard, Mr. P. B. H. Cuff, Group purchasing director, said that in his early years with the company Mr. Bolton had on several occasions stopped him to tell him of recent events that had no immediate bearing on his work but were of great interest to him in understanding the company's position. By 1958, annual management conferences were being held for all senior and junior executives, at which board members described the current state of affairs and plans for the future in their areas.

e) To avoid unnecessary status barriers, reserved spaces in the parking lot had been eliminated. On most memoranda the names of executives were alphabetized; the use of first names was encouraged; and all personnel, regardless of position and function, were expected to "clock in" at the same time.

f) Since 1954, the personnel selection and training functions had been entrusted to a director, Mr. Bowman Scott.

g) To assure attractive working conditions, a pension scheme had been established, as well as an employee restaurant, a health centre, a sports and cricket club, and a trend toward yearly or longer term employment contracts.

With respect to formal organization. "Our policy is to develop a number of virtually independent company units within the Group, each concentrating on either a specialized function such as research, or a logically grouped sales and production activity such as test instrumentation. . . . We envisage each individual company unit growing to a size of perhaps 500–700 personnel—a size which we believe will meet, on the one hand, the need to maximise personal satisfactions, and, on the other, to operate near to the optimum unit size for the technical requirements of our particular industry. The dangers of growing apart are apparent, but we are confident that through our group structure and because of the experience our senior executives have gained in working as a very closely knit team, we shall be able to achieve the principal benefits of centralized policy-making and the economics of joint services, without hampering the exercise of individual initiative in the separate companies."

Mr. Bolton was particularly desirous of avoiding what he termed a "peaky" organization, in which management thinking would be dominated by his personal views. In this regard he said he had found that people in an organization tended to create a pinnacle, even when the managing director was anxious not to become an all-powerful father-figure. People had come to him, for example, and suggested that he ought to buy a new car, since his Jaguar was not as new as it might be and therefore not fully appropriate to his position. He said that one of a number of problems that could arise in a peaky organization was the difficulty of hiring "number-two" men who were intimidated by the individual brilliance of their prospective bosses and feared being completely submerged by them.

In contrast with the "peaky" organization, "great-man" approach to management, Mr. Bolton expressed the opinion that managerial needs were, like vacuums, abhorred by nature, and that they would ultimately be filled of their own accord. For example, he indicated that if he and Mr. Eric Jones, Group commercial director, had not pushed product diversification, "two other chaps would have, and the result would have been the same." Similarly, he believed that if Solartron had not developed the reading machine or the radar simulator, some other firm would have done so.

With respect to finance. Objectives in finance were (1) to increase borrowed in relation to equity and preference funds on a 2:1 ratio; (2) to use company funds principally for working capital; and to use other sources, such as lease-back arrangements, for plant and fixed assets; (3) starting in 1958–59, to establish a progressive common stock dividend record against the possibility that in three to five years there might be opportunities for greater expansion than were visualized in 1958 (although profits had been sacrificed for balanced and rapid growth in the first ten years, increasing dividend payments were believed to be important ultimately because company executives considered that English companies were judged on a dividend rather than earnings-yield basis); (4) to achieve gross margins[5] on products in full production (beyond the initial progress-payment or pilot-production stage) of 60% or more; (5) to reduce overhead spending progressively, until it declined to approximately 33% of projected gross sales.

With respect to R.&D. (1) ". . . We have established a prime objective of achieving entirely new developments which show substantial improvements in contemporary design practice. As a rough rule of thumb, we have endeavoured to produce new designs which will be some three to five years ahead of the existing state of the art in other countries, and in this way we hope to achieve a breathing space in which our new products can become fully established before the pressure of competition might catch up with them." (2) "In contrast with many military organizations, where research funds are all too often taken as a symbol of power, and prevailing sentiment is to get as much as you can and to hell with the whole, we are attempting to build the feeling instead that R.&D. funds are a means by which a subsidiary or research team can make a contribution to the Group, and that this contribution, rather than the power involved, is the important thing." (3) "Eventually we are aiming for more and more new projects at SR.&D.[6]—tending more toward research and away from development —and we intend to have the development work done by the individual manufacturing subsidiaries."

Product planning

Early product history. The initial development of Solartron's product line was described by a company executive as follows:[7]

> The start and growth of the enterprise has followed a familiar pattern; at first a handful of men in a shed, and then a leap-frogging into larger and larger premises as the work prospered. In 1947 two young engineers, Mr. E. R. Ponsford and Mr. L. B. Copestick, scraped together a few hundred pounds, hired a disused stable, and set up as makers of electronic test instruments. Both had been apprenticed in the electronic industry and were aware of shortcomings in the available

---

[5] Sales price less "bought-out" materials and direct wages.
[6] Solartron Research and Development Ltd., a subsidiary.
[7] Solartron Research and Development Ltd., a subsidiary.

equipment. In 1948 they registered the name Solartron, but eighteen months were to pass before they were in a position to produce an electronic instrument of their own—the first proprietary laboratory amplifier on the British market. The main activity of the two directors and their three employees at first was the development, manufacture, and repair of equipment under government contract. This steady work enabled them to lease a small factory in Kingston, and additions to the board brought enough working capital to proceed with more ambitious plans. Two years after the introduction of their first instrument the company was invited to exhibit at the Physical Society's Exhibition, and this they regarded as a mark of acceptance in the sphere of electronics.

The early years were hard but rewarding in every sense except the material. Many of the founders' old associates and trainees were anxious to join the company, even at reduced wages, for the sake of opportunities to come.

Ploughing back of all profits was never adequate to finance the rapidly growing production and development, and substantial additional capital was introduced when Mr. John Bolton and Mr. John Crosse joined the company in 1951 and 1952, respectively.

Thus, by the 30th June 1953, at the end of the first five years of its corporate life, Solartron had become established with 110 personnel, 7,500 square feet of factory space, and a turnover of approximately £100,000 per annum. There were then two companies, Solartron Laboratory Instruments Ltd., with a growing product line of electronic test instruments, and Solartron Engineering Limited, which was responsible for the precision mechanical engineering and metalwork aspects of Solartron products. The stage was set for the broadening of the organizational and products base and substantial increase in sales volume during the second five years, 1953–58.[8]

Diversification. During its second five years, Solartron diversified into "systems engineered" products. The initial decision to do so was made in 1952–53 as a result of what were considered to be the limitations of laboratory instruments as a product line on which to base future growth. The reasoning of the company's board, as reported in 1958, was as follows (paraphrased):

> On the one hand, delivery periods must be kept short. For, once a customer has ordered an instrument, he expects rapid delivery (a month or less) or will seek an alternative source of supply. On the other hand, inventories must be kept at a minimum, because as a rapidly growing company our finances will be limited. Operations will therefore be continuously balanced between the risk of an inventory buildup if sales decrease and a scramble to increase production if sales increase.
>
> Solartron could safely base its expansion on laboratory instruments only if it specializes intensely in one type of instrument, as certain firms have done in the United States. Because of the size of the United Kingdom market, however, this will not be feasible.

[8] From a paper presented May 27, 1958, before a meeting of the Seminar on Problems in Industrial Administration at the London School of Economics and Political Science.

Our wisest move would be to seek additional "systems engineered" products with higher unit prices and longer delivery requirements. Such products would broaden our customer base and reduce the complexity of current operations. Because they would lengthen our order book, it would also be easier to obtain outside finance.

In order that we can make the maximum contribution and utilize our resources to the fullest, these new products should be in rapidly expanding sectors of the electronics industry where it will not be necessary to design somebody else out of the market.

Choosing new product areas.   In connection with this analysis, Mr. Bolton prepared a rough evaluation of the industry's future growth along the lines of Exhibit 6. This was based on the assumption that already developed sectors of the industry would remain a constant or decreasing proportion of the total, while undeveloped and as yet unknown sectors would become larger. Overall, a fivefold increase over 20 years was estimated, with particular segments changing in relative importance roughly as indicated in Exhibit 6.

Entering new fields.   As a consequence of this analysis, Solartron began slowly to diversify during its second five years. Impetus to enter new fields came from various sources: In 1953–54 a study was made of the business machine field, and it was concluded that the most important undeveloped requirements were (1) fast input devices for computers; (2) memories with large storage capacity and quick access; (3) equipment for sorting information. Of these, the first was selected for development and work was started on the reading machine (see Exhibit 7). In 1954 a decision to develop the checkweigher was made, based on the belief that accurate control of weight was a fundamental future need in automated processes—especially where packaged articles such as food were concerned, since such items are sold by weight. The choice of this field was also related to development and engineering skills already possessed by Solartron. With this product, work was started in the field of industrial controls. In 1955 evidence of strong interest by the Swedish Air Ministry touched off development of the company's radar simulator device. In 1957 "Anglicization" (adaptation to British components) of an American-designed "data-tape" recording machine was begun under license from the Consolidated Electrodynamics Corporation. During this same period the Group sponsored research and development in the field of data processing (chiefly analogue computers).

In speaking of the company's diversification, Mr. Eric Jones, Group commercial director, said: "Not everyone was agreed that we should go into systems, perhaps partly because when you look two or three years ahead in a new field, it looks more like science fiction than commercial reality. I think even J. B. [Mr. Bolton] thought that diversification might be premature. But I pushed radar simulators, he pushed business machines, we got agreement to develop the checkweigher, and here we are today."

Allocating R.&D. funds.   "We are compromising between forward research and spending on present products," said Mr. Bolton, "and we are doing it by eye." Mr. Bolton stated that this compromise involved making choices between "picking up basic principles at an early stage, or applying more intensive effort to remaining problems in already developed areas—such as increasing the reliability of a particular kind of oscilloscope." He explained that in the most recent operating year (1957–58) this choice had been made by allocating Group R.&D. funds to the various product groups in proportion to their estimated growth

Exhibit 6

SOLARTRON ESTIMATES OF FUTURE GROWTH
OF ELECTRONICS INDUSTRY

Market sector	Solartron rough estimates of sales of sector as a percent of the total electronics industry	
	1953	1973
1. *Domestic Radio and TV* Comments: Few export sales; domestic market will probably reach a plateau as in the U.S. Would have to compete with large, well-established firms. Not for us	25	10
2. *Communications* Comments: Major European networks already installed. Sales will be for improvement and replacement purposes. Industry cartelized; suppliers often affiliated with communications firms. Not our cup of tea	20	8
3. *Radar and Navigational Aids* Comments: A growing field which should have possibilities for us. Assume market percentage will remain the same. Total increase will thus be fivefold	5	5
4. *Military Requirements* Comments: Assume total static even though electronic share will increase, therefore ultimate percentage of the market down. Not so interesting as some other sectors	35	15
5. *Data Processing* (including business machines and industrial data processing equipment) Comments: Increasing use for computation as well as to reduce paper work. Digital computers have already been extensively developed by several large firms but analogue techniques and a number of other problems remain. An interesting field for us	*	20
6. *Industrial Controls* Comments: Ultimately will be larger than data processing. Since automation of production operations will come after the automation of paper work, however, this sector will develop more slowly. This deserves our attention	*	15
7. *Scientific Education* Comments: May never loom too large but relatively untouched. Has possibilities	*	5
8. *Atomic Energy* Comments: Insignificant at present but will grow	*	17
9. *Miscellaneous*	15	17

* Negligible.
Source: Company's records.

Exhibit 7

COMPUTERS OR CLERKS

The electronic computer is ten years old, a teenager among industrial machinery with a teenager's problems of adjustment to society. During its first decade, when it was being used largely as a research tool for resolving equations beyond the capacity of mathematicians, the decision to buy a computer or not depended on the straight-forward point whether a company or a Government research department had enough work of this kind to justify the investment of upwards of £150,000 in a single computer. There was no question of doing the work by other means. Such abstruse scientific, aerodynamic and even economic calculations were either done on a computer or not done at all. But now computers are being offered to a wider market as machines that will mechanise clerical work and control production processes, and they are being judged by different standards. Here a company does have a choice between two alternatives—it can choose between electronic computers and human clerks, or labourers.

The saving of labour by a computer can be exaggerated. The real gift it brings to management is the opportunity to cut through the red tape and the paper work that assumes alarming proportions once a company's operations reach a certain size. Much of this routine could now be transferred to computers, inside which it would be promptly assimilated, sorted, added to, subtracted from, pigeonholed, filed for future reference, while a neat printed record appeared at the other end. But is this worth doing?

The answer varies from company to company, depending on how vital it is to the sound management of the business to have quick access to day-to-day information. Boots, which is making a big change-over to electronic accounting, obviously sets great store by prompt reports on the changing level of sales and stocks for the 60,000 different items sold by the company's retail shops. Bibby's, manufacturing animal feeding stuffs, uses a computer to keep watch on rapidly changing raw material prices, so that the feeding-stuff formula can be varied to make allowance for them—a job that requires an unexpectedly large number of weekly calculations. Tube investments, selling products that vary from order to order, uses a computer to sort the orders, stipulate the most economical raw material, give manufacturing instructions and prepare cost figures, spending 30 seconds on planning and printing instructions about each order, against 35 minutes by ordinary methods. The Banco di Roma has just installed a computer to handle all the accounts of its 200–300 branches. Many other examples can be found among the 100-odd computers now in use in this country where resort to a fast-thinking computer has probably improved a company's efficiency. But users are noticeably reluctant to quote any estimate of the amount of money saved by electronic accounting. Boots calculate that the company's change to electronic book-keeping will stop the annual 10 per cent rise in clerical staff that has gone on now for several years. But even this type of saving is difficult to assess.

Computers still have obvious limitations; skillful handling is needed to make them earn their keep. Initial cost is the biggest single factor. At the first exhibition in the world devoted entirely to electronic computers, which has been open in London during the past ten days, the price of the 27 different models on sale ranged all the way from £20,000 to £800,000, the cheapest being made by Elliott and the dearest by IBM. A computer consists of two basic parts; one which does the arithmetic and is relatively cheap to make, and the other which acts as a "memory" and stores all the relevant data and instructions upon which the computer operates. There are several ways of building a "memory"; some of them are cheaper than others but unfortunately they are also slower-working. If the "memory" is slow, this tends to hold up the rate at which the computer works.

As a rough rule of thumb, the cheaper computers have small "memories"; the more expensive the machine, the bigger its memory and the faster it can get at the facts. In scientific calculations, calculating ability is frequently more important than capacious memory, so the small computers, many of which are only just on the market, are ideally suited for research purposes, providing the maximum computing ability for the minimum cost. For business accounting, however, a big "memory" is more important than calculating ability; the machine is required to hold data about stocks, or invoices, or temperature levels, or railway schedules, or insurance policies, and carry out one or two simple calculations on them when the need arises. The ideal computer for business accounting therefore tends to come in the £100,000 to £300,000 range.

It would be unfair, however, to blame the high cost of computers entirely on the electronics engineer. The computer itself frequently costs less than the mechanical equipment that goes with it. The second big limitation on the use of computers is in the design of this equipment. A computer cannot read—yet. Data have to be fed into it in a form it can understand, from punched cards, punched tape or magnetic tape, and fed out again in a form that the operator can understand. This requires tape readers, mechanical feeds and printing equipment, all of which operate at unnaturally high speeds. The purely mechanical difficulties created by these high speeds make all this ancillary equipment extremely expensive, considering the basic simplicity of its design. Some steps have been taken towards the development of electronic "readers" that could read type faces and transmit the results direct to the computer; the specification put out by the banks for a machine that would "read" magnetic characters printed on cheques has given a marked fillip to this type of research.

The first two "reading" machines of their kind were exhibited at the computer exhibition, one of them being Solartron's complex reader, which is now said to be able to decipher not only carbon copies but even handwritten characters. The cost is £25,000 for a machine "reading" three reasonably similar type faces; the much simpler apparatus developed by Electric and Musical Industries solely for "reading" a specially designed type printed in magnetic ink, and intended primarily for cheque sorting, might cost one-tenth of this amount when in production. These figures give some indication of the cost of the trimmings that go with a computer. Ferranti, the first company to make computers in this country, designing machines used mainly by laboratories for vast calculations, sells one basic computer for £50,000, but the full installation costs £160,000.

The third big limitation on the use of computers lies with the customer rather than the machine. Production engineering must be fairly well understood in industry by now, but the application of the same technique to office work is not. In most cases, wholesale changes in routine are needed to fit the job to the computer and it is doubtful whether this is always appreciated by the buyer. Commercial computers have a vast appetite for work, but they are not the "thinking machines" that scientists were discussing at the National Physical Laboratory a week ago. They cannot plan the way a job ought to be done; they can act only on data and in-

Exhibit 7—Concluded

structions fed to them by human operators and if the work is badly planned, the computer can do nothing to correct it.

Some experts have a shrewd suspicion that managements have found it more difficult to adjust their methods to computers than they had expected, rather in the way of those housewives whose pressure cookers sit unused on the top shelf. Their evidence is the large number of commercial computers used—on the admission of the owners—mainly for calculating wage packets. To put a computer to this work is like taking a steamroller to crack a nut—a useful way of filling odd moments but a sad under-employment of the machine's great capabilities. But wage calculations happens to be one of the easiest jobs to tailor for a computer—this is why manufacturers frequently use it for demonstrations purposes—and it gives both computer operators and management a breathing space to learn how to use their new toy.

Although manufacturers can supply computers with a plan of work built into them, this is essentially a job that can be carried out only by men who know and have worked in the company buying the machine and who understand its business. The planning of work for a computer goes far beyond the mere mathematics of working out a code of instructions telling the machine how to do the job. It calls for a certain amount of imagination to grasp the computer's potentialities for helping the company, and although the manufacturer's staff can give advice on what is or is not technically possible they cannot be expected to understand how each business works or the best way that it should be run. Management must be prepared to spend some time learning to do the job itself. It may take months, or even years, to learn how to get maximum value from a computer. In some cases, it is still going to be cheaper and less troublesome to do the job with clerks.

Source: *The Economist*, December 6, 1958, pp. 915–16. Reproduced by permission.

in sales over the subsequent five-year period. Mr. Bolton added: "To some extent we are still a little paternalistic in this regard, in that I am still doling the money out as from a family kitty, basing individual allocations on the individual family members' estimates of their needs, scaled down to fit the total budget."

Picking individual projects.   According to Mr. James Rothman, administrative assistant for SR.&D., the principal sources of ideas for new projects were as follows: (1) Company staff, which was the principal source of ideas involving logical extensions of existing products, either by simple adaptation (such as redesigning a machine to read in polar as well as X and Y coordinates), or by using new principles or components. These were the source of the largest number of new projects. (2) Outsiders who joined Solartron and brought new ideas with them. This was the main source of radically new developments. (3) Outside requests of the "we need help badly" variety. In this respect, senior engineers were encouraged to visit with customers and discuss their problems. The company's technical service engineers also turned in as many as 2,000 visit reports each month, in which they reported on unresolved difficulties they had encountered in the field.

Over 100 possibilities for new projects were generated by these various sources in the course of a year. Of these, approximately 10% were chosen to be worked on, and the remainder were either rejected or held in abeyance. In the case of SR.&D., decisions were made by Mr. L. Copestick, managing director, and Mr. R. Catherall, research director. In the case of SEBM, SIC, and Radar Simulators, decisions were made by the senior executives involved. Decisions were made on a basis of these criteria: the estimated sales and gross profits that would result from making a given investment, and the interest of the engineers involved in carrying out the project.

Although formal calculations were not always prepared in selecting projects, a work order stating the estimated completion date and cost was issued at the time a project was begun. During the course of the project, monthly comparisons of work-in-progress (labor, materials, and overhead) were made with the budgeted cost by the senior executives and project engineers involved.

In late 1957 Mr. Rothman had been asked to devise a formula so that the decision whether a proposed project should be financed with Group funds could be made by a representative committee on the basis of the project's profitability ratio (the ratio of present value of profits over three years to the initial investment). Efforts to formalize the research and development program had been under way for over five years. This formula was enthusiastically received by Mr. Bolton, but it had not been implemented because it had been viewed more coolly by senior SR.&D. executives, on the grounds that the present system worked well, and that the estimates needed to calculate the profitability ratio would be too sketchy to be of real value. Excerpts from the summary of Mr. Rothman's proposal follow:

NEW PRODUCTS ASSESSMENT SUMMARY

It is suggested that the decision whether a proposed development project should be financed by Group should be based very largely on its profitability ratio. . . .

In order to obtain a fair assessment of the profitability ratios, a representative committee would be formed to collate and agree upon the individual forecasts from which the profitability ratios would be calculated. . . . This committee would also draw attention to other intangible factors that might affect a decision on a particular product.

The Managing Directors of the development companies concerned could start development on any project approved by the Committee. However, in order to ensure that the Group's financial resources are not overstrained at any one time, a subcommittee of the Group Board will decide at three-monthly intervals the amount to be spent on development by each company in the next but two three-monthly period. This decision would be based on a consideration of projects under way and of projects approved by the New Products Committee.

It would then be the responsibility of the Managing Directors concerned to ensure that they did not overspend their budgeted allocation.

The aim has been to provide an agreed selection process and while providing short-term stability in development budgets, it is designed to give long-term flexibility in allocation of funds for SEG sponsored development.

Texas Instruments, Incorporated (A) (Condensed)

ON APRIL 17, 1959, Texas Instruments Incorporated (TI) of Dallas, Texas, merged with the Metals and Controls Corporation (M & C) of Attleboro, Massachusetts. One of the fastest growing large corporations in the country, TI had achieved a compound annual growth from 1946 through 1958 of 38% in sales and 42% in net income. The president had publicly predicted that volume would more than double in 1959 to a sales level near $200 million. Almost half this growth, he added, might come through mergers, with M & C contributing $42 million to $45 million. To date TI's principal business had been in electronic and electromechanical equipment and systems, semiconductors and other components, and exploration services for oil, gas, and minerals.

So highly was TI regarded by the market that in May 1960 its common was selling at about 70 times the 1959 earnings of $3.59 a share.

M & C ACTIVITIES

Itself the product of a 1932 merger and a postwar diversification, M & C had three major groups of products: clad metals, control instruments, and nuclear fuel components and instrumented cores. The company had grown steadily, and in 1959 had plants in two U.S. locations and five foreign countries. Reflecting predecessor corporation names, the clad metal lines were known as General Plate (GP) products, and the control instrument liens were known as Spencer products. Included in the former were industrial, precious, and thermostat metals; fancy wire; and wire and tubing. Included in the latter were motor protectors, circuit breakers, thermostats, and precision switches. Among these Spencer lines there were some that utilized GP products as raw materials; i.e., GP thermostat bimetals and GP clad electrical contacts.

Apart from a portion of GP's precious metal products which went to the jewelry trade (where appearance and fast delivery from stock were

key considerations), most GP and Spencer products had to be designed
to specific customer requirements and produced to customer order.
Thus engineering know-how and close coordination between the sales
and production departments on delivery dates were important. Owing
to the technical nature of the products and also to their fast-changing
applications, a company sales force with a high degree of engineering
competence was essential. To serve its several thousand customers,
many of whom purchased both Spencer and GP products, the company
maintained a force of 50 men in the field, divided into Spencer and GP
units.

With Spencer products facing important competition from four other
firms in the $10 million to $40 million annual sales bracket, tight control of costs was important for securing the large orders generally placed
by the kinds of customers to whom these products were sold. Buyers
included manufacturers of fractional horsepower motors, household appliances, air conditioning, and aircraft and missiles. In contrast, GP
industrial metals met no direct competition, although clad metals for
industrial uses met with competition from alloys.

M & C's PREMERGER ORGANIZATION

At the time TI took over M & C, a task force of four junior executives
had just completed, at the acting president's request, a critical study of
M & C's organizational structure. So far its nuclear activities had been
conducted by an entirely separate subsidiary, and the GP and Spencer
activities had been organized as shown on Exhibit 1.

Under the acting president at the top level came a tier of predominantly functional executives (the vice presidents for marketing, engineering, and finance, the treasurer, and the controller). At the third
and fourth levels of command, the structure increasingly showed a
breakdown by product lines. For example, at the fourth level in manufacturing there were four separate groups corresponding to the major
Spencer lines, and six separate groups corresponding to the major GP
lines. Approximately the same breakdown appeared among the fourth-
level product specialists in marketing. Although there was no profit
responsibility at this level, the controller had been sending marketing's
product specialists a monthly P & L by product line, in the hope of encouraging informal meetings among the people in marketing, engineering, and production who were working on the same lines.

Even at the second level, the predominantly functional division of
responsibilities was neither complete nor unalloyed. Thus the vice president for marketing was also the vice president of Spencer Products,
and in this capacity he had reporting to him the Spencer engineers. As
a result, the company's vice president of engineering was, in effect, the
vice president only of GP engineering, although he also served in an
other-than-functional role by acting as the vice president of M & C International. (In 1958 exports and other foreign sales totaled about $2
million.)

After confidential interviews with 140 people, members of the M & C

Exhibit 1

PREMERGER METALS AND CONTROLS ORGANIZATION

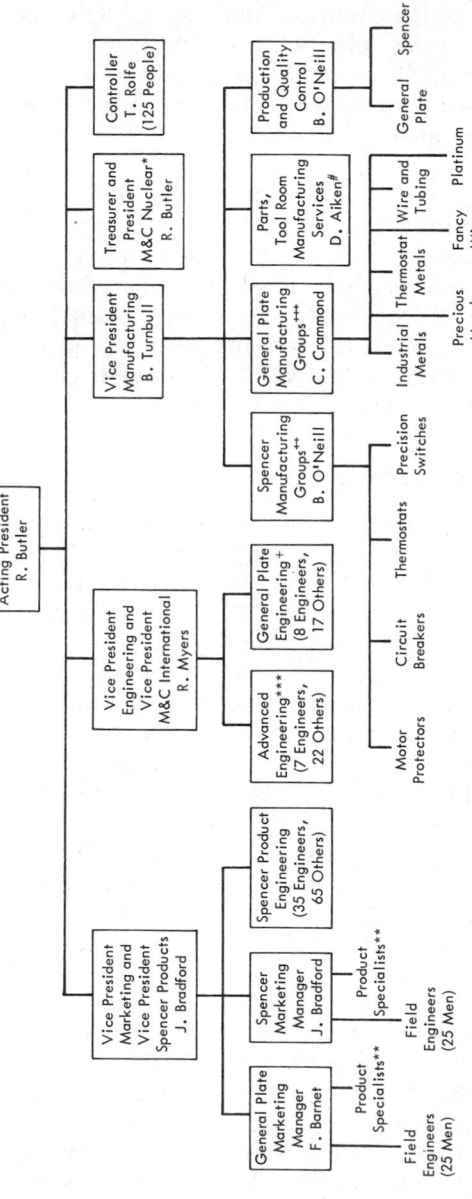

* Detail on M & C Nuclear not disclosed.

** Responsible for factory-customer coordination on specifications, prices, delivery, and new applications on different product lines (broken down about as shown in the manufacturing department).

\+ Responsible for long-range product development for GP lines.

*** Worked on new applications and process designs for GP lines.

\+\+ Principal operations in Spencer production departments were parts-making and assembly.

\+\+\+ Principal operations in GP industrial, precious, and thermostat metal departments were bonding and rolling; in GP wire and fancy wire departments, drawing; and in GP platinum department, melting and refining. Some GP facilities were shared, and roughly 5% of direct labor hours for each GP department were devoted to work for other departments.

\# Reporting to Aiken were units making two GP and three Spencer parts.

Source: Interviews and company records.

task force reportedly concluded that this organizational structure was causing or contributing to a number of company problems. Accordingly the task force recommended sweeping changes, first to the acting president by whom they had been appointed, then to his successor, Mr. Edward O. Vetter, a 39-year-old TI vice president brought in following the merger.

MR. VETTER'S REVIEW AND APPRAISAL

As soon as he arrived at M & C, Mr. Vetter spent most of four days in closed meetings with task force members. At the same time he scheduled public meetings with all executives; these sessions he devoted to general discussions of his aims for the organization and to reassurances that drastic changes would not be made.

From these discussions Vetter learned that a great many people at M & C felt that the three major functional departments were not cooperating well enough in the exploitation of new product opportunities based on existing markets and skills. Although in a few isolated instances, marketing, engineering, and production personnel concerned with a particular product had formed small informal groups to work on common problems, the three departments had not been seen as working together with maximum effectiveness, particularly in new product development. To blame, besides top management's inattention and the absence of a comprehensive plan, was a lack of clear-cut responsibility and authority.

Other problems, too, provided additional evidence of the failure of functional groups to work together harmoniously and effectively. Thus there was continued squabbling between process engineers and production supervisors, with neither group being willing to accept the other's suggestions for improvements in manufacturing methods. With both groups reporting to different vice presidents, conflicts too often came up for resolution at top levels. Here many times decisions were postponed and issues left unresolved.

Vetter was also told by many members of the organization that the personal influence of marketing's product specialists played too large a role in company decisions. Formally assigned to coordinate certain aspects of factory-customer relations (see notes to Exhibit 1), these specialists were said to determine the amount of R.&D. time given to particular lines, with the result that some lines had grown quite strong while promising opportunities elsewhere were neglected. Similarly personal relationships between product specialists and production personnel largely determined scheduling priorities.

After becoming familiar with these problems, Mr. Vetter decided that M & C provided a golden opportunity for applying TI's philosophy of organization by what TI called "product-customer centered groups." Basically this plan involved putting a single manager in charge of sales, manufacturing, and engineering on a particular product line, and making this manager responsible for profits. This type of structure, Mr. Vetter noted, was what had been proposed by M & C's own task force on organization. According to TI's president, it offered advantages not only in managing existing lines but also in finding new opportunities for discerning and serving new customer needs.

As he was collecting information on M & C's organizational arrangements, Mr. Vetter had dictated the following set of notes for his own use:

> It appears as if natural product groups already exist here. General Plate, Spencer and Nuclear have always been separate, and International sales are set apart under Richard Myers. Within these major groupings there is also a somewhat parallel division of the manufacturing and marketing facilities along product lines. There are ten production departments that are each organized to produce a particular product line, while there is an almost parallel organization of marketing product specialists under James Bradford.
>
> Bringing together product managers and production supervisors for similar product lines would seem to be the logical implementation of TI's management philosophy. Of course, one problem would be the rearrangement of some of the production facilities in order to locate all the equipment under a product manager's control in one area. While we do have ten product-manufacturing departments, some of these share facilities and perform work for one another. In addition, the parts department performs fabrication operations for several production departments. In spite of this, there are no major pieces of equipment that would have to be physically relocated. We estimated that some duplicate equipment will have to be purchased if we go ahead with product-centered decentralization; in order to accomplish this about $1.5 million will have to be spent almost three years before it would otherwise have been committed.
>
> I believe that the "inside" product specialist—the man at the factory who lives with both the manufacturing and the marketing problems for his line—is a key man. Our products are mainly engineered to customer order and, as such, require a great deal of coordination on delivery dates, specifications, and special applications. In addition to performing this liaison, the product managers could be the men who sense ideas for new product applications from their marketing contacts and then transmit these to the product engineering personnel at the factory.
>
> These men would not be salesmen. A field sales force would still be needed to make regular calls on all of our clients and to cultivate the associations with our customers' engineering staffs. One significant question here is how to organize the sales force. These men are highly skilled and quite expensive to employ—each salesman should enter commitments of at least $1 million yearly in order to justify his expenses. Since our customers are spread all over the country, it would appear economical to assign field salesmen by geographical areas, each to sell all, or at least a number of, our products. Unfortunately, this system might take a good measure of the responsibility for the sales supervision. Our problem here is to leave sales responsibility at the product group level without having an undue duplication of field sales personnel.
>
> The filtering down of responsibility and authority would mean that we would need more "management skill" in order for the product managers to be able to manage the little companies of which each

would be in charge. The product manager must be capable of making sales, manufacturing, financial, and engineering decisions. He is no longer judged against a budget but becomes responsible for profits. We would need talented men to fill these positions—a shift in the organizational structure would undoubtedly force us to hire some new people. Nevertheless, there are tremendous benefits to be gained in terms of giving more people the chance to display their talents and in just plain better functioning of the M & C division.

The organization of engineering personnel brings up a whole hornets' nest of questions. First of all, there are two distinct engineering functions: product engineers, those concerned with current product designs and new applications for existing products; and advanced engineers, those who work on long-term product development. There is little doubt that the new applications sales effort would benefit from placing the product engineering personnel in close organizational contact with the marketers. This would mean splitting engineering up among all the product groups and would probably make for a less efficient overall operation. Decentralization of the advanced engineering groups is easily as ticklish a problem. Again, it would probably receive more marketing-oriented stimulus if it were placed under the supervision of the product manager. I wonder, however, if he might not be motivated to cut long-term development more drastically than top management normally would in times of business recession. Furthermore, I wonder if the economies of centralized advanced engineering and research in terms of combined effort and personnel selection are not so great as to make decentralization of this function an extremely poor choice. The basic question we have to answer here is to what degree should we sacrifice operating economy in order to give our engineering personnel a greater marketing orientation.

*   *   *   *   *

Scheduling has long been a bone of contention here wherever facilities are shared. Conflicts for priorities between product specialists are always occurring. If we decentralize, however, the amount of facilities that are shared will decrease substantially and this problem should be alleviated. Again we have the basic choice of retaining the centralized scheduling groups or splitting the function up among the various product groups.

In addition to the above issues, Mr. Vetter was considering the proper timing for an organizational change. He was debating whether a change should be made by gradual steps or whether the transfer in corporate ownership provided a convenient opportunity for making radical changes with a minimum of employee resentment. In general, the M & C personnel expressed some regrets because the family that had founded the company was no longer associated with it. They recognized, however, that the continual top management conflict of recent years necessitated a change and were pleased by the fact that a recognized leader in the industry had taken over the company.

Texas Instruments, Incorporated (B)

IN MAY 1960 Tom Pringle, the manager of the Industrial Metals product department at Texas Instrument's Metals & Controls division, was considering several courses of action in the face of his department's failure to meet forecasted sales and profits during the first four months of 1960. The rebuilding of inventories by M & C's customers, which had been expected as an aftermath of the settlement of the 1959 steel strike, had not materialized and shipments from Pringle's product department were running about 12% below forecast. Furthermore, incoming sales commitments during these four months were 15% below expectations. The product department's direct profit, according to preliminary statements, was 19% below plan.

In light of these adverse developments, Pringle was studying the advisability of three specific moves which would improve his profit performance: (1) eliminating his $30,000 advertising budget for the latter half of 1960, (2) postponing the addition of two engineers to his engineering group until 1961, and (3) reducing further purchases of raw materials in order to improve his department's return on assets ratio. Until now, Pringle had been reluctant to make any concessions in his department's scale of operations since there was a very strong accent on rapid growth throughout the Texas Instruments organization. This attitude toward expansion also appeared to prevail in the new top management group in the Metals & Controls division. The enthusiasm of the Texas Instrument's management had caught on at Metals & Controls with the formation of the product-centered decentralized organization.

THE 1959 REORGANIZATION

In June 1959, just three months after Metals & Controls Corporation had become a division of Texas Instruments Incorporated, Mr. Edward

O. Vetter, the division vice president, instituted a product-centered organization. This decentralization was carried out in accordance with Texas Instruments' policy of placing ultimate responsibility for profitable operation at the product level. The framework that emerged was similar to that which existed elsewhere in the company.

Mr. Vetter organized four major product groups at Metals & Controls: General Plate, Spencer Controls, Nuclear Products, and International Operations. To augment these groups, six centralized staff units were organized at the division level: Research and Development, Legal, Industrial Engineering, Control, Marketing, and Personnel (Exhibit 1).

Exhibit 1

ORGANIZATION CHART, METALS & CONTROLS DIVISION

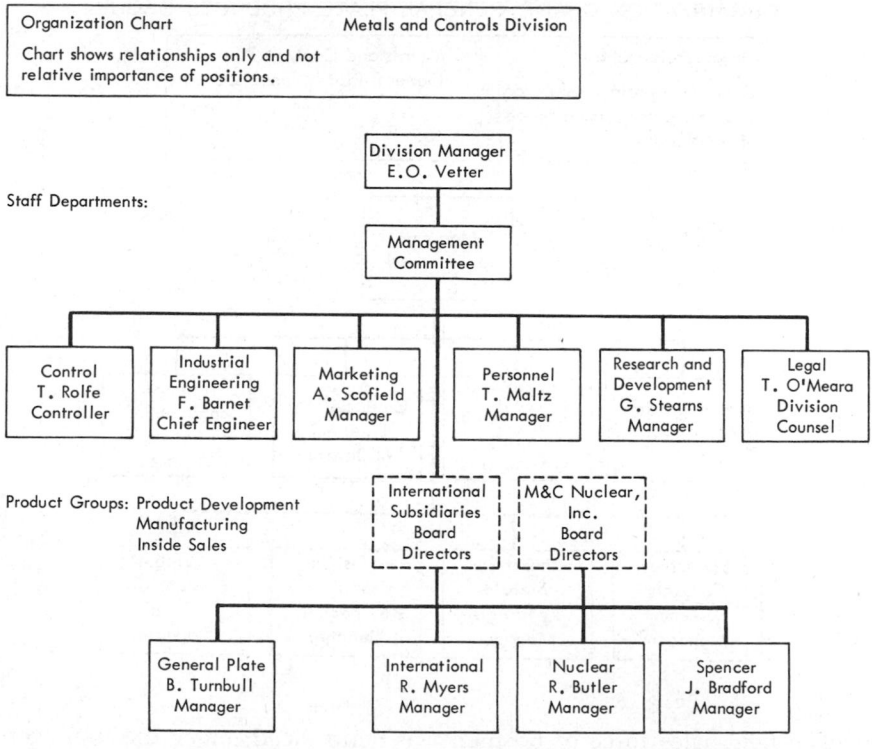

The four managers of the product groups and the six managers of these staff departments, along with Mr. Vetter, comprised the management committee for the Metals & Controls division. This committee was a sounding board for helping each responsible manager make the proper decision as required by his job responsibility. In the case of profit performance, the ultimate responsibility for the division was Vetter's.

Within each product group, several product departments were established. The General Plate products group, for example, included the Industrial Metals, Electrical Contacts, Industrial Wire, and Precious

Metals departments (Exhibit 2). The manager of each of these departments was responsible for its "profit performance." He was supported by staff units such as Industrial Engineering and Administration which reported directly to the group manager (Burt Turnbull for General Plate products). The expense of these staff units was charged to the individual product departments proportionally to the volume of activity in the various departments as measured by direct labor hours or by sales dollars less raw materials cost. The product departments were also charged with those expenses over which the manager and his supervisory group were able to exercise direct control, such as labor and materials.

Exhibit 2

ORGANIZATION CHART, GENERAL PLATE PRODUCTS GROUP

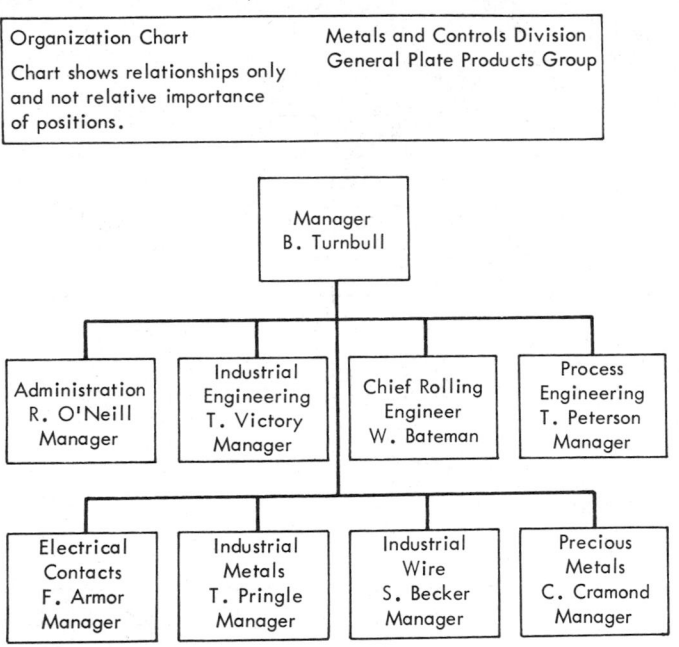

The field sales force of 50 men was centralized under the manager for marketing, Al Scofield (Exhibit 1). These men were divided about evenly into two major selling groups: one for General Plate products, and the other for Spencer products. The 25 salesmen assigned to General Plate and the 25 salesmen assigned to Spencer were shared by the four General Plate and four Spencer product departments. Each individual product department also maintained "inside" marketing personnel who performed such functions as pricing, developing marketing strategy, order follow-up and providing the field sales engineers with information on new applications, designs, and product specifications for its particular line.

The Industrial Metals department

Tom Pringle was manager of the Industrial Metals department of the General Plate products group. Sales of this department in 1959 were approximately $4 million.[1] Pringle was responsible for the profitability of two product lines: (1) industrial metals and (2) thermostat metals. His department's sales were split about evenly between these lines, although industrial metals had the greater growth potential because of the almost infinite number of possible clad metals for which an ever increasing number of applications was being found. He was in charge of the marketing, engineering, and manufacturing activities for both these lines and had six key subordinates:

INDUSTRIAL METALS DEPARTMENT

Years of Service with the Metals and Controls Organization

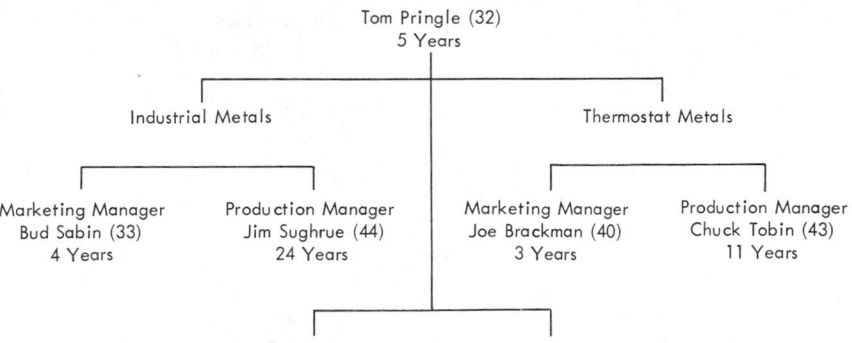

The function of the marketing managers in the Industrial Metals department (Bud Sabin and Joe Brackman) was to supervise the "inside selling units." These units were responsible for developing marketing strategy, pricing, contacting customers on special requests and factory problems, for promotional activities, and for coordinating product development and sales. In May 1960, in addition to its regular work, the Industrial Metals inside selling unit was developing a manual of special applications for its products which it hoped would improve the ability of the field sales force to envision new uses. The production managers had line responsibility for the efficient use of manufacturing facilities, for meeting delivery promises to customers, and for expenses incurred in producing the department's products. The product and process engineering group had responsibility for designing new products and devising new production processes. The production control manager formulated guidelines to aid the foremen in scheduling work through the

---

[1] All figures have been disguised.

plant, supervised the expediters and clerks who served as a clearing-house for information on delivery dates, and was responsible for ordering raw material and maintaining a balanced inventory.

In accordance with Texas Instruments' policy of placing ultimate responsibility for profitable operation at the product level, Tom Pringle's performance was measured, to a large extent, by the actual profits earned by the Industrial Metals department. The old M & C system of evaluating performance according to fixed and variable department budgets had been supplemented by the establishment of these "profit centers." Although the system passed actual profit responsibility to the product department manager level, the Texas Instruments' top management had always retained some control over the profit centers by requiring each manager to formulate a one-year plan which was subject to review by higher management. As a result, profit planning was instituted whereby each manager set forth a detailed plan for the year's operations under the direction of the management committee. His actual performance was continually being evaluated against the plan.

Formulation of the profit plan.   In October 1959, Tom Pringle began to prepare his department's profit plan for 1960. This was part of a company-wide effort in which all department managers participated. The first step in the process was to prepare a detailed estimate of expected sales for the year. These estimates were gathered from two sources: the inside selling units and the field sales force. Management felt that one would serve as a good check on the other, and, furthermore, believed that widespread participation in preparing the plan was one way to insure its effectiveness. Bud Sabin and Joe Brackman, then, began to prepare estimates of 1960 sales by product lines with the help of the individual product specialists within the inside marketing group. Sabin and Brackman were also aided by the Texas Instruments central marketing group which prepared a report which estimated normal growth for their product lines. Pringle suggested that they prepare their estimates by subdividing the market into three parts: sales resulting from normal industry growth at current levels of market penetration; increased sales resulting from further penetration of the market with existing products; and increased sales from new products detailed by specific customers. At the same time, Herb Skinner, the manager of the General Plate field sales force, asked the field engineers to predict the volume of orders that each Industrial Metals customer would place in 1960, without referring to the reports being readied by the product marketing groups. In this way, the marketing managers made forecasts by product line and the field force made forecasts by customer.

The field selling force came up with estimated thermostat metal sales of $2,350,000 for 1960, and the inside group estimated sales of $2,420,000. Pringle felt that these two estimates were in reasonably good agreement. On the other hand, Bud Sabin, the Industrial Metals marketing manager, estimated sales of $3,050,000, while Skinner's group predicted only $2,500,000. Sabin predicted that 20% of the increase would come from normal growth, 50% from increased market penetration with existing products, and 30% from new products. Sales for Sabin's group had been $1,400,000 in 1958 and $2,100,000 in 1959. Pringle felt that the disparity between the two estimates was significant and he discussed the matter with both men. All three men finally decided that the sales force had submitted a conservative estimate and agreed that Sabin's figure was the most realistic goal.

Once the sales estimate of $5,470,000 was agreed upon by Pringle and his marketing managers, the process of estimating manufacturing costs began. The manufacturing superintendents, Chuck Tobin and Jim Sughrue, were furnished the thermostat and industrial metals sales estimates and were instructed to forecast direct labor costs, supervisory salaries, and overhead expenses. These forecasts were to be made for each manufacturing area, or cost center, under their supervision. Sughrue was responsible for five cost centers and Tobin for four, each of which was directly supervised by a foreman. These expenses were to be forecast monthly and were to be used as a yardstick by which the actual expense performance of the manufacturing personnel could later be measured.

Jim Sughrue had previously calculated the hourly labor cost and the output per hour for each of his cost centers for 1959. To estimate 1960 salaries and wages, he then increased 1959 expenses proportionately to the expected sales increase. He followed the same procedure in determining 1960 overhead expenses, such as expendable tools, travel, telephone, process supplies, and general supplies. Chuck Tobin's task was somewhat simpler since the sales projection for his cost centers required a level of output that exactly matched the current production level. For salaries and wages, he merely used as his 1960 estimate the actual cost experience that had been reported on the most recent monthly income statement he received. For overhead, he applied a historical percent-of-sales ratio and then reduced his estimate by 3% to account for increased efficiency. In discussing the overhead estimate with his foremen, Tobin informed them that he had allowed for an 8% efficiency increase.

Since this was the first time any attempt at such detailed planning had been made at M & C, and since the M & C accounting system had recently been changed to match Texas Instruments', very little historical information was available. For this reason, Pringle did not completely delegate the responsibility for the various marketing and manufacturing estimates to his subordinates. Instead he worked in conjunction with them to develop the forecasts. He hoped that his participation in this process would insure a more accurate forecast for the year. Furthermore, he hoped to develop the ability of his supervision to plan ahead.

Pringle estimated direct materials cost and consumption factors himself. Since it was impossible to predict what all the various strip metal prices would be, he calculated the ratio of materials expense to sales for 1959 and applied it to the 1960 sales projections for each of the product lines in his department.

The marketing, administration, and engineering groups that serviced Pringle's Industrial Metals group forecast their expenses by detailing their personnel requirements and then applying historical ratios of expenses to personnel to estimate their other expenses. From these dollar figures, Pringle was able to estimate what proportions of these amounts would be charged to his department.

With the various forecasts in hand, Pringle estimated a direct profit of $1,392,000 on a sales volume of $5,470,000. Once this plan had been drawn up, it was reviewed by the division management committee in relationship to the specific profit and sales goals which it has established for the division. In reviewing the plans for each product department in terms of the specific group goals, it became obvious that the combined plans of the General Plate product departments were not sufficient to meet the overall goal, and that based on market penetration, new product developments, and other factors, the planned sales volume for Industrial Metals should be revised upward to $6,050,000 and direct profit to $1,587,000 (Exhibit 3). This was discussed among Vetter, Turnbull, Scofield, and Pringle and they agreed that it was a difficult but achievable plan.

Exhibit 3

INDUSTRIAL METALS DEPARTMENT

Initial and Revised Profit Statements for 1960*

	Initial	Revised
Sales........................	$5,470,000	$6,050,000
Direct labor..................	435,000	480,000
Direct material...............	1,920,000	2,115,000
Overhead.....................	875,000	968,000
Marketing....................	305,000	346,000
Administration...............	161,000	161,000
Engineering..................	382,000	393,000
Direct profit...............	1,392,000	1,587,000

* All figures have been disguised.

Actual performance, 1960. On May 10 Tom Pringle received a detailed statement comparing the actual performance of his department for January through April with his budget (Exhibit 4). Sales were 12% below plan, and direct profit was 19% below plan.

In addition to these figures, manufacturing expenses by cost centers were accumulated for Pringle. He passed these along to the production superintendents after he had made adjustments in the budgeted expense figures to allow for the sales decline. Pringle had devised a variable budget system whereby he applied factors to the forecast expenses to indicate what an acceptable expense performance was at sales levels other than the planned volume. Chuck Tobin and Jim Sughrue then analyzed the actual expenses and, one week later, held meetings with their foremen to discuss the causes of both favorable and unfavorable variances. The most common explanation of favorable manufacturing variances was either extremely efficient utilization of labor or close

Exhibit 4

COMPARISON OF ACTUAL AND
BUDGETED PERFORMANCE,
JANUARY–APRIL 1960*

	Budgeted	Actual
Sales	$2,020,000	$1,780,000
Direct labor	160,000	142,400
Direct material	704,000	593,000
Overhead	322,000	287,000
Marketing	100,000	116,400
Administration	54,000	55,800
Engineering	126,000	136,600
Direct profit	554,000	448,000

* All figures have been disguised.

control over overhead. Unfavorable variances most frequently resulted from machine delays which necessitated overtime labor payments.

Specific problems. Pringle was currently faced with three specific problems. In light of his department's poor performance these past months, he was considering the effects of eliminating his $30,000 advertising budget for the remainder of 1960, postponing the addition of two new engineers to his staff for six months, and reducing raw materials purchases in order to decrease inventory and thus improve his department's return on assets performance.

He had discussed the possibility of eliminating the advertising budget with Bud Sabin and Joe Brackman but had not yet reached a conclusion. Advertising expenditures had been budgeted at $30,000 for the final six months of 1960. The Industrial Metals department ads were generally placed in trade journals read by design engineers in the electrical, automobile, and appliance industries. Pringle did not know for certain how important an aid these advertisements were to his sales force. He did know that all of his major competitors allocated about the same proportion of sales revenue for advertising expenditures and that Industrial Metals ads were occasionally mentioned by customers.

In late 1959, Pringle had made plans to increase his engineering staff from eight men to ten men in mid-1960. He felt that the two men could begin functioning productively by early 1961 and could help to revise certain processes which were yielding excessive scrap, to develop new products, and to assist the field engineers in discovering new applications for existing products. Pringle estimated that postponing the hiring of these men for six months would save $20,000 in engineering salaries and supporting expenses.

Pringle also knew that one of the important indicators of his performance was the department's ratio of direct profit to assets used. This figure had been budgeted at 40% for 1961, but actual results to date were 31%. Pringle was considering reductions in raw materials purchases in order to decrease inventories and thus improve performance. He had discussed this possibility with Phil Waterman, the production control manager for Industrial Metals. Pringle knew that significant improvements in the overall ratio could be made in this way since raw materials inventories accounted for almost 20% of total assets and were at a level of ten months' usage at present consumption ratios. He recognized, however, that this course of action required accepting a greater risk of running out. This risk was important to assess since most customers required rapid delivery and Pringle's suppliers usually required four months' lead time to manufacture the nonstandard size metals in relatively small lots required for the Industrial Metals' cladding operation.

The purpose of the profit plan.   The degree to which the plan was used as a method for evaluating performance and fixing compensation was not completely clear to Pringle. Everyone seemed to recognize that this first effort was imperfect and had errors built in because of inadequate historical data. He had never been explicitly informed of the extent to which top management desired product department decision making to be motivated by short-run effects on planned performance. Pringle stated that during the months immediately following the initiation of the plan he had concluded that short-term performance was much less significant than long-run growth and that he had preferred to concentrate on the longer run development of new products and markets.

Pringle knew that the Metals & Controls operating committee met every Monday to review the performance of each product department from preliminary reports. Customarily Burt Turnbull, the manager of the General Plate group, discussed both Pringle's incoming sales commitments and actual manufacturing expenses with him before each meeting. Pringle also knew that each manager was given a formal appraisal review every six months by his superior. It was common knowledge that the department's performance in relation to its plan was evaluated at both these sessions. Furthermore, Pringle was aware of the fact that Turnbull's performance as product group manager would be affected by his own performance with Industrial Metals. Over a period of months, Pringle had learned that the management committee utilized the comparison of actual and planned performance to pinpoint trouble spots. On occasion Vetter had called him in to explain any significant deviations from plan but normally he was represented at these meetings by Burt Turnbull. It was Pringle's impression that Vetter had been satisfied with the explanation he had given.

In their day-to-day decisions, Pringle's subordinates seemed to be influenced only in a very general way by the profit plan. They reviewed their monthly performance against plan with interest, but generally tended to bias their decisions in favor of long-run development at the expense of short-run deviations from the plan. More recently, however, Pringle realized that top management was not satisfied with his explanations of failure to meet plans. The message, though not stated explicitly, seemed to be that he was expected to take whatever remedial and alternate courses of action were needed in order to meet the one-year goals. He was certain that real pressure was building up for each department manager to meet his one-year plan.

In commenting on the use of planning at M & C, Mr. Vetter, the division vice president, stated four major purposes of the program:

> To set a par for the course. Vetter believed that performance was always improved if the manager proposed a realistic objective for his performance and was informed in advance of what was expected of him.

> To grow management ability. Vetter believed that the job of manager was to coordinate all the areas for which he was given responsibility. He saw the planning process as a tool for improving these managerial skills.

> To anticipate problems and look ahead. Vetter felt that the planning process gave the department managers a convenient tool for planning personnel requirements and sales strategy. It also set guideposts so that shifts in business conditions could be detected quickly and plans could be altered.

> To weld Texas Instruments into one unit. The basic goals for each division were formulated by Vetter in recognition of overall company goals as disseminated by Haggerty, the company president. These were passed down to the product department level by the product group manager at each Texas Instruments division. Profit planning was thus being carried out by the same process by every department manager in the corporation.

Vetter recognized, however, that many reasons could exist for performance being either better or worse than planned. He stated that in his experience extremely rigid profit plans often motivated managers to budget low in order to provide themselves with a safety cushion. In his view, this made the entire profit planning process worthless.

Dennison Manufacturing Company (A & B)

A RECENT MAGAZINE ARTICLE introduced the Dennison Manufacturing Company as follows:

> Only a few years ago, Dennison Manufacturing Company of Framingham, Massachusetts, looked the very model of the sleepily staid old New England company. Its rambling red brick plant was picturesque, but little else. . . . About all it had to show for 120 years of corporate existence was $2 million a year in profits and a clutter of thousands of paper products—boxes, tags, labels, ribbons, wrappings, coated papers and stationery items—along with labeling and punching machines. (To generations of school children Dennison was best known for its gummed rings for reinforcing looseleaf notebook pages). . . .
>
> Yet in 1964, Dennison suddenly jumped into the modern world, and with gusto. Knowing that something needed to be done for its growth, and believing that the answer was to get some new products, Dennison management went all the way. It came up with a machine for the red-hot office copier market based on electrostatic technology it had licensed a few years before from Radio Corp. of America. . . .
>
> At the same time, Dennison's basic business has been booming thanks to a strong economy and President [Phillip] Hamilton's reorganization of the business along modern lines. For all of its small size and complex product line, Dennison has a strong position in its speciality field. . . .[1]

The change which had occurred in the decade 1957–1967 had been dramatic. Instead of a "paternalistic, sleepy firm," Dennison was regarded as a growth company. The investment community backed up this analysis by trading Dennison common stock at 29 times its previous year's earnings.

Dennison was one of the oldest converters of paper products in the United States. Founded in 1844 to manufacture quality paper boxes

---

[1] *Forbes*, February 15, 1967, p. 64.

for the jewelry trade, it had expanded its product line to include a wide variety of paper products (4,000 made for stock, plus made-to-order items), numerous gummed and coated papers, and several machines to facilitate efficient use of paper products. Included among the latter were pinning machines, and machines for high-speed printing of price and inventory data on tags. The latest addition to this line was the Dennison high-speed electrostatic copier, with a capability of 1,800 copies an hour.

Dennison's corporate goals, as stated in internal publications and by members of management, could be summarized as follows:

1. Growth through invention and acquisition, and through obtaining exclusive distributorships in the paper-product field.
2. Development of useful paper products and machines which give those products their full meaning.

One top manager described the distinctive competence of the company as being its ability to obtain a "product edge." Cited as examples were the development of a paper patch tag around the turn of the century, and the more recent development of the therimage process[2] for labeling plastic bottles (1958) and the low-cost, high-speed copier (1967).

As of 1966, Dennison revenues were divided as follows:

	Percent
Dennison brand-name products sold to resale outlets	33
Made-to-order tags, tickets, labels, industrial crepe paper, and set-up boxes	31
Plain and coated or gummed paper	21
Machinery and equipment sales and rental	15

Total revenues had expanded from $41.0 million in 1957 to $87.4 million in 1966. Net earnings had gone from 5.1% of sales or $2.1 million to 6% of sales or $5.3 million in the same period. Return on equity improved from 10.8% in 1957 to 17.8% in 1967. The expansion had resulted from both internal growth and acquisitions. Three new divisions—Therimage, Copier, and Holiday (paper specialities)—had been formed during this 10-year period. In 1966 the Copier Division alone accounted for over $13 million in sales. (See Exhibit 1 for financial details.)

There was an explicit commitment among members of top management to internal growth and profits. The president, Phillip Hamilton, said, "I believe that earnings is the best measurement of how you are doing." This sentiment was amplified by Mr. Frank Swisher, the treasurer, who stated, "I think one of the key values here is that we as managers should be making a fair return on the stockholders' investment. Of course this is within the framework of not milking the con-

---

[2] A heat sensitive dye which allowed four-color printing in a single pass on most types of plastic and cellophane.

sumer. I know that Dennison has always been very socially-conscious. I just don't think that social responsibility is incompatible with profit. Wages and fringes, profits, and a good return on investment are not incompatible. In fact, for long-run success they must exist together."

In addition to growing from within, Dennison had been actively acquiring other companies. Its acquisitions had all been oriented toward paper products. In 1960 the company acquired a manufacturer of ribbons. In 1961 it acquired Eastman Tag and Label Manufacturing Company, and thus effectively expanded its made-to-order business to the west coast market. This acquisition, which added $3.5 million sales in its first year, had grown substantially since. Dunn Paper Company, acquired in 1965, was the first entry by Dennison into the manufacture of paper. Less than 10% of Dunn's output was sold to other Dennison divisions, but the acquisition added to Dennison's sales and profits.

In 1967 a merger was consummated between Dennison and National Blank Book. National's 1966 sales were $24.6 million. This merger added a broad line of commercial and school supplies to Dennison's product list. National produced over 3,500 stock items, including looseleaf ring and post binders, data processing binders, indexes and fillers, spiral-bound notebooks, bound blank ledger and columnar journal books, analysis and worksheet pads, diaries, and other personal books. In 1966 National's sales by end use were 68% to commercial users, 25% for schools, and 7% for personal use.

Dennison's strategy had remained relatively constant from 1957 to 1967. The main variations in the operation of the company which had led to rapid development were thought by management to be the changes in organizational structure and the change in the bonus system. Mr. Dana Huntington, the chairman of the board, said, "I am convinced that the biggest single factor in our recent success was the assignment of profit responsibility for a product line to a well-trained group of managers in a single operating unit. The second biggest factor was that we began paying management based on results."

ORGANIZATIONAL STRUCTURE

The 1955 organization. Until 1955, Dennison was organized along functional lines. Except in merchandising, there were no managers whose responsibility related to particular product lines. Thus a single sales department was responsible for selling the whole range of products, and the same held true for each salesman in a territory.

Based on his experience as manager of Dennison's Box Division, where he had been responsible for both production and sales, Mr. Huntington decided to move in the direction of decentralized product-line division. He described as follows the changes which he and Mr. Hamilton, then sales manager, effected in 1955:

> Phil Hamilton and I started to rearrange the sales organization so that we were organized by markets served, and geographically within markets served. With the old structure, we just couldn't keep abreast of the various lines. The salesmen were scattered too thin. Just the problems of keeping the price book up-to-date, making changes as products

were introduced or became obsolete, were horrendous. As a district sales manager at the time, I couldn't possibly direct my men intelligently. There was no rhyme or reason to the associations which we had between salesman, markets, and customers.

In 1955 we established national sales managers here at Framingham for each product. We were convinced that the key to future success was marketing. We then got the sales manager and the merchandising manager for each product line to work together as a team.

Much later, after this step was well understood, we did away with the general works manager [production manager] and set up production units which corresponded to the marketing units. It was a big job teaching new techniques and new ways of thinking. Not all of the people we had in managerial positions were capable of making the switch.

The change to profit consciousness and a growth orientation required a difficult educational effort. Many of the people within the company at all levels commented on the past orientation of the Dennison organization. Typical of such comments was the following:

> The orientation of the old management was to high principles, proper treatment of employees, and to making Dennison a nice place to work. The thought of making money beyond a certain regular profit was not important. . . .

A division manager talked of the old Dennison as follows:

> I guess we were smug and inclined to produce and create at our own convenience. We were fortunate—or unfortunate—in having a marketing position which would allow us to do that. We had never really had a purge, nor was the management inclined to be a hard pusher of people. We were steady, and anything but aggressive. We just weren't keeping up with progress in management techniques.

The 1960 organization.   After the initial process of reorienting managers to think like general managers was under way, it was decided to introduce a product-group form of organization. The company's seven product lines were divided into three groups of two to three lines each, and three vice presidents were appointed to supervise each group. To these vice presidents there reported separate sales, merchandise, and production managers for each line.

Mr. Huntington recalled that the assignment of product responsibility to particular individuals necessitated changes in personnel:

> We had to change some personnel. Three years ago we set a policy of compulsory retirement at 68. Previous to that time we had many people working into their 70's and even some into their 80's. Now, at management's option, people can be required to retire anytime after they are 65.
>
> We have been slow in making changes. I think that out of the whole company we have not gotten rid of more than 25 or 30. We forced out four or five so far this year, six or eight last year, and six the year before that. I can remember back in 1939 when one of the former presidents fired 32 people in one day to "make a clean sweep in the organization." That isn't the way it should be done. The fear, disruption, and self-protection that result are too harmful. Since I have had anything to say in the matter, we only take a few at a time. In each case we try to

remember our responsibility. For long-service employees, we attempt to make adjustments in their jobs, get them to retire early, or at the very worst give them six months to find a new position. I think more and more executives are thinking this way.

Mr. Hamilton talked about the change which he and Mr. Huntington had originated in the following terms:

> People continued to work here because it was a low-pressure organization. It was a pleasant place to work, and they were satisfied. There weren't many ambitious, driving men in positions of power in the company. There were always a few people who thought we could be doing better, but the type of organization we had tended to attract people who were satisfied with the climate.
>
> Our changes were evolutionary. It had to be. We had a shortage of qualified people and we had a complicated task in disentangling the production process. Of the top 40 people here 10 years ago, about one-third have become motivated, and the rest have given no great resistance or assistance to the changes which we were trying to accomplish.

The 1963 organization. In 1963 it was decided to make a general manager responsible for each product line. This move was implemented gradually, and by 1967 Dennison's formal organization had evolved into a profit-center divisional organization. There were profit-center divisions in the following businesses:

Resale Products...................... Paper products sold through distributors and retailers, stock tags, labels, crepe paper and streamers, notebook fillers, diaper liners.

Copier............................ The Dennison line of copiers, including a large office copier, a desk-top office copier, a coin-operated rental machine, a high-speed copier, and several specialized electrostatic copiers. Sold direct.

Industrial Products.................. Made-to-order tags and labels sold directly to the end user.

Marking Systems.................... Machines, tags, and attaching devices which formed a complete system allowing the user to print variable information on a tag near its point of use, and mechanically to attach the tag or label to an object. Distributed mainly to soft goods manufacturers and to retailers.

Therimage......................... Machines and supplies for a Dennison-developed process for labeling plastic bottles. Sold direct mainly to manufacturers of branded consumer items and to contract packaging firms.

Holiday........................... Decorated wrapping paper and ribbons sold through distributors and retail outlets. In smaller markets, Holiday Division products were sold by Resale Division salesmen.

Box............................... Set-up and folding speciality boxes, sold mainly to the jewelry and high-priced novelty trade.

Gummed and Coated Paper.......... All types of coatings applied to paper purchased outside the company. About 45% of this division's sales were made to other Dennison divisions.

In addition to these divisions, Dennison had three active subsidiaries which it treated as separate profit centers. Their activities were paralleled to the mainstream of Dennison's business:

Dennison Eastman.................. A west coast manufacturer of made-to-order tags and labels. This company merchandised the products of Dennison's Marking Systems Division as well as its own line of products.

Dunn Paper...................... A speciality paper manufacturer. Of the production of its three paper machines, about 10% was sold to Dennison divisions.

National Blank Book............... Manufacturer of loose-leaf ring and post binders, data processing form binders, indexes and fillers, spiral-bound notebooks, bound blank ledgers and columnar journal books, analysis and worksheet pads, and diaries and other personal record books.

Besides the divisions and subsidiaries, there were three other main cost centers. These were the financial office, including the treasurer's and controller's staff; the service department including industrial engineering, facilities, mechanical maintenance, warehousing, and facilities planning; and the R&D center. The 1967 Dennison organization chart appears as Exhibit 1.

THE BONUS SYSTEM

Until 1956, the Dennison Company had a history of paying year-end bonuses at the discretion of the board of directors. These bonuses had generally been thought of as relating most closely to salary level and seniority with normal payment based on a percentage of salary, but the exact determination was not fixed.

In 1956, the executive committee decided to develop a formula to determine bonus payments for each of three levels of employees: wage and weekly salaried personnel (Plan 1), middle management (Plan 2), and top management (Plan 3). For the Plan 1 group, the formula was such that payments went up and down slowly as company profits changed. For the middle management group (Plan 2) there was a one-to-one correspondence between changes in overall company profit and the group bonus (for example, doubling profits would double this group's bonus). For top management, the Plan 3 bonus fund (1)[3] was tied to return on investment and peaked sharply as profit increased. (See Exhibit 2.) The formula for the fund was as follows:

Plan 3 bonus fund$^{(1)}$ =

$$\left(\frac{\text{Pretax prebonus earnings}^{(2)}}{\text{Stockholders' beginning equity}^{(3)}} - .11^{(4)} \right) (.13)^{(5)} \left(\begin{array}{c} \text{Pretax}^{(2)} \\ \text{prebonus} \\ \text{earnings} \end{array} \right)$$

---

[3] The numbers in parentheses are keyed to statements in the text explaining their origin and to the sample calculation shown below.

PARTIAL ORGANIZATION CHART, MAY 1967

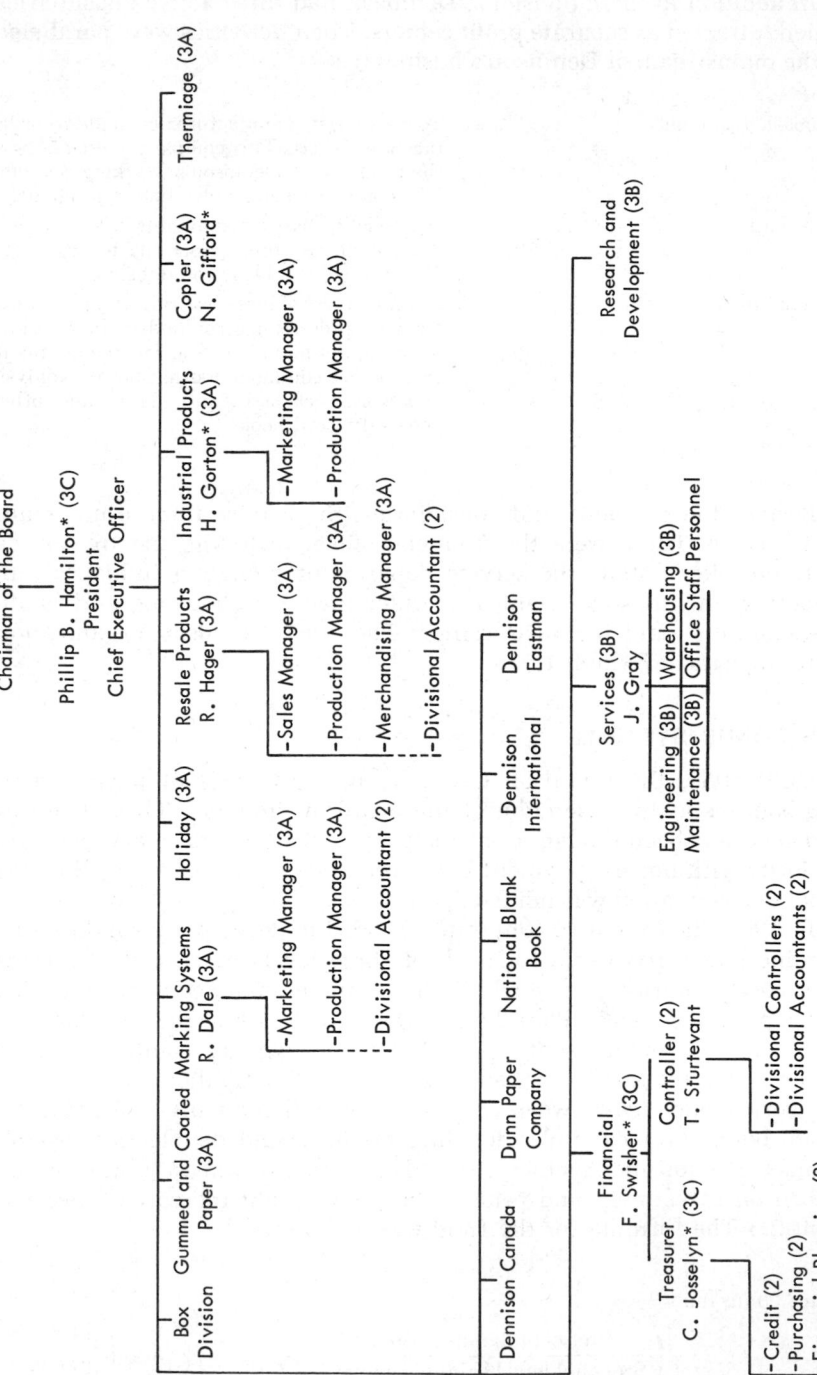

Dana C. Huntington* (3C)
Chairman of the Board

Phillip B. Hamilton* (3C)
President
Chief Executive Officer

Box Division

Gummed and Coated Paper (3A)

Marking Systems
R. Dale (3A)
-Marketing Manager (3A)
-Production Manager (3A)
-Divisional Accountant (2)

Holiday (3A)

Resale Products
R. Hager (3A)
-Sales Manager (3A)
-Production Manager (3A)
-Merchandising Manager (3A)
-Divisional Accountant (2)

Industrial Products
H. Gorton* (3A)
-Marketing Manager (3A)
-Production Manager (3A)

Copier (3A)
N. Gifford*

Thermiage (3A)

Dennison Canada

Dunn Paper Company

National Blank Book

Dennison International

Dennison Eastman

Financial
F. Swisher* (3C)

Treasurer
C. Josselyn* (3C)
-Credit (2)
-Purchasing (2)
-Financial Planning (2)

Controller (2)
T. Sturtevant
-Divisional Controllers (2)
-Divisional Accountants (2)

Services (3B)
J. Gray

Engineering (3B)
Maintenance (3B)

Warehousing (3B)
Office Staff Personnel

Research and Development (3B)

* Inside director.
Note: The numbers in brackets refer to the bonus plan to which the individual belongs.

Within this formula, the 11% reduction (4) in the earnings/equity percentage reflected the belief that stockholders should earn a "normal" 11% return before any bonus at all would be paid. The .13 (5) was simply an arbitrary figure, inserted because it served the function of relating bonus levels under the new plan to levels under pre-existing arrangements.

With the fund computed, the next step was to see how many months of salary it would cover for all members of the Plan 3 group. Subject to the limitation that no one could receive bonus payments equal to more than six months' salary, each individual's bonus then became his monthly salary figure multiplied by the number of months that the bonus fund could support:

$$\begin{matrix}\text{Individual}\\ \text{Corporate bonus}\\ \text{payment}\end{matrix} = \left(\frac{\text{Fund}^{(1)}}{\text{Participants' aggregate monthly salary}^{(6)}}\right) \times \left(\begin{matrix}\text{Individual's}\\ \text{monthly}\\ \text{salary}\end{matrix}\right)$$

Although by 1966, this original plan had been supplemented by other arrangements, it was still used to compute at least a portion of the bonus payable to all Plan 3 executives. When applied to the year's adjusted RoI for the 41 persons covered at that time, the formulas detailed above yielded the following results:

CORPORATE BONUS CALCULATION, 1966

Pretax earnings as reported................................	9,754,000
Plus bonuses under Plans 1, 2, 3........................	+$ 1,484,000
Pretax prebonus earnings (2)............................	$11,238,000
Stockholders' beginning equity (3).....................	$28,884,000
Rate of return on investment (ROI) (2) ÷ (3)...........	38.9%
Less normal return (4).................................	−11.0%
Adjusted ROI..	27.9%
Bonus rate (adjusted ROI times .13) (5)................	3.627%
Bonus fund plan 3 (earnings × rate) (1)...............	$ 407,600
Participants' aggregate monthly salaries (6)...........	$ 80,000
Individual's bonus-corporate (7) = (1) ÷ (6) ($407,600/$80,000).................................	5.01 months salary

Under the original corporate bonus plan, all Plan 3 executives, whether headquarters or divisional and whether line or staff, had their bonuses computed alike. Subsequently, in 1964 the executive committee decided that this formula alone did not sufficiently tie incentive payments to profit improvement, or to individual performance in the area for which each executive was especially responsible. To overcome these difficulties, it was decided that only part of each executive's bonus should henceforth be computed under the general corporate plan. Getting the rest would be made dependent on moving toward attainment of a profit target, and payments would be made on a different basis for divisional executives, the corporate staff men who advised them in their work, and the top headquarters line. Plan 1 and Plan 2 calculations were unaffected.

Plan 3 was divided into 3 parts; Plan 3A, Plan 3B, and Plan 3C. Plan 3A was for division executives. This group comprised 24 men in 1966. (See organization chart on page 726 for those who participate in this plan.) Two-thirds of the bonus payment for members of Plan 3A now became dependent on a new formula shown below—still, however, subject to the limitation that bonus from whatever source would not go above six months' salary:

$$\text{Divisional bonus calculation}^{(8)} = \left(\frac{\text{Actual divisional profit improvement}}{\text{Budgeted divisional profit improvement}} \right) (0.3) \left(\text{Participant's annual salary} \right)$$

This formula meant that if a division made none of its projected profit improvement, no divisional bonus would be paid. If the division reached its target, then the Plan 3A divisional bonus calculation (8) would yield a figure of 30% of the combined yearly salary payments to participating executives. Since, however, the divisional bonus was weighted by multiplying by two-thirds, reaching target would yield a bonus payment of only 20% of salary (equivalent to 2.4 months). On the other hand, the larger the corporate bonus was, the sooner divisional executives would reach this six months' salary cut-off point, beyond which extra performance resulted in no higher bonus payment.[4]

The new Plan 3B was for staff executives. (Twelve participants in 1966—see organization chart for some of their positions.) One-third of the Plan 3B bonus was computed under the original Plan 3. The rest was then based on the average divisional figure (i.e., an average of the number of months of salary paid out to the managers of each of Dennison's eight divisions as calculated in Plan 3A). For corporate executives and inside directors who were not division managers, Plan 3C was developed (five men in 1966). As with Plan 3A and Plan 3B, Plan 3C provided that one-third of a man's bonus would be based on the old Plan 3 calculations while the remaining two-thirds (9) was dependent on how much was realized of a budgeted increment in consolidated corporate earnings. The formula under which this two-thirds portion was computed was the same as the formula for the divisional bonus:

$$\text{Individual's bonus}^{(9)} = \left(\frac{\text{Actual profit improvement}}{\text{Budget profit improvement}} \right) (0.3) \left(\text{Individual's annual salary} \right)$$

IMPACT OF BONUS SYSTEM

According to Dennison's treasurer, more managers had been hurt than helped by tying bonus payments so closely to individual achievements. Thus, in 1966, of the 41 executives included in Plan 3, only 11

---

[4] In 1966, for example, when all divisional executives would attain 1.67 months' salary from their one-third of the 5.01 months' corporate figure (1), divisional executives could increase their bonus no further by reaching more than 173% of target.

earned as much as or more than the corporate bonus alone would have permitted. Of these 11, 7 earned the maximum of 50% of annual salary and 4 earned 44%. For the rest, four earned a relatively low 14%; the rest lay between 28% and 36%.

Mr. Hamilton commented on some aspects of this bonus plan as follows:

> There is always a question about the division between base pay and bonus. How much of a man's total compensation should be left to bonus? My view is that we should hold the base salary level even with the market. A bonus is payment for the accomplishment of a reasonably hard task. If a man has been successful in the past, this should be reflected in his base pay. The bonus should be the payment for current extra effort.
>
> One trouble Dennison had in the past was that bonuses came to be regarded by some people as a part of the base pay. The fact that there can be broad swings from year to year now tends to discourage thoughts like that.
>
> We are paying for profit improvement. With the bonus system as currently formulated, we direct our general managers at that goal. I have told the fellow that the principal ways to get profit improvements are first through increasing sales volume, second through improving our gross margins, and third through cost reduction. I expect them to get results in all of these areas.

Mr. Huntington commented that he believed the bonus system gave a new freedom to top management. He said, "Whereas once the major advantage of working for Dennison was working conditions and security, we are now able to say, 'If you are not up to the job, we will have to get someone who can handle it!' Of course this is true only with the younger men. With some of the older men, we have to have compassion. We in top management are more responsible than they are for what they are now."

A division manager indicated that people at his level wanted to be judged on the basis of performance only within areas over which they had complete control. He therefore looked forward to having each division become self-sufficient over time:

> They want to have the managers assume a corporate outlook. This is why one-third of the bonus is based on corporate profits. This new system, however, makes the manager want to split up the skills and make certain that he is judged only on what he controls. I think that more and more we shall see each division pull into itself and become self-sufficient. The further this process goes, the less of a problem we will have.

BONUS DETERMINANTS

With bonus payments to each participant dependent on such factors as salary, departmental profit, and realization of profit targets, Dennison operated under clearly defined policies regarding salary levels, allocation of shared costs, transfer pricing, and forward budgeting.

Salary levels. Several members of management commented that in the past Dennison's salaries had been low in comparison to other firms in the area. It was observed at all levels in the organization that Dennison had made a conscientious effort to catch up and become competitive in the salary structure.

At the divisional level, the general manager requested a pool of funds for salary increases during the following year when budgets were made up. The division manager then divided up this pool among the employees, subject to review by the salary committee composed of Messrs. Hamilton, Huntington, and Swisher. The managers interviewed said that in general all specific requests for salary increases had been granted. One manager stated that he believed requests were granted because they were well documented. For each job, the standard procedure manual set a salary range. (See Exhibit 3.) The division general manager then determined where in the range a particular manager should fall.

Shared costs. One of the most constantly troublesome problems in the accounting system was the problem of joint costs. According to the controller, almost every cost category for which the divisional general manager was held responsible included some joint costs. Only cash discounts, wage increases, travel and expense, advertising samples, and selling were unaffected by the performance of other departments; 21 other lines on the profit and loss statement all represented shared costs. The system of cost allocation within manufacturing was described as follows:

> Overhead costs and other shared costs are allocated to the various production departments based on some standard, such as number of orders processed, orders received, square feet of floor space, number of employees or historical usage of a particular service department. These estimated allocations are then built into the standard cost rate for the department.

Transfer prices. Besides being affected by shared costs including overhead charges, divisional profits reflected the prices at which materials or services were transferred from division to division. The company's practice in respect to transfer prices was described as follows:

> Each department . . . makes goods and transfers them to other divisions at the standard industrial engineering cost. Any variances for a department are then automatically allocated by the computer to the divisions which use the output from that particular department. This allocation is made on the basis of the percentage of total hours used in the previous year. In other words, if department 22 worked 1,500 hours for division X and 7,500 hours for division Y and 1,000 hours for division Z, 15% of any variances would be absorbed by division X, 75% by division Y and 10% by division Z.

Exact figures on transfers among divisions were not readily available, but the controller gave the following estimate for each division as to what percentage of its work was done for others and whether it was, on balance, a buyer from or maker for other divisions:

Division	Percent of work done for other divisions	Net buyer − Net maker + Equal balance =
Box	25	+
Copier	0	0
Gummed paper	45	+
Industrial products	25	=
Holiday	0	0
Marking systems	2–3	−
Resale	10	=
Therimage	15	+

Budgets. The profit targets used in calculating bonus payments at Dennison were established through the operation of the company's budgeting system. This system, of course, also set targets for sales and costs, and in effect provided a plan for each upcoming year. The budgeting process was described as follows by Mr. Swisher:

> In September each year, I issue a letter to all general managers forecasting the general business climate by quarters. Wherever this information is relevant, they use this letter as the basis for their forecasts of activity. They follow the pattern of economic activity predicted in order to make a breakdown of sales by months. The divisional accountants and controllers prepare facts and figures regarding the historical seasonal patterns and trends. These are then given to the product managers who make the actual forecasts. Although we don't do our forecasts by items, we do look at the differentiation between the old, staid item, the new dynamic ones with proven potential, and the new items with unknown potential.
>
> All of our forecasting is based on customer charges and not on orders received.[5]
>
> Once these steps are carried out, the results are consolidated and submitted to the policy committee which approves the sales budget.
>
> Since we change our standard costs every two years, it is easy to prepare a profit figure in the years when the standard costs don't change.
>
> Once the sales and profit figures are set, we go after the marketing and administrative budgets. We determine an expense budget for each group in the company. Once a budget for R&D, maintenance, or advertising had been determined, the manager is charged that figure. He can't improve his bonus by cutting down these areas which could have had long-run effects.
>
> The budget for each year is worked out as precisely as possible. The improved budgetary process which has been worked out over the past few years has made the targets we set more realistic. The fact that the budget is prepared in exactly the same format as the monthly profit and loss statements aids the manager in understanding both the need for and use of the budgets.

---

[5] Because a high percentage of business in some divisions was made to order, there could be a considerable time lag between receipt of an order and billing the customer. Hence the distinction between "charges" and "orders."

When Phil Hamilton and I review the budgets, we want them to be realistic as possible and to be firm plans. This system will work only if the verp top management is extremely committed to making it work.

Mr. Hamilton indicated that one of the most difficult problems in this process lay in assigning to each division a task that would be both fair and challenging:

It's difficult to make sure that the tasks for each of the divisions are equally hard. This is really the purpose of setting the budget. We try to set goals which will be difficult to achieve but well within the potential of the division.

One of the most difficult problems is to set a stiff enough task. We have tried to make it so that the divisions don't compete with each other, and are just competing with themselves and their own past performance. Of course we do let the managers know which divisions have done well. We recognize that money isn't the only motivation among our managers. In mnay cases, pride is as important a motivator as money.

Mr. Hamilton further indicated that the major role in setting targets was played by himself and Mr. Swisher:

The targets for each division are set by Swisher and me. We make up the budget based on projections and estimates furnished by the individual divisions. These estimates are placed within the context of the guidelines established by the executive committee and adjusted to give the over-all company its required growth.

A divisional manager gave the following account of the budget-setting process as it appeared to him:

By and large the budgets come up from the bottom of the organization. On the sales side, the marketing manager and his product managers are well-equipped with data on past sales, market activity, the economy, and new product introductions. They make predictions for one year in advance, broken into major product categories. In this way they arrive at their expected volume. Meanwhile, production, accounting, engineering services, etc. attempt to determine our production costs. From there we go into a little wilder speculation on the variances which we might get in such areas as primary material costs, labor and overhead charges, and warehousing costs. These are all put together to get the forecasting for the division.

I would say that the figures are generally accepted if they are reasonably in line with the economic projections made by Mr. Swisher, the expected new product growth, and with realistic profit improvement possibilities within the division. I would say that top management people have a very good seat-of-the-pants understanding of the business we are in.

ACCOUNTING AND CONTROL

Mr. Swisher, the chief financial officer of the company, indicated that all accounting at Dennison was handled centrally through seven divisional accountants and three divisional controllers, all of whom reported to the corporate assistant controller. Although physically located in the divisions these men's salaries and promotions were determined by the accounting department. The accountants and their staffs, he said, recorded divisional sales and costs, examined the latter to "make certain their division does not get overcharged," set up standard costs, "made up the price book based on standard costs," and analyzed and interpreted control figures for management. The controller's functions were, Mr. Swisher added, "more managerial." Their responsibilities included plans and budgets, inventory control, ROI analysis, internal auditing, and comparative studies of divisional performance.

Mr. Swisher added the following comments on relationships between the accountants and controllers and the divisional executives with whom they worked:

> Centralized accounting has been the system in this company for 40 years. In the early days there was some conflict of interest between divisional loyalty and corporate loyalty. I think now that the situation is accepted by everyone.
>
> There is still a slight tendency to be loyal to the operating people in the area in which you are working. This is only natural. At times we find minor areas where the accountants and controllers are able to give a break to the operating area. For example, with our standard cost system, items are credited at standard with a variance and charges are made at actual. We have an excess cost category which is for occurrences beyond the control of the manager. We keep a pretty careful watch on this account, and I am sure that it is not abused.

A divisional accountant had the following to say of his relationships with divisional and corporate executives:

> Information in Dennison goes all the way to the top. Mr. Hamilton likes to get all the information that he can. Any piece of data gets good exposure. His favorite question is "Where are the wild ones?" I have made it a point, however, never to say anything to the president that I hadn't said to the general manager of my division. However, I will make the same strong arguments for a position in Mr. Hamilton's office that I will in the division manager's office.

Mr. Sturtevant, the assistant corporate controller, said by far the most eagerly awaited report was the monthly divisional P&L statement. Distributed on the 9th of the month, this was analyzed at once by a group composed of the divisional general manager, his major functional executives, and the divisional accountant. Next day, or as soon as schedules permitted, Mr. Hamilton met with the group to review their analysis.

Although Mr. Hamilton did not have a background in finance, he was known among members of management for his determined use of the numbers generated by the control system. He said:

> The control function is one of closing loopholes. In the past we had some problems such as payment of invoices without checking on delivery of goods, slow claims adjustment, and poor internal control on work-in-process and finished-goods inventory. I think that this is in the process of being corrected. We have just hired an internal auditor, a policeman to see that the practices set down are observed.

The general manager of a division is at the mercy of his accounting information. Cost reduction takes a positive attitude. You have to keep at it. The whole process of improving profits is one of re-energizing and restimulating the manager. Proper information allows the corporate management to do this. If I have any complaint about our present accounting system, it is that not all of the accountants and controllers are as bold as they should be. They tend to keep quiet rather than give the independent analysis needed by management.

THE MONTHLY PROFIT REVIEW

At all levels, executives at Dennison manifested keen interest in what the top officers were thinking. Many talked in personal terms about requests made by Mr. Hamilton, opinions expressed by Mr. Swisher, or other clues which the individual felt he had to the workings of the Dennison corporate mind.

Perhaps the chief source of this vertical communication was the monthly profit review sessions held by Mr. Hamilton with the managers of each division. Generally the division general manager, the marketing, production, and sales managers, the divisional accountant, divisional controller, and company controller would attend these sessions. It was only when a special question of fact existed that other members of the divisional staff were brought in. A partial transcript of one meeting is provided in Appendix A.

Mr. Hamilton spoke of these meetings as being one of his most important management tools. Before each meeting, he received the monthly profit and loss statement for all divisions. (See Exhibit 5 for a sample monthly P&L statement and examples of supporting data.) He generally spent a weekend reviewing both the over-all figures and supporting data before holding the meetings. He said of these meetings:

> The monthly P&L offers me a timely tool for management. In addition to the divisional figures, I get a lot of supporting data. In addition to reviewing the figures, we talk about problems and planning. I found that may questions have caused some of the managers to have group meetings beforehand to go over their own results and prepare. I now make the general managers make statements and lay out the problems at the beginning of the meeting. They should welcome the opportunity to discuss the problems and not to sweep them under the table.
>
> I am apt to be rough on people whose skin is a little tender. I tend to lean heavily on those areas that I feel need emphasis.

APPENDIX A

DENNISON MANUFACTURING COMPANY (A & B)

Profit Review Session Excerpts—Resale Products Division[1]
Those present were:
Phillip Hamilton—President Dennison
Thomas Sturtevant—Corporate Controller

---

[1] All internal numbers have been disguised in order to preserve confidences.

Ray Hager—General Manager, Resale Products Division
John Redmond—Sales Manager, Resale Products Division
Robert Hawkins—Production Manager, Resale Products Division
Spurgeon Condo—Merchandise Manager, Resale Products Division

HAMILTON: Well, Ray, will you please start out the quarterly profit review, emphasizing particularly the March results?

HAGER: As you can see, the results were not good. Sales are not meeting budgets. Customer charges are not as high as orders received, and generally the results are down. Our course we all know the budget did not follow our normal seasonal pattern, and the sales are not as healthy as they were forecast to be when we made our budget considerations. John, do you want to say why?

REDMOND: Well, we lost at least $60,000 volume on the diaper-liner deal which wasn't introduced as it normally is in the last part of March. This volume will be made up when we run the promotion in April.

HAGER: How is that volume coming in now?

REDMOND: It's a little late; there are some problems in bringing it in. International Paper Company and P&G are both promoting their disposable diaper liners heavily.

HAGER: Is Johnson & Johnson still pushing disposable diaper liners?

REDMOND: I never hear about them—not in the market place, but I think Curity is taking as much as before.

Our government business is off $30,000 in orders received. This is due to some GSA bids we didn't get. We got a new bid in, though, on $40,000 to $80,000 worth of polyethylene envelopes.

CONDO: We got the order!

REDMOND: Oh, I didn't now that! It hadn't come in yesterday . . .

General business conditions have really been off. We have been suffering, along with Detroit. Also, if you remember, we had the budget adjustment so we took $250,000 from the normal seasonal pattern, and moved it forward. The expectation was for a good first quarter with a poorer last quarter.

HAGER: Do you think we are getting a more healthy picture now?

REDMOND: Yes, the "Polyethylene" envelopes are coming in strong. We have got an $11,000 new account and a lot more attention. Our reports are indicating that we have been a lot more aggressive and a lot more successful in holding on to distribution.

HAGER: Another cause for alarm is our credit problem.

REDMOND: Yes, that cost us $48,000 in sales. If credit problems continue the way they have, we are going to be in a real bind.

HAMILTON: Let me ask a question that has me disturbed. Even if the sales budget was deliberately increased $250,000, it only produced a slightly greater profit than last year. Unless we increase our sales more substantially, we are going to have a decrease in over-all profit.

STURTEVANT: We had two objectives in changing that $250,000 from the last quarter to the third. First, we thought that the first half was going to have a greater percentage gain over 1966 than the second half. Second, we want to reflect in Line 49 earnings what they should be at that time of the year.[2]

HAMILTON: We were wrong when we increased the budget for that reason. We had to stretch to get a volume-profit relationship which would get

---

[2] "Line 49 earnings" refers to line 49 of the divisional profit report shown in Exhibit 5. The bonus for divisional personnel was determined by "Line 49 earnings" improvement.

us an 8% increase in over-all profit. We had to get the $600,000 increase in sales just to get hold even in profits . . . .

*   *   *   *   *

HAMILTON: O.K., Ray, go on with your discussion.

HAGER: We have to make a certain percentage increase in each line. If we reach our budget in orders received, we will not be doing too badly. If we had had the promised volume, we would have had $690,000 increase in Line 49. Our basic problem is sales.

STURTEVANT: Right. But you realize one rather shocking fact is that to make our sales budget, we will have to bill over $2 million a month for the rest of the year.

HAGER: We will have the new West Coast warehouse on-stream.

STURTEVANT: How will that help?

HAMILTON: Yes, we want an orderly opening of the warehouse—we don't want to push it if it is going to create problems later.

HAGER: Incidentally, how is the warehouse going to be charged to me? Nobody has told me.

STURTEVANT: You're being charged as a parent company is being charged.

HAGER: Who is controlling the cost there?

HAMILTON: This isn't the place to go into this. Tom, explain it to Ray later. If he doesn't like it, he can write me a letter, and we will adjudicate the matter later.

We are not going to worry about this monthly figure right now. . . . [Discussion proceeded on several items such as changes in transportation terms, and cash discounts.]

*   *   *   *   *

I notice there are some commodity variations.

HAGER: Before you get down there, how about the wage cost? [There was then some discussion of the wage costs.]

HAMILTON: Well, really, in the whole scheme of things, that is rather insignificant. I am adverse to any further monkeying with the secondary variation. I am not sure that the philosophy of allocation is completely right. But this way, at least, we maintain comparability. You are charged according to the budget. The budget was set on this basis so that you should be willing to accept the result.

STURTEVANT: Ray [Hager] would be interested. We are now trying to get standard costing for the warehouse. We could then get it so that you could plan on what your actual costs would be, and not have to worry about things hidden under the rug at the end of the year.

HAGER: This would be great. This is perhaps the area I feel most hazy on. . . . [Discussion proceeded on the warehouse costs and other allocated costs.]

HAMILTON: Let's look at this volume variation account. Why don't we have more here now than last year? Last year we had a $15,000 volume gain. I don't think it's been less busy. It must be the change in standards that now shows above the line.

HAGER: In two areas outside of the division, in Department 3, Industrial Products, and Department 25, we are working only 40 hours a week. Our new color presses are down to 40 hours as well. We have been trying to work them the 45 hours. We are having to absorb their negative variances.

HAMILTON: To what extent has the inventory and build-up in the West Coast warehouse helped to absorb the hourly rate?

STURTEVANT: That was last year.

HAWKINS: Department 5 has a $2,020 loss in efficiency and a $1,000 gain in wages. It doesn't take into account the problem of the incentive bonus, and getting production back up to standard.

HAMILTON: I noticed you had $366 loss due to off-standard work[3] in the corner-cut and double-scoring machine. Why? I thought these were good. [See Exhibit 6.]

HAGER: It is always better to make an efficiency gain. But we can't with the rates in those machines. The standards from Department 42 [not under the control of the division] really don't apply to Resale. We can't get the same production rate.

HAMILTON: What about 21 B? This department always had a gain. It has now got a substantial loss.

*   *   *   *   *

You fellows have a sizable profit improvement plan going. How is it coming along?

HAGER: We are not getting the factory engineering we expected. If I don't get the service I think we should be getting from the engineering department, can I cut my engineering expense?

HAMILTON: If it is clear-cut that you are not getting what you should get, you can hire outside. The fact is that we have so many bodies with a salary that we have a million dollars budgeted in that department. So either they deliver some results or we are going to have to cut back on the number of bodies. Let's say it's clear that they are unable to deliver the results to your division; then I would say that you will have to hire outside, but they will have to drop one, two, three, or more people. Of course factory engineering is now in new hands and we will have to see the results. I want to make this judgment in terms of factual reports. Can you do this for me? What have they been doing—time, date, number, etc.

HAGER: The place we are getting results from in factory engineering is in installation. Of course if I had an engineer in my department, we could do it ourselves. We don't need the high-priced talent in the factory engineering department. What we really need is their help in the area where originality is required. . . .

HAMILTON: All right. Let's move on to the expenses. We have some special work to do.

HAGER: Before we move on, I think we should take another look at having an engineer assigned to our department.

HAMILTON: It is entirely possible to assign an engineer. Hawkins, you call a meeting with you and me, Hager, and Gray. . . . [Two engineers and a methods man were later assigned.]

*   *   *   *   *

Having gone through all this, it is as clear as crystal that we need billings. We can't make the dollar profit if we don't get the sales. Let's see now. Have we covered all the soft spots and special situations? [General agreement.]

HAGER: As we get a clearer picture of the economy, we can lay plans, and move forward in both the engineering efforts and in cleaning up the product line.

HAMILTON: John [Redmond], you should figure which areas you could get the mileage out of in your sales program. It is that sort of thing that I am willing to pay for. Not only should you provide some incentive for the salesmen to push, but you have got to develop some incentive for the customers to buy. . . .

---

[3] Off-standard work was second or discards which were produced as the result of machine difficulties.

CONDO: This might call for a dealer-jobber type promotion. Also, I think we need some incentive for the salesmen. We have just put out a promotion on Color Brite crepe paper which seems to be going well. With a six-carton order we will give a rack free. I think this is what will get the customer to buy.

HAMILTON: No question, business has softened. We have to get an answer and figure a way to make the customers move the product off our shelves. We mustn't wait for government programs to take hold. We must do far better than average if we are going to equal our past performance. [At this point, Mr. Hamilton made some statements about some of the economic measures which President Johnson was taking to improve the economic situation in the United States. He listed several factors, enumerating the cut in the discount rate, releasing of the highway funds, etc.]

*   *   *   *   *

When they want to suppress business, they can push it down easily. But it takes the public time to respond to a stimulus. We as a company have to build up the stimulus for our own customers. We can't rely on the government to do it. Too, we can't just put pressure on the men. Neither Ray nor I just sit out here and say, "Get more sales," and expect that we will have more sales. We have got to find ways to make the customer want our products and make our salesmen want to sell them. We have to be constantly on the look-out for either small businesses, and some way of reviving interest. Also another way is through judicious acquisition. . . .

This line from time to time needs new items. We should be looking. There are over 700 members in the National Stationery Manufacturers Association. Maybe one of them would provide us with an opportunity for an acquisition which would "beef up" our line. We are not alone in this area, and we must keep looking.

*   *   *   *   *

John, [Redmond] I am glad to see the monkey is on your back, and you, Condo, as merchandising man, you must give him the meat to cook in the kitchen. Are there any vacancies or problems that you have in your salesmen line-up? What about the "weak sisters"?

REDMOND: Well, basically, I don't think a "strong sister" up there in ———would do us any good.

HAMILTON: What about in———?

REDMOND: I don't think we are weak there.

HAMILTON: Are you satisfied with your line managers?

REDMOND: Yes.

HAMILTON: What about your capital equipment program? Can you use up your budget?

HAWKINS: Why, sure, I could use up all the budget even before you took 40% away.

*   *   *   *   *

HAMILTON: How's the MacAdams press doing? O.K.? We have the follow up on our expenditures. . . .

About this inventory problem, it says here that we have $4,200,000 compared to $2,955,000 last year. Where did this come from?

STURTEVANT: Well, crepe and dealer labels and some of the other products have been produced according to budget not according to sales.

HAMILTON: Well, what control have we got to prevent this going merrily on? Can I rely on you to control this?

ALL: Yes, sir, yes, yes, yes.

HAGER: I disagree partially with what you said. I think a lot of the inventory that we have now is just simply necessary inventory versus the inadequate inventory that we had last year.

HAMILTON: Well, on the other hand, this division has its own controls on inventory. But the inventory committee is advisory—you have got to take the responsibility for the results. So, when you are long on inventory, just don't let Hawkins, your production manager, make any more of it. Right?

HAGER: Right.

HAWKINS: I never thought I'd hear it. We have got too much inventory in our finished goods.

HAMILTON: Tom, do you have anything to add. Ray, John, . . . Phil. Well, thank you, gentlemen, for a good report. I think the answer is obvious —just get the sales.

In reviewing this meeting with the casewriter, Mr. Hamilton said:

> As you saw, I was trying to make certain that the soft spots were recognized and explained. Of course the obvious thing is sales, but as I said we can't just ask for more sales, we have got to get new products and new plans.
>
> I think that the expenses are generally well-contained. If we are going to get profit improvement, we are just going to have to blast it out. In that one place where I talked about the $300 plus expense variation, I was trying to make them all aware of the fact that it is the small variation which makes the difference between great performance and mediocrity. . . .
>
> We worked hard with this division to get a budget which would absorb the increased costs. They have got to meet the budget, but I recognize that they need the help of the staff groups. In at least one case, they haven't been getting what they have been paying for. I'll have a status report tomorrow on that problem. We've got to get support for the divisions.

Exhibit 1

DENNISON MANUFACTURING COMPANY (A & B)
Ten Year Summary
(dollar amounts in thousands)

	1966	*1965*	*1964*	*1963*	*1962*	*1961*	*1960*	*1959*	*1958*	*1957*
Sales and equipment rentals	$87,410	$69,835	$57,173	$53,795	$52,366	$47,501	$45,523	$43,391	$40,545	$40,992
Taxes on income	4,502	2,505	2,036	2,523	2,096	1,760	1,875	2,170	1,784	1,999
Net earnings	5,252	2,913	2,193	2,354	1,982	1,829	1,983	2,219	1,839	2,103
As a percent of sales	6.0%	4.1%	3.8%	4.4%	3.8%	3.9%	4.4%	5.1%	4.5%	5.1%
Per share of common stock*	2.20	1.18	.87	.94	.77	.70	.77	.87	.70	.82
Cash dividends	1.545	1,371	1,367	1,366	1,371	1,373	1,379	1,325	1,152	1,324
Debenture stock	235	235	235	235	235	235	235	235	235	235
Common stocks	1,310	1,136	1,132	1,131	1,136	1,137	1,144	1,090	917	1,089
Per share*	.575	.50	.50	.50	.50	.50	.50	.48	.40	.48
Stock dividend—common	100%	—	—	—	—	—	100%	—	—	—
Settlement of prior years' tax claims	244	—	—	—	—	—	320	—	282	—
Earnings reinvested										
This year	3,706	1,542	826	988	611	456	924	894	969	779
Total to date†	18,347	20,426	18,884	18,058	17,071	16,460	16,004	15,837	14,943	13,975
Current assets	35,949	27,854	22,677	21,570	19,973	20,334	18,758	19,007	17,969	16,875
Current liabilities	17,546	12,598	7,945	6,344	6,802	7,974	3,785	3,166	2,595	2,606
Working capital	18,403	15,256	14,732	15,226	13,170	12,360	14,973	15,841	15,374	14,269
Working capital ratio	2.0 to 1	2.2 to 1	2.9 to 1	3.4 to 1	2.9 to 1	2.5 to 1	5.0 to 1	6.0 to 1	6.9 to 1	6.5 to 1
Plant and equipment—net	20,787	17,192	12,635	11,611	11,953	11,926	9,045	7,423	7,017	7,137
Added this year—gross	7,500	7,942§	2,580	1,658	2,068	4,388‡	2,799	1,613	1,055	1,931
Provision for depreciation	3,568	2,685	1,780	1,831	1,845	1,301	1,123	1,142	1,151	1,045
Long-term debt	6,334	3,515	—	—	—	—	—	—	—	—
Stockholders' equity	32,860	28,884	27,386	26,426	25,430	24,911	24,536	23,788	22,883	21,914
Equity per common share*	12.36	10.61	10.00	9.60	9.17	8.89	8.73	8.32	7.93	7.50
Shares of stock outstanding										
Debenture stock	29,420	29,420	29,420	29,420	29,420	29,420	29,420	29,420	29,420	29,420
Common stocks	2,278,552	1,138,886	1,134,261	1,131,041	1,130,666	1,136,226	1,139,086	573,608	573,238	573,238
Market price range*										
"A" common stock high	43	25¼	42	27¼	14¾	20½	14¼	9⅝	8	10
"A" common stock low	23¼	13⅞	15¼	9½	7½	13¼	8⅜	7¼	5¾	5⅝

* Based on number of shares outstanding at end of each year and adjusted for stock splits in 1966 and 1960.
† Reflects $6,029,000 in 1966 and $757,000 in 1960 transferred to "Common Stock" in connection with stock splits.
‡ Includes net value of plant and equipment of Dennison Eastman Company.
§ Includes net value of plant and equipment of Dunn Paper Company.
Source: Dennison 1966 Annual Report, pp. 6–7.

Exhibit 1—Continued

DENNISON MANUFACTURING COMPANY
AND WHOLLY OWNED SUBSIDIARIES

ASSETS Current assets	December 31, 1966	December 31, 1965
Cash...	$ 1,374,145	$ 1,958,338
Trade accounts receivable, less allowances of $594,000 ($326,000 in 1965) for discounts, etc..............	15,926,869	12,368,287
Merchandise materials and supplies		
Finished merchandise.........................	$ 5,613,901	$ 3,547,741
In process.................................	7,853,738	5,457,951
Raw materials..............................	3,836,947	3,451,541
Supplies...................................	710,129	627,142
	$18,014,715	$13,084,375
Prepaid expenses.............................	633,337	442,805
Total current assets......................	$35,949,066	$27,853,805
Other assets		
Investment in British subsidiary, not consolidated— at cost....................................	$ 169,775	$ 169,775
Miscellaneous receivables, investments, etc., less allowances of $133,723 ($97,120 in 1965)..........	563,997	514,673
Good will....................................	1	1
	$ 733,773	$ 684,449
Property, plant and equipment—on the basis of cost		
Land..	$ 401,421	$ 397,252
Buildings and building equipment................	7,688,087	7,068,412
Machinery, equipment, etc......................	35,744,490	31,851,381
Construction in progress (estimated cost to complete—$2,348,000)............................	1,544,353	
	$45,378,351	$39,317,044
Less allowances for depreciation..................	24,591,044	22,125,427
	$20,787,307	$17,191,617
Total assets............................	$57,470,146	$45,729,871

Exhibit 1—Concluded

LIABILITIES AND STOCKHOLDERS' EQUITY	December 31, 1966	December 31, 1965
Current liabilities		
Notes payable..................................	$ 6,700,000	$ 4,430,000
Accounts payable..............................	4,996,250	2,898,987
Accrued compensation and related taxes...........	3,007,911	3,562,964
United States and Canadian income taxes..........	2,329,463	1,576,888
Current maturities on long-term debt..............	512,637	128,700
Total current liabilities....................	$17,546,261	$12,597,539
Deferred federal income taxes......................	730,000	734,000
Long-term debt (less current maturities)		
4½% notes to bank............................	$ 2,700,000	$ 3,000,000
4¾% notes to bank............................	3,000,000	
4½% notes payable to former stockholders of acquired subsidiary in equal annual installments to 1970.....	386,100	514,800
6½% equipment notes due in equal monthly install- ments to 1971...............................	247,607	
	$ 6,333,707	$ 3,514,800
Stockholders' equity		
Debenture stock, $8 cumulative, par value $100 per share (entitled in liquidation to and callable at $4,707,200):		
Authorized and issued 29,420 shares..............	$ 2,942,000	$ 2,942,000
"A" common stock, par value $5 per share: Authorized 3,000,000 shares (1,200,000 in 1965); issued 2,335,127 shares (1,145,470 in 1965).........	11,675,635	5,727,350
Voting common stock, par value $5 per share: Authorized 200,000 shares (80,000 in 1965); issued 106,449 shares (75,318 in 1965).................	532,245	376,590
Capital in excess of par value......................	22,330	74,646
Earnings reinvested............................	18,346,813	20,425,688
	$33,519,023	$29,546,274
Less treasury stock at cost—146,642 shares (51,081 in 1965) of "A" common stock; 16,382 shares (30,821 in 1965) of voting common stock.................	658,845	662,742
Total stockholders' equity................	$32,860,178	$28,883,532
Total liabilities and stockholders' equity.....	$57,470,146	$45,729,871

Exhibit 2

DENNISON MANUFACTURING COMPANY (A & B)

Bonus Plans Compared

(basis: months of bonus to participants)

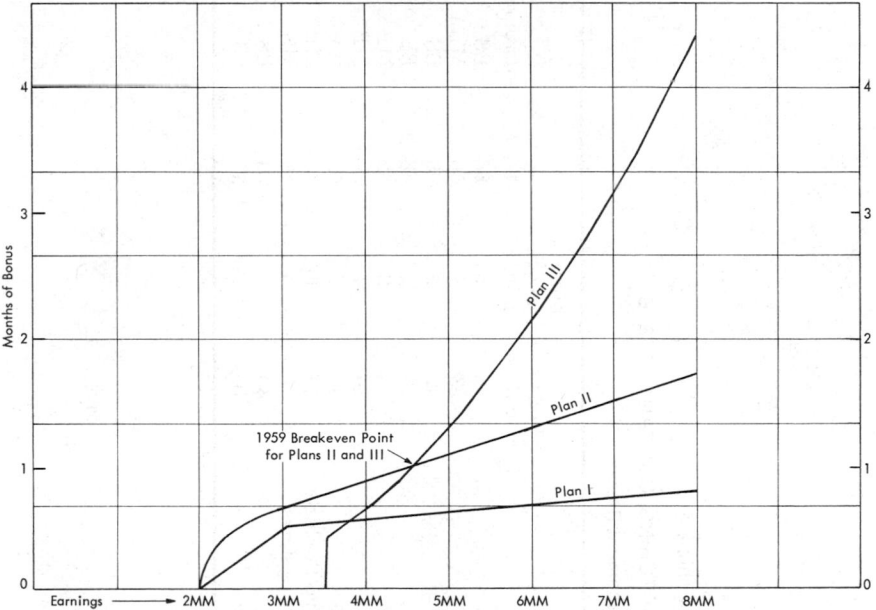

Note: (a) Plan I curve based on average participant.
      (b) Plan III curve based on 1960 opening capital (23,788M).
      (c) All curves based on November 1959 participants and pay levels.

Exhibit 3

DENNISON MANUFACTURING COMPANY (A & B)

Dennison Salary Ranges

1967

	Low	High
Foreman....................................	7,200	10,000
Salesman...................................	7,200	18,000
District sales manager.......................	13,000	20,000
Division marketing manager..................	13,000	22,000
Division production manager.................	13,000	22,000
Division manager...........................	17,500	35,000
Corporate staff manager.....................	17,500	35,000

Exhibit 4

DENNISON MANUFACTURING COMPANY (A & B)

Management Profile

Name	Position	Years with Dennison	Years in present position	Age	Education	Functional background
Dana C. Huntington	Chairman of the Board	48	6	68	BS	Marketing
Phillip B. Hamilton	President	33	1	56	MBA	Marketing
Francis Swisher	V.P. Finance	42	9	68	BS	Control
Calvin Josselyn	Treasurer	26	2	48	BS	Control
Thomas Sturtevant	Assistant Controller	3	2	32	MBA	Control
John Gray	General Manager Service	16	1	39	MBA	Production
Howard Weeks	V.P. International Business	39	7	62	BA	Marketing
Howard Gorton	General Manager Industrial Products	36	6	65	MBA	Marketing
Robert Dale	General Manager Marking Systems	7	3	49	MS	R&D
Ray Hager	General Manager Resale	30	3	52	BS	Sales
Nelson Gifford	Operations V.P.	10	1	37	BS	Control

Exhibit 5

DENNISON MANUFACTURING COMPANY (A & B)

Resale Line

(March—three month report final 1967)

		Monthly budget	Percent	Monthly actual	Percent	YTD budget	Percent	YTD actual	Percent	Previous year	Percent
01	Gross sales	1,431,000		1,192,431		3,950,000		3,380,197		3,323,971	
02	Returns and allowances	27,000–		29,752–		81,000–		82,341–		70,532–	
04	Net sales	1,404,000	100.0	1,162,679	100.0	3,869,000	100.0	3,297,856	100.0	3,253,439	100.0
05	Primary cost	733,400–	52.2–	616,231–	53.0	2,039,200–	52.7–	1,757,635–	53.3–	1,660,327–	51.0–
06	Secondary cost	153,600–	11.0–	116,470–	10.0	420,000–	10.9–	381,179–	11.5–	342,311–	10.5–
07	Transportation	51,900–	3.7–	42,193–	3.6–	139,700–	3.6–	101,743–	3.1–	116,733–	3.6–
08	Total 05–07	938,900–	66.9–	774,894–	66.6–	2,598,900–	67.2–	2,240,557–	67.9–	2,119,371–	65.1–
09	Secondary revenues	465,100	33.1	387,785	33.4	1,270,100	32.8	1,057,299	32.1	1,134,068	34.9
10	Cash discounts	30,000–	2.1–	24,766–	2.1–	81,700–	2.1–	70,112–	2.1–	64,721–	2.0–
11	Wage increases	5,736	0.4–	6,532–	0.6–	16,850–	0.4–	16,431–	0.5–	20,033–	0.6–
12	Soc. Sec. dep. var.	200	0.0	74–	0.0–	500	0.0	102–	0.0–	3,103–	0.1–
13	Commodity var.	1,650	0.1	1,403–	0.1–	1,650–	0.1–	823	0.0–	310	0.0
14	Service var.	805	0.1	80–	0.0–	3,200	0.1	160–	0.0–	17,795–	0.5–
15	Secondary var.	26,821–	1.9–	30,363–	2.6–	71,563–	1.9–	86,417–	2.6–	432	0.0
16	Trans. var.	27,034–	1.9–	44,921–	3.9–	70,491–	1.8–	84,319–	2.6–	64,491–	1.9–
17	Price var.	3,240	0.2	15,346	1.3	9,000	0.2	29,421	0.9	7,296	0.2
18	Volume var.	20,000	1.4	15,211	1.3	50,000	1.3	17,117	0.5	37,087	1.1
19	Mfg. P&L	12,000–	0.9–	18,379–	1.6–	36,000–	0.9–	41,223–	1.3–	48,253–	1.5–
20	Acc. year end diff.	4,800–	0.4–	3,582–	0.3	12,450–	0.3–	10,002–	0.3–	21,821–	0.7–
21	Profit improvement	8,000	0.6	6,349	0.6	20,000	0.5	13,995	0.4	13,005	0.4
28	Total 10–21	72,496–	5.2–	86,030–	7.4–	208,004–	5.4–	249,056–	7.6–	182,087–	5.6–
29	Net before mkting	392,604	27.9	301,755	26.0	1,062,096	27.4	808,243	24.5	951,981	29.3

Researcher's Note: The figures on this and the following page have been disguised and as such are not placed here for detailed analysis. It is important to note the detail available to Mr. Hamilton before the meeting and the tone of the meeting in light of the fact that Line 49 profit was 35% below budget.

Exhibit 5—Continued

		Monthly budget	Percent	Monthly actual	Percent	YTD budget	Percent	YTD actual	Percent	Previous year	Percent
30	Admin. salaries	10,900 –	0.8 –	10,950 –	0.9 –	32,800 –	0.8 –	31,743 –	1.0 –	30,321 –	0.9 –
31	Travel and expense	3,200 –	0.2 –	6,593 –	0.6 –	23,500 –	0.6 –	17,137 –	0.5 –	19,593 –	0.6 –
32	Miscellaneous	100 –	0.0 –	1,700 –	0.1 –	2,200 –	0.1 –	4,053 –	0.1 –	5,737 –	0.2 –
33	Estimating	12,000 –	0.8 –	8,354 –	0.7 –	4,000 –	0.1 –	3,011 –	0.1 –	4,978 –	0.2 –
34	Trade associations	1,500 –	0.1 –	4,533 –	0.4 –	7,500 –	0.2 –	5,191 –	0.1 –	5,130 –	0.2 –
35	Advertising samples	38,000 –	2.7 –	35,791 –	3.1 –	120,000 –	3.1 –	90,311 –	2.7 –	111,131 –	3.4 –
36	General and mkting. ovhd.	15,000 –	1.1 –	15,000 –	1.3 –	45,000 –	1.2 –	45,000 –	1.4 –	42,371 –	1.3 –
37	Selling	102,000 –	7.3 –	100,193 –	8.6 –	306,125 –	7.9 –	294,312 –	8.9 –	263,321 –	8.1 –
38	Sketches and orig.	8,000 –	0.6 –	12,341 –	1.1 –	24,000 –	0.6 –	25,112 –	0.8 –	25,677 –	0.8 –
39	Excess and dropped	5,500 –	0.4 –	6,331 –	0.6 –	16,241 –	0.4 –	12,219 –	0.4 –	17,833 –	0.5 –
40	Research and eng.	16,700 –	1.2 –	8,294 –	0.7 –	51,350 –	1.3 –	29,227 –	0.9 –	48,117 –	1.5 –
41	Accruals	11,500 –	0.8 –	11,500 –	1.0 –	34,500 –	0.9 –	34,500 –	1.0 –	20,100 –	0.6 –
48	Total 30–41	224,400 –	16.0 –	221,580 –	19.1 –	667,216 –	17.2 –	591,816 –	17.9 –	594,309 –	18.3 –
49	Revenue after mkting	168,204	11.9	80,175	6.9	394,880	10.2	216,427	6.6	357,672	11.0
50	Ind. research	5,750 –	0.4 –	2,831 –	0.2 –	16,500 –	0.4 –	16,325 –	0.5 –	13,073 –	0.4 –
51	General and admin.	21,000 –	1.5 –	20,752 –	1.8 –	63,000 –	1.6 –	62,243 –	1.9 –	53,138 –	1.6 –
52	Interest	10,971 –	0.8 –	11,947 –	1.0 –	33,127 –	0.9 –	37,100 –	1.1 –	23,192 –	0.7 –
53	Year-end bonus	12,000 –	0.8 –	10,001 –	0.9 –	36,000 –	0.9 –	30,419 –	0.9 –	24,497 –	0.8 –
58	Total 50–53	49,721	3.5 –	45,531	3.9 –	148,627 –	3.8	146,087 –	4.4 –	113,900	3.5 –
59	Earn. before tax	118,483	8.4	34,644	3.0	246,253	6.4	70,340	2.2	243,772	7.5
60	Income taxes	59,241 –	4.2 –	17,322 –	1.5 –	123,126 –	3.2 –	35,170 –	1.1 –	121,886 –	3.7 –
69	Profit after taxes	59,242	4.2	17,322	1.5	123,127	3.2	35,170	1.1	121,886	3.8

Exhibit 6

DENNISON MANUFACTURING COMPANY (A & B)

To: Mr. R. C. Hawkins   Date: April 13, 1967

From: P. J. Mahoney   Page 2 of a six-page
                                           report sent to Mr. Hamilton
Subject: March 1967 Departmental   before the meeting
         Variations

4. Department 4

Efficiency—$463 Gain

Only problems are on the Kluge Dieout & 9 × 12. Delays are very
heavy on the Kluge and low efficiency is the problem on the
9 × 12.

    Indirect—Stock—Ship—Jog—Continue to op-
erate at more hours than budgeted.

    Adjustor—Same story.

    Misc Expense—$451 Loss

    Die Sharpening $1275.
    Misc. Small Exps. $36.

5. Department 5

	Efficiency Loss	$2,020	
Label Pkg.		$ 286	Low efficiency
Wire "		178	" "
Quad Run		130	Off Std. work and delay
2H Ace		79	" " " " "
Roc Die		148	" " " " "
150 Ct.		70	Delay
2H 150		141	"
*Corn Cutting Machinery		169	" and off Std. work
*Double Scoring Machine		198	" " " " "
S. H. Machine		94	" " " " "
410 Env.		173	Off Std. work

Misc. Expense — $466. Loss

Manpower	$516
CH Bus Stab	70
	$586

* These items discussed during monthly profit review.

Dennison Manufacturing Company (C)

IN MAY 1967, Mr. Phillip Hamilton, president of Dennison Manufacturing Company, was faced with a recurrence of the question of a transfer price between divisions on a new product. By the time the issue was presented to him, it was clear that no settlement could be reached through direct negotiations among the division managers involved. Although at the time the issue arose only two divisions were involved, the nature of the product made it clear that this decision would affect a third division and could potentially set a precedent for handling other questions of this type.

The product. The new product had been developed through research and design efforts on attaching devices. Called Secur-A-Tach, it was a substitute for string or wire in tying items together. Secur-A-Tach was a piece of molded nylon with specially molded end-pieces which locked together. Once joined the Secur-A-Tach ends could not be separated without destroying them, thus making the attachment tamperproof. Secur-A-Tach was designed to withstand a strain of 20 lbs. pressure. It could be made in a variety of lengths and colors. (See Exhibit 1 for an illustration of the Secur-A-Tach device.)

Priced to sell for $2.40 per thousand with a 50% gross margin[1] Secur-A-Tach was thought to have a very large potential market. Total realizable potential was believed to be between $1 million and $3 million sales per year. Retail stores could use them to attach price tags and stock tags to high-ticket items such as purses, jewelry, etc., without fear of customer switching. Also, items in pairs, such as shoes, could be securely and easily joined for display. Another major use was thought to be with shipping tags and stock tags used by manufacturers. Ease of attachment, tamperproof design, strength, and appearance were thought to be the major advantages which Secur-A-Tach enjoyed. It was also believed

---

[1] All internal cost, sales and expense data are disguised; however, essential relationships have been preserved.

748

Exhibit 1

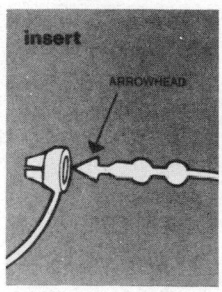 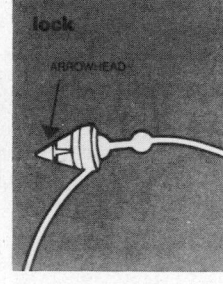 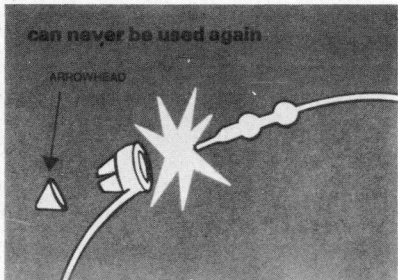

1. Simply pass the pointed end of Secur-A-Tach through the loopholes of the item and tag(s) you want to join together.

2. Insert arrowhead firmly into socket. You can *feel* it snap into place.

3. When Secur-A-Tach bond is pulled apart, the arrowhead breaks off and hook-ing-holding power is lost forever. Can't be used again!
Two lengths (5″ and 9″) meet most attach-ing needs.

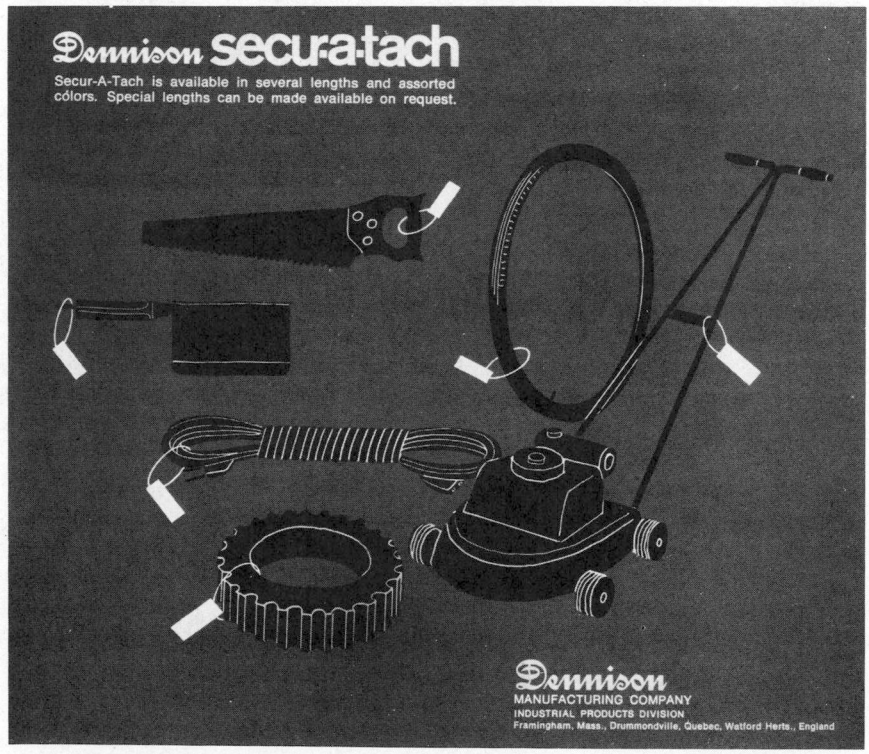

that the fact that tags could be bought without being prestrung would eliminate one of the major problems faced by the purchaser of tags. Tangled strings were often a nuisance.

History of the product.   Secur-A-Tach had been developed by Mr.

Exhibit 1—Continued

Source: Company records.

Gerry Merser, a product manager in the marketing systems division in cooperation with one of Dennison's outside suppliers. The idea for the product and its subsequent development had resulted from the success enjoyed by the Dennison Swiftach system, also developed by Mr. Merser. Swiftach was a device for attaching tags to soft goods by putting a molded nylon fastener through the garments with the aid of an attaching

Exhibit 2

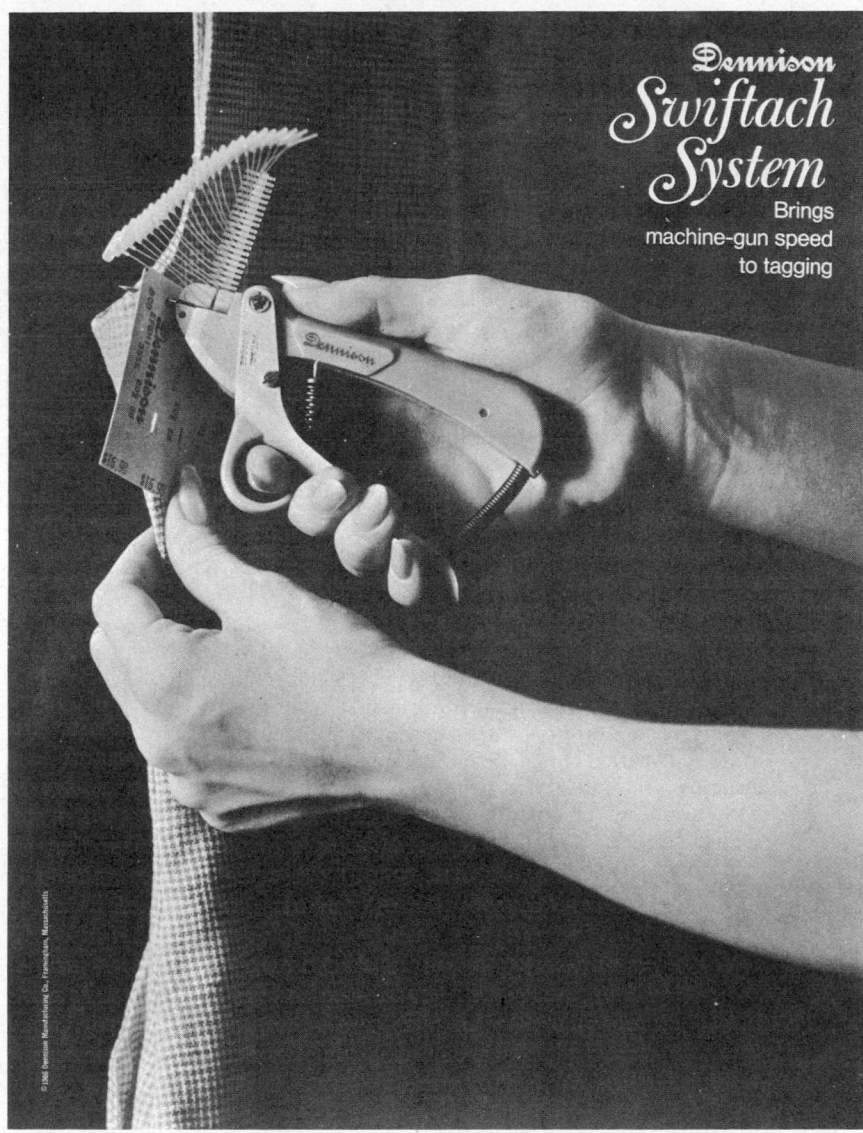

gun. The marking systems division had achieved 85% saturation in the major retail chains with Swiftach. Sales of guns and fasteners approached $1.2 million per year. (See Exhibit 2 for pictures and literature on the Swiftach system.)

Mr. Merser and others in the marking systems division believed that the Secur-A-Tach market was potentially even greater. They thought that the wider appeal of Secur-A-Tach would be an opening wedge to cus-

tomers who were unacquainted with Dennison's tags and marking machines. Initially it was believed that the marking systems, industrial
products, and resale divisions had the greatest potential for selling Secur-
A-Tach. The question which had been sent to Mr. Hamilton was an issue
raised between the industrial products division and the marking systems
division.

The division's proposals.   Mr. Howard Gorton, manager of the industrial products division, wrote the following letter to Mr. Hamilton:

Industrial Products Needs for Secur-A-Tach

The proprietary aspects of Secur-A-Tach by the marking systems division are well understood and appreciated by industrial products personnel. However, by the nature of the product, industrial products
division has a vital interest and must be given completely parallel
consideration in all regards for the industrial products markets.

Delineation of the industrial products needs are:
1.   Simultaneous launching date.
   a)   Secur-A-Tach is even more suited to industrial products than
        Swiftach. Hence industrial products sales force must not be
        denied the product until marking systems has made market
        coverage.
   b)   Lead time of even 30 days would be a serious disadvantage
        to industrial products.
   c)   Aside from any or all of the above reasons, a lead time for
        market coverage by marking systems division would cut into
        industrial products division tag sales volume by the cost of
        strings or wires if nothing else.
2.   Orders to be accepted and filled according to date of receipt.
3.   Market coverage must be along normal lines as between marking
     systems and industrial products.
   a)   "Raiding" of customers by selling the attachment only to the
        customers of the other division must not be permitted in either
        the retail or industrial markets.
   b)   Sale of the attachment for use on competitors' tags to be per-
        mitted and encouraged by both divisions.
4.   Secur-A-Tach must be transferred from marking systems to in-
     dustrial products according to normal procedures, i.e., without
     profit or discount arrangement just as pressure sensitive labels and
     dial-set tags are transferred in reverse. Credit for production and
     thereby contribution to the corporation to be shown statistically
     on the records of the marking systems division.

In reply, Mr. Robert Dale, manager of the marking systems division,
wrote this letter to Mr. Hamilton:

   I have been in a discussion with Mr. Gorton on this subject. As we
   are at opposite points and have not reached agreement, he felt he
   would like to refer it to you for a decision. In view of my heavy travel
   schedule I wanted to put the following in writing.
   As you know, this product fits the product line of marking systems,
   industrial products and resale. It should be spread across as broad a
   distribution front as possible. Industrial products, less than resale,
   can probably do much with it. However, two questions concerning this
   product and the interdivisional handling are:

1. Time of launching.
2. Cost to industrial products or resale.

My feelings on this matter are as follows:

1. It is not practical to contemplate simultaneous launching as requested by industrial products. There is only one mold on order, due July 15. It would be foolhardy to order additional molds until the first is proven out. The capacity of the one mold is insufficient to handle the business we see on demand from marking systems division customers alone, let alone that from other divisions.

   The earliest that sufficient capacity would be available for industrial products is probably September, at which time additional molds would be delivered. During this interval I see no major problem as most of what marking systems division sells will be in retail channels.

2. Cost: As we have handled Swiftach successfully by allowing 35% secondary revenue, so I would suggest Secur-A-Tach be handled. Transferring at cost does not provide means of recovering mold cost, development expense, and other miscellaneous expenses incurred. Transferring at sell less 35% provides for recovering of expenses to the producing division and also gives a higher than normal return to the selling division.

THE DIVISIONS

Industrial products. The industrial products division was the second oldest division in Dennison. Its basic charter was to sell paper products to manufacturers. Based on this charter, it made tags and labels to order for large customers. Its activities included designing, printing, collating, stringing or wiring, and in many cases storing the tags or labels which would serve to identify the products of the manufacturer. In addition to this business the industrial products division produced and sold industrial crepe for electrical insulation purposes. (See Exhibit 3 for disguised financial data on the industrial products and marking systems divisions, and Exhibit 4 for a partial organization chart.)

Mr. Gorton described his division's basic strength as the ability to put together almost any combination of paper with printed information in

Exhibit 3

DISGUISED DIVISIONAL FINANCIAL DATA

(dollars in thousands)

| | Marking systems division | | Industrial products division | |
	1966 actual	1967 budget	1966 actual	1967 budget
Sales	$9,500	$11,100	$6,010	$6,900
Cost of goods sold	5,800	6,600	4,420	4,950
Secondary revenue	$3,700	$ 4,500	$1,590	$1,950
Marketing, G&A	1,800	2,100	1,140	1,350
"Line 49" profit (profit after marketing)	$1,900	$ 2,400	$ 450	$ 600

Source: Company records.

Exhibit 4

PARTIAL ORGANIZATION CHART

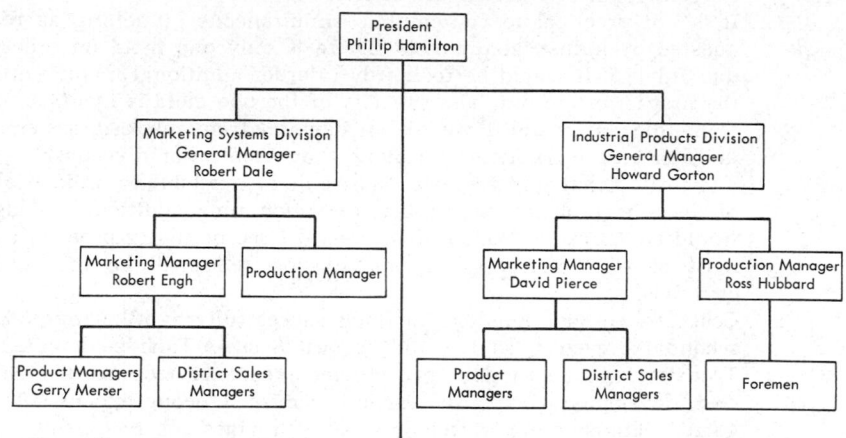

Source: Company records.

an attractive way. The major sales strategy of the division was to go into a customer's operation, to analyze his needs for tags and labels, and to design a final product which would eliminate insofar as possible the need for hand inscribing data and multiple handling of the tags.

Mr. Gorton's division had to rely on its ability to do complicated things to paper such as multiple color printing of both sides, production of manifold tags, special wiring or stringing, or special paper combinations. Simple tags were often sold on a basis of low price and rapid service. In these cases, the division was competing against small one-man shops which could produce simple tags on a $2,000 Heidelberg press. It was deemed almost impossible for a large company to compete for the smallest low-price end of the business. Dennison tended to specialize in the more complicated tag and label products, produced on machines which cost up to $100,000 each. It was in the area of solving complicated problems or delivering large quantities that Dennison had an advantage.

This division had not made any breakthroughs with totally new products. Mr. Gorton said that a new product for the industrial products division meant an adaptation or minor adjustment in an existing product idea to make it solve customers' problems. He believed that much of the division's ingenuity had been aimed at the development of the complicated devices which produced the tags and labels more cheaply, rather than at new consumer applications. He also added, "Although some might think that we didn't keep up with progress, it has to be remembered that two of the most glamorous and profitable divisions of the company are offshoots of the industrial products division. Both marking systems and thermiage were spawned from this group." Another member of the division management echoed these feelings and said, "For many years the money which might have gone to developing a couple of divisions which are now the senior citizens has gone to promoting the more glamorous machine-oriented divisions. From a corporate point of view this is probably right, but now as these new developments pay off, I hope we get a chance to enjoy some of the benefits."

The targeted increase in profits for the industrial products division in 1967 was roughly $150,000. Mr. Gorton and his managers believed that they had a difficult task to accomplish if they were to meet that goal and obtain their 30% divisional bonus. Mr. Gorton said of this goal:

> Phil Hamilton thinks there is a great deal of room for profit improvement through cost reduction. I am less sure. There is quite a difference in obtaining a reduction in stock goods line versus obtaining a cost reduction when the products are made in short and medium production runs on general purpose machines. With some of the changes which we have made to get increased volume, with the constant attention to our estimating procedures, and with the help of new products, I think we have a fighting chance.

A major cost reduction program in the past had reduced indirect labor from 22 people to 15 in a three-year period, while sales had increased by $2 million.

The industrial products division was organized into two separate parts, marketing and production. Marketing, under Mr. David Pierce, was then divided into six regions, each with a district sales manager. In addition, three product groups, industrial crepe, tags, and labels, reported to Mr. Pierce. The salesmen were given a quota and received a commission on sales. Salesmen were guaranteed 90% of the commissions which they would receive if they reached quota. In addition, they were guaranteed 90% of their previous year's earnings. Owing to an 8% commission rate after the quota was reached, this provision frequently caused their base salaries to rise.

The bonus paid to district managers was equal to the average of the commissions paid to his salesmen on sales in excess of quota. As a percentage of total compensation, the bonuses received by the district managers were the lowest in the sales line.

Secur-A-Tach was thought of by the personnel in the industrial products division as being of great potential value in their division. By eliminating prestringing and wiring of tags, it would simplify the made-to-order production process. At the same time it would be a great convenience for the customer. Unless the industrial products division could sell Secur-A-Tach, the division's revenues would be cut by the cost of wiring. As one man said, "Although attachment isn't an end in itself, Secur-A-Tach should give us an important plus over competition. We can offer something that no one else can." Another man said, "This product is really a natural for our division. We should eventualy be able to sell as much as, if not more than, the marking systems division."

The whole question of divisionalization was raised during discussion of Secur-A-Tach. One man said: "Dennison is so divisionalized that sometimes we get into problems. I have seen very few transfers of personnel among the divisions. I personally think it would be hard to get anyone to transfer out of our division. The division managers are somewhat jealous of the experience developed in the people under them. I really don't think that divisionalization has meant greater opportunity for the people in the company. The opportunity comes through growing in your own division. There is a lot less cooperation here across division lines than there used to be. I think the sense of responsibility which managers have developed precludes them asking for help."

Another man echoed these feelings, but less strongly, in saying, "The tendency is for divisions to draw into themselves. If our division were moved across the street, given control over all its own production and services, we would do better." One middle manager said, "If we are going to have profit responsibility, I think we should have it at each level. I don't think it should stop at the division level."

A final factor that Mr. Gorton saw as relevant to the diputed transfer-price issue was the fact that materials as well as finished products were to some extent transferred between divisions. Industrial products made about $1.25 million for the resale division and about $500,000 for marking systems. On a dollar basis, trade with the resale division about balanced out, but Mr. Gorton believed that currently a substantial amount more was produced for the marking systems divisions than was purchased from it. He believed that the percentage of industrial products' output sent to other divisions had been relatively constant for the past five years.

Marking systems division.   The marking systems division's basic charter was the development, production, and marketing of machines which could print variable information on tags or labels at a customer's site, and machines which could attach tags or labels to the end products. The development of Swiftach and Secur-A-Tach had simplified the customer's task of attaching tags and labels considerably. Before Swiftach, tags and labels had to be hand-sewn to garments, or hand-tied or wired to hard goods. These new developments speeded up the process considerably.

The marking systems division had been split off from the industrial products division in 1955. It grew quickly until 1959 when its growth tapered off. One member of the division's management said:

> We were a sleeping giant. We had lots of technology that was not being used. For years this division wasn't marketing oriented. Marketing was looked at as an expense rather than an investment. Our salesmen were selling 50% more per man than our competitors which meant they were so busy with their current customers they couldn't make cold calls and find new customers.

Mr. Robert Dale, the current general manager of the division, took over in January 1965. Since that time he had increased the sales force from 38 men to 56. In the two years of his management, profits were up 38%.

Mr. Dale believed that with the new product introductions which had been made since 1965, the marking systems division was at least equal to and in most cases better than any of his competitors.

In raising the issue of pricing transferred products at a figure other than cost, Mr. Dale recognized that he was going against past practice.

He felt, however, that this was justified because the product development costs had cut into his division's profits, and his division was buying the molds and paying for the sales promotion literature. The industrial engineering costs did not provide for recovery of these expenditures. He furthermore believed that the lead time in introduction which he requested for his division was the most fair solution. Until the first mold had proven itself at production rates, there would be a capacity constraint on the production of the Secur-A-Tach and he did not believe his division should suffer.

The marketing people in the marking systems division felt strongly on the issue as well. One man said:

> We realize that this new product has a very broad market which certainly is over and above this division's charter. It will give us and the other divisions a powerful lever to open new doors for Dennison.
>
> We were frankly disappointed in the way Swiftach was handled by the other divisions. We achieved 85% penetration, but it was by hard door-to-door sales effort. If we handled Secur-A-Tach exclusively for a few months, I am sure that we could make a large impact. I worry about two divisions calling on the same customers with the same product. In the case of some large department stores and chains, our two sales forces overlap. Industrial products makes all their tags and labels while we supply their marking and pinning machines. Although this won't occur often, it has been a serious source of friction in the past.

Another worry was expressed about the transfer at cost. "Without giving the division any profit, what incentive is there for our product manager to work with the other division's salesmen."

At the very least, marking systems was anxious to assure that there be a clear-cut division of customers between the industrial products division and the marking systems division.

Further complications. In addition to the question of the transfer price between marking systems and industrial products, there was the problem of the discount structure. Marking systems would be selling directly to the end user, and therefore wished to establish as high a price as possible, allowing full markup. The industrial products division would also be selling to end users, but when the resale division started to sell the product, it would be through its normal channels of distributors and wholesalers. Included among their customers would be small printing shops. These channels would expect their normal discounts. Some within the marking systems division were worried that allowing the Secur-A-Tach to be sold through all of these channels would enable their own customers to buy through third parties at a lower price than would be charged by marking systems. It was believed that small printing houses often passed material on at cost in order to keep their presses full. A typical discount structure was as follows:

Printing shops . . . . 10% off list
Wholesalers . . . . 35% off list
Distributors . . . . 40% off list

It was believed that different packaging would help mitigate the problem of parallel sourcing, but marking systems personnel could not see why they should be placed at any disadvantage in selling their own product. Others within the company discounted the possibility of any difficulties arising in this fashion.

Another potential problem was the question of special packaging, colors, or sizes. If the other divisions wanted Secur-A-Tach packaged in lots of less than 1,000 or with the other division's own label, the marking systems division personnel felt that special charges would have to be made.

Corporate viewpoints.   Mr. Frank Swisher, financial vice president of Dennison, said:

> I see no valid susbtitute for transfer at cost. We have operated on this basis successfully and although we have had many discussions in the past, no argument for change has seemed compelling. Cost is a definite figure upon which we can get agreement. We don't spend our energy arguing about market value, etc. Transferring at cost has the added advantage of putting the emphasis on marketing. The selling division gets measured by its results.

Mr. Thomas Sturtevant, the assistant corporate controller, said:

> I believe that we must maintain our policy of transferring goods at cost. If we change that, we will devote far too much energy to arguing about the rules of the game rather than playing it.
>
> I do believe, however, that the division which develops a product should have first crack at the production capacity. They should be allowed to sell all they can; they spent the time and money to develop the product. Once they have sold all they can to their own market, I believe the products should be transferred to the other divisions at cost without a statistical measure of what the profit might have been. Our system is set up to measure the selling force. Production is simply a cost center for the divisions.
>
> I can't see that the divisions should have a valid complaint if they are measured and paid on the basis of the rules set down at the beginning of the year. They will be judged on the basis that they were told they would be.
>
> The individual product manager shouldn't really worry about his success being recognized. The commodity report will show both sales and gross margin received throughout the company on the sales of his product. When corporate officers want to know how much he has contributed to the company, they can easily find out.

Effect on managers' bonuses.   Regardless of the decision reached on the transfer-price dispute, it appeared unlikely bonus payments to managers below the division level, including the product manager, would be noticeably affected. However, changes in profit distribution between the divisions did have a slight impact on the bonus of the divisional general managers, the divisional marketing managers, and the divisional production managers. In the case of industrial products, each $7,500 profit after marketing but before corporate expense ("Line 49" profit on Exhibit 3) meant an increment in bonus of 1% of their annual salary. In the case of marketing systems, a $25,000 change would have the same effect. If for example, the industrial products division sold as little as $200,000 worth of Secur-A-Tach, the difference between transfer at cost and transfer at 35% off list as suggested by marking systems division would amount to 4% of the division management's annual salary. This would be from $600 to $1,000 per man.

The accomplishment of purpose: Organizational processes and behavior

OUR study of strategy has brought us to the prescription that organizational structure must follow strategy if implementation is to be effective. We have seen that structural design involves inevitably (1) a suitable specialization of task, (2) a parallel provision for coordination, and (3) information systems for meeting the requirement that specialists be well informed and their work coordinated. We have seen that a variety of structures may be suitable to a strategy so long as the performance influenced by structural characteristics is not diverted from strategic ends.

We turn now from structural considerations to other influences upon organizational behavior. A logical structure does not ensure effective organized effort any more than a high degree of technical skill in individual members insures achievement of organizational purposes. We suggest the following proposition for testing in your analysis of cases: *Organizational performance is effective to the extent that (in an atmosphere deliberately created to encourage the development of required skills and to provide the satisfactions of personal progress) individual energy is successfully directed toward organizational goals.* Convergence of energy upon purpose is made effective by individual and group commitment to purpose.

Man-made and natural organizational *systems* and *processes* are available to influence individual development and performance. In any organization the system which relates specific influences upon behavior to each other (so as to constitute an ultimate impact upon behavior) is made up of some six elements: (1) standards, (2) measures, (3) incentives, (4) rewards, (5) penalties, and (6) controls. The distinguishing characteristic of a system, of course, is the interaction of its elements. This interdependence will vary from organization to organization and from situation to situation and cannot always be observed, controlled, or completely analyzed.

The familiar processes which bear on performance are (1) measurement, (2) evaluation, (3) motivation, (4) control, and (5) individual development. The most important aspect of a process is the speed and direction of its forward motion and the nature of its side effects. So far as the uniqueness of each company situation allows, we shall look at combinations of these organizational systems and processes in the following order:

1. The establishment of standards and measurement of performance.
2. The administration of motivation and incentive systems.
3. The operation of systems of restraint and control.
4. The recruitment and development of management.

These processes have been studied in detail by specialists of several kinds. We shall not attempt to extract all the wisdom or expose all the folly which, over the years, has accumulated in the study of human relations and organizational behavior. We are now concerned, as always, with the limited but important ways in which specialized bodies of knowledge can be put to use in the implementation of strategy. The idea of strategy will dominate our approach to the internal organizational systems which animate structure, just as it dominated our discussion of the factors that determine structure itself. It may be desirable to point out that our aim is not to coerce and manipulate unwilling individuals. It is instead to support and direct individuals who are at least assenting to or, more desirably, committed to organizational goals. Commitment to purpose remains in our scheme of things the overriding necessary condition of effective accomplishment.

ESTABLISHMENT OF STANDARDS AND MEASUREMENT OF PERFORMANCE

If progress toward goals is to be supervised at all, it will have to be observed and measured. If it is to be measured, whether quantitatively or qualitatively, there must be some idea of where an organization is compared to where it ought to be. To state where an organization ought to be is to set a standard. A standard takes shape as a projection of hoped-for or budgeted performance. As time passes, positive and negative variances between budgeted and actual performance are recorded. This comparison makes possible, although it does not necessarily justify, relating incentives and controls to performance as measured against standards. For example, managers in the Hilton Hotels group prepare detailed forecasts of their anticipated revenues, costs, and operating profits, all based on past records and future projections that take growth targets into account. The reward system recognizes not only good results but accuracy of forecasting.

It is virtually impossible to make meaningful generalizations about how proper standards might be set in particular companies. It can be said, however, that in any organization the overall strategy can be translated into more or less detailed future plans (the detail becoming less predictable as the time span grows longer), which permit comparison of actual with predicted performance. Whether standards are being set at exactly the proper level is less significant than the fact that an effort is being made to raise them steadily as organizational power and resources increase. External events may, however, invalidate predictions. It must be recognized that for good reasons as well as bad, standards are not always attainable. Hence the need for skill in variable budgeting.

By far the most important problem of measurement is that increased interest in the measurement of performance against standards brings increased danger that the executive evaluation program may encourage performance which detracts from rather than supports the overall strategy.

The temptation to use measurement primarily for the purpose of judging executive performance is acute. The desire to put management responsibility in the ablest hands leads to comparing managers in terms of results. Failure to meet a standard leads naturally to the assignment of blame to persons. The general manager's most urgent duty is to see that planned results are indeed accomplished. Such pressure, unfortunately, may lead to exaggerated respect for specific measures and for the short-run results they quantify, and thus to ultimate misevaluation of performance.

The problems of measurement cluster about the fallacy of the single criterion.[1] When any single measure like return on investment, for example, is used to determine the compensation, promotion, or reassignment of a manager, the resultant behavior will often lead to unplanned and undesired outcomes. No single measure can encompass the total contribution of an individual either to immediate and longer term results or to the efforts of others. The sensitivity of individuals to evaluation leads them to produce the performance that will measure up in terms of the criterion rather than in terms of more important purposes. Since managers respond to the measures management actually takes to reward performance, mere verbal exhortations to behave in the manner required by long-range strategy carry no weight, and cannot be relied upon to preclude undesirable actions encouraged by a poorly designed measurement and reward system.

Faith in the efficacy of a standard measure like return on investment can reach extreme proportions, especially among men to whom the idea of strategy is apparently unfamiliar. Thus a visiting top manager from a major automobile manufacturer told a class that the company being discussed could solve its apparently bothersome problem of designing an effective relationship between the home office and the branches by giving the branch managers a great deal of autonomy and then judging their performance solely on the basis of return on the capital employed by

---

[1] See John Dearden's "Limits on Decentralized Profit Responsibility" and "Mirage of Profit Decentralization" in E. P. Learned, F. J. Aguilar, and R. C. K. Valtz, *European Problems in General Management*, pp. 570–97. These articles first appeared in the *Harvard Business Review*, July–August 1962, pp. 81–89; and November–December 1962, pp. 140–54.

each. A student who was not convinced answered this argument as follows:

> Although this solution to the branch-home office relations problem had merit, it overlooked the fact that the company was dependent for a great deal of its capital on bankers who evaluated the company on bases other than return on investment. If the proposed solution was accepted, the branch manager might increase his return on investment by allowing his delinquency percentage to rise. Rising delinquency percentages might cause the bankers to withhold new credit from the company. The condition could therefore arise in which the branch manager, though carrying out policies which make his performance appear good under the evaluation system being used, would actually be acting in a manner destructive to the welfare of the company as a whole.[2]

Instances in which performance is measured in terms of just one figure or ratio are so numerous as to suggest that the pursuit of quantification and measurement as such has overshadowed the real goal of management evaluation. If we return to our original hypothesis that profit and return on investment are terms that can be usefully employed to denote the results to be sought by business, but are too general to characterize its distinctive mission or purpose, then we must say that short-term profitability is not by itself an adequate measure of managerial performance. Return on investment, when used alone, is another dangerous criterion, since it can lead businessmen to postpone needed product research or the modernization of facilities in the interest of keeping down the investment on the basis of which their performance is measured. Certainly we must conclude that evaluation of performance must not be focused exclusively upon the criterion of short-run profitability or any other single standard which may cause managers to act contrary to the long-range interests of the company as a whole.

As you discuss the cases that follow, you will be concerned with developing more adequate criteria. Our concern for strategy naturally leads us to suggest that the management evaluation system which plays so great a part in influencing management performance must employ a number of criteria, some of which are subjective and thus difficult to quantify. It is easy to argue that subjective judgments are unfair. But use of a harmful or irrelevant criterion just because it leads itself to quantification is a poor exchange for alleged objectivity.

Against multiple criteria, it may be argued that they restrict the freedom of the profit-center manager to produce the results required through any means he elects. This may of course be true, but the manager who does not want his methods to be subject to scrutiny does not want to be judged. Accountants, sometimes indifferent to the imperfections of their figures and the artificiality of their conventions, do not always make clear the true meaning of an annual profit figure or the extent to which a sharp rise from one year to the next may reflect to make investments needed to sustain the future of a product line.

---

[2] David J. Dunn, "Evaluation of Performance" (unpublished student paper). Reproduced by permission.

If multiple criteria are to be used, it is not enough for top management simply to announce that short-term profitability and return on investment are only two measures among many—including responsibility to society—by which executives are going to be judged. Such an announcement did not prevent violation of the antitrust laws by managers in the electrical industry, who believed it was more important for them to produce the expected profit than to inform their superiors that the basis for conducting business both honestly and profitably had disappeared. To give subordinates freedom to exercise judgment and simultaneously to demand profitability produces an enormous pressure which cannot be effectively controlled by endless talk about tying rewards to factors other than profit.

The tragedy of men, honorable in other ways, working for seniors who were apparently unaware of price-fixing practices, should dramatize one serious predicament of the profit-center form of organization, where, characteristically, management expects to solve the problems of evaluation by decentralizing freedom of decision to subordinates, so long as profit objectives are met. Decentralization seems sometimes to serve as a cloak for nonsupervision, except for the control implicit in the superficial measure of profitability. It would appear to preclude accurate evaluation, and the use of multiple criteria may indeed make a full measure of decentralization inappropriate.

To delegate authority to profit centers and to base evaluation upon proper performance must not mean that the profit center's strategic decisions are left unsupervised. *Even under decentralization, top management must remain familiar with divisional substrategy, with the fortunes —good and bad—that attend implementation, and with the problems involved in attempting to achieve budgeted performance.* The true function of measurement is to increase perceptions of the problems limiting achievement. If an individual sees where he stands in meeting a schedule, he may be led to inquire why he is not somewhere else. If this kind of question is not asked, the answer is not proffered. An effective system of evaluation must include information which will allow top management to understand the problems faced by subordinates in achieving the results for which they are held responsible. And certainly if evaluation is to be comprehensive enough to avoid the distortions cited thus far, immediate results will not be the only object of evaluation. The effectiveness with which problems are handled along the way will be evaluated, even though this judgment, like most of the important decisions of management, must remain subjective.

To quote Dunn once more:

> In effect then, subordinates will not only be judged on the results, but on the effectiveness with which they overcome problems of known magnitude. This involves subjective judgment that raises the question of fairness. I submit the responsibility of top management is to *be fair,* not to evolve a system that proves its fairness beyond the question of a doubt. It is nice to be nice and to establish evaluation systems by which everyone is relieved of fears of personal prejudice and favoritism. It is much more important, however, that an evaluation system con-

tribute to the long-range welfare of the company. If this need neces-
sitates management's requiring subordinates to accept subjective judgment in good faith, then this is what has to be done. If making these
judgments requires management's time, then the time will have to be
spent.[3]

The process of formulating and implementing strategy, which is
supervised directly by the chief executive in a single-unit company, can
be shared widely in a multiunit company. Preoccupation with final results need not be so exclusive as to prevent top management from working with divisional management in establishing objectives and policies
or in formulating plans to meet objectives. Such joint endeavor helps to
ensure that divisional performance will not be evaluated without full
knowledge of the problems encountered in implementation.

When the diversified company becomes so large that this process is
impracticable, then new means must be devised. *Implicit in accurate
evaluation is familiarity with performance on a basis other than through
accounting figures.*

The formula of evaluation most consistent with the concept of strategy
that is outlined in these notes is what is called "management by objectives." Instead of simply evaluating "traits," like some of the older
appraisal systems, this process entails at all levels of management a
meeting between subordinate and superior to agree on the achievements
which the subordinate will try to accomplish during the forthcoming
period. The subordinate's suggested objectives are modified if, after discussion, they appear either impractical or understated. They are checked
for the contribution they will make to the larger strategy of which they
must be a part. They are designed to include quantitatively nonmeasur-
able items as well as items budgeted in the formal short-term and long-
range plans. The problems of successfully designing such a system are
easier to see than to solve. Nonetheless, an acceptance of the imperfections and inexactness of such a system, plus a shared interest in the
problems to be overcome in serving strategy, make possible a kind of
communication which cannot be replaced by the application of a single
criterion. Certainly, it is the quality of his objectives and of his attempts
to overcome obstacles posed by circumstance and by competition that is
the most important thing to measure about a manager's performance.

MOTIVATION AND INCENTIVE SYSTEMS

The influences upon behavior in any organization are visible and invisible, planned and unplanned, formal and not formal. The intent to
measure affects the performance which is the object of measurement;
cause and effect obscure each other. The executive who refuses to leave
the implementation of strategy to chance has available diverse means of
encouraging behavior which advances strategy and deterring behavior
which does not. The positive elements, always organized in patterns
which make them influential in given situations, may be designated as

---

[3] Ibid.

motivation and incentive systems. The negative elements, similarly patterned, can be grouped as systems of restraint and control. Organization studies have led their authors variously to prefer positive or negative signals and to conclude that one or the other is preferable. The general manager will do well to conclude that each is indispensable.

Whatever the necessity for and the difficulties of performance evaluation, the effort to encourage and reward takes precedence over the effort to deter and restrain. Thus, properly directed, motivation may have more positive effects than control. Certainly, the general manager-strategist, whose own prior experience is likely to have made him intensely interested in the subject of executive compensation, should welcome whatever guidance he can get from researchers or staff assistants working in the field of job evaluation and compensation. Unfortunately, here also the prevailing thinking is often oriented less toward the goals to be sought than toward the requirements of the systems adopted.

The human relations movement has developed convincing evidence that executives, like workers, are influenced by nonmonetary as well as financial incentives. At the same time, it is no longer argued that financial rewards are even relatively unimportant, and much thought has been given to equitable compensation of executives.

Unfortunately for the analyst of executive performance, it is harder to describe for the executive than for the man at the machine what he does and how he spends his time. The terminology of his job description is full of phrases like "has responsibility for," "maintains relationships with," and "supervises the operation of." The activities of planning, problem solving, and directing or administering are virtually invisible. And the activities of recruiting, training, and developing subordinates are hardly more concretely identifiable.

In any case, it is fallacious to assume that quality of performance is the only basis for the compensation of executives. Many other factors must be taken into account. The job itself has certain characteristics that help to determine the pay schedules. These include complexity of the work, the general education required, and the knowledge or technical training needed. Compensation should also reflect the responsibility of the job-incumbent for people and property, the nature and number of decisions he must make, and the effect of his activities and decisions upon profits.

In addition to reflecting the quality of performance and the nature of the job, an executive's compensation must also have some logical relationship to rewards paid to others in the same organization. That is, the compensation system must reflect in some way a man's position in the hierarchy. On any one ladder there must be suitable steps between levels from top to bottom, if incentive is to be provided and increased scope recognized. At the same time, adjustments must be made to reflect the varying contributions that can be expected from individuals in the hierarchy of the staff versus that of the line.

Furthermore, in a compensation system, factors pertaining to the individual are almost as important as those pertaining to performance, the job, or the structure of the organization. A man's age and length of service, the state of his health, some notion of his future potential, some idea of his material needs, and some insight into his views about all of these should influence either the amount of total pay or the distribution of total pay among base salary, bonuses, stock options, and other incentive measures.

Besides the many factors already listed, still another set of influences —this time coming from the external part of the environment—ordinarily affects the level of executive compensation. Included here are regional differences in the cost of living, the increments allowed for overseas assignment, the market price of given qualifications and experience, the level of local taxation, the desire for tax avoidance or delay, and the effect of high business salaries on other professions.

Just as multiple criteria are appropriate for the evaluation of performance, so many considerations must be taken into account in the compensation of executives. The company which says it pays only for results does not know what it is doing.

In addition to the problem of deciding what factors to reward, there is the equally complex issue of deciding what forms compensation should take. We would emphasize that financial rewards are especially important in business, and no matter how great the enthusiasm of a man for his work, attention to the level of executive salary is an important ingredient in the achievement of strategy. Money, it is said, cannot buy happiness. On the other hand, happiness, valuable as it is, cannot buy food, shelter, access to culture, travel, or college educations for one's children. Even after the desired standard of living is attained, money is still an effective incentive. Businessmen used to the struggle for profit find satisfaction in their own growing net worth. Even though taxes may limit asset growth severely, the income is still important. As Crawford Greenewalt says in his *Uncommon Man,* the salary figure provides satisfaction by indicating the worth of the contribution made, even if most of it is paid out in taxes.[4]

There is no question about the desirability of paying high salaries for work of great value. Yet until recently, it was clearly social policy in the United States, as elsewhere, that executive take-home pay be kept at a modest ceiling. As a consequence, profit sharing, executive bonuses, stock options, stock purchase plans, deferred compensation contracts, split-dollar insurance, pension, group term insurance, savings plans, and other fringe benefits have multiplied enormously, and they have been directed not so much toward providing incentive as toward enabling executives to avoid high taxes on current income. It is as incentives, however, that these various devices should be judged. Regarded as incentives to reward *individual* performance, many of these devices encounter two immediate objections, quite aside from the ethics of their tax-avoidance features. First, how compatible are the assumptions back of such rewards with the aspirations of the businessman to be viewed as a professional person? The student who begins to think of business as a

---

[4] C. H. Greenewalt, *The Uncommon Man; the Individual in the Organization* (New York: McGraw-Hill), 1959.

profession will wonder what kind of executive will perform better with a profit-sharing bonus than he would with an equivalent salary. He may ask whether a doctor should be paid according to the longevity of his patients and whether a surgeon would try harder if given a bonus when his patient survived an operation. Second, how feasible is it to distinguish any one individual's contribution to the total accomplishment of the company? And even if contribution could be distinguished and correctly measured, what about the implications of the fact that the funds available for added incentive payments are a function of total rather than of individual performance? In view of these considerations, it can at least be argued that incentives for individual performance reflect dubious assumptions.

If, then, incentives are ruled out as an inappropriate or impractical means of rewarding individual effort, should they be cast out altogether? We believe not. There is certainly some merit in giving stock options to the group of executives most responsible for strategy decisions, if the purpose is to assure reward for attention to the middle and longer run future. There is some rationale for giving the same group current or even deferred bonuses, the amount of which is tied to annual profit, if the purpose is to motivate better cost control—something surprisingly difficult to do in a business environment marked by booming sales and high income taxes. Certainly, too, incentive payments to the key executive group must be condoned where needed to attract and hold the scarce managerial talent without which any strategy will suffer.

In any case, as you examine the effort made by companies to provide adequate rewards, to stimulate effective executive performance, and to inspire commitment to organizational purposes, you will wish to look closely at the relation between the incentive offered and the kind of performance needed. This observation holds as true, of course, for nonmonetary as it does for financial rewards.

The area of nonmonetary incentive systems is even more difficult to traverse quickly than that of financial objectives. Executives are as much members of the human race as other employees; they are thus as much affected as anyone else by pride in accomplishment, the climate for free expression, pleasure in able and honest associates, and satisfaction in work worth doing.

They are said to be moved also by status symbols like office carpets, thermos sets, or office location and size. The trappings of rank and small symbols of authority are too widely cultivated to be regarded as unimportant, but little is known of their real influence. If individual contribution to organized effort is abundantly clear, little attention is likely to be given to status symbols. For example, the R.&D. executive with the greatest contributions to the product line may favor the "reverse status symbol" of the lab technician's cotton jacket. This is not to say that symbols have no potentially useful role to play. Office decor, for example, can be used to symbolize strategy, as when a company introduces abstract art into its central office to help dramatize its breaks with the past.

Very little systematic work has been done to determine what incentives or company climate might be most conducive to executive creativity, executive commitment to forward planning, executive dedication to the training of subordinates, or executive striving for personal development and growth. All these are of utmost value, but their impact is long-run and peculiarly intangible. It is well known, however, that the climate most commonly extolled by men in upper management positions is one where they have freedom to experiment and apply their own ideas without unnecessary constraints. This type of positive incentive is particularly suited for use in combination with the "management-by-objectives" approach to the problem of executive evaluation. Given clear objectives and a broad consensus, then latitude can be safely granted to executives to choose their own course—so long as they do not conceal the problems they encounter. In other words, the executive can be presumed to respond to the conditions likely to encourage the goal-oriented behavior expected of him.

We may not always know the influence exerted by evaluation, compensation, and advancement, but if we keep purpose clear and incentive systems simple, we may keep unintended distractions to a minimum. Above all, we should be able to see the relevance to desired outcomes of the rewards offered. The harder it is to relate achievement to motives, the more cautious we should be in proposing an incentives program.

SYSTEMS OF RESTRAINT AND CONTROL

Like the system of incentives, the system of restraints and controls should be designed with the requirements of strategy in mind, rather than the niceties of complex techniques and procedures. It is the function of penalties and controls to enforce rather than to encourage—to inhibit strategically undesirable behavior rather than to create new patterns. Motivation, as we have said, is a complex of both positive and negative influences. Working in conjunction, these induce desired performance and inhibit undesirable behavior.

The need for controls—even at the executive level—is rooted in the central facts of organization itself. The inevitable consequence of divided activity is the emergence of substrategies, which are at least slightly deflected from the true course by the needs of individuals and the concepts and procedures of specialized groups, each with its own quasi-professional precepts and ideals. We must have controls, therefore, even in healthy and competent organizations manned by men of goodwill who are aware of organization purpose.

Like other aspects of organizational structure and processes, controls may be both formal and informal, that is, both prescribed and emergent. Both types are needed, and both are important. It is, however, in the nature of things that management is more likely to give explicit attention to the formal controls that it has itself prescribed than to the informal controls emergent within particular groups or subgroups.

Formal and informal controls differ in nature as well as in their genesis. The former have to do with data that are quantifiable, the latter with subjective values and behavior. Formal control derives from accounting; it reflects the conventions and assumptions of that discipline and implies the superior importance of what can be quantified over what cannot. Its influence arises from the responsiveness of individuals—if subject to supervision and appraisal—to information that reveals variances between what is recorded as being expected of them and what is recorded as being achieved. If the information depicts variances from strategically desirable behavior, then it tends to direct attention toward strategic goals and to support goal-oriented policy. But if, as is more often the case, the information simply focuses on those short-run results which the state of the art can measure, then it directs effort toward performance which, if not undesirable, is at least biased toward short-run objectives.

To emphasize the probable shortcomings of formal or quantifiable controls is not to assert that they have no value. Numbers do influence behavior—especially when pressures are applied to subordinates by superiors contemplating the same numbers. Numbers are essential in complex organizations, since personal acquaintance with what is being accomplished and personal surveillance over it by an owner-manager is no longer possible. As we have seen, the performance of individuals and subunits cannot be left to chance, even when acceptance and understanding of policy have been indicated and adequate competence and judgment are assured. Whether for surveillance from above or for self-control and self-guidance, numbers have a meaningful role to play, and well-selected numbers have a very meaningful role. We in no way mean to diminish the importance of figures, but only to emphasize that figures must be supplemented by informal or social controls.

Just as the idea of formal control is derived from accounting, the idea of informal control is derived from the inquiries of the behavioral sciences into the nature of organizational behavior. In all functioning groups, norms develop to which individuals are responsive if not obedient. These norms constitute the accepted way of doing things; they define the limits of proper behavior, and the type of action that will meet with approval from the group. In view of the way they operate, the control we have in mind is better described as *social* rather than *informal*. It is embedded in the activities, interactions, and sentiments characterizing group behavior. Sentiments take the form of likes and dislikes among men and evaluative judgments exercised upon each other. Negative sentiments, of great importance to their objects, may be activated by individual departure from a norm; such sentiments can either constitute a punishment in themselves, or can lead to some other form of punishment.

The shortcomings of formal control based on quantitative measurements of performance can be largely obviated by designing and implementing a system in which formal and social controls are integrated. For example, meetings of groups of managers to discuss control reports can facilitate inquiry into the significance of problems lying behind variances, can widen the range of solutions considered, and can bring pressure to bear from peers as well as from superiors. All these features can in turn contribute to finding a new course of action which addresses the problem rather than the figures.

One of the most vexing problems in attempting to establish a functional system of formal and social controls lies in the area of ethical standards. In difficult competitive situations, the pressure for results can lead individuals into illegal and unethical practices. Instead of countering this tendency, group norms may encourage yielding to these pressures. For example, knowing that others were doing the same thing undoubtedly influenced some electrical industry division managers to flout the antitrust laws when they could not otherwise meet the sales and profit expectations of the home office. On a lesser scale, group norms can be supportive to suppliers making expensive gifts to purchasing agents, or to salesmen offering extravagant entertainment to customers.

Where top management refuses to condone pursuit of company goals by unethical methods, it must resort to penalties like dismissal that are severe enough to dramatize its opposition. If a division sales manager, who is caught having arranged call-girl attentions for an important customer, against both the standards of expected behavior and the policy of the company, is not penalized at all, or only mildly, because of the volume of his sales and the profit he generates, ethical standards will not long be of great importance. If he is fired, then his successor is likely to think twice about the means he employs to achieve the organizational purposes that are assigned to him.

But there are limits to the effectiveness of punishment, in companies as well as in families and in society. If violations are not detected, the fear of punishment tends to weaken. A system of inspection is therefore implicit in formal control. But besides its expense and complexity, such policing of behavior has the drawback of adversely affecting the attitudes of an individual toward his organization. His commitment to creative accomplishment is likely to be shaken, especially if he is the kind of person who is not likely to cut corners in the performance of his duties. To undermine the motivation of the ethically inclined is a high price to pay for detection of the weak.

The student of general management is thus confronted by a dilemma: if an organization is sufficiently decentralized to permit individuals to develop new solutions to problems and new avenues to corporate achievement, then the opportunity for wrongdoing cannot be eliminated. This being so, a system of controls must be supplemented by a selective system of executive recruitment and training. No system of control, no program of rewards and penalties, no procedures of measuring and evaluating performance can take the place of the individual who has a clear idea of right and wrong, a consistent policy for himself, and the strength to stand the gaff when results suffer because he stands firm. This kind of person is different from the human animal who grasps at every proferred reward and flinches at every punishment. His development is greatly assisted by the systems, standards, rewards, incentives, penalties, and controls which permit the application of qualitative criteria and avoid the oversimplification of numerical measures. It is always the way systems are administered that determines their ultimate usefulness and impact.

RECRUITMENT AND DEVELOPMENT OF`MANAGEMENT

Organizational behavior, in the view we have just taken of it, is the product of interacting *systems* of measures, motives, standards, incentives, rewards, penalties, and controls. Put another way, behavior is the outcome of *processes* of measurement, evaluation, motivation, and control. These systems and processes affect and shape the development of all individuals, most crucially those in management positions. Management development is therefore an ongoing process in all organizations, whether planned or not. As you examine cases which permit a wide-angled view of organizational activities, it is appropriate to inquire into the need to plan this development, rather than to let it occur as it will.

In days gone by, before it was generally realized that relying on a consciously designated corporate strategy was far safer and more productive than simply trusting to good luck, a widely shared set of assumptions operated to inhibit the emergence of management development programs. These assumptions have been described as follows:

1. Good management is instinct in action. A number of men are born with the qualities of energy, shrewdness of judgment, ambition, and capacity for responsibility. These men become the leaders of business.
2. A man prepares himself for advancement by performing well in his present job. The man who does best in competition with his fellows is best qualified to lead them.
3. If an organization does not happen to have adequate numbers of men with innate qualities of leadership who are equal to higher responsibilities, it may bring in such persons from other companies.
4. Men with the proper amount of ambition do not need to be "motivated" to demonstrate the personal qualities which qualify them for advancement.
5. Management cannot be taught formally—in school or anywhere else.[5]

The ideas that we have been examining here suggest that these assumptions are obsolescent. Men are, of course, born with different innate characteristics, but none of these precludes acquiring knowledge, attitudes, and skills which fill the gap between an identifiable personality trait had executive action. Good performance in lesser jobs is expected of men considered for bigger jobs, but different and additional qualifications are required for higher responsibility. Thus the most scholarly professor, the most dexterous machine operator, and the most persuasive salesman do not necessarily make a good college president, foreman, and sales manager. The abilities that make the difference can be learned from experience or to some extent from formal education. As a substitute for training and supplying the requisite experience internally, com-

---

[5] K. R. Andrews, *The Effectiveness of University Management Development Programs* (Boston: Division of Research, the Harvard Graduate School of Business Administration, 1966), p. 232.

panies can import managers trained by competitors, but this approach, though sometimes unavoidable, is risky and expensive. The risk lies in the relative difficulty of appraising the quality of outsiders and estimating their ability to transfer their technical effectiveness to a new organization. The cost lies chiefly in the disruption of natural internal incentive systems.

The supply of men and women who, of their own volition, can or will arrange for their own development is smaller than required. Advances in technology, the internationalization of markets, and the progress of research on information processing and organizational behavior all make it absurd to suppose that a person can learn all he will need to know from what he is currently doing. In particular, the activities of the general manager differ so much in kind from those of other management that special preparation for the top job should be considered, unless it is demonstrably impossible.

The multiplication of company-sponsored and university management training programs is evidence that the old idea that managers are born not made has been displaced by the proposition that managers are born with capacities which can be developed. In the process of seeing to it that the company is adequately manned to implement its strategy, we can identify training requirements. In other words, strategy can be our guide to (1) the skills which will be required to perform the critical tasks; (2) the number of persons with specific skill, age, and experience characteristics who will be required in the light of planned growth and predicted attrition; and (3) the number of new individuals of requisite potential who must be recruited to ensure the availability, at the appropriate time, of skills that require years to develop.

No matter what the outcome of these calculations, it can safely be said that every organization must actively recruit new talent if it aims to maintain its position and to grow. These recruits should have adequate ability not only for filling the junior positions to which they are initially called, but also for learning the management skills needed to advance to higher positions. Like planning of all kinds, recruiting must be done well ahead of the actual need.

> Men with the ultimate capacity to become general managers should be sought out in their twenties, for able men today in a society in which the level of education as well as economic means is rising rapidly are looking for careers, not jobs. In this same spirit companies should recruit—not meeting the needs for clerk, field salesman, or laboratory technician alone but making an investment in the caliber of executive who in 25 years will be overseeing an activity not even contemplated today.[6]

One of the principal impediments to effective execution of plans is shortage of management manpower of the breadth required at the time required. This shortage is the result of faulty planning, not of a natural scarcity of good raw material. Consider the bank which wishes to open 50 branches overseas as part of its international expansion. It will not

---

[6] Ibid., p. 240.

be able to export and replace 50 branch managers unless, years earlier, deliberate attention has been given to securing and to training banker-administrators. These are not technicians who know only credit, for example; they must know how to preside over an entire if small bank, learn and speak a foreign language, establish and maintain relationships with a foreign government, and provide banking services not for an exclusively American but for a different group of individual and corporate customers.

After successful recruitment of candidates with high potential, speeding the course of management development is usually the only way to keep manpower planning in phase with the requirements of strategy. Thus the recruit should be put to work at a job which uses the abilities he has and challenges him to acquire the knowledge he lacks about the company and industry:

> For men educated in this generation sweeping out the stockroom or carrying samples to the quality control laboratory are inappropriate unless these activities demand their level of education or will teach them something besides humility. To introduce the school-trained men of high promise to everyday affairs may mean the devising of jobs which have not existed hitherto. Expansion of analytical sections and accounting and financial departments, projects in market research, rudimentary exploratory investigations in new products departments, process control or data processing projects are all work which will use school-taught techniques and yet require practical and essential exposure to the company and solutions to the problem of establishing working relationships with old hands. Any recruit, no matter how brilliant his academic achievement, has of course much to learn that schools cannot teach him. His seasoning should be accomplished while he works with the power that he has, not doing a sentence of indeterminate length in clerical work of no difficulty.[7]

The manpower requirements imposed by commitment to a strategy of growth mean quite simply that men and women overqualified for conventional beginning assignments must be sought out and carefully cultivated thereafter. Individuals who respond well to the opportunities devised for them should be assigned to established organization positions and given responsibility as fast as capacity to absorb it is indicated. To promote rapidly is not the point so much as to maintain the initial momentum and to provide work to highly qualified individuals which is both essential and challenging.

The rise of professional business education and the development of advanced management programs make formal training available to men and women not only at the beginning of their careers but also at appropriate intervals thereafter. Short courses for executives are almost always stimulating and often of permanent value. But management development as such is predominantly an organizational process which must be supported, not thwarted, by the incentive and control systems to which we have already alluded. Distribution of rewards and penalties will effectively determine how much attention executives will give to the

---

[7] Ibid., pp. 240–41.

training of their subordinates. No amount of lip service will take the place of action in establishing effective management development as an important management activity. To evaluate a manager in part on his effort and effectiveness in bringing along his juniors requires subjective measures and a time span longer than one fiscal year. These limitations do not seriously impede judgment, especially when both strategy and the urgency of its implications for manpower development are clearly known.

In designing on-the-job training, a focus on strategy makes possible a substantial economy of effort, in that management development and management evaluation can be carried on together. Thus a "management-by-objectives" program, already characterized as a most appropriate approach to evaluation of performance, can be simultaneously administered as an instrument of development. For example, in Texas Instruments, Inc., Mr. Pringle could use his conference with his superiors not only to discuss variances from budgeted departmental performance, but also to discover how far his suggested solutions are appropriate or inappropriate and why. In all such cases, discussion of objectives proposed, problems encountered, and results obtained provide opportunities for inquiry, for instruction and counsel, for learning what needs to be done and at what level of effectiveness.

Besides providing an ideal opportunity for learning, concentration on objectives permits delegation to juniors of choice of means and other decision-making responsibilities otherwise hard to come by. Throughout the top levels of the corporation, if senior management is spending adequate time on the surveillance of the environment and on the study of strategic alternatives, then the responsibility for day-to-day operations must necessarily be delegated. Since juniors cannot learn how to bear responsibility without having it, this necessity is of itself conducive to learning. If, within limits, responsibility for the choice of means to obtain objectives is also delegated, opportunity is presented for innovation, experimentation, and creative approaches to problem solving. Where ends rather than means are the object of attention and agreement exists on what ends are and should be, means may be allowed to vary at the discretion of the developing junior manager. The clearer the company's goals, the smaller the emphasis that must be placed on uniformity, and the greater the opportunity for initiative. Freedom to make mistakes and achieve success is more productive in developing executive skills than practice in following detailed how-to-do-it instructions designed by superiors or staff specialists. Commitment to purpose rather than to procedures appears to energize initiative.

A stress on purpose rather than on procedures suggests that organizational climate, though intangible, is more important to individual growth than the mechanisms of personnel administration. The development of each individual in the direction best suited both to his own powers and to organizational needs is most likely to take place in the company where everybody is encouraged to work at the height of his ability and is rewarded for doing so. Such a company must have a clear idea of what it is and what it intends to become. With this idea sufficiently institutionalized so that organization members grow committed to it, the effort required for achievement will be forthcoming without elaborate incentives and coercive controls. Purpose, especially if considered worth accomplishing, is the most powerful incentive to accomplishment. If goals are not set high enough, they must be reset—as high as developing creativity and accelerating momentum suggest.

In short, from the point of view of general management, management development is not a combination of staff activities and formal training designed to provide neophytes with a common body of knowledge, or to produce a generalized good manager. Rather, development is inextricably linked to organizational purpose, which shapes to its own requirements the kind, rate, and amount of development which takes place. It is a process by which men are professionally equipped to be—as far as possible in advance of the need—what the evolving strategy of the firm requires them to be, at the required level of excellence.

Although the processes of recruiting, training, and providing successive job opportunities and challenges are less formal than systems of compensation, control, and performance measurement, they have their own canons and precepts. Their claims to attention and to deference for their own sake must also be subordinated to the requirements of strategy.

The chief executive will have a special interest of his own in the process of management development. For standards of performance, measures for accurate evaluation, incentives, and controls will have a lower priority in his eyes than a committed organization, manned by people who know what they are supposed to do and committed to the overall ends to which their particular activities contribute. The general manager is not blind to the needs of his subordinates to serve their own purposes as well as those of the organization, any more than he is blind to the need, under the rules of accounting, for total assets to equal total liabilities. Wherever conflicting claims are made upon his attention, he requires that they be reconciled in a way which does not obscure organizational objectives or slow down the action being taken to attain them.

*   *   *   *   *

In examining the cases that follow, try to identify the strategy of the company and the structure of relationships established to implement it. Note the standards that have been established for measurement purposes. Are they appropriate for measuring the progress of the organization toward its goals? Is the way performance is measured likely to assist or impede constructive behavior? What pattern of possible incentives encouraging appropriate behavior can be identified? Do they converge on desired outcomes? What restraints and controls discouraging inappropriate behavior are in force? What changes in measurement, incentive, and control systems would you recommend to facilitate achievement of goals? If your analysis of the company's situation suggests that strategy and structure should be changed, these recommendations should, of course, precede your suggested plans for effective implementation.

The Rose Company

MR. JAMES PIERCE had recently received word of his appointment as general manager of the Jackson Plant, one of the older established units of The Rose Company. As such, Mr. Pierce was to be responsible for the management and administration at the Jackson Plant of all functions and personnel except sales.

Both top management and Mr. Pierce realized that there were several unique features about his new assignment. Mr. Pierce decided to assess his new situation and relationships before undertaking his assignment. He was personally acquainted with the home office executives, but had met few of the Jackson personnel. This case contains some of his reflections regarding the new assignment.

The Rose Company conducted marketing activities throughout the United States and in certain foreign countries. These activities were directed from the home office by a vice president in charge of sales.

Manufacturing operations and certain other departments were under the supervision and control of a senior vice president. These are shown in Exhibit 1. For many years the company had operated a highly centralized-functional type of manufacturing organization. There was no general manager at any plant; each of the departments in a plant reported on a line basis to its functional counterpart at the home office. For instance, the industrial relations manager of a particular plant reported to the vice president in charge of industrial relations at the home office, and the plant controller to the vice president-controller, and so on.

Mr. Pierce stated that in the opinion of the top management the record of the Jackson Plant had not been satisfactory for several years. The Rose board had recently approved the erection of a new plant in a different part of the city and the use of new methods of production. Lower costs of processing and a reduced manpower requirement at the new plant were expected. Reduction of costs and improved quality of products were needed to maintain competitive leadership and gain some slight product advantage. The proposed combination of methods of manufacturing and mixing materials had not been tried elsewhere in the company. Some features would be entirely new to employees.

According to Mr. Pierce the top management of The Rose Company was beginning to question the advisability of the central control of manufacturing operations. The officers decided to test the value of a decentralized operation in connection with the Jackson Plant. They apparently believed that a general management representative at Jackson was needed if the new experiment in manufacturing methods and the required rebuilding of the organization were to succeed.

Prior to the new assignment Mr. Pierce had been an accounting executive in the controller's department of the company. From independent sources the casewriter learned that Mr. Pierce had demonstrated analytical ability and general administrative capacity. He was generally liked by people. From top management's point of view he had an essential toughness described as an ability to see anything important through. By some he was regarded as the company's efficiency expert. Others thought he was a perfectionist and aggressive in reaching the goals that had been set. Mr. Pierce was aware of these opinions about his personal behavior.

Mr. Pierce summarized his problem in part as follows:

> I am going into a situation involving a large number of changes. I will have a new plant; new methods and processes but most of all I will be dealing with a set of changed relationships. Heretofore all the heads of departments in the plant reported to their functional counterparts in the home office. Now they will report to me. I am a complete stranger and in addition this is my first assignment in a major "line" job. The men will know this.
>
> When I was called into the senior vice president's office to be informed of my new assignment he asked me to talk with each of the functional members of his staff. The vice presidents in charge of production planning, manufacturing, and industrial relations said they were going to issue all headquarters instructions to me as plant manager and they were going to cut off their connections with their counterparts in my plant. The other home office executives admitted their functional counterparts would report to me in line capacity. They should obey my orders and I would be responsible for their pay and promotion. But these executives proposed to follow the common practice of many companies of maintaining a dotted line or functional relationship with these men. I realize that these two different patterns of home office plant relationships will create real administrative problems for me.

Exhibit 2 shows the organization relationships as defined in these conferences.

Exhibit 1

THE ROSE COMPANY

Old Organization

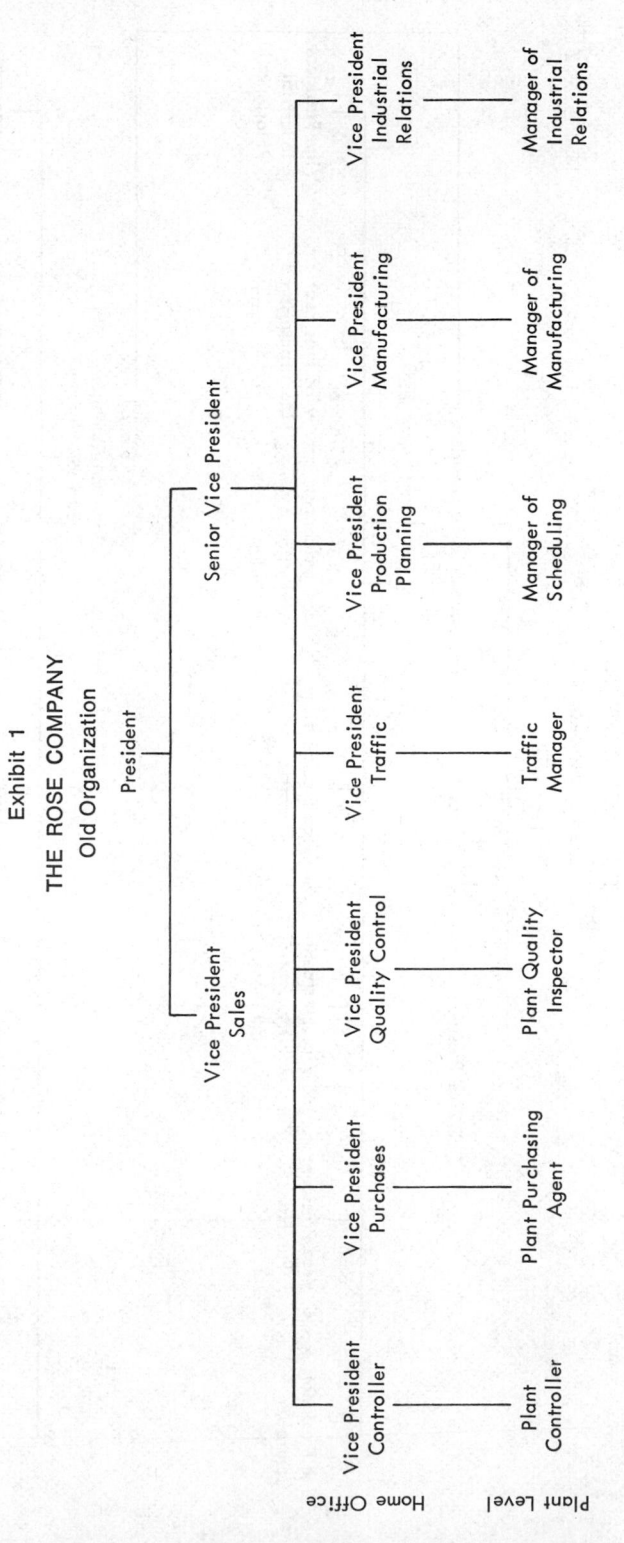

Exhibit 2
THE ROSE COMPANY
New Organization

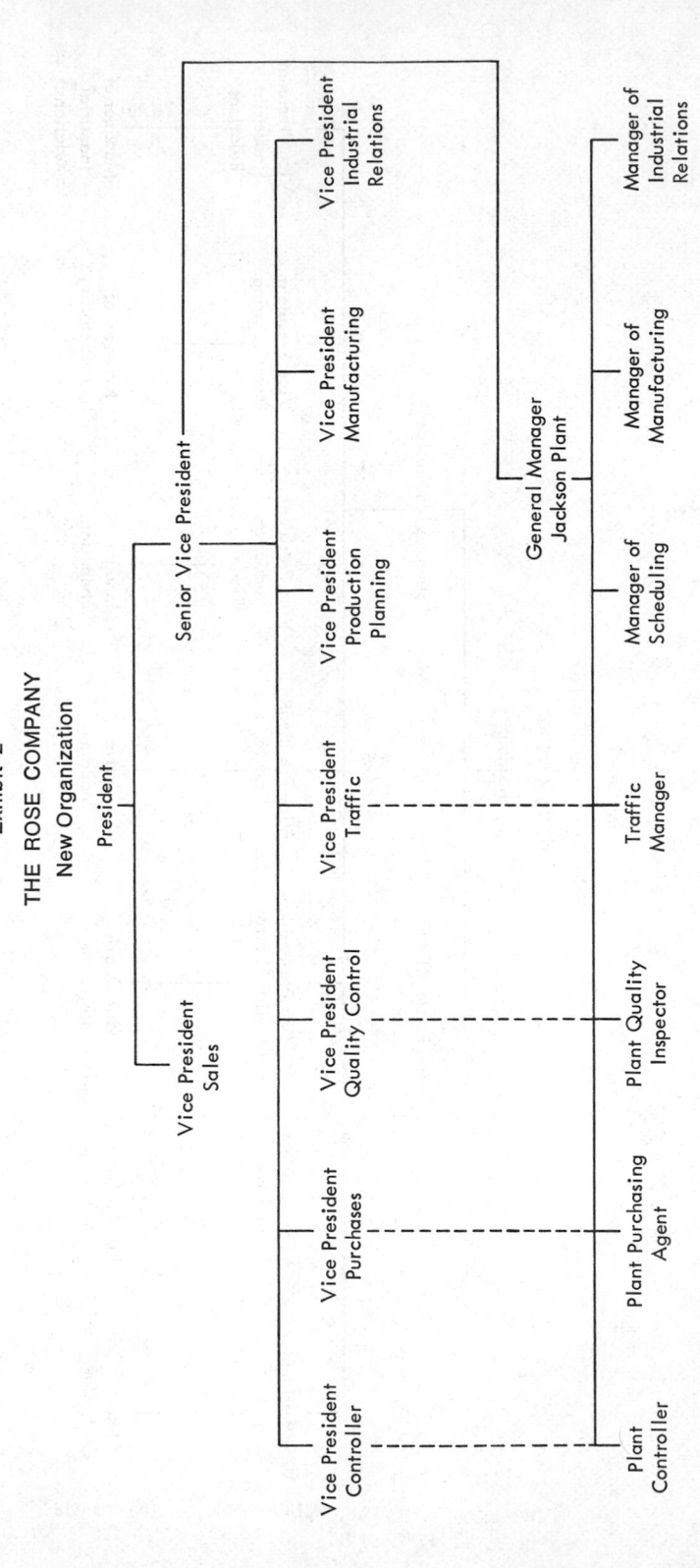

Northeastern Food Company (A)

IN THE EARLY May of 1970 the Northeastern Food Company, a regional chain of supermarkets, took possession of Sadler's Inc., a chain of 10 soft goods discount houses. The act symbolized a major decision. While soft goods of "general merchandise" had been sold in Northeastern stores for several years, the acquisition of Sadler's marked Northeastern's entry into the field of soft goods retailing on a large scale.

Northeastern had grown rapidly between 1950 and 1960, more than doubling sales and earnings. The pace of growth in sales and profit was even faster during the 1960s. By 1970 there were Northeastern stores in all the northeastern states from Massachusetts to Maryland.

The rapid growth of Northeastern was attributed by industry experts primarily to the quality of its management, considered nationally to be among the most competent in food retailing. The company's management prided itself not only on its technical ability, but on its analytical approach to policy and operations and on its encouragement of new ideas and executive talent. (See Exhibit 1.)

Top management. The senior officers of Northeastern Food, William Shae (president) and Harold Norfield (executive vice president) in particular, took time, whenever they felt the need, to re-examine their situation and determine Northeastern's place in its changing industry. One such study resulted in an orderly decentralization of the company over a period of five years beginning in 1960. The role of the store manager, to cite one consequence, was greatly increased.

Each line and staff vice president at the home offices was encouraged to set general objectives five and ten years ahead. Detailed plans for the opening of new stores and the entry into new markets were made three years in advance. In addition, an estimate of the personnel requirements which the future would impose and training programs geared to filling projected needs were included in the plans.

The keystone of Northeastern policy was said to be William Shae's oft-quoted statement that "the most important asset in a business is people." Decentralization, planning, and training were the means by which Northeastern leaders said they sought to create an environment in which "interested, able, productive, and dedicated people" would operate to produce a growing, profitable, ethical, and flexible business. One professional student of the industry noted that "working at Northeastern seemed to mold any man into a professional manager."

A great deal of effort was exerted to make certain that Northeastern's approach to business was reflected in its stores. The image of the Northeastern store in the community was kept under close scrutiny. Competitive prices, quality merchandise, and "friendliness" were the objectives toward which operating policy was oriented. A frank and smooth working relationship with the Union of Retail Clerks was carefully nurtured in a further attempt to administer company policy through cooperative people. Most important, decentralization had made the store manager a key man in translating the company's objectives into satisfied customers.

The store manager.   The Northeastern store manager was expected to (1) make good local merchandising decisions, (2) foster more storewide spirit among employees, (3) develop the supervisory potentials of store personnel by better on-the-job training, and (4) carry out smoothly the transfer of employees from one department to another. To accomplish these objectives, an organization was developed which attempted to give the store manager the local merchandising advantage of the independent as well as the purchasing power of the big chain.

The store manager was given responsibility (1) for all personnel in his store, (2) for control and conservation of all property in his store, and was held accountable for (3) control of operating expenditures, and (4) for the conduct of store operation and sales programs. In a number of areas, security, maintenance, store layout, and store organization, the central office provided help for the manager in the form of policy guidelines and staff organizations. The place of the store manager in the formal organization is presented in Exhibit 2.

ENTRY INTO SOFT GOODS MARKET

The thinking which led Northeastern management to acquire Sadler's represented an evolving consensus of executive viewpoint. Mr. Shae noted that:

> Over the years, and especially recently, we have been watching other retailing business. The general-merchandise field has lured some supermarket operators into big experimental undertakings. We have gone along on a modest scale in our own stores. On the other hand, we have felt that in certain strategic locations it was advantageous to us to have a discount house next to our supermarket or almost adjacent to it. We have encouraged and sought to attract discounters. We have had satisfactory sales results in our supermarkets from this neighborly relationship. We like it. So do others. In whatever course we follow, we are interested in doing only those things which will help *our* supermarkets.

Other executives reported the development of Northeastern's decision to enter soft goods as follows:

Mr. Harold Norfield, executive vice president and general manager, said:

> We began our connection with the discount business by locating next to them in various centers. It soon became apparent that the strength of our neighbor was going to have a lot to do with our own volume.

Noting that the discount house was a permanent revolution, Mr. Harmon Stoddard, vice president, finance, went on to say:

> The average discount department store is a hard thing to finance. The lease umbrella given by the supermarket as financial support to the discounter is basically a guarantee of the discounters. That means that if the discounter goes under we are in the discount business anyway. It seemed as if we might as well be in the discount business ourselves and do it the proper way.
>
> Another reason to consider discounters is diversification out of the food business. The potential for horizontal expansion is extended by entry into the nonfood business. There is a single criterion as to where we will expand—return on investment.

Mr. Goldman, vice president of sales, noted that:

> In a 1966 speech to an industry association William Shae set what is still our policy. "We are not going to go into the nonfood business in our supermarkets any more than we already have. It doesn't seem right for us. Basically, it's not our business."
>
> During the '50s and '60s we got evidence on the various ways of handling the nonfoods problem. The problems arising from being under one roof seem to outweigh the possible savings. The answer for us was having discounters as neighbors, and we proceeded to move into centers and experienced good volume.
>
> However, all this time we never closed our eyes to the *acquisition* of an existing discount chain if it was available at the right price. We were looking for a small chain (so that the price wouldn't be out of our range) which was reasonably successful.

SELECTION OF SADLER'S

At the time William Shae was making his speech, Northeastern was already involved in serious negotiations with Sadler's, a Connecticut chain of 10 department stores. Each store was an attractive well-built structure in a shopping center outside a principal city or town. The stores had 14 departments including hardware, men's and women's clothes and furnishings, children's and teenage clothes, shoes, domestics, cosmetics and drugs, toys and automotive equipment. All but the women's department were leased[1] to concessionaires who specialized in retailing a specific line of merchandise.

---

[1] Historically, the owner of the soft goods discount house has been a specialist in the retailing of clothing only. Rather than extending his own capital and merchandising experience to such diverse lines as hardware, millinery, shoes, or

Sadler's had been started in 1961 as a family enterprise by Sol Feinman. Northeastern management later reported that, as the number of stores and sales volume grew, Mr. Feinman's merchandising acumen and the capital resources of his relatives were gradually being stretched to the breaking point. The management of the stores was theoretically delegated to store managers, but Mr. Feinman himself took part in virtually all operating decisions. In addition to running the stores, he controlled buying and merchandising for Sadler's women's department, planned the layout of new stores, and took a major part in negotiations with shopping center owners and Sadler's lessees.

Mr. Norfield described the Sadler situation as follows:

> We were considering an acquisition and Harmon Stoddard came to us with a proposal to buy Sadler's. Sadler's was near us in seven centers and was going to be next to us in five more. Their company had been run by a family group. In fact there was only one active manager, Feinman.
>
> As soon as they began to expand Feinman found himself out of his depth. He simply had too much to do. As far as we saw it, it appeared that he began to want a change from the situation where his partners were milking the business and acting as a drain and a source of confusion while he did all the work.
>
> Now Feinman came in contact with Harmon Stoddard in some location negotiations and it seems that they talked together and the idea came up. Harmon presented it to a group of us and the first time around, we said no. The next time we got one of our directors who has a broad background in nonfood retailing to go out and look at the stores and make a careful study. This time we decided it was O.K.

According to Mr. Stoddard, "the price was right" (see Exhibits 3 and 4).

> At the time of our first negotiation the stock was selling in the low 50s. When the number of shares was set, we were selling in the 80s. So each day the number of shares came down.

As an outcome of the acquisition, certain plans, described by Mr. Goldman, were developed:

> Our plan is fairly clear. We just don't know the time schedule. The job is, first, building an organization. Then, once that's done we can step out and build new stores.
>
> Our long-range plan is not to use Sadler's as a neighbor until they are organized and running. I would guess that by the end of this year they'll be organized.
>
> You know, decisions here don't get made in an authoritarian way. We think you can't operate with any effectiveness in that way. There are 12 or so men here who constitute a top echelon. Each of us operates as if nobody owns the company but himself. Then if I believe some-

---

even food, he usually leased space and fixtures to specialists in those lines. The lessee usually provided his own stock, promotion, department manager, and paid through rent for services provided by the store. The store owner's control over the operations of leased departments varied according to the terms of the individually negotiated leases.

thing, I will get others to recognize the issue and we will have a meeting. Then when we reach a consensus, we move. You see, no one of us has that power and we won't make a decision unless there is compatibility. That is the key thing—we all operate together.

BUILDING AN ORGANIZATION

The acquisition of Sadler's created new responsibilities and problems for Northeastern management. In early April, Mr. Norfield indicated the most important of these were the need to establish policies and create a store image:

> We are building an organization from scratch. We don't know how to run this kind of a store and we will have to learn. We are now in the process of deciding what we want. . . .We took over from the sellers only one man *really*, their general manager [Sol Feinman]. He is a good merchant and will be the only man among us with real soft goods experience. Under him we plan to build an organization something like this:

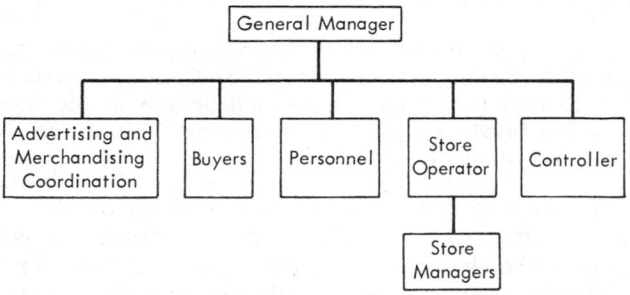

> We will put two of our men in, one as the store operator and the other as the controller. Results will come out of this group, and we will just have to learn what is right. Our management group will work together on settling policy matters, such as what we should stand for, what relations Sadler's should have to Northeastern, and what type of concessionaires we should have. They will be: William Shae, president and chairman; Harold Norfield, executive vice president and general manager; Robert Fitz, vice president of development; Richard Goldman, vice president of sales; Harmon Stoddard, financial vice president; John Gorman, vice president of mergers and acquisitions [see Organization Chart, Exhibit 5].

Appointment of a stores superintendent. In April 1970, Mr. Daniel Kraft, 30, a graduate of New York University, was assigned to the position of stores superintendent within the Sadler organization. (See Exhibit 6 for the formal organization under which he was to function.) Before joining Northeastern four years earlier, Kraft had worked for a leading New York department store as a department manager. At Northeastern he was originally hired as a nonfoods buyer and was later promoted to nonfoods sales manager. In the fall of 1969 he was detached from sales activities for training in store operations. During the month of May he visited the stores to acquaint himself with Sadler's discount operations.

Approach of the stores superintendent.   In determining his own responsibilities, as well as where Sadler's should fit into the Northeastern organization, Daniel Kraft attempted to identify areas in which policy was needed. (See Exhibit 7 for the list Kraft prepared in March.) He believed that there were two major requirements: (1) the need for Northeastern management to learn the discount business and (2) the necessity to teach Sadler personnel how to operate in an organized and effective manner. The job was complicated by the lack of experienced Sadler management.

The limited Sadler organization comprised Mr. Feinman, the general manager; Mr. Parnas, in charge of advertising and promotion; and Mr. Levy, the controller. Mr. Levy was later replaced by Ronald Arnold from the Northeastern organization.

Establishing policy.   Mr. Kraft stated that policy making at Northeastern involved a discussion of diverse ideas until the group agreed upon a common view. He said:

> I do not set the objectives when planning policy. That is for Mr. Harold Norfield to decide. I don't really have a policy of my own. My only objective is that I want Sadler's to be to the discount business what Northeastern is to food marketing. This means aggressiveness, flexibility, competitiveness.

Mr. Kraft acknowledged that top management was faced with a number of unresolved policy questions, one of which was how Sadler's and Northeastern should work together. He said, however, that he himself was really concerned only with his immediate objective, "to increase the responsibility and authority of Sadler's store management. These men work long hours and don't have the help we can offer them, but on the other hand, they aren't handling the problems that we think store managers ought to handle. I want to upgrade the operating effectiveness of the store managers."

Developing store managers.   Mr. Kraft began his task of developing store managers by attempting two forms of action: (1) to relieve managers of some of the operating detail through the use of Northeastern staff divisions and (2) to broaden their perspective and widen their opportunity for taking initiative and assuming responsibility.

STORE MANAGERS' MEETINGS

Mr. Kraft early instituted regular store managers' meetings. The first of these was held June 5 at the Hartford Sadler offices. The meeting was attended by all 10 Sadler's store managers and by Mr. Feinman, Mr. Parnas, Mr. Cronin (Sadler's security officer), Mr. Smith (Northeastern New York office, construction and maintenance department), Mr. Bonder (Northeastern Yankee division maintenance), Mr. Arnold (Sadler's controller), and Mr. Richardson (Northeastern Yankee division, personnel). Mr. Kraft announced at the opening of the meeting that its purpose was to gain understanding. Future meetings were to be scheduled on a monthly basis with a planned agenda, and it was hoped that the store managers would be active participants who determined the agenda. Continuing, Kraft stated, "We are trying to feel our way through what is a very complicated situation. In particular, we want to learn how we can help you. We feel we can help you today by setting a few policies."

Maintenance.   Mr. Kraft introduced Mr. Pete Smith who first described the organizational structure of the Northeastern construction and engineering division and then presented Mr. Robert Bonder from the maintenance supervision office in New Haven. Bonder passed out a copy of maintenance policy procedures and read from it.

BONDER: One thing I didn't write in this policy statement was about preventive maintenance. Once a month we have a maintenance mechanic come to check up on each store. We want to be sure that maintenance is not being handled by the store manager. Sometimes when you will ask us to do something via the communications form, we are going to be slow—we have to be. We have to see what the landlord's responsibility is in the leases. I hope, I know, we'll get your cooperation.

KRAFT: Thanks, Bob. Just to get our thinking straight on this, let me explain. Our service arm is a truly magnificent organization. If you work with them, they'll break their back for you. However, their services *are not free,* and some time in July you will be on a store profit and loss basis.

Very specific questions were raised by the store managers. The discussion of vendors provides an example.

BELL (Groton):   What is the procedure going to be with vendors? A man came into my store the other day with a mop and said that this was the authorized mop in the stores.

BONDER: We have tried to test all mops and find which are the best mops for you to have in your store. We'd like to use the one we have for a few more weeks.

FEINMAN: The question is not answered. The fact is, we will do the buying at the home office. But if we're going to get into detail, we're not going to get anywhere.

KRAFT: Let me clarify this. Nothing is authorized for store managers until you get it in writing in this area of purchasing. Another point—there are to be no interviews or pictures unless Sol approves. This is a tested policy by which we live happily.

SHULBERG (Windsor):   What is going to be your policy on window washers? When are we going to have to get rid of our people, or are you going to approve special people, or what?

BONDER: We never throw people out. If you are happy with the man you have, O.K. We will look at their price; if it is too high, they are notified and given a chance to meet what we consider a competitive price.

KRAFT [breaking into the conversation]:   On this point of the windows, I want to say something. We at Northeastern keep our floors and windows clean and I think maybe it is a fetish with us. Larry, can you say something in this area of cleanliness?

SHULBERG (Windsor):   Well, the porter service is inadequate as it stands now. If the major problems are going to be handled by you, then I think everything will be O.K.

FEINMAN [breaking into the conversation]:   The details will be handled; we don't have time to talk about them. Until such time as people get to you, keep things reasonably O.K.

SMITH: We have to learn your type of organization in order to get our service organization functioning in a useful way to help you.

Discussion continued, covering floor washing, broken fixtures, rest rooms, and other areas of maintenance. Feinman repeatedly asked the store managers to stay out of details.

Personnel policy.   Dan Kraft brought up the matter of personnel policy. He mentioned that trouble had arisen with the State of Connecticut over certain hours and hiring details.

A general discussion of personnel followed. Problems considered, other than violations of the labor laws, included (1) lack of customer service and suggestive selling and (2) the inadequate number of people filling stock. Mr. Feinman stressed the importance of personal appearance. At one point he said heatedly:

> We have to control the personnel of the departments. Their appearance and the appearance of help in general is very important. We run fairly decent stores; our personnel have to look right. What kind of people are we letting into our stores to work there? What kind of impression are we giving? [There was a deadly quiet in the room.] We can write all the bulletins in the world and it won't help. You have got to look at your employees. Every time I come into the store I see dreadful things. I see some boys in dungarees. I was in one store the other day and saw a woman clerk who had terry-cloth bedroom slippers on. Maybe the girl with the apron on behind the snack bar changes it every day. Maybe she ought to be changing it twice. We can't have employees in this store wearing terry-cloth bedroom slippers! Part of the problem is that your employees don't know what to do. You have to tell them. We can't be your eyes!

Mr. Hofstein, of the Torrington store, observed that "representatives of the leased department [were] the chief offenders," to which Feinman replied:

> If they argue with you, you have the authority. If you tell them what you want to do—run a store right—and they argue with you, I want to know about it.

During the coffee break which followed Mr. Feinman's speech, Mr. Kraft spent most of his time chatting with store managers. At one point Mr. Carnot expressed to Mr. Kraft his annoyance with Mr. Feinman's behavior at the meeting. He said, "Christ, Feinman's a tough nut." Kraft said, "You've got to admire him. He is certainly going to get more out of this operation than you or I ever will. He started as a poor boy with a candy stand and look where he is today!"

The remaining discussion covered security practices, two cashiers who had been apprehended in tests at three stores, and labor laws. In closing his discussion, Mr. Richardson of the Northeastern personnel office said that he thought "all Northeastern policies could be summarized by the Golden Rule and by Mr. William Shae's statement that 'Our most important asset is people.' You can buy a lawn mower at the Topp's store, but it's the people who bring the customers into Sadler's."

At this juncture Mr. Kraft turned the meeting over to Mr. Feinman who said:

> Well, boys, we've got to do more business. Last week nobody made plan. Some of you came so close that if you had just put in a little more effort I'm sure you could have made it. It's just terrible that you can come that close to plan and not make it. I don't know what the answer is but I think we're going to have to do a lot more in-store promotion. It's necessary! We've got to get the concessionaires to cooperate. You've got that speaker in the store and you've got to use it.

He noted that Mr. Jones of the Hartford store was very successful at selling over the loud-speaker. Referring to the concessionaires, Feinman went on, "We don't make enough use of the people in the stores, the values they can offer."

Promotion.   General discussion followed among Mr. Feinman, Mr. Parnas, Mr. Kraft, and the store managers concerning effective types of promotion. Arguments ensued over specific promotional points; for example, the number of items to be broadcast over the speaker each day, the kind of items, and the number of times the same item could be promoted:

> SHARF (Bristol):   Would it be possible for us to see the numbers on other stores? I don't really mean numbers, specific numbers, but perhaps our ranking. I want to know where things are better, and then maybe we can find out which approaches are working and why.

Neither Mr. Feinman nor Mr. Kraft nor the store managers liked the naming of specific stores. Mr. Feinman went on to say:

> We don't want specific numbers. Some stores should be low and we can't criticize them because they are. It's natural that because of size and location one store outsells another consistently.
>
> But let's have six specials six days a week. It will work. You can use the same item more than once during the week. On Saturday and after five o'clock you can break the fair-trade laws. I don't think they're enforced except by complaint, and those inspectors aren't in the stores after five. They don't work the same kind of week that we do.

Mr. Kraft summarized the discussion concerning promotion and stated that if the store managers wanted to see a departmental ranking within stores for all the stores this could be arranged. Following, Ronald Arnold described the objectives for accounting in the new organization.

Summation of meeting.   Mr. Kraft then noted that the official agenda had been completed and threw the floor open for questions. A variety of subjects were brought up. Mr. Feinman continued to emphasize specifics of merchandising, while Kraft sought to draw out the store managers.

At 4:30 the meeting closed. Afterwards, Mr. Kraft said that he thought the meeting had gone reasonably well, although it had been an hour and a half too long. He was of the opinion that Mr. Feinman's urge to make specific decisions made his task of encouraging feedback from the store managers more difficult.

SOLUTIONS TO SPECIFIC PROBLEMS

On June 6, Mr. Kraft attended a series of meetings at Northeastern headquarters in New York scheduled to work out solutions to specific problems, function and organizational, involving a variety of Northeastern staff divisions. During the course of the day Kraft spoke with John Gorman, Jim Brown (personnel), Irving Holland (grocery sales manager), Dick Goldman, and the key men controlling store supplies and store security.

Discussion covered the organization of Sadler's personnel operation, personnel policy for Sadler's, the possible unionization of Sadler's store employees, liaison between Northeastern's and Sadler's merchandising operations, central purchasing of store supplies, and the conflict between store security and customer convenience as criteria for new store layout. In each case the result of discussion was a decision to handle a specific problem in a given way, or the establishment of a policy or procedure to cover future questions arising in a given area.

Following his meetings, Mr. Kraft described what he conceived his role to be. He explained that as he saw it his task was to get the Sadler's organization *moving*.

> Mr. Norfield told me that there is no doubt that I will not be able to get perfect policies set up everywhere. If I am able to set things up so that there is a 5% savings in supplies, it is very possible that a 10% savings will eventually be realized. But my job is to get things organized and going immediately while still building towards long-range Northeastern goals. In fact, if it turns out that we have to take a loss in supplies in the short run, two to six months, we will do this as long as it is expected that by centralizing in the long run we will save 5% or 7%. So that in each area I feel that I am making compromises and just coming out with a working solution that approaches what I expect Northeastern will be doing in the future. You know an awful lot of nice pretty policy decisions are being made in the home office, but the messy condition that the Sadler's organization is in makes this job—well, I am working regularly 10 to 15 hours a day and I still can't get everything done. There is just so far that one can overextend oneself.

Exhibit 1

NORTHEASTERN FOOD COMPANY (A)
Northeastern Consolidated Balance Sheet June 1, 1969
(in thousands)

Current assets			Current liabilities		
Cash	$	5,661	Accounts payable	$	9,221
Accounts receivable		1,973	Accrued expenses		4,508
Inventories		23,242	Other accruals		3,122
Prepayals		813	Total current liabilities	$	16,851
Total current assets	$	31,689	Deferred taxes		818
Net fixed assets		74,675	Long-term debt		54,345
Other assets		1,063	Capital stock and surplus		
Total assets		$107,427	2,018,072 of 6,500,000 shares		
			authorized are outstanding		11,894
			Retained earnings		23,519
			Total liabilities		$107,427

Northeastern Consolidated Statement of Earnings for 52 Weeks Ending June 1, 1969
(in thousands)

Retail sales	$387,308
Costs and expenses	
cost of sales, etc.	370,711
Depreciation and amortization	4,146
	$374,857
Earnings before taxes	$ 12,451
Estimated federal taxes	5,751
Net earnings	$ 6,700

Other Information

	Sales	Earnings	Earnings per share
	(in thousands)		
1930	$ 22,400	$ 544	$0.28
1940	33,858	418	0.21
1950	81,000	1,409	0.70
1954	133,537	1,626	0.81
1955	159,066	2,185	1.09
1956	199,432	2,790	1.38
1957	246,872	3,677	1.81
1958	314,285	5,017	2.48
1959	387,308	6,700	3.32

Source: Company records.

Exhibit 2

NORTHEASTERN FOOD COMPANY (A)

Typical Organization Chart

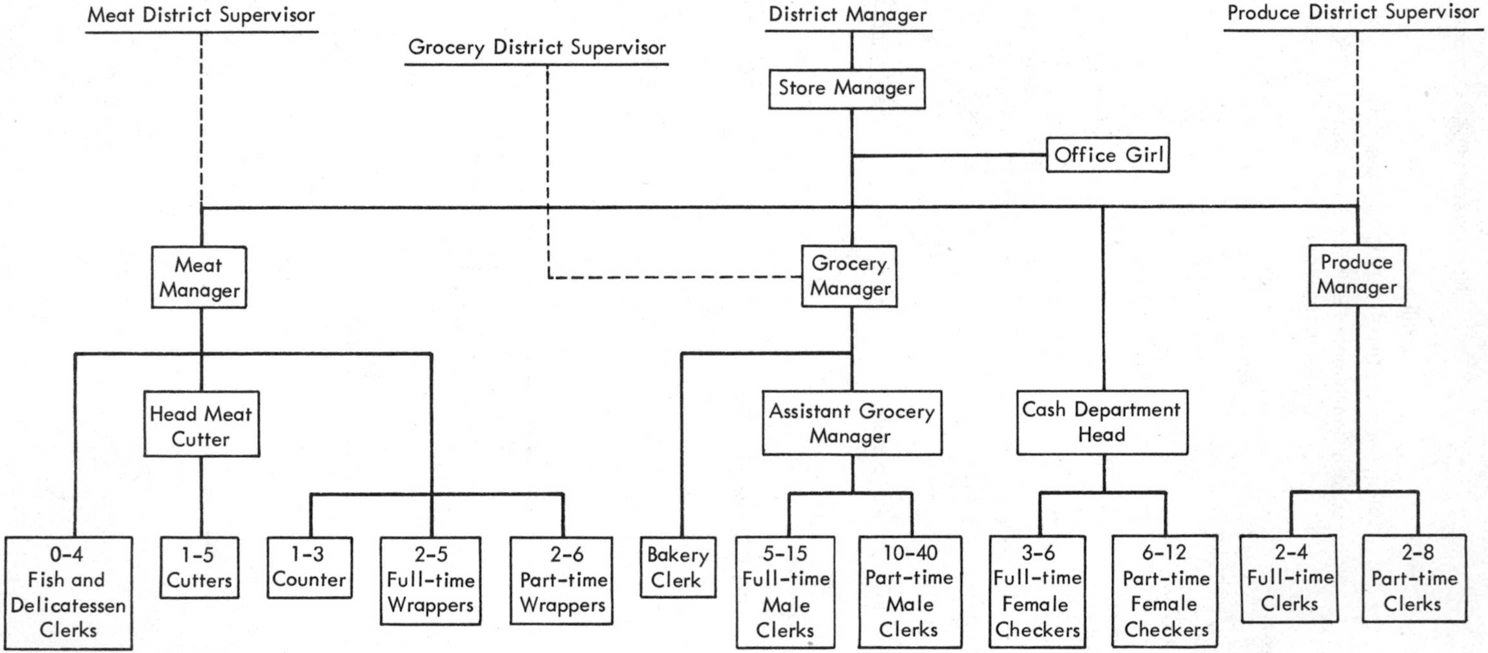

Meat District Supervisor

Grocery District Supervisor

District Manager

Produce District Supervisor

Store Manager

Office Girl

Meat Manager

Grocery Manager

Produce Manager

Head Meat Cutter

Bakery Clerk

Assistant Grocery Manager

Cash Department Head

0–4 Fish and Delicatessen Clerks

1–5 Cutters

1–3 Counter

2–5 Full-time Wrappers

2–6 Part-time Wrappers

5–15 Full-time Male Clerks

10–40 Part-time Male Clerks

3–6 Full-time Female Checkers

6–12 Part-time Female Checkers

2–4 Full-time Clerks

2–8 Part-time Clerks

Note: Usual range of total employees—50–100.
Source: Store opening manual.

Exhibit 3

NORTHEASTERN FOOD COMPANY (A)

Sadler's Inc., et al. Consolidated Balance Sheet, Dec. 21, 1969
(in thousands)

Current assets		Current liabilities	
Cash	$1,040	Accounts payable	$2,024
Accounts receivable (net)	1,281	Accrued expenses	476
Inventory (cost or market		Other accruals	2,093
"retail method")	2,422		
Prepayals	340	Total current liabilities	$4,593
Total current assets	$5,083		
Fixed assets (net)		Long-term Debt	1,163
Furniture and fixtures	1,333		
Automobiles	42	Capital	
Leasehold improvements	287	Common stock	170
	$1,662	Preferred stock	81
Other assets (including $80,000		Capital surplus	115
in U.S. Govt. Bonds)	227	Earned surplus	850
Total assets	$6,972	Total liabilities	$6,972

Sadler's Inc., et al. Consolidated Income Statement for Calendar Year 1969
(in thousands)

Net sales (Sadler's owned departments)	$7,653
Cost of goods sold	5,223
	$2,430
Rental income	1,685
Gross profit	$4,115
Operating expenses (see Schedule 1)	3,984
Operating profit	$ 131
Depreciation and amortization	96
Net operating profit	$ 35
Other income	18
Net profit before taxes	$ 53

Schedule 1
Operating Expenses

Direct salaries (including officers' salaries of $135,000)	$1,719
Rent, electricity and water	841
Taxes	117
Insurance	97
Repairs	58
Advertising	632
Interest	96
Other	424
Total	$3,984

Source: Company records.

Exhibit 4

Mr. Gorman's Pro Forma Operating Statement for
Sadler's,* Calendar Year 1970
Rental Operations Only
(in thousands)

Total income...	$3,588
Total direct expenses (see Schedule 1).....................	3,314
	$ 274
Managerial salaries......................................	72
	$ 202
Taxes at 40%..	81
Estimated net after taxes................................	$ 121

Schedule 1
Operating Expenses

Direct salaries..	$ 825
Rent, electricity and water..............................	1,040
Taxes†..	19
Insurance‡..	50
Repairs...	62
Advertising...	787
Interest§...	19
Other...	512
Total..	$3,314

* The opening of three Sadler stores was planned for calendar 1970.
† Real estate taxes not payable until second year.
‡ $700,000 of life insurance on officers with cash surrender value of $130,000 was surrendered on purchase.
§ The greater part of Sadler's debt to be retired or renegotiated by the parent.
Source: Company records.

Exhibit 5

NORTHEASTERN FOOD COMPANY (A)

Partial Organization Chart of the
Northeastern Food Company

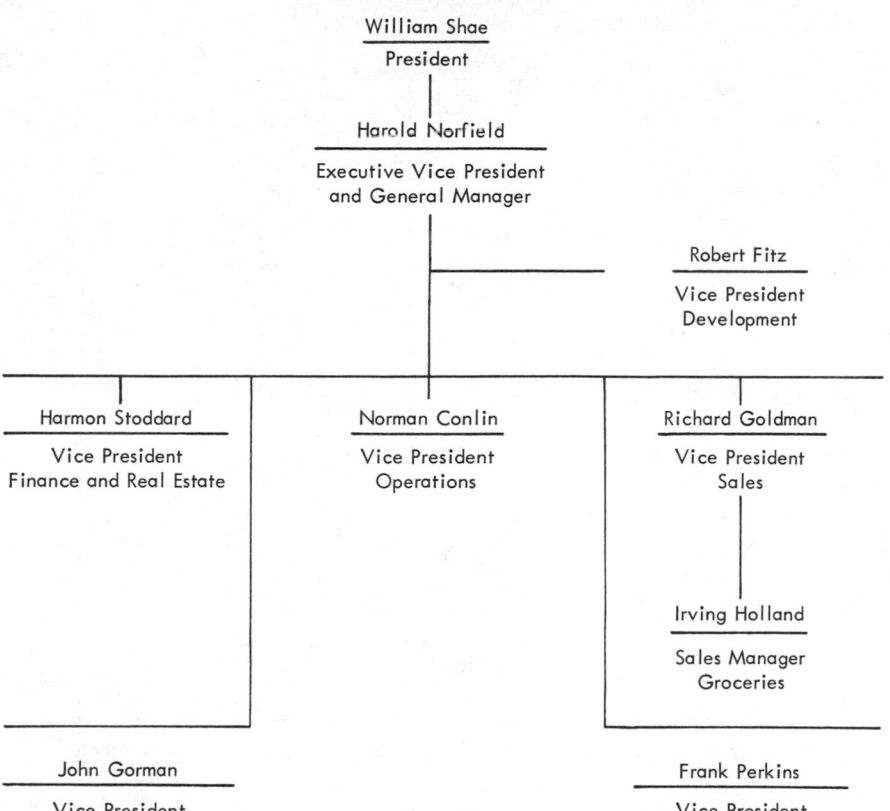

William Shae
President

Harold Norfield
Executive Vice President
and General Manager

Robert Fitz
Vice President
Development

Harmon Stoddard
Vice President
Finance and Real Estate

Norman Conlin
Vice President
Operations

Richard Goldman
Vice President
Sales

Irving Holland
Sales Manager
Groceries

John Gorman
Vice President
Mergers and Acquisitions

Frank Perkins
Vice President
Yankee Division
(Office in New Haven)

Exhibit 6

NORTHEASTERN FOOD COMPANY (A)

Partial Organization of Sadler's Division Including Working
Relationships of Sadler's, May 6, 1970 to the Parent Company*

Northeastern New York Office

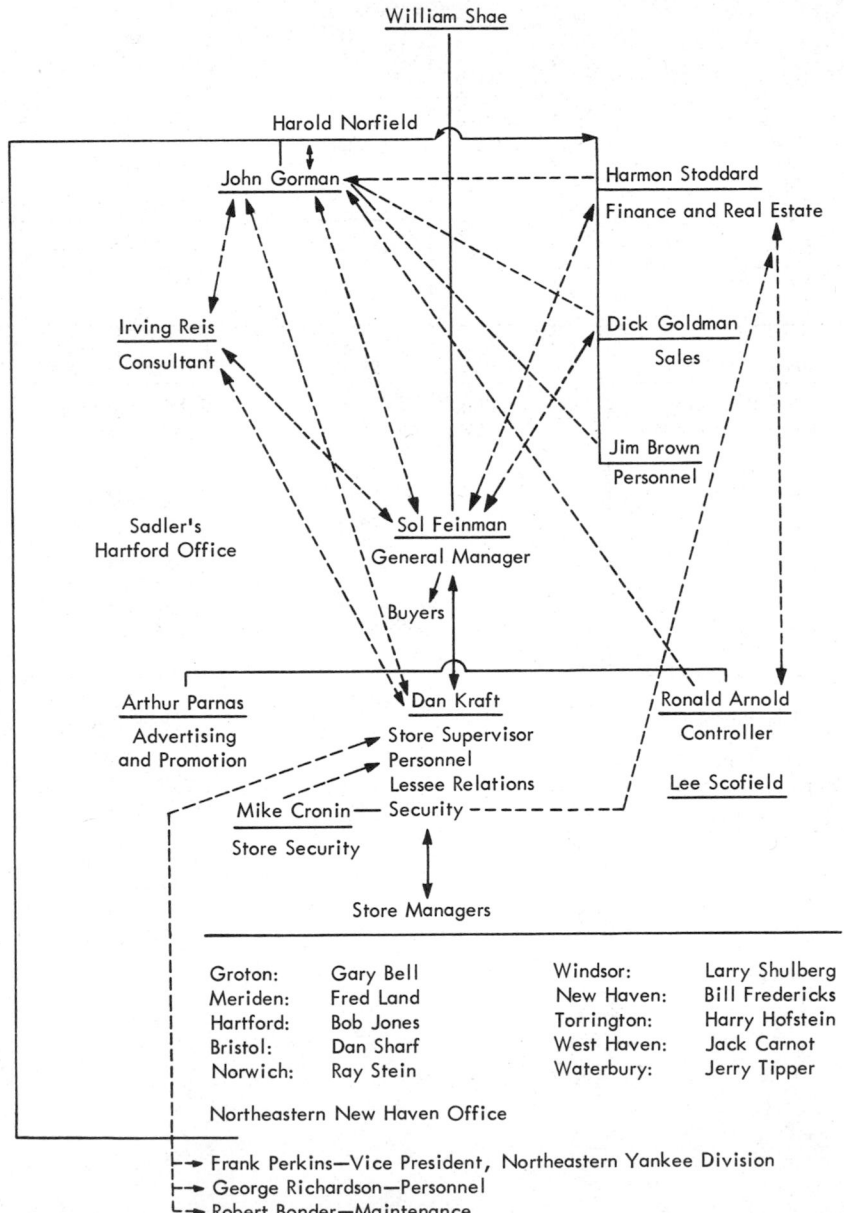

* Dotted line denotes working rather than formal relationships.
These relationships evolved during the month of April 1970.

Exhibit 7

NORTHEASTERN FOOD COMPANY (A)
Memorandum from Messrs. Kraft and Arnold
to Mr. Gorman Based upon Their First Exposure
to the Sadler's Organization
March 28, 1970

Outlined below is a brief summary of points which we are presently in the process of scheduling and studying.

1. Issuance of weekly merchandising reports, i.e., "Open to Buy" and Sales Reports showing actual vs. planned.
2. Preparation of quarterly merchandising and expense budgets.
3. Reporting on a 4-week basis plus periodic profit and loss by stores.
4. Write up of a uniform, standardized set of instructions and procedures for merchandising, accounting, security, operations, personnel, etc.
5. Preparation of a predetermined check list of what is to be accomplished in a store visit by merchandising personnel.
6. Schedule of meetings of buyers and store managers—generally once a month.
7. Evaluation of advertising controls and the necessary follow-through.

Northeastern Food Company (B)

In early May of 1970 the Northeastern Food Company, a regional chain of supermarkets, took possession of Sadler's Inc., a chain of 10 soft goods' discount houses. The act symbolized a major decision. While soft goods or "general merchandise" had been sold in Northeastern stores for several years, the acquisition of Sadler's marked Northeastern's entry into the field of soft goods' retailing on a large scale.

The thinking of Northeastern top management which led to the acquisition and its view of the problems posed by the acquisition is summarized in the Northeastern Foods (A) case. Northeastern (A) introduces Mr. Daniel Kraft's first steps to resolve some of these problems. He described what he was doing as "getting things organized and going immediately while still building towards long-range Northeastern goals."

In the Northeastern (B) case, attention is focused on Mr. Kraft as he worked at his job during a period of six weeks beginning in early June and ending the second week of July. The casewriter spent nearly all of this time with Mr. Kraft through what John Gorman termed "the theoretical break-even point" in the integration of Sadler's and Northeastern.

As the following pages make clear, this was a difficult period for Mr. Kraft. To begin with, he was not certain what his job was. He operated at three distinctly separate levels of the Northeastern organization. His liaison role in the establishment of useful Northeastern-Sadler relationships brought him into regular contact with the top echelon of Northeastern management. As a key member of the developing Sadler management group, and as Northeastern's sole operating representative, Mr. Kraft worked closely with Mr. Feinman and Mr. Parnas in keeping the business running. It was not until late June that Mr. Kraft thought he understood what was expected of him at this level of the organization. Finally, his formally assigned job, stores

798

superintendent, brought him in constant contact with the first echelon of the management group, the store managers. The series of incidents and meetings described below, in which larger issues became apparent in the midst of endless, time-consuming details, reveals the development of these jobs and relationships. They made the spring an exhausting and often confusing one for Mr. Kraft.

WORKING WITH MR. FEINMAN

Mr. Kraft devoted most of his time during the month of May to learning about Sadler's, visiting the stores and becoming acquainted with their managers. He helped them become acquainted with each other, as in the June 5 store managers' meeting, the first ever held in Sadler's. He began work with Northeastern staff divisions to bring maintenance and security up to Northeastern standards. At the same time, he gradually got to know Mr. Feinman, Sadler's general manager.

A typical sequence of events involving this relationship took place on June 7. At 10 o'clock Mr. Kraft and the casewriter drove to the Northeastern Yankee Division offices in New Haven for Frank Perkins' weekly division meeting. The meeting dealt with experiments in trading traffic between neighboring Northeastern and Sadler's stores and the need for an advertising format which would be consistent with and strengthen the quality image of the Northeastern stores in the consumer's mind.

At lunch following the meeting, Mr. Feinman, Mr. Parnas, and Mr. Kraft discussed competitive problems the Sadler stores were facing with promotion of advertised items by other stores below cost. Mr. Feinman asked Mr. Kraft to help with the problems. When Kraft explained that he had other things to do, Mr. Feinman complained that he was "upset," and added:

Look Dan, I know that you have a lot to do, but some things come first. You've got to give more time to *sales*. I'm not knocking personnel or security; those things are important. But we've got to have *sales* and I wish that we could get some of your help in this area.

KRAFT: Sol, weren't you in on the discussion which determined my place in the organization? No? I really assumed that you were.

Later, the three returned to the division offices where they looked over plans for the new Stamford store. At the same time they discussed Mr. Kraft's plan to hire a new man to manage the West Haven store in order to replace Jack Carnot who (all three felt) was doing a poor job. Mr. Kraft was due back in Hartford for an afternoon meeting with Mr. Gorman but delayed his return 45 minutes in order to interview a candidate for the West Haven position. As a result he returned to Hartford too late to catch Mr. Gorman. Later that evening, on the way back to New York, Kraft's driving reflected his exasperation with the way "events" interfered with his work of organization building. He would become familiar with this problem as time passed.

A DAY IN THE HARTFORD STORE

Mr. Kraft planned to concentrate his efforts of Thursday, Friday, and Monday, June 8, 9, and 12 on organization and planning in such "tool" areas as personnel and security, but was interrupted numerous times by small crises in the stores and by the problems in merchandising in the three departments for which he was responsible. The events of Tuesday, June 13, for example, forced Mr. Kraft to devote his entire day to such problems.

The week of June 12 was the time of Sadler's 6th Anniversary Sale. One million copies of a 24-page "circular" had been mailed to the population surrounding the Sadler's stores. It contained a number of "bargains" which were used to highlight values available "throughout the store." Experience had shown that this kind of direct mail advertising substantially increased sales. Mr. Feinman had little confidence in the Hartford store manager's ability to exploit the expected increase in traffic, and a visit to the store on Monday had confirmed his suspicions.

Tuesday morning, Mr. Kraft was working in his office checking the progress which James Little (Northeastern New York office personnel staff) was making in organizing Sadler's personnel procedures. At 9:30 he received a call from Mr. Feinman telling him to "Drop everything, and get out to the Hartford store."

Mr. Kraft went immediately to the Hartford store, said hello briefly to Jones, the manager, and then went methodically through the store with a copy of the circular in his hand. At each department he asked the department manager if he "could have five minutes" and would the department manager "show him where the circular items were." Mr. Kraft looked in each case to see whether the merchandise in question had been signed properly, whether there was a specific "as advertised" sign on it, and then gave general merchandising tips. He said to the women's department manager, for example, "Nylons should be arranged by sizes in clear plastic boxes. Why don't you get some from the hardware department? You can borrow them. It makes it easier for the customer to buy and when it is easier, she buys more."

At each department he asked what was moving from the circular, what was not, what was in stock, and why something was not in stock. He checked the floor, the back rooms, and the stock rooms for cleanliness. He looked for price tags and register tapes on the floor (a security hazard) and counted 56 carriages in use for storing or displaying stock.

After a check of the entire store he returned to the front and asked Jones if he would have lunch. For privacy he suggested Jones' cash office. While eating, Mr. Kraft began reviewing his observations. He covered general store appearance, service, security, and the carriage problem. Only "50% of your carriages are available for use," he said at one point. "Now how can we lick this? What are *you* going to do about it?" Mr. Kraft recounted to Jones the details of his store tour.

Mr. Kraft then discussed the results of the circular with Jones, item by item. He noted that some department managers had allowed themselves to run out of stock on advertised items by the second day of the seven-day circular week and urged Mr. Jones to follow up on their promises to get more merchandise.

Immediately after lunch Mr. Kraft returned to his office to begin again on the accumulated work awaiting him there. Within an hour, however, Mr. Feinman called. Kraft summarized his morning's activities for Feinman. The latter was not satisfied with Kraft's reliance on the store manager to resolve the problems Kraft had observed and asked Kraft to return to the Hartford store at once.

A half-hour later, Mr. Kraft was back in the store. He began immediately to look for trouble spots in the store's appearance and operation. For example, when he reached the hardware department he found what he considered an entirely unsatisfactory situation. He said to the hardware department manager:

> You are not merchandising. You are not doing the job that has to be done to sell. Why are you out of stock on this? . . . This is advertised and is good value; why hide it? Where is the sign? . . . What the hell does DWW mean? You have got to make the advertising dollars produce what *you* paid for it. It is your money [lessee pays for the advertisement of his items] not mine. . . . We can't be your eyes. This aisle looks like an outhouse.

The department manager admitted the charge. Mr. Kraft continued to point out other faults—bad signs, out-of-season seasonal items; e.g., storm windows and a radiator. "Bird seed doesn't sell. Why give it three feet? Why only two and one-half feet available in a five-foot aisle? . . . Get this crap off the floor. . . . I don't know what to tell you. Can I help you? Can I call your boss to get you some support?" Obviously upset, the department manager explained that he knew he was in the wrong but that he was getting no support or money from his boss. Mr. Kraft left without further comment.

The shoe department was found still to have carriages holding stock. In one of the stockrooms Kraft took a little rubbish out of a large cardboard box and then emptied the contents of one of the carriages into it. He then took the carriage and pushed it out on the floor.

Walking through the store, he spoke of the hardware department manager's problems. "How much can you do with a guy who is working 77 hours a week and then Sunday? How mad can you get?" Later in the day, Kraft made a truce with the department manager. He in no way accepted the situation, but made it clear that he understood that the department manager had not been operating under ideal conditions. The department manager promised to have the department shipshape by the next day.

A NORTHEASTERN-SADLER'S MANAGEMENT MEETING

Apparently Kraft's rather sensational visit brought results, for by the next week he was able to move beyond the immediate problems at the Hartford store and concentrate on some personnel and advertising matters crucial to the Northeastern and Sadler's organizations. On Wed.

June 14, Mr. Kraft began the day with a nine o'clock visit to the Hartford store. A quick check showed that the hardware department was now clean and orderly. The principal purpose of Mr. Kraft's visit, however, was to introduce Mr. Edward Roth to the store manager. Roth was to assist in managing the store before taking on the job of field supervisor for Sadler's. At ten o'clock Mr. Kraft returned to the Hartford office with Roth for a "meeting with Sol, Art, and two of the Northeastern vice presidents to discuss advertising policy." At this meeting a pattern of relationships between the Northeastern and Sadler's managements evolved.

The meeting was held in the conference room off the main office area. Sadler's advertisements of recent years were tacked up on the walls, along with those of major competitors and department stores. John Gorman (Northeastern vice president, mergers and acquisitions), Richard Goldman (Northeastern vice president, sales), John Shalleck (director of the advertising agency used by Northeastern), and Messrs. Feinman, Kraft, Parnas, and Roth attended the meeting.

Following the introduction of John Shalleck, the meeting began with a discussion of the store image which Sadler's advertising created in the consumer's mind. It was finally decided that Sadler's weekly newspaper advertising should emphasize the image of *value* so that Sadler's would gradually become synonymous with value in the customer's mind. One or two items would be highlighted per ad in order to focus attention on a specific department.

In a typical exchange, Dick Goldman responded to a remark of Mr. Feinman by saying:

But you are talking about merchandising, not advertising policy.
FEINMAN: Aren't they intertwined?
GORMAN: The purpose of this meeting today is to hammer out concepts. You have got to do this before you can get to the details of the coordination of store merchandising.
ROTH: You have a reliable store, you can back your goods.
GORMAN: You have a convenient, beautiful store.
GOLDMAN: These are themes which make up *you*. Use them and repeat them.
Later Feinman said:
Let's summarize. We've decided that we need more planning and an institutional approach.
GORMAN: Sol, that's not strong enough. If I were Art Parnas I wouldn't know what to do. You should say, "This is the format; this is what we are going to do."
KRAFT: But you've got to tie the merchandising into the ad, you have to be in stock.
GORMAN: Absolutely, otherwise it's unethical. We decided at management meetings on Saturday and Monday that we are going to adopt the following policy: We are going to be a true discount department store built upon the principles of fair merchandising. We're going to strive to have values in each concessionaire's department comparable to the rest of the store.

*   *   *   *   *

GOLDMAN: In the future, your key man will have to be a well-paid and well-motivated manager.

ROTH: You have to feed the manager information.

* * * * *

GORMAN: We cannot have a man who will try to operate with the goal of pleasing Sol Feinman. He's got to have his own ideas and fight for them, that's the sort of man we need in this organization.

* * * * *

GOLDMAN: You have to consider the long run versus the short run. What is good? How good are results? The average sale is good and this means that we need more business in every store. Where do the customers come from? And how are we going to get more?

Sandwiches and coke were served; the discussion continued and may be summarized as follows:

The women's departments in our stores are as good as any in the country. If we get the customer coming to Sadler's for her regular type of staple item which is bought frequently, we can marry the customer right there. We might then investigate the layout of the stores. Then we can consider the proper place of gimmicks. The very carnival atmosphere which is so good for promotion may contradict the image of value.

FEINMAN: Gimmicks work and build traffic.

GOLDMAN: The gimmick *idea* is right and OK, but you have to be careful how you do it.

SHALLECK: You want as an objective to build your customer count. To do this, you ought to get a little sophisticated and break down your market, then aim your advertising at segments of the market. For example, you can put a little thing in an ad that really gets the teenage girl going, that says the store is for her.

FEINMAN: We can do this, but these clever little things that you're talking about, we just don't know how to do. Can we get an agent?

GORMAN: It's our philosophy at Northeastern that you own the mechanic but that you hire the special talent.

During the next few minutes Gorman, Goldman, and Kraft discussed what steps would have to be taken in order to establish a sales plan. A general discussion of organization followed, with considerable attention being given to the problems of the store managers.

GORMAN: Part of the problem here is that we would not give anybody a straight answer until last week because we didn't know until last week what policy would be. We really didn't know what the nature of the animal we bought was and what sort of thing we wanted from it. Now that a policy has been set we can get going on how to build. At times during this building process, Dan is going to have to do more than his assigned task.

FEINMAN: I've been trying to say this. Sometimes Dan is going to have to be more than store superintendent.

GOLDMAN: Yes, but Dan will be the only man who answers questions about the stores.

FEINMAN: You know, I will have to learn how to run this way and so will Art Parnas. I am not used to this.

* * * * *

At 4:30 P.M., Dick Goldman and John Shalleck left the meeting for New York. A Sadler's staff meeting was held, and Ron Arnold joined the discussion of a variety of problem areas. As conversation proceeded, Mr. Gorman drew on his pad a chart as shown below of the organization which had been planned during discussions with the Northeastern management group the previous Saturday and Monday.

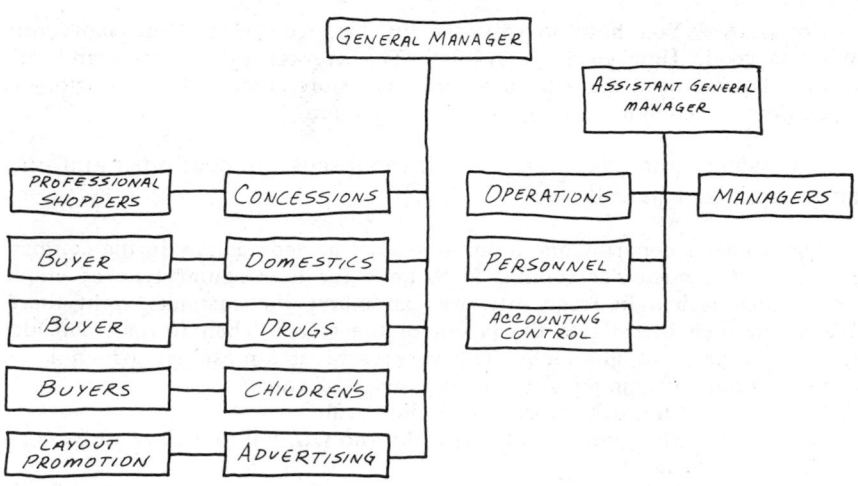

GORMAN: Let me give you my ideas on organization and the thoughts of those who were at the meeting Monday. Since the store manager is going to be God Almighty in his store, a supervisor may remind and suggest but not give him orders. Art's total responsibility, therefore, will be coordination at the store level of all concessionaires' operations. He will be doing merchandising, not worrying about cleanliness and so on. The store operating superintendent, Kraft, is going to take care of all the operating details. Then the advertising manager will handle that area.

Mr. Gorman then laid out on the table the organization chart which he had prepared.

This is the organization as it was set up Monday. (1) There will be a very competent general manager in this organization. We have one but he needs a backer-upper. You know how we believe in backing up at Northeastern. We believe that you can't depend upon just one man. An assistant manager must be available to relieve Sol of the operating detail. That will leave him free for the area in which he is superb, merchandising. Immediately we are going to get a drug man and then once there is an advertising man, Art will move in and handle the concessionaires. We don't even know whether the assistant general manager exists or not. He may simply be a combination of Art and Dan. . . .

You see, we're not sure that "operations" here at Sadler's are the same thing we think of at Northeastern.

FEINMAN: Maybe operations means more than at Northeastern and it seems to me, Dan, that this is what John is trying to tell you.

GORMAN: Operations in a discount department store such as Sadler's may mean more than the purely technical detail of "operations." In particular it requires a flare for sales and a willingness to shape activities so that they are directed toward producing sales through proper use of operations techniques.

KRAFT: Yes, this is what I've been trying to do all along. I've been trying to tell you this.

FEINMAN: Dan, I know you've been trying to help me and I make a lot of noise now and then, but I hope you can ignore it.

KRAFT: *You know,* John, I love sales, this is what I love to do.

GORMAN: Sure, Dan. The operations man with the store managers has to have a sales flare to keep Art's suggestions going and to implement Sol's ideas.

We can take off as soon as the advertising man gets here. All we agreed to do at the meeting was to put down something on paper which we hoped was right. Maybe we will change. Certainly Northeastern is a flexible organization.

The discussion which followed was at first confined to the company's future organizational structure. Later, it broadened to include other aspects of planning for the future. Mr. Kraft noted that a promotional plan for the Fourth of July had yet to be developed, and the focus of the meeting narrowed to take up this more immediate question.

The discussion was lengthy turning on the policy problems of whether to open the stores on holidays. Northeastern stayed closed as a matter of policy, but Sadler's competitor was open for business. Eventually the problem was resolved when Feinman and Kraft estimated that with a volume of $15,000 per store for the day, labor, overhead and advertising would eat up the gross margin.

Instead of staying open for July 4, the group planned a "Salathon" for July 3, and a pre-July 4 sale to begin Thursday, June 29. The meeting continued until 7:15 when the entire group went out to dinner at one of the best restaurants in Hartford. Dinner was excellent and the conversation lively shop talk. At 8:30 the group returned to the office. During a discussion primarily concerned with control area problems, Mr. Gorman distributed a "cleaner" copy of the organization chart he had prepared (see Exhibit 1).

MORE WORK WITH THE STORE MANAGERS

In response to the urgings of Mr. Feinman and Mr. Gorman, evident above, Mr. Kraft began to spend more of his time in the Sadler's stores, helping with merchandising aspects of store operations. At the same time he tried not to let his work at building the Sadler's organization fall behind. A second New Haven meeting illustrated the development of Northeastern's program for decentralized store management and reflected the shifts in relations between Northeastern and Sadler's, and Mr. Feinman and Mr. Kraft.

On Wednesday, June 21, Mr. Kraft drove directly from New York to the Yankee Division Office in order to attend another of Frank Perkins' weekly management meetings. Sadler's was also represented by Mr. Parnas, its acting advertising director. After a review of divisional sales

Exhibit 1

NORTHEASTERN FOOD COMPANY (B)

Tentative Organization for Sadler's
(neat draft)

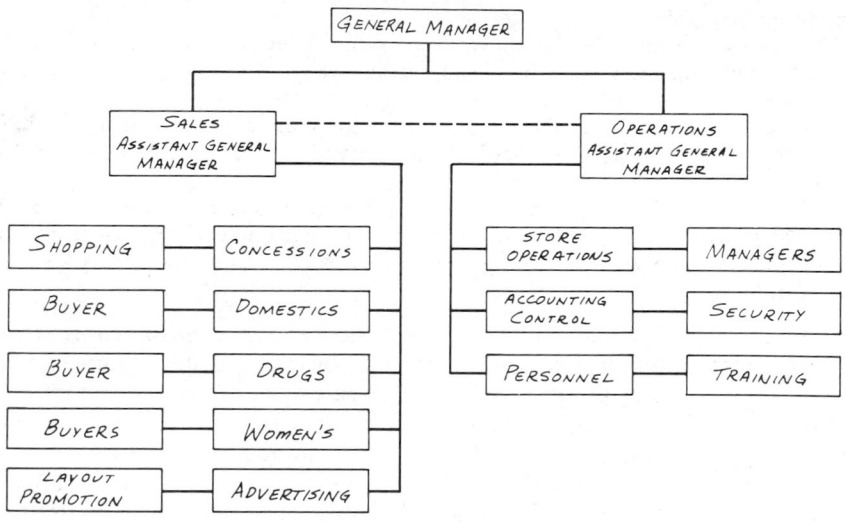

and gross profits, the discussion turned to advertising. Sadler's had marked sales increases following distribution of its anniversary circular but Northeastern did not, even though its stores were adjacent to Sadler's (in the Waterbury area, for example, sales were +$40,000 for Sadler's and −$1,300 for Northeastern relative to expectation). An experiment in traffic tracking was planned. Later, a Northeastern store manager from Greenwich described his use of a form letter to develop traffic among the "rich shore people."

Following the meeting, Mr. Parnas wondered at the responsibilities expected of a store manager. He seemed impressed when Mr. Kraft told him that, in the future, the Sadler's store managers would have to do things like write a personal form letter and be responsible for a plan which included rent, overhead, and labor. Parnas commented, "I'm still just a little amazed."

KRAFT: I think Frank Perkins put his finger on it when he said that Sears Roebuck has the right idea. They pay a man a $20,000 salary and then make him one billion per cent responsible for everything under him.

PARNAS: But he has to be a master of detail in order to run a store properly.

KRAFT: No, he has to *control* the details.

Shortly thereafter Mr. Feinman arrived. After lunch Feinman, Parnas and Kraft hammered out a solution to the various problems raised by the rearrangement of the fixtures in the West Haven store. Mr. Feinman dominated the 1½ hours of heated argument, working on 3 copies of the floor plan and making some changes on each.

As Kraft and the casewriter drove to the West Haven Sadler's store following this incident, Kraft exploded:

This is just typical of the way Feinman operates. As far as I am concerned I will be surprised if this plan isn't changed another 10 times before we get the store reset. Feinman insists on operating by making decisions on the spur of the moment. He is always running off on a hundred things. I have been trained to operate in an organized and deliberate manner and Feinman's approach is driving me frantic. In the areas which I control I'll be damned if I'm going to let Feinman get his fingers in, since by myself I am able to get things done in an organized and rational way and am coming along nicely.

THE SECOND STORE MANAGER'S MEETING

Mr. Kraft had a chance to run things his way five days later. Monday, June 26, was the occasion of the second store managers' meeting. Present at the meeting were Kraft, James Little and Ned Hammond (both of Northeastern New York personnel department), George Richardson (Yankee division personnel department), Fritz Hansmann (Sadler's women's clothes buyer), nine Sadler's store managers and Joe Rooney, Harry Hofstein, manager of the Torrington store and Mr. Feinman were absent.

A wide range of problems was presented to Mr. Kraft in the morning session, with lessee relations the recurring theme. Statements of difficulties between the store managers and the managers of leased departments ranged from the general (Hammond called the relationship a "long-range fundamental problem") to the specific (Roth cited such lessee complaints as "They didn't like the pickles we put up by the registers in the store."). Again in a later discussion of promotion details, talk tended to focus on the lessees. Mr. Kraft complained about the lack of stock in staple lines: "Whenever I'm in the store, they always tell me, 'it's coming in.' They never say 'we've goofed' or 'we're out of stock.' I get no answer and with all due respect to Mr. Feinman he often gets no answer from the lessees." In this, as in the other situations mentioned during the morning, the crux of the problem was felt to be that "the department manager is the man in the middle."

After lunch Mr. Kraft announced that he would work with Jerry Tipper to "create a short checklist of common problems which came up with lessees. We will try and work these out." He then moved the meeting on to consider the question of "customer consciousness." Stein, of the Norwich store, stressed the need for working through the employees to make sure the "employees treat the customer the way they would like to be treated." He emphasized the necessity for "repetition" in driving home this "golden rule" policy, while Kraft suggested a more personal approach to the employees: "You can comment about a girl's hairdo over the mike. It will make her blush like hell, but she will love you for it." Kraft concluded that "the store manager sets the tone."

The managers also had requests concerning their own working conditions. Most were now working 60 hours a week (at least 9 hours a day with several 13½ hour days in a 6 day week). They proposed a schedule that would allow them one day off, three nights a week off, and a late morning after a late night. Mr. Kraft agreed that their requests were reasonable but warned that "since we are crazy enough to go into retailing, you realize that what we are working on isn't going to go for the period Thanksgiving to Christmas."

Mr. Kraft noted that even with shorter hours and a good assistant manager, the store was the manager's responsibility. He closed by stating,

> Look, I am staking my and my family's future on Sadler's and Northeastern's Sadler's division. In the future we are going to be the best discount house in the business. So I think you are betting your time and your effort on a good thing. I have one job here, to build up the store manager until he runs that store. If you give me the cooperation you have been giving, I am sure we will finish my job soon.

NORTHEASTERN-SADLER'S RELATIONS

On Tuesday and Wednesday, June 27 and 28, Mr. Kraft and Mr. Robert Fitz made a swing of the Sadler's stores and some of those of Sadler's competitors in order to evaluate merchandising aspects of the Sadler's operations. Kraft described the trip tersely by noting that "Mr. Fitz was not happy with what he saw." It seemed to the casewriter that as a result of Mr. Fitz's report to Northeastern top management, the morning of June 30 began with everyone touchy. In fact it was a normal work day in the Sadler's Hartford office. Mr. Gorman was up for the day and a merchandising consultant, Irving Reis, came in around 9:30. Mr. Kraft spent the first two hours of the morning working out solutions to a variety of operating problems in the stores. Mr. Gorman talked privately with Mr. Feinman about the latter's adjustment to the integration of Sadler's into Northeastern Foods. When Mr. Reis arrived, discussion shifted to technical matters related to inventory control and warehousing, two problems which were to take up most of the day.

At 11 o'clock, Kraft was called into Mr. Feinman's office to meet a Mr. Cantor. Mr. Feinman introduced Cantor as an old friend and neighbor and the "doughnut king" in New England. Kraft was informed that Feinman had arranged for Cantor to lease space in the new Stamford store for a doughnut stand. Outlining the terms of the arrangement, Mr. Feinman explained that he had found a space for the doughnut man on the floor. The discussion concerned details and Kraft closed by saying that he was delighted to have Mr. Cantor come in but that he, Mr. Cantor, would understand if Kraft checked with the Northeastern bakery organization to see if they thought his operation was acceptable. Mr. Cantor accepted this reservation to the agreement.

After Cantor left Mr. Feinman's office, Mr. Feinman explained to Mr. Kraft that he thought the introduction of the doughnut stand involved pushing the cash registers over to the left side of the store. Cantor was to get 28 x 14 feet and pay 10% rent on sales of $150 a week. Feinman estimated that it would cost $2,000 to put Cantor's fixture in, but that beyond that there would be no investment. Mr. Kraft noted that the doughnut stand would replace the registers in the natural exit point. The registers were now to be at the far side of the store. In addition, after Mr. Kraft and Feinman took a scale to the Stamford floor plan, it appeared that one register would be lost. Mr. Kraft questioned whether they could afford to lose one register on the grounds that if the store developed well there would be a substantial tie-up at peak traffic times.

Mr. Feinman explained that the discussion worked out in such a way that he had found himself in a bad bargaining position. He noted that an offer to let the doughnut man in to future stores and all existing ones might prove to be a strong enough inducement to make Cantor shift his position on the floor.

Mr. Kraft was clearly unhappy about the decision but chose not to dispute it. Rather, he argued that Northeastern surveys had found that one of the things which irked customers was to wait in line. Mr. Feinman responded that it seemed to him "instinctively that a customer in a discount house might feel a little different." She would want to feel that she was buying at a place where there was traffic, where everybody came for bargains.

Somewhat later, with John Gorman and Irving Reis in the office, conversation shifted to the question of Raymond Hoffman, the man being considered for the position of assistant general manager in charge of merchandising. Mr. Hoffman was expected in Hartford that morning for a final interview. Reis noted that:

He has a very fine reputation, a tremendous potential for growth, and, for his age, a marvelous merchandising background.

GORMAN: You know a problem we face is that before we hire him, we are going to have to spell out clearly his responsibilities and his future. It is one thing to ask one of our own people to come down to a rather undefined situation and quite another thing to *hire* a good man on this basis.

With Mr. Gorman leading, it was decided that the new man would be called "assistant to the general manager." He would be in control of the buyers and their operations and work as an assistant to Mr. Feinman.

GORMAN (to Feinman): You are the merchant, and he will be your assistant. This will push you upstairs away from the details which you dislike. You just have to recognize, Sol, that the details aren't your cup of tea. You set the policy and decide what you want and then it's up to him to see that it gets done. Is that all right with you?

FEINMAN: That's precisely what I want.

GORMAN: Then you have to be the same thing with this man here, [pointing to Kraft] who will be your operations assistant. You will tell him how you want those stores to look and he'll have to get it done. The same thing with Art and the concessionaires. You tell him what arrangements you have made, what the formal agreements are, and what promotions are coming, and it will be up to Art to get things done.

Now what I'd like to do is set up a framework of time within which I can come down here regularly and help clear out the pipeline. I have time freed up now and I'm going to schedule things so that I can get down here on a regular basis. If I can handle some of the detail and some of the leg work and just follow up on things, then it will free you so that you can start looking ahead and building.

Is there a place for me?

FEINMAN: Yes. I'll tell you what we can do. We have to be salesminded. Personnel is very important; so is security and maintenance and so on. But they are number two, and sales is number one. Let me give you an example. Dan, you were in the store the other day in West Haven. You saw some towels there which you thought were priced badly. You know much more about domestics than I ever will. You know what you should have done, you should have changed the price right then while you were in the store.

KRAFT: Before I left the store, I called Art and told him about the situation. Domestics is one of his assigned departments. He promised me that he would follow up on it but I know that he's been over his head with work.

FEINMAN: He doesn't have the *time*. When you see something wrong when you're in a store, whether it's my department or Art's, you have to handle it right there and then.

GORMAN: Dan, I don't agree with Sol in principle, or for the long-run, but in the short-run we can't be as straight laced about organization as we might like. We're going to have to cross lines. You'll have to let each other know about it, but until we get set up, when you see a fire, put it out whether or not it's in your bailiwick.

KRAFT: OK, this is perfectly fine with me. I'd like to make one request though, that you relieve me of all my specific duties involving the co-ordination of advertising in my assigned departments and I'll take as my responsibility trouble shooting in all departments.

FEINMAN [laughing]: I can't relieve you of that responsibility. Who else will do it? I don't have the time. What I'm trying to do is give you this job in addition to what you're doing.

GORMAN: What we're saying, Dan, is this. You came out of a very highly and well-structured organization. If you had crossed lines back there, you'd have gotten spanked unless you had a very constructive contribution to make. In this organization you're going to have to be a Jack-of-all-trades, at least for a while. Maybe in a few months you can firm up lines, after we get the new men with their feet on the ground. I know that you people have too many things to do, but all we can do at this point is give you more. You people have to have some time to get the bees out of your bonnet, but that's going to have to wait for a while.

Soon after this discussion Messrs. Feinman and Gorman left the room to interview Raymond Hoffman. Mr. Kraft spent the rest of the morning (1) discussing the sales presentation made the previous day by the Sweda representatives (cash registers which would produce more data for inventory and merchandising control) with Irving Reis; (2) talking with several of his store managers on the phone about their problems; (3) interviewing an applicant for a job; and (4) planning sales for the next quarter.

At about 1:30, Dan Kraft and Ron Arnold stopped their work for a few minutes to chat. It appeared that Kraft was very depressed. He said, "As far as I am concerned this was a *terrible* week; everybody is jumping on me, and I'll be glad when it's all over." Telling Arnold of his experience in Mr. Feinman's office, he said, "You know, I've been working at 190% of my capacity. Well, if they want me to work 200%, I guess I'll have to."

At 2:00 P.M., Messrs. Gorman, Feinman, Kraft and Arnold had a meeting in Mr. Feinman's office. Areas covered were payroll control; problems with some of the Northeastern divisions which were as Mr. Gorman put it, "holding themselves back as if you fellows have the plague instead of pitching in and helping wherever they can"; lessee cooperation on circulars; other methods of promotion, particularly reciprocal couponing; the possibility of a central warehouse and Dan Kraft's warehouse expense report; and finally the presentation of Kraft's sales forecast for the quarter.

The casewriter sensed a very pleasant spirit at this meeting. Everybody was happy and working well together. The sales plan was revised in the best of spirits. Mr. Feinman tactfully explained his objections, and Mr. Gorman was able to enter the discussion only on those occasions when he felt that technical advice was needed. There was much joking and no friction. Mr. Kraft remarked to the casewriter that Mr. Feinman had eagerly awaited the institution of a sales plan. He thought that one reason for the success of the meeting was the fact that his and Mr. Feinman's goals had "finally" coincided.

After the meeting, and in private, Mr. Arnold noted:

> It was a great meeting. Everybody was relaxed. It just had to come. Everything has been gloomy for so long that this meeting was a godsend.
>
> The fact that Sol is going to go on vacation for three weeks on Monday and is looking forward to his first relaxation in well over a year probably helped. So does the fact that it's Friday. The sun came out today, I guess that was it. It can't rain all the time.

LESSEE RELATIONS

The turn in the weather, coinciding with Mr. Feinman's departure for a vacation in Europe, also marked a turn in the Sadler's organization. While the type of problems they faced had not changed, the Sadler's executives expressed the feeling that at least things had "settled down." Monday, July 3, was spent getting responsibility for specific matters shifted from Mr. Feinman to Mr. Kraft and making sure that Mr. Feinman and his family got off on their trip pleasantly. By the end of the day spirits were soaring as news from the stores indicated that the July 3 Salathon was going to be a smashing success. On top of very good pre-4th sale days—Thursday, Friday and Saturday—the average Sadler store did $40,000 on Monday, a 12-hour day, as opposed to the usual $6,000 day.

On Wednesday, July 5, Mr. Kraft spent the better part of his morning out planning for the formalization of personnel procedures with Jim Little. The rest of the day was consumed handling a mountain of memoranda and letters left for him by Mr. Feinman. He came across a group of problems which were to be prime trouble spots during the next weeks. They were all in the area of lessee relations. He previously had had contact with lessees through his store managers, but now, because of Mr. Feinman's absence, he had to handle several problems at top management level. The situation concerning shoes in West Haven was a typical example of the problems Sadler's was experiencing.

a) On June 28, when Kraft visited the West Haven store, he found the shoe department in an appalling state. The merchandise was dirty, worn, and consisted of unappealing styles. He gave the department manager a bad time and notified Mr. Feinman of the state of affairs.

b) Negotiations by Messrs. Shae, Norfield, and Stoddard with Mr. Hirsch, the owner of American Footware (the concessionaire in West Haven), resulted in an agreement which gave American the shoe concession in the new Stamford store and the right to prove themselves in all their present locations over the following 365 days. In return, Northeastern had a unilateral right to cancel all American's leases at the end of that time.

c) On Monday, July 10, Kraft received a call from a very upset Joe Rooney, complaining about the intolerable state of the shoe department in his store. Kraft called Mr. Hirsch and told him that the shoes were dirty, old, out of style, and a detriment to the store. He elicited from Mr. Hirsch a promise to get all the inferior goods out of the store by markdowns.

d) On July 14, Joe Rooney called Mr. Kraft at Hartford to say that American had fulfilled its promise and that he thanked Mr. Kraft for getting such prompt action. But, he noted that at the same time that the markdown goods went out of the store, in came an assortment that made the original merchandise look beautiful.

e) Kraft then called Hirsch. Hirsch at first protested that the situation could not exist but then admitted that he had closed one of his stores in the Midwest and was "scattering the merchandise around the country."

f) Kraft then noted to Parnas who had listened to the conversation on a second wire that "as the agreement stands, Hirsch has the occasion and the incentive to give Sadler's a real screwing which he can do as long as he does not break the lease. This can continue for 365 days."

g) Kraft called New York and described the situation to Mr. Gorman in a conversation including problems with the hardware and domestics concessionaire.

h) Within an hour, Kraft got a call from American Footware. Gorman had brought Harmon Stoddard into the picture and Stoddard had called Hirsch. The result was that the new goods which were inferior were going to be marked down that day and there would be no more dumping.

i) Kraft hung up the phone and in a slightly incredulous voice said, "Boy, when I call New York, I get results. I find it strange to be working regularly with vice presidents, but the problems I am facing are such that it seems to be the only effective way of getting them resolved." He then noted that he had been getting increasingly involved with the relationship of Northeastern to the concessionaires at the top management level, "not by my own design, but seemingly by accident, I guess that it is mostly because I am the only figure down here all the time who is a liaison with Northeastern."

The Adams Corporation (A)

IN JANUARY of 1972, the Board of Directors of The Adams Corporation simultaneously announced the highest sales in the company's history, the lowest dollar after-tax profits in a twenty-year period, the retirement (for personal reasons) of its long-tenure President and Chief Executive Officer.

Founded in St. Louis in 1848, the Adams Brothers Company had long been identified as a family firm both in name and operating philosophy. Writing in a business history journal, a former family senior manager comments, "My grandfather wanted to lead a business organization with ethical standards. He wanted to produce a quality product and a quality working climate for both employees and managers. He thought the Holy Bible and the concept of family stewardship provided him with all the guidelines needed to lead his company. A belief in the fundamental goodness of mankind, in the power of fair play and in the importance of personal and corporate integrity were his trademarks. Those traditions exist today in the nineteen sixties."

In the early 1950s, two significant corporate events occurred. First, the name of the firm was changed to The Adams Corporation. Secondly, somewhat over 50 percent of the corporation shares were sold by various family groups to the wider public. In 1971 all branches of the family owned or "influenced" less than one-fifth of the outstanding shares of Adams.

The Adams Corporation was widely known and respected as a manufacturer and distributor of quality, branded, consumer products for the American, Canadian and European (export) markets. Adams products were processed in four regional plants located near raw material sources,[1] were stored and distributed in a series of recently constructed or renovated distribution centers located in key cities throughout North

---

[1] No single plant processed the full line of Adams products, but each plant processed the main items in the line.

America and were sold by a company sales force to thousands of retail outlets—primarily supermarkets.

In explaining the original long-term financial success of the company a former officer commented, "Adams led the industry in the development of unique production processes that produced a quality product at a very low cost. The company has always been production-oriented and volume-oriented and it paid off for a long time. During those decades the Adams brand was all that was needed to sell our product; we didn't do anything but a little advertising. Competition was limited and our production efficiency and raw material sources enabled us to outspace the industry in sales and profit. Our strategy was to make a quality product, distribute it and sell it cheap."

"But that has all changed in the past 20 years," he continued. "Our three major competitors have outdistanced us in net profits and market aggressiveness. One of them—a first-class marketing group—has doubled sales and profits within the past five years. Our gross sales have increased to almost $350,000,000 but our net profits have dropped continuously during that same period. While a consumer action group just designated us as 'best value,' we have fallen behind in marketing techniques, e.g., our packaging is just out of date."

Structurally, Adams was organized into eight major divisions; seven of these were regional sales divisions with responsibility for distribution and sales of the company's consumer products to retail stores in their area. Each regional sales division was further divided into organizational units at the state and county and/or trading area level. Each sales division was governed by a corporate price list in the selling of company products but had some leeway to meet the local competitive price developments. Each sales division was also assigned (by the home office) a quota of salesmen it could hire and was given the salary ranges within which these men could be employed. All salesmen were on straight salary and expense reimbursement salary plan which tended to be under industry averages.

A small central accounting office accumulated sales and expense information for each of the several sales divisions on a quarterly basis, and prepared the overall company financial statements. Each sales division received, without commentary, a quarterly statement showing the number of cases processed and sold for the overall division, sales revenue per case of the overall division, and local expenses per case for the overall division.

Somewhat similar information was obtained from the manufacturing division. Manufacturing division accounting was complicated by variations in the cost of obtaining and processing the basic materials used in Adams' products. These variations—particularly in procurement—were largely beyond the control of that division. The accounting office did have, however, one rough external check on manufacturing division effectiveness. A crude market price for case lots goods to some large national chains did exist.

Once a quarter, the seven senior sales vice presidents met with general management in St. Louis. Typically, management discussion focused on divisional sales results and expense control. The company's objective of being number one the largest selling line in its field, directed group attention to sales vs. budget. All knew that last year's sales targets had to be exceeded—"no matter what." The manufacturing division vice president sat in on these meetings to explain the product availability situation. Because of his St. Louis office location, he frequently talked with Mr. Jerome Adams about overall manufacturing operations and specifically about large procurement decisions.

The Adams Company had a trade reputation for being very conservative with its compensation program. All officers were on a straight salary program. An officer might expect a modest salary increase every one or two years; these increases tended to be in the thousand-dollar range regardless of divisional performance or company profit position. Salaries among the six divisional vice presidents ranged from $32,000 to $42,000 with the higher amounts going to more senior officers. Mr. Jerome Adams' salary of $48,000 was the highest in the company. There was no corporate bonus plan. A very limited stock option program was in operation, but the depressed price of Adams stock meant that few officers exercised their options.

Of considerable pride to Mr. Jerome Adams had been the corporate climate at Adams. "We take care of our family" was his oft-repeated phrase at company banquets honoring long-service employees. "We are a team and it is a team spirit that has built Adams into its leading position in this industry." No member of first line, middle or senior management could be discharged (except in cases of moral crime or dishonesty) without a personal review of his case by Mr. Adams. As a matter of fact, executive turnover at Adams was very low. Executives at all levels viewed their jobs as a lifetime career. There was no compulsory retirement plan and some managers were still active in their mid-seventies.

The operational extension of this organizational philosophy was quite evident to employees and managers. A private family trust, for over 75 years, provided emergency assistance to all members of the Adams' organization. Adams led its industry in the granting of educational scholarships, in medical insurance for employees and managers, and in the encouragement of its "members" to give corporate and personal time and effort to community problems and organizations.

Mr. Adams noted two positive aspects of this organizational philosophy. "We have a high percentage of long-term employees—Joe Girly, a guard at East St. Louis, completes 55 years with us this year and every one of his brothers and sisters has worked here. And it is not uncommon for a vice president to retire with a blue pin—that means 40 years of service. We have led this industry in manufacturing process innovation, quality control and value for low price for decades. I am proud of our accomplishments and this pride is shown by everyone—from janitors to directors." Industry sources noted that there was no question that Adams was number one in terms of manufacturing and logistic efficiency.

In December of 1971, the annual Adams management conference

gathered over 80 of Adams' senior management in St. Louis. Most expected the usual formal routines—the announcement of 1971 results and 1972 budgets, the award of the Gold Flag to the top processing plant and sales division for exceeding targets and the award of service pins to executives. All expected the usual social good times. It was an opportunity to meet and drink with "old buddies."

After a series of task force meetings, the managers gathered in a banquet room—good naturedly referred to as the "Rib Room" since a local singer "Eve" was to provide entertainment. At the front of the room, in the usual fashion, was a dais with a long, elaborately decorated head table. Sitting at the center of that table was Mr. Jerome Adams. Following tradition, Mr. Adams' vice presidents, in order of seniority with the company, sat on his right. On his left, sat major family shareholders, corporate staff, and—a newcomer—soon to be introduced.

After awarding service pins and the "Gold Flags" of achievement, Mr. Adams announced formally what had been a corporate "secret" for several months. First, a new investing group had assumed a "control" position on the board of Adams. Secondly, that Mr. Price Millman would take over as President and Chief Executive Officer of Adams immediately.

Introducing Mr. Millman, Adams pointed out the outstanding record of the firm's new president. "Price got his MBA in 1959, spent four years in control and marketing and then was named as the youngest divisional president in the history of the Tenny Corporation. In the past years, he has made his division the most profitable in Tenny and the industry leader in its field. We are fortunate to have him with us. Please give him your complete support."

In a later informal meeting with the divisional vice presidents, Mr. Millman spoke about his respect for past Adams' accomplishments and the urgent need to infuse Adams with "fighting spirit" and "competitiveness." "My personal and organizational philosophy are the same—the name of the game is to fight and win. I almost drowned, but I won my first swimming race at eleven years of age. That philosophy of always winning is what enabled me to build the Ajax Division into Tenny's most profitable operation. We are going to do this at Adams. I want to show progress by the June 30th Directors' meeting."

"The new owner group wants fast results. They have suggested I develop a new format for Adams' operations. They want an organizational plan that will shake this company up. Once we get that new format, gentlemen, I have but one goal—each month must be better than the last. I didn't give up a good job at Tenny to lose at Adams."

Exhibit 1

THE ADAMS CORPORATION (A)

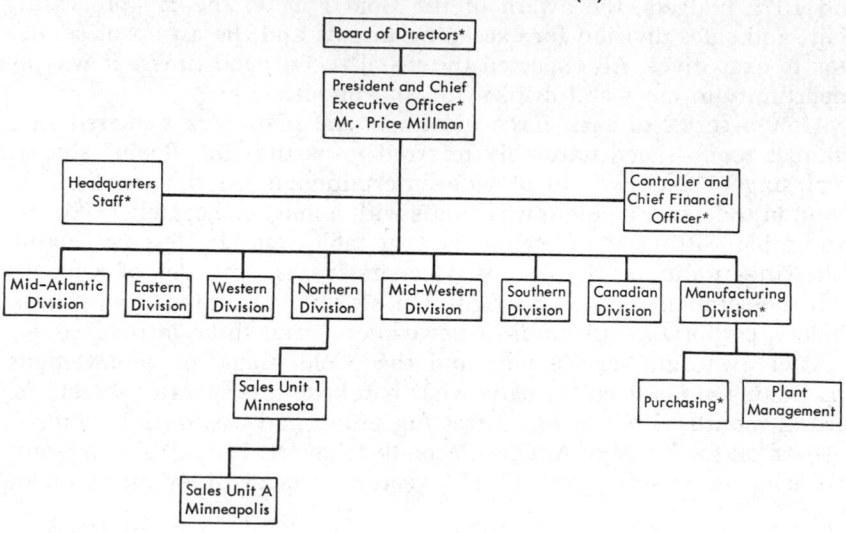

* Located in St. Louis.

Basic Industries

IN MAY 1966, Pete Adams, plant manager of Basic Industries' Chicago plant, was worried about the new facilities proposal for toranium. His division, metal products, was asking for $1 million to build facilities which would be at full capacity in less than a year and a half (if forecasted sales were realized). Yet the divisional vice president for production seemed more interested in where the new facility was to go than in how big it should be. Adams wondered how, as plant manager, his salary and performance review would look in 1968 with the new facility short of capacity.

BASIC INDUSTRIES, METAL PRODUCTS DIVISION

Basic Industries engaged in a number of activities ranging from shipbuilding to the manufacture of electronic components. The corporation was organized into five autonomous divisions (see Exhibit 1). In 1965 these divisions had sales totaling $500 million. Of the five, the metal products division was the most profitable. In 1965, this division realized an after-tax income of $16 million on sales of $110 million and an investment of $63.7 million.

This position of profit leadership within the company had not always been held by metal products. In fact, in the early 1950s, Basic's top management had considered dropping the division. At that time, the division's market share was declining owing to a lack of manufacturing facilities, high costs, and depressed prices.

A change in divisional management resulted in a marked improvement. Between 1960 and 1965, for example, the division's sales grew at 8% a year and profits at 20% a year. The division's ROI during this period rose from 12% in 1960 to 25% in 1965.

Ronald Brewer, president of metal products division since 1955, explained how this growth had been achieved:

Exhibit 1

ORGANIZATION CHART FOR BASIC INDUSTRIES

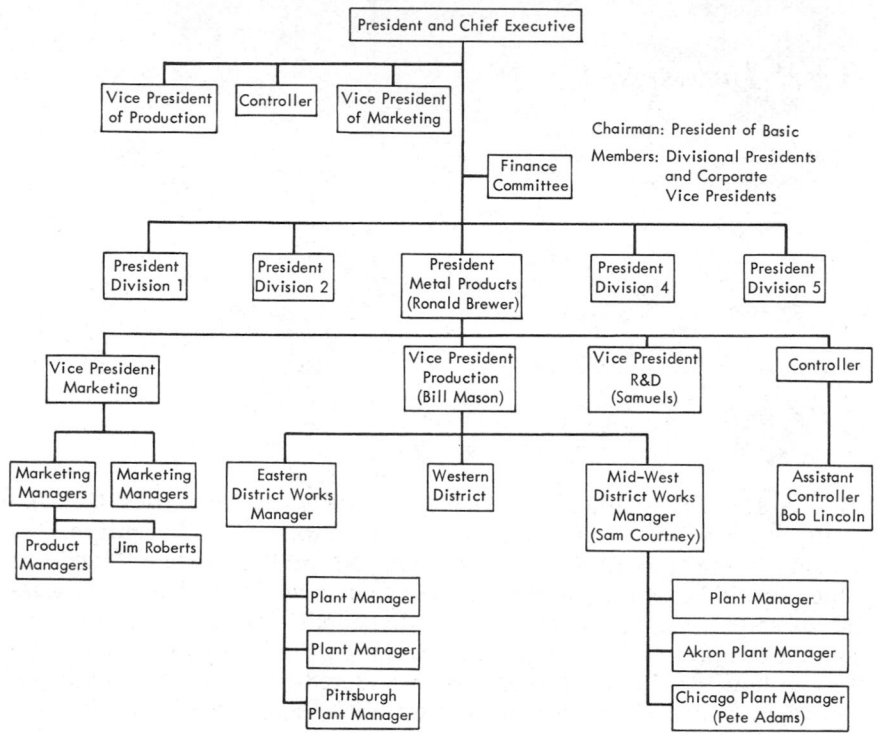

Source: Casewriter's notes.

Planning goes on in many places in the Metal Products Division, but we do go through a formal planning process to establish goals. We establish very specific goals for products and departments in every phase of the business. This formal and detailed planning is worked out on a yearly basis. We start at the end of the second quarter to begin to plan for the following year.

We plan on the basis of our expectations as to the market. If it's not there, we live a little harder. We cut back to assure ourselves of a good cash flow. Our record has been good, but it might not always be. Some of our products are 30 years old. We've just invested $5 million, which is a lot of money for our division, in expanding capacity for a 25-year-old product. But we're making money out of it and it's growing.

Along with detailed planning for the year to come, we ask for plans for years three and four. Our goal is to make sure that we can satisfy demand. Any time we approach 85% of capacity at one of our plants, our engineers get busy.

They will give the plant manager the information as to what he needs in the way of new equipment. The plant manager will then fit the engineer's recommendation into his expansion plans. The plant manager's plan then goes to our control manager. The marketing people then add their forecasts, and by that time we have built up the new facilities proposal. On the other hand, the marketing people may have spearheaded the project. Sometimes they alert the plant manager to a rapid growth in his product and he goes to the engineers. In this division, everyone is marketing minded.

* * * * *

We measure plants, and they measure their departments against plan. For example, we have a rule of thumb that a plant must meet its cost reduction goals. So if one idea doesn't work out, a plant must find another one to get costs to the planned level. We make damned sure that we make our goals as a division. Our objective is to have the best product in the market at the lowest cost. It's a simple concept, but the simpler the concept, the better it's understood.

Well, on the basis of his performance against plan, a man is looked at by his superior at least once a year, maybe more. We take a pretty hardnosed position with a guy. We tell him what we think his potential is, where he is going to go, what he is going to be able to do. We have run guys up *and* down the ladder. In this division, it's performance and fact that count. We have no formal incentive plan but we do recognize performance with salary increases and with promotions.

You know, we have divisions in this company which are volume happy. We here are profit conscious. We had to be to survive. What I'd like to see is interest allocated on a pro rata basis according to total investment. I grant you that this would hurt some of the other divisions more than us, but I think that treating interest as a corporate expense, as we do, changes your marketing philosophy and your pricing philosophy.

For example, most new facilities proposals are wrong with respect to their estimates of market size—volume attainable at a given price—and timing. You can second-guess a forecast though, in several ways, and hedge to protect yourself. There is a feeling at Basic Industries that there is a stigma attached to coming back for more money. That means that if you propose a project at the bare minimum requirement and then come back for more, some people feel that you've done something wrong. Generally, this leads to an overestimate of the amount of capital required. It turns out that if you have the money you do spend it, so that this stigma leads to overspending on capital projects. We at metal products are trying to correct this. First, we screen projects closely. We go over them with a fine tooth comb. Second, internally, we set a goal to spend less than we ask for where there is a contingency.

Also, when a project comes in at an estimated 50% return, we cut the estimate down. Everyone does. The figure might go out at 30%. But this practice works the other way too. For example, in 1958 Bill Mason [metal products' vice president of production] and I worked like hell to get a project through. Although it looked like 8% on paper, we knew that we could get the costs way down once it got going, so we put it through at 12%. We're making double that on it today. We haven't had a capital request rejected by the finance committee [see Exhibit 1] in 8 years.

Of course, every once in a while we shoot some craps, but not too often. We are committed to a specific growth rate in net income and ROI. Therefore, we are selective in what we do and how we spend our money. It's seldom that we spend $500,000 to develop something until we know it's got real market potential. You just don't send 100 samples out and then forecast a flood of orders. New products grow slowly. It takes six or seven years. And given that it takes this long, it doesn't take a lot of capital to develop and test our new ideas. Before you really invest, you've done your homework. Over the years we've done a good job in our new products, getting away from the aircraft industry. In 1945, 70% of our business was based on aircraft. Today it's 40%. The way we do things protects us. We have to have a very strong sense of the technical idea and the scope of the market before we invest heavily.

The metal products division's main business was producing a variety of basic and rare nonferrous metals and alloys such as nickel, nickel-beryllium, and titanium in a myriad of sizes and shapes for electrical, mechanical, and structural uses in industry. One of the division's major strengths was its leadership in high-performance material technology. Through patents and a great deal of proprietary experience, metal products had a substantial technological lead on its competitors.

TORANIUM

In the late 1950s metal products decided to follow its technological knowledge and proprietary production skills into the high-performance materials market. One of metal products' most promising new materials was toranium, for which Jim Roberts was product manager (see Exhibit 1).

Roberts was 33 years old and had a Ph.D. in chemical engineering. Prior to becoming a product manager, he had worked in one of metal products' research laboratories. Roberts explained some of toranium's history:

> Developing toranium was a trial-and-error process. The lab knew that the properties of the class of high performance materials to which toranium belonged were unusually flexible, and, therefore, felt such materials had to be useful. So it was an act of faith that led R.&D. to experiment with different combinations of these materials. They had no particular application in mind.
>
> In 1957 we developed the first usable toranium. Our next problem was finding applications for it. It cost $50 a pound. However, since a chemist in the lab thought we could make it for less, we began to look for applications.
>
> In 1962, I entered the picture.
>
> I discovered it was an aerospace business. When the characteristics of our material were announced to the aerospace people, they committed themselves to it. Our competitors were asleep. They weren't going to the customer. I went out and called on the customers and developed sales.
>
> In 1963, we decided to shift the pilot plant from the lab and give it to the production people at Akron. We decided that we simply were not getting a good production-oriented consideration of the process problems. The people at Akron cut the costs by two-thirds and the price stayed the same.
>
> In 1963, I also chose to shut off R.&D. on toranium because it

couldn't help in the market place. We had to learn more in the market place before we could use and direct R.&D.

I ought to mention that under the management system used by Mr. Samuels [vice president of R.&D.], the product manager, along with R.&D. and production, shares in the responsibility for monitoring and directing an R.&D. program. This arrangement is part of an attempt to keep everyone market-oriented.

From 1962 to 1965, sales of toranium increased from $250,000 a year to $1 million a year just by seeking them, and in 1965 we put R.&D. back in.

This material can't miss. It has a great combination of properties: excellent machinability, thermal shock resistance and heat insulation. Moreover, it is an excellent electrical conductor.

We can sell all that we can produce. Customers are coming to us with their needs. They have found that toranium's properties and our technical capabilities are superior to anything or anyone in the market.

Moreover, pricing has not been a factor in the development of markets to date. In fact, sales have been generated by the introduction of improved grades of toranium at premium prices. Presently, General Electric represents our only competition, but we expect that Union Carbide will be in the market place with competitive materials during the next few years. However, I don't expect anyone to be significantly competitive before 1968. Anyway, competition might actually help a little bit in expanding the market and stimulating the customers as well as in educating our own R.&D.

Now, if one assumes that no other corporation will offer significant competition to toranium until 1968, the only real uncertainty in our forecasts for toranium is related to metal products' technical and marketing abilities. R.&D. must develop the applications it is currently working on, and production will have to make them efficiently.

This production area can be a real headache. For example, R.&D. developed a toranium part for one of our fighter bombers. However, two out of three castings cracked. On the other hand, we've got the best skills in the industry with respect to high pressure casting. If we can't do it, no one can.

The final uncertainty is new demand. I've got to bring in new applications, but that shouldn't be a problem. You know, I've placed toranium samples with over 17 major customers. Can you imagine what will happen if even two or three of them pay off? As far as I'm concerned, if the forecasts for toranium are inaccurate, they're underestimates of future sales.

NEW FACILITIES PROPOSAL

Sam Courtney, district works manager (to whom the plant managers of the Chicago, Akron, and Indianapolis plants reported) explained the origin of the new toranium facilities proposal:

The product manager makes a forecast once a year, and when it comes time to make major decisions, he makes long-range forecasts. In January 1965, we were at 35% of the toranium pilot-plant capacity. At that time we said, "We have to know beyond 1966, we need a long-range forecast. Volume is beginning to move up."

The production control manager usually collects the forecasts.

> Each year it is his responsibility to see where we are approaching 85% or 90% of capacity. When that is the case in some product line, he warns the production vice president. However, in this instance, toranium was a transition product and Akron (where the pilot plant was located) picked up the problem and told the manager of product forecasting that we were in trouble.

The long-range forecast that Courtney requested arrived at his office about March 1, 1965, and clearly indicated a need for new capacity. Moreover, Roberts' 1966 regular forecast, which was sent to production in October 1965, was 28% higher than the March long-range projection. It called for additional capacity by October 1966.

Courtney's first response was to request a new long-range forecast. He also authorized the Akron plant to order certain equipment on which there would be a long lead time. The district works manager explained, "It is obvious we are going to need additional capacity in a hurry, and the unique properties of toranium require special, made-to-order, equipment. We can't afford to lose sales. Producing toranium is like coining money."

At the same time, Courtney began discussions on the problem with Bill Mason, vice president of production for metal products. They decided that the Akron plant was probably the wrong location in which to expand the toranium business. Courtney commented, "There are 20 products being produced in Akron, and that plant cannot possibly give toranium the kind of attention it deserves. The business is a new one, and it needs to be cared for like a young child. They won't do that in a plant with many important large-volume products. We have decided over a period of years that Akron is too complex, and this seems like a good time to do something about it."

The two locations proposed as new sites for the toranium facilities were Pittsburgh and Chicago. Each was a one-product plant which "could use product diversification." While Pittsburgh seemed to be favored initially, Mason and Courtney were concerned that the toranium would be contaminated if it came in contact with the rather dirty products produced at Pittsburgh. Therefore, Courtney asked engineering to make studies of both locations.

The results of these initial studies were inconclusive. The Pittsburgh plant felt that the problem of contamination was not severe, and the economic differential between the locations was not substantial.

After the initial studies were completed, Roberts' new long-range forecast arrived. The following table compares this forecast with Roberts' previous long-range forecasts:

ACTUAL AND PROJECTED SALES
(dollars in millions)

Date of forecast	1965	1966	1967	1968	1969	1970	1971
March 1964.........	1.08	1.30	...	...	2.20	...	...
March 1965.........	1.17	1.40	1.60	...	...	2.80	...
March 1966.........	...	1.80	2.50	3.40	...	...	5.60
Actual.........	1.00	...	...	...	...	...	...

In response to this accelerating market situation, Courtney and Mason asked Adams (plant manager at Chicago) to make a "full-fledged study of the three locations" (Akron, Pittsburgh, and Chicago). At the same time, Mason told Brewer (president of metal products), "We're now about 90% certain that Chicago will be the choice. Associated with the newness of the material is a rapidly changing technology. . . . The metal products R.&D. center at Evanston is only ten minutes away. . . . Another important factor is Adams. Titanium honeycomb at Chicago was in real trouble. We couldn't even cover our direct costs. Adams turned it around by giving it careful attention. That's the kind of job toranium needs."

Peter Adams was 35 years old. He had worked for Basic since he graduated from college with a B.S. in engineering. After spending a year in the corporate college training program, Adams was assigned to the metal products division. There he worked as an assistant to the midwestern district manager for production. Before becoming Chicago plant manager in 1963, Adams had been the assistant manager at the same plant for two years.

In working through the financial data on the toranium project, Adams chose to compare the three sites with respect to internal rates of return. He made this comparison for the case where capacity was expanded to meet forecasted sales for 1967 ($2.5 million), the case where capacity was expanded to met forecasted sales for 1971 ($5.6 million) and the case where capacity was expanded from $2.5 to $5.6 million. The results of Adams' analysis are summarized in the following table:

		Chicago	Pittsburgh	Akron
			(dollars in thousands)	
1.	Incremental capital investment for capacity through 1967.....	$ 980	$1,092	$ 765
	Internal rate of return......	34%	37%	45%
2.	Incremental capital investment for capacity through 1971.....	$1,342	$1,412	$1,272
	Internal rate of return......	52%	54%	55%
3.	Incremental capital investment to raise capacity from $2.5 to $5.6 million................	$ 710	$ 735	$ 740
	Internal rate of return......	45%	47%	46%

While the economics favored Akron, Adams was aware that Mason favored Chicago. This feeling resulted from conversations with Courtney about the toranium project. Courtney pointed out the importance of quality, service to customers, liaison with R.&D., and production flexibility to a new product like toranium. Furthermore, Courtney expressed the view that Chicago looked good in these respects, despite its cost disadvantage. Courtney also suggested that a proposal which asked for enough capacity to meet 1967 forecasted demand would have the best prospects for divisional acceptance.

By the end of April 1966, Adams' work had progressed far enough to permit preparation of a draft of a new facilities proposal recommending a Chicago facility. Except for the marketing story which he obtained from Roberts, he had written the entire text. On May 3, Adams brought the completed draft to New York for a discussion with Mason and Courtney. The meeting, which was quite informal, began with Adams reading his draft proposal aloud to the group. Mason and Courtney commented on the draft as he went along. Some of the more substantial comments are included in the following excerpts from the meeting.

Meeting on the draft proposal

ADAMS: We expect that production inefficiencies and quality problems will be encountered upon start-up of the new facility in Chicago. In order to prevent these problems from interfering with the growth of toranium, the new facilities for producing toranium powder, pressing ingots, and casting finished products will be installed in Chicago and operated until normal production efficiency is attained. At that time, existing Akron equipment will be transferred to the Chicago location. Assuming early approval of the project, Chicago will be in production in the first quarter of 1967, and joint Akron and Chicago operations will continue through September 1967. The Akron equipment will be transferred in October and November 1967, and Chicago will be in full operation in December 1967.

MASON: Wait a minute! You're not in production until the first quarter of 1967, and the forecasts say we are going to be short in 1966!

ADAMS: There is a problem in machinery order lag.

MASON: Have you ordered a press?

ADAMS: Yes, and we'll be moving by October.

MASON: Well, then, say you'll be in business in the last quarter of 1966. Look, Pete, this document has to be approved by Brewer and then the finance committee. If Chicago's our choice, we've got to *sell* Chicago. Let's put our best foot forward! The problem is to make it clear that on economics alone we would go to Akron . . . but you have to bring out the flaw in the economics: that managing 20 product lines, especially when you've got fancy products, just isn't possible.

COURTNEY: And you have a better building.

MASON: All of this should be in a table in the text. It ought to cover incremental cost, incremental investment, incremental expense, incremental ROI, and the building space. And Sam's right. Akron is a poor building; it's a warehouse. Pittsburgh is better for something like high-pressure materials. But out in Chicago you've got a multi-story building with more than enough space that is perfect for this sort of project.

COURTNEY: Pete, are we getting this compact enough for you?

MASON: Hey, why don't we put some sexy looking graphs in the thing? I don't know, but maybe we could plot incremental investment vs. incremental return for each location. See what you can do, Pete.

COURTNEY: Yes, that's a good idea.

*   *   *   *   *

MASON: Now, Pete, one other thing. You'll have to include discounted cash flow on the other two locations. Some of those guys [division and corporate top management] are going to look at just the numbers. You'll show them they're not too different.

*   *   *   *   *

MASON: The biggest discussion will be, "Why the hell move to Chicago?"

COURTNEY: You know, Pete, you should discuss the labor content in the product.

MASON: Good. We have to weave in the idea that it's a product with a low labor content and explain that this means the high Chicago labor cost will not hurt us.

ADAMS: One last item: Shouldn't we be asking for more capacity? Two-and-one-half million dollars only carries us through 1967.

MASON: Pete, we certainly wouldn't do this for one of our established products. Where our main business is involved, we build capacity in five-and ten-year chunks. But we have to treat toranium a little differently. The problem here is to take a position in the market. Competition isn't going to clobber us if we don't have the capacity to satisfy everyone. If the market develops, we can move quickly.

After the meeting, Courtney explained that he and Mason had been disappointed with Adams' draft and were trying to help him improve it without really "clobbering" him. "Adams' draft was weak. His numbers were incomplete and his argument sloppy. I've asked him to meet with Bob Lincoln [assistant controller for metal products] to discuss the proposal."

The result of Adams' five meetings with Lincoln was three more drafts of the toranium proposal. The numerical exhibits were revised for greater clarity. The text was revised to lessen the number of technical terms.

Adams, however, was still very much concerned with the appropriate size of the new facility. "Mason is only interested in justifying the location of the new facility!" Adams exclaimed. "We plan to sell $5.6 million worth of toranium in 1971. Yet we're asking for only $2.5 million worth of capacity. It's crazy! But, you know, I think Mason doesn't really care what capacity we propose. He just wants 'sexy looking graphs.' That's O.K. for him, because I'm the one who's going to get it in the neck in 1968. So far as I can see, Brewer has built his reputation by bringing this division from chronic under-capacity to a full-capacity, high ROI position."

The next step in the toranium facilities proposal was a formal presentation to the top management of metal products on June 2, 1966. There were two capital projects on the agenda. Brewer began the meeting by announcing that its purpose was to "discuss the proposals and decide if they were any good." He turned the meeting over to Mason, who, in turn, asked Adams to "take over and direct the meeting."

Adams proceeded by reading the draft proposal, after first asking for comments. He got halfway down the first page before Brewer interrupted.

BREWER: Let me stop you right here. You have told them [the proposal was aimed at Basic Industries' finance committee] the name, and you have told them how much money you want, but you haven't told them what the name means, and you haven't told them what the products are.

At this point a discussion began as to what the name of the project was going to be. The meeting then continued with Adams reading and people occasionally making comments on his English and on the text.

BREWER: Look, let's get this straight. What we are doing in this proposal is trying to tell them what it is we are spending their money on. That's what they want to know. Tell me about the electronic applications in that table you have there. I have to be able to explain them to the finance committee. I understand "steel" and "aerospace" but I don't understand "electronic applications" and I don't understand "electronic industry." I need some more specific words.

SAMUELS: [vice president of R.&D.]: Let me ask you a question which someone in the finance committee might ask. It's a nasty one. You forecast here that the industry sales in 1971 are going to be about $7 million, or maybe a little less. You think we are going to have 75% or 85% of this business. You also think we are going to get competition from G.E. and others. Do you think companies of that stature are going to be satisfied with sharing $1.5 million of the business? Don't you think that we may lose some of our market share?

This question was answered by Roberts and pursued by a few others. Essentially Roberts argued that the proprietary technology of the metal products division was going to be strong enough to defend its market share.

BREWER: Let me tell you about an item which is much discussed in the finance committee. They are concerned, and basically this involves other divisions, with underestimating the cost of investment projects. I think, in fact, that there was a request for additional funds on a project recently which was as large as our entire annual capital budget.[1] Second of all, as a result of the capital expenditure cutback, there was a tendency, and again it has been in other divisions, to cut back on or delay facilities. Now it's not really just the capital expenditure cutback that is the reason for their behavior. If they had been doing their planning, they should have been thinking about these expenditures five or six years ago, not two years ago. But they didn't do the estimates, or their estimates weren't correct, and now they are sold out on a lot of items and are buying products from other people and reselling them and not making any money. It's affecting the corporate earnings, so the environment in the finance committee today is very much (1) "Tell us how much you want, and tell us *all* that you want," and (2) "Give us a damned good return." Now I don't want us to get *sloppy*, but, Bill, if you need something, ask for it. And then make Pete meet his numbers.

ADAMS: Well, on this one, as I think you know, the machinery is already on order and we are sure that our market estimates are correct.

BREWER: Yes, I know that. I just mean that if you want something, then plan it right and tell them what you are going to need so you don't come back asking for more money six months later.

*   *   *   *   *

BREWER: I am going to need some words on competition. I am also going to need some words on why we are ready so soon on this project. We are asking for money now, and we say we are going to be in operation in the fourth quarter.

SAMUELS: Foresight (*followed by general laughter*).

MASON: Well, it's really quite understandable. This began last October when we thought we were going to expand at Akron. At that time, it was obvious that we needed capacity so we ordered some machines. Then as the

---

[1] Metal products division's capital budget in 1965 was $7.9 million.

thing developed, it was clear that there would be some other things we needed, and because of the timing lag we had to order them.

BREWER: OK . . . now another thing. Numerical control is hot as a firecracker in the finance committee. I am not saying that we should have it on this project, but you should be aware that the corporation is thinking a lot about it.

* * * * *

BREWER: [Much later on in the discussion.] There are really three reasons for moving. Why not state them?

1. You want to free up some space at Akron which you need.
2. There are 20 products at Akron, and toranium can't get the attention it needs.
3. You can get operating efficiencies if you move.

If you set it out, you can cut out all of this crap. You know, it would do you people some good if you read a facilities proposal[2] on something you didn't know beforehand. You really have to think about the guy who doesn't know what you're talking about. I read a proposal yesterday that was absolutely ridiculous. It had pounds per hour and tons per year and tons per month and tons per day and—except for the simplest numbers, which were in a table—all the rest were spread out through the story.

* * * * *

Adams indicated that he was disappointed with the meeting. Brewer seemed to him to be preoccupied with "words," and the topic of additional capacity never really came up. The only encouraging sign was Brewer's statement, "Tell us all that you want." But it seemed that all Mason "wanted" was $2.5 million worth of capacity.

Adams saw three possibilities open to him. First, he could ask for additional capacity.

This alternative meant that Adams would have to speak with Courtney and Mason. The Chicago plant manager viewed the prospect of such a conversation with mixed feelings. In the past, his relations with Courtney and Mason had been excellent. He had been able to deal with these men on an informal and relaxed level. However, the experience of drafting the toranium proposal left Adams a little uneasy. Courtney and Mason had been quite critical of his draft and had made him meet with Bob Lincoln in order to revise it. What would their reaction be if he were to request a reconsideration of the proposal at this late date? Moreover, what new data or arguments could he offer in support of a request for additional capacity?

On the other hand, Adams saw a formal request for additional capacity as a way of getting his feelings on the record. Even if his superiors refused his request, he would be in a better position with respect to the 1968 performance review. However, Adams wondered how his performance review would go if he formally requested and received additional capacity and the market did not develop as forecasted.

As his second alternative, Adams believed he could ask that the new facilities proposal specify that metal products would be needing more money for toranium facilities in the future.

---

[2] The finance committee reviewed approximately 190 capital requests in 1965.

This alternative did not pose the same problems as the first with respect to Courtney and Mason. Adams felt that saying more funds might be needed would be acceptable to Courtney and Mason, whereas asking for more might not be. However, the alternative introduced a new problem. Brewer had been quite explicit in insisting that the division ask for all that was needed so that it would not have to come back and ask for more in six months. To admit a possible need for additional funds, therefore, might jeopardize the entire project.

In spite of this problem, Adams felt that this alternative was the best one available. It was a compromise between his point of view and Mason's. If top management felt that the future of toranium was too uncertain, then why not ask for contingent funds? This would get Adams off the hook and still not actually increase metal products' real investment.

As his third alternative, Adams decided he could drop the issue and hope to be transferred or promoted before 1968.

Richardson Corporation

On August 15, 1968, Thomas Sutherland was asked to manage the Richardson Corporation's effort to win the development contract for the Air Force's Sauron Missile System.[1] Sutherland, who was 51 years old, had a doctorate in aeronautical engineering and had worked for Richardson since 1945.

By May 5, 1969, the competition for the Sauron development contract was in its final months. Richardson and two other defense contractors had survived an elimination process that had begun with five contestants. In two months, these firms would have to submit comprehensive bids to the Air Force.[2] In six months, a winner would be chosen.

Yet in spite of the success he had experienced to date, Sutherland could not help being nervous about what lay ahead. The Sauron project was a critical one for the program manager. His career at Richardson had been exclusively in engineering and product development, and Sauron was his first opportunity to manage a major program.

In addition, Sutherland knew that winning the Sauron contract was important to the Richardson Corporation. Large, prime defense contracts were becoming scarcer and scarcer. And, since some of Richardson's major contracts were almost completed, the corporation needed to win a large contract in the near future in order to maintain its engineering force and make full use of its facilities.

On the other hand, some of Richardson's most recent projects had been experiencing substantial overruns on their budgeted cost. In addition to being an embarrassment to the firm and a possible liability for future contract competitions, these overruns were costing Richard-

---

[1] The Sauron Missile System described in this case is fictitious. The management problems and all other aspects of the case, however, are a disguised description of an actual business problem which did face the management of Richardson.

[2] The actual bids were each expected to be in excess of 30,000 pages and were described by one member of Richardson's management "as enough paper to fill a room 8 ft. × 10 ft. to the ceiling."

son considerable money due to the fixed price provisions of the firm's contracts with the government. Moreover, these losses on government contracts were coming at the same time that Richardson needed funds for its extensive diversification into commercial ventures (see Exhibits 1 and 2 for income statements and balance sheets).

In short, Richardson's management wanted to *win* the Sauron development contract at a price which reflected *realistic* cost estimates. It was Sutherland's job to see that this happened.

AIR FORCE PROCUREMENT AND THE SAURON MISSILE SYSTEM

Before exploring the problems facing Tom Sutherland in early April 1969, it is necessary to briefly describe the environment in which he operated. And one of the most influential aspects of this environment was the Air Force procurement process, which consisted of a time sequence of four activities: concept formulation, contract definition, engineering development, and system production.

Concept formulation. For the Sauron program, the activities of concept formulation began in the mid-1960s when the Air Force became dissatisfied with existing systems for air base defense. New developments in radar and missile technology and the poor test record of the existing system convinced Air Force personnel that a new system was needed. As a result, the Air Force funded a number of research and development contracts with aerospace firms to study the techniques and hardware required to build a new air base defense system. These contracts were given to about five firms, including Richardson.

Contract definition. In August 1968, the Air Force sent a request for proposal (RFP) on the development of a Sauron missile system to a number of aerospace firms. Five contractors submitted proposals in which they outlined their firm's capabilities to design and develop a system that would satisfy the specifications of the RFP. In December 1968, the Air Force asked three of the contractors, including Richardson, to submit a comprehensive bid on the development work for the Sauron system. Each of these contractors was awarded an $8 million fixed price contract[3] to cover the expenses of developing the bid, which was due by July 11, 1969.

Engineering development. From July 11 to November 1, the Air Force would review the bids, negotiate any changes in them it felt necessary, and accept one as the winner of the competition. The engineering development contract for which the three contractors were competing was to be fixed price incentive. The contractors and the Air Force would agree on a target cost for the development and tentative fee for the contractor. In addition, a ceiling price would be established for the contract. Any costs in excess of the target and less than the ceiling would be shared by the contractor and the Air Force. Any costs

---

[3] Richardson estimated it would spend about $20 million on the Sauron competition. However, a substantial part of $12 million difference between this figure and the amount of the contract definition contract would be charged to overhead on other government contracts.

in excess of the ceiling would be assumed entirely by the contractor.

For example, the Sauron development contract was expected to cost about $500 million. If one assumes that figure to be the target cost, the contractors fee to be 12% of target, the ceiling to be $640 million, and the cost sharing ratio to be 80% Air Force—20% contractor to $600 million, the pricing arrangement for the contract would be that diagrammed below.

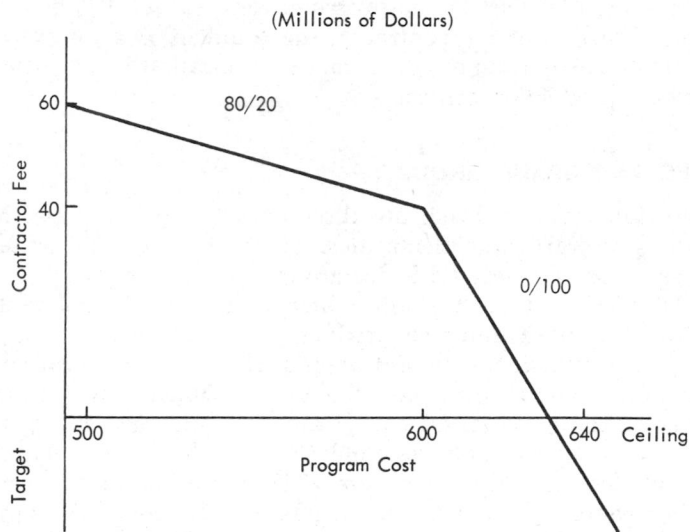

System production. The goal of the engineering development contract was to develop a Sauron missile system and demonstrate that it was ready for production. While the production contract was often awarded with the engineering development contract, this was not the case with Sauron. However, the Air Force wanted to protect its future production price while still in a competitive stage and, therefore, asked the contractors to guarantee maximum production prices for a period of five years longer than the engineering development program. Unlike commercial production options, the Air Force paid no fee to hold the option.

THE RICHARDSON CORPORATION

In 1968, the Richardson Corporation had sales of $2.1 billion and net earnings after taxes of $58 million. As of December 31, 1968, Richardson's net worth was $528 million and the firm had $235 million of long-term debt outstanding. (See Exhibits 1 and 2 for Richardson's income statement and balance sheet.) Aerospace analysts on Wall Street considered Richardson to be a well-managed firm relative to other firms in its industry.

The Sauron program represented an excellent opportunity and a substantial risk for Richardson. If cost overruns on the Sauron development contract approached some recent industry overruns (in excess of 100%), Richardson could lose a great deal of money. For example, a 50% overrun on a $500 target cost (see the example above on page 833) could result in a loss to Richardson of $110 million or almost ⅕ of the firm's net worth. A 100% overrun would result in a $360 million loss.

While past experience indicated that contractors rarely absorbed the entire impact of overruns of this magnitude (due to the contractors' ability to show that part of the overruns were caused by the customer through redirection of the contract), the trend in weapon system procurement was away from easy contract renegotiation and "getting well" on follow-on production contracts.

MISSILES AND SPACE GROUP

Richardson was organized into three basic product groups: Missiles and Space; Aircraft; and Electronics. The Sauron missile system program was in the Missiles and Space group.

The Missiles and Space group, which had sales of $585 million in 1968, was organized into five product divisions, with 10 major programs, and 10 functional support areas (see Exhibit 3). Program managers had direct control over the following activities: program planning, program marketing, program cost estimating and budgeting, management of major subcontracts, assembly and test of developmental units, and product testing of delivered items. The control of all other activities was either shared by program managers and functional executives or given entirely to functional executives.

Finance and contract administration were under the joint control of programs and group support organizations. Personnel in these areas reported directly to a group functional manager. However, finance and contracts men were located in the program or division (some programs were too small to justify their own finance and contract staff) and there was a "heavy" dotted line between these functional men and the program and/or division manager.

Manufacturing, purchasing, personnel, administration, facilities management, research and development, and engineering were under the control of group functional managers. Program managers "contracted" with the group for the services they wanted and "paid" for "mutually agreed statements of defined work or services" out of budgeted contract or product development funds. Due to security problems, the large size of programs being served, or geographic remoteness of facilities, these functional personnel were often located with a program rather than at the group headquarters.

The management of the group's engineering activities warrants individual comment. The program manager was in direct control of project engineering which included the top engineering managers assigned to a project. However, during the life of a project a varying level and kind of engineering effort was needed, and this engineering effort was supplied by group engineering "on contract" to the program.

One senior manager described the management environment in the Missiles and Space group's network of joint and separate powers in the following manner.

> Promotion in this group is in a functional line. Men identify with their function and the salary structure is keyed on the function. Contract lawyers, engineers, finance types rarely do the right thing for the program.
>
> On the other hand, program management is not always a dead end. Rather, it is a high risk strategy. Program managers step out of the functional line and its steady promotional ladder. If they are successful —that is, if they win a large program and/or manage one so that it meets its performance, schedule, and cost goals—the route to the top is direct and fast. However, if a man fails as a program manager, he usually returns to his functional area—in almost all cases, engineering,— with the bloom considerably off the rose. This is not to say that future promotion in his functional area is blocked but rather to say that if you try for the brass ring and miss it's not easy to get another chance.
>
> Management in the Missiles and Space group is by popularity contest. It's tough to measure anything else. Every quarter the functional managers get 3% of their budget to hand out in merit raises. Well, they just sit around the table and compare one man to another, and give out the merit raises on the basis of who's popular.
>
> The philosophy around here is that jobs get done by a bunch of nice guys working in harmony together. For example, one program spent $400 million last year. Yet no one knew if the managers were heroes or bums. There was a lack of any standard with respect to what reasonable cost and performance were for that program.
>
> Moreover, with programs that last more than six years from the start of contract definition to the end of system production, it is rare that the same program manager or for that matter program management team stays with a program for its entire life. Thus a guy might win a contract competition and get rewarded with a promotion. Another guy might then take over the engineering development, and still a third might manage the production of the system. If costs overrun, is it bad cost control, poor cost estimation, or faulty design? With so many variables and such a changing management team, it is really difficult to fix the blame for any problem. Thus, everything around here is short range. The heroes are the doers. You get to be a vice president by putting out fires.
>
> In addition, the extreme fluidity of new business effort means that a man might move three times a year every year he's at Richardson. With all this shuffling, you never know about inversion—that is, the guy you fire might be your boss on the next project. Moreover, since you might be moving from a program at any time, you need to keep lots of friends so that when you do need a job, you can call one of them up and ask whether you may come to work for him.
>
> Then there is this damn seniority. For some jobs, a ten-year Richardson man is not good enough. You need a fifteen-year man. There's some sort of a thing about service pins. And the damn fringe benefits are tied to service with a particular company. Yet given the fluidity of the industry, this penalizes the guy who moves where the action is.
>
> Also a man's status around here seems to be measured by the

number of men reporting to him—that appears to be a measure of worth. For example, every manager has a certain rating in terms of his level of supervision. If he loses a number of people reporting to him, he might lose his parking space.

Thomas Sutherland, program manager for Sauron, took exception to this description of Richardson's organizational environment. The following are excerpts from his comments on the subject.

The program manager's job is a reasonably responsible one. It's certainly much stronger than that implied in the comments I've just read. Plays are called from here.

*   *   *   *   *

I've worked with Richardson for 24 years now, and I have had seven different bosses. It's far less than three every year.

*   *   *   *   *

Personal loyalties at Richardson are a combination of two things: functional loyalties, and, due to the long-term nature of some of our programs, we get program loyalties. For example, the people who worked on our early missile program were brought up under our current president's [he was the program manager] management approach. That program has lasted 10 years and generated considerable loyalties. I think these program loyalties are as strong and important as functional loyalties in understanding how Richardson operates. It is true that at the lower levels functional loyalties are stronger; but at the higher levels of management program loyalties seem to be more important.

*   *   *   *   *

I think this guy is right when he mentions popularity—but popularity in the sense that people are convinced of the merit of a person's performance.

*   *   *   *   *

I think he's off base when he says that it's our philosophy to get things done with nice guys. That certainly can and has happened on particular programs, but it certainly is not planned that way.

*   *   *   *   *

This program of seniority has some truth in it, but again I believe it's somewhat exaggerated. The man who is program manager of our largest missile program has only been with Richardson for seven years, and he has been manager of this program for the last three years.

*   *   *   *   *

The critical measure of a program manager's performance is how the projected earnings to the end of the program have changed during the year. In my case, I expect that if we are successful with Sauron, I will be managing the program in its engineering development and perhaps production phases. Part of Richardson's selling job to the customer is that we sell the management team, so we do not as a policy take the proposal manager out after the contract is won.

*   *   *   *   *

About 250 of the top executives (including Sutherland) at Richardson are on a salary incentive plan. A certain amount of company profits—10% of profits after taxes—is distributed among these men. The criteria is threefold. The profit of the organization of which the man is a part is one-third of his score. The second one-third is a man's contribution to getting new business. How well does he set the stage for long-term survival and growth of his organization? However, because of the five- to ten-year nature of our business, and the one-year nature of the measure, this is a difficult segment of the incentive plan to calibrate.

The final one-third of an individual's rating is his own performance. This is rated by his superior as being either outstanding, average, or poor. An outstanding rating is often worth twice what a poor rating is worth. For example, the first two-thirds of the incentive plan determines what is called the nominal compensation. An outstanding rating might mean that an individual gets 130% of nominal. A poor rating might mean 70% of nominal. The rating system, of course, is quite subjective. However, a man usually knows why he is rated as he is, and very rarely do men object to ratings.

THE SAURON PROGRAM

The Sauron program was established as a separate organization within the Missiles and Space group in January 1969. By the end of April 1969, 700 people were working on Sauron, and 350 of these people reported in a direct line to Thomas Sutherland, Sauron program manager (see Exhibit 4).

Before becoming program manager, Sutherland had been manager of advanced development for the product development division. When the Air Force requested a proposal on the Sauron development contract in August 1968, Sutherland was assigned full time to manage the program. From August to October, Sutherland worked with a small group of men and the output of this effort was a proposal to develop the Sauron which was delivered to the Air Force on October 7, 1968. In December, Richardson was asked, along with two other aerospace firms, to submit a comprehensive bid on the development of Sauron. The bid was due on July 11, 1969.

The basic tasks before Sutherland's team during the period from December 1968, to July 1969, were the following: (1) design an air base defense system that would satisfy the performance specification detailed in the Air Force's Sauron RFP;[4] (2) estimate the cost and time required to develop the Sauron system that was designed; (3) write a contract which contained the hardware and systems specifications for the Sauron system and a price-incentive arrangement for the development work. (See Exhibit 5.)

Sutherland commented on his job during contract definition.

> As I see my job during contract definition it is to apprise the top management of the risks involved in the Sauron program, and to establish an attitude in lower level personnel that the program can be done for a cost that will allow us to win. I also must create an industrial team and build a relationship with the Air Force program office.
>
> While doing all this, I must insure that we develop an approach to the problem that is acceptable to the Air Force both technically and

---

[4] The RFP was over 1,000 pages.

from a cost point of view. I also must conduct my relationship with the Air Force in an orderly and effective manner so that I build the proper image of Richardson in the Air Force's mind.

The week of May 5th

The activities of the Sauron program team during the week of May 5, 1969, were representative of the kinds of problems involved in performing these tasks. An initial distribution of expected contract costs was being generated. Design specifications on the major hardware components were being finalized. And presentations to Richardson's top management and to high level Air Force personnel were being prepared.

Monday

Sutherland met with Art Schoen, contracts manager, to discuss a presentation Schoen was preparing for top management on an approach to pricing the Sauron contract. The assistant program manager, the subcontracts manager, and the chief engineer also attended the meeting.

Schoen began the meeting by projecting a vu-graph of a presentation outline on the wall. This was accepted and Schoen then proceeded to go through a pile of vu-graphs, arranged in the order of the outline. After about 50 vu-graphs, Sutherland was getting upset.

SUTHERLAND: Art, everything you've said so far is of the how to save Richardson's tail variety. It's fine. That's your job. That's how you earn your living. The main issue, however, is how to price this contract.

ASSISTANT PROGRAM MANAGER: We started this meeting at 8:30 A.M. and now it's after 11 A.M. and we haven't gotten to the meat of the matter yet.

SCHOEN: I figured I was supposed to analyze my contract.

SUTHERLAND: We're trying to develop a one- to two-hour briefing on the subject of pricing and incentives to top management. You were asked to bring what you felt was an appropriate outline. What we've seen is an appendix to the guts of the issue. The presentation as I see it is that I explain how the program manager proposes to price the proposal and what kind of a contract he proposes the company sign and why. I've got to give reasons, and I ought to start with the pricing strategy first. It's killing me to sit here and listen to all this crap.

SCHOEN: Well, if we're going to give the pitch—

SUTHERLAND: Damn it. I'm going to give the whole God-damn pitch. What I'm trying to do today is get some data that I can use.

The pricing meeting finally ended after 12 P.M. and another meeting on the subject was scheduled for the following day at 3 P.M.

Sutherland commented (to the researcher):

> For a week before this meeting I have been trying to find out if my contracts man and my finance man could put together a presentation which I could give to the group and corporate managers. I am finding out that they cannot.

These preparations for presentations to top management were critical, as well as time-consuming, activities. While Missiles and Space group management seemed to be committed to winning the Sauron contract, recent overruns on some Missiles and Space contracts made them sensitive to the quality and reality of the cost estimates. Thus, Sutherland felt that he would have to defend his cost estimates and pricing recommendations with some convincing arguments at the group level.

The attitudes of corporate management to the Sauron project were mixed. The financial squeeze on the firm due to its commercial ventures and the public criticism for overruns on recent government contracts had some corporate managers reluctant to expose the firm to the additional financial risk inherent in a program of Sauron's magnitude and technical uncertainty. On the other hand, the corporation had given the Sauron project considerable support to date and Sutherland was hopeful that it would continue to do so in the future.

On Monday afternoon, Sutherland observed the first full rehearsal for the February 13–14 Air Force review. All major subcontractor representatives, equipment engineers, and top program executives made brief presentations. In addition, the full scale mock-ups of the ground system and a Sauron missile were explained in some detail. The rehearsal began at 1:00 P.M. and ended about 8:15 P.M.

The Air Force review was critical in the selection process, for although many government contracts were competitive in name only (the winner was reasonably certain of getting the contract before contract definition), the Sauron competition was thought to be wide open. The in-process review was an opportunity to sell Richardson's concepts and capabilities to the Air Force as well as to get any negative reaction the Air Force might have to Richardson's approach.

Tuesday

Sutherland met with the top program engineering managers to discuss progress on system design and estimation of development program cost. One issue that Sutherland was anxious to resolve was missile size. At the rehearsal on Monday, the missile equipment engineer implied that a decision had been reached to use the large model. Since that was the first time Sutherland learned about the decision, he wanted to discuss it with the engineers:

> I see this as an important tactical problem. Theoretically I guess I should delegate the decision. However, on a similar sizing problem with our radar design the engineering group proposed a smaller size than the Air Force had requested. The Air Force is notorious for downgrading a contractor if he departs from their original notions of system. The radar proposal got us a great deal of flak.

In response to Sutherland's question about the missile size, the missile equipment manager explained that the "large" missile would cost $33 million more than the "small" model called for in the Air Force RFP.

SUTHERLAND: Why that much more?
MISSILE EQUIPMENT MANAGER: Principally due to the motor weight and the structural weight.

SUTHERLAND: How much is the propellant?
AN ENGINEER: 500 pounds.
SUTHERLAND: How much per pound?
THE ENGINEER: $5 a pound.
SUTHERLAND: OK, go on.
MISSILE EQUIPMENT ENGINEER: That's it.
SUTHERLAND: What intercept range are we going to guarantee?
MISSILE EQUIPMENT MANAGER: I'd like to know that, too.
SUTHERLAND: I'm talking about numbers. What numbers are we going to guarantee in the systems specs?
SYSTEMS ENGINEERING MANAGER: We don't really have our first pretty good cut on how the systems specs will read, and we won't have it for a few weeks.
SUTHERLAND: I can't accept that.
CHIEF ENGINEER: The thing just isn't done yet, Tom.
AN ENGINEER: What do we mean by intercept?
CHIEF ENGINEER: That's the problem.
THE ENGINEER: What we've got is a measure of vehicle performance.
SUTHERLAND: Right, but we don't guarantee vehicle performance. We have to guarantee systems performance. [As prime contractor, Richardson was required to guarantee the performance of the complete system. For example, if the missile worked perfectly and the radar failed, the system failed. Thus, Sutherland was explaining that Richardson had to guarantee that the missile would intercept the enemy target not that the missile would intercept the enemy target given that all other systems worked perfectly.]
MISSILE EQUIPMENT MANAGER: Well, we're still trying to define a success factor in regard to the missile performance.

At this point the researcher had to leave the meeting. He was informed later that it had been decided to bid on the basis of a small missile and offer the large missile as an option. Moreover, even though further study of the missile size problem showed that there was no cost differential between the models, Richardson still decided to offer the large missile as an option.

The group president's staff meeting scheduled for Tuesdays was canceled. Sutherland normally attended these meetings and reported on the status of the Sauron program. He used this free time to dictate a number of letters.

On Tuesday afternoon, Sutherland met with the leaders of the program review teams. These teams consisted of men from group function organizations. Their tasks were to critically review Sauron system design, engineering development cost estimates, and pricing proposals. Most of the review team work was scheduled for June.

Sutherland also attended the continuation of Monday's pricing meeting. In addition to those who attended Monday's meeting, the manager of finance for Sauron, the manager of finance for the group, and two review team leaders attended the continuation. One of the central topics of conversation at the meeting was subcontract costs. A recent Missiles and Space group program was experiencing subcontracts costs that were 65% greater than originally estimated and Sutherland was determined to avoid a similar situation with Sauron.[5] When Sutherland

---

[5] 70% of Sauron's components were to be developed by subcontractors.

asked John Tyler, subcontracts manager, to explain his (Tyler's) approach to estimating costs, Tyler responded by discussing the "degree of definition" of the subcontracts.

TYLER: We're trying to define risks. If we have not fully defined the performance specifications to our subcontractors, then they have the opportunity to charge us with any changes we make after we win the contract. The degree of definition is simply my appraisal of how far we are along in defining performance specifications to our subcontractors.

ASSISTANT PROGRAM MANAGER: Question—Would you agree to putting in a degree of subcontract definition?

TYLER: OK.

ASSISTANT PROGRAM MANAGER: Then I think we're in agreement.

SUTHERLAND: But you're not including hardware definition. Is that right?

TYLER: Let me talk to this point again. Tom [Sutherland], if we have a decimal point wrong, we can be wrong by $200,000. If the hardware performance specifications do not stand, then the subcontract does not stand.

ASSISTANT PROGRAM MANAGER: The issue is what will it cost to develop a subsystem for Sauron. As prime contractor we'll have to bid the lowest bid possible to win the competition. But the cost is always greater. We must assess our subcontractor's capabilities, the accuracy of our specifications and the quality of his management. You want to predict the actual final cost of the subsystem. How much will it cost to design, develop, and deliver the subsystem you need?

Subcontracts were fixed price incentive. As long as the performance and hardware specifications remained unchanged, Richardson knew its maximum financial exposure. However, if Richardson changed a specification, the subcontractor could change his target cost. Moreover, the magnitude of the change in the target cost often exceeded the cost of making the technical change. In this way, subcontractors could compensate for added cost due to their own mistakes. Thus, if a subcontract's specifications were not fully defined, Richardson would be exposed to contract changes and added cost.

Sutherland commented on the problem.

During contract definition we are pricing a product before we have fully designed it. Thus the problems we have with respect to the government are simultaneously experienced by subcontractors with respect to pricing to us. In early missile programs we tried to have real competition for subcontracts—signed and sealed bids. But we were kidding ourselves. The subcontracts we were getting were just not realistically priced.

On the other hand, the company has just gone through a large program where it had only a rough understanding of what the subcontract costs would be and sold the product on a fixed price based on these rough subcontract estimates. Then we found that we could not negotiate satisfactory arrangements with the subcontractors to do the work that we had expected them to do.

Thus, we're trying to do two things with Sauron. By improving our degree of contract definition in the subcontract area we hope to develop realistic prices—not drive our subcontractors to unrealistic estimates.

Lack of understanding can have two effects on cost estimates;

(1) if the contractor is trying to be overprotective, he will overprice the work to be done, (2) if he does not understand the full scope of his work, he can underprice. Both situations are damaging.

It's my problem to assess what the "fudge" factor is in each subcontract situation. Are they low or high because of ignorance? What motivates their management? Electrotech, for example, came in with a $20 million bid. If that were overrun by 50%, we are talking about an overrun in excess of $10 million on our contract.

Wednesday

In the morning, Sutherland attended a demonstration for the Air Force of Richardson's new long-distance communication system. This activity took about two hours.

Sutherland then attended the beginning of an engineering review meeting called by the radar equipment manager to discuss problems he was having with a subcontractor for a component of the radar system. Present at the meeting were Dan Graham, chief engineer for Sauron; Tyler, subcontracts manager; Bill Williams, system engineering manager; and the engineers working for the radar equipment manager. The chief engineer began the conversation by responding to the equipment manager's request to change contractors.

GRAHAM (chief engineer):   I don't see why we don't just leave it alone.

RADAR EQUIPMENT MANAGER: We've got one helluva interface problem with Electrotech.

GRAHAM: Why is it any different than when we were going to do that part of the system? [Richardson was going to develop a subcomponent which was to fit into a major subsystem being built by one of Richardson's subcontractors. However, during the contract definition part of the competition, Richardson decided to ask Electrotech to build the subcomponent. Graham's question, therefore, was in effect "how had the problem of interface with a major subcontractor changed merely because Richardson was no longer producing the subcomponent and Electrotech was?"]

RADAR EQUIPMENT MANAGER: It's quite different.

GRAHAM: Have you got any data to show me?

RADAR EQUIPMENT MANAGER: Yes. (The equipment manager then got up and pulled out five or six large drafting sheets and spent 10 to 15 minutes showing Graham what he meant.)

GRAHAM: Well, that move would certainly simplify the situation. But I don't think it would make Electrotech very happy. And this could hurt the other stuff they're doing for us.

AN ENGINEER: Electrotech is not really cooperating with us—they're not putting their nose to the grindstone. I think that might be a relevant consideration in this instance.

RADAR EQUIPMENT MANAGER: That's right. When the Electrotech people are here, they sometimes get up and leave before the meetings are finished.

GRAHAM: If the subcomponent hadn't been allocated to Electrotech and we weren't going that way, I might consider your proposal a little more.

TYLER: Dan [Graham], I think Electrotech can do the job. We can get their attention. You and I can lay a bull whip on their back if necessary. But the change now could result in significant problems with two of our subcontractors.

GRAHAM: Right, it's too late to change now. If we do not get satisfactory response from Electrotech, we haven't closed the door on a change.

RADAR EQUIPMENT MANAGER: Well, we could bring it back in-house. It's a pretty important piece of equipment.

WILLIAMS (systems engineering manager): Don't forget we're just designing and pricing the equipment at this point—we're not bidding on a production contract. We can always go to another source for production or for engineering development, if that's necessary.

GRAHAM: I'll ask them to break out the cost of this item separately. In that way we'll be able to see if their cost estimates are high.

TYLER: I'm happy.

GRAHAM: You're probably the happiest guy in the room (*laughter.*)

After the meeting Sutherland made the following remarks to the researcher:

> Graham had a meeting with Tyler prior to the meeting with the engineers. He and Tyler had developed what they thought to be a satisfactory program approach. The purpose of the meeting was to sound out any opposition to their approach, listen to the complaints, and then motivate the engineers to move in the direction they had charted. They asked me to attend part of the meeting.

The issue of subcontractors also occupied much of Sutherland's afternoon. One subcontractor was insisting on the use of a particular display at the Air Force Review. Sutherland felt the display was inappropriate and asked that it be changed. During the course of the afternoon, Sutherland spoke on the telephone with the subcontractor's program manager three times. Part of the last conversation follows:

> I'm sorry you called. You've got more important things to work on than this display, and I think you're just wasting your time on it. We're on the spot—we've got to make a presentation to the Air Force next week, and we've got to call all the shots. What you sent us was 90% OK. Why argue about the other 10%. Tell your guys to be flexible and constructive. The schedule that they have on display is inconsistent with our master schedule. All I can figure out was that your guys are doing it just to irritate us. Also you've changed the design on one of the components so that the model you're describing is not the same as the model that we're describing. You know you've got to clear all design changes with Graham [chief engineer] before they're made.

On the same afternoon, Sutherland got a call from one of three companies competing for the contract to develop the propellant for the missile. The caller explained that he wanted to remain in the competition but that due to lack of available funds, he would not be able to continue unless Richardson was able to help him out financially. Moreover, he said he would be unable to submit the cost estimates that were due the following week. After a 20-minute conversation. Sutherland referred the caller to Tyler, subcontracts manager. After speaking with this subcontractor, Tyler told the researcher that the subcontractor was just bluffing and after some discussion had agreed to remain in the competition and submit the required cost estimates on time.

Sutherland commented on dealing with subcontractors.

> The military environment requires that we team with other companies on programs such as Sauron. What is needed, however, is one

major consistent strategy if our effort is to be effective. That requires the endorsement of the top managers of all companies involved.

It's my role to see that this happens. We have top management meetings to discuss proposal strategy. Subcontracting organization managers as well as our managers attend. As you see, occasionally we do have some friction and short tempers.

Sutherland's last appointment on Wednesday was at 6:00 P.M. with Art Schoen, the contracts manager. The two men discussed alternate approaches to pricing the contract and Sutherland asked Schoen to work out the two most promising ones.

Thursday

Sutherland's entire day was devoted to the second full rehearsal for the Air Force Review.

Friday

The regularly scheduled Sauron program review meeting was cancelled in order to continue the rehearsal for the Air Force Review. Sutherland then met briefly with the manager of operations for Sauron to review the preliminary cost estimate for the entire development program.

Following this meeting, Sutherland met with the Sauron engineering managers to discuss their part of the presentation to group and corporate management. When they presented their material to Sutherland, the program manager was visibly upset and the following exchange took place.

SUTHERLAND: There's no title on the chart. What are you talking about? [The engineers present explained the analysis to Sutherland.] No, that's not what I wanted to say. Who drew this chart?

AN ENGINEER: I did.

SUTHERLAND: Well, it doesn't have the data that I asked for last week. Where's that chart that I drew last Sunday? I'm sure that's exactly what I wanted.

THE ENGINEER: Well, I took the liberty—

SUTHERLAND: No, that's not what I wanted. I'm sorry that's just not what I wanted plotted. You put a completely different subject on the chart.

THE ENGINEER: OK, we'll redo it for you.

SUTHERLAND: All right, let's get back to the engineering man-month chart. [See diagram below.] I'm worried about converging on this one. How did you arrive at these numbers? [The engineer explained the analysis to

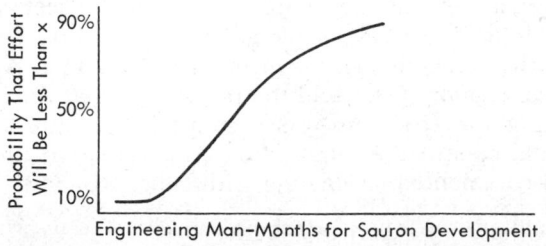

Engineering Man–Months for Sauron Development

Sutherland.] No, that's not a 50% confidence level. I'd say it's more like a 10% confidence level.

ASSISTANT PROGRAM MANAGER: Why don't you take a look at the S73 pricing analysis? The 100% figure should include everything that could possibly happen.

SUTHERLAND: Even at the 90% confidence level, I'd say your analysis is off by at least 100%. Why don't you put a probability curve on the schedule completion. I want some degree of couth. [About five or ten minutes of discussion among people at the meeting followed.] OK, let's not work that problem here.

After the meeting with the engineers, Sutherland rewrote his one-page, weekly Program Status report and tried to catch up on the week's mail.

He also made the following comments to the researcher:

> I was trying to do two things at the meeting. First, I had spent some time before telling these engineers the kind of format I wished. I wanted to know the impact of program delays and underestimation of the size of the program on the manpower. Overhead rates change a number of times every year at Richardson. Therefore, performance can be better tracked against man-months of labor.
>
> The main thing that I was trying to get in this, and a number of other meetings, was a degree of sophistication in our analysis. The material that I was getting simply was not of a quality that I felt I could use with group or corporate people.

Sutherland's last meeting of the day was with Art Schoen to discuss the status of preparation for the top management presentations. After the meeting the program manager made the following comments to the researcher.

> The Sauron project did not exist a year ago. It's a new project: it's got new people. There hasn't been time to retrain or to change old habits and styles. Our problem is, given these constraints, to find out what kind of poker game we're in, and then determine how much the chips are going to cost us.
>
> A number of years ago I established my technical ability within and outside of the Richardson Corporation. I think it's fair to say that I am considered one of the top engineers in Richardson. The jobs I have held have been predominantly engineering and concept oriented.
>
> I was aware that if I was to get ahead any further, I would have to convince top management here that I was a capable manager. This did not necessarily mean that I wished or will make program management my career.
>
> Demonstrated capability to manage a program of major importance to the company is a critical attribute. I think I am doing a good job. The objective way to measure this, of course, is whether I win the contract. However, if I lose, it is important that I know why I've lost.
>
> I have accepted this job for a number of reasons, one is personal pride—I'm sure I can do any job in Richardson. Secondly, I sincerely think that Richardson can do a good job for the Air Force on the program, and I know that Richardson needs the program to continue to employ the technical talent that we have.

Exhibit 1

RICHARDSON CORPORATION

Income Statement

($ millions)

	1968	1967	1966	1965	1964
Sales					
Military aircraft..................	$ 955	$ 846	$ 737	$ 795	$ 682
Missiles & space..................	585	670	445	409	421
Commercial......................	622	508	270	211	137
Total......................	$2,162	$2,024	$1,452	$1,415	$1,240
Earnings before taxes................	$ 103	$ 102	$ 98	$ 105	$ 63
Earnings after taxes.................	58	59	53	55	32
Earnings per share..................	2.69	2.87	2.89	6.69	3.95
Stock price range...................	63–36	78–43	57–31	73–42	50–25

Source: Richardson Annual Reports.

Exhibit 2

RICHARDSON CORPORATION

Balance Sheet

($ millions)

	1968	1967	1966	1965	1964
ASSETS					
Cash............................	$ 42	$ 46	$ 50	$ 69	$ 33
A/R............................	112	140	141	165	164
Inventories......................	716	550	351	151	137
Total current..............	$ 870	$ 736	$542	$385	$334
Fixed assets.....................	721	640	470	269	219
Less: depreciation.................	282	219	171	149	129
Net...........................	$ 439	$ 421	$299	$120	$ 90
Total......................	$1,309	$1,157	$841	$505	$424
LIABILITIES					
A/P............................	$ 420	$ 350	$171	$120	$ 94
Accrued expenses.................	119	104	84	73	64
Current part L.T. debt............	7	6	4	3	3
Total current..............	$ 546	$ 460	$259	$196	$161
Long-term debt..................	235	240	233	47	55
Stockholders' equity...............	528	457	349	262	208
Total......................	$1,309	$1,157	$841	$505	$424

Source: Richardson Annual Reports.

Exhibit 3

RICHARDSON CORPORATION
Missiles and Space Group
Organization Chart
January 1969

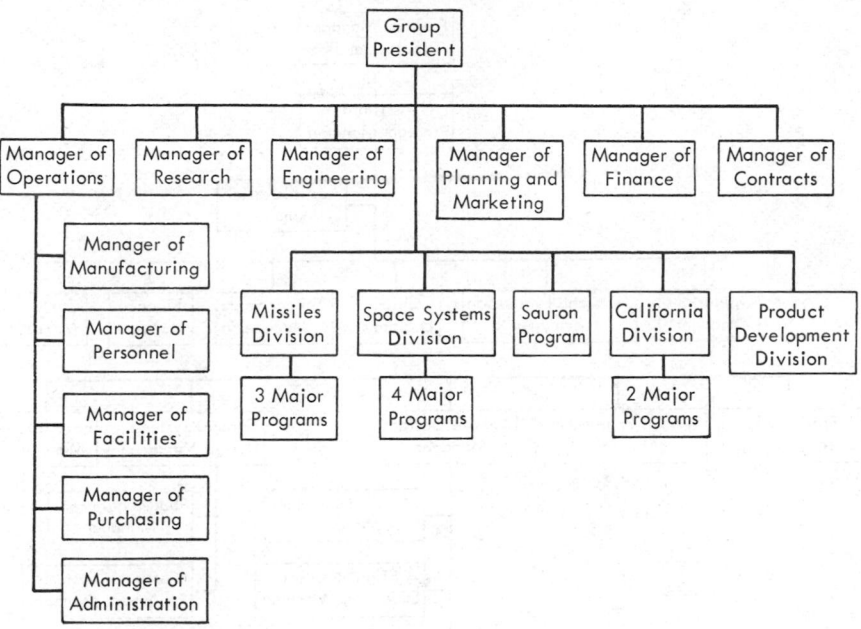

Source: Missiles and Space group organization manual.

Exhibit 4

RICHARDSON CORPORATION
Sauron Program
Organization Chart
January 1969

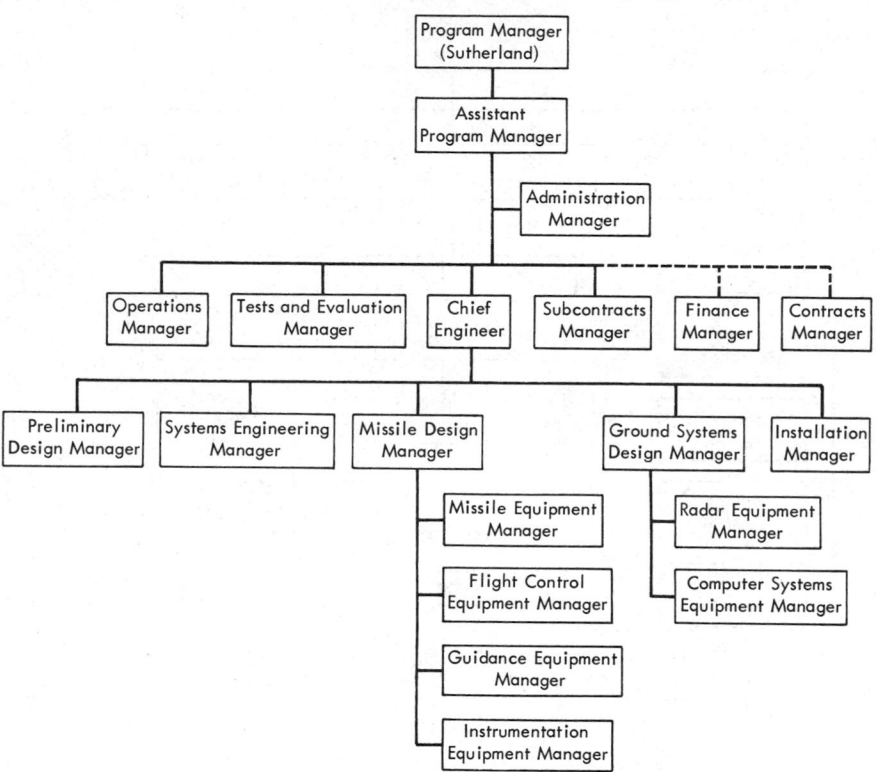

Source: Missiles and Space group organization manual.

Exhibit 5

RICHARDSON CORPORATION
Key Contract Definition Tasks and People
Involved in Their Performance

TASKS:	Design of hardware and software to meet Air Force performance specifications	Estimate probable cost distribution for engineering development work	Write engineering development contract
	What technology will be needed? What approach will we take to the solution of the technical problems?	How much will it cost and how long will it take to solve the technical problems and build a prototype system?	What price and incentive arrangement should we commit Richardson to?
PEOPLE INVOLVED:	Subcontractors Engineering Contracts Air Force Program officers	Subcontractors Engineering Finance Program management	Contracts Corporate management Group management Program management Air Force Program officers

Source: Casewriter's notes.

Industrial Products, Inc.

ON APRIL 5, 1967, the finance committee of Industrial Products, Inc. approved its Equipment Division's capital request for $5.8 million to build a new plant for FIREGUARD, a line of fire protection equipment. However, in October 1967 Mr. Robert Kendall, Manager of the Chemical Process Department (see Exhibit 1), the department in which FIRE-GUARD was produced, was considering the possibility of killing the expansion project. Divisional pressure for improved departmental earnings and FIREGUARD's continued record of substantial operating losses argued for not using the appropriated capital funds. On the other hand, Kendall was well aware that many people in his department were committed to growing the FIREGUARD business and would be quite upset if the project were killed. The context in which Kendall had to make his decision was the following.

EQUIPMENT DIVISION, INDUSTRIAL PRODUCTS, INC.

Industrial Products, Inc. was founded in 1949 as a producer of refrigeration equipment. Since that time, the company had diversified its activities into areas such as material handling systems, machine tools, heavy industrial equipment, and laboratory instruments. In 1966, the company's sales were in excess of $350 million.

The Equipment Division was the largest of Industrial's divisions measured in terms of sales revenue. In 1966, the Equipment Division's sales were $135.4 million and its net income before taxes was $31.2 million on an investment of $96.5 million. FIREGUARD, the division's new fire protection line, contributed sales of $2.2 million but produced a net loss before taxes of $1.1 million in 1966. However, with forecasted potential sales in excess of $30 million per year and forecasted net income before taxes in excess of $6.0 million per year, FIREGUARD was considered one of the most promising new products in the Equipment Division.

FIREGUARD

In its continuing work on refrigerants, the Equipment Division's Refrigeration Department had developed a number of new plastic materials that exhibited superior fire extinguishing properties. At the same time, the division already produced some of the kind of equipment needed to extinguish fires. Because both the equipment and materials required were readily available in existing businesses, experimental and then commercial sales soon followed. The brand name under which the division developed this business was FIREGUARD.

The division management was highly optimistic concerning FIREGUARD's commercial prospects. Whereas all automatic fire extinction equipment required extensive piping to create a system, FIREGUARD was able to operate with a number of physically independent modules. Thus the size of a FIREGUARD system depended principally on the number of module units in the area to be protected.

The source of FIREGUARD's advantage lay in the chemical process used to extinguish fires. The Equipment Division's scientists had discovered a relatively inexpensive chemical substance they called NO-OX that expanded with explosive speed when exposed to air, reacting with the oxygen to free a heavy inert gas. The fire extinction properties of the gas were immediately recognized as superb.

The attack on the fire protection and extinguishing market called for early sales of single module equipment to the "traditional" market for portable extinguishers (local governments, schools, fire departments, industrial plants, commercial offices). Sales of automatic fire protection systems to the same users would follow. Finally, the strategy called for expanding primary demand by eventually introducing automatic residential systems. Exhibit 2 shows sales of the portable units from 1961 to 1966. The automatic systems market was entered for the first time during 1966.

The FIREGUARD business was the responsibility of Mr. Robert Kendall, Manager of the Equipment Division's Chemical Process Department (see the organization chart, Exhibit 1). The department manufactured and sold equipment for chemical manufacturing processes. In 1960, the division's General Manager, Mr. Lon Fischer, had become concerned with the quality of performance in the manufacturing and construction of chemical process equipment while it was part of the general refrigeration area and had reorganized the activity in a new department—chemical processes—so that "the chemical phase of the business could get separate attention." Because FIREGUARD was a "chemical" business, it was moved into the Chemical Process Department at the time of its formation.[1]

The Equipment Division's assessment of the market was described by George Kramer, Product Manager for FIREGUARD.

> When we went into FIREGUARD we thought we knew a great deal about the fire protection business. However, we discovered that we

[1] The NO-OX business remained in the Refrigeration Department. The Chemical Process Department "purchased" the chemical from the Refrigeration Department at a negotiated "market" price.

knew very little and our customers knew less. They couldn't have cared less about the product. They were protected because they had to be according to the law or the insurance company. So we have had to study the job for the customer. The result has been that we have had a big learning and education program.

Commenting on Mr. Kramer's description, Mr. Kendall observed:

We got into the FIREGUARD business because we knew how to build some equipment and we had superior extinguishing materials. In fact we know how to build the containers very well. We make them at our Akron, Ohio factory. But we're still learning how to put together the support equipment.

The difficulty in engineering has been to learn the requirements of different applications. We are marketing a system, not equipment, and not extinguishing material. Thus, most of our learning has to be in the field in a sequence of trial and error steps.

Out of the first 300 units, we had to take back 100 over time. Now it's 200 out of 3,000. The engineers are still worried: they can explain what happens after the fact but the problem of responding in a controlled way to undesired fires or explosions is still there.

The other aspect of FIREGUARD planning has been market definition. It has been going on for five or six years as we have tried to move from fire departments to industrial plants, to office building systems, to homeowners. Each area is a different problem in the field. Different costs can be cut, different customers have to be educated, and in some instances different parts of our division have to be educated.

For example, we have had an endless series of arguments with our automatic systems design group trying to define what fire protection was. When we finally got it settled, we found that we needed a larger container unit.

However, the decision to build a larger container posed an important facility problem for us. We knew we were going to have to expand because FIREGUARD was already using 250,000 out of 750,000 production man-hours available at Akron. By 1970, the forecasts indicated that FIREGUARD would require 650,000 man-hours. And our other lines were growing.

Add to this the problem of the large containers and it's clear we needed a new facility. We really weren't up to handle them in the existing facility. Therefore, I asked Steve Matthews, facilities planner for FIREGUARD, to study the Akron plant and make recommendations.

Steve Matthews' career at Industrial Products had begun at Akron. He left the company only to rejoin it later to work on a task force which introduced a new data processing system to the Cleveland facility. His performance on that job led to his assignment in February 1966, to head a team put together to study the organization and operation of the Equipment Division's activities at their Cleveland and Akron locations. This assignment was later expanded to cover a study in depth of the FIREGUARD facilities at Akron. Matthews commented on his approach to the study.

My problem was to get a feel for each of Akron's businesses out of marketing. I wanted a definition of the way we did business in each of these markets. It was not easy. For example, in FIREGUARD, George

Kramer's forecast was the greatest problem. It was absurdly conservative. I needed to know everything about the business, the way it was going to grow, the role of the parts business, the nature of customer service, and exactly how the business was going to be run so we could design a facility that would meet these needs.

We started the study on the assumption that the business would expand at Akron (location) because it appeared economic to do so. It seemed that the question of relocation costs, the problem of building a new building, and the location of the market indicated that we stay at Akron.

So we were evaluating existing facilities in the light of the markets of 1970 and beyond. If our product managers didn't give us the forecast, we interpolated as best we could. We wanted to build a facility which would enable us to do business the right way in 1970.

Matthews had found the major elements of his problems to be (1) Akron was poorly run, the data available were poor and the manpower available to gather data not always adequate; (2) problems at Akron resulted from the way in which the relationship between engineering and production were organized, an issue outside the scope of the study; (3) many of the study group's findings reflected unfavorably on Akron management and therefore raised political problems; and (4) the group came to feel that the need was for a "mass production" type activity although Akron was typically "job shop" oriented. As a result, the facility being planned looked as if it would be a radical departure from existing facilities both in terms of physical design and the mode of operation.

In fact, by November 1966, when Matthews was to meet with Kendall for a final review of the FIREGUARD project, he had been ready to recommend a new plant in the Carolinas.[2] It was Matthews' judgment that it would be easier to implement the critical nonfacility[3] part of the FIREGUARD expansion project in the new location. He had explained to Kendall that "failure to undertake and effectively implement nonfacility programs would negate the effects of the proposed physical facility plan."

The last part of the meeting with Kendall held November 15 had concerned the size of the capital investment and its timing. An excerpt from that conversation is reproduced below:

MATTHEWS: . . . And, I may be wrapping it up too soon, but we strongly recommend going to South Carolina. The existing manufacturing facilities are theoretically adequate to meet the FIREGUARD market demands through 1969. But, practically, we believe that conditions demand the acceleration of this project. Expanded production to meet 1967 and 1968 forecasts plus inventory build-up in anticipation of moving the production

---

[2] While Matthews formally reported to the Akron plant manager, he kept in close contact with Kendall throughout the FIREGUARD study. The Akron plant manager attended many of these meetings and was aware of Matthews' assessment of the Akron facility and its management. However, since the demand for Akron's other products was growing and their production caused less problems than FIREGUARD's, the Akron plant manager was not upset at the prospect of losing FIREGUARD.

[3] Accounting and information systems, inventory and production control systems, and material handling systems.

lines will be very difficult to achieve under the existing conditions. The new factory will be needed as soon as it can be constructed. We prefer to schedule the physical construction program to fit into the program for an orderly transfer of personnel, equipment and procedures. Systems and procedures are to be completely worked out before this move is made. Our schedule calls for completion of the plant in the late fall of 1968, assuming that authorization to proceed is obtained in the first quarter of 1967.

KENDALL: There is no way we can invest incrementally?

MATTHEWS: I don't really think so.

KENDALL: What are we going to do when they won't give us $5.8 million?

MATTHEWS: You either bet on a business or you don't. You either believe the forecasts or you don't.

KENDALL: What if you believe half a forecast?

MATTHEWS: You couldn't build half a plant. You save some, but not a lot. What's a half? What forecast are you going to hang your hat on?

KENDALL: Half: I'll commit myself for half but want to be able to make the whole thing. Can't you build one plant for 1971 and then another just like it for 1975? Or what about some added subcontracting? Why can't we do more subcontracting since our manufacturing process isn't that unique?

MATTHEWS: As for two plants, you put machines in for the product and you don't need more than one, even for peak volume. As for subcontracting, our make or buy analysis shows that if we realize forecasted sales, we can improve our return by manufacturing some parts that we now subcontract.

KENDALL: Well, yes, but if we really don't have a proprietary position in terms of knowledge and so on, why can't we subcontract our expansion in this area?

MATTHEWS: The trouble with subcontracting is that you never make your delivery promises. It's just impossible to get yourself organized so that you can produce the kind of customer service you need.

Bob, I know your problem. You're thinking about our original estimate of $1.9 million back in June. The original facility was just a factory. This is also a warehouse and a service center. And given the nonfacility expenditures for systems, the investment per unit of capacity is the same as the original proposal.

Kendall had accepted Matthews' argument and arranged to have the FIREGUARD project presented to a meeting of the Equipment Division's executive committee[4] on December 16. Matthews began that meeting by describing the basic strategic assumptions of the FIREGUARD business. He described it as "a business selling hardware at a profit, based on warehousing, service, and parts." He noted that at the rate the business was growing, by 1969, they would be handling five million parts. That meant, he argued, that FIREGUARD was a large-volume production-oriented operation rather than the traditional job shop kind of business typical of Akron.

Excerpts from the meeting included the exchange below:

BRIGGS (Gen Mgr.):   The rumor mill had it that the new facility at Akron was going to cost only $2 million. Why is it that your proposal is so expensive?

---

[4] The divisional executive committee consisted of the division's general manager, assistant general manager, department managers, and top functional managers.

KENDALL: The original facility the people were talking about was simply a plant for the large containers. This is a much larger operation with many more products.

MATTHEWS: Also, the original facility was just a factory. Not only are there more products but this is a warehouse and service center.

A substantial discussion of labor costs and related problems led to the question of systems.

HUGHES (Mgr. Eng.): What about systems, do you have any allowance for the cost of all these systems you are installing?

MATTHEWS: You have $175,000 project costs and $185,000 engineering and that ought to cover it.

HUGHES: That's not enough, how many programmers do you have?

MATTHEWS: Five, I think.

HUGHES: I think that is low. We had 10 programmers at East St. Louis [an earlier project] if I am not mistaken.

GOLDEN (Asst. Gen. Mgr.): How many accountants do you have?

Matthews looked the figure up in his back-up notebook. He explained that the nature of the FIREGUARD operation was such that it would produce for a full warehouse rather than on the basis of meeting customer demand. Therefore, the demand on accounting was different from traditional equipment businesses.

GOLDEN: I think traditionally we have had our overrun (spent more than budget) on systems and accounting.

MATTHEWS: I think I understand your point, Bill, and we will do our best to take care of it.

After this discussion, Matthews presented the project summary shown below.

	1967	1968	1969	1970	1975
			(millions of dollars)		
Sales	$ 3.6	$ 9.0	$17.7	$24.5	$41.5
Net income before taxes	(1.1)*	(.4)*	.8*	3.9	7.5
ROI	—	—	7.4	26.0	32.0
Fixed investment	1.0†	1.2†	4.3†	6.9†	8.0‡
Working capital	2.5	4.7	6.5	8.1	15.5
Total investment	3.5	5.9	10.8	15.0	23.5

* Includes $1.1 million for noncapital items associated with the move: i.e., costs of transfers, lay-offs, training, equipment moving, and project management.

† Will provide space to satisfy forecasted sales through 1975 and equipment to satisfy forecasted sales through 1970.

‡ $1.1 million additional equipment will be needed to satisfy 1975 forecasted sales.

On April 5, 1967, Briggs presented the FIREGUARD project to the corporate finance committee. While questions of subcontracting, poor current performance, and future ROI were raised, the general feeling of the group was that the project was a good one and the business very promising. Therefore, after a short discussion, the project was approved.

SECOND THOUGHTS

However, Kendall was still uneasy about the FIREGUARD project. Matthews argued that the future market for FIREGUARD products was large and lucrative. Yet the earnings record of FIREGUARD since its inception in 1961 had been poor. Moreover, as sales for the product grew, so did the losses.

Kendall's concern was intensified when the review of his department's 1968 Business Plan was conducted in October 1967.[5] Divisional executives had expressed concern with the department's recent earnings record (see Exhibit 4). Moreover, Kendall was well aware that the corporation had specifically asked about the FIREGUARD business the previous fall. Since corporate requests for detailed information on an individual business were quite unusual, Kendall knew that FIREGUARD was in the limelight and that most likely there was pressure on the division officers to see that the business' performance improved.

In an effort to secure some guidance in this matter, Kendall asked Mike Richards, Corporate Director of Planning, to discuss FIREGUARD with him. While Richards reflected corporate thinking he did not represent it. Therefore, the meeting between Kendall and Richards was in the nature of "informal advice" rather than "formal corporate review."

The October 27 meeting began with Kendall expressing his concerns to Richards.

KENDALL: Mike, Briggs is putting pressure on me to raise the department's profits. But if FIREGUARD goes ahead with the approved expansion, earnings are not going to get much better. On the other hand, Matthews has some convincing arguments for FIREGUARD's market potential. To tell the truth, I'm perplexed.

RICHARDS: Well, . . . from my point of view, FIREGUARD doesn't fit with the rest of our products. We make machine tools, material handling systems, and refrigeration equipment. We enjoy a close relationship with our customers so that we can understand and help solve their technical problems.

On the other hand, FIREGUARD is a mass-produced, standard design product. Moreover, compared to our existing product line, FIREGUARD is mass marketed. That means problems of distribution and service that we haven't faced before.

KENDALL: OK, but FIREGUARD's got a fantastic future potential. Its sales in 1975 could easily exceed the total department's sales today.

RICHARDS: Look, I'm not arguing that you drop FIREGUARD completely. I'm merely saying that you don't really know how to market or produce the

---

[5] The Equipment Division's Business Plan attempted to answer the questions "What will happen to our products next year and the year after that?" and "What do we plan to do about it?". Departmental Plans were reviewed each fall by the division. (Performance against current plan was reviewed quarterly.) This plan review was a formal meeting in which departmental managers made presentations of their Business Plan to divisional officers. Officers were free to make comments and often did.

Plans were typically concerned with market size, market share, product volume, product price, and profit. Return on investment was sometimes used as a tool to measure the quality of a "business," but the business plans did not include specific investment planning. At most, a crude forecast of "capital requirement" was included.

product very well. If I were you, I would be inclined to concentrate on improving FIREGUARD's profits and then grow the business after you've learned how to run it profitably.

KENDALL: That's easier said than done. We've already asked for and received approval for a new plant. The division will not be too pleased if I now say that FIREGUARD should not be expanded for a while. Moreover, I'm sure Matthews will hit the roof.

RICHARDS: Mike, you asked for my opinion and I've given it to you. I think it's better to retrench now rather than sacrifice current earnings to a project that has yet to make a profit.

Following his conversation with Richards, Kendall decided to speak with Matthews about the FIREGUARD project. Kendall began the meeting by explaining his concern over FIREGUARD's past and current performance and expressing pessimism about its future performance. To support this view, Kendall used many of Richards' arguments. Matthews responded quickly.

MATTHEWS: First, it seems to me that the issue is closed since the corporation approved our request for capital funds. Moreover I think their decision was a wise one. It takes money to build the marketing and systems capabilities we need to take advantage of the FIREGUARD opportunity. If we don't spend money today, we'll surely fail in the years to come.

Anyway, we've carefully timed our expenditures for capital and noncapital items so that we can cut back if the assumed market doesn't develop. For example, by December we will have ordered about $1.1 million in equipment and spent about $160,000 on noncapital items. Yet since the penalty for cancelling the equipment order is only $290,000, our total exposure as of the beginning of 1968 will be $450,000. (Cancellation of equipment was not allowed after January 1, 1968.) Moreover, while the entire capital budget of $5.8 million will be irrevocably committed by the end of 1968, we will have spent only $650,000 of our $1.1 million noncapital budget by that time. In fact, we wouldn't spend our entire noncapital budget until September 1969.

Also, even if FIREGUARD doesn't make it, you've always got a new plant even though most of the machinery is specially designed for the FIREGUARD product line. (The plant represented 70% of the capital budget.)

But this isn't going to happen. FIREGUARD has an enormous business potential. Moreover, the division will make as much on the NO-OX as it does on the equipment. But we both know that FIREGUARD is a new kind of product for the Equipment Division. It depends on the sales and servicing of hardware. This coupled with distribution are major factors to cope with. It's just going to take time and money to develop the capabilities we need.

KENDALL: But we haven't done very well in the six years we've been trying to date.

MATTHEWS: That's because we've been producing at Akron. Our new plant in South Carolina will solve many of our problems. Bob, it takes time to develop a new business. The payoff doesn't come right away.

KENDALL: Steve, that all sounds very good but have you looked at Kramer's monthly reports for the first seven months of this year (see Exhibit 5)? After six years it still sounds as if we just began.

MATTHEWS: Even a great business can do poorly if it's mismanaged. We haven't been coordinating design with production. We haven't had a production line suitable for high volume manufacturing. We haven't had adequate part standardization. We haven't put nearly enough money into developing the needed management and production control systems. Bob, I could go on like this for 10 minutes, but you know these problems as well as I do. How do you expect to make money given this situation? And you certainly can't blame Kramer for a manufacturing problem.

KENDALL: You've got a point, but then where the hell does Kramer get his forecasts? Doesn't he take the production constraint into consideration?

MATTHEWS: OK, you've got a point. However, I don't think that should influence your view of the future of FIREGUARD. A lot of people[6] here have spent a lot of time on this project. We have finally got it out from under Akron and have the resources to make it. I don't see how you can even consider changing it at this late date.

---

[6] While Matthews and about a dozen other men had spent over a year and half on the project, the possibility of moving the operation to South Carolina had been kept highly confidential because of its potential impact on the Akron work force. Thus, in addition to the people planning the facility, only the top division and corporate officers were aware of the decision to move the FIREGUARD production operation.

However, while the construction of the new plant had not begun by the time of the Matthews-Kendall meeting, some equipment had been ordered and options had been taken on a piece of land. The cost of cancelling the equipment order and the land option would be $105,000. Moreover, $114,500 had already been spent for non-capital items.

Exhibit 1

INDUSTRIAL PRODUCTS, INC.

Equipment Division

Partial Organization Chart as of March 1966

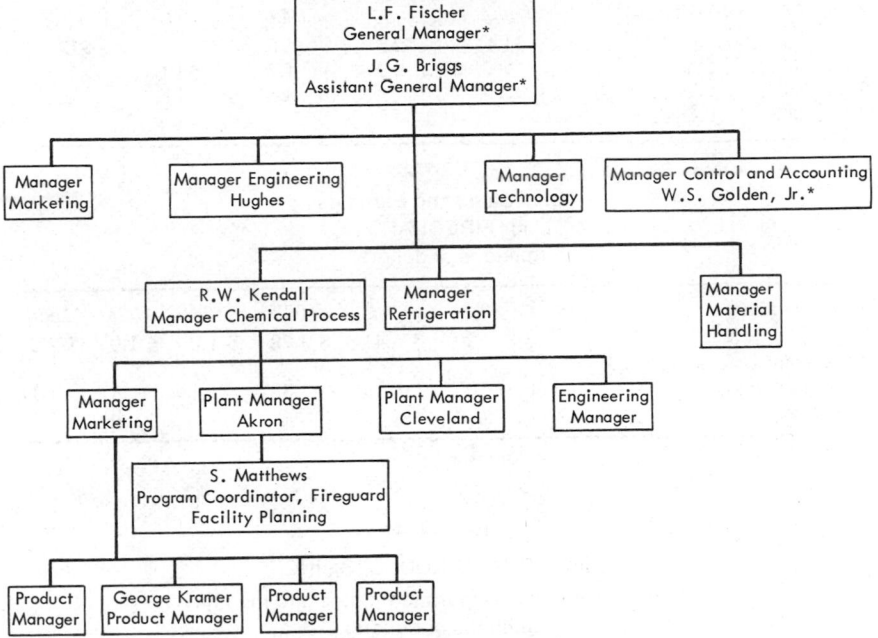

* After the promotion of Mr. Fischer to a position as a corporate officer, in July 1966, Mr. Briggs was made Division General Manager and Mr. Golden, Assistant General Manager.

Exhibit 2

INDUSTRIAL PRODUCTS, INC.

Sales of Portable FIREGUARD Units

1961–1966

(in number of units)

```
1961......................... 400
1962......................... 820
1963......................... 1,450
1964......................... 1,985
1965......................... 3,775
1966......................... 4,362
```

Exhibit 3

INDUSTRIAL PRODUCTS, INC.
Forecasted Sales for FIREGUARD
(millions of dollars)

Date of forecast	1964	1965	1966	1967	1968
September 1964................	$1.1	$2.5	$4.3		$13.3
July 1965.....................		2.2	4.2	$8.1	
July 1966.....................			3.4	4.8	9.2
April 1967....................				3.6	

Actual Sales and Earnings
for FIREGUARD
(millions of dollars)

Year	1961	1962	1963	1964	1965	1966
Sales........................	$ .20	$ .41	$ .73	$ 1.0	$ 1.9	$ 2.2
Net income before taxes						
Actual.....................	(.05)	(.15)	(.38)	(.45)	(.8)	(1.1)
Plan					(.3)	.1

Exhibit 4

INDUSTRIAL PRODUCTS, INC.
Chemical Process Department Sales and Income
(millions of dollars)

	1960	1961	1962	1963	1964	1965	1966
Sales........................	$ 12.4	$13.4	$15.1	$16.2	$17.8	$20.4	$23.2
Net income before taxes........	(.50)	.04	.75	1.72	2.3	3.0	3.1

Exhibit 5

INDUSTRIAL PRODUCTS, INC.

Product Manager's Written Comments on the Monthly
Progress Reports for FIREGUARD

January 1967: Equipment sales are 49% of plan because of large factory backlog ($790,000 on 1/31/66 from $439,000 on 12/31/65).

February 1967: Total equipment shipments are only 46% of plan. While Akron backlog has risen $500,000 this year, part of this is the customary seasonal build-up. It appears we may well be 20% below plan.

March 1967: Total shipments continue to lag with year-to-date sales at 50% of plan, up only 4% from February. We continue to have new equipment production difficulties as represented by a backlog of orders at Akron $850,000. Backlog as a result of shipments withheld due to production difficulties is $450,000 leaving sales to date substantially below plan as reflected by the latest yearly forecast.

April 1967: Sales continue to lag due to a continuing sales failure to penetrate the commercial market. Automatic systems sales have been delayed due to a lack of production of the new sensing device. Year-to-date total sales have improved 7% from March due to heavy overseas shipments. This foreign business is accomplished at significantly lower margins accounting for the continuing higher manufacturing cost versus sales.

May 1967: Sales continue to lag as reported in April with only slight improvement (0.4%). Equipment backlog is $725,000, about $300,000 above normal for sales to date. All costs to date are in line with the latest forecast except for development where there will be an overrun of $120,000 for 160% of plan due to automatic systems problems.

June 1967: The above listed low sales have been reflected in our 1968 Business Plan. Our entry into the industrial systems market has been set back at least one year for lack of satisfactory sensing equipment and is reflected in our 1968 Business Plan by a 94% reduction in plan sales in this area.

July 1967: The high manufacturing costs were due to accounting errors at Akron. One group of costs was cleared prior to sales clearing. Another group was cleared to cost of product when it should have been transferred to an inventory account. When these are corrected in August, the net effect will be to increase our August gross margin by about $75,000.

Managing the strategic process

THE LAST SET of cases in this book presents an opportunity to observe the range, unity, and interrelation of the concepts and subconcepts essential to the conscious formulation and implementation of a strategy governing the planned development of a total organization. The idea and its components have now been quite carefully and separately explored. It becomes appropriate at this point to reexamine corporate strategy not so much as a concept complete and still but as an organizational process forever in motion, never ending.

STRATEGY AS A PROCESS

For the purposes of analysis, as you have already noted, we have presented strategy formulation as being reasonably complete before implementation begins, as if it made sense to know where we are going before we start. Yet we know that we often move without knowing where we will end at last; the determination of purpose is in reality in dynamic interrelation with implementation. Implementation is itself a complex process including many subprocesses of thought and organization which introduce into prior resolution tentativeness and doubt and lead us to change direction.

That strategy formulation is itself a *process of organization*, rather than the masterly conception of a single mind, has been less clear till now. Yet the sheer difficulty of reconciling uncertain environmental opportunity, unclear corporate capabilities and limited resources, submerged personal values, and emerging aspirations to social responsibility suggests that at least in complicated organizations strategy must be an organizational achievement and may often be unfinished. Important as leadership is, the range of strategic alternatives which must be considered in a decentralized or diversified company exceeds what one person can conceive of. As technology develops, the chief executive cannot usually maintain his own technical knowledge at the level necessary for accurate personal critical discriminations. As a firm extends its activities internationally, the senior person in the company cannot himself learn in detail the cultural and geographical conditions which require local adaptation of both ends and means.

As in all administrative processes, *managing the process becomes a function distinct from performing it.* The principal strategists of technically or otherwise complex organizations therefore manage a strategic decision-making process rather than make strategic decisions. When they "make" a decision approving proposals originating from appraisals of need and opportunity made by others, they are ratifying decisions emerging from lower echelons in which the earliest and most junior participants may have played importantly decisive roles.[1] The structure of the organization may predetermine the nature of subsequent changes in strategy. In this sense strategy formulation is an activity widely shared in the hierarchy of management, rather than being concentrated at its highest levels. Top management, indeed, may bear the same relationship to divisional management as an outside board of directors does to top management. Unless it meddles improperly, such a board does not itself originate or conceive of the corporate strategy it has the ultimate responsibility of approving. The chief recourse of executives or directors ratifying strategy is not to second-guess proponents of specific alternatives but to make sure that the process is working right, that the quality of judgment applied to uncertainty is good, and that the context of strategic decision is conducive to adaptations of strategy of the magnitude required by changing opportunity and risk.

Participation in strategy formulation may thus begin with the market manager who sees a new product opportunity or the analyst who first arranges the assumptions that make possible a 30 percent return on investment in a new venture. But strategy may be influenced by organization structure as much as by individuals. The strategic alternatives generated in a functionally organized integrated company will be different in kind and scope from those maturing in divisionalized and diversified companies. The organization form of Solartron, you will remember, had influence on its strategy—in part, because organizational goals were part of Solartron's strategy, but even more significantly because autonomous corporate units inevitably compete for resources with a wide variety of unrelated new product ideas to ensure their own survival and growth. Opportunities requiring joint exploration of several of these autonomous organization units may be doomed by separation to neglect.

Similarly the cement plants in Rugby, all units in a functionally organized cost-controlled company are not going to suggest daring diversifications. We have seen that structure should follow strategy in organization design. What is important now is that in part structure *is* strategy. If, in short, the process of strategy formulation, as it must be, is distributed throughout an organization, the shape of that organi-

---

[1] See Joseph L. Bower, *Managing the Resource Allocation Process* (Boston: Division of Research, Harvard Business School, 1970).

zation and the influences that motivate it will be reflected in the strategy it produces. The strategic decision must, of course, be made in the light of organization and human consequences. Furthermore, it must be arrived at recognizing the constraint of structure and systems derived from previous strategy which influence the generation of new alternatives. Context is both supportive and inhibiting. It may be necessary to change organization before certain strategic alternatives can be fully explored or experimentally attempted.

The subunits of an organization established to implement a given corporate purpose soon are developing divergent strategies to support their own growth and development, especially if responsibility for profit and growth has been assigned to those units. It is true, therefore, that the organization processes and measurement systems by which the functioning of the structure is evaluated will influence strategy. When an international company once tried to interest its Latin-American subsidiaries in profit rather than in the number of sewing machines sold, the country managers, inexperienced but responsive, began making ice cream, selling insurance, and manufacturing stove grates in unused plant space. These diversifications, all aimed at increasing profitability within one year, changed, at least for a time, the local strategy of this company. The structure—geographically discrete and relatively autonomous profit centers—and the incentive system—reward for short-run profitability—together could ultimately have changed the strategy of the entire company. As it happens it was the corporate intention that the company go through a transition emphasizing profitability while its future strategy, too difficult a question for anybody in a company unused to strategic planning to settle, became a problem which could be managed.

In the course of a never finished process in which corporate strategy may be changing only imperceptibly in response to changing capabilities and changing market environments, sudden opportunity or major tactical decision may intrude to distract attention from distant goals to immediate gain. Thus the opportunity for a computer firm to merge with a large finance company may seem too good to pass up, but the strategy of the company will change with the acquisition or its ability to implement its strategy will be affected. A strategy may suddenly be rationalized to mean something very different from what was originally intended because of the opportunism which at the beginning of this book we declared the conceptual enemy of strategy. The necessity to accommodate unexpected opportunity in the course of continuous strategic decision is a crucial aspect of process. Accepting or refusing specific opportunity will strengthen or weaken the capability of an organization and thus alter what is probably the most crucial determinant of strategy in an organization with already developed market power.

MANAGING THE PROCESS

Study of the cases and ideas of this book usually leads to acceptance as the basis for management action of the need for a continuous process of strategic decision. This process extends from the origin of a discrete decision to its successful completion and incorporation into subsequent decisions. With this need established in an organization, the next step is to initiate the process and secure the participation first of those in senior management position and then of those in intermediate and junior positions. The simplest way for the chief executive of a company to begin is to put corporate objectives on the agenda of appropriate meetings of functional staff, management, or directors.

Consider, for example, a large, long-established, diversified, and increasingly unprofitable company. Its principal division was fully integrated from ownership of sources of raw materials to delivery of manufactured products to the consumer. Its president, after a day's discussion of the concept of strategy, asked his seven vice presidents, who had worked together for years, to submit to him a one-page statement expressing each officer's concept of the company's business, a summary statement of its strategy. He had in mind to go on from there, as users of this book have done in handling these cases. After identifying the strategy deducible from the company's established operations and taking advantage of their participation in resource allocation decisions, the vice presidents would be asked to evaluate apparent current strategy and make suggestions for its change and improvement. This first effort to establish a conscious process of strategic decision came to a quick recess when the president found that it took weeks to get the statements submitted and that, once collected, they read like descriptions of seven different companies.

When discussion of current strategy resumed, a number of key issues emerged from a study of a central question—why so successful a company was seeing its margins shrink and its profits decline. The communication of similar issues to those assigned responsibility to deal with the function they affect is an obvious next step. The soundness of the company's recent diversification was assigned as a question to the division managers concerned. They found themselves asked to present a strategy for a scheduled achievement of adequate return or of orderly divestment. The alternative uses of the company's enormous resources of raw material was examined for the first time. The record of the research and development department, venerable in the industry for former achievements, was suddenly seen to be of little consequence in the competition that had grown up to take away market share. Decisions long since postponed or ignored began to seem urgent. Two divisions were discontinued and expectations of improved performance began to alert the attention of division and functional managers throughout the organization to strategic issues.

Getting people who know the business to identify issues needing resolution, communicating these issues to all the managers affected, and programming action leading to resolution usually leads to the articulation of a strategy to which annual operating plans—otherwise merely numerical extrapolations of hope applied to past experience—can be successively related. It is not our purpose here, however, to present a master design for formal planning systems. This is a specialty of its own, which like all such other specialties, needs to be related to corporate strategy but not allowed to smother or substitute for it.

When formal plans are prepared and submitted as the program to which performance is compared as a basis for evaluation, managers in intermediate position are necessarily involved in initiating projects within a concept of strategy rather than proceeding ad hoc from situation to situation. Senior managers can be guided in their approval of investment decisions by a pattern more rational than their hunches, their instinct for risk, and their faith in the track record of those making proposals, important as all these are. They have a key question to ask: what impact upon present and projected strategy will this decision make? As you look at Heublein you will be asking what would the acquisition of Hamm's Brewery do to Heublein's original business? The latter will have to be accurately defined before the question can be answered or the consequences of any answer be made into a program of action or decision not to act.

Sustaining the strategic process requires monitoring resource allocation with awareness of its strategic—as well as operational—consequences and its social, political, as well as financial, characteristics. Seeing to it that the process works right means that the roles of the middle-level general manager be known and appropriately supported.

As Hugo Uyterhoeven has pointed out,[2] the middle-level general manager occupies a role quite different from that of the senior general manager, relevant as is his experience as preparation for later advancement. With strategic language and summary corporate goals coming to him from his superiors and the language and problems of everyday operations coming to him from his subordinates, he has the responsibility of translating the operational proposals, improvisations, and piecemeal solutions of his subordinates into the strategic pattern suggested to him by his superiors.

Faced with the need to make reconciliation between short-term and long-term considerations, he must examine proposals and supervise operations with an eye to their effect on long-term development. As he transforms general strategic directions into operating plans and programs, he is required to practice the overview of the general manager under the usual circumstance that his responsibility for balanced attention to short- and long-term needs and for bringing diverse everyday activities within the stream of evolving strategy far outruns his authority to require either change in strategy or to alter radically the product line of his division.

The general manager at middle level, certainly in a crucial position to implement strategy in such a way as to advance it rather than depart from it, needs to be protected against such distractions as performance evaluation systems overemphasizing short-term performance and to be supported continually in his duty of securing results which run beyond his authority to order certain outcomes. He needs to learn how to interpret the signals he gets as proposals he submits for top-management approval are accepted or turned down. His superiors will be de-

---

[2] See Hugo E. R. Uyterhoeven, "General Managers in the Middle," *Harvard Business Review*, March–April 1972, pp. 75–85.

pendent upon his judgment as they receive his proposals for new investment and will often be guided more by their opinion of his past performance or their desire to give him greater responsibility than by the detailed content of his proposals. They will do well then to realize the complexity of his position and the necessity of his being equal to the exigencies of making tactical reality subject to strategic guidance and to directing observation of operations toward appropriate amendment of strategy.

Developing the accuracy of strategic decision in a multiproduct, technically complex company requires ultimately direct attention to organization climate and individual development. The judgment required is to conduct operations against a demanding operating plan and to plan simultaneously for a changing future, to negotiate with superiors and subordinates the level of expected performance and to see, in short, the strategic implications of what is happening in the company and in its environment. The capacity of the general manager, outlined early in this book, must as part of the process of managing the strategy process be consciously cultivated, if the firm is to mature in its capacity to conduct its business and to be able to recognize in time the changes in strategy it must effect.

Executive development, viewed from the perspective of the general manager, is essentially the nurturing of the generalist capabilities referred to throughout the text portions of this book. The management of the process of strategic decision must be concerned principally with continuous surveillance of the environment and development of the internal capabilities and distinctive competence of the company. The breadth of vision and the quality of judgment brought to the application of corporate capability to environmental opportunity are crucial. The president who keeps his organization involved continuously in appraising its performance against its goals, appraising its goals against the company's concept of its place in its industry and in society, and debating openly and often the continued validity of its strategy will find corporate attention to strategic questions gradually proving effective in letting the organization know what it is, what its activities are about, where it is going, and why its existence and growth are worth the best contributions of its members.

The president of a company has as his highest function the management of a continuous process of strategic decision in which a succession of corporate objectives of ever-increasing appropriateness provides the means of economic contribution, the necessary commensurate return, and the opportunity for the men and women of the organization to live and develop through productive and rewarding careers.

Heublein, Inc. (A & B) (Condensed)

WITH GROWTH in sales and profits since 1959 far outstripping the liquor industry's "Big Four," Heublein, Inc., producer of Smirnoff vodka and other liquor and food items, had moved up to become the fifth largest liquor company in the United States by 1965. (See Exhibit 1 and 2 for Heublein financial statistics.)

Table 1*

Industry rank in 1965	Company	1964 Liquor sales (millons)	1965 Total sales (millons)	Total sales gain 1959–1965 (percent)	Profit gain 1959–1965 (percent)
1	Distillers Corporation.......	$718	$1,005	37	52
2	Hiram Walker.............	498	530	28	46
3	National Distillers.........	430	829	44	24
4	Schenley Industries (est.)....	390	461	0	33
5	Heublein, Inc.............	123	166	89	259

* Derived from various company annual reports.

Mr. Hart, Heublein's president since 1960 and a former executive vice president of international marketing for the Colgate-Palmolive Company, commented on the company's business as follows:

> Although liquor products account for most of our sales at the present time, we consider ourselves in the consumer goods business, not the liquor business. Liquor is a consumer good just like toothpaste and is sold the same way.
>
> To be successful in this business, you need three things: a good product, distribution, and advertising. You must have a good product. If you don't, the consumer will find you out and you will not get any

868

repeat purchases. You also need good distribution so the consumer will be able to get your product easily and conveniently. Finally, you must have a good convincing story to tell the consumer about why he should buy your product and you tell it through advertising.

In 1965, Heublein's management had three long-range goals: (1) to make Smirnoff the number one liquor brand in the world; (2) to continue a sales growth of 10% a year through internal growth, acquisitions, or both; and (3) to maintain Heublein's return on equity above 15%.

As one means of meeting these goals, a major specific acquisition opportunity was being considered in the fall of 1965. The potential acquisition (Hamm's Brewing Company) raised a number of short-term as well as strategic issues, however, which Mr. Hart wanted to consider carefully. Hamm's was almost as large as Heublein in sales, and therefore the impact of the acquisition on Heublein was certain to be significant. The beer and liquor industries were in many respects similar, but Heublein had had no direct experience in the beer industry. Mr. Hart emphasized that the kinds of companies being sought were not just profitable financial deals, but rather firms in which Heublein's management believed it could improve operations. Heublein's acquisition policies had been explained more fully by Mr. Hart in a 1965 presentation before the Los Angeles Society of Security Analysts:

> Frankly, we take a long hard look at any potential acquisition. We ask ourselves: "Will the new product or company we acquire have a potential at least equal to existing Heublein products, in order not to dilute present equity? Will new products lend themselves to our channels of distribution and marketing techniques? Will these products have sufficient gross margin to allow for our type of distribution, advertising, and merchandising?"

The question of the potential Hamm's acquisition will be explored in more detail following a description of Heublein's current position, strategy, and the trends in their basic markets.

Market. Between 1955 and 1964, U.S. consumption of distilled spirits[1] increased from 199 million wine gallons to 277 million, or 39% (see Exhibit 3). By the latter year, some 60 million Americans—about 53% of the adult population—drank some sort of alcoholic beverage. These Americans spent about $6.5 billion for liquor, about one-third of the amount spent for public elementary and secondary school education. Excise taxes[2] on these sales provided the Federal Government with about $2.5 billion in 1964, more than any other single source of revenue except for personal and corporate income taxes.

Rising sales of liquor could be attributed to various causes, including a rising population, increased personal discretionary income contribut-

---

[1] Several terms in common use in the industry require definition:

Proof is a term used to specify the proportion of alcohol in a product. The proof number is equal to twice the percent of alcohol (by volume) in the product.

A *proof gallon* is any volume which contains the same amount of alcohol as a gallon of 100 proof spirits.

A *wine gallon* is a gallon by volume (regardless of proof). Thus a gallon (five fifths) of 80 proof vodka would be one wine gallon but only 8/10 proof gallons.

[2] The federal excise tax on distilled spirits was $10.50 per proof gallon in 1965.

ing to a slightly higher per capita consumption; changing social mores; the declining proportion of people in "dry" states; and changes in the population make-up by age group. Mr. Edward Kelley, Heublein's executive vice president, felt the growth in liquor consumption between 1955 and 1964 was primarily the result of the increase in per capita consumption, which appeared to be related to the growth in personal discretionary income, and the spread of drinking to more segments of the population and on more occasions, resulting from the trends of social living habits.

Predicting the future in relation to income and demographic changes, industry sources looked forward to an even faster growth in consumption from 1965 to 1970 than from 1955 to 1964: 4.5% or more a year, compared with 3.6%. Since the Bureau of the Census forecast that the 25 to 54 age groups would increase an average of nearly 17% between 1970 and 1980, many industry observers felt the picture beyond 1970 looked better than that between 1965 and 1970.

Market changes.   Demand for the various categories of liquor was changing as well as growing between 1955 and 1964 (see Exhibits 3, 4, and 5). Thus there was a dramatic shift in consumer preference to straight whiskeys, imported whiskeys and the nonwhiskeys, and away from the blended and bonded whiskeys. While some observers felt this represented a return to the pre-World War II relationship which provided straight whiskeys with a slight edge over blended whiskeys, most industry sources felt the shift in consumption reflected a trend toward lightness in liquor taste. According to Roger Bensen:

> The most probable reason [for the trend toward lightness] is that people drink mainly to satisfy social and status needs and for effect and not inherently for taste. The taste of many liquors is something which new drinkers find difficult to assimilate. Hence, they turn to various cocktails or mixed drinks to disguise the original flavor of the liquor product. And to complete the pattern, people achieve further fulfillment of social and status needs by using the newer, more current, more exotic liquors and cocktail formulations as a vehicle for their drinking.[3]

Some of the most important of these changes are reflected in the following figures for distilled spirits entering trade channels:

According to many industry observers, one of the more important developments in the liquor industry between 1960 and 1965 was the growth of bottled cocktails. Although bottled cocktails had been on the market for over 50 years, they had shown little growth until 1960. In that year, Heublein, which had almost 100% of the market at that time, developed a new product formulation, package, and promotional campaign for its line of bottled cocktails. By 1965, volume had increased 100% to an estimated 1.9 million wine gallons, as Distillers Corporation, Hiram Walker, Schenley, and others entered the market. Nevertheless, Heublein, whose volume increased 60% during the period, still had 55% of the market in 1965. The convenience, low consumer price

---

[3] Roger Bensen, *Heublein, Inc.*, Investment Research Dept., Glore Forgan, Wm. R. Staats Inc., December 1965, p. 21.

Table 2

Product type	Volume 1955 (millions of wine gallons)	Volume 1964 (millions of wine gallons)	Market share 1955 (percent)	Market share 1964 (percent)	Change in vol. 1955 to 1964 (percent)
Whiskeys					
Bonded...............	12.9	7.9	6.3	2.8	(39)
Straight..............	46.1	69.6	22.7	24.3	51
Blend...............	81.5	74.7	40.0	26.1	(8)
Scotch...............	12.3	28.3	6.0	9.9	130
Canadian............	9.2	17.2	4.5	6.0	87
Total all whiskey..	161.5	197.9	79.5	69.1	22
Nonwhiskeys					
Gin*.................	20.7	31.1	10.2	10.9	50
Vodka*..............	7.0	28.1	3.4	9.8	302
Rum.................	2.7	5.9	1.3	2.1	119
Brandy..............	4.6	8.7	2.3	3.0	89
Other...............	6.6	14.6	3.3	5.1	121
Total nonwhiskeys.	41.8	88.4	20.5	30.9	111
Total distilled spirits..........	203.3	286.3	100.0	100.0	41

* Gin and vodka were unique among the distilled spirits since they required no aging. The principal distinction between gin and vodka was that the juniper berry flavor was added to grain neutral spirits to produce the former, while as many flavor-producing ingredients as possible were filtered out from grain neutral spirits to produce the latter.

(only a few pennies more than comparable drinks mixed at home), and trend toward lightness caused one liquor authority to predict that bottled cocktails might represent close to 10% of the industry's volume by 1975.

Trends in competition. Between 1955 and 1965, the majority of the companies in the liquor industry followed one of two broad strategies. Most of the medium-sized companies aggressively marketed their products in traditional ways. They did not increase, decrease, or change their product line, nor did they attempt to diversify out of the liquor business. None of these companies had a complete line of liquor products, and some had only one or two products. Several of these companies, however, experienced extremely rapid grwth during this period. Their success could generally be attributed to having a leading product in one or two of the more rapidly growing segments of the liquor market.

The four major distillers also marketed their products in traditional ways. However, with the exception of Hiram Walker, each of these companies attempted to diversify out of the liquor industry through acquisitions between 1955 and 1965. Even with this diversification, however, liquor accounted for the major portion of the sales of each of these companies in 1965. Moreover, with the possible exception of National Distillers, the major distillers no longer seemed to be interested in further diversification outside of the liquor business in the middle 1960s. Rather they began to compete more vigorously in all segments of the liquor market during 1964 and 1965, particularly the more rapidly growing segments. This increased competition, coupled with the trend toward lightness, caused John Shaw of Equity Research Associates to predict that:

Marketing efforts will become more consumer-oriented, stressing "appetite appeal" in much the same way as the food industry. Over all, advertising and promotional costs can be expected to trend higher, as brand competition remains intense.[4]

Thumbnail sketches of a few of the companies that have grown rapidly or that competed directly with Heublein are given below.

James B. Beam Distilling Company was a medium-sized liquor company that specialized in the production and marketing of premium Kentucky straight bourbon whiskey. Nearly 80% of Beam's $92 million sales in 1965 were derived from its Jim Beam brand, which was the second largest selling straight bourbon whiskey in the country. As a result of the expansion of the straight whiskey market, Beam was able to increase its profits by over 20% per year between 1953 and 1965.

Paddington Corporation[5] was the exclusive importer of J & B Rare Scotch whiskey, the number two brand of Scotch in 1964. Although J & B was Paddington's only product, the company sales and earnings growth were the highest in the industry between 1960 and 1964. In the latter year, Paddington earned 37.5% on its stockholders' equity, and gross sales reached over $125 million.

Distillers Corporation-Seagram's, Ltd., a Canadian-based corporation, was the largest worldwide producer and marketer of distilled spirits in 1965. Although 80% of Seagram's $897 million in 1964 gross sales came from whiskeys, the company also had a complete line of the nonwhiskeys. The breadth of its product line allowed Seagram's to take advantage of changing consumer preferences. Seagram's VO, for example, was the major recipient of the growing demand for Canadian whiskey. However, the company also changed old products or introduced new products in response to changing consumer preferences. When sales of Calvert Reserve had declined for over seven consecutive years, Seagram's replaced it with a restyled "soft whiskey," Calvert Extra, in the spring of 1963, and experienced an immediate sales gain of over 17%. In 1964, Seagram's withdrew Lord Calvert, a premium blended whiskey, and replaced it with Canadian Lord Calvert, a moderately priced Canadian whiskey bottled in the United States, to take advantage of the trend toward bulk imports. In addition, Seagram's introduced nine new liquor products between 1961 and 1964 to capitalize on the trend toward lightness. Among these were two Scotches (100 Pipers and Passport) and four liqueurs as well as a gin, a vodka, the first Hawaiian rum, and a line of Calvert bottled cocktails.

Schenley, the fourth largest liquor company in 1964 with gross sales of $406 million, had one of the lowest growth rates in the liquor industry between 1955 and 1964. The company's gross sales decreased about 3%

---

[4] John Shaw, "Trends in the Liquor Industry," *Equity Research Associates,* August 30, 1965, p. 6.

[5] Paddington Corporation was acquired by Liggett & Myers Tobacco Company in April 1966. L & M also acquired Star Industries, a wholesale liquor distributor, liquor importer, and owner of 40% of Paddington's voting securities, at the same time. In 1964, Star's net sales (sales less federal and state excise taxes) were $82 million. During the same year, L & M had net sales of $293 million and total assets of $401 million.

during that period, even though Schenley had three of the top 10 straight whiskey brands and had made several nonliquor acquisitions. However, in 1964, Schenley acquired Buckingham, the importer of Cutty Sark, the number one brand of Scotch, and introduced a line of bottled cocktails. As a result of these actions, several industry observers were predicting a turn around at Schenley by 1967.

Methods of distribution. Distribution of liquor took two basic forms at the beginning of 1966. In 18 "control states," a state-regulated agency was responsible for the distribution and sale of distilled spirits. In these states, the marketer usually sold the product to the state agency at the national wholesaler price and allowed the state to distribute the products as it saw fit. These states often had laws which restricted the type of point-of-promotion advertising that a company could undertake. In the other 32 states, called "open states," distribution was accomplished through wholesalers who redistributed the product to the retailers who sold the product to the ultimate consumer. From 1958 to 1964, the number of these independent wholesalers declined almost 43%, so there were only 2,305 wholesalers left in 1964 who were licensed by the Federal Alcohol Administration to deal in distilled spirits. This trend, which was similar to that in other consumer-product industries, was primarily caused, according to industry observers, by a serious profit squeeze on the wholesaler as his costs of operation increased while the retail prices of inexpensive liquors declined because of intense competition—a situation which was aggravated by the spread of private labels. While distillers had not felt the effects of this squeeze by 1964, there was a feeling among some industry observers that distillers might have to lower their prices to wholesalers or lose lower volume lines if the trend continued.

Cost structure. The cost of producing liquor products, excluding federal and state taxes on the raw materials, was relatively low compared to the retail selling prices. For example, high-quality vodka reportedly cost about 61 cents a fifth to produce, and retailed at $5.75. Federal taxes on raw materials, were often not much different for high-priced and low-priced liquors, even though they were often made by different processes. The different methods of production resulted in differences in taste and quality between the high-priced and low-priced liquors, however.

HEUBLEIN'S HISTORY

The House of Heublein was founded in 1859 in Hartford, Connecticut, by Andrew Heublein, a painter and weaver by trade. At that time, the House of Heublein was a combination restaurant, cafe, and small hotel. By 1875, Andrew's two sons, Gilbert and Lewis, were running the business. They branched out by conducting a wholesale wine business in addition to expanding the original operations. In 1892, through a combination of fortuitous circumstances, Heublein invented the bottled cocktail. From this time until the start of national prohibition, Heublein's principal business was the production and sale of distilled spirits.

In 1907, Heublein began importing Brand's A-1 steak sauce and later, when World War I disrupted the importation, acquired the manufacturing rights to the product in the United States. When prohibition forced Heublein to close down its liquor plant in 1920, the company transferred key personnel to food operations. Until the repeal of prohibition in 1933, A-1 steak sauce was Heublein's principal product.

In 1939, John Martin, Heublein's president and one of the company's principal stockholders, acquired the rights to Smirnoff vodka from Mr. Rudolph Kunett. Although Heublein sold only 6,000 cases of Smirnoff that year, a carefully planned promotional campaign, which was put into operation immediately after World War II, aided in boosting the sales of Smirnoff to over one million cases per year by 1954. As the vodka market expanded, Heublein introduced Relska vodka in 1953 and Popov in 1961 to have entries in the middle- and low-price segments of the market.

Although Smirnoff's remained Heublein's principal product from 1959, when it accounted for over 67% of sales, to 1965, when it accounted for 51% of sales, Heublein began to diversify its product line and to expand its international operations in the former year.

Heublein used both internal growth and acquisitions to broaden its product line. In 1960, Heublein began a campaign to increase the sales of its bottled cocktails by introducing new kinds of cocktails and promoting the entire line more heavily. As Heublein's sales began to increase, other distillers, principally Distillers Corporation, began to market their own cocktails. By 1965, bottled cocktails sales exceeded 850,000 cases a year, more than double the 1960 sales. At that time, Heublein still claimed 55% of the market.

In 1961, Heublein made two acquisitions which strengthened its specialty food line. Timely Brands, which manufactured and marketed a complete line of ready-to-use, home dessert decorating products including Cake-Mate icing and gels, was acquired in June. In July, Heublein acquired Escoffier, Ltd. of London, England, makers of 23 famed gourmet sauces and specialties.

Heublein made two more acquisitions during this period, both of which were designed to broaden and strengthen Heublein's liquor line. In April 1964, Heublein acquired Arrow Liquors Corporation for an estimated cost of $5.7 million. Arrow's principal products were its line of cordials, including Arrow Peppermint Schnapps, Arrow Blackberry Brandy, and its domestically bottled, bulk-imported Scotch, McMaster's. According to Mr. Edward Kelley, the three principal reasons for the Arrow acquisition were that Heublein expected the cordial and Scotch markets to grow in the future, that Arrow had products that were among the leaders in these markets in the control states, and that Arrow had a small but extremely competent management.

In January 1965, Heublein acquired Vintage Wines for approximately $2.2 million. Vintage, whose sales were about $4 million at the time of the acquisition, was integrated with the Heublein Liquor Division. Vintage's principal product was Lancers Vin Rose, and imported Portuguese wine that accounted for about 50% of the company's sales.

The expansion which occurred in Heublein's international operations consisted primarily of the establishment of franchise operations in 21 additional foreign countries. This raised the number of such operations from 11 in 1959 to 32 in 1965.

HEUBLEIN'S RECENT OPERATIONS

Financial situation. During the 1965 fiscal year, Heublein earned $7.4 million on sales of $166 million, which represented about a 19% return on stockholders' equity. Between 1959 and 1965, Heublein's sales growth, profit growth, and return on equity far exceeded the average of the four major distillers (see Table 1). In addition, even though Heublein was spending nearly twice as much (as a percentage of sales) on advertising as the average of the four major distillers, and had increased the company's dividend payout ratio to 50% of earnings, the company had a cash flow of $8.6 million in 1965, about 22% on equity, which compared favorably to the 9% average of the four major distillers.

Product line. At the end of 1965, Heublein was marketing well over 50 products through its four divisions. While vodka was the company's principal product, accounting for 62% of 1965 sales, the company's product base had been broadened considerably since 1960 by acquisitions, internal growth, and new marketing agreements (see Exhibit 6 for sales mix trends). Heublein's product-line strategy was to market high-quality consumer products which provided the high margins necessary to support intensive advertising. Heublein aimed its promotions of these products at the growing, prosperous, young adult market. The company was also interested in phasing out some of its less profitable lines whenever possible.

The liquor products division accounted for over 80% of Heublein's 1965 sales. Its principal product was Smirnoff vodka, the fourth largest selling liquor brand in the United States in 1965, with estimated annual sales of 2.3 million cases. Company officials expected that Smirnoff, with its faster rate of growth would move ahead of the third place brand (Canadian Club: 2.4 million cases) and second place brand (Seagram's VO: 2.5 million cases) within three years.

In 1965, Smirnoff had 23% of the total vodka market and outsold the second place vodka brand by over four to one. In addition, Smirnoff was the only premium-priced vodka on the market in 1965, since Wolfschmidt, formerly another premium-priced vodka, had lowered its wholesale price in 1964 in an effort to stimulate sales. After considering this action, Mr. Hart decided the appropriate response was to raise Smirnoff's wholesale price $1 per case and to put the additional revenue into advertising. Although Wolfschmidt's sales more than doubled, this increase appeared to come from the middle-priced segment of the vodka market, since Smirnoff's sales also increased 4% over the previous year and was running over 10% ahead in 1966. Smirnoff also appeared to be immune to the spread of the hundreds of private-label vodkas, since company officials felt that these products obtained their sales from the 15% to 30% of the vodka market that was price conscious.

As a result, many industry observers expected Smirnoff to dominate the vodka market well into the future, particularly since Smirnoff could, on the basis of its sales volume, afford to spend $7 million to $8 million on advertising, while its closest rival could afford to spend only $2 million before putting the brand into the red.[6,7]

Relska, a medium-priced vodka, and Popov, a low-priced vodka, were produced and sold primarily to give Heublein's distributors a full line of vodka products. They accounted for 11% of company sales in 1965. They were cheaper to produce than Smirnoff but were not as smooth to the taste, according to company officials.

Heublein bottled cocktails sold an estimated 500,000 cases in 1965, about 55% of the bottled cocktail market. Nevertheless, Heublein was beginning to receive competition from the national distilling companies, particularly Distillers Corporation, whose U.S. subsidiary, Seagram's, was marketing a similar line. Mr. Hart, however, welcomed this competition. He commented to the Los Angeles Society of Security Analysts in 1965:

> We believe the idea of bottled cocktails has not been completely sold to the American public. We were therefore delighted when we learned that one of the major companies in the liquor industry was introducing a new line of cocktails and that there would be heavy expenditures in advertising and merchandising to promote their usage to the public.[8]
>
> We are of the opinion that, as the cocktail market expands, our share will decrease, but Heublein cocktails will continue to be the leader and that our cases will show remarkable increases.

Mr. Hart explained to the casewriter that distribution was one of the principal reasons Heublein would keep its number one position:

> We secured distribution in 1960 when the other companies weren't too interested in cocktails. Since a distributor will usually carry only two or three lines, this means that he will have Heublein and Calvert or Heublein and Schenley: in other words, Heublein and somebody else. . . . In addition to being first, Heublein's wide line will also help us get and maintain distribution.

In 1965, Heublein's bottled cocktail line included Manhattans, Vodka Sours, Extra Dry Martinis, Gin Sours, Whiskey Sours, Side Cars, Vodka Martinis, Daiquiris, Old Fashioneds, and Stingers.

During 1964, the liquor products division re-introduced Milshire gin. For years, Milshire had been a regional gin selling about 100,000 cases a year. However, in 1963 the promotional budget was deemed sufficient to devote some real attention to Milshire. To prepare for this, the old inventory was sold off, the product was reformulated, and the package was redesigned. The principal difference in the product was that its botanical

---

[6] Roger D. Bensen, *Heublein, Inc.*, Glore Forgan, Wm. R. Staats Inc., December 1965, p. 25.

[7] In 1963, according to the *Liquor Handbook*, Heublein spent $1.4 million to advertise Smirnoff, while total advertising for all other vodka brands during the same year was $1.2 million.

[8] Heublein spent $2 million advertising its line of bottled cocktails in 1965. Seagram's spent $1.5 million advertising its Calvert line the same year.

and aromatic content was lowered since it was filtered through activated charcoal in a process similar to that used to make Smirnoff. The net effect of this was to make the gin "lighter." Sales for 1964 increased to 150,000 cases, a significant jump, but still very far behind the 2.1 million cases of Gordon's, the leading brand.

In 1966, Heublein reached an agreement with Tequila Cuervo S.A. to be the exclusive U.S. marketer of Jose Cuervo and Matador tequilas and a cordial based on the same spirit. Heublein planned to market these products on a nationwide basis through the liquor products division.

The liquor products division also marketed Harvey's sherries, ports, and table wines; Bell's Scotches; Gibley's Canadian whiskeys; Byrrh aperitif wine ("Byrrh on the rocks, please"); and the products of Vintage Wines, Inc.

The Arrow division accounted for about 10% of Heublein's sales in 1965. The division's principal products were Arrow cordials, liqueurs, and brandies, and McMaster's Scotch. Arrow's distribution system was particularly strong in the control states. In addition, Arrow's distribution in the open states was strengthened in 1965, when Heublein discontinued the production of its line of Heublein cordials and substituted the Arrow line.

Although the sales of the food division more than doubled between 1961 and 1965, it accounted for only 8% of the company's 1965 sales. Nevertheless, A-1 steak sauce was the company's number two profit producer in 1965, second only to Smirnoff vodka. Other food products included Cake-Mate icings and gels, Escoffier sauces, Grey-Poupon Mustard, and Maltex and Maypo cereals. In 1965, Heublein reached an agreement with the Coastal Valley Canning Company of California to distribute and market Snap-E-Tom Tomato Cocktail. Snap-E-Tom was a tomato juice flavored with onion and chili pepper juices. It was designed for the pre-meal juice and the cocktail mixer markets, both of which had high profit margins.

Marketing. The casewriter felt that Heublein's unique advertising and promotion policies and campaigns set Heublein apart from the other liquor companies (see Exhibit 7 for the advertising expenditures of various liquor companies). Heublein considered liquor to be a branded consumer product, and viewed itself as a marketer of high-quality consumer products rather than as a liquor company. As a result, Heublein developed intensive advertising campaigns to sell its products for the growing, affluent young adult market, since it believed it was easier to get a new customer in this market than to get a 40-year-old Scotch drinker to switch to vodka. Because of the importance attached to advertising, Heublein spent 10.6% of sales for advertising in 1965, nearly double the 5.7% of Distillers Corporation.

In addition, Heublein was an aggressive innovator among liquor industry advertisers. In the 1950s, industry self-regulation prohibited depicting a woman in an advertisement for a liquor product. In 1958, Heublein advised the Distilled Spirits Institute that it believed this ban on the portrayal of women was "obsolete, hopelessly prudish, and downright bad business." Finally, The DSI agreed, and Heublein became the first liquor company to portray women in its ads under the new DSI self-regulation, an advertising practice later followed by nearly every major distiller. Heublein also pioneered a change in DSI regulations to permit liquor advertising in Sunday supplements. At the end of 1965, Heublein was pushing for the use of liquor advertisements on radio and TV similar to beer and wine advertisements.

Another unique feature of Heublein's marketing was the promotions it used. These were designed to appeal to the young adult group and used celebrities and off-beat approaches to gain attention (see Exhibit 8). An example of this approach was the Smirnoff Mule promotion launched in May 1965. The promotion, Heublein's largest for a single drink, was designed to catch the discotheque popularity on the upswing. The total investment was about $2.0 million for advertising, merchandising, and sales promotion. *The New York Times* commented that:

> Included in the Smirnoff advertising mix are a drink, called the Smirnoff Mule; a song and dance, called simply The Mule; a recording called Skitch Plays "The Mule"; a copper-colored metal mug in which to drink the Smirnoff Mule and a recent phenomenon called the discotheque. . . [Heublein's advertising agency] the Gumbinner-North Company has recruited such vodka salesmen as Skitch Henderson, Carmen McRae, and Killer Joe Piro to put it over. . . . In addition to Smirnoff ads, The Mule will be featured in local advertising by the 7-Up people.[9]

Distribution.   Heublein sold its products directly to state liquor control boards in the 18 control states and to approximately 235 wholesale distributors in the 32 open states and the District of Columbia. Food products were sold through food brokers and wholesalers. It was Heublein's policy to strive to create mutually profitable relationships with its distributors. For example, one of the reasons for the creation of Popov vodka was to give Heublein's distributors a low-priced vodka brand to sell.

International operations.   At the end of 1965, Heublein was involved in three types of overseas activities. The largest and most important was its licensing operation. Distillers in 32 foreign countries were licensed to manufacture and market Smirnoff vodka. Among the countries in which Heublein had such franchises were Austria, Denmark, Greece, Ireland, New Zealand, South Africa, and Spain. When selecting a franchise holder, Heublein looked for a local distiller who had good production facilities and who was a good marketer in his country. Heublein felt this policy allowed them to get established faster than if Heublein tried to set up its own plant. Heublein also felt it improved relations with the local government.

Under these franchise agreements, the distiller produced the neutral spirits in the best way possible in his country. To maintain quality control, however, Heublein installed and owned the copper filtration units and shipped the charcoal to these locations from Hartford. This was done at cost. The contracts called for a license fee (about 10% of sales) and

---

[9] Walter Carlson, "Advertising: Smirnoff Harnesses the Mule," *The New York Times,* June 27, 1965.

also stipulated that certain amounts be spent by the franchisee for advertising. Usually, during the first three or four years, Heublein would add its 10% license fee to these advertising funds in order to help build up the business. Plans were under way at the end of 1965 to begin operations in six more countries, including Ecuador, India, and Nigeria.

Heublein also exported Smirnoff, primarily to military bases overseas. In addition, Heublein opened an operation in Freeport, Jamaica, in 1965, to produce Smirnoff and other Heublein liquor products, and to market these products to customers such as ship's chandlers and diplomatic agencies who could purchase tax-free liquor.

Between 1961 and 1965, Heublein's export sales increased 99%, royalties from licenses 145% and profits from international operations 458%. In 1965, net export sales stood at $1.2 million and profits before taxes from international operations, including license fees, were $880,000.

Production. At the end of 1965, Heublein owned and operated three plants throughout the United States, with an annual capacity of 20.0 million wine gallons for all product lines, and was building a plant in Detroit to replace the old Arrow plant. This plant was to cost $4.5 million and to have an annual capacity of 5.5 million wine gallons. When completed, this plant would give Heublein a total annual capacity of 25.5 million wine gallons. All these plants were highly automated.

Heublein had about 975 employees in 1965, of whom slightly less than half were hourly employees. In 1965, labor costs were only 3% of the total cost of sales.

Heublein did not produce the grain neutral spirits for its gin and vodka production, but rather purchased these requirements on contract and the open market from four distillers. Heublein maintained facilities in the Midwest for the storage of 8.0 million proof gallons, however, in case none of these suppliers could meet Heublein's stringent quality requirements. At 1965 consumption rates, this represented about a one-year supply.

According to Heublein, even the high-quality grain neutral spirits it received from its suppliers contained too many impurities for direct use in Smirnoff. The first step in Smirnoff production was, therefore, to redistill these grain neutral spirits. At the end of the redistillation, the alcohol was 192 proof. It was then blended with distilled water to reduce the mixture to 80 proof. This mixture was then filtered slowly through 10 copper tanks which contained over 14,000 pounds of activated charcoal. The filtering process required eight hours. According to company officials, it was during this process that the vodka became smooth and mellow and acquired its mild, but distinctive taste. The only remaining step was to bottle the finished product, since vodka required no aging.

Heublein also redistilled the grain neutral spirits used in the production of its charcoal filtered Milshire gin. However, the company did not redistill the liquors (purchased on the open market) used in the production of Heublein cocktails.

Most of the food products were manufactured at Hartford or at the plant in Burlington, Vermont. Heublein insisted on the same high-quality standards in the purchase of raw materials and production of its food products that it required in its liquor production.

THE PROPOSED HAMM ACQUISITION

Early in the fall of 1965, Heublein's top management was seriously considering the possible acquisition of the Theo. Hamm Brewing Company. They were particularly interested because they felt Hamm's could profit immensely from what they felt was Heublein's major strength— the ability to market a consumer product extremely well. If the acquisition were consummated, Heublein would become the first company to engage in the production and sale of both beer and liquor.

Under the proposed agreement Heublein would acquire all of the outstanding shares of Hamm's common in exchange for 420,032 shares of Heublein's 5% preferred, and 200,031 shares of Heublein's 5% convertible preferred. Both preferreds had a par value of $100; the latter was convertible into three shares of Heublein common, subject to certain provisions against dilution of earnings. Although Hamm's stock was held by a family group and did not have a market price, Heublein's board estimated that the aggregate fair value was in excess of $62 million, or book value (see Exhibit 9). The proposed agreement stipulated that each class of preferred would have the right to elect one member to Heublein's board. In addition, it was provided that the $25 million of securities indicated on the Theo. Hamm Brewing Company consolidated balance sheet as of 9/30/65 would be liquidated and used to buy out dissident Hamm's stockholders prior to the acquisition by Heublein. This would have the effect of reducing Hamm's working capital and stockholder equity before the purchase by about $25 million.

Hamm's history and competitive position.   Hamm's was a family-owned brewing company. During the five years preceding the proposed acquisition, sales and profits had remained relatively stable (see Exhibits 10 and 11). However, since industry sales had increased slightly more than 11% during this period, Hamm's market share had declined from 4.5% to 3.7%. In addition, Hamm's return on sales had lagged behind the industry leaders (see Exhibits 12 and 13).

Hamm's sold three brands of beer at the end of 1965: Waldech (premium price), Hamm's (premium and popular price), and Buckhorn (lower price). The 1964 sales breakdown among these brands had been 17,800 barrels[10] for Waldech, 3,624,700 barrels for Hamm's, and 57,800 barrels for Buckhorn, for a total of 3,700,300 barrels. In addition, Hamm's had produced some beer for sale to F. & M. Schaefer Brewing Company under the Gunther brand in 1964.

In 1965, Hamm's beer was sold in 31 states and the District of Columbia. Most sales, however, were made in the midwestern, western, and southwestern parts of the United States. Hamm's relied exclusively on 479 independent wholesalers for its distribution, most of whom carried other brands of beer. Although any of these wholesalers could terminate his relationship with Hamm's at will, none of them accounted for more than 2.5% of Hamm's 1964 sales.

---

[10] A barrel was equivalent to 31 U.S. gallons.

According to some industry observers, Hamm's four breweries were one of its principal assets. Three of these were owned outright, while the fourth was leased. The location and annual productive capacity of each of these plants was as follows:

Location	Annual productive capacity (barrels)
St. Paul, Minnesota	2,550,000
San Francisco, California	1,000,000
Los Angeles, California	500,000
Houston, Texas (leased)	450,000
	4,500,000

According to industry estimates, the cost of replacing Hamm's 1965 capacity would be about $135 million, or more than double the proposed purchase price. This estimate was based on the industry rule of thumb which set the costs of new plant construction at $30 to $35 per barrel at the end of 1965.

Like Heublein, Hamm's purchased most of the raw materials needed for its production—malt, barley, hops and corn grits—from various independent suppliers. About one-fourth of the malt and hops requirements were met by wholly owned subsidiaries, however.

The brewing industry.   At the end of 1964, the beer market was approximately the same size as the distilled spirits market, or about $6.4 billion a year (see Exhibit 14). In addition, from 1960 to 1964, the beer market had grown at approximately the same annual rate as the liquor market, i.e., at about 2.5%. Per capita beer consumption had increased moderately during the period.

Since people began consuming beer at a younger age than liquor, industry observers expected beer consumption to increase as much as, if not more than, liquor consumption through 1970. Most of this increase was expected to be in the sale of packaged beer since the sale of draught beer had decreased from 22% of total beer sales in 1955 to 19% in 1964.

The same observers felt that brand loyalty was not as strong for beer as for liquor. Nevertheless, the economies of high-volume production and the use of high dollar advertising (see Exhibit 15) seemed to be causing a gradual concentration of the beer industry, for the number of breweries operated in the United States decreased from 329 to 211 between 1953 and 1963. Moreover, the percentage of sales accounted for by the largest brewing companies had recently been increasing (see Exhibit 16).

RECOMMENDATION

Mr. Hart knew that the negotiations with Hamm's had been proceeding for some time, and that any significant modifications in the proposed terms were unlikely. He also felt that there was little additional information available which would be important, and that the Heublein directors would be expecting his recommendation soon.

Exhibit 1

HEUBLEIN, INC. (A & B) (Condensed)
Consolidated Balance Sheets as of June 30
(dollars in thousands)

ASSETS	1955	1960	1963	1964	1965
Current assets:					
Cash	$ 2,298	$ 3,925	$ 2,744	$ 3,357	$ 3,338
Time deposits	—	—	6,000	1,750	—
Marketable securities	9	4,883	1,000	—	4,048
Investment in whiskey certificates	—	593	1,069	150	—
Accounts and notes receivable	5,157	12,426	17,835	18,668	19,010
Inventories	5,825	8,269	9,127	13,347	16,323
Prepaid expenses	297	382	356	325	548
Total current assets	$13,586	$30,479	$38,130	$37,597	$43,267
Long-term assets					
Property, plant and equipment-net	$ 3,254	$ 5,793	$ 6,363	$ 7,339	$ 7,502
Deferred charges, other assets and goodwill	223	416	1,068	3,659	5,383
Total long-term assets	$ 3,477	$ 6,209	$ 7,431	$10,998	$12,885
Total assets	$17,063	$36,688	$45,561	$48,595	$56,152

LIABILITIES AND STOCKHOLDERS' EQUITY	1955	1960	1963	1964	1965
Current liabilities:					
Notes payable to banks	$ 2,000	—	—	—	—
Accounts payable	687	$ 1,933	$ 2,078	$ 2,417	$ 3,584
Federal income tax	531	2,857	3,607	4,129	4,701
Accrued liabilities	513	2,688	4,044	5,175	5,774
Cash dividends payable	98	299	733	721	986
Long-term debt due within one year	301	631	777	850	1,013
Total current liabilities	$ 4,129	$ 8,408	$11,239	$13,292	$16,059
Long-term liabilities					
Long-term debt due after one year	$ 4,699	$ 5,388	$ 3,239	$ 2,416	$ 1,403
Deferred federal income tax	—	—	154	248	316
Minority interest	—	—	—	272	—
Total long-term liabilities	$ 4,699	$ 5,388	$ 3,393	$ 2,936	$ 1,719
Stockholders' equity	$ 8,235	$22,892	$30,929	$32,368	$38,374
Total liabilities and stockholders' equity	$17,063	$36,688	$45,561	$48,595	$56,152

Source: Heublein records.

Exhibit 2

HEUBLEIN, INC. (A & B) (Condensed)

Consolidated Statement of Income for Year Ending June 30
(dollars in thousands)

	1955	1956	1957	1958	1959	1960	1961	1962	1963	1964	1965
Net sales	$37,222	$68,543	$82,064	$87,839	$87,647	$103,169	$108,281	$116,142	$121,995	$135,848	$165,595
Cost of sales*	29,503	53,219	63,234	67,231	67,276	78,028	80,419	85,793	89,500	99,575	121,503
Gross profit	$ 7,719	$15,325	$18,830	$20,608	$20,372	$ 25,140	$ 27,862	$ 30,349	$ 32,495	$ 36,273	$ 44,092
Expenses:											
Selling and advertising	$ 4,650	$ 8,013	$10,617	$12,613	$12,710	$ 14,276	$ 16,089	$ 16,444	$ 18,271	$ 20,477	$ 24,551
Administrative and general	1,479	2,288	2,699	2,822	2,561	2,783	3,205	4,111	3,710	3,485	4,257
	6,130	10,301	13,315	15,434	15,271	17,060	19,293	20,555	21,981	23,962	28,808
	1,590	5,024	5,515	5,176	5,100	8,080	8,569	9,794	10,514	12,312	15,284
Other†	189	316	407	519	638	293	168	199	(339)	(18)	(112)
	1,401	4,708	5,109	4,654	4,462	7,788	8,401	9,595	10,852	12,330	15,397
State and federal income taxes	733	2,531	2,697	2,524	2,399	4,232	4,587	5,188	5,830	6,516	8,021
Net income	$ 667	$ 2,177	$ 2,411	$ 2,130	$ 2,063	$ 3,556	$ 3,814	$ 4,407	$ 5,022	$ 5,814	$ 7,376

* Cost of sales includes federal excise taxes on the withdrawal of distilled spirits from bond. For the fiscal year 1965, these totalled $90 million.
† Interest income, interest expense, and miscellaneous.
Source: Heublein records.

Exhibit 3

HEUBLEIN, INC. (A & B) (Condensed)
Liquor—Consumption vs. Population

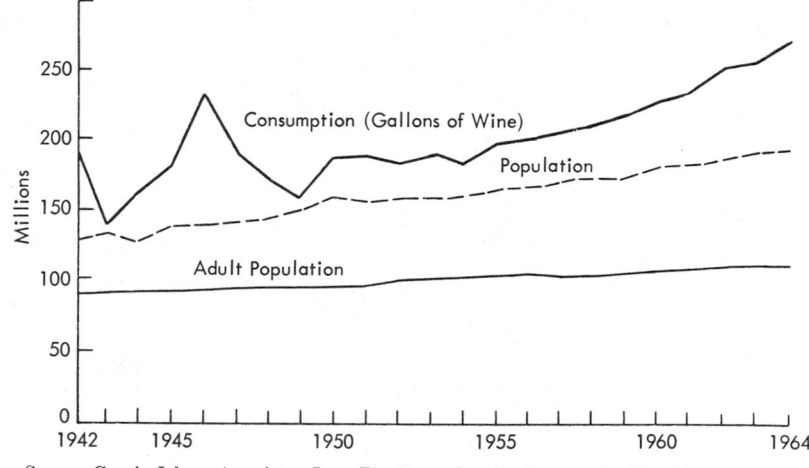

Source: Garvin Jobson Associates, Inc., *The Liquor Handbook, 1965;* cited by Glore Forgan, Wm.
R. Staats Inc., in *Heublein, Inc.*, December 1965.

Exhibit 4

HEUBLEIN, INC. (A & B) (Condensed)
Whiskey Consumption Trend, 1955–1964
(expressed as a three-year moving average)

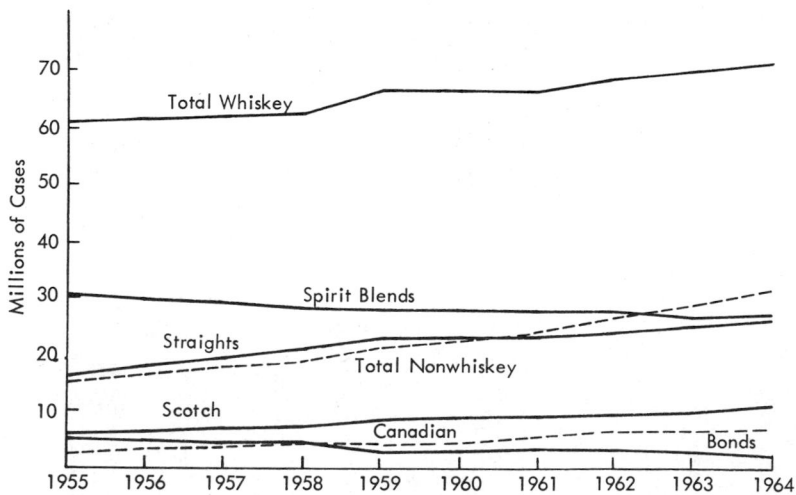

Exhibit 5

HEUBLEIN, INC. (A & B) (Condensed)
Nonwhiskey Consumption Trend, 1955–1964
(expressed as a three-year moving average)

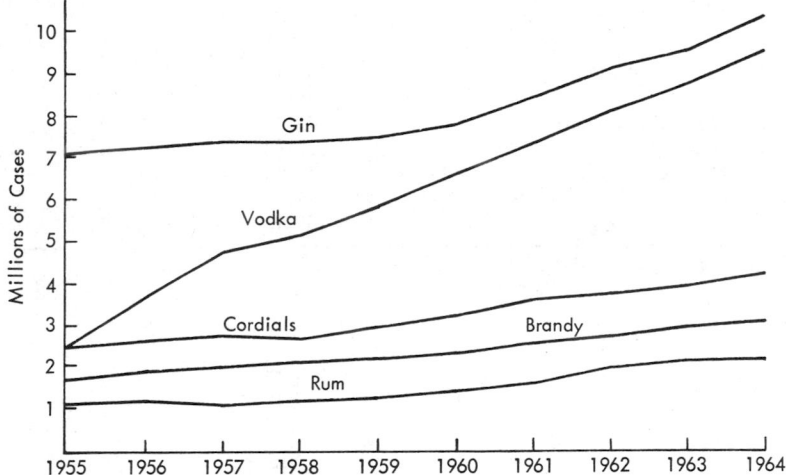

Source: Gavin Jobson Associates, *The Liquor Handbook*, 1965; cited by Glore Forgan, Wm. R. Staats Inc., in *Heublein, Inc.*, December 1965.

Exhibit 6

HEUBLEIN, INC. (A & B) (Condensed)
Heublein Sales Mix for Selected Years

Year	Smirnoff vodka	Other vodka	Total vodka	Other alcoholic beverages	Food	Total
1965	51%	11%	62%	30%	8%	100%
1964	58	12	70	21	9	100
1963	62	12	74	16	10	100
1962	63	11	74	16	10	100
1961	64	11	75	19	6	100
1960	67	9	76	18	6	100
1955	61	2	63	32	5	100
1950	27	—	27	63	10	100

Source: Heublein records.

Exhibit 7

HEUBLEIN, INC. (A & B) (Condensed)

Advertising Expenditures of Major Liquor Companies for 1965

Company	Advertising (million)	Sales (million)	Advertising as a percent of sales
Distillers Corp. Seagram's Ltd...............	$43,750	$762,520	5.7%
Schenley Industries.........................	23,100	380,200	6.1
National Distillers & Chemical Corp..........	19,668	810,900	2.4
Hiram Walker-Gooderham & Worts, Ltd.......	17,750	498,174	3.6
Heublein, Inc..............................	17,495	165,522	10.6

Source: *Advertising Age*, January 3, 1966, p. 46.

Exhibit 8

HEUBLEIN, INC. (A & B) (Condensed)

Smirnoff Mule Ad

THE SMIRNOFF MULE—SKITCH HENDERSON MADE IT A SONG. "KILLER JOE" PIRO MADE IT A DANCE.

NEW DRINK...SMIRNOFF® MULE
It swings!

Taste the new party favorite that's sweeping the country, the swingingest drink since Smirnoff invented vodka. It's the Smirnoff Mule, made with Smirnoff and 7-Up®. Just pour a jigger of Smirnoff over ice. Add juice of ¼ lime. Fill Mule mug or glass with 7-Up to your taste. *Delicious!* Only smooth, flawless Smirnoff, filtered through 14,000 pounds of activated charcoal, blends so perfectly with 7-Up. That's why the fuel for your Mule must be Smirnoff! *It leaves you breathless®*

SMIRNOFF VODKA 80 AND 100 PROOF. DISTILLED FROM GRAIN. STE P·ERRE SMIRNOFF FLS. (DIVISION OF HEUBLEIN). HARTFORD, CONN.

Exhibit 9

HEUBLEIN, INC. (A & B) (Condensed)
Theo. Hamm Brewing Company Consolidated Balance Sheets
(dollars in thousands)

	Nov. 30 1964	Sept. 30 1965
CURRENT ASSETS		
Cash...	$ 3,475	$ 3,153
Certificates of deposit..........................	2,000	500
Commercial paper and marketable securities (at cost)*.................................	26,560	24,044
Accounts receivable (net)........................	5,452	7,959
Inventories...................................	5,352	6,479
Prepaid expenses.............................	898	891
Total current assets......................	$43,737	$43,027
Investments and other assets......................	6,467	6,536
Property, plant, and equipment (net)...............	26,381	26,930
	$76,585	$76,493
CURRENT LIABILITIES		
Trade accounts payable........................	$ 2,639	$ 2,926
Salaries and wages............................	1,207	1,304
Customers' deposits...........................	932	1,151
Miscellaneous accounts payable and accrued expenses............................	470	1,301
Taxes other than taxes on income................	2,038	2,299
Federal and state taxes on income...............	2,657	2,559
Dividends payable............................	1,538	660
Sinking fund deposits due in one year............	100	100
Total current liabilities....................	$11,580	$12,302
Eight percent debenture bonds...................	1,400	1,400
Stockholders equity		
Capital stock.................................	55,083	26,432
Capital surplus...............................	—	26,273
Earned surplus...............................	8,521	10,086
	$76,585	$76,493

* The market value of these securities was $28.1 million in 1964 and $25.7 million in 1965.
Source: Heublein Acquisition Study.

Exhibit 10

HEUBLEIN, INC. (A & B) (Condensed)

Theo. Hamm Brewing Company Consolidated Statement of Income
(dollars in thousands)

	Years ended November 30,					(Unaudited) ten months ended September 30	
	1960	1961	1962	1963	1964	1964	1965 §
Revenues:							
Sales less allowances	$119,881	$115,874	$114,885	$119,584	$124,233	$106,109	$109,449
Interest	161	240	270	575	958	748	941
Dividends	81	62	50	51	61	58	42
Other	283	95	175	196	351	301	359
	$120,407	$116,272	$115,380	$120,405	$125,602	$107,217	$110,791
Costs and expenses:							
Cost of goods sold*	$89,843	$86,314	$86,595	$90,878	$95,388	$81,004	$84,597
Selling, delivery, advertising, general and administrative expenses	16,263	17,065	16,200	18,534	21,423	18,196	19,026
Interest:							
Long-term debt	235	164	120	120	120	100	100
Other	8	159	2	16	13	12	
	$106,349	$103,702	$102,918	$109,548	$116,945	$99,312	$103,723
Earnings before taxes on income	$14,057	$12,570	$12,462	$10,857	$8,657	$7,905	$7,068
Taxes on income:							
Federal	$6,750	$6,150	$6,100	$5,100	$3,900	$3,550	$3,000
State	450	400	400	275	300	275	522
	$7,200	$6,550	$6,500	$5,375	$4,200	$3,825	$3,225
Net earnings (excluding the operations of the Eastern division and related distributing subsidiaries)	$6,857	$6,020	$5,962	$5,482	$4,457	$4,080	$3,843
Loss on operations of Eastern division and related distributing subsidiaries less applicable income tax benefits†	1,092	1,717	2,124	1,408	—	—	—
Net earnings	$5,765	$4,303	$3,838	$4,074	$4,457	$4,080	$3,843
Preferred stock dividend requirements	210	210	210	210	210	175	142
Earnings applicable to common stock	$5,555	$4,093	$3,628	$3,864	$4,247	$3,905	$3,701
Per common share (dollars)							
Earnings applicable to common stock‡	$2.14	$1.57	$1.40	$1.49	$1.63	$1.50	$1.40
Cash dividends declared			.40	.95	1.25	.50	.75

* Cost of goods sold includes federal and state excise taxes of between $32 and $38 million for each of the above periods.

† In 1960, the company acquired brewing facilities in Baltimore, Maryland, which were sold in 1963 for $6 million, the approximate net carrying amount of the facilities. Applicable income tax benefits ranging between $1.2 and $2.1 million have been netted against loss on operations of Eastern division and related distributing subsidiaries for the years 1960–1963 inclusive.

‡ Earnings applicable to common stock are based on the number of shares outstanding at the end of each period as adjusted for the recapitalization during the year ended November 30, 1961.

§ Earnings for the 10 months ended September 30, 1965 were adversely affected by nonrecurring legal and centennial expenses aggregating approximately $400,000.

Source: Heublein Acquisition Study.

Exhibit 11

HEUBLEIN, INC. (A & B) (Condensed)
Heublein, Inc. and Theo. Hamm Brewing Company
Pro Forma Combined Statement of Income
(dollars in thousands)

	Heublein Hamm June 30, 1960 Nov. 30, 1960	June 30, 1961 Nov. 30, 1961	June 30, 1962 Nov. 30, 1962	June 30, 1963 Nov. 30, 1963	June 30, 1964 Nov. 30, 1964	Ten months to Sept. 30, 1965
Net sales	$223,050	$224,156	$231,027	$241,579	$260,082	$249,056
Cost of sales	167,872	166,732	172,389	180,378	194,963	187,059
Selling, general and administrative expenses	33,323	36,359	36,755	40,515	45,385	43,164
Other income (deductions):						
Interest and dividend income	352	417	444	865	1,287	1,217
Interest expense	(560)	(595)	(363)	(344)	(342)	(215)
Miscellaneous—net	198	85	93	503	308	320
	(10)	(93)	174	1,024	1,253	1,322
Income before income taxes	21,845	20,972	22,057	21,710	20,987	20,155
Provision for income taxes	11,432	11,137	11,688	11,205	10,716	9,966
Net income before loss on discontinued operations of Hamm	10,413	9,835	10,369	10,505	10,271	10,189
Loss on discontinued operations of Hamm, less applicable income tax benefits	1,092	1,717	2,124	1,408	—	—
Net income	9,321	8,118	8,245	9,097	10,271	10,189
Deduct pro forma adjustments						
Interest and dividend income	219	275	290	591	981	950
Interest expense	1,209	983	975	501	122	85
Income taxes	(738)	(638)	(652)	(549)	(496)	(418)
	690	620	613	543	607	617
Pro forma net income	8,631	7,498	7,632	8,554	9,664	9,572
Preferred dividend requirements:						
Heublein:						
5% preferred stock	2,100	2,100	2,100	2,100	2,100	1,750
5% convertible preferred stock	1,000	1,000	1,000	1,000	1,000	833
	3,100	3,100	3,100	3,100	3,100	2,583
Pro forma earnings applicable to common stock	$ 5,531	$ 4,398	$ 4,532	$ 5,454	$ 6,564	$ 6,989
Pro forma earnings per share (dollars):						
Assuming no conversion of convertible preferred stock	$1.15	$ .91	$ .93	$1.12	$1.37	$1.43
Assuming full conversion of convertible preferred stock	1.21	1.00	1.01	1.18	1.40	1.43
Actual Heublein earnings per share*	.74	.79	.91	1.03	1.21	1.30

* Heublein shares outstanding in June of 1965, 4.9 million; approximate market price/share in 1965 (to September) $26–$27.
Source: Heublein Acquisition Study.

Exhibit 12

HEUBLEIN, INC. (A & B) (Condensed)

Beer: Larger Markets, Tougher Competition*

The bigger it gets, the rougher it gets. That sums up the brewing industry, which has just had its best year ever. But no one brewer had an easy time of it, and the competition will get even stiffer in the years ahead.

by Kenneth Ford, Managing Editor

No one in the brewing industry had anything but kind words last week for the nation's growing number of young adults.

Not only were they quaffing their share of brew and more besides, but even more significant, they appeared willing to cast aside some old-fashioned concepts about beer being a "blue-collar" drink.

For the nation's 190 brewers (four fewer than the year before) the moral was that patience pays off. All during the long, dry decade of the Fifties the industry watched total consumption lag behind population growth and per capita consumption remain static at a low level. Brewers pinned their hopes on the vast crop of war babies of the Forties, hoping that when they reached drinking age they would set off a beer boom, but also fearing they might move from the innocence of Coke to the decadence of Martinis in one easy step.

They didn't. When the 1963 figures were totaled up at this time last year, there were clear signs that the brewing industry was on the move at last. No one outside the industry realized how fast it was moving until the 1964 totals came in last month.

The results: total sales (consumption) climbed to 98.5-million barrels, up five per cent from 1963s 93.8-million barrels. Per capita consumption, the more meaningful measure of marketing effectiveness, jumped to 15.7 gallons, up 2.6 per cent from 1963s 15.3 gallons. Both gains were the best year-to-year increase posted by the industry since 1947.

It is a certainty that the industry will cross the 100-million barrel barrier in 1965. The only question is whether it will reach 101-million or 102-million barrels. No one will be unhappy if it doesn't go that high—the industry's most optimistic forecasters hadn't expected it to reach the 100-million barrel level until 1967.

But though the over-all industry outlook is sudsy, neither leaders nor laggards are finding it easy selling.

Competition has never been fiercer. The nation's top 10 brewers have staked out 57.7 per cent share of the total market, selling 56.6-million barrels of that 98.5 million total. The next 14 ranking brewers take 25.4 per cent of the total, or 25-million barrels. All together, the top 24 brewers, each doing better than one-million barrels apiece, account for 82.9 per cent of total sales, some 81.6-million barrels.

But even what would be a normally respectable gain was not enough to hold the previous year's position, much less advance, in the top 24 standings.

Losses and gains

Carling dropped in 1964 from fourth to fifth; Hamm from seventh to eight; Rheingold from tenth to 11th; Lucky Lager from 13th to 16th; Pearl from 17th to 18th; Narragansett from 19th to 21th and Jackson from 23rd

* *Printer's Ink*, February 12, 1965. Reproduced by permission.

Exhibit 12—Continued

to 24th. Yet five had made sales gains—Carling's posted a 1.7 percent increase; Rheingold a 3.1 percent increase; Pearl a 5.4 percent increase; Narragansett a 2.8 percent increase; and Jackson a 2.2 percent increase.

The leading brewers had set such a blistering pace that merely running to keep up just wasn't fast enough.

First-place Anheuser-Busch (Budweiser Busch Bavarian-Michelob) achieved a 10.1 percent gain that carried it across the 10-million-barrel level, an industry record, and gave it a 10.5 percent share of the total market. A-B phenomenal performance was the culmination of marketing programs set in motion as long as a decade ago. Basically, these concentrated on development of marketing executives, achieving the best possible communication with its 900 wholesalers throughout the country and expanding plants into growing markets. (Its new Houston brewery will be ready next year.)

Though A-B is one of the heaviest advertisers in the industry, it makes only evolutionary changes in its advertising program from year to year. "Where There's Life There's Bud" (1963) became "That Bud, that's beer" (1964) and now becomes "It's Worth It, It's Budweiser" (1965).

Expansion-minded Schlitz, eyeing the heavier-beer-drinking Canadian market (per capita consumption 16.4 gallons) tried to migrate north by buying control of Canada's Labatt Brewing, but found itself ensnarled in anti-trust actions and other legal complications. The time and attention it had to devote to these were reflected in only a 5.3 percent gain, in contrast to 1963s 13 percent gain.

Another 11.6 percent gain like the one Pabst made last year might well knock Schlitz out of second-place. And fast-rising Falstaff is a factor that Schlitz and Pabst marketing executives both must reckon with in the year ahead.

Falstaff surprised everyone by clipping Carling out of fourth place in the brewing industry. Carling had made sixteen consecutive sales gains that brought it up from 19th in the industry and was generally conceded to be the brewer to watch. Controlled by Canadian entrepreneur E. P. Taylor, its marketing strategy is based on two rules: build plants where the markets are growing (it now has nine in the U.S.) and advertise heavily.

But it was Falstaff's ambition and innovation that carried it ahead. It markets only one brand of beer, Falstaff, in 32 states westward from Indiana. These states have 45 percent of the nation's population but consume less than 45 percent of total beer production.

A competitor to respect

"If we were in the other 18 states, we'd be selling 10.5-million barrels instead of 5.8-million," says George Holtman, vice president, advertising. Holtman's boast is not idle. That Falstaff is a competitor to respect is attested to by Hamm's decline of 2.5 percent. Both collided competitively in the Midwest generally and the Chicago market in particular. Falstaff began moving into Chicago three years ago and the 1964 figures reflect its arrival. Similarly, it began moving into the West Coast in recent years where traditional beer sales patterns are changing, too. Lucky Lager, long the leading West Coast brand, slumped 15.1 percent, dropping below the two-million barrel level under the impact of competition from Falstaff and other interloping brewers. Among them: the Schlitz-Burgemeister brand team, Falstaff, Budweiser, and Carling. The latter is going to build its own brewery in the San Francisco area, which should make conditions in the important California

Exhibit 12—Continued

market (it accounts for about 7.5 percent of total consumption alone) even more competitive.

But the moral is not that the big bad national brands come in and knock off the poor little locals. Washington-based Olympia, strong in the Northwest, and Denver-based Coors both are making significant progress on the West Coast. Olympia scored a 22.1 percent increase, and Coors, long the strong man of the Rocky Mountain empire, boosted advertising budgets by 11 percent and barged into California. Result: a 12 percent sales increase.

In the big New York market it was a locally-based brewer that led the pack—Brooklyn's F&M Schaefer Brewing. Schaefer soared to 4,250,000 barrels up 10.1 percent, while Newark-based Ballantine dropped 3.9 percent and Rheingold, up 3.1 percent, slipped out of the to ten and found its claim to being top brand in the New York metropolitan area under severe pressure.

Ballantine, long handled by the Wm. Esty Co., is now looking for a new advertising agency. Rheingold, sold by the Liebmann family to Pepsi-Cola United Bottlers, switched agencies again. In recent years it has gone from Foote Cone & Belding to J. Walter Thompson, back to FCB, and is now at Doyle Dane Bernbach. Rheingold, under the aegis of its new management, reportedly was moving ahead at year's end behind a barrage of television and radio spots.

Competition keen in East, too

Throughout the East, competition was similarly strong. Philadelphia-based Schmidt (Schmidt-Prior-Valley Forge) gained 13.3 percent, Baltimore-based National climbed 21.5 percent, and Manhattan-based Ruppert, strong in New England, moved ahead 22.5 percent. Rochester-based Genessee (up 20.2 percent) cemented its already strong position in upstate New York.

One result of this fierce competition was increased ad budgets. With most brewers offering what economists call "poorly differentiated products" i.e., sameness—images were the most important function in marketing. Most brewers, in *Printer's Ink's* annual marketing survey, of course declined to give data on ad expenditures, though a few admitted increases ranging from 4 to 6 percent. However, the industry operates on a so-much-per-barrel basis in its ad budgeting. *Printer's Ink's* study of beer advertising expenditures (October 2, 1964, page 25) found the industry average was 96-cents a barrel for the four measured media. This would put total spending in a 98.5-million barrel year at $94.4-million in those media. This, however, is only about one-third of total expenditures. Big chunks of money go for "rights" to broadcast sports events, a staple of beer marketing. For instance, Schlitz, now building a new brewery in Texas, paid out $5.3-million for rights to the Houston Colts games.

"It's all part of becoming a new resident of the area," a Schlitz spokesman explained. "We want to get known fast and this is how you do it."

So important are sports sponsorships that they significantly influence marketing strategy. For example, Schmidt's bought the old Standard Beverage plant in Cleveland from Schaefer (which then bought the old Gunther plant in Baltimore from Hamm). Schmidt originally intended to use the Cleveland brewery to supply its markets in Western Pennsylvania and Western New York state and had no immediate intention of entering the northeastern Ohio market. But the opportunity arose to buy a participation in radio-sponsorship of the Cleveland Browns games. Schmidt's bought it and entered the market immediately.

Exhibit 12—Continued

Can U.S. compete abroad?

For the past few years, American brewers have enviously watched the success of imported European beers in the U.S. The European imports sell less than 1 percent of the total sold in the U.S. but their profit margins are far better than the domestic brewers achieve on a unit basis. Would the same not hold true for U.S. and Canadian beers overseas? It is also a way to rise above the cannibalistic competition in the U.S. The other way is to increase the beer consumption of the American drinker. Though 1964s 3.3 percent increase in per capita consumption was the best in recent years, the industry lags far behind the high of 18.7 gallons set in 1945 or even the post-war 18.4 gallons quaffed in 1947.

New products may help. Schlitz, Pabst and National are now strongly promoting malt liquor brands. A-B's Michelob and Hamm's Waldech in the super-premium class are upgrading beer's image and adding a new group of customers.

But it is a packaging development that may be of the most far-reaching significance. This is the home keg or draft beer that fits neatly into the family refrigerator. In the consumption battle, beer's increase in share must come from soft drinks, coffee, tea, and such—not merely from population growth or competitors' customers.

In the decade ending in 1963, beer consumption increased only 12 percent while the population grew 19 percent. Soft drinks shot up 48 percent, soluble coffee 158, and tea 20 percent.

The confirmed beer drinker guzzles about six quarts a week on a yearly averaged-out basis. That's about two and a half 12-ounce cans at a time.

What the industry must attract is the glass-at-a-time sipper. That's not much at a time, but there are an awful lot of them and enough sips by enough people can boost beer back near the 20 gallons per capita consumption level of pre-World War I days.

It will take a revolution in American beer-drinking patterns to do it, but it could happen.

Exhibit 13

HEUBLEIN, INC. (A & B) (Condensed)
Returns on 1964 Sales of Leading Brewers

	Total revenues (000)	Pretax net (000)	Profit margin (percent)	Barrels sold (000)	Pretax returns/ barrel
Anheuser-Busch	$491,384	$39,312	8.00	10,235	$3.84
Schlitz	311,394	28,277	9.08	8,266	3.42
Pabst	227,610	20,421	8.97	7,444	2.74
Falstaff	211,943	13,604	6.42	5,815	2.33
Hamm	125,602	8,657	6.89	3,719	2.33

Source: Company annual reports.

Exhibit 14

HEUBLEIN, INC. (A & B) (Condensed)

Alcoholic Beverages—Consumer Expenditures, 1942–1964

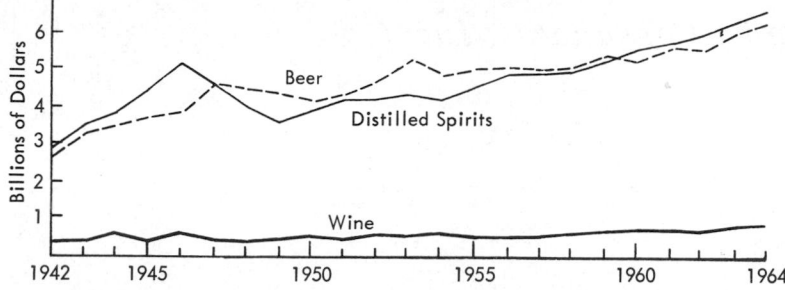

Source: *The Liquor Handbook, 1965;* cited by Glore Forgan, Wm. R. Staats Inc., in *Heublein, Inc.,* December 1965.

Exhibit 15

HEUBLEIN, INC. (A & B) (Condensed)

Advertising Expenditures of Major Brewers
in 1965

Company	Advertising (000)	Sales (000)	Advertising percent of sales
Jos. Schlitz Brewing Co.	$34,200	$311,375	11.0
Anheuser-Busch, Inc.	32,500	491,384	6.6
Pabst Brewing Co.	15,900	227,610	7.0
Carling Brewing Co.	15,500	412,306	3.8
Falstaff Brewing Corp.	15,000	211,943	7.0

Source: *Advertising Age,* January 3, 1966, p. 46.

Exhibit 16

HEUBLEIN, INC. (A & B) (Condensed)

Market Share of Major Brewers
(percent)

	1964	1963	1962	1961	1960	1959	1958	1957	1956	1955	1954	1953	1952	1951
Top 25	83.7	82.2	79.9	77.4	75.1	73.8	70.5	69.2	67.5	64.3	62.1	61.3	60.2	57.5
Top 10	57.7	56.8	55.0	52.8	51.4	50.0	45.9	45.2	44.4	42.7	40.8	40.1	40.8	39.2

Source: Research Company of America.

Sigma Consultants, Inc. (A)

EDWARD ROBSON put down the two memoranda he had been reading and wondered what conclusions he should draw about the best way to develop health care consulting at Sigma Consultants, Inc. Sigma was a large research and management consulting company with headquarters on the West Coast and offices in a number of major United States cities and various foreign countries. At the August 6, 1969, meeting of Sigma's Executive Committee, two weeks earlier, the senior management of the company had concluded that Sigma would like to support the health care field as one of its primary development areas in the near future. Edward Robson, Executive Vice President of Sigma, had been given the responsibility for determining how this development should be effected.

The main question, thought Mr. Robson, was: What should Sigma management do to encourage development of this area?

> Do we try to respond to, and encourage, individual efforts by staff members, and leave it at that? Do we try to identify the areas we think are of interest, decide what action seems indicated, and try to take it? Or do we announce our interest to the staff and then sit back and let individual efforts determine what will happen?
>
> Several issues have to be faced. First, our operating process is set up essentially to keep our existing activities going rather than to develop new ones. Second, any new development cannot depend on unilateral "management" action; it needs professional staff participation. Third, health care activities are widely scattered in Sigma at present; some like to keep an area this way—others dislike it. Finally, any proposed management action with visibility and impact is going to be met with some resistance from individual staff members and managers because of the threat to individual freedom, support of an activity the person does not understand or is not interested in, concerns over exclusion or loss of control of business, and because of the need to make choices about what to support.

BACKGROUND INFORMATION

Sigma Consultants, Inc. had annual revenues in 1969 of $50 million and was widely recognized as one of the leading organizations in its field. It provided professional services to industrial, commercial, not-for-profit, and government organizations in the United States and abroad. Its full-time professional staff of approximately 1,000 persons (a great number of whom were based on the West Coast) included specialists with training and professional experience in such varied fields as economics, engineering sciences, chemistry, physics, mathematics, biology, operations research, behavioral sciences, business management, finance, marketing, and many other areas. In addition, Sigma had contract relationships with a number of independent individual consultants, many of whom were internationally known specialists and faculty members of prominent academic institutions. Top management at Sigma believed that one of the company's major assets was the range of diverse, outstanding talents it could marshall for a client and considered the firm's capacity to attract and engage the interests of such high caliber staff to be a principal corporate strength.

The official Sigma statement of corporate goals indicated that the objective of Sigma was to operate profitably by:

1. applying our technical and managerial competence to social, economic, technical, and business issues of significance to our clients;
2. maintaining a corporate environment that will attract and develop the best people, encourage enterprise, excellence and high ethical standards;
3. operating throughout the world; and
4. achieving pre-eminence in our fields of activity.

Hierarchical organization was kept to a minimum at Sigma; hence there were very few official titles. As one observer remarked, "A lot of people at Sigma—and the lucky ones everyone agrees—are simply, uncomplicatedly, staff. Staff is rank enough." There was no official organization chart at Sigma; however the professional staff responsible for client assignments were divided into six divisions, each of which had a division head who was a Sigma vice president. (A list of the divisions, together with the names of the various persons mentioned in this case, is given in Exhibit 1.)

In the words of one division head, "The divisions are profit centers—but they are more political entities than rational groupings; and there is substantial overlap and competition between divisions." Within each division there were usually departments. "In a very rough sort of way, staff members of the same profession, or primary professional interest, tend to cluster together," said one senior professional, "but this is not stated as a requirement in principle, nor is it followed in practice. Sometimes people who can serve a particular type of client are grouped together. But, in fact, one cannot make any general statement on how these departments have come to have their current composition, except to say that personal empathy and current expediency have apparently each played a large part."

"More important than in many organizations," observed another professional, "is the need—in describing Sigma—to stress the separation and coordination of the work and administrative organizations and the individual's multiple membership in both. The most important organizational unit at Sigma is the 'project team'," he explained:

> These teams are created for each new client assignment and consist of the staff specialists required to handle the project problem. The leader of a project team need not be a designated member of the organizational hierarchy (that is, a division head, department head, etc.). In fact, some members of a project team are often more senior in some area of experience or higher in the administrative organization than the project leader; but for the purpose of that assignment, they subordinate themselves to the technical and administrative direction of the project leader. The project is the basic unit of Sigma's work; and the agreement to conduct an assignment is normally arrived at by negotiation between the project leader and the client. It is the project leader who chooses the team to work with him, often with advice from other staff members. It is company policy, however, that an individual's participation on a team is a matter of choice and agreement between himself and the project leader. A staff member is ordinarily active in two to four or more projects at any given time. The average project lasts about six months, at which time the team dissolves and the members become involved in other activities; sometimes, of course, a team member is used only in a particular aspect of a project and for a short time. Another aspect of the limited role of the formal structure is that it is expected that the members of a department will work anywhere in the organization that particular project problems require, and that most individuals will be able to generate business and lead projects with clients as soon after joining Sigma as they are reasonably integrated through experience on others' projects.

"A problem—and a strength—in the Sigma organization is that the system requires independence, initiative and self-control on the part of the staff," observed one senior executive. "The problem is general but it shows up particularly in the kind of situation the organization is currently facing. For example, in health care, one of the main issues which has to be considered is the extent to which corporate initiative and professional independence can be combined."

THE EARLY DEVELOPMENT OF HEALTH CARE CONSULTING AT SIGMA

Laboratory-based, health-related work had been a part of Sigma's activity for some years. The analysis, development and testing of drugs had been lodged primarily in the Life Sciences Division, with significant efforts in the design and evaluation of medical equipment conducted in the Engineering Division. In recent years, however, there had been another, growing set of activities in health *care* work. This was not centered in lab-based work; it included consulting on hospital organization, medical instrument marketing research, design of health care delivery systems, and so forth.

Many individuals were involved in this growing activity. Fairly typical of Sigma's entry into health care work, however, were the experiences of four particular Sigma professionals who had become active in health care. It should be noted that many other individuals became involved in health care work—to an equal or lesser degree than the four cited. However, the four persons were among the small number who were most prominently involved and their experience, since it was typical, is an illustration, and offers some understanding, of the process of entry into health care work.

Peter Dowell. After graduation from Stanford Business School in 1962, Mr. Dowell joined Sigma and began his career there in market research. In 1963, Sigma was asked to conduct a diversification study for a business firm, and in connection with this, Mr. Dowell did a study of the medical electronics market. His work in this relatively new field established Mr. Dowell as something of an expert on medical electronics and he co-authored a paper on the subject in 1964 for one of Sigma's publications. A second assignment on the subject for another client was subsequently conducted.

In 1966, a letter came to the Sigma contracting office requesting a feasibility study of a hospital merger in Oregon. The request was passed on to Mr. Dowell's division head, who asked Mr. Dowell to undertake the study. The day before the inquiry came in, Mr. Dowell had been introduced to a new staff member, Mr. Hobart; remembering their discussion and Mr. Hobart's ideas on organizational behavior, Mr. Dowell invited Mr. Hobart to work on the project with him. The $20,000 project was a success: the hospitals merged, client-relationships were good, and Mr. Dowell and Mr. Hobart were asked to make two or three presentations to their professional peers at Sigma. Mr. Dowell was "turned on" by the challenge of handling the human problems: "It blew my mind. It became obvious to me also," he said, "that health care could be a gold mine." From this point onwards, Mr. Dowell became increasingly involved in health care assignments, particularly ones which involved some aspect of organizational development or change, and he shifted the medical electronics work to another professional.

Norman Williams. Mr. Williams was a vice president without portfolio and had had a long and varied career at Sigma, which he joined after graduating from Harvard Business School in 1935. In 1940 when Sigma started its first biological research, Williams was asked to serve as a guide to the newly formed work group. Later, in 1950, Mr. Williams had taken on the task of developing Sigma's Operations Research work. During the 1950s this involved him in leading a couple of projects on the marketing of drugs for two business firms. During the 1960s other health-related work came to Mr. Williams in connection with Congressional investigations of the drug industry and government studies of the relationship between smoking and health.

In 1966, a client inquiry came to the contracting office from Western Blue Cross; it was brought to Williams who became the project leader. Williams sought out Dowell, who suggested Hobart join them; and so the three, together with three faculty members from prominent schools of Medicine and Public Health, began work on a planning study for the largest carrier of health insurance in its market. "For me," said Williams, "that project was the turning point. The work required that I learn about the trends in health care and I became convinced of the opportunities in the field and the importance of the field." After this experience, Williams became involved in further health care assignments.

Wynn Day.   Mr. Day joined Sigma's Engineering Division in 1964 with a Ph.D. in applied mathematics from Berkeley. His first years were devoted to mathematical, simulation, and systems analyses for the Air Force. After two years of full-time military-oriented cases, Day concluded he wanted to spend the major part of his time on a permanent basis in nondefense areas and he moved into a small, newly formed Systems Engineering department in the same division, which did some defense work but was making attempts to develop business outside the military sphere.

His first introduction to hospitals and health care came as a result of an acquisition study done in 1966 by Sigma for Eastex Corporation, as a result of which Eastex purchased a foreign firm which manufactured automated materials delivery systems for hospitals. After the purchase, Sigma provided some assistance in re-engineering the systems for the American market. When the engineers were faced with possible bottleneck and material shortage problems in the complicated automated system, Day suggested they might use a simulation program. As a result he ran a $19,000 case in 1967 to develop a simulation model suitable for many hospital configurations.

Although he continued doing military projects, Day was interested by hospital problems and proceeded, on his own initiative (and with the concurrence of his department head), to write proposals for studies advertised in the government's *Commerce Business Daily*. Some of this was done in his own time. The first project was for Walter Reed Hospital in Washington, D.C.; the Sigma proposal ranked seventh out of the twelve submitted and Day observed that he later saw that "it was a naïve job." A second proposal, in 1968 to the Public Health Service for a Dallas public hospital, was also unsuccessful. (Another top consultant firm got the job at two-thirds the Sigma price.) Meanwhile Mr. Day was also engaged in some engineering work on artificial heart equipment. Early in 1969, he submitted a third proposal, to the Department of Defense; in June, Sigma was awarded a large contract for a major study of a new military hospital system.

Nicholas Vogel.   Mr. Vogel joined Sigma's Operations Research staff in 1960 after obtaining his Ph.D. in chemical engineering from the Massachusetts Institute of Technology. His early work involved him in the development and application of computer models to problems as diverse as antisubmarine warfare, the feasibility of national centralized facilities for the storage and retrieval of scientific documents, and inland waterway transportation.

In July 1963, the switchboard operator at Sigma received a call from a professor of preventive medicine at the Los Angeles College of Medicine who wanted some help from an applied mathematician. The professor, Dr. Baxter Warren, subsequently visited Sigma and talked with a couple of professionals about developing quantitative planning methods for cancer control. The Los Angeles institution had funds from the U.S. Public Health Service and planned to develop a general model for use in local health departments. Mr. Vogel was brought into the discussion because he had been trained to apply mathematical sophistication to similarly messy problems, had shown marked adaptability, and had a computer background. The result of the meeting was a $17,000 project. The relatively unplanned nature of Mr. Vogel's involvement in health care was compounded by the fact that the original team leader resigned from Sigma shortly after the contract was signed and Mr. Vogel, whose qualifications were comparable, was made team leader in his place. As a result of this project, Vogel was retained as a consultant by the Los Angeles College and a series of further projects for Sigma followed. During this period Vogel became extremely interested in epidemiology[1] and public health as a fertile area in which to pursue his general career interest in the interactions of theory and practice. As a consequence he had been engaged almost exclusively on health care assignments since 1963.

Mr. Vogel's work with the Los Angeles College of Medicine also led to Sigma's later employing Dr. Baxter Warren in 1966, when Warren decided to leave his Los Angeles post. "We were taking a risk with Baxter Warren," said the head of the division that had engaged him, "because he had a very specialized skill; but Warren brought a union card. Also, he has a very broad knowledge at a detailed level, knows who is doing what in the field and where, helps the company get jobs, knows who to call if a specialized consultant is needed, and has an ability to review and edit the output of Sigma staff to ensure that nonmedical staff do not make inadvertent errors." Since joining Sigma, Dr. Warren had worked entirely on health care projects.

In addition to the four persons discussed above, many other individuals at Sigma also entered the field and activity in health care continued to increase during the period from 1966 through 1969. Some indication of the development of health work is given in Exhibit 2, which lists some of the major projects conducted during the four-year period, and in Table 1 which summarizes the increase in the total dollar volume of business.

Table 1

HEALTH CARE AND RELATED PROJECTS SOLD ($000)

Size of project	1966	1967		1968		1969 (est.)
$1–$100..................	440	453		716		930
$100–$250...............	—	—	(3)	544	(3)	575
Subtotal................	440	453		1,260		1,505
Over $250...............	(1)* 415	—	(2)	825	(1)	835
Total.................	855	453		2,085		2,340

* Figures in parentheses represent the number of projects.
Source: Prepared by Sigma staff from company records.

---

[1] Epidemiology: a science that deals with the incidence, distribution, and control of disease in a population.

INITIAL STEPS TOWARDS THE ORGANIZATION OF HEALTH CARE ACTIVITIES

As one member of Sigma observed, "Health-care work in the initial years involved a variety of individuals in many divisions; development was the result of individual initiatives and chance circumstance; communication and coordination was purely at the personal level." Some first steps towards formalization, however, began to be taken.

Monday lunches.   In the fall of 1967, Norm Williams suggested that those interested in health care might meet informally over lunch on a regular basis. The practice of Monday lunches was launched that November. A table for seven was reserved every Monday and each week Williams' secretary would call up some of those on the list of professionals interested in health care. The group would vary from week to week and provided a convenient opportunity for colleagues to discuss common interests.

Health care brochure.   During 1967, Pete Dowell had the idea for a health care brochure. From a practical standpoint a brochure was envisaged as an aid to public relations with clients. It was also described by Mr. Dowell as a tangible way of moving things along, and a way of consolidating health care activities. "This idea took a long time to move to fruition," commented Mr. Dowell; "it was 1969 before a brochure was finally produced by the Sigma Public Relations Office—and many professionals have serious reservations about the document and its usefulness. The development of a brochure, however, automatically raised other issues: practical problems, such as the development of a mailing list and the identification of a place or person in Sigma to whom potential clients should direct their inquiries."

Client Inquiry Committee.   The problem of who should receive the client inquiries evoked by a brochure posed a difficulty. As one professional put it, "No one person should be selected because any individual is identified with one viewpoint and because one person should not capture the inquiries." A solution emerged one day as four professionals (Jackson, Thompson, Evans, and Dowell) discussed what to do about the problem, while walking back after one of the Monday lunches: Why not form a group to handle inquiries? Subsequently, a discussion between three men (Lewis, Hobart, Dowell) generated the notion of rotating the membership of the group. The idea was discussed at a Monday lunch, then with the head of the contracting office, then at a larger meeting of professionals convened by Mr. Dowell. Edward Robson and Stephen Bayne, the president of Sigma, were apprised that the proposal had the agreement of the contracting office and the health care people and so the Client Inquiry Committee was formed in May 1969.

At a group meeting (to which everyone working on any kind of health care task was invited) the first three committee members were selected informally: Mr. Williams for a 2-month term, Mr. Dowell for 4 months, and Mr. Lewis for 6 months. It was anticipated that subsequently a more formal voting system and, occasionally, a mail ballot would be used. At the same time, meetings for all professionals interested in health care were planned to take place every two months.

THE DECISION TO SUPPORT HEALTH CARE

During the spring of 1969, the Executive Committee of Sigma had been considering possible areas of new business which the company might develop. Management had concluded previously that a growth rate of 15% per year was a desirable corporate objective. The subject of the spring meetings was to consider, out of the vast number of alternatives, which new business areas should be selected and developed in order to achieve the company's growth objectives.

"Health care was an obvious candidate," said one executive. "Merely from one's reading of the newspapers and so forth—one knew that health care was a large market, with many problems, and ripe for change." (An example of material which bore out this executive's remarks and data on the growth of the multibillion dollar health care business are shown in Exhibits 3, 4, 5 and 6.) "In addition," he continued, "our people had been doing health care work and the opportunities for growth were apparent from their experiences. A strong factor in our thinking, too, was the fact that Sigma appeared to have a tremendous opportunity—because of its wide range of expertise in laboratory work on drugs, facilities planning, systems design and management consulting—to make a unique contribution to a field that required a broad interdisciplinary approach."

As executive vice president of Sigma, Ed Robson had specific responsibility for the planning of overall corporate development at Sigma. He had also had contacts with some of the persons involved in health care work; for example, two or three years earlier, when Robson had been head of the Management Division,[2] he had encouraged the efforts of some of his staff who were doing health care work. Later he had supported Pete Dowell's proposal for a health care brochure. In choosing health care as a field for special development, it had been agreed at the Executive Committee meeting that Mr. Robson would accept responsibility for determining how this development should be brought about. Consequently, following the Executive Committee's decision on health care, Mr. Robson decided to call a meeting of six Sigma professionals who had been active in health care work, ensuring that he had one person at least from each of the divisions with an active interest in the field.

The brief memorandum that Mr. Robson sent out to the six professionals described the reason for the meeting as follows:

> The senior management of the company, in a recent discussion, concluded that Sigma would like to support the health care field as one of its primary development areas in the near future. It seemed appropriate to take to the addressees the question of how this can best be done.
>
> In brief, I would like to discuss with you the development of a program involving financial investment, organization, recruiting, promotion, training, or whatever other steps ought to be taken to get maximum corporate thrust in the development of health care as a significant Sigma professional activity, and recognized as such in the outside world.

---

[2] In 1969, there was no longer a division of this name; the former Management Division had been split up into three units: Public Management Division, a Corporate Management Division, and a Management Sciences Division.

THE HEALTH CARE MEETING

The six persons Mr. Robson invited to the meeting in his office on August 12 were Pete Dowell, Wynn Day, Frank Jackson, Sam Lewis, Nick Vogel and Norm Williams. During the three-hour meeting, it was apparent to Mr. Robson that different members of the group held widely differing views about which would be the best way to develop health care work at Sigma. Although the discussion raised many significant issues and identified a number of alternative possible courses of action, there was no agreement about what would be the best thing to do. In light of this, it was agreed that the group should meet again in ten days' time and that meanwhile two or three members of the group would each write up draft memoranda outlining some alternatives and their relative merits. As a result, on August 19 Mr. Robson had received two memoranda from two members of the group, Frank Jackson (an urban affairs expert who had become involved in health work) and Pete Dowell. Excerpts from these memoranda are reproduced in Exhibits 7 and 8.

After Mr. Robson had carefully read these two memoranda, he wondered what conclusions he should draw from them about the development of health care—and what position he should take at the next meeting with the six professionals.

Although there were a number of points of contact between Mr. Jackson's memo and Mr. Dowell's, Mr. Robson thought that they could probably be viewed as representing two of the opposed positions that had come up in the August 12 meeting—a conflict between those who, in Mr. Jackson's phrase, favored "a centralized, organized development strategy" and those who, like Mr. Dowell, favored a more evolutionary, grass-roots effort in which "the constituency of the [health care] business development organization should be the professional staff."

ALTERNATIVE VIEWS OF THE PROBLEM

Although it was useful to examine the dichotomy represented by Mr. Jackson's memo and Mr. Dowell's, Mr. Robson realized that the viewpoints expressed by the two men represented more than the opinions of two individuals. Strong views were held by many individuals and genuine differences of opinion existed at many different points in Sigma.

One of those who favored a more organized approach was Nick Vogel. In Mr. Vogel's view, "We've been staggering along like a drunken man for five years. Maybe we've had some glimmering of the goal we wanted to reach five years down the road, but we've wandered off—been diverted by something—and could really get where we want to far more rapidly if we developed a plan. We need to decide what kinds of business we should do and which projects we should and should not accept. Of course I may be a Victorian," he said with a smile; "I think one has to consider what is of value to the corporation, not just what is of interest to myself. At a personal level I'm interested in epidemiology. But that doesn't have to be the focus of our work—epidemiology has many ramifications and I can do the same thing in a number of different areas of health care. One thing we need, though, is a health care department—for a whole variety of reasons."

Another aspect of the situation was mentioned by another Sigma professional, who pointed out some of the problems of leadership in health care:

> Leadership at Sigma is a tricky thing. For the individual, you have to want leadership—but you also have to know how to get it . . . and how to cope with the rugged independents—you know, the guys who will say to themselves, "If someone's going to be my boss, he's going to have to prove that he is suitable for the position better than I have done." I suspect also that some kinds of resistance, competition, call it what you will, have resulted in some guys' talents not being used fully —you know, they just weren't included in things. From management's standpoint too, developing leadership is difficult since there would almost certainly be a rejection on the part of the staff of any unilateral management action to establish a leader.
>
> In the case of health care there is the added difficulty of whether the area needs to be headed up by somebody with professional qualifications in the field of medicine. I guess some of the staff feel that, if you bring someone in on the basis of medical qualifications, he may hold all the old vices that we have discovered in the health care field— and that clients pose enough trouble on this score without having someone on the staff who represents the same ingrained traditions. Of course it's conceivable you could find a maverick. But from our standpoint, which of us could judge a good maverick from a bad one?

Another perspective on the development of the health care area was that of Nelson Hobart, a professional whose special field was human relations and organizational development. Hobart described what he thought were some common misconceptions of how development occurs in an organization:

> The business of asking questions about whether the firm should enter, or develop, health care consulting is in one sense a top management game! It reminds me of a situation I once heard of which arose in one of the large contract research organizations about twenty years ago. The president of the organization invited a friend (who was then a vice president of one of the top management consultants) to take a look at his organization and see whether it should go into management consulting. After six weeks of talking to people and analyzing the figures, the friend returned to the president and asked him to repeat the first question that he had asked him to investigate. When the president had repeated his question about whether the organization should move into management consulting, his friend replied that, from his analysis of the figures, 37% of the work that they were doing at that time represented what he and other management consulting firms would describe as management consulting!
>
> When some of these questions came up at Sigma, you know, about whether we should enter health care, or how to develop health care, it's very tempting to respond, "Damn it, we are in health care. Can't you see? Do we have to hire tired experts before people around Sigma see us as legitimately in health care?"

He added:

> I know the cry goes up to "organize" health care or another area—
> but the development process needs to be seen as an evolutionary process
> . . . the process has its own logic but it is not the logic of conventional
> "planning." The real problem with defining the health care field, for
> example, lies in the risk that one may proscribe other fields and also
> limit the new field you are trying to get at . . . that is, your definition
> may be comprehensible to you but shut off other people whose perspec-
> tives might provide a richer insight into, or even a new conception of,
> the newly emerging area. It's one thing to buy some experts, who allow
> you to compete in an established field. It's another to go into a field
> that really doesn't exist, and in which your own behavior is necessarily
> a shaping force.

Mr. Hobart's colleague, Chuck Ryder, joined in on this point:

> In fact the best decision about defining a field in a case like health
> care may be to decide not to make a decision on definition at this time.
> Instead, let the process develop . . . recognize the risks of formaliza-
> tion . . . acknowledge the organization's possible incapacity to select
> the right new people until more experience has built up . . . and
> avoid, for example, not recognizing new things, new developments in
> the field, because one has focused on growing, say, through buying
> existing hospital consulting firms.
>
> You can't preconceive the nature of a change process. In developing
> a new area the real force lies in the vital juices of human beings . . .
> their interests and their commitments. Commitment is never in organi-
> zations—it's in people. So the way growth in an area is accelerated is
> by doing work in it . . . not by "establishing an organization" but by
> letting the organization be defined operationally by which guys are on
> board.

One who held a contrary view of what was required was Zach Kennedy, who had joined Sigma two months earlier, having been chief administrator for nine years of a major urban hospital with 700 physicians
on its staff and an annual budget of approximately $85 million. Mr.
Kennedy had originally come to know Sigma as a client when he had
asked them to conduct a small study. Later, when he decided to move
from his hospital post, and had been invited to join Sigma's professional
staff through the initiative of Sigma staff he had met previously, Mr.
Kennedy's views on health care were direct:

> The health field is really not a field at all—it needs an agglomera-
> tion of talent . . . and that is Sigma's great strength. There is no one
> who is good in the health field anywhere . . . and that is what helps
> make it such a ripe field for development. What Sigma lacks, of course,
> is health credibility . . . and health is a very close field; everybody
> knows everybody and if you make a boo-boo you're out—but if you do
> two or three good projects, you're in. If Sigma gets credibility one could
> make a killing. We're doing $2 million of health care business at pres-
> ent—but we could be doing $10 million—the Sigma name is gold and
> so are the people and talents we have here. The trouble is that all
> they've been doing is scratching at the market, when what is required
> is discipline and boldness.

Within two weeks of getting here I saw that what we needed was a small, powerful, talented group. We would have top people in the field —risk not having them chargeable for a while—and do a major project or two at cost. Maybe we'd even have to spend $350,000 or $500,000 on them. In this way we could make a name for ourselves and perhaps publish a book on our experience. But we must have quality control. The trouble is that an expert here is a guy who has done a project on a subject. But we need a core of people who know how a hospital operates, and how a board of trustees operates, and what motivates doctors. There's no mystery to these things—but it requires exposure.

A different view of the role of and need for health specialists, however, was indicated by Mr. Dowell who had noted in a memo to Mr. Robson in late 1967:

I am not at all dismayed about our lack of experience. . . . I can think of at least three cases over the past year where our lack of "hospital expertise" has been no drawback—Belvue, S. F. General, and Western Blue Cross. Current possibilities with two other potential clients carry that same flavor.

Different viewpoints about the organization of health care were also held by different division heads. Thorley Elliott, the head of Management Sciences, for instance, had read a copy of Dowell's latest memo and commented:

In reviewing Pete Dowell's memo, I find that I am disappointed with the approach taken to-date. . . . I feel it will be inadequate to do what we ought to do. The most important issue, to my mind, centers around the question of whether the overall activity requires that some small group of Sigma staff be highly specialized, dedicated, and committed to that given activity with no other real alternatives available within the Sigma framework. If this is necessary then I think the rather loose, traditional methods described in Pete's memo are far from adequate. Our normal approach simply leaves such people much too vulnerable to decision-making in which they have limited participation even though it is vital to their future; at the same time, I don't believe it establishes an adequate framework for budgeting and business development.

As far as I can see, sooner or later we will have to either form a formal core group or we will never do more than dabble in the health care field. I know this is a hard issue to face, but I don't think you can dodge it. From my point of view, incidentally, almost exactly the same needs are encountered in the fields of transportation, education and regulatory economics. In each case we have an area that sounds as though it was a market—but is really a series of separate and somewhat interrelated different markets—and in each case we have subject matter that cuts broadly across the divisional activities of Sigma.

George McDonald, head of the Public Management Division, disagreed with Elliott's view though:

Forming a department is by no means an automatic way of developing an area. In fact forming a department might insulate health care . . . tend to encourage a cloistered approach. I would prefer to see some stronger coordination—possibly a coordinator, someone with some tools, someone who could report progress in the field. But the proposal for a department is gutless; it doesn't innovate . . . or encourage a man to show how he can get round organizational obstacles. Health care is always going to require talents from all parts of the company and we can't avoid the reality of dealing with that problem by forming a health care department.

CONCLUSION

Mr. Robson smiled as he recalled a recent visitor's description of Sigma as "one of the world's most varied assortments of prima donnas." Clearly there were strong differences of opinion on what should be done —and some of these differences reflected different views of consulting (as Pete Dowell had put it once: "Who owns the problem: the client or the consultant?") and concerns for different types of health care work, as well as basically different approaches to the issue of how to develop a new business area at Sigma.

The health care market, it seemed to Robson, had great potential and Sigma's range of skills was eminently suited to it. However, it was an area, he realized, in which a number of firms were very interested. One of Sigma's staff had reported to Robson what he had heard about the efforts of one of the large systems-oriented aerospace companies to move into nondefense work:

> The Civil Systems Division is about five years old now. . . . From meagre beginnings it has grown to about 55 full-time people with various others from the organization spending occasional time on specific assignments and projects. The Department is organized on a project area basis with Transportation, Health, Pollution, Urban and Other being the five departments.
>
> The most striking difference between the activities of the people with whom I talked and our own efforts is the scale upon which they are basing their involvement as it compares with ours. Having the aerospace orientation has led them into the civilian area looking for large efforts of years' duration involving millions of dollars and many, many people and much development and proposal-writing expense (they price people differently when they are working toward an accepted proposal than they do when the proposal becomes a contract). They are not yet sure to what extent such a market exists but they have become involved in it enough to make the future look fairly bright and they have a couple of years to continue to spend considerably more than they make.
>
> Another difference is their exclusive reliance on the technical skills of physical sciences and engineering to perform the task. Their "systems" orientation up to this point includes every component but people and they are skeptical of the place into which someone with a social science orientation would fit.

Two days earlier Mr. Robson had received another indication of potential competitor activity in a memo from Norm Williams. Mr. Williams had reported that one of Sigma's senior outside medical consultants on a major current project had told Williams privately that one of the smaller top-quality management consulting groups was to announce shortly the formation of a new Institutional Consulting Subsidiary and that he and "some friends" of his had been invited to become affiliated with it and been offered stock options as an inducement.

In light of all this, thought Mr. Robson, "What direction should Sigma take?"

Exhibit 1

SIGMA CONSULTANTS, INC. (A)

List of Persons Referred to in Health Care Case

Sigma Corporate level:
Stephen Bayne, President
Edward Robson, Executive Vice President

Corporate Management Division: (5)*
Zach Kennedy
Charles Young

Engineering Division: (7)
Wynn Day
Paul Isaac
Henry Turner

Life Sciences Division: (5)
Robert Stringer (Division Head)
Samuel Lewis

Management Sciences Division: (7)
Thorley Elliott (Division Head)
Harold Satterlee
Nicholas Vogel
Baxter Warren
Norman Williams

Public Management Division: (16)
George McDonald (Division Head)
Luther Evans
Frank Jackson
Murray Long
Frederick Norton
Lee Thompson
Cooper Todd

Research & Development Division: (8)
Peter Dowell
Nelson Hobart
Ben Kimber
David Newlin
Chuck Ryder

* The number in parentheses indicates the number of individuals in the division who had served as team leader on a health-related project during the period 1966 through mid-1969.

Exhibit 2

SIGMA CONSULTANTS, INC. (A)

Major Health Care Projects, 1966–1969

1966	*Project description*	*Team leader*	*Amount*
Belvue.................	Merger of Oregon hospitals	Dowell	$ 20,000
L.A. College of Medicine..	Facilities development	Norton	60,000
Western Blue Cross.......	Organizational development	Williams	72,000
Eastex, Inc..............	Automated material delivery system design	Isaac	415,000
1967			
S.F. General Hospital.....	Administration, organization and operation of the radiology dept.	Dowell	67,000
W. Johnson Gen. Hospital..............	Establishment of a regional radiation therapy center	Long/ Norton	52,000
Medical Data Bureau, Chicago..............	Computer network	Young	59,500
City of Boston...........	Merger of two independent public health organizations	Todd	55,900
1968			
Public Health Service, North Carolina.........	Quantitative planning tools for national cancer program	Warren	236,084
Eastex, Inc..............	Pilot model of delivery system	Isaac	133,000
Regional Medical Program (HSMHA).....	Analysis of programs	Newlin	535,000
HSMHA (NCHSR&D)....	Financing of chronic leukemia treatment expense	Williams/ Satterlee	175,200
HEW..................	Systems analysis—artificial heart	Turner	290,000
1969			
New York Clinic.........	Computer applications	Warren	170,485
Department of Defense....	New military hospital system plan	Day	836,000
Univ. of Cal., Berkeley Medical Center.........	Medical center development	Dowell	220,000
NASA [proposal drafted]..............	Drug effects in space	Kimber	185,000

Exhibit 3

SIGMA CONSULTANTS, INC. (A)

Press Report on U.S. Health Care Situation

AILING HEALTH SYSTEM NEEDS MORE THAN MONEY

WASHINGTON—The Federal dollar looms large in American health care and is likely to loom larger, but the Government seems caught in the classic Alice-in-Wonderland predicament— the more money the Administration puts in, the more is needed. In short, as the Red Queen said to Alice: It takes all the running you can do to keep in the same place.

In large measure that was the central finding of the report made public last week from the task force on Medicaid and related problems. The task force, headed by Walter J. McNerney, president of the Blue Cross Association, was appointed a year ago by the Secretary of Health, Education and Welfare.

"It is a central conclusion of the task force that money is needed, but that money alone will not guarantee either capacity or effectiveness of the system," the report said. In that context, it was not discussing simply Medicaid, but the entire system of American health care.

Indeed, the clear implication of the report was that neither Medicaid nor any other major health program can be put in proper working order without making basic changes in the whole complex system by which Americans get health care when they need it.

The extent of the failure is apparent to the person with adequate income who nevertheless finds it hard to reach a doctor except by long waiting and who may go from specialist to specialist with little continuity of care. It is apparent to the doctor who may regularly work 60 to 80 hours a week and still may not have enough time for all he wants to do. It is probably less apparent, but more tragically real, to the poor and near-poor, many of whom get no care at all until it becomes a matter of life and death.

The report offered no concrete solution to the problem; indeed it said there is no simple solution. But it did suggest directions. These included less dependence on individual and isolated transactions between a doctor and a patient, more voice for the consumer, and more leadership by government to promote change. Since Medicare and Medicaid already exert a big influence on the system, they were cited as access points where the leadership can be applied.

Exert Leverage

Medicare, a Federal program of medical insurance for persons over 65 years of age, and Medicaid, a state-Federal medical welfare program designed to help the poor and the near-poor of all ages, exert great leverage on the whole health-care situation. In turn, they are powerfully affected by the changes they cause in the private sector.

Today health care in the United States is a roughly $64-billion enterprise, heavily hit by inflation. It is estimated that 26 cents of every health dollar comes from Federal sources. Medicare and Medicaid together form the main component of the Federal share. In size and proportion they have been increasing steadily in recent years and have been complicating the rest of the picture.

Neither program does the full job for which it was designed. Medicare helps virtually all Americans in the age group it covers, but, on the average, it pays only about half of their health bills; that still leaves a hardship for many of the elderly. Medicaid, at present, helps only about one-third of all the poor and near-poor for whom its benefits were intended.

Yet the cost of these programs is already large and growing. The one point on which there is hardly any disagreement among the experts is that the dollar growth cannot continue indefinitely without some other changes.

"If a benevolent and affluent government were to begin to pay for all the basic health care needed by all those who can't pay for it themselves, but no other changes were introduced into the existing system, the result would be a disastrous rise in the cost of services that are already scarce," the task force report said.

Community Affair

In its recommendations, the task force made it clear that health care must become a community affair where it has been an individual affair in the past. The Department of Health, Education and Welfare was singled out as the agency on which the greatest responsibility must rest for exerting leadership and achieving change.

Among the specific new directions that the group sees as desirable is greater emphasis on group practice of medicine and, in particular, on more extensive use of prepaid health plans that emphasize preventive care. Other study groups have come to much the same conclusions in the past; but it appears now that government is becoming more and more inclined to accept many of those conclusions and that the voice of organized medicine is less adamant and less powerful in opposition.

HAROLD M. SCHMECK Jr.

Source: © *The New York Times*. Reprinted by permission.

Exhibit 4

SIGMA CONSULTANTS, INC. (A)

Consultant's Report on Health Care Conference

MEMORANDUM

TO: (18 professionals)

FROM: Luther Evans

RE: Insurance Companies & Health Care

At the recent American Public Health Association meeting in Philadelphia a Mr. Howard Ennes, Vice President of Equitable, gave a talk on the insurance companies' role in health care.

Three hundred companies are covering 100 million people with "some type of health care insurance." These 300 companies account for 80% of the total health insurance business. In 1968 this amounted to 6.7 billion dollars.

There is a crisis in health care. $60 billion spent in 1968 with probably $100 billion a year within 5 years. If both President Nixon and Walter Reuther agree that there is a "health crisis," then *there is one.*

. . . . [Equitable] feel(s) that a complete revision of the present order of priorities is needed. Organized health care service will be the order of the day, and the GP will soon be out.

Systems of group practice such as Kaiser* should be carefully looked at. When they talk, as they do, about 2 beds per 1,000 population under group practice versus 4½ beds per 1,000 in communities, then we are talking of big money savings.

Action in the health care field is crucial for survival of insurance companies. Therefore, the conservative insurance companies are *now on the move.* If you are not part of the solution, you are part of the problem.

* Casewriter's note: The Kaiser Foundation medical care program conducted a prepaid comprehensive group practice health care program for more than 1.75 million persons on the West Coast through 18 hospital-based health centers and 45 out-patient facilities. (1968 data).

Exhibit 5

SIGMA CONSULTANTS, INC. (A)
Data on the Growth of Health Care Expenditures
National health care expenditures: selected years, 1950 to 1975
(1969 and 1975 estimated)

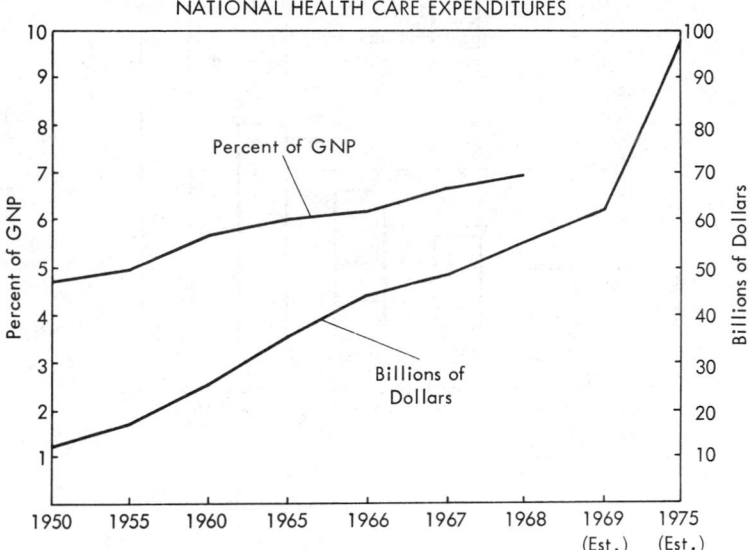

NATIONAL HEALTH CARE EXPENDITURES

Source: Insurance Industry Task Force.

Per capita personal health care expenditures, 1960–1968
(public and private)*

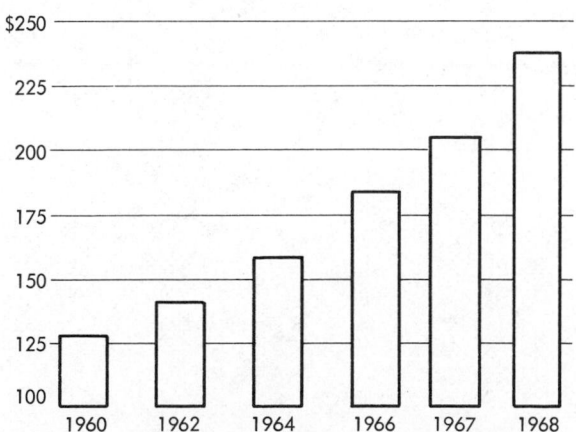

* Does not include expenses for prepayment; expenditures of private voluntary agencies for other health services; government public health activities and identifiable administrative expenses under public programs.

Sources: The Committee for National Health Insurance; data from the U.S. Department of Health, Education and Welfare.

Exhibit 5—Continued

Public and private expenditures for health and medical care
(1950–1969 fiscal year)

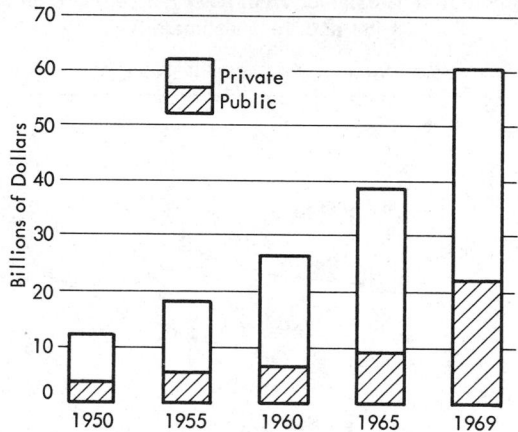

Sources: The Committee for National Health Insurance; data
from the U.S. Department of Health, Education and Welfare.

Exhibit 6

SIGMA CONSULTANTS, INC. (A)

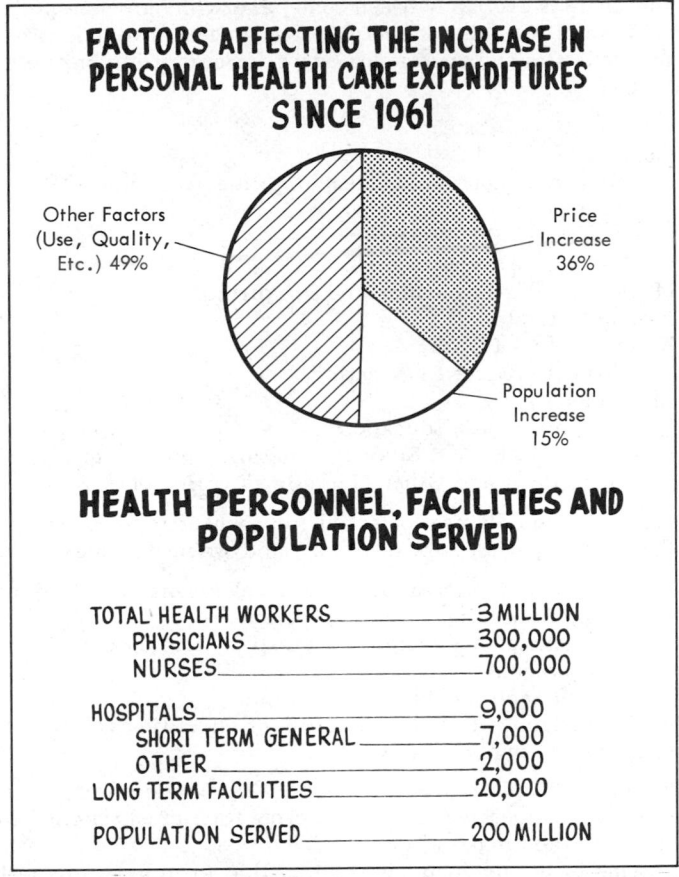

FACTORS AFFECTING THE INCREASE IN PERSONAL HEALTH CARE EXPENDITURES SINCE 1961

Other Factors (Use, Quality, Etc.) 49%

Price Increase 36%

Population Increase 15%

HEALTH PERSONNEL, FACILITIES AND POPULATION SERVED

TOTAL HEALTH WORKERS	3 MILLION
PHYSICIANS	300,000
NURSES	700,000
HOSPITALS	9,000
SHORT TERM GENERAL	7,000
OTHER	2,000
LONG TERM FACILITIES	20,000
POPULATION SERVED	200 MILLION

Source: Chart presented by Mr. Wilbur Cohen, Secretary Designate of HEW to Senate Subcommittee chaired by Senator Abraham Ribicoff, April 26, 1968. Reported in *Health Care in America: Hearings before the Subcommittee on Executive Reorganization of the Committee on Government Operations*, U.S. Senate, 90th Congress, 1968.

Exhibit 7

SIGMA CONSULTANTS, INC. (A)

Excerpts from F. Jackson Memorandum of August 18, 1969

Subject: HEALTH BUSINESS DEVELOPMENT

There appears to be little doubt that "Health" can be one of the significant growth areas for Sigma. The diversity of opportunities and the breadth of skills required demand the participation of all Divisions. It will also demand the broadening of skills as well as increasing depth in a number of areas.

Exhibit 7—Continued

The field of health is actually a number of categories for business development. While there is overlap between some, and while any one project might incorporate several, we think it useful to recognize a distinction for forming both an umbrella strategy and tactical steps for organizing business development activities.

1. Health Care—Overseas
2. Health Facilities
    (a) Hospital (community; teaching; medical centers)
    (b) Others
3. Community Health Projects
4. Bio-Medical Research
5. Medical/Health Economics and Financing
6. Industrial Health
7. Environmental Health
8. Bio-Medical Product Engineering
9. Epidemiology
10. Medical and Health Education
11. Policy and Evaluation Studies (federal, regional, etc.)
12. Pharmaceutical and Other Marketing for Health Care.

In order to develop Sigma's potential for each of these a centralized, organized development strategy is necessary and would include:

— determination of priority business development opportunities for the immediate future and three-year period
— establishment of a strategy for prospect *development* and *response*
— staff development
— staff recruitment, including consultants
— inquiry assignment, with evaluation of effectiveness
— publicity and public relations

The execution of this strategy must be a corporate effort, supported in significant part by corporate funds. The Corporation must sanction the effort, give it legitimacy, and make it accountable.

There seems to be much in the Sigma ethic to mitigate against strong, centralized direction. Certainly the strategy should not undercut Sigma's basic strengths stemming from its flexible mechanisms for response. However, our current flexible mechanism for business development is too dependent upon the interest and availability of individual staff members, or of loose coalitions among them, to likely lead a strong enough effort to make a relatively fast impact. The answer would seem to lie in an approach which allows the Sigma basic form of desired staff independence, while at the same time tightening and directing business development.

Five general models for organizational structures may be noted:

1. *Continued operations in the present form.* This is characterized by an essentially *ad hoc* response to opportunities which are brought to our attention.
2. *The appointment of one person,* well-qualified and generally knowledgeable about the entire health field, to have responsibility for directing all business development efforts.
3. *The establishment of a clearly identified Health Group* (Division, Subdivisional Department, or informal coalition) whose members devote their time almost exclusively to health.

Exhibit 7—Continued

4. *Expansion of the role of the present Client Inquiry Advisory Committee* to include responsibility for coordinating business development.
5. *Establishment of a new committee structure* to draw across Sigma Divisional lines. To be composed of people who would *commit* a certain part of their time to a business development effort. The committee would draw upon others in Sigma—organized informally or in some subcommittee structure—to carry out business development efforts with them.

None of those basic alternatives need be viewed as exclusive options. Indeed, the organizational structure which I pose below for discussion would include each of these components. This would include:

— *A Sigma Health Director,* appointed on the corporate level, who would function as a team leader for a Sigma project, "Health Business Development." The Director would orchestrate, and participate in, Sigma's business development thrusts. The Director would draw his legitimacy and backing from corporate management, through which he would relate to the Division V.P.'s. At this time no separate Health Department is envisioned, rather the Director would draw "staff" from the existing Sigma structure.
— *The Advisory Committee would continue* with its same charge and composition. However, rather than reporting to Contracting, it would report to the Director who would share project assignment responsibility with Contracting.
— *A rather elaborate Advisory Committee structure for business development* is called for to advise and assist in the task of initiating action (building project prospects, staff, and image). Working committees would be established for the major business development categories. These would be informal committees (composed of people with mutual interest for each area) and each chairman would work with the Director to articulate development opportunities and to involve people from the larger group.

   Throughout the initial years, it is not likely Sigma will have all the senior staff required to build our image and pursue our goals for a number of the business development areas. To overcome this, Sigma could retain the *exclusive consulting services of a cadre of senior people* of the calibre required. Such consultants would work with the Director and his business development groups as well as with project teams.

The structure outlined above would in part depend upon the strength and ability of the Director. However, to an even greater degree, its success would depend on the willingness of Sigma staff to cooperate and to commit at least part of their time to business development activities. Such commitment could be encouraged by the judicious use of the Health Business Development project funds to serve as an inducement: it would be understood that further funds would not be forthcoming if commitment was not carried out. Assignment of such funds, in all cases, should be expected to entail the same responsibility by staff as project work for clients.

As a first step, until a Director is appointed, or as an alternative to his appointment, a five-man committee might be established to play the coordinating, leadership role. The committee members should commit a required

Exhibit 7—Concluded

proportion of their time to the task—to be charged to project funds. It would be advisable to have one member of the corporate central staff sit as chairman of this group to strengthen its legitimacy and provide continuity of leadership. This group might well be built around the existing Client Inquiry Advisory Committee.

Exhibit 8

SIGMA CONSULTANTS, INC. (A)

Excerpts from P. Dowell Memorandum of August 18, 1969

Subject: ORGANIZING FOR BUSINESS DEVELOPMENT IN HEALTH CARE

At a recent meeting of corporate management and division heads, it was agreed that the company should put its chips on what looks like a winning area. Development activities financed from corporate funds might include things like:

1.   increased contact with high-level health people in HEW, DOD, etc;
2.   identification of people and skills Sigma should recruit;
3.   coordinated public relations to get most mileage from our work;
4.   identification of new areas to develop;
5.   internal staff development;
6.   articles;
7.   time to coordinate health activities among divisions by keeping division heads and business managers up to date.

If corporate money is going to be available, there needs to be some organization through which to channel it and to be accountable for its use to Sigma management.

We have the Client Inquiry Steering Committee whose primary function is to recommend assignment of client inquiries to Contracting and suggest staffing resources to other people who would like to use the Committee. The Steering Committee operates primarily in a responsive mode. It sets the agenda for our large bi-monthly health care meetings. The Committee is becoming generally recognized throughout Sigma as a major organizational innovation in response to the problem of how to handle client inquiries in a large, diffuse, interdivisional field such as health.

The job now is to organize ourselves in a way that goes beyond the response function into the active area of business development. Corporate management recognizes the desirability of having the people who are involved professionally in health care work organize their own business development function, rather than having an organization imposed from top management.

We may be able to agree that the organization we evolve should possess certain characteristics and take into account certain organizational and interpersonal realities in Sigma. For example, the bulk of the people who have an interest in health care do not view it as their only or even their primary commitment. These people, as well as many we don't even know about yet, are and will be vital to the growth and development of health care consulting at Sigma. Any organization that we do develop should accommodate the fact of varying commitment. It should allow commitment and access to the health care projects to be as easy as possible.

The business development organizations should also be capable of change so that resources can be focused and refocused in a timely manner, to be responsive to market conditions and professional interests of particular people in Sigma. It should be able to operate across all of the existing divisions in a way that does not compete with them but rather uses those organizations, augments them, and draws strength from them. The organization should be capable of developing some reasonable focus or series of focuses to the health care field in a way that is believable, understandable and relevant to people who are professionally interested in health care as well as the management structure of the company. The business development organization should also be in close touch with what's going on in the health care field in Sigma and outside. Probably the best mechanism for doing the former is to have close touch with the Steering Committee.

We would like to suggest some alternative models.

Model #1

One person tapped by the group to head up our business development activities in health care.

This is a traditional way and it has the advantages of continuity and of having a single person accountable to top management. It provides an organizational nucleus with some stability around which people could cluster. It could provide recognition for a particular person. On the negative side, the notion of a czar might shut out a lot of people around Sigma. No one person completely embodies all of the interests of the health care people in Sigma, either with respect to particular functional areas (such as hospital administration, medical care financing, systems analysis, etc.) or with respect to basic philosophy of how to do consulting in the health care field. The person chosen to perform that business development function might find himself quickly out on the periphery or otherwise isolated from a substantial segment of the professionals interested or potentially interested in health care at Sigma.

Model #2

Having the Steering Committee take over the duties of business development as well as its existing functions.

In favor of this idea is the fact that the committee is an established body. It is continually energized by inquiries from the contracting office and others so that the members of the committee have to talk with one another frequently. Because it is in touch with the client inquiry assignment activity, it is also in touch with what is going on in health care generally in Sigma. On the negative side, business development is a basically different function from what the Steering Committee was originally set up to do. Also the combination of inquiry assignment and business development might be too heavy a burden on the members of the Steering Committee, even if it were funded by corporate money. Third, it would concentrate substantial power in the Steering Committee which might be viewed by some people as unwise. Fourth, the Steering Committee is only three people and probably should be kept to only three because of the need for rapid communication in the assignment function. Consequently it takes a long time to directly involve much of the professional staff.

Model #3

Form a separate business development committee consisting of three to four people operating parallel and similar to the Steering Committee.

On the positive side, it would be an additional organizational innovation

Exhibit 8—Concluded

patterned after one which has worked already. It would enable more people in the larger health care group to be involved in important aspects of our health care business. Because of the rotation feature, there would be built-in change and new ideas. But, there would also be built-in continuity. On the con side, there is probably feeling against the proliferation of committees. Decision making "by committee" is suspect to a greater or lesser degree by many people. Also unless this business development committee is activated in some way from the outside, it might do nothing. This perhaps could be overcome by requiring it to meet periodically with the Steering Committee to find out what is going on in the health care field, and also by making it accountable for a report to the larger health care group at the bi-monthly meeting of that group. Finally, it will be energized from time to time as it needs to consider potential health care applicants and bring these applicants to the attention of our personnel department, or various divisional people and staff members.

Model #4

Do not organize business development. We're doing pretty well as it is. Let it continue to evolve.

We hope that this memo can serve to stimulate some thoughts so that we can decide on our business development function in a way we can all live with and which can get the job done.

We would like to urge that we innovate, that we not be bound by past methods and ways of doing things. The organization should be made *primarily* responsible to the professional staff. We are not denying the responsibility and accountability needed to top management; but rather the constituency of the business development organization should be the professional staff.

Sigma Consultants, Inc. (A)
(Supplement)

THE INFORMATION below describes practices and procedures at Sigma important to understanding Sigma Consultants (A).

THE GENERATION OF CLIENT ASSIGNMENTS

Prospective client assignments come into Sigma in a variety of ways according to one corporate officer:

> By and large business flows to Sigma; and much of it appears to be a result of previous projects. . . . you know—former clients, people who have heard of a project we did or who have been referred by former clients. There are also those that seem to come out of a general awareness of Sigma or the reputation or writings of one of our staff. I would say, therefore, that less than 25% of projects are developed purely on staff initiative.
>
> Some project possibilties start with a phone call to a Sigma office; some may be initiated by a general letter of inquiry or a government RFP (request for proposal); other inquiries come in the mail to individual professionals. One way and another, though, I would say 80%–90% of prospects come to us through members.
>
> Staff are encouraged to bring client inquiries along—to develop them —and then report them to management. The Contracting Office (which is responsible for registering prospects, reviewing contracts, and en-suring that the firm avoids conflicts of interest) can sometimes suggest relevant people for a project team. And in a case where there is doubt about whom an inquiry should go to, a management committee, which meets briefly every day, may be asked to decide. However, by the time they are reported to Contracting, three quarters of the prospects are being handled by the person who becomes project leader.

THE RECORD OF USAGE OF PROFESSIONAL TIME

As a research and management consulting firm, the largest single expense incurred by Sigma was the salary cost of the professional staff employed to conduct client assignments. The record of how consultants' time had been spent was built up from time reports submitted every Friday by each staff member on which every hour spent during the week was to be recorded. The basic workweek for accounting purposes was assumed to be 40 hours; all calculations of individual, group, division, and corporate activity were computed on this basis. The categories into which staff time was analyzed, with an indication of a typical breakdown for one division, are shown in the table below.

Table 1

TYPICAL DIVISIONAL USAGE OF DISTRIBUTABLE STAFF TIME

Administration—General....................................	1.5%
Hiring......................................	2.0
Prospect charges—Nontransferred commercial................	2.7
Government.............................	4.1
Business development..	5.7
Professional activities......................................	2.0
	18.0%
Chargeable time..	82.0
Total..	100.0%

The categories of "General Administration" and "Hiring" are self-explanatory. Other categories were used as follows:

Prospect charges. When a staff member got a promising project inquiry at Sigma, where the problem had been clearly identified and Sigma was sure that it wanted to write a proposal, the professional would usually request a "prospect number" or account. Any time that he spent pursuing this "prospect" such as making an initial study of the problems or writing a project proposal for the client would be charged to the prospect account number. Where a prospect turned into a firm project contract, in the case of commercial clients, it was Sigma's contract practice to charge the client the cost of developing the project (i.e., the time spent on writing the proposal, visiting the prospective client, etc.). The amount in Table 1 for commercial prospect charges, therefore, represents work charged to "prospect" accounts that has not resulted in a project contract. In the case of government projects, federal regulations did not permit firms to bill the government for time spent on a project in advance of a contract; hence this figure represented the total prospect cost for prospective government projects.

Business development. This was a very general category that covered business development and sales efforts that could not be identified with a particular serious prospect. For example, a campaign of formal calls on key organizations (e.g., federal and state agencies, professional, institutional and commercial organizations) would be charged to this category. Time spent on writing letters to prospective clients about matters of potential interest, inquiry follow-up (where it was necessary to investigate an inquiry to determine just what a client wanted Sigma to do), and possibly a visit to a trade convention might be charged to business development.

Professional activities. This category might be used for time spent by staff on educational and professional society affairs, on writing a paper for a professional journal, or attending a national, annual professional meeting.

Chargeable Time. This consisted essentially of time charged to clients for work on project assignments. As indicated earlier, this category also included transferred commercial prospect charges.

"The point of view taken by the professional staff to complete time cards," remarked one division business manager, "varies somewhat according to the individual. My particular hobby-horse though, is the time worked, over and above the basic 40 hours, which is not recorded." He continued:

> Occasionally some of this time may get on the record—but on the whole it doesn't. Many of the staff resist recording this time; they view it as "conscience time," time perhaps to bring a project or a report up to the quality that they will be happy with, but this can lead to unusual results. A little while ago, for example, we had a computer installation job and when the final time report came in I noticed that the project leader had finished the job and recorded charges which were billed to the client were about 5% under the original estimate. Yet I knew our men worked twelve hours a day for several weeks on that job—it's inevitable on a computer installation job—but the client didn't pay for the overtime!
>
> Of course, the way our business is set up, Sigma carries the risk on most jobs; you see we agree to bill the client only for the time recorded. So that, if it comes out less than the project budget, the client saves; but if it's over budget we carry the loss—unless we can, and wish to, negotiate an increase. But our firm policy is not to do so at the end of a project.
>
> In addition to ensuring quality, a project leader at Sigma is concerned to meet his project budget. What happens is that many leaders like to leave themselves a little cushion for the end of an assignment. Sometimes something can crop up at the last minute; so they like to have something available so that they won't go over their project budget. There's no particular credit to finishing under budget. But where nothing does crop up, however, one finishes up the project under budget—as happened in the computer case! As a result I'm experimenting in my division with methods of getting time over 40 hours a week recorded.

CORPORATE PROJECT DEVELOPMENT FUNDS

The net total of all the divisional profit margins represented the total Sigma "professional service margin." In preparing the annual budget two items were deducted from this total before arriving at the corporate income from operations: The first item was central service costs (e.g., corporate officers' salaries and expenses and general services like accounting, the computer lab, purchasing, etc.); the second was an amount for corporate funded development projects.

The amount of divisional new business development funds for Sigma as a whole totalled approximately $2.0 million at direct salary cost. At normal client billing rates (i.e., including overhead and profit markup) this represented say $6.0 million. In addition to these funds there was an amount of $600,000 (valued at billing rates) budgeted at the corporate level to fund what were termed "corporate projects." This amount was budgeted as a lump sum at the beginning of the year and was allocated during the year by Edward Robson, the executive vice president, to individual professional staff or small groups who approached him for support of activities they (and Mr. Robson) judged to be in the corporate interest. The median project size had tended to be about $15,000 and their nature was quite varied.

By valuing these funds at billing rates it was possible for a staff member to charge his time up to a corporate project without either him or his division suffering a drop in reported chargeable time levels or divisional profit. However, some staff members referred to corporate project money as "funny money" and, as one staff member observed, "Given a choice, a professional will always prefer to work on a client's assignment rather than a corporate or divisional project."

Erikson Industries

Introduction

ESTABLISHED in the late 1930s through the merger of three industrial manufacturing companies, Erikson Industries was a large, diversified industrial company with headquarters in Chicago. Although the largest proportion of the company's business was concentrated in the manufacture of heavy industrial machinery, electrical equipment, and fluid power controls, in 1966 Erikson's activities ranged from the production of power units for small boats and the manufacture of hospital X-ray equipment to short-haul trucking. By that year, too, a number of Erikson department managers were engaged in the process of formulating new strategy to exploit a trend toward underground distribution of power. While the precise dimensions and place of the movement from overhead to underground distribution were not yet determinable (in 1963 only about 10% of either transmission or distribution plant was underground equipment), many managers believed that the traditional businesses supplying utility customers were about to experience a revolutionary transformation. This case examines this trend, especially in relation to several departments at Erikson, and provides data on the industry and the company which permit analysis of the question, "What should Erikson Industries do to exploit the opportunities presented by changing markets?"

The U.S. electric power industry

As demonstrated by the 1965 "blackout" in the Northeastern power grid, electric power played a critical role in the economic and social life of the United States. That year nearly 23% of the energy used in the highly industrialized U.S. economy was consumed in the form of electricity, and this figure was expected to rise. Household electricity was especially important: 99.8% of all homes were wired in 1965, and while only 4.2% of these used electricity for heat, its use for lighting and a host of appliances made electricity a virtual necessity.

Power for residential, industrial and other uses was supplied by four groups of producers. Industrial plants supplying their own needs accounted for slightly more than 10% of electricity generation. Government-owned utilities accounted for about 20% and cooperatives for another 7%. The remaining 60% was supplied by investor-owned electric utilities. There were 220 generating companies in 1963 with operating revenues over $1 million each. While power companies were engaged in the complete process of bringing electricity from energy source to the consumer, the demands for equipment at various stages of this process were traditionally viewed as separate ones. Many manufacturers therefore organized their production and marketing efforts as if the markets for generating, transmission, and distribution were independent, the market for distribution plant facilities being the largest in recent years.

Generally, the financial relationships evident in the electrical industry followed from the nature of the industry. In sharp contrast to the situation in most manufacturing industries, annual operating expenses here were only 58% more than construction expenditures (1963). Electricity typically was *generated* in giant automated plants requiring heavy capital investment and relatively little operating labor—fuel being the major cost and labor less than 10% of total cost. *Transmission,* the transportation of high voltage power from the generating source over wires to transformers at local distribution centers, and *distribution,* the local transportation of middle-range voltage power to the consumer, required as much labor per dollar of capital as the production of electricity but involved far lower total operating costs, with transmission being even more capital-intensive than distribution. (See Exhibits 1–3.)

From the point of view of equipment manufacturers selling to these three segments of the industry, different factors determine the level of activity. By and large, production and transmission equipment sales were a function of the growth and movement of a population and industry over long time periods and of improvements in equipment technology. In contrast, distribution equipment sales were closely tied to short-term movements in residential and industrial construction and to per capita increases in load. Of even greater importance to the growth of distribution equipment sales were increases in load due to new kinds of electrical products. Even a single new appliance had considerable impact, and the *average new all-electric* home used 25,000 kw.-hr. annually, 3⅓ times as much as the *average new* home.

Competition

Competing in the electrical equipment market were a number of firms ranging from the giant General Electric, across large diversified firms such as Allis Chalmers and Erikson Industries, to small specialty manufacturers such as the Maloney Corporation or Kuhlman Electric Company. Except where a company possessed a major technological product advantage, competition was fierce and low manufacturing costs were critical to survival and competitive success.

The trend toward underground

The paragraphs above probably would have been an accurate picture of electric power equipment markets during the 1960s were it not for a marked trend toward underground distribution equipment. In the late 1950s in an upper income development in suburban St. Louis, Missouri Power began to experiment with underground residential distribution, trying to deliver power to a suburban area by underground cables rather than by unsightly overhead wires.

The first idea was to put a pole-type transformer system underground in a kiosk. Very few were installed because of water and soil erosion problems and also high cost. The utility companies then decided to try putting a transformer above ground, in a pad-mount. All wiring, however, was underground. There seemed little initial industry enthusiasm in the development of pad-mounted equipment and none of the major manufacturers invested much effort on the problem, although Missouri Power and some small suppliers remained interested. (Exhibit 4 reproduces excerpts from a pamphlet by a major electric utility which was opposed to underground systems.)

In the market, the concept of underground picked up a good deal of support in many of the more beauty-conscious communities in California, and by the early 1960s numerous local ordinances had appeared requiring that new homes be served by underground distribution. Responding quickly to this trend, the Electric Utility Sales Division in Erikson's Electric Utility Group organized itself to sell underground products. By February of 1963, Erikson held the first of a series of conferences for electric utility companies on Underground Distribution Systems.

For a variety of reasons the trend began to accelerate. Most important, perhaps, an affluent population could afford the approximately $200 which underground distribution added to the cost of the home. As more systems were installed and improvements in equipment and manufacturing techniques effected, this cost was reduced. Nevertheless, in late 1964, Erikson management estimated that an underground system cost about $150 more per home than an overhead system; about $80 extra was required for the cable and the remainder for the transformer, protective equipment and subsidiary devices. On the other hand, the operating and maintenance problems of these systems were found to be less serious than expected. Taste in homes and rising aesthetic concerns (evident in Mrs. Johnson's May 1965 White House Conference on the appearance of the U.S. landscape) also contributed to the demand for underground distribution. Exhibit 5 reproduces part of a typical article on the subject of underground distribution networks, and even more startling were proposals to bring high voltage transmission underground. By 1965 any question as to the pace or importance of the trend had disappeared, but underground distribution still posed problems for manufacturing companies which had profitable overhead component businesses and for utilities which had heavy investment in above-ground facilities.

Implications of underground systems for Erikson Industries

Like most of its competition, Erikson's efforts to serve the electric utility industry were organized into a number of product departments. Because of broad impact of the trend toward underground systems, however, the departments in a number of divisions and groups were being affected by the trend. (Exhibit 6 shows an abbreviated organization chart illustrating the various units involved in underground power equipment.) The impact of the new development, however, was quite uneven. The Outdoor Lighting Department was faced primarily with having to design and market new types of standards for street lights, given the probability that utility poles would no longer be available to hold street lamps. At the other extreme, the Distribution Protective Equipment Department found that underground distribution would render a major portion of its existing product line obsolete.

The remainder of this case is devoted to discussing the manner in which some of the more deeply involved units had analyzed their opportunities and were responding to the challenge. These units are the Electric Utility Sales Division, the Distribution Transformer Department, the Distribution Protective Equipment Department, the Wire and Cable Department, and the Business and Technical Planning Operation of the Power Distribution Division. Each was a profit center measured against annual budget goals. Incentive compensation for division and department management was tied closely to annual profit.

ELECTRIC UTILITY SALES DIVISION

In some respects, the Electric Utility Sales Division (EUSD) was confronting the problem of underground systems on the broadest front. EUSD was a pooled sales organization, selling products produced by the Electric Utility Group product departments and certain other items. This arrangement reduced the number of sales calls made by Erikson representatives and was considered a tremendous asset because it permitted the company to devote resources to selling a customer in whatever way was appropriate to the specific case. The customers were in a position to demand what they wanted, and a pooled force helped to provide it.

Because of the variety of pressures described earlier, the utilities were becoming more receptive to the idea of underground distribution. The EUSD, which had been making periodic surveys of utility industry attitude toward underground systems, found this impression strongly reflected in these surveys. Exhibit 7 provides the results of the survey for the years 1960, 1962, and 1964.

Selling underground systems and equipment

The EUSD was concerned primarily with competing for the expected demand for underground installations in new residential developments. Timing was critical in the choice of emphasis. While conversion would be important in the future, in 1965 it was one-sixtieth the size of the new home market. Pressure was becoming extremely strong for new residential developments to install underground systems. Housing starts in 1965 were running about 1,000,000 for single-family housing and about 600,000 a year for other types of dwellings. EUSD management expected that approximately 10% of the family homes started in 1965 would be serviced by underground networks. They expected the number of underground installations in 1970 to have increased to 355,000[1] and by 1975 to have risen to 750,000, roughly two-thirds of all family home starts projected for that year.

Although the number of new underground installations constituted a rich market, it was small relative to the potential conversion market. If and when conversion opportunities opened up, they would be huge. For example, one customer had estimated that to convert its entire system (including transmission) to underground would require an additional investment of $5.6 billion as compared with its total existing investment (including generation equipment) of $3.2 billion. The utility indicated that rates would have to be increased by 50% or more to pay for the new facilities. As a consequence of problems of this magnitude and sensitivity, EUSD executives were inclined to view the conversion market as one with long-range potential, but without much immediate relevance to the problems confronting them.

In 1966, the EUSD was not planning to accelerate the trend toward underground distribution systems by openly stimulating primary demand or by aggressively trying to sell such ideas to the utilities. EUSD management had three reasons why they believed aggressive promotion by Erikson was not advisable.

In the first place, the larger companies supplying power equipment were sometimes accused by their customers of adopting a "know-it-all" attitude. Some of the small firms took advantage of this feeling and used sales strategies which contained a measure of "give the business to us to maintain competition and protect yourselves against the inflexibility of the large firms." Moreover, although no one knew very much about low-cost underground systems—and, indeed, for a change the manufacturers might know somewhat more than the utilities—EUSD management thought it ill-advised to flaunt what insight they had in patronizing terms. The "know-it-all" problem might best be overcome, EUSD executives indicated, by anticipating the customer's needs and having products ready when they were wanted: "Nothing but ill will can come from promoting something the customer does not want. We want to help utilities look as good as possible."

Second, pressure for innovation was being generated by the public. In retrospect, EUSD managers thought, the industry, including Erikson, had been slow in accepting the idea. The result was that equipment design and production capacity were just emerging. "Too rapid a rate of growth in demand before we have equipment designs would have meant that the customer would dictate product configuration. In such a situation, the little guy has the advantage, for he is set up to make tailor-

---

[1] As of early 1966, this estimate had been raised to 575,000.

made products. From our point of view, the trend was as fast as we could handle it."

Finally, EUSD managers were concerned about the possible effect of rapid and expensive development of underground systems on the ability of utilities to compete with other forms of power. A short-run bonanza in expensive underground systems could mean substantial long-run loss in all types of electric utility equipment if the industry lost market share to gas and oil.

EUSD managers also pointed out that some internal corporate reasons existed for progressing cautiously. Present product lines in the distribution area were profitable. Premature obsolescence and termination of these product lines could mean lost profits. Profits on underground systems had not yet shown returns of the sort which were available in existing lines. Until these requirements and the situation in general had become somewhat more firmly defined, there appeared to be little sense in rushing headlong into what was considered to be a relatively risky venture.

Selling underground systems and equipment: Short-term tactics

Because underground systems were a new and relatively unfamiliar development, the EUSD had found that a key element in securing orders was the group's and the division's skill in designing and in planning the installation of underground networks. This development, which represented a significant change from the problems in selling overhead systems to customers who knew—or thought they knew—more than the suppliers about the characteristics and problems of the equipment, offered the various product departments a chance to leapfrog competition and design equipment and systems which had a chance of becoming industry standards. For the moment, the high degree of individual attention required by each system and Erikson's ability to provide both the attention and the complete system appeared to provide some price protection. At the same time, the EUSD was banking on generating a reservoir of good will and a reputation for cooperative expertise which would persist even in a mature and more competitive market. Advanced and sound products were obviously preconditions for the success of this strategy.

Erikson's competition was considered to be good and they were not expected to remain passive while major products were changing or becoming obsolete. In fact, some of the smaller firms had been the most willing to engage in early experimental operations at a time when the potential returns appeared unattractive to the market leaders.

Once the major firms had made the commitment to compete strongly for underground sales, the smaller companies were put at something of a disadvantage because they each offered some particular items but were not able to offer a utility an integrated package, including any needed engineering. EUSD managers had, therefore, anticipated that the smaller firms would cooperate to develop products which could be sold on the basis that they were compatible but easily separable. This approach would be an attempt to combat the overall system emphasis of the larger companies with a full product line.

The expectations were being borne out by late 1965. Advertisements had appeared in trade publications promoting the combined products of several companies, emphasizing their nature as separate but compatible components. EUSD managers indicated they would not be surprised if some formal mergers developed as a result of the market trends.

An appraisal of the future

The comments EUSD executives made about the future of underground systems and of the opportunities for Erikson may be summarized as follows:

> Underground distribution systems, and underground systems of all types, are new, undeveloped, and rapidly changing. This provides a tremendous opportunity for a company such as Erikson to bring together its resources of management, money, sales ability, technical ability, and skill in planning for the future, to secure an important position in the market. In taking advantage of this opportunity, the company must develop products which are so outstanding they will be accepted as the industry standard, and they should be part of an integral system.

The executives noted that the utility industry was confronted with a major problem which Erikson and the other equipment suppliers were not equipped to solve—the need for some system to assess charges on underground equipment. The utilities could charge the extra cost of installing underground systems to the promoters of the new developments (who would then recover their cost from the ultimate purchaser of the home), or the utilities could bill at higher rates those customers supplied through underground systems. However, neither alternative was considered completely satisfactory because differential billing and/or higher costs to the customer might be involved.

DISTRIBUTION TRANSFORMER DEPARTMENT

The Distribution Transformer Department (DTD) was the product department with one of the greatest dollar volume of sales at stake in the change from overhead to underground systems. DTD also held a large market share in the distribution transformer industry, a position which company management believed to be essential to the department's other objectives of maintaining a competitive cost, profit, and technological position. Its departmental return on investment was high for the company.

The overhead distribution transformer industry was very competitive, with 15 to 18 firms offering distribution transformers to utility companies. The market was also characterized by a large variety of highly standardized products. DTD manufactured and stocked approximately 750 catalog items, but each item was a well-established, mature product. The typical pole transformer served 8 to 10 older type homes.

Production of transformer coils and cores involved a surprising amount of hand labor, considering the basic stability of product design. Mechanization of various types had been investigated, but in many instances the return on investment in such mechanization had not been found adequate to justify the projects. Nevertheless, the DTD plant in Arkansas was one of the most highly mechanized low-cost plants in the industry. The coil and core components did not differ significantly between overhead and underground units.

The growth of the underground transformer market

The DTD had been involved in early experiments with underground transformers, but these units were expensive and not sufficiently successful to have encouraged the department to enter the underground market at an early date. Once the potential had become more fully recognized, the department began to design new units. In 1965, transformers for underground systems accounted for 14% of DTD dollar volume exclusive of network transformers. (Approximately 16% of new homes constructed in 1965 were serviced by underground systems, according to DTD estimates.) DTD produced about 7,500 pad-mounted units and only 380 completely underground below-grade units. These latter were eventually expected to account for most of the underground business.

Department executives estimated that about half of Erikson's competition, including all major firms, had entered the underground transformer market.

Impact of underground systems

According to DTD management, the immediate impact of the growth of underground distribution systems on the DTD's overhead transformer market would not be severe for three to four years. Until major conversion efforts developed, the DTD's market for replacement transformers would probably remain quite stable. In fact, if the conversion movement began to be serious, it would quickly outstrip the facilities capable of supplying it. Underground transformers were expected to account only for about 55% of new housing installations by 1970. Thus, even in 1970, underground distribution would not be available in vast areas of the country.

On the other hand, the costs of competing in the underground market could have a severe effect on DTD profits in the near term. Although the basic components of a transformer, the coil and core, were the same in all three major transformer types (pole, pad-mounted, and below-grade units), major differences were created by the need to package the underground units and their related equipment safely and effectively. Moreover, transformer manufacturers had been unable to promote standardization because the utilities had failed to settle on common operating procedures and components. Competition was severe, particularly in the area of developing solutions to customer problems. These innovations were usually mechanical in nature and external to the transformer tank and often took the form of an accessory.

Compounding the variety of sizes and capacities of the basic unit components with a custom package had thus proved to be an expensive task. Moreover, the techniques for manufacturing the new packages were not at all similar to those used for the "can" style of pole transformers, so that new machinery was required to produce the product.

Hopefully, the introduction of below-grade units would give the suppliers a new opportunity to standardize the industry. Because below-grade transformers were designed for permanent implacement in underground vaults, with no access except to controls on the top, the problem of design was left much more to the manufacturer. In addition, because of the need to plan carefully for adequate ventilation and for protection from immersion and soil and water corrosion, the manufacturers and not the utilities had the knowledge to specify what would be an adequate unit. Thus, the manufacturers were in a position to make major contributions to the design of the units and of the associated hardware, vaults, and gratings.

DTD management saw a substantial opportunity for the company to capitalize on its skills and engineering talents to sell the underground units and associated products. Stronger and closer customer relations would be required in order to assist both the utilities and the ultimate customer to plan their investment wisely. In addition, because the suppliers would have the technical knowledge, more emphasis would have to be placed on applications engineering. Management thought, therefore, that substantial opportunities would accrue to companies which developed complete systems, *provided* the systems incorporated technological advantages not present in the individual units. Erikson's most severe competition in the future might come from such companies, provided any of them recognized and were able to exploit the opportunity.

In order to prepare to supply the demand for underground distribution transformers, DTD management had to allow for a three- to four-year lag in the development of plant facilities. In late 1965, all parts of the DTD operation were working at full capacity. Complete plans for the future were not yet available, but two expansion projects had been started. Over the next three to five years, department management estimated the DTD might require up to a total of $23 million to build the facilities required to manufacture underground units.

DISTRIBUTION PROTECTIVE EQUIPMENT DEPARTMENT

Of all Erikson's distribution equipment, the traditional products of the Distribution Protective Equipment Department (DPED) were those most seriously threatened by the trend toward underground distribution systems. DPED products, which consisted primarily of lightning arresters and cutouts, overvoltage and overcurrent protection devices and fuses, served to protect electrical systems from overloads and power surges caused by natural elements such as lightning as well as by mechanical or system failures. Many of these threats would no longer be serious for underground systems and even those products likely to remain in demand would have to be completely redesigned in order to meet the requirements of underground service. The cost of redevelopment had at first looked quite high in terms of the potential revenue the products would generate. The department was experiencing losses and as much as $10 million was required for research on the new products required for underground systems.

The department's future had looked particularly dark until 1964, when a corporate study group suggested concentrating certain aspects of the company's protective apparatus business into more logical patterns. At that time, a decision was made to put both the protective and switching aspects of distribution systems into the DPED and to define the scope of the department's operations to include all phases of the distribution system current switching problem. Certain switchgear production was transferred to DPED in Chicago from the High Voltage Switchgear Department in Newark, New Jersey.

Department management indicated that more recently the prospects for the department had further improved when new estimates of the underground market suggested that the returns offered DPED by that business might be higher than originally expected. Moreover, in some respects, the quality of protection provided for underground components would have to be greater than for overhead units because of the difficulty in repairing a system which had suffered electrical damage. As a result, the DPED was expected to generate a profitable underground business —although perhaps not until the late 1960s.

Although the DPED had diagnosed the type of high quality, reliable, safe, and compact switching equipment it should have ready for the new underground market, it had been unable, as of December 1965, to secure a production model which could be manufactured at a price considered essential for market acceptance. The principal product required was a small vacuum switch, a unit which would interrupt an overloaded circuit and reclose when the load returned to normal. The department had agreed with a contract research and development organization to spend $80,000 to develop the unit. The results were still unsatisfactory and development of other products was being delayed until the vacuum switch had been perfected. There was no way of knowing how long it would take to perfect the switch. Until that happened, the DPED would not have any products particularly acceptable for underground use.

Future actions

The department was progressing to develop the new products required. Nevertheless, there still remained the problem of how fast to spend development money. Radical changes were taking place in the industry, requiring radically different products and skills from DPED, but management indicated that it was not at all certain how fast the trends were progressing and was not sure how rapidly development money should be used.

Competition was active in the field and had produced some very satisfactory products, although none of them had as much potential as DPED management believed their new product line would possess. Some executives wondered, therefore, whether it might be wise to proceed as rapidly as possible with the development of Erikson's new line in order to introduce a product so outstanding it might become an industry standard. This course of action seemed to imply rapid development of as many products as possible despite the fact that profitable volume might be several years in the future.

WIRE AND CABLE DEPARTMENT

In the late 1940s, the Wire and Cable Department terminated its paper-insulated power transmission and power distribution cable business in order to focus its competitive resources on the 25% of the wire and cable market which required relatively higher inputs of engineering and technological talent. Paper-insulated cables carried very little markup over material and direct fabricating costs and did not offer significant economies of scale. As a result of these conditions, the major profits in that business were retained by the copper producers. In addition, Erikson's sources of copper supply were relatively restricted. Much higher profits could be gained by using the material available in wire products other than paper-insulated cable.

Because of the development of nonpaper solid insulations and advances in insulating techniques, the Wire and Cable Department was ready with a product which could be plowed directly into the ground up to a depth of six feet without preliminary trenching, which gave protection from soil, weather, and animal damage, and which was not unreasonable in price. Department executives believed this product was ideally suited for competing in the underground market, and for those utilities which were particularly concerned about potential maintenance problems and protection of the cable and circuit, the department created Procor, a coated cable placed in a conduit at the time of manufacture so that the problem of pulling cable into a conduit during installation was eliminated.

The department's market research and planning staff had been actively exploring the prospects in the underground cable business for some time but had concluded that these products would be a relatively small part of the Wire and Cable Department's future business. Since department management had found the same lack of enthusiasm among its potential customers for underground products that other executives in the company had noted, they had tended not to promote the products strongly, either to the public or the utilities.

Market research projected a tripling of the amount of direct burial cable used in underground systems between 1965 and 1970. Procor's use would grow much more slowly, only doubling in the same period. The slower growth of Procor was expected because management believed that many utilities already had decided, and more would undoubtedly reach the same conclusion, that Procor's advantages were not worth its extra cost. The split between primary and secondary applications (55%/45%) would not change significantly by 1970. The department planned, however, for Erikson to increase its share of the market from 7% to 15% by the end of the period.

In order to attain this goal and capitalize in the department's existing resources, the department would continue to promote its cable to new real estate developments. In the majority of instances, where price was a dominant factor, the use of direct burial cable would be suggested and Procor would be recommended only in those instances where there was an extreme concern for reliability and flexibility. Customers worried about these problems would undoubtedly be willing to pay the extra price necessary to obtain the highest quality product.

Prospects for the future

The department was constantly searching for ways to improve its existing product line, as typified by its development of a plastic-coated steel jacket to replace the plastic jackets formerly used on Procor. One important project currently under way was the effort to develop solid insulation cable capable of carrying higher voltages. Such cable was extremely difficult to design and produce with the high-quality electrical properties it required for satisfactory operation. If quality products could be developed to sell at competitive prices and margins, the potential profits would be extremely attractive in the event that total underground systems and conversion of all overhead wiring were undertaken.

The department's operations were sufficiently flexible to permit it to absorb the demand which could be created if residential underground distribution grew faster than anticipated. An increase in demand of 25% to 35% above levels projected for 1970 would require the assignment of only one additional cable machine to underground products. The department's operations did not benefit from significant economies of scale—the only problem would be where to put the additional machine. The major irrevocable decision, management noted, was the allocation of research and development expenditures. These were currently assigned to the development of large-cable, high-voltage transmission lines. If this business did not develop as expected, the talent might have been more profitably used to work on the problems remainingg in the residential underground phase of the market.

Although the Wire and Cable Department was in the Construction Group, its management kept in close touch with departments in the Electric Utility Group on problems of common concern, of which underground networks was one. The department nonetheless relied primarily on its own salesmen to provide information of the state of the market and to set the direction for product planning. Management indicated that the department appeared to have its share of the responsibilities for underground residential distribution well under control.

BUSINESS AND TECHNICAL PLANNING OPERATION, POWER DISTRIBUTION DIVISION

The Planning Operation, with its responsibilities for evaluating major trends and opportunities that might confront the Power Distribution

Division (PDD), had become interested quite early in the problems of underground distribution systems. The Operation's task was to take a systems approach to these opportunities (rather than a product viewpoint) in order to bring together whatever information might be useful for decisions confronting the division and its departments and to assist the operating managers in charting their courses of action. Fulfillment of this responsibility required the Operation to explore the major aspects of the trend toward underground networks, including the nature of the markets, the type of products required, and the manufacturing problems which they would create.

Commenting on the history of the distribution business, Operation executives noted that the power distribution supply business had long been considered a stable one.

> Demand increased slowly along with the population and with growth in the per capita kilowatt-hour usage. The market was characterized by a great variety of highly stable products. The result was that after the price-fixing case in the early 1960s, the pressure on prices became intense as all firms struggled to maintain their positions in the market. Prices dropped about 30%, enough to eliminate completely the gross margin these products had formerly enjoyed.
>
> Imaginative management and extremely strict control over costs permitted the division to remain profitable, but the emphasis on cost control did not provide much incentive for management to invest in the development of products for underground systems which would make existing lines obsolete and which were being fairly actively resisted by most of the company's major utility customers. The atmosphere at that time was simply not conducive to the growth of a new business. "When you've been squeezing the buffalo on the nickel, it's hard to turn around and spend to grow new product markets." In 20/20 retrospect, common knowledge of the amount of money being spent on landscaping, swimming pools and the like should have been taken as a warning that underground systems would become a social necessity.

As some of the smaller manufacturers began to introduce underground products and the variety of pressures increased on utilities to put distribution systems underground, PDD management established an "Underground Council" to develop recommendations for the course Erikson should set in this new area. The Council included representatives of the product departments most concerned with underground distribution systems (Distribution Transformer, Distribution Protective Equipment, Outdoor Lighting, Wire and Cable, and Meter), the Electric Utility Sales Division and the Planning Operation.

The Council, which began meeting in 1964, presented its report in February 1965. The report, in essence, pointed out that a significant opportunity was available for Erikson in this area and recommended steps to take advantage of it. Based on long-range forecasts, however, it did not appear that in the near term the overhead business would suffer substantially as a result of the underground trend.

During the summer, Planning Operation executives restudied the subject and issued a revised opinion in November 1965. This study suggested that earlier estimates had been on the conservative side. The underground market was likely to grow much faster than anticipated earlier, and the effect on the company's present business was likely to be much more dramatic.

The remainder of this section will summarize the contents of these two studies and conclude with comments by Planning Operation management about the situation as of December 1965.

Underground Council report: February 1965

The Council's report in February concluded that by 1970 Power Distribution Division sales of underground system equipment would represent a net sales increase of $10 million from its existing (relatively) low level. The forecast assumed that the number of new homes to be equipped with underground distribution facilities would increase from 108,000 a year in 1965 to 380,000 in 1970. As a second critical assumption, the forecast projected an increase in Erikson's share of the underground market on the basis of targets established by the various departments.

The report noted that in many respects the underground business would not materially erode the PPD's planned sales level of existing products. The Distribution Transformer Department, for example, would in 1969 lose only about $1.2 million of business in its total replacement market of $32.0 million if it did not have adequate underground transformers available and would be severely affected only when conversion began to be a significant factor in the demand for underground equipment.

The Council went on to suggest that the methods required to take advantage of the opportunities in underground systems would be significantly different from those required for present operations. Whereas the company's strategy in the overhead business was directed to maintaining cost leadership and maximum profits in a situation which did not permit much product innovation or design improvement, the critical element of the underground strategy would be design leadership. A leadership position could be obtained by pushing rapidly into advanced products, by having the products available in the market ahead of competition, and by introducing new marketing trends.

In order to obtain product and market leadership, the Underground Council recommended several steps which would represent substantial changes from existing practice. With respect to organization, the report stated:

> The ability to increase Erikson's market share will require a dramatically superior product and time leadership. The ability to work with a system rather than a single product requires a variety of competences not heretofore needed in the [product departments]. The need to innovate and work toward an ultimate design requires a quantity of engineering effort that is greatly in excess of that needed for a standardized product [in which a favorable profit position hinges importantly on cost control]. These unique requirements suggest that they consider an underground product development section.

The Council also recommended a new marketing approach:

1. There is no other area of distribution where our customers are as open to suggestion and guidance as in the underground area. To give this guidance, Erikson sales engineers should be schooled in depth. This schooling should follow the IBM pattern, making each Erikson salesman capable of becoming an important contributing factor, in the selection of both products and systems.

2. It is essential that as the innovative "leapfrog" products come into the market the merchandising and sales efforts be sufficient to be heard above the hue and cry by three audiences:

   a) Purchasing,
   b) Engineering and operating,
   c) Top management and sales.

Bold advertising, road shows, meetings, speakers, convention displays, training meetings for customer engineers will all have to be employed.

There was one relatively immediate product of the report. The Underground Council, in its recommendation, had suggested that Erikson Industries enter the terminations[2] business. This opportunity had previously been examined by several departments, but no firm decisions on an appropriate course of action had been reached. Terminations were an important factor in the underground system because they had to be allowed for in the design of the components and because they offered an excellent place to locate sensors for indicating voltage and faulty current. In September of 1965, the Planning Operation arranged a multidepartmental technical meeting to challenge a group of 25 engineers with the question, "Can Erikson Industries make an innovative contribution in the termination business?" The answer was a resounding "yes," and it was subsequently backed up by several patent dockets filed to protect the outcome of the ideas generated. With a solid engineering base having thus been established, a business plan was drafted and presented to DPED management in November of 1965. The project was funded and hiring began in January 1966. The project team approach to this group of products was retained. The first product introduction was scheduled for September 1966—a year from the feasibility conference in 1965.

In the course of preparing the report, the Underground Council secured a set of ratings which compared Erikson's position in the underground market to those of its competition on a number of factors considered critical to Erikson's success in the business. The ratings are shown in Exhibit 8. All ratings except the "Innovative Posture" were made by Erikson employees. An outside consulting firm was retained to develop the "Innovative Posture" rating.

The revised appraisal: November 1965

In November 1965 a revised appraisal of the underground market was prepared by the PDD Planning Operation, which undertook a reexamination of the program. The reappraisal was necessary because

---

[2] Terminations are devices for connecting cables to any piece of equipment, such as transformers and sectionalizing switches.

the change to underground systems (both in new developments and in conversion of existing facilities) appeared to be progressing faster than originally expected. In addition, Planning Operation management wished to take account of the progress made within the company toward exploitation of underground opportunities and new product possibilities that had appeared since February. (See Exhibit 9 for details.)

Although the reasons for public enthusiasm were essentially non-economic, company-sponsored surveys had shown that homeowners were very much aware of the value which underground systems gave to their property. Seventy-five per cent of those questioned indicated they would be willing to pay $400 for a total underground system.

The trend toward restrictive legislation was also important. The report noted that at the state and national level, measures were being introduced to require the conversion of all transmission and distribution systems to below-ground networks. Although easily defeated so far, the fact that they had been introduced at all was adduced as evidence of the interest and increasing ferment the problem was causing. The construction industry was beginning to put pressure on the utility industry to act and to absorb the cost. Some utilities, anticipating new regulations on the subject, had begun to propose alternatives which they believed would lead to orderly and economical conversion of electric systems.

Given the new atmosphere, the revised report looked with enthusiasm on the steps which had been taken to implement the February proposals. A new and separate group had been established in the Distribution Transformer Department to develop underground transformers. On the other hand, some of the most important and most immediately needed new products had fallen behind their development schedules. Furthermore, profits had been lagging. In response, the reappraisal urged the development of new low-cost units as a way to restore an adequate profit rate while serving customers' requirements. Finally, the reappraisal noted that renewed efforts were required to develop total systems rather than components. The report suggested exploring interconnectable modular components, designing integral vault and installation kits and investigating cooperation with other types of utilities such as CATV in an effort to reduce or share installation costs.

Evaluation of progress

In reviewing, late in 1965, the progress Erikson had made in taking advantage of the underground opportunity, Planning Operation executives noted that the company had so far achieved better market penetration in underground products than it had established in overhead systems. This factor was encouraging, given the rating the Underground Council's report had made of the company's competitive posture.

On the other hand, the price structure for the underground products had been disappointingly poor. Despite the fact that the products were not standard commodity items, but rather contained a high proprietary element, the prices were not sufficiently high to maintain a very satisfactory profit. The fact that prices had not been good was ascribed in part to the general ignorance and confusion among companies trying to enter the underground industry about the potential costs of such systems, the potential volume, and the response of the utilities to different prices. In addition, latecomers seemed to be willing to bid at low prices merely to gain experience with underground problems and equipment.

Furthermore, because design had not yet been standardized for most products, it had not been economically feasible to invest in efficient tooling. Underground products and designs were still subject to substantial change. In one case, where the DTD had developed a product with measurably superior features, which was priced competitively, and on which prompt delivery could be given, the product had virtually been accepted as an industry standard. The profit on this line was considered to provide a satisfactory return. This example gave further support to the argument that the company had a substantial amount to gain by expending the funds and effort to develop rapidly superior products which could become industry standards.

Planning Operation management thought that Erikson still had the opportunity and the capability to develop products of a superior nature and achieve a position of product leadership which the Council had recommended the company attempt to attain. They thought, however, that the delays which had been encountered certainly endangered the effort.

A BASIC QUESTION

In addition to their interest in specific products, the men who had been exploring the development of Erikson's attack on the underground market were concerned about the proper method of organizing multiproduct, multidepartmental, multidivisional, and multigroup innovations in a climate of radical social, product, and market change. Their comments were in the following vein:

> The existing organization focuses the company's efforts on satisfying an established system of product and market relationships. Product departments have the responsibility for developing and producing the goods required to satisfy the demand of the market. Product or pooled sales organizations maintain contact with the market and supply the product departments with information about these demands. But, when a market opportunity arises which cuts across established lines, it becomes a major problem to gather the necessary information about the opportunity, to identify and recommend actions designed to capitalize on the opportunity, and to implement these actions. Groups such as the Underground Council can provide a mechanism for identifying an opportunity and planning its development. Nevertheless, study groups such as the Council are usually advisory, may consist of staff men in lower ranks of their respective departments, and have no real innovating force other than the power of their prose. This, at times, may be very weak by comparison with the difficulties a department manager has solving the day-to-day problems of his department.
>
> In effect, we are asking where the company should put the re-

sponsibility for innovation. Does our current system adequately allow for major changes? If not, then what should we do to improve our ability to respond to the environment? If so, is there any way to give the department managers a better opportunity to make use of the innovative forces they may discover?

Are there any lessons on these topics which could be drawn from the efforts to obtain a position for Erikson Industries in the underground distribution systems market?

Exhibit 1

ERIKSON INDUSTRIES

Selected Categories of Electrical Utility Plant Investment
for Privately Owned Electric Utilities with
Operating Revenue over $1,000,000
(billions of dollars)

	1963	1962	1961	1960	1959	1955	1953
Production plant.................	$21.5	$20.7	$19.6	$18.4	$16.9	$12.0	$ 9.5
Transmission plant..............	8.3	7.7	7.2	6.8	6.3	4.5	3.6
Towers and features............	0.8	0.7	0.6	0.6	0.5	0.4	0.4
Poles and fixtures..............	0.9	0.9	0.8	0.8	0.7	0.5	0.4
Overhead conduit and conductors.................	0.5	0.4	0.4	0.4	0.4	0.3	0.2
Distribution plant...............	20.0	18.8	17.7	16.7	15.5	11.3	9.4
Poles, towers and fixtures.......	3.3	3.2	3.0	2.8	2.6	1.9	1.6
Overhead conductors..........	3.2	3.0	2.8	2.6	2.5	1.8	1.5
Underground conduit..........	1.1	1.1	1.0	1.0	0.8	0.6	0.5
Underground conductors........	1.2	1.1	1.0	1.0	0.9	0.7	0.6
Line transformers.............	3.7	3.5	3.3	3.1	2.8	1.9	1.5
Street lighting................	0.8	0.7	0.7	0.6	0.6	0.4	0.3
Total plant in service............	51.3	48.6	45.8	43.2	39.9	28.7	23.4

Source: Federal Power Commission. *Statistics of Electric Utility in the United States*, 1963, *Privately Owned.*

Exhibit 2a

ERIKSON INDUSTRIES

Construction Expenditures, Electric Utilities
(millions of dollars)

	1964	1963	1962	1961	1960	1959	1955	1953
Investor-owned utilities								
Production............	$1,114	$1,165	$1,078	$1,267	$1,342	$1,519	$1,064	$1,391
Transmission.........	824	644	609	579	537	554	434	442
Distribution..........	1,424	1,323	1,305	1,265	1,300	1,163	1,093	938
Other................	189	187	162	145	152	147	128	105
Total................	3,551	3,319	3,154	3,256	3,331	3,383	2,719	2,876
Federal appropriations....	495	482	447	446	416	356	310	482

Source: Edison Electric Institute, *Statistical Yearbook of the Electrical Utility Industry,* 1964.

Exhibit 2b

ERIKSON INDUSTRIES

Electric Utility Construction
Forecast of Expenditures

1960–1970...................... $51.9 billion
1970–1980...................... 91.4 billion

Source: Edison Electric Institute, *Meeting Tomorrow's Power Needs.*

Exhibit 3

ERIKSON INDUSTRIES

Operation and Maintenance Expenses of Privately Owned Electric Utilities with
Operating Revenues over $1,000,000
(millions of dollars)

	1963	1962	1961	1960	1959	1955	1953
Production expense.............	$2,975	$2,825	$2,664	$2,509	$2,381	$1,898	$1,726
Transmission expense............	165	161	151	152	145	110	101
Maintenance.................	72	71	66	53	51	41	38
Distribution expense............	811	779	749	762	720	587	534
Maintenance.................	392	377	353	292	271	222	203
Total operating expense......	5,249	5,001	4,725	4,531	4,289	3,379	3,060
Operations and maintenance expense as percent of operating revenues....................	43.7	43.9	44.3	44.8	45.2	46.9	49.6

Exhibit 4

ERIKSON INDUSTRIES

Excerpts from a Pamphlet of the Disguised Utility Company

Have you ever wondered why more of the wires that bring electricity to you and your neighbors aren't underground? They could be. But there are many reasons why they shouldn't. One important reason is cost. Most of the people we've asked tell us they wouldn't want all lines underground if it meant their electric bills would double. And that's what it would mean. . . .

Why doesn't the Disguised Utility Company put its wires underground? . . . Basically it is a matter of cost. The expense . . . varies . . . but it is always several times the cost of putting the same wire overhead. In a typical residential district, the cost . . . is three to four times that of overhead. . . . The only way we could put wires underground, and still stay in business, would be to increase our rates. Putting all our lines underground would mean present rates would have to be almost doubled. And in addition, the owner of an average home located, say, 75 feet from our lines would have to pay about $175 to have an underground connection installed to his house.

An independent survey organization recently polled a sample of our customers. Nine out of ten said they wouldn't want underground lines if it meant that their bills would be doubled. . . . With doubled power costs we could expect a drastic slowing down of industrial expansion. . . . One of the biggest reasons for rapid growth of this area . . . has been . . . electric power at reasonable rates. Another drawback . . . is . . . the mess and in-

Exhibit 4—Continued

convenience when streets, sidewalks, and trees and lawns are dug up to install or repair the wires underneath.

But don't underground lines justify the added cost by providing trouble-free service? This is certainly not the case. . . . Underground wires are by no means trouble free. There have been explosions. . . . Workers . . . dig into buried lines . . . Decay through electro-chemical action, and corrosion of various kinds. Underground wires mean fewer outages but the interruptions last longer, because it takes much longer to repair an underground line—usually from two to eight times as long. . . . You can't see a break in an underground wire. . . . In these days of home freezers and other vital appliances, one long service cutoff can do much more damage than several short ones.

A few of the communities we serve have passed laws, or are considering them, which would compel us to bury high-voltage lines within their borders. The company believes such laws are not in your best interests because: . . . extra cost of construction is greatest. . . . Simple fairness dictates . . . standards of facilities and construction must be uniform. Enormous costs . . . [Cannot make selective charges.]

We have been working on improving our overhead service for many decades. . . . Trees are our biggest problem; they cause about ⅔ of all power interruptions. . . . We've had a large-scale tree program in operation for many years . . . without charge or obligation.

To sum it up Underground wires are extremely expensive to install. Customers' bills would have to be approximately doubled to pay for them. They are by no means the cure-all that many people think. Maintenance and repair work . . . is difficult, costly, and lengthy.

Exhibit 5

ERIKSON INDUSTRIES

Excerpts from an Article in *House & Home*

Costs, the perennial problem in underground wiring, are coming down, but they are still a major roadblock.

It would be hard to find a builder who doesn't appreciate the sales value of an uncluttered skyscape like the one pictured below. "We feel strongly that underground utilities are a definite sales advantage," says Wesley Mohr, project manager for Del Webb's Clear Lake City in Houston. Adds Joseph Eichler of Palo Alto, Calif.: "I'm sure underground wiring has increased the sales of our homes."

But it would be even harder to find a builder of medium-priced homes (e.g., $20,000) who in today's hard-sell markets would risk spending $400 to $500 a house to avoid wirescapes. . . . And that, a HOUSE & HOME survey shows, is the premium now paid by the average builder who wants underground wiring instead of unsightly poles and wires.

There are hopeful signs for the future. Less than three years ago many of the power companies queried by HOUSE & HOME said they simply weren't doing underground wiring. Today most of them at least offer underground service, and those that still don't are finally giving the subject serious thought.

The big reason for this changed attitude is the changed policy of the Bell Telephone System, which operates 81% of the nation's telephones. Bell

Exhibit 5—Continued

has asked its 22 operating companies to bury their cables wherever possible, and expects that by 1970 virtually all new service will be underground.

"This puts us in a very sensitive position," says one electric company executive. "With all the other utility lines out of sight, we're the only ones left messing up the landscape, and we're really beginning to feel the public pressure. It's good public relations for us to go underground as fast as we can."

Mounting public pressure has already led some power companies to cut their charge to builders

Arizona Public Service Co. charges about $120 a lot for underground wiring—down 80% from five years ago. Southern California Edison Co. charges about $150 a lot—roughly half as much as five years ago. San Francisco's Pacific Gas & Electric Co. which charged as much as $1,000 a lot 15 years ago and $600 a lot three years ago, now charges less than $400 a lot. And Houston Lighting & Power Co., which has just begun to offer underground service, already charges less than $200 a lot.

But most builders around the country have to pay much more. In St. Louis, the underground premium is $1,000 a lot; in San Antonio and Memphis $500; and in Seattle up to $500.

Charges like these don't rule out underground wiring just for low- and medium-range builders. They also make high-priced builders think twice. Says Denver Builder Marcus Bogue, whose underground charge for his new Eastridge Homes was $400 a house: "At these prices I wouldn't put underground wiring in any site where I wasn't trying to capitalize on the view. It's just too expensive—even for our $35,000 houses."

Are high underground charges necessary? Not according to Chicago's Commonwealth Edison Co.

Comm Ed has found that under normal ground conditions, with today's equipment and engineering know-how, it can provide underground wiring for subdivision builders at less than $100 a lot.

To be eligible for this rate, a builder must have at least 24 houses in his development, and lot frontages must not exceed 125'. If he meets these qualifications, Comm Ed will bury his wires for a basic charge of $50 a lot, plus 75¢ per trench foot for service lines. (The average service length is 60', costs $45.)

Moreover, if a builder puts at least two major electric appliances in each of his houses, Comm Ed will usually rebate enough to cover the entire underground cost.

Unsurprisingly, Commonwealth Edison is doing far more underground wiring than any other electric utility in the country. This year the company expects to bring underground service to 4,000 to 5,000 new houses.

Comm Ed's underground methods—detailed on the following two pages—require only standard manufactured equipment and involve techniques that have been thoroughly tested in actual service. They are worth study by builders and developers who want more attractive—and more saleable—subdivisions and by other power company executives who recognize the growing public pressure for underground service.

Note: The professional information contained in this reprint from *House & Home* is not to be construed as the magazine's endorsement or recommendation of any product, service, company or individual.
Source: *House & Home*, August, 1963. © 1963 by *Time Inc.*, New York, N.Y.

Exhibit 6

ERIKSON INDUSTRIES

Partial Organization Chart Showing Departments
Mentioned in Case

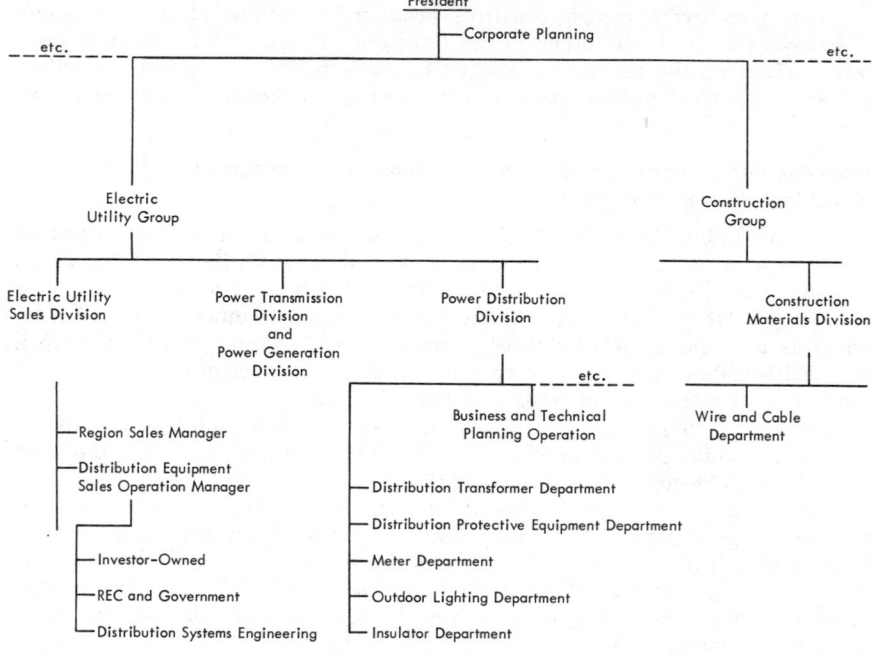

Exhibit 7

ERIKSON INDUSTRIES

Electric Utility Sales Division
Survey of Utility Attitudes toward
Underground Residential Distribution Systems

Prevailing attitude toward residential underground
(51 utilities)

Attitude	1960	1962	1964
Opposed	17	1	0
Negative	14	14	4
Open-minded	16	27	9
Favorable	2	5	26
Enthusiastic	2	4	12

Attitudes toward underground residential distribution within
utility managerial groups—1964 survey of 51 utilities

Group	For	Indifferent	Against
Executive Office	41	6	4
Engineering	44	4	3
Operating	32	11	8
Sales	46	4	1
Rate	27	17	7

Exhibit 8

ERIKSON INDUSTRIES

Comparative Ratings on Critical Competitive Factors

	Ability to integrate products	Aggressiveness in marketplace	Design competence	Innovative posture	Total
Allis Chalmers	5	3	5	3	16
Delta Star	5	3	4	5	17
Erikson	7	7	7	5	26
General Electric	7	7	8	5	27
Kuhlman	3	4	3	3	13
Line Material	8	7	6	8	29
Maloney	4	3	3	2	12
RTE Corp	6	7	6	10	29
Wagner	3	3	3	2	11
Westinghouse	7	6	7	6	26

Note: Ratings 0–10 (arbitrary scale). All internally prepared except "Innovative Posture." While the numerical rankings may not be exact, they provide a look at who the lively ones will be in the pursuit of underground business. It seems significant that Line Material and RTE Corp., who receive half or less of the pole-type business that Erikson receives, should manage to equal, let alone lead, in this kind of appraisal. Another factor in the appraisal of competition is performance in the market. The following table gives estimated 1964 market percentages.

	Estimate of market participation summer 1964
General Electric	29%
Erikson	27
Westinghouse	19
Line Material	7
RTE Corp	5
Maloney	4
Pennsylvania	3
Allis Chalmers	3
Kuhlman	2
Wagner	1

Exhibit 9

ERIKSON INDUSTRIES

Comparison of the Underground Distribution Transformer
Market Projected for 1970
(millions of dollars)

	Estimate in February report	Estimate in November report
Total underground distribution transformer market	$21.2	$70.0
Erikson share of UDT market	5.8	15.8
Overhead DT market replaced by UDT	8.6	32.2
Erikson overhead DT lost to UDT	1.4	5.5
Net increase in Erikson distribution transformer sales if objectives met	4.4	10.3

Stone Petroleum International: Functional Products Group

IN SEPTEMBER 1966, Jim Robbins was getting increasingly worried about the new capital request for iso-chlorathane. As manager of the Industrial Chemicals Division's functional chemicals product group, Mr. Robbins was responsible for providing adequate quantities of iso-chlorathane at competitive quality and cost. Normally, providing such capacity presented few problems. In this instance, however, everything seemed to be going wrong.

The forecasted market for iso-chlorathane was exploding. Whereas the October 1965 forecast showed no capacity problem until 1969, the June 1966 forecast showed sales capacity constrained by middle 1967. Moreover, the process technology of iso-chlorathane was changing. A new low-cost process was being developed but would not be "on line" before 1969. Finally, there were shortages of the raw material on which the current process was based.

"I think I could handle this mess," Mr. Robbins explained, "if it weren't for all my other products. You know that our new facility for Plexon is running 60%–80% over the planned cost of $10 million. Given the atmosphere in the golden tower [the general manager's office] that's not too good."

Stone Petroleum was an international firm engaged in all aspects of the oil industry. The company's operations were organized into six areas: exploration and production, transportation, refining, marketing, chemicals, and research. The chemicals area, whose operations were principally domestic, was divided into three divisions: petrochemicals, industrial chemicals, and synthetic fibers and resins. In 1965, the chemicals group contributed $452 million in sales revenue, which represented 16% of the corporate total.

Each division in the chemicals area was self-supporting and contained its own research and staff groups. Division executives were held responsible for planning the future of their divisions and for operating them successfully. Although plans and problems were discussed regularly with headquarters personnel, central management's greatest influence arose through performance appraisal based on such measures as ROI.

INDUSTRIAL CHEMICALS

Industrial Chemicals was the largest chemicals division, with market sales of $212 million in 1965. Basically, Industrial Chemicals was organized into the traditional functional areas of marketing, production, engineering, and R&D (see Exhibit 1). However, in 1964, the division added a fifth area called operations. The operations area was designed to serve a central, coordinating function for the division's activities. The other two chemicals divisions did not have operations areas, nor did they plan to adopt them at the time of the case.

The reason for the creation of the operations function sheds light on the nature of its task. Industrial Chemicals sold its products to other Stone divisions as well as to outside industries. Moreover, these products served as raw materials in some cases and as end products in others. For example, one chemical compound might have been sold to 20 outside customers in six different industries and to two other Stone divisions for use as raw material in four instances and as complementary end products in three others. Since this variety of application and use was multiplied by the hundreds of products that Industrial Chemicals produced, the need for a formal planning and coordinating function was apparent.

It was this function that the operations department was to perform. To do this, the area was divided into product groups, each of which was responsible for coordinating the production, engineering, and sale of a group of products. Product groups were created around different stages in the production process: that is, one product group was responsible for a group of basic "first-stage" chemicals while another had more complex, intermediate products. One of a group's most critical tasks was planning capacity requirements. Thus the group played a key role in the capital planning process.

Product groups were responsible for perceiving the need for additional capacity and developing a detailed proposal asking for this capacity. This proposal, which specified volume, kind of process, capital needed, and timing, was submitted to the divisional management. If they approved the proposal, it was submitted to the corporate finance committee for final approval. Projects that satisfied cost of capital requirements and were consistent with corporate strategy were usually accepted.

The relationship between the product groups and the functional departments in Industrial Chemicals was not that of "staff" vs. "line." For example, both product group managers and plant managers were held responsible for satisfactory output and cost. Both marketing managers and product group managers were held responsible for achieving budgeted sales levels.

However, this joint responsibility was not always accompanied by joint authority. The product group manager could "hire and fire" only four men: the functional coordinators reporting to him. Any other personnel that worked for the product group had to be obtained from a functional area on a project basis. For example, the engineering department decided on the number and allocation of engineers in Industrial Chemicals.

Rewards and punishments

Bill Stalzer, general manager of Industrial Chemicals, explained how men were measured and rewarded in the division.

> We certainly have the data to measure a man against present and past performance, but we don't have an automatic or mechanical examination. There are just too many interrelationships in this company to put the finger on someone on the basis of one set of numbers.
>
> Performance against plan is only a starting point. Did a man meet his planned market share, net income, and ROI? If not, why not? Every man is bound to have some bad luck. We want to know how he dealt with the adverse conditions. Did he cut back or take a gamble? Does he see the broad, corporate issues, or is he myopically fixed on the details of the problem? These are the important questions. We're interested in future performance, not past glories or mishaps.
>
> In this regard, we also place great emphasis on what one might call interpersonal skills. For example, we feel that a key part of a manager's job is developing and training his subordinates. You can't measure whether or not a man has adequately performed this key task in terms of dollars but, nevertheless, it is a critical aspect of a manager's overall evaluation.
>
> However, let me make one point perfectly clear. While we place emphasis on subjective criteria for evaluation, we do not ignore actual performance against plan. We'd be poor managers if we forgot to make profits. It is always a natural assumption that a man who makes plan consistently is doing the rest of his job well also. I know this may not be the case, but if a man makes plan, examination of other aspects of his performance tends to be less intense. On the other hand, if a man doesn't perform well again plan, we will most likely look into his total performance in greater depth. However, not making plan is not a personal disaster for a good manager.

FUNCTIONAL CHEMICALS

Mr. Robbins was the manager of the functional chemicals product group. Mr. Robbins was 42 and had been an assistant manager of Industrial Chemicals engineering before becoming group manager in January 1965. Four men reported directly to Mr. Robbins: Lee Fifer, production coordinator; Ralph Miller, marketing coordinator; Bob Scott, R&D coordinator; and Sam West, engineering coordinator (see Exhibit 1). The functional chemicals group operated from a set of offices in the corporate headquarters building in Houston, Texas.

In 1965, the group's 10 products accounted for 424 million pounds (total output) of production valued at over $50 million (including internal product shipments transferred at market price.)

Iso-chlorathane

In April 1966, Mr. Robbins, manager for functional chemicals, explained that one of his products, iso-chlorathane, was "taking off" (see Exhibit 2).

> There are 12 firms producing and selling iso-chlorathane in the United States. Six of these account for over 75% of industry sales, which are currently at the rate of 1,280 million pounds a year. We're selling at the rate of 265 million pounds a year, which is our capacity level. In fact, we are turning down outside sales. While our anticipated need in 1969 is 300 million pounds, I think we can get the additional 35 million pounds by using our expense budget.[1]
>
> The problem, however, is that 300 million pounds in 1969 is a low forecast. That forecast came out last October, and now the market is going wild. I expect that in his June forecast Ralph Miller [marketing coordinator for functional chemicals] will predict a considerably greater need.
>
> In the past, they have built the iso-chlorathane capacity in bits and pieces because this division seems to have a great fear of overexpansion. In 1950, Stone built a plant at Baton Rouge. In 1953, the plant was up to 134 million pounds and they put in 16 million more. In 1954, there was a report proposing expansion of the plant by 40 million pounds. The proposal was refused by division officers on the basis of a weak marketing story. A 60-million-pound expansion was finally carried out in 1957 and brought the plant up to 210 million pounds. In 1962 they built a second plant at Philadelphia which was rated at 35 million pounds. Since then, they have gradually brought its theoretical capacity up to 55 million pounds.
>
> Today, however, we see a tremendous market for iso-chlorathane and we are determined to build a facility that will meet our *long-term* needs. It's just good economics to do it.

Sam West, engineering coordinator for functional chemicals, pointed out that the iso-chlorathane capacity problem had another important dimension: the process for making the product was in transition. The process by which Stone made iso-chlorathane was based on a raw material called prime gas. However, in 1962, a new type of technology was developed that used another raw material, feed gas, to make the product. West explained the situation as follows:

> Feed gas sells for 2 to 4 cents per pound, which means an iso-chlorathane cost of 5.5 to 7 cents per pound. Prime gas costs 6 to 8 cents per pound, which yields an iso-chlorathane costing 7.5 to 9 cents per pound. Furthermore, since investment per pound is about the same for both processes, the ROI picture is even more dramatic.
>
> I think this article sums up the situation. [Excerpts from the article follow.]

---

[1] Capital expenditures under $100,000 did not require corporate management's approval. Such expenditures were included on an expense budget which was approved by divisional management.

The demand for iso-chlorathane with its broad market base has flourished in the U.S. economy. Its end products are incorporated in a wide variety of plastics and foam products.

However, slowing the expansion of industry capacity is the producers' indecision about whether iso-chlorathane process technology is sufficiently developed to permit a switch from prime gas to feed gas raw material. Feed gas's compelling attractiveness can be summed up succinctly: manufacturing costs of feed gas are 2¢ to 4¢/lb. vs. 6¢ to 8¢/lb. for prime gas.

But feed gas technology is new and untried and a choice of processes is limited.

*   *   *   *   *

There seems to be little argument that the future, be it sooner or later, does belong to feed-gas-based iso-chlorathane production. Vested interest in prime gas and untested technology appear to be only short-term deterrents.

In April 1966, the Research and Development Department of Industrial Chemicals was still unable to transfer its feed-gas-based process from the laboratory to a pilot plant. Therefore, the functional chemicals group arranged to meet with representatives of R&D to discuss the situation. A transcript of part of that meeting follows:

R&D: The problem facing us is that of basically inappropriate pilot plant equipment. During the first phase, the instrumentation broke down under the high pressure. We are now experimenting with a different kind of sensing device and coupling.

WEST: But, as far as you know, high pressure is going to be a problem regardless of what you do?

R&D: That's right.

ROBBINS: Now wait a minute! Let's not leave the problem with the sensors. What kind of material do you want?

R&D: It has to be a special bonded metal. We've been told that it will take six weeks to get it.

ROBBINS: What! Can't we get that for you in the shop?

WEST: Sure. What are the specifications? [He obtained them, went out and returned with confirmation of the fact that the plant had the metal and the appropriate sensors could be constructed that afternoon.]

ROBBINS: OK. Now what about the other equipment you need? You want a four-gallon container. That is what you going to use when you're scaling up, isn't it?

R&D: Yes. That's right—four gallons. But it has to be made from super-strength steel. We've been told that it takes 14 weeks to get it.

ROBBINS: Can't we make that also? [West, Fifer, and Robbins decided that the plant could make it.]

R&D: But aren't bonded metals on allocation? [When a material was on allocation, the government had deemed it to be scarce and was controlling its use.]

WEST: I told them it was in the national interest. [At this point in the meeting the men from R&D left.]

ROBBINS: Don't they know that we are in a *hurry*? How can they contemplate 14 weeks?

WEST: Well, it's the way they think about this kind of thing. Whenever someone says that something will take 10 weeks they wait 10 weeks. That is the way they have been trained.

Robbins: But they sounded like business as usual.

Fifer: Well, they don't know about things like this. I didn't know that we had that steel in the shop.

Robbins: Sure, I didn't either, but on a thing like this we'll move heaven and earth. If a corporation like Stone really wants something, we can get anything we want in a month.

After R&D's discouraging report, Robbins started negotiations with certain U.S. chemical firms (not in the iso-chlorathane business) in an attempt to secure licenses on their feed-gas-based processes. Stone's major competitor in the iso-chlorathane market had already purchased exclusive rights to one of the new processes from a Japanese firm. However, this competitor was having problems with quality and was rumored to have lost over $2 million in equipment and materials.

Mr. Robbins' negotiations resulted in more frustration and little accomplishment. Most of the processes were still in the laboratory stage. Moreover, those firms with the most promising results seemed interested in entering the iso-chlorathane market themselves.

From May to September, Mr. Robbins' life as manager of the functional chemicals group was chaotic.

May

Mr. West, Mr. Robbins' engineering coordinator, reported that he desperately needed engineering help. "I've got seven major projects on the fire, and I need 100 man-months of engineering more than I've got, and I can't get that damn engineering department to move," he said.

At the end of April 1966, year-to-date sales for functional chemicals were only 70% of plan. (Year-to-date sales for Industrial Chemicals were 82% of plan.) However, Mr. Robbins was philosophical about the situation: "The important thing around here is to update your plan and have a reasonable explanation for why you are under. You have to be able to put on a good dog and pony show for divisional management."

June

In June, Miller's forecast for iso-chlorathane came out (see Table 1). Mr. Robbins explained the implications of rising sales as follows:

> The June forecast really puts the pressure on. As a basic chemical, iso-chlorathane faces strong price competition. Price cutting has already resulted in a price decline from 13 cents per pound in 1963 to 10 cents per pound this year. Moreover, I see no let-up in this slide. In fact, we project a price of 7 cents per pound for 1971.
>
> Now, the problem is that these sales forecasts are based on our meeting these price cuts. Given current prices on raw materials, a new plant with the prime-gas-based process means a decline in iso-chlorathane ROI from last year's 14% to 10% in 1971. However, if we get a new feed-gas-based process plant to replace Baton Rouge, ROI should jump to about 21% in 1971.

Table 1

Iso-clorathane Forecasts, 1966–1970

(millions of pounds)

	1966	1967	1968	1969	1970
Market sales	164	210	270	310	352
Internal use					
Industrial	60	60	75	80	90
Fibers	50	60	65	75	80
Other	10	10	15	23	22
Total	284	340	425	488	544

Yet all I hear from R&D is that the feed-gas process is great but it is far from being commercial. You know, it's OK for a little guy not to have the leading technology. But for Stone, it's impossible. Our strategy is to compete with the largest oil and chemical companies by staying ahead of their laboratories and being first with low-cost plants.

Moreover, how the hell am I going to plan ahead when I get forecasts like Miller's? Look at the Synthetic Fibers and Resins Division. They're one of our biggest customers. Yet we can never tell how much they will need. Last October, they told us they wanted 40 million pounds in 1966 and saw a need for 50 million pounds in 1970.

Sales for the functional chemicals group as of June were 81% of plan for the year to date. (Divisional sales were 85% of year-to-date plan.) Mr. Robbins indicated he was pleased.

July

R&D came up with a "promising" breakthrough on the feed-gas process. However, their best estimate for getting a plant "on line" (if things worked out) was late 1969.

The iso-chlorathane problem was further complicated by a shortage of prime gas, the raw material for the present process. Prime gas was produced by Stone's Basic Chemicals Division. In addition to its use as a raw material for making iso-chlorathane, prime gas was the basic input in making Nylostyrene, a product produced by the Synthetic Fibers and Resins Division (see Exhibit 3).

However, Fibers' need for prime gas would be reduced considerably in 1968. In that year, the division was scheduled to open a large Nylostyrene plant using a new process based on a new raw material. A representative of the Basic Chemicals Division commented on the situation. "Long term we are going to have prime gas coming out of our ears (see Exhibit 4). Everyone wants to switch from prime gas to feed gas, and prime gas is a by-product of the process for making feed gas. However, today we're short because we don't have enough stills, and the ones we have are running into technical problems. Right now we're doing our best work with Fibers and Industrial to allocate what we've got."

Purchasing offered no help. A representative of Stone's Corporate Purchasing Department explained that "the world is short of prime gas. There is some capacity at Monsanto but they won't sell to a competitor like Stone. And the problem is that no one will build new capacity in the face of feed gas. Everyone's afraid of the new feed gas technologies."

On July 11, the functional chemicals group met to discuss the alternatives open to them with respect to iso-chlorathane.

ROBBINS: Let's see. Long term we're looking for a plant that will replace Baton Rouge. How big shall we build this thing, or study it anyway?

WEST: For what year do you want it?

ROBBINS: 1973 or '76? What is our forecast? We have one for 1976, don't we?

MILLER: Yeah, '76. I figure about 750 million pounds.

ROBBINS: OK. If we keep Philadelphia that means about 700 million pounds. So why don't we study 700 million and half of that? The marketing people have been telling us 500 isn't big enough. Let's throw 700 at them and see what they do.

FIFER: I think we should put out a white paper on iso-chlorathane which states all the problems we are facing, and send it to engineering. I just don't think they know what our problems are.

MILLER: You might also send it to R&D.

ROBBINS: OK, Sam, when can you do it? While you are on vacation?

WEST: Yes.

*   *   *   *   *

WEST: In the short term, we have a prime-gas shortage at Baton Rouge and Philadelphia. There is competition between iso-chlorathane and Nylostyrene. Lee [Fifer] and Tom McWilliams [production manager for Nylostyrene] get together periodically to negotiate priorities.

ROBBINS: Who is the stumbling block to making modifications needed to get additional output?

FIFER: Nobody.

ROBBINS: Well, who is going to do this?

FIFER: We are hoping to get McWilliams to.

WEST: They are as anxious to get it going as we are, and we hope we can use their engineering time to do it.

*   *   *   *   *

ROBBINS: Another alternative is to buy iso-chlorathane from Grace. Also, Ralph [Miller], you were going to look overseas. Did you find anything?

MILLER: No, I started, but then this thing with Fibers started and you went on vacation and everything else went on vacation.

ROBBINS: Another thing is that Japanese company. Purchasing swears they have 100 million pounds of iso-chlorathane capacity. My calculations indicate that if this is true, they may have 15 million pounds to sell.

FIFER: But we can't make any money if we buy iso-chlorathane at their prices.

ROBBINS: Hell, short term, our problem is to meet our commitments. I don't give a damn about the economics.

*   *   *   *   *

ROBBINS: I think we've had enough on this goddamned iso-chlorathane. We've got to worry about that $2-$2.5 million overrun on the Plexon facility.

FIFER: Want to hear about real short-term problems?

ROBBINS: Can we do anything?

FIFER: No, but maybe you should be informed. Because of the strike at the Houston plant and the war in Vietnam, there is now a shortage of the chemicals which we need to run at low pressures. However, running at higher pressures means we are using 10,000 more pounds of prime gas per day to get the same output.

ROBBINS: Well, one thing we know is that Fibers is a source of a great deal of trouble. They're taking a great deal more iso-chlorathane than their commitment. [Fibers and Resins Division was able to draw on whatever iso-chlorathane it wanted from the storage tanks. There were accounting records but no control numbers.]

MILLER: I think we're heading for real trouble. Our inventories of iso-chlorathane are at the danger level, and with Baton Rouge running at 60% of capacity because of the prime gas shortage, things look bad.

ROBBINS: Look, I agree, but the problem is the process. Our current process based on prime gas yields a low-cost iso-chlorathane. In fact, I think we're the lowest in the industry. So we could expand using prime gas and still show a pretty good return, particularly since prime gas is going to be an almost "free" commodity after Nylostyrene stops using it. But Stalzer is "hooked" on feed gas and it's not very easy to change his thinking. And you can't use equipment designed for the prime gas process for the feed gas process.

MILLER: But the damn feed-gas process is at best years away, and given R&D's speed, perhaps we'll never see it. What's this going to do to our plan?

ROBBINS: Ralph, I don't want to go through the plan because it will scare us. If we look at what we said we were going to do and compare it with where we are, we'll be so upset we won't be able to operate.

August

Not much progress was made on the iso-chlorathane problem. Vacation schedule and problems with other products left little time for iso-chlorathane. Stone was contemplating a major acquisition and Mr. Robbins was giving a great deal of his time to an evaluatory task force to which he had been assigned.

In other areas, Industrial chemicals had acquired a small chemical manufacturer, and the iso-chlorathane group was working on the problems of assimilation. Moreover, it was becoming apparent that the new facility for Plexon would overrun its planned cost of $10 million by much more than 20%–25%.

On the other hand, year-to-date sales for functional chemicals were now 83% of plan (year-to-date sales for Industrial Chemicals were now 87% of plan), and West finally obtained an engineer for the group to work specifically on iso-chlorathane.

September

The overrun on the new facility for Plexon was now approaching 60%–80% and was occupying most of Robbins' time.

R&D work on the feed-gas process proceeded with some success. However, because of equipment problems and critical material shortages, the estimate for getting a plant "on line" was still late 1969.

The new engineer for iso-chlorathane had studied the possibility of an "interim" expansion of iso-chlorathane facilities. His figures showed that a $5.2 million addition to Baton Rouge could provide needed product capacity through 1968. (Existing facilities could not be expanded beyond the 425 million-pound level. Additional capacity would necessitate a new plant to replace Baton Rouge.) However, the project ROI depended on the cost of prime gas.

While the prime gas shortage was relieved (through improved efficiency of the stills) to the point where the functional chemicals group could meet its 1966 iso-chlorathane commitments, there was not going to be enough prime gas to satisfy projected iso-chlorathane needs for 1967. Since other companies were not selling the raw material, Mr. Robbins saw only two ways of getting additional prime gas: (1) to increase output of current prime-gas facilities (by improving the stills, etc.), or (2) to build an incremental new prime gas facility. However, according to the new engineer, existing equipment was already being overworked and, therefore, the first alternative would result in expensive prime gas (7 cents per pound). The engineer's analysis is included as Exhibit 5.

Mr. Robbins was perplexed. Obviously, Stone's management would not accept a project with a 6% ROI, but it was equally clear to Mr. Robbins that, with the uncertainty surrounding the new feed-gas technology and the behavior of competitors, the management climate was not conducive to expenditures for additional prime-gas facilities of new plants. Moreover, the decision to build new prime facilities belonged to the Basic Chemicals Division not to Industrial Chemicals.

Mr. Robbins saw three alternative courses of action:

1. Put more pressure on his group and other interested organizations within Stone Petroleum to settle the iso-chlorathane issue. While there were many specific actions that could be taken along these lines, the following came to Mr. Robbins' mind:

> a) Have the new engineer write up an official proposal for the incremental investment in new prime gas facilities. This action was certain to meet opposition, given top management commitments to the feed gas technology. However, it made the most economic sense.
>
> b) Meet with people outside the product group and get some help on the long-term process problem. Over six months had passed since Mr. Robbins realized that iso-chlorathane capacity was going to be a problem. Yet he had not even begun to draft a new capital proposal. Mr. Robbins considered meeting with some people from other divisions or from R&D. But the problem was whom to meet and what to ask. Meetings with R&D didn't seem to get anywhere at all. Moreover, Mr. Robbins was concerned about developing his subordinates. He was used to letting a man learn by doing, even if it took a long time. If he assumed the task of coordinating R&D, for example, Mr. Robbins felt he would impede Mr. Scott's [coordinator for R&D] development as a manager. Besides, if he gave his men a little more time, he was hopeful they would resolve the problems themselves, an occurrence that would put two feathers in Mr. Robbins' cap.

In any event, the product group manager was sure that a great deal of his and his group's problems were due to the nature of Stone's organization and he certainly couldn't change that.

2. Shift the emphasis of the group's activity from iso-chlorathane to the group's other nine products. Iso-chlorathane had already diverted the group's attention and effort to the point that the Plexon facility was going to run more than 100% over its planned cost. If the group couldn't show a few bright spots, better than planned performance, its 1967 plan review in November was going to be a nightmare. At any rate, being out of capacity on iso-chlorathane wouldn't be that big a tragedy. The product's market share would not be hurt because competitors were also out of capacity and uncertain about the new feed gas process.

3. Get assigned to manage the new acquisition that was being studied by the task force of which he was a member. Barring a minor miracle, Mr. Robbins saw a rather grim performance for his group in 1966, and future prospects did not look much better. Given such a record, he felt that his chances for advancement would not be particularly good. However, the task force was going to recommend acquisition, and assignment to the new operation would provide a graceful exit from a messy situation.

Exhibit 1

STONE PETROLEUM INTERNATIONAL: FUNCTIONAL PRODUCTS GROUP

1965 Organization Chart (abbreviated)

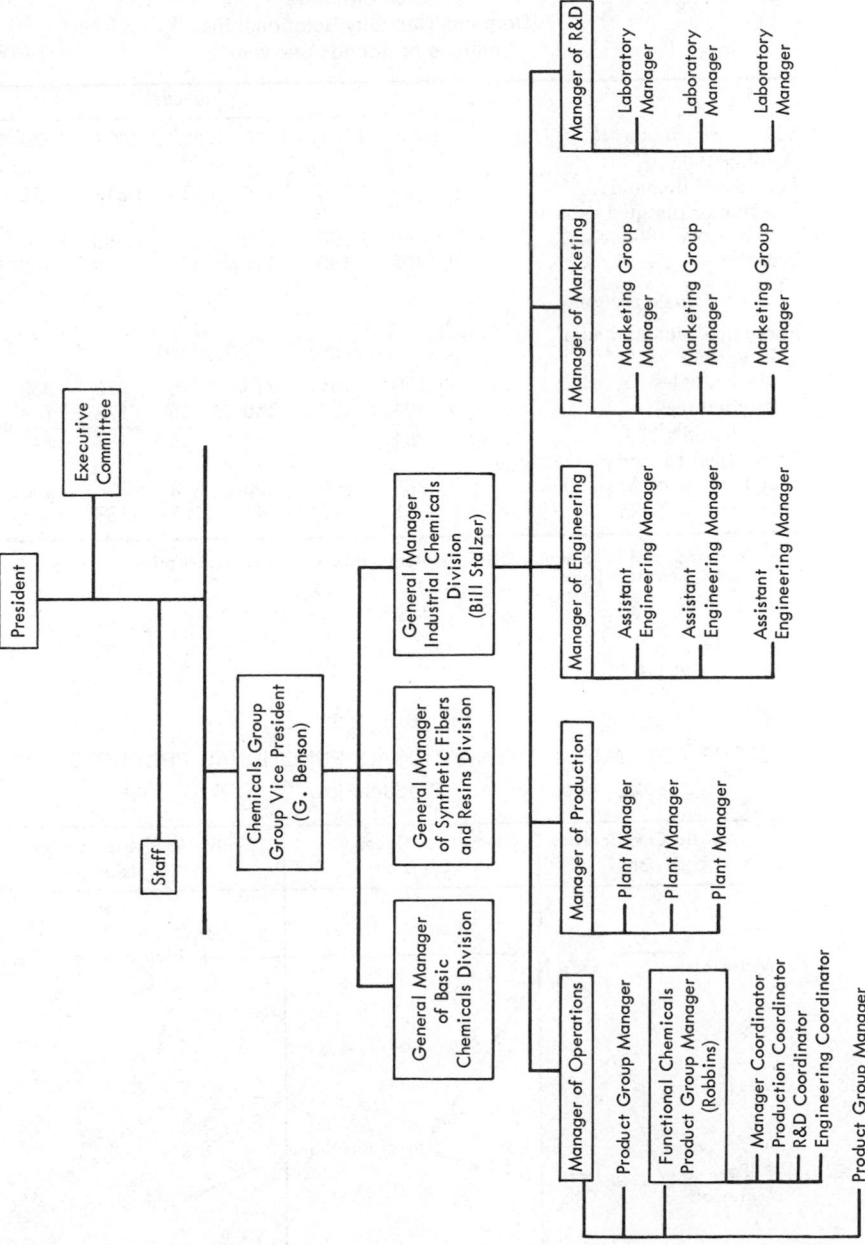

Exhibit 2

STONE PETROLEUM INTERNATIONAL: FUNCTIONAL PRODUCTS GROUP

Iso-chlorathane
Demand/Capacity Relationships
(millions of pounds per year)

	Forecast						
U.S. market	*1965*	*1966*	*1967*	*1968*	*1969*	*1970*	*1971*
October 1965							
Forecasted demand..............	940	1,040	1,124	1,214	1,312	1,416	1,630
Existing or planned capacity as of April 1966..............	1,340	1,220	1,240	1,330	1,350	1,350	1,350
Balance......................	400	180	116	116	38	(66)	(280)
Stone's position							
Forecasted demand as of June 1966							
Market sales.................	150	164	210	270	310	352	
Internal use.................	104	120	130	155	178	192	
Total*...................	254	284	340	425	488	544	
Theoretical capacity existing or planned as of April 1966.......	265	300	300	300	300	300	
Balance......................	11	16	(40)	(125)	(188)	(244)	

* Total sales used to determine ROI. All internal sales valued at market price.
Source: Casewriter's notes.

Exhibit 3

STONE PETROLEUM INTERNATIONAL: FUNCTIONAL PRODUCTS GROUP

Product Flow

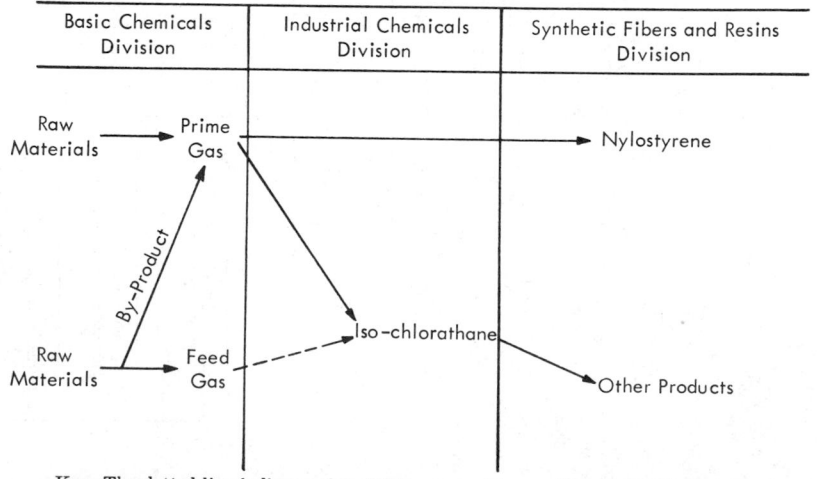

Key: The dotted line indicates that R&D was working on feed-gas-based processes for iso-chlorathane.
Source: Casewriter's notes.

Exhibit 4

STONE PETROLEUM INTERNATIONAL: FUNCTIONAL PRODUCTS GROUP
Prime Gas Supply and Usage for Nylostyrene and Iso-chlorathane Production
for Period from January 1, 1967, through 1970
(thousands of pounds per day)
(average)

	1967 (1st half)	1967 (2nd half)	1968 (1st half)	1968 (3rd qtr.)	1968 (4th qtr.)	1969	1970
Philadelphia Supply............	108	108	108	108	108	108	108
Desired usage							
Nylostyrene...............	62	69	75	50*	45*	0	0
Iso-chlorathane...........	58	58	58	58	58	58	46†
Total.................	120	127	133	108*	103	58	46
Baton Rouge Supply...........	213	213	213	213	213	213	213
Desired usage							
Nylostyrene...............	126	126	126	90*	74*	65	55
Iso-chlorathane...........	105	102	89	85	115	115	0†
Total.................	231	228	215	175*	189	180	55

* Fibers and Resins Division expected its new Nylostyrene process on line in late 1968.
† Feed-gas-based process for iso-chlorathane "scheduled to be on line" in late 1969.
Source: Casewriter's notes.

Exhibit 5

STONE PETROLEUM INTERNATIONAL: FUNCTIONAL PRODUCTS GROUP

Engineer's Analysis

Alternatives	Cost of raw material to industrial chemicals	Cost of iso-chlorathane	Average selling price of iso-chlorathane 1967–1971	Incremental investment		Total investment	
				Dollars (millions)	ROI	Dollars (millions)	ROI
1. "Interim" expansion							
New prime gas facility..........	6¢	7.5¢	8.5¢	$ 5.2	23%	$40.5	10.3%
Squeeze existing facility..........	7¢	8.25¢	8.5¢	$ 5.2	6%	$40.5	8.1%
2. New 500-million-pound plant to replace Baton Rouge— prime gas process (ROI based on 425-million-pound sales) ...	6¢	7.0¢	8.5¢	$40.0	13.2%	$40.0	13.2%
3. New 500-million-pound plant to replace Baton Rouge— feed gas process (ROI based on 425-million-pound sales)	2¢	6.0¢	8.5¢	$40.0	25%	$40.0	25%

Source: Casewriter's notes.

Stone Petroleum International (A)

Look at this report, Jack! What in hell are we going to have to do in this company to get our capital expenditures program under control? We've been planning to get at least $325 million for our Group during each of the next two years, but this morning I got this damn report from Adams saying we would receive less than $215 million each year! How can I get more profit without capital?

Mr. John Rhodes, an assistant to Mr. William Alexander, entered the latter's office in response to a seemingly urgent telephone call and was greeted with this outburst as Mr. Alexander thrust a paper in his direction.

As Mr. Rhodes glanced at the memorandum from Mr. Adams, the Manager of Corporate Development, dated November 11, 1969, he saw the data which had stimulated Mr. Alexander's remarks.

Of direct relevance to Mr. Alexander was a detailed table showing the

Stone Petroleum International's Projected Capital Expenditures and Resources
(000,000)

	1970	1971	After
Capital expenditures			
Approved for U.S. & Foreign Investment	$427	$344	$120
Priority for U.S. & Foreign Investment	223	348	310
Total "Indicated" Program	$650	$692	$430
Available resources			
Net cash generation (estimated)	$314		
Short-term borrowing (estimated)	120		
	$434		
Excess of "indicated" expenditures over resources available	$216		

"projected excesses" within his Chemicals Group of $110 and $162 million during the next two years:

Group	Present approved		Indicated program (approved and priority)		Suggested ceiling		Excess of indicated over ceiling	
	1970	1971	1970	1971	1970	1971	1970	1971
Chemicals	$217	$180	$325	$377	$215	$215	$110	$162

Although the "present approved" total of $217 million was already slightly in excess of the $215 million "suggested ceiling," the Chemicals Group also had $108 million in "priority projects" for the following year. Of this $108 million, $73 million was designated for 128 projects in support of regular product lines.

The difficult process of trying to select projects for deletion or deferral was made even less palatable by the somewhat arbitrary allocation decision described in the memorandum from Mr. Adams to the Corporate Vice President of Finance:

> The suggested approach might best be labeled "pragmatic." It is simply an allocation by groups to achieve a forced choice situation. I [Mr. Adams] arrived at allocations by arbitrarily[1] pinning some figures down and arriving at a target by difference (i.e., by subtracting fixed obligations from the projected funds available). . . .
>
> The above are arbitrary but they serve to clearly illustrate the major force choice position of the Chemicals Group involving trade-offs between the Trinidad complex and alternative Chemicals Group investments. . . .

Mr. Alexander had been vice president of the $800 million Chemicals Group only a few months, but he was becoming very anxious to try to identify and remedy the causes of major strategic problems which were continuously demanding his attention and undermining the Chemicals Group's performance. The recently appointed president of Stone Petroleum International [Mr. Wright] was looking to Mr. Alexander for improved performance in the short run and substantially better results in the long run.[2]

Following brief comments regarding the chemical industry and the company's background, this case will describe the initial explicit recognition of the problems of strategic planning and the corporation's preliminary responses, which preceded the crisis indicated above. Stone Petroleum International (B) will discuss various activities and events which unfolded during the ensuing winter and spring of 1969–1970.

---

[1] The allocation was not literally "arbitrary," but was roughly proportional to the Groups' present asset bases adjusted for recent trends in profitability.

[2] The Stone Petroleum: Functional Products Group case presents problems facing a middle manager in the Stone organization during 1966. Stone Petroleum International cases (A) and (B) describe the problems facing Stone executives as they attempted to cope with major strategic problems taxing their company. Specifically, the cases consider management's attempts to develop and implement a formal system of strategic planning in the large chemicals group of a major petrochemical firm.

THE INDUSTRY

During the late 1950s and early 1960s, the expanding domestic and international chemicals markets had attracted a number of aggressive new competitors. A few manufacturing firms had diversified into the market, but the most significant new entrants were the large petroleum companies with huge cash flows available for research and plant expansion.[3] Increasing diversification by individual chemical firms plus the entrance of new competitors led to excess capacity and declining prices in a number of market segments. As large new facilities with relatively low unit costs were added to the market, many companies began to feel strong pressures on profits. (The projected growth rates for petroleum, chemicals, plastics and some other industries are presented in comparative form as Exhibit 1.)

In addition to an increased number of competitors, many of the industry's markets were beginning to stabilize, and increasing R&D expenditures tended to decrease the competitive advantages held by firms in certain market segments.[4] The impact of these market developments on individual firms varied significantly for companies that had a majority of their resources devoted to markets similar to those of Stone's Chemicals Group. (See Exhibits 2 and 3 for a comparison of performance.) Some of these companies, as well as Stone, were reevaluating their corporate strategies and reorganizing their management structures in preparation for an increasingly competitive economic environment in the 1970s.

THE COMPANY

Several problems which were quite common throughout the chemical industry had been affecting Stone's Chemicals Group during the 1960s. The company's somewhat ineffective accounting and information system and peculiar transfer pricing system led to an inadequate and/or inappropriate analysis of business lines, which in turn had had a detrimental impact on the planning and control processes.[5] The financial planning process had largely centered around the annual budgets, and planning of operations had reflected strong engineering and production, as opposed to marketing and financial considerations. In addition, salaries and promotions within the company had been more closely associated with tenure than with economic performance. As a result of these several conditions, nearly 90% of the profit centers had failed to meet their "annual plans" during the past few years.[6]

---

[3] Although Stone had a large petroleum products group, it did not have nearly the cash flow available from that source that some of the larger and more recent entrants into the chemicals markets were able to generate.

[4] During this period, "packaged technology" became available, whereby a company could buy the technological specifications for a given product at a reasonable price and have the necessary facilities built accordingly.

[5] In this transfer pricing system, goods were transferred from one division to another at cost, and the book value of the related investment was transferred as well.

[6] See, for example, "Stone Petroleum International: Functional Products Group."

The history of the Chemicals Group during the 1960s had been filled with various reorganizations which were intended to relieve the problems. In 1960, the Group was restructured in an effort to make the chemical operations more marketing-oriented. The functional divisions were broken up and marketing-technical teams and operating teams were established to try to improve performance. By 1963, after a series of financially disastrous new plant investments had been undertaken, corporate management again began to be concerned about the company's organizational structure. During that year, two types of permanent committees were established in an effort to improve the coordination of activities throughout the corporation. At the corporate level, the Executive Committee (ExCom) was formed to bring the group vice presidents and corporate officers together, and within each group, Operating Committees were formed composed of the group vice president and the presidents and executive vice presidents of each of the divisions. (The abbreviated corporate organization chart in Exhibit 4 includes these committees.) There were no substantial improvements in either the information and measurement process or the reward system to accompany these organizational changes.

Early in 1965, the Executive Committee (ExCom) again became very anxious about the economic performance in the Chemicals Group. This dissatisfaction led to the appointment of a task force to study the organizational problems and related matters in the Group. At the recommendation of the task force, the Group's business lines were analyzed and subsequently rearranged. Although some progress had been made, many felt that it was not until after the departure of Mr. Benson, the Chemicals Group vice president, in 1968, that Mr. Fred Wright was able to direct the Group's attention to the sources of the strategic problems and to begin to eliminate some ineffective personnel.

By mid-1969, the organizational and environmental problems facing Stone had manifested themselves in a number of ways. Between 1964 and 1968, the company had undertaken a $2.5 billion construction program. Many technical breakdowns had frustrated this building effort; unanticipated problems at the Chemicals Group's Houston plant alone had cost $0.33 per share in 1968.[7] Another $0.12 per share decline that year was attributed to declining prices and rising costs in the petroleum markets. The company's basic research program had created few new business areas in recent years, although process developments had been reasonably fruitful. The size and breadth of these problem areas suggest the seriousness of the problems facing Stone's management.

In the spring of 1969, after reading an outside researcher's report regarding some of the company's strategic planning problems and talking with Mr. Chambers from the company's planning staff, Mr. Wright, then the Chemicals Group's vice president, hired the Business Consultants Associates (BCA) to study the Group's strategic planning process and product/market strategy and to make recommendations for improvements. The consultants analyzed the Group's several dozen busi-

---

[7] These problems included the Plexon facility discussed in the Stone Petroleum International: Functional Products Group case.

ness lines and classified each of them according to the expected relative growth rate of the market and the relative share of market the Group might reasonably seek. This classification scheme also provided a basis for relating the various business lines to broad product/market categories ranging from "defensive cash generators" to "sources of significant growth." (See Exhibit 5 for a more complete list of these classifications.) This consulting report combined with executive promotions during 1969 provided the background for more comprehensive changes in the strategic planning process later in the year.

Mr. Wright and Mr. Alexander, both of whom had joined Stone after graduation from college, had moved up the company's hierarchy rather rapidly in recent years. In 1965, Wright was president of Stone's International Petroleum Group and Alexander was one of his three senior vice presidents. Mr. Wright was appointed chairman of the newly organized Eastern Group during 1966[8], and Alexander moved into domestic operations to become president of the Chemicals Group's Basic Chemicals Division. Mr. Wright was moved to the Chemicals Group as a vice president in 1967, thus assuming responsibility for a large portion of Mr. Benson's group, including Mr. Alexander's division. When Benson resigned in 1968 after 35 years' service, Wright picked up the balance of the Chemicals Group's activities, and Alexander moved across from Basic Chemicals to a newly formed Chemicals Operations Division as its president. Again the stage was set for further promotions.

Following the 1969 retirement of Mr. Reid, the president of Stone, Mr. Wright was promoted from vice president of the Chemicals Group to president of the company, and Mr. Alexander was promoted from president of the Chemicals Operations Division to vice president of the Chemicals Group. At this point, these two executives each had extensive in-depth operating experience within the company, but had had rather brief exposure to the problems of general management. Although both the men were acutely aware of the existence of strategic problems throughout their respective organizations, they were somewhat uncertain about the specific causes of the problems and about how to begin strategic planning so as to overcome the problems within an acceptable period of time. At the same time, they were in the organizational positions responsible for the development and implementation of improved strategic planning processes.

Six months after his promotion to vice president of the Chemicals Group, Mr. Alexander had the opportunity to make further changes in the division top managements. He chose to replace the president of the Polymers and Specialties Division as well as the man who had been appointed his successor. His choices, Richard Wentworth and Donald Brown, both represented double jump promotions; that is both were promoted from vice president to president, past executive vice presidents. Both were regarded as tough, capable, energetic, young managers. The other two division presidents were retained in their positions.

---

[8] The Eastern Group, encompassing Asia and the South Pacific, was one of the regional groups within the International Group.

AN APPROACH TO STRATEGIC PLANNING

The first explicit effort by the new company president to encourage corporate management to reconsider Stone's strategic posture came in a letter dated July 1, 1969, addressed to the corporation's ExCom. In that letter, Mr. Wright outlined several urgent problems facing the ExCom in areas related to strategic planning. Wright's concern centered on the problems of articulating corporate objectives, organizing to meet such objectives, analyzing competitors' positions and actions, selecting capital investment levels consistent with corporate objectives, and anticipating competitive responses.

During July and August, the serious interest of the new president in improved planning and performance became increasingly obvious when he announced to his subordinates a desire to push Stone's earnings per share from an estimated $4.20 for 1969 to $5.00 in 1970. Partly as a response to his perception of the problems facing him, Mr. Alexander hired an assistant, Jack Rhodes, a 1960 graduate of the Harvard Business School who had worked as a consultant to petroleum and chemical companies including Stone, and asked him to assist with the development and implementation of an organizational structure to encourage and support strategic planning within his Chemicals Group.

At the same time, Mr. Wright began to probe the problems of his corporate office. Inasmuch as he felt the problems of Stone were partially attributable to an historical inability to tie salary and promotion to performance, he had hired the consulting firm of Knight & Co. to study the company's management compensation program. After four weeks of intensive study, the consultants concluded that no realistic proposals could be presented until the company made substantial improvements in its information system which would permit some quantitative evaluation of individual managers' performance. This conclusion highlighted the role of the information system, noted above, as a serious obstacle to the identification of strategic problems.

As Mr. Wright took hold of the Stone company, the developing climate in the weekly ExCom meetings left Mr. Alexander with no doubt that he needed immediately to develop plans for better short-run economic performance and for much better performance in the long run. His Group represented about 40% of the corporate investment, but provided less than 25% of the total corporate revenue and profit. He would have to improve or he would be cut back.

Mr. Alexander spent the summer discussing the problems of his Group with a wide range of interested parties. For example, he asked three members of the corporate planning staff who were known for their critical views, as well as their intelligence, to propose a program of activity to him. These men—operating as a task force—were deeply involved in reorganizing the management information system of the company on a charge from Mr. Wright. Their work had as its premise a view of what strategic planning should be like at Stone. Implicit were a concept of organization based on profit centers, transfer prices to help with the measurement of businesses, and a performance-oriented reward system. They were delighted to have a chance to influence directly the thinking of so important a line manager.

Mr. Alexander also called the Business Consultants Associates back to his Group and asked them to make in-depth analyses of two of his major businesses and two of his competitors. In addition, he continued to talk extensively among his widespread network of friends in the chemical industry.

His basic conclusion was that Stone's Chemicals Group required much more sophisticated general management. Resources that had been diffused over a number of businesses in the past had to be focused. Operations that had been managed with a high degree of slack needed to be tightened considerably.

For help on the specifics of these matters, he turned to the members of his Group Operating Committee, the presidents of the three product divisions that made up his Group and the pooled functional divisions that provided operating support. In September he began a series of intensive meetings with these officers to consider the future of the Group. A task force of planning and control staff was set up to support the Group in its work. (This use of staff was regarded by lower levels of management as nearly revolutionary, for Stone's Chemicals Group had a strong tradition of "bottom-up" line management. In fact, lower level management was delighted by the change, for it implied, they thought, that the Operating Committee might be able to deal with their plans on an informal, substantive basis. In the past, Operating Committee inputs had tended to reflect philosophy and corporate politics. The burden of the task of review on a non-staffed, under-informed group was too great to permit economic analysis.)

In mid-September, about ten days after these meetings began, Mr. Rhodes sent a memo to Mr. Alexander in which he outlined some basic problem areas and suggested a few preliminary steps to begin remedying them.

> During our discussion last week, we identified three major classes of interacting problems:
>
> 1. Need for better planning.
> 2. Need for better measures of both businesses and managers.
> 3. Need for better managers.
>
> In order to begin thinking about these problems you might consider them in terms of a two-phase program. The initial phase should include "tightening the ship" through gradual adjustments, not major restructuring, in the organization. This adjustment process should include such steps as:
>
> a) Defining businesses along lines that make sense in economic and technical terms as a basis for strategy formulation.
> b) Developing a system of information and measurement for use in planning and controlling business lines.
> c) Making preliminary plans for improving the quality of managers at both functional and general levels.

The second, and much more formidable phase, should include the preparation of major analytical studies as a basis for developing SPI's posture for profitable performance during the 1970s and early 1980s.

Inasmuch as your task force has tentatively divided the business lines into "loser," "winner," and "marginal" categories, I would encourage you to first focus your attention on the "loser" category by trying to eliminate those businesses and managers who are clearly hurting Chemicals Group. This step will serve the dual purposes of eliminating detractors from the Group and providing a clear signal to other managers that substantive changes are in progress. In addition, you should try to avoid making major irreversible commitments at this time if there is a chance that improved information in the near future might change the worth of the business proposal.

Your time might be best spent by concentrating your efforts on a limited number of businesses in need of help. This time should be spent assisting with the development of an integrated process of strategic planning, evaluating businesses, and measuring general managers as they interact with superiors, subordinates, and staff experts.

By working with the managers on a one-to-one basis, you should be able to discourage much of the existing ritual in the planning process and encourage substantive planning. Such a change in the planning process and the subsequent development of 3- to 5-year plans should yield two distinct benefits:

1. The number of operating problems demanding top management's time should be reduced.
2. Annual budgets and capital budgeting proposals should be more meaningful.

Although the above paragraphs contain many time-consuming suggestions, there are two related points which should be considered as well. You should think about a process for permitting upper management to intervene meaningfully in major long-range planning activities. Secondly, efforts must be made to insure that Chemicals Group managers think in terms of *profit;* it is essential that your signals transmit that objective.

After Mr. Alexander read and pondered Mr. Rhodes' memo, he called his assistant to his office.

ALEXANDER: I've just finished reading your memo, Jack, and I get the impression you don't fully appreciate the fact that I've been at this desk only sixty days. Don't you realize I've been an officer in this Group for only three years, and that many of my subordinates have been here for ten years?

RHODES: Yes, I realize these things, but I think we must start on some of these problems.

ALEXANDER: I'm convinced we must begin separating businesses from their present managers for purposes of evaluation and then we must make some decisions about both businesses and managers. But that takes time. I'm not sure I have the ability yet to move so fast and I certainly don't have the data. Eliminating many of the "planning rituals" which have existed around here will take time, and the idea of "chopping heads" is certainly inconsistent with the company's tradition.

RHODES: I know these changes are substantial, but don't Wright and Burns want to see some dramatic improvements?

ALEXANDER: Sure they want to see improvements, but they don't want to see the organization in chaos! I'm not positive about just how fast Wright is prepared to move, and I don't know exactly what Burns expects to have happen either. I do know that Burns doesn't like bloodlettings.

I know that I've got to begin taking some big steps or I'll never get this mammoth organization off the old track and moving on a new course at an increased rate! Maybe the meeting at Copper Creek will be a good time to initiate the new tack and see how things move from there.

Two weeks later, Mr. Rhodes accompanied Mr. Alexander to the Chemicals Group Operating Committee's meeting at Copper Creek, Texas, to observe and listen to their discussion of the categorization of business lines and related problems concerning the strategic planning process. At that meeting, the Business Consultants Associates, hired earlier by Mr. Wright, made a major presentation regarding the classification scheme for the business lines which they had developed during their summer's work at Stone. Members of the consulting firm also discussed the basic elements of the strategic planning process before a meeting of all those present.

Although the consultants' presentation was an important part of the agenda, Mr. Alexander had hoped a large part of the meeting time could be spent making choices about business lines which had been classified as "winners" and "losers" by the Business Consultants Associates. Mr. Alexander and Mr. Rhodes also thought the meeting would provide a good forum for Mr. Alexander to emphasize the growing necessity for the Chemicals Group to become more selective in choosing the business lines on which it wanted to focus its energies and resources.

The process of trying to analyze the several dozen business lines was severely hampered by the paucity of useful information available to those in attendance. Exhibit 6 presents the format of the data available to the committee, and Exhibit 7 summarizes information from supporting documents for one of the divisions. These exhibits were prepared from the same sources which Knight & Co. had found to be inadequate to use as a basis for a revised compensation plan. The lack of accurate and comprehensive analytical data contributed to the committee's inability to discuss and make decisions about the complete list of business lines. As a result, the chief dialogue at the Copper Creek meeting centered on an attempt to select a posture for the Group in the styrene monomer market. Although the full objectives of the meeting were not attained, the consultants' presentation and the subsequent debate provided some common basis for understanding the trade-offs to be made among divisions and business lines within the Group during the ensuing months.

Mr. Alexander was also able to make clear his view of the situation's urgency: "Wright has gone on the line for $5.00 a share and I think we have to back him up. That's a 25% earnings increase for us."

One of Mr. Alexander's vice presidents responded, "Will, nobody in the organization believes that we can make $5.00, and I'm not sure we can either—at least not without wrecking the company."

In the evening, over drinks, the work continued. Mr. Alexander noted in closing the discussion at 11:30 P.M.: "Wright has made it clear to me that I have a limited amount of time to get this situation turned around. I want to be sure that each of you understands that that means your division has less time!"

A week later, in a memorandum dated October 5, Mr. C. W. Monroe, Chemicals' Operations Division vice president, presented a tentative classification of all the business lines in Chemicals Group as he had interpreted the discussion at the Copper Creek meeting. (See Exhibit 8 for a summary of the classifications.) The closing paragraph of his memorandum, quoted below, contained his recognition that there were additional problems to be resolved before a "portfolio" of business lines could be selected.

> We have no way at this time of relating the make-up of this list [largely Exhibit 8] to the necessary "Portfolio" that must represent the Chemicals Group investments to achieve the stated objectives of 9.5 per cent per year sales growth and 9 per cent per year growth in income before taxes. In order to get from where we are today to the planned environment we seek will take time and a great deal of effort. I have asked the Controller's Group, which includes the Control Manager of the Industrial Products Group, to address the problem of establishing a timetable and work program to achieve the goal of a "Portfolio" evaluating. I anticipate that several months will elapse before we can quantitatively relate the "Portfolio" to our Chemicals Group objectives. This, however, should not deter us and we may develop some qualitative benefits as we go along.

While Mr. Monroe had been working on the classification scheme for the business lines, Mr. Rhodes had been trying to think about what had and what had not been accomplished at the Copper Creek meeting a few days earlier. In a private discussion on October 6, Mr. Rhodes and Mr. Alexander exchanged some thoughts regarding the meeting.

RHODES: In many ways, the meeting wasn't too different from many in the past because each division—except, perhaps, Basic Chemicals—was still a bit enchanted with the future.

ALEXANDER: On the other hand, some began to realize that because of past mistakes within the company, we don't have the necessary resources to pursue all profitable market opportunities. The central question we finally reached at the meeting seemed to be, "What position do we want to take in plastics?" And that's a key question.

RHODES: Will, I wasn't as happy. It seemed to me as though the officers did not have clear criteria to use in selecting postures, much less strategies, for different markets.

ALEXANDER: Yes, but I thought we were able to get a much better understanding of why we are losing money in some of our businesses. Where we have underinvested in the past, old plants are clobbering our margins. If we choose to respond by making major capital commitments, depreciation kills us for five years before market penetration begins to pay off. With capital short, we can't stand the drain on cash flow.

Another thing I noticed was that although the vice presidents began to face some of the hard trade-offs *in context*, most weren't yet ready to sacrifice their own favorite markets or projects. . . .

RHODES: Will, what would happen, for instance, if you said to a manager: Tell us what you need to make this a profitable business, and how long it will take. If you convince us, you've got the money, and it's your head if you're wrong. If you don't convince us, we adopt a "milking" strategy with minimum new money.

ALEXANDER: I can do that, but while I'm emphasizing thorough analysis and commitment, I think it's important that men perceive the differences in circumstances that will cost a business line its life as opposed to those that will cost a man his job. I'm not sure what will happen when I push for both today, but I think we need to move in that direction. In the meantime, as we continue the analysis of businesses and then projects, it will be essential that effective staff analysts be available, and it will be helpful to have standardized formats for developing analyses, and, perhaps, computer models to assist with the numerical work. Monroe isn't really geared up to help us yet. I'd like you to be of whatever help you can to him.

Following the Copper Creek meeting of September 24–25, Mr. Barrett, the Chemicals Group's planning coordinator, was formally assigned the responsibility for coordinating the Group's business planning activities. Mr. Rhodes had argued that development of a formal, structured format for data collection and analysis should await the completion of the new information system then being implemented, but Mr. Alexander was anxious for Mr. Barrett to prepare a system for collecting and analyzing data in a comparable manner, even though the initial input might be somewhat inaccurate. He hoped such a standardized analytical format could be developed in time for the Group's capital expenditures presentation to the ExCom in December.

The concerns expressed by various managers at the Copper Creek meetings about the organizational implications of the changes planned within the Group over the ensuing few months led Mr. Alexander to prepare a memo reviewing the need for specific profit centers and a formalized transfer pricing mechanism. That memorandum, which follows, accompanied a schedule of the specific profit centers which were to be incorporated into the new management information system.

Gentlemen: October 7, 1969

The Chemicals Group has been handicapped in the past year and a half by operation under a management system that has been expensive, complex, and often inaccurate. Problems arising from computing return on the basis of the entire upstream investment and costing of variances have led to inefficient and costly study and analysis. As a consequence, there has been a great deal of discussion at all levels of the Chemicals Group concerning Profit Center Definition and Transfer Pricing and the attendant development of a management information system that would allow us to operate more knowledgeably and definitively within the Divisions of the Group.

On May 5, the Group's Operating Committee first sanctioned the idea that we should proceed with the development of the above-mentioned system. We reviewed the implications of the new system in conjunction with our discussions at the recent meetings in Copper Creek however, it is obvious that there is still much concern on the part of a number of people within the Divisions of the Group who are involved.

I detect the main sources of concern as reorganization, redefinition of many peoples' responsibilities, loss of market orientation, and lack of confidence in broad applications of transfer prices. I am convinced that none of these is valid.

In order to accomplish the objectives of the Profit Center concept, a reorganization of the Group is neither necessary, nor desirable; however, the responsibilities of individuals will be given much greater clarification.

It is evident that in establishing the present Chemicals Group organization, a great deal of thought was given to definition of business divisions and the general manager groupings. We would anticipate some gradual planned change in the content or alignment of these groups that would appear logical and can occur over a period of time. Providing information necessary to those people involved in managing their areas of responsibility, however, requires some refinement and elucidation. This is one of the key areas to which Profit Center Definition and Transfer Pricing address themselves.

*   *   *   *   *

Transfer prices on materials moving between Profit Centers are considered a necessary requirement to effect strategically sound business judgments and plans for a specific Center. The transfer prices will be utilized only to satisfy management's determination of the way it would like to see our businesses developed; they are not necessary from a custodial accounting standpoint.

Sufficient time and care will be taken to make sure that we do not disrupt the effectiveness of the present progress of the Group. Your cooperation and assistance are sought—indeed are necessary—in helping us to accomplish this objective.

Very truly yours,

The five weeks following the Copper Creek meeting were terribly busy ones for Mr. Alexander, as he tried to handle daily operations and complete the year's budgeting cycle. Every Monday he met with the ExCom to discuss problems facing the other groups and to try to analyze the capital expenditure proposals being presented by the other group vice presidents. Defending his own proposals at such meetings was always a taxing experience because the weak performance in his Group provided impetus for close scrutiny by other group vice presidents.

In addition to the rather "routine" tasks demanding his attention, Mr. Alexander was confronted with two crises which took him out of his office for several days. Early in the second week of October, an explosion rocked the Group's plant at Wood River, Illinois, and destroyed a huge compressor which had supported several million dollars of annual profit. Capital rationing in the company several years earlier had precluded the installation of back-up equipment during the plant's construction, so the process of replacing the compressor and repairing the facilities met with numerous delays. Within ten days of the explosion at Wood River, a hurricane toppled a large ethylene tower at the Group's Houston complex. These problems, combined with his continuing concern for the instability of prices in the chemical industry, kept Alexander quite preoccupied throughout a period of weeks when he was also trying to implement new planning concepts within his Operating Committee.

Although these emergency conditions demanded much of his time and attention, Mr. Alexander's most time-consuming activities were his regular Tuesday and Thursday meetings with his Operating Committee. This committee, sitting with their executive vice presidents, usually spent Thursdays discussing problems arising from interdivisional transactions, personnel policies, and operating matters. The same people met every Tuesday to consider plans for major business centers in the Group. Often during these planning sessions, the lower level managers responsible for specific business activities would present the business plans while various members of the committee asked questions.

The presentation for Pydraul 213 was typical. The product had been a weak but promising new business area for many years when, twelve months earlier, Mr. Frank Drummond had been asked to take it over to see if he could make it profitable. The following are excerpts from his presentation.

DRUMMOND: You can see on the chart in front of you how our sales have continued to climb over the past year—from $430,000 per quarter in the third quarter of 1969 to $870,000 for the same quarter this year. . . .

The chart indicates the superior technical characteristics of our product under extreme operating conditions. . . .

Our sales for 1970 are projected to be 4.4 million pounds—10% in excess of our current production capacity. . . .

Our present facility is too small to meet our projected needs and too small to permit the economies of scale which will permit us to cut our selling prices from $1.00 per pound to $0.70 per pound. . . .

We have presented essentially two options for consideration. The first is to expand our capacity from the present 4 to 10 million pounds over the next two years at a $1.9 million investment and stay at that size, and the second is to plan to expand to 60 million pounds capacity over the next seven years for an investment of $53 million. . . .

At one point during the discussion, Mr. Alexander asked,

Frank, what makes you think we can take the market away from Celanese and Dow? We've been in here for five years now with a great product, but no business.[9] Why will things change?

Mr. Drummond responded by summarizing the optimistic premises on which growth could be anticipated. He conceded the risks involved, but concluded, "This is the only way in which we can grow this into a profitable business."[10]

Mr. Alexander replied:

Then Frank, why don't you go back to your group and work out a plan that involves no new capital and see what that looks like. With

[9] Dow, Celanese, Du Pont, General Electric and a few other companies were then selling products for many of the same markets and had combined annual sales of about 150 million pounds.

[10] The product had lost money since its inception, including a projected loss of $800,000 in 1969 and $300,000 in 1970 after assigned overhead. The existing gross margin of 9% was projected to increase to 24% in 1970.

the major investments we're going to have to make in Trinidad,[11] I don't see how we can spend $2 million on this one in the next two years.

In contrast, at another meeting the Operating Committee approved plans that involved spending $100 million over five years to capture a major share of the rapidly growing market for styrene monomer.

Mr. Rhodes had accompanied Mr. Alexander to all the Chemicals Group Operating Committee meetings following the sessions at Copper Creek. After seven meetings in October, Mr. Rhodes felt he had seen enough to provide some basis for presenting some explicit ideas to his boss. The following are excerpts from their discussion:

RHODES: Will, your staff people don't understand that they should be working twenty-four hours a day until this series of reviews is over. Your managers don't understand they have the right to demand that the staff produce. . . . I was somewhat astonished by Barrett's comment that he could not have capital funding totals for your committee until more than ten days after the meeting. . . . The company is facing a crisis and yet the idea is not fully understood by the organization. . . . I think this is because your committee is accepting "business as usual" answers from the staff.

ALEXANDER: That's right, Jack, but I have better support today than any manager of this Group ever had, and it's getting better.

RHODES: OK, we're all learning. We are beginning to understand how to pick specialty businesses. But in addition to seeking logical groupings of specialty products, we have to emphasize the importance of early payout, high ROI after market acceptance and before competition develops, and acceptable ROI after competition appears.

We also need a well-developed strategic plan for a logical group of products. That depends upon expert knowledge of the market, of the competition, of the customer, and how he buys.

ALEXANDER: You're my hair shirt, Jack. I thought the most impressive part of the Silicone business proposal was not the financial success of the business, but the complete knowledge of the business demonstrated in the presentation. That presentation was certainly different from the "extraordinary new products" and "need to fill out the product line" type.

RHODES: That's because Paul is a good manager. Will, given the existing capital shortage, how are we going to analyze the questions of "What is the pay-off?" and "What is the commitment?" Often at the meetings I've felt that men seemed to feel the company had to invest or retrench in every product line. Perhaps the new "name of the game" must be "focus."

ALEXANDER: I'm sure that's right. If we stop trying to do everything, if we take what's left after Trinidad and put it into our best businesses, if we get good plans and pay off for good performance, I'm just convinced we'll get progress, although I can't say how.

RHODES: Well, we have to have better review sessions. Forecasts of progress simply don't do. It is important that we begin to get analytical answers to the questions raised in these meetings. The results may be crude,

[11] The company, under the leadership of Wright's predecessor, had committed itself to a several hundred million dollars investment in an off-shore production facility complex in Trinidad based on natural gas there. By 1969 the investment was 50% completed and most managers were convinced it had been a poor decision.

and it may be important to concede at the start that the answer may be crude, but given the kinds of decisions that you are being forced to make, I would think that we ought to get as much information as we possibly can, with some feeling that individuals are committed to the judgments they are providing.

It was not until November 10 that Mr. Alexander and Mr. Rhodes could find time to sit down and talk again about planning. While Mr. Alexander did not disagree with the substance of Mr. Rhodes' comments, he still did not see how he could "push" or "pull" his managers to get them moving in the desired directions at an adequate pace. Toward the end of their discussion, Mr. Rhodes broached a few additional topics.

RHODES: Does the Group need fewer but better lower level general managers? Perhaps some of the managers need bigger jobs and others apparently can't handle what they've got now.

ALEXANDER: I'm beginning to think those may be real problems. Some of my managers seem to be doing little more than shuffling paper. . . .

RHODES: . . . do you have any second sources of information which permit you to check on the quality of the "new plans" you are getting? I know that in practice all you could do is hope to shake things up and create a better climate, but you might want to press hard on the specifies in at least one or two instances that you think are critical.

ALEXANDER: We've talked about this problem before. We may have to add some staff to help us get at some of these critical areas. But right now outside faces would be unsettling.

Two days later, Jack Rhodes heard his phone ringing as he returned from his mid-morning coffee break. The irritated voice on the other end of the line was obviously Mr. Alexander's: "Jack, come down to my office and see what that blasted Adams sent out in the morning mail!"

As Mr. Rhodes headed for Mr. Alexander's office, he knew anything from the Manager of Corporate Development that produced such a response from his boss had to mean "bad news."

Alexander (pointing to the memo mentioned on page 967 of this case) said, "Look at this report, Jack! What in hell are we going to have to do. . . ."

Exhibit 1

STONE PETROLEUM INTERNATIONAL (A)

Industrial Growth

What do all these trends mean in the way of U.S. production? Charts 1, 2, and 3 show how much production will grow by 1982 in key major industry groups. On the average, industrial production will more than double in 15 years, keeping pace with the gain in industrial capacity.

In our industry forecasts, five factors were considered:

1. Past growth trends, as measured by the Federal Reserve Board's indexes of production, which often do not have any direct relationship to tons, pounds, gallons, feet or other unit of measurement of production of specific products.
2. The amount and trend of research and development spending.
3. Prospects for development of new products.
4. Prospects for use of new technology and cost-cutting machinery.
5. The implications of projected trends in GNP expenditures by sectors and components for output of specific industries.

The fastest growing industries, such as plastics, man-made fibers, chemicals, appliances and aluminum ranked high in all five of the above factors.

Chart 1

U.S. INDUSTRIAL GROWTH, 1967–1982

	Percent increase						
	0	*25*	*50*	*75*	*100*	*125*	*150*	*175*
Utilities.. 176								
Manufacturing.......................... 107								
Industrial production average............. 107								
Mining............... 37								

* Source: "The American Economy," McGraw-Hill Publications, Economics Dept., 1967.

Exhibit 1—Continued

Chart 2

GROWTH OF MAJOR INDUSTRIES, 1967–1982

Industrial Production Average

Percent increase

Industry	Percent increase
Chemicals	+227%
Rubber and plastic products	+206%
Electric utilities	+188%
Instruments	+165%
Electrical machinery	+138%
Gas utilities	+130%
Furniture	+117%
Non-ferrous metals	+111%
Paper	+110%
Transportation equipment	+109%
Non-electrical machinery	+91%
Printing and publishing	+89%
Fabricated metals	+83%
Stone, clay and glass	+82%
Textiles	+80%
Stone and earth minerals	+78%
Apparel	+75%
Petroleum	+72%
Food and beverages	+58%
Steel	+49%
Metal mining	+43%
Tobacco	+39%
Crude oil and natural gas	+35%
Bituminous coal mining	+29%
Lumber	+25%
Leather	+17%
Defense products	−17%

(Scale: 0 25 50 75 100 125 150 175 200 225)

Exhibit 1—Continued

Chart 3

THE BIG GAINERS, 1967–1982
Selected Product Lines

Percent increase

	0	50	100	150	200	250	300	350	400	450	500	550	

Plastics materials... 568

Plastics products.. 378

Man-made fibers... 290

Electric housewares... 255

Inorganic chemicals.................... 221

Basic organic chemicals............... 200

Aluminum refining............... 196

Aluminum mill shapes............ 196

Man-made fabrics.......... 176

Laundry appliances......... 173

Kerosene............ 172

Tufted and hard surface rugs........ 150

Asphalt, waxes...... 147

Electrical equipment and parts.... 140

Synthetic rubber... 133

Sanitary paper products... 127

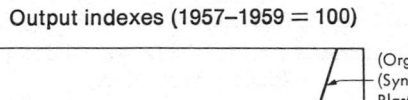

Exhibit 1—Concluded

Output indexes (1957–1959 = 100)

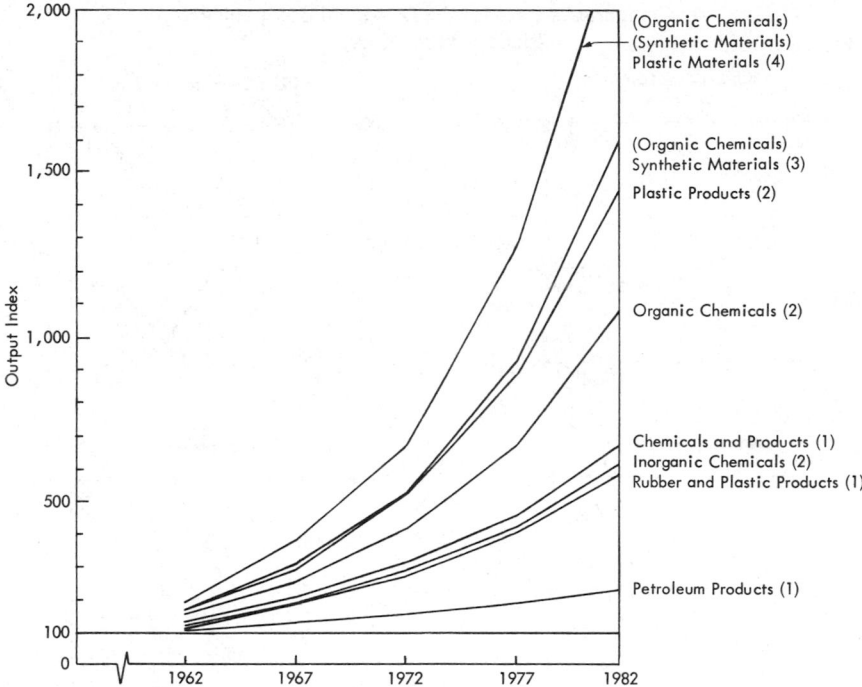

Legend:
(1) Primary product class
(2) Secondary product subclass
(3) Tertiary product subclass
(4) Fourth product subclass

Exhibit 2

STONE PETROLEUM INTERNATIONAL (A)

Comparative Data for Six Chemical Companies
(dollars in millions)

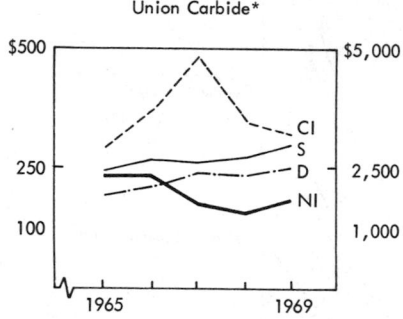

Union Carbide*

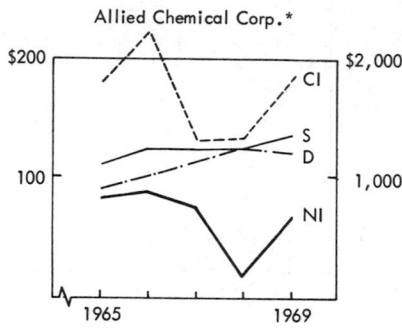

Allied Chemical Corp.*

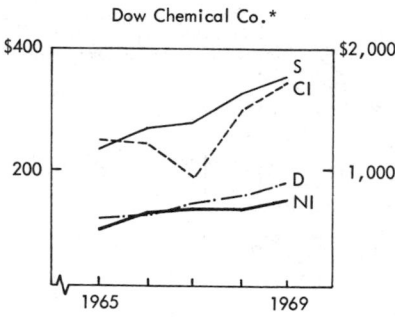

Dow Chemical Co.*

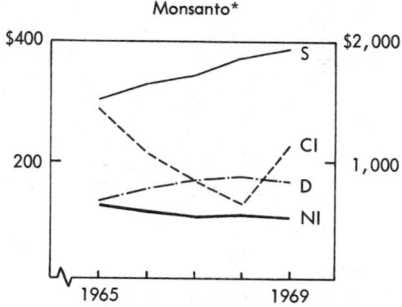

Monsanto*

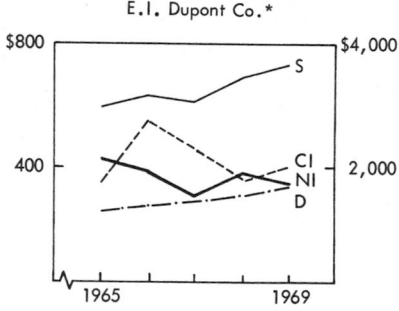

E.I. Dupont Co.*

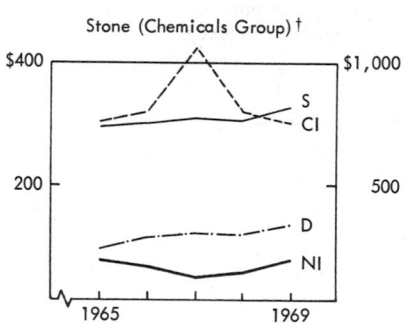

Stone (Chemicals Group)†

Note: NI = Net income
      CI = Capital investment
      D = Depreciation
      S = Sales
* Source: Annual reports.
† Source: Internal documents.

Exhibit 3

STONE PETROLEUM INTERNATIONAL (A)

Consolidated Statements of Income, 1965–1969

(dollars in millions)

	1969	1968	1967	1966	1965
REVENUES:					
Sales and other operating revenue....	$3,810	$3,570	$3,398	$3,466	$2,774
Dividends, interest, and other income.........................	41	32	15	14	13
	$3,851	$3,602	$3,413	$3,480	$2,787
COSTS AND EXPENSES:					
Purchased oils and chemicals........	$1,347	$1,239	$1,190	$1,250	$ 912
Costs and operating expenses........	737	739	710	680	526
Selling, general, and administrative expenses.......................	356	332	317	295	227
Income, operating, and consumer taxes..........................	780	751	672	674	564
Depreciation, depletion, and dry hole costs..........................	316	286	256	237	228
Interest on long-term debt...........	62	46	38	21	20
	3,598	3,393	3,183	3,157	2,477
Net income...................	$ 253	$ 209	$ 230	$ 323	$ 310

Consolidated Balance Sheets at December 31, 1965–1969

(dollars in millions)

	1969	1968	1967	1966	1965
ASSETS:					
Current assets					
Cash and short-term securities.....	$ 259	$ 325	$ 172	$ 174	$ 195
Receivables and prepayments......	553	555	473	470	403
Inventories of oils and chemicals...	281	250	246	218	199
Other.........................	36	37	37	36	29
Total current assets..........	$1,129	$1,167	$ 928	$ 898	$ 826
Investments and long-term receivables, etc................	62	44	38	36	34
Properties, plant and equipment (net).	3,195	2,857	2,460	1,940	1,841
Total assets....................	$4,386	$4,068	$3,426	$2,874	$2,701
LIABILITIES AND SHAREHOLDERS' INVESTMENT:					
Current liabilities					
Payables and accruals............	$ 466	$ 497	$ 409	$ 359	$ 313
Income, operating, and consumer taxes.......................	156	165	152	156	131
Other.........................	28	16	10	13	9
Total current liabilities.......	650	678	571	528	453
Long-term debt.................	1,106	995	814	476	520
Deferred credits—federal income tax...........................	228	205	182	170	155
Shareholders' investment..........	2,402	2,190	1,859	1,700	1,573
Total liabilities and shareholders' investment........	$4,386	$4,068	$3,426	$2,874	$2,701

Exhibit 4

STONE PETROLEUM INTERNATIONAL (A)
Organization Chart (abbreviated)

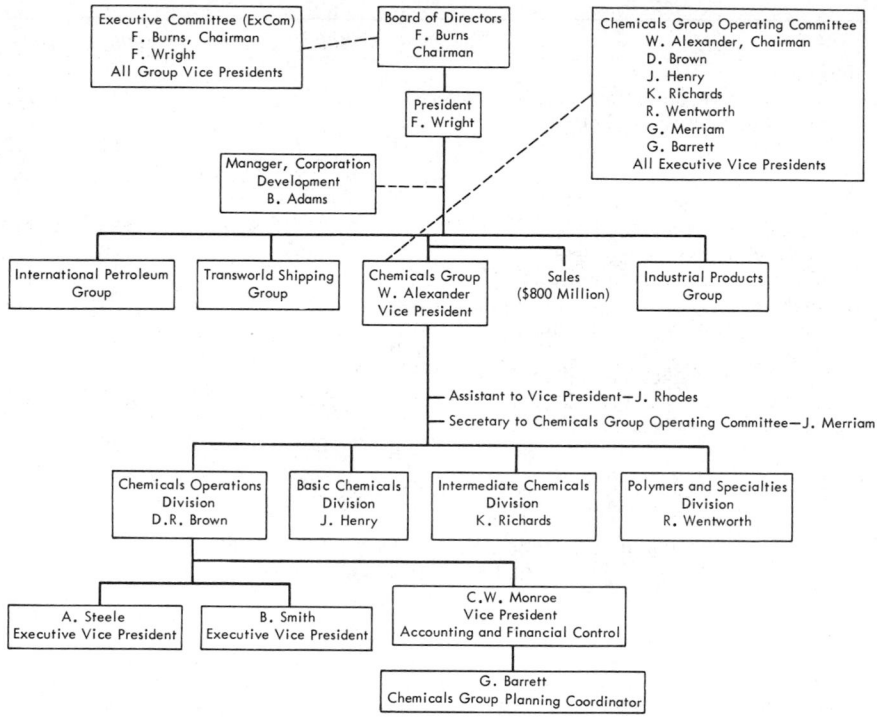

Exhibit 5

STONE PETROLEUM INTERNATIONAL (A)
Categorization of Business Lines

Consulting firm's classification by market growth rate and Stone's market share:

Lg = Low growth (in total market size)
Hg = High growth
Ls = Low share (of total market for Stone)
Hs = High share
Classification examples by divisions

Number of business lines	Class	Description
		Chemicals Operations Division
4	A	Positive operating income; want to support
1	B	Negative operating income, but good potential
5	C	Questionable
		Basic Chemicals Division
7	A	Must be supported
3	B	Support to maximum available cash
2	C	Withdraw
		Polymers and Specialties Division
20	A	Must be supported
9	B	Support to maximum available cash
7	C	Withdraw
		Intermediates Chemicals Division
10	A_1	Untouchables; defensive cash generators (Hs Lg)
	A_2	Strategic decision made
12	B	Offensive cash generators (Hs Hg)
6	C	Opportunities (Ls Hg)
3	D	Sell out facility
4	E	Phase out

Exhibit 6

STONE PETROLEUM INTERNATIONAL (A)

Profit Center Analysis

Division: polymers and specialties profit center No.	Name	Stone's 1969 total sales (000)	Stone's 1968 total production (000 lbs.)	Stone's 1968 total sales (000 lbs.)	Gross fixed invest-ment (direct) (millions)	1970 Assigned Overhead* (dollars in thousands) Home office adminis-tration	R&D	Marketing	Other costs
703	Phthalic anhydride	$33,900	880,000	419,000	$42.0	$ 275	$ 627	$ 484	$149
753	Acrytontile	8,300	30,100	30,100	10.2	908	259	154	24
738	Therminol	12,700	128,000	90,000	15.0	0	800	198	0
	Total category A (20 P.C.'s)					$ 766	$ 6,818	$4,889	$593
	Total category B (9 P.C.'s)					1,515	4,169	1,716	323
	Total category C (7 P.C.'s)					169	2,586	1,106	69
	Division totals					$2,450	$13,573	$7,711	$985

* Includes only overheads assigned directly to profit center (not aggregate, dept., etc.).
† High growth/Low sales, etc.
§ A, B, or C.
Note: Net income and cash flow implications of the projects are presented in Exhibit 7.

Fixed capital requirements (dollars in millions)						Percent share Stone 1968		Percent pounds growth 1970–74				Cash flow	
1970	1971	1972	1973	1974	Total 1970–74	Market- ing	Produc- tion	SPI	In- dus- try†	Category	Priority cate- gory§	1968	5-yr.
$ 7.1	$ 24.0	$ 3.9	$10.0	$17.6	$ 62.6	38	32	9.3	10	Lg Hs	A	+	−
2.0	20.5	9.0	0	0	31.5	8	8	30.0	15	Hg Ls	B	+	−
3.2	0.8	0	0	0	4.0	3	5	13.5	11	Hg Ls	C		+
$44.5	$ 86.2	$53.0	$29.0	$34.7	$247.4								
4.5	36.4	28.9	3.3	7.5	80.6								
4.0	1.2	2.4	6.5	0.3	14.4								
$53.0	$123.8	$84.3	$38.8	$42.5	$342.4								

Exhibit 7

STONE PETROLEUM INTERNATIONAL (A)

Polymers and Specialties Division: Analysis of Capital
Expenditure Requirements by Business Line Category

(dollars in millions)

Business line category	5-year cumulative		Net income after tax			Fixed capital requirements			Net cash flow		
	Net income after tax	Net cash flow	1970	1974	1970–74	1970	1974	1970–74	1970	1974	1970–74
A.........	+	+	$21.7	$36.2	$134.6	$31.6	$ 4.0	$ 94.1	($12.8)	$33.2	$48.3
	+	–	12.6	15.4	69.6	10.7	30.6	123.9	(1.1)	(3.1)	(38.9)
	–	–	(.6)	(.8)	(5.8)	2.2	.1	29.4	1.6	1.5	(31.5)
	Subtotal		$33.7	$50.8	$198.4	$44.5	$34.7	$247.4	($15.5)	$31.6	($22.1)
B.........	+	+	$ 1.3	$ 5.4	$ 19.7	$ .8	$ 4.2	$ 13.1	$ 5.3	$ 3.7	$17.3
	+	–	3.0	4.5	17.8	1.8	2.4	62.0	.7	3.1	(40.3)
	–	–	(1.3)	.2	(3.1)	1.9	.9	5.5	(2.4)	.2	(5.9)
	Subtotal		$ 3.0	$10.1	$ 34.4	$ 4.5	$ 7.5	$ 80.6	2.2	$ 6.6	($28.9)
C.........	+	+	$ 1.8	$ 5.2	$ 20.3	$ 3.6	$ 0.1	$ 11.4	($ 2.7)	$ 6.1	$11.3
	+	–	.2	.4	1.7	.4	—	2.6	—	.6	(.4)
	–		(.3)	—	(.8)	—	.2	.4	(.1)	.4	(1.8)
	Subtotal		$ 1.7	$ 5.6	$ 21.2	$ 4.0	$ .3	$ 14.4	($ 2.8)	($ 6.3)	($ 9.1)
Division totals...			$38.4	$66.5	$254.0	$53.0	$42.5	$342.4	($16.1)	$31.9	($60.1)

Exhibit 8

STONE PETROLEUM INTERNATIONAL (A)
Classification of Business Lines

Memorandum
Confidential

To: Operating Committee—   Date: September 30, 1969
             Chemicals Group
             Messrs. M. A. Hill
                     T. D. Miller
                     J. W. Merriam

From: C. W. Monroe

Subject: Subdivision of Businesses

Gentlemen:

Following my return from the meeting in Copper Creek last week, I sat down and tried to organize my understanding of the sense of the meeting as it related to the rating of the businesses. The following is the result of this effort, and you may find it useful as a preliminary exercise. Certainly the categories in which I have placed businesses is not sacred. Also, I took the liberty of lumping certain groups together. I have given copies of this to the Control Managers, and any corrections you wish to make to this list should be handled through them.

  I—BUSINESSES SELECTED FOR MARKET DOMINANCE
      Intermediate Chemicals (5 businesses)
      Basic Chemicals (5 businesses)
      Operations (3 businesses)
      Polymers & Specialties (10 businesses)
  II—BUSINESSES SELECTED TO MAINTAIN MARKET SHARE
      Intermediate Chemicals (6 businesses)
      Basic Chemicals (1 business)
      Polymers & Specialties (10 businesses)
 III—BUSINESSES SELECTED AS POTENTIAL FOR MARKET
        DOMINANCE
      Intermediate Chemicals (no businesses listed)
      Basic Chemicals (no businesses listed)
      Operations (no businesses listed)
      Polymers & Specialties (2 businesses)
  IV—BUSINESSES SELECTED AS POTENTIAL FOR DISPOSAL*
      Intermediate Chemicals (3 businesses)
      Basic Chemicals (3 businesses)
      Operations (1 business)
      Polymers & Specialties (2 businesses)
   V—BUSINESSES WHOSE STATUS IS UNDECIDED
      Intermediate Chemicals (6 businesses)
      Basic Chemicals (1 business)
      Operations (5 businesses)
      Polymers & Specialties (4 businesses)

* Through sale or draining off income.

Stone Petroleum International (B)

"Jack, what am I going to have to do to get this ship off the rocks? Gross margins for the first quarter were catastrophic—40% *under* forecasts; completion of our new management information system has been delayed until early October; the managers continue their resistance to organizational changes. Look at our Willow Flats meeting. . . . I can't tolerate approaching the end of another fiscal year with such an unresponsive organization!"

In April 1970, Mr. William Alexander, vice president of the Chemicals Group, and his assistant, Mr. Jack Rhodes, had just returned from a two-day meeting of the Group's Operating Committee at Willow Flats, Texas. Both were more than anxious to try to clarify their reactions to that meeting and develop Mr. Alexander's next moves before he met with Mr. Wright, Stone's president, the following Wednesday.

As background to this situation, Stone Petroleum International (A) described the company's declining corporate performance and the appointment of a new president with a strong desire to increase the corporation's earnings. From June through early October 1969, the corporation's Executive Committee (ExCom) and the Chemicals Group Operating Committee began to focus their attention on the strategic planning requirements for the corporation. (See Stone Petroleum International (A), Exhibit 4, for an abbreviated organization chart.) During the latter part of September, Mr. Alexander, vice president of the Chemicals Group since June, had met with his Operating Committee in Copper Creek for two days to begin analyzing the Group's business lines and to initiate a new organizational context for strategic planning.

Mr. Alexander's weeks following Copper Creek had been filled with meetings, personnel problems, and operating crises. On November 11 Mr. Bob Adams, manager of Corporate Development, issued a report detailing the enormous differences between the Group VP's "approved" and "priority" capital expenditure proposals and the funding levels planned by the corporation. This report served to jolt the several Groups into realizing there was a crisis in the processes of capital expenditures budgeting and strategic planning throughout the corporation, including Mr. Alexander's Chemicals Group.

After the initial reverberations from Mr. Adams' memo had echoed through the plush halls of his Group's executive suit, Mr. Alexander still faced the very real problem of eliminating the differences between his prior expected level of funding and the corporation's new plans— amounts of $110 million and $162 million for 1970 and 1971, respectively. In order to cut his capital expenditure requests by such amounts, Alexander knew his Operating Committee would have to shift some of its priorities dramatically during the next two months and continue the re-analysis throughout 1970.

ALEXANDER: Jack, we've got to develop a crash program to improve our planning process around here. We don't have time to do the planning right, I know, and our information won't be as accurate as we'd like, but we've got to get moving!

RHODES: OK, what can I do to help get this process underway?

ALEXANDER: I'd like you to prepare a rough timetable of critical activities for my office during 1970 and to sketch some guidelines for the preparation of a strategic plan once a "posture" has been selected for a market segment.

Mr. Rhodes' days and evening through the Thanksgiving weekend were devoted primarily to considering the actions Mr. Alexander had taken thus far, and those he had been unable or unwilling to take, as a basis for scheduling the future activities and recommending guidelines for strategic planning. By the end of November, he had developed some thoughts on the topics and was prepared to discuss them with Mr. Alexander.

RHODES: You told me to begin *given* a 1970 budget. As I understand it, the budget will consist of a one-year program of objectives to which a named individual has committed himself on items, such as sales, margins, cost improvements, new capacity, new product developments, and so on, that can be *measured* at specific dates. Where incentive arrangements can be made for performance, I think we agreed that it would be a good thing.

ALEXANDER: That's right, I think reaching that point will be a real step.

RHODES: We also agree that these objectives have been set in a context that is gradually changing. If problems arise, they should not be interpreted as immediate evidence of an individual's faults, or the lousy organization. Just the opposite. Part of the profit center manager's job is to bring hard problems to the attention of the division or group.

ALEXANDER: What I would like, too, to see coming to us are: the severe scheduling problems; trade-offs across profit center lines; and major shifts in technology, the market, politics or competition, that change "the name of the game."

RHODES: Right, it seems important that the individuals responsible for businesses understand that you need to know about questions of this sort, even if the action you take is to refer the problem back to them.

ALEXANDER: I feel we're also beginning to make some progress in this area, though not nearly enough. But what about after the budget is set? What sort of schedule do you propose for 1970?

RHODES: There are two main tasks: (1) making good on 1970; and (2) developing a strategic plan for 1970–1975. They ought to be the two principal activities of the profit centers. Here's one page of proses (Mr. Rhodes gave Mr. Alexander a memo including the paragraphs below):

> In late December or early January, each of the individuals who has signed a plan should be asked to prepare for his profit center a strategic plan consisting of two cases:
> How Stone should move in the business with unlimited funds?
> How Stone should move with funds limited? In this second case *you* should specify how limited depending on the preliminary discussions of the ExCom this fall, e.g., no new money; no net cash drain in any year; or no net cash drain for the total five-year period, but some drain in any given year.
>
> *   *   *   *   *
>
> A strategic plan should provide a definition of product and market scope. These definitions will need to be improved over time and the lines along which you aggregate may change, but at first the plan ought to state, "We are producing a, b, and c, to serve markets x, y, z." Given an initial definition of scope, the plan should answer a number of major questions about the market and Stone.

ALEXANDER: What are some of those questions? Do you have them written down anywhere? Better yet, work them out with Barrett.

In what form should we expect to get the replies to all these questions?

RHODES: Wherever possible, the analysis of Stone and the market should be quantitative, but given the kind of data available, much will not be. Even so, the goal ought to be as many hard numbers as possible—not because life is like that, but because it's easier to make assumptions clear when everything is out on the table. The goal, also, ought to be as much personal involvement and commitment of the relevant management as possible.

ALEXANDER: How much time do you think this process will take?

RHODES: The first draft will probably take at least two months. During this time, staff assistance should be provided by engineering, management information systems, market research, Stone specialists, and outside consultants—when appropriate.

ALEXANDER: More important, I want to know when they're resisting help. You know this process is going to be quite a change for many of the managers. We must do everything we can to get things off on the right foot in this planning cycle.

RHODES: Well, I think it would make sense at the beginning of the planning period, to take a day or two—or more—to develop an awareness in the planning teams of what a strategic plan looks like, and how they can get help in preparing one. Discussions of cases, or examples of "good plans" might be the right idea.

ALEXANDER: Coaching is fine, but I also want to be sure that during January and February we are keeping operations moving forward. No explosions!

RHODES: Right. The review of profit center progress against the 1970 budget needs to begin at the end of January. Variances should be noted and severe ones flagged for early attention. But not many meaningful trends will have emerged by then.

But in contrast, by the end of February, there may well be serious problems.

ALEXANDER: I want to schedule reviews for those businesses in trouble. I've put the idea on the Operating Committee agenda. This process has often been so poorly handled as to be useless. It will take a lot of time and effort to change this history. We'll all have to learn.

RHODES: Won't we be starting our review of the strategic plans at about the same time.

ALEXANDER: Yes, why?

RHODES: Well, my thought is that when review of the strategic plans begins, your options become incredibly widespread. How you run the review process can have a great deal to do with how the staff is used at different levels of the organization; with how the organizational structure evolves; and with how the role of division officers evolves, as well as the quality of the plans. You can get at them all.

ALEXANDER: I'm listening. What do you have in mind?

RHODES: It's a long story. Let's take the last point first. It is critical to the whole process that reviews of the plans be thorough. Right now planning and measurement take too much time and accomplish too little. The main reason is that each event, each review or discussion, tends to be too superficial. This means that better preparation by all parties at a review and fewer reviews are both desirable.

One implication may well be that in 1970 only "25," or some such number, big businesses can be included in the strategic planning process. But it's a certainty that better preparation means that your office needs help, either from Barrett if he is prepared to help, or from Merriam, or from others. They ought to be as critical as possible in the analysis of plans they provide for *you* and provide questions that cut deeply. Who else sees their work is a different question. You wield a subtle needle, but with staff to help, you can feel surer that you can probe directly toward the soft spots.

Whom you use for your staff raises an interesting question. Personally, I believe that the people you rely on for detailed criticism of the strategic plans, should not be the same souls who ought to be committed to helping the profit centers produce the plans. Objectivity is great, but I'm not sure I like to trust the thoroughness of completely objective managers. Moreover, and this comment bears on the first organizational point we mentioned, it seems to me that the staff contributing to the plans ought to be located at lower levels, probably reporting to the divisions as a service function.

Turning to the other organization questions, the review process will provide you many opportunities to adjust the boundaries of profit centers, as well as to rearrange groupings, and to change the role of division officers. The first point is straightforward. The second is touchy.

ALEXANDER: Jack, I'm not sure just what I want to do about some of the division officers. It's not always easy to see which ones are really doing a good job.

Since I moved Brown and Wentworth up to head their respective divisions, they seem to be catching on and trying to do what we have in mind. I'm still disappointed in some of the others though; they just don't seem to want to change any of their old habits. Trying to determine just what the executive vice presidents are contributing is really a thorny problem too.

RHODES: I'll agree the task is not easy, but how you proceed with the review process can substantially increase or decrease the importance of the division officers and /or the Operating Committee. For example, "because time is so scarce," you could conduct the reviews by visiting the divisions yourself without the Operating Committee along. You can also affect the status of the executive vice presidents.

ALEXANDER: Well, that's useful. You know my uncertainties about how fast we can push things. I want to talk to Barrett and then to some of the Operating Committee to see what their ideas are. I believe, though, that we'll end up with something like your proposed schedule.

Most of the topics discussed by Mr. Alexander and Mr. Rhodes during their conversation concerned important activities for 1970, but Alexander had some tasks associated with 1970's budget to finish prior to the year's end. An indication of the position of the Chemicals Group planning late in November was presented in a memorandum from Mr. Wentworth regarding the November 26 capital planning meeting. Some of the topics discussed in that meeting were as follows:

— The need to stay within capital expenditure limits of $215 million annually for 1970 and 1971.
— The need to reevaluate some of the business plans if proposed capital expenditures were deferred.
— The need for managers to avoid getting "shook up" as the cycling of product/market analyses stretched out over a period of several months.

The Group's Operating Committee had thus been formally apprised of the capital constraints and the probable ramifications for some of the specific business plans and the planning process in general.

During the last Operating Committee meeting in November, Alexander had occasion to describe the pressures he was receiving from the ExCom to get his Group moving.

BROWN: Will, is it really necessary for us to spend all this time reviewing so many proposals in such detail? Much of it seems like a waste of time.

ALEXANDER: It may seem like a waste of time to some of you, but it's damned important to me! The reputation of our plans in the ExCom is terrible. We have a real credibility problem. And I don't blame them. We're asking for half the available capital and our recent record is full of mistakes. The company has invested hundreds of millions of dollars in Chemicals during the past few years, and there has been no return. Our earnings are lower than in 1964. If we don't increase our ROI and develop our proposals more thoroughly, our investment capital will be cut even more!

RICHARDS: Don't you think the ExCom is trying to push some of these changes too fast? We can't change everything overnight.

ALEXANDER: It may seem as though they're rushing things, but they don't think so, and that's what counts! And I can't deliver results to them until I get them from you . . . .

By early December the divisions began submitting the "blue sheets" containing business plans for the forthcoming year. (Exhibit 1 presents an example of the four-page "blue sheets.") Working with the revenue and expense data and cash flow projections in these "blue sheets," the Chemicals Group Operating Committee classified and ranked their related capital expenditures proposals under the following categories before submitting them to the ExCom late in December:

A. Projects which were projected to be excellent cash generators.
B. Small projects which were not anticipated to have positive net cash flows for several years, but which seemed like desirable long-range investments.
C. Huge projects which represented major strategic commitments.

After extended discussion and debate with the ExCom during the last week of December and first week of January, Mr. Alexander finally received approval for $213 million of capital expenditures during 1970, $2 million less than "suggested" in the November 11 memo. From this total, he managed to have $7 million set aside for later allocation largely at his discretion, and he assumed primary responsibility for one of the Category C projects.

The continuous state of flux throughout the company regarding the handling of business and facility planning combined with Mr. Bob Adams' new responsibilities in those areas raised a number of questions with Alexander for which he felt clarification was needed. In order to get a specific and direct reply to these questions, he asked the president, Mr. Fred Wright. The views exchanged in their conversation were later recorded in a memorandum to the entire Stone management group.

Mr. Wright notes that Mr. Adams has been given the task of coordinating the capital budgeting between the divisions and the ExCom for the years 1970 and 1971. In addition, Adams' group would immediately have its charter expanded to look at Stone's total business from a standpoint of better planning, better measures, and better input to each of the business centers. Mr. Adams' group was to work between the business divisions and the ExCom, not as a decision-making group, but rather one that would take an impartial and unbiased attitude in raising questions on things to be done, and problems to be avoided.

His first task would be to study, with the operating groups involved, those major segments of the business which appeared to be in some difficulty, and to explore and recommend those avenues which the corporation should take in maximizing the growth and profitability of these businesses. He was to work closely in this area both with the operating people, staff people and the ExCom.

Mr. Alexander noted wryly to Mr. Rhodes, that there might well be more "gifts from Mr. Adams."

While the Chemicals Group Operating Committee members were spending January finalizing the 1969 operating results and assembling business plans for the "1970 Business Plan—Chemicals Group" document, Mr. Rhodes took some time to discuss the spring's planning activities with Mr. Barrett and Mr. Adams. The following excerpts from a discussion with Mr. Alexander later that month regarding the planning program reflect his reactions to Mr. Barrett's and Mr. Adams' plans:

ALEXANDER: What were you able to learn from Barrett and Adams about their plans for the spring?

RHODES: Barrett's program for planning this spring is in keeping with the spirit of our discussions last fall. I'll help him any way I can. . . .

The problem of coaching managers regarding the strategic planning process is still ahead of us though I might be able to help with the process, but others will have to work on the technical considerations. I'm not much of a chemist. . . .

ALEXANDER: Do they think the managers feel any more committed to their plans than before?

RHODES: I don't think so. They say most of the managers still seem to feel they are just signing numerical forecasts rather than commitments against which they will actually be evaluated. I feel we need to work harder on this. Group sessions seem to be a place for exploratory planning, whereas one-to-one meetings might be more useful for establishing strong commitments. The role played by your executive vice presidents in this process will certainly influence their status in the organization. . . .

ALEXANDER: It's tough to get real commitments when our internal information and control system is so lousy, but I know we've got to start sometime. . . .

The "1970 Business Plan—Chemicals Group," presented late in January, contained a formal summary statement of Mr. Alexander's thoughts on the 1969–1970 restructuring within his Group.

> During 1969, the Chemicals Group was sorted into over 70 defined "major" businesses. A principal 1970 objective is to develop an optimum allocation of available resources among these businesses so that strategic plans can be developed for the parts which are consistent with the plans for the whole. This is expected to be a drawn-out process involving a significant portion of the time of top group management. After this optimization process has gone through several iterations, strategic plans will be developed for each business. A planning mechanism will also be established to keep the strategic plans up to date.

This published compilation of business plans for each of the divisions and the departments within them for the Group showed a wide variation in the level of understanding of strategic planning reached by various managers throughout the Group. Although many of the plans included appropriate jargon, probably absorbed during the many meetings, and some contained reasonably complete strategic plans, several of the statements from the profit centers read like budget variance analyses written by engineers or accountants or like volume forecasts from optimistic salesmen. This planning document provided evidence that there was a substantial amount of coaching still needed during the forthcoming year. As a matter of fact, one observer said the 1970 Plan was "not much better than the prior ones had been!"

Although Mr. Alexander realized his "1970 Business Plan" left a great deal to be desired, he felt by the end of January that the Group was making some progress toward improving its strategic planning process. However, his developing satisfaction was crushed on February 9 when he received the Group's performance data for the first month's operations, Gross margins were 60% less than both expectations and plans. As he attempted to locate the sources of the apparent confluence of poor planning and poor performance, he was further frustrated by the gross characteristics of his data collection system. The shortcomings were of such magnitude he could identify some broad problem areas, but neither he nor anyone else could attribute specific portions of the deteriorating gross margins to particular business lines or management failures. At the same time, he was aware of the fact that the staff working on the new management information system had encountered difficulties which promised to delay completion of that desperately needed system. With this pressing situation in mind, Mr. Alexander called a meeting of his Operating Committee for the purpose of discussing the need to reassess the Group's business plans in light of the continuing capital constraints. The following are excerpts from that meeting:

ALEXANDER: All of you have seen our performance data for January, and I'm sure you'll agree these are terrible. Fred has seen them and he is very unhappy. If our first quarter looks like January, the stockholder's meeting will be chaotic and we'll really be "under the gun."

STEELE: Will, doesn't Wright realize we've been working almost continuously on our analyses of business plans? There are bound to be some setbacks during this transitional period.

ALEXANDER: Yes, Fred knows very well what we've been doing, but he wants current earnings to go up, not *down*. We must start today to reassess both our short and longer term problems and opportunities in the light of current developments as well as our discussion of the past several weeks. It's important that we think carefully about the ways in which we use all our resources, not just our capital.

HENRY: You said we must start this reassessment today, Will, but do you have a schedule for when specific phases are to be finished? I don't know about the others, but I've been so tied up with all these planning meetings, I haven't had the time to begin working on some of my operations the way I would like.

BROWN: I've had somewhat the same problem, but I think I'm slowly getting more things under control.

ALEXANDER: I know it seems like we all have a lot to do, but we must keep up the pace, or we'll never really get both our current operations and our future plans fully under control.

Going back to Henry's question about a schedule, let me outline briefly the deadlines I think we must meet. By May 1 I want to have all the revised profit center plans completed. These plans must specify any business or functional programs that are necessary to maximize short-term performance, that is, for 1970 and 1971. In addition, I want to see statements of potential problems for 1972 and beyond, so we can begin to develop programs to minimize those problems.

RICHARDS: Will, isn't this somewhat repetitious of what we were doing in November and December?

ALEXANDER: In a way, that's right. But all of you have seen the complete set of plans now, and you also know what our recent performance has been. Moreover, managers are going to be held responsible for their plans. That means the quality of the plans had better be much better. Monroe has given us all the evidence we need that the first pass plans were soft. Let's get them hard!

OK, by July 1, we will have a good chance to review our current performance. I will also expect to see the programs for short-term improvement implemented by that date. Three months later, about October 1, we should have all of our 1971 business and functional department plans completed and defined in terms of our 1971 budget.

SMITH: Will, do you think we'll need to spend as much time reviewing these plans next fall as we did during this past one?

ALEXANDER: I don't know for sure, but I sincerely hope it's not necessary.

I expect we will all have better plans to begin with and that we'll also have a better overall idea of the Group's direction by that time.

During October, we'll consolidate our various plans, review them thoroughly, and prepare them for presentation to the ExCom.

From the looks on your faces, I know what some of you are thinking, "That's one hell of a lot of work!" I don't deny that, but we're all going to have to push very hard to get this operation back to a satisfactorily profitable position again.

The afternoon of the same day that Mr. Alexander had met with his Operating Committee, Mr. Barrett, the Group's planning coordinator, distributed an extended statement entitled "Guidelines for Quantitative Description of Chemicals Group Profit Center Strategies." This series of "Guidelines" provided the standardized format for profit center planning on a comparative basis that had been sought at the Copper Creek meeting in September, and as such, marked another step in the formalization of the planning process within the Group. In addition to presenting the "Guidelines," Mr. Barrett's memorandum mentioned an available computer program to assist with the analyses and warned that some of the gross margins in the December plans looked overly optimistic. (Exhibit 2 contains more detailed excerpts from Mr. Barrett's memo.)

As part of his effort to encourage the managers in the service departments to begin improving their planning processes, Mr. Barrett included with his "Guidelines" an exemplary planning report from Mr. J. J. Smith of the R&D staff in Houston. Smith's report presented information regarding the various operating functions his staff would be supporting during the forthcoming year, the division of their work between "products" and "processes," and a further breakdown according to "new" and "existing" categories. Although the contents of his report had measurable substantive worth, of even greater significance was the fact that his staff had assumed the initiative and developed and submitted the plans without explicit encouragement from the Chemicals Group management.

After Mr. Barrett circulated his report with the attached R&D plans, he began "waiting patiently" for the marketing staff and other departments to take the hint and begin to formalize their planning processes. Rather than attempting to force various people to follow their suggestions for strategic planning, Mr. Alexander, Mr. Barrett, and others were trying to demonstrate the value and importance of the planning activity as a basis for encouraging managers' interest in, and willingness to seek assistance with, a formalized strategic planning process.

The information in Mr. Barrett's memorandum was not intended to be the final step toward improving the planning process, but it did provide a basis for coordinating and standardizing more of the data being submitted. Planning information available to the Group's Operating Committee up through February had consisted mostly of the profit centers' "blue sheets" plus the individual profit centers' business plans. The summary character of the documents and the occasionally offhand approach to their preparation by the profit centers were sources of frustration to the Operating Committee's efforts to compare the business lines and projects and to really understand the bases for choosing one alternative in preference to another.

Between mid-February and mid-April, Mr. Alexander and the Chemicals Group's Operating Committee spent a great deal of time attending meetings and attempting to encourage the development of revised profit center plans in time for the review which he had previously stated would begin on May 1. The standardized planning forms and procedures presented in Mr. Barrett's "Guidelines" report provided direction for the coaching process as well as a basis for developing generally comparable data for substantive analyses. By focusing attention on strategic problems through the use of specific questions, the "Guidelines" served as a valuable tool during the learning process. Although the data being analyzed were acknowledged to be less accurate and consistent than was desirable and some of the forecasts seemed somewhat optimistic, the process of raising and seeking answers to strategic questions was deemed by most participants to be a valuable and integral addition to the company's planning cycle.

As the managers of the major profit centers approached the completion of their revised plans, Mr. Alexander tried to meet with some of them individually to impress upon them that their new plans were more nearly commitments than forecasts and that they would be evaluated largely in terms of their performance vis-à-vis those commitments.

The Group's unsatisfactory gross margins persisted through February, and as a result, the Group was faced with growing pressures for improvements in current operations. March's results subsequently provided some relief by exceeding the 1970 Plan, but the first quarter's combined results still registered well under earlier projections. Such performance seemed destined to cause some embarrassment for the corporation's officers at the approaching stockholders' meeting.

The stockholders' meeting proved to be a rather painful reminder to Chairman Burns and President Wright that the difficulties facing them were also quite visible to the stockholders. In addition to protesters who invaded the meeting, a few angry stockholders raised sharp points about the company's management and economic performance.

One of the leading financial journals reported the meeting as follows:

> NEW YORK—It was a rough annual meeting for executives of Stone Petroleum Int'l. First they had to weather complaints from stockholders, angry about a 19% decline in first quarter profit. Then they had to face an invasion of students, furious about increasing pollution. . . .
>
> Shareholder Edward Green, who described himself as "a private investor," declared, "you have repeatedly referred to this as a growth company. To me it seems to be a shrinking company. . . ."
>
> Mr. Burns, chairman, conceded that "performance hasn't been satisfactory over the past few years to shareholders or to us." He said, however, "We are finally getting some price stability in the chemical industry. It's a rough situation but we believe it's improving."
>
> Asked another shareholder, "How can it be that things are going so wrong? Is management remiss?" Stone has "made a few mistakes,"

said Mr. Burns. But he blamed the company's market performance on "go-go glamor treatment."

Earlier, Mr. Wright had told shareholders that despite the first quarter decline, the company expects 1970 earnings to "be better" than the $253 million earned in 1969. After the meeting, Mr. Burns declined further comment on this prediction. . . .

Wright blamed the first quarter earnings decline partly on an explosion at the company's Wood River, Ill., plant last October. He said the plant was delayed in getting back into operations until the first week in March, later than had been expected. Earnings were also affected, he said, by costs in some areas rising faster "than our ability to offset them through improvements in operating efficiency or through higher selling prices."

While the corporate officers were facing the stockholders in New York, Mr. Alexander had his Group's Operating Committee, including executive vice presidents, in Willow Flats, Texas, for a two-day planning session. His primary objective for the meeting was to develop plans for 1973 and the interim steps necessary to fulfill those plans. Although he realized short-run adjustments would be needed in the information system, operating relationships, and personnel assignments, it became apparent to him almost from the outset of the meeting that the majority of those in attendance were intent upon firmly resisting any further "reorganizations."

The Committee's discussions, however, eventually led to a consensus on a few points. They felt that smaller and more logical groupings of business lines would provide more manageable units of activity. This idea led to a suggestion for the creation of another division and the appointment of two additional general managers. The separation of the business lines into the four broad categories of specialty chemicals, specialty plastics, commodity chemicals, and commodity plastics was also thought to add some coherence to the business line arrangement. To help unify control over some business lines, it was recommended that jurisdiction over about 25% of the operating plants be transferred to the business line managers who had exclusive use for the output of those facilities.

During the meeting some managers expressed skepticism about the new transfer pricing system. They seemed to be concerned both about how it would operate and about its apparently mechanistic impact on the reward system.

As Mr. Alexander and Mr. Rhodes drove back to the office late Friday afternoon, they talked about how some of the planning and coaching efforts were beginning to show results, but Mr. Alexander was still perplexed about the alternatives facing him regarding his own actions and his managers' growing resistance to organizational changes.

ALEXANDER: Jack, Monroe told me that the divisions' forecasts of improved performance are empty. He said they are predicting better margins, but that there are no plans or programs to indicate that they will achieve them.

What can I do? I need better data, but I won't have it until October. I know I need capital, but the corporation won't give it to me until our credibility improves. How can they give me $100 million for styrene with our profits the way they look? I could fire some people, but in most cases the ones managing the weakest businesses weren't the ones who made the bad decisions. . . .

RHODES: Will, have you heard from Fred about the stockholders' meeting?

ALEXANDER: I'll say I have! The experience was worse than he had even expected. . . .

Exhibit 1

STONE PETROLEUM INTERNATIONAL (B)
"Blue Sheet" Example
Revenue and Expense Projections
(dollars in millions)

	1969	1970	1971	1972	1973	1974	1975
Sales outside Chemicals Group	18.0	20.1	26.1	37.1	64.1	114.1	159.8
Sales to Chemicals Group P.C.'s	4.5	4.8	5.1	5.3	3.6	2.6	1.3
Total sales income	22.5	24.9	31.2	42.4	67.7	116.7	161.1
Total sales pounds (millions)	155	180	240	350	550	895	1,280
Manufacturing cost	9.6	12.0	14.4	20.3	30.6	50.5	71.4
Home office additions	0.2	0.3	0.2	0.4	0.5	1.0	1.4
Distribution expense	3.0	4.1	5.2	7.4	10.6	14.6	16.8
Gross margin	9.7	8.5	11.4	14.3	26.0	50.6	71.5
% sales	43.1%	34.1%	36.5%	33.7%	38.4%	43.4%	44.4%
Assigned & shared overhead							
R.&D.	0.8	2.0	2.4	3.0	3.4	3.3	3.2
Marketing	0.5	1.3	1.6	1.8	2.5	2.8	3.6
Other	0.9	0.8	0.8	0.9	0.4	0.4	0.4
Allocated overhead	1.5	2.0	3.2	5.0	6.5	7.0	7.6
Operating income	6.0	2.4	3.4	3.6	13.2	37.1	56.7
% sales	26.7%	9.6%	10.9%	8.5%	19.5%	31.8%	35.2%
Depreciation	3.1	4.3	6.8	10.7	14.0	14.9	16.3
ROI income	2.9	-1.9	-3.4	-7.1	-0.8	22.2	40.4
% sales	12.9%					19.0%	25.1%
% total utilized investment	6.7%					10.9%	17.6%
Net income after tax	1.4	-0.9	-1.7	-3.5	-0.4	10.9	19.8
% sales	6.2%					9.3%	12.3%
% total utilized investment	3.3%					5.4%	8.6%
Gross fixed investment	37.5	49.6	79.1	124.8	162.6	173.9	189.5
Working capital	5.5	6.5	8.0	11.0	17.1	28.9	40.4
Total utilized investment	43.0	56.1	87.1	135.8	179.7	202.8	229.9
Turnover	52.3%	44.4%	35.8%	31.2%	37.7%	57.5%	70.1%
Incremental turnover						58.9%	74.2%

Profit Center 532 Maleic Anhydride
No.   Name

12/2/69

Cash Flow Projection—Profit Center 532
(dollars in millions)

	1970	1971	1972	1973	1974	1975
Net income after tax	-0.9	-1.7	-3.5	-0.4	10.9	19.8
Depreciation	4.3	6.8	10.7	14.0	14.9	16.3
Deferred income tax	0.4	0.6	1.0	1.3	1.3	1.5
Total cash generated	3.8	5.7	8.2	14.9	27.1	37.6
Dividend obligation	-0.6	-0.9	-1.8	-0.2	5.4	9.9
New direct fixed investment—major projects	9.1	21.3	35.0	27.8	5.5	7.6
New direct fixed investment—working budgets	0.6	0.7	1.1	1.8	2.3	2.6
New supporting plant investment transfers	1.6	5.6	6.6	5.7	2.8	4.4
New supporting non-plant investment transfers	0.8	1.9	3.0	2.5	0.7	1.0
Working capital additions	0.8	1.5	2.8	6.0	11.5	11.5
Total cash requirements	12.3	30.1	46.7	43.6	28.2	37.0
Net cash flow	-8.5	-24.4	-38.5	-28.7	-1.1	+0.6

Cumulative cash flow

	1970	1971	1972	1973	1974	1975
Total cash generated	3.8	9.5	17.7	32.6	59.7	97.3
Total cash requirements	12.3	42.4	89.1	132.7	160.9	197.9
Net cash flow	-8.5	-32.9	-71.4	-100.1	-101.2	-100.6

Approved: _____   _____

             Operations Manager   Date

           _____   _____

             Control Manager   Date

12-2-69

Exhibit 1—Continued

Positions and Objectives

Share and growth		Stone	Industry
Production			
Share—1969	%	51.0	xxx
Share—1976	%	53.0	xxx
Growth rate—1969 through 1976	%/yr.	13.5	13.0
Sales outside stone			
Share—1969	%	48.0	xxx
Share—1976	%	49.0	xxx
Growth rate—1969 through 1976	%/yr.	8.3	8.0

Major competitors	1969 Share—%	
	Production	*Outside sales*
1. Monsanto	23	24
2. Du Pont	12	14
3. Jefferson	6	6

Long-range profit center objective	Check One
Maintain or improve market share	x
Achieve dominant market share	
Withdraw from business	
Other (explain below)	

Issued: 12/2/69

Revised:

Profit Center 532   *Maleic Anhydride*
No.   Name

Major Transfers
(millions of pounds and transfer price)

	1969	1970	1971	1972	1973	1974	1975
From other Chemicals							
Group profit centers							
P.C. 507-quantity	7.8	8.0	11.5	15.0	24.0	40.0	53.0
P.C. 507-price	6.4¢	6.2¢	6.0¢	6.0¢	5.7¢	5.4¢	5.2¢
Total transfers *in* (pounds)	7.8	8.0	11.5	15.0	24.0	40.0	53.0
To other Chemicals							
Group profit centers							
P.C. 556-quantity	32.0	35.0	39.0	44.0	30.0	20.0	10.0
P.C. 556-price	14.0¢	13.8¢	13.0¢	12.0¢	12.0¢	13.0¢	12.6¢
Total transfers *out* (pounds)	3.2	3.5	3.9	4.4	3.0	2.0	1.0

Issued: 12–2–69

Revised:

Profit Center: *532*   *Maleic Anhydride*
No.   Name

Exhibit 2

STONE PETROLEUM INTERNATIONAL (B)
Excerpts from "Guidelines for Quantitative Description
of Chemicals Group Profit Center Strategies"
(February 13, 1970)

This report is intended to provide a standardized format for presenting "the current and projected competitive position and objectives, product flows, financial performance, growth, resource requirements, and cash flows of our businesses."

For this purpose, every Profit Center should be viewed as a separate business. Current competitive position and Revenue and Expense (R&E) performance should be stated, as well as a projection of performance for each of the next seven years. Cash requirements and flows should be similarly stated. Submittal of this information, if desired, for aggregates of two or more closely associated Profit Centers is appropriate, in addition to, but not in lieu of, information on each Profit Center separately.

Three types of forms will be provided for Profit Center information: Blue —to be prepared by each Profit Center for entry and submittal of R&E, cash flow, major transfers, and position and objectives data on its proposed business plans.

Green—to be prepared for submitting the description and impact of any desired alternative plan whose definition or feasibility is not yet sufficiently established for submittal as the proposed plan.

White—for classification of assigned R&D expenses in sufficient detail to permit planning of this function.

Input forms for a computer program to handle the Profit Center's R&E and cash flow data are included in this report.

In addition to the new forms and the computer program which have been developed, there are some past problem areas and future plans which deserve attention. The plans presented in December 1969 contained gross margin ratios which seemed unreasonably high in future years, and since financial performance is very sensitive to these ratios, they must be examined critically. Further, there is reason to assume there has not been adequate coordination of the transfer prices used, and as a result, some of the individual Profit Center data are considerably out of balance.

By next week a format will be provided for collecting data regarding long-term capital programs, and by April a procedure will be developed to provide investment and depreciation data for existing facilities by profit centers.

In addition, this report includes guidelines for the collection and manipulation of data, basic macro-economic assumptions including price-level indices, and a planning report from Mr. J. J. Smith which may provide some insight into the way planning data might be assembled.

Index of cases

Index of cases

This book has been set in 9 and 8 point Primer, leaded 2 points. Part numbers and chapter titles are 18 point Scotch Roman; part titles are 18 point Scotch Roman italic and case titles are 14 point Scotch Roman italic. The size of the type page is 27 by 46½ picas.